RURAL CHINA

Imperial Control in the Nineteenth Century

中國鄉村

THIS BOOK IS A PRODUCT OF THE MODERN CHINESE HISTORY PROJECT CARRIED ON BY THE FAR EASTERN AND RUSSIAN INSTITUTE OF THE UNIVERSITY OF WASHINGTON. MEMBERS OF THE GROUP REPRESENT VARIOUS DISCIPLINES IN THE SOCIAL SCIENCES AND HUMANITIES. THE WORK OF THE PROJECT IS OF A COOPERATIVE NATURE WITH EACH MEMBER ASSISTING THE OTHERS THROUGH CRITICAL DISCUSSION AND THE CONTRIBUTION OF IDEAS AND MATERIAL. THE RESPONSIBILITY FOR EACH STUDY RESTS WITH THE AUTHOR.

RURAL CHINA

Imperial Control in the Nineteenth Century BY

KUNG-CHUAN HSIAO

UNIVERSITY OF WASHINGTON PRESS

Seattle and London

RURAL CHINA is Number 8 of the Publications on Asia
of the Institute for Comparative and Foreign Area Studies,
formerly Far Eastern and Russian Institute Publications
on Asia.

PREFACE

This is a study of the rationale, methods, and effects of the system of control over rural China as exercised by the Ch'ing government during the nineteenth century. Owing to the limited availability
of relevant information and my desire to bring this study to a close
within a reasonable period of time, I do not propose to explore every
aspect of the subject or to give a full account of those aspects with
which I deal. Some omissions are in fact quite conspicuous. For instance, the ethnic minorities that dwelt in some parts of the empire
as well as the rural inhabitants of its outlying regions are not considered. I hope, however, that despite the lacunae that remain, the
results presented here will convey a tolerably clear impression of
the situation that prevailed in the empire during the period.

Such a study may serve some useful purposes. Imperial China was
an agricultural country in which rural inhabitants constituted the overwhelming majority of the population. No discussion of Chinese history or society can be adequate without taking into account the impact of the government upon the millions that lived in the villages
and the attitudes and behavior which the people exhibited under various conditions at various periods of time. The nineteenth century
is particularly interesting, for it was a period of dynastic decline
and political transition. A study of rural China during this period
will reveal some of the forces and factors that contributed to the decline of the imperial system and will perhaps also furnish useful clues
for interpreting the historical developments of later times.

Descriptions and narratives of Chinese rural life in the nineteenth
century are not lacking, but they are often not the results of careful
investigation. Few of them offer painstaking analyses of the phenom-
ena observed; some contain a variety of misconceptions and misin-
terpretations. The unresolved divergencies in interpretation that
abound in some of these writings often prove bewildering to the reader. There is a need for a more systematic treatment of the matter—
a need which the present study presumes partially to fill. Moreover,
although much has been written on the general administrative system of the empire, relatively little has been written either in Chi-

nese or in Western languages on its structure and functioning at the lowest administrative—or rather subadministrative—level. An important aspect of the imperial system has thus been neglected. By showing, as I have tried to do, how the imperial government undertook to maintain control over the inhabitants of the countryside, how these inhabitants reacted to that control, and how the natural and historical environment influenced both the operation of the system of control and the behavior of those that came under its sway, I have attempted to arrive at a more or less adequate view of the matter and at the same time to dispel some of the major misconceptions that have gained currency in certain quarters.

To approach this aim I have striven for concreteness and preciseness in presentation, even at the risk of burdening the reader with cumbersome details. I believe that only in this way can the picture be brought into sufficiently sharp focus to give an accurate impression. Such an approach has channeled my efforts into a historical rather than a theoretical treatment of the subject. I am concerned, in other words, with exhibiting the relevant situations and processes that had historical reality at a given time rather than with general concepts or inclusive schematisms for universal application. I have tried to scrutinize each set of facts from as many different angles and in as many different situations as the data permit. And as the full significance of any institution or set of institutions cannot be grasped without reference to the historical and social context, I have often found it necessary to deal with matters that transcend the subject of immediate concern or to allude to situations that extend beyond the period under consideration.

SOURCES

The use of source material requires care. Writings on China and things Chinese of the nineteenth century are readily available. However, information directly germane to the present investigation is not too ample nor is every bit of it trustworthy. How to treat such material constitutes a methodological problem.

Rural inhabitants of imperial China were mostly illiterate. Their workaday conditions and doings did not as a rule engage the attention of those who could write and therefore remained largely unrecorded. Officials and scholars who made frequent references to "the distress and sufferings of the people" were more likely to repeat generalities than to portray the concrete realities of rural life. Moreover, the relatively small amount of pertinent information which I have been able to muster from diverse Chinese sources does not always fully or directly serve my purpose. It has been said that the historian of primitive economic life must usually be content with documents preserved only in fragments and written by men who knew nothing of the

problems that interest us today. Dealing with a relatively recent period of Chinese history and having a comparatively large amount of accessible material to draw upon, I am more fortunate than the historian of primitive economic life. Nevertheless, I cannot help wishing
that the writers of Chinese documents had anticipated some of our
problems and needs. Writers of the nineteenth century often left behind them pieces of tantalizing information but stopped short of making
the matters sufficiently transparent to readers of a later age. Or, as
in other instances, useful data concerning one locality or one period
are found in a certain source, but comparable or matching records for
other localities or periods are unavailable anywhere.

Owing partly to an actual dearth of material and partly to the limited
amount of records to which I had access, the data used in this study
are not uniformly adequate or evenly balanced. The resulting view of
rural China is thus a mosaic of historical fragments, with better definition and fuller details at some places but with gaps or areas of hazi-
ness at others. To compensate for this defect and to guard against
misunderstanding, the following expedients were sometimes resorted
to. Whenever possible, the locality and time of each piece of information is indicated so that the reader may appraise not only the perti-
nence of the individual items cited but also the validity of the conclusions based upon them. In some instances a limited quantity of data
relative to conditions prevailing before or after the nineteenth century was used to help fill some of the inevitable gaps.

Allowance for possible biases or inaccuracies in the material used
presented another problem. Official documents, from which a considerable amount of information was drawn, were written almost exclusively from the government's standpoint. Moreover, officials in
the imperial days were prone to exaggerate, to tone down, or to whitewash matters as convenience or necessity dictated. They were inclined to regard the reports required of them as an annoying routine
to be dispatched with as little fuss about accuracy as possible. Documents that involved matters of grave consequence were given more
careful treatment, but with a view not to insuring exactitude or truth-
fulness but rather to making certain that the officials concerned might
not be implicated or contract greater responsibilities than they had to.

Local gazetteers, which furnished a good deal of indispensable information, were written often with little more objectivity or accuracy
than were government documents. Some of these records of local conditions, events, and personalities were more painstakingly or com-
petently done than others; but a considerable number are marred by
the partiality, dishonesty, or carelessness of contributors. The local
gentry and in some instances the local officials who dictated the actual
contents as well as the editorial policies of the works sponsored by
them, were too often not above prejudice or selfishness. The fact that

any single gazetteer was written by a number of persons whose scholarly qualifications were not uniformly high and who frequently executed their assignments with poor coordination and inadequate supervision,[1] points to the possibility of unintentional errors and omissions, even where willful misrepresentation was not practiced. A well-known Chinese historian went so far as to say that local gazetteers were among those categories of writings to which credence could not be lent.[2] Most of the gazetteers contain sections dealing with geographical and related matters. Even there the data are too often inadequate and inaccurate. In many instances later editions of a gazetteer reproduced entries from editions compiled decades or centuries earlier without making necessary provisions to reflect whatever changes may have taken place during the interval and without warning the reader of the fact. Occasionally, in small or remote localities, a dearth of reliable information prevented even the most conscientious compilers from producing satisfactory records.[3]

Private writings posed no less a problem. The authors of these belonged to the literate segment of the population, and many of them were gentry. Their views and attitudes were therefore similar to those of the writers who drafted government documents and compiled local gazetteers. Writing in a private capacity, they may well have been freer than the writers of government documents to state the truth as they saw it and to express their convictions as they wished. But there is no assurance that they were on that account necessarily free from bias or inaccuracy.

All this points to one conclusion: circumspection is required in using source material. I have avoided using any writing that appears to be of doubtful reliability; but in a few instances I had to choose between using doubtful information and having no information at all and took the lesser of the two evils. The margin of error was narrowed by checking such information against the known historical background and against accounts given by Western writers whenever available, and by making due allowance for biases or distortions where these were known to exist.

Western writers, particularly those of the nineteenth century who were in China to witness happenings and conditions of the empire, have furnished much useful information. The fact that they came from lands with widely different cultural traditions gave them certain advantages denied to native writers. They were free from the intimate prejudices of the latter and could observe the developments with some detachment. Furthermore, being in a strange land where even items of everyday life demanded reflection, they were likely to discern significant facts that easily escaped the notice of native writers. For instance, the vivid descriptions of rural scenes and activities found in some Western writings would have been regarded by Chinese writers as too commonplace to merit recording. This is not saying that Western writers of the nineteenth century did not have disadvantages of their own. They were often inclined to interpret Chinese ways and institutions in terms of their own societal background; few of them escaped entirely the distorting effects of what may be called "cultural apperception." And, owing to personal idiosyncrasies, prepossessions, or sheer incompetence, some of them gave accounts that are misleading or confusing.[4] I found it no less necessary to exercise caution in using Western writings than in using Chinese material.

I used information relative to conditions prevailing later than the nineteenth century when I felt that such information would shed light on the period under investigation or when data directly pertinent to that period were not available at the time of writing. Obviously there is some risk in using such material. But as the changes that occurred in rural life during the nineteenth century and in the opening decades of the twentieth do not appear to have been extensive or basic, any error that may result from inferring earlier conditions from accounts of later situations would not materially affect the accuracy of the picture.[5] It may be noted also that I made use of such accounts sparingly and in only a few instances.

ACKNOWLEDGMENTS

I wish to thank my colleagues in the Far Eastern and Russian Institute at the University of Washington who at various times took part in the Modern Chinese History Project. My thanks are due in particular to Chung-li Chang, Franz Michael, Vincent Y. C. Shih, George E. Taylor, and Hellmut Wilhelm. They overcame my initial hesitancy to undertake a challenging task and thus gave me an opportunity to acquaint myself with a field into which I had hitherto had no more than a casual glimpse. They offered me encouragement and advice at all stages of the preparation of this volume, and I found their words helpful and stimulating. Even when I could not bring myself to accept their opinion on some point, I was invariably persuaded by their searching criticisms to re-examine the case, and as a result was often able to present the evidence in a more suitable way or formulate the conclusions in a more careful manner. I alone, of course, am responsible for the shortcomings that still remain.

I am indebted to George E. Taylor, who read my lengthy manuscript several times through and made valuable suggestions toward its improvement, and to Gladys Greenwood, who edited the manuscript with admirable judiciousness and meticulous care. My thanks are due also to Mercedes MacDonald, who undertook the laborious task of checking the references, quotations, notes, and bibliography and prepared the manuscript for the printer. For their generous help I am very grateful.

Kung-chuan Hsiao

University of Washington
October 10, 1957

Prefatory Note to the Second Printing

This book is here reprinted without textual change. Since its publication six years ago the writer, drawn into another area of research, has gained no additional information pertinent to its subject matter significant enough to justify a revision. He must therefore apologize for all the faults and inadequacies that are inherited from the first printing.

K. C. H.

Seattle, Washington
May, 1967

CONTENTS

TABLES

Part One

THE DIVISIONS OF RURAL AREAS

Chapter 1

VILLAGES, MARKETS, AND TOWNS

THE PROBLEM OF CONTROL

Autocracies such as imperial China presuppose a sharp distinction between rulers and subjects and a consequent divergence of interests between them. [1] The first problem of an autocratic ruler is, therefore, how to maintain firm control of his subjects so that he and his heirs may sit securely on the throne.

The solution as it was worked out in China during the successive dynasties from Ch'in to Ch'ing consisted essentially in the development of an administrative apparatus which helped the emperors to assure obedience and forestall rebellions, partly by ministering to the basic material needs of their subjects so that few of them would be driven by unbearable hardships "to tread the dangerous path," partly by inculcating in their minds carefully chosen precepts (mostly from doctrines of the Confucian tradition) that tended to make them accept or acquiesce in the existing order, and partly by keeping constant surveillance over them so that "bad people" might be detected and dealt with in time. This administrative apparatus, reinforced at strategic points by a military apparatus, made it possible for a single dynasty to control a vast realm for a considerable period of time.

The basic principles of imperial control had undergone little modification over since the time of the first emperor of Ch'in. However, as a result of accumulated experience and the ingenuity of some of the emperors of subsequent dynasties, refinements and improvements in the details of the administrative apparatus were introduced from time to time—generally in favor of increased centralization, more minute regulations, stricter surveillance, and tighter control. When the Ch'ing dynasty established itself in 1644, it took over the highly sophisticated system left behind by the defunct Ming dynasty, added further refinements of its own, and thus brought the imperial structure to its final development. Understandably, to the Ch'ing rulers who were alien conquerors of China, the problem of control was even more urgent than it had been to their immediate predecessors, who replaced the alien rule of Yüan with a native dynasty.

3

The extensive territory and immense population of China made imperial control a formidable task indeed. To handle this task adequately an elaborate administrative hierarchy was evolved, with the emperor at the apex and a huge officialdom below. Directly under the emperor stood the central hierarchy with an impressive array of offices, including the Grand Secretariat *(nei-ko)*, the Grand Council *(chün-chi-ch'u*, established in 1730), and the Six Boards *(liu pu)*, to mention only a few of the most important. The ranking officials of these yamen, individually or in groups, advised the emperor on weighty matters when required, helped him to reach decisions, and, assisted by their subordinates, carried out his orders or transmitted them to lower administrative levels.

Through a system of "local government" the administrative arm of the imperial government extended from Peking to every part of the empire. Each of the eighteen provinces of China proper was subdivided into a varying number of administrative divisions, namely, prefectures *(fu)* and districts *(chou* and *hsien,* sometimes referred to as "counties"). [2] With a few exceptions a governor *(hsün-fu)* headed the provincial administration, and was flanked by a provincial treasurer *(pu-cheng-shih)* and a provincial judge *(an-ch'a-shih)*. In some instances, a governor-general *(tsung-tu,* sometimes referred to as "viceroy") was appointed for a single province (Chihli and Szechwan where no governors were appointed); in other instances, a governor-general presided over two or three provinces, each of which had its own governor. The chief official of a prefecture was the prefect *(chih-fu)* and that of a district, the magistrate *(chih-chou* or *chih-hsien)*. These officials were placed under the direct supervision of the provincial authorities and, in fact, were assigned to their respective posts by the governors or governors-general concerned. The magistrates occupied the lowest level of the regular administrative hierarchy and were often described as "local officials" *(ti-fang-kuan)* or as "officials in intimate contact with the people" *(ch'in min chih kuan)*. [3]

Diverse methods were employed to keep the gigantic, sprawling administrative apparatus under effective central control. For instance, to prevent any imperial servant from acquiring undue influence or excessive authority, every important post was shared by two or more officials of equal rank and powers and, at the same time, a single high-ranking official was often assigned to serve concurrently in more than one capacity. The functions of government offices were rarely defined precisely or demarked in any clear way; in fact, the powers and responsibilities of important officials were deliberately made to overlap. The appointments, promotions, and dismissals of all local officials, from governors-general down to district magistrates, were reserved for the central government in Peking. These functionaries were as a rule not allowed to serve in their home provinces; they were rarely permitted to remain in one post beyond a few years. Discretionary power was very sparingly given to officials, even those with great responsibilities. Every administrative decision and action had to be reported to Peking, including matters that were merely routine. These and other devices of a similar nature were so consistently and effectively applied that, as a noted Chinese writer of the nineteenth century observed, the entire officialdom remained placid during the two and a half centuries of the Ch'ing dynasty's existence. [4]

Control of officialdom, however, was only part of the task. There was also the problem of keeping peace and order in the numerous cities and towns and in the innumerable villages of the empire. In fact, while officialdom itself constituted an object of imperial control, it was at the same time an instrument of control forged by the imperial rulers to gain an administrative hold on the general population. Shaping this indispensable instrument in itself was no easy undertaking, but to apply it effectively over the common people presented to the emperors an even more challenging problem.

The immense geographical expanse of the empire and its limited facilities for communication and transportation, coupled with the illiteracy and political indifference of the overwhelming majority of the inhabitants, rendered it exceedingly difficult even to make known the laws and decrees of the government, to say nothing of enforcing them or carrying them out. The district magistrate, who was supposed to administer directly to the people's needs, had under his jurisdiction an area often over a thousand square miles in extent. With a total of roughly 1,500 magistrates in all types of *chou* and *hsien,* there was on the average one magistrate for 100,000 inhabitants (calculated on the basis of the 1749 official figures) or 250,000 (1819 official figures). [5] The magistrate was so overburdened with a wide range of vaguely prescribed duties that he had little time or facilities to do any of them well, if indeed he had the intention or capacity to do so at all. [6] It was perhaps not too difficult to achieve a semblance of efficient administration in the city, where the seat of the *chou* or *hsien* yamen was located; the same thing may be said of a *chen* (town), where a submagistrate assisted the magistrate of the district to keep order. But it was a different situation in the open countryside that surrounded the city and the town—the rural areas where the bulk of the people lived. The magistrate and his assistants could hardly keep in touch with all the villages and villagers, even in a comparatively small district, if indeed these officials took their duties seriously enough to attempt such contact.

The imperial rulers did not allow this partial administrative vacuum to remain unfilled. Since ancient times there had been groupings and divisions on a local scale and agents of the government in rural China. The subadministrative divisions set up by the Ch'in dynasty served as the first working model for subsequent regimes. [7] The

Ch'ing emperors took over the system as it existed in the Ming dynasty; they modified it in some significant details and made use of any additional local organizations that appeared to be helpful in subadministrative control. The resulting system, viewed in historical context, was remarkably comprehensive and ingenious.

Some of the basic principles that underlay this system and its chief problems should be examined briefly before we venture into description and analysis of its component parts. In the first place, realizing that it was impractical to extend the regular administrative arm further down than the district magistrate and his subordinates, the Ch'ing emperors drafted local inhabitants to assist in rural control as their predecessors had done. Thus, the headmen of the *pao-chia* (police) and *li-chia* (revenue collection) divisions and the managers of the rural granaries were selected from the inhabitants of the villages or neighborhoods where these institutions were to operate. The clans (groups held together by kinship bonds), which prospered especially in provinces south of the Yellow River, were sometimes made to serve as supplementary instruments of surveillance and indoctrination. The advantages of such arrangements are obvious. On the one hand, the local inhabitants were more likely than government officials to know the conditions and personalities of their own home places and were therefore in a better position to cope with local problems that might arise or at least to furnish information that the government might desire. On the other hand, by drawing assistance from local inhabitants to implement control—by imposing upon some of them the responsibility to inform the government of misdeeds and wrongdoers—villagers might be deterred from breaking the laws even where they were not directly under the watchful eyes of officials.

To prevent the development of undue power or influence in the rural groups or divisions, a number of restraining devices were employed. Every local agency or organization, whether sponsored by the government or of local origin, was placed under the control or supervision of the magistrate. The government always reserved the right to suppress any group or activity which it deemed pernicious. The hand of the government, acting through the magistrate, was ever ready to strike; and when circumstances demanded, the troops stationed in many strategic points of the empire could be called into action. Moreover, the selection of village headmen and rural managers was usually subject to the review of the magistrate, if indeed the appointments were not actually made by the magistrate himself. While historically-evolved rural groups and divisions were normally allowed to exist, artificial divisions were created by the government and were juxtaposed beside or superimposed upon them, so that the former might not grow into integral centers of local power. Thus, in the *pao-chia* and *li-chia* divisions the households of the countryside were regimented into units of ten and multiples of ten, regardless of village or other natural boundaries.

The idea of local self-government was alien to the system of rural control. Any local initiative or community life that was displayed in the villages was tolerated by the government either to facilitate control or because interference was deemed unnecessary. Villages and clans and other rural groups were, in the eyes of the government, so many convenient points through which subadministrative control might be extended into the countryside.

It is worth while to note that even in employing suppressive measures, the government drew upon the assistance of local inhabitants as far as was consistent with expediency or safety. The *pao-chia* system and to some extent the clan organizations, as we shall see later, were made to help in keeping records of the inhabitants, watching their daily doings, reporting suspicious characters and offensive deeds, and apprehending criminals wanted by the government. When local people were made to supply their own spies and sheriffs, they might be persuaded to act prudently even if no government officials were present; the possibility of criminals finding shelter in the neighborhoods or would-be rebels brewing seditious schemes in remote villages might thus be reduced.

The imperial rulers, however, were astute enough not to maintain control exclusively by means of suppressive measures. Attention was also paid to matters that tended to render the inhabitants less inclined to break laws or to defy the authorities. Steps were taken, on the one hand, to provide the minimum conditions for rural inhabitants to gain a livelihood and to provide against natural or man-made disasters. The imperial government undertook, among other things, to reclaim land, to promote or encourage irrigation and flood prevention, and to conduct famine relief work. On the other hand, methods of popular indoctrination were applied to various segments of the population, with a view to upholding a system of values that would prove advantageous to the imperial regime. Following broadly the tradition established in the preceding dynasty, the Ch'ing rulers lent official support to the accepted social and moral precepts of the "orthodox" school of Neo-Confucianism. Through the "examination and school" system they sought to instill the state ideology in the minds of scholars and officials; by relying upon the influence of these men and by means of a variety of institutions, including the rural schools, popular religion, and the clan organization, they undertook to extend this ideology to the untutored millions in the countryside.

It is difficult to evaluate precisely the efficacy of this system of rural control. It must have contributed, to an undetermined extent, to the stability of the Ch'ing regime—one of the relatively long-lived dynasties in Chinese history, but evidence indicates that it never operated in a manner fully satisfactory to the imperial rulers, who perhaps had never expected it to produce perfect results.

Indeed, it is quite clear that the rural control system of the Ch'ing dynasty was not without some grave shortcomings. In fact, the very merits that persuaded the emperors to adopt it proved in the long run to be the source of its weaknesses. As an inseparable part of the imperial structure, it shared the essential qualities of the total system and therefore had to stand or fall with it.

The first major difficulty of rural control was that its effective operation presupposed an administrative condition which the imperial government could not provide. As already noted, in an autocracy in which the interests of the rulers and subjects were assumed to be separate if not incompatible, the entire administrative system was built on the basis of suspicion. Imperial security was the primary concern of the rulers and their first axiom of security was to hold all power in their own hands, to keep the subjects habitually in awe of that power, and at the same time to discourage anyone—scholars and officials as well as common people—from developing independence and self-reliance. Applying this axiom to the practical conduct of administration, the emperors found it prudent not to give to any official opportunities for exercising the initiative, independent judgment, or unhampered authority necessary for proper performance of his prescribed duties. Political safety was deliberately stressed at the expense of administrative efficiency. Consistent and long application of this policy eventually demoralized the officialdom. Few public functionaries, from the highest ranking mandarins in Peking to the humble magistrates of remote districts, made efforts to do things that might bring true advantages to their sovereigns or give material benefits to the people; most merely sought to keep out of trouble and to look out for their personal advantage and profit. By the beginning of the nineteenth century loyalty to the dynasty had become a rare official virtue, and administrative indifference and ineptitude a common vice. A decayed officialdom not only lowered the prestige of the imperial regime but affected adversely every other aspect of the administrative apparatus. In particular, the degeneration of the administration at the district level rendered the proper operation of the various institutions of rural control practically impossible. For without the effective official prompting and supervision on which the whole system of rural control hinged, the *pao-chia, li-chia,* and other institutions inevitably deteriorated into empty routines or in the worst cases turned into standing opportunities for subadministrative corruption.

A further crucial difficulty of rural control was that it created conditions tending to weaken the rural foundations of the empire. The rural inhabitants of imperial China, mostly peasants and practically all illiterate, since ancient times had never been generally active or aggressive. Their attention and energy were devoted to eking out a meager livelihood. Driven by desperation and lured by promises of a change for the better, villagers had helped to topple dynasties on more than one occasion; but under normal conditions and when left to themselves, they were comparatively unambitious and politically ineffectual. Accordingly, the problem of controlling the peasant masses may appear to have been a relatively simple matter. But the characteristic "passivity" of the rural population imposed definite limitations on the effectiveness of control. The method of employing local inhabitants to implement subadministrative control, though theoretically sound, failed in practice because of the reluctance of the inhabitants to serve, their incapacity to do the tasks expected of them, and in many instances the readiness of those employed to use the machinery of rural control to further their private interests instead of to serve the imperial cause.

Moreover, official supervision, indispensable to keeping the control system in operation, precluded local pride or *esprit de corps*, equally indispensable to the continued effective operation of the various agencies or organizations. The magistrate, bound by rigid regulations (issued from Peking with little regard for divergent conditions in different parts of the empire) and given practically no discretionary powers, seldom took the trouble to adapt imperial policies to the requirements of local circumstances. As a result the inhabitants often came to regard anything that involved the government with indifference, suspicion, or fear. One cannot deny that the mere presence of the subadministrative instruments of control in the countryside must have exerted a deterrent influence on many a would-be troublemaker. One cannot suppose, however, that rural control as maintained by the Ch'ing rulers ever instilled in the minds of the villagers any sentiment of positive loyalty toward their sovereigns or toward their immediate community. The people of imperial China, to borrow a well-known phrase, were like "a dish of loose sand."

Popular indoctrination apparently brought some results, but here again they were essentially negative in character. Villagers were taught an ideology calculated to bolster up their "conservatism," to condition them mentally to obey authority without question rather than to prepare them to cope with the concrete problems of life by improving their personal capacities. Rural China was thus kept virtually stagnant, intellectually and economically unable to meet the challenge of changed circumstances; the inhabitants became helpless against grave disasters wrought by nature or against oppressions inflicted by local bullies and yamen underlings. The foundations of the empire, ironically, were weakened by the very process of control.

So long as conditions remained broadly favorable to the regime, things appeared tolerably quiet. But as soon as serious crises struck, as in the nineteenth century, the mortal flaws of the imperial structure began to show. Famines occurred frequently and over wide areas, at a time when the administration had deteriorated at all levels and was less capable than before to deal with these problems. The intrusion of Western powers at this critical juncture dealt damaging blows to imperial prestige and authority and played havoc with the native economy, especially in places where Western commerce and industry made substantial inroads. The rural masses, hitherto placid by force of habit, traditional inertia, and the restraining influences of imperial control, broke out into violent uprisings where the disturbing factors were most actively at work. Previously the imperial rulers had no more than an incomplete hold on rural China; now the complicated apparatus they had used to maintain that hold proved virtually useless. It would be inaccurate to say that the atrophy of the system of rural control brought about this state of affairs. The truth is that in the closing decades of the nineteenth century the entire imperial structure, of which this system was a part, was in a state of total degeneration. The Ch'ing dynasty, and with it the Chinese dynastic system, was in fact rapidly drawing to an end.

THE CONFIGURATION OF RURAL CHINA

Rural China was not closely organized but it was not amorphous. The vast countryside *(hsiang)* that lay outside the cities *(ch'eng,* seats of the provincial, prefectural, and district administrations),[8] contained a variety of divisions and centers of rural life. Some of these, which we shall call administrative divisions, were set up more or less arbitrarily by the imperial government for the purpose of control. Others were results of natural growth quite independent of government action, although the government might lend them official or semi-official recognition and thus weave them into the fabric of control.

Except for a few localities where rural families lived in scattered individual farmhouses, as in some parts of Szechwan, and some places where livelihood was extremely meager, as the hilly land of some provinces, the inhabitants of rural China distributed themselves in concentrations of diverse sizes and forms, namely, villages *(ts'un* or *chuang)*, rural markets *(shih, chi, ch'ang,* etc.), and towns *(chen)*. Local economic conditions were chiefly responsible for their appearance, although social and political forces may also have been at work. For instance, the presence of a river or stream near arable land, furnishing adequate water for irrigation and other purposes, might constitute the material basis for the origin and development of a village.

The number of villages in a given district, as well as the size, degree of organization, and amount of communal activities in individual villages, varied with density of local population, size of the district, and above all geographical and economic conditions of the locality.[9] The larger and more prosperous villages often displayed qualities of a "community. "[10] The village was in fact the basic unit of Chinese rural community life, as the family constituted the primary unit of Chinese social life.

The village, however, was not economically self-contained. The material needs of villagers might be quite simple and few, but they were likely to go beyond the limited resources of their own community. Some of the larger villages met part of these needs by having "business streets," strings of small stores. But these villages, together with smaller ones without such facilities, depended upon nearby rural markets or towns to exchange goods and services to satisfy their economic needs.

Rural markets varied in size and structure. They often developed from the "business streets" of prosperous villages; some were distinguished from ordinary villages mainly by the presence of periodic trading activities. A rural market was in reality a village that had acquired a specialized economic function. The assumption of such a function introduced certain changes into the village. A new name was sometimes given to a village which had become a market; a number of nonfarming inhabitants invariably moved into it. Rural markets, however, retained the essential features of rural communities, and their inhabitants remained predominantly agricultural.

Towns were usually outgrowths of rural markets. As the economy of a rural area expanded, the market serving the adjacent villages became a center of increasingly extensive trading activities. A point was eventually reached when this community lost much of its purely agricultural character and emerged as a town. The augmented trading facilities which it now afforded induced villagers from a wider area to come to buy or sell. In a few instances, however, towns resulted from the growth of native industries; Ching-te-chen (Kiangsi), where the finest porcelain was made, was an outstanding example.

There were therefore two types of towns—trading and manufacturing. Towns were no longer rural communities pure and simple; in fact, the more prosperous of them might possess walls and other characteristic marks of a city. Moreover, owing to the economic importance of a town, it might be chosen by the imperial government to serve as a subsidiary administrative center with a submagistrate assigned to assist the magistrate of the district concerned, or it might be made a garrison point where regular troops were stationed and held ready to meet any emergency that might arise in the area. Such a town could hardly be distinguished from a city except by its official name and by the absence of a magistrate's yamen.

Villages, rural markets, and to some extent towns constituted the chief aspects of the rural configuration. It will be necessary to describe them in fuller details in the subsequent pages, but for the moment we must pause to explain briefly the *Hsiang*, a rural division of

a different nature. (The word *Hsiang* is capitalized to distinguish it
from *hsiang*, "countryside.")

The *Hsiang* division, as it existed in the nineteenth century and
throughout Ch'ing times, was a segment of the countryside lying outside a city and containing a number of villages, rural markets, and
perhaps one or more towns. The number of such segments varied,
but in a large number of districts there were four Hsiang in each,
one outside each of the four gates of the walled city. A typical example
of such an arrangement was afforded by Wei Chou (Chihli) which had
its four *Hsiang* named as follows:[11]

	Villages
Tung (East) Hsiang	174
Hsi (West) Hsiang	70
Nan (South) Hsiang	153
Pei (North) Hsiang	89

The *Hsiang* division does not appear to have been the product of
natural growth, as its component villages were. It was known in ancient times and in all probability was originally an administrative
division made by the government.[12] In Ch'ing times it ceased to be
an official administrative division but was allowed to stand and frequently made use of in rural control. In fact, the *Hsiang* became in
a number of instances a unit of intervillage cooperation or organization; it had semiofficial recognition and occupied a definite place in
the pattern of rural life. *

THE PHYSICAL ASPECTS OF THE VILLAGE

Villages in different parts of the Chinese empire varied considerably
in their physical structure.[13] Indeed, the fact that villages were natural growths accounted for their lack of uniformity.[14] The situation was
clearly described by a Western writer:

> If, in certain respects, Chinese cities appear to be "laid out" with
> an attempt at uniformity, as much cannot be said of the villages.
> These are developed just as circumstances happen to make them. . . .

---

*The terms *hsiang*, "countryside," and *Hsiang*, a rural division,
both written in Chinese as 鄉 , should be distinguished from each
other and from the homonym 廂 , *"Hsiang"* (in quotation marks here
and hereafter), which indicates a suburban division made by the government to facilitate revenue collection (see chapters 2 and 4 on the
li-chia system).

> The first settler built his dwelling where he thought best; another fol-
> lowed his example. It was necessary to have a path to get to these,
> and soon. . . another path, or a continuation of the first, running,
> it may be, at sharp angles. Other houses, other paths, other streets;
> but no system about them. [15]

The formal arrangement of the village was after all not so important
as its content—its size and material conditions. The influence of geographical and economic circumstances on this aspect of the village
was too obvious to escape the attention of even casual observers.
M. Huc, though not always accurate in his descriptions, was broadly
correct in pointing out the difference in distribution and general appearance of villages in certain central and western provinces. He
wrote in the mid-nineteenth century:

> It is easy to form perfectly opposite ideas of the population of China,
> according to the route by which you traverse it. If, for example, in
> the central provinces you travel along the roads, you would be led
> to believe the country much less populous than it really is. The vil-
> lages are few and far between, the waste lands so considerable that
> you might at times fancy yourself in the deserts of Tartary. But trav-
> erse the same province by the canals or rivers, and the aspect of the
> country is entirely changed. Often you pass huge cities, containing not
> less than two or three millions of inhabitants, whilst smaller towns
> and great villages follow each other in almost uninterrupted succes-
> sion. [16]

His comparison of the villages in Hupeh and Szechwan provinces is
also illustrative of this point:

> The province of Hou-pé [Hupeh] is in all respects very inferior to
> that of Sse-tchouen (Szechwan). The land, which is not very fertile,
> is covered with a multitude of ponds and marshes, of which the Chi-
> nese, industrious and patient as they are, can make but little use.
> The villages have in general a very poor and wretched appearance.
> The inhabitants have an unhealthy and rather wild aspect, and are
> frequently affected by cutaneous diseases. . . . It is said that in the
> province of Hou-pé, the harvest of a year is seldom sufficient for a
> month's consumption. The great populations of the towns are supplied
> from the neighbouring provinces, and especially Sse-tchouen, which
> cannot in ten years consume the produce of one.
> It would seem as if the richness and beauty of Sse-tchouen had ex-
> ercised a great influence on its inhabitants; for the manners are much
> superior to those of the Chinese of the other provinces. The great
> towns are, at least relatively, clean and neat. The aspect of the vil-
> lages, and even of the farms, bears witness to the comfortable cir-
> cumstances of their inhabitants. [17]

The author may have exaggerated the opulence of Szechwan[18] or underestimated the productivity of the soil of Hupeh.[19] But he was not far from the truth in noticing the differences between the villages of these provinces and in attributing the cause of these differences to geographical conditions.

Similar if not more pronounced differences were found between villages of northern and southern provinces, where the geographical characteristics form such a clear contrast as to lead a modern authority to regard these general regions as "two Chinas."[20] Geographical environment together with historical background seemed to have shaped the rural communities of these regions into two distinguishable varieties. According to a modern Chinese writer, villages in the Yellow River Valley were generally formed by compact clusters of farmsteads, whereas in the Yangtze Valley the peasant households were often more loosely arranged. "Close-dwelling" villages were typical of North China; "loose-dwelling" villages, of South China.[21] Northern and southern villages were marked off also by a perceptible difference in their organization: the influence of the clan organization was more noticeable in many southern villages and was comparatively unimportant in the north.[22]

The influence of economic conditions on rural life is most clearly evident in the differences in distribution and size of the villages. A survey made of northeastern China in the 1870's and 1880's by some British military officers revealed the fact that villages were situated farther apart or closer together in proportion to the fertility of the soil. One of these officers reported:

> The villages are rarely more than 4 miles apart in barren districts; usually much closer, i.e., from 1/2 to 1 mile apart in fertile districts. . . .
> The above remarks apply equally well to all the fertile parts of north-east China.[23]

In areas where the soil was very poor, the villages were not only farther apart but also smaller. Another reported:

> None of the villages in this country have any depth; they consist of little more than a row of houses on each side of the street. There would probably be from 80 to 100 houses on each side of the road in the length of a mile.[24]

In many other places the villages were even smaller. According to another report concerning an area which showed "signs of occasional flooding," diminutive hamlets were encountered on the road leading from Chi-k'ou to Tsang-chou (Chihli):

Tsz-tsun; 10 houses, where there is a small pond of brackish water.
. . . Very scant cultivation near the village.
12 1/2 miles. —A village of three houses 1/4 mile to the north.
13 1/2 miles. —Ma-ying; a village of 25 houses.
At Ma-ying the appearance of the country improves, and some
signs of prosperity were visible in the shape of some cows, calves,
and ponies.[25]

Naturally, wherever conditions were better, villages were larger and
more prosperous in appearance. Further west on the same road:

22 miles. —San-chi-hu; a village of 100 houses, with a pond and
wells. . . .
38 1/4 miles. —Hsin-chuang; a village of 300 houses. This village
is more prosperous in appearance than any to the east. The houses
are better built, the people better clad, and many of them apparently
well-to-do.
The cultivated area in this neighborhood appears very considerable, as compared with the size and distance apart of the villages;
and it is said that in favoured years the produce of grain is somewhat in excess of the requirements of the population. During the
past years, 1873, 1874, 1875, the harvest had been average, but
scarcity was feared in 1876.[26]

Other factors, of course, influenced the physical aspects of the village. A convenient location that blessed it with immunity from floods,
or a government depot that lent it economic affluence, often enabled it
to grow beyond the average size. About sixteen miles west on the road
from Chi-k'ou to Tsang-chou, was Wang-hsü-tzu, "a village of 400
houses or 4,000 inhabitants, built on a mound raised about five feet
above the surrounding country, apparently to protect it from floods."[27]
Pay-tsang, located on the road leading from Peking to Tientsin, was
a large village on the Pei-ho. "There are numerous brick buildings
here in which rice is stored. . . . This is one of the depôts for the
storage of the rice tribute."[28] While various factors were decisive
in particular instances, the quality of the soil remained in general
the most important single factor in determining the physical makeup
of the villages.
Since the soil of some southern provinces was more fertile than
that of most northern provinces, the population of villages there was
often larger. Some villages in Kwangtung, where favorable agricultural conditions were reinforced by other economic advantages, were
said to have contained huge populations. For example, S. W. Williams
described the villages in Nan-hai Hsien in the 1880's:

The people are grouped into hamlets and villages. . . . In the district of Nan-hai, which forms the western part of the city of Canton, and the surrounding country for more than a hundred square miles, there are one hundred and eighty . . . villages; the population of each . . . varies from two hundred and upwards to one hundred thousand, but ordinarily ranges between three hundred and thirty-five hundred. [29]

The 1883 edition of the gazetteer of Ju-lin Hsiang (a part of Chiu-chiang, southwest of Nan-hai), afforded the following data:[30]

Villages	Households	Inhabitants
6 east-side	4,572	25,318
16 west-side	3,462	19,334
9 south-side	2,108	11,466
9 north-side	7,033	36,461
Total 40	17,175	92,579

The average number of inhabitants in this locality was about 2,300 per village and in the more densely populated east-side villages about 4,200. Moreover, the compiler of this gazetteer indicated that among the forty-one villages under consideration, the largest contained over 1,000 households each, while the smallest had forty. Since the average number of persons in each household was not less than five, the total number of inhabitants of one of the largest villages must have been well over 5,000.

Such oversized rural communities were by no means the prevailing type in South China. There were tiny hamlets in the south as in the north, and the majority of southern villages were much smaller than these Kwangtung specimens. For instance, L. Donnat, writing around 1860 about a village near Ningpo (Chekiang), discovered that "la population de Ouang-fou est d'environ 120 familles, qui, à cinq membres per famille, forment une total de 600 habitants. Cette population est entièrement formée de cultivateurs."[31] While villages with several hundred inhabitants like this one were common in South China, the exceptionally large villages with a population of 100,000 (like the one in Nan-hai) were significant because they showed that under especially favorable circumstances rural communities could become so prosperous that they were virtually towns, whether or not they were designated as such.

Regional differences should not obscure the differences within each of these general areas. The significant point is that the differences in the physical aspects of the villages—whether the comparison is made between villages in the same region or in different regions—illustrate the same point: the decisive influence of geographical and economic conditions. [32]

The amount of land under cultivation naturally varied with the size of the population. Among the few local gazetteers which supplied relevant figures, the 1875 edition of the *Cheng-ting hsien chih* (Cheng-ting was a district in western Chihli) gives some interesting data which show a general though not exact correlation between the amount of farm land and the size of village population. [33] The 1850 edition of the gazetteer of Ting Chou (Chihli) gives interesting details concerning the 321 villages, markets, and towns of this district. The size of these rural divisions varied widely; the largest of them had over 1,000 inhabitants, the smallest less than 100. The former group comprised about 9 per cent of the total, and the latter about 7 per cent. The greatest number of them, amounting to about 22.5 per cent, had a population of 100 to 199 persons each. [34] Tables 1 to 4 illustrate some of the conclusions suggested above. [35] Regrettably, we have no comparable data to show the conditions in South China.

TABLE 1
DESCRIPTION OF VILLAGES IN NORTH CHINA
(OVER 1,000 POPULATION)

Village	House-holds	Popu-lation	Regis-tered Land *(mow)*	Wells	Streets	Temples	Water Supply	Road
Lou-ti-ts'un	186	1,632	4,800	25	2	14	Creek	S. to Shen-ts'e Hsien
Ch'uan-ch'iu-ts'un	252	1,607	8,000	45	6	10		N. to Wang-tü Hsien
P'an-ts'un	297	1,570	2,300	17	2	5	River	S.E. 40 *li* to city
Tung-wang-ts'un	124	1,481	6,000	63	2	5		E. to Ch'i Chou
Ta-wang-lu-ts'un	232	1,469	9,400	9	4	2	Spring	E. to Ch'i Chou
Hsi-ting-ts'un	190	1,460	1,600	36	2	11	River	E. to Ch'i Chou
Hsi-shih-i-ts'un	225	1,370	6,300	15	4	3	River	S. 15 *li* to city
Pei-nei-pao-ts'un	200	1,353	5,600	20	3	10	Creek	S. to Shen-ts'e Hsien
Wang-ts'un	215	1,280	970	26	2	4	River	S.E. 40 *li* to city
Ta-hsi-chang-ts'un	274	1,236	4,200	15	7	25	River	S. 20 *li* to city
Hsiao-wang-lou-ts'un	136	1,235	5,400	5	2	2	Spring	S. to Ch'i Chou
T'ang-ch'eng-ts'un	214	1,223	4,900	23	3	5	River	S. 15 *li* to city
Kao-chiu-ts'un	210	1,223	9,140	30	5	12	River	E. to Wang-tu Hsien
Hsi-chang-ch'ien-ts'un	245	1,188	(?)480	15	4	14	River	S.E. to Shen-ts'e Hsien
Su-ch'üan-ts'un	209	1,173	3,100	40	3	18	River	S.E. 20 *li* to city
Hsin-chuang	166	1,168	6,100	35	3	4		E. to Shen-ts'e Hsien
P'ang-ts'un	214	1,149	3,300	34	5	19		E. to Ch'i Chou
Niu-tien-ts'un	213	1,047	4,500	24	4	2	River	W. to Hsin-lo Hsien
Tung-shih-i-ts'un	236	1,137	9,130	13	1	3	River	S.W. 15 *li* to city
Liu-chao-ts'un	220	1,120	4,900	23	3	5		S.W. 35 *li* to city
Hu-fang-ts'un	202	1,118	5,500	21	3	3		S. 30 *li* to city
Tung-liu-ch'un-ts'un	169	1,107	4,300	8	3	3	Spring	E. to Ch'i Chou
Ti-li-ts'un	179	1,104	3,200	10	7	3	Creek	E. to Ch'i Chou
Chai-ch'eng-ts'un	175	1,089	5,000	6	2	10		E. to Ch'i Chou
Hsi-ch'eng-ts'un	185	1,066	4,300	13	3	3	Creek	N. to Ch'i Chou
Tung-chang-ch'ien-ts'un	182	1,051	4,200	23	5	8	River	S.E. to Shen-ts'e Hsien
Yu-wei-ts'un	150	1,050	3,100	4	4	3	Creek	S.W. to Wu-chih Hsien
Pei-chü-yu-ts'un	161	1,008	6,000	28	3	7		S. to Wu-chih Hsien
TOTAL	5,561	34,724	134,620	826	97	203		

TABLE 2
DESCRIPTION OF VILLAGES IN NORTH CHINA
(100-199 POPULATION)

Village	House-holds	Popu-lation	Regis-tered Land (mow)	Wells	Streets	Temples	Water Supply	Road
P'i-chia-ts'un	15	103	500	12	2	3		N.E. to city
Ch'i-chia-chuang	17	104	400	9	1	2	Creek	
Pei-yang-chio	17	104	400	12	1	2	River	
Nan-ch'eng-ts'un	14	105	700	8	1	2		
Liu-chia-chuang	11	106	300	5	1	1		
Hsi-nan-ts'un	25	109	350	3	1	2		
Hsi-hu-ts'un	40	110	1,500	9	1	2		
Nan-shih-erh-li-p'u	4	113	500	30	1	4		
Pei-hsin-hsing	16	114	400	7	1	2		
Ting-ling-tien	16	115	1,200	19	3	2		
Tung-t'ung-fang-ts'un	29	117	300	12	1	8		S. to city
Wu-chia-chuang	30	118	300	7	1	6		to T'ang Hsien
Pei-ku-shan	23	118	1,250	18	2	3		
Lao-yeh-chuang	17	120	500	3	2	5		W. to city
Ling-pei-ts'un	24	123	500	7	1	3		
Ch'en-chia-chuang	29	124	1,300	7	1	4		
Hsin-ch'eng-ts'un	21	125	1,100	11	1	2		
Hsiao-chang-ts'un	24	125	1,000	8	2	2		
Mu-chia-chuang	24	125	1,500	3	2	2		
Ling-nan-ts'un	22	127	300	5	2	2		
Pai-chia-chuang	16	130	1,000	7	2	0		
Yo-liu-chuang	28	130	300	5	3	1		
Hsiao-hsin-chuang	30	131	2,000	2	2	7		
Chang-yao-chuang	22	133	300	14	1	1		
Ch'en-ts'un-ying	25	139	200	13	2	3		
Pa-li-tien	38	140	600	7	1	3		
Wu-ts'un-ts'un	29	141	300	3	2	4		
Ho-yang-p'ing-ts'un	35	144	600	9	3	2		
An-hui-t'ung-ts'un	27	145	800	15	2	4		
Hsin-chuang	38	148	500	0	1	2		
Hsi-shuang-t'un-ts'un	21	150	1,900	5	2	0		
Lu-chia-chuang	32	150	900	6	1	2		
Wang-chia-chuang	16	153	700	7	1	4	River	
Wang-shih-ying	28	153	400	3	2	2		
Fu-ts'un	31	153	900	8	1	2		
Ma-chia-ai	25	158	1,100	14	2	2		
Ch'en-chia-tso-ts'un	25	159	200	8	2	2		
Yen-chia-chuang	29	159	800	20	1	2		
Chung-p'ing-ku-ts'un	10	160	700	2	1	1		
Ta-hsing-chuang	15	160	500	5	1	2		
Li-chia-chuang	24	160	2,100	3	4	1		
Nan-ling-t'ou-ts'un	27	160	900	19	1	3		
Wei-chia-tung	30	163	1,000	2	1	3		
Yu-chia-tso	65	163	600	11	1	4		
Kao-chia-chuang	24	164	300	15	1	3		
Hu-kung-ch'eng-ts'un	23	170	600	8	1	4	River	
Tung-kan-te-ts'un	26	171	1,100	5	1	3		
Wang-hui-tung-ts'un	31	172	700	10	2	2	River	
T'i-ts'ui-ch'iu-ts'un	27	173	600	12	4	3		
Tung-chia-chuang	29	174	900	5	2	3	Creek	
Yin-chia-chuang	28	174	1,000	15	1	1		
Tung-han-ts'un	30	174	750	9	1	2		
Erh-lang-miao-ts'un	29	175	100	6	1	2		
Pei-erh-shih-li-chuang	34	176	400	5	1	4		
Ts'ao-ts'un	36	176	470	5	1	2		
Ts'ui-yüan-shih-ts'un	31	178	800	23	1	1		
Pei-erh-shih-li-p'u	34	178	400	6	1	4		
Wang-chia-chuang	38	178	400	0	1	4		
Pan-pi-tien	23	179	800	12	1	3		
Ho-chia-ying	31	179	600	5	1	2		
Yang-yao-ts'un	33	180	600	8	1	4		
Chung-ku-tung	33	183	200	8	3	5	Creek	
Liu-chia-chuang	38	183	600	8	1	2	River	
Hsin-ch'eng-ts'un	29	184	1,700	6	2	3		
Ta-chao-ts'un	36	184	500	4	2	4		S.W. to Wu-chih Hsien
Hou-hsin-chuang	44	184	200	5	1	6		N. to Wang-tu Hsien
Kung-chuang	73	184	600	8	1	2		
Ma-t'ou-ts'un	40	188	310	7	1	1		
Pei-ch'a-chi-ts'un	25	189	300	12	1	2		
Nan-hsüan-ts'un	35	189	800	8	2	2		
Li-yu-ts'un	80	195	800	11	1	3		
Pa-chio-lang-ts'un	30	197	1,200	19	3	2		
Kung-hui-t'ung-ts'un	34	199	600	9	1	2		
TOTAL	2,083	11,093	52,230					

TABLE 3
DESCRIPTION OF SMALL VILLAGES IN NORTH CHINA*
(LESS THAN 100 POPULATION)

Village	House-holds	Popu-lation	Regis-tered Land (mow)	Wells	Streets	Temples
Sung-chia-chuang	4	18	400	5	1	0
Hsiao-yang-yao-ts'un	5	20	100	5	1	2
Ch'i-chia-chuang	12	32	140	5	1	2
Hsia-chia-chuang	7	38	200	3	1	4
Nan-t'ung-fang-t'ung	8	38	700	3	1	1
Hsiao-wa-li-ts'un	11	50	350	7	1	1
Ch'ing-nan-hsüan-ts'un	20	51	300	4	1	2
Wu-chia-chuang	28	64	500	5	1	4
Hsiao-wa-fang-chuang	18	68	800	2	1	1
Nan-ho-ying-ts'un	12	70	1,100	9	1	2
Huang-chia-ying	24	70	500	3	4	4
Wang-yao-ts'un	15	72	300	9	1	2
Li-yao-ts'un	15	72	300	9	1	3
K'ang-chia-chuang	11	73	400	9	1	2
Ts'ai-chia-chuang	14	75	400	2	1	1
Liu-chia-tien	15	77	80	5	2	1
Yü-yün-shih-ts'un	18	84	800	8	1	4
Wang-yün-shih-ts'un	18	84	100	12	2	2
Liu-chia-tien	18	86	400	7	1	4
Pei-t'ao-ch'iu-ts'un	18	90	300	11	3	3
Kuan-chia-chuang	17	92	500	2	1	2
Wu-ting-chuang	9	93	1,100	11	1	1
TOTAL	317	1,417	9,770	135	30	47

*These villages had no thoroughfares leading directly to the district city or neighboring districts, and no adjacent body of water.

TABLE 4
PHYSICAL ASPECTS OF LARGE AND SMALL VILLAGES
IN NORTH CHINA

Population of Village	Average Land per Village (in mow)	Average Number of:			
		Wells per Village	Streets per Village	Temples per Village	Rivers, Creeks
Over 1,000	4,807.86	29.00	3.46	7.25	Usually present
100-199	715.48	8.84	1.51	2.73	Often absent
Below 100	444.99	5.11	1.36	2.13	Usually absent

RURAL MARKETS AND TOWNS

The general features of rural markets were summarized by A. H. Smith in the closing decade of the nineteenth century:

> The times at which village markets are held vary greatly. In large cities there is a market every day, but in country places this would involve a waste of time. Sometimes the market takes place every other day, and sometimes on every day the numeral of which is a multiple of three. A more common arrangement, however, seems to be that which is based upon the division of the lunar month in thirty days. . . . If a market is held every five days, it will occur six times every month. . . . The various markets will be designated by the days on which they occur, as "One-six," meaning the market which is held every first, sixth, eleventh, sixteenth, twenty-first, and twenty-sixth day of the moon. [36]

The rural markets went under different names in different parts of imperial China. Speaking generally, North China markets were known as *chi* (gathering), whereas those in South China were often called *hsü* and those in West China *ch'ang*. [37] Whatever their names, the functions and arrangements of these markets remained essentially the same.

It may be useful to cite a few descriptions contained in local gazetteers. According to the *Lu-lung hsien chih*, the rural markets of this locality were arranged as in Table 5:[38]

TABLE 5
RURAL MARKETS IN LU-LUNG HSIEN

Market *(chi)*	Market Days	Main Commodity
Yu-tsa-chen	1*, 11, 21; 6, 16, 26	Grain, livestock
Chiu-pai-hu-chen	4, 14, 24; 9, 19, 29	Grain, livestock
Heng-ho-chen	5, 15, 25; 10, 20, 30	Grain, fuel, meat, livestock
Lang-ko-chuang	2, 12, 22; 8, 18, 28	Unspecified
Yen-ho-ying	2, 12, 22; 7, 17, 27	Unspecified
Liu-chia-cheng †	3, 13, 23; 8, 18, 28	Unspecified
Liu-chia-cheng‡	1, 11, 21; 6, 16, 26	Unspecified

*Refers to first day of the Chinese month.
†Major market *(ta-chi)*.
‡Minor market *(hsiao-chi)*.

This situation was typical of North China, although markets in other northern localities varied slightly in the commodities exchanged and in the arrangement of market days. [39]

Markets were usually within walking distance of the home villages of their patrons. [40] Occasionally patrons might have to come from neighboring districts but the distance was never great. [41] The distances between markets and the district city varied, since the markets were distributed in accordance with the needs of the groups of villages they served. Rural markets were usually located at some distance from the city, which always had its own markets. [42]

The number of markets varied in different *chou* and *hsien*, from a dozen to several hundred. The following table, prepared from a number of local gazetteers done in the nineteenth century, shows the wide range of variation, due undoubtedly to the different degrees of economic prosperity attained in the localities in question. [43]

Number of Markets

Cheng-ting Hsien (Chihli)	17	(1875)
Fu-ning Hsien (Chihli)	14	(1877)
T'eng Hsien (Shantung)	420	(1868)
Nan-yang Hsien (Honan)	29	(1904)
Sui Chou (Honan)	47	(1892)
Yü-lin Chou (Kwangsi)	28	(1894)

The economic needs of villages were not served by the rural markets alone. There were towns which were in reality fully developed markets and villages with "business streets" which were embryonic markets. The following description of two such villages will give us a glimpse into the conditions of North China in the late nineteenth century. According to a survey made by some British military officers in the 1880's, Yen-ch'ao, lying on the road from Tsao-lin to Peking, was a village "thickly set in trees," with a street "500 to 600 yards long, lined by shops"; and Shaw-tyen-zwang, a large village on the road from Tientsin to Te Chou, had almost attained the commercial intensity of a small town. The observer reported, concerning the latter:

> Its general appearance indicates agricultural prosperity; when visited, a large market was being held. Carts drawn by 2 to 8 oxen, ponies or mules, laden wheelbarrows, carriers, etc., were making their way with supplies towards the town. Several temporary smithies had been established in its outskirts. [44]

The 1850 edition of the gazetteer of Ting Chou (Chihli) contained examples of all these places of rural exchange. [45] As Tables 1 to 4 will show, villages with business streets had fairly large populations and an apparently higher degree of prosperity than ordinary villages.

These seemed to represent a transitional stage between ordinary villages and the regular markets (which, as we are already aware, had
their sites also in villages). They differed from the markets not so
much in the size of population as in the fact that they were not, like
the latter, formally constituted as trading centers and that they served
more restricted areas than the latter. It should be admitted, however,
that occasionally it is somewhat difficult to draw the line of demarcation.

Conditions in South China were broadly similar to those in the north;
there were differences in nomenclature though not in substance. In
southern provinces, particularly in Kwangtung and Kwangsi, rural
markets were usually known as *hsü*, while in western provinces (Szechwan, Kweichow, and Yunnan) they were normally called *ch'ang*. [46]
In some localities they were referred to as *shih*, which simply means
"market." For instance, the 1877 edition of the gazetteer of Ch'u Chou
(Chekiang) stated that the *shih* of the various districts under the jurisdiction of this prefecture had schedules similar to markets of other
localities, following the 1-6, 2-7, and 3-8 patterns. [47] Even in Yunnan
where the name *ch'ang* generally prevailed, rural markets were sometimes called *shih*, as in the district of Nan-ning. [48] In Kiangsi, according to the 1901 edition of *Ch'ang-ning hsien chih*, "village markets
were customarily called *yü*, all of which had gatherings once every
three days." [49]

The number of rural markets varied from province to province, although in the south the variation was somewhat less: [50]

Number of Markets

Hsiang-shan Hsien (Kwangtung)	26	(1873)
Hua Hsien (Kwangtung)	26	(1890)
Hsing-i Hsien (Kwangtung)	22	(1889)
Ch'ing-yüan Hsien (Kwangtung)	40	(1880)
Po-pai Hsien (Kwangsi)	38	(1889)
Lu Chou (Szechwan)	86	(1882)
Chiang-an Hsien (Szechwan)	32	(1882)
Na-ch'i Hsien (Szechwan)	10	(1882)
Mei-t'an Hsien (Kweichow)	47	(1899)
Ch'ang-ning Hsien (Kiangsi)	24	(1901)

The commodities exchanged in the markets were mostly local produce. In markets of less populous and prosperous localities especially,
the exchange was limited to a few items, as for example in Ch'u Chou
(Chekiang), where "there was nothing beyond rice, grain, salt, fish,
cotton cloth, and thread." [51] In some of the wealthiest districts, however, especially in southern Kwangtung, the goods supplied by rural
markets went far beyond the simple needs of ordinary peasants. An

outstanding instance was afforded by Chiu-chiang Ju-lin Hsiang, one
of the major subdivisions of Nan-hai Hsien. The 1883 edition of the
gazetteer of this locality gave brief descriptions of its various rural
markets, among which *Ta-hsü* (Great Market) was the most remarkable. Its regular market-day schedule followed the familiar 3-6-9 pattern, but it differed from most other markets in being of immense
size. It had twenty-six streets and lanes and contained seven sub-
markets, where silk, cloth, silkworm eggs, poultry, fish, and so
forth were exchanged. The total number of stores was over 1,500, in
which "ten thousand sorts of goods were collected and stored."[52] This
was in reality a miniature town rather than a rural market; at any
rate it was a highly exceptional rural market made possible, in all
probability, by the phenomenal prosperity of coastal Kwangtung following the development of commerce after the Opium War.[53]

The last of the natural divisions of the rural areas was the *chen*,
the town. The towns in the various provinces were, of course, of
different sizes. The smallest were hardly distinguishable from the
rural markets, such as Ming-yüeh-chen and Tung-t'ing-chen of Ting
Chou (Chihli). The former had only two streets, whereas Tzu-wei-
ts'un-chi, a rural market in the same locality, had three; the latter
contained twenty-two stores, only seven more than Wu-nü-ts'un-chi,
another rural market there. The larger towns such as Fu-shan-chen
of Kwangtung and Ching-te-chen of Kiangsi were highly prosperous
and densely populated communities. According to William C. Milne,
writing in the mid-nineteenth century:

> [Fu-shan Chen] was perhaps the most remarkable for the exhibition
> of universal energy in business of every form. It may be named "the
> Birmingham of China." It lies twelve miles W. by S. of Canton city;
> is a large town without walls; reputed to contain 1,000,000 inhabitants.
> Both the canal and river through the town were crammed with boats;
> each side of the river thickly populated and built up with dwellings,
> shops, godowns, factories and hongs.[54]

Ching-te-chen, however, afforded a different example of the oversized town. According to the author quoted above, this large market-
town was "one of the four famous interior markets of the empire,"[55]
and was

> . . . famed for being the chief manufactury of porcelain. . . . It is
> described by those who have visited the place as an immense village,
> or unwalled town rather, stretching three miles along a beautiful
> river, and flanked by a semicircle of fine mountains, from which
> much of the earth required for the ware is brought. . . . If rumor
> is to be relied on, there are at least five hundred kilns constantly
> at work. . . . The population of the place, though given out to be quite
> one million, may be nearer the truth if set down at half a million,

which is borne out by the common saying, "At Kingtih [Ching-te] they daily consume 10,000 piculs of rice and 1,000 pigs."[56]

Towns of this dimension and type ceased to be genuine rural communities, although formally they still remained a part of the countryside and were not incorporated as cities.

Chapter 2

ADMINISTRATIVE DIVISIONS:
PAO-CHIA AND *LI-CHIA*

For the purpose of controlling the rural areas the Ch'ing government, following the general policy of the preceding dynasty and adopting in large measure its methods, instituted two systems of subadministrative divisions, which were superimposed upon but did not replace the natural divisions outlined in chapter 1. On the one hand, there was a system of *pao-chia* divisions to facilitate what may be described as police control, and on the other hand, a system of *li-chia* divisions originally intended as a help in the collection of the land and corvée imposts.

Owing partly to the lack of uniformity in the application of the official schemes and partly to the vicissitudes which these systems underwent during their existence, a good deal of confusion arose in their actual practice as well as in their nomenclature. In fact, this confusion led some writers to believe that the *pao-chia* and the *li-chia* were one and the same system with divergent names. One writer was aware of this confusion but did not succeed in freeing himself from it.[1] Like many others he failed to discern that the police control and revenue collection systems were *originally* separate ones with distinct structures and functions.

To show how bad this confusion was, two instances may be cited here. George Jamieson, an informed student of Chinese law, wrote in 1880:

> . . . the *chia* in many places is lost sight of, and the *Li* or *Pao*, for sometimes the one term and sometimes the other is used, is the only group between the family on the one hand and the *Hsien* or territorial district on the other. Other terms are used besides the above in different Provinces, but the thing indicated is the same.[2]

Hsiao I-shan, a well-known contemporary Chinese historian, wrote in 1945:

> The Ch'ing court put in force the *pao-chia* system in all parts of the empire. This originated in the reign of Shun-chih. At first it was the *tsung-chia* system; then it became the *li-chia* system. In both ten *hu* constituted a *chia,* and ten *chia* a *tsung.* It was called *fang* in the city, *"Hsiang"* in areas near the city, and *li* in the countryside. In the forty-

25

seventh year of K'ang-hsi it was decreed that a *p'ai-t'ou* be instituted
in every ten *hu*, a *chia-t'ou* in every ten *p'ai*, and a *pao-chang* in every
ten *chia*.[3]

Apparently aware of the confusion involved in his statement, this
writer confessed that the matter was far from clear to him and complained that "many persons of the Ch'ing dynasty discussed the *pao-
chia*, but they all were muddled and difficult to understand. "

The following section is an attempt to outline the structural features
of these two systems of subadministrative rural divisions and to dispel as far as possible confusion and misunderstanding that arose during and after the Ch'ing dynasty. We shall first describe these systems and then demonstrate that in spite of fluctuating and occasionally
overlapping nomenclatures they were originally two distinct systems
with clearly defined functions and not a single system with two sets
of interchangeable names.

THE *PAO-CHIA* DIVISIONS

The *pao-chia* was the simpler of the two. This system was officially
adopted at the inception of the dynasty,[4] although it had a much earlier
origin.[5] Some historians held that it had its archetype in the local system described in the *Chou-li* or the *Kuan-tzu*.[6] In the former it was
said:

> Five households constitute a *lin*, five *lin* a *li*, four *li* a *tsan*, five *tsan*
> a *p'i*, five *p'i* a *hsien*, and five *hsien* a *sui*. Each of these . . . has
> control of its own affairs, orders, prohibitions, and punishments.
> Each examines [the number of its] inhabitants and assigns land to
> them, inspects their implements, and teaches them agriculture.[7]

It is clear that the *Chou-li* divisions described above were intended
to serve a broader purpose than the strictly police functions of maintaining local order by keeping a close surveillance over the inhabitants.

The *Kuan-tzu* contained several schemes of local divisions,[8] but as
in the *Chou-li*, these were assigned wider functions, including military
organization and local peace.

The local divisions of Ch'in and Han and subsequent dynasties usually claimed direct descent from the *Chou-li* arrangement; however,
there were important differences in substance as well as in form. It
suffices to note here that the local system established in A. D. 589 by
Emperor Wen-ti of the Sui dynasty seemed to be the first to introduce
the idea of policing, a departure from the classical tradition.[9] It was
said:

Upon ascending to the throne Wen-ti of Sui ordered that every five households be constituted into a *pao*, every five *pao* into a *lu*, and every four *lu* into a *tsu*, each of these [divisions] to have its own *cheng* [head]. Outside the imperial capital, *li-cheng* who are to be the counterparts of the *lu-cheng*, and *tang-chang* who are the equivalents of the *tsu-cheng*, are to be instituted. [All these] are to inspect and oversee [their respective divisions]. [10]

The local system of the T'ang dynasty appeared to be the first to combine in the same hands the duties of census taking, revenue collection, and police supervision, with emphasis on the last. [11]

The real forerunner of the Ch'ing system, however, was the *pao-chia* of the Sung dynasty, set up by Wang An-shih in 1070. This Sung system, as it was first established, not only assumed the name *pao-chia* for the first time but was the first to make the detection and reporting of criminals its sole function. According to the *Sung-shih*, it was ordered that:

. . . among the inhabitants within the metropolitan area of the imperial capital, ten households be organized into a *pao*, for which a *pao-chang* was to be selected from heads of households who possessed ability and strength. Fifty households were to constitute a *ta-pao* [large *pao*], and one person was selected to be the *ta-pao-chang*. Ten *ta-pao* were to constitute a *tu-pao* (general *pao*), for which a person respected by the inhabitants was appointed as *tu-pao-cheng*. . . . In each of the *ta-pao* five inhabitants were to keep night watch by turns. Rewards were given to whoever reported or apprehended [criminals]. If inhabitants of the same *pao* committed robbery, murder, arson, rape, taught or practiced heresy, or manufactured or stored poison, and if their neighbors were aware of the crimes but failed to report [them], these latter were punished according to law . . . Wherever [the number of households in a given neighborhood] reached ten, a separate *p'ai* [placard] was provided on which the names of the heads of these households and the total number of the households were written. [12]

This system was soon applied to the whole empire, and about a year after its inception it was converted into a subsidiary military system, a sort of permanent local militia.

Wang Shou-jen, the well-known philosopher and official of the Ming dynasty, contributed something to the development of the *pao-chia* as a local police system. Between 1517 and 1520, when he was engaged in suppressing bandits and rebels in Kiangsi, he established a system requiring every ten households to register their members on a card and "to report promptly to the government any unfamiliar face or any suspicious action" that appeared in the neighborhood. The ten households were collectively responsible for any delinquency in performing such prescribed duties. This system, however, differed from the *pao-chia* of Ch'ing times in several respects. It was a local institution not applied to other parts of the empire. The heads of the ten households took charge of the records by turns; no permanent headmen were instituted. Even in 1520, when a *pao-chang* was appointed in each village, his duty was restricted to integrating local efforts at dealing with thieves and robbers. He had no jurisdiction over any matter that concerned the ten-household groups. The historical significance of Wang Shou-jen's system lies in the fact that it was designed exclusively for the purpose of detecting crimes and criminals through joint local responsibility. [13]

Whatever the historical origin of the *pao-chia*, it is plain that the Ch'ing dynasty used it as a device to watch and check the number, movements, and activities of the people, through agents selected from the local inhabitants themselves. The scheme as laid down by the imperial authorities was a relatively simple affair. Briefly, every ten *hu* (households) were arranged into one *p'ai*, for which a *p'ai-t'ou* (head of *p'ai*, sometimes called *p'ai-chang*) was set up; every ten *p'ai* constituted a *chia*, the head of which was known as *chia-chang* or *chia-t'ou;* and every ten *chia* formed a *pao*, which was placed under the care of a *pao-chang* or *pao-cheng*. [14]

One or two actual instances may be cited here. According to the gazetteer of Nan-ning Hsien (Yunnan), the *pao-chia* arrangement as it existed there in 1851 was as follows:[15]

Households:	21,232
P'ai:	2,096
P'ai-chang:	2,096
Chia:	209
Chia-chang:	209
Pao:	20
Pao-chang:	20

Similarly, the 1873 edition of the gazetteer of Liu-yang Hsien (Hunan) supplied this information:[16]

Households:	62,334
P'ai-chang:	6,143
Chia-chang:	611
Pao-cheng:	121

This *hsien*, like Nan-ning Hsien above, followed the official tithing or decimal arrangement fairly closely, as the numbers of the various divisions and heads of the divisions indicate.

It was the exception, however, to follow the official tithing system. As we shall see later, local practices usually deviated widely from

official regulations. For the moment it may be useful to make clear
the relationship between the *pao-chia* on the one side and the *Hsiang*
and the villages on the other. The village was not officially recognized as an integral element of the *pao-chia* system, but in practice,
village boundaries were respected. For instance, Liu Heng, a re-
putedly capable magistrate of the nineteenth century, informs us that
when he renovated the *pao-chia* in Pa Hsien (Szechwan), he allowed
the households in small villages, if numbering less than the official
quota in each village, to constitute a separate *p'ai* or *chia*.[17] The 1879
edition of the gazetteer of T'ung Chou (Chihli) indicated that there was
a total of 608 villages and towns in this locality, for which 567 *pao-
cheng* were instituted. The village was generally taken as a unit coextensive with the *pao*. [18] In Lin-chang Hsien (Honan) villages became the component units of the *pao* divisions; the number of villages
in each *pao* varied from about half a dozen to over twenty. [19]

The *Hsiang* also came into unofficial relationship with the *pao-chia*.
Occasionally the *Hsiang* appeared as a higher division over the *pao*
(or over villages which comprised a sufficient number of households
to become coextensive with the *pao*). This seems to be the meaning
of the dictum of an eighteenth-century writer that "the *pao-chia* becomes operative when villages are interlocked in the *Hsiang*. "[20]

The following example will illustrate this type of relationship. In
1669, shortly after the *pao-chia* system was launched, the magistrate
of T'eng Hsien (Shantung) renamed the eight *Hsiang* into which this
district was originally divided, and distributed the *pao* in this fashion:[21]

Ch'ien Hsiang (Northwest):	5
K'an Hsiang (North):	5
Ken Hsiang (Northeast:	7
Chen Hsiang (East):	5
Hsün Hsiang (Southeast):	9
Li Hsiang (South):	22
K'un Hsiang (Southwest):	7
Tui Hsiang (West):	12

In other instances a different relationship obtained. The picture
presented by Ch'ing-pien Hsien (Shensi) is especially interesting. In
1731 when this district was newly constituted, its countryside was
divided into three *Hsiang*. The number of *p'ai* in the city area and in
each of the *Hsiang* was given as follows:

City:	475
East Hsiang:	172
West Hsiang:	519
South Hsiang:	188

Curiously, neither *pao* nor *chia* was mentioned by the compiler of the gazetteer that supplied the above information. By the end of the nineteenth century this district was redivided, and two more *Hsiang* were added to the original three. The arrangement is shown in Table 6:[22]

TABLE 6
PAO-CHIA ARRANGEMENT IN CH'ING-PIEN HSIEN

Locality	No. Households	No. Villages	No. *Pang-ch'a*	No. *P'ai-t'ou*
City	776	121	10	76
East Hsiang	352	65	5	34
South Hsiang	561	153	5	50
Southwest Hsiang	397	110	5	38
West Hsiang	406	140	4	40
Northwest Hsiang	618	70	6	60

The *pao* remained conspicuously absent. The compiler of this gazetteer explained that "each *p'ai-t'ou* controlled ten registered households, and, besides *shan-shen* [assistant gentry], there were *pang-ch'a* [assistant inspectors] in place of *chia-chang*. Each *pang-ch'a* controlled ten *p'ai-t'ou*. There were several *shan-shen* in each *Hsiang* to supervise and check [the *pang-ch'a*]." These *shan-shen* presumably took the place of the *pao-chang* of the official scheme.

The *Hsiang*, however, was sometimes identified with or treated as an equivalent of the *pao*. An experienced magistrate who served in several districts in the north during the reign of K'ang-hsi, for example, regarded the *Hsiang* as the highest division in the *pao-chia* system. According to him, "the present *pao-chia* calls for a head in each ten households, to be known as *chia-chang*, and a head in each hundred households, to be known as *pao-cheng*. Each *Hsiang* is to have a head, bearing the title *pao-chang*."[23] Although his terminology deviated from the official, the pattern of organization remained substantially the same. This magistrate was not the only one who equated the *Hsiang* with the *pao*. Some nineteenth-century writers held practically the same opinion. According to one, "the method of *pao-chia* consisted in instituting *pao-chang* to supervise the *Hsiang* and *chia-chang* to watch over ten households."[24] Another observed that the method then in use was "one *chia-chang* for every ten households, one *pao-cheng* for every hundred households, and one *pao-chang* for each *Hsiang*."[25]

Actual instances may be produced to substantiate their opinion. According to the 1891 edition of the gazetteer of Li-p'ing Fu (Kweichow), the *pao-chia* arrangement obtaining in this prefecture was as follows: "for every ten households a *chia-chang* is instituted, and for every ten *chia,* a *pao-cheng.* A *pao-chang* is instituted in each of the four *Hsiang,* east, south, west, and north, who is to take general charge of [this division]. "[26] Likewise, in Nan-yang Hsien (Honan), so said the 1904 edition of its gazetteer, the *Hsiang* became the highest division in the *pao-chia* system, occupying the position of the *pao.* [27]

It is clear from the above that during the nineteenth century if not earlier there were in practice two versions of the official *pao-chia* scheme with reference to the *Hsiang:*

First Version	*Second Version*
Hsiang	
1,000 households *pao (pao-chang)*	*Hsiang = pao (pao-chang)*
100 households *chia (chia-chang)*	*(?) (pao-cheng) (pang-ch'a)*
10 households *p'ai (p'ai-t'ou)*	*chia (chia-chang) (p'ai-t'ou)*

It may be asked why the Ch'ing rulers did not make use of the natural and customary divisions of the rural areas, the *Hsiang* and the village, as a basis upon which to erect the *pao-chia* structure, since these divisions were found by local officials to be too useful to dispense with. One reason may have been that since the number of households in the villages varied widely, these natural divisions could not always fit in with the decimal system of the police divisions. It is probable too that since the purpose of the *pao-chia* was to watch and control the inhabitants of the countryside, the imperial government considered it safer to make it an entirely separate system, free from the influence of village organizations. Indeed, it might have been the intention of the Ch'ing emperors to use this system to counterbalance whatever strength the rural communities might develop. For that purpose, it would be much better to keep the *pao-chia* as separate as possible from the existing rural organizations.

Whatever had been the real motive for not incorporating the *pao-chia* into the *Hsiang* and villages, the emperors did not succeed in keeping this set of subadministrative divisions entirely distinct from the natural divisions. As we have just shown, local officials frequently found it expedient to avail themselves of the facilities afforded by the natural rural divisions. The *Hsiang* and villages therefore eventually became working divisions in the *pao-chia* system despite the imperial intention. This marriage of the administrative and natural divisions brought the former unavoidably under the influence of local exigencies, and this partially explains the discrepancies noted above. [28]

THE *LI-CHIA* DIVISIONS

The *li-chia* was a little more complicated than the *pao-chia.* It was officially set up by the Shun-chih emperor in 1648, four years after the inception of the *pao-chia*. It also had its origin in the past. As a system of subadministrative divisions for the purpose of revenue collection it could be traced directly to the *li-chia* of the Ming dynasty, which in turn was based upon the *li-she* of the Yüan dynasty.[29] Since the Ch'ing system was directly copied from the Ming with but slight modifications, it may be interesting to note briefly the arrangement adopted by Emperor T'ai-tsu in 1321. According to the *Ming-shih*, the emperor ordered that in compiling the *huang-ts'e* (yellow registers) for tax collection,

> . . . every one hundred and ten households be constituted into one *li*, from which ten with the largest number of *ting* [taxpaying adult males] and taxable land be selected to serve as *chang* [heads]. The remaining hundred households are to be organized into ten *chia*, with a total of ten *chia-shou* [heads of *chia*]. . . . [the division containing one hundred and ten households] is to be known as *fang* in the city, "*Hsiang*" in areas near the city, and *li* in the *Hsiang* and *tu* [rural areas].[30]

In spite of its defects this system persisted and late in the sixteenth century during the Wan-li reign became officially known as the *li-chia*.[31] In fact a few local gazetteers compiled in the Ch'ing dynasty still contain records of the *li-chia* divisions as they existed in Ming times.[32]

As already noted, the *li-chia* arrangement adopted by the Ch'ing rulers differed little from its immediate predecessor beyond a slight modification in nomenclature. According to the official regulations, every 110 households in the rural areas were to constitute a *li* in which the heads of the ten households that had the largest number of taxpaying adult males were to be elected *li-chang* (heads of the *li*). The remaining 100 households were, as in the Ming system, to be divided evenly into ten *chia*; each of the latter was to elect a *chia-chang* (head of the *chia*, the equivalent of the *chia-shou* in the Ming system). Similar groupings of households were to be made in the cities and suburban areas, but these groupings were to have different names. In the cities every 110 households formed a *fang* (instead of a *li*), whereas in the suburbs they formed a "*Hsiang*." A census was to be taken every three years. The *chia-chang* was assigned the duty of collecting the tax records of the eleven households under his supervision and of handing them over to the head of the higher division, *li-chang*, *fang-chang*, or "*Hsiang*"-*chang*, as the case might be, who in turn was responsible for sending the records to the local yamen.[33]

This official scheme was not strictly carried out, nor was it uniformly applied in all parts of the empire. Indeed, deviations from it were so numerous as to defy systematization. Only in a few instances was it followed more or less faithfully. There was much less conformity with the official scheme and nomenclature in the provinces along the Yangtze Valley and to the south than in the provinces of North China. Many causes brought about these discrepancies. Some of the irregularities in the south were inherited from previous dynasties and were allowed to persist partly because the imperial government did not find it necessary or feasible to enforce uniformity in those comparatively remote regions. Other deviations seem to have been the result of local economic or demographic changes; a substantial increase or decrease in the number of households in a given locality, for example, might eventually disturb the *li-chia* arrangement (see Appendix I). A bewildering variety of forms and nomenclatures thus came into existence, making the study of the rural tax collection structure of the Ch'ing dynasty a rather baffling task. [34] The question arises, if the government was unable even to establish a reasonable degree of uniformity in the *li-chia* structure, how could it achieve uniform results in the highly difficult task of collecting taxes in the vast countryside?

RELATIONSHIP BETWEEN THE *PAO-CHIA* AND THE *LI-CHIA*

We are now ready to settle the question whether the *pao-chia* and the *li-chia* were in fact two distinct systems or one system with two different names. The materials presented above have already shown that these were separate devices of imperial control, each with its own special purpose and functions. The following brief arguments may further clarify the issue.

In the first place, the *pao-chia* and the *li-chia* were treated by law as two systems serving distinct purposes. In the *Ta-Ch'ing lü-li*, [35] the legal provisions governing the operation of the *pao-chia* came under the *hsing-lü* (penal code dealing mainly with crimes and criminals) whereas the *li-chia* came under the *hu-lü* (laws concerning finance and population). While we cannot attribute scientific accuracy to this and other classifications made by imperial jurists, this demarcation between the police control and tax collection systems seems to be a sufficiently clear indication that the Ch'ing government regarded these systems as functionally distinct and independent of each other.

There was sufficient structural differentiation to mark the one system from the other. The *pao-chia* and the *li-chia* arrangements were roughly similar but not identical. Both had the *chia* as one of the lower divisions (which could be one cause of confusion) but it was differently constituted. In the official *pao-chia* (police control) system, the *chia* was made up of ten *p'ai*, each of which contained ten *hu*. The *hu*, therefore, was the basic unit and the *p'ai* the basic division. The tithing or decimal idea was consistently maintained. In the official *li-chia* (tax collection) system while the *hu* was also the basic unit, the *chia* was not really a basic division. According to the regulations, the *li* was made up of 110 *hu,* and subdivided into ten *chia,* each containing eleven *hu.* The decimal idea was to some extent modified. The *li* was the basic division rather than the *chia;* it was also the highest division, since there was none over it. The *pao-chia* as officially defined had a three-level, the *li-chia* a two-level, structure:

The *pao-chia* structure	The *li-chia* structure
10 *hu* = 1 *p'ai*	10 *hu* = 1 *chia*
10 *p'ai* (100 hu) = 1 *chia*	110 *hu* = 1 *li*
10 *chia* (1,000 hu) = 1 *pao*	

Remembering that these structures were officially set up at about the same time (1644 and 1648), one is led to think that they were intentionally made to differ so that they might remain separate systems with specifically assigned functions.

A number of local historians recognized a functional difference between the *pao-chia* and the *li-chia.* The compiler of the *Yung hsien chih* (1897 edition) in discussing the registration of households distinguished between what he called *li-i chih hu-k'ou* (households and inhabitants registered for the *li* service) and *p'ai-men chih hu-k'ou* (households and inhabitants registered from door to door). He went on to explain that the *hu-k'ou* registered in the first connection included households and inhabitants liable to the land and corvée taxes. In this case, "the *li* controlled the *chia,* the *chia* controlled the *hu,* and the *hu* controlled the *ting* [taxpaying adult male]." The *hu-k'ou* registered in the second connection included all the households and their members that dwelt in a given area. In this case, "a *ti-fang* [a *pao-chia* agent, see chapter 3] controlled ten *chia,* and each *chia* contained ten households." The *hu-k'ou* in the first, he added, were registered "on the basis of farm land," those in the second, "on the basis of residence."[36] This writer was speaking of the practice of his own time. The *pao-chia* structure he envisaged deviated from the original official scheme. But his distinction between the *pao-chia* and *li-chia* functions with respect to household registration was essentially valid.

Similar distinctions were made by other writers. Explaining the fact that Ch'ang-ning Hsien (Kiangsi) contained two *tu,* four *"Hsiang,"* and twelve *pao,* the compiler of the 1901 edition of its gazetteer wrote that *"ting-liang* [corvée and grain taxes] were controlled in the two *tu,* while the households belonged to the *'Hsiang'* and *pao."*[37] Making allowance for the somewhat confused terminology, we have no reason to doubt the correctness of the functional distinction made by this writer. The compiler of the 1890 edition of the *Ho hsien chih* also employed inaccurate terminology but maintained a cogent distinction between the tax and police divisions. He recorded that in 1865 the district magistrate rearranged the *liang-hu* (households paying the grain taxes) of this locality, so that they constituted eighteen *li* with a total of 18, 802 *hu*. About a quarter of a century later, in 1889, another magistrate revamped the *pao-chia* divisions, constituting thirty-one *t'uan* with a total of 31, 502 *hu*. [38] The term *t'uan* was here used as the name of a *pao-chia* division which in this instance contained an average of about 1, 000 households. Hence it was the equivalent of an official *pao*. Ko T'ao, in his preface to the section on the *pao-chia* in the gazetteer of Hsien Hsien, put the whole matter in a nutshell by pointing out that "the chief function of the *li-chia* was *i* [service, i. e., tax collection], while the chief function of the *pao-chia* was *wei* [protection, i. e., police surveillance]. [39]

As officially defined, these two systems did have functions that overlapped at one point. Both were assigned the task of counting and registering the number of households in a given area. But even here a distinction existed. The *li-chia* registration was made for the purpose of ascertaining the amount of taxes to be collected, whereas the *pao-chia* registration was designed to detect unlawful and subservient elements by keeping a reliable record of the households and inhabitants of the locality concerned.

In spite of their distinct purposes, the *hu-k'ou* registration task of the *li-chia* was transferred (early in the reign of Ch'ien-lung) to the *pao-chia,* and in many instances, even the matter of tax collection went into the hands of *pao-chia* agents. It was probably this transfer of functions that led a recent writer to believe that "the *li-chia* structure was in reality merely an antecedent stage in the formation of the *pao-chia* structure," and that, in other words, "the *li-chia* system before the Ch'ien-lung and Chia-ch'ing times together with the *pao-chia* after this period constituted, as a matter of fact, two successive stages which completed the development of the *pao-chia*. "[40]

Such a view does not square with the fact that the *li-chia* was officially instituted in 1648, four years after the official establishment of the *pao-chia* (1644). This view also overlooks the fact that in post-Chia-ch'ing times (when, according to the writer cited above, the *pao-chia* reached its "complete development") both the *li-chia* and *pao-chia* had deteriorated. The main functions of the *li-chia* were given over to the *pao-chia,* with or without express imperial approval, in the eighteenth century, simply because the *li-chia* had suffered a more advanced atrophy than the *pao-chia*. The transfer of functions was in reality the telescoping of two previously separate systems, instead of the transition from a lower to a higher phase in a single system. Indeed, there is every indication that the Ch'ing rulers purposely set up two separate systems with specific and independent functions, as a precaution against giving too much power to any one local agency.

What happened later, namely, the telescoping of functions into the same hands, went beyond their original intentions; if they acquiesced in this new situation (particularly in the matter of registration), they were merely acknowledging a *fait accompli* and not lending imperial blessing to any achievement of the *pao-chia* system.

Those who have regarded the *pao-chia* and the *li-chia* as a single system were probably led to this view by the way these systems were often handled by local officials, by the fact that the *pao-chia* and *li-chia* divisions as well as functions often overlapped, and by the careless manner in which the nomenclatures of the systems were employed. Moreover, some of the compilers of local gazetteers, through misunderstanding the true significance and functions of these systems, or through having insufficient and inaccurate data at their command, introduced confusions of their own. [41]

THE *SHE* AS A RURAL DIVISION

The *she* was another official division, conceptually distinct from both the *li-chia* and the *pao-chia,* though in fact somewhat related to at least one of them. It may be useful to explain briefly its form and functions here.

According to an early edition of the *Ta-Ch'ing hui-tien shih-li*[42] the imperial government approved in 1660 (Shun-chih 17) a proposal to set up *li-she* in the countryside of the empire. It was said that a varying number of adjacent households (between twenty and fifty were to constitute one *she,* so that the households in each division could extend "mutual assistance in farm work, in the event of death or sickness occurring in any of them during the farming season." Later editions of this compilation are silent on this matter, but a number of local gazetteers recorded that the *she* actually existed in many localities, testifying that this seventeenth-century government directive was not a dead letter.

The *Han-tan hsien chih* (1933 edition), for instance, citing from the 1756 edition of the same gazetteer, stated: "This district originally contained twenty-six *she* and four *t'un,* but sometime later the *t'un* were changed into *she,* making a total of thirty *she.* Each *she* was divided into ten *chia.*"[43] Similarly, the *Luan chou chih* (1898) describing the rural divisions of this locality in Chihli province, stated that at the time when a census count was made in 1896, there was "a total of 65 *t'un* and *she,* 1,347 *ts'un* and *chuang,* . . . with 75,697 *hu* and 561,667 *ting-k'ou.*"[44] Again, according to the 1892 edition of the gazetteer of Sui Chou (Honan), the villages of this locality were mostly designated as *she,* e.g., Liang-ts'un-she, An-hsiang-she, etc.[45] An almost identical situation existed in Lin-chang Hsien, another locality

in the same province, where the rural areas were divided into eight
she.[46]

The *she* were also found in some Central and South China provinces.
In some localities in Hupeh the *she* appeared to have replaced the *li*.
A typical instance was afforded by I-ch'eng Hsien where according
to the *Kuang-hsü yü-ti chi*[47] the rural divisions were arranged in the
following fashion:

she ts'un

	she	ts'un
Tung (East) Hsiang	6	28
Hsi (West) Hsiang	2	37
Nan (South) Hsiang	5	29
Pei (North) Hsiang	3	23

Comparable situations existed in Kuang-hua Hsien, Chu-shan Hsien,
and Chu-ch'i Hsien.[48] In South China the *she* appeared in Nan-hai
Hsien and Hsing-i Hsien (both in Kwangtung),[49] in T'ung-an Hsien
(Fukien),[50] and in Nan-ch'ang Hsien (Kiangsi).[51] According to the 1910
edition of the *Nan-hai hsien chih*, the countryside of Nan-hai was divided into fifty-eight *pao* (written in Chinese differently from the *pao*
of the *pao-chia*), some subdivided into *Hsiang* and others into *she*.
Both the *Hsiang* and the *she* were in turn divided into villages. The
Chiu-chiang ju-ling hsiang chih (1883) described a different arrangement in Chiu-chiang Pao (a division of the Nan-hai Hsien), where the
ts'un were subdivided into *she*.[52] The *she* was a subdivision of the
tu or *Hsiang* in Hsin-i Hsien.[53] Curiously, the *she* appeared only in
the city areas of Nan-ch'ang Hsien, where each *she* contained a varying number of *t'u*.[54]

What was the nature of this *she* division as exemplified by these
localities? We may begin by tracing the historical antecedents of
the *she*. One of the earliest occurrences of this term was in the *Tso-
chuan*. It was said that in the twenty-fifth year of Chao-kung (517
B. C.) the state of Ch'i presented 1,000 *she* to Lu. Tu Yü, an annotator
who lived in the third century A. D., explained that "twenty-five households constituted one *she*."[55] In the Sui dynasty (589-617) "twenty-five
households formed a *she*," which was primarily a unit for carrying on
the sacrificial rituals to the gods of land and grain.[56] As time went
on, the *she* acquired other functions. It came into relationship with
rural granaries in the Sui and T'ang dynasties,[57] and assumed the task
of local famine relief, which was to be important in the subadministrative schemes of practically all subsequent dynasties.[58] During the
Yüan dynasty the *she* became an officially instituted center of agricultural affairs. In 1270 Kublai Khan issued the *Nung-sang chih shih-*

ch'i t'iao (Seventeen Articles of the Agricultural and Sericultural System), which called for the organization of every fifty households in the villages into one *she,* and for the appointment of an elderly person versed in agricultural matters to serve as its head, whose duty it was "to teach and supervise the planting of farm crops and mulberry trees" and to guide the general conduct of the inhabitants belonging to his organization.[59] The size of the *she* was again increased in the Ming dynasty, and its function of rural control was further stressed. Emperor T'ai-tsu ordered late in 1369 (Hung-wu 1) that one *she* be established for every hundred households and that an altar be set up in each *she,* where sacrifices to the land and grain gods were to be offered. He retained, with some modifications, the Yüan system of *li-she,* and directed the inhabitants of North China to organize their *li-chia* divisions "on the basis of the *she.* "[60] This, of course, brought the *she* into relationship with the tax-collection divisions. In 1375 it was ordered that peasants who participated in the sacrificial ritual performed at the *she-t'an* (the rural altar) should pledge by oath "to suppress the strong and support the weak,"[61] making the *she* an instrument of imperial control through popular religion.

Such were the historical antecedents of the *she* division of the Ch'ing dynasty, stated in the briefest of terms. It is clear that the *she* as conceived by the Ch'ing government came nearest to the Yüan system, that is, it was intended primarily as an organization for promoting or facilitating farm production. The *she* of Ch'ing times assumed some other functions which its predecessors had at one time or another performed. For instance, the *she* in Ho Hsien (Kwangsi) was said to have been essentially a rural organization for performing sacrificial rites. According to the compiler of the 1890 edition of the *Ho hsien chih:*

> Seven or eight households, or as many as several tens of them, shared one *she*. Sacrificial offerings were made in the second, sixth, and eighth months of the year. On each occasion all persons belonging to the *she* assembled and brought with them the necessary articles to offer sacrifices. When the ritual was completed, they had a feast and drank wine.[62]

In Shansi province the *she* became virtually the center of village public affairs, as an 1883 memorial of Chang Chih-tung (then governor of that province) revealed:

> It has been ascertained that the inhabitants of Shansi province customarily form one *she* in each village. If there are two or three public temples in a village, two or three *she* are formed accordingly. Each *she* has its head, whose orders the villagers obey without exception.[63]

More often the *she,* as in Ming times, was wedded to the *li-chia*

(hence the appellation *li-she)* and became one of the tax gathering divisions, as in Hsiang-fu Hsien (Honan). The compiler of the 1898 edition of the gazetteer wrote: *"Li-chia:* a total of 79 *she.* In Yung-cheng
4 [1726] Hsin-an *she* was annexed to Ts'ao Hsien, Shantung; a total
of 78 *she* remained. A *ching-ts'ui* [tax prompter] was instituted in
each *li* to urge the payment of taxes."[64] Similarly, the *she* became
a tax-collection division in Han-tan Hsien (Chihli). In 1855 Lu Yün-
ch'ang, the magistrate, scrutinized the tax registers "from one *she*
to another," and was thus able to put a stop to the hitherto prevailing
corrupt practice of *ts'uan she t'iao chia* (sneaking off the *she,* jump-
ing across the *chia),* that is, of "registering the title of one's land in
a *she* in the east, whereas the land was actually in the west, or registering the title in a *she* in the north, whereas the land was actually
in the south."[65] In fact, in some instances the *she* was treated as the
equivalent of the *li,* as in Ch'ing-chou Tao (Shantung) in the seventeenth century[66] and Fu-ning Hsien (Chihli) in the nineteenth.[67]

The *she* was associated with the rural granaries in the Ch'ing dynasty as it was in Sui and T'ang times. The *she-ts'ang* (community
granaries) will be discussed later.

●

Part Two

**RURAL
CONTROL**

Chapter 3

POLICE CONTROL:
THE *PAO-CHIA* SYSTEM

THE THEORY AND PRACTICE OF THE *PAO-CHIA*

The founders of the Ch'ing dynasty appreciated the truth of an old Chinese axiom that the empire could be conquered but not ruled on horseback.[1] Instead of relying solely on military power, they undertook to maintain their rule by making use of the techniques and institutions of control that had been developed by previous dynasties. As soon as the new rulers entered Peking, they adopted the entire administrative and subadministrative structure left behind by the Ming dynasty, making whatever changes seemed necessary to render it safe and suitable for their own use. The *pao-chia* was one of the most important subadministrative apparatuses which constituted that structure.

It took a while, however, for the *pao-chia* of the Ch'ing dynasty to reach its definitive form. The initial step to establish that system was taken in 1644, the first year of Shun-chih when the Prince Regent, at the suggestion of Chin Chih-chün (a Chinese serving as junior vice-president of the Board of War), ordered local officials to set up *p'ai* and *chia* for all those who submitted themselves to the new regime.[2] According to an official compilation, "the method of the *pao-chia*" as it was instituted in 1644 was as follows:

> In the city and rural areas of the *chou* and *hsien,* every ten households institute a *p'ai-t'ou* [headman of the *p'ai*], every ten *p'ai* a *chia-t'ou,* and every ten *chia* a *pao-chang* [headman of the *pao*]. A *yin-p'ai* [seal placard] is given each household, on which are to be written the names of the adult males and other persons [that belong to it]. If any one of these inhabitants goes away, his destination is recorded; if a person comes into the household, the place from which he comes is ascertained [and recorded].[3]

Apparently, this was a system of registration adopted to facilitate control over the inhabitants of the regions of the empire that had been newly brought under the conqueror's sway. Meanwhile, another sys-

43

tem, roughly similar to the one just mentioned, was established:

> Shun-chih 1st year: establish the *chia-chang* and *tsung-chia* in the *chou* and *hsien*. In the villages of the *fu*, *chou*, *hsien*, and *wei*, every ten households institute a *chia-chang* and one hundred households institute a *tsung-chia*. Persons in the neighborhoods are to report cases of theft and robbery, the presence of fugitives, and criminal and offensive acts to their *chia-chang*, who will in turn report them to the *tsung-chia*. The *tsung-chia* will report to the *fu*, *chou*, *hsien*, or *wei* authorities, who, after having verified the reports, will transmit them to the Board of War.[4]

This system differed from the one above in two respects. In the first place, the *pao-chia-p'ai* system was under the supervision of the Board of Revenue, whereas the *tsung-chia* system was under the Board of War.[5] Secondly, there was a structural difference:

Pao-chia-p'ai system	*Tsung-chia* system
10 households - *p'ai* (with *p'ai-t'ou*)	10 households - *chia*
100 households - *chia* (with *chia-t'ou*)	(with *chia-chang*)
1,000 households - *pao* (with *pao-chang*)	100 households - *tsung-chia*

It is difficult to explain the simultaneous creation of two instruments of control operating on similar principles and serving identical purposes. They may well have been the results of inadequate planning and poor coordination that conceivably existed at a time when the imperial structure itself was in its formative stage. Later, when the new dynasty had firmly consolidated its conquest and completed its institutional organization, the *tsung-chia* as a postcampaign instrument of control dropped out of existence, leaving the *pao-chia* under the Board of Revenue to carry on the functions of registration and surveillance.

By the beginning of the eighteenth century, the *pao-chia-p'ai* structure had become definitely established. The following document issued in 1708 makes clear the form and functions of the *pao-chia* as envisaged by the government at that time:

> Each household is given a placard on which the official seal is affixed. The names and number of adult males are written on it. In case any of them go away, their destination is recorded; in case any come into the households, the places from which they come are ascertained. It is forbidden to take in strangers and suspicious characters, unless a thorough questioning of them has been made. Every ten households set up a *p'ai-t'ou* [placard-head], every ten *p'ai* a *chia-t'ou*, and every ten *chia* a *pao-chang*. . . . Hostels keep registers for the purpose of checking [the guests] and paper placards are also given to temples and shrines. At the end of each month, the *pao-chang* submits a *kan-*

chieh [willing bond], giving assurance that everything has been well in the neighborhoods, which *[kan-chieh]* is sent to the official concerned for inspection. Whoever fails to comply will be punished. [6]

This was the *pao-chia* system of the Ch'ing dynasty, which was to help the emperors gain control of the empire at a subadministrative level. Its distinctive features are readily seen. Its first function was the registration of the households and inhabitants in the neighborhoods and villages. Superficially, it resembled a census system, for it recorded the names of all inhabitants of a given place—all persons who dwelt in households, temples, and hostels—kept track of all the movements of individuals and households, made periodic recounts of the local population, and brought their registers up to date. [7] But it was more than a census system, for it imposed upon the persons registered and those who made the registration the duties of a constable or sheriff: to watch, detect, and report any crime or criminal that might be found in the neighborhoods. The registers facilitated the execution of these duties by providing records concerning the inhabitants and their movements. It was not designed, however, to furnish a complete count of the local population or to compile any vital statistics but merely to register adult males[8]—individuals who had the potential capacity and were the most likely to disturb the imperial peace.

The second and perhaps central function of the *pao-chia* was the detection and reporting of crimes—all acts that violated imperial law or disturbed the local order. Each inhabitant was required to report to his *pao-chia* head the presence of criminals and the commission of criminal or culpable acts; the *pao-chia* heads were responsible for reporting them to the local authorities. The failure of anyone to perform the required duty would bring punishment not only upon himself but upon all his neighbors who belonged to his ten-household group. [9] Since obviously the police duties of the *pao-chia* could be carried out only if records of the inhabitants were available, the imperial government imposed penalties on any person who failed to register. [10] Families of the gentry[11] were not exempt from registration. Since landowners had a stronger motive than other inhabitants to evade registration, the law provided heavier punishment for such delinquency among them: "The families of the gentry as well as those of the common people shall all be registered, subject to the inspection of the *pao-chang* and *chia-chang*. If any fail to register . . . a family liable for the land tax shall be punished by one hundred blows and one not so liable by eighty. "[12] Significantly, because the *pao-chia* dealt with police matters, it was placed without exception under the supervision of the *hsing-fang* (Crimes Division) of the magistrate's yamen. [13]

Another distinctive feature of the *pao-chia* that deserves notice is that local inhabitants themselves were made to operate it, while local officials supervised its operation without taking any direct part in it. Such an arrangement had its advantages. By enlisting the help of the local inhabitants, the government extended its control to the remotest hamlets without multiplying the number of government officials; by putting the *pao-chia* under the supervision of local officials, it prevented the *pao-chia* heads from acquiring undue power or influence. Under this system the people became potential informers against wrongdoers or lawbreakers among their own neighbors—in other words they were made to spy upon themselves. Such mutual fear and suspicion were instilled in their minds that few of them dared to venture into seditious schemes with their fellow villagers. Thus even if individual criminals could not be completely eliminated, the opportunity for instigating concerted uprisings was greatly reduced. The usefulness of the *pao-chia* as an instrument of control lay as much in its deterrent effects on the people as in whatever actual assistance it might render the government in suppression of crimes. A nineteenth-century Western writer correctly said of the Ch'ing dynasty that "what is ostensibly a paternal government ruling its subjects through their filial affection is in reality a tyrannical administration that maintains its power by *fear and distrust.*"[14] The *pao-chia* was one of the instruments employed by the emperors for this very purpose. To regard it as "an organization for census-taking,"[15] "the self-government of old China,"[16] or "a system of local government,"[17] as some writers do, is to misinterpret not only the function of the *pao-chia* but also the nature of the imperial system.

Such, then, was the theory of the *pao-chia* as it was accepted by the Ch'ing rulers. Practice, however, did not correspond exactly to theory; the efficacy of the system did not measure up to its theoretical usefulness. The government often found it difficult to enforce its operation; it was unable even to establish uniformity in its structure. Except perhaps for a few years at the beginning of the nineteenth century, when it was believed to have produced satisfactory results in some parts of the empire, the system became increasingly ineffectual until the middle of the nineteenth century, when "banditry" and rebellions broke out in more than one region, a sure indication that the police control system was not performing as it should. But the emperors attached great importance to it and had tried their best since its inception in the middle of the seventeenth century to make it function. The Yung-cheng emperor made a particularly earnest effort early in the eighteenth century to narrow the gap between *pao-chia* theory and practice. A 1726 edict reads:

> There is no better method of bandit suppression than the *pao-chia;* but local officials, being afraid that it is difficult and troublesome to work, regard it as an old formality and do not operate it with ear-

nestness. They fail to carry out inspection with rigor. Some of them resort to the pretext that it is difficult to arrange the villages into *p'ai* and *chia*, owing to the fact that the number of the households they contain is not always divisible by ten. Others in the frontier provinces use the pretext that it is inconvenient to apply the system of interior provinces there, since natives and ethnic minorities inter-mingle and dwell together.

Their views are exceedingly erroneous. The few households in a village, however small, may be arranged into one *chia*. The Miao and T'ung who submit themselves to our rule may be regimented together with all other inhabitants. If there is a sincere intention, there will be actual results.

The *chiu ch'ing* [nine ministers] are hereby directed to discuss in detail and report to me what severe punishments should be inflicted from now on upon governors-general and governors and all officials above the magistrates of the *chou* and *hsien* who do not perform their duties with real earnestness; and how those *pao-chang, chia-chang,* and persons in the *chia* who make factual reports [of crimes and crim-inals] should be rewarded, and how those who conceal [crimes and criminals] should be punished. [18]

One result brought about by this edict was the extension of the *pao-chia* to people who had hitherto remained outside its scope. Some of the ethnic minorities, especially the Miao and the T'ung, and several categories of inhabitants with special status, including the *p'eng-min* (shed people) of Kiangsi, Chekiang, and Fukien, and the *liao-hu* (shan-ty households) of Kwangtung, were for the first time placed under *pao-chia* control. The clan organizations, kinship groups which dominated many of the villages of South and Central China, were also integrated into the control system by turning them into supplementary units of the *pao-chia*.

In villages and walled rural communities where clans with one hun-dred or more members dwell together, and where the regular *pao-chia* cannot make thorough inspections, a *tsu-cheng* [clan head] is established in each clan, to be selected from members of the group concerned, who is upright in character and respected by members of the entire clan. He is required to report to the local officials the presence of wicked and criminal persons in order that they may be properly dealt with. If he allows himself to be influenced by personal feelings and conceals [their presence], he will be punished in the same manner as in the case of a *pao-chia* agent. [19]

The nomenclature used by the Yung-cheng emperor and his servants around 1726 differed somewhat from the one used in 1644 and 1708. The 1726 nomenclature, as we have just seen, included *pao-cheng* and *chia-chang,* but no mention was made of the *p'ai-t'ou,* whereas the 1644 nomenclature contained *pao-chang, chia-t'ou,* and *p'ai-t'ou.* The *pao-cheng* obviously was synonymous with *pao-chang*, while the *chia-chang* was synonymous with *chia-t'ou*. There is no ground for concluding that the omission of the *p'ai* division in 1726 indicated an actual change in the *pao-chia* arrangement. It is safe to say, however, that the imperial government was careless in its language and was therefore partly responsible for the confusion in terminology that puzzled many a later writer. The emperor himself may not have been clear about the exact arrangement of the system. He contended that "the few households of a village may be arranged into one *chia,*" apparently oblivious of the fact that according to the regulations, ten households constituted a *p'ai*, whereas a *chia* contained one hundred. The "few households" of a tiny village were hardly sufficient to constitute a *chia*.

The inclusion of special categories of the people referred to above set a new trend in the *pao-chia*, making it virtually a system of universal surveillance, a trend that continued down to Tao-kuang times. A 1729 edict ordered the banner households in China proper to set up *pao-chia*,[20] and another of 1841 extended the system to households belonging to the imperial clan.[21] Gentry and scholars, privileged in other respects, were not exempt from this all-inclusive control. By edicts of 1727, 1757, and 1758, their households were to join the same *pao-chia* units that included those of the commoners who happened to be their neighbors and were made equally subject to the inspection of the *chia-chang* and *pao-chang*.[22] Special categories of the common people, wherever conditions permitted, were likewise regimented. An edict of 1729 brought the *tan-min* (boat people) within the pale of *pao-chia* control;[23] the application of *pao-chia* control to *p'eng-min* and *liao-hu* was extended in 1739;[24] and additional ethnic minorities, including the Yao and Moslems, were ordered in 1731 and 1756 to discontinue the practice of selecting their own headmen and to organize themselves into *pao-chia* divisions.[25]

Renewed emphasis was placed upon the police system during the Ch'ien-lung and Chia-ch'ing reigns,[26] approximately from the middle of the eighteenth to the first quarter of the nineteenth century, when signs of unrest became increasingly evident in many parts of the empire. In a number of edicts and orders the rulers sought to extend and intensify the police control. Besides applying it to special categories of the people, it was made to operate in far-flung places of the empire. In 1733 (Yung-cheng 11) Taiwan (Formosa) was included in the *pao-chia* system. In 1743 (Ch'ien-lung 8) it was decided that "inhabitants in Mongolia who cultivated the land should be ordered to set up *p'ai-t'ou, tsung-chia,* and ten-household heads." This order was reiterated in 1757. Meanwhile farmers in Shansi and Shensi (then regarded as frontier territories) were required to do the same.[27] Inhabitants of islands off the coasts of Shantung and Chekiang provinces were ordered to arrange themselves into *pao-chia* divisions in 1793 and 1794.[28]

By far the most serious effort to render the *pao-chia* system effective in the provinces of China proper was made by the Ch'ien-lung emperor in 1757. Discovering that the personnel of the police system had deteriorated and that the local officials showed little interest in the matter, he ordered all the governors-general and governors to report the local conditions in detail and to suggest concrete measures of improvement. On the basis of these reports the Board of Revenue made a number of recommendations, including the selection of *pao-cheng* and *chia-chang* from "honest, literate, and propertied persons"; the institution of *ti-fang* to relieve the *pao-chia* heads of urging tax payments and making arrests of criminals, tasks which by then had been heaped upon their shoulders without imperial authorization; and the preservation of the original quota of personnel at the various levels of the system.[29] The *pao-chia* arrangement envisaged by the central authorities at this moment was of the three-level *(pao-cheng, chia-chang,* and *p'ai-t'ou)* pattern, taking, apparently, the *pao-cheng* and *chia-chang* from the 1726 nomenclature, and *p'ai-t'ou* from that of 1644. In 1775 an empire-wide checking of *pao-chia* registers was conducted. Apparently attaching a good deal of importance to these registers, the Ch'ien-lung emperor ordered provincial authorities to use them as the basis of all future reports on population.[30]

From the latter part of the eighteenth century to the opening decades of the nineteenth, the imperial peace was marred by the outbreak of a number of insurrections and revolts, the most important of which were the uprisings led by the various leaders of the White Lotus in Shensi, Hunan, and Szechwan, and in 1813 the daring plot of Lin-ch'ing, who was probably also a member of the White Lotus.[31] The imperial government made some use of the "village braves" in an attempt to suppress the "bandits," but it also banked its hopes on the efficacious operation of the *pao-chia* as a preventive measure. More than ever, the government tried to inject new life and vigor into this timeworn rural police system. In 1746 (Ch'ien-lung 11) the government had already sought to use the *pao-chia* as a weapon to fight "heretical doctrines" and secret societies.[32] But with the beginning of the reign of Chia-ch'ing imperial attention to the *pao-chia* was renewed and did not abate until it became obvious that the *pao-chia* was altogether unequal to the task of coping with widespread and large-scale social unrest.

An edict of 1799 (Chia-ch'ing 4, in response to the petitions of a number of central government officials) indicated the current imperial view concerning the rural police system:

The method of *pao-chia* . . . as a means of detecting wicked and criminal persons and suppressing banditry at its source, is truly an excellent way to maintain local order. Regulations were formulated a long time ago. But owing to the fact that local officials have allowed the matter to drift during many years past, they have come to regard it as a mere formality; or worse still, through their mismanagement they have made it a cause of trouble [to the people]. As a consequence robbers and bandits secrete themselves in the localities under the jurisdiction of these officials. There is no way of detecting [dangerous elements]. . . . Unless all the ill practices are swept away and a study of the matter is made with earnestness, how can we eradicate the root of wickedness and give peace to the good people? . . .

It is hereby especially ordered that all governors-general and governors instruct their subordinates to consult the regulations previously formulated and urge the people with a sincere heart, so that they will select upright *li-chang [sic]* and institute *men-p'ai* [door placards], with a view to making the number of persons, taxpaying adults, and households in every *chou* and *hsien* ascertainable by inspecting the *[pao-chia]* registers, thus depriving wicked persons and bandits of their hiding places. [33]

Not satisfied with merely requiring the local officials to follow the old regulations, the Chia-ch'ing emperor indicated in an edict of 1800 some guiding principles for improving the *pao-chia*. First, he stated that bylaws should be pertinent, simple, and easy to follow so that they could be really effectual; second, he stressed the importance of relying on "honest *chia-chang*" for compiling the registers, and of avoiding the intrusion of yamen underlings; third, he asserted that periodic inspection of the ten-households by local officials themselves was the only way to insure reliable records, and that such inspection necessitated frequent visits to the countryside; finally, he attached, like his predecessors, great value to suitable punishment for those who failed in their duties. [34]

As if anticipating the plot of Lin Ch'ing, an edict of 1801 ordered a more strict enforcement of the *pao-chia* control in the metropolitan area of the imperial capital, particularly over the temples where persons of various descriptions found lodging. This practice was now forbidden; only expectant officials or those awaiting imperial audience were permitted to make use of these makeshift inns. [35]

Despite reports that the *pao-chia* did not yield the expected results, the Chia-ch'ing emperor maintained his confidence in the practicability of the rural police system. Replying to a petition by Fukien provincial officials to reduce the responsibilities imposed on the *pao-chia* agents, he said in an edict of 1814 (Chia-ch'ing 19):

Wang Chih-i and others memorialized to the effect that persons in Fukien generally are afraid of and avoid being appointed to the offices of *p'ai-chang, chia-chang,* and *pao-chang,* all for the reason that

these offices easily draw resentment and hatred toward the incumbents. It was suggested that the duties of apprehending criminals and
urging tax payments be no longer assigned to the *pao-chia* agents who
are to be held responsible only for investigating bad characters.
Wherever such characters are found to hide in a neighborhood, they
are authorized to report secretly to the local officials; the latter are
to pretend that they discovered the facts through personal investigation, so that the former will not draw resentment.

If a person is impartial and upright in his heart, why should he be
solicitous about drawing resentment and hatred? On the contrary,
precisely because one cannot be free from selfish motives, he desires
to show favors to others and is afraid of drawing resentment. Recently this has become a common weakness of all officials, both in
and out of the imperial capital. These *p'ai-chang* in question are indeed too insignificant and too lowly to call for censure.

It is hereby ordered that the duties of arresting criminals wanted
by the government and of urging and collecting money and grain taxes
shall no longer be imposed upon [the *pao-chia*]. As to the matter of
supervising the household and the inhabitants, since these agents are
held responsible for supervision, they should be given the authority
of making reports. In case a neighborhood harbors wicked elements,
these agents should precisely be ordered to report the offenders by
name, so that criminals and their accomplices may be deterred and
dare not continue their clandestine activities. If, however, the *pao-
chia* are made to report secretly to the local officials who pretend to
have secured the information through their own personal investigation,
wicked elements will have no respect for the *chia-chang*. How can
they be effectual in their task of weeding out the wicked elements and
giving peace to the good ones?[36]

The emperor was convinced that thanks to his own zeal and to the efforts of some of his servants the *pao-chia* was yielding gratifying results. He redoubled his efforts at increasing its effectiveness. In
another edict of 1814 he said:

It is known that the *pao-chia* as an instrument for suppressing marauders and giving peace to the good, is a most excellent administrative measure. In the winter of last year, We, in an imperial edict,
ordered expressly that it be put into universal operation. This order
has been carried out in the metropolitan area and in the provinces,
one after another.

In the eleventh month of the present year, when We reverently visited the East Mausoleum, We perceived that in the *chou* and *hsien*
through which we passed on Our journey, the *men-p'ai* posted on the
doors of the households had all the relevant items written clearly and
in detail. Moreover, upon questioning, the officials of all ranks high
and low who came to the capital from the various provinces testified
unanimously that they have obeyed this order referred to above and

complied with the prescribed form in making the registration and investigation [in their respective localities] without any exception whatever. It is clear, therefore, that results are gradually obtained also in working the *pao-chia* system outside the capital. [37]

In an edict issued in the same year, the emperor spoke almost with elation over the success of the *pao-chia* in Kwangtung province:

> [Governor] Jüan Yüan memorialized that he arrested the principal and accomplices involved in a crime against the throne . . . including Hu Ping-yao . . . Chu Mao-li . . . etc. . . . Shortly after he arrived at his post, Jüan Yüan was able to direct his subordinates to register and check closely and rigidly the *pao-chia* in their respective localities. In consequence, he uncovered this monstrous crime immediately and dealt with the criminals without delay. He certainly deserves commendation. It is hereby ordered that the title of Junior Protector of the Heir Apparent be conferred upon Jüan Yüan, and the privilege of wearing the peacock feather be granted to him. [38]

The emperor did not become complacent, however. Realizing that any success so far achieved could be only temporary, he renewed his efforts to enhance the effectiveness of the *pao-chia*. In a number of edicts, including the ones already cited, he reiterated the necessity of checking the registers at suitable intervals and admonished his servants not to relax their vigilance. In the earlier 1814 edict he said:

> As the inhabitants of a given locality are likely to change their residence, the number of households and mouths varies accordingly. If the registers are not checked from time to time, the records will soon lose their accuracy and the entire system become an empty name. Owing to their sluggish habits, high and low officials of the provinces are generally diligent at the beginning but negligent afterwards. They are concerned merely with presenting a good appearance for the moment; after a while, they will regard the matter as a mere formality, to which little thought will be given. . . .
> If everyone of the local officials exerts himself energetically . . . all the inhabitants will be accurately counted and everything will come under the clear view of the government. Where, then, can wicked persons find a place to hide themselves? If, however, the officials obey ostensibly and actually disregard Our wishes, i.e., if they respond to a standing requirement with empty gestures, or if they take advantage of [the *pao-chia*] to make trouble for and impose burdens upon the good people, those governors-general and governors who thus fail to carry out Our orders with vigor shall be severely punished without mercy. [39]

The measures which the Chia-ch'ing emperor deemed necessary

for keeping the *pao-chia* in good running order included (1) checking the registers every year after the autumn harvest, (2) requiring the *pao-chia* heads to assume joint responsibility, and (3) relieving them of duties other than those essential to police control.

The idea of checking the registers after the autumn harvest originated with a high official. As explained by the emperor, its merits lay in that it took advantage of the time when farmhands and various types of hired laborers would presumably have returned to their home villages. A count made at this time of the year would be the most accurate attainable.

> After the autumn harvest officials of *chou* and *hsien* are first to issue directives to the *pao-chang* and other personnel in the villages and hamlets, instructing them to make a careful survey of the households and mouths in their respective communities and compile draft registers. These draft registers are to be sent to the officials concerned, who are then to go to the villages and make personal inspections. All this should be done in accordance with the promulgated regulations. A *hu-pao kan-chieh* [a willing bond of mutual guarantee] should be secured in each case. The *men-p'ai* should be revised and posted on the door of every household.
>
> Officials of the *tao, fu,* or *chih-li-chou* concerned are to go to the localities in person to make sampling inspections, upon the completion of which they should report the matter to the governor-general or governor. . . . The latter is to report to the imperial court at the end of each year. [40]

The *hu-pao kan-chieh* mentioned above (known also as *lien-ming hu-pao* or joint pledge and mutual responsibility) was a device calculated to forestall irresponsibility on the part of the *pao-chia* heads. The theory was that the *chia-chang* and *pao-chang,* being naturally afraid of the punishments threatened if lawbreakers were discovered among those whom they had guaranteed, would exercise greater than usual care in making the registers and be less inclined to cover up crimes or criminals. The emperor liked the device so well that he more than once insisted on its thorough application. The abortive plot of Lin Ch'ing more than any other incident probably impressed him with the necessity of tightening the *pao-chia* control by means of joint responsibility. Thus he said in an edict of 1815:

> In the *pao-chia* registers ten households make a *p'ai*. These ten households in the *p'ai* are ordered to maintain mutual surveillance one over another. If there are suspicious persons in the neighborhood, they should be reported immediately to the government. If seditious criminals are apprehended, not only will the person who makes the initial report be rewarded with money and official appointment, but the ten households in his *p'ai* will also be suitably rewarded. If, however,

seditious criminals are harbored and no report is made, and if these
are arrested through information obtained by local officials, the
households that harbor them will receive the same penalty as the
criminals. The ten households in the same *p'ai* will be held jointly responsible. [41]

A further step in this direction was taken in 1816 when the *pao-chia*
heads were required to furnish written bonds. An edict of this year
reads:

> At present the *pao-chia* is in operation in the provinces and the *men-
> p'ai* have been checked. But in the absence of definite responsibility,
> it is feared that some of the *li-chang[sic]* and *chia-chang* may resort
> to the evil practice of covering up [crimes and criminals]. It is or-
> dered that governors-general and governors of the provinces again
> issue strict directives to the local officials who shall, at the time of
> making *pao-chia* registration, require *li-chang* and *chia-chang* to
> furnish *lien-ming hu-pao kan-chieh* [willing bonds of joint pledge and
> mutual responsibility]. If there are in the neighborhoods persons
> whose origins are doubtful or whose ways are suspicious, and the
> *li-chang* and others concerned refuse to furnish bonds for them out
> of fear of being implicated [in case of crime], these should be im-
> mediately reported. On the other hand, if bonds are furnished and
> subsequently it is discovered that the persons for whom the bonds
> have been furnished have committed crime or offenses, or are fugi-
> tive-criminals of a seditious nature, the *li-chang* and *chia-chang*
> furnishing the bonds shall be held jointly responsible. The degree of
> punishment varies proportionally with the degree of gravity of the
> crime committed. [42]

Meanwhile, aware that overburdened *pao-chia* agents could not discharge their duties properly, the emperor endeavored to simplify and
lighten their work. The *pao-chang* and *chia-chang* had been given a
variety of irrelevant tasks to perform, which unavoidably distracted
them from their proper responsibilities as defined in 1644. The emperor therefore ordered in 1814 that "the tasks of arresting criminals
and of urging and collecting money and grain taxes should no longer
be assigned" to them. The same idea underlay the following edict,
issued in 1815:

> [*P'ai-t'ou* and *chia-chang*] should be entrusted solely with the task
> of investigating marauders and maintaining peace in the neighbor-
> hoods. All other miscellaneous services, including furnishing sup-
> plies, making arrests, and running errands, should not be imposed
> on them, in order that good people will not be deterred by possible
> losses and dread to enter these offices. [43]

As already pointed out, the Chia-ch'ing emperor's keen interest in the *pao-chia* was the outcome of historical circumstances rather than personal predilection. When he ascended the throne (1796), the dynasty had already passed its zenith. Growing social and political disturbances, while not yet serious enough to threaten the throne itself, were alarmingly widespread and so persistent that maintenance of imperial peace was difficult. How to cope with this situation of smoldering unrest and prevent it from breaking out into a conflagration of open revolt became an urgent question. It was in official parlance the problem of "bandit suppression" that claimed the foremost attention of the imperial government. In trying to meet this problem, the emperor found no better instrument than the *pao-chia* apparatus.

The emperor foresaw the impending danger. About thirty-five years after he issued the edict (1814) in which he made a desperate effort to rid the countryside of "persons practicing heretical religions" by means of the *pao-chia*,[44] a great rebellion led by leaders of a "heretical sect" broke out in South China and nearly overthrew the dynasty. But he was less accurate in estimating the efficacy of the *pao-chia* as an instrument of control in the face of the rising tide of "banditry." It appears that the *pao-chia* proved an effective deterrent only in times of relative tranquility when few of the rural inhabitants were driven by desperation to "tread the dangerous path"; but in a period of general unrest the *pao-chia* was no more able than any other instrument of imperial control to operate with its peacetime efficiency (or, more accurately, semi-efficiency). It was, in fact, outmoded by the changed circumstances.

The Chia-ch'ing emperor's successors showed comparatively little interest in the *pao-chia*. A survey of the official records reveals that from the Tao-kuang reign to the end of the dynasty (1821-1911) scant mention was made of it. The Tao-kuang emperor spoke of it occasionally; he still recognized the theoretical usefulness of the system, so much so that in 1850 he attributed the rampant "banditry" (especially in Hunan, Kwangsi, and Kwangtung) directly to the decay of the *pao-chia*.[45] But he was no longer sanguine about the practical usefulness of the police control system and had no suggestion as to how to revitalize it. Thereafter the *pao-chia* became except in isolated instances little more than a mere *ku-shih* (an antiquated formality). The editors of the official compilation, *Huang-ch'ao hsü wen-hsien t'ung-k'ao,* went so far as to conclude that the *pao-chia* had become totally and absolutely useless.[46]

Up to this point, we have been reviewing the action taken by the imperial government to implement the *pao-chia* as an empire-wide system of control. As official documents show, the emperors emphatically affirmed the importance of this system but at the same time complained that it often fell short in performance. The *pao-chia* was in fact beset with inherent weaknesses and confronted with difficulties that arose from social and political circumstances. But it was not an entirely unworkable system. In localities where competent or conscientious officials were able to adapt it to local conditions or to exercise ingenuity in operating it, the *pao-chia* showed a degree of effectiveness not observed in other parts of the empire. In such instances local practices always deviated in varying degrees from the official regulations. The imperial government, apparently more interested in getting practical results than in maintaining uniformity or strict adherence to law, allowed such deviations and even went so far as to give official approval.

Yü Ch'eng-lung, governor of Chihli in the 1680's, employed the *pao-chia* successfully in suppressing the bandits that were previously rampant in the province. [47] Huang Liu-hung, a younger contemporary of Yü and a magistrate of long experience, [48] Ju Tun-ho, a magistrate serving in Nan-lo Hsien (Chihli) late in the eighteenth century, and Wang Hui-tsu, magistrate of Ning-yüan Hsien (Hunan), [49] each in his own way achieved success with the *pao-chia*. Ch'en Hung-mou, an eighteenth-century official of renown, extended the usefulness of the *pao-chia* by enlisting "beggar kings" as *pao-chia* heads to supervise the vagabond households in Kiangsu province, thus bringing under control those whose very vagrancy defied registration by the usual method. [50] The name of Yeh P'ei-sun occupies an especially prominent place in the annals of the *pao-chia*. While he was provincial treasurer of Hunan (1781) he devised the *hsün-huan ts'e* (rotating registers), which operated as follows: A set of two registers was prepared for each *pao-chia* unit, one of which was placed in the hands of the local agent while the other was kept in the magistrate's yamen; by periodically rotating these records, additional entries and corrections could be made and official checking could be done without interruption. The imperial government was so pleased with this convenient device that it ordered (1813) all provincial authorities to adopt it. [51]

Some of the nineteenth-century local officials could vie with their predecessors in ingenuity or zeal in operating the *pao-chia*. The efforts of Liu Heng, magistrate of Pa Hsien (Szechwan), deserve special mention. In response to the imperial edict of 1814, he set up the *pao-chia* in conformity with the official decimal pattern. He also introduced some refinements of his own. In addition to the *men-p'ai* pasted on the door of the household concerned, he instituted a *shih-chia p'ai* (ten-household card) to be kept by the *p'ai-chang* (i.e., *p'ai-t'ou),* and a card for every hundred households to be kept by the *chia-chang.* The *pao-cheng* were responsible for the compilation of the *ts'ao-ts'e* (draft registers) which formed the basis for the *cheng-ts'e* (official registers) to be compiled by the local yamen. Adopting the *hsün-huan ts'e* system of Yeh P'ei-sun, he required the magistrate to prepare two sets of *ts'ao-ts'e.* One copy of the first set, known as the *hsün-ts'e* (current registers), was distributed to each *pao-cheng*. At the end of the lunar year the *pao-cheng* sent it, with proper entries, to the magistrate. At the same time, a copy of the second set, known as the *huan-ts'e* (rotating registers), was given him for making entries during the following year. At any given time one copy of one set of these draft registers was in the hands of every *pao-cheng*, while corresponding copies of the other set were in the ya-men. [52]

Successful utilization of the *pao-chia* in Hunan was claimed for Lu-fei Ch'üan, governor of the province. It was said that thanks to his efforts, the *pao-chia* of a number of districts became so efficient that its agents effectively assisted the government in detecting and suppressing dangerous *hui-fei* (secret-society bandits) in 1847. [53]

T'ao Chu, governor of Anhwei in the 1820's, made an attempt to extend the *pao-chia* to special categories of the people. In a memorial of 1825 he reported that he had arranged the *p'eng-min* (shed people) of that province into *pao-chia,* with a *p'eng-t'ou* (head of the shed) in each grouping serving as a *pao-chia* agent. [54] Thus, for example,

	No. Households	No. *p'eng-t'ou*
Hsi Hsien	156	17
Hsiu-ning Hsien	232	13
Ch'i-men Hsien	432	24
I Hsien	10	1

The *p'eng-t'ou* appear to have been roughly equivalent to the *p'ai-t'ou* in the regular *pao-chia* arrangement, at least so far as the number of households was concerned. About twelve years later (1837), when he was governor-general of Liang-Chiang, T'ao Chu again memorialized the throne that shed people in several other localities of Anhwei were similarly organized but in a modified and augmented pattern: "A *p'ai-chang [p'ai-t'ou* of regular *pao-chia]* was instituted for every ten households, a *p'eng-chang* for every ten *p'ai,* and a *p'eng-t'ou* for every mountain area. [All these heads] were required to investigate robbers and bandits. "[55]

T'ao also undertook to organize inhabitants of villages along the seacoast of Kiangsu. In a memorial of 1836 he reported:

At present all the villages along the coast have been inspected and registered. Ten households are made into one *chia* for which a *chia-chang* is instituted. As soon as ten *chia* have been arranged, a *tsung-chia* is set up [to supervise them]. If fewer than ten *chia* are obtained in a given place, three to five *chia* are placed under a *tsung.* If fewer than ten households are found in a given neighborhood, or if the households are scattered over a wide area, a *chang* is set up in each neighborhood.

Families living permanently in boats were arranged as follows:

> Functionaries in the *chou* and *hsien* have been charged with the task
> of arranging every ten boats into one *chia,* after the pattern of the
> *pao-chia.* . . . Fishing boats are also to be similarly arranged,
> namely, every ten of them into a *chia,* for which a *yü-chia* [fisher-
> man *chia-chang]* is instituted, who is assigned the duty of watching
> over them. [56]

In the same year Yao Ying, a functionary serving in Formosa, reported to the provincial authorities of Fukien that the 1,042 villages
of Chia-i Hsien were arranged into thirty-five *pao* and the 1,427 villages of Chang-hua Hsien into thirteen *pao,* pointing out that the population of these villages varied from under a hundred to several hundred persons. [57]

Another instance of trying to operate the police system in far-flung
parts of the empire was afforded by Shu-hsing-a, governor-general
of Shen-Kan, who memorialized in 1852 that in obedience to an imperial order he had formulated a set of rules governing the *pao-chia*
and applied them in practice. [58]

A third instance of this sort was found in Kuang-t'ung Hsien (Yunnan)
where Ho Shao-ch'i, the magistrate, organized in 1844 all the inhabitants, Chinese, Moslems, and the *I,* a total of 9,657 households, into
fifty-two *chia,* with an average of 185 households in each *chia.* [59]

Hsia Hsieh recorded two attempts at making the *pao-chia* an instrument for suppressing opium smoking and for maintaining order
during the Opium War. According to him, Huang Chüeh-tzu, a high-
ranking central official, sought to put a stop to the opium trade by
prohibiting opium smoking. He said in a memorial of 1838:

> It is humbly begged that governors-general and governors be ordered
> to instruct sternly the *fu, chou,* and *hsien* officials to make an inspec-
> tion of the *pao-chia.* The local inhabitants should be informed before-
> hand to the effect that at the end of one year every five households in
> the neighborhoods are to furnish written bonds for one another. If at
> the end of the period specified there are still offenders, permission
> for informing against them should be given and substantial rewards
> to informers be granted. On the other hand, if offenders are covered
> up or tolerated, and if these are found out, the offenders are to be
> punished according to the new law, namely, with death, and those who
> furnish the bonds punished according to law. [60]

The other attempt which Hsia noted was made in 1842:

> When the foreigners entered Hsia-kuan, Huang Fang-t'ung, the gov-
> ernor at Nanking, ordered that the *pao-chia* method be applied in the

city. Every fifty households and shops facing one another on a street were to establish a *cha* [palisade], and to each division was issued a *p'ai-ts'e* [placard register]. The gate of the palisade was open in the daytime but closed at night, to forestall plundering by wicked people who might take advantage of the general confusion. Inhabitants of Nanking were at first grateful to him. [61]

A few provincial and local officials endeavored to operate the *pao-chia* in post-Taiping times. Ting Jih-ch'ang, one of the enterprising members of the Li Hung-chang group, issued a number of directives to various magistrates of Kiangsu province, where he served as governor in the 1860's. With ostensible earnestness he indicated his determination to revive the *pao-chia* which he said had disappeared in many parts of the province during the rebellion. [62] Comparable attempts were made by Pien Pao-ti, governor of Hunan between 1881 and 1886. He memorialized that his subordinates were instructed to check the *pao-chia* registers every year after the autumn harvest, in accordance with the old regulations, and that he owed his success to the hearty support of the local gentry, in particular to those of Ch'ang-sha and Shan-hua. [63] As late as in the 1890's a magistrate in Ch'ing-pien Hsien (Shensi) made a number of suggestions to his superiors with a view to implementing the local police system. He proposed that the assistance of the gentry be enlisted to supply leadership in the upper ranks of the *pao-chia* personnel. Perhaps the most novel idea he offered was that if any of the households in a given *p'ai* was found to have concealed criminals or committed crimes, the *p'ai-t'ou* was to report the matter to the gentry agent in charge. The magistrate did not deal with it unless it could not be handled by the gentry leaders. [64]

It appears, then, that local interest in the *pao-chia* continued in some parts of the empire long after imperial interest had waned. One possible explanation is that *pao-chia* operation remained almost to the very end of the dynasty one of the yardsticks for measuring the service merits of local officials. The system had survived its actual usefulness, but as an "antiquated routine" it still possessed a ghost-like legal existence and a faded administrative significance. Some of the favorable reports concerning local *pao-chia* practice may have exaggerated the results attained, if any results actually were attained. One cannot be sure that ostensible local interest was a true index of local success.

Even if these reports are taken at face value, provincial and local officials had not followed faithfully the regulations of the *pao-chia* system as formulated by their imperial masters. In fact they deviated quite widely, adding substantially to the confusion in form and terminology that puzzled many a later writer. As early as the seventeenth century (not long after the establishment of the *pao-chia),* Huang

Liu-hung set up a *pao-chia* structure with a *chia-pao-Hsiang* instead
of the official *p'ai-chia-pao* pattern. [65] So much liberty had been taken
generally that by the end of the eighteenth century the official form
was mutilated almost beyond recognition in many parts of the empire. As a writer of this period summed up the situation,

> In the *chou* and *hsien* of the present time, some villages have *pao-
> chang* only, others *chia-chang*, and still others *p'ai-chang*. Some
> have all these, whereas others have only one of these. Where all
> three are present, the heads of superior divisions no longer have
> authority over those below, each having acquired independent or dif-
> ferent functions. [66]

Meanwhile, an even more important change took place: the assumption of the tax collection function of the *li-chia* by the *pao-chia*. We do
not know exactly when this happened, but it is certain that the change
had taken place in many parts of the empire by the middle of the eighteenth century.

This shift of function from *li-chia* to *pao-chia* was partly due to the
actions of the imperial government. For instance, the Ch'ien-lung emperor ordered, in a 1743 edict, the *pao-chia* in Shansi, Shensi, and
other "frontier regions" to report persons "who were behind in their
payment of land taxes, who committed theft, and those whose places
of origin were obscure."[67] Perhaps for the sake of convenience, the
emperor thus unwittingly threw together functions belonging to two
separate systems of imperial control. In other cases the change was
due to actions of local officials, without the knowledge or authorization of the imperial government. The most outstanding instances were
reported by Tseng Kuo-fan in the middle of the nineteenth century in
Heng-yang and Ch'ing-ch'uan (Hunan). In a memorial (1854) he said:

> Investigation shows that the *pao-chia* of Heng-yang Hsien and Ch'ing-
> ch'uan Hsien have recently been devoting their time exclusively to
> collecting the money and grain taxes, neglecting their duties of un-
> covering bandits. The origin of this practice is traced to Tao-kuang
> fifteenth year [1835] when Shen Hsieh, a former magistrate of Heng-
> yang, lightly changed the regulations. In so doing he had neither me-
> morialized the throne nor informed the governor and the finance com-
> missioner. He simply made the *pao-chia* collect all the taxes. The
> magistrate of Ch'ing-ch'uan followed him and did the same thing.
> Subsequently numerous evils have appeared. *Pao-chia* agents who are
> powerless suffer the crushing burden of making good the defaults of
> taxpayers, whereas those who are powerful connive with corrupt ya-
> men underlings to extort money from them beyond the amount of taxes
> for which they are liable. . . .
>   It may be recalled that in the ninth month of Tao-kuang thirtieth
> year [1850] Wu Jo-chun, an imperial censor, memorialized the throne

concerning malpractices of long standing. He pointed out that urging
tax payment is the responsibility of yamen underlings, while apprehending robbers is the duty of the *pao-chia*. An imperial edict had
been reverently received which ordered that all those who disturb the
pao-chia on the pretext of urging tax payment . . . be severely punished. . . . Heng-yang and Ch'ing-chuan have not yet obeyed this
order and the matter stands uncorrected. [68]

As Tseng's memorial indicates, the shifting of the *li-chia's* function to the *pao-chia* tended to prevent the latter from performing its
own proper functions. The imperial government therefore tried for
a while to keep the two systems functionally apart by threatening with
punishment those "who disturbed the *pao-chia*." But historical circumstances favored such a development, and some of the emperors
themselves unintentionally contributed to it.

At the time when the *li-chia* was set up (1648), it was assigned the
task of assisting in the compilation of the *huang-ts'e* (the yellow registers), the basis for tax assessment and collection. In 1656 the government changed the original practice of compiling the registers once
in every three years to once in every five. [69] Registration was further
simplified with the merging of the *ting-yin* (corvée tax on adult males)
into the *ti-liang* (land tax), a change which began late in the seventeenth century and was completed early in the nineteenth, [70] thus making the task of *li-chia* registration less formidable. And when the
K'ang-hsi emperor decided in 1713 to fix the *ting* tax quota permanently on the basis of the census returns of 1711 (to stop making new
assessments thereafter even though the population of the empire later
showed an increase), the compilation of the *li-chia* registers lost
much of its significance in the revenue system. [71]

The practice of compiling quinquennial registers was allowed to
continue for a while. It did not take the imperial government long to
see that as the "household and inhabitant" registers compiled after
1713 theoretically had little connection with the revenue system, it
was a useless duplication of function to have both the *li-chia* and *pao-
chia* compile separate registers. Consequently, the task of compilation
was officially taken away from the *li-chia* in 1740 (Ch'ien-lung 5) leaving the *pao-chia* the sole agent to perform it. A government order
said:

> Since *men-p'ai* [door placards] of the *pao-chia* have been instituted
> in the *chou* and *hsien* of the various provinces, on which native in-
> habitants and transient dwellers are all enumerated, [the population
> of any given locality] can already be ascertained in these records. If
> the number of the transients is deducted and the number of the in-
> habitants is reported, the actual number of the latter can readily be
> determined. The governors-general and governors are hereby ordered
> to send in, in the eleventh month of each year, reports of the actual

number of households and mouths and the amount of grain [in their respective provinces]. [72]

Thirty-two years later (1772), the task of revising the *hu-k'ou* registers every five years, a former *li-chia* task which had become by then "a routine formality," was officially abolished, [73] thereby putting an end to *li-chia* registration, one of the main functions originally assigned to the tax collection system. In an edict of 1775 (Ch'ien-lung 40) the emperor set forth the reason for relying on the *pao-chia* alone for *hu-k'ou* registration:

> Increases in the number of households and mouths in the various provinces have been reported to the *Hu-pu* [as the law requires]. After continued practice for a long time, however, officials have come to regard the reports as a routine formality and the higher officials have failed to supervise [their compilation] with any attention. . . . At present a general inspection of the *pao-chia* is being made in the provinces. The number of households and mouths in each province is ascertained and entered in the registers. It will not be difficult to count them by using these registers. From now on the governors-general and governors of the provinces are to direct their subordinates to obtain the actual number of the population and send the report to them who are in turn to send the reports to the imperial court. By perusing these reports We can not merely acquaint Ourselves with the prosperity of the millions but also determine whether or not the provinces are doing their utmost in *pao-chia* arrangement and inspection. [74]

Abolition of *li-chia* registration and official recognition of the *pao-chia* as the sole agent for furnishing census figures were generally speaking logical products of the historical circumstances. They were developments dictated by convenience. For, while the land tax was levied on the basis of the amount of registered land, the tax payments were made by the households that owned the land; while the quotas of the corvée tax were theoretically fixed once and for all, the names of adult males who had died or had passed the age of tax liability must be periodically deleted and the names of youths who had meanwhile come of age duly added. The *pao-chia* registers should have been able to furnish the required information as to the number of households and adult males in a given neighborhood or village;[75] they need not be accurate, but they served the revenue collection purposes perhaps as well as the *li-chia* registers formerly did.

There was, however, a drawback. The government soon found it impossible to keep the other main function of the *li-chia*, tax collection, from being imposed upon the *pao-chia*. Local officials now had to rely solely on the *pao-chia* for information concerning the number and location of tax-liable households and individuals and were readily persuaded to rely on it also for collecting tax payments in rural areas—to the detriment of the *pao-chia* as an instrument of police control. The situation in Hunan province reported by Tseng Kuo-fan was not the only instance.[76] In some cases, the *li-chia* divisions disappeared altogether and *pao-chia* divisions replaced them for tax collection purposes.[77]

Partly as the result of the assumption of *li-chia* functions by the *pao-chia,* a rural office known as *ti-fang* or *ti-pao* came into existence. We do not know when or how the *ti-fang* originated. By the middle of the eighteenth century it had become firmly established in many parts of the empire as an instrument of rural control, shouldering the responsibilities of police control *(pao-chia)* and tax collection *(li-chia)* at the same time. A statement taken from an official compilation explains the functions of the *ti-fang:*

> The service performed by the *ti-fang* is most important. Each of the *chou* or *hsien* is divided into a number of *ti-fang* [wards] and each *ti-fang* [agent] is in charge of a number of villages. He shares the responsibility for tax payments, disputes over land and homesteads, cases of litigation, occurrences of robbery and theft, and investigation of murder cases. Whenever there is any [government] service or undertaking, he is responsible for prompting the supply of the necessary implements and materials, and for supervising the drafted corvée laborers. If he makes any slight mistake or is slightly tardy in his action, flogging will be promptly administered to him.[78]

The *ti-fang* did not always replace the *pao-chia.* In many instances they existed side by side in the same localities, a highly confusing situation. The imperial government made some attempts to remedy the chaotic situation. In 1757 (Ch'ien-lung 22) the Board of Revenue decided to apportion the functions of rural control between the *ti-fang* and the *pao-chia.* The police functions were reserved for the latter, leaving to the former "matters concerning the households, marriage, urging tax payments, and arresting prisoners."[79]

It appears that this action did not bring much result. In many localities it remained difficult to keep the *ti-fang* and *pao-chia* functionally apart. For instance, a *ti-fang* agent was instituted (1763) in each of the villages of T'ung-kuan Hsien (Shensi) to supervise the *p'ai* divisions and to assist the *pao-chang* in carrying out his police control duties.[80] The *ti-fang* served as a *pao-chia* division in a number of districts of Yü-lin Fu[81] and in Yen-yüan Hsien (Szechwan)[82] in the nineteenth century. In some localities in Kwangsi province the *ti-fang* virtually replaced the *pao-chia* and, somewhat curiously, remained distinct from the *li-chia.* According to the *Yung hsien chih* (1897),

> The *hu-k'ou* [households and mouths] have two different aspects. On the one hand, there are the *hu-k'ou* of the *li-chia* service, which are registered on the basis of taxable land and adult males liable to the

corvée imposts. The *li* controls the *chia,* the *chia* controls the *hu*
which latter in turn controls the *ting*[adult males]. The *k'ou* here are
identical with the *ting.* On the other hand, there are the *hu-k'ou* of the
door-to-door registration system based on the households that dwell
in a given area. Each *ti-fang* controls ten *chia,* and each *chia* contains
ten *hu.* The *k'ou* here refers to all the male and female inhabitants
belonging to these households.

In the former case land forms the basis of division; in the latter,
residence. [83]

"The door-to-door registration system" mentioned could be only the
men-p'ai system of the *pao-chia.* In other localities the *ti-fang* after having been entangled with the *pao-chia* became a tax collection
apparatus pure and simple; the police function of the *pao-chia* was
completely forgotten. Thus, according to an ex-magistrate writing
late in the nineteenth century,

> Matters relating to labor draft and litigations were dealt with by the
> *ti-fang* and *chia-chang,* whereas the duty of expediting tax payment
> fell on the shoulders of the *chia-chang.* When I asked these local head-
> men about the method of apprehending thieves and robbers, and of
> pacifying the people, they looked foolish, making no response to my
> questions. They seemed to think, "These are not our duties!"[84]

There is no evidence that the imperial government made any attempt to stop such confusing practices. By the second half of the nineteenth century *"ti-fang"* had become widely used by Chinese and Western writers alike to refer to a headman of the *pao-chia.* Thus Robert
Coleman, writing around 1890, identified "the policeman of the village" in Shantung province as the *ti-fang,* who also served as a tax
collection agent. [85] About a decade later, A. H. Smith wrote that the
village "local constable" was called "the *ti-fang* or *ti-pao.* "[86] Even
in more recent times, "the policeman of the village" was still known
as *"ti-fang.* "[87]

The practice of referring to headmen of the police control system as
ti-pao (sometimes written by Western writers as *tee-pao* or *tee-pow)*
introduced a further cause of confusion. Emile Bard, agreeing with
A. H. Smith, spoke of the *ti-pao* as "the dean of the village" who was
"responsible for the conduct of the families in his domain."[88] H. B.
Morse identified the *ti-pao* as the head of the *chia* division, which
would have made him the equivalent of the *chia-chang.* [89] E. T. C.
Werner described the *ti-pao* as "the rural constable," the headman
of the *chia.* [90] Other writers regarded the *ti-pao* as a rural tax collection agent often acting at the same time as a police agent. This was
the view of George Smith who wrote in the 1840's about the conditions
of a village in Ningpo (Chekiang). [91] About twenty years later, Samuel

Mossman discovered that the *ti-pao* had the duty of registering land transfers, a duty more properly exercised by tax collection agents. [92] H. S. Bucklin, writing much later, held that the *ti-pao* had the duties of (1) collecting the taxes, (2) certifying land sales, and (3) reporting theft, robbery, murder, and other crimes. [93]

The term *ti-pao* may have been derived from *ti-lin pao-chia* (neighbors in the locality and the *pao-chia* heads). [94] According to the *Lü-li pien-lan* (1877), the imperial law required that in dealing with "grave cases involving murder or manslaughter" local officials "summoned *ti-lin pao-chia*" for questioning. [95] The term *ti-pao* was perhaps derived by shortening *ti-lin pao-chia* for the sake of convenience, in accordance with customary Chinese practice.

The *ti-pao* as a rural control agent appeared relatively early in the dynasty, probably before the middle of the eighteenth century. One of the earliest official references to it was made in a general directive issued in 1741 by Ch'en Hung-mou, governor of Kiangsi. It was said that "in the various localities of Kiangsi, whenever cases of theft turn up, the local officials do not make any serious effort to apprehend the thieves and to recover the stolen goods, but merely punish the *ti-pao*. "[96] The *ti-pao* of whom Ch'en spoke was therefore a *pao-chia* head.

Other officials in the eighteenth and nineteenth centuries also treated the *ti-pao* as a *pao-chia* agent. Ju Tun-ho, magistrate of Nan-lo Hsien (Chihli) around 1786, made the *ti-pao* in the villages perform the duties of *pao-chia* registration and inspection. [97] Wang Hui-tsu, a magistrate of long experience, wrote in the closing decade of the eighteenth century that it was necessary only to order the *ti-pao* to investigate "ordinary cases of theft."[98] Chang Ch'i, a magistrate serving in Shantung province, wrote early in the nineteenth century that "whenever serious incidents occurred in the ten-household neighborhoods, the *ti-pao* never failed to involve the *chia-chang* and *p'ai-t'ou*, "[99] thus implying that the *ti-pao* and *pao-chang* were the same. About fifty years later Ting Jih-ch'ang, governor of Kiangsu, instructed one of the magistrates that the *ti-pao* should be selected by elderly persons in the ten-*chia* division. [100] Apparently, Ting also took the *ti-pao* as the equivalent of the *pao-chang*. In another connection Ting required the *ti-pao* to assist local officials who went to the villages to investigate cases of murder. [101] Li T'ang-chieh wrote in 1847 that the *ti-pao* in some localities of Honan province were punished by the magistrates for their failure to prevent undeserving inhabitants from going into the city to receive government relief. [102] Weng T'ung-ho said in 1899 that when he lived in temporary retirement in his native village in Ch'ang-shu (Kiangsu), he summoned the *ti-pao* to bring an unfilial peasant to him so that he could reprimand him. [103]

It appears clear that the *ti-pao* was essentially a rural agent who was assigned the tasks proper to the heads of the *pao-chia*. But as the task of collecting taxes had eventually devolved on the *pao-chia*, the *ti-pao* became also known in many instances as tax collection agents. [104] As the terms *ti-fang* and *ti-pao* were often indiscriminately used by various writers, their precise meaning can be determined only by the ascertainable facts in each individual case. [105]

The imposition of the task of collecting taxes on the *pao-chia* was not the only important functional alteration of the police control system. During the turbulent nineteenth century it was given another function: local defense. In the middle of the century when the Taiping Rebellion broke out, the imperial government soon found that the banner garrison forces and the regular *lü-ying* troops could not meet the situation and was compelled to approve and encourage the organization of *t'uan-lien* (regiment and drill corps) in those parts of the empire infested by "banditry." Many local officials readily perceived the convenience of making use of the *pao-chia* structure as a basis for the organization of local corps. Some of them kept a distinction between the *pao-chia* and *t'uan-lien* but insisted that since the one supplemented the other, they should be operated jointly. [106] Others failed to see any practical distinction between the two at all and believed that *"t'uan-lien* was no other than the method of *pao-chia.* "[107] At any rate, the *pao-chia* of many localities became inseparably involved in *t'uan-lien* work. [108]

In one sense this development was natural. It was a relatively short distance from police control to local defense; both had to do with maintenance of order. As a compiler of the *Fu-shun hsien chih* (1911) put it, "the *pao-chia* was established in peaceful times. In time of emergency it was integrated to form *t'uan* and activated by *lien*. The titles *pao-cheng* and *pao-chang* were changed into *t'uan-tsung* (corps officer) and *t'uan-chang* (corps commander). "[109]

Superficially it appears that the *pao-chia*, which had suffered decades of deterioration, received a new lease on life in localities where it served as the basis of local defense organizations. However, precisely because the process involved an important functional transformation, the organizations thus created cannot be regarded as a resurrection of the police control system. In the new circumstances that characterized the second part of the nineteenth century the *pao-chia* system, which was conceived and developed under very different conditions, had lost much of its practical usefulness. The gravest internal crisis was passed in the 1860's, when the Taiping Rebellion was put down, but the former situation could never be restored. Half-hearted efforts were made to re-establish the *pao-chia*, especially in localities where it had virtually disappeared as a result of devastations of war, but these efforts were to no avail. [110] That the *pao-chia* ceased to operate even in the imperial capital may be inferred from the fact that the imperial government ordered the officials "to set up *men-p'ai* and *hu-ts'e*" after robbers plundered the residence of a secretary of the Board of Works in the winter of 1877. [111] When the empire began to recover from the shock of wars and rebellions with the so-called T'ung-chih Restoration, new ideas of administration were heard for the first time. Government planners began to talk about police control in terms of *ching-ch'a* or *hsün-ching* (Japanese- or European-style police system)[112] instead of the traditional *pao-chia*. Before the nineteenth century drew to an end, some observers had come to the conclusion that the *pao-chia* as an instrument of police control had "disappeared in reality as well as in name."[113]

THE RURAL GENTRY AND THE *PAO-CHIA*

The Ch'ing rulers, in line with their policy of according special consideration to the gentry and scholars (i. e., potential gentry), [114] granted certain immunities to them in the *pao-chia* system but did not exempt them from *pao-chia* control and, contrary to their general practice of enlisting gentry assistance in imperial control, they virtually excluded the gentry from *pao-chia* leadership. This is made especially clear in the following regulation, laid down in 1727 (Yung-cheng 5):

> All families of *shen-shih* [gentry and scholars] shall register [in the *pao-chia*] and submit themselves to the inspection of the *pao-chang* and *chia-chang*. Any that fail to register shall be punished in accordance with the law governing delinquency in household [registration].
> However, *pao-chia* regulations provide for various *i* [services] which are performed by the *pao-chang* and *chia-chang*, and for services in the form of night watch and guarding the street gates, which are performed by turns by the ten households [in the *p'ai* division]. As the gentry have already entered officialdom and scholars are studying in the schools, they, together with commoners that are aged or disabled, and the minor sons and grandsons of widows shall be exempted from these services. [115]

The reason for insisting on bringing the gentry and scholars under *pao-chia* control is obvious. These otherwise privileges persons, after all, were subjects of the imperial rulers. The fact that they were often called on to assist in administration did not dispense with the need for keeping them under surveillance. Indeed, by virtue of their literacy and prestige in their home localities, they often became centers of decisive influence in the villages. This made it all the more important for the imperial rulers to keep a watchful eye to make sure that they might not misuse their prestige and influence to lead their fellow villagers into actions detrimental to imperial interests.

The reason for according differential treatment to the gentry in the *pao-chia* system may also be readily surmised. While it was necessary to bring the gentry under *pao-chia* surveillance, it would have been unwise to obliterate the distinction between them and the commoners. [116] Such an action might have impaired the gentry's prestige to an extent that would render them unsuitable for their unique role in the imperial system and might also have aroused their resentment against the *pao-chia* system. But since the gentry already dominated the local scene, it would also have been unwise to give them the power that pertained to the offices of the *pao-chia* heads. By reserving the posts of *pao-chang* and *chia-chang* to commoners, a sort of balance of power between two segments of the population might be maintained.

This was apparently the theory underlying the policy of including the gentry in *pao-chia* control but excluding them from *pao-chia* leadership. It was a reasonable theory, from the imperial point of view, but it did not work out well in practice. It was easier to prevent the gentry from assuming the government-conferred power of the *pao-chia* heads than to induce them to submit themselves to *pao-chia* control. There are numerous instances in which the *shen-shih* obstructed the enforcement of the *pao-chia* regulations over themselves, or simply refused to comply with the requirement of registering their names and those of their relatives in the *pao-chia* records. Such opposition occurred most often in localities where influential clans or "big families" (almost invariably under gentry leadership) dominated the scene. An experienced magistrate of the seventeenth century explained that on account of the opposition of the gentry's "big clans and great families," the *pao-chia* failed to operate smoothly in certain parts of South China. "When," he said, "a *chou* or *hsien* launches an undertaking [i. e., the *pao-chia*] which is inconvenient to the gentry and scholars, they invariably argue against it and hinder it from being put into effect." [117] Later, in the middle of the nineteenth century, a censor called imperial attention to the fact that "in the provinces the big families consider the *men-p'ai* [door placards] suitable only for the common people to display and refuse to write the entries on the *men-p'ai* with any degree of accuracy. Local officials [who have the responsibility of enforcing the *pao-chia* regulations] overlook [the delinquency of] the big families and limit their inspection to the households of commoners." [118] Gentry opposition to *pao-chia* registration was so strong in Chihli, the province in which the imperial capital was located, that Yü Ch'eng-lung, governor in the 1680's, found it more prudent to allay it by recognizing the gentry's special status than to overcome it by strictly enforcing the law. Consequently, he adopted the following procedure of registration for the province:

> In places where among the ten households are [households of] the rural gentry, *kung-sheng, chien-sheng,* or *sheng-yüan* [scholars],

which cannot be conveniently registered and subjected to inspection like [the households of] the common people . . . a special register may be instituted for the rural gentry, another for scholars who have passed the two higher examinations, civil or military, and still another for the *kung-sheng, chien-sheng,* and *sheng-yüan.* . . . This is a method by which persons with high status are distinguished from those with low status.[119]

In other words, he sought to save the *pao-chia* by deviating from the prescribed mode of registration. The imperial government itself sometimes found it necessary to circumvent established regulations in the face of the practical situation in order to make the *pao-chia* work. The following order, issued in 1726, shows how the government sought to meet gentry opposition to *pao-chia* control by indirectly enlisting their cooperation through their clan organizations:

. . . in villages and walled communities where clans with over one hundred members each dwell together, and where the *pao-chia* cannot carry out the work of registration and inspection, a man of firm and upright character, respected and feared heretofore by all the clansmen, should be selected from each of the clans and be instituted as *tsu-cheng* [clan head]. In case wicked elements are found in the clan, he should report to the government so that they can be properly dealt with. If he conceals their presence out of personal feelings, he will be punished in the same manner as the *pao-chia.*[120]

We do not have sufficient information to estimate the total effect of the gentry's opposition upon *pao-chia* control. Perhaps it was not at any time flagrant enough to paralyze the *pao-chia;* but it probably prevented police control from being completely or consistently effective in every part of the empire. One should not, however, jump to the conclusion that the imperial rulers had committed a blunder in attempting to bring the gentry and scholars within the pale of *pao-chia* control. Obviously the system could not have worked appreciably better, even if the gentry had been exempted from its control. From the government's point of view, it was surely better to have some of the gentry under *pao-chia* control than none at all.

The imperial policy of excluding the gentry from pao-chia leadership fared somewhat better than that of including them in pao-chia control. As the gentry were often disposed to boycott the *pao-chia,* few were interested in assuming responsibility in *pao-chia* work. At the same time the government had less success in keeping the gentry's dominating influence out of the *pao-chia.* When unrest and disorder appeared with increasing seriousness in various parts of the empire in the nineteenth century, the local gentry, convinced of the necessity of protecting their own "property, families, and lives," gradually shed their aversion to the *pao-chia* and often lent active support to *pao-chia* as well as *t'uan-lien* work. Local officials who were responsible for implementing and supervising *pao-chia* operation learned from experience that the cooperation of the local gentry was indispensable to effectuating police control as it was to virtually every other government undertaking.

Even before the end of the eighteenth century, the feeling had prevailed in local officialdom that the gentry must be induced to help run the *pao-chia* system. [121] That feeling spread in the next century and, reinforced by the gentry's wish to defend their own interests, readily translated itself into action. Liu Heng, magistrate of Pa Hsien (Szechwan) in the middle of the nineteenth century, relied on the local gentry to operate the *pao-chia* and achieved much better results than his predecessors. [122] Hu Lin-i, a prefect serving in Kweichow province in the early 1850's, persuaded "persons possessing economic means and official ranks" to direct both the *pao-chia* and *t'uan-lien* work in their respective home localities. [123] Pien Pao-ti, governor of Hunan in the early 1880's, secured the assistance of the gentry to operate the pao-chia. [124]

Two instances illustrate the ways local officials availed themselves of gentry help to operate the *pao-chia*. According to the 1899 edition of the Ch'ing-pien Hsien (Shensi) gazetteer, Ting Hsi-kuei, the magistrate who assumed his post in 1896, employed the local gentry in the following fashion:

> In any given place where there are already two *tsung-shen* [chief gentry] and where the area is extensive, each of the *tsung-shen* should be requested to nominate one or two *shan-shen* [assistant gentry]. In addition [they are requested to] institute, after public deliberation, a number of *t'uan-tsung* and *p'ai-t'ou* to assist them. All these are to be selected from upright, conscientious and careful men who enjoy the confidence of the multitude. . . .
>
> The gentry leaders, when personally inspecting the households and inhabitants, must bring with them the *men-p'ai* [door placards]. They first select the *p'ai-t'ou*, to each of whom is given a *men-p'ai*. After having written on the *men-p'ai* the *p'ai-t'ou*'s name, address, occupation, and the number of adult males and other members of his own household, he is to enter on it similar items of the other nine households [in the *p'ai*]. A monthly register is to be compiled and sent to the *hsien* for reference. . . .
>
> From this time on, if there are unlawful activities, such as harboring robbers, housing gamblers, or practicing theft, in the ten-household division, each household is to report the matter to the *p'ai-t'ou* who, after making sure that the report is in accordance with the facts, brings it to the attention of the gentry leaders. These leaders are to deal with the matter by consulting one another. If the persons involved

refuse to yield to their decisions, the matter is to be reported to the official. [125]

As a result, the *pao-chia* arrangement shown in Table 7 emerged:[126]

TABLE 7
PAO-CHIA ARRANGEMENT IN CH'ING-PIEN HSIEN

	No. *Tsung-shen*	No. *Shan-shen*	No. *Pang-ch'a**	No. *P'ai-t'ou*	No. Villages	No. Households
City	1	5	10	76	121	776
East Hsiang	0	5	5	34	65	352
South Hsiang	0	4	5	50	153	561
Southwest Hsiang	0	5	5	30	110	397
West Hsiang	0	4	4	40	140	406
Northwest Hsiang	0	4	6	60	70	818

*Assistant inspectors.

The other instance was recorded by the compilers of the 1891 edition of *Li-p'ing fu chih*. After pointing out that imperial regulations disqualified scholars entitled to wear "the blue gown" *(sheng-yüan)* and men in yamen service, and required commoners to serve in the *pao-chia* posts, [127] the compilers went on to describe the local procedure of instituting the *pao-chia* heads:

> The local official . . . issues an order to *shen-ch'i* (gentry elders) of advanced age, who nominate [two candidates for] the *tsung-chia* of each ward and two [candidates for] the *li-chang* of each village. It does not matter whether the persons nominated possess any *ting-tai* [official ranks or titles]. They are selected on the basis of enjoying the confidence of the populace by virtue of their integrity and ability, of being owners of landed property, and of being able to read and write. . . . Of the two *tsung-chia* [candidates] nominated, one is appointed to take general charge of the *pao-chia* in each ward. . . . Of the two *li-chang* [candidates] nominated, one is appointed to head the *chia-chang* of the ten-household divisions [in the village], and is responsible for selecting the *chia-chang* [who are to serve under him]. . . . A list of the names [of these *pao-chia* heads] is sent to the yamen . . . no official appointment is necessary. [128]

This instance is particularly interesting. Here the imperial prohibition against imposing *pao-chia* service upon the gentry and scholars was knowingly set aside and *pao-chia* heads were appointed without regard to the social status of the candidates. Since the qualifications included the ability to read and write—an ability rarely possessed by commoners in the villages—a veiled preference for scholars and gentry was clearly indicated.

These instances point to one conclusion: gentry leadership was brought to bear on the *pao-chia* despite imperial regulations to the contrary. Somewhat curiously, the imperial government made no attempt to stop such practice, nor did local officials try to conceal the fact that they relied on gentry assistance to operate the *pao-chia*. Indeed, as early as 1863, Liu Shou-t'u, governor of Shun-t'ien Fu (Chihli) recommended to the imperial government that the practice of employing *shen-ch'i* (gentry elders) in *pao-chia* work be widely adopted. [129] Perhaps under the social conditions of the empire, it was physically impossible to exclude the gentry from *pao-chia* leadership; the imperial government realized this and acquiesced in a development that was virtually inevitable. The government's original reluctance to place the *pao-chia* under gentry leadership, however, was not without some validity. In addition to the undesirability of having local influence concentrated in one group, there was the likelihood that "bad gentry" might transform the apparatus of police control into an instrument of selfish interests. The necessity of guarding against such use of the *pao-chia* for ends that were detrimental both to the imperial interests and the welfare of the common villagers was recognized by more than one official who was able to see the other side of the question. [130]

TENTATIVE APPRAISAL OF THE *PAO-CHIA*

As the *pao-chia* was only one instrument of rural control, its value can be accurately measured only against the entire complex of imperial institutions. But it may be useful to venture a tentative appraisal by analyzing some of the circumstances and factors that directly or especially affected the *pao-chia*.

It appears that the Ch'ing emperors themselves appraised the effectiveness of the *pao-chia* from time to time and were on the whole pessimistic in their views. Thus, only a little over half a century after the inception of the *pao-chia*, the K'ang-hsi emperor complained (in 1708) that it was not working well because officials did not give sufficient attention to the matter. [131] Less than two decades later, in 1724, the Shun-chih emperor warned against the likelihood of "having the *pao-chia* in name but not in reality" and of "suffering its shortcomings without enjoying its benefits," and officially stated (1726) that "since the *pao-chia* was reactivated in K'ang-hsi 47 [1708] it has again become, through a long period of neglect, a mere name without substance."[132] In 1757 the Ch'ien-lung emperor said in an edict that the *pao-chia* regulations were honored merely as a matter of form. [133] In a number of edicts the Chia-ch'ing emperor (1810, 1812, and 1816) and the Tao-kuang emperor (1850) made known their disappointment in the *pao-chia*.[134] The latter, in fact, attributed the rampancy of the *hui-fei* (secret society "bandits") and other troublemakers in Kwangsi and neighboring provinces to the failure of the *pao-chia* in those parts of the empire where officials "treated the *pao-chia* as an antiquated routine" and made no effort to work it.[135]

Many officials joined their sovereigns in this chorus of disillusionment. According to an ex-magistrate writing around 1690, the *pao-chia* system in certain localities had broken down to such an extent that its heads virtually disappeared from the scene and that *Hsiang-chang* (village elders) had been taking charge of the affairs of the *pao* for a long while.[136] About eighty years later, a high functionary of Kwangtung province memorialized in 1769:

> . . . while officials of the various provinces ostensibly comply with the imperial edicts [concerning the *pao-chia*] as a matter of routine, it is still impossible to distinguish between the sheep and the goats among the local inhabitants. Even though there have been recent cases in which robbery and theft were discovered, very few of these were reported by the *pao-chia*.[137]

The Ch'ien-lung emperor, to whom this memorial was addressed, confirmed this view and complained that "officials have come to look upon [the *pao-chia*] as an impracticable, trite talk and treat it as a matter of mere formality."

A number of officials of the eighteenth and nineteenth centuries echoed the pessimistic views of their predecessors. Writing around 1870, Wang Hui-tsu, an experienced magistrate, asserted that few officials made any real effort at working the *pao-chia* despite the fact that its vigorous practice constituted a consideration for administrative merit.[138] Ho Shao-ch'i, a magistrate serving in Yunnan Province, made the following statement upon arriving at his post in Kuang-t'ung Hsien in 1844:

> In the *pao-chia* system of the present time, the placards pasted on the doors of the households are no more than sheets of paper. [Fugitives and criminals] can hide themselves without fear of being detected, and anybody can move in and out [of a neighborhood] without being questioned. Yamen clerks and runners surfeit themselves and sing praise to a "good administration." The people suffer and bandits are happy, while officials feel perfectly satisfied with themselves.[139]

It was said that even in provinces where the high officials endeavored to make something out of the *pao-chia*, local magistrates often responded with their customary method of "passive disobedience."[140] Wang Ting-an, writing in the 1870's, viewed the situation with such despair that he condemned the *pao-chia* as an impossible system which caused trouble whenever attempts were made to enforce it. [141] Liu Ching-tsao, compiler of a government reference work, commented retrospectively in 1911 (shortly before the outbreak of the revolution):

> Speaking of the *pao-chia* each [protagonist] had his own theory and each wrote his own book. Generally, however, [these persons] merely repeated the platitudes of the *Chou-kuan* or copied the model left behind by the minister of the Sung dynasty [Wang An-shih]. The *[pao-chia]* routine was kept up to some extent in the metropolises; but in out-of-the-way localities it was unknown even as a dead letter. [142]

Some of these judgments are perhaps too pessimistic. It is obviously unsafe to suppose that the *pao-chia* was of no use whatever to the imperial rulers. The presence of this system of police control in the countryside, even though it never yielded the theoretical results expected, must have had some deterrent effect upon the bulk of the peasantry and discouraged some of the potential troublemakers from actually breaking rural peace. This deterrent effect alone would have rendered it a useful instrument of control.

The statements quoted above were not, however, wholly groundless. The banditry and rebellions that occurred in the nineteenth century in wide areas of the empire (as the Tao-kuang emperor indicated) are positive evidence that whatever efficacy the *pao-chia* may have had previously, the system had become so impaired by this time that it was no longer able to keep the rural populace generally obedient and peaceful. Originally designed as an instrument of control for use in times of peace, the *pao-chia* could operate effectively only when certain favorable conditions continued to exist. The peasantry need not be economically prosperous, but the bulk of them did not suffer dire destitution; the common people need not obey imperial laws invariably and to the letter, but they held the established authority in general awe and respect; officials need not all be efficient or incorruptible, but many of them endeavored to prevent the living conditions from becoming intolerable for the inhabitants under their administration. These conditions, which had existed in the heyday of the dynasty, tended to disappear in the nineteenth century. By the middle of the century the situation had become critical. Recurrent floods and droughts brought about serious disasters in many parts of the empire. Humiliation in wars with "barbarian" countries damaged imperial prestige irreparably. The trend of official corruption which began in the last years of the Ch'ien-lung reign became increasingly widespread. The dynasty as a whole was in a process of disintegration; inevitably, the institutions of the imperial system—including the *pao-chia*—also rapidly deteriorated. It is not surprising that the *pao-chia,* an instrument which was only partially effective even in normal times, could not cope with the now changed and turbulent conditions. Its presence in the countryside no longer exerted any deterrent effect upon villagers in desperation and "bandits" who openly challenged the authority of the government. When the entire imperial structure was badly shaken, the police control system could not remain unaffected.

It should be stressed, however, that even before the nineteenth century the *pao-chia* was confronted with difficulties and obstacles which, in the given historical situation, were virtually impossible to overcome and which prevented it from measuring up to the expectations of the imperial rulers.

In the first place, the method of registration prescribed by law proved difficult to execute. Each household, we recall, was required to have a *men-p'ai,* or door placard, on which the names of the members were to be written. The average villager seldom was able to fulfill this seemingly simple requirement;[143] and the gentry often chose to sabotage the registration procedure altogether. [144] Some officials tried to remedy the situation by simplifying the requirement. Ch'en Hung-mou, for example, suggested in 1758 that the names of women and children be omitted. [145] Later, in the 1860's, Ting Jih-ch'ang required the registration only of the name and age of the head of the household on the door placard. [146] There is no evidence that such measures removed the fundamental obstacle to registration; the general unwillingness to register.

The compilation of the registers from the door placards presented further difficulties. The *pao-chia* heads were responsible for compiling the records of the various divisions and then sending them to the magistrate's yamen in the *chou* or *hsien* city. Few of the door-placard entries were accurately made; most of the *pao-chia* heads were illiterate commoners, unable personally to check the entries even if they intended to do so. The records compiled were therefore often not sufficiently reliable for the purpose of keeping track of the inhabitants. Moreover, when the records reached the yamen, they were transcribed into the official registers by clerks whose interests usually lay in matters other than police control. The registers which they compiled were frequently found to be "carelessly done."[147] According to the law, the magistrates were to check these registers to make sure that the figures and information they contained were accurate before sending them to the imperial government at the end of the fiscal year. However, owing to the facts that the number of villages in a district was usually very large, that the administrative area of an average *chou* or *hsien* was quite extensive, and that facilities for travel were very meager, even the most earnest magistrate found it impossible to make effective inspection of all the households and tithing divisions. Many magistrates simply sent out the registers without thorough checking. [148] It is conceivable, of course, that in some districts and during certain periods of time, exceptionally conscientious and capable magistrates produced *pao-chia* registers that were sufficiently accurate for the purpose of implementing imperial control in the localities concerned. But it can hardly be supposed that the majority of the local officials were of such caliber and that all the registers were uniformly and consistently reliable.

The expense of making the enormous number of door placards and registers must have been from the very beginning another stumbling block to the successful operation of the *pao-chia*. Strange to say, the imperial government was aware of the problem of financing the undertaking but never made any provisions for meeting it. It seems to have been content with leaving the matter to the resourcefulness of local officials and agents. An edict issued in 1799 is very revealing:

> The registers being numerous, a large amount of money is required. It is difficult for the clerks and underlings to make up the deficiency; contributions made by local officials are no more than nominal. The result has simply been that officials pass on the responsibilities to the clerks and underlings. [149]

The emperor was well informed on the matter but was hardly well advised in allowing the situation to continue. As late as the 1860's, when a governor of Kiangsu endeavored to use the *pao-chia,* he found no other method to finance it than to rely on the ingenuity of his magistrates! [150] The expenses fell eventually upon the villagers. Within half a century after the inception of the system, P'eng P'eng, a well-known magistrate of the time, discovered that "the paper used in making the placards was taken from the people,"[151] and rightly regarded the practice as a burden on them.

Such a practice not only added a financial burden to the villagers but opened wide a door to official extortion. An eighteenth-century writer pointed out:

> Since the *hsün-huan* registers are placed in each *Hsiang* and sent to the magistracy on the first day of each month, the officials and clerks of the *hsien* take advantage of this regulation to extort from the *Hsiang*. Since reports are made [by the *hsien*] to the *fu* at the end of each season, officials and clerks there in turn take advantage of this regulation to extort from the *hsien*. [152]

The governor of Shun-t'ien Fu testified that similar extortionary practices persisted down to the nineteenth century in 1862:

> Recently, the manner of operating the *pao-chia* is as follows: First of all, the *pao-chang* of each *Hsiang* is summoned to receive the door

placards; he is charged a certain sum of money. Afterwards he is ordered to hand in the household registers; again he is charged a certain sum. The yamen clerks and underlings take the money from the *Hsiang pao,* the *Hsiang pao* from the *chia-chang,* and finally the *chia-chang* from the various households. . . . Nothing is accomplished, but immense expenses are involved. [153]

Under such circumstances, the rural inhabitants could hardly be expected to support *pao-chia* operations willingly or enthusiastically.

The imperial regulations which required periodic reports from the *pao-chia* to the magistrate's yamen posed another set of difficult problems. According to an early regulation, *pao-chia* heads were required to go on the first and fifteenth day of each month to the *chou* or *hsien* yamen to answer roll call and to report the conditions of their respective neighborhoods, even when no untoward incidents had occurred. To the imperial rulers these semimonthly visits afforded a convenient means for local officials to check the work of the *pao-chia.* As the magistrate could not possibly make a trip to the villages twice each month, the only way to bring the *pao-chia* heads under this direct review was to require them to go to the city. This procedure unavoidably worked hardship on the *pao-chia* heads. A magistrate of the seventeenth century explained the situation thus:

. . . hundreds or thousands of these men crowd before the gate of the yamen. It usually takes them several days to make the round trip from their home villages to the city and to wait [for the officials to receive their bonded reports]; the price of food in the city, owing to profiteering, rises suddenly on these days. Thus in this single matter of sending the bonded reports the people of the rural areas are made to suffer twenty-four times every year. [154]

Moreover, as another magistrate of the same period pointed out, the semimonthly visits to the yamen gave rise to extortionary practices, thus inflicting further hardships on the *pao-chia* heads. The Hsing-fang (Crimes Division) clerks in charge of *pao-chia* matters regularly demanded money from them; those who paid the bribes had their reports accepted without delay or question. None of them dared to ignore the demand. [155]

We do not know to what extent this regulation was strictly enforced. It may have been relaxed or silently dropped not too long after its adoption, for writers of the eighteenth and nineteenth centuries rarely discussed the problem of the semimonthly reports. However, the regulation which required the *pao-chia* to report the presence of criminals and commission of crimes as soon as discovered remained in legal force down to the last days of the dynasty. The enforcement of this regulation was also confronted with difficulties.

Inhabitants of rural areas had the legal obligation to report crimes and criminals to their own *pao-chia* heads. Failure to report was an offense punishable according to law. This requirement appears simple, but in practice it was not at all easy to fulfill. Crimes serious enough to merit government attention were seldom committed by timid men; on the contrary, they were likely to be the work of persons who had little respect for the lives and property of their fellow villagers. The average householder, knowing that the vengeance of such men was fearful and that whatever protection the government might offer was uncertain, far away, and slow to come, found it more prudent not to incur the wrath of desperadoes than to fulfill a legal obligation which the government often failed to exact. Keeping silence therefore was less risky than reporting what one knew. In fact, bitter experience taught that the lot of the informer was far from enviable. According to Chang Hui-yen, writing late in the eighteenth century, an informer usually got himself into trouble without rendering any service to the imperial government:

> If the information is not acted upon [by the local official], he is immediately visited with calamity [as a result of vengeful actions taken by the lawbreakers]. If it is acted upon [thus temporarily removing the offenders from the scene], he suffers the terrible vengeance of the offenders later on, [when the latter are again at large]. . . .

Moreover, the informer had no assurance that his report would be supported by his fellow villagers and gain the attention of the local official:

> When the matter is brought to the notice of the *pao-chang*, he is not certain that the latter will not try to cover up the crime. If he appeals to the gentry of his own village, as gentlemen do not regard themselves as having any responsibility concerning such matters, none of them is willing to lend him support.

And "even if the evidence is beyond doubt and the case brought to the local official, the informer often got himself into great trouble by being thus involved in an affair of the yamen."[156] Eventually villagers learned to practice the axiom: "Each sweeps the snow in front of his own door and pays no attention to the hoarfrost on another man's roof." In all probability, the Chia-ch'ing emperor did not exaggerate matters too much when he complained in 1810 that "nobody had ever informed against inhabitants who harbored bandits and criminals."[157] It was said that in some instances local officials dared not make investigation trips into localities infested by robbers and bandits.[158] Perhaps the imperial government should not have blamed the ordinary villager for his timidity.

Officials seeking to encourage villagers to report crimes suggested that informers be protected from danger of retaliation or embarrassment by making their *pao-chia* reports "confidential."[159] The imperial government rejected this suggestion and tried instead to impose stricter responsibility on the *pao-chia*. An edict issued in 1799 said that "if the *Hsiang pao* are not held definitely responsible [for reporting crimes], who would be ready to take up a matter that does not concern himself and bring it to an official."[160] The problem of nonreporting was therefore to be met not by protecting the informer but by enforcing a system of *lien-ming hu-pao* (joint pledge and mutual responsibility).[161] This device, as a Western student of Chinese law pointed out, resembles the "frankpledge" of Anglo-Saxon England, by which neighbors "frankly" or "willingly" bound themselves for the conduct of each and all.[162] It did not prove effective in imperial China. The problem of nonreporting remained unsolved; the *lien-ming hu-pao* requirement in fact made the villagers more diffident and reticent than before. Instead of accepting the "mutual responsibility" imposed upon them, they shirked it by a conspiracy of silence.

Nonreporting was not the only problem; more serious still was the problem of extortionary practices, in which many a *pao-chia* head indulged. That the *pao-chia* afforded opportunities for petty extortion and blackmail to unscrupulous individuals was realized as early as Sung times. Ssu-ma Kuang, one of the leading opponents of Wang An-shih and his policies, alleged (not without ground):

> The *pao-cheng* and *chia-chang*, relying on their authority and abusing their power, demanded goods and extorted bribes [from rural inhabitants]. Those who failed to meet their wishes, even in the slightest degree, suffered unlawful whipping and beating [inflicted by these *pao-chia* heads].[163]

The *pao-chia* heads of the Ch'ing dynasty were not endowed with military power, but their extortionary practices were no less dreadful than those of their Sung predecessors. Appointment to a *pao-chia* position was regarded as a passport to illegal gains; the "willing bonds" afforded a lucrative source of semiofficial blackmail.[164] The occurrence of murder cases gave the *ti-pao* and other agents opportunities to exact money from their neighbors.[165] "When a man attempts to step out of the ordinary routine," according to a Western traveler in Shantung and Shansi in 1865, "an ill-disposed neighbor or a petty bailiff comes in and threatens to inform against him unless he gives him so much money."[166] The situation was noticed by the imperial government; it repeatedly insisted on selecting "upright persons" to fill the *pao-chia* posts.

This brings us to the crucial problem of recruiting suitable personnel for the *pao-chia*. The Ch'ing emperors tried their best to solve it, but their efforts produced relatively little result. They found it difficult to secure desirable persons to fill the *pao-chia* posts because, as an old Chinese saying goes, "those who are worthy do not serve, while those who serve are not worthy."

The difficulty was partly of the government's own making. Since the imperial rulers included the gentry in *pao-chia* control but excluded them from *pao-chia* service, local officials responsible for operating the *pao-chia* were compelled to look for candidates among commoners in the villages—people who lacked prestige, were mostly illiterate, knew little about the ways of government, and being busy with farming or other callings, had little leisure. As there was really little choice among such men, many local officials simply made the inhabitants in the households of each *pao-chia* division serve by turns. And as the able-bodied among them had to attend to their respective occupations, the men that became *pao-chia* heads were often "ignorant, decrepit old men, without adequate family backgrounds or means of living."[167] In some instances, the result of "designating the head of the first household of the first *chia* division as *chia-chang*" was even worse; the failure to take into consideration the personal qualifications of these men frequently put "illiterate, greedy, and mean scoundrels" in the *pao-chia* posts.[168]

Sometimes it happened that the commoner *pao-chia* heads showed a certain degree of intelligence, good sense, and willingness to serve. Their best intentions and honest efforts, however, were often frustrated. The very fact that they were commoners tended to prevent them from commanding the respect of the gentry householders in their neighborhoods; it was likely also that their authority might be questioned by their fellow commoners.

The Ch'ien-lung emperor made an attempt in 1757 to solve the problem of *pao-chia* personnel by a sort of compromise. Recognizing that ordinary villagers were unqualified to serve and upholding the regulation that the gentry should not be required to serve, he instructed local officials to find candidates among persons described as "honest, literate, and in possession of property." No "rascally elements of the neighborhoods," he said, should be permitted to become *pao-chia* heads.[169]

It is interesting that the emperor made no mention of the social status of the qualified candidates and that he included literacy as one of the qualifications. Apparently, he had in mind those persons who had studied (presumably for the examinations) but had not earned any of the examination degrees, "literati" or scholars who did not have gentry status. Persons with the qualifications specified by the emperor should indeed be able to serve creditably. But the problem was to find a sufficient number of such persons in the villages. Very few households in an average village could boast of members that were at once "literate and in possession of property"—even granting that there was no dearth of "honest" inhabitants. Moreover, there was no assurance that inhabitants with such qualifications were willing to serve. The situation in some parts of South China, described by a writer early in the eighteenth century, is particularly revealing:

> Most of the persons engaged as scholars teach school elsewhere, leaving in their own homes two or three women and minors. The poor who engage themselves as hired laborers or peddlers leave their homes early in the morning and return late in the evening. They hardly find time to earn enough to keep themselves alive. The wealthy lead a cautious life, refusing to have anything to do with matters outside of their doors. The traders likewise prudently attend to their own business, being afraid of the youthful bullies of the neighborhood as if they were tigers. To expect such persons to control the villages and neighborhoods, to inspect during the day and to keep watch during the night . . . no wonder they do not feel happy about it all![170]

This situation persisted until the nineteenth century, when most rural inhabitants still avoided being appointed *p'ai-chang* or *pao-chang*.[171]

The problem of recruiting suitable *pao-chia* personnel was further complicated by the maltreatment of *pao-chia* heads at the hands of local officials and yamen underlings. Besides being liable for satisfying their extortions and for supplying materials and labor in sundry government requisitions,[172] *pao-chia* heads were often subject to wanton beating or other punishments.[173] Many of them naturally tried hard to get out of the service. Those not yet drawn in did their best to avoid being drafted. Few went so far as to injure their eyes or cut off their fingers to escape the service as had been done in the Sung dynasty,[174] but some *pao-chang* and *chia-chang* were known to have secured permission to resign by "engaging influence" or "begging favor."[175] So many of them did this that the *pao-chia* personnel remained in a state of flux or, as a seventeenth-century magistrate put it, "where a person named Chang served, all of a sudden it was a person named Li."[176] A fluid *pao-chia* personnel could hardly be expected to be efficient or reliable.

Sporadic attempts were made to remedy the situation but they produced little result. The government limited the term of service of the *pao-chia* heads so that none of them would be compelled to shoulder the burden interminably;[177] it sought to lighten their burdens by relieving them of all functions irrelevant to police control;[178] some of the local officials tried to improve the treatment of the *pao-chang* and *chia-chang* by showing them studied courtesy[179] or honoring them with laudatory tablets commending their "meritorious services."[180] There is no evidence that these remedial measures were generally or consistently applied.

Closely related to the problem of the reluctance of "honest persons" to serve was that of the influx of undesirable characters into the *pao-chia* service. Local bullies and "bare sticks" were often as anxious to get into the *pao-chia* as simple, harmless villagers were anxious to stay away from it. Chang Ch'i, writing early in the nineteenth century, put the matter this way: "Since prudent persons who pursue scholarly studies cannot perform these functions [of the *pao-chia*] and well-to-do householders dare not perform them, those who both can and dare must be overbearing, violent, and aggressive persons."[181]

A sort of Gresham's law, therefore, operated in the process of *pao-chia* personnel recruitment—a phenomenon widely noticed since the eighteenth century and down to the end of the dynasty. For example, the Ch'ien-lung emperor complained in 1757 that "rascals" as a rule became *pao-chang* and *chia-chang* in the villages.[182] A host of officials called attention to the same fact. Early in the eighteenth century, Shen T'ung observed that those who served as *pao-chia* heads were "usually commoners with an eye on money but without shame or self-respect."[183] In the next century, Wu Wen-yung, governor-general of Yün-Kuei, wrote that the *pao-chia* heads in the provinces under his jurisdiction "generally were absolutely illiterate, base, and greedy 'sticks,' upon whom the local officials trampled at will and who in turn oppressed their respective villages and neighborhoods at will."[184] Chang Sheng-chieh summed up the situation:

> The *pao-chang* and *chia-chang* of today [nineteenth century] are recruited from lowly and unprincipled elements of the villages and neighborhoods. They go about the households in "service" to the yamen, namely, pursuing profits and gains to supply their superiors from day to day; and taking advantage of the opportunities thus afforded them, they extort money from simple-minded villagers to fatten themselves. . . . This state of affairs has existed for a long time.[185]

It may be added that to those persons whom Chang Sheng-chieh described as "unprincipled elements," *pao-chia* service was not an onerous burden but a source of illegal profits. Many of them scrambled for the *pao-chia* posts and once they had them endeavored to keep them as long as they could. In fact, some of them succeeded (at least in the closing decades of the dynasty) in making these posts virtually hereditary, handed down from father to son.[186]

With the problem of personnel unsolved and with the difficulties confronting registration and reporting unremoved, the *pao-chia* system could not have operated with the efficiency which the founding emperors of Ch'ing expected. This is not saying that it was not a useful and necessary instrument of rural control. Under the historical circumstances and against the institutional background of imperial China, the *pao-chia* was perhaps the only feasible instrument that could have served the purpose for which it was intended. However, the same circumstances that rendered the *pao-chia* indispensable to the imperial rulers also limited its actual usefulness to them. This is a conclusion that applies not only to the *pao-chia* but also to other instruments of rural control, as subsequent discussions will show.

Chapter 4

TAX COLLECTION
IN RURAL AREAS:
THE *LI-CHIA* SYSTEM

THE ROLE OF THE *LI-CHIA* IN TAX ASSESSMENT AND REGISTRATION

The *Fu-i* Revenue System of the Ch'ing Dynasty

Whatever truth lies in the statement that the sole purpose of the government of China after the "Three Dynasties" of antiquity was to collect the *fu* and *i* (land and labor imposts)[1] it cannot be doubted that taxation was one of the most urgent concerns of the imperial administration of the Ch'ing as well as previous dynasties. The land and labor imposts in particular constituted the main sources of the imperial revenue for a considerable part of the dynasty. [2] The emperors gave much of their attention to these taxes—to their assessment and collection, and to suitable machinery with which to secure the largest possible amount of income from them. The *li-chia* was that part of the revenue machinery which operated at a subadministrative level in the countryside, originally to assist in the registration of rural inhabitants with a view to facilitating the assessment of the labor service imposts and later to help in the general task of tax collection in rural areas. In order to explain the working of the *li-chia* and to gain a clear view of its significance, it is necessary to acquaint ourselves briefly with the *fu-i* system as a whole.

The land and labor imposts of the Ch'ing dynasty were generally defined for the first time in the original edition of the *Fu-i ch'üan-shu* (Complete Text of the Land and Labor Imposts) compiled in 1646 (Shun-chih 3). [3] This and subsequent editions[4] contained the quotas of *ti* (land) and *ting* (labor) imposts to be levied in the various provinces, the amount of cultivated land, the number of persons liable to the labor imposts, and the quotas of the revenue to be sent to the imperial coffers. A copy of each edition was distributed to every *chou* and *hsien* for the reference of the magistrate and another copy placed in the local Confucian temple so that "scholars and the common people could examine it. "[5]

The regular land tax *(fu)* was assessed on cultivated land owned by

the people, which was officially known as *min-fu ti* or simply *min-ti*.
The rates were fixed according to the degree of fertility of the soil,
the *mow* being taken as the unit, although the size of the *mow* varied
in different places. [6] Naturally, the rates varied in different localities, [7] the heaviest burdens falling on certain regions of Kiangsu and
Chekiang. [8] The imposts were paid either in kind or in money equivalents. [9] In some provinces rice tribute was levied which like the ordinary land tax might be paid in money. [10]

The original rates as fixed in Shun-chih times were not exorbitant. [11]
Surtaxes, however, were invariably imposed, which often amounted
to several times the amount of the regular levy. The most important
of these surcharges were the *huo-hao* (allowance for melting wastage),
originated in the Ming dynasty, [12] and the *hsien-yü* (allowance for grain
wastage);[13] these together became known as *hao-hsien*. Originally illegal, these were later tacitly legalized when official rates were fixed
for them by the government. [14] It was then illegal to practice *hao-wai
fou shou* (levying in excess of the fixed wastage allowance), an offense
punishable by law. [15]

Owners of all productive *min-ti*, including officials, gentry, and
scholars, were liable to the land taxes and surtaxes. In some cases
and under certain conditions, however, the imposts might be temporarily or permanently waived. Land other than *min-ti*, such as that
used for sacrificial and educational purposes, that owned by the government and by temples, and that allotted to bannermen, was perpetually exempt from the regular taxation. Odd bits of *min-ti*, too
small to be worth the trouble of assessment, were also exempt. [16] Ordinary *min-ti* usually was granted a temporary remission during periods of natural calamities or on occasions of imperial celebration. [17]

While the *Fu-i ch'üan-shu* remained the basic official text for revenue collection, it was supplemented by a number of other compilations, the most important of which included the *chang-liang ts'e* (land-
measurement registers) and the *huang ts'e* (yellow registers). [18] These
were directly concerned with the collection of the land and labor imposts. The land-measurement registers, known also as *yü-lin ts'e*
(fish-scale registers), showed the amount of land in each locality;
they were compiled from figures supposedly derived from actual measurement of the land. [19] It is doubtful that the measurement, wherever
made, was accurate; it is quite certain that the "bow" or measuring
frame used varied widely in different places so that the *mow* became
a highly variable quantity. [20] With some exceptions, measurement was
probably not actually made in the Ch'ing dynasty. The figures were
largely based on the registers of the previous regime, since the expenses involved in a nationwide survey were clearly prohibitive. [21]
The official land registers were therefore not accurate to begin with;
as time went on, fraudulent practices and inevitable changes wrought

by nature and men further vitiated these registers which became in some localities a source of inequity and corruption. [22]

The i levies or labor service imposts (sometimes translated as "corvée"), [23] like the fu, had their origin in the past. [24] These constituted that part of the registration system with which the li-$chia$ was directly concerned. The Ch'ing system of i was modeled mainly after the Ming, in form as well as in substance. [25] The basic concept of the i was perhaps most succinctly stated by the compiler of an official work: "Generally speaking, the functions performed by $shih$-$ta\ fu$ [scholar officials] in their own native places constitute $chih$ [official duties]; the services rendered to the government by the common people constitute i [compulsory labor]. "[26] Theoretically, the people were all required to render a certain amount of labor service to the government, but since the Sung dynasty persons liable to the labor conscription were allowed to pay the government a sort of quitrent, sums of money in lieu of actual services. [27] As a result, the labor imposts eventually amounted to the payment of money in addition to whatever actual labor service the government deemed necessary to require of the people who legally speaking had already paid their i obligations.

As in previous dynasties, persons liable to the i were designated $ting$–adult males between sixteen and sixty sui (between fifteen and fifty-nine years of age in Western reckoning). [28] There were various categories of $ting$. Most of the common villagers were classified as min-$ting$, which of course constituted the most important category. Rates of the impost varied according to the locality, from 0.001 tael in some places in Chekiang province to 4.053 taels in some places in Shansi. [29] The labor taxes were relatively light in some southeastern provinces where the land taxes were heavy; and conversely, where the people had to pay higher rates in the i, they were taxed somewhat less on their land. [30] In all localities an extra sum was levied when an intercalary month occurred in a year. [31] Since the i was a duty of the common people, persons with special status—officials and titled scholars—were exempted from it. [32] And since labor service theoretically could be performed only by able-bodied persons, commoners above sixty and below sixteen were also exempted from paying the $ting$ money. [33]

Theory to the contrary, [34] additional labor services were often required of the people who had completed the payment of their $ting$ money. Some of these additional services could not be fulfilled by the payment of quitrent. The pao-$chia$ and li-$chia$ services were two outstanding instances of this type of i. [35] Other additional services beyond the $ting$ imposed by the government were often referred to as $ch'ai$ or $ch'ai$-yao and might be paid with money. [36] The burdens were apportioned to those liable in direct ratio to the amount of land or the number of oxen and donkeys owned, [37] or were imposed on individual households or entire villages by assigning to each unit a fixed quota.[38] No definite regulations were laid down by the central authorities. Strictly speaking, these levies were illegal; they were usually called into existence by the logic of actual exigencies. For while the regular *ting* imposts were legally supposed to cover all labor services, the money collected was often found insufficient to pay for the hired labor engaged in government construction or transportation work.[39] The most obvious way for local officials to meet this deficit was simply to impose further burdens on the inhabitants. Furthermore, military campaigns invariably demanded services from inhabitants of the areas concerned, particularly in supplying manpower for transportation and miscellaneous materials. These necessitated additional labor service or additional quitrent.[40]

Two types of *ch'ai*, however, enjoyed a measure of legality. The imperial courier system maintained for the transmission of official dispatches employed, at numerous stations throughout the empire, varying numbers of couriers and horses. According to the regulations formulated in 1668 (K'ang-hsi 7), each of the couriers was paid *kung-shih* (labor-food) money, varying from 0.01 to 0.08 tael per day. The money was to come from the revenue collected from the regular taxes. Boat-trackers serving on water routes were similarly paid.[41] If additional couriers or trackers were necessary, they were to be hired at wages proportionate to the distances they had to travel. The additional expenditure thus incurred had to come from extra levies. The other type of *ch'ai* sanctioned by the government and supported by funds from the regular revenue was the services rendered in river conservancy work. At the beginning of the dynasty, fixed quotas of *ho-fu* (river laborers) were set up, and "labor-food" payments to them were included in the budget as an item in the *Fu-i ch'üan-shu*.[42] In practice, however, special imposts were made to meet the expenses that the regular funds failed to cover. When the Ch'ien-lung emperor ascended the throne in 1735, he expressly forbade such imposts, reiterating the rule that conservancy work should be financed with "the regular funds."[43] There is no evidence that this prohibition put a stop to illegal levies.[44]

In order to gain a knowledge of the total number of subjects available for labor services and the number of them in any given locality, it was necessary to compile special *hu ts'e* or *ting ts'e,* registers to show the number of taxable individuals in the numerous households, just as the *chang-liang ts'e* showed the amount of taxable land. The former were the equivalents of the *huang ts'e* of the Ming dynasty and often called by that name. Like the Ming registers, they contained information concerning taxable land owned by the households registered therein,[45] evidently because labor service levies were eventually collected in connection with land taxes. The general features of the two series of basic tax registers and the relation between them were explained by an early nineteenth-century Chinese writer:

> The *huang ts'e* [yellow registers] and the *yü-lin ts'e* [fish-scale registers] are the only documents upon which officials rely to collect the taxes. The *huang ts'e* have the households as their main entries, to which [information concerning] land is appended; the *yü-lin ts'e* are basically a record of [taxable] land, to which information concerning the households is appended. Being the warp and woof each to the other, they are mutually supplementary in their use.[46]

The *Li-chia* and the Compilation of the *Huang Ts'e*

The procedure of compiling the *ting ts'e* or yellow registers, known in official parlance as *pien-shen* (to compile and to inspect), adopted by the Ch'ing government largely resembled that of the preceding dynasty.[47] Once in every three years a census of the households and inhabitants in the empire was made, and the *chou* and *hsien* magistrates were held responsible for compiling the local registers. The method was as follows:

> Every 110 households are to constitute a *li* in which the heads of the ten households having the largest number of *ting* are to be the *[li-] chang*, and the remaining 100 households are to be arranged into ten *chia*. [The 110-household divisions] in cities are designated *fang*, those immediately outside the cities, *"Hsiang,"* and those in the countryside, *li*.
> When the time for compiling the registers arrives, each household is ordered to list its members in accordance with the prescribed form. This list is then handed to the headman of the *chia* concerned. The *chia-chang* compiles a list of all persons in the ten households [under his supervision] as well as those in his own household, and turns it over to the *fang-*, *"Hsiang"-*, or *li-chang*, as the case may be. These latter then compile their lists and send them to the *chou* or *hsien* [magistrate]. The magistrate compiles a register from the original lists and, after affixing the official seal, sends it to the *fu*. The prefect of the *fu* makes a general register in accordance with the prescribed form and, after having signed it and affixed the official seal, sends it to the provincial treasurer.
> In comparing the registers, subjects who are sixty are omitted from the list and those reaching sixteen added to it.[48]

Such was the basic regulation that defined the registration procedure and set up the *li-chia* system. It is obvious that this system, as originally conceived, was merely a device for assisting the government to complete the *ting* registers.

Between 1648, when the *pien-shen* registration was officially es-

tablished, and 1772, when it was abolished, supplementary regulations intended to improve the efficiency of the *li-chia* apparatus were
issued by the imperial authorities. A law enacted in 1654 required that
in the taking of the triennial census the lists of every *li* and *chia* were
to be checked in detail, to ensure that the original totals, the names
of those deleted and recently entered, the current number of persons
liable to the *ting* imposts, and the amount of tax assessed upon each
person were clearly shown. Falsifying the records was punishable
by law.[49] By an order of 1657, rewards were to be given to *chou* or
hsien magistrates who in compiling the registers showed an increase
in the number of *ting* amounting to at least 2,000 above the previous
figure. Three years later, provincial authorities were instructed to
take the increase or decrease of population reported as a yardstick
for measuring the merits of local functionaries.[50]

The task of empire-wide registration was burdensome and difficult,
and for this reason was never satisfactorily carried out. To reduce
the amount of work, the imperial government in 1656 modified the
original procedure, ordering that the census be taken once in five
years rather than once in three.[51] No remedy was found, however, for
the fundamental problem—the inaccuracy of the registers, which resulted from the failure of the *li-chia* to put the names of all tax-liable
persons on the *ting* lists. Unfilled labor service quotas often resulted,
a default which the government designated as *ch'üeh-e jen-ting*. Efforts were of course made to fill the quotas. In 1686 the imperial government threatened with punishment all magistrates who failed to report persons recently becoming liable for the *ting* imposts. In the
year following, provincial governors were ordered to fill all vacant
quotas in the next registration.[52] Matters did not improve. As late
as 1716 the government, still wrestling with the same problem, went
so far as to make inhabitants of the same *chia* or *t'u* shoulder the
burdens of "defunct" *ting*.[53]

The imperial government took a decisive step in 1712 (K'ang-hsi
51). It permanently froze the *ting* quota as it was established in the
registers of the current year. Emperor Sheng-tsu said in a well-
known edict:

> In looking over the reports concerning the number of inhabitants and
> tax-liable persons made by the governors-general and governors of
> the various provinces, we perceived that they have not included all
> the population increases currently accrued. The empire has enjoyed
> continued peace for a long time, and the number of households and
> inhabitants has been multiplying daily. If additional taxes are assessed
> on the basis of the current population figures, it is really quite im-
> proper. For although there is an increase in population, there is no
> increase in the amount of cultivated land. We deem it fit, therefore,
> to instruct governors-general and governors of the provinces to take

the number of registered *ting* listed in the current registers, which
number is not to be augmented or diminished, as the permanent, fixed
quota [for collecting the *ting* imposts]. All inhabitants born hereafter
shall be exempted from [additional] imposts. In taking the census it
will be necessary merely to ascertain the actual amount of population
increase and report it in separate registers. [54]

This drastically reduced the significance of the *li-chia* as an agency
for assisting in the compilation of the yellow registers. The process
of counting the inhabitants had thus become a sort of general census
instead of a method to ascertain tax liability.

Meanwhile, another crucial change was taking place. Since about
1672 (K'ang-hsi 11) the *ting* imposts had begun to be collected in conjunction with the land taxes in one locality after another. The former
were soon legally merged into the latter. As a result, the yellow registers lost much of their former usefulness. [55] The quinquennial *pien-
shen* procedure continued for a while; in fact, before its abolition in
1772, some efforts were made to insure accuracy in the registers,
as evinced by the edicts of 1736 (Ch'ien-lung 1) and 1740 (Ch'ien-lung
5). [56] It was soon realized, however, that the utility of the registers
hardly justified the trouble involved in making the special *li-chia* records. On the recommendation of the *Hu-pu*, the imperial government
decided to drop the process of *li-chia* compilation and to make use of
the *pao-chia* records as a basis for the annual reports, a preliminary
step toward the preparation of the registers. An order issued in 1740
to provincial authorities said:

> Reports on the number of inhabitants [in the provinces] are made
> annually. The interval is quite brief, and the number of households
> and individuals, from metropolitan cities to remote hamlets, is very
> large. If reports are made yearly in conformity with the *pien-shen*
> procedure, it is feared that much trouble will be entailed. Since door
> placards of the *pao-chia* have been instituted in the *chou* and *hsien* of
> the various provinces, on which native inhabitants and transient dwell-
> ers are all enumerated, [the population of any locality] can already
> be ascertained in these records. Deducting the number of the tran-
> sients from that of the native inhabitants reported, the actual number
> of the latter can readily be determined. The governors-general and
> governors should be instructed to send in, in the eleventh month of
> each year, reports of the actual number of households and inhabitants
> and the amount of grain [in their respective provinces]. [57]

The logical conclusion of this development was drawn by the Ch'ien-
lung emperor who abolished the practice of compiling the quinquennial
ting registers altogether. In a 1772 edict he said:

The reason for instituting the old procedure of registering the in-

habitants and tax-liable persons was to forestall the fraudulent practice of leaving out households with a view to evading taxes. The making
of a census and compilation of registers in every five years afforded
[the government] a means of scrutinizing [the matter of the *ting* im-
posts]. But now since the money levied on the *ting* has been portioned
out on the grain taxes which are assessed on land, and since, in compliance with the gracious edict of the Imperial Grandfather issued in
K'ang-hsi 52, no additional *ting* taxes are levied on inhabitants born
after that date, the quinquennial compilation of registers has become
no more than carrying on an empty form, with no practical benefit
to administration. . . . The procedure of *pien-shen* is hereby ordered to be permanently discontinued from now on.[58]

This was the imperial *coup de grâce* that formally ended a practice
that had outlived its usefulness. From that time on the emperors gave
up all attempts at determining for revenue purposes the number of
inhabitants in the countryside of the empire.[59] While the *li-chia* was
not abolished with the *pien-shen*, it had lost its original and distinctive function of assisting in the compilation of the rural *ting* records.

Effects of the Merging of the *Fu* and *I* on the *Li-chia*

In the early years of the Ch'ing dynasty the land taxes and the labor
imposts were legally two separate sources of imperial revenue, although these tended in practice to merge one into the other. In fact,
in some localities the *i-t'iao pien* (single-whip) method of taxation
which prevailed late in the Ming dynasty[60] was allowed to persist.[61]
In the greater part of Szechwan province, for instance, the grain tax
on land had always "carried" the *ting* imposts.[62] The advantages of
assessing and collecting the *ting* with the land taxes were obvious. It
was a simpler way of handling the matter. By hitching the *ting* imposts to the land, tax evasion was rendered somewhat more difficult
than when the *ting* were assessed on and collected from the households irrespective of landownership. By placing the burdens on the
shoulders of landowners, the government avoided the exasperating
situation of trying to collect revenue from persons who could not pay
because they had no property.[63] This method was not necessarily an
equitable one; it was possible for wealthy families to remain exempt
from the labor imposts so long as they refrained from owning land,
or in so far as they managed by fraud to shield their land from such
liabilities.[64] But as the imperial government was interested less in
abstract justice and more in a convenient way of collecting revenue,
it was soon ready to give sanction to a hitherto unauthorized practice.

The first official move appears to have been made in 1716 (K'ang-
hsi 55) when the imperial authorities expressly approved the appor-

tioning of the *ting* imposts among payers of the land taxes in Kwang-tung province, at the rate of 0.1064 to 1.00 tael of silver.[65] In 1723 (Yung-cheng 1), this practice was approved for Chihli province.[66] One province after another received authorization, and by the early nine-teenth century practically all the provinces were applying this method of collection.[67] The rates obtaining in different localities varied wide-ly, from 0.001 (Kiangsu) to 0.861 (Hunan).[68] During the remaining years of the dynasty the *fu* and *i* had become for practical purposes one and the same tax.

The *li-chia* divisions, originally groupings for the purpose of regis-tering the number of *ting* in a given rural neighborhood, suffered changes as a result of the integration of the land and labor imposts. As we have seen in an earlier chapter,[69] the *li-chia* divisions were originally made on the basis of a prescribed number of households that dwelt in a given place. They were not made on the basis of land.[70] As, however, the *ting* imposts were sometimes collected, since the early days of the dynasty, in conjunction with the land taxes, the amount of taxable land became in some localities the basis for making the *li-chia* divisions. A revealing example was recorded in the *Hang-chou fu chih* which indicated that in 1671 (K'ang-hsi 10) "the gentry and common people" of the prefecture of Hang-chou (Chekiang) petitioned that the size of the *li* be standardized so that each would comprise a total of 3,000 *mow* of land.[71] The situation in Yen-ch'eng Hsien (Kiang-su), according to the *Huai-an fu chih*, was in part as follows:[72]

Amount of Land *(mow)*

P'ei-ch'iao Li	25,447
T'iao-ho Li	19,978
Ch'üeh-hsiang Li	32,424
Ch'ing-kou Li	6,251
Hsin-chuang Li	9,280

A comparable situation existed in Shan-yang Hsien, though the *li* di-vision there came under the appellation *t'u:*

Amount of Land *(mow)*

Jen-tzu 1st T'u	7,318
Jen-tzu 2nd T'u	6,594
Jen-tzu 4th T'u	5,512
Jen-tzu 6th T'u	2,957

. . .

An instance which reflected most clearly the change after the in-tegration of the *ting* and *ti* imposts was afforded by the 1886 edition of *Ch'ang-p'ing chou chih*.[73] From some time late in the seventeenth century the *li-chia* divisions in this locality in Chihli province had no longer been made on the basis of households. The arrangement, according to the compiler, was the following:

	Amount of Land *(mow)*	Number of *Ting*
Te-hsin Li	2,900	153
Hsin-ning Li	6,400	141
Chü-an Li	3,600	81
I-ch'ang Li	8,000	190
Tsung-shan Li	6,700	244
Yü-ch'ing Li	4,800	168
Hui-ch'ien Li	11,100	132
T'ai-p'ing Li	5,700	72
An-jen Li	6,400	171

Effectiveness of the *Li-chia* as a Supplementary Apparatus of Registration

Since the *li-chia* officially ceased to perform the tax registration function in 1772, this evaluation is limited to the period between 1648 and that date. Regrettably, available records are generally silent on the actual operation of the *li-chia* in this respect. We can do no better than to draw some inferences from fragmentary evidence.

Anticipating the possibility of falsifying the records, the imperial government specifically forbade "fraudulently concealing taxable land" and illegally claiming exemption from labor imposts.[74] But no amount of legal prohibition could entirely overcome the desire to evade taxes. The heads of the *li-chia* often had a private interest in not supplying accurate records to the government; sometimes they might have found it difficult to prevail against the desire of influential households in the neighborhoods to shirk their tax liabilities. The difficulty was aggravated by the fact that the Ch'ing dynasty inherited the jumbled registers of the preceding regime and was not in a position to inaugurate an entirely new empire-wide registration. According to a circuit censor in the early years of the dynasty:

> . . . when census and registration of households and inhabitants were made in the *chou, hsien,* and *wei* of the provinces, the old figures were used without exception. Youths who came of age were not registered as *ting,* whereas the names of aged persons were not deleted from the registers. Labor services thus became inequitable.[75]

Judging from the experience of the *pao-chia,* it is safe to assume that the *li-chia* registration system did not improve matters in later years.

An assertion made by a nineteenth-century Chinese writer, though referring especially to Shansi province, may throw some light on the general conditions under which the *li-chia* had to operate during and before that century. He pointed out several widespread evils in the registration procedure:

> The *fu* and the *i* have fixed rates. But big households, either through clandestine bribery or overt favoritism, often manage to reduce assessments where these should really be increased. Wherever big households enjoy a reduction, inconsequential ones suffer an increase. Exempting the rich and encumbering the poor: this has been an evil since ancient times. . . .
> The three categories [i. e., the theoretical classification of *i* into *li-chia; chün-yao;* equalized labor service, a euphemism for quitrent; and *tsa-fan,* miscellaneous labor services] and the nine [official land tax] rates were originally instituted for the reason that there is disparity in the people's wealth. [The actual assessment] however, is completely in the hands of the supervising official. When he wishes to make a higher assessment, one person is required to supply the labor service of several; when he wishes to make a lower one, several tax-liable persons do not pay even the quitrent of a single one.[76]

It is difficult to imagine that the *li-chia* records, prepared under such conditions, represented the actual number of households and inhabitants, or the actual amount of land owned by these households in the various neighborhoods; even if these records were mathematically accurate, it is also doubtful that they served as the basis for equitable tax assessments.

Nor can we assume that local officials and yamen clerks treated the *li-chia* records and the yellow registers based on them with genuine respect. Quite possibly the experience of the Ming dynasty was repeated in the Ch'ing. According to the *Ming-shih,* "the *huang ts'e* later became a mere form. When officials assessed land taxes and levied labor service imposts, they made registers themselves, calling them *pai ts'e* [white registers]."[77] At any rate, it is certain that by the second half of the nineteenth century whatever tax registers based on the *li-chia* records were formerly available had largely disappeared as the result of wars and calamities. Local revenue collection often depended on the transcribed records privately made and possessed by yamen clerks.[78] After all, since the quotas of the *ting* were permanently fixed in 1712 and since the *ting* imposts were first officially hitched to the land taxes in 1723, the *li-chia* records had little significance for the revenue system. The greatest amount of evil came from the confused and juggled land registers for which the *li-chia* system was not responsible at all.

After the abolition of the procedure of *li-chia* registration, the population registers made on the basis of the *pao-chia* records were no more accurate than the previous registers compiled from the *li-chia* reports. According to the editor of an official reference work, the household reports (supposedly based on actual *pao-chia* figures), which were annually sent to Peking, were generally manufactured in the following fashion:

> . . . the provincial treasurer instructed the *chou* and *hsien* to furnish [records], and the *chou* and *hsien* magistrates instructed the wolfish yamen clerks to do the same. The clerks had merely to gather themselves in one room and produce the required documents.[79]

THE *LI-CHIA*'S ROLE IN TAX COLLECTION

The original function of the *li-chia* was to assist the local officials in the periodic compilation of the yellow registers, which recorded the number of inhabitants liable to the *ting* (labor service) imposts in the various parts of the empire. Eventually, however, the *li-chia* became involved in the process of tax collection and ceased for all practical purposes to perform its original function. To examine the functional transformation of the *li-chia,* it is helpful to know some of the features of the process of tax collection in imperial China that have bearing on our inquiry. The general process of tax collection fell into three distinguishable phases:[80] (1) officially reminding the taxpayers of their obligations, a procedure usually known in imperial times as *ts'ui-k'o* (which for lack of a more suitable word may be tentatively rendered as "prompting tax payments"), (2) receiving the taxes which might be paid in kind or converted into money equivalents, and (3) sending the taxes collected in the various localities to the imperial government. The *li-chia* was made to serve only in the first two of these procedures.

The complicated *ts'ui-k'o* procedure was important because default in tax payment was a persistent and widespread practice. The government found it necessary to remind, repeatedly and forcefully, all taxpayers of their obligations as owners of land. The procedure began with the official announcement of the dates on which payments were due in each locality. Imperial law required the payment of the land and labor service taxes each year during two collection periods, which varied from province to province.[81] About one month before the first day on which taxes were due, a document known as the *i-chih yu-tan* (easy-comprehension notice) was issued by the local yamen to each of the taxpayers in the district concerned, so that they knew exactly how much and when they had to pay the government.[82] The *yu-tan* adopted in 1649 proved to be a source of extortionary practices,[83] and was abolished officially in 1687.[84] The imperial government sought to improve the situation by taking a number of remedial measures.[85]

It permitted taxpayers to voice protests against malpractices. [86] In place of the *yu-tan* it instituted early in the eighteenth century the *kun-tan,* a document issued by the local yamen to the head of the *chia* division, who saw to it that it circulated among the five or ten households in his neighborhood, thereby reminding each of its tax obligations. [87] Any household that failed to pass the document to the household next in order (thus causing a bottleneck in the *ts'ui-k'o* procedure) was punishable by law. [88] This new device, it was said, did away with some of the most flagrant malpractices, but many more persisted well into the nineteenth century. [89] The *kun-tan* itself did not turn out to be more than a mixed blessing to the taxpayers, [90] who continued to suffer in silence as before. [91]

The procedure of receiving the tax payments as prescribed by law was a simple one. A government order issued in 1661 required that all tax money be deposited by the taxpayer personally in wooden chests placed in front of the yamen gate and that all tax grain be delivered to designated storehouses. [92] This method, which made personal delivery mandatory, was reaffirmed again and again, for it was believed that it was the only way to forestall fraudulent tampering with public revenue by clerks, underlings, and headmen of the *li-chia*. [93] A small taxpayer, however, whose tax was under one tael in silver, was permitted to request a taxpayer of more substantial sums to make the payment for him. [94] (This afforded a pretext for a notorious malpractice known as *pao-lan.*) [95] Receipts were issued to persons who had completed their payments. Withholding such receipts or issuing them without specifying the sums received was an offense punishable by law. [96] Except for brief periods, [97] these receipts contained three identical sections, one for the yamen files, the second for the use of the agents authorized to receive the payments, and the third for the taxpayer. [98] Hence these documents were known as *san-lien ch'uan-p'iao* (three-section string-receipts, the Chinese equivalent of triplicate copies), or simply *ch'uan-p'iao;* since they carried the official seal and had to be cut for the appropriate sections to be distributed, they were sometimes called *ying-p'iao* (seal receipts) or *chieh-p'iao* (cut receipts). [99] The possession of *ch'uan-p'iao* constituted legal proof that the person had fulfilled his tax obligations for the current year. Many a taxpayer, however, received this all-important document only after much delay or paying extortion money to the yamen underlings in charge of tax collection.

The district magistrate was legally the tax collector who dealt directly with the taxpayers of the locality concerned. It was his duty to take in all the taxes due and transfer the revenue to the provincial treasurer, who in turn sent the proper portion of the revenue thus realized to Peking. [100] The magistrate, however, was authorized to appoint assistants to help him carry out the various tasks of collection and to avail himself of the assistance of the submagistrate or the educational officer if the locality had no submagistrate. [101]

Of course the magistrates made extensive use of their own underlings, the yamen clerks and runners. One of the clerks, popularly called *tsung-shu* (chief recorder), figured most prominently in tax collection. While the quotas given in the *Fu-i ch'üan-shu* constituted the official basis for making the collection and this compilation was always available for the magistrate's reference, it lacked detail and often was not up to date. The magistrate had to depend upon the recording clerk for concrete information concerning the local rates, payments currently due, taxpayers in arrears, etc. The *tsung-shu* was the first person to go to for such information. [102]

Much of the process of tax collection on the *chou* and *hsien* level was done through paper work. But the task of *ts'ui-k'o* involved trips to the villages where many of the taxpayers lived. It was physically impossible for the magistrate or his yamen underlings to go there and "prompt" payment of taxes; he naturally called into service a swarm of minor assistants, the *li-chia* heads, yamen runners whose regular duties lay outside of tax collection, and other persons whose legal status was not clear. Practices differed in different localities. According to a semiofficial publication, the *ts'ui-k'o* procedure might be carried on in three different ways: (1) by sending a yamen runner to each of the *li* divisions where he remained until all taxes were paid, (2) by enlisting the services of the *li-shu* (i. e. , *li-chang)* or *chia-tsung* (i.e. , *chia-chang)*, or (3) by designating some of the heads of the taxpaying households as *ts'ui-t'ou* (prompting chief). [103]

The practice of using the *li-chia* as a subsidiary apparatus for tax collection may be directly traced to the Ming dynasty. Since the *ting* imposts of Ming times were very heavy and difficult to collect, the *li-chia* was instituted for the express purpose of "prompting" tax payments. The heads of the households with the largest number of *ting* and the largest amount of land were always appointed *li-chang*. The fact that in Ming times the *li-chia* was popularly known as *ching-ts'ui* (prompting agency)[104] justifies the supposition that its main function was *ts'ui-k'o* instead of registration. To facilitate the collection of land taxes the Ming government instituted, in addition to the *li-chia*, four *liang-chang* (grain-tax collectors) in every *ch'ü* (ward), who were selected from among owners of large amounts of land. [105] Thus during a part of the Ming dynasty at least the process of tax collection may be described as "the *li-chia* reminded the taxpayers of their obligations, the households paid their taxes, the *liang-chang* received the payments, and the *chou·* or *hsien* magistrates supervised the collection. " As time went on, both the *li-chia* and *liang-chang* became sources of corruption; the former were often compelled by the magistrate and his underlings to supply materials and render services far beyond their legal duties. [106]

The Ch'ing rulers abolished the *liang-chang* and made the magistrate the sole official tax collector;[107] they retained the *li-chia* but changed its function from "prompting" tax payments to household registration. These moves were apparently calculated to remedy some of the worst evils of the Ming system. However, the *li-chia* of Ch'ing times soon ceased to perform its function as a rural registration agent and was made to serve substantially the same function as the *ching-ts'ui* of Ming times. In other words, a functional transformation of the *li-chia* took place which was tantamount to a reversion to the Ming practice.

This transformation took place early in the Ch'ing dynasty. By the middle of the seventeenth century many a local official had hailed the practice of using the *li-chia* to help in collecting taxes as "a fine method."[108] "Prompting and receiving tax payments" soon were recognized as the proper function of the *li-chia*;[109] eventually, it was regarded as the only rural agent authorized by law "to demand and handle tax payments."[110] As one might expect, the resumption of the function of *ts'ui-k'o* by the *li-chia* brought back many of the malpractices prevailing in the Ming dynasty, the worst of which was the illegal imposition of heavy burdens on its personnel and indirectly on the taxpayers of the neighborhood divisions.

The 1881 edition of the *Wu-hsi Chin-kuei hsien chih* gives us a revealing account of the *li-chia* in these two districts of Kiangsu province during the latter part of the seventeenth and the early part of the nineteenth century:

> Each *li* constituted a *t'u* which contained 110 households; each *t'u* was divided into 10 *chia*. Inhabitants having the largest number of *ting* and the largest amount of land were selected to serve as *li-chang;* . . . those households possessing moderate amounts of property were appointed *chia-shou* [i.e., *chia-chang*]. . . .
>
> The *li-chang* served by annual turns, in an endless cycle. But because one *li-chang* could not be adequate to the burdensome services incumbent upon him, a *tsung-chia* [chief of the *chia*] and a *shui-shu* [tax recorder] (the latter also known as *hu-shu* [recorder of the households] or *ch'ü-shu* [ward recorder]) were instituted. The person who served in the current year as *li-chang* had already served as *tsung-chia* in the previous year and would serve as *shui-shu* in the year following. One person thus served for three consecutive years [in three different capacities]; for the remaining seven years [of a ten-year round], he performed no services. In any given year, three persons from three different *chia* served concurrently [as *li-chang*, *tsung-chia*, and *shui-shu*]; the remaining seven *chia* performed no services.

The *li-chang* was in charge of the taxes, paid in kind or in money equivalents, in his *t'u*. He was held responsible for any surplus, deficit, or arrears in the payments; for "prompting" and pressing for the payments; and for answering to the yamen on the days when reckoning was due.

The *tsung-chia* managed the business of the *t'u*. He was held responsible for any unjust or unlawful dealings among the inhabitants, and for any robbery or theft that had occurred therein. . . .

The *shui-shu* kept the tax records of the *t'u*. He was responsible for recording all transfers of land titles [within the division].

The above situation continued until 1686. Obviously because the existing arrangement had given rise to serious abuses, T'ang Ping, governor of Kiangsu, introduced some minor changes. He prohibited the appointment of *li-chang* to serve in the capacity described above. As a result, the duties hitherto incumbent upon the *li-chang* devolved upon the *tsung-chia*.

Another change took place in 1820:

In Chia-ch'ing 25, Governor Li Hsing-yüan issued a stern directive, saying in part . . . "From now on the person who performs the services of the *ti-pao* shall be publicly nominated by the scholars and common people of each *t'u* . . . and the nominees shall report to the local government for appointment. . . . In case any household [in a *t'u*] fails to pay its taxes or is overdue in its payments, a *liang-ch'ai* [a yamen runner] shall be held responsible jointly with the *ti-pao* for compelling [the defaulting households] to make the payments.[111]

This lengthy account is particularly interesting because it epitomizes some of the developments that occurred not only in these districts of Kiangsu but in slightly different ways in other localities as well. It reveals that as early as in the middle of the seventeenth century, when the dynasty was newly established, local practices had already deviated from the provisions of imperial law. The duties assigned to the *li-chia* clearly went beyond the limits set by law. The official function of the *li-chia*, registration of the taxpaying households, gave place completely to the function of tax collection. By the time Li Hsing-yüan introduced his measures of reform, the *tsung-chia*, following the *li-chang* and *shui-shu*, had disappeared from the scene, leaving the *ti-pao* to shoulder the burdens that formerly fell upon these *li-chia* heads, a trend of change to which reference has already been made in connection with the *pao-chia*.[112]

The following passage from the 1872 edition of the *Nan-hai hsien chih* not only describes another mode of operation but also explains some of the hardships that befell those in the *li-chia* who were involved in the process of tax collection:

In collecting the taxes in our district, the *tu* controls a varying
number of *pao;* each *pao* controls a varying number of *t'u* . . . and
each *t'u* controls ten *chia.* By annual turns, [the head of] one of the
chia takes charge of matters connected with tax payment. The person
currently responsible for these matters is called *tang-nien.*

In the first month of the lunar year, the person serving as *tang-
nien* invites all the [heads of the] ten *chia* in the *t'u* to a party at which
wine and food are served. He examines the tax receipts in the possession of the guests, in order to ascertain if any of them have not paid
their taxes in full. If one of them has failed to pay, he is punished in
accordance with the established practice. . . . Hence a proverb persists to the present day . . . to the effect that a wedding does not
take place in the household of a *tang-nien.* The reason is . . . being
pressed by public services . . . he has no time to attend to private
affairs.

Each *chia* controls a varying number of households, one of which
was designated *tsung-hu* [general household] and the rest *tzu-hu* [mem-
ber households]. . . . [The *tang-nien* of the *chia]* checks [the tax
payments of] the *tsung-hu* which in turn checks [those of] the *tzu-hu.*
[Under such an arrangement] there is no way to evade the taxes.

But as the tax registers of the district are kept in the yamen, village elders and *li-chang* cannot see them. . . . Consequently, yamen
clerks and runners are free to practice *fei-sa* [fraudulent transposition
of tax burdens from one household to another]. [113]

The lot of the *li-chia* heads thus became hardly enviable. In many
cases they were held responsible not only for making their fellow villagers pay the taxes but for making good any taxes that the villagers
failed to pay. "As a consequence," a local historian informs us, "the
entire clan of the person serving his one-year turn [as *li-chang]* had
to postpone all weddings, and some of the inhabitants were thus compelled to forsake their home villages [to escape the burdens placed
upon them]. "[114]

In some localities efforts were made to ameliorate the situation.
The experiences of Chin-ch'i Hsien (Kiangsi) are illuminating. According to a Chinese writer:

In provinces south of the Yangtze River, a *hsien* is invariably divided into a number of *Hsiang.* A *Hsiang* is subdivided into *tu,* each
of the latter with a number of *li;* and each *tu* contains a number of *t'u,*
each of the latter with a number of households. There are ten *chia* in
each *t'u.* Each *chia* furnishes by turns the labor services of the *hsien.*
These services are always incumbent on the heads of the *li,* known as
li-chang and *liang-chang.* These two heads divide the responsibility
of "prompting" the payment of taxes due in the summer and autumn
collection periods, and they are replaced at the end of the year. On
specific days fixed beforehand by the local official, they report [to
the yamen] in the morning, a procedure known as "answering the

roll call. " Failure to report is punished by flogging. Yamen clerks and runners use numerous pretexts to extort money from them on the appointed days; the money is always paid as demanded.

Chin-ch'i has six *Hsiang* and over forty *tu*. Kuei-cheng Hsiang is one of the six. It contains nine *tu*, each with four *t'u*. The distance of these to the city varies between thirty and forty *li* [about ten English miles]. Payment of the summer taxes is made in the city, where [these two *li-chia* heads] have to pay for their lodging and food and go to the yamen clerks and runners. A fee is agreed upon, usually not less than seventy or eighty taels annually. Autumn taxes are paid in rice, which has to be delivered to the tribute granaries at Hsü-wan. A comparable fee is exacted.

Households of the gentry are designated *huan* [official] and those of scholars *ju* [literati], and their status is indicated in the registers. The local official permits any of these that refuse to pay taxes to pass unquestioned. He merely demands [the two *li-chia* heads] to hand in the full amount of revenue specified in the registers. As a result, the latter have to make payments for [the defaulters], the sum amounting to no less than twenty or thirty taels each year. In addition, they are flogged and imprisoned every month, practically without exception. Those who perform the services [of the *li-chang* and *liang-chang]* frequently go bankrupt.

A change for the better came in 1708:

Feng Meng-k'un, a *sheng-yüan* of this district, was a native of the Second T'u of the Ninth Tu. . . . The tax he was liable to pay amounted to about one-third of the total quota of his *chia*. Having pity on those who had to perform the troublesome and onerous services [of the *li-chang* and *liang-chang]*, he devised a method of "service-exemption. " The posts of the *ts'e-shu* [recorder], *t'u-chang[li-chang]*, *chia-chang*, and *hu-chang* [head of household] were filled by honest persons of adequate property. It was agreed that half of the summer taxes were to be paid during the fourth month of the lunar year, and the remainder cleared in the eighth month. At no other time was it necessary [for the *li-chia* heads] to go into the city. Roll call and extortionary fees were abolished.

Furthermore, [he persuaded] the "official" and "literati" households to lead the neighborhoods in paying the full quotas of their taxes ahead of time. As to the taxes of the other registered households, the *t'u-chang* held the *chia-chang* responsible [for their payment] and the *chia-chang* in turn held the *hu-chang* responsible. The *ts'e-shu* was responsible for recording any change in the amounts.

This method was first adopted in K'ang-hsi 47 [1708]. By now [1720] it has been in operation for more than ten years. The total amount of fees saved was over 2,000 taels.

Feng died in the year *ting-yu* [1717]. At that time the other *t'u* of Kuei-cheng Hsiang had all adopted his method. Shortly afterwards, three or four out of the ten *t'u* in the six *Hsiang*[of this district] heard of it and adopted it also.[115]

Whatever benefits accrued from this reform in Chin-ch'i were bound to be limited in geographical extent. The evils which Feng Meng-k'un remedied in Chin-ch'i were observed in many other localities of the empire and usually remained unchecked. The situation was so bad that it attracted imperial attention, as an edict of 1724 indicates. The Yung-cheng emperor instructed the governor of Kiangsi:

> The labor service imposts and land grain taxes are to be paid by the people in person. This is the established practice. We have heard that in Kiangsi province inhabitants of the *li* are required to "prompt" the tax payments. Each of the ten *chia* in the *li* serve by one-year turns. . . . Making petty villagers render this service is not only to expose them to the exactions of corrupt yamen clerks but also to force them to neglect their farming, owing to the necessity of running about [in order to carry out the duty thus imposed upon them]. . . . Investigations shall be immediately made and the said practice be generally abolished.[116]

We do not have concrete information concerning the effect of this imperial edict on the *li-chia* of Kiangsi, but we have some data to show that similar practices prevailed in a number of other provinces, including Hunan, Kwangsi, Kweichow, and Shantung. In Tao Chou (Hunan), for example, *hu-shou* (i.e., *hu-chang)* were set up, each serving by turns within the *chia* division. These households were ordered to take out the *kun-tan* (rolling bills) from the local yamen and to go with the yamen runners to press every household in the neighborhoods for payment of taxes. Flogging was readily administered to *hu-shou* whenever somebody failed to pay on time. Occasionally, some of the households were located so far away from the dwellings of the *hu-shou* that it was physically impossible to go to them and demand the tax payments. Or, in other instances, the defaulters were too closely related to the *hu-shou* for the latter to perform their duties as tax collecting agents effectively. These circumstances increased the *hu-shou*'s chances of being punished by flogging. As a result, many of them sought to escape the hardship either by bribing the yamen runners, who would find substitutes to receive the flogging, or by getting yamen clerks to shift the burden to some other household. The fact that in 1853 the magistrate granted special exemption from this service to the households of young scholars actively engaged in the local examinations[117] indicates that the general situation just described persisted well into the nineteenth century.

The condition that prevailed in Yung Hsien (Kwangsi) during the late seventeenth and early eighteenth centuries, illustrates another type of misuse that plagued the *li-chia:* imposing other extralegal services upon the *li-chang*–services which were hardly related to *ts'ui-k'o* or to any other phase of tax collection. According to a local historian:

> During K'ang-hsi times, one household in each *li* served by turns as *li-chang* in a ten-year cycle. One person from each household served, also by turns, as *tung-t'ou* [i.e., *chia-chang*]. The *li-chang* performed "public" services, while the *tung-t'ou* was chiefly responsible for "prompting" tax payments.
>
> The so-called public services included welcoming new magistrates and seeing departing officials off; mending and repairing furniture and furnishings for officials; and providing utensils, tools, and ceremonial paraphernalia of the yamen. Materials of all dimensions and values required every year in connection with these services came exclusively from the *li-chang*. In addition, the *li-chang* on duty for the current month sent to the yamen chests of sweetmeats, two every night (a total sum of two taels silver was sent in lieu of the food); this was spent over and above other fees. . . .
>
> Moreover, expenses for the annual repair of the yamen of the provincial, circuit, and prefectural officials also came from the *li-chang;* similarly, expenses for the annual repair of the local examination booths, the city walls and moats, and all other public structures. . . . It is impossible to enumerate all the miscellaneous services that descended upon the *li-chang*. . . . Nor is it possible to trace the exactions demanded by the local yamen clerks and runners. . . .
>
> Consequently, once a villager was appointed *li-chang* he had to be prepared virtually to give up his life. Even a wealthy household with savings accumulated for nine years could be ruined by one year's expenses [entailed in *li-chang* services]. Some sought to escape destruction by becoming fugitives, others by pretending death or extinction. . . .
>
> The services remained, even though the land [upon which the liabilities fell] was allowed to become uncultivated. Unpaid services then devolved on members of the same families; if these also fled and could not be found, the burdens fell upon households of the same *li-chia* division. [118]

This was by no means a unique instance. Comparable situations existed in other parts of the empire. [119] Illegal practices persisted as long as the *li-chia* system operated, despite express imperial prohibition of the imposition of extralegal services upon the *li-chang*. As early as 1660 (Shun-chih 17) local officials were sternly forbidden to assign unauthorized duties to the *li-chia*, "such as supplying rice and fuel for [their] daily use, expense and labor for repairing or building yamen, for [making] furniture or [procuring] various gifts, or for [furnishing] carriers, horses, or bodyguards." This interdiction was reiterated in 1669 and again in 1700. [120] Such extralegal services, however, proved exceedingly convenient if not exactly indispensable to the local officials. They were therefore disinclined to pay due regard to imperial wishes or to respect the proper functions of the *li-chia*. As a result, many a *li-chang* or *chia-chang* was put in a virtually impossible position, to the detriment of the *li-chia* as an auxiliary instrument of tax collection.

One should not imagine, however, that the *li-chia* agents were above reproach. Many of them were known to have shifted the extralegal burdens to the taxpayers. [121] In other instances *li-chia* agents developed corrupt practices of their own, oppressing the taxpayers under their jurisdiction and making unlawful profit by capitalizing on their authority as tax collection agents for the government. One particularly striking instance will illustrate the worst type of such subadministrative corruption. According to a Chinese source, this was the situation in Ch'ang-an Hsien (Shensi) in the second half of the nineteenth century:

> Investigation shows that the taxpaying inhabitants of Ch'ang-an are arranged into forty-nine *li*, each *li* being divided into ten *chia* (some into eleven or twelve *chia*). . . . Since the earliest times those paying the taxes are *hua-hu*, while those in charge of the taxes are *li-chang*. This is the generally established practice.
>
> Matters, however, are different in Ch'ang-an. . . . Being *hua-hu* these households dare not look into the account books of the *li-chang*, nor are they permitted to inquire about the account books of the *li*. They allow the *li-chang* freely to shift and tamper with the tax quotas [incumbent upon them]; they are afraid to find the least fault with [the *li-chang*]. The latter would promptly raise a mob and insult any offending taxpayer. If, as a last resort, a taxpaying household brings the matter to the attention of the magistrate . . . the *li-chang* would maneuver with the yamen runners in charge of tax collection. [Under such circumstances] even if the household in question does not stint on expenses, it would be outnumbered and outmaneuvered [by the *li-chang* and his connivers]. It may go bankrupt without obtaining redress. Hence generally the taxpayers choose to suffer injuries without giving vent to anger or raising any protest.
>
> When the *li-chang* reckons the accounts, he sits in the center of the hall, while taxpayers stand outside the door. The *li-chang* dines in the hall, while taxpayers eat their meals below the flight of steps leading up to the hall. The *li-chang* is treated with the deference due to a parent, whereas taxpayers are regarded as his inferiors, as his sons or grandchildren. A distinction between the superior and inferiors is thus set up. Recently there has prevailed a sentiment that the *li-chang* should not demean himself by entering into marriage relationships with any household of taxpayers [under his jurisdiction]. A line between honorable and dishonorable is thus drawn. . . .
>
> Even after having sold his land to another person, a taxpayer remains liable for his original taxes. Even the gentry cannot remove this liability. . . .
>
> Careful investigation reveals that all these evils have arisen from

two or three corrupt *li-chang* who, with yamen runners as their accomplices, avail themselves of every opportunity to fish for illegal gains, to oppress and maltreat peaceful, timid villagers. . . . These *li-chang* are persons who have been in charge of tax matters for a long time. [122]

Understandably, the *li-chia* office became highly lucrative in many parts of the empire, so much so that it virtually had to be bought by those who sought it. In Tung-kuan Hsien (Kwangtung), for example, where the *li-chia* recorder was locally known as the *shu-suan,* the district magistrate sold that office at a handsome price. According to local historians:

This district has 127 *t'u,* each of which has a *shu-suan* who keeps the registers in his private home. When a landowner seeks to clear his tax payment, he has to hand to [the *shu-suan]* a bribe, which is calculated on the basis of the number of *mow* he owns, before his payment is accepted and the receipt for it issued to him.

A new *shu-suan* is appointed at the end of five years. The incumbent presents 1,000 taels to the magistrate in accordance with established practice. [123]

Under such circumstances, the *li-chia* could hardly assist the government to collect the taxes honestly and efficiently, or deal with the taxpayers fairly and in accordance with law. Indeed, it appears that the *li-chia* repeated the story of the *pao-chia,* at least in one respect: the agents recruited from honest villagers became the victims of yamen underlings; while those drawn from rascally elements victimized the taxpayers through a variety of subadministrative malpractices.

GENERAL APPRAISAL OF THE *LI-CHIA*

Problems of Tax Collection

The *li-chia* constituted but one cog in the imperial revenue machinery. Obviously, no appraisal of the *li-chia* can be properly made without viewing it in the context of the entire revenue system; we must know something of the problems confronting the *fu-i* system in general. While the *li-chia* apparatus was not free from inherent defects, its failure to function adequately and properly either as a rural registration agency or as a rural tax collection agency was due largely to the circumstances under which it operated.

The Ch'ing revenue system, though more refined than that of any previous dynasty, could not overcome or cope adequately with the historical conditions inevitably concomitant with the imperial system. An officialdom which became increasingly inept and corrupt as time went on, a populace that remained generally helpless and indifferent, ready victims of official and gentry corruption, a vast countryside with very few facilities for communication and transportation—all these conditions posed problems that were practically impossible to solve and rendered the operation of the *fu-i* system a frustrating task for the imperial rulers. On the one hand, the imperial government seldom received the full amounts of the taxes that were legally due; on the other hand, taxpayers in the villages often had to pay much more than was due, suffering losses far beyond the tax burdens that were legally imposed upon them. Unbearable oppression sometimes drove villagers into riots. or other acts of violence, endangering the peace and security of the empire.

The registration of households, the assessment of taxes, and the collection of taxes all were confronted with a multiplicity of problems and gave rise to a host of malpractices. [124] These can conveniently be discussed under two main headings: (1) malpractices in connection with assessment and registration, and (2) malpractices in connection with *ts'ui-k'o* and other procedures of tax collection. The bahavior of local officials and yamen underlings, who were directly responsible for these malpractices, and the participation of the local gentry will be discussed. It is hoped that this discussion will throw light on the operation of the Ch'ing revenue system in the nineteenth century.

Malpractices in Assessment and Registration

The original assessment made at the inception of the Ch'ing dynasty was based mainly on the Ming assessment, which was far from equitable. Subsequent fraudulent practices aggravated the situation, turning inequities into injustice. Even in comparatively early times of the Ch'ing dynasty it was reported in some localities that the tax registers were falsified to facilitate defalcation by yamen underlings and tax evasion by landowners. One result of such practice was the shifting of the tax burdens from those who should have carried them to those who did not own the land in question. [125] Malpractices of this type became so widespread that a sort of trade jargon developed in time. Perhaps the most revealing are the terms *fei* (to fly), *shai* (to sprinkle), *kuei* (to falsify), and *chi* (to lodge). These are succinctly explained by a recent Chinese writer:

> What was known as *fei* was to shift the tax quotas of those households from which payments could be easily collected, to those which were no longer liable for taxes, and change the registration accordingly. The payments received went into the private pockets [of persons in charge of the matter].
> What was known as *shai* was to defalcate the payments [made by some of the households] and to make up the resulting deficit by parcel-

ing the amount to other households [which as a consequence had to pay more than their legal quotas].

What was known as *kuei* was to make false reports, such as reporting land already under cultivation as newly reclaimed land, or partial famine as total famine. . . . In every instance unlawful gains accrued to the persons [making such reports].

What was known as *chi* was to report taxes already collected as still due and defalcate the revenue. The quotas incumbent on households of one tax division were "lodged" in households of another division, and this procedure was repeated, so that the original [liabilities] could not be traced. [126]

An actual example of falsifying the registers was supplied by a nineteenth-century governor of Kiangsu. In a reply to the petition of the magistrate of Fu-ning Hsien, dated 1868, he said:

Wang Hsiao-chen, the *tsung-shu* [a yamen clerk] of the said district, has left no evil undone. For any peasant who pays him a fee, he reports productive land as waste land. Conversely, he who does not bribe him will suffer the consequences of having barren land reported as productive. The people hate him deep in their bones. [127]

The ingenuity of some of the yamen clerks went beyond the ordinary practices of *fei, shai, kuei,* and *chi;* in fact, their application of these fraudulent methods was not limited to existing households. The device of "ghost households" is especially striking. According to a well-known nineteenth-century Chinese writer,

. . . when the *liang-shu* [yamen clerk in charge of tax registers] made up the registers, he put on record, for each actual household [suitable for his purpose] an imaginary one, which was supposed to be located in the same *t'u* and to have a head bearing the same name as the former, but which was liable for a different tax quota. This imaginary household was known as *kuei hu* [ghost-household]. Suppose a real household under the name Chao Ta was liable for one *shih* of rice; the *liang-shu* would make up a ghost-household, also under the name Chao Ta, but with liability for one *shen* [1/100 of one *shih*]. When the time of collecting the taxes arrived, this *liang-shu* paid one *sheng* for the imaginary taxpayer, altered the figure "one *sheng*" to read "one *shih*" on the receipt, and demanded from Chao Ta [the real taxpayer] the money equivalent of one *shih* of rice. [128]

The *i* or corvée presented an equally somber picture. The greatest hardships connected with the *i* arose from the fact that the original avowed intention of the imperial government to integrate all the labor service imposts of the Ming dynasty into one levy, the *ting,* was not—and perhaps could not be—carried out. Practical exigencies often de-

manded various sorts of services beyond what was covered by the
ting; the money collected from the *ting* was often found to be insufficient to pay for services theoretically covered by it. Official graft
and extortion stretched further the demand for extra imposts. All
these factors played havoc with the *i* and brought ruinous consequences
to many rural inhabitants. In one sense, the burdens of the *ting* were
even more difficult to bear than those of the land taxes. As a nineteenth-century governor of Shansi pointed out, [129] deferment could be
granted to payers of the land taxes, whereas the *ting* imposts were
exacted whenever it was due, no consideration being given to famine
or calamities. When one illegal levy was added to another, the *ting*
burdens could become truly crushing.

How extralegal imposts arose may be seen from the conditions in
Chihli province where the *i* was fairly heavy. A magistrate writing
from ten years' experience stated that owing to their propinquity to
the imperial capital many districts were required to furnish labor
and expenses toward repairing roads and bridges, taking care of the
imperial hunting grounds, transportation and other services in connection with the emperor's yearly visit to the mausoleums, and so
forth. Local officials shifted the burdens to the people. Magistrates
and their underlings took advantage of the labor conscriptions to extort money, often double the necessary sums, from taxpayers. But
since they were afraid of the gentry, they victimized the commoner
villagers almost exclusively. [130] In 1822 the treasurer of the same
province explained the matter in these words:

> While the land taxes are regular and clearly defined, the extra-
> legal labor imposts are without fixed quotas. Evil practices grow
> up as time goes on, until pretexts for imposing additional services
> become countless. . . .
> Since the amount officially established is insufficient to defray the
> actual expenses . . . circumstances compel [local functionaries]
> to exact additional money from the people. As soon as the order to
> collect the money is issued, yamen clerks, runners, and rural agents
> rush in to fish for gains, each at his suitable level: submagistrates
> and petty officers rise as a group to divide the spoils; and wicked
> scholars, *sheng-yüan* and *chien-sheng,* indulge freely in manipulating
> [the collection].

Some of the most shocking evils, however, came from unjust distribution of these extralegal tax burdens. The treasurer continued:

> The labor imposts [beyond the *ting]* for which the people are liable
> have hitherto been assessed evenly on land. The matter, however,
> is done in a bad way. At first exemptions are granted to those be-
> longing to gentry families or big clans; then scholars of various grades

are exempted; and finally even yamen clerks, doorkeepers, soldiers, runners, and all persons in yamen service claim exemption, on the pretext that they are already performing labor service. The number of *pai-i* [unauthorized yamen runners] increases daily. Moreover, persons bearing the same family name contribute money and purchase a petty official title for one of them who is clever and eloquent, so that the entire group enjoys exemption from the labor service imposts. The amount of land paying such imposts decreases in proportion as the amount of land exempted from them increases. Each taxpayer, in other words, has to pay proportionally more. As a result, a hard-working peasant has to pay as much as two to four hundred copper cash per *mow* of land, several times the regular tax [authorized by law] which is about one-tenth of a tael. [131]

The very fact that such imposts were extralegal prevented the as-sessments from being made according to definite regulations. The resulting chaos in turn precluded the possibility of supervision. Un-limited opportunity was thus given to yamen underlings to extort and to embezzle. According to another nineteenth-century writer, this was the situation in Chihli:

. . . assessments are sometimes made on the basis of the number of oxen or donkeys owned [by the households]; sometimes villages are taken as units or households registered in the *pao-chia* are held individually responsible. The situation is confused and no definite rules are followed. Consequently, superior officials have no way of keeping a check on [their subordinates]. The manner in which the inhabitants pay their taxes also varies from locality to locality. Spe-cial exemptions are sometimes granted to city dwellers, sometimes to the gentry, and sometimes to persons in yamen service. The com-mon people are placed at a decided disadvantage: they are made to bear the entire burden. [132]

In a memorial of 1882, Chang Chih-tung, then governor of Shansi, made the following revealing statement concerning the general prac-tice in that province:

In the *chou* and *hsien* of Shansi province the government measure that oppresses the people the most is not the collection of the regular taxes but the imposition of extra labor services. What is called *ch'ai-yao* [labor conscription] is in reality not a measure to make use of their labor but a method of exacting their money.

Hitherto the customary quotas assigned [to the various localities] amounted to fifty or sixty thousand strings of copper cash in a large district, and several thousand to ten thousand in a small one. The amount to be collected in each locality is apportioned to the people on the basis of their regular tax quotas. The amount collected is shared by the local magistrate and his subordinates.

In those *chou* and *hsien* through which thoroughfares pass, toll-chests are set up [to collect money from those who use the roads]. Owners of beasts of burden in the four rural areas are called together and horses and carriages of travelers are detained, from whom payments are demanded, either according to annual rates or in lump sums. A donkey, for example, is assessed one hundred copper cash per month, while a carriage is assessed several thousand. In consequence, porters of other provinces are reluctant to enter Shansi.[133]

Even in southern provinces where the regular *ting* tax was relatively light, illegal impositions were often observed. For instance, in a report to the emperor, a supervisory censor said that the labor and expenses incurred in building boats for government use in the various *chou* and *hsien* of Chekiang were exacted from the *li-chia*. The amounts exacted by local officials were fairly substantial; for example, the magistrate of Sui-an collected over 1,700 taels, that of Wu-ch'eng over 12,000 taels, and that of Chu-chi over 7,000 taels.[134]

Military campaigns made conditions worse in localities through which the supply lines passed. A circuit censor, memorializing the Chia-ch'ing emperor in 1800 concerning Kwangsi, said:

> In Ch'ien-lung 53 [1788] when a military campaign was in progress against An-nan, conscript laborers were drafted from every household in the prefectures of Szu-nan, Nan-ning, T'ai-p'ing, Chen-an, and Szu-ch'eng, and were employed at various points to transport military material. . . . Peasants were daily assigned to these points to await work. The inhabitants of any given district lived in villages some of which were located at distances varying from several tens of *li* to as many as two hundred *li*. Those drafted had to bring with them their own food; they slept in the open to wait for their turns. They were prevented from attending to their own work. . . .
>
> The campaign was successfully concluded more than ten years ago, but labor conscription remains. . . . Yamen clerks and runners as well as attendants of local officials all desire to have conscript laborers at these points in the countryside so that they can continue to gratify their avarice. . . . Sometimes when villagers are unable to perform the services, they secretly bribe the record-keeper who connives with clerks, runners, and attendants and shares the booty with them. . . . In fact, some of the magistrates receive monthly "presents" from the record-keeper, which are called "the monthly fees." For this reason these officials dawdle, allowing the conscription to remain long after the order to abolish it has been received.[135]

Another instance was reported in two northern provinces. In a memorial of 1879, Yen Ching-ming made the following observation:

> Labor conscription weighs hard on the people. This is universally

true in all northern provinces, but especially so in Shansi and Shensi. Formerly, when military campaigns were in progress, labor services from the people were indispensable to transportation. Hence for every tael of silver levied as land tax, additional labor service imposts were assessed, amounting to several times the regular quotas. . . . In recent years labor services are seldom required for military purposes; there are only occasional demands for [nonmilitary] labor services. But the imposts in localities along the courier roads have not been materially reduced, while those in secluded places remain as heavy as before. At present every tael of money in payment of the regular taxes carries a labor service surcharge which varies from 800 to over 1,000 copper cash. Ostensibly [the government] has not increased the tax burden; but in reality the burden bears heavily [on the people]. The regular taxes are occasionally remitted; but labor service imposts are exacted even in years of famine. [136]

The courier system, one of the regular services maintained by the imperial government for the transmission of official dispatches, became another source of inequitable imposition. A regulation of 1668 fixed the quota of couriers to be engaged in the land and water courier posts and expressly provided that their "labor and food expenses" were to come from the regular revenue receipts. [137] It was unlawful to incur additional expenses or demand services beyond what was necessary for strictly government purposes. Officials from governors-general down were forbidden to require magistrates to supply labor and materials for transportation, even when they were traveling on official missions. [138]

These regulations and prohibitions, however, were more generally ignored or circumvented than obeyed. Indeed, the Ch'ien-lung emperor was unwittingly responsible for incurring extralegal labor services when he made the famous imperial tours to Chiang-nan. According to an eyewitness:

Boat-trackers for the imperial vessel were river-soldiers of Huai-an. The boatmen on ships following the imperial vessel were drafted from local inhabitants. Each t'u [= li] was required to supply about forty boatmen and five boats and to have them ready for use. In addition, about twenty carriers were furnished by each t'u. The hsien did not issue written orders but made the conscription through oral instructions. The reason was that there was an explicit law which forbade conscription beyond the authorized labor services. Each person thus drafted was given one-fifth of a tael for his "labor and food expenses." The inhabitants, however, paid two taels for each of these laborers who were hired by them [to meet the conscription]. . . . An order to commandeer boats was issued as early as the spring of 1750. Boats from the countryside were seized by yamen runners when they approached the city. Those who paid the bribes demanded of them, however, could have their boats released. [139]

Local officials were the most frequent offenders. Willingly or un-willingly they made illegal use of the courier system (and of whatever rural agencies were available) to provide transportation services for their superiors or central officials passing through their localities. The general state of affairs was described in a memorial of 1803 by a former grand secretary who had retired in the previous year. After pointing out that the transportation facilities authorized by existing regulations were adequate for the actual needs of officials on imperial missions, he continued:

> Since the *chou* and *hsien* have been given charge of the courier system, it is possible for the magistrates to employ the *li-chia* to supply services. As a result, nothing hinders them from increasing the number of horses and riders [beyond the authorized limits]. . . . Sometimes the increase amounts to several tenfold. . . . A further result of this is that yamen attendants in charge of the courier posts and clerks and runners responsible for providing the transportation services take the opportunity to extort money. . . . Peasants have to stop their farming, bring their own food and fodder, and wait ahead of time [at the designated places]. The sufferings are indescribable. [140]

Comparable conditions prevailed where the transportation services were rendered on waterways. An eyewitness describes the following scene:

> A certain high official is traveling through the district. His ship moves very slowly along the river. I am curious about its slow speed, as it is pulled by a large number of boat-trackers. Upon closer inspection I discover that among the several hundred persons pulling the boat, nine out of ten are hunchbacks, cripples, one-eyed persons, men with swollen shins, men whining or crying from illness, hunger, or cold. Some of them fall to the ground after taking a few steps; some, not being able to walk, rest their elbows on the towrope and let others carry them along; some disengage themselves from the pulling cord, run down the embankment, and disappear from view. Two foremen, each with a whip in his hand, supervise the gang. They whip those who fail to pull hard, and chase vociferously those who run away. But when too many fall down and run away, these foremen with their whips also flee—being themselves afraid of punishment. . . .
> After a long while the ship passes out of sight. Some of the fugitives come out from their hiding places. I inquire their conditions. With knitted brows they make this reply: "We are all hungry people. Official boats passing through this district are, as an established practice, furnished with boat-trackers, the number varying with the rank of the official [to whom the service was offered]. Each of us is supposed to receive fifty or sixty copper cash daily, which is barely enough for food. But fees have to be paid in order to get the money. After fees are deducted, one after another, the sum each receives

is less than twenty cash, not enough for one meal. The servants, attendants, and boatmen of high officials, relying on the official influence of their masters, usually carry a great amount of miscellaneous commodities in their ships. with a view to evading taxes and making handsome profits. . . . Employing underfed people to pull overladen boats—this is the reason why the ships do not go fast and trackers often run away before the services are completed.[141]

Illegal conscriptions or levies were made in other types of labor services, including those connected with flood prevention, water conservancy, and repair of city walls. The general situation was quite similar to that in the courier service. As is well known, the Ch'ing government abolished the Ming practice of annual draft and established fixed quotas of laborers in the various regions liable to inundation, such as those on the banks of the Yellow River. These quota laborers were given "labor and food expenses" from funds provided for regularly in the *Fu-i ch'üan-shu*.[142] The imperial regulations, however, were not universally applied,[143] nor were they followed for very long. As early as 1690 (K'ang-hsi 29) extra levies were made in various *chou* and *hsien* to raise funds for hiring laborers to work on river dikes.[144] In Chekiang, Hunan, Hupeh, and Szechwan special levies were made to finance flood prevention work along the seacoasts or on rivers.[145] The practice of drafting laborers for "emergency repair" of city walls, government granaries, and yamen buildings had become so widespread that it eventually received tacit authorization by the imperial government.[146]

In short, in matters connected with assessing and drafting labor services a wide gap existed between imperial law and local practices. Local officials and their subordinates were directly responsible for this gap. It would be unreasonable to expect the *li-chia*, the agents of which were at the mercy of yamen underlings, to fulfill the requirements of the imperial law.

Malpractices in Tax Collection

An examination of the many malpractices that appeared in connection with the various procedures of tax collection underscores further the difficult situation in which the *li-chia* operated. As has been mentioned, the *ts'ui-k'o* procedure differed in different localities.[147] Obviously, the greatest hardships were sustained by the taxpayers when yamen runners assumed the task. A seventeenth-century governor of Chekiang stated that the *t'u-ch'ai*, one of whom was assigned to "prompt" payment of taxes in each *li* division, were accustomed to making a noisy entrance into the villages and demanding food, wine, and money from the inhabitants.[148] A circuit intendant of Ch'ing-chou (Shantung) of the same period described the fearful effects of the practice of *tso-ts'ui* (sitting down to demand payment), in a report to the governor-general and governor:

> [Ch'ing-chou] Fu controls more than ten *chou* and *hsien*. In each of the latter is a special yamen runner to whom is assigned the duty of supervising *ts'ui-k'o*, at the yamen every day throughout the year. Each *hsien* controls several dozen of *she* divisions; in each of the latter is a special yamen runner who is responsible for "prompting" tax payments in that division, every day throughout the year. Hence arises the name *tso-ts'ui* [sitting down to prompt payments]. These runners regard their assignments as a passport to extortion. An authorized runner often brings with him several hangers-on. As soon as they arrive at a village, they demand service fees, travel expenses, fees for clearing the accounts, both when payment notices are served and when tax receipts are issued. . . . If these runners really can effectively make the inhabitants pay their taxes to the government, they perhaps may be excused for having placed the welfare of the people below the interest of the state. Unfortunately, however, they are merely concerned with fattening themselves . . . [and perform doubtful services to the government]. When tax payments remain overdue, other runners are sent in their place—and the entire routine is repeated once more. [149]

Well-intentioned officials sometimes sought to curb the flagrant activities of yamen runners in charge of tax collection (often called *liang-ch'ai)*. An eighteenth-century governor of Shensi, for instance, went so far as to try to abolish the practice of sending yamen runners into the countryside to "prompt" payment of taxes. [150] But the practice persisted in this and other provinces down to the nineteenth century and even later. A Chinese writer depicted the conditions of a district in Shensi in the 1860's as follows:

> To each of the forty-nine *li* divisions of Ch'ang-an, a yamen runner is assigned to supervise *ts'ui-k'o*. Persons assigned to this duty are heads of the *min* [guards], *k'uai* [constables] and *tsao* [lictors] bands. These heads, however, feel themselves too important to go to the countryside. They send a few of their rank and file to answer the duties, who are called "runners-on-errand."
>
> Runners-on-errand as well as head runners receive "official" food expenses. . . . Aside from this, fees in the form of "fan money," "carriage fare," "fees for flogging received," "fees to acknowledge favors shown," etc., are exacted [from taxpayers]. . . . On the average, a head runner received over ten thousand strings [of copper cash each year]. Hence a head runner upon appointment as *liang-ch'ai* is congratulated by all [his friends], for it is a way to riches. . . .
>
> Investigation shows that in all the *li* divisions the *liang-ch'ai* is called "the housekeeper." Nothing can be safely done without first asking the permission of "the housekeeper." . . . Wicked *li-chia*

heads are on good terms with him. Whenever the magistrate, out of pity on poor inhabitants of the *li*, shows willingness to postpone collection of their taxes, "the housekeeper" invariably encourages them to default. When eventually the runner on duty is to be punished [for failure to collect the taxes overdue], a substitute is hired to appear in the yamen to receive the flogging. Every time a flogging is administered, inhabitants of the *li* have to pay a certain sum of money as a "flogging fee."

Furthermore, regarding receiving the flogging as doing a "favor" [to the defaulters], the latter are required to show their appreciation of the favor done them. Sometimes, on the pretext of a wedding or funeral [in the runner's family], wicked *li-chia* heads invite for him all the inhabitants in the *li-chia* divisions to a feast. After it is over, the *li-chia* heads begin their maneuver. One of them proposes that each should present "the housekeeper" with a certain number of strings [of cash]; his accomplices voice agreement. . . . "The housekeeper" departs with a full load [of money]. [151]

A different form of extortion was practiced jointly by yamen clerks and runners in Kwangtung province. The following situation was revealed by some members of the local gentry early in 1834 in a petition to the magistrate of Hsiang-shan:

> In our district there are altogether fourteen *tu* . . . divided into forty-four *t'u*. Tickets are issued every year to start the general prompting of tax payments, and are called "golden flower tickets." Yamen clerks in charge of tax matters usually "sell" these tickets to yamen runners, [at prices] varying with the relative degree of wealth or poverty of the *t'u*. The runners then extort money from the households that are serving their one-year turns [in the *li-chia*]. . . . Households with medium means or with little property are greatly distressed when their one-year turns come. . . .
>
> According to regulations, detailed figures showing the amount of taxes paid by or due from the households should be prepared by the *li* recorder every year. After having been sent [to the yamen] and audited, these are to be publicly exhibited in the *li* divisions concerned. This is to show that [the figures] have been found to be correct and to enable the taxpayers to get the payments ready beforehand. But at present the figures showing unpaid taxes in the ten-*chia* divisions are given to the runners alone. . . . All of a sudden, the runners make arrests and extort money [from the inhabitants]. [152]

The same practice, according to a local historian, prevailed in Kwangtung, as did other equally sordid forms of extortion. In an 1836 memorial a censor of Hu-kuang circuit said:

> In the localities under the jurisdiction of this circuit, the various *t'u-ch'ai* [yamen runners in charge of tax "prompting" in the *t'u*], when

urging payment of tax money and grain, do not ask the householders who are actually in arrears to make payments, but choose some other wealthy persons in the neighborhood and arrest them on charges of supposed nonpayment of taxes. If the extortions they demanded are not met to the fullest extent, these persons are subjected to beating and maltreatment, on the further charge of resisting tax collection by force. Sometimes it happens that when one family fails to pay taxes on time, several families are ruined. [153]

The general situation in the last decades of the nineteenth century was perhaps best summarized by a reader of the Hanlin Academy in a memorial of 1884:

Officials find it advantageous to have all taxes collected promptly; but yamen runners find it profitable to have much of them remain unpaid.

In any given district there are many sorts of yamen runners who undertake to "prompt" tax payments, viz . . . "head prompters," "general head prompters," "runners of the *tu*," "runners of the *t'u*," "runners of the *pao*," runners to assist runners, runners to advance payments, and counterfeit runners to receive floggings for runners who are punished for failure to meet the deadline. All these hope that the people have their taxes overdue so that they can make profit for themselves out of their default.

When runners of the *t'u* or the *pao* go to the countryside to exact tax payments, the first thing they do is to demand bribes which are called "parcel money." The giving of "parcel money" brings to the taxpayer the privilege of delaying the payment of his taxes. When a formerly wealthy household becomes suddenly insolvent, the "head prompter" will go and demand the payment in person. Wearing sumptuous garments and riding in a sedan chair, and followed by a large number of attendants, he extorts "parcel money" from the household in question, amounting to as much as several tens of thousand [copper cash]. The payment of the money brings, of course, the privilege of deferring the taxes.

When the final date of collecting the taxes has passed and only a small fraction of the revenue has been collected, the magistrate as usual punishes the yamen runners. The latter hire some worthless fellows with payments of money, send them to the yamen to receive the flogging, or to carry the cangue—as a warning to the multitude. The "head prompters" and other runners do not suffer anything at all. In fact, they use the flogging and cangue-carrying as a pretext for further extortions. . . .

At the beginning of the collection period, yamen runners who keep the records often make payments for households of moderate or great wealth that are able to pay their taxes. They take out the receipts for the payments made and, on presenting the receipts, demand from these households repayments doubling the amounts of the taxes for which they are legally liable. These receipts are called "proxy-receipts." [154]

In some localities of southeastern China yamen underlings took advantage of default in another manner. According to a *chü-jen* scholar writing in the last decades of the nineteenth century:

> Default in tax payments is what the people cannot always avoid but yamen underlings are glad to have. For when taxes of a previous year are paid in the subsequent fiscal year, these are called "stale payments." Those who make "stale payments" are required to pay surcharges ranging from 30 to 40 per cent [of the regular taxes]. If payment is again slightly delayed, ruthless yamen runners bring the receipts to the payers' homes, claiming that they have made payments for them. They noisily demand extortions from whomever they wish. The money demanded may amount to as much as twice the legal quota [for which the taxpayers are liable]. It goes without saying that they have to be entertained with wine and rich food. . . . This malpractice prevails in the southeastern provinces.[155]

Extortioners sometimes overestimated the financial capacities of their victims. In such cases villagers who were unable to meet their exorbitant demands might resort to the only way out—suicide. For instance, a governor of Hunan (nineteenth century) reported that a "defaulting" taxpayer took his own life after being beaten up by disappointed tax exactors from the yamen.[156] These were some of the malpractices connected with *ts'ui-k'o*, the tax-prompting procedure, which made it too often a scourge to the taxpayer. Other abuses were connected with the next stage of tax collection—the receiving of tax-payments by the local officials and their assistants. The most widely noticed malpractice directly connected with receiving tax payments was *chung-pao* (satiation at the middle, i.e., the realizing of illegal gains by officials and their underlings at the expense of both the government and the taxpayer). This malpractice was made possible partly by defects in the revenue system and partly by the corruption of local officialdom. The *li-chia* itself had little to do with it.

Chung-pao was most succinctly explained by a Western observer writing in the 1890's:

> The grave point of weakness and danger in the Chinese financial system, or lack of system, lies, so far as the government revenues are concerned, in the free opportunities which are afforded for extortion, illegal exactions from the people, and every form of official robbery. It is safe to say that no tax is collected and paid over to the treasury in the exact amount stipulated by law. The subject invariably pays more than he ought, and the Emperor as invariably receives less than his due. And if the exact total of all sums collected from every source in any year could be compared with the corresponding total annually devoted to public purposes in the same period of time, the enormous divergence between the two sums would astonish the world.[157]

The magistrate, as the official in immediate charge of tax collection, was in an advantageous position to engage in *chung-pao*. Many methods were available to him, some of which were described by another Western writer of the same period:

> His most important, or at least his most profitable duty, is the collection and remission of the land tax, for which purpose he pays a liberal salary to a highly-trained conveyancer kept permanently on the premises. The Board [of Revenues] at Peking never asks for more than the regulation amount of this, and is uncommonly glad to see even "eight-tenths" of it paid. But by means of juggling with silver rates and "copper cash" rates, by drawing harrowing pictures of local disasters and poverty, by legerdemain in counting and measuring, charging fees for the receipts, notices, tickets, attendance, and what not, it has come about in the course of time that the actual amount of the land tax collected is anything between twice and four times the legal amount, whilst under no circumstances is the full amount even officially due ever admitted to be in hand. Say the land tax of the district is 10,000 taels, a profit of this sum . . . would evidently bring the man back to his native village, after twenty years of work, with a handsome fortune. But he does not get all this for himself; many superiors have to be squared in a fixed, decorous, and it may be said, imperially-recognized way. [158]

Of course, not all magistrates were corrupt. Some of them were honest though ineffectual men; a few tried to introduce honesty into tax collection. For instance, thanks to the action of a magistrate of Nan-hai (Kwangtung), a set of regulations was worked out in 1777 indicating clearly the dates, places, and procedure of making tax payments and prohibiting all forms of illegal exaction. These rules were engraved on stone tablets erected in every *t'u* division of the countryside so that villagers could see them. If any yamen underlings attempted to harass taxpayers, the latter were authorized to send a petition to the government. The local official promised immediate attention if the petition was undersigned by responsible persons of the ten *chia* in the *t'u* concerned. The local historian who recorded this fact noted that these rules "had been followed without exception." [159]

Magistrates like this one, however, were relatively few. Even if we lend full credence to the claim of the historian cited above, we may still be sure that the influence of the conscientious official whom he describes was limited. The good work of a few could not counterbalance the harm done by many.

Here as elsewhere the practices of corrupt magistrates were aggravated by the tricks of yamen underlings. In fact, official corruption was impossible unless subordinates acted as accomplices. Some of the posts of yamen clerks became so lucrative that they had to be bought with substantial sums of money. Concrete instances were discovered by a nineteenth-century governor of Kiangsu:

> In the *chou* and *hsien* of Kiangsu, there is the post of *tsung-shu* [chief
> recorder] who is in charge of collecting tax money and grain. When
> a new magistrate takes up his office and just before the collection
> of the land and tribute taxes begins, clerks in the various divisions
> [of the yamen] intrigue to get this position by presenting to their su-
> perior a "gift" amounting to over 1,000 taels. . . . After a clerk
> is once appointed to this post . . . he feels free to engage in illegal
> dealings.[160]

What the people thought of the yamen tax collectors is reflected in a
popular Chinese story retold by a missionary. In this story, the god
of wealth was originally a tax gatherer.[161]

It is impossible to describe all the diverse ways in which local officials and yamen underlings fleeced rural taxpayers on the one hand
and defrauded the imperial government on the other, in order to accomplish "satiation at the middle." A few of the most glaring examples
will suffice.

One of the most obvious methods of realizing unlawful gains was to
overcharge taxpayers at the time they made their payments, by adding unauthorized surcharges to the regulation amounts, by demanding
fees on items officially free of charge, or by exacting money on whatever pretext seemed pertinent. In Nan-hai, before the well-meaning
magistrate mentioned above drew up the regulations of 1777, villagers
had to pay, over and above the money and grain legally due to the
government, fees for notices and receipts, "food expenses" for yamen
runners assisting revenue collection, and a penalty fee for delayed
payments.[162] The simplest and perhaps the most outrageous method
of extorting illegal payments from taxpayers was described in the
gazetteer of Tung-kuan:

> There are one hundred and twenty-seven *t'u* in this district. A *shu-
> suan* [recorder-accountant] is assigned to each *t'u*, each of whom
> keeps the local tax records in his private home. When the taxpaying
> households make their payments, a bribe is demanded, at a certain
> rate per *mow*. The payments are certified as completed only after
> the bribes have been paid. [The post of the *shu-suan* is so lucra-
> tive that] when the term of five years expires it is the custom to
> make a "present" of 1,000 taels to the yamen.[163]

A more subtle method of "satiating the middle" was to juggle and
manipulate the tax receipts. One such method was confessed by a veteran yamen underling.[164] The yamen clerk in charge of revenue collection received payments in advance, at reduced rates, from wealthy
households with which he was on good terms and indicated that they
had cleared their payments. The resulting deficit in revenue was made
up by juggling the receipts of households paying small amounts of
taxes. When these households paid their taxes, they were given fal-

sified receipts, either with irrelevant dates or with incorrect names
of taxpayers, though with the correct amounts of taxes. Despite the
fact that they had paid their taxes and were in possession of receipts,
they appeared in the official records as defaulters.

Less refined versions of the above method were exposed by a well-
known Chinese writer of the nineteenth century. Referring to conditions in Kiangsu he said:

> The standard practice had been that the receipts were given a few
> days after the tax money or grain was delivered. At present, however,
> tax money is sometimes collected in advance but no receipts are is-
> sued until several months later. In some cases, money is collected
> and no receipts are given at all. Worse still, some of the taxpayers
> make advance payments or pay their taxes on time, but the yamen
> sends another tax collector who denies any knowledge of their pre-
> vious payments and demands payment again.
>
> There are households that are accustomed to being in arrears and
> do not care to have receipts. These pay about 10 or 20 per cent of
> the amount legally due, merely to stay out of trouble. The yamen
> underlings are glad to pocket the money collected as their extra earn-
> ings and repeat the transaction year after year. How much money is
> involved in such fraudulent practices is entirely beyond human calcula-
> tion. [165]

An entirely different type of malpractice arose from the fact that
local officials often disregarded the imperial regulation requiring taxpayers to deliver payments in person and to deposit the money in official chests placed in the yamen. As a result taxpayers were exposed
to various methods of indirect extortion. A striking case was recorded
in the gazetteer of Yung Hsien (Kwangsi):

> Formerly, there were four money shops established by the local
> official to receive tax payments; these were Chung-hsin, Kung-ho,
> I-ch'ang, and Yü-ho. At that time, no fixed standard was set up to gov-
> ern the wastage allowances. [These shops] levied surcharges as their
> whim dictated. The surcharge on tax payments of over one tael was
> 70 or 80 per cent of the total amounts due. The rate on amounts under
> one tael was about 150 per cent. Households paying taxes amounting
> to 0.02 or 0.03 tael had to pay surcharges ranging between 0.20 and
> 0.30 tael. The people suffered, having no way of making known their
> grievances.
>
> In Chia-ch'ing 5 [1800] an imperial edict was received which pro-
> hibited the establishment of unauthorized money shops in the *chou*
> and *hsien*, with a view to putting a stop to overcharges. Governor
> Hsieh accordingly issued a directive to all localities under his juris-
> diction, requiring that in collecting the taxes, chests be placed in
> the principal hall of the yamen, that the people wrap the money and

deposit it in person in one of the chests, and that clerks and runners be prevented from defalcating [the revenue]. This directive was received, but the magistrate did not make it known. In the fourth month of the eighth year [1803], local gentry petitioned the prefectural authorities [concerning the money shops]. Although the "government" money shops were abolished by order of the prefect, the required chests were placed [not in the principal hall of the yamen but] in the yamen treasury where [taxpayers] suffered overcharges through inequitable steelyards and other forms of foul dealings as before.

In the fourth month of the ninth year, the gentry petitioned the provincial judge. By his order the chests were placed in the principal hall for the first time. But a roving "stick" [rascal] from Kwangtung, conniving with local yamen underlings, secured an appointment as chest-keeper. Overcharging became even worse. In the eighth month, the gentry petitioned the provincial treasurer to no avail.

The same situation continued till the eleventh year [1806]. When the time for collecting the taxes arrived, the chest-keeper resorted to a new trick. He decided that no receipts were to be given to those who had completed their payments, the purpose of this move being to facilitate defalcation. Shortly afterwards, the gentry got hold of his secret account showing the amount of overcharges he had made in the past. They made copies of it and petitioned the governor as well as the provincial treasurer and judge. Notice of trial was already issued, but the chest-keeper enjoyed powerful patronage, and the case was hushed up. . . .

In the sixth month [of the same year], the gentry again went to petition the governor. It was only then that the prefect was directed to try the case. . . . After two hearings by the magistrate of Huai-chi, twenty-two hearings by the magistrate of Ts'ang-wu (both being instructed by the prefect to do so), and one hearing by the prefect himself in the twelfth month, the fact and circumstances concerning the corrupt practices of the past years were fully uncovered. The offending underlings were duly punished.

In consequence of this, regulations concerning wastage allowances were drawn up after deliberation. A surcharge of 0.42 tael was to be collected on every tael of tax payment. The same rate was to be maintained irrespective of the amount of the tax collected from each payer. . . . The gentry . . . had these regulations engraved on stone tablets in order that they might be handed down to posterity.[166]

This instance may not be typical, but it is highly illuminating. It reveals the fact that yamen underlings, lowly as their position was, could command powerful influence under special circumstances. No *li-chia* could ever hope to work against such a formidable evil force.

It should not be assumed that dropping tax payments in chests placed in the yamen or fixing the rate of wastage allowances solved the basic problems of tax collection. In many instances making payments in the yamen itself became a hardship on the rural inhabitants. The compiler of the 1896 edition of the gazetteer of Tz'u-li (Hunan) wrote:

> Villagers are afraid to go into the city. When the time for making
> tax payments arrives in summer and autumn, they sometimes allow
> their payments to become overdue or sometimes ask other persons
> to make payments for them. These persons may forget the matter.
> . . . Yamen clerks often make payments [for those who fail to pay
> on time] and withhold the receipts which are sold to rascally "bro-
> kers. " These brokers visit the defaulters and charge them with the
> crime of resisting tax collection. Even women and chickens and dogs
> can have no peace. The villagers can do nothing but satisfy whatever
> demands the brokers care to make. One household after another is
> thus reduced to financial ruin.[167]

Still another type of malpractice arose from the officially approved
practice of collecting money in lieu of grain. The rate was fixed in
terms of silver taels.[168] But as the income of taxpayers, especially
the small ones, was in copper cash, they were compelled to change
their copper into silver, usually at specially designated places. This
afforded local officials and yamen underlings ample opportunity to
"juggle with silver rates," as noted by the Western writer cited above.
The situation became more serious when the value of silver reached
unprecedented heights after the beginning of the nineteenth century.
According to a well-known high-ranking official, the exchange rate
at the beginning of the dynasty was about 700 copper cash to one tael
of silver. It fluctuated during Yung-cheng and Ch'ien-lung times, but
it did not rise much above 1,000 cash per tael. Early in the nineteenth
century it jumped to 2,000 and reached peaks as high as 5,000 or
6,000 in Hsien-feng and Tung-chih times.[169] Whatever may have been
the causes for the rise,[170] it was bound to work hardships, especially
on those villagers who paid relatively small amounts of taxes. Tax
assessments were fixed in terms of silver; depreciation in the value
of the copper cash amounted to increasing the burdens of taxpayers.
An early practice which permitted the payment of 30 per cent of the
tax money in copper cash, established in 1657 (Shun-chih 14) and indicated on the official tax notices, was shortly afterwards discarded.[171]
Taxpayers therefore had to absorb all the losses incurred from the
rising exchange rate. Tax collectors, on the other hand, whether to
reap gains or merely to protect themselves, seldom failed to apply
the rate most favorable to themselves in collecting the revenues.
A few instances will illustrate the point. An edict of 1828 (Tao-
kuang 8) quoted the following report made by an imperial censor:

> Recently, when taxes are collected in Shantung province, the exchange
> rate has been steadily raised. Thus in Ning-hai Chou, 4,000 Peking
> cash [= 2,100 regulation cash] are collected for each tael; in Chu-

ch'eng Hsien, 4,260 Peking cash. In the present year trouble has broken out in Huang Hsien as a result of raising the exchange rate. The pretext offered [by the local official] is that the value of silver has gone up. The same pretext is heard in other *chou* and *hsien*. The rates are raised day after day, and there is no limit to the process.[172]

A year later, the emperor stated in another edict:

We hear that in Honan province the current exchange rate [in the open market] is 2,800 Peking cash to one tael of silver. Local officials, such as those of Hsin-cheng Hsien, Yu Chou, Hsü Chou, and Ling-pao Hsien, fixed the rate as high as between 4,000 and 4,600 cash to a tael, a rise of about 400 cash per tael over last year.

About sixty years later, an American diplomat observed a particularly bad instance of juggling exchange rates which resulted in local resistance. The customary rate in a district not far from the imperial capital was 2,000 cash per tael. At an unspecified date it was raised by a magistrate to 4,000. Sometime later, trouble began to brew.

A new incumbent increased the rate to 5,000, and this was quietly paid. Misunderstanding the temper of his constituency, after a few months, he raised the rate of exchange to 6,000. Then they grumbled, but they paid. A further increase to 7,000 provoked talk of organized opposition, but nothing practical resulted from it. Before the first half of his term of office had expired, he raised the rate again, demanding 8,000 cash for an ounce of silver, or about four times the legitimate amount.

This brought matters to a crisis. A mass meeting was held, at which it was decided to present a petition to the emperor, through the censorate. . . . The documents were accordingly prepared and a committee of three influential literati carried them to the capital. . . . It was returned to them unread, they were each favored with fifty blows of the bamboo, and fined a small sum for contempt of court. They returned home sore and crestfallen, and the local magistrate . . . signalized his victory by increasing the official rate of exchange to 9,000 pieces of cash for an ounce of silver. . . . Another meeting was at once called, papers were more carefully drawn up . . . and another deputation bore them to the capital. This time they were successful. The offending official was degraded, stripped of his rank, and forbidden to apply for future official employment.[173]

Similar malpractices were sometimes reported in South China. In a district in Kiangsi, for example, the official rate of exchange for tax collection purposes was 1,000 cash per tael, but revenue agents exacted 1,885 cash for each tael due. Since grain was under 800 cash per *shih* during the late 1830's, a taxpayer had to sell two to three *shih* of grain to pay one tael of tax.[174]

The profits from juggling exchange rates were so attractive to local functionaries that some of them sought to extend the practice by demanding payment in money equivalents where grain was the authorized form of payment. The following instance was reported in the 1854 edition of the gazetteer of T'ung-jen Fu (Kweichow):

> Investigation shows that . . . the people of P'o-t'ou Hsiang have always paid their grain taxes promptly. When the time for collection arrives, the inhabitants go to the granaries and deliver their grain. Keepers of the granaries, however, resort to obstructive tactics, refusing to receive the grain. The people are asked to hand in money in place of grain so that they can embezzle the money collected in excess of the value of the grain. [175]

The outbreak of the Taiping Rebellion introduced additional difficulties into an already unsatisfactory situation. Recognizing that the ability of taxpayers to meet their tax obligations was greatly reduced because of disturbances and devastation brought about by war, the imperial government authorized local officials to collect half of the taxes in copper cash and half in silver taels. [176] But magistrates continued to demand payment in silver.

Confronted with such varied and widespread malpractices, in which local officials and yamen underlings freely indulged, what could the *li-chia* heads do to keep the procedure of tax collection within the bounds of law? They were after all merely ordinary taxpayers in subadministrative service. We recall that a law promulgated early in the dynasty authorized the *li-chang* and *chia-chang* to lay charges against magistrates who imposed illegal burdens on taxpayers. [177] This law remained very largely a dead letter.

Local Gentry and the Revenue System

The local gentry constituted another disturbing factor which prevented the revenue system in general and the *li-chia* in particular from operating properly. By making use of their privileged status, members of the gentry who owned land and were liable for taxes were usually able to protect themselves against the trespasses of tax collectors, leaving the commoner taxpayers to bear the main brunt of extortion. By misusing their privileges they could even shift their tax burdens to unprivileged payers or join officials and underlings in oppressing the common people. [178] Scholars who had not passed any of the examinations or purchased any official titles or ranks were not, strictly speaking, members of the gentry. But the very fact that they studied for the examinations and aspired to gentry status usually induced local officials to treat them with special courtesy and fellow villagers to regard them with a measure of respect. Naturally, they were inclined to capitalize on whatever special consideration or treatment was accorded them to gain advantages in tax matters.

While all land under cultivation was liable for taxes, not all taxpayers were equal in the eyes of the imperial government. Differences in social status gave rise to two different categories of taxpayers. The Ch'ing government granted from earliest times a number of special immunities and privileges to officials and the gentry, putting them in a position of advantage over other segments of the population. [179] As taxpayers, the privileged groups were treated with more consideration by the government than their less favored fellow payers. Scholars who had attained the grades of *kung-sheng, chien-sheng,* or *sheng-yüan* and who were liable for the land taxes, were granted periods of grace from two to six months if they found it inconvenient to pay on time, whereas ordinary landowners had to complete payment on the officially fixed dates. [180] All members of the gentry were furthermore exempted from labor services of all forms. [181] Continuing a Chinese tradition of ancient origin, [182] the Ch'ing rulers exempted from the corvée all *sheng-yüan* who submitted themselves to the newly established authority, even before the dynasty was formally inaugurated at Peking. A few years after the initial action, corvée exemptions were extended in 1635 to all *chü-jen* to the extent of four *ting* each. Immunities were further expanded by the Shun-chih emperor in 1648, when regulations were formulated to govern the treatment of various categories of officials and scholars. Under these regulations officials of the highest rank enjoyed as many as thirty exemptions each, while scholars of the lowest grade had two each. This generous arrangement remained until 1657 when the regulations were changed; thereafter privileged persons were to have only one exemption each, that is, only the person himself was exempted, not any of the members of his family. [183] With a view to stopping the misuse of this privilege, a governor sought to abolish it in 1726. But the law of 1657 was reaffirmed by the imperial government, [184] and remained unaltered to the end of the dynasty.

The merging of the *ting* (labor) into the *ti* (land) taxes, which resulted in the assessment of the former on the basis of land instead of on the person and in making it a surtax on land, had some effects on the above-mentioned privilege. Legally, the gentry retained their personal exemption from the regular *ting* imposts and miscellaneous *ch'ai* services; it made no difference whether they owned land or not. In practice, all landless persons were free from the liability for the *ting*;[185] It made no difference whether they possessed privileged status or were commoners. This change in taxation therefore had little practical meaning for members of the gentry who owned no land. Landowning gentry, on the other hand, although still liable for the land taxes, enjoyed an advantage over landowning commoners in being exempted from the *ting* surtax and in fact often from all other labor imposts. In other words, they were privileged to pay less tax than a commoner with the same amount of land and liable for the same quota of land tax. For gentry who had extensive landholdings the financial advantage was evidently substantial. Since the quotas of the *ting* in any given locality were fixed since late K'ang-hsi times, the exemptions allowed to gentry landowners put additional burdens on the commoner landowners. This situation gave an incentive for commoner landowners to acquire privileged status and for members of the gentry to acquire land. [186]

From the very beginning the emperors were aware that the gentry might misuse the privileges granted to them. Almost immediately after granting these privileges, they took steps to keep those enjoying them from going beyond the bounds of law. But since many of the privileged persons were bent on misusing their privileges, imperial taxation became in part a struggle between the government, which endeavored to curtail tax fraud, and the gentry, who tried to stretch their privileges to the widest possible extent. Fraudulent practices resorted to by members of the gentry consisted mainly in outright nonpayment of taxes, in shifting their liabilities to other payers, or in giving shelter to tax evaders who did not enjoy legal exemptions. [187] A number of social circumstances facilitated these practices. The differential treatment of the two sorts of taxpayers contributed directly to the situation. Without any authorization by the government, households liable for taxes were distinguished into *shen-hu* (gentry households), *huan-hu* (official households), and *ju-hu* (scholar households) on the one hand, and *min-hu* (commoner households) on the other hand; between *ta-hu* (big households) and *hsiao-hu* (small households); and between *ch'eng-hu* (city households, i.e., absentee landowners) and *hsiang-hu* (rural households, i.e., taxpaying peasants. [188] Different treatment was accorded to each category of these households, special consideration being given to those enjoying social prestige, political influence, or economic power. In extreme cases these households became oppressors of the rest. Furthermore, despite occasional conflicts of interest between them, local gentry in general stood in a more or less close relationship with local officials. Gentry with relatively high official ranks possessed a good deal of prestige and influence; and most of the gentry as well as scholars aspiring to gentry status understood the ways, good and evil, of officialdom. Magistrates often found it necessary to invite the assistance or cooperation of these persons in a wide variety of undertakings, and were therefore more ready to disregard or circumvent imperial regulations than to incur the gentry's enmity. Officials often shut their eyes to unlawful acts committed by the gentry or even connived with them in questionable transactions. Persons with gentry status were thus in a position to defraud the government of its regular revenues or to exploit their fellow taxpayers with commoner status. Against such persons the *li-chia* agents, who were commoners like the majority of rural householders, could do nothing at all to uphold the legally prescribed procedures of tax collection.

The Ch'ing emperors began their campaign against gentry malpractices by trying to put a stop to outright default in the payment of the land taxes. In 1658, exactly ten years after the inauguration of the *li-chia* system, the imperial government decreed:

> . . . all local gentry [including *chin-shih, chü-jen, kung-sheng, chien-sheng,* and *sheng-yüan,* both civil and military], and persons in yamen service, who have persistently failed to make payments of their taxes shall be punished; the penalty in each case shall be determined by the amount of taxes unpaid. [189]

Two years later, because nonpayment of land taxes was especially prevalent in Chiang-nan, the government instructed local officials to indicate in their annual reports the precise amounts of taxes which the gentry had failed to pay on time, so that the culprits could be duly apprehended and dealt with. [190]

The first drastic measure against gentry defaulters was adopted immediately after the K'ang-hsi emperor ascended the throne in 1661. According to official historical records, [191] Chu Kuo-chih, governor of Chiang-ning, memorialized that punishment should be given to 13,517 members of the gentry with civil or military ranks or titles in the prefectures of Su-chou, Sung-chiang, Ch'ang-chou, and Chen-chiang and in the district of Li-yang, because these had repeatedly refused to pay their taxes. Punishment was promptly meted out. Thousands were dismissed, deprived of their titles or ranks, imprisoned or flogged. The case was not closed until the middle of 1662 when all offenders, whether already sent to the imperial capital as prisoners or still incarcerated in local jails, were set free by an imperial order. [192] The immediate effect of this well-known "Tax Clearance Case of Chiang-nan" was summarized by a prefect serving in Chekiang province:

> In addition to local officials demoted or dismissed, local gentry and *sheng-yüan* who have their ranks or titles taken away from them amount to about one hundred in small districts and almost one thousand in large ones. After the occurrence of the Clearance Case, not only does the number of persons with gentry status dwindle to no more than a handful and the tracks of their carriages no longer mark the entrances to the yamen but the number of scholars also diminishes to such an extent that when the educational authorities arrive to conduct the examinations, no more than a few appear to take them. [193]

The general deterrent value of this move, however, seems to have been insignificant. The government had to apply disciplinary measures more than once to the gentry who remained tax defaulters in other localities. A mid-seventeenth-century magistrate of Kan-ch'üan (Shen-si), for example, petitioned the educational authorities to cashier "bad scholars" for the same offense:

> In this small frontier district the deportment of *sheng-yüan* reminds one of the gentry and officials. Once a person enters the local government school, he takes delight in acquiring cultivated land but is accustomed to paying no taxes whatever. Rural agents, being unable to deal with him, have to pay for him or receive punishment [for failure to collect the revenues]. Many such cases are reported. . . . The magistrate, considering the fact that the culprits are scholars on whom punishment cannot be forthwith inflicted, either issues notices [to urge them to pay] or sends yamen runners to demand payment. The result is either that the runners get pummeled or the notices are burned or torn to shreds. [194]

The general situation continued to be so bad that in 1679, less than two decades after the Clearance Case, the imperial government found it necessary to take special steps to discipline tax evaders of gentry status. In a 1679 edict the emperor laid down the following rule:

> Wherever members of the gentry and titled scholars refuse to pay their taxes, the magistrate of the *chou* or *hsien* concerned shall make a list of such defaulting households, indicating the percentages of their unpaid taxes, and send a separate detailed report to his superior official. The governor-general or governor shall report to Us, indicating the names of the offenders. All persons possessing ranks or titles, whether they are gentry or scholars, whether they are *chin-shih, chü-jen, kung-sheng, chien-sheng,* or *sheng-yüan,* civil or military, shall be deprived of their ranks or titles in accordance with established precedents, punished by wearing the cangue, and compelled to make good whatever portions of the taxes they have failed to pay. [195]

Detailed regulations to prevent tax evasion were soon worked out. In 1728 (Yung-cheng 6) the imperial government ruled that the gentry status of taxpayers should be clearly indicated in the official registers and string receipts and that all payments should be collected on the officially fixed dates. The old privilege of special deferment was thus abrogated. Two years later it was ordered that *chou* and *hsien* magistrates should compile quarterly lists showing the tax quotas for which civil and military *sheng-yüan* and *chien-sheng* were severally liable and the amounts they had paid, and send the lists to the local educational officials, who were thus informed of the conduct of the

scholars so that undutiful ones among them might be duly punished. [196]
About the same time a scale of punishment was worked out, the penalties varying with the amounts of taxes overdue from all grades of
titled scholars including *chin-shih* and *chü-jen*.[197] Local officials responsible for collecting the taxes were also required to indicate in the
registers the gentry status of taxpayers and the amounts of taxes overdue. Defaulters were to be properly punished. Persons who suffered
punishment could have their ranks or titles reinstated only after full
payment of their dues. [198]

We have no way to ascertain the extent to which these imperial regulations and orders were carried out. It may be reasonably assumed
that their enforcement depended on the ability and determination of
individual local officials and that since such officials were not many,
privileged landowners must have found it not too difficult to evade their
taxes. Wang Hui-tsu, who served in Tao Chou (Hunan) in the 1870's,
found that taxpayers there were used to nonpayment of taxes because
gentry owners took advantage of their status to resist collection. Persons who did not actually belong to the gentry—yamen clerks and
scholars who had not yet acquired the *sheng-yüan* degree—registered
themselves as "scholar households," thereby claiming gentry privileges and actually receiving special consideration. This malpractice
became so firmly established that in 1775 when a wealthy person was
appointed magistrate of Tao Chou, he found it more expedient to make
good the outstanding arrears with his own money than to compel the
defaulters to pay. Later magistrates who attempted to collect overdue
payments often found their revenue agents beaten and their authority
openly challenged. However, in the autumn of 1786 Wang Hui-tsu put
pressure on the so-called "scholar households," and after having
jailed those who owed the most taxes (including a *chien-sheng* and a
scholar aspiring to the *sheng-yüan*), he was able to persuade most
of the defaulters to pay. [199]

So far the imperial government was concerned only with the collection of the land tax from gentry owners. Its attention was soon
drawn to the evasion of *i*, the labor service imposts. The first action,
taken in 1662, was calculated to improve the conditions in some localities in Kiangsu province. One year after the tax clearance case
a supervisory censor memorialized the throne that in the two prefectures of Su-chou and Sung-chiang the established practice of assigning *li-chia* service on the basis of land ownership was not followed
and glaring inequities resulted.

> Nominally, only persons possessing adequate property are inducted
> into the service. Actually, land is not taken into consideration at
> all. Instances exist in which persons who have sold all their land
> are reported for the *li* services; whereas in other instances persons

owning extensive tracts of land are entirely exempted from such services.[200]

As a remedy, the imperial government reorganized the *li-chia* divisions on the basis of land. It was decreed:

> . . . the land in the districts [of Wu-hsi and Chin-kuei, both situated in the above-mentioned region] is to be evenly divided so that each *t'u [li]* contains about 3,000 *mow* and each *chia* about 300 *mow*. [All owners of land] irrespective of whether they are of gentry, scholar, or commoner status, are to be registered in the *li-chia* and each and every one of them is liable for all labor service imposts.[201]

We have no information concerning the effect of this drastic measure. It is known, however, that by the mid-nineteenth century this novel arrangement had ceased to operate and "the amount of land in each *chia* no longer had any significance" in determining liabilities for the *i* imposts.[202]

The first action that concerned the empire as a whole was taken by the imperial government in 1690 when it ordered that "in all provinces the land of gentry as well as that of the common people shall be liable for labor service imposts." This decision was called forth by a memorial of the governor of Shantung:

> . . . all land belonging to the gentry, including *kung-sheng* and *chien-sheng*, has hitherto enjoyed exemption from miscellaneous labor services, with the result that burdens fall exclusively on the common people. Moreover, since influential and wealthy households with vast tracts of land do not render labor services, crafty commoners "lodge" their land under the names of gentry . . . in order also to evade labor services. Such practices should be vigorously stamped out.[203]

This action, however, produced no tangible effect. An imperial edict issued a decade later, in 1700, reiterated the necessity of eradicating the same evil, which continued to exist, and added that yamen underlings and ordinary soldiers, "following bad examples," managed also to evade labor service liabilities.[204]

The imperial government again undertook in 1726 "to draw up detailed regulations governing the practice of gentry exemptions" from labor services. Evidently exasperated by the flagrant misuse of this privilege, the governor of Szechwan recommended the abolition of all exemptions as an effective way to forestall evasion. After thorough deliberation by the Board of Revenue and the Nine Ministers, the imperial government came to this conclusion:

> Each person of gentry or scholar status shall be granted one exemption, namely, one *ting* for himself. The households of any of his sons, grandsons, or other members of his family that claim unauthorized exemptions or adopt the unauthorized appellation *ju-hu* [scholar house-

hold] or *huan-hu* [official household], with a view to sheltering tax evaders or concealing tax liabilities, shall be apprehended and punished.[205]

This did not mean that the government revoked the 1690 decision, but merely that the imperial authorities clarified a somewhat confusing situation. In the early days of the dynasty when the *fu* was assessed on land and the *i* on persons, it was easy to keep a clear line of demarcation between these two basic taxes and to determine the liabilities for the latter incumbent upon persons of various status. But because these taxes had tended to merge in practice since very early times, that is, the taxes on persons had actually become surtaxes on land, this line was no longer clear. Meanwhile, the regular *ting* quotas had remained stationary since 1712, but miscellaneous *ch'ai-yao* imposts kept on multiplying. The amount of the latter increased and that of the former eventually became a relatively small portion of the total revenue collectible from all labor service imposts.

A practical question arose from this development. Should landowners of gentry status pay all these imposts, the miscellaneous *ch'ai-yao* as well as the regular *ting?*

Such landowners had no doubt as to the correct answer to this question. They knew that imperial laws had granted them special immunities which legally entitled them to one exemption in the *ting*. The law was silent on miscellaneous labor imposts, but they felt justified in holding fast to the basic principle that persons with gentry status should be exempted from labor service of all forms, regardless of how much land they owned. Hence they tried hard to keep and often succeeded in keeping these liabilities from falling on their land. In fact, some of them went beyond this and took advantage of their status to obtain illegal gains.

Local officials took a different view of the matter. Looking at it from a practical rather than a legal point of view, they held that since all labor service imposts were actually assessed on land, whoever owned land should pay them, regardless of personal status. To exempt the gentry, who were often substantial landowners, was to lose more revenue than the government (or they themselves) could afford. They often argued, not without cogency, that to give special consideration to gentry landowners was to overburden ordinary taxpayers.

When the imperial government ordered in 1690 that miscellaneous *ch'ai-yao* imposts should be collected from all landowners regardless of their status, it favored the view of the local officials. In so doing, it authorized the collection of these imposts from gentry landowners. When it reaffirmed the privilege of *ting* exemption in 1726, it lent support to the gentry view stated above, but with an important though implied reservation. While gentry landowners claimed exemption from all labor service imposts—the numerous forms of *ch'ai-yao* as well as the regular *ting*—the imperial government insisted, in agreement with the old regulation that each gentry landowner was entitled to no more than the exemption of one *ting;* that, in other words, he was liable for all forms of *ch'ai-yao*. Since *ch'ai-yao* theoretically was also *i* in the same sense as the *ting* was, the government was perhaps slightly inconsistent in granting exemption from the one but collecting the other. But it was shrewd in choosing to forego the limited revenues from the *ting* in order to insure the more extensive revenues from the *ch'ai-yao*. At any rate, it made clear the extent of liabilities for labor service imposts incumbent upon gentry landowners.

Offenses committed by some of the privileged persons went beyond the simple evasion of their own tax liabilities. One of these that bothered the government most was the practice often known in official parlance as *pao-lan ch'ien-liang:* taking the responsibility of tax payment (and default) for others with the intention of getting unlawful profit out of the transaction or, in other words, misusing the privilege of exemption of the *ting* to shelter taxpayers who did not possess this privilege and who desired to evade part or all of their tax liabilities. Some early examples occurred in Shantung province, according to an official statement made in 1690:

> Land belonging to gentry households in Shantung does not fulfill labor services. . . . Moreover, some of the gentry engage themselves in *pao-lan ch'ien-liang*. They take the responsibility of receiving money and grain in payment of the taxes and of delivering these [for commoner taxpayers to the government]. They put all the surcharges into their private pockets, thus causing losses both to the government and the people. [These members of the gentry] should be dealt with in accordance with the law governing fraudulent concealment of taxable land. [206]

At about the same time, similar instances were reported in Hunan. The imperial authorities said in an instruction issued in 1696:

> It has been an evil practice to distinguish between *ta-hu* [big households] and *hsiao-hu* [small households]. The former freely oppress the latter, compelling them to hand over their tax payments to the *ta-hu*. The *hsiao-hu* are not allowed to drop their payments into the [official] chests. In extreme cases they are compelled to render services [to the *ta-hu]*.
>
> Henceforth all *hsiao-hu* are to be taken out of the *chia* division which contain *ta-hu* and are to constitute separate *chia* of their own, with separate tax registers. The *hsiao-hu* are to pay their taxes in person. The governor-general and governor shall report any who practice *pao-lan*, refuse to pay taxes, extort money or demand overcharges [from taxpayers] so that they may be punished for their crimes. [207]

Pao-lan, of course, was not limited to these two provinces, nor to wealthy gentry landowners. The following edict issued by the Yung-cheng emperor in 1724 is revealing:

> We have been informed that there are degenerate *sheng-yüan* and *chien-sheng* who do not possess much taxable land themselves but who, relying on their scholarly titles, have the audacity to assume tax responsibilities for persons bearing the same family names as theirs by falsely registering the land of these persons as their own. Such *sheng-yüan* call themselves *ju-hu* [scholar households] while *chien-sheng* call themselves *huan-hu* [official households]. They invariably delay payment of all taxes. . . . Their payments are always overdue when the time of collection arrives. Many such *[sheng-yüan* and *chien-sheng]* are in large cities; the situation is worse in hilly country, in small secluded districts.
>
> Governors-general and governors are ordered to report [such culprits] and to abolish the appellations *ju-hu* and *huan-hu*. *Sheng-yüan* and *chien-sheng* who persist in disobeying [the law] shall be promptly and severely punished. [208]

In some localities yamen runners found it impossible to deal with powerful scholar-gentry defaulters. An imperial edict of 1818 (Chia-ch'ing 20) said that "bad scholars and big households of Ch'ao-yang and Chieh-yang [Kwangtung] assumed tax responsibilities for others and refused to pay taxes. In the worst cases, yamen agents dared not go to the villages to urge payment."[209] According to another source, taxpayers in Tung-kuan (another district of the same province) often evaded payment of labor service imposts by putting themselves under the "protection" of "powerful villagers." The magistrate succumbed to the influence of the local gentry and made no attempt at adjusting tax burdens. [210]

The collection of the rice tribute occasioned special methods of *pao-lan*. Dishonest practices, including unauthorized surcharges, extortions made in connection with collection and transportation, had beset the rice tribute system ever since the beginning of the dynasty. [211] In some localities the situation became worse after the 1760's. [212] No amount of government regulations could put an end to the malpractices. By the end of the eighteenth century the problem appeared extremely serious to some high-ranking officials. One made the following alarming report to the emperor around 1800:

> Your servant has learned through investigation that the rice for which members of the gentry assume responsibility is called "scholar rice," that for which *chü-jen, kung-sheng, sheng-yüan,* and *chien-sheng* assume responsibility is called "examination rice," and that for which pettifoggers assume responsibility is called "litigation rice." Among

these three categories [of persons who fraudulently assume responsibility for payment of the tribute rice] the gentry merely refuse to pay more rice than they wish; perverse *sheng-yüan* and wicked *chien-sheng*, together with pettifoggers, pay less than is due. Nobody dares find fault with them even when the quantity and quality of their rice fall below the official standard. . . .

Chou and *hsien* magistrates, intimidated by these bad scholars and pettifoggers, make up the deficit [caused by the latter's default] by exacting extra payments from meek taxpayers and law-abiding common people. The additional levies imposed upon law-abiding *chü-jen, kung-sheng, sheng-yüan,* and *chien-sheng* vary in amount, roughly between 20 and 30 per cent [of the legal quotas for which they are severally liable]. The greatest hardship falls on innocent peasants and small taxpayers who dare not resist even when the overcharges amount to 50 or 60 per cent. . . . Ignorant peasants of secluded villages, however, do not endure despoiling perpetually. After a while they also become shrewd; they bribe the *pao-hu* [households that assume tax responsibilities for others] and entrust the matter of payment to them. The fees they have to pay are much less than if the taxes are paid by themselves. . . . As a result, during recent years the number of *pao-hu* increases daily, while the number of *hsiang-hu* [rural households] that pay their taxes directly daily decreases. [213]

Government agents were particularly baffled by those *pao-hu* that were in a position to use litigation as a weapon of defense (or offense). This high official continued:

The amount of [tribute] rice paid through the *pao-hu* has been quite large. When the rice arrives at the granaries, a little inquiry on the part of the official or clerk in charge provokes refusal to deliver it. Sometimes [the carriers] dump outside the granaries the rice which is wet, of inferior quality and insufficient amount, and scurry away; they repair to the yamen of the superior official to bring charges [against the collector] who meanwhile is compelled to take care of [the rice] for them. [214]

An illuminating if not typical example of gentry *pao-lan* was afforded by Kiangsu province. In two memorials of 1846 (Tao-kuang 26), the governor reported that in Chao-wen and Ch'ang-su, two districts in Su-chou prefecture where the practice had been especially notorious, a charge of tax fraud was brought against a *chü-jen* who had previously served as magistrate in a district in Chihli, two *chien-sheng,* and three military *chü-jen.* The facts were as follows:

The territories of these two districts are very extensive. Small taxpayers living in remote villages find it difficult to make the journey [to the designated places] to deliver their tribute rice. Some of them ask large taxpayers who own great amounts of land to make payments for them. Hence arises the distinction between *ta-hu* [big households] and *hsiao-hu* [small households].

Ts'ai T'ing-hsiung (a magistrate living in his home locality on leave of absence due to sickness) and Ts'ai T'ing-hsün (his brother), together with P'u Teng-k'uei and P'u Teng-piao (military *chü-jen* and sons of P'u Ta-t'ien [a *chien-sheng])* have been making payments for rural households for some time. Since the rice produced by rural households is dry and clean (the land being cultivated by the peasants themselves), whereas the rice from the land of Ts'ai and P'u is wet and impure (their land being cultivated by tenants), they substitute the rice they receive from their tenants for the rice which the rural households ask them to deliver for them. They force the granaries to accept [the inferior rice]; quite often they fail to make payments on time.[215]

Matters were already bad enough. The worst happened when for some reason Ts'ai T'ing-hsiung stopped handling the transactions and when the two military *chü-jen* went to the imperial capital to take the metropolitan examinations. Ts'ai T'ing-hsün and P'u Ta-t'ien took over the business and began to exploit the rural taxpayers, charging fees for their services. In order to augment their unlawful profits, they assumed false names and got themselves appointed tax recorders of the localities concerned so that they could engage in fraud without fear of being discovered. Their tricks might have remained unnoticed had not a disgruntled tax defaulter brought them to light. The net outcome of this case was that all the local gentry involved were deprived of their ranks and titles, some received the additional penalty of being flogged with the heavy bamboo, and an interdiction was issued against further practices of *pao-lan*. All households were required to pay taxes in person. But the authorities did not make clear how the rural households were to overcome the physical difficulty of transporting their grain from their far-flung villages to the government storehouses.

In the mid-nineteenth century, riots traceable to gentry malpractices were reported in several parts of the empire. In 1846 the attention of the Tao-kuang emperor was called to the fact that the oppression of "small households" by "big households" through *pao-lan* had become a cause of widespread unrest in Kiangsu.[216] A writer of the same period substantiated this alarming view by pointing out that persistent oppression through misuse of gentry privilege during a period of many decades had driven the people to extremities, with the result that "demolition of granaries, wrecking of yamen, resisting arrest by force, and wounding officials were reported every year and occurred in every city."[217]

The riot of 1842 in Ts'ung-yang (Hupeh) is especially instructive. Chung Jen-chieh, a *sheng-yüan* scholar, together with several other *sheng-yüan,* undertook *pao-lan* in the collection of tribute rice and suddenly became rich. A newly appointed magistrate endeavored to ameliorate the plight of small taxpayers. Chung suspected his rivals, especially Ts'ai Shao-hsün (another *sheng-yüan),* of having instigated this move. After having murdered Ts'ai's family members (who lived in the countryside) and burned down his house, Chung led several hundred of his followers into the city in pursuit of his enemy. The magistrate was taken prisoner and killed. Villagers of the district were forced to join the riot; the mob eventually numbered over ten thousand men. The uprising was not quelled until a month later, when the provincial commander in chief personally led troops to recapture the city. Chung and about ten other *sheng-yüan,* some civil and some military, who took part in the riot were severely punished. [218] The imperial government responded to this unhappy incident by issuing an order that thereafter any magistrate of Ts'ung-yang who failed to discover and deal properly with *sheng-yüan* or *chien-sheng* practicing *pao-lan* would be cashiered in accordance with the law. [219] Meanwhile, similar riots of smaller dimensions broke out in other localities, including Kuei-an, Jen-ho (Chekiang), Tan-yang, Chen-che (Kiangsu), Hsin-yü (Kiangsi), and Lui-yang (Hunan). [220] Such riots were of course part of the general unrest prevailing between the Opium War and the Taiping Rebellion, but gentry malpractices in tax collection were one of the factors contributing to that general unrest.

The situation did not materially improve after the Taiping Rebellion. Some attempts were made during the busy days of military campaigning to ease the burdens on common taxpayers, particularly in South China. Li Hung-chang (governor of Kiangsu) memorialized in 1862[221] and Tso Tsung-t'ang (governor of Chekiang) in 1863[222] for reduction of excessive tax burdens in their provinces and abolition of the distinction between "big" and "small households." These moves may have yielded limited benefits to taxpayers in these regions, but the age-old malpractices generally remained. In edicts of 1865 the T'ung-chih emperor was reiterating the same old injunctions that no person should be permitted to assume responsibilities for the tax payments of others and that no distinction between big and small households should be permitted to stand. [223] Late in the 1860's a governor of Kiangsu noted that households of commoners were still paying much higher rates than gentry landowners; in extreme cases the commoner rate was eight times as high as the gentry rate. [224] As late as 1882 the Kuang-hsü emperor found it still necessary to issue an edict to prohibit *pao-lan.* [225]

Diverse factors contributed to this fraudulent and harmful practice, which continued despite express legal prohibition. [226] One was the recognition of the gentry as persons possessing special status and therefore deserving special consideration. The emperors had good reasons

for singling them out for favored treatment. In return for the privileges granted them, they were expected to become loyal assistants
of the imperial administration or at least not to oppose its interests.
Some of the gentry fulfilled this expectation to some extent. In many
cases they helped the government to maintain local order, to strength-
en imperial control, and even to defend the regime against its enemies. But for every one of such gentry there were a number of others
who were more concerned with self-interest than with the interest of
the government, and more anxious to realize immediate gains than
to render useful service. Indeed, the enjoyment of special consideration as taxpayers whetted their greed; the possession of special
privileges afforded means of gratifying this greed. They became the
worst of taxpayers, whose fraudulent ways could not be stopped by
any amount of legislation. [227] A well-known Chinese writer was not
far from the truth when he asserted that "the only remedy lay in the
equal and uniform treatment of the gentry and the people. "[228]

It would be inaccurate, however, to lay the blame exclusively on
the gentry. Without the encouragement or connivance of local officials
and yamen underlings, the gentry could not have gone as far as they
did. Sometimes local officials encouraged fraudulent practices by
compelling the local gentry to engage in *pao-lan*. It was reported in
1754 that some of the magistrates, afraid that they would show a poor
administrative record by failing to collect full tax payments in their
chou or *hsien*, resorted to the unlawful expedient of "forcing" wealthy
households to assume complete responsibility for the other taxpayers
in their *tu* or *t'u* divisions.[229] In instances reported in the nineteenth
century officials and yamen clerks encouraged *pao-lan* in a flagrant
manner. Government granaries in the *chou* and *hsien* to which tax payments were to be delivered were kept open for only three to five days
during the period of collection. Taxpayers arriving after the granaries
were closed had to pay money in lieu of grain and thus incurred additional expenses. Rural taxpayers suffered the most. After having transported their grain to the designated granaries, they were dismayed
to find the storehouses shut. Only those households that engaged in
pao-lan were informed of the dates when the granaries were open;
these alone managed to deliver their grain without trouble. [230]

Quite often local officials and yamen underlings became partners
of the gentry-scholar elements in the highly lucrative though unlawful
enterprise of *pao-lan*. The lion's share of the profit (according to a
nineteenth-century writer) usually went to yamen underlings. The
scholars who participated "received the least amount of profit but
were most easily exposed to hazards and suffered the gravest consequences. " He explained:

> For every hundred parts of illegal gains derived from tribute rice

that go to clerks and runners, the local official takes ten parts, the gentry receive two or three, and the scholars do not get more than one part. . . .

The authority of the magistrate is not great enough to harm the gentry, but it can easily ruin scholars. . . . To deprive a *sheng-yüan* or *chien-sheng* of his title, the magistrate sends an official dispatch in the morning, and in the same evening he receives the word of approval. . . .

When members of the gentry are involved in matters of tribute rice [they do not have to visit the yamen]; those who go are either their assistants in business or members of their households. But when scholars are so involved, they must go to the yamen in person. Hence says a proverb: "One hundred *mow* of land in the family brings one every day of the year to the magistrate." . . . The more days a scholar spends running around [to arrange tax matters], the less time he has for scholarly pursuits. It makes little difference whether he is a *chü-jen, kung-sheng, sheng-yüan,* or *chien-sheng*. He is bound to ruin his literary career and to block the road to official honors and achievement.[231]

The explanation seems quite plausible. But we are not concerned here with determining the relative degree of advantage enjoyed by local officials, yamen underlings, gentry, and scholars;[232] nor are we interested in ascertaining the relative degree of guilt with which each of these groups should be charged. All of them participated, in different capacities and to different extents, in an empire-wide "racket" and social inequalities reinforced by official corruption rendered the evils of the revenue system beyond remedy.

Other conditions also contributed to tax fraud in general and to *pao-lan* in particular. The distance that separated remote villages from the city offered a constant difficulty to tax collection. The situation was described in a letter from an eighteenth-century *chin-shih* scholar to the magistrate of a district in Kiangsu:

In I-hsin the distances from the city to the borders measure over one hundred *li* in the west and south, and just under one hundred *li* in the east and north. When one person goes to the city to pay taxes, some of his clan members and relatives ask him to make payments for them [in order to save them the long trip]. Households without able-bodied men and sick persons who cannot walk are compelled by the circumstances to ask others to make payments for them. Yamen clerks and runners, however, detain these persons who make payments for others and try to blackmail them, saying, "Why do you engage in *pao-lan?*" The local official, failing to make an investigation of the actual situation, places these persons under arrest and upbraids them, saying also, "Why do you engage in *pao-lan?*"

When the gentry make payments for others with a view to securing private gain at the expense of the common people, their action constitutes *pao-lan* and should be prohibited. Is it right to punish common people who extend mutual help with a view to fulfilling their public duties ? It is obvious that when the prohibition of *pao-lan* becomes overstrict, those who cannot deliver the tax payments themselves will invariably entrust the matter to yamen runners who will avail themselves of the opportunity to defalcate the revenue. [233]

Difficult as it was to distinguish between *pao-lan* and bona fide mutual help, it was equally difficult to prevent gentry elements from using mutual help as a pretext to engage in sheltering tax defaulters. The emperors therefore required taxpayers to deliver their money and grain in person. But they were not able to find an effective method of collecting revenue from rural taxpayers in a vast countryside with poor means of transportation. The *li-chia* in itself might have proved useful to some extent. But it was frustrated or vitiated by two potent forces: corrupt local officials with their underlings on one side and greedy local gentry on the other. To expect the *li-chia* heads, who were themselves taxpayers with a commoner status, to overcome these forces—to curtail default, extortion, and oppression which were so profitable to these privileged persons—was to invite disappointment, even more so than to expect the *pao-chia* heads to detect and report crimes. For while the *pao-chia* had to work against outlaws, the *li-chia* had to fight against the vested interests of powerful and influential segments of society. [234]

Effects of Malpractices on Imperial Revenue

The net result of the malpractices in which local officials, yamen underlings, and local gentry indulged and which rendered the proper operation of the *li-chia* apparatus impossible was, so far as the imperial government was concerned, a reduction to varying extents of its actual revenue from the land and labor taxes. It may be of some interest to note briefly how nonpayment of taxes and official defalcation actually affected the revenue of the imperial government.

Nonpayment of taxes, either in the form of simple default *(ch'ien-liang)* or in the more troublesome form of resisting collection by force *(k'ang-liang)* existed since the earliest days of the dynasty. The extent of nonpayment varied in different periods and in different provinces. Nonpayment was quite extensive during the reign of Shun-chih, when the government was engaged mainly in consolidating the fruits of conquest and the administrative machinery was not as yet running at its peak of efficiency. Nonpayment of taxes was perhaps even more extensive during and immediately after the turbulent mid-nineteenth century when wars and other calamities impoverished many of the taxpayers and weakened the prestige and administrative efficiency of the imperial government. Tax evasion became more widely practiced than ever[235] and riòts against tax collectors were frequently reported in many parts of the empire. [236] Nonpayment of taxes was less extensive during the relatively prosperous reigns of K'ang-hsi, Yung-cheng, and Ch'ien-lung, and later during the reigns of the T'ung-chih and Kuang-hsü emperors, at least in some of the provinces.

From the earliest days to the end of the dynasty, local officials seldom sent to Peking (through the provincial authorities) the full amount of the taxes which they were supposed to collect in their respective districts. [237] In some instances the dereliction may have been due to the default of the taxpayers; in others it was simply the result of defalcation by local officials and their underlings, who often falsely accused taxpayers of defaulting. [238] Their ruse did not remain undetected; the Yung-cheng emperor on one occasion attributed the main cause of revenue losses to "satiation at the middle" and took a comparatively lenient view of the general run of taxpayers. [239] Unlike nonpayment of taxes by the people, the extent of which fluctuated with changing circumstances, official defalcation continued steadily and tended to increase as the dynasty declined.

The extent of official embezzlement may be illustrated by Table 8, composed of instances reported in Shensi and Kiangsu:[240]

TABLE 8
OCCURRENCES OF EMBEZZLEMENT

Locality	Status of Official	Amount Embezzled		Date
		Money (taels)	Grain	
Mei Hsien (Shensi)	Magistrate	8,240	Valued at 8,160 taels	1843
Hua-t'ing Hsien (Kiangsu)	Acting magistrate	17,588	465 *shih*	1845
Ch'ing-p'u (Kiangsu)	Acting magistrate	19,296	693 *shih*	1845

The official quota for the land and labor imposts in Shensi (with 76 districts) for this period was about 1,675,000 taels and that in Kiangsu (with 65 districts) was about 3,626,000 taels. The amount embezzled in each of these districts represented a considerable percentage of the revenue collected annually. The situation varied in different periods and different provinces, but it may safely be said that there was almost no year in which the imperial government received in full the land and labor taxes, for the collection of which the *li-chia* was partially or indirectly responsible.[241]

Nonpayment of taxes and official defalcation did not in themselves mean fiscal ruin for the imperial government. The total revenue of the government was not derived from the *ti-ting* and *ts'ao-liang* alone, but came also from a number of other levies including customs, salt gabelle, taxes on special commodities such as tea, and fees for licenses (e. g. , brokers' permits). [242] Two important new sources of revenue, maritime customs and the *likin,* were added in the nineteenth century. During the eighteenth and nineteenth centuries the size of the income from these old and new levies steadily increased, and the importance of the regular *ti-ting* correspondingly decreased. The incomplete figures in Table 9 will suffice to demonstrate this trend. [243]

TABLE 9
REVENUE FROM *TI-TING* AND OTHER LEVIES*
(In 1, 000 taels)

Levy	1720	1735	1865	1885	1895
Ti-ting	33, 910	34, 695	22, 000	23, 023	23, 737
Other	6, 370	9, 620	37, 000	46, 915	52, 102

*Where grain receipts were originally entered as separate items, the figures are converted into silver at one tael per *shih.*

These figures cannot be regarded as accurate; they cannot be checked, and specialists do not agree. [244] They serve, however, to indicate the general trend: the land and labor imposts in the first quarter of the eighteenth century yielded over 80 per cent of the total imperial revenue; by 1865 receipts from these sources had shrunk to less than 40 per cent and to just a little over 30 per cent in the closing decade of the nineteenth century. As the *ti-ting* became less important, the *li-chia,* which was an auxiliary instrument to assist in the collection of these taxes, was bound to lose much of its original significance in the imperial revenue system. As we have shown before, the *li-chia* eventually ceased to exist as a distinct system of rural control and its functions of registration and revenue collection passed into the hands of some of the *pao-chia* personnel.

The dynasty did not suffer financial ruin as a result of the eclipse of the *li-chia,* but it was not spared other grave difficulties. The land and labor taxes occupied a less and less important place in the imperial revenue system, but they remained a constant source of hardship for many a taxpayer. Local officials and their underlings and the rural agents who carried on the original *li-chia* duties continued to exploit or oppress the villagers; local gentry continued to take advantage of their special status to advance their interests at the expense of their fellow taxpayers. When the empire as a whole was confronted with repeated crises and the government lost much of its prestige, the resentment induced by unjust methods of tax collection eventually gave rise to local unrest, which in turn contributed to the general turbulence of the nineteenth century. The Taiping Rebellion, the most momentous upheaval of the period, gained its initial strength partly by appealing to the general dissatisfaction with the tax system. According to a contemporary account:

> When the rebels achieved their first successes, they foraged for food supplies and money in the *chou* and *hsien* of western Kwangsi through which they passed. Whenever they came upon wealthy families or influential households, they [plundered these so thoroughly as to] dig three feet into the ground. The gentry of western Kwangsi went to the imperial capital to present their grievances to the throne. . . . When the rebels advanced from Ch'ang-sha [Hunan] and captured Wu-ch'ang and Han-k'ou [Hupeh], their method changed several times. At first they plundered cities only. In fact, they distributed clothing and other articles [which they had previously looted elsewhere] to poor people of the countryside. They made it generally known that they would in future exempt all taxes for a period of three years. . . .
>
> The rebels never indulge in killing in the villages. . . . But they plunder most thoroughly households in which families of officials, their private secretaries, or yamen clerks and runners have sought shelter, as well as residences of gentry families. They slaughter the occupants and burn down the buildings. Households that give shelter to such families are charged with "harboring ogres," and also have their members killed and their buildings burned down. . . . As a result, where the rebels pass, no household dares take in families of officials or of their secretaries. Such families often have to spend the night in pine groves or sleep in abandoned temples. [245]

The rebels evidently were shrewd in capitalizing on the mistakes committed by the Ch'ing government in its revenue administration. But they committed mistakes of their own and failed to work out satisfactory solutions of the problems of tax collection. Their utopian "land system of the Heavenly Dynasty" remained on paper. After the establishment of their government at Nanking, public revenue became for them an urgent administrative problem. To insure full collection of taxes they instituted a hierarchy of *hsiang-kuan* (rural officials) selected from propertied households of the various divisions, who were assigned substantially the same duties as those of the old *li-chia*: registering taxpayers and prompting tax payments. [246] In this new arrangement some of the old, familiar malpractices of the *li-chia*, including extortion and embezzlement, were repeated. [247] That the Taiping rebels were unable to set up a workable revenue system is not surprising. Their regime was too short-lived and too full of difficulties in itself to effect any real reform in social and political habits. In fact, considering the quality of leadership of the Taiping rebels, it is doubtful that they were in a better position than the Ch'ing rulers to solve the all-important and very difficult problem of tax collection at the rural level. [248]

Chapter 5

FAMINE CONTROL:
SHE-TS'ANG
AND OTHER GRANARIES

THE GRANARY SYSTEM OF THE CH'ING DYNASTY

The Ch'ing emperors could not operate their administrative system without adequate revenue, but they were aware that the best way to insure adequate revenue was to conserve the people's ability to pay taxes. The imperial government therefore took care to nurse the agrarian economy, chiefly through measures of land reclamation[1] and water conservancy, the latter including irrigation and flood prevention work.[2] At the same time, it endeavored to alleviate the hardships that peasants frequently suffered and to help them make provisions against natural disasters. It regularly granted deferment or exemption to taxpayers in localities suffering from calamities;[3] and it developed a network of local granaries from which grain could be dispensed in times of stress to those who needed it, in the form of sale, loan, or outright relief. Famine control became so important an element in the general system of rural control that it claimed no less imperial attention than the *pao-chia* or *li-chia*.

The measures of famine control adopted by the Ch'ing government proved useful up to a certain point but were never free from the effects of official ineptitude, indifference, and corruption. As time went on, whatever degree of effectiveness they had had diminished with the decline of the dynasty. This was particularly true of the empire-wide system of local granaries which were an essential part of the system of famine control. This chapter examines the structure and functioning of the granary system, with special attention to the storehouses in the countryside. Other phases of famine control that did not involve rural organization will be touched upon only incidentally; no attempt will be made to survey the system of famine control as a whole.[4]

The system of local granaries of the Ch'ing dynasty, which should be clearly distinguished from the imperial granaries,[5] comprised three distinct though related sets of granaries known respectively as *ch'ang-p'ing-ts'ang* (ever-normal granaries),[6] *i-ts'ang* (charity or town granaries) and *she-ts'ang* (community or rural granaries). Speaking generally, these three types of storehouses were distinguishable by their location and mode of management. With respect to their location it was said, "All *ch'ang-p'ing* and *i-ts'ang* are established in the cities of *chou* or *hsien*, but *she-ts'ang* are built in villages. Hence all granaries built in the countryside are *she-ts'ang.*"[7] While all *she-ts'ang* were located in the countryside, not all *i-ts'ang* were built in cities. According to a regulation of 1679 (K'ang-hsi 18), local inhabitants were encouraged to institute *i-ts'ang* in towns and markets outside the walled cities.[8] A government decision of 1742 (Ch'ien-lung 7) required the construction of *i-ts'ang* in "great towns" and "populous rural areas" as well as in district cities.[9]

The *ch'ang-p'ing* differed from the other two types of granaries in that part of their grain reserves came from government sources, mainly through purchase with government funds, although contributions from wealthy persons were accepted.[10] The reserves of *i-ts'ang* and *she-ts'ang*, on the other hand, were supported by private contributors, the former by merchants of towns or markets,[11] and the latter by inhabitants of the rural neighborhoods.[12] Another and perhaps more crucial difference between the *ch'ang-p'ing* on the one side and *i-ts'ang* and *she-ts'ang* on the other was that the former were essentially government granaries and were therefore directly managed by local officials,[13] whereas *i-ts'ang* and *she-ts'ang* were left to the management of local inhabitants though always subject to official supervision and inspection.[14]

Like all other Chinese institutions, the granary system did not maintain strict uniformity in its structure. The *she-ts'ang* of some provinces, for example, Shensi and Kwangsi, were known as "government-established *she-ts'ang*" because their grain reserves were purchased with government funds or came from *ch'ang-p'ing* granaries.[15] Moreover, despite express regulations, the distinction between *i-ts'ang* and *she-ts'ang* often became blurred. These names were sometimes used interchangeably as if they were synonymous,[16] although generally the distinctions obtained (see Appendix II for a historical survey of the Ch'ing granary system).

STRUCTURE AND OPERATION OF THE LOCAL GRANARIES

Ch'ang-p'ing-ts'ang

The chief concern of the present chapter is the *she-ts'ang* (community granaries) of the countryside, but they can be better understood if the structure and operation of the entire network of local granaries, which included also the *i-ts'ang* and *ch'ang-p'ing*, are outlined.

The *ch'ang-p'ing-ts'ang* (ever-normal granaries) were first established in 1655 by the imperial government. According to regulations, formulated at this and later times, one or more government-storehouses were to be built in every *chou* and *hsien* and managed by the local magistrate. The grain, which might be rice, wheat, sorghum, or other foodstuff,[17] was procured by purchase with government funds as well as by contributions from all who cared to make them. In certain provinces, including Chihli, Chiang-nan, Kiangsi, Shensi, and Shansi, a *ts'ang-ta-shih* (commissioner of granaries) was appointed to oversee the operation of the granaries in each province. The grain reserve was lent to needy peasants or sold at "normal" (below current market) prices, as the situation required. Whatever amount was taken out of the granaries was replenished as soon as feasible. An annual account was rendered by the local official and was eventually sent to the imperial government.[18] Quotas were fixed for all parts of the empire.[19] Regulations adopted in 1691 specified a storage of 5,000 *shih* in a large district, 4,000 and 3,000 in smaller ones. The amounts fluctuated at different times so that the total quota for the whole empire varied between roughly 30,000,000 and 48,000,000 *shih*.[20]

The operation of the *ch'ang-p'ing* was governed by detailed regulations,[21] a few of which may be noted here. Purchases of grain were to be made each year after the autumn harvest, either locally or in neighboring districts where the prices were relatively low. If the market supply was short, the routine purchases might be postponed until the next calendar year.[22] Special funds were set aside for making the purchases. "Local gentry and wealthy persons" were invited to make contributions to the government grain reserves.[23] The scholarly title of *chien-sheng* was awarded to those contributing specific quantities of grain.[24]

Disbursement of the grain reserve took the forms *p'ing-t'iao* (sale at normal prices) and *chen-chieh* (relief loan). To avoid rot through long storage, a fixed portion of the grain, usually 30 per cent of the reserve, the proportion varying in different provinces, was sold below market prices each year in the spring and summer months and replenished after harvest. In case of famine, the amount of grain sold might go beyond the regular percentages. When there was an oversupply of grain on the free market, the amount might be reduced or the sale suspended altogether for the season. Reduction of the selling price varied with circumstances. In years of good harvest the grain was sold at 0.05 tael per *shih* below the market price; in a year of famine, at 0.10 tael. Further reductions could be made upon special imperial authorization, which however could never exceed 0.30 tael per *shih*.[25] "Relief loans" were made to peasants who were short of seed or food.[26] Borrowers were required to repay the granaries after the autumn harvest. In about ten provinces, including Shantung, Chiang-nan, Kwangtung, and Szechwan, no interest was charged. Even in those provinces where a 10 per cent interest was charged, the government waived it whenever a loss of crops amounting to 30 per cent or more was reported. [27] Persons, including the gentry, who fraudulently took advantage of the grain sale or grain loans to profiteer, and officials who allowed the grain reserve to dwindle or storehouses to go out of repair, were threatened with punishment. [28]

The *ch'ang-p'ing* system was never very effective. The success of a government-operated undertaking depended directly upon the attitude of the local officials who were responsible for its operation. There were instances of conscientious efforts to render the *ch'ang-p'ing* a useful institution, [29] but official apathy generally prevailed. It was quite possible that the edicts and regulations issued by the imperial government in the earlier days of the dynasty remained largely a dead letter. [30] It is at any rate doubtful that even in the heyday of the regime the *ch'ang-p'ing* were free from official corruption. Indeed, according to a well-informed seventeenth-century writer, [31] official fraud and defalcation prevented many of the government granaries from procuring the prescribed quantities of grain reserve. Actual instances were reported in which magistrates stole the local grain reserves and frustrated imperial efforts to stamp out their malpractices. In 1726, one year after he threatened defalcators with the death penalty, the Yung-cheng emperor had to admit that when he sent special high commissioners to investigate the conditions of the granaries in Fukien province where defalcation was reported to be extensive, "undutiful officials" forestalled the proceedings by borrowing grain from rich families and putting it into the depots just before the commissioners arrived. [32] An imperial investigation of malpractices in the *ch'ang-p'ing* granaries of Chekiang province in 1746 ended almost in failure. The extraordinary action of a local *chien-sheng* scholar brought an offending magistrate to justice; but thanks to the higher provincial officials who had an interest in not exposing the wrongdoings of their subordinates, all other culprits went free. [33] One emperor after another deplored the fact that despite their vital importance, the *ch'ang-p'ing* granaries had become "an official form devoid of substance. "[34]

The most tangible evidence of the degeneration of the *ch'ang-p'ing* system was the progressive depletion of the grain reserves. As early as 1766 the imperial authorities were informed that reserves in the various provinces fell below the official quotas. By 1831 it was reported that "in the *chou* and *hsien* of the provinces the *ch'ang-p'ing* granaries usually showed in their account books that funds for making purchases were available but no grain was actually in store."[35] An official source indicated that in 1835 the actual amount of deficit in the granaries amounted to almost one half of the total quota. [36] When a Western writer made a survey in the 1870's he found that local officials had "allowed their granaries to remain empty." In the "very many public granaries" he visited, he "seldom, if ever, found one containing more than a measure of rice." Many of the storehouses were "in a ruinous condition."[37] A Chinese student of the granary system pointed out that information concerning the *ch'ang-p'ing* ceased in 1898 (Kuang-hsü 24);[38] he drew the likely conclusion that they had virtually gone out of existence before the dynasty came to an end.[39]

I-ts'ang

The *i-ts'ang* and *she-ts'ang* of the Ch'ing dynasty were simultaneously inaugurated in 1654 (Shun-chih 11),[40] a year before the inception of the *ch'ang-p'ing*. The basic features of these granaries were made clear by a government order issued in 1679: "Local functionaries shall persuade officials, gentry, scholars, and common people to contribute grain and to build *she-ts'ang* in villages and *i-ts'ang* in towns and markets. [Contributors] shall be considered for suitable reward.[41] Supplementary regulations were drawn up from time to time.[42] As already noted, while the *ch'ang-p'ing* were managed by local magistrates, both *i-ts'ang* and *she-ts'ang* were left to the management of local inhabitants.[43] The imperial authorities often stressed that rural and town granaries should exclusively serve the peasants of the localities which instituted them. Transferring the grain reserve of one place to give relief to neighboring towns or cities or lending grain to scholars, soldiers, yamen runners, and other persons not engaged in farming was expressly forbidden.[44]

The following regulations governing management and operation of *i-ts'ang* were formulated for Chihli and Shansi, and those in other provinces were probably similar.

> Scholars and common people of the two provinces Chihli and Shansi who contribute grain to *i-ts'ang* shall be given official commendation proportionate to the amount donated, in accordance with the rules governing *she* grain contribution.
>
> In the *chou* and *hsien* of the two provinces Chihli and Shansi, the business of the *i-ts'ang* . . . shall be managed by *ts'ang-cheng* [granary managers] and assistant managers, openly nominated from scholars or commoners who are upright, prudent, and in possession of adequate property. These shall serve a term of three years. . . .
>
> The grain stored in the *i-ts'ang* of the two provinces Chihli and Shansi shall be loaned out in spring and repaid in autumn [each year], with an interest charge of 10 per cent. . . . Those whose harvests suffer a loss of 30 per cent or more shall have the interest charge waived . . . those who sustain a loss of over 50 per cent may postpone the payment of the loan till autumn of the next year.[45]

A special type of *i-ts'ang* was maintained by merchants and was therefore located in populous towns or large markets.[46] Salt merchants appear to have been most active in this enterprise. Those of the Liang-Huai region contributed during the first quarter of the eighteenth century, a sum of 240,000 taels which was used to finance the establishment of a number of granaries designated as *yen-i-ts'ang* (salt granaries). Naturally, these were managed by the salt merchants themselves.[47] Similar granaries were set up in other regions, including Kiangsi and Chekiang.[48] In certain districts of Shantung the reserves of the salt granaries were raised by compulsory pro rata subscriptions.[49] Special regulations to govern these granaries were issued by the imperial government.[50]

It is difficult to evaluate in any precise manner the effectiveness of the *i-ts'ang* as an instrument of famine control. It is safe to say, however, that whatever measure of success these granaries may have attained in the prosperous years of the dynasty, they tended to disappear from the scene during the nineteenth century, especially after the Taiping Rebellion. Like other imperial institutions, the *i-ts'ang* was influenced by the quality of local administration. Just as official enthusiasm imparted strength to these local granaries, official negligence never failed to impair their vitality. When negligence became the rule and enthusiasm the exception, the very existence of the reserve system was threatened. It is true that as late as in 1825 the efforts of an energetic governor resulted in a renewal of *i-ts'ang* activities in Anhwei province.[51] Between 1839 and 1844 an ingenious governor increased the number of *i-ts'ang* in Kweichow.[52] But these were two exceptional instances. The general run of governors of this period had to be reminded of the importance of the matter, as the Hsien-feng emperor did remind them in an edict of 1852.[53] With uprisings and rebellions rife in the empire during the mid-nineteenth century, even well-meaning local officials found it difficult to attend to the task of famine control. The T'ung-chih emperor did not exaggerate when he said in an edict of 1867 that "after military campaigns began and the land was devastated by bandits, most of the formerly existing *i-ts'ang* were abandoned and went to ruin."[54] The experience of the Sui dynasty, which witnessed the creation of the *i-ts'ang* system, was thus repeated in a different manner.[55]

She-ts'ang

We are now ready to take up the *she-ts'ang* (community granaries of the countryside). It should be noted that while the *she-ts'ang* and *i-ts'ang* of the Ch'ing dynasty were different types of local granaries, officials and writers sometimes confused them, calling rural granaries *i-ts'ang*.[56] Such storehouses should be treated as *she-ts'ang*, despite their misnomer.

As already indicated, the *she-ts'ang* system was begun in 1654,[57] although its distinctive features were not made fully clear until a quarter of a century later. The first of these rural granaries were established in Chihli province. Others followed in practically all parts of the empire.[58]

The primary purpose of the *she-ts'ang*, according to an edict of the K'ang-hsi emperor issued in 1703, was to supplement the *ch'ang-p'ing*, whose reserves might not always be adequate.[59] Like the *i-ts'ang* these rural granaries were as a matter of principle placed in the hands of local inhabitants and their reserves normally raised through voluntary contributions. In response to an imperial directive, the government worked out the following basic regulations in 1703:

> Wherever a *she-ts'ang* is established, the grain contributed [by the inhabitants of] a rural area shall be stored in that same rural area; it shall be managed by honest persons of that locality. In a year of good harvest increased efforts shall be made to accumulate the reserve; in a year of modest harvest, the reserve shall be sold and replaced with fresh grain; in a year of bad harvest [the reserve shall be used] to give relief, the amount varying with the number of persons [in the households] requiring help.[60]

To induce wealthy inhabitants to make contributions, the government issued the following regulations:

> Local officials shall, at the harvest time of each year, persuade the gentry, scholars, and common people to contribute to the grain reserve of the *she-ts'ang*. Each shall contribute according to his ability; no definite amount shall be fixed and it is forbidden to resort to enforced subscription or annoying impositions. . . .
>
> When the gentry, scholars, and common people contribute grain to the *she-ts'ang*, the quantities contributed shall be examined and recorded. . . . The local official shall reward a person who contributes ten *shih* or more, with red silk; thirty *shih* or more, with a commendatory tablet . . . if a person contributes during many years a large quantity amounting to three or four hundred *shih*, he shall be awarded the Button of the Eighth Rank upon petition to the emperor.[61]

A regulation of 1715 extended the scope of reward to commoners who contributed less than ten *shih*. A five-*shih* contribution brought the donor exemption from miscellaneous labor services for one year; a contribution of 250 *shih* was rewarded with an official button and permanent exemption from labor services.[62]

These regulations applied to all *she-ts'ang* established through voluntary contributions, a method adopted in most of the provinces. Shensi and Kwangsi, however, subscribed to another method. In Kwangsi the *she-ts'ang* grain reserves came from the surplus of the *ch'ang-p'ing* granaries accrued from interest on grain loans, and in Shensi from purchases with government revenue. [63] The *she-ts'ang* in these provinces were appropriately designated as "government-established *she-ts'ang*. "[64]

The rural granaries were usually left to local management and placed under government supervision. This basic policy was explicitly stated on more than one occasion. In an edict of 1729 (Yung-cheng 7) Emperor Shih-tsung said:

> We think that when *she-ts'ang* are established by the state, the original intention is to make the people accumulate a reserve by themselves, so that urgent needs of the people may be met by their own resources and provisions. Hence each *she* should manage and keep records of the spring loans, autumn repayments, and increments realized from interest charges. Local officials have the responsibility for making inspections and auditing [the accounts] only; they should not infringe upon its authority to receive and disburse [its grain reserve]. [65]

The *she-chang* (granary manager) and assistant manager were appointed from persons who qualified themselves by "upright conduct and adequate property," for a term of three years (except in Kiangsu province where the term was at different times ten years, three years, and one year), which could be extended to another three years upon petition by members of the community. A manager who served creditably for three years was rewarded with a commendatory tablet; unimpeachable service of five years entitled him to exemption from labor service for life. The government apparently assumed that managers of the rural granaries were nominated from the common people. In Shensi province managers were given an annual stipend of twelve *shih* of grain; creditable service was rewarded with additional quantities of grain. Managers who failed in their duties were to be promptly dismissed and subject to punishment by the government. Any deficit in the grain reserve was to be made good by the outgoing manager. [66] In Shensi and Kwangsi, however, the local magistrate was held responsible for mismanagement of *she-ts'ang*. [67]

The grain reserves of the *she-ts'ang* like those of the *i-ts'ang* could be used only to give relief to peasants living in the villages where the granaries were located. Law prohibited assistance to neighboring communities or to persons not tilling the soil. [68] The procedure of securing grain loans as prescribed by law was as follows:

> For the purpose of making loans from the *she* grain reserve, local officials shall prepare beforehand detailed registers of all households, indicating names of the householders and their addresses. These records shall be kept in the yamen files. . . . Qualified peas-

ants who desire to apply for loans shall so report to the *she-chang*, who shall collect all the applications and present them together to the local official. [The amount of grain] dispensed [to each applicant] shall be determined by the number of persons [in his household]. [69]

Since the grain distributed was in the nature of a loan, it had to be repaid with interest by borrowers who were able to do so. In years of famine the interest charge was generally waived. [70] Anticipating the possibility that substantial increments might result from interest on loans, the government fixed quotas for different provinces and stipulated that surplus grain should be sold each year during the "green-yellow gap," the spring and summer months when the new crop was yet to come and the old crop was practically exhausted. Funds realized from such a sale could be used, with imperial authorization obtained through the provincial authorities, to finance irrigation work or any other project beneficial to peasants but beyond the capacities of individual villagers to undertake. [71] Detailed accounts of the grain were kept by the rural managers and by the local magistrate. At the end of each fiscal year a report was made to the provincial authorities who in turn reported to the imperial government. [72]

One significant fact emerges. While the Ch'ing rulers insisted on the principle that rural granaries were the people's own and should be managed by the people themselves, they never failed to impose stringent government control upon these storehouses. Even the routine procedure of making loans could not be completed without official scrutiny and approval. Under such an arrangement the rural managers were denied any measure of discretion. Their actual responsibilities did not go much beyond taking care of the grain reserves and recording routine transactions. The granaries were subject not only to the supervision of local officials but to central, imperial control.

The imperial government had good reasons for regarding the rural granaries as a vital concern. Past experience had shown that a grain reserve was one of the best means of maintaining imperial peace in times of stress. In the Sung dynasty the *ch'ang-p'ing* and *she-ts'ang* were said to have helped in averting imminent uprisings or riots. [73] The T'ung-chih emperor of the Ch'ing dynasty stated that the lack of local grain reserves was an immediate cause of the failure of his servants to withstand the onslaught of rebels and bandits. In an edict of 1864 (T'ung-chih 3) he said:

The *ch'ang-p'ing* established in the *chou* and *hsien* of various provinces are designed to provide against natural calamities in times of peace and against emergencies in times of unrest. . . . Recently, military affairs have become a constant concern. Localities have fallen to invading bandits, often because food supplies were exhausted. The sole reason for this is that [grain reserves] have been wantonly depleted by *chou* and *hsien* officials who heartlessly drained away the food supplies, leaving nothing to fall back upon in an emergency.[74]

The very fact that the imperial government had a keen interest in the granary system induced it to keep as much control over it as was consistent with the practical situation. The *ch'ang-p'ing* were placed under official management because their reserves came from government sources. Local inhabitants were allowed to manage their *i-ts'ang* and *she-ts'ang* because the resources of the government could not adequately answer the imperial need, and the people themselves had to be induced to contribute the necessary grain, The government had no intention of making any concession to local autonomy. From the imperial point of view there was therefore no essential difference between the *ch'ang-p'ing* on the one side and the *i-ts'ang* and *she-ts'ang* on the other: they all served the same purpose of famine control for the sake of imperial security.

The local granaries, however, did not fulfill the expectations of the imperial rulers. We have indicated in very broad terms that both the *ch'ang-p'ing* and *i-ts'ang* tended to degenerate and disappear as time went on. We shall now in more concrete terms show the degeneration of the *she-ts'ang*. The conditions of *ch'ang-p'ing* and *i-ts'ang* as they existed in the nineteenth century will also be mentioned, for the sake of comparison and to give us a more comprehensive view of the conditions of the *she-ts'ang*.

DECAY OF THE LOCAL GRANARY SYSTEM

We have little information concerning the operation of the local granaries. From many local gazetteers, however, we can ascertain the conditions of the storehouses as they existed in the nineteenth century. The general picture is one of decay and degeneration, although in some instances local granaries were said.to have been kept in running order or revived after a period of virtual extinction, by well-meaning and enterprising local officials. Ironically, granaries in localities where the economy was less stringent tended to fare somewhat better than those in localities where the inhabitants stood in greater need of them as a result of general poverty or frequent calamities.

To begin with North China. According to the *Yen-ch'ing chou chih* (1880), the *i-ts'ang* and *she-ts'ang* located in five different places in the city and countryside were restored in 1815 and again in 1826 by order of the governor-general, and a total of 4,099 *shih* of grain was contributed at various times.[75] This was one of the few instances in which grain stores were revived in Chihli. In other localities of this province the granary system tended to fall into decay. In Wei Chou the grain reserve of the eleven *ch'ang-p'ing* storehouses (reconditioned in the 1850's) dwindled rapidly in the following manner:[76]

Original quota: 35,000 *shih*
Actual amount stored: 14,553 *shih* (c. 1856)
Actual amount stored: 4,554 *shih* (c. 1857)

The eight *i-ts'ang* of the same locality, built in 1753 by order of the governor-general, disappeared at an unspecified date. In 1850, however, a local official rebuilt six of them distributed in the city and rural areas as follows:[77]

Grain reserve *(shih)*

City:	13,978
Hsi-ho Ying:	2,997
Li-lin Chuang:	1,633
Pei-shui Ch'uan:	926
T'ao-hua Pao:	608
Luan-ch'uan Pao:	879

Apparently, the *i-ts'ang* of Wei Chou did exceptionally well. The four *she-ts'ang* were much less prosperous. Repairs were made in 1842 and again in 1849. But at the time when the local historian was writing (c. 1870), the total reserve had diminished from a total of 1,488 *shih* to 729 *shih*, less than half of the original amount.[78] The grain reserve of the *ch'ang-p'ing* and *i-ts'ang* of Han-tan Hsien was said to have been helpful in the famine of 1846. As late as 1880 a magistrate renovated the *i-ts'ang* storehouses, but of the 14,000 *shih* originally stored in them this official was able to replenish only a little over 9,000 *shih*. This reduced reserve was later completely exhausted.[79] Even in localities around the imperial capital, many of the *ch'ang-p'ing* and *i-ts'ang* were reported to have collapsed in ruins.[80]

Other northern provinces repeated the experience of Chihli. Many of the local granaries of Shantung, the compiler of the provincial gazetteer wrote in 1890, were allowed to fall into disrepair.[81] The *ch'ang-p'ing* of Feng-chen Hsien (Shansi), first built in 1763, were repaired in 1853 and in 1881, and were reported to have contained over 12,000 *shih* of grain.[82] But in I-ch'eng Hsien the grain reserve of one of the two *ch'ang-p'ing* storehouses decreased from over 6,000 *shih* in Ch'ien-lung times to less than 200 in Hsien-feng. At the close of the dynasty the total reserve of both granaries was less than 2,000 *shih*, scarcely one third of the original amount.[83] T'ung-kuan Hsien (Shensi) had three *ch'ang-p'ing* storehouses and six *she-ts'ang*, with a total reserve of over 6,000 *shih* in Ch'ien-lung times. By 1901 all the rural granaries had disappeared, leaving only two of the three city storehouses.[84] In Lu-i Hsien (Honan) a magistrate rebuilt in 1893 the *ch'ang-p'ing* granaries, which had collapsed a long time before. The *i-*

ts'ang and *she-ts'ang,* however, were not restored. [85] The *ch'ang-p'ing* of Sui Chou in the same province were rebuilt in 1872 and again in 1898. Nothing was said of the rural granaries;[86] presumably they had been out of existence for some time.

Similar conditions prevailed in provinces south of the Yellow River. The *ch'ang-p'ing* of Hsing-kuo Chou (Hupeh), according to a local historian, were rebuilt by the magistrate in 1730. These were burnt down later and never restored. The *she-ts'ang,* which were first instituted in 1725, also disappeared in the fire of 1730. In 1879 a large number of rural storehouses, with a total reserve of 20,000 *shih,* were built by order of the governor-general. [87] A general survey made in 1861 revealed that in thirty of the seventy-five *chou* and *hsien* of Hunan province the contents of the local granaries were completely drained, and no attempt at replenishment was reported. In the remaining thirty-five localities the grain reserves generally fell below the official quotas. [88] The decline of the rural granaries is also shown in accounts in a number of local gazetteers. It was recorded that all the nine granaries of Tao Chou, one in the city and eight in the countryside, went out of existence in the 1870's.[89] Pa-ling Hsien formerly boasted a *ch'ang-p'ing* reserve of over 27,000 *shih* and a total of thirty-five *she-ts'ang* with a reserve of over 2,900 *shih.* In 1852, however, the city granaries were destroyed by "bandits," and only a fraction of the rural grain reserve remained during the closing decades of the nineteenth century. [90] The *ch'ang-p'ing* reserve of Tz'u-li Hsien, according to official records, was depleted in the following manner:

> Original reserve: 10,246 *shih*
> Reserve in 1815:   6,662 *shih*
> Reserve in 1861:   2,056 *shih*

The compiler of the gazetteer containing this information pointed out that from what he heard, the 2,056 *shih* supposedly available in 1861 existed on paper only; in fact, "not a spoonful of grain remained" in the storehouses. [91] The five *she-ts'ang* of this district fared no better. The original reserve of 6,000 shih was exhausted at an unspecified date and only partially replenished in 1863 at the order of the governor of the province. The reserve was soon drained again. In 1881 a reserve of over 7,000 *shih* was raised by pro rata contributions imposed on landowners. About a decade later it gradually disappeared again, "through embezzlement or theft."[92]

In the provinces of southeast China where agricultural production was relatively high, it was easier for local granaries to survive but they seldom enjoyed consistent prosperity. The picture in some districts of Anhwei as shown in Tables 10 and 11, indicated the relatively favorable conditions of this region:[93]

TABLE 10
LOCAL GRANARIES IN LU-CHOU FU, 1883

Locality	Ch'ang-p'ing	I-ts'ang	She-ts'ang
Ho-fei Hsien	4	0	5
Lu-chiang Hsien	2	0	6
Su-ch'eng Hsien	1*	0	4
Wu-wei Chou	6†	0	10
Ts'ao Hsien	4†	2†	4†

*Abandoned.
†In ruins.

TABLE 11
GRAIN RESERVES IN LU-CHOU FU

Locality	Reserve, 1737 (shih)	Reserve, 1884 (shih)
Ho-fei Hsien	2,843	5,546
Lu-chiang Hsien	2,463	4,352
Shu-ch'eng Hsien	2,400	5,488
Wu-wei Chou	3,200	4,036
Ts'ao Hsien	3,200	6,975

The situation in some localities of southeastern China, however, was little better than the worst in North China. In Chien-ch'ang Hsien (Kiangsi) the ch'ang-p'ing storehouses, which formerly contained a reserve of over 10,000 shih, went out of existence in the closing years of the dynasty. [94] Similarly, most of the ch'ang-p'ing, i-ts'ang, and she-ts'ang in the districts of Hang-chou Fu (Chekiang) had ceased to operate before the end of the nineteenth century. [95] An enterprising governor of Kiangsu, with the assistance of other officials and local gentry, set up a number of granaries in 1831, which continued to function for several decades. The local historian explained that these new storehouses were instituted because "the ch'ang-p'ing had been destroyed and could not be restored, while the she-ts'ang were prone to give rise to troublesome complications." [96]

Kwangtung province also showed an uneven record. According to a local historian:

In that year [1723] an order was received and contributions to she-ts'ang were solicited. In most instances the order was only nominally carried out. Chang Hsiang-ch'ien, magistrate of Ho-p'ing Hsien, however, afforded an exception. He did his utmost to solicit contributions and was able to build 102 storehouses, with a total grain reserve of over 13,000 shih. [97]

We do not know how long the plentiful reserve of this district lasted. Judging by the experiences of other localities of this province, Ling-shan, Ch'ing-yüan, and Tung-kuan, it probably did not remain intact for very long. In Ling-shan Hsien a magistrate sometime in the K'ang-hsi reign established a number of *ch'ang-p'ing* storehouses in the city. In Ch'ien-lung times another magistrate set up a number of *she-ts'ang* in the countryside. We hear no more of the *ch'ang-p'ing;* it was said that at the beginning of the Tao-kuang reign (1821), all the *she-ts'ang* had only a nominal existence. [98] Ch'ing-yüan Hsien had an unspecified quantity of *she-ts'ang* grain reserves procured through contributions made in 1725. In 1743 (Ch'ien-lung 8) the total amount of grain in store was over 9,000 *shih*. This was wiped out in 1854 as a result of the rebellion. Funds for purchasing grain amounting to over 4,000 taels also disappeared when the provincial treasury was destroyed by fire in 1857. [99] This catastrophe presumably brought the existence of local granaries in this district to an end.

The vicissitudes undergone by the rural granaries of Tung-kuan Hsien may serve to epitomize experiences of other localities. According to a local historian:

> In this district . . . four granaries established by the gentry and common people in the Ming dynasty . . . were abandoned at the beginning of the present dynasty. A number of *she-ts'ang* were instituted in Yung-cheng times. . . . The Board *[Hu-pu]* fixed, in Ch'ien-lung times, a quota for the grain to be stored in the granaries of Tung-kuan, which was as high as over 97,000 *shih*. . . . Although evil practices arose as time went on and although [the granaries] suffered pillage by the Red Bandits, the records still showed in T'ung-chih times a reserve of over 22,000 *shih*. At the end of the Kuang-hsü reign [1908] high provincial authorities ordered the magistrate to sell all the grain and assign the buildings and grounds to a middle school. A fine institution of the dynasty was thus done away with, root and branch. [100]

The same picture obtained in southwestern provinces. In Lu Chou (Szechwan) the *ch'ang-p'ing* grain reserve specified in the *Fu-i ch'uan-shu* was 41,005 *shih*. According to a local historian, the actual reserve at one time reached 58,000 *shih* but dwindled to 8,275 *shih* during the last quarter of the nineteenth century. The *she-ts'ang* reserve, however, showed an increase, from 9,139 to 15,564 *shih*. [101] In Fu-shun Hsien only a few of the original sixty-five rural granaries survived at the end of the nineteenth century. New granaries were built between 1880 and 1883 by order of the governor-general. About forty years later, of the ninety-nine storehouses located in the city and countryside, sixty-six showed a decrease in their reserves, and eight had their reserves completely drained away. [102] In Chiang-ching Hsien, the *she-ts'ang* established in 1754 were virtually forgotten before long. When in 1817 the government again found it necessary to procure a reserve for the inhabitants, a different name (relief granaries) was adopted for the new storehouses. In 1880 a third new set of rural granaries was instituted and a third name (reserve granaries) adopted. [103] This confirmed the impression that even in places like Szechwan, where the economic circumstances were relatively favorable, local granaries were a highly perishable institution. It is no wonder that they more frequently died an early death in the less friendly environment of Yunnan and Kweichow. [104]

The imperial government, then, intended the various types of local granaries to constitute a comprehensive system of famine control. Time and circumstances reduced it to a mosaic of varying patterns with divergent degrees of effectiveness. The fortune of individual granaries was greatly affected by the willingness or ability of local functionaries to undertake a delicate and difficult task. The granaries survived or prospered only under the administration of conscientious magistrates, and there was no assurance that their successors could maintain an administration of the same quality. As dutiful officials were relatively rare, the majority of local granaries were short-lived, at least in the later part of the nineteenth century. A Western observer came very near to the truth when he wrote in the 1870's:

> In all walled cities as well as in many towns and villages, there are imperial [i.e., local] granaries, in which rice is supposed to be stored by the government, so that it may be retailed at a reduced price in times of war or famine to the soldiers of the garrison and the poor. These institutions owe their origin, not so much to benevolent feelings as to those of self-preservation. Mandarins are well aware that few things are more dangerous to the peace of the state than a half-starved population. . . . [But] they are very apathetic, and allow their granaries to remain empty. I have visited very many public granaries, and have seldom, if ever, found one containing more than a measure of rice. I found many in a ruinous condition. [105]

Such a state of affairs, of course, was not brought about in one day. It took years of negligence to put local granaries completely out of commission. The experience in some parts of Kiangsu province may be cited as an illustration. In 1770 an acting governor memorialized the throne as follows:

> . . . although the official quota of grain reserves of the *she-ts'ang* in Su-chou, Sung-chiang, Ch'ang-chou, Chen-chiang, and T'ai-ts'ang . . . amounts to over 269,000 *shih*, a careful investigation reveals that of this total over 163,000 *shih* has been loaned to the people in many years past and has not been repaid, over 600 *shih* has been

defalcated by local managers, and over 60,000 *shih* remains to be purchased (funds for making the purchase being on hand). The actual reserve in the storehouses is less than 50,000 *shih*. . . .

The total quota of grain reserves in Chian-ning, Huai-an, Yang-chou, Hsü-chou, and T'ung-chou . . . is over 116,900 *shih*. Of this, over 13,800 *shih* has been loaned to the people in years past and has not been repaid, over 440 *shih* has been embezzled by local managers, and over 5,600 *shih* remains to be purchased (funds on hand). The actual reserve in the storehouses amounts only to less than 69,000 *shih*. [106]

In other words, before the end of the third quarter of the eighteenth century, the *she-ts'ang* grain reserve of this generally wealthy province fell short of its official requirement by over 60 per cent. That was far from encouraging, but worse was to come during the subsequent century. The local granaries were so completely drained of their reserves that when a severe famine occurred in some localities of Chen-chiang in the 1880's and again in the 1890's, the prefect had to rely on emergency contributions by the local gentry and wealthy persons and on relief grain diverted from the tribute rice storehouses. [107] Thus, in about one hundred years the regular reserve system of this prefecture broke down completely through a process of gradual depletion. The same process was at work in many other localities of the empire.

DIFFICULTIES OF THE GRANARY SYSTEM

The unsatisfactory conditions of the local granaries, briefly described in the preceding section, resulted from a variety of difficulties. These fall into four main categories: (1) those connected with the procurement of the grain reserve, (2) those connected with its dispensation, (3) those connected with the supervision of the storehouses, and (4) those connected with the appointment of local managers.

Procurement

Government-operated *ch'ang-p'ing* granaries suffered more from the first set of difficulties than did either the *i-ts'ang* or *she-ts'ang*. According to imperial regulations, the *ch'ang-p'ing* reserves were obtained through purchase with government funds and through contributions from wealthy people. These methods of procurement afforded corrupt officials ready opportunities for making illegal profits. As early as 1766, imperial authorities were notified that some *chou* and *hsien* magistrates in Kweichow province fixed a quota on every household, rich or poor, and required it to supply and transport the prescribed amount of grain to the city where the storehouses were located. The burden thus illegally imposed upon the inhabitants almost equaled that of the regular land tax.[108] Another form of corruption was noted by the Chia-ch'ing emperor. Quoting from a memorial, he said in an 1800 edict:

> . . . when local officials purchase grain for the granaries, they often resort to the evil practice of paying money short of the selling prices, of compelling [the sellers] to give them receipts [even though the specified sums were not received], and of juggling payments and prices.[109]

In one sense, these offending officials were not wholly to blame, since they were not given adequate funds to make the necessary purchases. A memorial presented to the Chia-ch'ing emperor in 1802 contained these revealing words:

> The purchase price fixed in the various provinces varies from five to seven mace [0.5 to 0.7 tael] per *shih*. Compared with market prices, this is really too low. As a consequence, most of the *chou* and *hsien* magistrates prefer to hand over money to their successors at the end of their terms, after they have previously sold the grain reserves. The newcomers, thinking it convenient to have cash on hand, gladly accept the money, without inquiring whether it is sufficient for making the purchases. This procedure is repeated, with the result that funds for purchasing the grain remain, but no grain is stored in the granaries. In the worst cases even the storehouses are allowed to deteriorate. . . . If, however, it is decided to buy the grain, the fact that the official price is below the market price leaves only one way open to the local functionaries, namely, to fix a quota for each household and compel the people to sell [their grain at the official price]. The more scrupulous among these officials, for this reason, desist from making purchases. . . . Under such circumstances, to order that the purchases be made within a fixed time limit is to work hardship either on the people or on the officials.[110]

Some magistrates, scrupulous or otherwise, discovered a way to avoid embarrassing themselves or harassing the people too much. They hit upon the idea of "soaking the rich." A nineteenth-century writer reported the following practice in Hunan province:

> [The *ch'ang-p'ing*] granaries are controlled by local officials. The grain which they are supposed to contain has long been depleted. Some officials use government sale and dispensation as a pretext for settling the accounts. When it is time to make the prescribed purchases for replenishing the reserves, they send some money to wealthy households and compel them to supply the grain. These households dare

not accept the money [which is not sufficient to cover the cost anyway],
but bribe the officials with a view to getting future exemption [from
such compulsory sale]. This has now become a customary practice.[111]

It may be noted also that aside from facilitating official corruption,
the practice of government purchase of *ch'ang-p'ing* grain brought
with it an economic problem unforeseen by the earliest imperial rulers. In an edict of 1731 the Yung-cheng emperor pointed out that while
it was important to store as much grain as possible in the local granaries, it was undesirable to occasion any undue rise in grain prices
through excessive buying:

> Grain reserves involve the food supply of the people. Formerly, ef-
> forts were made to fill the quotas of the granaries of all provinces.
> The purpose was to give relief in localities suffering occasional flood
> or drought. Hence in addition to [the regular purchases for] the *ch'ang-
> p'ing,* contributions were collected to augment the reserves. . . . All
> these are for the sake of the people. Later on, owing to the fact that
> too much grain was bought [for the granaries], the market price of
> grain rose every day. We are genuinely afraid that this may have an
> adverse effect on the people's food supply. An imperial edict has
> therefore been issued, ordering a temporary suspension of all pur-
> chases so that grain may circulate freely in the market and its price
> go down. This is also calculated to benefit the people. We hear, how-
> ever, that high officials in the provinces treat the suspension of pur-
> chases as a measure to save trouble for themselves. . . . The gov-
> ernors-general and governors of all provinces are hereby instructed
> to take into account local conditions and carefully manage the matter.
> They should make purchases wherever suitable and suspend them
> whenever necessary.[112]

There is no evidence that excessive government buying of grain remained an important problem. On the contrary, local officials tended
to suspend purchases whenever they found it convenient and to make
them only when compelled. This edict is interesting because it reveals the generally lax attitude of local officials toward measures
adopted by the imperial government, especially those that required
sustained effort to execute. It is interesting also because it illustrates
the impossibility of exerting imperial control without an efficient
local administration.

Government purchase was not the only avenue to corruption. The
practice of raising grain reserves through voluntary contributions
also made possible some forms of fraud. For example, the *chien-
sheng* title, which theoretically admitted the bearer into the Imperial
College at Peking, could be obtained by contributing a certain quantity of grain, varying in different localities, to the *ch'ang-p'ing* granaries. Influential persons who desired to acquire privileged status but

were unwilling to pay the full price (if anything at all), often prevailed upon local officials superior in rank to the *chou* or *hsien* magistrates to recommend them to the latter. A request was made to the effect that so-and-so would be pleased to purchase the scholarly title in question. The subordinate officials who were concurrently managers of the *ch'ang-p'ing* knew full well that it was safer to let the granaries forgo contributions than to incur the displeasure of their superiors. But in order to safeguard themselves against possible charges of defalcation, especially when inspection of the storehouses was impending, they usually made a report indicating that the old grain had recently been sold to make room for a fresh stock to be purchased sometime later. The shortage resulting from failure to collect the full amounts of contribution by prospective *chien-sheng* scholars was thus concealed. [113]

Dispensation

Even more serious difficulties were encountered in dispensing the grain reserves of both the government-operated and locally managed storehouses. One of the most usual malpractices in the *ch'ang-p'ing* was defalcation by local officials in charge of the reserves. The situation became so alarming that the imperial government found it necessary to take action in 1799. The Chia-ch'ing emperor approved the following decision:

> With the lapse of time, evil practices appear in the *ch'ang-p'ing* of the provinces. Even in years when there is no need to give relief, [local officials] use the routine replenishment of old reserves with new grain and disburse the grain in order to derive illegal gains from the transactions. Hereafter [they] are forbidden to make loans in years not affected by calamities, so that the people may be spared a burdensome practice. [114]

About a century later, the following passage appeared in an 1897 issue of the *Peking Gazette:*

> The Censor Chang Chao-lan denounces the practice, prevalent among the magistrates, of speculating with the cereals stored in the public granaries, with the result that they become bankrupt and are unable to settle their accounts with the government. . . . The Censor accuses them of allowing the old grain to mould in the granaries and of selling the fresh for their own profit. It is easy to foresee what the result of such a course would be in time of need. We seriously exhort the various viceroys [governors-general] and governors of our provinces to look into this matter and order the entire stock of cereals to be sold, the proceeds to be placed at interest. Furthermore, We order each

magistrate to submit to Us each year an exact account of the amounts
so placed and of the contents of the public storehouses. [115]

Some of the most crucial difficulties connected with dispensation
arose from the great size of the population and the prevalence of inefficient, corrupt local administration. Speaking of the granary system in general, a well-known official said in a gubernatorial directive
at the turn of the eighteenth century:

> In recent times those who talk about making provision against famine
> do not go beyond accumulating and storing grain in storehouses. They
> fail to see that . . . [even if] a grain reserve amounting to over a
> million [shih] were distributed to the people, this would not suffice
> to give relief to one administrative division in a year of serious fam-
> ine. Moreover, [they fail to recognize] the existence of vexatious
> procedures connected with going to the city to receive [the grain], of
> evil practices arising from defalcation by yamen clerks, runners, and
> rural headmen, and of the annoyance of being later pressed for re-
> payment to the granaries. Indeed, grain reserves can no longer be
> depended upon. [116]

Another formidable difficulty was that official red tape often made
it impossible to give timely succor to those urgently in need of it.
The *ch'ang-p'ing* storehouses, being located in cities, proved especially ineffectual. As a twelfth-century advocate of the *she-ts'ang*
cogently argued:

> . . . in the *chou* and *hsien* wherever flood or drought occurs and aid
> is given either in the form of famine relief or grain sale, the benefits
> usually go to dwellers of cities and urban areas, but seldom extend
> to inhabitants of villages. The latter live in the worst of circum-
> stances; some of them fail to secure one single copper cash after a
> whole day's toil. Even when they manage to get some cash, they find
> that not many well-to-do households in their own villages [have grain
> to spare]. They have to go [elsewhere] to buy the grain, at distances
> from several *li* to several tens of *li*. [When they arrive at these
> places, they discover] that it is already too late. As a result, [their
> family members] old and young, lament and sigh; they begin to think
> of abandoning their homesteads, to escape disaster and to seek a
> more friendly soil. The strong and brawny among them refuse to die
> sitting down and are ready to do everything—theft, robbery, banditry.
> . . . Inhabitants of the cities usually are not driven to such extrem-
> ities. I am therefore of the opinion that the distress of city-dwellers
> is relatively light and easily perceived, whereas that of peasants is
> grave and difficult to discern. [117]

The *she-ts'ang* and *i-ts'ang*, widely instituted by the Ch'ing emperors, to some extent took care of the needs of the countryside. But
in so far as these were government-supervised institutions, they did

not entirely escape the evils of official red tape. An eighteenth-century governor, noted for his exceptional enthusiasm for the granary system, pointed out that during times of famine managers of rural granaries dared not touch the reserves without having first obtained official authorization, which was often given only after considerable delay. The same situation prevailed in the nineteenth century. [118] In some localities matters were even worse, as an example from eighteenth-century Shensi shows, since *chou* and *hsien* magistrates were expected to secure permission from provincial authorities before they decided to authorize disbursement by local managers. [119]

It was always difficult to ascertain the degree of need in order to give equitable or adequate relief to destitute families. The procedure of distributing the grain, even with the best of intentions on the part of persons in charge, was in itself a toilsome and vexatious task. When those who doled out the grain were less than honest, the result could be appalling. A particularly bad if not necessarily typical case was recorded in one of the local gazetteers. A serious famine occurred in Lu-lung Hsien (Chihli) in the spring of 1833, and the local official decided to give relief with the grain reserve of the town granaries. He authorized rural headmen *(hsiang-chang)* to distribute rice certificates entitling the bearer to a stated quantity of grain to those thought deserving. These relief agents, however, gave the certificates to persons who presented them with bribes instead of giving them to the really needy. On the day the rice was to be dispensed to those holding certificates, more than a thousand outraged persons gathered to air their grievances. The matter was settled only through the intercession of a prominent member of the gentry. [120] Moreover, local magistrates themselves might misappropriate relief funds, as some of the nineteenth-century magistrates in Shensi regularly did. Their misdeeds were uncovered only when a particularly "upright" commissioner was sent to investigate a famine in the early 1860's. [121]

The difficulties of extending relief to the peasants of far-flung villages were almost insurmountable. It made little difference whether the grain came from the local granaries or other sources. A noted official, writing in the first half of the nineteenth century, pointed out:

> . . . people who live in obscurity in the countryside fear government officials as if they were deities. If, unluckily, calamities occur, they often remain where they are, waiting to starve to death. Those who hold petitions in their hands and make tearful entreaties [for relief] and those who gather a mob in the market place to stage noisy demonstrations are certainly not bona fide peasants. [122]

This writer failed to say who these articulate individuals were. Other sources tend to indicate that some of them must have been local scholars or gentry.

Curiously, the imperial government authorized local functionaries to give relief to "poor scholars," including those who had made the *kung-sheng, chien-sheng,* and *sheng-yüan* grades. Specific regulations were drawn up and relief quotas were fixed for various localities. [123] Thus, according to an eighteenth-century writer, the educational official of the *chou* or *hsien* was responsible for preparing a list of scholars under his direction deserving aid. The number of such scholars, however, could not exceed one third of the examination quota of the district concerned. The amount of relief given to each scholar was within prescribed limits proportionate to the number of persons in his family and to the extent of the famine. Anticipating the possibility of the misuse of this privilege by unprincipled scholars, the government made it clear that

> . . . any who were shameless enough to pretend to be ordinary calamity-stricken people and cause disturbances, or to pretend to be members of ordinary households would, besides having their names deleted from the official relief list, receive joint admonition by the local magistrate and educational official if their offense was light, and suffer deprivation of title if their offense was grave. [124]

Despite such preventive measures, privileged persons did not cease to exploit famine relief to secure themselves unwarranted advantages. The culpable ways of some members of the gentry are described by a governor of Anhwei in a memorial of 1895:

> Unworthy members of the gentry [appointed to assist in making surveys] are accustomed to conniving with yamen clerks and runners to practice fraud. They institute registers beforehand and "sell relief" to the common people who must pay fees before their names are entered in the registers. Those who do not have the money have to pay the taxes as usual, even though they have suffered real calamities. Influential persons, on the contrary, are not only exempted from the taxes, but feed themselves on relief funds. If *chou* or *hsien* magistrates question or object to what they do, even in a mild way, they promptly send a joint petition to superior officials, using "the people's distress" as a pretext [for their doings]. In extreme cases they may gather a mob to cause disturbances or obstruct transportation [of the relief grain]. . . . Since local officials cannot put a stop [to such practices], they usually report the famine conditions as presented [by these rascals], either out of consideration for their record of administrative merits or perhaps for gains which they clandestinely receive. [125]

No special reference was made here to the granary system. But the situation may well have prevented the grain reserve from helping destitute peasants.

The annual grain sale and loan, a routine procedure apart from emergency relief, also gave rise to official fraud. Corrupt magistrates took advantage of it to cover up deficits in the stores or to realize illegal profits. These malpractices became so flagrant that they evoked a 1799 edict forbidding the making of grain loans from the *ch'ang-p'ing* reserves during normal years, "in order to remove an annoyance to the people."[126] Meanwhile, corrupt managers of *i-ts'ang* and *she-ts'ang* joined local officials in the racket, though operating in a different manner. Some of them profiteered by selling the grain at prices two or three times higher than the market rates, "to line their own private purses at the expense of community charity."[127]

In their failure to repay the grain loans local inhabitants themselves contributed to the decay of the granary system. A 1770 memorial to the Ch'ien-lung emperor reported that in five adjacent prefectures in Kiangsu where the land was comparatively fertile, the original grain reserve in the *she-ts'ang* amounted to a total of over 260,000 *shih*. Of this, more than 160,000 shih was lent out to persons who never repaid. In six other prefectures (including Chiang-ning) bad loans amounted to more than the quantities defalcated and sold put together.[128] Many of the defaulters failed to repay because they had nothing to pay with. Most of the peasants were hard pressed even in normal years.[129] It was no surprise that they could not honor debts incurred during a famine. In Pa-ling Hsien (Hunan), for example, none of the loans made in years of famine was ever repaid.[130] Whatever had been the cause, the net result of persistent and widespread default was to drain the local granaries of their reserves. Indeed, a dilemma was involved in the practice of granting loans to destitute peasants. They were the most worthy of help but the least able to repay. The best solution would have been to give them outright relief instead of giving them grain loans. But a new problem would have arisen: how to replenish the reserves thus expended? Even without official or local corruption the granary system was confronted with a formidable obstacle.

All these difficulties eventually decayed the local granaries. Despite imperial intention and insistence, the numerous storehouses that once dotted all parts of the empire often had their contents depleted or their buildings dilapidated. In edicts issued in 1792, 1800, 1802, 1831, and 1835 the emperors deplored the fact that the granaries, especially the *ch'ang-p'ing*, had become another "official form devoid of substance."[131] In the last-mentioned edict it was pointed out that, according to reports of provincial authorities, of a total quota of over forty million *shih* of grain, less than twenty-five million *shih* remained, a shortage of almost 40 per cent. This was the official account; the real situation may have been worse. Thinking that official corruption and negligence were responsible for this unhappy state of affairs, emperors tried more than once to ameliorate it by threatening undutiful officials with punishment. Their efforts usually proved futile.[132]

Supervision

Special difficulties plagued the *she-ts'ang* and *i-ts'ang*, local granaries not directly operated by the government. The fundamental idea underlying them appears sensible enough: a community effort to render assistance to all who needed it, by provisions made beforehand through contributions from those who could afford them; or, as stated by a local historian, "to make the wealthy contribute more and the poor contribute less; to use the grain reserve of one neighborhood to succor the inhabitants of the same neighborhood."[133] The imperial rulers could hardly have allowed such an important institution to be free from administrative control. Under the circumstances that prevailed in the empire, it is doubtful that many granaries would have been established or would have been operated in a manner acceptable to the government if not for government action. Local inhabitants were for the most part too diffident or indifferent to initiate community enterprises such as *she-ts'ang* and *i-ts'ang* and too inexperienced to conduct such enterprises properly. As a governor of Kiangsu said in the nineteenth century:

> The *she-ts'ang* instituted by the ancients were designed to supplement the *ch'ang-p'ing*. The basic principle [governing the former] is that the task of auditing [the accounts], collecting and distributing [the grain reserves] should devolve on the local managers and that officials should not interfere with these matters. . . . But matters relating to drawing up regulations and making appointments [of the managers] should be placed in charge of government officials who thus make up for the inadequate capacities of the people.[134]

In other words, local management and government supervision were the magic formula with which the imperial rulers hoped to insure the proper operation of the local granary system.

But the formula did not measure up to expectations. Reasonable as it appears, its practical usefulness was seriously impaired by the fact that local officials, upon whom the government depended for effective supervision of the granaries, too often proved inept or corrupt. In fact, it sometimes happened that local officials and their underlings fought with local managers over the lion's share of the spoils from fraudulent practices.[135]

Instances were known in which "inspectors" sent by the local yamen to check the grain reserves once or twice each year had to be entertained with feasts, bribed with "gifts," and provided with travel expenses. Villagers were compelled to share the cost even though the benefits that might come from the granaries were meager and uncertain. [136] In other cases yamen clerks extorted money from rural inhabitants when they went to villages or towns to help check the grain reserves. [137] In still others local officials using a law requiring borrowers to pay 10 per cent interest as a pretext, demanded this interest from local managers, even though the grain had not been lent. [138] Government supervision thus turned out to be at best a necessary evil. It gave rise to official corruption without stopping the malpractices in which many of the managers indulged.

Precisely because government supervision of local granaries proved profitable to local officials, some went beyond their legal authority and encroached upon the right of local management. Time and again the imperial government had to point out the line of demarcation between official supervision and local management and to forbid unlawful interference with the latter. In an edict of 1729 the Yung-cheng emperor said:

> We think that when the government established *she-ts'ang*, the idea was to instruct the people to accumulate grain reserves by their own efforts, so that provisions of the people might be used to give relief to themselves in an emergency. Spring loans and autumn repayments as well as interest accrued [from the loans] are to be managed and recorded by rural managers themselves. Local functionaries shall have the responsibility of inspection and supervision only; they are forbidden to infringe upon the right to receive and distribute [the grain]. [139]

This edict referred specifically to Shensi province. Encroachment on the right of local management was also reported in other parts of the empire. In an edict of 1799 the Chia-ch'ing emperor pointed out some of the undesirable consequences:

> The original idea of the *she-ts'ang* is to have charitable, wealthy households of a given locality contribute [grain] and to lend it to needy people. Recently, officials have taken over the management [of these granaries]. Most of these officials have embezzled [the grain] on some pretext. Long periods of time have elapsed, but no replenishment is made. If some [grain] remains [after official defalcation], headmen in charge [of the storehouses] as well as yamen clerks are allowed to sell it fraudulently. When a famine occurs, not a single grain of rice is available [in the granaries]. As a consequence, wealthy households are no longer willing to make contributions, and honest persons refuse to serve as managers. [140]

It is not our opinion that official supervision could be dispensed with or that it constituted the sole source of evil. Local managers were equally capable of fraud and peculation, with or without official supervision. It was said by one nineteenth-century writer that *she-ts'ang* reserves seldom lasted over twenty years, and were usually "misappropriated piecemeal by keepers of the storehouses."[141] The point is that in a political environment in which honesty did not generally prevail among persons in charge of public matters, no administrative device, official management (as in *ch'ang-p'ing*) or local management under official supervision (as in *she-ts'ang* and *i-ts'ang*) could insure a grain reserve system that adequately served the imperial purpose of famine control.

A dilemma, in fact, confronted the imperial rulers. If the local granaries were not placed under official supervision, local indifference and corruption would soon put them out of commission; but if government officials interfered, local leaders that might have some interest in them would be deterred from supporting them, and a host of malpractices would appear as a result of that very interference. This dilemma is stated in very frank terms by a noted writer of the nineteenth century, speaking from his experience as an official in Shensi province in the 1870's:

> If this move in the public interest [i.e., establishing and operating *she-ts'ang]* is entrusted to government officials, yamen clerks and runners will reap gains through embezzlement. . . . If officials do not play a leading role, the gentry will shirk their responsibilities and the undertaking will not last any length of time.
>
> The business of the *she-ts'ang*, from accumulating the reserve to its disbursement, from collecting [the contributions] to keeping and guarding [the stores], is so burdensome and intricate that unless [persons in charge are] nominated with the backing of official authority, who is willing to shoulder the task? Furthermore, evil influences and malpractices (including defalcation and careless disbursement by headmen of the *she*, and borrowing [the grain] by force and refusal to make repayments by local bullies) are so rampant that unless culprits are dealt with and punished by the authority of government officials, who dares incur the resentment of the former? . . .
>
> The situation calls for official interference. Evil consequences, however, follow closely on this very interference. Wealthy householders are timid; honest persons are usually cautious. Even learned gentlemen are not necessarily versed in government affairs, nor acquainted with the local official. Local bullies, on the other hand, generally form alliances with yamen underlings and are skilled in the art of making trouble. If any of the above-mentioned malpractices appear, the official is inevitably notified. This step involves the further steps of waiting for the official rescript, for the summons and for the trial. The expenses entailed are already enormous. If [the defendant] by luck wins the case, he can continue to operate [the gran-

ary] and extend its usefulness. But if unluckily he encounters some
bullies who have unearthed some of his faults or mistakes, or who
simply fabricate some charges against him, he may be rebuked by
the local official. As soon as he is so repudiated, he faces the un-
palatable prospect of having to make good [whatever deficit exists
in the grain reserve]. In that event, the only course open to him is
to keep silence and remain out of sight. The bullies, however, gather
their comrades far and wide, seizing the opportunity to intrude into
[the granary system]. . . . Under such a circumstance, the fate of
the *she-ts'ang* can readily be foreseen. [142]

Appointment of Managers

Selection and appointment of local managers presented a baffling
problem. This was true of the *i-ts'ang* as well as the *she-ts'ang*, but
for the latter the problem was especially acute because they were
located in the countryside where material conditions were generally
less favorable and community leadership was more difficult to secure than in towns and cities.

Well-informed officials seldom failed to underscore the axiomatic
truth that the success of the rural granaries hinged as much upon satisfactory local management as upon effective government supervision.
One nineteenth-century writer put it:

> In establishing *i-ts'ang* and *she-ts'ang* among the people . . . there
> must be loyal, honest, and charitable individuals of excellent char-
> acter, who alone can shoulder the responsibility of receiving and
> dispensing the grain . . . there must be clean, uncorrupt officials
> of fine quality, who alone can fulfil the duty of supervision. [143]

Officials were sometimes credited with paying scrupulous attention
not only to the selection of local managers but to ways and means of
enhancing their prestige or giving them encouragement. One outstanding instance was afforded by Ch'en Hung-mou who endeavored to make
effective use of the *she-ts'ang* system in Hunan and Kiangsi. In regulations he drew up for Hunan, where he was governor between 1755 and
1756, he said:

> The *she-chang* [manager of *she-ts'ang*] manages the granary for the
> entire *she*. He performs toilsome tasks and bears the brunt of crit-
> icism in order to render beneficial service to his neighborhood. His
> motivation is highly commendable, and he should not be compared to
> the *hsiang-yüeh* or *lien-chang* [head of village corps]. Whether he is
> gentry, scholar, or elder, the local official should make the appoint-
> ment with trust and show the appointee more than ordinary courtesy.
> Even though he is a commoner, he should be exempted from miscel-
> laneous labor services and not be required to genuflect before the
> official. [144]

We have no information as to how well the *she-ts'ang* of Hunan and Kiangsi fared under Ch'en's governorship. But even if they were well ordered and well managed, their success would constitute no proof of the success of their counterparts in other provinces and in other periods of the dynasty. On the contrary, evidence indicates that the problem of local management prevented most of the rural granaries from attaining their goal. The basic difficulty lay in the lack of suitable candidates for the office of *she-chang*. This was succinctly stated by a writer versed in the granary system:

> Proper functioning of the *she-ts'ang* depends solely on getting suitable persons to manage it. Not all rural neighborhoods, however, have inhabitants who are qualified for the responsibilities. Those who are interested in the task are not necessarily suitable for it, while those who are suitable are not necessarily interested. [145]

The same opinion was voiced by many writers in different periods of the Ch'ing dynasty. Before the end of the eighteenth century it was established that, as in the *pao-chia* system, the same dilemma usually occurred when nominations for *she-ts'ang* managers were made: "The virtuous don't do it, while those who wish to do it aren't virtuous." One official memorialized the Ch'ien-lung emperor in 1756.

> . . . scholars who are honest, cautious, and unimpeachable in their conduct, cultivate their own persons in their own homes; they do not enjoy meddling in business outside their doors. Those willing to perform this service [i.e., management of rural granaries] are usually persons who desire to use it as a pretext to meddle [in public matters]. [146]

Another memorialized in 1762:

> When nominations for managers of *she* are made, some who are nominated are willing to serve, while others are not. The reason [for this difference], so far as can be ascertained, is that upright persons are afraid that if they make mistakes in management, they and their families may suffer the consequences. Crafty persons, on the other hand, regard appointment to the manager's office as an honor and an opportunity to manipulate [the grain reserve]. [147]

A third, writing in the closing decades of the century, pointed out that when new managers were nominated to replace those whose term had expired, "those who were shy of public service dodged the nomination as best they could, whereas those who had an eye on [illegal] gains sought it with all their might."[148]

Innocent villagers had good reason for avoiding the draft. Testimonies of the eighteenth century, when the greatest efforts were made to operate the *she-ts'ang*, show that the responsibilities incumbent on the manager were not merely onerous but virtually crushing. Under

the historical circumstances, they constituted an impossible task.
This was admitted by the K'ang-hsi emperor himself. In response to
a petition of Chu Shih, president of the imperial censorate, to establish *she-ts'ang* and promote irrigation in Shansi province, the emperor said in 1720:

> Concerning the matter of establishing *she-ts'ang*, Li Kuang-ti had
> memorialized Us, when he was serving as governor [of Chihli]. We
> gave him this instruction: "It is easy to speak of *[she-ts'ang]*, but the
> undertaking is difficult to accomplish. You may try it." Li Kuang-ti
> tried it for several years without accomplishing any result, while
> the people grumbled a great deal. Chang Pai-hsing also memorialized
> Us, claiming that the *she-ts'ang* was helpful. We ordered him to try
> it in Yung-p'ing. Whether it has produced results really beneficial to
> the people he has so far failed to report.
>
> As to whether the *she-ts'ang* is useful, We have for a long time
> gathered information carefully. In general, whenever *she-ts'ang* are
> established, it is axiomatic that persons with sufficient property are
> selected to manage them. Such persons, not being government of-
> ficials, are without authority or attendants. When the grain loaned
> out is to be collected from the borrowers, whom then can they send
> to demand the repayments? Even in a year of good harvest, if the
> borrowers refuse to pay, the managers have no way of dealing with
> them. If the harvest is bad, who would repay the grain? At first,
> grain belonging to many persons is exacted from them and stored
> [in the granaries], but nobody watches the stores. Later, when the
> grain is found to be wanting, the managers will invariably be ordered
> to make good the missing reserves. This is tantamount to throwing
> away the grain of many persons for no perceptible use. The managers,
> on the other hand, face bankruptcy for being compelled to make good
> the missing reserves, and for no justifiable reason.
>
> The *she-ts'ang* originated with Chu Hsi, the [Sung] philosopher.
> What he said [concerning this institution] may be found in the collec-
> tion of his literary works. This institution can operate in villages of
> small districts only. If, as a result of this memorial, it is established
> as a fixed precedent [for the whole empire] and its promotion is en-
> trusted to government officials, the people would receive little ben-
> efit.[149]

When we recall that empire-wide operation of the *she-ts'ang* had
been authorized in 1679, the emperor's pessimistic view becomes the
more remarkable. After giving the system a trial during the closing
quarter of the seventeenth and the opening decades of the eighteenth
century,[150] the astute ruler was convinced by experience that it could
not fulfill its high promise. That he was justified in holding such a
view is borne out by the fact that Chu Shih, the official who petitioned
to establish the *she-ts'ang* system in Shansi, retracted his proposal
and begged his sovereign to rescind the order which assigned him the

thankless task of operating rural granaries in the said province. [151] Not
long after this incident, one report after another from local officials
of various parts of the empire confirmed the K'ang-hsi emperor's
opinion that managers of *she-ts'ang* were inevitably placed in most
perplexing circumstances. Ch'en Hung-mou, one of the most enthusiastic advocates of this institution, memorialized the Ch'ien-lung emperor in 1745 with these disheartening words:

> The *she-ts'ang* in Shensi province did not possess much reserve.
> Since Yung-cheng 7 (1729), thanks to the bounty of Emperor Shih-
> ts'ung, surplus revenue from wastage allowances . . . for two fiscal
> years was used to purchase grain for the people. . . . *Chou* and *hsien*
> magistrates, knowing that they were responsible [for the granaries],
> regarded [the reserves] as government property. . . . The local
> managers had no power of discretion; even the magistrates could not
> make decisions of their own. Whenever the grain was to be loaned to
> the inhabitants, approval of superior officials had to be secured. . . .
> The people's need was urgent, but rescripts from the superior of-
> ficials were tardy in coming. . . . Sometimes a directive was issued
> that it was not mandatory to lend out the grain. When the reserve be-
> came moldy and spoiled, the managers and assistant managers were
> held responsible. As a result, all were afraid to serve [as managers].
> Persons with adequate property were absolutely reluctant to serve. [152]

The lot of local managers was hardly better even in localities where
the grain reserves were raised by contribution. In the same year in
which Ch'en Hung-mou reported conditions in Shensi, Yen Ssu-sheng,
governor of Hupeh, submitted several memorials concerning local
granaries, one of which said:

> The grain stored in the *she-ts'ang* comes from contributions by the
> people and is lent to the needy among them. [Some of the borrowers]
> have fled their home villages or have long since died. As there are
> no regulations covering such cases, the recorded quantities of grain
> stored in the *she-ts'ang* do not correspond to what is actually avail-
> able. *Chou* and *hsien* magistrates hold the managers responsible [for
> the differences between the actual and recorded amounts]. . . . The
> latter cannot escape flogging or whipping for failure to make good the
> deficits. . . . All consider serving as a granary manager a "dread-
> ful path"; eventually it will become impossible to get persons to man-
> age [the granaries]. [153]

In another memorial he said:

> In a year of good harvest, most of the families have sufficient grain
> and the price of grain drops. As a result, the grain reserves of the
> *she-ts'ang* cannot be lent out, completely or in part. *Chou* and *hsien*
> magistrates often reckon only with the quantities fixed by law. They
> require [the local managers] to report an interest of one hundred
> *[shih]* for every thousand *[shih]* of the grain reserve. They refuse

to consider whether or not the grain has been lent out, completely or in part. For no fault of their own, managers may have to pay up [interest on loans which are never made]. [154]

Conditions in Kiangsu province were revealed by Li Hu, acting governor, in a memorial submitted in 1770:

> Recently, in various localities of Kiangsu all cautious villagers are reluctant to serve as *she-chang* [managers of *she*]. For in managing the collection and distribution of the grain, the managers not only are liable to incur their neighbors' censure and spite but also face the difficulty of dealing with recalcitrant debtors who refuse to repay [the grain loans]. They may have to make good the deficits thus resulting. The most troublesome and painful duties, however, are checking the reserves and rendering the monthly and quarterly accounts . . . for which the local official holds them solely responsible, because the grain reserves are placed under their management. They have to run between the villages and the city, incurring many expenses. Besides this, they suffer the heckling of yamen clerks and runners. . . . As soon as they are appointed *she-chang* there is no respite from drudgery. [155]

The same acting governor pointed out that rural inhabitants were often appointed to serve as managers, whether or not they wished to do so. Such persons could hardly be expected to act with enthusiasm or a sense of responsibility. The original practice in Kiangsu required an incumbent to serve for a term of ten years. Since it seemed unfair to burden a villager for so long a period, the tenure was shortened to three years in 1757 and to one year in 1758. Instead of improving matters, the shorter term reduced the procedure of appointment to a sheer farce. Li Hu continued:

> In recent years incumbents of the office of *she-chang* treat it as a wayside inn; one yields the post to another in rapid succession. Both predecessor and successor avoid touching the actual business, and co-operate to hide the true state of affairs. The result is that the business of making spring loans and collecting autumn repayments becomes a sham, an utterly empty formality. Moreover, within each *she* division there are not many who are upright and qualified for the office of *she-chang*. Since the one-year term involves a large number of candidates, these are nominated from the households by turns, by the rural headmen. As a result, those appointed are usually unsatisfactory. [156]

It cannot be concluded, however, that all would have been well if official interference had been removed. The lack of official supervision also created difficulties, as the same document emphasized:

According to the original regulations, receiving and disbursing the grain of *she-ts'ang* are the duties of the *she-chang*. . . . When spring loans are made and autumn repayments are collected, however, local officials fail to supervise and to press defaulters for payments. Consequently, *she-chang* indulge in favoritism and lend out the grain without discrimination; local bullies borrow the grain by force and refuse to pay their debts. It is inevitable that such evil practices arise.

Some inhabitants found the office of manager so lucrative that they sought it eagerly. It goes without saying that their willingness made them even worse managers than the reluctant ones. [157] Squabbles over the spoils sometimes arose, and mismanagement necessitated official intervention of doubtful benefit. According to a local historian:

Cunning *she-chang* reported fictitious amounts [of grain reserves to supervising authorities] and embezzled large quantities [of the grain]. Waspish villagers used their mismanagement as a pretext and fought ceaselessly for the spoils. Thereupon the local magistrate, desiring to put an end to their harmful ways, transferred all the grain reserve to the city storehouses by government order, and took the management into his own hands. . . . Official management transformed the grain virtually into government property . . . the value of which diminished each day. [158]

THE GENTRY AND RURAL GRANARIES

Rural granaries like other local institutions were susceptible to the influences of local gentry and scholars. While such influences could be beneficial, they often introduced a disturbing element into the granary system. As we recall, the *she-ts'ang* owed its revival in the twelfth century largely to the efforts of well-intentioned gentry. Chu Hsi, who contributed most to this revival, related the circumstances that led him to establish the first of the storehouses of this period:

Between the spring and summer of the *wu-tzu* year of Ch'ien-tao [1168], the people of Chien suffered a serious famine. I was then residing in K'ai-yao Hsiang of Ts'ung-an [Hsien, Fukien]. Mr. Chu-ko T'ing-jui, the district magistrate, sent a letter to me, addressing Mr. Liu Ju-yü, an elderly retired official living in his home village, and myself, saying: "The people are starving; please persuade wealthy inhabitants to take out the grain in their stores and sell it at reduced prices in order to give relief to the destitute."

Upon receiving this letter, Mr. Liu and I did what we were asked to do. But while inhabitants of the neighborhood were rejoicing over their escape from starvation, bandits suddenly rose in P'u-ch'eng, barely twenty *li* from our locality. The inhabitants were greatly frightened, and the grain supply was nearly exhausted. Mr. Liu and I were worried, not knowing what to do. We sent a letter to the district and prefectural authorities. Mr. Hsü Chia, who was then the prefect, ordered government functionaries to send us six hundred *hu* [i. e., *shih]* of rice on the same day [he received our letter]. . . . The people were again saved from starvation. . . .

In autumn [of the same year], we again petitioned the prefect, saying . . . "Please establish *she-ts'ang* patterned after the ancient model to store [the grain intended for famine relief]. " Thereupon we built three granaries. . . . Liu Fu and Liu Te-hsing, both *kung-sheng* scholars, and Liu Jui, a native of the neighborhood, were in charge of accounts and supervised the construction [of the storehouses].[159]

This experiment proved so gratifying that a number of *she-ts'ang* sprang up in various localities in Fukien, Chekiang, and Kiangsi provinces due to the efforts of local gentry inspired by Chu Hsi's idea and method. [160] These granaries also proved more or less successful. Convinced of the practicability of this institution, Chu Hsi proposed in a memorial of 1811 that the *she-ts'ang* be considered for empire-wide adoption, and described the operation of the Ts'ung-an *she-ts'ang*:

In Ch'ien-tao fourth year [1168] when Hsi, your servant, was residing in K'ai-yao Hsiang of Ts'ung-an, the rural inhabitants suffered a shortage of food. Six hundred *shih* of rice from the *ch'ang-p'ing* was obtained from the prefectural authorities upon petition. This was used to give relief or lent to the people, all of whom were loud in their expression of joy. [Additional] grain was later stored in the countryside. Inhabitants were allowed to borrow grain from the storehouses in summer and were instructed to repay their debts in winter with an interest charge of 10 per cent. In case of unsatisfactory harvest, one half of the interest was waived; in case of serious famine, all of it was waived. These granaries were jointly managed by officials residing in their home villages, a few local scholars, and your humble servant. After a period of fourteen years, the six hundred *shih* of grain [borrowed from the *ch'ang-p'ing* to start the rural granaries] was returned to the prefectural government. At present, the local grain reserve amounts to 3,100 *shih*, which is being used to operate the *she-ts'ang*. Interest is no longer charged [on loans]. Famine still occurs in some years, but no inhabitants of this rural area are without food. [161]

The most significant point to note here is that the *she-ts'ang* which Chu Hsi and his admirers brought into being owed their success almost exclusively to the action of local gentry and scholars. The institution did not emerge originally as an imperial device, and there is no evidence that the system produced many fruitful results when it was adopted throughout the empire. One is tempted to conclude that the *she-ts'ang* was essentially a local institution for famine relief, unsuitable for the purpose of imperial control.

What was the precise motive behind the action of Chu Hsi and his followers ? Sir Henry Gray, speaking of the *i-ts'ang* and *she-ts'ang* of Ch'ing times, asserted:

> Like the others [*ch'ang-p'ing* granaries], these granaries are erected to prevent uprisings from a starving population. Villagers, oppressed either by the gods or men, are very ready to band themselves together as pirates or highwaymen to obtain the common necessities of life. [162]

From this observation he drew the conclusion that the psychological origin of all local granaries could be traced "not so much to benevolent feelings as to those of self-preservation" on the part of those who established and maintained them. This view was echoed by Chinese writers. One argued:

> Poor and rich people usually are at odds one with the other. The rich oppress the poor, while the poor harbor envy and malice toward the rich. In normal times poor people already are prepared to make trouble when occasion arises. Then they are goaded by hunger, it becomes inevitable that they create disturbances. At first they will probably loot rice [wherever they find it]; then they will plunder the rich; finally, they will openly band themselves together and become full-fledged bandits. [163]

A similar line of reasoning underlay the familiar argument that wealthy people should contribute generously to the *she-ts'ang*, for "to protect the poor is tantamount to protecting the rich. "[164] These writers were convinced that wealthy and privileged persons showed interest in the granary system because it constituted an investment in their own safety and peace.

Whatever may have been Chu Hsi's prime motive, he made it amply clear that rural granaries were an effective means of averting social disorder:

> There are three *li* divisions in the southern part of Chien-yang [Fukien], being all designated "Chao-hsien." These border on [the districts of] Shun-ch'ang and Ou-ning. The land is difficult of access, and the inhabitants are violent in their disposition. In past years wicked elements were not weeded out after military campaigns. These elements promptly rose in swarms to indulge in violence whenever a small famine occurred, once every few years. . . . In a certain year of the Shao-hsing reign [1131-62], a serious famine occurred. Wicked people everywhere gathered themselves into bands; they drank wine, gambled, whistled, and shouted—ominous signs that they were about to repeat what they had done before. Inhabitants of the *li* were much frightened.
>
> Mr. Wei Yüan-li, renowned scholar of the *li*, made a request to Mr. Yüan Fu-i, the *ch'ang-p'ing* commissioner; he obtained a quantity of rice [from the *ch'ang-p'ing* reserve] and lent it [to the destitute inhabitants]. The situation promptly quieted down. Evil designs

were thereby frustrated. When autumn came and the harvest was about to be gathered in, Wei Yüan-li again obtained [some grain] and built granaries in Ch'ang-t'an [to store it]. . . . Since that time, whenever the harvest was bad [the grain stored in the granaries] was distributed [to those who needed relief]. . . . For a number of years the inhabitants of the three *li* enjoyed an adequate food supply and a peaceful life, free from disorder and destruction. [165]

There is no doubt that this view of Chu Hsi's was accepted, tacitly or expressly, by all who had faith in the granary system. Without denying the presence of humanitarian sentiments on the part of some of the gentry and scholars, one can safely assume that "the feelings of self-preservation," to which Sir Henry Gray referred were normally at work when they devoted their energies to promoting local grain reserves.

It is therefore no surprise that some of the gentry of the Ch'ing dynasty, like their counterparts in Sung times, showed a great deal of interest in the granaries, especially in provinces south of the Yellow River. In Kwangtung, for example, a considerable number of *she-ts'ang* and *i-ts'ang* owed their existence to gentry action. [166]

Local officials were quick to recognize the helpful if not indispensable role of the gentry in operating the rural granaries. In the mid-eighteenth century, Ch'en Hung-mou enlisted the assistance of the gentry in his attempt to operate the *she-ts'ang* in a number of provinces. [167] In the closing decade of the nineteenth century, a prefect of Chen-chiang Fu (Kiangsu) worked out an ingenious method of insuring cooperation between members of the gentry living in cities and those dwelling in villages. He entrusted the former with receiving and the latter with disbursing the resources of the granaries. [168] A nineteenth-century writer advocated that the gentry be employed to supervise the management of *she-ts'ang* and that the actual chores of handling the reserves be left to managers nominated by the villagers concerned. [169] But gentry participation did not guarantee success. Much depended upon the quality and personal prestige of the individuals who took part. After having laid down the broad principle that "the first requisite for operating *she-ts'ang* was to secure suitable personnel," the writer continued:

> Suppose that a person, after attaining success in officialdom and achieving renown, retires to the countryside and operates *she-ts'ang* wholeheartedly in his home village or neighborhood. Since his fame and prestige are sufficient to impress both the local official and the people, what he plans and carries out would stand the test of time. . . . [But] if *kung-sheng, chien-sheng,* or *sheng-yüan* scholars take charge of the matter, [the situation would be different]. Not all scholars have fine character and superior erudition. Even if every one of them is a gentleman who practices virtue, it is not certain that the

official has respect for them or confidence in them and that the people are ready to obey them. [170]

This writer made a useful comment on the difference in prestige between two segments of the gentry, the retired officials and the titled scholars who had not held office. He was probably correct in placing less confidence in the scholars than the officials as operators of local granaries. Prestige, however, was not the only factor relevant to the situation. Personal character often had important if not decisive influence. The members of the gentry, *shen* as well as *shih*, did not exhibit uniform behavior, nor were all of them of the same quality. Just as some scholars were "perverse" *(tiao-sheng)*, in the parlance of the time, so were some retired officials "bad" *(lieh-shen)*. "Perverse scholars" and "bad gentry" could hardly be expected by their fellow villagers to operate the granaries with strict probity. Members of the gentry were often said to have treated local storehouses as a source of personal gain. The once ample grain reserve of the *i-ts'ang* of Fu-shan Chen (Nan-hai, Kwangtung), for example, was embezzled by "relatives of a certain influential member of the gentry." The reserve was replenished only after determined efforts by a native *chü-jen* scholar in the last quarter of the nineteenth century. [171] The situation in Ling-shan Hsien (Kwangtung) is even more revealing. Each of the *she-ts'ang* of this locality was placed under the management of a "wealthy gentry-elder," who was subject to the supervision of the local magistrate. The managers were far from interested in the welfare of their communities:

> When they heard that some villagers wished to borrow some grain, they declared that it belonged to the government [and therefore they could not grant the loan]. After they collected the grain and put it in store, they made profit out of it. When famine occurred, they not only refused to sell the grain at reduced prices but sometimes realized a profit three times the original price. In other words, they took advantage of an institution established by farsighted predecessors, a charitable undertaking supported by many people, to line their own purses. [172]

SUMMARY AND CONCLUSIONS

In the present section an attempt has been made to explain why the local granary system did not live up to its promise as an instrument of imperial famine control. No one can deny that accumulating a grain reserve to provide against disaster was a sound idea; no one questions the necessity of giving relief to hungry villagers, either to conserve the rural economy or to stave off peasant uprisings. A survey of some of the available records, however, compels the conclusion that

like other devices of rural control, whatever benefits the local granaries may have produced were partly, of not largely, neutralized by
the ill effects with which they were attended.

We may assume that in the earlier days of the dynasty, when the
regime exhibited its maximum vigor, the granaries fared somewhat
better than after the eighteenth century. Even during the comparatively
prosperous days, the government had found the *ch'ang-p'ing* inadequate and had to supplement them with *i-ts'ang* and *she-ts'ang*. Early
experiences with the rural granaries were so disappointing that the
K'ang-hsi emperor was led to condemn them as an institution for empire-wide adoption. The Yung-cheng emperor, his immediate successor, disregarded his warning that the *she-ts'ang* was suitable for
limited application only, and found the difficulties of their operation
baffling. [173] Subsequent experiences were even less encouraging. [174]
Many of the granaries that existed in the first two centuries of the
dynasty failed to weather the wars and rebellions of the nineteenth
century. [175] In T'ung-chih and Kuang-hsü times some of the storehouses, especially those in the cities, were revived, [176] but they did
not ease the convulsions of a dying regime and were eventually liquidated together with the imperial throne itself by the revolution of
1911. [177]

The three main types of local granaries were susceptible to mala-
dies of various descriptions, most of which sprang from the historical
conditions of imperial China. This system of famine control was prevented from successful operation by an officialdom which was often
as corrupt as it was incompetent, and by a peasantry whose material
destitution was perpetuated by its inability to exert itself against an
unfavorable social and natural environment. The importance of the
latter factor cannot be overstressed. The grain reserve system was
called forth by the necessity of giving relief to helpless villagers, but
their very helplessness, ironically, precluded them from receiving
real benefits from it. Needy peasants were either denied the succor
promised by the stores or turned into permanent debtors by loans
which they could not repay. Rapacious elements of the countryside,
on the other hand, preyed upon the grain reserves, playing havoc
with their management. The generally desperate situation observed
in the latter part of the nineteenth century was well summarized by
the compiler of a local gazetteer:

> When granaries were built in cities, benefits could not reach all rustic
> corners; when the grain was stored with rural managers, bullies
> often appropriated it for their own profit. Summer borrowing and
> winter repayment opened the way to default by persons without means;
> official red tape and government auditing rendered [the granaries] a
> dreadful path for persons who were in charge of them. . . . In addi-
> tion, "fuel expenses" for gentry-directors, wages of watchmen, wast-

ages resulting from drying the grain in the wind and sun, all these entailed expenditures which exceeded the receipts. Bankruptcy was a
real worry. Consequently, wealthy gentry, after having suffered the
bitter experience of being implicated [in the mess] and compelled to
pay up the losses, kept scrupulously away from the granaries. Those
that lacked the financial resources, on the other hand, could not bear
the burden incidental to the management, [even though they were willing to serve].[178]

It was almost impossible to ameliorate this perplexing situation,
because in addition to malpractices resulting from social conditions
there existed a set of economic circumstances which rendered the
creation and maintenance of an adequate grain reserve a Herculean
task. Inadequate agricultural production, recurrent natural disasters,[179] and population pressure[180] combined to condemn the bulk of
the rural inhabitants to eternal scarcity. Despite intensive cultivation China did not produce enough food to feed her millions, especially
with the substantial increases of population after the middle of the
eighteenth century.[181] A Western expert on famine relief in modern
China was undoubtedly right when he asserted:

One often hears statements about the "margin of livelihood" in China,
but facts show that there is no margin at all if the population be regarded as a whole. The bare food requirements for a normal year
are greater than the present production and importation of edibles.
. . .
It is this lack of any margin of livelihood that is one of the fundamental causes of famine.[182]

Another modern Western writer, an authority on Chinese agrarian
economy, concurred substantially with this opinion: "The small in-
comes reduced most of the farmers and their families to a mere subsistence basis. In fact the people feed themselves in winter, just as
one "roughs" labor animals through the winter, by consuming as little
and as poor food as possible."[183] Both observations were made in the
first decades of the twentieth century and also apply, in a slightly
lesser degree, to the nineteenth century.

It was futile to expect the peasants to set aside part of their produce
to provide against hard times. They had no surplus and hard times
were constant. If they borrowed from the local granaries, they were
required to repay their loans, often with interest charges. But since
needy farmers could barely subsist even in normal years, a grain
loan in a bad year was little better than "quenching thirst by drinking
poison," as a Chinese saying goes. It should be admitted that the
Ch'ing emperors did not count on the average villager to sustain the
granary system. Grain reserves in various localities came from purchases made with government funds and contributions from well-to-do

gentry or common people. But this fact did not remove the basic economic difficulty: total production of food was insufficient to meet the requirements of the nation as a whole. Moreover, gentry bounty could not be depended upon. As owners of land wealthy householders had an interest in keeping tillers of the soil alive and in extending them some help whenever it was necessary. But not all of them were sufficiently enlightened or farsighted. For every one who lent active material or moral support to the local granaries, there might be more than one who refused to cooperate with local officials in an undertaking of vital importance, or who took part in the matter merely in order to plunder the stores. [184]

The Ch'ing emperors were in no special way responsible for the unsatisfactory functioning of the local granary system. Like their predecessors in previous dynasties, they were confronted by essentially similar historical circumstances which prevented them all from fully carrying out their intentions. At any rate, they did not accomplish any less than the emperors of the Ming dynasty. A Chinese historian commenting on the Ming granaries remarked that "although the institution was a good one, no person had seriously tried to put it into practice."[185] The following description of the conditions of a locality in Hupeh province in the same dynasty might well be a portrayal of those obtaining in Ch'ing times:

> [Grain] received from the forty-three *li* divisions was put into a few storehouses. No attempt was made at separating the chaff from the rice, nor at keeping an account of gains or losses. The managers collected surplus grain from [inhabitants of] the various *li*. When the annual quotas were filled, further collection was made in money equivalents of the grain to facilitate defalcation. Moreover, the amount embezzled by yamen underlings and lost through default in repayment by borrowers in the neighborhoods was impossible to ascertain. [186]

The worst that may be said of the Ch'ing rulers is that they employed traditional methods to solve the age-old problem of famine control and were not able to touch the crux of that problem or to rise above the historical circumstances posing the problem.

We are not arguing that the grain reserve system was not a useful institution. Generation after generation of emperors had no better method to provide against famine, and the granaries were helpful within certain limits in reducing the dangers arising from widespread starvation. An unsatisfactory method of famine control was better than no method at all, and it was possible that the Ch'ing rulers never had expected the granaries to function with perfect results. But the reserve system, like any other imperial institution, did not operate in a historical vacuum. Its performance was conditioned by circumstances—physical, economic, and political. For this reason it could not produce all the results of which it was theoretically capable when other major factors in the historical situation tended to undermine the imperial structure as a whole, or when other elements in the imperial system did not work satisfactorily. It had to stand or fall with the entire dynastic complex. The local granary system fared better in times when general conditions were better and the regime itself healthier and became proportionally ineffectual or harmful when the historical situation took a turn for the worse. In these times the granary system itself became a contributing factor to the general process of disintegration.

It may be noted that leaders of the Taiping Rebellion offered a somewhat novel solution of the problem of famine control. In the *T'ien-ch'ao t'ien-mou chih-tu* (The Land System of the Heavenly Dynasty), their utopian social scheme, they envisaged a system of land distribution and property ownership which promised to meet this problem by pooling all agricultural resources for the benefit of all.

> All land under heaven will be cultivated in common by all who live under heaven. . . . [The produce from] all land under heaven will circulate to equalize abundance and scarcity. The produce of one locality where the harvest is good will be transported to give relief to another place where famine occurs. . . .
>
> At harvest time the *liang-ssu-ma* [headmen of twenty-five households] will supervise the *wu-chang* [headmen of five households] and will, after deducting [quantities of grain] sufficient for food for each of the persons belonging to the twenty-five households until the next harvest, [collect] the surplus and send it to the state granaries. [187]

The novelty of the Taiping scheme consisted mainly in the changed conception of landownership, resulting in a different conception of famine control. Famine relief was not a charitable undertaking sponsored by the government and supported by wealthy individuals but an integral part of the social system itself. This was a definite departure from famine control through a network of local granaries.

The Taipings, however, did not put their "land system" into practice. It is idle to speculate whether or not it was more feasible than the traditional grain reserve system. It is doubtful that with their limited administrative experience they could have carried out their quasi-communistic plans successfully, even if their "heavenly dynasty" had managed to withstand the onslaught of the forces led by Tseng Kuo-fan. One thing at least is certain. Without a substantial increase in the total agricultural production resulting from decisive improvements in the material environment, "an equalization of abundance and scarcity" between different parts of the empire might have done away with economic inequity but could hardly have ended famine and economic want for the population as a whole.

Chapter 6

●

IDEOLOGICAL CONTROL:
THE *HSIANG-YUEH*
AND OTHER INSTITUTIONS

THE *HSIANG-YÜEH* LECTURE SYSTEM

Following the footsteps of their predecessors in previous dynasties, the Ch'ing rulers tried to maintain a firm hold on their subjects
by ideological control. They found Sung Confucianism of the Ch'eng-
Chu school, which stressed social duties and human relationships, a
most serviceable instrument for this purpose. Ostensible reverence was consistently paid to Confucius by the emperors themselves.
Scholars of the past whose utterances and conduct were considered
useful to the purpose of imperial control were canonized from time
to time.[1] Emperors from Shun-chih to Ch'ien-lung undertook to
prepare commentaries on Confucian classics, dissertations on Sung
Confucian philosophy, and editions of the works of Chu Hsi—enlisting the help of Chinese scholars whenever they deemed it feasible
or wise.[2] With "imperial Confucianism"[3] thus established as the
absolute criterion of thought and conduct, the immediate practical
task for the new rulers was to win over the scholars, especially
those who had survived the Ming dynasty and remained loyal to it.
The builders of Ch'ing were fully aware that for a long time in the
past scholars as a class had occupied a key position in the social
and political structure of China, and that to control the scholars
was virtually tantamount to controlling the entire population. The
most important move they made was the revival of the examination system. Almost immediately after the Shun-chih emperor entered Peking, the first provincial examinations were held by imperial
order in the autumn of 1644. The first metropolitan examinations
followed in the spring of 1646, and the first full-dress "examinations
for scholars of wide learning and great literary attainment" were
conducted by the order of the K'ang-hsi emperor in 1679.[4] By this
and other devices the Ch'ing rulers sought to secure the support of
the native scholars, to direct their minds and energy to the "proper
channels" and to keep them out of mischief.

The astute rulers did not overlook the importance of controlling
the minds of the masses. Realizing that most villagers were illiterate

and hence that the methods used to control scholars were unsuitable for them, they resorted to a variety of means of popular indoctrination, the most interesting of which was the *hsiang-yüeh* lecture system.

The *hsiang-yüeh* lectures appear to have been inaugurated by the Shun-chih emperor with the promulgation of his *Liu Yü* (Six Maxims of a Hortatory Edict), urging his subjects in the provinces and banners to practice virtue and to lead a peaceful life. [5] In order to make clear the meanings of these maxims to the people, a *hsiang-yüeh* was appointed in each locality, to give lectures on them at fixed intervals. The Board of Rites decided in 1659 that the *hsiang-yüeh* and his chief assistant should be nominated by the local inhabitants from among the *sheng-yüan* scholars who were over sixty *sui* (59 years of age) and noted for their unimpeachable character; and that if no such scholars were available, commoners of good reputation over sixty or seventy *sui* would also be eligible for the posts. On the first and fifteenth day of the month the *hsiang-yüeh,* assisted by his deputy, was required to expound the imperial maxims and to record all good and evil deeds performed by inhabitants of his neighborhood. [6]

A new development of the *hsiang-yüeh* lecture system occurred in 1670. Eighteen years after the Shun-chih emperor issued the *Liu Yü,* his successor, K'ang-hsi, wrote a new set of maxims for the instruction of his subjects, the well-known *Sheng Yü* (The Sacred Edict of K'ang-hsi). The sixteen maxims of this edict were henceforth to be the text for the neighborhood lectures, superseding the original six maxims. [7]

About half a century later, in 1724, the Yung-cheng emperor, apparently thinking that even the sixteen maxims of the Sacred Edict were too brief for the comprehension of "ignorant rustics," wrote the *Sheng-yü kuang-hsün* (The Amplified Instructions of the Sacred Edict), a lengthy document of about 10,000 words. [8] In order to make the system work more effectively, the imperial government increased the *hsiang-yüeh* personnel in 1729. In addition to the *yüeh-cheng (hsiang-yüeh* heads) three or four "honest and prudent persons" were to be nominated to serve as *chih-yüeh* who, as their title indicates, were to assist the *yüeh-cheng* by monthly turns. Every rural area *(Hsiang)* and every village where population was particularly dense was to have a fixed place for delivering the *hsiang-yüeh* lectures, to be known as *chiang-yüeh so.* A meeting was to be called, on the first and fifteenth days of the month, which all the elders, scholars, and commoners of the neighborhoods were expected to attend. If the *yüeh-cheng* and *chih-yüeh* proved successful in their work or honest in their efforts after three years of service, they were to be suitably rewarded on the recommendation of the provincial authorities. Negligent ones were threatened with punishment. [9]

The *hsiang-yüeh* were responsible for recording the culpable as well as the praiseworthy conduct of persons living in their neighborhoods. At an early date in the dynasty, structures known as *shen-ming t'ing* (exposition pavilions) were erected in all provinces for displaying imperial edicts issued for the edification of the people. [10] Names of persons guilty of some misconduct, especially offenses against filial and fraternal duties, were to be posted in these pavilions and removed as soon as the culprits had mended their ways. [11] This procedure was intended to strengthen the effects of the *hsiang-yüeh* lectures. It was a spiritual pillory with which the authorities hoped to shame villagers and townsfolk into better behavior or at least to deter them from straying from the prescribed path of duty.

The Ch'ing rulers attached so much importance to the *hsiang-yüeh* that they commanded their servants again and again to redouble their efforts to make it a really potent educational influence. For example, the Ch'ien-lung emperor decreed in 1736, 1737, and 1743 that the lectures should be conducted with the utmost enthusiasm. [12] It was ordered in 1753 that in addition to the regular semimonthly lectures officials should take every opportunity to instruct villagers in Confucian moral precepts, employing local dialects and colloquial speech, so that all could comprehend. [13] A little later, when the activities of secret societies became alarmingly widespread, the imperial government made desperate efforts to make effective use of the *hsiang-yüeh*, as a series of edicts issued by the Tao-kuang emperor bears witness. [14] As late as 1865 the T'ung-chih emperor showed interest in the neighborhood lecture system. [15]

The Contents of the Lectures

The *Liu Yü* of the Shun-chih emperor promulgated in 1652 was a comparatively simple affair. The six maxims which it contains may be rendered as follows:

1. Perform filial duties to your parents.
2. Honor and respect your elders and superiors.
3. Maintain harmonious relationships with your neighbors.
4. Instruct and discipline your sons and grandsons.
5. Let each work peacefully for his own livelihood.
6. Do not commit wrongful deeds. [16]

These six maxims deal with four separate matters: maxims 1, 2, and 3 with family and social relations, maxim 4 with education, maxim 5 with livelihood, and maxim 6 with general order. They represent as a whole the substance of the Confucian ethic reduced to the barest essentials.

The Sacred Edict of K'ang-hsi, with its sixteen maxims, was of course a more elaborate document than the *Liu Yü*. [17] The relation between these two edicts may be made clear by the following table:

Comparisons of the Maxims in the *Liu Yü* and *Sheng Yü*

Liu Yü   *Sheng Yü*

Social Relations

1. Perform filial duties to your parents.

2. Honor and respect your elders and superiors.

3. Maintain harmonious relationships with your neighbors.

1. Perform with sincerity filial and fraternal duties in order to give due importance to social relations.

2. Behave with generosity to your kindred in order to demonstrate harmony and affection.

3. Cultivate peace and concord in your neighborhoods in order to prevent quarrels and litigations.

9. Manifest propriety and courtesy in order to make manners and customs good.

Education

6. Extend the schools of instruction in order to make correct the practices of scholars.

7. Reject false doctrines in order to honor learning.

4. Instruct and discipline your sons and grandsons.

11. Instruct your sons and younger brothers in order to guard them from evil-doing.

Livelihood

5. Let each work peacefully for his own livelihood.

4. Recognize the importance of husbandry and the culture of mulberry trees in order to insure a sufficiency of food and clothing.

5. Hold economy in estimation in order to conserve your money and goods.

10. Work diligently at your proper calling in order to give settlement to the aims of the people.

Peace and Order

6. Do not commit wrongful deeds.

8. Explain the laws in order to warn the ignorant and obstinate.

12. Put a stop to false accusations
    in order to protect the innocent
    and good.
13. Abstain from the concealment of
    fugitives in order to avoid be-
    ing involved in their punish-
    ment.
14. Pay your taxes fully in order to
    dispense with official urging.
15. Combine in the *pao-chia* in or-
    der to suppress thieves and
    robbers.
16. Resolve animosities in order to
    value your lives duly.

While the *Sheng Yü* was essentially an elaboration of the *Liu Yü*, it differs from it in at least one significant respect: it places a greater emphasis on the prevention of unlawful and antisocial conduct. One is tempted to surmise that whatever had been the attitude of the Shun-chih emperor, imperial Confucianism had become, in the hands of his successor, less an influence to make men good than a method to dissuade them from becoming elements dangerous to the security of the empire. [18]

This shift of emphasis was even more pronounced in the Yung-cheng emperor's Amplified Instruction of 1724. [19] In this lengthy document he dwelt persistently upon the cultivation of those personal attitudes and conduct that were conducive to the good order of the empire, even in places where the Edict was dealing with other matters, such as social relations, education, and livelihood. He argued, for instance, that filial duty implied not merely the love of one's own parents but also unswerving loyalty to one's sovereign and punctilious fulfillment of all social obligations. A filial son, in other words, should at the same time be "a dutiful and fine subject when he tills the soil and a loyal and brave soldier when he fights on the battlefield" (maxim 1). Each person, he contended, was assigned a vocation by heaven, so that even though men were not equal in their individual capacities, none would be without their own proper callings. Such callings, high and low, constituted the proper duties of men. He added: "There are no callings that are easy to accomplish, nor are there tasks that cannot be accomplished. For if each man keep and pursue his own occu-pation, there will be no unaccomplished missions" (maxim 10).

Special advice was offered to farmers. The emperor urged them with these encouraging words:

Never abandon your land lightly on account of occasional natural calamities, and never change your original occupation merely because

you hanker for spectacular gains and big profits. . . . Even though not much is left after paying public [taxes] and private [rent], yet by gradual accumulation day after day and month after month, you can achieve an ample living for yourselves and your families, with property for your sons and grandsons to inherit [maxim 4].

All persons, he counseled, must be frugal in order to be prepared for adversities. Lavishness would leave them helpless in a year of disaster when "the weak die of starvation in ditches, whereas the able-bodied do evil and commit crimes" (maxim 5). All must, however, be unstinting in paying their taxes. It would be sheer ingratitude to withhold financial support from one's own government. The emperor addressed all taxpayers in these words:

If you realize that what the court worries over and concerns itself with day and night is nothing but the affairs of the people—that dikes are built when there is a flood, prayers are offered when there is drought, and when locusts appear efforts are made to extirpate them; that you enjoy the benefits if fortunately calamities are thus warded off, and your taxes are exempted or you are given relief by your government if calamities ensue—do you then have the heart to allow your taxes to remain unpaid, thus delaying the fulfilment of your government's needs?

In spite of his cultivated suavity in language the emperor spoke here like an exacting parent, a father who never forgets his own interests and never feels sure of his son's devotion. As we pass on to those portions of the Amplified Instructions which deal directly with the prevention of crimes and preservation of order, we find that at many places not even the language is suave. Punishment is promised to all who transgress the laws and injunctions of the government. The *pao-chia*, the rural police system, must be tightened so that "thieves and robbers shall have no place to shelter their bodies." All are warned against subscribing to "false doctrines," the falsity of which has been demonstrated by imperial proscription. He wrote:

Lascivious and villainous persons . . . from brotherhoods; bind themselves to one another by oath; meet in the night and disperse at the dawn; violate the laws, corrupt the age, and impose on the people; and behold! one morning the whole thing comes to light, they are seized and dealt with according to law. What they vainly thought would prove the source of their felicity becomes the occasion of their misery. So it was with the White Lotus and Incense Burning societies whose fate may serve as a beacon to all others [maxim 7].[20]

Supplementary materials for the *hsiang-yüeh* lectures issued from time to time by various emperors showed the same engrossment in imperial security. Aside from a few instances to the contrary, notably the edicts of 1713,[21] 1746,[22] and 1891,[23] the imperial authorities were predominantly interested in the reinforcement of those maxims of the Sacred Edict which have to do with the maintenance of order and obedience to laws. Thus it was ordered in 1737 that an explanation of the main provisions of the imperial code was to be made at the close of every lecture session, and that provincial officials were to compile a handbook of law and to distribute copies of it to all villages and hamlets.[24] Another government order required that *hsiang-yüeh* lecturers should bring to the attention of their audience those provisions of the law which a villager would transgress if he disobeyed the injunctions of the Edict. Laws prohibiting feuds and fights became in 1739 supplementary materials for the *hsiang-yüeh* lectures.[25] Governors-general and governors were instructed in 1744 to proclaim in "a clear and earnest manner all criminal acts that were readily committed under given local conditions and certainly punishable by law," including robbery, rape, tomb-leveling, and all degrees of murder, and to direct the *hsiang-yüeh* lecturers to warn their listeners against them.[26] This order was reiterated in 1777, making the provincial judge responsible for the selection and publication of relevant legal provisions.[27]

Specific forms of lawbreaking received attention in the lectures. Since an early date the Ch'ing rulers had been awake to the danger of secret societies and unauthorized religious sects. Whatever ambiguity might have arisen from the term "false doctrines," which maxim 7 of the Sacred Edict urged the people to shun, was dispelled by the Yung-cheng emperor who identified them in his Amplified Instructions with the teachings of the White Lotus, Incense Burners, and the Catholics. Increasing attention was bestowed on this maxim as the threat of subversive religious groups became ever more alarming. In 1758 the government ordered the *hsiang-yüeh* to add to the regular lectures elucidation of laws governing cases that involved "heretic creeds."[28] In the same year imperial approval was given to a proposal that laws concerning false doctrines and heretical beliefs be printed and distributed to inhabitants of all localities.[29] In 1839 the Tao-kuang emperor, complying with the request of some provincial officials, directed *han-lin* scholars to prepare a metrical composition on maxim 7 for distribution to all villages.[30] The Hsien-feng emperor, alarmed by the rampancy of the "religious bandits" and hoping to offset their influence with counterpropaganda, copied this *Szu-yen yün-wen* (Tetrametrical Composition) in his own handwriting, engraved it on a stone tablet, and distributed rubbings of it to all village schools. Ten years later, in 1861, because the Taiping rebels were still unsuppressed, he ordered provincial officials to enlist the service of local gentry and scholars in the *hsiang-yüeh* system. *Sheng-yüan* scholars in particular were engaged to give lectures on the "Tetrametrical Composition" in towns and villages with a view to making its meanings clear "to every family and household. "[31] As late as 1877 the imperial government indicated that *hsiang-yüeh* lectures on the Amplified Instruction still constituted the most suitable measure to stem the tide of "heretical teaching. "[32]

The Extent of the Lecture System

To make all subjects obedient to its autocratic rule the Ch'ing government sought to indoctrinate them thoroughly with the basic precepts of imperial Confucianism. Although no serious attempt was made to eradicate illiteracy through universal education, great pains were taken to render the *hsiang-yüeh* an empire-wide institution.

The lectures were intended primarily for the edification of "ignorant rustics, "[33] but people of every social status and ethnic origin were given opportunities to attend them. The system was expanded rapidly. In 1686 military officers and soldiers in all army camps were required to read and expound the sixteen maxims of the Sacred Edict. [34] In 1729, when the boat people of Kwangtung were permitted to settle on the shores, it was decreed that a suitable number of *yüeh-cheng* be appointed for them from among elderly *sheng-yüan* scholars who were noted for their respectability and learning. [35] The Fan people, an ethnic minority dwelling in Szechwan province, were to have the Sacred Edict, current laws, and government regulations explained to them at places especially reserved for this purpose. Language barriers were to be surmounted with the help of interpreters. [36] The Hui people (Moslems) of Shensi and Kansu, [37] and the Miao of Kwangsi were brought under the influence of *hsiang-yüeh* in 1797. [38] Although the Bannermen, the most privileged of all ethnic groups, were spared the formalities of the semimonthly meetings, they had to learn by heart the Six Maxims, the Sacred Edict, and the Amplified Instructions. [39] Even youthful scholars, not "ignorant" from the imperial point of view, were not considered beyond the doctrinal influence of the hortatory edicts. A government order of 1690 obliged all scholars who had not as yet obtained the *chü-jen* degree to be present at all the lectures given by local educational officials. Actions contrary to the precepts of these edicts were punishable by law. [40] Aspirants for the *sheng-yüan* title had to be able to write from memory some sections of the Amplified Instructions when they took the local examinations, to prove that they had studied this formidable document. [41]

The *Hsiang-yüeh* in Operation

The lecture system attained a measure of success, thanks to the

support of some local officials who either wrote popular expositions
of the imperial documents or took pains to keep alive the institution
of semimonthly lecturing. For example, Fan Hung wrote the *Liu-yü
yen-i,* in which he explained the six maxims of Shih-tsu in everyday
language.[42] Eleven years after the promulgation of the Sacred Edict
of K'ang-hsi, Liang Yen-nien, magistrate of Fan-ch'ang district (Anhwei), published a work entitled *Sheng-yü hsiang-chieh,* containing
nearly 250 pictorial illustrations of individuals distinguished in history by the display or neglect of the virtues enjoined in the imperial
maxims. Each maxim was followed by a lengthy exposition "in a style
midway between the classical and colloquial."[43] A governor of Chekiang in 1679 compiled the *Sheng-yü chih-chieh* (Direct Explanations
of the Sacred Edict); this was printed and copies distributed to all
villages by imperial order.[44] The Amplified Instructions also received their share of attention. Wang Yu-p'u, a salt commissioner
in Shensi, produced *Sheng-yü kuang-hsün chih-chieh,* a paraphrase
of the Instructions in the northern vernacular.[45] This was widely ac-
claimed by many officials. Han Feng for instance used it as the text
for all *hsiang-yüeh* lectures in his province. He claimed that "the
people thronged round to hear it."[46]

Some local officials helped to spread the influence of the edicts by
taking the *hsiang-yüeh* system seriously. Huang Liu-hung, an experienced magistrate of the seventeenth century, said that in the district under his administration "every village and every clan held lecture meetings on the appointed days of the month." To facilitate matters he modified the prescribed method of selecting *hsiang-yüeh* heads.
Instead of appointing separate *hsiang-yüeh* personnel, he made the village and clan heads serve and gave them a free hand in choosing their
assistants.[47] Yü Ch'eng-lung, governor of Chihli (1678-1700), stressed
the educative importance of the *hsiang-yüeh* system and endeavored
to make it work.[48] A mid-seventeenth-century magistrate of T'ung-
kuan (Shensi) induced the local gentry to attend the semimonthly meetings.[49] When Fu-an-k'ang took up the post of governor-general of
Shen-Kan in 1785 he required all inhabitants of the two provinces,
Moslem as well as Chinese, to listen to the regular *hsiang-yüeh* sermons.[50] About a decade later, a magistrate of Ning-yüan (Hunan) believed that his efforts in reviving the *hsiang-yüeh* had yielded gratifying results in improving the morals of the inhabitants.[51] A mid-
nineteenth-century educational official of Ch'en Chou (Honan) increased
the effectiveness of the *hsiang-yüeh* by giving lectures jointly with
local gentry.[52] As late as in 1896 a magistrate of Ch'ing-pien (Shensi)
reported that he had never failed to hold the semimonthly lecture
meetings, so that "everyone of the poverty-stricken inhabitants of
this frontier land might bathe in the educative influence of the saga-
cious emperors."[53]

Comparable instances occurred in provinces south of the Yellow River. Realizing that the *hsiang-yüeh* lecturers had lost their prestige, a magistrate of Hua-yung (Hunan) in 1812 invited scholars and commoners of the towns and villages who enjoyed a fine reputation among their neighbors to fill the posts of the *yüeh-cheng*.[54] The magistrates of Meng-ch'eng (Anhwei) regularly conducted lecture meetings every month, expounding on each occasion one or two of the sixteen maxims and one or two provisions of the imperial code, a practice which persisted down to the middle of the nineteenth century.[55] Ting Jih-ch'ang appears to have made the most serious attempt at working the *hsiang-yüeh* in Kiangsu. To make sure that all the magistrates in the province did not neglect their duties of popular indoctrination, the governor in an 1868 directive required them to send him monthly reports on the semimonthly lectures. Official merits were determined by the degree of diligence the magistrates displayed in this work.[56] In addition he directed local educational officials to ride the circuit periodically to supervise *hsiang-yüeh* meetings in the countryside.[57] Lecturers were paid salaries and had to preach once in every five days instead of once in fifteen as scheduled in the original regulations.[58] A few years later Liao Lun, a magistrate of the same province, built on his own initiative a *sheng-yü t'ing*, a pavilion where lectures on the Sacred Edict were delivered.[59] Li Ch'un-ho, acting magistrate of T'ung-hsiang (Chekiang) appointed in 1872, revived the *hsiang-yüeh* by selecting a number of *sheng-yüan* scholars to expound the Sacred Edict.[60] Juan Yüan, governor of Kwangtung, in 1831 ordered all submagistrates *(hsün-chien)* to conduct the semimonthly lectures in addition to those delivered by the regular *hsiang-yüeh* personnel.[61] Huang An-tao, prefect of Kao-chou Fu (Kwangtung), in 1825 formulated a series of *hsiang-yüeh* regulations for the guidance of his subordinates. Among the most interesting of these were (1) that the chief official of each city, assisted by two lecturers, should expound the contents of the Amplified Instructions, using the local dialect to insure complete understanding on the part of the listeners, and (2) that each submagistrate, assisted by four lecturers, should give similar lectures in rural markets three times a month.[62] Sung Hao, acting magistrate of Ch'i-chiang and later magistrate of Hsin-ching and Chiang-ching (Szechwan), hit upon the idea of selecting "persons with a clear voice" to deliver roadside lectures on the Sacred Edict.[63] Nan-kung Hsiu, magistrate of Po-pai (Kwangsi) in the later 1730's, appointed a *sheng-yüan* scholar noted for his "upright character" to the post of *yüeh-cheng* to take charge of the semimonthly lectures "for the instruction of the people of his neighborhood."[64] A magistrate of Ch'ien-yang (Kweichow), who served from 1838 to 1841, conducted the lectures so effectively that "all untutored people were moved and encouraged" to behave themselves properly.[65] Of-

ficials in Li-p'ing Fu (Kweichow) were credited with a somewhat ingenious method of conducting the lectures. They put the responsibility
of the *hsiang-yüeh* meetings on the *pao-chia* heads, believing that
they could thereby "reap the complete fruits of the *pao-chia.* "[66] These
heads expounded, in simple language, the maxims of the Sacred Edict
and selected provisions of the imperial code to villagers who gathered
in the various rural markets. At the sound of a gong the market-goers
assembled around a platform, temporarily set up with a few tables,
and listened to the sermons "in respectful silence." Business could
be attended to only after the completion of the lectures. [67]

In many instances local gentry offered their cooperation. The gentry of the thirteen rural areas of P'an-yü (Kwangtung) contributed
funds and in 1777 built a *kung-so* (public meeting hall) in which a copy
of the Sacred Edict was "reverentially kept" and where villagers old
and young gathered to listen to the sermons. [68] A wealthy member of
the gentry of Nan-hai (Kwangtung) contributed money to establish in
1871 a *shan-t'ang,* a charity organization which, besides maintaining
free schools and engaging in charitable activities, sponsored periodic
lectures on the Sacred Edict. [69] Chung-i Hsiang, a prosperous rural
area of Fu-shan (Kwangtung), had several *shan-t'ang* among which
was Wan-shan T'ang (Hall of Ten Thousand Charities) built in 1881
by cooperative efforts of the local gentry. This organization engaged
lecturers to expound the Sacred Edict and other texts on the practice
of Confucian morality. [70] In Hua Hsien (Kwangtung) a retired official
established the T'ung-shan Hsiang-yüeh and erected a building to be
used for giving the semimonthly lectures. [71]

An Appraisal of the *Hsiang-yüeh* Lecture System

There is no doubt that the *hsiang-yüeh* as an instrument of popular
indoctrination produced some desirable results—desirable, that is,
from the imperial point of view. When the person giving the lectures
was endowed with the gift of felicitous expression or could impress
his listeners with his sincerity or zeal, the sonorous platitudes of the
imperial maxims might acquire concrete meaning and strike a re-
sponsive chord in the breast of the average peasant. An instance recorded by a local historian will serve to illustrate how effective a
hsiang-yüeh lecture could be. Chiang Pai-li, a peasant of T'ien-p'an
village in the district of Yang-chiang (Kwangtung), had five sons. He
did not amount to anything and the straitened circumstances of his
family forced the younger generation to live apart from their parents.
Chiang Chung-yeh, a child of his fifth son, inherited the family profession and its lack of prosperity. A turn in his life came on the fifteenth day of the eighth month of the fifth year of Chia-ch'ing (1800),
when he attended a *hsiang-yüeh* lecture in his native village. The

preacher told the story of the Ch'en clan of Chiang-chou, one of the illustrations used in the Amplified Instructions, according to which some members of this clan achieved wealth by honest work and made it possible for its seven hundred kinsfolk to live together. The young peasant was moved to the depths of his heart and said to himself, "Can I not also achieve what the Ch'ens accomplished?" From that day on he worked harder than ever and accumulated a moderate wealth to bring together and support all his kin. [72]

In other instances *hsiang-yüeh* lecturers by the force of their personality or enthusiasm exerted tangible moral influence upon their neighbors. Ch'en Kuei, son of a village scholar and a regular *kung-sheng* of the year 1698, served as *hsiang-yüeh* for more than ten years in his home village. "He encouraged good men and instructed his neighbors so successfully that there was not a single case of quarrel or litigation." Fang Tien-ching, a *kung-sheng* of the year 1710, was a man of great probity and integrity. "He took charge of *hsiang-yüeh* for more than thirty years, during which period the neighborhoods remained in tranquil harmony. There were at first a few rogues who tried to bully the villagers. But after patient and persistent persuasion, he made them change their conduct."[73] Li Chao-nien, a scholar unsuccessful in the examinations who purchased his official title, conducted *sheng-yü* lectures with such regularity and effectiveness that "few quarrels or litigations arose in his neighborhood."[74]

Under the historical conditions of the Chinese empire, the *hsiang-yüeh* was an attractive method of ideological control. It was perhaps the only possible method by which the influence of imperial Confucianism could be brought to bear on the vast rural populace.[75] But like other imperial institutions of rural control the *hsiang-yüeh* did not operate as effectively as the imperial rulers may have wished. For every claim that it operated well (as in the instances cited above), there were many that it did not. Allowing for the likelihood of official exaggeration in both directions, it is difficult to entertain any optimistic view of the effectiveness of the lecture system in the face of the predominant number of unfavorable statements concerning its operation.

Officials and some of the emperors repeatedly complained that there was a tendency for the rural lectures to degenerate into an empty formality. Western observers of the nineteenth century, who obviously had no reason to exaggerate either the merits or the demerits of the *hsiang-yüeh,* did not find it an effective institution. Huc, writing in the 1850's, conceded that "this custom, if seriously carried out, can only be laudable and useful"; but he added that "as it is done now, it is merely a vain ceremony." He continued:

. . . there are indeed in all the localities places appointed where the

Mandarins ought to instruct the people; they are called *Chan-yu-ting*
[shang-yü t'ing, Hall of Holy Instructions.] . : . but on the appointed day, the Mandarin does just walk in, smoke a pipe, drink a cup
of tea, and walk out again. [76]

W. E. Geil, an American traveler, remarked at the beginning of the
twentieth century that "the practice of reading the Maxims by the Mandarins had relapsed into 'innocuous desuetude.'"[77]

Opinions of many Chinese officials were no more encouraging than
those of Western writers. As early as 1694, shortly after the inception of the *hsiang-yüeh,* a retired magistrate of long experience recorded that most local officials of his own day treated the prescribed
lecture meetings as "an outworn routine," and conducted them only
occasionally. In some instances, he said, they did not bother to secure a regular place for the purpose and often made use of Buddhist
or Taoist temples. [78] It may be supposed that as a retired magistrate,
this writer was likely not only to have an intimate knowledge of the
actual situation but also to be in a position to appraise the institution
more or less disinterestedly. Another local official, writing early
in the eighteenth century, described the *hsiang-yüeh* of his time in
these words:

> On the morning of the first and fifteenth day of the month . . . [the
> local official] goes to the temple of the god of the city walls and moats.
> He wears his official vestment and sits gravely still, uttering not a
> single word—hardly distinguishable from a wooden idol. The master
> of ceremony, joined by the gentry and scholars, requests him to read
> the Sacred Edict once. The lecturer talks without making clear the
> meaning of the text; the audience listens without comprehending what
> is said. [At the close of the session] official and people disperse in
> a noisy jumble. [79]

Such scenes were witnessed in cities; the lectures were taken probably even less seriously in the countryside, if indeed they were given
at all.

Some of the emperors complained loudly that all was not well with
the *hsiang-yüeh.* The Ch'ien-lung emperor said in a rather lengthy
edict of 1740, "The semimonthly lectures amount to no more than a
mere formality. Words pass from the mouth [of the lecturer] to the
ears [of the listeners], but hardly is there genuine comprehension."[80]
Three years later, he said in another edict that although the Sacred
Edict and the Amplified Instructions were expounded to the people,
few persons actually practiced what was enjoined.

> When the semimonthly lectures are given in some corner of a city,
> the inhabitants of the nearby neighborhoods who gather to listen amount
> to no more than a few tens or a hundred persons; in the towns and vil-

lages where definite places are occasionally reserved for giving the lectures, the institution itself suffers remissness as time goes on. [81]

The Chia-ch'ing emperor, his immediate successor, lamented in an edict of 1809 that "during recent years local officials have come to regard [the *hsiang-yüeh*] as a matter of mere routine. In the worst cases they have allowed it to fall into disuse altogether."[82] The Tao-kuang, T'ung-chih, and Kuang-hsü emperors expressed the same sentiment in edicts issued in 1833, 1865, and 1876. [83] T'ung-chih was convinced that "the deterioration of the people's hearts and customs," observed especially during the turbulent mid-nineteenth century, was due to the fact that local functionaries had allowed the *hsiang-yüeh* to fall into desuetude.

Whatever may have been the intrinsic merits of the *hsiang-yüeh*, the majority of Chinese officials and quite a few of the emperors expressed disappointment in its performance. If we have to choose between this view and the view of the apparently optimistic minority, it seems safer to subscribe to the former, even if we do not care to go as far as some writers in saying that the lecture system had virtually ceased to function before the dynasty came to an end. [84] Moreover, even if we take the favorable reports at their face value, it is doubtful that we can regard the operation of the *hsiang-yüeh* as a success. The usefulness of any instrument of popular indoctrination has to be measured by the general effects it produces on the entire area of its operation and not by a relatively small number of instances. Judging by the conditions that prevailed in rural China of the nineteenth century and by the general pattern of behavior of rural inhabitants the *hsiang-yüeh* cannot be considered a success from the imperial point of view. A survey of some of the difficulties that confronted the *hsiang-yüeh* will partially explain why it could not operate effectively in general. One of the most obvious of these was the ineptitude or lack of time or interest on the part of the average official who had the direct responsibility of operating it. Officials of imperial China were rarely blessed with eloquence. Their efforts at spreading the influence of imperial Confucianism through oral discourses must have often proved futile. To many a magistrate who was burdened with hundreds of onerous official duties, the *hsiang-yüeh* must have appeared an unavailing nuisance. He could pay scrupulous attention to matters such as tax collection, banditry, murder, and litigation, but he was prone to neglect the semimonthly lecturing.

The difficulty of securing suitable persons to serve in the *hsiang-yüeh* in the thousands of towns and villages throughout the vast empire cannot be exaggerated. According to the regulations the *yüeh-cheng* and their assistants had to be literate and respectable individuals whose character was sufficiently fine to inspire confidence in their audiences. Obviously, such individuals, if any, could be found only among the gentry. This was the reason why *"yüeh-cheng* and *chih-yüeh* were originally selected from among *chü-jen, kung-sheng,* and *sheng-yüan, "*[85] although the law did not forbid commoners to serve as *hsiang-yüeh* heads. Experience showed that it was not easy to secure the service of titled scholars. For one thing, the inducement offered to the *hsiang-yüeh* personnel did not seem to be worth the trouble involved in the office. Citations for merit,[86] commendatory tablets, and material remuneration were promised as rewards for creditable service.[87] In a district of Kwangtung province *hsiang-yüeh* lecturers were decorated with an official button (probably of the lowest rank) and paid one or two candereens of silver for each lecture delivered.[88] In another, the *yüeh-cheng* received one tael for every month's service.[89] Gentry and scholars, particularly those who had achieved the *chü-jen* or *kung-sheng* degrees, usually had better ways of gaining prestige and riches; naturally, they were not attracted by the small honors or pittances dealt out to the village lecturers.[90] Those who offered their services therefore frequently must have been men of lesser calibre, whose social and moral influence on their fellow villagers or townsmen was limited or negligible. As an eighteenth-century writer said:

> *Yüeh-chang [yüeh-cheng]* nominated by the neighborhoods are either vulgar persons who own much property or decrepit elderly individuals of the countryside. None of these have any interest in public affairs. . . . This is the reason that the *hsiang-yüeh* has come to be regarded as a mere routine and nobody has attempted to effectuate it.[91]

The service of gentry or scholars in itself, however, did not constitute any guarantee of success. According to a nineteenth-century official who memorialized the throne regarding the proposal that *sheng-yüan* scholars be appointed in all rural localities to expound the Amplified Instructions:

> It has been ascertained that at the beginning of the present dynasty *yüeh-cheng* and *chih-yüeh* were instituted to take charge of the lectures. At first *chü-jen, kung-sheng,* or *sheng-yüan* were appointed to these posts. Soon afterwards, however, imperial approval was given to the recommendation of the Board of Rites that [untitled] scholars and commoners be equally eligible to these posts and that no definite number of lecturers be fixed for each rural area. . . . For in each local school scholars whose character and knowledge are both excellent do not number more than a few. These either study in the academies or make a living as private tutors. If a number of scholars are appointed to every rural area and each of these scholars is required to give several lectures every month . . . they would thereby suffer hardships.[92]

This official spoke expressly on behalf of scholars of excellent character and knowledge. At the same time he warned the imperial government of the existence of scholars of questionable character and doubtful learning who far outnumbered scholars of the "better" sort.

The problem of securing suitable personnel was perhaps most succinctly explained by Shen Yüeh-lin:

> At first gentry and scholars were appointed to the posts [of *hsiang-yüeh*]. These often relied on their immunities and privileges to indulge in outrageous behavior. When, in order to correct the mistake, common people were appointed instead, loafers and worthless persons took advantage of the posts to oppress rural inhabitants. [93]

Even waiving the question of personal character, the problem of selecting satisfactory lecturers was far from easy. The Ch'ing rulers, so far as available records indicate, were genuinely interested in inculcating basic precepts of imperial Confucianism on the minds of the rural populace. Obviously, their wishes could be carried out only when the lecturers were able to make their listeners understand what they said, or able at least to make their sermons interesting enough to attract a large number of people to the sessions. But the general run of lecturers did not show such ability. The traditional Chinese literati might be experts in composing "eight-legged essays," but seldom were they good speakers that could help "ignorant rustics" to appreciate what they said. It is no wonder, then, as one of the emperors admitted, that very few villagers presented themselves at the *hsiang-yüeh* meetings.

The fundamental obstacle that stood in the way of successful ideological control, however, was the unsatisfactory condition under which the bulk of the Chinese peasantry was condemned to live. The dire want and glaring inequities that were the lot of many villagers silently but indisputably controverted almost every one of the injunctions of imperial Confucianism. The Edict counseled harmony, diligence, economy, patience, and observance of good customs and laws. In a supplementary *hsiang-yüeh* text, one of the emperors urged wealthy subjects of his empire to have some consideration for the needs of their less fortunate neighbors. [94] But the fact remained that in a country where economic production was seldom sufficient to sustain all its inhabitants, where privileged families enjoyed prosperity at the expense of the unprivileged (even though it was only a limited prosperity), and where calamities often brought misery to many of the people, the practice of "virtue" and performance of duty became a luxury which not many could afford. On the other hand, believers in "false doctrines"—the White Lotus, the Nien, or the God-worshippers—promised "ignorant rustics" food for their empty stomachs and "heavenly kingdom" for their superstitious minds. Even though the promised material and spiritual comforts eventually were not fulfilled, the shibboleths of the insurgent "bandits" must have had in the ears of many villagers a truer ring than the lofty precepts of imperial Confucianism.

This is no mere conjecture. The Tao-kuang emperor noted in an edict of 1835 that "religious bandits" of Chihli, Honan, Shantung, Hunan, Kiangsi, and Kwangsi gathered themselves into marauding hordes, giving to their activities the attractive name *chün liang* (food equalization).[95] A leader of one of the rebel bands in Kwangtung presented their case in these words:

> We plebians were born in times of plenty and were once loyal people; our families are respectable in our village, and we practiced well-doing, and regarded property. Owing to a succession of rainy seasons, the farmers were unable to save the crops, and we had no capital for our business, so that people of all occupations were obliged to join the bandits. We came into the west province seeking a place to remain, when we met fellow townsmen in the same trouble as ourselves. So that we were forced to become bandits to save ourselves from starvation.[96]

The writer of this passage was presenting a petition to the government, not making a revolutionary manifesto; hence the rather conciliatory tone. The language of other insurgents could be quite violent, as is exemplified by the following declaration of a band of the Hung Society in Shao-chou (Kwangtung):

> The present dynasty are only Manchus, people of a small nation, but the power of their troops enabled them to usurp possession of China and take the revenue, from which it is plain that anyone may get money from China if they are powerful in warfare. . . . The Manchus get the revenues of the eighteen provinces and appoint officers who oppress the people; and why should we, natives of China, be excluded from levying money?[97]

The wrath of insurgent villagers was as often directed against land-owners as against government officials. An eyewitness of the occupation of Nanking by the Taipings pointed out that while peddlers, merchants, scholars, and people of other walks of life who were forced to join the rebels frequently ran away, those who remained loyal to the end were invariably rural inhabitants. He recorded the following conversation with some villagers dwelling in the vicinity of Nanking after the coming of the Taipings:

> People of the countryside are illiterate and hate government officials. When I asked them, "Were the officials corrupt? Did they misapply the laws?" they replied, "We don't know." "Why do you hate them?"

"Because they collected land taxes. " "Do the Long Hairs not collect taxes also ?" "We pay taxes in kind or money equivalents to the Long Hairs, but we no longer pay rent to our landlords. " "The land you till belongs to your landlords; why don't you pay them rent ?" "If we pay them rent, we shall not have enough. We have so many sons and grandsons each; how can we have enough ?" . . . "If you do not have enough, you should seek support by other means. " Answer: "There are too many people and there is no other means of making a livelihood; moreover, we do not have the money to make another livelihood. "[98]

The writer added: "I recall when I was in the Ts'ai village of Ch'en-hsü-ch'iao, I could not find a single copy of the official almanac; the presence of the Four Books and Five Classics must have been a rare phenomenon of the hoary past. The inhabitants were all illiterate. "

"To pacify the Yellow Turbans with the Book of Filial Piety" was an old Chinese pleasantry. To preach to half-hungry people, "Pay your taxes in order to dispense with official urging," "Hold economy in estimation in order to conserve your money and goods," "Cultivate peace and concord in your neighborhoods in order to prevent quarrels and litigations," was worse than a joke; it was sheer mockery.

It may be added that clever enemies of the government occasionally turned the *hsiang-yüeh* system to serve their own purposes. In an edict of 1865 the T'ung-chih emperor stated that in some districts of Hupeh province villagers and townsmen collected money, organized meetings, "burned incense and bound themselves by oath, under the pretext of conducting *hsiang-yüeh* lectures to expound the Sacred Edict. "[99]

Metamorphoses of the *Hsiang-yüeh*

In previous sections of the present study it has been shown that the *pao-chia* and *li-chia*, two other systems of imperial control, had a curious way of turning into something they were not originally designed to be. The *hsiang-yüeh* showed a similar tendency; at one time or another and in different localities, it assumed diverse functions other than the indoctrination of villagers and townsfolk.

The *hsiang-yüeh* was not an invention of the Ch'ing rulers; the name may be traced back to 1076, when a Confucian scholar wrote the *Lü-shih hsiang-yüeh* in which he laid down a plan for organizing a sort of village self-government. [100] He was influenced by the *Chou-li*, but his basic conception differed from that of the *Chou-li*. His *hsiang-yüeh* was to be a spontaneous, voluntary association of villagers for the fourfold purpose of common endeavor in morality, education, social intercourse, and economic assistance. It was not to be government-sponsored, as were the local units described in the *Chou-li*.

The Neo-Confucianist Chu Hsi liked the idea so well that he wrote an improved version of it about a century later. [101] Fang Hsiao-ju, a well-known scholar, and Wang Shou-jen, the famous philosopher-states-man, both of the Ming dynasty, echoed the *hsiang-yüeh* idea with important variations. [102] Wang's scheme, in particular, reverted to the ancient conception. [103] Whatever vicissitudes the *hsiang-yüeh* had undergone prior to its adoption by the founder of the Ch'ing dynasty in the middle of the seventeenth century, it was never intended to be exclusively a method of ideological control through popular indoctrination. [104] The *hsiang-yüeh* of the Ch'ing dynasty as it was originally instituted, while not an invention, was therefore a radical departure from tradition.

Historical circumstances, however, introduced changes in the Ch'ing system. Functions not directly related to indoctrination were assumed by the *hsiang-yüeh* and as time went on the original purpose which was assigned to it by the Ch'ing rulers was often forgotten.

In a few instances *hsiang-yüeh* heads were known to have gone beyond their duties as local preceptors and become arbiters of local affairs. This development seems to have been especially common in southern provinces. In Kwangtung, for example, villagers of certain localities gathered in the offices of the *hsiang-yüeh* to decide matters of common concern. [105] *Hsiang-yüeh* heads who displayed qualities of leadership sometimes acquired considerable influence among rural inhabitants. In one case the *hsiang-yüeh* head handled local matters with so much candor and ability that for several decades "he was feared and respected by villagers and his clansmen."[106] In certain localities of Kwangsi province the power and influence of the *hsiang-yüeh* outweighed those enjoyed by village elders and rural headmen—so much so that "they made arbitrary decisions concerning affairs and monopolized access to local affairs."[107]

A more frequent and important change was the assumption of *pao-chia* functions by the *hsiang-yüeh*, which thus turned from an instrument of ideological control into one of police control. This transformation, as noted by a well-known official, began to take place quite early—in some localities before the eighteenth century. The following passage from an essay on "The Careful Selection of *Hsiang-yüeh*," was written by Yü Ch'eng-lung around 1679:

> The imperial government instituted the *hsiang-yüeh*, expecting that virtuous elderly persons would be selected [to operate it]. . . . In each village there is a building for the *hsiang-yüeh* where the sixteen maxims of the Sacred Edict are to be expounded on the first and fifteenth days of the month. The purpose is to persuade men to do good and to forbear from doing evil. As to matters of crime detection and suppression, night watch, and village protection, the *pao-chia* is to be chiefly relied upon.

Unfortunately, however . . . when local officials order some villagers to be placed under arrest, yamen underlings, without [taking the trouble] to ascertain the addresses of the plaintiffs and defendants, usually go directly to the homes of the *hsiang-yüeh,* who are thus obliged to supply these agents with food and drink. If in any way they incur their displeasure, abusive language follows immediately. Furthermore, [the *hsiang-yüeh]* are regularly browbeaten and maltreated when they answer rollcall on the first and fifteenth days of the month. [In criminal cases] the *hsiang yüeh* are held responsible for any failure to bring in the culprits. . . . To make matters worse, in cases of petty litigation they are invariably designated as witnesses. . . . One case follows another . . . without one moment's peace. . . . As a consequence, respectable persons of ripe age despise the *hsiang-yüeh* as a servile office, and wealthy families regard it as a path to ruin. Whenever these are called to serve, they try every means to get themselves out [of the unacceptable appointments] by personal influence or bribery. On the other hand, shameless "bare sticks" seize every opportunity to get it, so that they can, working in collusion with yamen underlings, prey upon their fellow villagers. [108]

The process of the transformation of the lecture system into a police apparatus went on with quickened pace in the nineteenth century. Before long many local officials spoke of the *hsiang-yüeh* as if it had been the *pao-chia* and treated it accordingly. [109] The imperial government itself eventually forgot the lecturing function of the *hsiang-yüeh* and came to think of police surveillance as its "original" function, as the Tao-kuang emperor did. In an edict issued in 1830 he said:

The original purpose of setting up *hsiang-yüeh* in *chou* and *hsien* is to control the rural neighborhoods and to inspect the *p'ai* and *pao* registers [i.e., the *pao-chia* records]. If there are thieves, robbers, or bandits that break laws, heads of the *hsiang-yüeh* [in the localities concerned] are to report them to the authorities, so that they may be dealt with. [110]

It is understandable that a modern Chinese historian has found it impossible to say with certainty whether the *hsiang-yüeh* and the *pao-chia* were actually two distinct institutions or one system with divergent names. [111]

Another important change was the *hsiang-yüeh's* assumption of the defense functions of the *t'uan-lien,* the "regiment and drill" corps organized in villages, or as was often the case, the use of the *hsiang-yüeh* framework in organizing *t'uan-lien.* Such changes occurred in some localities quite early in the dynasty, and became increasingly prevalent in the middle of the nineteenth century. In Fu-shan Chen (Kwangtung) a number of elders organized a rural militia in 1647 to protect their villages against *Huang-t'ou tsei* (Yellow-head bandits).

This local force, the "Loyal and Righteous Corps," was disbanded
after a while and revived in 1655 to fight sea pirates. It was reorganized in 1662 and assumed the new appellation, the *"Hsiang-yüeh* of
the Loyal and Righteous."[112] When the British demanded the privilege of entering the city of Canton in 1842, the *hsiang-yüeh* around the
provincial capital enlisted volunteers to defend the city against the
"English barbarians." These volunteers were known as *yüeh-yung*,
a contraction of *ke yüeh hsiang-yung* (village braves of the several
yüeh).[113] In his campaign against the Taiping rebels Tseng Kuo-fan
found the *pao-chia* an indispensable foundation on which to build the
t'uan-lien. But as "men of upright character and honored status" did
not wish to demean themselves by assuming the titles of *ti-pao* or
pao-chia, Tseng decided to use the name *hsiang-yüeh* instead.[114] About
a generation later, Chang Chih-tung instructed inhabitants of Shansi
province to launch a system of rural self-defense against bandits,
which was also in effect a fusion of *hsiang-yüeh, pao-chia,* and *t'uan-
lien.*[115]

Fusion of *hsiang-yüeh* and *t'uan-lien* was reported in other provinces. In Po-pai (Kwangsi) the following arrangement was said to
have existed in the nineteenth century. A number of *ch'ang-kan* (permanent servicemen) were placed under the direction of *hsiang-yüeh,*
whose duty it was "to watch for roving bandits," and a number of
lien-yung (drilled braves) under the command of a *lien-tsung* (drill
general), who was responsible for "protecting the villages." The city
and rural areas were manned as follows:[116]

	City	Rural
Hsiang-yüeh	35	70
Ch'ang-kan	135	272
Lien-tsung	35	70
Lien-yung	328	656

In Lo-ch'uan (Shensi), according to a local historian, "Each *Hsiang*
appointed a *t'uan-tsung* [corps commander], popularly known as *lao-
tsung.* Later on the *t'uan-tsung* was changed to *hsiang-yüeh.*"[117]

In the overwhelming majority of instances in which the *hsiang-yüeh*
metamorphosed into rural self-defense organizations called *t'uan-
lien* or otherwise, the original function of expounding the Sacred Edict
and Amplified Instructions dropped out of sight. Occasionally, however, it was retained, as in some of the organizations in Kwangtung.
In Hua Hsien a local scholar with a purchased official title, "Upon
receiving an order to organize *t'uan-lien* . . . united more than ten
rural areas to form the T'ung-an Hsiang-yüeh. . . . He caused a
shan-t'ang [hall] to be built near the Lan-p'an Temple and invited

persons with clear voices to lecture on the Sacred Edict in the hall. "[118]

Perhaps the most curious change that took place in the rural lecture system was that reported by a contemporary sociologist in Taitou, a village in Shantung province:

> The *hsiang-yüeh* was the tax collector. Originally his chief duty was to convey to the villagers the Emperor's instructions as to how to be a filial son and to see that social customs and the people's daily life were in conformity with the Confucian ethics. Gradually the *hsiang-yüeh* became merely a political orderly for transmitting orders from the county government to the village and returning reports to them on village affairs. Finally even these circumscribed duties stopped and he became merely a tax collector, a position which did not command much respect. [119]

This, we believe, epitomized the functional transformation of the *hsiang-yüeh*.

HSIANG-YIN-CHIU AND OTHER WAYS OF HONORING OLD AGE

Lao-min and Lao-nung

Confucianism called for respect for old age. The Ch'ing emperors perceived in this tradition another useful means of ideological control. Elderly men are less prone than young ones to be revolutionaries. Persons who have genuine affection and respect for their elders are less likely to be interested in overthrowing the established order. Consequently, in addition to preaching veneration in the *hsiang-yüeh* lectures, the imperial authorities themselves undertook to display in a variety of ways their own attitude toward age, hoping thus to set an example to their subjects.

In the first place, the imperial government adopted a consistent policy of distributing material benefits to subjects who had attained a certain age. Such people were referred to in official language as *lao-min* (aged subjects) or *lao-jen* (aged people) who, as the records show, must have been at least over seventy *sui* to qualify for imperial munificence chiefly in the form of special gifts and exemption from labor services. The practice was definitely established by the K'ang-hsi emperor and kept up by his successors until a comparatively late time. [120] Provincial and local gazetteers usually recorded instances of such acts of beneficence in which elderly villagers and townsmen were given silver, silk, grain, and meat. According to the gazetteer of En-p'ing (Kwangtung), grain and silk were distributed to aged persons on seventeen occasions between 1688 and 1831. [121]

We have a few figures showing the extent of such imperial bounty. According to an official report submitted in 1726 by the *Hu-pu* to the emperor, 1,421,625 men and women between seventy and one hundred *sui* received silk and other goods with a total value of 890,000 taels, and rice amounting to 160,000 *shih*.[122] These recipients were all commoners. Officials, scholars, merchants, and Buddhist or Taoist bonzes were excluded. Obviously, the amount of benefit enjoyed by each recipient could not be very substantial but was enough to arouse the interest of local inhabitants. The following figures were supplied by the gazetteer of I-ch'eng (Shansi):[123]

Date	Recipients	Taels
1723	aged men	860
1724	aged women	1,030
1736	aged men	710
1752	men over 70 *sui*	583
1762	men over 70 *sui*	550

Whatever may have been the amount of material benefit to the recipients, the gifts bestowed upon *lao-min* served to give evidence of imperial consideration for age. The emperors never failed to exploit the propaganda value of this gesture of studied munificence by praising the "profound love and plenteous generosity" of their predecessors, resting assured that they themselves would later on be similarly glorified by their successors.

Unfortunately for the imperial rulers, however, the task of distributing the gifts was not always done properly by their servants. The institution of honoring age was soon spoiled by corrupt local officials and yamen underlings. Early in the eighteenth century the situation had become bad enough to come to imperial attention. The Yung-cheng emperor said in an edict of 1723:

> The purpose of presenting gifts to elderly persons is to honor age. The money expended in each *chou* and *hsien* amounts to several thousand [taels]. But officials from provincial treasurers down to magistrates deduct sums from this money [to line their own purses] and yamen underlings extort [bribes from the beneficiaries], with the result that each elderly person receives less than one-tenth of the allotted share.[124]

A method of demonstrating imperial benevolence thus became a source of official corruption. It is doubtful that the people were always convinced of the avowed high purpose of the gifts or that the recipients felt genuine gratitude toward the donors. Despite imperial injunctions to stop official malpractices and to ensure full delivery of the gifts, the situation did not improve. The institution of honoring age by distributing gifts became less and less significant as the dynasty wore on, and seems to have become no more than "an empty formality" by the middle of the nineteenth century.

Imperial consideration for age was also shown by bestowing non-material honors upon elderly subjects. One of the most common practices was to confer official titles or ranks on those who were able to secure the recommendation of local officials. [125] Other manifestations of imperial favor included the privilege of hanging *pien* (honorific tablets) over the gates and erecting *fang* (arches of commendation) in front of the houses of their recipients. Regulations were drawn up by the Board of Rites defining the qualifications, procedures, and ceremonial forms of *ching-piao ch'i-shou* (giving distinction to longevity). [126] Local gazetteers recorded numerous cases in which aged persons received such honors from the imperial, provincial, or local governments. In Pa-ling (Hunan), for example, a nonagenarian received an official button during the reign of Ch'ien-lung; another received an eighth-rank button in the same period; while a grand old man of 105 *sui* was accorded in 1837 the privilege of erecting a *fang* to celebrate his birthday anniversary. [127] In Hsiang-shan, (Kwangtung) a large number of aged persons received honors and distinctions of various descriptions, the latest instances occurring in 1911. [128]

Special categories of aged persons were sometimes singled out for imperial honors. Beginning with the reign of Ch'ien-lung, aged scholars who had failed to attain their aspirations were awarded suitable degrees or official titles. [129] Aged farmers, too, became objects of imperial grace. The practice of honoring *lao-nung* (aged or senior farmers) was inaugurated by the Yung-cheng emperor in 1724 when he decreed that "one or two elderly farmers in each village who are noted for their diligence be selected for suitable rewards."[130] Later in the same year the emperor ordered that "one such farmer should be recommended by the magistrate of each *chou* or *hsien* concerned, and an official button of the eighth rank be conferred upon him."[131] His immediate successor, the Ch'ien-lung emperor, kept up this practice, [132] which eventually became an established institution defined by imperial regulations. [133]

We have not been able to ascertain whether these devices had produced the desired effects upon inhabitants of the countryside. The institution of "senior farmers" seems to have fallen into desuetude after the reign of Ch'ien-lung. At any rate we have evidence that during the period of their existence both these devices gave rise to fraudulent and corrupt practices. The most common fraud resorted to be frustrated scholars was to report themselves much older than they actually were in order to qualify for the degrees or titles granted by special imperial favor. Since there were no birth certificates to prove their true ages, the attestation of local educational officials was often sufficient to turn a middle-aged scholar into a septuagenarian. This attestation could be readily obtained by bribery or personal influence.

The imperial authorities sought to put a stop to such fraudulent practices by raising the age qualification from seventy to eighty *sui* and later by requiring that a *sheng-yüan* scholar must have failed in at least three successive examinations before he was eligible for a *chü-jen* degree by grace.[134] These measures made deception more difficult but could hardly eradicate it altogether.

The nomination of senior farmers also afforded opportunities for local corruption. The Yung-cheng emperor said, in an edict of 1729:

> When we ordered *chou* and *hsien* [magistrates] to recommend aged peasants who are to receive official buttons to honor their persons, Our intention was to encourage the people to devote their energies to agriculture, which is their basic occupation, and to return to a state of simplicity and prudence. . . . But We hear that in the provinces when senior farmers are recommended, *chou* and *hsien* magistrates rely solely on the recommendation of gentry and scholars; the latter receive bribes from dishonest persons [who seek their recommendation]. . . . After having obtained the honors appertaining to official buttons, these persons capitalize upon them to consolidate their powerful, rascally influence. Such practices go directly contrary to Our intention. . . . Governors-general and governors of the provinces are hereby ordered to investigate thoroughly, to dismiss all senior farmers who do not deserve the honor and who have engaged themselves in undesirable conduct, and to replace them with worthy persons selected anew.[135]

A few months later, the imperial government decided at the suggestion of a provincial official that beginning in 1729 the appointment of senior farmers was to be made once in three years instead of annually as originally planned.[136] The reason offered for this move was that it would make the honor more attractive by making it more difficult to obtain. The real motive may have been to reduce opportunities for fraud.

The institutions designed to honor age thus proved somewhat disappointing to the imperial rulers. Whether the honor conferred was economic or nonmaterial, it was often vitiated by fraud. When elderly persons themselves participated in the deception, which was often widely known to local inhabitants, the imperial maxim, "honor and respect your elders and superiors," must have sounded rather hollow in the ears of many a young man.

Hsiang-yin-chiu

The *hsiang-yin-chiu* (or simply *hsiang-yin*), the community drinking ceremony, was a ceremonial affair required by law to be held at regular intervals in various *chou* and *hsien* of the provinces. It should be distinguished from the imperial feasts occasionally held in Peking to which aged people were invited to help celebrate the birthdays of some of the earlier emperors. [137] The latter were intended mainly to enhance the festive spirit of the occasion, whereas the former was at bottom a device of ideological control. Although the drinking ceremony was not held in villages, nor were its "guests" restricted to rural inhabitants, its theory and practice reveal some interesting aspects of imperial control.

Like many another institution adopted by the Ch'ing rulers, the drinking ceremony had its origin in classical Confucianism and was practiced by dynasties long before them. [138] The Ch'ing system as set up in 1644[139] was as follows:[140] On the fifteenth day of the first month and the first day of the tenth, the *hsiang-yin* ceremony was to be conducted in all the provinces. The chief official of the locality was to act as host. An elderly person of eminent virtue was to be invited as *Ta-pin* (Grand Guest, sometimes known as *Cheng-pin*, Principal Guest), others of lesser eminence as *Chieh-pin* (Intermediate Guests), and persons of still less eminence as *Chung-pin* (Ordinary Guests) or *Ch'i-pin* (Elderly Guests). The local educational official served as *Szu-cheng* (master of ceremonies), and a number of *sheng-yüan* scholars were present to announce the ceremonial items, to pour wine into the ritual cups, and to read aloud the imperial edict relevant to the occasion. The master of ceremonies opened the meeting with these prescribed remarks:

> Respectfully considering that the Imperial Court following an ancient tradition established the *hsiang-yin-chiu* in order to emphasize the importance of instruction through ceremonial practice but not to enjoy food and drink, we, old and young, should persuade and encourage one another so that subjects will be perfectly loyal and sons completely dutiful; seniors and juniors will maintain proper order among themselves, and elder brothers will be friendly while younger ones deferential; kinsmen will be affectionate, and neighbors on good terms with one another. We shall never neglect [these duties] lest we bring shame upon our forefathers.

After the host and guests had emptied their first cup of wine, a *lu-ling an* (decree desk) was placed in the center of the hall. One of the *sheng-yüan* scholars stepped forward and read aloud this imperial decree:

> . . . [The object of] *hsiang-yin-chiu* is to show the proper respect for the aged and consideration for the virtuous, and to keep away the unrighteous and the perverse. Persons of advanced age and outstanding virtue are to occupy seats of honor, and others are to have places proper to their ages. Men who have committed offenses against the law are not allowed to intrude upon the seats intended for good and obedient subjects. [141]

The whole affair was artificial and stiff to the utmost degree; the ban-
queters could hardly mistake it for a convivial gathering. In spite of
its name there was not much drinking and the food was frequently bad.
The only enjoyment the guests might derive from the occasion was
the prestige of being invited by the local official. But even this sometimes became a doubtful privilege. The banquet was to be held, according to regulations, in the city where the local yamen was situated,
although villagers might be invited as guests. The original rule of
selecting the guests was modified in 1753 so that the Grand Guest was
to be chosen from among elderly and virtuous *shen-shih* (gentry).
Commoners could be honored as Intermediate and Ordinary Guests.
Government officials who happened to be in their own native cities
or villages might attend the banquet, not as guests but as *tsun* (honorary hosts) to assist the official host "to entertain" the guests. [142]
This rule, especially the part concerning the social status of the
guests, was variously interpreted by local officials, resulting in divergent criteria of selection. Some chose the Grand Guest from the
gentry, Intermediate Guests from local scholars, and Ordinary Guests
from Commoners. [143] Others thought[144] that only retired officials and
titled scholars were qualified for Grand and Intermediate Guests. [145]
Still others dispensed with the gentry qualification altogether, making
commoners eligible for all the banquet seats. [146]

As a result, the line drawn by the imperial government between
gentry on the one hand and commoners on the other became blurred.
In some instances commoners actually achieved the honor of Grand
Guest. [147] A distinction in costume, however, was maintained between
guests of different social status. Only persons with official rank or
titles could wear official vestments, whereas commoners must be
contented with "bright-hued ordinary dress,"[148] irrespective of the
seats they occupied in the ceremony.

We have no data to determine the exact proportion of guests with
gentry status to those with commoner status. Evidence seems to indicate that while the former outnumbered the latter among the Grand
Guests, [149] in some localities the latter gained in number among the
Ordinary Guests. [150] Table 12 for Hsiang-shan (Kwangtung)[151] may
support a further conjecture that while the gentry often participated in
the ceremony, most of those who did were not of the highest status.
Here the number of persons possessing gentry status exceeded those
whose status was not indicated and who presumably were commoners.
It is interesting to note that among the former group a number were
petty officials, one was *chü-jen,* and none was indicated as having attained *chin-shih,* the acme of scholarly success. Exactly half of the
scholars were *chien-sheng,* a status which could be purchased and
did not carry much prestige.

Hsing-an Hsien (Kiangsi) presented another illuminating picture.

TABLE 12
STATUS OF *HSIANG-YIN* GUESTS IN HSIANG-SHAN

Reign	Petty official	Retired official	*Chü-jen*	*Kung-sheng*	*Sheng-yüan*	*Chien-sheng*	*Wu-chü*	*Wu-sheng*	Unspecified	TOTAL
Shun-chih									5	5
K'ang-hsi				2	3				8	13
Ch'ien-lung		2		2		3	1	1	7	16
Chia-ch'ing	9		1		1	7			2	20
Tao-kuang	1			2		1			3	7
TOTAL	10	2	1	6	4	11	1	1	25	61

Between 1644 and 1862, 124 guests were invited to the ceremonial
banquet, among whom only twenty-nine were said to have possessed
kung-ming (merits and titles). These included ten *kung-sheng*, five
sheng-yüeh, ten *chien-sheng*, and four *wu-sheng*. [152] While we cannot jump to the conclusion that an overwhelming majority of the guests
in this district were commoners, it seems quite sure that the majority of them did not enjoy great scholarly or official eminence. We
should note that it was not because this locality suffered from such
a dearth of scholars that few of them could be invited to the banquets.
A local historian informs us that during the period under consideration Hsing-an boasted no less than 227 scholars who had attained the
higher degrees, among whom were two *chin-shih*, 71 *chü-jen*, and
154 *kung-sheng* of various categories. [153] The number of these scholars was almost double that of all the guests of *hsiang-yin;* the number of *chü-jen* amounted to more than half. But none of the *chin-shih*
or *chü-jen* participated in the ceremony. Ch'ang-ning, another district of the same province, showed a similar tendency: among all the
49 guests invited at different times, only three were *chien-sheng*, five
were fathers of *chien-sheng*, and one was the son of a *sheng-yüan*. [154]
In other words, less than 20 per cent of the guests had scholarly status
or were members of scholarly families. In Po-pai (Kwangsi) among
the 165 guests only six were scholars; two *sheng-yüan*, three *chien-
sheng*, and one *wu-sheng*. The rest were mostly described as "elderly
men," "scholars seeking no government office," and "offspring of local
worthies." [155] A reasonable guess is that all these were commoners.

Even in Nan-ch'ang (Kiangsi), where unusually keen interest in the
drinking ceremony was manifested, the distribution of guests of different social status told a similar story (Table 13). [156]

TABLE 13
HSIANG-YIN GUESTS IN NAN-CH'ANG HSIEN

Reign	Number of Guests	Guests with Ranks or Titles	No Ranks or Titles Indicated
Shun-chih	5	1	4
K'ang-hsi	31	6	25
Yung-cheng	1	0	1
Ch'ien-lung	159	19	140
Chia-ch'ing	34	16	18
Tao-kuang	102	26	76
Hsien-feng	74	13	61
T'ung-chih	11	4	7
Kuang-hsü	119	60	59
Hsüan-t'ung	92	29	63
TOTAL	628	174	454

Guests with ranks or titles, in other words, amounted to less than one third of the total, although there was an exceptionally high proportion of persons with scholarly degrees above the *chü-jen* among the guests invited in the earlier years of the dynasty.

Table 14 shows the social status of the Grand Guests of this district:

TABLE 14
STATUS OF *HSIANG-YIN* GRAND GUESTS IN NAN-CH'ANG HSIEN

Reign	*Chu-shih* or *Nei-ko chung shu*	Magistrate	Local Educational Official	Ass't Instructor, Imperial College	Petty Official	Miscellaneous Titles	*Han-lin*	*Chü-jen*	*Kung-sheng*	*Sheng-yüan*	*Chien-sheng*	Unspecified	TOTAL
Shun-chih												1	1
K'ang-hsi			4						1	1			6
Yung-cheng													0
Ch'ien-lung		1	2				1	2	13			1	20
Chia-ch'ing		1		1				2	4				8
Tao-kuang	1		4			1	1		5			4	16
Hsien-feng		1	1						1		1	5	9
T'ung-chih									2				2
Kuang-hsü	1				4	1	1		11	2		3	23
Hsüan-t'ung								1	4	4		2	11
TOTAL	2	3	11	1	4	2	3	5	41	7	1	16	96

The presence of a few officials above the seventh rank (*chu-shih*, sixth rank; magistrate and educational official, seventh rank) and some scholars above the *chü-jen* indicates that the drinking ceremony was more highly regarded in this district than in many others. But these local celebrities constituted a minority of the total number of guests invited, as well as of the total number of scholars holding such degrees. Between 1647 and 1910 no less than 159 scholars in this district attained *chin-shih;* between 1646 and 1909, 752 earned their *chü-jen;* and between 1644 and 1910, 592 were awarded *kung-sheng* of various categories. [157] Thus only three out of 159 *chin-shih*, five out of 752 *chü-jen*, and forty-one out of 592 *kung-sheng* participated in the *hsiang-yin*.

The paucity of guests of higher social status was not due to mere accident. It seems symptomatic of some weakness in the institution itself. We have already indicated the lack of a uniform standard for selecting the guests. This would not have been a bad thing if the selections were carefully made. However, from a comparatively early time local officials often allowed the ceremony to degenerate into a farce. In a directive issued in the mid-seventeenth century a provincial educational official of Chiang-nan pointed out that the selection was currently made in the most careless manner:

> Local magistrates rely on the nominations made by the district educational official, who in turn leaves the choice entirely to the *sheng-yüan* scholars. Bonded recommendations open the door wide to bribery, and despicable fellows are honored as guests. As a result, persons who have self-respect are ashamed to associate themselves [with such guests], while onlookers laugh at [the ceremony]. [158]

Another official described conditions in a prefecture of Kiangsi province:

> I am informed that hitherto in nominating the Grand Guest wealth has been the only consideration and virtue completely neglected. A person with substantial property is selected and honored in this ceremony. Yamen underlings of the prefecture and district, gatekeepers of the local educational official, and unscrupulous *sheng-yüan* scholars all treat this man as a piece of profitable property, from whom they can freely extort money. . . . Therefore, whenever a wealthy person hears [that he is considered for nomination], he avoids it as if running away from a fire. [159]

Huang Liu-hung, a well-known magistrate, described the general situation in the second half of the seventeenth century:

> Regulations call for giving [the banquet] twice in every year. . . . But officials usually regard it as a mere formality. They conduct the ceremony at irregular intervals; some of them do not bother to conduct it once in their entire term of office. As is known, expenses for the banquets are legally included among the items of local budgets, to be met by revenue allotted to local governments. Do these officials, then, put the funds into their own pockets and let this important cer-

emony lapse into oblivion? As to those officials who occasionally conduct it, they allow yamen clerks to dictate the choice, and *hsiang-yüeh* and *ti-pao* to draw up the lists [of guests]. No regard is paid to the personal character of the participants in this ceremony. Only persons whose families are in affluent circumstances are chosen. After the banquets are over [the guests] have to present substantial gifts to the officials, educational as well as administrative, in order to "express their gratitude." Meanwhile, other persons who have helped in the ceremony and yamen clerks, every one of them, extort money from the guests. . . . Consequently, when a villager hears that his name is included [in the list of guests], he feels as if he is falling bodily into fire and hot water. Some of them make open confession of their sins, or take off their clothing and show the scars left on their bodies as a result of punishment by blows, [thus to disqualify themselves for this doubtful honor]. Is not all this very ridiculous? Persons who have a modicum of self-respect, therefore, consider the *hsiang-yin* a matter of no importance and are ashamed to attend it. [160]

This state of affairs seems to have persisted in the eighteenth century. A governor of Shensi said in a 1746 directive:

Some [magistrates] receive bribes and make nominations indiscriminately; others demand money from persons whose names they include [in the list of guests]; still others who desire gains make supernumerary nominations and do not report their superiors. They also permit assistant magistrates, jail wardens, educational officials, clerks, servants to extort money. The food and wine are bought at below-market prices. [161]

A provincial educational official of Chekiang memorialized the throne in 1762:

In the populous and wealthy localities of the provinces [local officials] regard [the *hsiang-yin*] as a matter of little account. They do not conduct it for a period of several decades. In one or two obscure, small districts it is held twice a year, and a few guests are invited on each occasion. . . . Persons who have criminal records, or are well known for their strong appetite for litigation, or are noted for their mean conduct, are allowed to attend it, provided they belong to fairly rich families. [162]

A few years earlier, in 1737, the Board of Rites itself acknowledged the general decay of the banquet institution and offered an explanation for official remissness:

If the local officials concerned select unworthy guests out of personal consideration, they have of course failed in their duties. But when sometimes persons who really are seniors in virtue as well as in years receive the invitation, depraved individuals make plans to extort money from them before the ceremony takes place, and try

> further to blackmail them after it is over, by pointing out whatever
> blemishes may mar the character of the guests and charging that the
> selection has been incorrectly made. As a result, local officials who
> anticipate the troubles that may be entailed, prefer not to give the
> banquet. [163]

The Board did not specify who these "depraved individuals" were.
It is difficult to ascertain whether the practices described occurred
only in some localities or were common throughout the country. It
is obvious, however, that long before the eighteenth century came to
an end the *hsiang-yin* had little attraction for persons of moderately
high social status. Gentry of some consequence avoided the ceremony
because it was beneath their dignity to attend. [164]

This is not saying that the *hsiang-yin* did not appear tempting to
some other individuals. Obscure townsmen and villagers who aspired
to local eminence and possessed no better means to attain it were
glad to accept an invitation to this official exercise, making the most of
it to open the first door to their goal. [165] These were usually persons
without *kung-ming* (merits and titles), to whom any sort of official
honor, real or imaginary, spelled distinction. Their anxiousness to
climb the social ladder is evinced by the fact that some of the commoner guests arrogated to themselves the privilege of wearing official buttons. For example, it was reported in the 1760's that all
elderly persons invited to the *hsiang-yin* in Chekiang province wore
gold buttons of the eighth or ninth rank, even though such a privilege
was not granted to them by the government. [166] The imperial authorities thereupon forbade all commoners attending the drinking ceremony
to wear official buttons or costumes. [167] We do not know what effect
this new ruling had upon the commoner guests. It is fairly certain
that in so far as invitations to the banquet were extended to that type
of person who enjoyed wearing unauthorized official insignia, its at-
tractiveness to persons of higher social status must have been further diminished. Moreover, the food and drink it offered hardly whetted the appetite of persons who did attend. [168] The Yung-cheng emperor said in an edict of 1723 that the banquet was in general "very
carelessly prepared."[169] The funds provided for it were very meager,
seldom exceeding ten taels in any given locality; in some places the
amount was less than one tael for the two banquets to be given each
year. The following table, containing figures culled from a few local
gazetteers, will give us a glimpse into the situation:[170]

Hsiang-yin Funds (in taels)

Nan-ch'ang Hsien (Kiangsi)	15.69
Pa-ling Hsien(Hunan)	12.00
Cheng-ting Hsien (Chihli)	12.00

Hsiang-yin Funds (in taels)

Hsiang-fu Hsien (Honan)	9.51
Yen-ch'ing Chou (Chihli)	8.25
Wei Chou (Chihli)	8.00
Hun-yüan Chou (Shansi)	8.00
Ch'u Chou (Anhwei)	8.00
Po-pai Hsien (Kwangsi)	7.00
Jung Hsien (Kwangsi)	7.00
Ch'ang-ning Hsien (Kiangsi)	5.10
Hsin Hsien (Shantung)	2.19
T'eng Hsien (Shantung)	1.64
T'ung-kuan Hsien (Shensi)	1.54
Lo-ch'uan Hsien (Shensi)	.95

It may be noted that the imperial government itself betrayed its decreasing interest in the ceremony by reducing its expenses or sometimes by making them unavailable altogether. For example, the original quota for Nan-ch'ang Hsien was 31.38 taels. This was cut in half at an unspecified date. The quota for Pa-ling Hsien was originally 24.00, similarly reduced around 1657.[171] The funds provided for Hsiang-fu Hsien were canceled in 1675 and were not restored until eight years later.[172] In Jung Hsien the *hsiang-yin* funds were permanently abolished.[173] During the years of unrest in the nineteenth century the money available for the banquet in various parts of the empire was generally turned over to the provincial treasurers, to be used for military expenditure. That this practice had received imperial approval is shown by an 1843 memorial submitted by the Board of Rites.[174]

It is not surprising, therefore, that local officials were often unenthusiastic about the drinking ceremony. In many places it was not held at all for long stretches of time. One local historian writing at the close of the nineteenth century, said: "Hitherto we have no knowledge of the *hsiang-yin;* ever since the period of turbulence it has not been practiced, and this is a long while."[175] Another, writing in the last years of the dynasty, expressed his regret that even in Kwangtung province, "a celebrated and cultured country," this ceremony was seldom witnessed.

> During the reigns of Chia-ch'ing and Tao-kuang of the present dynasty, local officials used the axiom "better to default than to abuse" as a pretext and ceased to conduct this ceremony. . . . After Tao-kuang times, we have not heard that anyone has ever performed this ceremony in our Kwangtung.[176]

Even in provinces where the *hsiang-yin* seems to have been better established, it was still not practiced consistently. In Kiangsi, for instance, a mid-eighteenth-century provincial official discovered that the magistrates were mostly negligent. [177] In localities like Nan-chang where the situation was better than average, actual practice still fell short of the legal requirements. This may be seen from the number of guests invited in this district at various times, from the beginning to the end of the dynasty, as indicated in Table 15:[178]

TABLE 15

NUMBER OF *HSIANG-YIN* GUESTS IN NAN-CH'ANG HSIEN

Reign	Number of Years	Number of Guests	Average Number of Guests per Year
Shun-chih	18	5	0.28
K'ang-hsi	61	31	0.50
Yung-cheng	13	1	0.07
Ch'ien-lung	60	159	2.65
Chia-ch'ing	25	34	1.36
Tao-kuang	30	102	3.40
Hsien-feng	11	74	6.72
T'ung-chih	13	11	0.84
Kuang-hsü	34	119	3.50
Hsüan-t'ung	3	92	30.66
TOTAL	268	628	2.34

Remembering that regulations called for at least two ceremonies a year and that one Grand Guest, at least one Intermediate Guest, and a number of Ordinary Guests were to be invited on each occasion, the average for over two and a half centuries was 2.34 guests per year (namely, 1.17 guests per occasion if two banquets were given each year); for 190 years the average number of guests per year was below three. Curiously, the average for the last three years of the dynasty suddenly jumped to an unprecedented high of 30.66. A reasonable guess is that this was the result of laxity in selection.

Other localities showed even less interest in the *hsiang-yin*. Table 16 shows the situation in Hsing-an (Kiangsi). [179] Hsiang-shan (Kwangtung) made an even poorer showing (Table 17), where for a period of almost two centuries the average number of guests per year remained below one. [180]

It should not be supposed that the actual number of guests attending each ceremony in a given locality necessarily approximated the average number of guests present in all ceremonies conducted in one reign period or in the entire dynastic period. Quite often local magistrates failed to give the banquet according to the schedule twice each year. The small numbers of guests by periods reported in these and

TABLE 16
HSIANG-YIN GUESTS IN HSING-AN

Reign	Number of Years	Number of Guests	Average Number of Guests per Year
Shun-chih	18	4	0.22
K'ang-hsi	61	2	0.03
Yung-cheng	13	4	0.31
Ch'ien-lung	60	15	0.25
Chia-ch'ing	25	5	0.20
Tao-kuang	30	79	2.63
Hsien-feng	11	4	0.36
TOTAL	218	113	0.52

TABLE 17
HSIANG-YIN GUESTS IN HSIANG-SHAN

Reign	Number of Years	Number of Guests	Average Number of Guests per Year
Shun-chih	18	5	0.27
K'ang-hsi	61	13	0.21
Ch'ien-lung	60	16	0.26
Chia-ch'ing	25	20	0.80
Tao-kuang	30	7	0.23
TOTAL	194	61	0.31

other localities may have been partly due to this failure. The actual number of guests invited to some of the occasions may have been larger than is suggested by the averages. We have, however, a concrete example in which the number of guests who took part in each of the *hsiang-yin* banquets was not more than three or four. Table 18 shows the situation in Jung Hsien (Kwangsi), from 1738 to 1763.[181]

Nor should we presume that the records contained in many of the local gazetteers (our main source of information) are necessarily complete. The compiler of the 1897 edition of the gazetteer of Jung Hsien (Kwangsi) made no reference to the drinking ceremony after 1763 (Ch'ien-lung 28). The 1880 edition of the gazetteer of Yen-chou Fu (Chekiang) supplies some data on this institution in the localities of this prefecture. Many of the instances recorded, however, were undated; a few of them were said to have taken place during or before the Ch'ien-lung reign. No record was made for two of the six districts.[182] It is difficult to say whether the silence of these and other local historians was due to inadvertent omission or to the fact that

TABLE 18
HSIANG-YIN GUESTS IN JUNG-HSIEN

Year, Day, Month	Number of Guests			Total
	Grand	Intermediate	Ordinary	
1738 1st of 10th	1	1	1	3
1747 15th of 2nd	1	1	1	3
1748 15th of 2nd	1	1	1	3
1st of 10th	1	1	1	3
1749 15th of 2nd	1	1	1	3
1st of 10th	1	1	1	3
1750 15th of 2nd	1	1	1	3
1751 15th of 2nd	1	1	1	3
1st of 10th	1	1	1	3
1752 15th of 2nd	1	1	1	3
1st of 10th	1	1	1	3
1753 15th of 2nd	1	1	1	3
1st of 10th	1	1	1	3
1754 15th of 2nd	1	1	1	3
1st of 10th	1	1	1	3
1755 date unspecified	1	1	1	3
1758 date unspecified	1	1	1	3
1762 date unspecified	1	1	2	4
1763 15th of 2nd	1	1	2	4
1st of 10th	1	1	2	4

no ceremony was actually conducted. Occasionally, compilers confessed that the records were incomplete. The 1932 edition of the gazetteer of Chao-p'ing (Kwangsi) furnishes information concerning the *hsiang-yin* up to 1760. The compiler indicated that "no records were made after the twenty-sixth year of Ch'ien-lung" (1761). [183] In fact, a large number of local gazetteers merely gave the *hsiang-yin* regulations without indicating whether the ceremony was actually held. Figures derived from the gazetteers cannot therefore be regarded as accurate indices to actual conditions. We may reasonably surmise, however, that in all probability the dwindling significance of the drinking ceremony in many localities had persuaded some compilers that to make a record was hardly worth the ink.

In some instances the *hsiang-yin* became virtually a private affair, financed by the local gentry on their own initiative or at the request of local officials. When the government funds for the ceremony were diverted to military purposes in 1843, the Board of Rites, unwilling to let the institution die out, ruled that "any local official that desires to keep up the tradition in order to stress the importance of propriety and courteousness may provide the banquet with funds contributed by himself."[184] We do not know how many officials carried out this rule. But in some places the continuation of the "tradition" had already become one of the gentry activities. As early as 1702 the gentry of Fu-shan, a town in Kwangtung, initiated the drinking ceremony, which was enacted once every year. It was revived in 1799, conducted regularly in a hall built by some members of the gentry, and continued until early in the nineteenth century.[185] A mid-nineteenth-century village scholar of Nan-hai (Kwangtung) contributed several hundred taels to finance the *hsiang-yin* banquets and the village school.[186] The ceremony was introduced into Chen-hsiung Chou (Yunnan) in 1838 by the local gentry at the suggestion of the magistrate.[187]

Whatever may have been the extent of gentry promotion of *hsiang-yin* banquets (it seems to have been quite limited), the results were negligible. Since villagers generally did not regard participation in the banquet ceremony as a true honor, the ideological influence which it might exert on the countryside was bound to be slight. It could not have any important meaning to the majority of the peasants, tillers of the soil, who had matters other than "honoring age" to worry about. To the village elite, who already possessed prestige greater than that of occupying seats in a feast which offered little wine to quench their thirst and not much food for thought, the *hsiang-yin* was without attraction even if it did not entail extortion or blackmail. By the very nature of the case, this time-worn imperial institution at its very best could have only a limited appeal to the people. At its worst, it lowered the prestige of the government, imperial and local, in the eyes of the rural inhabitants, instead of enhancing it.

TZ'U-SSU: LOCAL SACRIFICES

The Purpose and Forms of Official Sacrifices

The most subtle attempt at ideological control made by the Ch'ing rulers was their extensive application of the ancient principle, "instruction through worship." Whatever had been the attitude of the emperors themselves toward religion, there is ample ground for believing that they made use of religious sacrifices to reinforce other methods of influencing the minds of their subjects. Besides building temples and shrines in the imperial capital and personally performing sacrificial rites, they instituted various sacrifices in every *chou* and *hsien* of the empire, requiring government functionaries and encouraging the people to participate. The number of such sacrifices was quite large. They were classified officially into *ta ssu* (grand sacrifices), *chung ssu* (middle sacrifices), and *ch'ün ssu* (miscellaneous sacrifices). The first category included the worship of Heaven and Earth; the second, over 180 emperors of previous dynasties, Confucius, Kuan-ti (the god of war), and *ming-huan hsiang-hsien* (celebrated officials and local worthies) of the past; the third, gods of wind, clouds, thunder, rain, mountains, rivers, city walls and moats, spirits of "the loyal and righteous," and "neglected spirits."[188] Five or six different grounds were officially given for including these objects of worship in the imperial pantheon,[189] which may be grouped into (1) those worshiped for the purpose of expressing human gratitude or veneration, such as Confucius and Kuan-ti; (2) those worshiped for the beneficial or protective influences which they were supposed to exert over human beings, such as the gods of wind, clouds, land, and grain; (3) those worshiped for their outstanding virtues or services, such as "celebrated officials and local worthies"; and (4) those worshiped for fear that they would bring calamities to the people if not suitably appeased, such as the "neglected spirits."

The establishment of the sacrifices in categories (1) and (3) was intended to buttress with religious sentiment those values that were conducive to the security of the empire. Canonization of officials and scholars of bygone days who displayed Confucian saintliness, and gentry and commoners who demonstrated their loyalty in sacrificing their lives to defend the imperial order, was calculated to set up appropriate spiritual exemplars for the living to admire and imitate.[190]

Sacrifices in category (2) served the imperial purpose in a different way. By showing veneration to gods and spirits supposedly responsible for human welfare or miseries, the rulers hoped to convince their subjects that the government was deeply concerned with their interests[191] and at the same time to hint to them in a subtle manner that whatever hardships might befall them were beyond human power and therefore must be patiently borne.[192] The inculcation of the idea that man proposes but God disposes would exert a quieting influence upon the suffering masses. The Ch'ing emperors were no doubt glad to strengthen the already prevalent belief that human beings "depended upon Heaven for their daily rice" *(k'ao t'ien ch'ih fan)*. Even though religion could not remove the pain of an empty stomach, it tended to dull the edge of any resentment that hungry people might harbor against their government.

Sacrifices in category (4) reveal a most curious use of religion as an instrument of ideological control. The *li-t'an*, altars for making offerings to *wu ssu kuei shen*, "neglected spirits and ghosts," i.e., those not already included in the regular official sacrifices, are especially noteworthy. This institution was established early in the Ming dynasty. Emperor T'ai-tsu decreed in 1375 that an altar be erected in every *li* division and that sacrifices be offered twice a year to the otherwise slighted spirits of the locality. An invocatory text was read by elders at the ritual, beseeching the spirits to report evil and good

persons to the local gods so that they could be duly punished or rewarded. [193] The Manchu rulers adopted this ritual at the very inception of
the regime. A *li-t'an* altar was to be erected in the north suburb of
each city, where the local magistrate performed sacrificial rites on
three prescribed days of the year. [194] On top of the altar was placed
the tablet of *Ch'eng-huang* (god of the city walls and moats) and below
this, one on each side, were the tablets of the local "neglected spirits." [195] Additional altars were erected in villages where rural inhabitants held their own sacrificial rites. [196] The official invocatory text
was as follows:

> Although the ways of men and spirits differ, one being tangible and
> the other unseen, the basic principle behind them is the same. A ruler
> must be instituted to be the lord of myriads of people and of the wide
> world. He takes charge of matters of the greatest import and appoints
> various functionaries to fill different offices. He appoints an official
> to head each *fu, chou,* and *hsien.* He authorizes the appointment of a
> *li-chang* in every hundred households that inhabit these *fu, chou,* and
> *hsien,* to guide these households. In this way the functions of the su-
> periors and inferiors are well ordered. This is the method of ruling
> men. . . .
>
> The emperor has ordered functionaries in the realm to make peri-
> odic offerings [to the spirits]. There are to be sacrificial rites for
> *t'ai li* [grand unpropitiated spirits] in the imperial capital, for *kuo li*
> in the principalities [provincial capitals], for *chün-li* in *fu* and *chou,*
> for *i-li* in *hsien,* and finally for *hsiang-li* in the villages. . . . The
> god of the walls and moats is the supervisor [of local spirits].
>
> This is the order which we have respectfully received. We dare
> not disobey this order. We reverently set up an altar north of our
> city, and . . . we make special offerings to you, spirits of this dis-
> trict.
>
> If among our people there be persons who are unfilial toward their
> parents, or disrespectful toward their relatives; who commit acts of
> theft, robbery, or fraud, in defiance of imperial law; who make the
> crooked appear straight, or oppress good and honest people; who
> evade taxes and corvée, thus exhausting and injuring poor people—
> if there be such perverse, villainous, and wicked persons, we be-
> seech you, spirits, surely to report their evil deeds to the god [of the
> city walls and moats], so that he will expose them and cause them to
> meet with official punishment. If their offenses be light, they shall be
> sentenced to flogging or whipping; they will forfeit their claims to be
> regarded as law-abiding subjects. If their offenses be grave, they
> shall be condemned to imprisonment, exile, hanging, or decapitation,
> never to return alive to their native villages. If you, spirits, choose
> not to expose them, please surely make them suffer the Unseen Pun-
> ishment, causing their whole families to be inflicted with pestilential
> diseases, their domestic animals, silkworms, and agriculture to suf-
> fer losses and disasters.

If there be persons, on the contrary, who practice filial duties toward their parents; who maintain harmonious relations with their kin; who respect the authority of government, refrain from committing evil deeds and are good, upright individuals, [we beseech you,] spirits, surely to commend them to the god who will extend to them unseen protection and blessings, causing their families to live in peace and prosperity, their farming to run smoothly, their parents, wives, and children to dwell together with them securely in their native neighborhoods.

If among the officials of this entire district there be some who deceive the imperial court above and wrong good subjects below, who out of their greed after money resort to corruption, thus polluting the government and injuring the people, [we beseech you,] spirits, surely to be impartial and give them unmistakable retribution, in the same way [as given to other persons]. [197]

The *li-t'an* was not a very important item in the sacrificial system, but a minor object of local worship without any prominent place in the religious experience of rural inhabitants. In many parts of the empire it had ceased to exist long before the nineteenth century.[198] The invocatory text is highly interesting, however, because it throws an illuminating sidelight on the true purpose of official sacrifices. It shows that the imperial government made use of local sacrifices of every description to condition the minds of townsmen and villagers in such a way that they would be willing to submit to the commands and laws of their rulers and to observe the code of conduct that was most conducive to imperial security. This invocatory text formed a carefully worked-out counterpart to many of the maxims which made up the Sacred Edict of 1670.

There can be no doubt that the imperial authorities attached to the sacrifices an importance sufficiently great to induce them to set aside relatively large sums of money to defray the expenses.[199] To insure a steady source of funds, sacrificial land was reserved in many provinces, the amount of which ranged from 1,313 *mow* (in Anhwei) to 52,055 *mow* (in Fukien).[200] The following figures taken from local gazetteers may be regarded as fairly representative:

	Annual Expense (in taels)
Ch'ing-yüan Hsien (Kwangtung)	202.50
Ch'u Chou (Anhwei)	184.43
Nan-ch'ang Hsien (Kiangsi)	177.12
Ch'ang-ning Hsien (Kiangsi)	176.38
Mien-yang Hsien (Hupeh)	168.75
Yen-ch'ing Chou (Chihli)	166.69
Lo-ch'uan Hsien (Shensi)	135.95

Annual Expense
(in taels)

Pa-ling Hsien (Hunan)	133. 70
Cheng-ting Hsien (Chihli)	126. 66
Hun-yüan Hsien (Shansi)	114. 79
T'ung-kuan Hsien (Shansi)	94. 00
Po-pai Hsien (Kwangsi)	75. 00
T'eng Hsien (Shantung)	35. 51

The following table, prepared from the same sources, shows the distribution of the funds (in taels) among six local sacrifices that permit comparison:

TABLE 19
DISTRIBUTION OF FUNDS FOR SIX SACRIFICES
(In taels)

Locality	Confucian Temple	Celebrated Official and Local Worthy	Wen-ch'ang "God of Letters"	Kuan-ti "God of War"	Gods of Land, Wind, Clouds, etc.	Li-t'an
Ch'u		84. 70	45. 00	47. 83		
Ch'ang-ning		83. 58	26. 00	40. 00	16. 00	10. 00
Ch'ing-yüan		50. 99	26. 00	40. 00	25. 78	14. 80
Cheng-ting		50. 00	26. 66	40. 00		10. 00
Mien-yang	49. 27	7. 00	35. 74	35. 74	20. 00	11. 00
Pa-ling		47. 00		35. 00	23. 00	18. 00
Nan-ch'ang	43. 04	6. 11	20. 00	30. 00	2. 00	
Yen-ch'ing		40. 00	26. 66	40. 00	30. 00	10. 00
Po-pai		40. 00			-35. 00-	
Hun-yüan	40. 00	11. 18	15. 78	20. 83	-27. 00-	
T'ung-kuan	26. 00			16. 00		
T'eng	23. 13	4. 00			4. 00	4. 38

Forty or fifty taels was not a very large sum, nor indeed was one or two hundred. But remembering that the imperial government allowed no more than a dozen taels for the *hsiang-yin* ceremony, very little for the *hsiang-yüeh* lecture, and nothing at all for the vital *pao-chia* system, the expenses it provided for the local sacrifices were relatively speaking quite generous. It indeed spent large sums on gifts to elderly subjects. But these were occasional expressions of special grace and did not entail a fixed annual expenditure. Viewed in this light the system of local sacrifices appears to have enjoyed high priority among the major devices of imperial control, ideological or otherwise.

Effects and Difficulties of Religious Control

It is not easy to appraise the effectiveness of the official sacrifices as a method of ideological control. Doubtless the system achieved a certain amount of success. The people, commoners and gentry alike, accepted some of the sacrifices that were under imperial auspices.

The gentry and scholars often joined in efforts to help building or restoring temples dedicated to Confucius and his followers, maintaining sacrifices offered to Wen-ch'ang, the patron saint of literature, and honoring persons of outstanding virtue, including "celebrated officials, local worthies," "loyal and righteous men," and "chaste and filial women."[201] Commoners showed interest in other sacrifices which were sponsored or approved by the government. As a Western scholar put it:

> In villages and in other localities they have temples for the worship of mountains, streams, rocks, stones, etc. The God of Earth in particular enjoys much veneration. . . . In the chief cities of the provinces, departments [i.e., prefectures], and districts, the people are used to resort to certain state temples to worship the gods, especially those of the Walls and Moats and of the Eastern Yoh [i.e., Mount T'ai in Shantung], who are regarded as rulers of hell.[202]

The inhabitants of the empire showed the greatest reverence to those deities whom they believed had power over their own daily existence. Most of the peasants believed that rain was controlled entirely by certain gods.[203] Their superstitious zeal in praying for rain during a drought might sometimes prove annoying to local officials.[204] They all feared the god of city walls and moats.[205] In northern provinces bereaved sons "reported" the death of their parents to this deity.[206] Those who lived at a distance from the city might make the report to the temples of the land god *(t'u-ti tz'u)*[207] or to temples of dragon kings *(lung-wang miao)*.[208] Indeed, it may be said that many a villager or townsman was more afraid of the invisible sway of the local temples than the tangible authority of the local yamen. Persons in litigation who did not hesitate to perjure themselves in court were horror-stricken if required to substantiate their lies by swearing before some deities.[209]

Crude polytheism was thus a way of life with the masses.[210] It gave rise to a psychological attitude which made them easy material for ideological molding.[211] In so far as the government-sponsored sacrifices coincided with the religious needs of the inhabitants, they served to strengthen the ideological influences of the imperial government.

The needs of the people, however, did not always coincide with imperial purposes. While it is true that the religious motives of both the rulers and their subjects were permeated with "materialistic selfishness,"[212] the contents of their selfish interests were so divergent as to render their motives quite incompatible. The government hoped that sacrificial rites would help keep the people "good," obedient and peaceful, whereas the average worshiper was convinced that offerings to gods and genuflection before altars constituted a

method of bringing to himself or members of his family private advantages, good luck, personal protection, or cure of bodily ailments.
When he felt that the officially established sacrifices did not supply
deities that could answer his prayer or supplication, he never hesitated to go beyond them and worship gods of his own choice,[213] quite
irrespective of imperial purposes.

As time went on, a considerable number of popular sacrifices, distinct and different from the official ones, appeared in various sections
of the empire.[214] These were not necessarily directly contrary to the
official system, but they tended at least to detract the people's devotion from the official sacrifices. How much hold such unofficial sacrifices had on the populace may be seen from the fact that many otherwise niggardly persons turned generous when it was a matter of building shrines for or making offering to popular deities. As one local
historian said:

> If houses of worship are to be built or repaired, the larger ones of
> which entail an expense of a thousand taels and smaller ones sev-
> eral hundred, so many persons make contributions that the work is
> accomplished easily. . . . But when Confucian temples or temples
> for venerating the loyal, filial, chaste, and righteous, or other tem-
> ples that have to do with sustaining good morals [are to be built or
> repaired], nobody cares even to ask a question [concerning the mat-
> ter].[215]

Official sacrifices therefore did not always compete successfully
with popular sacrifices. Moreover, the malpractices and corrupt
ways of some local officials so discredited the government-sponsored
sacrifices that these were further alienated from the people. As early
as the seventeenth century the situation was already quite deplorable.
It was said that the temple keepers and yamen clerks in charge of the
sacrificial offering in the various temples and altars often embezzled
the funds set aside by the government and turned the rituals into a ver-
itable farce. "The whole thing was most perfunctorily done, and it
came quite near to being sacrilegious."[216]

The rites designed to honor "worthy" persons of the empire also
suffered desecration at the hands of local officials and their underlings. According to a regulation laid down in 1644, shrines of "celebrated officials and local worthies" were to be built in the *chou* and
hsien of all provinces. Names of persons deserving the honor were
to be proposed by local educational officials on the strength of the
merits or virtues of the deceased, the "consensus of local opinion"
being supposedly a decisive criterion for measuring such qualifications. Upon imperial approval, tablets bearing these names were
placed in the shrines, to be venerated by townsmen or villagers of
the localities concerned.[217] As early as 1652, however, fraudulent

practices had already been brought to imperial attention. Unworthy names were "indiscriminately recommended" and the institution was on the verge of becoming a mockery. [218] Despite threats of punishment, descendants of individuals of uncertain character through bribery or pressure managed to get tablets of their forefathers into these shrines. The K'ang-hsi emperor noted in 1668 (fourteen years after the establishment of this institution) that in one locality alone the educational official dealt out the honor so freely that within three years no less than 658 "local worthies" were enshrined and over a thousand official buttons were granted to their offspring. [219]

The emperor's wrath apparently did not stop the practice of promiscuous canonization. In 1724 and again in 1728 the Yung-cheng emperor found it necessary to order careful scrutiny of names recommended. Suspecting that officials serving in the imperial capital who came from the same province as the persons under consideration were inclined to indulge in favoritism, the emperor required local officials to assist in conducting the investigation. Having discovered that the institution was not operated in good faith, the Ch'ien-lung emperor sought remedy in more stringent regulations. He noted in 1748 that "celebrated officials and local worthies" were "lately selected from individuals whose descendants held high offices." In 1755 he mentioned concrete instances of such official favoritism: fathers of a board president and a chief censor had received the coveted honor, whereas the otherwise deserving father of a low-ranking official was denied it. Thereupon he ordered that grandparents and parents of those who were currently holding high offices above the "nine ministers" (third rank) or their equivalents, were to be barred from consideration, as long as their high-ranking offspring lived. [220] This move failed to ameliorate the situation; a well-known scholar who served in the Board of Rites early in the nineteenth century complained that all the recommendations received authorization with no question ever asked. [221] At about the same time, the Chia-ch'ing emperor reiterated the importance of making proper selection of "the celebrated and worthy" and pointed out that "in the various provinces many of the recommendations for local worthies were made on the basis of personal favor." One of the last efforts made by the imperial government to improve the situation was a new regulation drawn up in 1879 to the effect that no person was qualified for consideration until he had been dead for more than thirty years. [222]

The root of the trouble lay in the fact that wealthy and influential families of gentry and scholars regarded the temples of the "celebrated and worthy" as desirable places in which to honor their forefathers and ultimately to enhance their own social prestige. As a seventeenth-century writer put it:

In recent times once a family gains wealth or a person attains official rank, vainglory immediately becomes a concern and the desire to push dead progenitors into the company of "local worthies" is irresistible. Substantial bribes are appreciated by the local teachers and neighborhood elders, while personal influence induces the local educational and administrative officials to comply [with this desire]. [223]

Sometimes, however, when the practice became too flagrant or perhaps when some scholars failed to receive their share of the hush money, vehement protests would be raised against the undeserving candidates who in fact might be no more deserving than some of those already in the temple. A local gazetteer recorded that a wealthy merchant with the help of local gentry succeeded in placing the tablet of his father in the temple of local worthies. A number of *sheng-yüan, chü-jen,* and *chin-shih* petitioned the government to rescind the authorization. The case was eventually brought to the attention of the imperial government through a censor. [224]

The institution of honoring filial and chaste women was afflicted with similar malpractices: those accorded the honor were mostly members of wealthy or influential families, or individuals whose descendants had access to such families. [225] The imperial authorities were not unaware of such practices. The Ch'ien-lung emperor, for example, said in an edict of 1749:

> In isolated hamlets and remote areas of the countryside, deserving individuals who are without help and resources are unable to present their cases [to the proper authorities]. These are most easily forgotten. Special attention therefore should be paid them. . . . But if the customary procedure is followed—if the matter is relegated to neighbors and clansmen who are expected to propose [the candidates] and to yamen underlings who are authorized to investigate, with the result that those recommended do not deserve the honor, whereas deserving persons without money or influence are left out—then all who are responsible [for such mistakes] shall be punished according to the law. [226]

From the imperial point of view the influence exerted by local gentry upon these temples in which supposedly virtuous persons were immortalized was not necessarily salutary. The emperors' primary aim in establishing these shrines was to inculcate upon their subjects a philosophy of life that tended to make them dutiful, reverent, and above all impervious to seditious thought. In actual practice, however, these sacrificial rites aroused little interest among the peasant masses who naturally were more seriously concerned with material subsistence than with the glorification of departed ancestors. The gentry and scholars showed more interest in them but often with motives quite different from the imperial purpose. They were more anxious to enhance their own personal or family prestige than to strengthen the moral values for which the shrines were supposed to stand. They had little scruple in employing dishonorable means to obtain "honor" for their progenitors. The entry of one's parents or grandparents into one of these shrines was often more a matter of displaying one's wealth and influence than of manifesting affection for the deceased or belief in the sanctity of the official sacrifices.

How far the abuse of local sacrifices could go was illustrated by an incident in mid-nineteenth-century Kwangtung. The Confucian temple of En-p'ing Hsien required extensive repair, and it was decided in 1867 that something should be done immediately. Finding it very difficult to raise sufficient funds for the work, the local magistrate and gentry proposed that a *shu-yüan* (academy) be built to serve as a shrine to honor departed native sons. Contributors to the building funds (both for the Confucian temple and this shrine) were entitled to put their ancestors' tablets in the shrine, places of greater or lesser honor being determined by the amount of money contributed. No question about the character or status of the persons so honored was to be asked. This plan proved so successful that it was again adopted in 1885 to finance another building project. [227] It appealed readily to the gentry, scholars, and wealthy commoners; for it was apparently a shrewd application of the idea of purchasing official honors. Instead of buying official ranks or titles for living persons, enshrinement was bought for dead ones.

"Heretical Sects"

The greatest difficulty confronting the Ch'ing government and frustrating its attempts at religious control lay in the appearance of *hsieh-chiao* (heretical sects) from time to time in many parts of the empire. It is rather difficult to draw a line between orthodoxy and heresy among the countless sacrifices in the polytheism of the Chinese people. The imperial rulers, however, made a clear distinction between the two, based on political considerations. In so far as any form of worship or religious creed appeared harmless to imperial security, it was tolerated by the government, even though it was not included among the official sacrifices or did not conform strictly with the basic Confucian tenets. On the contrary, if any religious activity of the people tended to disturb the peace or was found to have been carried on with seditious intentions, it was branded as an "heretical sect" or *yin-ssu* (indecent worship) and therefore promptly forbidden.

The imperial government kept an especially vigilant eye on local religious festivals (usually known as *ying-shen sai-hui*), [228] pilgrimages to shrines beyond the provincial boundaries (often referred to as *yüeh-ching shao-hsiang),* and the propagation of unauthorized creeds to votaries *(ch'uan-chiao shou-t'u).* Such activities were allowed to go on unmolested for a while. But as soon as the government saw that they afforded opportunities for defrauding innocent people, tended to cause disturbances, or above all facilitated the fostering of insurrectionary movements, it took prompt action to stamp them out. The resulting inquisitional measures may appear to have been religious purges or persecution, but at bottom the imperial rulers were more interested in safeguarding their own political security than in upholding purity of religious faith or protecting the consciences of their subjects. [229]

Other important steps were taken by the Ch'ing government to suppress subversive religious activities. The earliest injunction against interprovincial pilgrimages was issued in 1739. In an edict of this year the Ch'ien-lung emperor described such practices in several northern provinces:

> The journey is sometimes as long as over one thousand *li* or even two or three thousand, and the time required is from one to three months. . . . This holds true in general for Chihli, Shantung, Shansi, Shensi, and particularly Honan. During the first and second months of the year, hundreds and thousands of people gather in groups [for the pilgrimage]. They first go to the *ch'eng-huang* temple of the provincial city, where they burn incense and a letter of invocation, calling the procedure "registration." They then begin their journey, going in various directions. . . . Men and women mix promiscuously, and it is impossible to tell the good from the bad. Fights, kidnapping, and thievery occur, and other incidents crop up in the dark. Such a vile practice constitutes at present a waste of money and is liable to give rise to heretical sects in the future. [230]

Knowing that this was already a widespread custom, the emperor instructed his servants not to prohibit it outright by threat of punishment but to stop it gradually through persuasion.

The practice continued; it was not limited to northern provinces, and the "evils" accompanying it went beyond "a waste of money." A governor of Shensi reported in 1746 that increasing interprovincial pilgrimages were made to certain places in Hupeh, and that these gave opportunities to smugglers of salt, gambling equipment, raw materials for making gunpowder, and other contraband goods. [231] The Chia-ch'ing emperor was informed that "thousands of people resorted twice a year, in spring and autumn, to a temple in Keängnan [Chiang-nan], to burn incense and give thanks to the gods; and also that similar meetings occurred in Keängse [Kiangsi], Nganhwuy [Anhwei], and Chekeäng [Chekiang]."[232] Thereupon he instructed the officials concerned "to disallow all such meetings and prohibit people going beyond their own district for religious purposes, because all such meetings occasion a waste of time and money, are injurious to morals, and afford pretexts for illegal associations."

A governor of Shantung found it necessary in 1827 to prohibit such pilgrimages, because "unlawful elements" were involved at every instance,[233] and, as the Ch'ien-lung emperor had anticipated, secret societies made use of them to cover up their insurrectionary plans. A number of pilgrims journeying from Chihli, Honan, and Shantung to the imperial capital in 1824 were arrested and charged with suspicious movements. Ten years later similar arrests were made. The practice was formally outlawed by an edict of 1824 and another of 1834.[234] That the imperial government had good reasons for suppressing such practices may be seen from the fact that in 1860 some rebels were reported to have made use of a local pilgrimage to lay siege to the city of Hangchow.[235]

The Ch'ing emperors were for a time careful not to suppress popular religious festivals. As late as 1743, when the Ch'ien-lung emperor proscribed heretical sects in Szechwan province, he expressly directed local officials not to interfere with the invocatory and thanksgiving exercises of "ignorant rustics," in order to avoid causing unnecessary trouble.[236] But when it became evident that such apparently innocent gatherings were often conducive to disturbances[237] or were connected with "heretical sects,"[238] the government banned them absolutely.[239]

The most urgent imperial concern, however, was with the heretical sects themselves. In his Amplified Instructions of 1724, the Yung-cheng emperor had already launched an ideological war against the White Lotus and Incense Burning societies, whose members he stigmatized as "lascivious and villainous persons." This warfare was renewed in 1839 by the Tao-kuang emperor, who contributed the Tetrametrical Composition as additional ammunition against *chiao-fei* (religious bandits). Realizing that persuasion had not reaped the desired results, the emperor decided to fight "heresy" with persecution, including legal interdiction, criminal punishment, and eventually military expeditions. Any religious activity that might contribute to the growth of heretical sects (usually through establishing an "indecent worship" or recruiting votaries) was sternly prohibited. Even here the imperial government seems to have maintained for a while a distinction between "heretical sects" that were seditious and those that were not. The Chia-ch'ing emperor revealed in an edict of 1800 the basic imperial point of view:

> The teachings of Confucius are honored forever. Other doctrines, such as Buddhism and Taoism, though not orthodox, have not been eradicated since Han and T'ang times to the present. . . . In the case

of [believers in] the White Lotus of recent times, they do not differ from the common people in their mode of living and dressing. . . . [Officials] fail to distinguish the good elements from the bad among them, and thus force them all into rebellious conduct. . . . As a matter of fact, when Liu Sung, Sung Chi-ch'ing, and Liu Chi-hsieh were arrested, it was because they secretly hatched seditious schemes, and not because they belonged to the White Lotus. I have made known the reason for punishing Liu Chi-hsieh yesterday and written in my own hand an essay "On Heretical Sects," in which I reiterated the principle that believers in heresies who obey laws will not be placed under arrest, but only those who herd themselves together and break laws will be punished. [240]

This distinction between law-abiding and law-breaking heretics was drawn on political rather than religious grounds, a fact which lends some support to our suspicion that in attempting to control religion, the imperial rulers were more concerned with dynastic security than purity of faith.

Whatever may have been the motive of the emperors in suppressing "heretical sects," they did not find the task an easy one. The Chia-ch'ing emperor complained in 1812 that "religious bandits" were still at large because local officials regarded the activities of such disturbing elements in the towns and villages "as a matter of course" and seldom attempted investigation or suppression. [241] "Law-breaking" heretics often managed to escape the meshes of imperial law, and did not come to official attention until their unlawful doings had flared into local disorder. One particularly bloody instance occurred in the mid-nineteenth century in western Yunnan where the inhabitants had the "bad habit" of "burning incense and binding themselves by oath." [242] In some cases "heretics" advanced startling religious tenets and made fanatics of some of their followers. According to a local historian summarizing an account given by a magistrate of Luan Chou (Chihli), certain writings of the White Lotus (which he seized in a raid on the society's local quarters), suggested the following story:

> Taking advantage of the turmoil at the end of the Yüan dynasty, Wu-sheng lao-mu (Old Mother Uncreated) married P'iao-kao lao-tsu (Old Grandfather Whirlwind-high) and gathered their followers in the T'ai-hang mountains. Their disciples dispersed and became founders of twenty-eight subjects, among whom Shih-fu (Stone Buddha) of Luan Chou was one. They seduced young men and women, several thousands of them, and taught them the aphrodisiacal art. . . .
>
> It was also said that before there were heaven and earth there was [Mother] Uncreated. The four hundred and eighty thousand children, whom [Mother] Uncreated procreated, were banished to the dusty world, owing to their impure thoughts. The Old Mother pined for

them. She therefore came down to the world to bring about their salvation.

Those [members of the society] who were decapitated [by order of the government] were said to have "ascended to heaven with the Red Decoration," and those condemned to die by mutilation, "ascended to heaven wearing the Great Red Robe." The latter [mode of death] was regarded by their comrades as the highest glory.

This was why [the magistrate commented], when persons converted to this sect were brought to trial, they confessed their membership willingly and were morbidly unafraid of death. [243]

Such a psychology, abnormal as it was, is not at all difficult to explain. The beliefs and attitudes that the imperial rulers undertook to cultivate through popular sacrifices could appeal only to persons who found their earthly lot unsatisfactory but tolerable. But to those who found their existence unbearable and longed for a better life, the "heretical teachings" of the White Lotus and other sects (which promised change for the better) were much more acceptable than the time-worn orthodoxies which lent support to the *status quo*. With the worsening of the conditions of the empire in the nineteenth century the heretical sects were bound to gain a firmer hold among people driven to desperation by their immediate circumstances. Leaders of insurrections saw in heresy a devastating weapon against the established authorities; government officials discovered that imperial law and the executioner's sword were virtually impotent against the emotional appeal of heresy to the fanatics. Feeble indeed became the Yung-cheng emperor's argument (in the Amplified Instructions) against the White Lotus that "what they vainly thought would prove the source of their felicity became the occasion of their misery." For what he regarded as "their misery" was to the heretics the very way to their "salvation."

The White Lotus sect had come to be very widespread by the time the Tao-kuang emperor launched his drive to stamp out heresy. In 1839 no less than thirty-nine temples of Old Mother Uncreated were discovered and destroyed by the government in Honan province alone, while similar temples were demolished in Chihli, Shantung, and Shansi. [244] The White Lotus ceased to operate for a time. About a decade later, however, another uprising of "religious bandits" with a widely different "heresy" was to take place—a large-scale rebellion which threatened to wipe out the dynasty root and branch. The regime was temporarily saved from destruction, but the deep-seated heretical infection of the body politic was never completely cured. As late as 1871 the imperial authorities were still speaking of "villainous subjects in the provinces who actually propagated and practiced *Teng-hua* (Wick Blossom), *Pai-lien* (White Lotus), *Ch'ing-lin* (Green Forest), and other sects." [245]

Nor were even the less dangerous "indecent sacrifices" effectively stamped out. The imperial government did not pay much attention to them in the earlier years of the dynasty, but efforts to suppress them increased when it became apparent that they might add fuel to the insurrectionary "heretical sects." The Tao-kuang emperor especially gave little quarter to those who indulged in unauthorized sacrifices.[246] But despite such efforts many superstitious sacrifices, subversive or otherwise, survived the dynasty.

Local gentry often lent a seemingly helpful hand to the government. Local gazetteers contain many instances in which retired officials and well-to-do scholars were said to have built temples or shrines or maintained local sacrifices. The local gentry may not have been sincerely concerned with imperial security; it is entirely possible that their actions were selfishly motivated. It was easier to raise funds to build or repair houses of popular worship, where deities were supposed to dispense unseen favor or afford supernatural protection to the worshipers, than to secure donations for erecting "Confucian temples or temples for venerating the Loyal, Filial, Chaste, and Righteous, or other temples that had to do with sustaining good morals." Unscrupulous individuals practiced fraud in connection with some of the institutions that the government established to honor the "worthy" dead; some of the local gentry were reported to have used the promotion of religious sacrifices as an opportunity for making illicit gains or furthering selfish interests. For this reason the Ch'ien-lung emperor issued an edict in 1766 which prohibited *chien-sheng* and *sheng-yüan* scholars from meddling with management of temple finances because, it was said, they too often treated temple property as if it had been their private possession.[247] On the other hand, influential local inhabitants might resent it bitterly if they were denied participation in temple affairs, as was reported in Jung Hsien (Kwang-tung) in 1872.[248] Such conduct and attitude on the part of the local gentry could hardly have proved helpful to the imperial government in its attempt to implement religious control.

We should not, however, minimize the importance of the effects of the general historical circumstances on that control—circumstances which in the declining years of the dynasty contributed to make every aspect of imperial control a frustrating task. In spite of its avowedly transmundane significance, religion could not completely transcend the material conditions under which the bulk of the people lived. When general poverty and social instability prevailed, the religious beliefs which had been upheld by the established authority tended to lose their hold upon the people and new or "unorthodox" religious movements appeared among the masses, who fervently embraced various eschatological concepts[249] whose very bizarreness rendered them attractive to the illiterate, desperate inhabitants of the countryside. The effectiveness of religious control, in short, hinged upon the ability of the government to achieve or preserve a minimum degree of economic and social stability. This simple truth explains not only the rampancy of "religious banditry" in the nineteenth century but the fact that the problem of religious control remained unsolved to the very end of the dynasty.

RURAL SCHOOLS

Shu-yüan, She-hsüeh, and I-hsüeh

The "examination and school" system *(k'o-chü hsüeh-hsiao)* of the Ch'ing dynasty, of which *shu-yüan* (academies), *she-hsüeh* (community schools), and *i-hsüeh* (charity schools) may be regarded as parts, was designed by the imperial rulers for the ideological control of the scholar-gentry *(shih ta-fu)*, and through them of the countless illiterate inhabitants of the countryside. We cannot describe the whole system in detail here but will review those aspects of it that bear directly on our inquiry, examining the three types of local schools mentioned above with a view to showing their structure and operation as well as their effectiveness as instruments of rural control.

The various schools that actually gave instruction to students and that were established or authorized by the Ch'ing government, fell into two general categories, *kuan-hsüeh* (official or government schools) and *hsüeh-hsiao* (nongovernment schools). The former category included special schools for children of the imperial clan, the Eight Banners, families bearing hereditary titles, etc., while the latter included *shu-yüan* (academies), *i-hsüeh* (charity schools), and *she-hsüeh* (rural or community schools). [250]

The *shu-yüan* had their origins in the T'ang dynasty. [251] The academies of the Ch'ing dynasty were at first private or semiofficial institutions established by local gentry or officials serving in the localities concerned. The first of them appeared in 1657 when a governor secured imperial approval to revive the Shih-ku Shu-yüan at Heng-yang (Hunan). [252] As time went on the emperors, especially Yung-cheng, seem to have been wary of giving their subjects and servants a free hand in educating young scholars. [253] Instead of trying to suppress the existing *shu-yüan*, however, they sought to gain control of them and use them as an instrument of imperial control by giving them limited financial support and laying down regulations for their operation.

Two edicts of the Yung-cheng emperor issued in 1733 reveal the imperial attitude; the first of these reads in part:

> High-ranking local officials in the provinces often establish academies in addition to the [government] schools. . . . We have heard that few of these academies have been of real benefit. . . . We have therefore withheld authorization that [the establishment of academies]

be made a general practice in the provinces. . . . Recently, however, we observe that high-ranking officials of the provinces have gradually realized the importance of paying attention to practical matters and of avoiding actions that buy fame and invite praise. . . . Let [one academy] be established in the place where the governor-general or governor has his official residence. . . . Let one thousand taels be given [to the institution]. . . . Later on, when scholars study in it . . . let a stipend be granted to each of them. [If the fund prove] inadequate, additional money may be drawn from the public coffers. [254]

In pursuance of this edict, twenty-one academies were established in the eighteen provinces. [255] The emperor apparently wished to limit the number of such institutions, but a large number of them appeared in district cities and rural communities as well as in provincial capitals. [256] Trying to make the best of the situation, the emperor issued the following edict in the same year: "In the various *fu, chou,* and *hsien,* all *shu-yüan,* whether established by the gentry who contributed the building funds or by local [officials] with public funds, shall be reported to the appropriate authorities for scrutiny."[257] This edict officially inaugurated the imperial supervision of local academies. A number of edicts and regulations followed. It was laid down in 1736 that headmasters of the academies should be selected according to carefully determined criteria and that rules governing the institutions should be modeled after the pattern set up by the Sung Confucianist Chu Hsi. Eight years later, scholars attending local academies were required to undergo examinations conducted by government officials with a view to distinguishing "the delinquent" from "the deserving." Provincial educational authorities were instructed to make periodic inspections to insure that such screening tests were properly carried out. The Board of Rites recommended in the same year that standard texts, including the Confucian classics and other works that had received imperial approval, be distributed to local academies. [258] How far imperial control was extended may be inferred from the fact that even the title of the headmasters was standardized in 1765. [259]

Later emperors tightened the control still further. The Chia-ch'ing, Tao-kuang, and Hsien-feng emperors showed their anxiety about the "degeneration" of the academies and ordered provincial authorities to remedy the situation, which was described by an official compiler in these words:

> The posts of headmaster were filled by tired, decrepit persons; scholars vied with one another in frivolities. What the latter read day and night did not go beyond eight-legged essays. But the general run of them [stayed] merely for the tiny allowances; some of them even refused to leave when their hair had turned white. [260]

This writer perhaps exaggerated matters, but if there was some ground for his statement, perhaps imperial control of the local academies brought about the general effect desired by the rulers: immunizing scholars against seditious thought and undue ambition and thus keeping them from becoming a danger to imperial security.

With effective control assured, the emperors made no further attempt to limit the number of local academies, as Yung-cheng apparently had done in 1726. Local officials often joined hands with local gentry in promoting and supporting such institutions of learning. Seldom could one find a prefecture or district without one of them. Some localities boasted more than a dozen each. [261] While many *shu-yüan* were in cities and towns, some had their sites in the country. [262] They were usually endowed with estates, in the form of "school land" or cash funds, from which salaries for instructors and allowances for scholars were paid. Those with better endowments commanded far greater resources than the thousand taels donated by order of the Yung-cheng emperor to the government-established institutions. [263] During the heyday of the reform movement of 1898, a few enterprising governors sought to use *shu-yüan* to introduce "new" or Western learning. [264]

There is little doubt that local academies, especially during the long period before the closing decades of the nineteenth century when the examination system began to crumble rapidly, did some useful service to the dynasty. By affording scholars opportunities to study—places to live, financial assistance, and in some cases competent instruction—they were thereby brought into the orbit of the examination system, within the pale of direct ideological influence. In some exceptional instances, *shu-yüan* served the government in matters even more directly conducive to imperial peace than ideological control. An academy in Kuang-chou Fu (Kwangtung), built in the mid-nineteenth century, for example, was intended to be at once "a place for scholarly instruction, moral discipline, resolution of quarrels, and cultivation of friendliness."[265] It should not be imagined, however, that the usefulness of the *shu-yüan* to the imperial government was unlimited. In the long run imperial control of these institutions produced results that were other than desirable to the rulers, as we shall see later.

The other two types of local schools generally had a lower scholastic standing than the academies. *She-hsüeh* (community schools) owed their immediate origin[266] to a government order of 1652, which required that "every rural area shall set up a *she-hsüeh* and select persons of honest and sincere character to serve as *she-shih* (community teachers).[267] These teachers were paid salaries and exempted from corvée duties. Their names were submitted to the educational authorities for scrutiny. [268] The purpose of these schools was made clear in subsequent orders. The Board of Rites was authorized in 1723 to decree:

> Schools established in *chou* and *hsien* are usually located in cities
> and towns. Villagers who live in remote places cannot attend them.
> In pursuance of a law of Shun-chih 9 [1652, it is hereby decreed that]
> a *she-hsüeh* be established in each of the larger rural areas in the
> various *chou* and *hsien*. . . . All youths of nearby villages between the
> ages of twelve and twenty who wish to study, are to attend [these
> schools] and carry on their scholarly works therein. [269]

This decree did not indicate who was to supply the funds necessary
for the establishment and operation of the rural schools. An edict of
1737, which required the establishment of such schools in the remote
regions of Kweichow province, authorized the provincial authorities
concerned to draw money from the tax revenues to meet the expenses. [270] This suggests that some if not all *she-hsüeh* were maintained with government funds.

The first *i-hsüeh* (charity schools) were started in 1702, when the
Board of Rites received imperial approval to establish them outside
the Ch'ung-wen gate of the imperial city. Three years later similar
institutions were authorized for Kweichow province for the benefit
of the "sons and younger brothers" of the chieftains of tribal groups.
In 1713 all provinces were ordered to build *i-hsüeh,* so that "youthful scholars without family connections and personal means" could
be given opportunities to study. [271] Special efforts were made during
the reigns of Yung-cheng and Ch'ien-lung to educate the ethnic minorities in Yunnan, Szechwan, Hunan, and Kwangtung. [272] Since "the
dialect of Fukien was incorrect and few inhabitants of that province
understood and spoke the Mandarin dialect," the government ordered
in 1737 that an *i-hsüeh* be set up in every district, which presumably had dialectal correction as a feature of its curriculum. [273] Thus it
appears that *i-hsüeh* were often used to give instruction to special
categories of the population or to inhabitants of special regions of the
empire. In general, however, the basic purpose of both *i-hsüeh* and
she-hsüeh was the same: to provide educational facilities for those
who could not otherwise afford them. As the Board of Rites put the
matter in 1736:

> The establishment of *i-hsüeh* has for its primary aim the educa-
> tional accomplishment of those who lack the means to study. . . .
> All who are willing to attend schools, whether they are adults or chil-
> dren, whether they live in the city or country, will be allowed to enter
> *i-hsüeh* and study. [274]

As this account shows, *she-hsüeh* and *i-hsüeh* did not differ very
much,[275] and sometimes the nomenclature was indiscriminately used.[276]
There may be some justification for the statement that "all the country schools for the Chinese [Han] students were generally called *she-
hsüeh,"*[277] implying that those for ethnic minorities were *i-hsüeh*. But

this distinction was not consistently maintained. It was disregarded, for example, in a government decree of 1713, which ordered the establishment of *i-hsüeh* in all provinces; by the K'ang-hsi emperor in 1715 when he instructed the governor of Chihli to set up *i-hsüeh* for ordinary villagers dwelling in the vicinity of the imperial capital;[278] and by the Ch'ien-lung emperor in an edict of 1751, which required the establishment of *she-hsüeh* in all localities inhabited by the Miao people.[279] Another and apparently legitimate distinction between these two types of schools was that *she-hsüeh* were rural institutions, while *i-hsüeh* operated both in cities and in the countryside. Even this distinction was not always observed.[280]

Whatever differences existed between the *she-hsüeh* and *i-hsüeh*, their basic aim remained essentially the same: to bring as many persons as possible under the influence of imperial Confucianism, especially those whose desire and capacity for literary education showed them to be individuals of ambition and potential leaders of their communities.

Through the efforts of dutiful local officials and cooperative gentry a large number of schools of both categories were established throughout the empire. In one district of Honan province there were at one time more than 120 *she-hsüeh*.[281] In a district of Kwangtung twenty-one *she-shüeh* were built with funds contributed by villagers.[282] The compiler of the 1878 edition of the prefectural gazetteer of Kuang-chou said that "every village had a *she-hsüeh*, " which also served as a place for neighborhood literary contests.[283] Big clans sometimes promoted rural schools. One notable example was Lien-yün She-hsüeh of P'ing-shan village (Hua Hsien, Kwangtung), established jointly by the Chiang, Liang, Liu, and Wei clans, the members of which constituted the overwhelming majority of a population of 8,000.[284] The local gentry were often interested in such schools,[285] some of which were said to have been quite successful. In one flourishing rural area of Nan-hai (Kwangtung), it was said, "When children attained the age of six or seven they all began to attend schools and study the Confucian classics. Even those of families of modest means entered one of the schools for several years and were taught to read.[286] Sometimes *she-hsüeh* extended their influence beyond the sphere of classroom instruction and became centers of local activities,[287] ceremonial occasions, or local defense.[288]

I-hsüeh fared also tolerably well under favorable circumstances. In the city of Wei Chou (Chihli), for example, an *i-hsüeh* established by a member of the gentry in 1739 was supported with an endowment of over 261 *mow* of land.[289] An *i-hsüeh* in Lu-lung (Chihli) was so successful that more than twenty of its pupils passed the examinations for the *sheng-yüan*.[290] As with the *she-hsüeh*, the enthusiasm of local officials and local gentry were directly responsible for the construction or institution of *i-hsüeh* in numerous places even in some not particularly noted for economic prosperity, such as Hsing Hsien (Shantung),[291] Feng-chen (Shansi),[292] Ch'üeh-shan (Honan),[293] and Yen-yüan (Szechwan).[294] When not enough funds were raised to build schoolhouses, temples or shrines were sometimes used, as in Ch'ing-pien (Shensi).[295] Other more or less similar instances may be multiplied almost indefinitely.[296]

It may be noted that the Yung-cheng emperor showed an unmistakable preference for *i-hsüeh* to *shu-yüan*, at least on one occasion. In 1723, three years before he turned down a governor's request to establish *shu-yüan* in Kiangsi,[297] he ordered all provinces to convert *shu-yüan* into *i-hsüeh* "in order to extend education."[298] No reason was given for this order. It may be surmised that the emperor wished to avoid the recurrence of a situation prevailing in the Ming dynasty, when some of the leading *shu-yüan* became centers of bitter political strife.[299] He preferred therefore to replace *shu-yüan*, which were attended by advanced students, with *i-hsüeh*, which were institutions of elementary instruction. We have no information regarding the effect of his move. Presumably, it may have stimulated local interest in *i-hsüeh*; it is doubtful, however, that any of the numerous *shu-yüan* were reorganized into *i-hsüeh* as a result.

Local Schools as Instruments of Control

Whatever may have been their personal attitude toward learning and Confucianism, the Ch'ing emperors could hardly fail to see that the local schools were useful instruments of ideological control. Accordingly, they undertook to encourage the establishment of certain types of local schools and to place them all under careful official supervision. It was their intention that such institutions should serve to extend the influence of "imperial Confucianism" to many persons beyond the pale of scholar-officialdom and perhaps also to help prepare some of them for serving the imperial cause.

The government allowed the schools almost no liberty in formulating their programs of instruction. Practically everything was regulated so that the instruction given would be subservient to the interest of the dynasty. Curricula were determined largely by the subject matter covered by the state examinations.[300] Official textbooks were selected, compiled, and distributed by the government, which virtually fixed the circumference as well as the center of literary instruction. A regulation issued in 1652 reads:

> From now on all provincial educational officials shall see to it that their subordinates make scholars read, study, and expound the Four Books, the Five Classics, the *Hsing-li ta-ch'üan*, the *Tzu-chih t'ung-chien kang-mu* . . . until they have mastered them so thoroughly as

to be able to discourse on them fluently in the examinations, to gain [from them] a broad knowledge of the past and present, and to apply them to practical use. Any who indulge stealthily in unorthodox learning and false doctrines, make a merit of strange [tenets] or innovate anomalous ones, shall not be allowed to pass [the examinations]. [301]

This set the keynote for imperial policy. Since then imperially approved texts were distributed to schools of the various provinces, [302] including the *i-hsüeh*. [303] The basic texts, the Four Books and Five Classics, had to be interpreted according to the commentaries of the Sung Confucianists, those who constituted the Ch'eng-Chu school. [304] The Sacred Edict of K'ang-hsi was distributed to schools in all provinces in 1700, and all students were expected to listen to the semimonthly *hsiang-yüeh* sermons conducted by educational officials. [305] Twenty-four years later the Amplified Instructions of Yung-cheng were issued to all schools. Any young student who aspired to the *sheng-yüan* but could not write the text from memory was disqualified, irrespective of his literary attainment. [306]

To make doubly sure that the authority of imperial Confucianism remained unchallenged, the emperors undertook to suppress publication of unauthorized books. The literary inquisition of K'ang-hsi and Ch'ien-lung times, camouflaged as an effort to encourage learning, is well known. [307] Scholars were not permitted to publish their own writings, not even the essays which had earned for them the *chü-jen* or *chin-shih* degrees. [308] Novels were thought to be capable of exerting dangerous influence on the minds of the people and were therefore forbidden. The Board of Rites ordered in 1652 that booksellers should print only "books on Sung philosophy" and those that dealt with methods of administration or were useful for literary studies. Those who published or sold books containing "trifling talks or indecent sayings" would receive severe punishment. This interdiction was repeated in 1663, 1687, 1714, 1725, 1810, 1834, and 1851. [309] The Tao-kuang emperor explained in 1834 that many novels were not fit for his subjects to peruse, because they taught their readers "to regard violent persons as heroic." [310] Scholars and commoners alike were cautioned in 1836 against composing doggerel to give vent to their ill feelings against obnoxious officials. [311]

The imperial authorities endeavored to make their control over scholars still more complete by issuing from time to time regulations and prohibitions calculated to keep them harmless in action as well as in thought. [312] Following a Ming dynasty practice of 1382, the Shun-chih emperor formulated in 1652 eight rules for all scholars to obey. Horizontal stone tablets bearing these rules were erected in every Confucian temple. Among other things scholars were enjoined to show respect to their teachers by listening attentively to their discourses and by refraining from "arguing unreasonably" with them.

They were forbidden to organize factions or associations, to publish their writings without authorization, to exert pressure upon local officials, or to hector or dictate to fellow villagers. They were expressly prohibited from meddling with political and judicial matters. Punishment after dismissal was promised to those who petitioned the government concerning the welfare or sufferings of soldiers and common people, even though what they said was well grounded. They were barred from having contact with local officials except in matters concerning their own education or the examinations. It was unlawful for scholars to involve themselves in lawsuits, even in matters that concerned themselves. In the latter event members of their own families could act on their behalf. The prohibitions, as the preamble of that document explained, were to be enforced for the scholars' own good: for by obeying the prescribed rules they should be able "to develop their talents and qualify themselves for government employment."[313]

Half a century later, in 1702, the K'ang-hsi emperor issued "An Essay for the Instruction and Discipline of Scholars" (Hsün-ch'ih shih-tsu wen). After urging them to behave in accordance with the best principles of imperial Confucianism, the emperor went on to enumerate a number of unscholarly misdeeds and condemned these in severe terms:

> As to those who harbor intentions that are not virtuous and commit acts that are erroneous: some who spread calumnious utterances and flying rumors, with a view to intimidating their officials and superiors; others, going in and out of yamen gates, lend assistance to tax evasion and realize profits by instigating lawsuits; still others prompt vicious, crafty persons to oppress the helpless and bully the weak; still others, summoning together their relatives, organize societies and bind themselves by oaths—scholars like these are insufferable to persons of good name and morals, despicable to fellow villagers and neighbors. Even if they luckily escape lawful punishment and continue unworthily to wear the scholarly vestment, should they not feel ashamed of themselves, if they consult their own consciences?[314]

Subsequent rulers issued additional instructions more or less in the same vein, although the historical context meanwhile changed. The most notable of these were the Yung-cheng emperor's "Essay on Partisanship" (P'eng-tang lun), written in 1725, and the Ch'ien-lung emperor's "Essay for the Instruction and Discipline of Scholars," written in 1740. The former was distributed to all local schools; the latter was originally addressed to students of the Imperial College but later issued also to local schools.[315]

The Yung-cheng emperor was primarily concerned with combatting the factional strife promoted by rival princes before his accession

to the throne, but in his essay he took up the general question of political loyalty and laid it down that "those who serve as ministers and
subordinates should recognize their own sovereign alone." The Ch'ien-
lung emperor shrewdly perceived that the resentment of a large number of scholars frustrated in the examinations constituted a real danger to the dynasty and attempted to allay their disappointment by directing their thoughts away from "title or fame." He argued in his
essay that since according to Chu Hsi "learning was for the sake of
one's own self," to expect any ulterior reward, whether title or fame,
was to misconstrue the legitimate aim of scholarly pursuits. It was
not wrong, of course, to take part in the state examinations. However, a true scholar should regard the passing of the examinations
as a by-product of learning, not as its purpose. The emperor continued:

> If you gentlemen really can put your thoughts beyond the examinations
> and envisage the reason that ancient scholars devoted themselves to
> learning, you will not be able to cease pursuing [knowledge for its own
> sake], even if you wished to do so. . . . Thus, by forgetting gain and
> loss, one will not be troubled by the examinations, even if he takes
> one each day. Indeed, in the present age, even Confucius himself could
> not avoid taking the examinations. But would [success or failure in]
> examinations trouble him at all?

"Not to be troubled by the examinations" was the medicine prescribed by the emperor for frustrated scholars. Those who accepted
it would remain content to engage themselves indefinitely in polish-
ing their "eight-legged essays," ruminating the themes of imperial
Confucianism—irrespective of their fortunes in the examination halls.
In other words, they would remain perfectly innocuous. The examination system, which was designed by the imperial founders to har-
ness the elite of the Chinese population, began to present a serious
problem as time went on. After more than a century of Manchu rule,
so many scholars were anxious to enter the privileged circle of scholar-officials that there was not enough room for them all. The Ch'ien-
lung emperor tried to meet the baffling problem of attracting scholars
with the tantalizing fruit of scholar-officialdom through the examinations and, at the same time, preventing those who failed to realize
their ambitions from feeling resentment against the dynasty. The fact
that Hung Hsiu-ch'üan, leader of the Taiping rebellion, was a frustrated scholar shows the practical significance of the emperor's move.
It also suggests that this attempt fell short of complete success.

The imperial government took concrete steps to effectuate its control of scholars. A few notable instances may be cited here. In 1651
the Board of Rites prohibited meetings of ten or more *sheng-yüan*
scholars who might demonstrate against local officials, an offense

punishable by exile and deprivation of titles. The K'ang-hsi emperor prohibited in 1652 and 1660 the forming of associations and meddling in yamen affairs. [316] This interdiction was repeated by the Yung-cheng emperor in 1725 with added severity. [317] To make sure that scholars could have no access to local officials on the pretext of seeing them on matters of learning, the Board ruled in 1651 that whenever a scholar visited the local official, he must enter his name on a "gate register," specifying the object of his visit. This requirement was reiterated in 1666 and 1673. [318] Scholars who allowed their essays to be published without government authorization were liable to punishment, suspension of the privilege of taking the metropolitan examinations for *chü-jen* offenders, deprival of their scholarly titles for *sheng-yüan,* and flogging for students eligible to compete in the local examinations. This regulation, issued in 1670, was not relaxed until 1736, when the Ch'ien-lung emperor ascended the throne. [319] Scholars who collectively refused to take examinations in order to embarrass local officials were to be punished, by an imperial edict of 1673, with suspension of the privilege of participating in subsequent examinations. [320] Between 1661 and 1801 the imperial authorities repeatedly ordered punishment of scholars who refused to pay taxes or helped others to evade them. [321] In fact, the personal liberty of scholars was so carefully circumscribed that even the matter of adopting personal names came under government scrutiny. Early in the dynasty it was ordered that adoption of personal names that might be suggestive of seditious sentiments be strictly prohibited. An individual with the family name Liu (the surname of the founder of the Han dynasty) was not permitted to adopt Hsing-Han (Reviving Han) or Shao-Han (Continuing Han) as his given name, nor was one with the family name Li (the surname of the founder of the T'ang dynasty) permitted to adopt Szu-T'ang or Chi-T'ang (Succeeding T'ang). The authorities, however, remained diplomatically silent on Chu, the surname of the founder of the Ming dynasty. [322]

Effects of Control on Rural Life

An appraisal of the effects of ideological control exercised by the Ch'ing government through the control of schools may be conveniently made by estimating separately its impact on those who were directly susceptible to indoctrination through books and on those who were not so susceptible, in other words, on scholars who were literate and on the bulk of rural inhabitants who were illiterate.

Assuming that the primary purpose of ideological control was to render scholars serviceable or at least harmless to the dynasty, the various measures adopted by the Ch'ing emperors attained a certain degree of success. An overwhelming majority of literate persons sub-

mitted themselves to the long years of "grind" involved in a scholar's life. [323] Some of them became so steeped in the traditions of imperial Confucianism that they became impervious to ideas of reform
or revolution. The boisterous ways of scholars of the Ming dynasty,
including outspoken criticisms of the government, political factional-
ism, and unrestrained doctrinal disputes, were replaced by a general
reticence concerning practical questions of social life, which was
characteristic of many a scholar of Ch'ien-lung and Chia-ch'ing times.
The intellectual atmosphere of the late eighteenth and early nineteenth century was strikingly depicted by a well-known literary man
of this period in these words:

> Recently, high officials possess no power and are timid; censors
> stop remonstrating and are accustomed to silence; doctrinal disputes
> do not rise and the world no longer speaks of learning; men in inferior
> positions cease to pass judgment [on their superiors] but devote their
> sole attention to the examinations or money-making, concerning them-
> selves not even remotely with moral principles or public affairs. [324]

Another writer of the same period observed:

> Many scholars of the Ming dynasty engaged themselves in instruc-
> tion and study. But now we no longer hear of anyone who gathers pu-
> pils around him or organizes learned societies. Ming scholars passed
> independent judgment [upon their government]. At present all scholars
> occupy themselves solely with the examinations. As a matter of fact,
> scholars who touch on current political affairs in their essays are
> excluded from consideration in the examinations. Speaking generally,
> it was the fashion during the Ming dynasty for officials to be unruly
> and scholars proud. The present dynasty perceives this dangerous
> tendency and undertakes to correct it thoroughly. Hence during the
> one hundred and several tens of years of its existence, the dynasty
> has witnessed many a disturbing incident. Every one of the uprisings,
> however, has been instigated by villains from the farmlands or spadas-
> sins of the streets. It has been peace and tranquility at the court and in
> the schools. [325]

While these writers may have somewhat exaggerated the torpidity
of officials and scholars or may have been too sweeping in their statements, the difference one of them noted between scholars of the Ming
and Ch'ing dynasties undoubtedly existed. This obviously represented
the net result of successful ideological control exercised by Ch'ing
emperors through the examination and school system.

The ideological control exercised by the Ch'ing government over
scholars through the examination and school system, however, did not
produce all the results expected of it by the imperial rulers. The
government was unable to enforce effectively all the regulations and
instructions laid down by the emperors. In so far as they were en-

forced, a number of effects were produced which proved to be highly undesirable from the imperial point of view.

There is ample evidence that the imperial regulations and instructions issued from time to time were as often disobeyed as honored. An increasing number of scholars departed from the prescribed pattern of behavior by flagrantly breaking imperial laws or doing violence to the precepts of imperial Confucianism. Such scholars became known in official parlance as *lieh-sheng* (bad scholars), or *tiao-sheng lieh-chien* (perverse *sheng-yüan*, bad *chien-sheng*). Despite stern interdiction,[326] they kept on pestering local officials with requests or petitions concerning matters irrelevant to scholarly pursuits. The requirement that scholars enter their names and indicate the purposes of their visits in the "gate registers" furnished by the local director of studies to the yamen became "an outdated formality" late in the seventeenth century,[327] and "a dead letter" in the middle of the eighteenth.[328] Frequently scholars presented their requests or petitions to the magistrates when the latter made their routine appearances in the local Confucian temple,[329] thus circumventing the law prohibiting yamen visits. The imperial government admitted in 1835 that despite repeated injunctions, scholars in all provinces persisted in "frequenting the yamen" and in "oppressing their fellow villagers or neighbors."[330]

Sometimes scholars debased themselves by illegally performing services below their status. The imperial government exempted them from corvée services and barred them from military service. But it was reported in 1735 that a number of civil and military *sheng-yüan* were enlisted among the troops of Shensi province.[331] Scholars of Chekiang province often served as local agents who kept tax records and certified transfers of land titles—services usually known as *li-i*, a form of labor service.[332] It was discovered in the 1880's that scholars of Shansi province frequently accepted appointments to the post of *li-chang* or took part in tax collection and litigations.[333]

Furthermore, when scholars were at odds with local officials, they might become boisterous or violent. By far the most common cause of friction between scholars and local officials was disappointment in the local examinations. Despite the advice of the Ch'ien-lung emperor, most scholars studied primarily for the purpose of obtaining titles and privileges. To fail in the examinations was a direct blow to their ambitions. Even if the examiners were truly impartial and discerning, defeated aspirants seldom were ready to admit their literary inferiority. Unfortunately for the imperial government, not many of the examiners were impartial or discerning. Young blood boiled easily and troubles promptly flared up. The K'ang-hsi emperor noted in an edict of 1673 that "young scholars in the provinces often went on strike in the local examinations, as a result of their quarrel with local functionaries."[334] The same behavior was noted by the Yung-cheng emperor in 1734.[335] Heavy punishment did not put a stop to disorderly strikes which sometimes ended in riots, as in the case reported in Feng-ch'eng (Kiangsi) in 1863 and in Chih-chiang (Hunan) in 1886.[336] Causes other than disappointment in the examinations sometimes brought about local strikes. In 1851 a number of *sheng-yüan* in Tung-kuan and pupils of a *shu-yüan* in Nan-hai (districts in Kwangtung) refused to take the prescribed local examinations as a protest against the magistrates' actions concerning tax and money matters.[337]

Other offenses were noted by the imperial government. "The worst" among the *sheng-yüan* of the provinces capitalized on their status and "took possession by force of land belonging to others" (1653).[338] "Bad scholars" were known (1729) to have "given shelter to outlaws, resisted tax collection, fabricated evidence to cause troubles, instigated lawsuits to ruin innocent men, or committed acts that were destructive of human relationships and contrary to reason."[339] The government was informed (1730) that scholars in eastern Kwangtung extorted money from the boats that passed through their villages and illegally levied tolls in rural markets.[340] Reports came from Chekiang (1766) that *sheng-yüan* and *chien-sheng* fought among themselves for control of temple properties, with a view to appropriating them eventually.[341] The imperial government learned (1739) that some of the young scholars of various localities of Changsha (Hunan), who gathered in the prefectural city for the examinations, insulted women and caused a near riot.[342] Taking advantage of their privileged status, scholars of Hsing-an (Kiangsi) lent cover to salt smugglers and persons engaged in other unlawful business. The practice became flagrant enough to invoke imperial action in 1835.[343] Pettifoggery remained a favorite "racket" of "bad scholars," despite imperial prohibition in 1771.[344]

"Bad" or "perverse" scholars sometimes became leaders of violent mobs. The imperial government found it necessary (1739) to prohibit gatherings of scholars, even for harmless purposes, because "bad scholars" in various provinces were reported to have frequently "gathered mobs and challenged the authority of officials."[345] In 1739 scholars of Fu-an (Fukien) insulted the magistrate and desecrated the local Confucian temple by painting its doors black; those in Ch'ang-li (Chihli) barricaded the yamen gate because they thought ill of the magistrate.[346] Three years later, the imperial government received reports that under the leadership of "bad scholars" inhabitants of several districts in northern Kiangsu staged a general strike of merchants *(pa-shih)* and caused disturbances in the yamen to voice their disapproval of the way the local official conducted the relief work after a flood.[347] A *sheng-yüan* of Yang-ku (Shantung) incited villagers to refuse to serve in river-dredging work and organized a mob to storm the prison and demolish the tax collector's office (1781).[348]

Two incidents that occurred in the middle of the nineteenth century deserve special mention. In 1841 the magistrate of Ch'ung-yang (Hupeh), suspecting that some of the *sheng-yüan* and yamen clerks were accomplices in corrupt practices, began a thorough investigation; the culprits promptly organized a riot and murdered the magistrate.[349] Four years later, a number of unsuccessful competitors in the local examinations held in the previous year (1844) in Feng-hua (Chekiang) charged the magistrate with favoritism and receiving bribes. On the first day of the examinations the assembled scholars rose against the magistrate (who was in charge of the examinations) and put him to flight with the help of the local inhabitants. "The tumult," it was said, "speedily grew into a regular rebellion," which had to be crushed by government troops.[350]

The scholars were not alone to blame for having been "bad" and "perverse." The ineptitude of local officials and the degeneration of the examination and school system itself must have exerted a demoralizing influence on many a scholar, making him cynical toward imperial Confucianism and its institutional ramifications. Fraud and deception beset the examinations.[351] Minute regulations did not put a stop to the widespread malpractices.[352] Despite punishments inflicted on culprits who were caught, bribery, favoritism, and cheating persisted and spread.[353] Opportunities for sons of poor peasants to enter the brotherhood of scholars were slim indeed. In some localities there was even a property qualification for obtaining the requisite "residence," thus barring scholars of modest means from the opportunity to compete in the local examinations.[354] A paraphrast of the Amplified Instructions wrote: "The general and the premier become such by no accident of birth; let every young man therefore press strongly forward. If you would learn well yourselves, and teach the younger members of your families, there is not a family that might not have a master or a doctor in it."[355] To many of the destitute villagers and frustrated scholars, this must have sounded hollow indeed.

The situation hardly favored the production of scholars who had genuine faith in Confucianism or true respect for the imperial government. To make matters worse, local educational officials, supposedly teachers and monitors of youthful scholars, often behaved in such a way as to inspire neither reverence nor confidence. In an edict of 1862, the imperial government took notice of their glaring shortcomings:

> . . . recently educational officials in the provinces do not carry out energetically their duties of instruction and supervision. They concern themselves solely with demanding gifts from the scholars, thus betraying an insatiable greed. Some of them even meddle in local af-

fairs, exploit the scholars when occasion arise, and pay court to wealthy gentry. [356]

This condemnatory view of educational officials was echoed by provincial authorities. A governor of Kiangsu writing at about the same time said:

> At present the educational officials are not only useless but also harmful. They are wont to receive as guests and friends *sheng-yüan* scholars with substantial gifts in their hands, and treat as enemies those who bring meager ones. They will subsequently petition to dismiss the latter, on the charge of absence from the examinations. If, however, bribes are sent to them, they will petition again to reinstate these scholars. When requested to recommend names for the "chaste and filial" citation, they will not comply unless money is given them. The worst among them collude with pettifoggers and bring lawsuits against scholars so that they can bite where there is plenty of meat. [357]

"Bad scholars" could render absolutely no assistance to the imperial government in matters of ideological control. .Indeed, their presence in the villages and towns of the empire tended to neutralize somewhat the ideological impact of those scholars whose influences the imperial rulers regarded as useful. The Ch'ing government, in short, achieved only an incomplete ideological control over scholar-officialdom, and for that very reason could not maintain a fully effective ideological control over the general populace.

This is not all. Somewhat ironically, ideological control over scholars and officials, in so far as it was effectively exercised, produced other results, which proved equally undesirable from the imperial point of view.

One of the central aims of ideological control was to render scholar-officials innocuous. However, precisely because they were lured by special status and privileges into conforming to the prescribed ideological pattern, they were prevented from developing anything like intellectual verve or moral strength. After generations of indoctrination and seeking "merits and fame" in the examinations, they finally became resigned to a philosophy of life that attached little significance to anything beyond personal advancement and gains. Many of the scholars emerged as obedient officials, but few of them became loyal servants of the imperial cause or faithful defenders of imperial Confucianism. They were harmless in ordinary times, but in times of emergency few of them were prepared to help their sovereigns to face the crises. Long-continued ideological control, in other words, ended in the moral and intellectual atrophy of the bulk of scholar-officials—the very individuals upon whom the dynasty relied to assist in the administration and to extend ideological control to the remote corners

of the vast realm. Ideological security was thus bought at a high price:
the eventual weakening of the moral foundation of the regime.

It may be contended that the remarkable services to the Ch'ing dynasty performed by Tseng Kuo-fan, a highly successful scholar-official, indicate that ideological control was not without some very
substantial results. The answer to this argument is simple. Tseng
was not an ordinary scholar; he and his close associates were in fact
very exceptional men. Their appearance at a crucial moment affected
the course of imperial history to some extent, but did not appreciably
alter the general situation that the examination and school system had
helped to create. Their conduct certainly was not typical of scholars
of the nineteenth century. It can easily be shown that during the Taiping Rebellion for one scholar (titled or otherwise) ready to fight for
the preservation of Confucianism and the dynasty, there were many
scholars who fled to safety at the first alarm, who compromised with
"bandits" to protect their "lives, families, and property," or who
cast in their lot with the rebels, as those who competed in the examinations conducted by the Taiping government at Nanking apparently
did.

So much for the effects of ideological control on persons directly
susceptible to indoctrination through the written word. To estimate
precisely the effects of ideological control on the bulk of rural inhabitants, who were largely illiterate, is impossible, but a general
view may be gained by surveying briefly the actual operation of the
rural schools. From the fragmentary data at hand we gather the impression that few of the local schools enjoyed real or sustained prosperity. The *shu-yüan,* which were often located in cities or towns
and were in a better position to command the support of local officials
or gentry, fared better than the *i-hsüeh* or *she-hsüeh,* especially in
localities that enjoyed a certain degree of economic prosperity. [358]
But academies in other localities did not present a uniformly encouraging picture. [359]

Our special concern here is of course with the *i-hsüeh,* which might
be located in the countryside, and with the *she-hsüeh,* which were
rural schools par excellence. Records concerning both types of schools
suggest the conclusion that these local institutions did not have much
impact upon the rural population. There is little evidence that "charity schools" were well managed or well attended. Many of them were
said to have gone out of existence shortly after their establishment.
In Han-tan (Chihli), for instance, none of the dozen *i-hsüeh* set up between 1685 and 1871 existed at the end of the dynasty, and some of
them disappeared long before its downfall. [360] In the comparatively
less flourishing districts of Yang-chou Fu (Kiangsu), very few of the
original *i-hsüeh* were in operation by 1810. [361] A governor of this province undertook to revive the local schools but was chagrined at his

failure. He discovered in 1868 that in one particularly disappointing district "there were more schools than pupils," and in another only four pupils were reported.[362] In T'ung-jen Fu (Kweichow) all *i-hsüeh* within its boundaries had disappeared before 1890.[363]

She-hsüeh, the rural schools calculated to teach youths of the countryside to read and write, fared no better. The authorities noted as early as 1686 that many of the rural schools were "improperly" conducted.[364] As time went on, these schools disappeared in one place after another, whether they were properly or improperly conducted. In Ts'ang-chou and Yen-ch'ing (both in Chihli), for example, all the *she-hsüeh* had ceased to operate by the mid-nineteenth century.[365] Practically the same thing happened in many other localities north and south of the Yellow River.[366] The 1919 edition of the gazetteer of Nan-ch'ang (Kiangsi) informs us of the situation in that locality:

> . . . from Ming times to the present, a period of more than five hundred years, rulers and officials of two dynasties had paid their attention to *she-hsüeh*. But altogether one could count no more than eleven of them built in the Ming dynasty and no more than two in the Ch'ing dynasty. Moreover, these schools had gone out of existence for so long a time that even their foundations cannot now be identified.[367]

While many *she-hsüeh* died from lack of care or support, some of them were closed down by the government for reasons of security. A revealing instance occurred in 1751 when the Board of Rites decided to close schools in rural areas inhabited by the Miao people of Kweichow province. The government have this explanation for its action:

> When *she-hsüeh* were established in localities in Kweichow inhabited by Miao people, it was originally expected that these would serve to civilize their fierce and wild natures and to enable them gradually to appreciate culture and morality. . . . But scholars with even a slight amount of self-respect are definitely reluctant to go into the Miao regions to teach, whereas those who are willing to make the adventure not only are unable to teach them good, but tend, it is feared, to allure them into evil deeds. Moreover, the Miao people are by nature stupid. It would be very difficult to make them comprehend the meanings of the Four Books. But, after they are taught to read, they can very easily peruse novels and other vile books. This merely encourages vicious persons to plot, without producing the desired results of educational influences. Therefore it is proper to dismiss at once all rural instructors who have served for three years in *she-hsüeh* located in the Miao regions and who have not shown any accomplishment, and to send back all others [to their native places] as soon as their terms expire, so that the schools will be gradually suspended and dissolved.[368]

This document is interesting not merely because it reveals the failure of a special type of the *she-hsüeh*, but because it lays bare the basic aim of the imperial government in setting up these rural schools: to use education as a means of ideological control. When it became a choice between illiteracy and danger to imperial peace, the authorities had no hesitation in choosing the former.

One reason that many schools operated inefficiently, if they operated at all, was that local officials were too often lukewarm toward such educational undertakings. The imperial government did not provide adequate funds for *shu-yüan*, *i-hsüeh*, or *she-hsüeh*. Magistrates often had to rely on financial support offered by local gentry or on contributions from their own pockets. Moreover, the average magistrate was too busy with urgent official chores, especially tax collection, criminal trials, and bandit suppression, to pay much attention to rural education, and too much concerned with balancing the official or personal budget to bother with financing rural schools. As a result, only a minority of local officials showed enthusiasm in *she-hsüeh* or *i-hsüeh*. In localities where the economy was more or less affluent, it was not difficult to find members of the local gentry who undertook to promote schools. But it was a different story where no such favorable circumstances existed.

Another closely related reason is the general poverty of the rural population. A nineteenth-century Chinese writer made this observation concerning rural private schools in Lu-i (Honan):

> The population grows daily. Those who till the soil manage to keep themselves alive with congee and gruel. Even if they have talented sons and younger brothers, they cannot prevent them from losing the chance to attend school. In the private schools a teacher gathers several tens of children and teaches them, in an ancient building. . . . These children usually give up their studies during harvest time. Those who come back in the ninth month [of the lunar year] are no more than 30 to 40 per cent of the original numbers. Owing to the fact that the fees the teacher receives are insufficient to support himself, he often has to announce that the school is temporarily closed. This state of affairs may continue for several years. Eventually, parents and elder brothers are discouraged by the lack of accomplishment [on the part of the pupils] and order them to take up farming or become artisans or peddlers. [369]

It is fairly certain that this description held true for rural schools in many other parts of the empire where the inhabitants lived in a tight economy. A Western author of the same period confirmed this view. "It is a current saying," he remarked, "that the rich never teach school, and the poor never attend one."[370]

It is significant to note that in imperial China where scholarship was "a primary social value and therefore an ideal of the villages,"[371] and where the government made attempts to extend educational opportunities to the countryside, so many of the rural inhabitants had to remain outside the door of learning. Imperial determination to extend ideological control could not remove the roadblock of rural poverty which rendered schooling a costly venture, even though it was offered free of charge. One is reminded of a saying of Mencius concerning the plight of peasants:

> In good years they engage themselves perpetually in bitter toil; in bad years they do not escape death and destruction. In such circumstances they only try to save themselves from death and are afraid they will not succeed. What leisure have they to cultivate propriety and righteousness. [372]

Substituting "imperial Confucianism" for "propriety and righteousness," we have here an explanation of the fact that the Ch'ing emperors made little headway in exercising ideological control through rural schools and repeated the experience of the founder of the Ming dynasty. [373] A Chinese local historian attributed the lack of effectiveness of local schools to official meddling. "Whatever should be done by the people themselves," he argued, "is for that very reason outside the proper sphere of governmental enterprise." [374] While there is truth in this contention, it is doubtful that a rural populace who lived from hand to mouth could do much in matters of education, even if they were left alone by the government. It is doubtful also that in an autocratic system as it existed in imperial China, where ideological control was a vital concern of the government, education could be left to the people themselves.

The conclusion is that the Ch'ing government did not obtain sufficient results from ideological control through the examination and school system to insure security in the countryside. At any rate, the difficulties and shortcomings of that system became increasingly evident in the nineteenth century. On the one hand, the attempt to control the rural inhabitants through the local literati did not produce a large enough number of reliable scholars to assist in ideological control at the rural level; nor did it succeed in preventing the appearance of "bad scholars," who virtually undermined imperial control by acting in ways that tended to impair the prestige of the existing order or to disturb the precarious peace of the villages. On the other hand, the rural schools did not bring the influence of ideological control to bear on a sufficiently large number of rural inhabitants, owing to the fact that these schools were often not properly operated and partly to the fact that few of the inhabitants were able or willing to send their children to study in these institutions. Broadly speaking, therefore, an ideological vacuum existed in the vast countryside of imperial China. The bulk of the rural inhabitants paid little attention to anything beyond the immediate exigencies of their everyday living. They were neither positively loyal to the existing regime nor opposed to it. Generally resigned to fate and to the dispensation of Heaven and the deities, they toiled patiently, trying to make a living as best as they could. Under ordinary circumstances, they remained placid and peaceful, even though the ideological control which the imperial government attempted to exercise hardly reached them.

Such a peace, which rested more upon the absence of disruptive motives or forces than upon the people's loyalty or positive support of the existing order, gave no assurance of permanence. As soon as the circumstances changed for the worse—as a result of grave calamities or crises—many of the rural inhabitants might be driven by desperation to alter their accustomed attitudes and behavior. The ideological vacuum to which we just referred made it easy for "heretical teachings" to sway the minds of illiterate villagers who might thus suddenly be lured by promises of better things to come into challenging the existing order. They did that, not because they rejected the imperial ideology (which in fact they had not in any real sense accepted), but simply because they found it impossible to live under the existing conditions. So far as the villagers were concerned, the riots or insurrections in which they took part did not represent a climax of ideological conflicts between the dynasty and the rebels but merely a last resort to escape insufferable hardships or to save themselves and their families from imminent starvation.

Ideological control as exercised by the Ch'ing rulers thus gave rise to a dilemma. In so far as it exerted little influence over the rural population, it contributed little to imperial security through rural control. In so far as it was effectively exercised over scholar-officials, it tended to weaken the imperial system at some of its vital points. The dilemma was inherent in the system and therefore permitted no real solution within the framework of that system.

LIMITS OF RURAL CONTROL

We have seen how the various institutions of rural control operated (or ceased to operate) in the nineteenth century and why they failed to attain the results which they were theoretically capable of producing. It remains here to attempt a broad appraisal of their usefulness to the dynasty and to explain briefly the factors that conditioned their performance.

The institutions of rural control appear to have contributed materially to the relative stability of the Ch'ing dynasty during the seventeenth and eighteenth centuries, when the imperial administration was more efficient than in later years and when the historical circumstances were comparatively favorable. In so far as these institutions

helped to keep the various segments of the population generally submissive to the existing order, they served the imperial purposes
fairly well. It cannot be supposed, however, that the system of rural
control, even during the period of its optimum effectiveness, operated
with the full efficiency upon which the imperial rulers time and again
insisted. It did not immunize the inhabitants of the countryside against
unlawful behavior or "heretical teachings." Riots, insurrections, or
"banditry" occurred in all periods of the dynasty; tax evasion and
fraudulent practices connected with tax collection had always plagued
the imperial government; the local granaries, rural schools, and
the *hsiang-yüeh* lecture system never worked really successfully in
all parts of the empire at any given moment or in any part of it for
a considerable period of time. All the evidence we have shows incon-
testably that rural control was serviceable to the Ch'ing rulers without being completely effective.

The partial efficacy of that system did not last indefinitely. When
the imperial administration deteriorated and the conditions of the
empire changed for the worse in the nineteenth century, the imperfect
peace that once prevailed was quickly disrupted. The prestige of the
imperial government rapidly declined. Local uprisings broke out
with increasing frequency and magnitude, some of them developing
into full-scale rebellions that threatened the existence of the dynasty
itself. One can hardly resist the conclusion that by the middle of the
century the system of rural control had for practical purposes completely broken down. Whatever useful service it may have previously
rendered to the dynasty and to imperial security proved now of little
avail. Police, ideological influence, famine relief, and other instruments of control were utterly ineffective against the rising tide of
poverty and unrest. Half-hearted efforts to revive the system made
since the period of the "T'ung-chih Restoration" brought little tangible
result.

It appears that the same circumstances which necessitated rural
control also set limits to its effectiveness. The existence of a vast
population in an extensive realm, with exceedingly poor means of
communication; the general prevalence of poverty and "ignorance"
among most of the rural population; the stratification of the inhabitants into two major groups, one of which supplied the rulers with
administrative servants while the other remained merely subjects;
the rule of an alien dynasty over subjects whom the rulers did not
trust—all these circumstances made rural control a particularly
important task for the Ch'ing emperors. They adopted a system
of rural control in which they sought to enlist the services of local inhabitants to assist in its implementation, but took care to prevent the emergence of local autonomy, chiefly by means of strict
government surveillance. They adopted, in other words, a system

which fitted the logic of the circumstances and met the requirements of the situation perhaps better than any other system that might have been devised.

Two crucial factors limited the operational effectiveness of rural control. In the first place, the imperial government had to enlist the assistance of local inhabitants to operate the institutions of control, but owing to the firmly set attitudes of these inhabitants and, somewhat ironically, to the basic aims of the government itself, it could not make them render really useful assistance. Rural control was designed with the general passivity and civic indifference of the inhabitants in view, and its primary aim was to perpetuate these mental attitudes so that the vast countryside might be made safe for the dynasty. The system of control operated partly on the psychology of fear and suspicion, and partly on the assumption that one way to insure obedience was to make the subjects dependent upon their government for physical subsistence or social advantages. No attempt was made by the government to develop in the villagers capacity or willingness to render active, positive service to their immediate communities or the empire. Indeed, one has good reason to suppose that the emperors really had no desire to make the institutions of control operate with complete efficiency by paying the necessary price—promoting the active participation of local inhabitants—lest local independence might thus be generated to the detriment of autocratic centralization. It appears that between a partially effective system of rural control and the risk of local autonomy the emperors made the inevitable choice. That choice, from the long-range view, was hardly fortunate. As a result rural control was condemned to rely largely on the passive resignation of those over whom it was exercised. The political stability which was thereby maintained consisted merely in the contingent absence of disorder; it did not rest on the solid foundation of positive obedience. When crises and disasters struck, when the prestige and power of the government were seriously damaged, the habitual diffidence of the villager quickly gave way to desperation, and the uncertain, imperfect imperial peace was rudely disrupted, despite the presence of the ramifying system of rural control.

Another factor worked even more directly to limit the effectiveness of that system. The imperial rulers could not trust the rural inhabitants with the institutions of control; they were thus compelled by the logic of the situation to rely on local officials to see to it that these institutions operated in a proper and safe manner. Competent and conscientious supervision by local magistrates was therefore an indispensable condition for successful rural control. But the theory and practice of the imperial government virtually precluded the development of a local officialdom that could carry out such supervision. From the earliest days of the dynasty the rulers were consistently more interested in making officials obedient and subservient than in evolving an efficient administration. Real authority was seldom delegated to any of the officials; no attempt was made to foster the capacities of making intelligent decisions in normal times or meeting crises with practical wisdom. Almost every regulation adopted by the emperors to govern officialdom aimed at rendering it innocuous—just as practically every measure of rural control was calculated to make the peasantry peaceful and harmless. Thus the "examination and school" system encouraged literary skill (in so far as it operated properly), but it did not train men of administrative competence. The system of universal check and surveillance forestalled open disobedience but at the same time ruled out the emergence of a proficient, energetic bureaucracy. The practice of paying inadequate salaries to government officials and permitting them financially to shift for themselves virtually forced them into graft or corruption. The resulting situation was hardly conducive to the lasting stability of the regime—a vast, often underfed rural population, controlled by an underpaid local officialdom of doubtful aptitude, with a somewhat overprivileged local gentry interposed between government and people, a group whose interest and motivations often differed materially from those of both. Already reduced in its usefulness for want of positive support from local inhabitants, rural control was further impaired by officials who proved themselves incapable of exercising effective supervision over its operation.

The quality of Ch'ing officialdom was not uniformly or consistently inferior. Speaking broadly, magistrates of the early years of the dynasty were somewhat more conscientious than those of later times. A Chinese writer observed from his personal experience that magistrates serving in the opening decades of the eighteenth century were usually concerned about the chores of their office; but within twenty or thirty years the fashion had so drastically changed that most of the magistrates talked about little except the amount of money which their posts might yield to them personally.[375] The corrupt influences of Ho-shen helped to bring about a further deterioration of local administration in the closing decades of that century.[376] Matters did not improve in the nineteenth century. In fact, imperial administration itself showed definite signs of deep-seated malady, especially after the stormy mid-century. According to a well-known high official who served in Peking for forty years, the state of affairs in the closing decades of that century was deplorable indeed. Officials of the various boards and courts often failed to appear in their offices; on some occasions, not a single soul was around to transact official business.[377] In the 1870's a number of the storehouses of the Board of Revenue for keeping newly minted currency collapsed for want of repair. Portions of the walls enclosing the mint were missing.[378] An inventory revealed that quantities of copper cash minted by the Board had been defalcated by officials whom the imperial authorities (for reasons unknown) made no efforts to apprehend.[379] In the metropolitan examinations held early in 1876 (Kuang-hsü 2), persons in charge of the preparation of the examination questions dated the document bearing them "T'ung-chih" (reign name of the recently deceased emperor) instead of "Kuang-hsü" (reign name of the ruling sovereign). This inexcusable error was discovered too late to make correct copies of the document and the questions had to be distributed to the contestants with part of the paper bearing the wrong date simply cut off.[380] Other instances of negligence, incompetence, or downright corruption can be readily added.[381] If, one may ask, officials at the highest administrative levels behaved (even if only occasionally) in such an irresponsible manner, how could the average district magistrate be expected to carry out his prescribed duties conscientiously or efficiently?[382] How could he be expected to exercise effective supervision over rural control, which was but one of a number of burdensome duties devolving upon him?

Thus it appears that the unsatisfactory quality of local officialdom (due partly to the effects of imperial control) set another limit to the usefulness of the system of rural control. It is probable that under the prevailing circumstances even an excellent local administration (if there could have been such an administration) could not have solved completely the problems of rural control. But it is certain that without a reasonably competent local administration rural control could not be fully effective under any circumstances.

We have attempted to explain in the foregoing chapters the theory and practice of the rural control system as it existed in the Ch'ing period and to estimate its usefulness to the imperial government. In the remaining chapters we shall undertake to trace the effects of control on rural inhabitants and on the patterns of their lives and to describe their reactions to control. It is hoped that we shall thus be able to show more fully the impact of rural control on the empire as a whole and arrive at a more accurate appraisal of such control as a means of securing political stability under autocratic rule.

●

Part Three

**THE
EFFECTS
OF
CONTROL**

Chapter 7

THE EFFECTS OF CONTROL
ON THE VILLAGE

THE VILLAGE AS COMMUNITY

We must acquaint ourselves with the patterns of rural life before
we can ascertain the effects of rural control upon the millions that
lived in the imperial countryside. The preliminary task is as challenging as the main inquiry itself. A contemporary Chinese historian,
who fully recognizes the importance of rural organizations, decided
to postpone writing on the subject because the information available
to him was meager. [1] As the data we are able to muster are still far
from adequate, we can attempt here no more than a tentative survey
and some provisional conclusions.

Chapters 7 and 8 delineate the patterns of rural life in those parts
of the empire where the inhabitants developed more or less well-
defined organizations and engaged in a variety of concerted activities,
and as far as possible trace the effects of control upon their organizations and activities. Our attention will be centered on the two major
rural organizations, the village and the clan. Chapters 9 and 10 discuss patterns of behavior exhibited by rural inhabitants in general,
without reference to organizations or organized activities, and show
the effects of control upon these inhabitants.

It may be useful to begin our investigation by tentatively explaining
the general nature of the village, before going into its structure and
functioning and some of its major activities. Two conflicting views
have been offered by various writers. According to one school of
thought, the Chinese village as it existed in imperial times was a
community that was "self-governing," "democratic," or, as some
put it, "autonomous." A Western writer of the nineteenth century
characterized Chinese village organization as "the self-government
of small communities" because "the management of the village is in
the hands of the people themselves. "[2] A modern Indian student of
political institutions believed that the Chinese village was a "com-
munalistic democracy" because it was left free to carry on a wide
variety of undertakings, including education, sanitation, defense, and

other matters of local interest. [3] As some modern Chinese writers
saw it:

> The village has perfect freedom of industry and trade, of religion,
> and of everything that concerns the government, regulation, and pro-
> tection of the locality. Whatever may be required for its well-being
> is supplied, not by Imperial Edicts or any other kind of governmental
> interference, but by voluntary associations. Thus, police, education,
> public health, public repairs of roads and canals, lighting, and in-
> numerable other functions, are managed by the villages themselves. [4]

Other writers, not so enthusiastic about the "self-governing" feature
of the village, nevertheless stressed the spontaneous character of its
organization. [5] H. B. Morse in particular held that the absence of the
consciousness of governmental interference in the minds of villagers
rendered the bulk of China's rural inhabitants essentially "free." In
connection with his discussion of the district magistrate, he wrote:

> . . . under the paternal government of this "Father and Mother of
> the people" [the magistrate] the ruled might be expected to be a body
> of abject slaves. This is far from being the case. . . . The Chinese
> are essentially a law-abiding people, and, in the country at least,
> are guilty of few crimes below their common recreations of rebellion
> and brigandage. These they indulge in periodically when the harvest
> is in, if for any reason, such as flood or drought, the crops have been
> deficient; but, apart from this and apart from the regular visits of
> the tax-collector, it is doubtful if the actual existence of a govern-
> ment is brought tangibly to the notice of a tenth, certainly not to a
> fifth, of the population. The remaining eighty or more per cent live
> their daily life under their customs, the common law of the land, in-
> terpreted and executed by themselves. Each village is the unit for
> this common-law government, the fathers of the village exercising
> the authority vested in age, but acting under no official warrant, and
> interpreting the customs of their fathers as they learned them in their
> youth. [6]

A different and far less rosy view of the Chinese village than any
of the above was taken by other observers, both Chinese and Western.
Thus J. S. Burgess wrote in his well-known study of Chinese guilds:

> The representation of the Chinese village as a democracy has been
> greatly overdone. As a matter of fact, it is a little oligarchy, con-
> trolled by the heads of the more important families. Among these
> heads there is a large degree of co-operation and counsel, but the
> people as a whole have practically nothing to say about the affairs of
> the village. In dealing with officials, the village headman represents
> the entire village unit. [7]

Martin C. Yang, a recent Chinese investigator, substantially concurred:

Many people believe that China is a democratic country, but its democracy is of a negative sort. It is true that the villagers, after they have paid their taxes and fulfilled other occasional obligations, are almost completely independent of governmental administration, and to this extent can be considered self-governed. But a closer view of the public life of the village shows it to be far from democratic. Local affairs have always been dominated by the village aristocracy, the clan heads and the official leaders. Individual villagers, or individual families, have never taken an active role in initiating, discussing, or making plans. By and large, the people have been ignorant, docile, and timid as regards public affairs. [8]

T. S. Ch'ien, a student of Chinese government, wrote recently:

. . . it is not to be suggested that the old China had local self-government in the sense that there were local self-governing bodies who enjoyed an authority with which the higher agents of the central government were not allowed to interfere. In the first place, the gentry who were active in local affairs owed their influence neither to election nor to formal appointment, but to a recognition, perhaps informal, of their local responsibility by the agents of the central government. In the second place, the gentry had to defer in whatever they did, to the wishes of the officials above them in the same way that inferior local officials deferred to the wishes of superior local officials or of the central government. They had no domain of their own, protected by constitutional or customary rights. [9]

These are the two views concerning the nature of the Chinese village as an organized local unit. On the one side, the village was regarded as autonomous or democratic because (1) it suffered virtually no governmental interference; (2) its community affairs were in the hands of the people themselves; and (3) its leaders acted under no direct official warrant. On the other side, the village was considered to have fallen short of democratic autonomy because (1) it was subject to potential or actual governmental interference; (2) its affairs were conducted by "oligarchical" or "aristocratic" elements, viz., the gentry, rather than by villagers in general; and (3) its leaders were recognized by and had to defer to government officials. The present investigator is inclined to think that the second view comes nearer to the actual conditions of village life, although he does not necessarily accept this view in all its details.

Where the government abstained from interfering with its affairs the village enjoyed a measure of autonomy. It enjoyed autonomy, however, not because the government intended to give it something like self-government, but because the authorities were unable completely to control or supervise its activities. Such "autonomy," in other words, was a result of incomplete centralization; the government never hesitated to interfere with village life whenever it deemed it necessary or desirable.

Even where government control was absent, the village as an organized community was not a democracy under the self-government of all the inhabitants. Village affairs were almost invariably directed or promoted by the rural gentry who often had interests distinguishable from those of the nongentry elements.

In localities where the clan organization was strong, it usually dominated the village. Although the clan membership included peasants and other nongentry elements, the clan leadership was usually in the hands of the local gentry. Ordinary villagers had little voice in deciding village or clan affairs, even though they were members of some clan.

Villagers, being long accustomed to despotic rule and very largely illiterate, displayed a decidedly passive mentality. They were usually more anxious to avoid personal troubles than to promote general well-being. Moreover, they seldom knew economic prosperity. Many of them lived from hand to mouth and had thus neither the means nor leisure to be interested in community affairs. There might be a limited amount of associated activities in which individual villagers participated, but these were sporadic and of limited scope, insufficient to constitute "self-government" in any true sense of the term.

Larger and more prosperous villages were likely to have a somewhat better organization and more community activities than villages in less favorable circumstances. Such organization and activities normally served as stabilizing influences in the countryside and were therefore tolerated or even encouraged by the government. But when the economic and political equilibrium of the empire was seriously disturbed, the behavior of the villagers—gentry as well as commoners—changed as a result. The former might make use of the village organization to protect local interests, even to the extent of challenging the authority of the government; the latter might out of desperation take part in riots, banditry, or outright rebellions. An insurrectionary potential lurked behind the normally placid villages. In times of unrest, village organization might change its orientation and actually contribute to the unrest. Viewed from the standpoint of imperial control, village organization was a variable quantum.

With the general nature of the village thus briefly indicated, we may now look into the realities of village organization and activities. The former is most conveniently dealt with by describing the characteristics of village leadership and the manner in which it emerged.

VILLAGE LEADERSHIP

Types of Leaders

Many observers noticed the presence of leaders in Chinese vil-

lages, [10] but few of them took care to distinguish between leaders instituted through formal procedure and those emerging from the local
inhabitants without such a procedure. This important distinction is
made by a modern writer, Martin C. Yang:

> Village leaders can be divided into the official and the lay leaders.
> Official leaders are elected by the villagers or appointed by the lo-
> cal or county government. They have specific duties to perform and
> are supposed to function not according to their own option but accord-
> ing to the fixed regulation. Under the old system there were four of-
> ficial leaders in a village of any size: the *she-chang*, the *chwang-
> chang*, the *hsiang-yüeh* and the *ti-fang*. . . .
>
> In each village there are a number of persons who are in a sense
> leaders though they hold no official position. Their influence in public
> affairs or in the community life may be much greater than that of the
> official leaders, but it may not be evident. They are known essentially
> as respected laymen. The most notable of these are the village elders,
> those who have performed special services for the village as a whole,
> and the school teachers. These persons comprise the village gentry,
> so to speak. . . .
>
> A layman leader is not elected or appointed and is usually a man of
> a kind entirely different from an official leader. He is a leader largely
> because he is admired and respected or because he holds an important
> position in the social life of the village. [11]

The distinction maintained by Yang is a valid one which must be
accepted as a basis for any intelligible discussion of village leadership, although it is unnecessary to commit oneself to every detail of
his argument or to follow his nomenclature.

Let us begin with what he called "official leaders," those instituted
through formal procedure. In the locality under his observation (a village in Chiao Hsien, Shantung) these included the *she-chang*, *chwang-
chang*, *hsiang-yüeh*, and *ti-fang*, who were respectively "head of the
rural district," "village head," "tax collector," and "policeman." [12]
The last two mentioned were obviously survivals of the lecture and
pao-chia systems.

Similar "leaders" existed in other parts of imperial China long
before the modern period. According to Huang Liu-hung, a seventeenth-century magistrate, there were in the district in which he
served a variety of rural headmen, including *hsiang-yüeh*, *ti-fang*,
chen-chang (head of town), *chi-chang* (market headman), *ts'un-chang*,
and *chuang-t'ou* (village headman). All these were appointed by the local official on the recommendation of the inhabitants of the towns,
markets, or villages concerned, and were "to work with the *pao-
cheng* and to supplement his functions." [13] With the exception of *chen-
chang* and *chi-chang*, the rural leaders identified by the two writers
cited above were essentially the same. Huang made an implied but

clear distinction between *pao-chia* heads and these rural agents,[14] although the latter were equally "official" in the sense that their appointments were authorized by the local government and that they served in the capacity of government agents in their respective localities. In addition to these, Huang recognized a *hsiang-chang* who was not to be confused with the *pao-cheng*, a *pao-chia* head controlling the same rural area. "The *Hsiang*," Huang wrote, "had its own distinct *chang* [head] to take charge of money and grain [i.e., tax] matters. The *hsiang-chang* should be chosen from elderly virtuous persons whose conduct had earned the respect of their fellow inhabitants."[15] The *hsiang-chang* in this case was roughly the equivalent of the *she-chang* of the Shantung village noted above.

A nineteenth-century instance may be cited for the sake of comparison. According to a set of regulations issued by a magistrate of Ting Chou (Chihli) early in 1847, the "public affairs" of each village were conducted by *li-cheng, hsiang-chang, ti-fang,* and *ts'ui-t'ou,* who were nominated by the villagers themselves and appointed to their posts after their qualifications were scrutinized by the magistrate. "The *li-cheng* took general charge of the affairs of the entire village." The *hsiang-chang* and *ti-fang* were responsible for detecting and reporting disorderly conduct, crimes and criminals, and in conjunction with the *ts'ui-t'ou,* for collecting the land and corvée taxes.[16] The setup here did not differ materially from the other two examples cited above, although the nomenclature was not uniform.

Arthur H. Smith, writing in the closing years of the nineteenth century, discovered that village headmen served the local government in the following manner:

> Of the affairs which concern the government, the most important is the imperial land or grain-tax. . . . Calls are constantly made by the local officials [for the headmen] for government transportation, provision for the entertainment of officers on government business, materials for the repairs of the banks of rivers, work on riverbanks, patrols for the Imperial roads . . . and many similar subjects.[17]

Village leaders, however, did not serve the local government exclusively; they often took charge of matters of a strictly community character and on some occasions acted as an administrative link between their own communities and the local government. Martin C. Yang's description of what he called "official leaders" of a village in Shantung was based on observations made in recent times, but it may very well reflect conditions of the previous century.

> The most important duty of the official leaders is dealing with the local or county government on behalf of the villagers. When a government order arrives, the local authority summons the *chwang-*

chang of all villages in the district to the market town where they are informed of their duty. The local *chwang-chang* returns to his village, sees the important laymen [leaders] first, and discusses with them the way in which the order will be carried out. . . .

Occasionally a *chwang-chang* is required to make petition or explanation of certain matters to the government on behalf of the villagers—an appeal for exemption from paying of land tax when famines occur, or an appeal for protection when there are threats from bandits. In respect to neighboring villages, the *chwang-chang* is delegated to take up a federal defense project among a group of villages or in the whole market-town area; to discuss with one or two neighboring villages a collective sponsorship of opera practicing or religious parade; and to act on behalf of the villagers in controversies with neighboring villages. Within the village the *chwang-chang* and his assistants are active leaders in inviting an opera company to the village for a three-day practice session during the slack season; they are leaders in conducting a religious parade when there is a drought. They are also the responsible persons when collective action is needed to combat locusts, or to meet crop crises caused by hail, flood, or storm. . . . The official leaders, especially the *chwang-chang*, are mediators when two families or two clans get into a dispute. The official leaders are also charged with the protection of the village: night patrolling to guard against petty theft and fire; crop watching to prevent animals or thieves from damaging the fields; and also surveillance to keep gambling, opium smoking, and prostitution from becoming too serious. [18]

It seems clear that a variety of rural headmen were found in the countryside during and before the nineteenth century who came to their positions through a formal procedure, local nomination, with or without official appointment. Some of them were survivals of, or connected with the decayed *pao-chia, li-chia,* or *hsiang-yüeh* system, and were charged with substantially the same duties that the personnel of those systems had. For this reason and also because these headmen were appointed by the local official on the recommendation of their fellow villagers, they were in reality subadministrative government agents, serving largely the purpose of rural control. Others among them were not specifically connected with any of the systems of rural control and might even be instituted without official appointment, but they might serve the local government at least part of the time in capacities similar to those of the headmen. To that extent they may also be considered subadministrative agents rather than strictly local leaders. Leaders of both these kinds might concurrently or on different occasions serve as leaders in community affairs or as "representatives" of their communities in dealing with the government and other communities. In such capacities they assumed the character of local leaders. But in whatever capacity they served, these "official" leaders remained distinct from those prominent individuals of a village whose leadership was informally recognized by the inhabitants.

We are now ready to take up the leaders of villages who came to their status not by official appointment but by general recognition. It is clear that while the official leaders were in a limited sense leaders in local activities, they were to a large extent subadministrative agents in the service of the government and therefore can hardly be considered as genuine community leaders. On the other hand, the informal or "layman" leaders of the village owed their prestige and influence not to the local magistrate but to their fellow villagers. It is interesting to see what sort of persons became such leaders and what role they played in village life.

Martin C. Yang's description of such leaders in Shantung is illuminating:

> In each village there are a number of persons who are in a sense leaders though they hold no official position. . . . The most notable of these are the village elders, those who have performed special services for the village as a whole, and the school teachers. . . .
>
> A layman leader is not elected or appointed and is usually a man of a kind entirely different from an official leader. . . .
>
> The layman leaders remain in the background, but their role is so important that without their advice and support the *chwang-chang* [an official leader] and his assistant are unable to accomplish anything. The village gentry are also heads of the chief clans or families. If they object to a program, or even if they merely take a negative attitude, the administration faces an impasse. Layman leaders do not, as a rule, deal with the government authorities directly. Sometimes the district leader or the county government invites them to a conference to hear their opinions regarding a certain case; not infrequently their advice influences government policy. [19]

J. S. Burgess' brief statement is also useful: "In the internal life of the village common affairs, such as the lesser legal disputes and providing the village teacher for the children, are in the hands of the village elders, an informal group of the older family heads who act as advisers of the headman of the village." [20]

Daniel H. Kulp discerned three types of informal leaders in South China, namely "the elders," [21] "scholars," and "natural leaders." Concerning the first type he wrote:

> They are not the oldest men in the village but the oldest effective men. They belong to the moieties or branch-families that are strong numerically and, more recently, financially. . . . Given natural competence the gray-haired men of each moiety can readily hold positions of leadership and control.

Leaders of the second type "have attained their position through natural capacity and achievement. They are traditionally looked up to because scholarship and official preferment by the hierarchy of the national government are social values long correlated."

The third type, the "natural leaders," were "those who have won their influence by sheer force of personality and cleverness. . . . [But] these natural leaders are formally recognized as leaders."[22]

Arthur H. Smith's observation, though not sufficiently precise, indicates the conditions of the nineteenth century: "In those regions where the method of selection is most loose . . . the headmen are not formally chosen, nor formally deposed. They drop into their places—or perhaps climb into them—by a kind of natural selection."[23]

Generally speaking, informal village leaders enjoyed more of the confidence of their fellow villagers and were treated with more courtesy by local officials than the "official leaders" who depended more or less upon the government for their positions. These persons were in a sense the village's own leaders and might exert greater influence on community affairs than those headmen who were formally instituted. What Martin C. Yang observed in modern China reflects also the general situation in the previous century:

> Laymen share a number of functions with the official leaders. . . . In mediating conflicts between families or clans, the laymen play a more important role than does the *chwang-chang;* they are more respected and consequently more influential. . . . The relations between the laymen and official leaders is definitely a supraordinate-subordinate one. This was uniformly true in the past and is still largely true in the present. In public affairs the official leaders do the active work but laymen direct them. The official leaders are generally the functionaries or even messengers of the gentry and the clan heads. When the *hsiang-chang* [an official leader] and his assistants receive orders from the government, they cannot make any decision until they have consulted with the influential laymen, and in these conferences the official leaders are usually expected to be completely acquiescent. They relay the orders but their own opinions on how they should be carried out is of minimal importance. . . . Traditionally, the magistrate or his secretaries paid respect to the village gentry, schoolteachers, and the large clan heads [who were informal village leaders], but would assume an air of superiority toward the official leaders.[24]

The predominant influence of the informal leaders was due to their social and personal prestige rather than to any articulate popular mandate. They were not voted into their leadership by their fellow villagers any more than they were commissioned by government officials, but while unofficial leaders often came from the rural gentry, official headmen were recruited from persons of lower social backgrounds.[25] Since the bulk of the villagers had in reality little power to make or unmake leaders of either type, the Chinese village may be described as democratic only in a very loose sense.

Official leaders were often given monetary remuneration for their services, supposed or real, or were allowed to "squeeze" with the tacit consent of all concerned, provided the graft did not become too flagrant or hurt too much. S. W. Williams, writing in the 1880's, observed that a headman in the vicinity of Canton received "such a salary as his fellow villagers gave him." The village of Whampoa, containing about 8,000 inhabitants, paid the "elder" a $300 salary.[26] Yang noted the following practice in a modern village in Shantung:

> The *chwang-chang* and his chief assistant receive compensation for their services in money or in entertainment and gifts. Formerly, the *chwang-chang* and other officers were not paid. Expenses were paid out of the public funds and the officers made a commission which took the place of a regular salary. If the actual expenses were ten dollars, for example, they would collect twelve and keep the difference for themselves. No villager ever bothered to make a fuss about this as long as the amounts were small.[27]

Such practices naturally lowered the prestige of the official leaders in the eyes of the villagers. Informal leaders, being members of the village gentry, would be inclined to avoid receiving direct remuneration, especially when the sum was a mere pittance, even though there was no assurance that these respectful leaders could not be tempted to engage in graft if the prize was comparatively substantial. Arthur H. Smith recorded an instance in which a scholar-headman obtained money by fraud. During one of the years in the late nineteenth century when the Yellow River made breaks in central Shantung, the districts in the province accessible to the river were required to furnish a certain quota of millet stalks to be used in the repair of the riverbanks. These stalks were to be paid for from special funds set aside for that purpose. The author was informed as follows:

> . . . the business of providing and delivering the stalks was put by the District Magistrate into the hands of an elderly headman, a literary graduate. This man naturally called about him some of his former pupils who did the practical part of the work. They . . . received in payment about 70,000 cash. Taking advantage of the general uncertainty which prevailed in regard to payments, these managers rendered no accounts to the village, but proceeded to appropriate a certain part of their receipts to their own use. . . . Matters continued in this way for more than a year, when some of those who were dissatisfied called a public meeting in a village temple, and demanded a clear account of receipts and expenses. . . . The graduate got some residents of the same village to "talk peace." . . . Their argument was this: "If we press this matter and take it before the District Magistrate, the old graduate . . . will lose his button and will be disgraced. The others concerned will all be beaten, and this will engender hatred and feuds which will last for generations."[28]

The upshot of this affair was a feast for all who cared to participate and the matter was thereby amicably settled or rather allowed to go unsettled. Smith failed to specify the status of those "who were dissatisfied" and who called a public meeting, but it is reasonable to surmise that they were not ordinary peasants.[29]

Selection of Leaders

Official leaders of the village were usually appointed by the local official upon recommendation of the rural inhabitants concerned. We must not suppose, however, that "recommendation" or "nomination" constituted a process of democratic election, in the sense that the candidates were freely chosen by a popular vote. Practices observed by some writers faintly suggested popular selection of village headmen. Such an instance was reported by Francis H. Nichols at the beginning of the present century:

> A Shensi village seldom consists of more than two hundred inhabitants, or forty families, according to Chinese methods of estimating. The only person in the entire community possessed of any authority is the "head man," who is appointed by the mandarin of the district. The head man carries no badge of authority, but is simply a farmer, like the rest of the villagers. His appointment to office is usually the result of his popularity with his neighbours, who have informed the mandarin of his especial intelligence and virtues.[30]

Observations made by other writers, however, indicate that the nominations were often made from a restricted candidacy or by a limited "constituency." A Western writer depicted conditions prevailing in the mid-nineteenth century:

> It is well known that the people in general, throughout China, dwell in villages . . . every village must have its head man. . . . This head man is chosen by the resident villagers . . . by the consentaneous voice of *the principal persons* in the place. The selection of this chief is done without the electioneering and strife which attend elections to higher offices in some other countries; it is the more easy, because the inhabitants of any village being in general all of one family, or at least one family predominating, it is necessary only to choose out *the most eminent branch of that family* as the chief man.[31]

Samuel Mossman, writing in the 1860's, found a substantially similar situation:

> The great mass of the population in China dwell in villages, in many of which there are no government officials. Yet every village has its "headman," elected by the resident villagers. . . . Generally the head-

man elected is chosen from *the most powerful family* in the village, or he is the most opulent and influential person of the single family of which the village is composed. [32]

S. W. Williams, writing about two decades later, said:

> The eldership of villages has no necessary connection with the clans, for the latter are unacknowledged by the government, but the clan having the majority in a village generally selects the elders [i. e., official headmen] from among their number. [33]

The observations of these writers are not accurate in every detail, but they indicate that the selection of the formal leaders of a village was far from a matter of free popular election.

This is confirmed by Martin C. Yang in his description of the "election" procedures prevailing in a modern village in Shantung:

> At the beginning of every year a meeting is held to elect a *hsiang-chang* [in republican times the equivalent of *chwang-chang*], his chief assistant, and other subordinate officers. Those who attend are the senior members of the families . . . though the heads of the upper-class families do not attend the meeting. Many farmers are uninterested in village matters and assume that there is no necessity for them to go to these meetings. . . . The election is conducted very informally. There is no ballot casting, no hand raising, and no campaign for candidates. The meeting is held in the village school or in some other customary meeting place. When several members of each clan have arrived, the person who presides over the meeting will stand up and say: "Uncles and brothers, now we are here to discuss the public affairs of our village. As you know, our *Chwang-chang*, Uncle P'an Chi, has served us very well in the past year. . . . Now is the time to conduct a new election of our *Chwang-chang* and other officers. " . . . This opening address is followed by a moment of silence. Then one of the electors, usually a partially recognized village leader, will say: "Since, as Uncle Heng Li has just said, Uncle P'an Chi has served us well in the past, I cannot see why we should let him retire. . . . " Other officers . . . are elected at the same meeting, but in a still less dignified manner. . . . The *chwang-chang* chooses one or two assistants, generally the persons who have already been his aides in the past. [34]

The qualifications for an official leader, according to this writer, were leisure, ability, personality, and tact. The *chwang-chang* of the village under observation was neither a tiller of the soil nor a craftsman. He was a fluent talker, a sociable person, a man who did not balk at petty deception when the situation warranted it and was willing to admit that he was subordinate to the village gentry and to serve them readily. [35]

Some Western writers indicated that an "elected" village headman might be disposed by the villagers and another substituted.[36] This was true theoretically, but actually it was often possible for the incumbent to occupy his office as long as he wished. Even dismissal consequent upon unsatisfactory service was usually effected by the voice of the village elite instead of a popular vote. According to Yang:

> Once such a person is elected, the probability is that he will remain in office for a long time. Some villagers may not be satisfied with him, but as long as he does not make serious mistakes they will not bother to elect someone else. If he himself really wants to retire, he informs the important villagers of his intention, so that the chairman of the election will make a different kind of opening address and the villagers will not reelect him. If he has done something inexcusable, then either he himself would not have face to hold office any longer or the influential layman leaders would suggest his dismissal. In this case, the chairman of the meeting would also hint that a new *chwang-chang* should be elected and the villagers would follow the cue. The result of the election is therefore to some extent prearranged and the meeting is a routine matter. The real authority lies in the hands of the layman leaders.[37]

Let us now turn to the informal leaders. According to James S. Burgess:

> The head men [informal leaders] of the villages are chosen from the heads of the family groups because of their general standing or "tse ke." This Chinese expression denotes a combination of age, wealth, learning and general effectiveness. The village heads are not elected in any mechanical way, but when a head man resigns or dies it is generally apparent which outstanding person would naturally assume control of the village affairs. This person is appointed at an informal conference of the important family heads.[38]

Informal leaders or "elders" of villages therefore emerged into leadership by virtue of their special qualification: age, wealth, learning, kin status, and personal capacity.[39] They were recognized rather than elected.

It was not necessary for any one leader to possess all these qualifications,[40] nor did the various qualifications have equal weight in determining leadership. Informal leaders even more than official ones had to be persons of leisure, prestige, and ability. Leisure and prestige usually came with wealth and learning. These were seldom if ever the privileges of individuals who had to work with their hands. Even age, though an asset, was not a decisive factor. It was said:

> Age is not of itself a qualification for leadership, but it is usually true that the essential qualities manifest themselves in later life and people believe that aged persons have much valuable experience. . . .

> A leader's successful functioning depends to a great extent on his knowledge of the people of the village, and such knowledge is more easily attained by those with the leisure to frequent wine shops and while away hours in conversation. . . . Formerly, as at present, leadership was something that was not sought but generally became the accompaniment of certain other attributes—age, wealth, scholarship. [41]

A scholar, on account of his literacy and possession of a title, could readily attain leadership, provided that he had sufficient acumen besides book-learning or that he was more or less affluent. According to a nineteenth-century writer, "the literary graduate" with a practical bent invariably took the lead among village headmen. [42] As he was in a position to come into contact with the district magistrate, he became thereby a notable person among his fellow villagers. He would be frequently requested to assist in the settlement of disputes or promotion of local undertakings although he might not monopolize the direction of community affairs. [43]

In short, the village leaders who came to their positions through the unwritten ballot of tacit recognition were none other than prominent and effective village gentry or scholars, who were also heads of families with appreciable influence.

Even the meager data we have been able to glean indicate that so far as leadership is concerned, the Chinese village of the nineteenth and early twentieth centuries was not exactly an autonomous democratic community. Its "official" or formal leaders, though distinct from and independent of the *pao-chia* (police) and *li-chia* (tax collection) heads, were not free from government control, as their appointment required government authorization and they were subservient to the local government. They were ostensibly nominated by their fellow villagers, but in actual practice they owed their positions more to the pleasure of "the principal persons" of the neighborhoods than to the free choice of the majority of the inhabitants. The "unofficial" or informal leaders of the village, while they owed no sponsorship to the local magistrate and were more or less independent of governmental interference, did not acquire the direction of village affairs as a result of any popular mandate or public election. They assumed leadership as the result of general recognition or "public opinion"; but "as a rule public opinion was created not by the small farmer but by the rural gentry and clan heads. "[44] All this followed from the fact that the general stratification of Chinese society reached down to the villages, [45] a stratification which did not have the rigidity of a caste system but still exerted important influences on many aspects of social life.

Clearly, the imperial government could exercise control over the village only by gaining control of its leaders, particularly the "informal" leaders, who had a much better hold on their fellow villagers than the "official" headmen. The control of the village, in other words, hinged largely upon the government's ability to control the rural gentry. How far it succeeded in doing so will be discussed after we have surveyed the main types of activities in which villages at one time or another were known to have engaged.

VILLAGE ACTIVITIES

We must remember that the type and intensity of village activities varied widely with the size, locality, and general environment of the village. In many cases, instances gathered from various sources may represent the maximum degree of activities which some of the villages attained, and we should not therefore assume that the average Chinese village was a well-organized, energetic community. Many of the activities were more or less negative in their purposes, calculated more to protect or defend local interests than to promote common welfare or improve neighborhood conditions.[46] It should also be noted here that since village leadership often remained in the hands of the gentry or literati, the participation of the bulk of the villagers in community undertakings rarely went beyond the contribution of manual labor or perhaps modest sums of money. It was the gentry or scholars who usually initiated the ideas, drew up the plans, directed the enterprises, and supplied or collected the necessary funds. The peasants did not play a prominent role in any work that called for organizing ability or for personal prestige.

The limited materials at our command do not permit a full discussion of all the phases of community activities. Only a few salient aspects will be dealt with, and these are grouped for the sake of convenience under four headings: religious activities, economic activities, maintenance of order and morals, and village defense.

Religious Activities

The religious activities of a village usually centered around one or more temples, although there were some villages which had no temple at all. The situation in Ting Chou (Chihli), though not necessarily typical, shows that the distribution of temples in various villages was far from uniform. Some villages of this locality had over thirty temples each, whereas others did not have even one (see Table 20).[47]

The lack of correlation between the number of temples and the size of the villages seems puzzling, but some explanation may be ventured. First, not all rural temples were of the same size. One sumptuous *Kuan-ti miao* (temple of the god of war) or *Lung-wang miao* (temple of the dragon king) might outweigh half a dozen tiny *T'u-ti miao* (tem-

TABLE 20
TEMPLES IN 35 VILLAGES, TING CHOU (CHIHLI)

Locality	No. Temples	No. Households	Amount of Land (in *mow*)
Hsi-pan-ts'un*	37	418*	1, 800
Ta-hsi-chang-ts'un	25	274	4, 200
Ting-ts'un	20	150	2, 100
Tzu-tung-ts'un	20	96	1, 700
Feng-ts'un	19	214	3, 300
Liu-tsao-ts'un	17	220	6, 000
Pei-tsung-ts'un	17	117	5, 100
Lien-t'ai-ts'un	16	180	6, 900
Hsi-chien-yang-ts'un	15	132	3, 900
Lou-ti-ts'un	14	186	4, 800
Kao-chin-ts'un	12	210	9, 140
Hsi-ting-ts'un	11	190	1, 600
Pei-nei-pao-ts'un	10	200	5, 600
Tung-chang-ch'ien-ts'un	8	182	4, 200
Tung-t'ung-fang-ts'un	8	29	300
Pei-chü-yu-ts'un	7	161	6, 000
Hou-hsin-ts'un	6	44	200
Wu-chia-chuang	6	30	300
P'an-ts'un	5	297	2, 300
T'ang-ch'eng-ts'un	5	214	4, 900
Wang-ts'un	4	215	970
Yu-chia-chuang	4	65	600
Pei-erh-shih-li-p'u	4	34	400
Tung-shih-i-ts'un	3	236	9, 130
Ta-wang-lu-ts'un	2	232	9, 400
Hsiao-wang-lu-ts'un	2	136	5, 400
Ma-ts'un	1	83	2, 200
Ma-t'ou-ts'un	1	40	3, 100
Liu-chia-tien	1	15	80
Hsiao-wa-li-ts'un	1	11	350
T'ai-t'ou-ts'un	0	193	3, 300
Chuang-t'ou-ts'un	0	141	2, 800
Hsi-shuang-t'un-ts'un	0	21	1, 900
Pai-chia-chuang	0	16	1, 000
Sung-chia-chuang	0	4	400

*Seat of a rural market; of the 418 households 7 were stores.

ples of land gods) in the cost of construction and religious importance.
The number of temples alone, therefore, does not necessarily indicate
the real extent of the religious activities of villages. The local gazet-

teer from which we derived our information did not specify the size of
the temples. It is possible that in some of the villages where the number of temples seems rather large in relation to the size of the population (e. g. , Tung-t'ung-fang-ts'un, twenty-nine households, eight
temples), the temples were diminutive "joss houses," whereas the
one or two temples in a village of over a hundred households (e. g. , Ta
Wang-lu Ts'un, 232 households, two temples) were comparatively
imposing structures. Second, it may be that the actual number of temples counted in a village at a given point of time did not necessarily
reflect the degree of prosperity of that community. A large number
of temples in a small village might mean that these were built in former days when it had a larger population. Villages with relatively
large populations but few or no temples (e. g. , T'ai-t'ou-ts'un, 193
households, no temple) may have been communities of recent growth.
Whatever may have been the real reason for the lack of exact correlation between the size of the village and the number of temples, we
can draw one useful conclusion: villages did not display equal amounts
of religious activities and in dealing with this aspect of rural community life it is not safe to generalize.

The religious needs of villages were partially met by the local temples.[48] They were places where prayers were said, votive offerings
made, family deaths reported, religious festivals held, or other religious exercises performed. Practices of course varied in different
parts of the empire. *She* sacrifices in some localities of Kwangsi
were noted by a local historian:

> In performing the *she* sacrifices seven or eight or as many as sev-
> eral tens of families formed into one *she,* which performed rites in
> the second, sixth, and eighth months. All belonging to the *she* as-
> sembled and contributed materials for the rites; they drank wine to-
> gether upon completion of the rites. . . . [Families that owned or
> tilled] land with common ditches or paths established one temple or
> one *she.* On the second day of the second, sixth, and eighth months
> of the year, all who were engaged in farming performed sacrificial
> rites together.[49]

Not all religious activities took place in temples. Rain prayers, for
instance, were usually said in shrines of "dragon kings" or other appropriate deities, but in some localities recourse was sought at other
spots. The rain prayers in a village in Shantung are described by
Martin Yang:

> When there is a drought, the local leaders organize a religious
> parade to the Dragon King, who is supposed to dwell in an old spring
> or well. If rain comes within ten days after the parade, the farmers
> feel that the Dragon King has answered their prayers. In giving thanks,
> a sacrifice is made to the god and the date for an opera is set. . . .

After several months, when the farm does not require so much attention, the village, or villages, have an opera which lasts three
days and is attended by people from neighboring villages. [50]

Theatrical performances were given on other religious occasions, in
some localities more than once a year. According to a provincial
director of studies, people of Shansi province indulged so much in
religious fairs and theatrical shows that evil consequences were bound
to appear. According to this official, "in prosperous areas six or
seven performances are organized each year, and as many as three
or four hundred [cash?] are assessed on each *mow* of good land. This
is to drain the resources of the little people, in order to supply the
managers with wine and meat."[51]

In some instances, fairs were promoted by rural temples to raise
funds for their maintenance. As Arthur H. Smith observed in the
1890's:

> Fairs are to be found in the largest Chinese cities, as well as in
> towns of every grade down even to small hamlets. . . . It appears to
> be a general truth that by far the larger part of these large fairs owe
> their existence to the managers of some temple. The end in view is the
> accumulation of a revenue for the use of the temple, which is accom-
> plished by levying certain taxes upon the traffic, and by the collection
> of a ground-rent. [52]

Besides serving religious purposes, rural temples sometimes became centers of nonreligious activities or served nonreligious purposes. According to a Chinese writer, in a well-organized rural community where the inhabitants belonged to more than one clan,

> The headquarters of the village organization is . . . a temple. . . .
> The village temple also owns property as does the ancestral hall, and
> is administered by a board of elders. . . . It also has festivals as
> does the ancestral hall. It maintains schools for the children of the
> village. In a word, it exercises all the rights and discharges all the
> duties toward the inter-group life as does the ancestral hall toward
> the inter-family life. [53]

According to a local historian, the temples in Luan Chou (Chihli) in
the late nineteenth century functioned as follows:

> Each of the *she* organizations had one temple. All the villages,
> large and small, within the *she* supported the incense fire of this
> temple. . . . Persons who managed [the affairs of the temple] were
> called *hui-shou* [headmen of the association]. The temple fairs were
> usually held sometime during the fourth and fifth months. . . . On
> the appointed days opera performances were given and all sorts of
> goods displayed in a bazaar. Men and women mixed confusedly, all
> going into the temple with incense and flowers to pray for good for-

> tune. . . . In addition to [this common temple] each village had its
> own temple, the deity of which had his date of birth. . . . Sometimes
> the village gave opera performances on this date and held a fair. This
> occasion was used also to make known village regulations, such as
> [prohibition against] permitting chickens, lambs, and oxen to harm
> the green crops, or the pilfering of crops by women and children.
> These prohibitions were written in large characters. Any who violat-
> ed them were liable to punishment.
>
> This was true only in the majority of wealthy and populous villages.
> [Even in these the festivals] were not necessarily performed every
> year. Occasionally, when prayers were said in a temple on account
> of drought, excessive rain, or the presence of locusts, and no ca-
> lamity ensued, opera performances were given as an expression of
> thanksgiving. No regular dates were fixed for these. [54]

Similar arrangements were found in Shansi province, where, according to the provincial authorities, each village formed itself into
as many *she* as it had temples. Each *she* had a *chang* (headman) from
whom "all villagers took orders."[55] The scope of the *she-chang*'s
authority was not specified, but it is reasonable to suppose that it
extended to matters that were not strictly religious.

The needs of different segments of the village population might be
answered by different temples located in the area. In a village of
modern Shantung, for example, such a situation existed:

> There are two temples . . . which are frequented by villagers of
> the whole district. One temple is located at the northeastern end of
> the market town. The deities in it are Kuan kung [i. e., Kuan-ti] and
> Tseng-sun [one of Confucius' immediate disciples]. . . . This tem-
> ple is not frequently patronized by the farmers but rather is a meeting
> place for the rural scholars. At the second large temple, which is
> Buddhist and is located near the market town, farmers seek divine
> blessing and protection. . . . The two shrines are located on the
> northern mountain and the southern hill. One is a shrine to the King
> of Cattle, the other is visited once a year on the ninth day of the ninth
> month, mostly by women. [56]

Temples were sometimes built by individuals, but more often they
were the results of community cooperation. Arthur H. Smith, writing
in the closing decade of the nineteenth century, described one form:

> When a few individuals wish to build a temple, they call the headmen
> of the village in whose charge by long custom are all the public mat-
> ters of the town, and the enterprise is put in their care. It is usual to
> make an assessment on the land for funds; this is not necessarily a
> fixed sum for each acre, but is more likely to be graded according
> to the amount of land each owns, the poor being perhaps altogether
> exempt, or very lightly taxed, and the rich paying much more heavily.

> When the money is all collected by the managers, the building begins
> under their direction. . . . When the temple has been built, . . . the
> managers select some one of the donors and appoint him a sort of
> president of the board of trustees. [57]

Building funds were not necessarily difficult to raise. When the temple in question had popular appeal, contributions came readily from
willing donors, even though the cost of construction or repair amounted to hundreds of taels. [58] The building and management of temples
were very often in the hands of the gentry or scholars, [59] who would
feel slighted if they were not asked to participate in the task. [60] A temple that owned land might become a bone of contention between influential persons. A government order issued in 1766 (Ch'ien-lung
31) illustrates this situation:

> All temples and shrines in Chekiang province are managed by *sheng-
> yüan* or *chien-sheng* who are designated "patrons." The patrons of one
> temple may belong to one or several families, but they all regard the
> land or hills [that belong to the temple] as if these were their own fam-
> ily property. They quarrel among themselves and each tries to snatch
> away [the management] from another, each possessing private ev-
> idence [to support his contention]. . . . They covet gains and en-
> gage in endless litigation: it is a most despicable practice. All pro-
> vincial authorities should be instructed to issue notices and make it
> clearly known that the title "patron" shall hereafter be abolished, and
> that no person is permitted to base claims on private evidence and
> engage in disputes or lawsuits. Landed property donated by gentry or
> commoners and temples built by them may be managed only by Bud-
> dhist bonzes, nuns, or Taoist priests. [61]

The text of this order was supposed to have been engraved on stone
tablets so that it could be "forever obeyed," but we have no evidence
that the practice in question actually stopped in Chekiang or other
provinces. It may well have persisted in some localities at least,
as an investigation made in modern times suggests. It was found that
"there are in the northern districts [of Kiangsu province] huge tracts
of land nominally belonging to temples, but actually owned by the few
people who manage them."[62] We are not informed of the social status
of these "few people" who managed the temple lands in northern Kiangsu, but it is reasonable to suppose that they were, like the patrons
of the temples in Chekiang, not ordinary peasants or commoner inhabitants of the countryside.

Nor did ordinary villagers have much voice in the various religious
activities that took place in or out of the temples. Religious fairs and
theatrical performances in Shansi, according to an apparently well-
intentioned official, afforded benefits to "the managers" at the expense

of "the little people." Similar abuse was said to have prevailed in more than one province during the nineteenth century. According to one Ch'ien Yung:

> In localities both south and north of the Yangtze, religious proces-
> sions and fairs have been known for a long time, but these have be-
> come especially extensive in recent times. What are known as "head-
> men" are mostly clerks or runners of *fu, chou,* or *hsien* yamen in the
> cities, and *ti-fang, pao-chang,* or loafers in the countryside. Gen-
> erally speaking, persons who have the slightest idea of what is prop-
> er and lawful and who have some esteem for their personal and fam-
> ily status do not take part [in these activities]. [63]

Thus, according to this Chinese observer, while the promotion or management of village fairs was below the dignity of the gentry, it afforded diversion and probably profit to a few persons who did not belong to the common peasantry and who in fact often proved them-selves to be predatory elements of the countryside.

The various religious activities that were found in Chinese villages, then, usually owed their existence to the leadership or direction sup-plied by a minority of the rural inhabitants. The bulk of villagers de-rived amusement or religious satisfaction from these activities but had no control over them.

Economic Activities

While there was little positive effort made by villagers at "com-munity welfare or betterment," there was a noticeable number of activities calculated to make their economic existence more tolerable and secure.

One of the most widely observed of such activities was the con-struction or repair of bridges and roads indispensable to villagers for intervillage travel and transportation to and from the nearby mar-kets and towns. Sometimes the work was undertaken collectively by the inhabitants, as was the construction of six bridges used by some villagers of Lin-chang Hsien (Honan). [64] Huc noted in the mid-nine-teenth century in Hupeh province a quaint way of raising funds for road repair, a method probably not widely used in other parts of the empire:

> The government does in fact never concern itself about the roads,
> except those which the Emperor has to traverse when he takes the
> trouble to travel. . . . As to the people, they must manage as well as
> they can. . . . There are some districts in which the public have en-
> deavored to supply for themselves a remedy for this deplorable neg-
> ligence of the government. In all lawsuits, disputes and quarrels, it
> is customary only to have recourse to the tribunals at the last extrem-

ity; most people prefer choosing as arbiters some old men of tried integrity and long experience, whose decisions they respect. In such cases it is very common to condemn the party declared to be in the wrong to mend a certain piece of the road at his own expense by way of fine, and in these districts the good state of the road is in a direct ratio with the quarrelsome and litigious spirit of the inhabitants. [65]

Quite often the rural gentry endeavored to provide fellow villagers with bridges, roads, and ferry services. Local gazetteers are full of such instances. For example, a self-made merchant-official of Hua Hsien (Kwangtung) contributed more than 3,000 taels to construct a stone-paved road leading from his village to the nearest market. The road was completed in 1893. [66] Numerous instances are recorded in which bridges and ferries became objects of gentry "beneficence."[67] In some localities the number of bridges credited to the rural gentry was quite large. [68] In these instances, however, the projects appear to have been undertaken by members of the gentry in their individual capacities instead of collectively by their fellow villagers under their leadership.

Ch'a-t'ing (tea pavilions) were often built at convenient places along country roads to serve rural travelers. The Rev. George Smith made the following observation when he visited a village outside the city of Ningpo (Chekiang) in September, 1845:

> Every three or four miles there was a building in which travellers are permitted to rest, and tea is supplied gratuitously at the expense of some wealthy and benevolent individuals. . . . The benevolent supporters of these institutions find their reward in the respect entertained towards them during life, and in the honor paid to their memory. [69]

Similar structures were found in almost all parts of the empire, especially in southern provinces. For example, the Lo-shan Ch'a-t'ing (Happy Benevolence Tea Pavilion) in Fu-shan (a Hsiang of Nan-hai, Kwangtung), built in 1871, was made possible by the *shih shang* (scholars and merchants) of this prosperous community. [70]

By far the most important economic activities undertaken by villagers were those connected with "water benefits" (irrigation) and flood prevention. The former was effected chiefly through the construction of ditches or watercourses, ponds, reservoirs, and dikes, while the latter was done mainly through the building of dikes or embankments.

The imperial government did not undertake to construct irrigation sluices or dikes in the villages, but it encouraged such work by giving legal protection to "water benefits" resulting from private efforts. Drawing water from private reservoirs, ponds, or ditches without authorization by the owners was a punishable crime.[71] Despite government encouragement or protection the extent of local irrigation work varied quite widely in different villages. In some localities, especially in northern provinces, villagers were often rather apathetic toward irrigation work. According to an eighteenth-century governor of Shensi:

> Water benefits could be realized everywhere if dikes and drains were built to conduct water of these rivers [in the province]. But on the one hand government functionaries do not take into their consideration the people's sufferings, and, on the other hand, the people [even] knowing what is beneficial to themselves, fail to accomplish anything in the absence of definite plans. Even in places where water ditches originally existed, these are allowed to fall into disuse.[72]

It was said that in one of the districts of this province, villagers did not enjoy any water benefits until 1872, when a well-intentioned magistrate took the initiative in promoting construction work.[73]

In other localities villages were more active in irrigation work. In Chihli, Anhwei, Kiangsu, Kwangtung, and Kwangsi construction work of various types was said to have been undertaken, apparently on the initiative of the local inhabitants concerned and was kept up until comparatively recent times.[74] Some of the projects were fairly extensive. The Shui-nan Hsin-tsung (New Drain of Shui-nan Village) in Tung-kuan (Kwangtung), which was constructed in 1901 with funds raised by the villagers, conducted water through a distance of over 1,100 *chang* (about 4,400 yards), and irrigated more than 700 *mow* of farm land. The amount contributed by each person was in direct ratio to the amount of land irrigated.[75] In another district of the same province minor repair work of irrigation dikes was done by villagers themselves, including landowners and tenants.[76] Inhabitants of Ch'ao Hsien (Anhwei) dug ponds "with their own private labor" to irrigate their fields.[77] Peasants living along the banks of Pao-chiang and Lang-ch'i-chiang, in Yung Hsien (Kwangsi), built embankments with wood and stone to divert water from these rivers to irrigate their farms.[78] Inhabitants along the banks of Ling-chiang, in Ho Hsien, "stopped the river water with a dike, which was used to irrigate farmland on which the major portion of grain produced by this district was grown."[79]

Irrigation work was sometimes accomplished and maintained with a certain degree of formal organization. In I-ch'eng (Shansi), in the late nineteenth century, a number of *ch'ü-chang* (drain headmen) were instituted by villagers to take charge of irrigation matters.[80] In Hua Hsien (Kwangtung) a *p'i-shui hui* (reservoir-water association) was formed to control an irrigation dike which served more than 6,000 *mow* of land. According to a local historian:

There was a *p'i-shui hui* [reservoir-water association] to control [the dike]. It was repaired as soon as breaks occurred during each flood season. The funds required for the work were raised by assessing an amount of money on each farmer in proportion to the amount of land irrigated. The quota of water allotted to each was in proportion to the quantity of rice produced. In recent years [late nineteenth century] Chiang Hao-jan and Chiang Ju-nan of Hsiang-shan village proposed that a thorough repair be made of the dike. They strongly urged all landowners who were members of the reservoir-water association to contribute money in proportion to the quotas of rice they produced. Chiang Ling-chuang, Chiang Jih-hsin, and Chiang Yün-tsao were put in charge of the matter. A sum of 1,400 cash was to be contributed for each *shih* [picul] of rice quota. . . . Modern methods were adopted in the construction. *Hung-mao ni* [cement] was used and the total cost amounted to 10,000 dollars. [81]

This association continued to exist for some time after the fall of the Ch'ing dynasty.

It is quite certain that irrigation work, especially that which involved organized efforts, was promoted by landowners. It is highly probable that some of the promoters belonged to local gentry families or powerful clans. The persons named in the above instance were evidently members of one clan, although their social status was not specified. In other instances it is beyond doubt that the work was accomplished under gentry leadership. In Han-tan (Chihli) a number of water locks were constructed sometime between the sixteenth and seventeenth centuries. One of these locks, called *Lo-ch'eng-t'ou cha*, irrigated over 8,000 *mow* of land cultivated by inhabitants of fifteen villages. Thanks to the guidance of Li Kuo-an, "a *shen-ch'i*"(gentry-elder) the usefulness of this sluice was extended to irrigate an additional 20,600 *mow* of land. [82] In Hua Hsien (Kwangtung) a retired merchant, who was awarded an official title of the fifth rank around 1870, was said to have been responsible for initiating the building of a system of locks which gave substantial water benefits to his home village. [83] Teng Ying-hsiung, a *chin-shih* of the year 1805, who later served as magistrate in Honan province, proposed and pushed through the rebuilding of an irrigation dike in his home village, [84] in Tung-kuan (Kwangtung). Even in cases in which the initiative came from local officials, the actual work was often carried out by the gentry. Without the collaboration of the latter, official initiative could not go very far. Thus, the magistrate of Ho-fei (Anhwei) found it necessary "to go personally to the village and discuss the matter with *shen-shih* and *ch'i-lao* [gentry and elders]" in order to effect the completion of a number of water reservoirs. [85]

For obvious reasons the village gentry were keenly interested in water benefits. Since most if not all were landowners, they readily grasped the importance of assuring harvests to the peasants who cultivated their land. Tillers of the soil also understood the importance of irrigation, but since they did not possess the prestige, means, or knowledge of the gentry, they naturally had to allow the latter to play the leading role.

The situation was essentially the same in flood prevention work, although here the hand of the government was somewhat more evident. In some localities, especially in North China, villagers prepared against flood by choosing a favorable site for their communities, as noted by some British officers in 1882: "Wang-hsu-chuang-tzu; a village of 400 houses or 4,000 inhabitants, built on a mound raised about 5 feet above the surrounding country, apparently to protect it from floods, to which the district appears liable."[86]

A more usual method of flood prevention was to build dikes or embankments. Emergency repair of such structures might be done by the rural community concerned. According to a nineteenth-century Western writer, "As soon as the danger of a flood became apparent, the village headmen ordered relays of men to work on a bank, which was made of whatever soil was at hand."[87] But ordinarily the intervention of the local government was indispensable. Many dikes were actually constructed and maintained by the joint efforts of the local inhabitants and government. In a rural area of Fu-shan (Kwangtung), the flood dikes were kept in repair by the villages protected by them, but extensive construction work was undertaken with the assistance of the local authorities.[88] Official subsidies might be granted to rural communities for the purpose of flood prevention work, and the local gentry were frequently responsible for securing such subsidies, as was the case in the construction of a dike in Hua Hsien (Kwangtung) in 1886.[89]

Indeed, gentry-official cooperation was responsible for the success of many a project. In 1820 three members of the gentry of high standing in Nan-hai (Kwangtung) contributed 75,000 taels to match the 80,000 taels "lent" by the provincial government for repairing and reinforcing an important dike.[90] In the same district, the magistrate in 1879 gave official approval to a gentry proposal that two taels of silver be assessed on every *mow* of land (60 per cent to be paid by the owner and 40 per cent by the tenant) for the construction of a dike protecting two villages. Later, when a flood damaged this dike, a *chü-jen* scholar obtained the permission of the magistrate to assess one tael on each *mow* of land (70 per cent of the sum to be paid by the owner, and 30 per cent by the tenant).[91] In Cheng-ting (Chihli), the government decided in 1873 that a flood dike be built at Ts'ao-ma-k'ou. It spelled disadvantage, however, to one particular village. The work was successfully completed after suitable adjustments were made under the leadership of a local *sheng-yüan* scholar. Other dikes

were repaired at the same time, the work being supervised by "deputies and gentry appointed" by the magistrate. [92] Another interesting
type of cooperation was observed in Mien-yang (Hupeh), where the
flood dikes enclosed areas of varying dimensions locally known as
yüan (literally, a court). According to a local historian, because the
land of this district was generally low,

> . . . the inhabitants built dikes to protect their land. . . . The long-
> est of these measured several tens of *li,* while the shorter ones were
> over ten *li.* [The areas enclosed by these dikes] were known as *yüan.*
> There were over one hundred such areas [in the entire district]. . . .
> Each *yüan* had a *chang* [headman] who directed the laborers engaged
> in the repair work [on the dikes]. [93]

As in many other cases, the expenses incurred were met partly by
assessing cash payments on the land protected by the dikes, partly
by gentry contributions, and partly by grants from the government.
The gentry alone, however, were responsible for supervising and
managing the projects. [94]

Local officials were not always cooperative. Some shirked their
duties, leaving the villagers, gentry and commoners alike, to shift
for themselves. In such cases any work done was without official help
or supervision, thereby giving rise to the distinction between *kuan yü*
(government dikes) and *min yü* (people's dikes). According to a local
historian in Kiangsi:

> [Dikes were built] to prevent floods. . . . Some of them measured
> several hundred *chang;* others formed circles of one or two *li.* . . .
> After repeated breaks and crumbling, the usual practice was to pe-
> tition the government for [repair] funds. Being afraid that the govern-
> ment treasury could not meet all the expenses, it was decided that all
> those that were listed in the old records be classified as "dikes to be
> repaired by the government," whereas those constructed in later
> times should be classified as "dikes to be repaired by the people."
> Dikes in the latter category might be registered [with the magistrate],
> but the government did not inspect them . . . nor supply funds for
> their repair. . . . Hence appeared the classification into "govern-
> ment dikes" and "people's dikes." [95]

Evidence indicates that the distinction between government and nongovernment dikes made in this part of Kiangsi held good also for other
localities. [96] The "people" referred to, however, must be taken to mean
"villagers under gentry leadership," as in irrigation work, even though
such leadership was not indicated. The term was evidently used in
contradistinction to "government" or "official" and not to mean "commoners" in contradistinction to persons with special status.

This point, obvious as it is, is important for correct interpretation of data. A dike in Nan-ch'ang (Kiangsi) with an over-all length of 4,800 *chang* (about 19,200 yards) was said to have been built in the last years of the Ch'ing dynasty "by the village people themselves."[97] It is improbable that ordinary peasants, with their limited means and knowledge, could have accomplished such a task without the direction of the rural gentry. On the contrary, the peasantry usually played a subordinate part in flood prevention work of any considerable extent. Many recorded instances show that retired officials and titled scholars were credited with carrying out such projects.[98]

The rural gentry who undertook flood prevention or irrigation work were not necessarily honest. Some of them took advantage of the situation and their status to practice graft. The deeds of such gentry were not always recorded, but occasionally they were intentionally or unwittingly exposed. A proclamation issued by the prefect of Lu-chou Fu (Anhwei), who was appointed to his post in 1873, is most revealing. This official made known his intention "to put a stop to habitual malpractices in river-dike work," and required all "gentry-managers of the various dikes" thereafter to submit their plans to the prefectural government, threatening severe punishment for anyone who fattened himself through fraudulent methods in connection with dike construction or repair work.[99]

Not all villages were able to take care of themselves in serious inundations. Huc's account of futile attempts made by villagers of a locality in Chekiang province in the mid-nineteenth century serves to illustrate this point:

> In 1849, we were stopped for six months in a Christian community of Tche-kiang [Chekiang], first by the torrents of rain that fell, and then by a general inundation over all that part of the country. It had the appearance of a vast sea, on the surface of which trees and villages were floating. The Chinese, who foresaw already the destruction of the harvest, and all the horrors of famine, displayed the most remarkable industry and perseverance in struggling against the misfortune from which they were suffering. After having tried to raise dykes round their fields, they next attempted to drain off the water by which they were filled; but just when they seemed on the point of succeeding in their difficult and toilsome undertaking, the rain again came pouring down, and their fields were once more covered. For three whole months we witnessed their unceasing industry; their labors were never discontinued for a moment. . . . The inundation could not be mastered, however; and after all their exhausting labor, the poor sufferers were compelled to abandon the cultivation of their fields, and found themselves in a complete state of destitution. Then they began to assemble in great bands, and wander about the province with bags on their backs, begging here and there for a little rice. . . . Whole villages were abandoned, and numerous families went to seek a subsistence in the neighboring provinces.[100]

Crop-watching was another type of village activity related to the economic welfare of persons engaged in farming. Crops were liable to theft by men or destruction by beasts, and for that reason required protection. Consequently, in some rural communities villagers organized themselves to watch crops collectively. For example, it was said that in the nineteenth century in Lu-i (Honan):

> During the time when barley and wheat were being harvested, women and girls of poor families flocked into the fields to pick up the ears that the harvesters overlooked and that lay on the ground. Cunning ones might pluck some [that were not cut], when no one was looking. Quarrels often resulted. Consequently, when harvest time approached, an explicit prohibition against picking up the ears was issued through common agreement [among the inhabitants]. Punishment was also definitely provided for anyone who grazed horses and cattle [in the fields] or who pilfered ears of wheat or rice. [Such an arrangement was] known as *lan-ch'ing hui* [association for protecting green crops]. [101]

Cooperative crop-watching benefited every tiller of the soil, but the task of organization and direction naturally fell on the shoulders of village leaders, who presumably owned land. As a Western writer observed:

> Certain activities are engaged in by the villagers under the direction of the elders. The most common of these is the organization and work of the "Ch'ing Miao Hui," or "Society for the Protection of the Growing Crops." Each family is requested to supply a certain number of youths to watch in turn over the growing crops. [102]

According to another Western observer writing at the end of the nineteenth century, the expenses entailed were borne by the landowners:

> [Crop-watching societies] are by no means of universal occurrence, but . . . are to be met with in some districts. . . . When a fixed number of persons is employed [to watch the crops], the expense is shared by the village, being in fact a tax upon the land, paid in the direct ratio of the amount of land which each one owns. [103]

In some instances offenders were very severely punished. A governor-general in the late nineteenth century reported that a luckless person in an unspecified part of Yunnan province plucked some ears of corn belonging to a neighbor. The watchman gave the alarm and he was caught. "According to custom a meeting of the village elders was summoned and the case laid before him." The pilferer was condemned to death, after his mother was compelled to sign a paper consenting to the sentence. [104]

Villages without crop-watching organizations were powerless against robbers and had to depend upon the government for whatever protection it chose to give. An interesting instance was afforded by

Shensi province. In a 1745 order, Governor Ch'en Hung-mou said:

> I have heard that there is a type of roving rowdies or vicious ma-
> rauders who lodge at deserted temples and abandoned kilns. When
> the autumn crops are ripe and pending harvest, they group them-
> selves, three or five in a batch, and furtively cut [the crops] in the
> darkness of the night. The stolen crops were sold in nearby places.
> A few of the landless households harbored such persons, deriving
> profits in reselling [the goods] thus sharing the booty [with them]. [105]

This shows how useful were the crop-watching organizations. The
fact that they were not "of universal occurrence" will not appear
strange if we remember that not all Chinese villages were well-organized communities, and that the smaller ones among them were
hardly communities at all.

In order to forestall the extortionary and evil practices adopted by
many a tax collector, some villages were known to have devised measures of self-protection, which consisted in helping or requiring fellow villagers to be ready for their tax payments and thus reducing
opportunities for extortion to a minimum. In a memorial submitted
in 1885 the governor of Kiangsi reported the following interesting
system:

> It has been ascertained that in Kiangsi there was formerly a method
> to insure prompt payment of the grain and labor taxes by enlisting
> volunteers who reminded the taxpayers of their obligations. Upright
> gentry and elders nominated a headman for each Hsiang and *tu* di-
> vision. . . . In addition to the headman, there were persons [ap-
> pointed to assist him] known as *tsung-ts'ui, kun-ts'ui,* and *hu-t'ou.*
> The appellations differed in different districts and the time set for
> completing the payments varied. But in all cases strict regulations
> were drawn up and all taxpayers urged one another to complete the
> payment of taxes on the appointed dates. Seldom was there a default-
> er. [106]

The governor continued to say that the system had broken down as a
result of the devastations of war. The number of defaulters increased
and the revenue from the grain and labor taxes decreased. But in those
districts where the system survived, the inhabitants continued to pay
their taxes in full or even in the worst cases never below 90 per cent
of the quota.

The *modus operandi* of such volunteer systems, according to another official of the period, was briefly as follows:

> One of the *chia* [headmen] served voluntarily to remind the inhabitants
> of their tax obligations; the term of service was one year. A person
> of ability and diligence was then selected by the inhabitants of the

chia to serve and was designated as "person in current service." . . .
Yamen runners were not allowed to go to the households [to demand
tax payments] in those *t'u* and *chia* divisions where such persons had
been appointed. [107]

A few similar instances were reported in other provinces. A governor of Kiangsu who held the post in the 1860's said in a directive
that as the current method of pressing for tax payments was onerous
to the "little people," it was better to adopt the method of "volunteer
agents of the *t'u*," the method prevailing in Wu-yang. In another document it was revealed that this method was adopted in Kao-yu Chou. [108]
This differed from the system in Kiangsi described above in at least
one respect: it was the result of government action instead of local
initiative. In Nan-hai (Kwangtung) an elderly person who was granted
by imperial grace the *chü-jen* title in 1862 and the title of Tutor of the
Imperial Academy the following year, built a hall for the sole purpose
of affording a meeting place for all the *chia-chang* in his own *t'u* division and a place where the regular taxes could be received by them.
As a result, "no tax agents [of the government] ever went to that rural
area." [109] However, this arrangement, which had the same effect as the
volunteer system in Kiangsi, was due to the generosity of one man
rather than to the cooperation of villagers in general. Another variation was found in Ju-lin Hsiang (Nan-hai, Kwangtung), where the
clan undertook to protect taxpayers against unscrupulous collectors.
According to a local historian writing in the 1880's, the situation was
so unbearable that the clans in this rural area authorized managers
of the ancestral halls to urge and receive tax payments of the households, thus sparing them the malpractices customarily resorted to
by government agents. [110]

Activities Connected with Local Order

Apart from the *pao-chia* heads, who were agents of the government
charged with the task of detecting crimes and criminals and preventing undesirable persons from hiding in the neighborhoods, many villages had their own leaders upon whom the inhabitants depended for
maintaining a certain degree of peace and order. These leaders supplemented the duties of the local official to some extent, especially
in settling local disputes, keeping villagers from drifting into improper conduct and in times of unrest defending their own communities against banditry. Sir Robert K. Douglas observed in the closing years of the nineteenth century that "a vast amount of business"
which should have fallen on the shoulders of the local official, was
"borne by his unofficial colleagues," the village leaders. [111] This is
substantially true, although the phrase "vast amount" may imply an
overestimate of the role of village leaders.

The settlement of local disputes was one of the functions of these leaders. No formal organization was instituted for the purpose, but as a rule the persons qualified to act as arbitrators in each community were recognized by their fellow villagers. These men were usually noted for their integrity, impartiality, and good sense. They were likely to belong to families of means and status, or as in many instances in South China, they were the heads of clans. Gentry status was not an indispensable qualification, but literacy was a definite advantage.[112] In some cases the arbitrators were village headmen.[113] Whatever may have been the personal qualifications and status of the arbitrators, their decisions were generally respected by the disputing parties.

The scope of arbitration ranges from settling petty squabbles between individuals to resolving clashes between groups. The following is a good instance of the successful settlement of an intraclan feud by Han Chao-ch'i, who acquired the *kung-sheng* status in 1878, in a village in P'an-yü district (Kwangtung):

> The Han clan of Ku-pa [village] was divided into two big *fang* [branches]. The members of these *fang* quarreled over a gate tower at Chung-tso . . . resulting in armed conflict. Fellow villagers ran for safety. Clan regulations failed to restrain them and the local official was unable to stop them. Three or five upright members of the gentry . . . begged him [Han Chao-ch'i] to return to his native village to effect a conciliation. Disregarding difficulties as well as danger, he personally went to the place where the fight was raging and by calm, impartial reasoning made both parties listen to him.[114]

Ordinarily the situation was not so spectacular. Many community disputes and neighborhood quarrels were settled in the village or town teahouse where the disputing parties, arbitrators, and onlookers assembled. The arbitrators listened to the arguments of both sides and rendered their judgment. The party adjudged to be at fault was supposed to pay for all the cups of tea served to those present, if no other penalties were imposed in addition.[115]

In a country where litigation in court was usually costly and troublesome, if not altogether ruinous to both defendant and plaintiff,[116] there was great value in settling disputes out of court. Well-intentioned officials often discouraged lawsuits and sent litigants to their home villages to seek the arbitration of their fellow villagers.[117] Grateful villagers might repay the services of effective arbitrators by rendering them assistance in return, as in the case of a *sheng-yüan* who apparently had more literary talent than financial resources:

> Mr. Yü Huan-mu of Hsin-ch'ang [Chekiang] was a poor scholar. In Tao-kuang Chi-hai [1839] he desired to take the examinations in the provincial capital, but he did not have sufficient money [to make the trip]. He remembered that in a past year he had helped a certain

> village settle a dispute; he visited this village [expecting the inhab-
> itants to render him some help]. Upon his arrival, the villagers gladly
> welcomed him; they were eager to entertain him with dinners and gave
> him more than twenty taels [as a gift]. . . . [With this money] he
> journeyed to Hangchow [the provincial capital] . . . where he took
> the examinations . . . and came out first on the list of successful
> scholars. [118]

Arbitration, however, was not always efficacious. Generally it could
not be resorted to in very grave incidents. Cases involving *jen-ming*
(human death) were seldom settled out of court, even where no crime
(manslaughter or murder) was committed. Villagers thus implicated
seldom escaped the blackmail and extortion of yamen underlings or
rural bullies. The suicide of a daughter-in-law in a southern village
in the nineteenth century reduced a well-to-do family to ruin. [119] Moreover, so long as lawsuits were a source of income for *sung-kun* (litigation sticks, i.e., pettifoggers) and for those who connived with
them, arbitration could never supplant yamen justice. [120]

Perhaps the greatest misfortune was that village arbitration did
not always insure equity or impartiality. The following description
of conditions in a village in South China is revealing:

> Justice is not always rendered in an even-handed manner in Phenix
> Village. There have been cases where the leaders have been under
> the influence of large branch-families or sib moieties *[fang]* that have
> been able to pervert or miscarry justice. If the offended party be-
> longs to a decadent line of the sib [clan], if his immediate relatives
> are few and *his financial resources and his learning limited,* he hardly
> dares to demand absolute justice from the offender who may have the
> support of a powerful familist group. Should he insist upon absolute
> justice, the leaders may grant it, but members of the strong familist
> group may subject the plaintiff to unending persecution in all sorts of
> indirect ways. [121]

Justice therefore proved powerless against the dominant influences
of clan, wealth, and "learning" in this modern village. It is reasonable to suppose that this held true in some of the rural communities
of earlier times.

Village order was maintained in a more positive way by formulating and enforcing *hsiang-kuei* (village regulations). According to the
compiler of a modern gazetteer, the earlier editions of this gazetteer contained a section which recorded the rules and prohibitions
calculated to promote the welfare of the community. These rules
were formulated by the gentry and commoners of the rural areas and
approved by the local official. [122] Another local historian recorded a
case in which a wealthy merchant of Tu-hsing village (in Hua Hsien,
Kwangtung, population about 1,200 persons), who had purchased a

fifth-rank official title, "brought together a number of rural gentry and drew up a set of *Hsiang-kuei* for the guidance of all."[123]

The effectiveness of village regulations depended much upon the quality of the persons who enforced them. It was said that when Hung Hsiu-ch'üan, the Taiping leader, lived in his home village in the 1830's, he set up five rules for his fellow villagers to follow. He promised flogging to anyone who committed adultery, seduced women, proved himself undutiful to parents, indulged in gambling, or loafed and "did evil." He wrote these rules on wooden tablets and distributed copies of them to heads of families. His commandments were so greatly respected by the villagers that two persons who committed adultery fled from the village for fear of his punishment.[124] In another rural community in South China, a *chü-jen* scholar (a contemporary of Hung Hsiu-ch'üan) succeeded in "purifying the morals" of his community by forbidding all wrongdoing. He enforced the prohibition against gambling so thoroughly that "no gamester dared to gratify his desires." His prestige was so great that he even altered an undesirable custom of long standing. According to a local historian:

> It was an old custom of Chiu-chiang [in Nan-hai, Kwangtung] that [misogamist] women loathed to live in their husbands' houses. They often committed suicide, if they were compelled to do so. . . . [Feng] Ju-t'ang [the titled scholar in question] sternly prohibited this practice, making it known that should any woman violate his interdiction [and put an end to herself], her husband's family might bury her corpse with nothing but straw to cover it, and her own parents' family would not be allowed to interfere. Thereafter this custom disappeared.[125]

Indeed, the prestige of some elderly villagers was so overwhelming that it exerted a direct, decisive moral influence upon their neighbors. It was said of one Yeh Sung-ling (status not specified), an inhabitant of a village in Hua Hsien (Kwangtung):

> In his last years he lived in his native village. When his fellow villagers were involved in private quarrels, a word from Sung-ling immediately stopped all wrangling. One time, a neighbor of his violated the village regulations through carelessness. Fellow villagers were about to meet in the temple to discuss punitive measures. The offender pleaded with them that he was perfectly willing to receive his due punishment, but the matter must not reach the ears of Sung-ling.[126]

Huc recorded a curious instance of a repentant gambler who stopped gambling in his community through concerted efforts:

> Gaming is [legally] prohibited in China, but it is nevertheless carried on everywhere with an almost unequalled passion. One large village, situated near to our mission, and not far from the Great

Wall, was celebrated for its professional gamblers. One day, the chief of a considerable family, who himself was in the habit of playing, made up his mind to reform the village. He therefore invited the principal inhabitants to a banquet, and towards the end of the repast he rose to address his guests, made some observations on the evil consequences of gaming, and proposed to them to form an association for the extirpation of this vice from their village. The proposal was at first received with astonishment; but finally, after a serious consultation, it was adopted. An act was drawn up and signed by all the associates, in which they bound themselves not only to abstain from playing, but to watch the other inhabitants, and seize upon all gamblers taken in the fact, who should be immediately carried before the tribunal to be punished according to the rigor of the law. The existence of the society was made known in the village, with the warning that it was resolved and ready for action.

Some days afterwards, three most determined gamblers, who had not taken the manifesto in earnest, were surprised with the cards in their hands. They were bound and carried before the tribunal of the nearest town, where they were severely beaten and heavily fined. We stayed some time in this part of the country, and can testify to the efficacy of this measure in correcting the prevailing vice of the village. So striking, indeed, was the success of the association that many others were organized in the neighborhood with the same object. [127]

Local Defense

Another important activity was exhibited by many villages. During times of disorder some of the rural communities threatened by bandits or rebels organized themselves for self-defense, either upon official encouragement or on their own initiative. The local defense forces were usually known as *hsiang-yung* (rural braves) or *t'uan-lien* (regiment and drill corps). While normally the government jealously guarded its military power, making it illegal for private subjects to possess weapons, it was compelled, especially in the middle and late nineteenth century, to enlist the help of rural inhabitants to cope with widespread insurrections and rebellions. Local officials were instructed to urge the inhabitants to organize *t'uan-lien* or *hsiang-yung*. [128] The government often employed local corps to fight beyond their native places (the Hunan *t'uan-lien* being of course the most outstanding instance) especially where the corps were organized under government auspices. Those formed on local initiative, on the other hand, were usually intended for the defense of the respective communities and seldom operated outside of them.

Local initiative frequently came from the gentry, who had more at stake than the average commoner, but commoners were not excluded from leadership. Hsieh Hsien-liang, a farmhand who lived in

a village of Ho-fei (Anhwei), was probably one of the most successful among commoner leaders in local defense. When Taiping troops
invaded northern Anhwei in 1853, local bandits sprang up almost everywhere. Hsieh was the first to propose *t'uan-lien* and was responsible for building earthen walls to defend his community. The rebels,
it was said, never broke through the defense lines he set up. [129] Shen
Chang-ta, a vegetable gardener, initiated local defense in the town of
K'an-p'u (Hai-yen, Chekiang) against the Taipings in 1861. [130] Pao Li-
shen, a peasant of Pao village in Chu-chi (Chekiang) led his fellow
villagers in a brave though futile defense of their home community.
According to a memorial submitted to the imperial government in
1864 by the acting governor, over 14,000 inhabitants and refugees,
including gentry and commoners, lost their lives when the village fell
in 1862 (T'ung-chih 1). [131] Nevertheless, the majority of leaders in
local defense were gentry or scholars with or without titles, who by
virtue of their status and literacy were better qualified for the task
than the average peasant.

Instances of gentry and scholar leadership in rural self-defense
are numerous. [132] Two types (or levels) of leadership can be distinguished. On the higher levels were persons who organized the militia,
financed and directed the operations. These were usually persons of
special status and comparatively ample financial means. On the lower levels were persons who actually commanded the forces. Gentry
and scholars quite often served as field commanders and fought with
the rank and file, but the majority of the commanders of the smaller
units were commoners. [133] It seems reasonable to assume that wherever the government was interested in *t'uan-lien,* it naturally showed
preference for gentry leadership. [134]

Practices and nomenclature varied in different localities. Commanders of smaller units were often called *t'uan-chang* (regiment heads) or
lien-chang (drill chiefs) or *t'uan-lien chang* (regiment drill chiefs).
Those of larger units frequently bore the title *t'uan-tsung* (regiment
generals) or *lien-tsung* (drill generals). [135] Managers or directors of defense organizations set up their offices in a village or town; such offices
were sometimes called *t'uan-lien chü* (regiment-drill bureaus). Sometimes one general manager was appointed and designated *chü-chang*
(head of bureau); or a number of persons served as *shen-tung* (gentry-
directors). Finance, supplies, drill, and other important matters were
discussed, decided, and managed by managers or directors. [136] In some
instances *t'uan-lien* bureaus also undertook to settle disputes between
villagers, as in the case of Hua-feng Chü (Flower Peak Bureau) in Hua
Hsien (Kwangtung) during and after the Taiping period. [137]

Villages and towns, not being blessed with the security of the walls
and moats of cities, usually strengthened their defense by building
wooden stockades or more often earthen or stone walls around them-

selves. These became known as *chai, pao,* or *yü.* If the terrain was not defensible, more suitable locations might be chosen for the *chai* or *pao,* in which valuables were kept and to which villagers repaired for safety. Such strongholds were known in practically all periods of imperial China and in all parts of the empire which bandits or rebels threatened to overrun. [138] A few nineteenth-century examples will serve to illustrate. In T'ung-shan (Kiangsu), a total of 133 *chai* were constructed between 1858 and 1865 by the inhabitants of 98 villages to defend themselves against the Yüeh-fei (Kwangsi bandits). [139] A *sheng-yüan* scholar living in a village west of the city of Ho-fei (Anhwei) led his fellow villagers in a successful defense against local bandits, the Nien-fei, and the Taiping troops between 1846 and 1860. "Walls and moats were constructed. . . . Nearly ten thousand households sought protection. [The inhabitants] fought when bandits came, and tilled their soil when they departed. The western countryside was thus able to live in comparative tranquility."[140] Villages of Yü-lin (Kwangsi), realizing the futility of fleeing before the oncoming bandits and convinced by the arguments of local officials, began in 1854 to erect defense walls. "Each village built a wall around itself, with mud or sun-baked bricks. The more prosperous villages sometimes used *san-ho* earth [a sort of cement]. All these walls were high enough to screen a man standing."[141] Villages in Honan often found safety in their *chai* or *yü* during the years when the province was threatened by the Nien rebels. [142] A Westerner journeying through the province in the late 1860's was impressed by the large number of these walled villages, which were "about six feet or more in thickness."[143] About the same time similar fortifications were seen in some parts of Shansi, in one district "as many as twenty being sometimes in sight at once."[144] It was said that between 1851 and 1898 no less than seventy-four *chai* were built in the countryside of Fu-shun Hsien (Szechwan), the largest of which was San-to Chai. Some 70,000 taels and seven years (1853-59) were required for its completion. It measured 1,300 *chang* (about 5,000 yards) in circumference and enclosed 4,000 *mow* of land (about 600 acres). The stone walls reached a height of about three *chang* (some thirty feet) and were eight or nine *ch'ih* (about ten feet) thick. [145]

The usefulness of the village defense organizations, up to a certain point, cannot be denied. They afforded some protection to the rural inhabitants, and helped the government to reduce local disorder and to curtail the movements of "bandits."[146] In fact, the Ch'ing government was quick to recognize the value of local corps. As early as 1797 it was proposed that local defense forces be organized to cope with the White Lotus, who were then rampaging in a considerable part of the empire. [147] The imperial government made much more extensive use of *hsiang-yung* or *t'uan-lien* in the Taiping period, first by re-

lying on high officials appointed especially for the task and later on
local gentry who cooperated with the government.[148] But the imperial
authorities were not without misgivings in allowing rural inhabitants
to arm and organize themselves. They were compelled by circumstances to resort to local corps, but they tried to keep a vigilant eye
on them. The following edict issued sometime in 1863 is particularly
revealing:

> Defense work along the northwestern borders of Hupeh province is
> at present urgent. Kuan-wen [then governor-general of Hu-Kwang in
> charge of the campaign against the Taipings] and Yen Shu-sen [gov-
> ernor of the province] should order all *chou* and *hsien* [magistrates]
> not to slacken their efforts in *t'uan-lien* work. They must select ca-
> pable local officials who shall supervise and guide the gentry and com-
> mon people to carry it out earnestly and in a proper way. The aim is
> not only to secure mutual assistance in defense but to prevent the pow-
> er of control from slipping into the hands of the people.[149]

Another difficulty confronting the government was that the motives
of local *t'uan-lien* leaders did not always coincide with imperial purposes. The local gentry were more directly interested in protecting
their homes and communities than in helping the government to put
down "banditry" in general. Such divergence of interests is revealed
in an edict issued by the Hsieng-feng emperor in the spring of 1860.
After stating that he had ordered the provincial authorities to encourage the local gentry and people to set up *t'uan-lien* organizations and
that it was necessary to extend *t'uan-lien* work in areas affected by
the Taiping Rebellion, the emperor continued:

> We hereby order all officials, both high and low ranking, who are
> now serving in the capital and whose native places are in Kiangsu,
> Anhwei, Chekiang, and Honan, to memorialize us to express their
> opinions and state what they know concerning the methods of estab-
> lishing *t'uan-lien* to assist the military campaigns and defense. It is
> imperative that [these officials] should take into consideration the gen-
> eral situation as a whole [i.e., the imperial interest] . . . and should
> not take into account [the immediate safety of] their respective home
> communities.[150]

The safety of their home communities, however, often constituted
the primary motive of those who organized *t'uan-lien*. This basic attitude was tellingly described by a local historian. Commenting on
the government's attempt in 1796 to use local defense forces to suppress a White Lotus rebel band led by Wang San-huai in certain parts
of Szechwan, he wrote:

> When rural volunteers are used to defend their respective villages

or neighborhoods, their effectiveness is readily demonstrated. But if
they are made to fight elsewhere in a general campaign, they are
quite unwilling [to serve]. For in the latter case there are no families, homesteads, farmland, and ancestral graves which have a hold
on their hearts.[151]

To some extent the government was correct in its estimate of the
usefulness of the local defense forces. The phenomenal successes of
the *t'uan-lien* of Hunan and Anhwei hardly need recalling. In other
instances the local defense forces may have proved to be better soldiers than the regulars of the Lü-ying. According to a Western witness writing in the closing years of the Hsien-feng reign:

> During the progress of the Rebellion, we have seen that the Govern-
> ment soldiers have been of little use, and that the chief checks sus-
> tained by the rebels have been from bands of *volunteers,* induced, by
> the high pay of wealthy men, to engage themselves against the enemies
> of the Emperor. At Tien-tsin it was the volunteers who saved Peking.
> . . . It was these "braves" who routed the Canton rebels, and inflict-
> ed their chief disasters. . . .

Describing the situation in Canton, this writer remarked:

> At intervals we had to crush through the barricades formed in the
> streets. At each was a guard of picked men in the pay of the house-
> holders in the neighborhood. They were by far the best-looking of all
> the soldiers. The village braves were the next best; long lanky fellows
> they were, poorly armed and badly dressed—the leg naked to the
> thigh, but dashing-looking men. And how different from the ragamuffin
> vagabonds that were rankled as *soldiers,* hang-dog, cutthroat, coward-
> ly wretches, better fitted for a massacre than a fight.[152]

This writer's opinion of the fighting qualities of "the village braves"
is borne out by the fact that their counterparts in many other parts
of the empire were credited with fine performances.[153]

Not all localities, however, formed defense organizations. Many
villages were too small or too impoverished to be able to afford them,
if indeed they needed any defense against the "bandits" who often
robbed the wealthy and promised a better lot to the poor. Even in
rural communities where protection was necessary, those who had
much at stake did not necessarily have enough will power to organize
a defense force. In some localities the gentry fled before the advanc-
ing rebels or bandits, leaving their communities to the mercy of the
invaders. An edict of 1853 reveals such occurrences in Kiangsi.[154]
When the danger seemed remote, local leaders had to be strongly
urged by magistrates or higher officials before they took any action.
A case in point was encountered in I-ch'eng (Shansi):

Since the beginning of the campaign, all governors-general and governors of the provinces have ordered their subordinates to organize volunteers for defense purposes, calling [these forces] *hsiang-t'uan* [rural corps]. At the beginning of the T'ung-chih reign [1862], conditions in Shansi province became turbulent. Magistrate Ch'eng of this district received orders to call a meeting of the gentry to discuss a plan for enlisting two hundred volunteers. The gentry indicated that it was a difficult task. The magistrate wrote them three or four times, urging [them to take action]. When they finally went to the yamen, the official dispatch was shown them. The magistrate added: "This matter absolutely cannot be delayed. " The gentry were thus compelled to comply. . . . In the winter of *ting-mao* year [1867], the Nien bandits marched westward from Chi Chou [Shansi]. Magistrate Chao sent a flying dispatch to the gentry, saying, "The enemy is very near: What should be done ?" After hesitating for a long while, agreement was reached with the gentry to enlist an additional three hundred volunteers. [155]

Situations like this lent force to the argument for government intervention. At any rate, official supervision or control of local defense organizations was highly desirable from the viewpoint of the imperial government. It was believed by some contemporary writers that the outstanding success of the *t'uan-lien* under the general direction of Tseng Kuo-fan and Tso Tsung-t'ang was due principally to ingenious government supervision. [156] Tseng himself said that the effectiveness of *t'uan-lien* hinged upon the service of "intelligent, capable magistrates and upright gentry" who could transform the ordinarily timid villagers into an effective fighting force. [157] Another official of the same period voiced the opinion that while local wealth and imminent danger were among the conditions that produced virile *t'uan-lien* organizations, the presence of capable local functionaries was the crucial factor. [158]

Official intervention was not always a help. Inept magistrates often prevented local defense organizations from operating satisfactorily, just as capable ones made them yield desirable results. *T'uan-lien* work was a difficult task that had to be undertaken with a great deal of skill and caution. Frequently local circumstances did not permit the government to do what it wished. Makeshift measures were often resorted to, resulting in unhappy experiences for both the government and the local inhabitants.

In some cases the *t'uan-lien* was simply grafted on the old *pao-chia* system. [159] In others the local corps were employed in connection with the regular troops, an arrangement usually unfavorable to the local corps. One revealing, though not necessarily typical, situation was observed by an imperial censor in 1800. He memorialized the throne that commanders of the government troops, knowing that their troops

could not fight and yet being suspicious of the "village braves," used
the latter alone to bear the brunt of the enemy's attack and the former
as their bodyguards. As a consequence,

> . . . the soldiers treated the village braves as slaves, who during
> quiet hours performed the chores of digging mud, cutting weeds, chop-
> ping firewood, and carrying water. In the evening [the village braves]
> stood guard while the soldiers slept. When bandits came and the vil-
> lage braves fought, the soldiers supervised them behind the lines. The
> village braves suffered all the casualties, whereas the soldiers claimed
> all the merits. Those among the former who had the slightest trace
> of physical strength took to their heels, leaving behind them those
> who were helpless and starving and had to submit themselves to their
> immediate needs. But eventually these also ran away when they were
> [again] confronted by bandits. [160]

The problem of suitable coordination of *t'uan-lien* with *pao-chia*
and government troops was not the only difficulty. Official interference sometimes made the financing of local defense appear burdensome to the villagers. The Ch'ing government resorted to *t'uan-
lien,* as a nineteenth-century writer pointed out, not only to supplement the degenerated regulars but also to shift a part of the military
expenses to its subjects. [161]

However, villagers who might be willing to contribute money for self-
defense were understandably reluctant to pay the expenses entailed
in government-controlled local corps; or they might be so destitute
that they could not make any contribution. Tseng Kuo-fan was so convinced of this difficulty that he hesitated for some time to push his
t'uan-lien program. In a letter to a friend he gave this word of warning:

> The matter of *t'uan-lien* is very difficult to talk about. In the villages
> and neighborhoods the inhabitants are poor and resources have been
> drained. . . . When these persons rise in the morning they do not
> know how they will keep themselves alive till the evening. They have
> hardly any money to contribute [to the *t'uan-lien* funds]. Moreover,
> when they see that those in charge [of the *t'uan-lien* funds] are not
> above embezzlement, they become even more disgruntled and refuse
> to co-operate. [162]

Difficulties sometimes arose between local officials and gentry.
Even in Hunan province where the *t'uan-lien* were particularly suc-
cessful, things were not always what the government desired. One of
Tseng Kuo-fan's contemporaries had this to say:

> Capable local officials . . . are seldom met with. An incompetent
> functionary refuses to go out [of his yamen] and leaves everything to
> the gentry and people. The latter are glad that he is easy to deal with;

they contribute funds and begin to drill. They catch a robber or bandit and send him to the official. [When they] say "flog him, " the official flogs him accordingly; [when they] say "execute him, " the official kills him accordingly. . . . But if the official is arrogant . . . friction will develop between him and the local gentry, and quarrels [between them] will arise. . . . Then there is the corrupt official who never has . . . the intention of defending against bandits. Covetous and cunning, he whispers with crooked gentry every day; with [tax] registers in their hands, they study the relative financial means of the inhabitants, saying, "This one should contribute so much to the *t'uan* funds, that one so much to the *lien* funds. " If contributions are not forthcoming, the persons defaulting will be put in jail. The [crooked] gentry ostensibly ask mercy for the prisoners. But when they come out of the yamen, they declare, "The official is now angry; he is going to impose fines doubling the original amounts [which the prisoners were required to contribute]. " Then they go into the yamen again and tell the official, "So and so is really not very rich; he wishes to present a personal gift to you, desiring that his name be removed from the list. " The official, glad of the "convenience, " [readily accepts the offer], with the consequence that the gentry receive 70 per cent or 80 per cent, while the official receives 20 per cent or 30 per cent of the "gift" money. [163]

Naturally, arguments for local autonomy were often heard. Commenting on the case of a Hunan *t'uan-lien* leader who initiated defense organization in his home village in 1854, a contemporary writer remarked:

I am of the opinion that village defense against bandits should be left entirely to the people themselves, without official interference, for the reason that they certainly understand the imperativeness of [protecting] their own lives and families. . . . But if it is made a matter of laws and regulations and the people are forced [to do it], then the people would meet [the government's orders] with empty words, while crafty individuals might exploit their neighbors by bullying and dictating to them. [164]

The root of the difficulty, however, lay deeper than government interference. Not all rural communities and village leaders were adequate to the task of self-defense. The will to fight was sometimes conspicuously lacking. In the spring of 1861, T'ung-ch'uan (Szechwan) was invaded by the insurrectionary forces of Lan Ta-shun. It was said by a local writer that the *t'uan-lien* corps in the locality proved to be entirely useless:

. . . villagers were secretly concerned with their own safety, and were unwilling [to join *t'uan-lien]* when the disaster was not yet personally experienced. Thus, while *t'uan-lien* [units were organized] to defend against the bandits and prepare for their coming, the units fell apart before the bandits had actually arrived. [165]

Another Chinese writer who witnessed the occupation of Nanking by the Taipings said, "regimenting and drilling native inhabitants were done by the natives with a view to defending their own villages. [Such units] could hardly defend [the communities] against powerful elements from other villages; still less [could they defend them against] the bandits. "[166]

Some of the difficulties that confronted rural *t'uan-lien* were described by a retired official who attempted to establish local defense against the Nien "bandits" in Ho-nei (Honan). In his diary for 1853 the *kuei-ch'ou* year of Hsien-feng, he wrote:

> 5th month, 19th day: Bandits reported as having passed the provincial capital and arrived at Chu-hsien Chen. . . . I wished to join neighboring villages together in order to defend ourselves. But no agreement was reached, no result obtained.
>
> 22nd to 23rd day: The bandits send their men to P'ing-kao, Ch'en-chia Kou, Chao-pao Chen and other villages to plunder. . . . Alarms were sounded several times a day in Yü-nan, Pao-feng [the writer's own village] and other villages.
>
> 24th day: Today all village volunteers have fled. I also sent my family members to live temporarily in the household of relatives in another village. Our village is very poor and lacks the means of defense; nor is there any consensus of opinion.
>
> 25th day: Friends in Ch'en-chia Kou [village] signed my name for me, to make an agreement with neighboring villages . . . to help each other in defense.
>
> 26th day: In the morning I led villagers to the foreshore. The men from the different villages did not show any discipline. Men from certain villages who were supposed to be present failed to come to the place. . . . When we arrived at Liu-lin, the bandits marched out in a pincer movement. . . . As soon as the villagers heard gun shots they all fled and returned [to their homes].
>
> 27th day: The bandits plundered South [Chang], North Chang, and Ch'iang villages. The inhabitants could not defend themselves and all fled. [167]

Apparently not discouraged by the fiasco of 1853, this well-intentioned retired official made an attempt to fortify his home village late in 1861:

> 10th month, 20th day: Invited several villages to discuss the matter of building defense walls. It was agreed that a survey of the land be made, that [funds be raised] by making assessments on the basis of the number of *mow* of land, the number of persons in each household, the size of the houses, the number of domestic animals, etc. An initial

assessment of 300 cash to be made; additional sums to be collected when this proves insufficient. . . . In other villages, assessments to be made only on the basis of land and population, 100 cash on every *mow* of land or each person. In our village wealthy households to contribute money, while poor households to supply labor in lieu of money. . . .

11th month, 1st day: A public bureau for defense construction was set up. . . .

2nd to 6th day: Reported that P'ing-kao and Chao-pao [villages] will build defense walls [of their own]. I am afraid that manpower will be short, owing to the fact that [neighboring] villages sharing our defense walls will be few; it will be difficult to defend our village. . . . In the evening I discussed the matter with fellow villagers, proposing that it is safer to abandon our plan before the construction work has actually begun.

7th day: Fellow villagers again in public discussion decided to carry out [the plan].

(1862) Last day of 3rd month: Construction of defense walls completed. But we lack the means to buy weapons and ammunition. [168]

Divergent or conflicting interests among rural as well as city inhabitants also often rendered local defense a difficult task. According to the Chinese writer quoted on page 302 who witnessed the fall of Nanking:

The difficulty of *t'uan-lien* [lies in the fact] that wealthy persons do not contribute funds, hoping to apportion [the expenses] to households of moderate means; poor people, on the other hand, while having regard for their own lives, wish to take advantage of [the disorder created by] bandits to rob wealthy families. Members of families of moderate means are invariably mediocre men who seek safety in doing nothing and are afraid to incur the enmity of the bandits. When [however, all these categories of persons] are compelled by the government [to organize for local defense], they reluctantly hoist a cloth flag to satisfy perfunctorily the official requirement. As soon as the official is gone, the flag is lowered and concealed. This is the state of affairs at present. [169]

Selfish interests sometimes led persons to actions detrimental not only to imperial order but also to rural peace. In 1854:

There was in An-ch'ing [Anhwei] a barber who went by the name Ting San and who was known for a long time to be a worthless person. He was commissioned to lead five hundred village braves [to fight the Taipings]. When his corps was defeated and fled to Hsiuning [Anhwei], he demanded a bounty of 500 taels. The magistrate of Hsiu-ning refused to give it. Thereupon Ting led his men in a loud protest; they painted their faces, changed their garb, and engaged themselves in large-scale looting. [170]

Persons with better social status might also do things to discredit *hsiang-yung* or *t'uan-lien,* ranging from petty graft to outright "banditry." It was said that during the short period before Nanking fell to the Taipings, many unscrupulous "literary men" (i. e., scholars titled or otherwise) became directors of *hsiang-yung* (village braves) bureaus. Practically all the 10,000 village braves recruited in the vicinity were local riff-raff.

> [The directors] extorted and intimidated the native inhabitants, in order to get money. Using solicitation of funds as a pretext, they secretly received bribes. . . . Meanwhile, they urged men on the streets or in the markets and timid, emaciated scholars to become village braves. These at first were unwilling to enlist, thinking that they were to be real village braves [and had to fight]. But soon they learned from cunning persons [that this was not the case]. All then gladly "served," receiving a daily pay of 300 cash. When afterwards the rebels came, all of them promptly dispersed. . . . Their homes were in nearby rural areas which could be reached in no more than a half day's journey. They threw away their weapons and became plain villagers again. [171]

The gentry of Chin-hua and Lan-ch'i (Chekiang) monopolized *t'uan-lien* leadership. For a time the local corps served their avowed purposes, but eventually they became a curse to the countryside. In a number of villages the armed forces used inspection as a pretext and engaged in robbery, with the result that these localities were regarded by travelers as "a dreadful road."[172] The gentry of some places in Kwangsi province, realizing that titles and ranks granted them as rewards for their contributions to local defense work gave them no material benefit, preferred "to nourish the bandits and share profits with them."[173] A wealthy *sheng-yüan* scholar of a district of Kweichow, who led *t'uan-lien* during the 1850's and was rewarded with the rank of prefect, secretly paid tribute to the "bandits." All persons and families that placed themselves under his "protection" were spared by the invading hordes. The protection, however, was extended only to those who could pay the price—contributions to his *"t'uan-lien* funds."
So many sought it that he did a roaring business.[174] The head of a wealthy family in a Kiangsu district organized a rural defense force. He received titles both from the Ch'ing government and the Taiping, thus sitting safely on the fence.[175] A *t'uan-lien* commander in Shang-lin (Kwangsi) who facilitated the occupation of that city by Shih Ta-k'ai (a Taiping prince), was made a "marquis" by the rebels, as a reward for his "exceptional service."[176] The best known instance of this sort was afforded by Miao P'ei-lin who began his career as a *sheng-yüan,* organized an effective village defense force against the Nien rebels, received high official ranks from the Ch'ing govern-

ment for his services, and ended as one of the most powerful "bandit" commanders. [177] A mid-nineteenth century Chinese writer summarized the situation prevailing around 1858 in Kwangsi:

> We need not dwell on those who use *t'uan-lien* as a pretext for collecting money and grain. There are others who call themselves *t'uan-lien*, but as a matter of fact have friendly intercourse with the bandits . . . who take advantage of their positions to reap immense profits . . . and worse still, who vie with one another in exerting power and influence, instigating angry conflicts and making trouble, or who lead their comrades to engage in open brigandage. [178]

Similarly, Seng-ko-lin-ch'in, the ill-starred commander of government troops against the Nien "bandits," depicted the conditions of the localities under his observation thus:

> The original purpose of setting up *t'uan-lien* and building walls or barricades in the various provinces is to help local defense against robbers and bandits. . . . But the *t'uan* [leaders], emboldened by the possession of these strongholds, frequently set their officials and superiors at naught, and arrogate to themselves the right to decide lawsuits. Some of these gathered around themselves large numbers of persons and refused to pay the grain taxes. Others among them perpetrated armed conflicts to give vent to personal spite. The worst of them even harbored rebellious designs, occupying cities and murdering officials, such as Liu Te-pei of Shantung, Li Chan of Honan, and Miao P'ei-lin of Anhwei, who started insurrections one after the other. [179]

Making allowance for likely official biases, this utterance may be accepted as a fairly reliable indication that local defense organizations did not invariably afford protection to those rural inhabitants who honestly desired it. In fact, some of these organizations proved to be a worse foe to the countryside than the "bandits." A well-known Chinese writer who lived to witness the White Lotus uprisings made a striking comparison of the "religious bandits," the government troops, and the "village braves":

> The *chiao-fei* [religious bandits] kill and plunder but do not violate women; soldiers kill, plunder, and violate women, but do not commit arson. Village braves indulge in all these [crimes]. Therefore, along with the White Lotus Sect, the people call government troops the "Green Lotus Sect" and village braves the "Red Lotus Sect," thus giving rise to the jocular reference to *san chiao t'ung yüan* [three sects with one identical source]. [180]

This discussion of village defense suggests a few conclusions. Impending danger often called forth a higher degree of community co-

operation and organization in villages than was exhibited in more normal times. Even under exceptional conditions, however, the village
did not always show the solidarity of a well-integrated community.
Cross-purposes sometimes rendered local defense organizations
impotent or even harmful. The government was often more directly
interested in suppressing "banditry" at large than in protecting any
given rural community, whereas villagers were more often interested
in local self-defense. The average rural household might be concerned
with its own safety and protection and therefore welcomed or accepted
the inconvenience and expenses entailed in "regiment and drill," but
in local defense selfish gentry households or local bullies might see
an opportunity for reaping illicit gains or extending unlawful influence.
Often the activities displayed by some villages in connection with self-
defense did not benefit the communities as a whole. And as in other
types of activities, leadership more often went to the gentry than to
the commoners.

When some of the gentry leaders took advantage of the unusual power
given them as *t'uan-lien* managers or commanders, the rural corps
afforded the villages defense against neither banditry nor official
corruption. They merely added another form of oppression. Occasionally, the gentry's game of flirting with the "bandits" ended in
tragedy, for both the innocent and the guilty. A Western observer reported in 1874 that a village in Ch'ang-lo (Kwangtung) was laid in ruins
and all its inhabitants massacred by government troops, on the charge
that an influential man of the community had joined the Taipings. [181]
This incident makes ridiculous the assertion that the Chinese village
was "self-governing" or "autonomous."

INTERVILLAGE ACTIVITIES

If the Chinese village as it existed in the nineteenth century was not
exactly a self-governing or autonomous community, neither did it appear to be a self-sufficient unit of rural life, even when it attained a
considerable degree of organization. In many cases the village proved
to be too small a unit to meet adequately the economic and other needs
of its inhabitants, either in normal times or during periods of turbulence. Village activities often transcended the boundaries of a single
community whenever situations arose in which its best efforts were
unequal to the exigencies.

There were two distinguishable types of activities involving more
than one village. In some cases, a number of villages discussed matters of common concern through their leaders, but plans were decided upon and executed separately by the individual communities.

When the local government proposes some desirable but not man-

datory program, leaders of all villages of the area will be called to
the market town to confer with the authorities and offer their opinions.
Back in the villages the official leaders go to the important laymen
leaders and the villagers to tell them what has happened in the market town. Villagers are not in a position to propose anything definite.
. . . On the following market days, the official leaders find out from
each other the opinions of their respective villages regarding the particular matter. . . . After two or three weeks, when the case has been
discussed again and again, the local authority summons the leaders of
the villages and important men of the local area to the market town for
a final decision. Then each village starts to make plans for the program. [182]

In other cases, villages cooperated in undertakings that affected
their common welfare or answered their common needs, making plans
and executing them jointly, often under the general direction of a
common organization. It is this type of intervillage activity that concerns us here. The following few examples show the nature of such
activities.

We have already mentioned the extensive irrigation locks in Han-
tan (Chihli), one of which served the farms of no less than fifteen
villages. [183] Obviously, these were the result of intervillage cooperation. Two adjacent villages in Hua Hsien (Kwangtung) decided in 1898
to improve their irrigation dike. After having agreed upon a plan, the
villages appointed two *sheng-yüan* scholars, one from each community, to take charge of the promotion and management of the project. [184]
A number of villages in Ho-nei (Honan) cooperated in 1848 to lessen
the danger of flood by dredging a river. According to the diary of a
retired official residing in one of these rural communities, the inhabitants proceeded in this way:

> 7th month, 13th day: Heard that the villages are discussing [the
> matter of] dredging the river; very glad. Everywhere water over-
> flows and farms are flooded. Officials pay no attention [to the situa-
> tion]; but [they] press hard for payments of the taxes. . . .
>
> 15th day: In the evening our village publicly discussed the matter
> of dredging the river.
>
> 23rd day: Feng, Ling, and other villages [sent representatives to
> our village] to discuss the matter of dredging the various rivers dur-
> ing the winter and spring months. Maps were ordered to be drawn
> first; *ti-pao* were urged to go to Pei-pao-feng [village] to make a
> survey. [185]

Over thirty bridges were built in 1748 by eight neighboring villages
in Ting Chou (Chihli), which formed themselves into an organization. [186] An important bridge in the countryside of Lin-chang (Honan)
was kept in constant repair by four villages which made use of it. [187]

Crop-watching was sometimes done on an intervillage level. According to a Western investigator writing in the closing years of the nineteenth century,

> . . . the arrangement for guarding standing crops is entered into by a single village or more probably by a considerable number of contiguous villages. The details are agreed upon at a meeting called for the purpose in some temple convenient to all the villages, and the meeting is attended by representatives of each village interested. At this meeting are settled the steps to be taken in case of the arrest of offenders. . . .
>
> To provide an adequate tribunal to take cognizance of cases of this sort, the representatives of the several villages concerned, in public assembly, nominate certain headmen from each village, who constitute a court before which offenders are to be brought and by which fines are to be fixed. [188]

This narrative is particularly illuminating, because it describes the form and procedure of cooperative action, which with suitable modifications may have served other types of intervillage activities.

Pavilions offering free tea and a few moments of rest to travelers were sometimes the result of intervillage cooperation. *Ma-an-kang Ch'a-t'ing* (Tea Pavilion of Horse Saddle Ridge), located in Hsi-ch'iao village (Nan-hai, Kwangtung), was built in 1875 with funds by Chients'un and Chin-ou, two walled villages. *Pai-ho-chi Ch'a-t'ing* (Tea Pavilion of White Crane Embankment), located in Shih-kang village, was built in 1892 jointly by Shih-kang and Shih-ching, two villages in the same district. [189]

Rural markets that served a group of nearby villages were established either by influential individuals of one village or by the communities which made use of them.[190] An actual case in which a market was established by a number of villages in North China was cited by a modern Chinese investigator. The procedure, as recorded on a stone monument set up in 1865 in the village where the market was situated, was as follows:

> It is said that, from time immemorial, markets had been established to facilitate exchange of what one possessed for what one lacked.
>
> Yiaochuang, Chaochiachuang, Tayuli, Lichiachuang and Taipingtsun being neighboring villages and always in agreement over common affairs, now jointly decide to establish a communal market. The market site is to be at Yiaochuang. Market dates are to be on the fifths and tenths. The *tou* [a dry measure] is regulated at the equivalent of twenty *sheng*. Scales will be sixteen or twenty taels to the catty, depending on the kind of commodity. Participating villages will take turns to measure with the *tou*. Public expense accounts will be settled once a year, and will be shared equally among the five participating villages. . . . Any hoodlum disturbing the order, disobeying the old rules and hampering the market, will be reported to the government authority for trial and punishment. . . .

Tayuli and Lichiachuang take *tou* measuring during the first ten days of the month, sharing two-fifths of public expenses. Yiaochuang and Taipingtsun take *tou* measuring during the second ten days of the month, sharing two-fifths of public expenses. Chaochiachuang takes *tou* measuring during the last ten days of the month, sharing one-fifth of the public expenses. [191]

Intervillage cooperation was not limited to economic activities, but frequently extended to religious affairs and matters concerning local order and defense. [192] There is some information concerning intervillage efforts at maintaining order and organizing defense. The *Chinese Repository* described an intervillage organization in the vicinity of mid-nineteenth-century Canton:

. . . of late years, owing to the alarming increase of crime, and especially to the dangerous ascendancy of the Triad Society, an additional arrangement has been made by the people, which, according to the testimony of our informant, works well. Twenty-four different villages have joined together to build a large house for purposes of general consultation; this stands at the market town on the south of the island of Honan. A keeper or president is appointed over this public hall, where the head men of these twenty-four villages meet, and in conjunction with the president deliberate and decide on any cases upon which either one may ask advice. . . . At this hall, once a month, all who desire it of the students in these twenty-four villages assemble before the president, and are examined on a theme proposed by him. [193]

The organization of these twenty-four villages was fairly comprehensive in its scope of activities. Comparable organizations seem to have existed in other parts of the empire. According to a local historian, upon the proposal of a *chin-shih* scholar of Chia-ch'ing 24th year (1819), who retired to his native village in P'an-yü (Kwangtung), two adjacent rural communities were organized into the *Shen-shui She* (Deep-water Association). "Unimportant matters were settled by each village; important matters were decided upon in public discussion by the entire association." [194] Another local historian recorded that a person noted for his ability to deal with exigencies was elected during the Kuang-hsü reign (late nineteenth century) to serve as *tsung-tung* (general director) of sixteen villages. "When the sentiments of people could not agree, [he] skillfully conciliated and adjusted them, so that no conflict of opinions arose." [195] Those sixteen villages obviously had some sort of intercommunity organization.

Settlement of disputes between inhabitants of different villages usually called for intervillage arbitration, even though no permanent intervillage organization existed. In a group of five villages in Hui Chou (Anhwei) the following practice prevailed: "In quarrels involving persons of two of these villages the *shen-shih* [gentry-scholars] of the town communities gather to listen to the statements of the two parties and try to effect a satisfactory settlement. In case the settlement cannot be arrived at, the dispute is taken to court."[196] Perhaps by far the most important undertaking was local defense. As a matter of fact, the *hsiang-yung* or *t'uan-lien* organizations called into being by the large-scale insurrections that shook nineteenth-century China, often went beyond the frontiers of a single village. A fairly extensive intervillage *t'uan-lien* organization was established in 1843 by a *ling-sheng* scholar, which was supported by over eighty villages of Tso Chou (Kwangsi).[197] A much larger organization was formed in 1854 in Yü-lin Chou of the same province under the leadership of several titled scholars (a *chü-jen*, *fu-kung-sheng*, and *tseng-sheng*) and a ninth-rank official, with headquarters in one of the participating villages. The defense forces were divided into ten units and afforded protection to 203 neighboring villages, covering an area of approximately fifty by sixty *li*.[198] When Taiping troops threatened north Kiangsu in 1858, villages in T'ung-shan Hsien, Hsiao Hsien, P'ei Hsien, Su-ch'ien Hsien, and P'i Chou built walls around themselves and set up defense organizations, many of which operated on an intervillage basis.[199] As late as 1900 eleven villages in the eastern part of I-ch'eng Hsien (Shansi) established a common *t'uan-lien* organization which so successfully defended these communities that while other localities affected by the Boxer uprising suffered disorder and other misfortunes, I-ch'eng was spared the punishment of suspension of the privilege of holding the local examinations, because its inhabitants "regarded Boxer-bandits as enemies and killed them."[200]

Huc, the well-known Lazarist missionary, recorded an intervillage defense organization set up by inhabitants of communities near the Great Wall. The circumstances under which it was established were exceptional, but the case may be cited here to illustrate the method of forming rural defense organizations and to throw some light on the attitude of the government toward such organizations when their activities were compatible with imperial purposes.

> This part of the country . . . is intersected by mountains, valleys and steppes. The villages scattered amongst them have not been considered of sufficient importance by the Government to be confided to the care of Mandarins. Deprived of the restraint of authority, this wild region had become the resort of many bands of robbers and miscreants, who exercised their trade with impunity throughout the neighborhood, both by day and night. . . . Many times had the Mandarins of the nearest town been petitioned for assistance, but none had dared to engage in a conflict with this army of banditti.
>
> But that which the Mandarins dared not attempt, a simple villager undertook and accomplished. "Since the Mandarins either cannot or

will not come to our assistance, " said he, "we must protect ourselves;
let us form a *houi [hui]*. " The *houis,* or societies of the Chinese, are
always inaugurated with a feast. Regardless of expense, the villagers
killed an old bullock, and sent letters of invitation to the villages
all round. Everybody approved the idea, and the society was entitled
Lao-niou-houi, or "Society of the Old Bull, " in remembrance of the
inauguration feast. The regulations were brief and simple.

The members were to enroll as many people as possible in their
ranks. They bound themselves to be ready to aid each other in the
capture of any robber, great or small. . . .

It was not long before all the brigands of the country were extermi-
nated or intimidated. . . .

These rapid and sanguinary executions [of robbers] began to make a
noise in the neighboring towns. The relations of the victims besieged
the tribunals with their complaints, and loudly demanded the death
of the assassins, as they called the Associates. Faithful to their oath,
the society presented themselves in a body to answer all accusations,
and contest the actions brought against them. . . . The trial was carried to the Criminal Court of Pekin, which approved the proceedings
of the Society, and banished a number of the functionaries whose negligence had caused all the disturbance. It was thought desirable, nevertheless, to bring the society under the authority of the Mandarins,
and legalise its existence: the regulations were modified, and each
member was required to wear a badge, delivered by the Mandarin of
the district. The name of *Lao-niou-houi* was replaced by that of *Tai-
ping-che [T'ai-p'ing she]* or "Agency for the Public Peace, " and this
was the title which the society bore when we left the country on our
way to Thibet [in 1844].[201]

Before we close this section, it may be interesting to note an example of intervillage organization established by a number of prosperous
villages which constituted a *Hsiang* in Lu-ling Hsien (Kiangsi), on the
west bank of the Kan River.

According to a local historian, these villages established in 1844
a *kung-so* (public bureau) to take charge of matters of common concern. Regulations were drawn up defining the activities of this organization, which centered around two projects, the *i-chuang* (community grain reserve) and *ping-hsing* (scholar aid). Funds required for
financing these projects were contributed by the households of each
village. Only those families that had sent in the designed quota, uniformly 5,000 cash from each, could enjoy the advantages offered by
the organization.

Originally, the grain reserve and the scholar aid were administered separately. The reserve was completely drained between 1855
and 1856; the empty storehouses were not fully replenished with grain
until 1876 when new contributions were made by the households and
clans, the amount to be contributed by each unit being then determined
by the ability to pay. The manager was nominated from *sheng-yüan*

scholars of the participating villages, who were known for their honesty and uprightness. At the end of each year, the manager rendered
accounts jointly with the directors *(shou-shih)*. Those directors who
were in charge for the current year were required to stay in the granaries and report monthly inspection of them. Census records were
prepared so that whenever famine occurred, relief was given to those
who needed it, "evenly and equally."

The scholar-aid project was initiated in 1845 by twenty-four persons, all of whom possessed academic degrees. A temple honoring
"native celebrities" was built in the district city, and a hostel for
scholars taking examinations in the provincial capital. In the home
office (located in one of the villages) four managers were nominated
by common consent from scholars who had attained at least the *kung-
sheng*. Once a year these managers submitted accounts of income and
expenditure for the entire fiscal period. Two managers were selected
by lot from *sheng-yüan* scholars who remained in the capital, to serve
in the hostel. Cash bonuses were given to scholars of these villages
and special premiums to those who passed the examinations or obtained official appointments. Native scholars who went to the provincial capital to take the examinations could find lodging in the hostel on the payment of a "registration fee," amounting to 2,000 cash.

An annual sacrificial ceremony was held in the temple of native
celebrities. It was conducted by scholars who had qualified for the
provincial examinations and was attended by representatives of families that had made the initial contribution of 5,000 cash, that had
subsequently contributed 100 taels to the grain reserve fund, or that
had among their members officials and scholars.[202] This remarkable
intervillage organization was probably exceptional, but it reveals the
extent to which the organized activities of rural communities might
be dominated by the gentry.

COOPERATIVE ACTIVITIES OF VILLAGERS

Cooperative activities of villagers who did not possess any special
status or privilege may be distinguished from what we have described
above as "village activities" by differences in their scope and in the
circumstances or status of those who promoted them. Speaking generally, "village activities" were carried out on a community basis
even where no formal organization was involved, and affected all the
inhabitants of a given village, even though not to the same extent and
in the same manner. And because these activities were normally initiated or directed by the rural gentry, they had village-wide implications even if a large number of villagers did not take an active part
in them. This was true in temple building, dike repairing, local
defense, etc. Even in organized crop-watching, which directly af-

fected only owners and cultivators of the land, all inhabitants of a village were expected to respect the "rules" laid down by the *lan-ch'ing-hui* or *ch'ing-miao hui* and were thus negatively affected by it. "Cooperative activities" of villagers, on the other hand, did not have such wide implications. They were carried on by a number of villagers to fulfill some specific needs of their own. These activities were never intended to embrace the community as a whole, or even to include other fellow villagers who did not have such needs. These were, in short, cooperative undertakings of private villagers instead of community enterprises. Moreover, those who participated in them were almost invariably persons of modest means and status, persons who were impelled by circumstances to pool their efforts or resources for the attainment of some limited ends.

Data on such cooperative activities are meager. The peasants probably had few such activities, and local historians were inclined to attach little significance to them. We shall, however, describe briefly three types of cooperative activities observed in different parts of the empire by Chinese and Western writers.[203]

"Incense" or "pilgrimage societies" constituted the first type. We have seen in an earlier part of this study that many of the Chinese people, believing that unseen forces brought them good luck or ill fortune, spent money on a variety of superstitious practices without stint, even though they could hardly afford to do so.[204] Local temples and religious festivals, usually the results of community efforts under gentry leadership, met some of the ordinary needs of the inhabitants, but did not satisfy all of them. Villagers often believed that the spirits or deities that held sway in distant places were for some reason mightier than those that were worshiped in the local shrines; to these persons a pilgrimage to one or more of such "holy places" was a religious act of the highest merit. To make such a pilgrimage, however, entailed many days of journey from the home village and expenditures far beyond the modest financial resources of many a villager. In order to make it possible, therefore, a number of the inhabitants organized themselves into *hsiang-hui* (incense societies) or *shan-hui* (mountain societies).

The organization established by certain villagers in Nan-ch'ang Hsien (Kiangsi) affords us a fine example of such societies. In order to finance and facilitate a pilgrimage to a temple which was regarded as especially hallowed, these villagers organized the *Ch'ao-hsien Hui* (Society for Visiting Immortals). Each of the members contributed money to the common fund; when sufficient money was thus raised, the members were ready for the trip which they had taken much time and effort to plan. They began their activities on the first day of the eighth month, going toward their destination in groups of a dozen to several dozen. One person in each of the groups was designated *hsiang-*

t'ou (incense head) to lead the procession; another was appointed *hsiang-wei* (incense tail) to bring up the rear. A red banner was carried, on which were inscribed the characters *wan shou chin hsiang* (ten-thousand longevity offering incense). During the season, up to one hundred such groups walked on the roads every day.[205]

An example of *shan-hui* was found in Shantung. To enable themselves to make a pilgrimage to one of the "sacred mountains," villagers who did not have sufficient funds to make the journey organized what were locally known as "mountain societies." Each member of a given society made a fixed monthly payment to the manager who usually lent out the common funds at interest. At the end of three years when enough money had been accumulated, the members went on the pilgrimage in a group.

In some cases, "mountain societies" were organized not to finance a distant pilgrimage but to promote some religious activities in the home community, including theatrical exhibitions in thanksgiving ceremonies. In such cases the societies were known as *tso shan-hui* (sitting or stationary mountain societies) in contradistinction to the *hsing shan-hui* (walking or traveling mountain societies).[206] The activities of the traveling variety sometimes became so extensive, that they alarmed the imperial authorities and called forth a series of injunctions against "interprovincial pilgrimages."[207]

A second type of cooperative activities in which commoner villagers engaged was financial in nature. The economy of rural China was so stringent that even honest and hard-working peasants were frequently compelled to take out loans for which grain was sometimes used as security.[208] Landowning farmers were in many instances forced to mortgage their property.[209] The interest rates were usually too high for the borrowers, to whom the temporary relief effected by the loans was like "drinking poison to quench a thirst."[210] It was so difficult for the average commoner to save money and accumulate capital that expenses beyond daily needs had to be met by borrowing. Villagers and townsmen in practically all parts of China invented an ingenious device whereby hard-pressed families could satisfy their needs and at the same time avoid the tiger's grip of usurers, provided of course they could muster enough friends or relatives to help them out. This was the "loan club" or association, known by a variety of names and given divergent forms in different parts of the empire.[211]

A nineteenth-century writer gives the following account:

> This [loan] society is temporary and voluntary. . . . The leader in
> the formation of the company is its president. . . . The occasion of
> its formation may be the buying of a field or a coffin or a wife, the
> setting up of a shop, the paying of a debt, or the expense of a lawsuit. The one who wants to use a certain sum of money goes among
> his friends and finds who will join the loan-society. He gives informa-

tion to each, concerning the names of others who will join, the amount of each share, and the time of payment. He then makes a supper to which all the members of the society are invited, and each guest lends the host one share. In a month, a half-year, or whatever time has been agreed upon, every member except the president, bids on the next loan, and he who bids highest gets it . . . and every member then pays to this highest bidder a sum equal to what each paid before to the president. So the loan continues to circulate, each who has not yet received it being allowed to bid. . . . Those who have once had the loan receive no interest, and the one who receives it last pays no interest, in the form of a bid, to the others. [212]

The third type of cooperative activity was really a variation of financial aid organization but was promoted by interested parties for the exclusive purpose of financing burials. Like the loan club, the burial association also assumed different names and forms but was invariably established by persons of limited financial means. According to the 1891 edition of the gazetteer of Pa-ling (Hunan),

> Poor families usually organized associations called *hsiao-i hui* [filial-duty associations] to finance funerals [of departed parents]. The procedure was to invite ten persons who had parents of advanced ages, each participant agreeing to put a certain sum of money [into a common fund]. When [one of the parents] died, the funeral expense was paid out of this fund. Consequently, even when a death occurred unexpectedly, the bereaved could fulfill to some extent the requirements of propriety. [213]

A Western observer wrote in the closing years of the last century:

> Societies for the assistance of those who have funerals are of common occurrence, and are of many different kinds. . . .
> Sometimes each family belonging to the league pays into the common fund a monthly subscription of 100 [cash] a month. Each family so contributing is entitled upon occasion of the death of an adult member of the family (or perhaps the older generation only) to draw upon this fund, say 6,000 cash, to be used in defraying the expenses. If there is not so much money in the treasury . . . the deficiency is made up by special taxes upon each member. . . .
> Another form of mutual assistance . . . is the following: A man whose parents are well advanced in life knows that he may at any time be called upon to spend upon the ceremonies at their death an amount which it will be difficult to raise. He therefore "invites association" *(ch'ing hui),* each member of which is under obligation upon occasion of the death of a parent to contribute a fixed sum. [214]

Another Western writer described a more elaborate form of this device:

. . . in order to prepare for the inevitable, those who have aged parents organize themselves into a Parental Burial Association with the definite intention of supplying for one another, as needed, money and labor. . . .

Upon organizing anywhere from ten to thirty people in such an association, the members establish an entrance fee of two dollars per person. This money is then loaned out at the best interest rates available. . . . When a parent dies . . . each member will contribute two dollars to the bereaved son. . . . Each member will send two persons who are to render assistance in any capacity. . . .

The association continues until the last parent of all the members is properly buried."[215]

THE ROLE OF THE GENTRY IN RURAL COMMUNITIES

The gentry (persons with official or academic titles) seem to have constituted the most active element in whatever community life was displayed by the Chinese village, although conditions varied in different parts of the empire. There is some indication that the gentry were more active and exerted more influence in the southern villages than in the northern ones.[216] We have no quantitative data to support this conclusion, but it may be reasonably conjectured that the gentry throve better where the rural economy was less stringent and that the presence of a flourishing elite might in turn augment rural prosperity. In small and impoverished villages there was little room for gentry activities, if indeed persons of special status chose to remain there. The gentry of such communities might become almost as inert as the commoners who inhabited them and virtually give up the functions performed by their counterparts in more prosperous communities. The scholars in one northern district were so throttled by their unfavorable environment that they lost much of the characterisitc aggressiveness of an elite group. According to a local historian:

. . . they were accustomed to a simple life, some of them having to wield the hoe and plough personally. None of them were known to have used undue influence over their fellow villagers and neighbors, or to have indulged in discussing current politics. It had been a practice of long standing not to encourage young family members to advance further after they had acquired the blue gown [the *sheng-yüan* degree].[217]

With this caution in mind we may proceed with the role of the gentry in villages.

Villages owed a great deal to the leadership supplied by the gentry—retired officials and titled scholars—for their limited organization and activities. Men with literary training and special social status were frequently active in the promotion of community

projects, including irrigation and flood-prevention work; the building
of roads, bridges, and ferries; the settlement of local disputes; and
the promotion of local defense organization.[218] It is not an exaggeration to say that the gentry constituted the keystone of rural organization. The village could and did exist without the gentry; but villages
without gentry could hardly show any high degree of organized community life or any considerable amount of organized activity. In so
far as the gentry had an interest in keeping their own communities
orderly and prosperous, their leadership and activities broadly contributed to the welfare of their fellow villagers as a whole. They might
in fact attempt to defend local interests against the encroachment of
the government, such as the extortionary or corrupt practices of local
magistrates and yamen underlings. Their literacy and special status often enabled them to make their protests known and even have
their grievances redressed.[219]

It is a mistake, however, to infer from this that the rural gentry
as a group was antagonistic to the government. On the contrary, retired officials and titled or aspirant scholars usually had an interest
in upholding the existing regime. As scholars they ordinarily prepared for or participated in the competitive examinations; their attitudes and views were therefore conditioned in varying degrees by
the precepts of imperial Confucianism. They were in general loyal
to the empire, even though they held no offices and had no political
responsibilities. Officials temporarily or permanently retired to their
home villages had no desire to antagonize the government or to challenge the authorities. And while scholars did not have exactly the
same status as officials they were potential officials; or, in the words
of a nineteenth-century Western writer, "they were expectants."[220]
Unless a scholar was bitterly disappointed in his aspirations, he generally preferred political stability to political upheaval. Even the persons who acquired gentry status merely "with the purpose of protecting their own kin and local people from the encroachment of the absolute power,"[221] could accomplish their purpose only if the government
which granted them their status commanded the general obedience of
the populace. They too were inclined to uphold the existing order.

Under normal circumstances, then, the gentry exerted a stabilizing
influence on the countryside. It was with good reason that the emperors of the Ch'ing dynasty made use of the gentry in exercising rural control; in fact, they tried to gain control of the village partly by
controlling its gentry.

Unfortunately for the rulers, however, normal circumstances did
not always obtain. Sometimes the rural gentry proved itself more of
a disturbing than a tranquilizing element. Privileged persons were
too often blinded by short-sighted, selfish interests and behaved in
such a way as to injure, perhaps unknowingly, the interests of both

their fellow villagers and the imperial rulers. Since comparatively early times the rural gentry had been known for their exploitation and oppression of the commoner inhabitants of the countryside. Speaking of conditions of the Ming dynasty, an eighteenth-century Chinese historian remarked that "many of the gentry who lived in their home communities relied on their personal power and treated the little folk as their prey."[222] That this tendency persisted in the Ch'ing dynasty may be gathered from the fact that the K'ang-hsi emperor found it necessary in 1682 to order some of his high-ranking servants to make circuit inspections and to report any *hao-ch'iang* (overbearing and powerful) elements that oppressed the common people.[223] A 1747 edict of the Ch'ien-lung emperor contains these revealing words:

> Formerly, the gentry in different localities relied on their power to act arbitrarily and oppressively in their home communities, and to abuse their neighbors. They wrought serious harm in the localities concerned. In the reign of Yung-cheng, special attention was paid to correcting this state of affairs and [the oppressive ways of the gentry] were sternly forbidden. The gentry began to learn to obey laws and regulations. . . . But recently their old habit appears again. Some of them even disregard decrees and laws, doing as their whims dictate. Such gentry are probably found in all provinces, but Fukien faces the worst [situation].[224]

Imperial interdiction and punishment, however, did not prevent some of the gentry from persisting in their undesirable ways. With the exception of a few who were especially notorious or luckless and were disciplined by *ch'i-ke* (unfrocking and dismissal),[225] the majority of *shen-shih* remained in their advantageous position, which they might exploit for their own benefit at the expense of commoner villagers. We have seen that they enjoyed special favor as taxpayers and were usually in a position to evade some of the burdens that legally fell upon them.[226] By force or fraud, privileged persons could secure material gains which often further extended their power and whetted their greed. Against the most powerful gentry elements, even scholars of lesser consequence could not always defend themselves.[227] The average commoner villager was often completely at their mercy.

Some of the ways of *lieh-shen* (bad gentry) have already been noted; a few additional instances may illustrate the part played by such gentry in the village. In some localities of Kwangtung, "powerful families" regularly sent armed bands to harvest by force the crops planted by villagers on tidal lands, calling the operation "seizing the sandflats."[228] Both Hsiang-ling and Ling-fen districts (Shansi) depended upon the water of P'ing-shui River for irrigation. Powerful families monopolized the "water benefits" with the result that no farmer could have water unless he purchased "water certificates" from them. This

inequitable situation continued until bitter feuds broke out, which eventually came to the attention of the imperial government in 1851.[229] A
military *chü-jen* of T'ai-hsing (Kiangsu), hearing that a villager hoarded a quantity of silver, falsely charged the latter with salt-smuggling
and robbed him of all his possessions. This titled bully did not receive punishment until sometime later in 1897.[230] Rural gentry sometimes took the law into their own hands. In some localities of Kiangsi
province, powerful individuals set up prohibitions or regulations in
villages or towns.

> Whenever poor people violated these, the cases were not brought to
> court. The offenders were wrapped up in bamboo baskets and drowned
> or buried alive in pits dug in the ground. Their relatives were com-
> pelled to sign statements to the effect that they had agreed to the pun-
> ishments, and were forbidden to make the matters known [to the gov-
> ernment].[231]

And as indicated in our discussion of rural *t'uan-lien,* privileged individuals were not above practicing graft in connection with local defense work. A governor-general of Liang-Kwang summarized the situation prevailing in the 1860's in these provinces as follows:

> Gentry who were virtuous took advantage of *[t'uan-lien]* to fish for
> gains. . . . Even tenant farmers, heads of the *li* divisions, military
> *sheng-yüan,* scholars aspiring to the *sheng-yüan* degree . . . gathered
> bands to dictate in a district. . . . High gentry used these as their
> talons and teeth; local officials showed them courtesy and respect.[232]

Nor did unscrupulous gentry hesitate to practice fraud in order to
realize illicit gains or to protect vested interests. An example of the
former was afforded by Hsiang-shan (Kwangtung). According to a local historian, peasants, including tenants as well as landowners, organized themselves to protect their land and crops against marauders.
Their self-defense organizations had operated since the last quarter
of the seventeenth century. Late in the nineteenth century, however,
two retired high-ranking officials of Shun-te (Kwangtung) were authorized to establish *t'uan-lien.* Using this as a pretext, they absorbed
the self-defense organizations of the villages of Hsiang-shan into one
extensive organization. Larger and larger contributions were demanded of the peasants. The total amount collected eventually reached
200,000 taels, but the total expenditure was less than 80,000 taels. No
clear account of the receipts and expenditures was ever rendered.[233]
Tung-kuan (Kwangtung) affords an example of the second point mentioned above, the gentry's use of fraud to protect their vested interests.
In 1889 a dispute occurred over rent for government land between the
local officials and some members of the gentry. The gentry called "a
general meeting of the entire district" to discuss measures against the

officials. Among the local leaders were a *chin-shih,* a *chü-jen,* and a *chien-sheng* who had purchased an official title of the third rank. Under their guidance the meeting resolved to petition the prefect, asking him to give due consideration to "common welfare." Apparently under their instigation, posters supporting their cause were issued, which were signed by *shih min* (scholars and people) of the entire district. The prefect replied:

> According to a long red poster sent to me by the magistrate, "all the charitable undertakings of this district depend on this [land]." . . . I definitely know that the posters issued "by the scholars and people" of the said district are the work of members of the gentry. They merely use the name of scholars and people as a pretext. If the district government should make them responsible for managing the matter, they would say, "Popular anger focuses on this matter; we dare not manage it," using this argument as an excuse to evade responsibility and postpone settlement. [234]

The prefect was perhaps not completely impartial but it is unlikely that his charge was entirely groundless, as further developments of the affair revealed. [235]

While not all gentry were selfish or oppressive, the stabilizing influences of "upright gentry" were bound to be neutralized by the deeds of "bad gentry." In so far as the rural elite oppressed their fellow villagers, they also became a disruptive force in their communities, tending in the long run not only to impair the "solidary social relationships"[236] that may have existed in them but also to undermine the economic equilibrium of the countryside. They enriched themselves at the expense of others and seldom invested their efforts and resources for the purpose of developing their villages. Many of them chose to reside in towns or cities, especially after having acquired considerable wealth and influence, where they found greater security, more prestige, and wider scope for their activities,[237] leaving their home communities to thrive or to decay as circumstances dictated.

In such a situation, the gentry ceased to be a reliable medium of rural control for the imperial government. On the contrary, this group tended to aggravate the discontent and unrest of the peasantry in bad times; they thwarted the imperial desire to maintain order in the countryside, even when they did not openly or directly come into conflict with local officials. When they became actually seditious—by secretly joining "bandits"[238] or actively inciting uprisings[239]—they constituted a direct menace to the imperial order itself.

SUMMARY

The evidence indicates that imperial control was never so thorough or complete as to render local organization impossible or local self-help unnecessary, or to immunize rural inhabitants against disobedience. Villages of a certain size and degree of prosperity displayed unmistakable evidences of community life and under different circumstances a variety of community activities calculated primarily to promote or safeguard local interests. In so far as these activities served the general interests of the villagers, they tended to exert a stabilizing influence on rural life and were therefore indirectly conducive to imperial peace. This partly explains why the imperial government did not experience serious difficulties in maintaining its control over the vast countryside until comparatively late times, even though its various institutions of subadministrative control did not function in a fully satisfactory manner.

The government usually refrained from interfering with rural organization and activities, but the Chinese village did not enjoy true autonomy or display the features of a genuine democratic community. Although organization appeared in many villages, it did not appear in all, and even in those where organizations existed, communal activities were limited in scope and were rarely if ever conducted by all the inhabitants on a basis of equality. It is difficult to find an instance in which associative efforts were coordinated by a village-wide organization for the welfare of all inhabitants. Most of the organizations were set up only for special purposes and often merely to meet temporary emergencies. Their membership usually included only a segment of the inhabitants of a given village. Commoners were not precluded from participation or even leadership in village undertakings, but the gentry usually dominated them. It was the gentry that determined to a large extent the pattern and direction of organized village life.

The control that the imperial government exercised over the countryside was an imperfect one. The practical situation rendered a complete control impossible; to a certain degree the government intentionally allowed a degree of freedom to villages and villagers so that some of their attitudes and organizations might be usefully exploited for the purpose of imperial security. The imperfect control thus maintained, however, constituted no guarantee of lasting imperial security. It left room for the appearance of attitudes and activities which were detrimental to security, as much as for the prevalence of those that were conducive to it. It allowed a social stratification and divergence of interests to exist, which may have been useful according to the principle of *divide et impera* but which at the same time prevented the village from developing into a well-knit community capable of meeting the practical problems of life in a none too friendly physical environment. The general tranquillity that normally obtained in the countryside was due much less to the positive will of the villagers to maintain a peaceful existence than to the absence of disruptive forces.

The fact that the population of rural China was not a homogeneous mass cannot be overemphasized. Socially, the inhabitants of a village often fell into two major groups, *shen* and *min* (the gentry and common people); financially, there was a flexible but distinct line between landowners who might be wealthy and tenant farmers who often were poor. The legal status of the gentry was not based on wealth, landed or otherwise; but since the gentry had better facilities to acquire wealth than the average commoner, [240] there was some affinity between social privilege and economic affluence. This is one reason why the organization in Chinese villages was seldom comprehensive and cooperation among their inhabitants usually limited. It is far-fetched to speak with the Marxist of a "class struggle" between the major segments of the rural population, but it seems evident that scarcely anything like "common social relationships" existed among them.[241] Cross-purposes and divergent interests appeared at all levels and the resultant "conflict relationships"[242] prevented the village from becoming a communal unit morally prepared to take care of itself in the face of adverse circumstances. Any serious crisis rendered the bulk of the rural inhabitants virtually helpless.[243] Instead of meeting emergencies with united mind and effort, they reacted to them differently; many of them were forced by the situation to alter their habitual attitudes and behavior. The precarious political and economic equilibrium was readily disturbed. Under such circumstances rural control, at best incomplete, was seriously impaired and became almost entirely ineffectual.

Certain special conditions, however, should be noted. In some parts of the empire, particularly in South China, the clan organization often served to bind rural communities into closer units than the villages of other localities. The presence of the clan in the countryside introduced a slightly different pattern of rural organization and presented a different set of problems for the imperial rulers. In the next chapter we shall examine the role of the clan as a rural organization and the effects and reactions of imperial control as it was exercised over the clan.

Chapter 8

THE CLAN
AND RURAL CONTROL

THE CLAN AND THE VILLAGE

The presence of the clan in a village introduced a principle of cohesion which would not otherwise have been present. For this reason the clan was useful to the imperial government as an instrument of rural control, but at the same time the control of the clan itself presented some baffling problems. The main purpose of this chapter is to ascertain the place of the clan organization in the system of rural control, but we must first examine the structure and functions of the clan itself.

The *tsu* or clan was primarily a kinship group;[1] but since ancient times it had had its roots in some territorial location.[2] As a recent investigator pointed out, "The *tsu* is a group descended from one ancestor who settled in a certain locality or neighborhood."[3]

The locality in which a clan originally settled might be a city or town, but more often it was a spot in the country from which a full-fledged village might spring. In fact, it was in rural areas that the clan usually attained its fullest development,[4] and the village often owed much to the clan. While rural communities were not always the outgrowth of clan settlement, the presence of the clan tended to give them a higher degree of cohesion than would otherwise have been possible. In many instances, as a modern writer said, "All the village organizations, except possibly those based on economic status, are determined directly or indirectly by clan relationships. . . . Neighborhoods are largely made up of families of the same clan."[5] In such cases, it is justifiable to regard the clan as "the solidary unit of the village."[6]

The reason for the strong affinity between the clan and village is obvious. The predominantly agricultural population of the village tended to be less mobile than city dwellers, and kinship ties were therefore better preserved in the villages than in the cities.[7] Hence different patterns of social organization obtained in cities and villages, guilds and "civic" associations being typical of the former as clans were characteristic of the latter.[8]

A nineteenth-century Western writer described the village as an outcome of clan settlement: "At some remote and generally unascertainable time in the dim past, some families arrived from somewhere else, camped down, made themselves a 'local habitation' . . . and that was the village."[9] Such a process probably took place at all times in almost all parts of the empire. San-p'o, a rural area in Cho Hsien (Chihli), was an example. This hilly locality was situated near the northeastern borders of Cho Hsien. Twenty-four villages of various sizes dotted a total area of about 55 by 30 *li*; the largest of these villages contained no more than 130 households each. According to a local historian:

> From the fact that most of [the inhabitants of] these villages had the same surnames and that most of these inhabitants bearing identical surnames belonged to the same clans, it may be gathered that at the beginning there were only a few households which, owing to their poverty, went without authorization into the hills and reclaimed the land. As time went on, a number of villages were gradually formed.[10]

Under special circumstances, large-scale migration and settlement might occur. In such cases not only was the approximate time of settlement known but the actual process could be observed. The repopulating of Szechwan province in the seventeenth century, after the extensive massacre of the original inhabitants by the "roving bandits" affords an illuminating example. According to a local gazetteer:

> In the reign of K'ang-hsi, inhabitants of other provinces were encouraged to populate Szechwan. . . . When [the immigrants] first arrived, all the land was without an owner; they were free to take possession and cultivate it. Sometimes one clan formed a village, and sometimes several clans formed a *pao* [village with defense walls]. In certain cases a single clan occupied as much land as several thousand *mow*. . . . But its members could not actually cultivate all of it.
>
> At the beginning of the Yung-cheng reign [1723], Hsien-te, governor-general of Szechwan [and Shensi], memorialized that immigrants into Szechwan were numerous enough to justify the establishment of the *pao-chia* system. . . . Each married couple was to constitute a *hu* [household], to whom was assigned thirty *mow* of irrigated land, or fifty *mow* of unirrigated land. If a couple had brothers, sons, or nephews living with them, fifteen *mow* of irrigated land or twenty-five *mow* of unirrigated land was given to each additional adult. . . . The emperor gave his approval, and the scheme was accordingly carried out. . . . When the *pao-chia* registers were checked in Ch'ien-lung eighth year [1743], there was a total of 4,470 *hu*, with 15,876 *ting* [adult males]. This was the result of growth in thirteen *[sic]* years, on a small territory of forty *li*.[11]

It is also occasionally possible to trace the history of the settlement of individual clans in a given locality. The *tsu-p'u* or *tsung-p'u* (gene-

alogical records) of some clans narrated the stories of their migration and growth. Information may also be culled from some local
gazetteers. A few instances from one of these latter may throw further light on the formative process of the clan-village.

The *shih-tsu* (first ancestor) of the T'an clan in Hsia-p'ai village
was a native of Heng Chou (Hunan). He went with his father in 1754
to Hsiang-shan (Kwangtung). His son settled in this village where,
early in the twentieth century, the clan grew into three *fang* (branches),
with a total membership of over two hundred. [12]

The first ancestor of the Cheng clan of I-men (Hsiang-shan, Kwangtung) was a native of Chekiang, who served as prefect of Kuang-chou
in the eleventh century. His grandson settled in Hsiang-shan, because
both his grandfather and father were buried there. He became "the
ancestor who established the Hsiang-shan Cheng clan." This clan became so large in the eighth generation that it divided into two branches,
each of the two brothers of this generation becoming the ancestor of a
branch clan. One branch was known as the P'ang-t'ou Cheng clan. Its
"ninth-generation ancestor" married a daughter of the Kao clan of
Hao-t'u Hsiang and moved to his wife's home village. His descendants numbered about 1,000 at one time. Most of those who remained
in the village were farmers, although some engaged in business in
the city and acquired considerable wealth. The other branch, headed
by the younger of the two brothers, gave rise to three subbranches.
(a) Cheng Tsung-jung, the elder son, had three male offspring (i. e.,
tenth generation): Cheng Ku-i, Cheng Ku-shun, and Cheng Ku-wen.
Ku-i and Ku-shun lived in one household; they became jointly the ancestors of one subbranch called the Hao-t'ou Cheng clan with about
5,000 descendants, among whom were the most eminent of the local
gentry. (b) Ku-wen lived with his father at Ch'ien-shan, thereby becoming the ancestor of the Ch'ien-shan Cheng clan, with about 600 descendants. (c) Cheng Tsung-te, Tsung-jung's younger and only brother, served as prefect of Feng-yang and Yen Chou at the beginning of
the fifteenth century. He settled in Ao-hsi and became the ancestor of
the Ao-hsi Cheng clan, with about 400 descendants. [13]

The ancestor of the Wang clan of Wang-yüan (in T'ung-kuan, Shensi)
was a grain-transport intendant in Shantung province, exiled to Shensi
on a charge of delinquency in official duties. He and his family lived
first in Hsi-ku Ts'un village, forty *li* west of the district city, but
later moved to Wang-chia Ho. One of his offspring attained the *chü-jen*
degree in the sixteenth century, and moved to the city. In the seventeenth century the clan moved back into the country, settling down
in Wang-yüan. In the opening decades of the twentieth century, members of this clan, numbering about fifty households, resided still in
the ancestral villages, Hsi-ku Ts'un, Wang-chia Ho, and Wang-yüan. [14]

These few examples show that a settler might take up his abode at some spot and eventually create both a clan and a village, or that he might locate himself in a village or town and generate a clan but not a village. This difference in the mode of settlement may afford a partial explanation of two different types of clan-villages, "monoclan villages," in which a number of families bearing the same surname dwelt, and "multiclan villages," in which two or more clans dwelt side by side.

Monoclan villages were more common in southern provinces. According to a recent writer:

> In the last six or seven centuries the centers of strongly developed *tsu* have lain in Central and Southeast China, that is the Yangtze Valley and the provinces of Fukien and Kwangtung. Here many villages are inhabited completely or predominantly by people of a single surname, recognizing a relationship among themselves. . . . In North China, however, villages composed of families of different surnames constitute the majority. [15]

A Western observer found the following situation in nineteenth-century Kwangtung: "Those of the same surname will in general be found inhabiting the same village, or neighborhood; the various branches of the original stock, like the limbs of the banyan tree, taking root around the parent trunk." [16]

The conditions of a village in Fukien were reported by another nineteenth-century writer: "The whole village was inhabited by persons having the same surname of Lim or Lin, who appeared to be united together by the ties of patriarchal law. This village clanship is a powerful bond of union." [17]

Such monoclan villages were less in evidence in North China, where villages were more often composed of "a cluster of families rather than of one clan," or of "groups of economic families rather than of single family-clans." [18] Monoclan villages, however, did exist in the north. The compiler of the gazetteer of T'ung-kuan (Shensi) wrote: "Formerly the people [of this district] used to collect themselves into clans and live together. Therefore most of the villages were known by the clan names, such as Feng-chia Ch'iao, Wang-chia Pien, Tung-chia Ho, Liang-chia Yüan, Li-chia Kou, etc." [19] The gazetteer of Ch'eng-ku (Shensi) supplied this information:

> During the earlier days of the present dynasty, there were few native inhabitants [in this district]. Bandit disturbances occurred at the end of the Ming dynasty; since then people had migrated from Kansu, Szechwan, Shansi, and Hupeh. Those of the same surnames who grouped themselves into clans and lived in separate villages used the surnames to designate their respective villages. [20]

Such instances, however, were comparatively few. Some of the villages which were formerly composed of single clans had in time lost their monoclan character. A nineteenth-century Western writer noted: "It often happens that in the changes, wrought by time, of the families for whom the place was named, not a single representative remains. In such cases the name may be retained or it may be altered, though all recollection of the circumstances of the change may be lost."[21]

We have no statistics to show the distribution of the two types of villages in the various parts of the empire, but the following figures, inadequate as they are, give us some impression of the situation. Kao-an (Kiangsi), a district neither particularly prosperous nor poor, was reported to have had 1,291 villages around the middle of the nineteenth century. The distribution of the two types of villages was as follows: monoclan villages, 1,121 (87 per cent); multiclan villages, 170 (13 per cent).[22] The villages of Hua Hsien (Kwangtung), a total of 398, however, showed a different distribution: monoclan villages, 157 (40 per cent); multiclan villages, 241 (60 per cent).[23] It appears that monoclan villages did not necessarily dominate all South China, but they were nevertheless more in evidence there than in the north. A modern investigator discovered that in Ting Hsien (Chihli), a predominantly agricultural area, only one of the sixty-two villages was of the monoclan type.[24] This may not be conclusive evidence, but it lends support to the general observation that in North China villages composed of different surnames constituted the majority.

It may also be noted that just as several clans might live in one village, one clan might dwell in several villages when the brood had outgrown the original homestead.[25] The Wang clan of Hsing-lin Ts'un in T'ung-kuan (Shensi) was a very good instance. At the downfall of the Yüan dynasty (1367), a certain Prince I found refuge in this village. His descendants became peasants and remained so during the Ming and Ch'ing dynasties, although some of them entered the brotherhood of scholars at the end of the Ch'ing dynasty. The clan kept no written genealogy, but the clan relationship among the more than eighty households that dwelt in six different villages was preserved unimpaired for centuries.[26]

The differences in composition between monoclan and multiclan villages was reflected in some difference in organization. In the former, where kinship group and rural community were virtually identical, village leadership was none other than clan leadership. For example, a village in Ningpo (Chekiang), inhabited by a single clan, "elected" an "elder" who "presided over the administration of community affairs" and at the same time served as clan head who took charge of clan matters.[27] Similar arrangements were found in other parts of the empire.[28] In multiclan villages the situation was somewhat different. Clan heads did not necessarily serve as village heads, although they often exerted noticeable influence on village affairs.[29]

The presence of more than one kinship group in one community might give rise to interclan rivalry or to open conflict, as we shall see later. For the moment it may be noted that there was no more social equality between different clans dwelling in one village than between individuals belonging to one clan. As gentry members of a clan dominated its commoner members, so some clans in a given community might be in a position to discriminate against others. Their discrimination might be based on seniority in residence, numerical strength, or the superior status of some of their own members. This was observed even in North China where the clan organization was comparatively weak. As a Western writer indicated, "There is . . . an emphasis on the status of the members of the old accepted families and a tendency to disregard the more recent immigrants into the community and to consider them as outsiders."[30]

Before taking up the question of clan organization, it may be useful to attempt some explanation of the different degrees of clan development in various parts of nineteenth-century China.[31] Some writers, such as J. S. Burgess, suggested that historical circumstances constituted a determining factor. He argued:

> In North China the successive invasions of the Manchus and the Mongolians have destroyed the continuity of the family clan system either by exterminating the members of the original clans or by forcing them to emigrate south. In the South, far distant from these waves of invasions, the same clans have had more permanent abode in their original towns and villages.[32]

This is a reasonable enough argument, but the writer could have gone further back to earlier periods of Chinese history. Long before the Mongolian invasion, which destroyed the Sung dynasty late in the thirteenth century, the fall of the Northern Sung dynasty in the first quarter of the twelfth century forced many large Chinese families and clans to migrate across the Yangtze River.[33] And before this there was another large-scale southward migration in the second decade of the fourth century of the Christian era. Upon the downfall of the Western Chin dynasty, some of the eminent native clans moved to localities south of the river, bringing with them much of old China's cultural and social tradition.

Economic factors may also have been at work. A modern writer was convinced that the clan did not play any important role in village administration in localities of North China where economic prosperity was unknown, but exerted stronger influences "in agriculturally rich sections" of the same general region.[34] Even in South China, according to some observers, the development of the clan was by no means uniform in all localities. It was stronger in Kwangtung, Fukien, and Kiangsi; and in certain parts of Kwangtung, especially where "the soil was fertile and population dense," the clan attained a size and vitality seldom equaled in other regions. Ch'ü Ta-chün, writing in 1700, gave the following picture:

> The prominent clans of Ling-nan center around Kuang-chou, and those of Kuang-chou center around the villages. There the soil is fertile and the population dense. Sometimes one village is inhabited by [households bearing] one surname, sometimes two or three surnames. Since T'ang and Sung times [these clans] have lived there continuously. Enjoying the bounty of their land and contented with their customs, very few of them have moved away to other places. [35]

The correlation between rural prosperity and strong clan organization is readily understandable. Without a sufficient amount of economic wealth no village could hold together and sustain a clan of any size. Poverty would preclude ancestral halls, ritual land, and so on, which were necessary if a clan was to perform the fullest measure of its functions. The situation in some localities of Shensi province lends support to these conjectures. According to a local historian, most of the inhabitants of Lo-ch'uan, I-ch'uan, and adjacent districts dwelt in caves or kilns. There were some small houses but none of the kind that would indicate any degree of wealth. As one would expect, in these poor districts no clan organization existed. [36] According to another historian, recording the conditions of T'ung-kuan (Shensi), "the families and clans used to live in groups. . . . But recently, owing to economic pressure, the number of families that dwelt apart from the kinship groups steadily increased." [37]

Sometimes the influence of the local economy was somewhat less decisive. In Ch'eng-ku (Shensi) clans managed to survive but in reduced sizes and simplified forms. It was said:

> Since the number of native inhabitants was small, no genealogy was in existence. A clan comprised no more than several tens of families. The situation was far different from that in Chiang-nan and Kuang-tung where one clan contained as many as several hundred families, the genealogical histories of which could be traced to the very beginnings. [38]

Similarly, in Ning-ch'iang (Shensi), another relatively poor locality, "Families come and go; most of which do not settle permanently. . . . Those that have settled down for some time and are regarded as notable clans . . . have lost their genealogical records. On the whole the inhabitants do not pay attention to clan organization." [39] Even in such cases the influence of economic factors was apparent.

MEMBERSHIP AND LEADERSHIP

The clan owed much of its development to its gentry members. The close association between the gentry and clan led some investigators to conclude that the clan was a gentry organization pure and simple. A Chinese writer, for example, made this remark:

> I think that both the big-family (or the house) system and the clan are the gentry's organizations. . . . I am sure that the clan is not universal in China and that the most effective and elaborate clans are found in the gentry. A clan organization among the landless or even petty owners is superfluous. [40]

Speaking generally, this is true, but the clan was "the gentry's organization" only in the sense that it was normally promoted and dominated by the gentry. The clan was obviously not composed exclusively of gentry members. As another Chinese writer correctly said, "Since the common descent group includes all of the families descended from the same distant ancestor, it comprises various social strata: the wealthy and prominent as well as the poor and the lowly, for the fortunes of individual families vary."[41] It was this inclusiveness that made it possible for some clans to attain enormous size under suitable conditions. A Chinese writer observed that some of the largest clans in Kwangtung province boasted a membership of 10,000.[42] It would be ridiculous to suppose that all the members were officials or titled scholars. Indeed, there were a few isolated instances in which clans were, probably during a limited period of time only, composed entirely of farmers. A recent writer quoted an informant:

> Our village is the only one inhabited by the *tsu* of Ch'u in our neighborhood. . . . It adjoins that of the *tsu* of Yü, but there is no community of interests or of administration between us, nor is there any ill-feeling. However, while we have been growing in number, they have been on the decline. . . . They are composed of farmers only, while our *tsu* possesses both farmers and educated people.[43]

Among these "farmers" of the Yü clan, however, there might well have been some landowners. It should also be pointed out that this clan was "on the decline" partly because it lacked gentry leadership, for the presence of scholar-officials in a clan tended to enhance not only its prestige but also its strength. The most eminent clans of Chia-hsing (Chekiang) counted among their members a large share of the scholars who attained the highest honors in the metropolitan examinations during the Ming and Ch'ing dynasties.[44]

It therefore seems clear that while clan membership usually included both gentry and commoners, clan leadership lay with the gentry. The gentry supplied the active, and the commoners the passive, components of the kinship group.

The intraclan differentiation of gentry and commoners and the domination of the latter by the former are well-established facts. In the

Ning clan of P'eng-lai (Shantung) members who had no wealth or social eminence did not attend the semiannual rites and the ensuing feast, nor did they have charge of the ritual land. The only privilege they enjoyed as members was the use of the common graveyard.[45] In the T'an clan of Nan-feng (Kiangsi) the status of scholar-officials was emphasized in the following ways: first, all the scholars were required to attend the annual sacrificial rites; second, on ritual occasions all the functionaries were chosen from the *shen-shih;* third, in distributing the meat used in the sacrifices an ordinary person was entitled to one catty (about 0.597 kg.), whereas any gentry member who attended the ritual received from two to eight catties, the amount being graded according to the academic degree he earned in the examinations; fourth, at the end of the rites all the *shen-shih* and elderly members participated in a big feast from which all other members were excluded; and fifth, only the tablets of members who had held official ranks or who had passed at least the examinations for the *chü-jen* degree were admitted into the ancestral hall free of charge, whereas fees were charged for the admission of tablets of all other members.[46] In the Chao clan of Wusih (Kiangsu) the line between gentry and commoner members was even more rigidly drawn. The genealogy records of this clan contain the following regulation:

> From now on it will be forbidden to contribute money in order to enter the ancestral hall. . . . One whose conduct is notable for loyalty, filial piety, fidelity to her husband [on the part of a widow] and the performance of duty, as well as one whose name is well known, whose career [as an official] is a success, and who has achieved the third degree in the civil examinations, elevates the reputation of his family and illuminates the virtues of former generation. Such a person after his or her death, naturally should enter the ancestral hall to enjoy the ritual.[47]

It should be noted, however, that while intraclan social differentiation resulted in intraclan social inequality, especially in clans with considerable wealth,[48] gentry members were usually satisfied with enjoying ceremonial privileges and control over the group. Their superior positions and prestige rendered them not only natural leaders of their group but often benefactors of their less fortunate fellow clansmen.[49] They were generally disposed to be charitable and helpful to the latter, not merely because a helping hand extended to kinsmen served to strengthen the solidarity of the group but also because charity, being traditionally regarded as a mark of virtue, was an effective method to enhance their own prestige.

Details of clan organization varied in different instances, but normally each kinship group recognized a suitable member as its head and set up a sort of clan government for managing or administering

its affairs. The clan head often bore the name *tsung-tzu* or *tsu-chang;*
he might be the ceremonial head, the chief executive, or both.[50] Sometimes a number of "executive members" might be selected to assist
the clan head to discharge his duties, particularly the management of
the clan property and ancestral hall.[51] In the larger clans subheads
were instituted, each to lead one of their branches *(fang),* and were
usually given the title *fang-chang* (heads of branches). In such cases
affairs concerning individual branches might be managed by the several *fang-chang,* but those involving the whole clan were managed or decided upon by the consent or with the cooperation of all these heads.[52]
Occasionally, the clan resolved itself into a sort of "direct democracy," when all its members under the leadership of *tsu-chang* and
fang-chang met in the ancestral hall to settle important matters. The
heads led the discussion and junior members voiced their assent.[53]

Age, seniority in generation, and personal ability were as a rule
the primary qualifications for clan leadership, but social and economic status were often equally decisive. In some clans the choice
of the *tsu-chang* was limited to members of the oldest living generation, although the person chosen did not have to belong to the oldest
line.[54] In others the choice was made on the basis of "merit," provided that the candidates were sufficiently advanced in age.[55] In most
cases gentry members were given preference, and the possession of
adequate property was sometimes regarded as a condition for holding certain offices. A recent writer summarizes the situation:

> In a Chinese village a *tsu-chang,* or head of a clan, has some in-
> fluence over a designated group of families. . . . He is usually an
> older member but sometimes may be the person who is the weal-
> thiest family head in that particular community, for his wealth al-
> lows him to do things others cannot afford.[56]

In the last analysis the criterion of "ability and virtue" tended to
merge into that of rank and wealth, for the simple reason that unlet-
tered peasants had little opportunity to demonstrate whatever personal capacities they may have possessed, and scholarly degrees,
official ranks, or substantial estates were easily taken to be ample
proof that those who had them were men of parts. Moreover, personal power often came with social superiority and financial influence,
and it was inevitable that clan members of lesser consequence should
acknowledge the leadership of their gentry kinsmen.

Social status did not play a uniformly important role in all clans.
As a recent investigator pointed out:

> The poorer the *tsu,* the less social differentiation. Under such cir-
> cumstances, age and generation are the proper determinants for the
> choice of a head. But as certain members acquire wealth and high
> social standing, social rank is more and more emphasized, and has
> to be taken into account in the selection of functionaries.[57]

This was true because the material and financial resources of clans invariably came from contributions made by their eminent and wealthy members. The wealth of the kinship group therefore depended upon the prosperity of its most successful members. In this sense it would be even more pertinent to say that the less social differentiation appeared in a clan, the poorer it would remain. But since clan organization could not develop to any great extent unless there was a certain degree of local prosperity and since wealth was unevenly distributed in imperial China, gentry domination of the clan must have been the normal state of affairs, at least during the Ch'ing dynasty.

CLAN ACTIVITIES

While different clans stressed different types of activities, all clan activities of any importance presupposed gentry leadership. The following were the most frequently undertaken:[58] (1) compilation and revision of genealogical records; (2) "ancestor worship" and the institution of ancestral halls, ritual land, and ancestral graveyards; (3) material assistance to clan members; (4) education of young clansmen; (5) punishment of misconduct and settlement of disputes; and (6) self-defense.

Genealogical Records

From its inception, probably in the third century of the Christian era, the compilation of genealogical records was essentially a gentry institution.[59] The *tsu-p'u* or *tsung-p'u* of more recent times differed from the *p'u-tieh* of the Wei and Chin dynasties in more than one respect, but they served substantially the same basic purpose of tracing and recording genealogical ties, and like the earlier genealogies, they were very largely the work of the gentry.

Not all clans possessed genealogical records. Those that did almost always had among their members a fairly large number of scholar-officials. Clans in more modest circumstances often were without such records, especially those in northern provinces where the clan phenomenon was less pronounced than in the south.[60] For instance, of the 208 clans that were found in T'ung-kuan (Shensi), only two had *tsu-p'u;* the rest either never had one or failed to preserve any that had been previously compiled.[61] Of the 168 clans in Lo-ch'uan (Shensi), only eight had genealogical records. Table 21 shows some relevant data concerning these eight clans.[62] Even in the south, some clans had no genealogical records; in Ching Chou (Hunan) only thirty-eight among a fairly large number of clans kept them.[63]

A glance at the contents of some of the genealogical records[64] will convince us that these were beyond the ability of clans with limited

TABLE 21
GENEALOGICAL RECORDS OF EIGHT CLANS
OF LO-CH'UAN (SHENSI)

Clan	Number of Clansmen	Number of Scholars	Date of Compilation	Location of Ancestral Halls
Li	4,838	37	1788	An-shih village
Chao	1,284	7	1811	Han village
Wu	836	3	1825	Ching-chao village
Han	1,168	15	1867	Ching-chao village
Tung	302	21	1906	Ch'iao-chang village
Ch'u	1,391	46	?	City
Fan	334	3	?	Ch'ing-niu village
An	594	1	1939	Huang-chuang village

means. Some of the more elaborate *tsu-p'u* contained not only accounts of the history (authentic or imaginary) of the clan since its
first appearance, growth of its membership, migration and settlement of its various branches (if any); descriptions and records of clan
property, ancestral halls, and ancestral graveyards; biographies of
eminent clansmen, rosters of men and women honored in one way or
another; but also such divergent items as "literary" or "scholarly
writings" done by clan members, "clan regulations," and "imperial
favors."[65] A work of such dimensions required a good deal of literary labor for compilation and considerable expenditure for printing. Even the simplest genealogical records required the cooperation
of the scholar's pen and landowner's purse;[66] ordinary peasants could
contribute very little, not even much data to enrich or embellish the
pages. The compilers could not exclude the names of nongentry clansmen or the vital statistics of their families, as the avowed aim of
tsu-p'u was to help keep kinship bonds intact. Behind such an aim,
however, there may have been a motive on the part of the gentry clansmen who promoted the undertaking to enhance their personal prestige
through the prestige of the clan—often by claiming descent from celebrities in the historical or mythological past or by giving boastful accounts of the lives and works of "illustrious clansmen" who were supposed to have "brought glory to their clan and ancestors." The ordinary villager-clansmen, whose chief concern was to keep themselves and their immediate families alive, probably had little interest
in this matter.

"Ancestor Worship"

"Ancestor worship" probably had a wider appeal than genealogical records, but it was not free from gentry domination or control. A distinction should be made between worship by the clan as a whole and worship by individual families which might or might not belong to a clan. The latter was quite often practiced even by commoner households in the village, but the former was definitely a gentry affair.

The reason is obvious. Clan worship involved the possession of an ancestral hall,[67] some ritual or sacrificial land, and perhaps also an ancestral graveyard.[68] These in turn presupposed the existence of some well-to-do clansmen who deemed it desirable to contribute money or land to make them possible. The *tsu-tz'u* or *tsung-tz'u* (ancestral hall, literally, clan hall) and *chi-t'ien* (ritual or sacrificial land) in particular were the chief objects of gentry attention. Officials, retired or otherwise, and titled scholars often willingly gave money or land to their own clans. Contributors naturally had a decisive voice in the management of ancestral halls and ritual land which were made possible by their generosity. The institution or augmentation of clan property was often regarded by successful men as the crowning achievement of their careers.

Local gazetteers are full of such instances. Ch'en Chang, a *sheng-yüan* scholar of Tung-kuan (Kwangtung), did not do well in the provincial examinations but had a good deal of success in business. When he had eventually amassed a considerable fortune, he remarked with satisfaction: "This will enable me to realize my ambition!" Thereupon he bought additional ritual land for his clan and built a new ancestral hall.[69] T'ang Yüan-liang, a trader who became rich and purchased an official title of the fifth rank, constructed in his native village in Hua Hsien (Kwangtung) a shrine for the "first ancestor" of his clan and gathered the village gentry to draw up a set of community regulations for the guidance of his kinsmen. The village was a monoclan community of 1,200 population.[70] K'ang Kuo-ch'i, a native of a village in Nan-hai (Kwangtung), rose from a poor young man to acting governor of Kwangsi in 1870. Upon retiring from office he contributed money to repair the ancestral tombs, build a new clan hall, and purchase an unspecified amount of ritual land.[71] Su Hsien-k'o, a *chü-jen* scholar of the year 1789 who had served as educational officer of Hsüan-hua, was chiefly responsible for building an ancestral hall and repairing all the ancestral graves in his native village in Yü-lin (Kwangsi).[72] Lu Hsi-p'o, a *chü-jen* of 1807 and magistrate of certain districts of Hupeh, built an ancestral hall for his clan with his savings and gave relief to all needy kinsmen.[73] Liu Shih-chia, a native of Lu-chiang (Anhwei) and a *chien-sheng* scholar who died in 1869, achieved moderate wealth in his late years and contributed 2,000 taels of silver to rebuild the ancestral hall which had been destroyed during the Taiping Rebellion. He gave an additional 500 taels for purchasing ritual land.[74] Ch'en T'ao, a wealthy villager of Hsia-i Hsiang in Such'ien (Kiangsu), built a clan hall, revised the genealogical records, and purchased a quantity of ritual land. [75] Shan Huai, a *chü-jen* of the year 1752, established a sumptuous ancestral hall, instituted ritual land of 1,000 *mow,* and bought a large number of houses in the city (a real estate investment) for his clan, in Fu-ning (Chihli). [76]

The ancestral hall and ritual land complex was correlated with the economic circumstances of the localities in question. One would not expect to see many halls built or much land possessed by clans in areas where the inhabitants were poor and the clans themselves had little more than a bare existence. Conversely, in villages where the kinship groups were more prosperous, ancestral halls (some of which were quite large) were more often found and extensive ritual land was more in evidence. The hall-land phenomenon was more pronounced in South China than in regions north of the Yangtze. [77] But this discrepancy was due directly to socioeconomic rather than to geographic differences; clan halls and ritual land were present in some northern localities and absent in certain southern ones. [78]

The ritual land constituted the economic basis of the clan organization. The possession of such property enabled the clan to display a variety of activities which might go beyond the maintenance of sacrificial rites. The amount of ritual land at the command of some kinship groups in South China, where their activities covered the widest scope, was quite considerable. A modern investigator was of the opinion that land owned by clans in a given locality might amount to as much as 75 per cent of all land under cultivation there, and ordinarily the proportion was between 23 per cent and 40 per cent. [79] We have no estimates for the nineteenth century, but a few figures from various sources, incomplete and presumably inaccurate as they are, may serve to give some idea of the situation. The ritual land referred to in Table 22 might be used also to extend material assistance to members of the clans; in fact, some of the clans chose to designate their land as *i-chuang* (welfare farm). [80]

The total amounts of land owned by these clans, assuming that these were the only ones that owned land in the localities mentioned, were quite small compared with the figures given by this modern investigator. But to the individual clans the possession of land amounting to 1,000 or more *mow* was certainly a considerable asset; even ritual land of a few hundred *mow* would enable the kinship group to perform some of the basic functions which would otherwise have been impossible.

The theory of the ritual land, as understood by earlier writers, was that the land remained as the permanent property of the clan and that the proceeds from the land were to be used for maintaining the sacrifices and for the benefit of the clansmen. The view as expressed in the following passage is representative:

The ritual land is popularly known as *chen-ch'ang t'ien*. Not only big clans and households but even the smaller families and branches often possess it. . . . I happened to read in the gazetteer of Hsin-ning [Kwangtung] that the local custom sets great store by the construction of ancestral halls, for which ritual land is generally provided. Three uses are made of the annual proceeds [from the land], namely, [1] on the first day of each month sons and younger brothers of the clansmen are summoned to the hall where exercises in literary composition are held for them; those who take part in the local elementary examinations are given "examination paper fees"; those who become government students are given subsidies and expenses in connection with the regular annual examinations; and those who go to take the examinations at the provincial or imperial capital are given travel expenses; [2] clan members who are sixty or over are given sacrificial meat and an annual rice subsidy; [3] those clansmen who are destitute, sick, or disabled are given grain, the amount varying with the size of their respective families; those who lack money to finance weddings or funerals are also given suitable assistance; and in case of famine, rice certificates are distributed to the needy members. . . . Similar practices prevail generally in Kwangtung province, although the amount of activities varies proportionally with the amount of land possessed [by the clans]. I think this institution accounts for the fact that inhabitants of this province are willing to study and attach importance to scholarly degrees. [81]

Other writers echoed this view. [82] While it was possible that persons who instituted the ritual land were prompted by the desire to perform duties toward their ancestors and to look after the welfare of their clansmen, there was nothing to prevent them from attaching a hidden utilitarian value to their action. According to a modern Chinese writer:

A piece of land is usually contributed to the [clan] organization by a member who is a governmental official, the pretext being that the products of the land may cover the expenses necessary in the keeping up of the ancestors' tombs and regular sacrifices. But, in fact, this common property is a common security with which the position of the clan may be maintained in the wider power structure of the community. It finances the education of the young members so that they may be able to enter the scholar class and attain high official position and protect the interest of their kinsmen. [83]

This is a plausible interpretation of the matter, although the writer seems to have oversimplified it. At any rate, two things are clear: first, ritual land was invariably instituted by members of a clan who enjoyed gentry status and possessed some wealth; second, the control or management of the clan property was usually placed in the hands of propertied and privileged clansmen. [84] It was the ritual land

TABLE 22
RITUAL LAND OF CLANS

Locality	Clan	Land (in *mow*)	Approximate Date
Wusih* (Kiangsu)	Hua	1, 590	1835
	Chou	1, 098	1804
	Ts'ai	1, 000	1810
	Ch'ien	890	1808
	Hu	660	1839
	T'eng	658	1877
	Ku	486	1810
Wu-chin† (Kiangsu)	Wang	over 1, 000	late 19th century
	Sheng	over 1, 132	late 19th century
Ho-fei‡ (Anhwei)	Li	over 1, 300#	1870
Lu-chiang§ (Anhwei)	Chang	over 3, 300#	early 19th century
Swatow‖ (Kwangtung)	Clan of 1, 400 persons	2, 300	1880
	2, 000 persons	1, 650	1880
	800 persons	785	1880
	400 persons	350	1880
	300 persons	240	1880

*Source: *Wu-hsi* (1881), 30/10a-15b.

†Source: Feng Kuei-fen (1809-74), *Chi*, 4/1b, 3b, and 5a.

‡Source: *Lu-chou* (1885), 17/23-24.

§Source: *Ibid.*, 16/9a-b.

‖Source: Adele M. Fielde, in *Journal of the Royal Asiatic Society*, North China Branch, N.S., XXIII (1888), 111.

#In terms of production of grain in *shih* or piculs. According to Li Tz'u-ming (1830-94), *Jih-chi*, v, 42a-b, and vi, *ping-chi*, 82a, one or two *mow* of land was rated in Hunan and Chekiang as capable of yielding on the average one *shih* of grain collectible as rent. There should be no wide difference between the practice in Anhwei and in other localities in Central China.

that gave many a clan its financial foundation, and it was ritual land also that rendered gentry domination a natural and perhaps inevitable consequence.

Material Welfare

Material welfare of the clan was promoted in a variety of ways. The

most common practice was to give subsidies or relief to aged and
needy clansmen, with proceeds accrued from clan property or grain
stored in clan granaries. A good instance of the former was afforded
by the Yang clan of Chiang-yin (Kiangsu). Part of the revenue from
the ritual land (a little over 1,000 *mow*) was used to set up a rice and
clothing allowance, to a share of which every descendant who was sufficiently old or destitute was entitled, the amount each received varying with the age of the recipient. Widows who did not remarry, orphans, and disabled clansmen were placed on the allowance list also.
Special subsidies were granted to pupils who studied in the schools,
apprentices in the trades or crafts, and persons who had funerals or
weddings in their families.[85] In some clans preference was shown to
members of the branch to which the founder of the ritual land or welfare farm belonged. In the Chao clan of Ch'ang-shu (Kiangsu), for
example, members of the "elder" branch were to receive more substantial aid from the *i-chuang* (welfare farm) than members of the
"younger" branch.[86] In the Hua clan of Chin-kuei (Kiangsu), one hundred *mow* of land was set aside in 1876 for the exclusive benefit of
the progeny of the ancestor from whom the founder of the *i-chuang*
himself was descended.[87] Clan granaries were less common than welfare farms, but a few instances were noticed in Hsiang-shan (Kwangtung). The Fang, Yang, and Miu clans each established in the mid-
nineteenth century an *i-ts'ang* granary for their own members, situated in the rural areas where they resided. The Yang clan granary
had an endowment of 950 *mow* which was calculated to insure a constant supply of grain for the storehouse.[88]

Clan aid was sometimes rendered to members in the form of loans.
It was an established practice in the Ch'en clan of Nan-hai (Kwangtung) that clansmen who desired it could borrow money from the funds
realized from the ritual land. If the borrower could not repay he
might lose his own land in order to make good his debt.[89] The Yang
clan of Wusih (Kiangsu) was so generous to its members that during
the Taiping uprising in the 1850's the clan mortgaged the ritual land
and lent the money thus raised to members in need.[90]

A curious example of clan aid was recorded in a local gazetteer.
Wang Cheng-yüan, a native of a village in Nan-hai (Kwangtung), organized an *i-hui* (welfare club), probably late in the nineteenth century, to help his kinsmen pay their taxes.

> His clan not being wealthy, the elders were repeatedly arrested
> for failure [of some clansmen] to pay taxes. Cheng-yuan asked those
> who were of the same mind each to contribute some private property,
> and established [with the resources thus obtained] an *i-hui* which un-
> dertook to pay in full all the taxes left outstanding by taxpayers [who
> for some justifiable cause had to default]. Thereafter his clansmen
> were spared the trouble of facing the tax collectors.[91]

Some clans helped their members to pay taxes in another way. The Feng clan of Nan-hai was said to have established the following practice:

> There was in Feng Ts'un [village] of Chuang-t'ou a *ch'ien-liang hui* [literally, cash-grain club, i.e., tax payment club] which undertook to collect the taxes [due the government] each year during the collection periods, at the village [ancestral] hall. All taxes [due from clansmen] must be handed in within three days . . . after which a penalty on the form of a 10 per cent surcharge was inflicted upon the defaulter. Family members of anyone who refused to pay taxes were held responsible [for the payment]. The rules were rigidly enforced, with the result that for three hundred years there was not a single inhabitant who failed to pay his taxes, not a single household that defaulted, not a single yamen underling who went to exact tax payment. . . . It was said that these were the clan regulations formulated by Feng Ch'ien-chai. [92]

Similar practices obatined in other clans of this region, [93] and in some cases the government found it convenient to recognize the clans as an agent of tax collection. [94]

Clans might undertake to build irrigation dikes, water reservoirs, and bridges. The Huang-t'eng-p'i dike, which was situated at T'ung-wa-k'eng in Hua Hsien (Kwangtung) and irrigated extensive rice land outside the south gate of the city, "was constructed by the K'uang clan and controlled by it throughout its existence. Its benefits were not shared by any other clan or village." [95] The Huang-chia-t'ang reservoir, which irrigated about 1,000 *mow* of land, belonged to the Huang clan of Fu-shun (Szechwan), where "water benefits for agricultural land came from reservoirs and not from rivers." [96]

"Water benefits" were sometimes promoted and enjoyed together by several clans. The Ta-hsia-p'i dike in Hua Hsien (Kwangtung) was built with contributions from the Chiang clan of Hsiao-pu village and the Miu clan of Wa-li-hsiang village, irrigating over eighty *mow* of land. The reservoir at Ya-chiao-hsiang, which irrigated 2,000 *mow* of land, was built jointly by the Chang and Lo clans in 1866. [97]

Instances of bridge building were fairly common, but the most remarkable one occurred in Lo-ch'uan (Shensi). The bridge at Shih-chia-chuang was first constructed sometime toward the end of the sixteenth century or the beginning of the seventeenth by a local inhabitant. His descendants kept up its repair, a task which became virtually a perennial clan project. In 1771 it was rebuilt with stone, and extensive repair work was done again in 1796. [98] Obviously, the convenience of this and other bridges built by clans was extended to all travelers.

Education of Clansmen

Clans were normally interested in educating their younger members, thus enabling them to participate in the state examinations which opened the path to academic degrees and official ranks. This interest was displayed in various methods of encouraging literary studies and in providing facilities for such studies.

Quite often financial assistance was given to budding scholars who had demonstrated aptitude or zeal in their studies. Such practices prevailed in some clans of Fang-kuo Hsiang (Chi-an, Kiangsi), Ch'a-k'eng (Hsin-hui, Kwangtung), and Hsiang-t'an (Hunan), [99] where scholarly distinction was put at a premium. The benefits given to clansmen were in proportion to the degree of scholarly advancement which they severally attained:

> . . . those young men who go to take the *yüan* examinations [at the district seat] . . . are to be given 1,600 cash for the expenses; those who take the *hsiang* examinations [at the provincial capital] are to be given 4,000 cash; those who take the *hui* examinations [at the imperial capital] are to be given 20,000 cash. Those who succeed in the first examinations are to be given 40,000 cash as a congratulatory gift; those who succeed in the second series are to be given 80,000; those who succeed in the last examinations are to be given 120,000. [100]

Consideration was sometimes given to the financial need of the recipients. In the Tseng clan of Hsiang-hsiang (Hunan), for example, families owning thirty *mow* or less of land were classified as "middle households," and those owning over thirty *mow* were called "upper households." Youngsters of "middle households" were given one *shih* of grain each per annum as soon as they entered school, and the allowance was continued until they "completed their scholarly achievements." Those of "upper households," however, received only four *tou*, 40 per cent of one *shih*. [101]

Many clans also made efforts to promote education by providing school facilities for their youthful members, especially those who belonged to families of modest means. They established *tsu-hsüeh* (clan schools) which were also known in different cases as *chia-shu* (family schools), *tz'u-hsüeh* (shrine schools), or simply *i-hsüeh* (welfare schools). A few examples will suffice to illustrate. The Chang clan of Lu-chiang (Anhwei) established a *chia-shu* "to instruct the sons and grandsons of the *tsu*," which was maintained with part of the revenue from 3,300 *mow* of "welfare land" donated in 1823 by a clansman who once served as provincial director of education in Hupeh. The Ko clan of Ho-fei established an *i-hsüeh* for the exclusive benefit of its children and youths, with an endowment of 300 *mow* of land contributed in the early nineteenth century by a clansman holding the *chien-sheng* title. [102] The Li clan of Huang-ts'un village in Hsing-an (Kiangsi) had the distinction of having maintained a clan school during a long period. This school, known as *Huang-ts'un i-shu,* was first established sometime in the Chih-cheng reign (1341-67) of the Yüan dynasty; its endowment in the form of land was increased in the Hung-chih reign (1488-1505) of the Ming dynasty. It was destroyed as a result of war at the end of the Ming dynasty but was rebuilt by the clan in the fifty-third year of K'ang-hsi (1714). Unfortunately, the local historian was silent concerning the subsequent story of this school. [103] Sometimes different branches of a clan established separate schools for their own members. An instance of this sort was found by a Western writer in Phenix village (Kwangtung), a monoclan community: "There are four buildings of a semipublic nature: the chief ancestral hall of the entire village . . . the ancestral halls and schools belonging to two different branches of the village group . . . and the small temple . . . south of the market center."[104] In fact, the clans of Kwangtung took so much interest in education that, according to a native writer, "everywhere ancestral halls were used for classrooms."[105]

Order and Morals

Large and well-organized clans often took pains to keep order and uphold morals in their own communities. Written codes of conduct echoing the basic principles of Confucianism (often known as *tsung-kuei*, "clan regulations") were sometimes formulated. The precepts were either repeated orally on suitable occasions[106] or posted in writing at appropriate places in the ancestral halls. [107] Sons were urged to be filial to their parents, wives dutiful to their husbands, brothers affectionate one to another. All were warned against laziness, extravagance, gambling, quarrels, violence, and other offensive conduct. [108] Adultery and failure to perform filial duties were pronounced grave offenses, often punishable by expulsion or even death. [109] In some instances infanticide and opium smoking were sternly forbidden. [110] One of the well-known clans of Hunan set forth a number of regulations, many of which echoed the maxims of the Sacred Edict, and reprinted in its genealogical records some forty articles of the Imperial Code, thus making clear to its members what was right and lawful in personal conduct, family relationships, and economic matters. [111]

Clan regulations were enforced by rewards and punishments, which were in some instances quite well defined and rigidly applied. For example, meritorious deeds performed by clansmen might be recorded in special "books of virtuous clansmen,"[112] or commemorated by petitioning the government for honorary plaques or arches. [113] Violations of clan regulations were dealt with by the heads of the clans. When the transgression was serious, the case might be heard in the ancestral hall, in the presence of clansmen, old and young. The purpose was not so much to elicit the verdict of public opinion as to pillory the victims and deter future offenders. The punishment inflicted on the erring clansmen might be open censure, flogging, fine, suspension of privileges, ostracism, or even death. [114] Such corporal and capital punishments were, of course, unauthorized by the government and therefore illegal. But seldom did they come to the attention of local officials.

In spite of clan regulations, disputes and quarrels frequently arose among clansmen. The settlement of disputes thus became also an important activity of the clans. Naturally, the leaders or heads of the kinship groups were charged with this task, and in some clans written rules were formulated to guide their leaders in exercising their authority. The genealogical records of the Wang clan of Cheng-chiang (Kiangsu), as revised in 1847, contain the following regulations:

> When quarrels arise in the *tsu* out of small resentments and disputes about landed property and money debts, the parties are to go to the ancestral hall and hand in a petition. The matter is to be brought to clarity and resolved in peace. Only when the decision is difficult is it permitted to bring a complaint before [the government] authorities, so that they may examine and decide the case. Should anyone bring action against another person by bypassing the head of the *tsu*, without petitioning him first, this person is to be fined five taels of silver to be added to the public funds of the ancestral hall. [115]

In the Feng clan of Nan-hai (Kwangtung), all clansmen were expected to attend the great sacrificial rites performed once every five years. On the day following the occasion, a general meeting was held in which all disputes were resolved and community affairs decided. [116]

Self-Defense

Rural self-defense against rioters, bandits, or other enemies of the community was sometimes undertaken by kinship organizations. An instance was reported in En-p'ing (Kwangtung) in the mid-nineteenth century:

> During the reign of Hsien-feng the Hakkas caused disturbances [in the countryside of this locality]. . . . The various clans that dwelt within a radius of ten *li* organized themselves into a group . . . calling itself Wu-fu Pao. Funds were raised and a building erected at Sa-hu-hsü . . . where meetings were called to discuss matters as they arose. [117]

The following account, while referring to a much later period, throws further light on the role of the clan in local defense:

> In Kwangtung the *tsu* is enlarged to include all those of the same

surname within the region, pooling their resources for aggressive and defensive purposes. When in the summer of 1944 the Japanese advanced to take the districts of T'ai-shan and San-shui, the county of L'ai-p'ing was menaced. The Chinese army had retreated, but the two *tsu* of Szu-t'u and Kuan organized themselves to fight for their homes. In the *tsu* of Szu-t'u the wealthy merchants and the landlords, realizing the great danger that threatened everyone, contributed all they had to buy munitions. As that was insufficient, the ritual land and other common property was auctioned off. [118]

Clans also defended themselves by force against government agents. The following incident occurred in a village in Fukien late in the nineteenth century:

> Once when Huang Dunglin's grandfather was still alive, a tax collector came to the village of Hwang and did some injustice to a family there. Dunglin's grandfather was a forthright man. He beat upon a gong to call up the men of the clan in order to resist the tax collector and his men. If apologies had not been made right then, there would certainly have been a bloody battle. Since then the Hwang village has had a title. It is called "the barbaric village."[119]

This survey of clan activities suggests one conclusion: clan activities duplicated to a large extent the village activities described in an earlier chapter. This is no surprise. The clan and village were intimately bound together, and both were dominated by virtually the same elements (the gentry) and composed of the same inhabitants (mostly peasants). There was little reason for any wide diversity in activities.

The presence of the clan in villages, especially in monoclan villages, of course introduced some differences into rural life. The clan tended to enhance the solidarity of its village and gave the rural community a tighter and more elaborate organization than in other cases. But the clan did not change in any material way the basic pattern of rural life. The differentiation between persons of different social and economic status remained, and the many problems which the village failed to meet remained unsolved by the clan.

CH'A-K'ENG, A NINETEENTH-CENTURY CLAN-VILLAGE

The picture of the clan-village given above is a composite one formed by the juxtaposition of facts gathered from various sources—facts which often had few connections among them in time or space. The following describes an actual clan-village. The writer, Liang Ch'i-ch'ao, personally observed conditions during the last decades of the nineteenth century; it is unnecessary, of course, to accept his interpretation of the facts.

The Liang clan with a membership of 3,000 dwelled along the slopes of hills on Ch'a-k'eng, a small island off the coast of Hsin-hui (Kwangtung). About 2,000 inhabitants did not belong to the Liang clan but dwelled in the same rural area. The entire settlement was divided into three *pao;* the Liangs constituted one of these. Matters that only concerned one *pao* were decided locally, but those that affected all the three *pao* were dealt with by a sort of federated organization known as the *San-pao Miao* [Temple of the Three Pao].

A government of the *pao* inhabited by the Liang clan was located in the *Liang-shih Tsung-tzu* [Ancestral Hall of the Liang Clan]. The highest authority was vested in the *ch'i-lao hui-i* [council of elders], composed of clansmen over fifty-one *sui*. Younger clansmen who possessed *kung-ming* above the *sheng-yüan* or *chien-sheng,* however, were eligible to participate in the deliberations of the council, even though they lacked the age qualification. The council was popularly called the *Shang-tz'u-t'ang* [Upper Ancestral Hall]. All matters, large and small, were decided by this organ.

In addition to the council there were four to six *chih-li* [attending managers], appointed from among younger clansmen, who carried out the decisions of the elders. Two of them were placed in charge of the accounts and were designated annually by the council. All the *chih-li* were required to present themselves at the meetings of the council.

There was a *pao-chang* whose duty was to deal with the local government. His social position was very low. Unless he was an elderly person, he could not attend the meetings of the council.

The elders and managers held honorary offices. The only tangible privileges they enjoyed were that they received double shares of the meat used in the sacrificial rites and that they took part in the ceremonial banquets given on special occasions. The *pao-chang,* however, was salaried. He received three *sheng* of rice from each household annually, known as the *pao-chang mi [pao-chang's* rice]. He collected it personally, from door to door.

The elders met regularly twice each year, just before the day on which the spring or autumn sacrificial rites were performed. In the spring meeting the most important item on the agenda was the nomination of the managers for the coming year. The most important business in the autumn meeting was the report of accounts by the retiring managers. Extra meetings were called whenever occasion demanded. On the average the council met more than twenty times each year, mostly during late winter and early spring when the peasants had some leisure. The total number of the elders exceeded sixty. Only a minority of them, however, attended the meetings. Decisions were occasionally made with a "quorum" of only a few elders. The meetings were open to clansmen who cared to attend and watch the proceedings; sometimes the "auditors" amounted to several hundred at one session. These were not offered seats. They stood on the floor of the meeting hall or on the steps outside it. They might voice their opinions, but if what they said was regarded as improper, the elders might censure them.

Among the questions brought up at the extra sessions of the council, those concerning disputes constituted the largest number. Whenever a dispute arose between clansmen, an attempt at settlement was made by elderly relatives of the parties. If the disputing parties were not satisfied with the decision, they might appeal to the *fen-tz'u* [branch ancestral hall] of the *fang* [branch] to which they belonged. And if they were still unsatisfied, they might then petition the council of elders which was a sort of supreme court for the clan. Beyond this, the only resort was litigation before the local magistrate. As, however, it was considered highly improper for any clansman to disobey the elders, litigation seldom occurred.

The "judicial functions" of the council also included punishment of offenders. Clansmen who violated laws of the imperial government, such as those against gambling and feuds, were punished by being whipped in front of the ancestral tablets, or by *t'ing-tso* [suspending the privilege of receiving the sacrificial meat] for a stated period. Tenants of rice land belonging to the ancestral hall who failed to pay their rent on time were punished by *t'ing-tso*. Clansmen who committed theft were tied with a rope and made to walk through the streets of the entire village, so that they would be insulted with shouting derision by children. This was called *yu-hsing* [the parading punishment]. Whenever adultery was discovered in the community, the inhabitants butchered all their hogs, distributing the meat to every household and made the families of the offending individuals pay the cost. This was called *tao-chu* [felling the swine]. A clansman who suffered the *tao-chu* treatment was punished officially by the council of elders with *ke-tso* [permanent suspension of the privilege of receiving sacrificial meat], which was tantamount to deprival of clan membership.

The main source of the income of the ancestral hall was the ritual land, amounting to about seven or eight hundred *mow*. Part of this land came from donations of clansmen; in addition, all alluvial land was regarded as clan property. The ritual land was rented out to clansmen, the tenants paying about 40 per cent of their crops to the ancestral hall. This arrangement was called *tui-t'ien* [converting land]. During famine years, however, whether a food shortage was caused by flood, drought, or storm, a reduction of rent was made, the amount being decided by the council of elders. The rates thus set up became the standard for private landlords. The chief outlay of the clan consisted of expenses incurred in the sacrificial rites and in keeping the ancestral hall and graves in repair. On every sacrificial occasion sacrificial meat was distributed to all clansmen not subject to the *t'ing-tso* penalty. The portions allotted to them during the New Year festivals were especially substantial, so that even the poorest families could have good meals.

A *hsiang-t'uan* [rural corps] was organized in each of the three *pao*. The rural corps of the *pao* inhabited by the Liang clan was placed under the direction of the council of elders. Young and able-bodied clansmen might volunteer for service; those who were accepted by the elders received double shares of the sacrificial meat. Weapons were distributed to the *t'uan-ting* [corps men], but munitions were kept by the *chih-li* [managers].

The small canal in front of the village was dredged every three or five years. Equipment and materials for the work were supplied by the ancestral hall, whereas labor came from all clansmen between eighteen and fifty *sui*. Elders and persons possessing *kung-ming* were exempt from the work. Among the rest, those who could not or were unwilling to work might obtain exemption by paying *mien-i ch'ien* [work-exemption fee], the money being used to hire men to work in their place. Whenever dikes had to be constructed or repaired, a similar arrangement was adopted. Persons who failed to report for work or pay the exemption fee were punished with *t'ing-tso*.

The village had three or four elementary schools which used the ancestral halls [general and branch] for classrooms. All the teachers were scholars native to the village. Tuition fees varied between thirty silver *yüan* [dollars] and a few *sheng* of rice, depending on the financial circumstances of the pupils' families. The teachers received double shares of the sacrificial meat. In return for the privileges of using the clan halls and receiving double shares of sacrificial meat, they gave free instruction to children of families who could not afford to pay any tuition fee.

The most important community amusement included *fang-teng* [the lantern festival] and *ta-chiao* [the ghost festival], held respectively in the New Year season and during the seventh month. The expenses were met by voluntary contributions; but if any deficit arose it was made good by the ancestral hall. A theatrical exhibition was staged once every three or five years, the expenses for which were taken care of by subsidies from *San-pao Miao,* the general ancestral hall, branch halls, and other village groups, as well as by contributions from individual clansmen.

The above were community activities. In addition to these, special groups were organized by some clansmen to realize special purposes common to themselves. One of the most interesting was the *Chiang-nan hui,* a sort of savings society planned to operate for twenty or thirty years. Each member was to deposit a certain sum of money with it; at the end of three or five years payment of interest to the members on their invested sums began. The members might agree to make contributions to community amusement expenses, which they often did. Members served in turn as *chih-li* and during their terms of office received double shares of the sacrificial meat. They received no other compensation. About thirty years ago three or four such societies operated in the village. Hard-working, frugal young clansmen often joined them. Quite a few of them who originally belonged to poor families eventually accumulated moderate fortunes. Another interesting organization was a sort of co-operative society for selling and buying agricultural products. Besides giving its members the benefit of lower cost or better prices, it contributed to various community expenditures, including funds for providing the sacrificial meat and financing festival activities.[120]

This account, given by Liang Ch'i-chao, one of the leaders of the 1898 reform movement, was based on first-hand information. His father served as *chih-li* of the general ancestral hall for over thirty years, and concurrently as one of the managers of the *San-pao Miao*. He also joined one of the savings societies and served as manager for a long while. The "self-government" (to use Liang's own phrase) of this clan-village reached the height of its development during his youth. As he was born in 1873, this must have been the 1880's or 1890's.

Liang spoke of what he saw or heard with unconcealed enthusiasm. He was anxious to point out that aside from paying taxes, "this rural self-government had almost nothing to do with the local officials." It may be doubted that the "self-government" or autonomy enjoyed by Ch'a-k'eng was as extensive as Liang imagined. His supposition that communities similar to it might be readily found in other parts of the empire may also be questioned. Ch'a-k'eng was favored by special circumstances, one of them being its location on an island off the coast of Kwangtung. But it is certain that his highly integrated clan-village shows clearly the extent to which the kinship group could contribute to the organization and activities of rural communities.

GOVERNMENT CONTROL OF CLANS

The importance of the clan was readily perceived by the imperial government. Being a well-organized group which tended to give villages a higher degree of community life, and being a gentry-led organization, the clan could be a very useful instrument of rural control. The imperial government therefore encouraged clan solidarity, made use of the clan organization as a means of rural control, and imposed rigid control upon clans when some of them proved unruly or detrimental to the order of the empire.

Both the K'ang-hsi and Yung-cheng emperors showed interest in the clan. Maxim Two of the Sacred Edict urged the people "to behave with generosity to your kindred, in order to demonstrate harmony and affection." In the Amplified Instructions all were exhorted to "establish *chia-miao* [ancestral shrines] to perform sacrificial rites, set up *chia-shu* [clan schools] to teach sons and younger brothers, institute *i-t'ien* [welfare farms] to succor destitute kinsmen, and revise *tsu-p'u* [clan genealogies] to bind together distant relatives."[121] Clansmen who had respect for their kinship ties, who were dutiful toward their ancestors, and who received instructions in the rudiments of Confucianism would naturally be inclined to be mild, "decent" individuals; and those who could rely on their kinship groups to give them aid and relief in misfortune would in all probability be prevented from "walking the dangerous path." The emperors obviously discerned in kinship groups a stabilizing influence that tended to make them a highly desirable institution. In fact some of the clans actually embodied the fundamental precepts of imperial Confucianism in their written regulations and even reprinted the complete text of the Amplified Instructions in their genealogical records, [122] although the stabilizing influence of the kinship organization as a whole fell short of imperial expectations.

Officials were not slow in responding to the emperors' interest. An eminent eighteenth-century governor proposed that the government assign to clan heads some of the responsibilities that pertained to the local magistrate, especially adjudication of minor offenses and settlement of disputes. He reasoned that such an arrangement would effectively reduce the chance of laws being broken by persons belonging to the clans. [123] He was so convinced of the soundness of his reasoning that he tried to put his ideas into practice. In a general directive issued by him in 1742 when he was a governor of Kiangsi, he required the clans in that province to elect elderly members to serve as *tsu-cheng* who were to be responsible for settling disputes and encouraging good conduct in their respective groups. In addition, these heads were expected to report feuds and other acts of violence to the local magistrates. [124] His ideas must also have appealed to the Ch'ien-lung emperor, for in 1757 imperial approval was given to the following regulation:

> [People] who group themselves into clans and dwell together shall, if their kinsmen are sufficiently numerous, select from their own respective groups persons of character and prestige and institute them as *tsu-cheng* [one for each clan], who shall be responsible for investigating and reporting the good and bad elements of the clans. [125]

The clan was thus formally given a legal status and brought under direct government control. As the *tsu-cheng* were given the essential functions of the *pao-chia* heads, the clan became to that extent a supplementary organ of the *pao-chia*. [126] This was made especially clear in a legal provision:

> In localities where there are villages and hamlets in which the inhabitants live together in clans, each with a membership of over one hundred persons, and where the *pao-chia* [heads] are unable to supervise adequately, a person of character and prestige shall be instituted [in each clan] as *tsu-cheng*. In case bad elements appear [in a clan] the *tsu-cheng* shall report them. If he allows himself to be influenced by personal feelings and conceals their presence, he shall be punished according to the law governing the *pao-chia*. [127]

A number of officials serving in the nineteenth century claimed that they used the clan organization to deal effectively with lawbreakers. For instance, Yao Ying, magistrate of Lung-ch'i (Fukien), wrote that in order to cope with the robbers and thieves that infested the district, he called together the *tsu-cheng* and family heads of the various villages and charged them with the task of registering their respective clansmen and disciplining any of them who committed offenses. Only when the culprits proved themselves incorrigible were they to be sent to the magistrate and punished by law. [128] Wu Kuang-yüeh, governor of Kiangsi around 1830, found the *tsu-cheng* useful in helping the government suppress banditry:

> *Tsu-cheng* have hitherto been instituted in this province. This is in itself a useful method of making and checking the *pao-chia* records, and it has been consistently employed. Recently, many of the bandits captured by the government are apprehended through information supplied by the gentry or sent by families or clans who made the arrest. [129]

Feng Kuei-fen, a well-known scholar of the period, was so convinced of the usefulness of the clan that he proposed to make it a basis for some of the major institutions of rural control, the *pao-chia, she-ts'ang,* and *t'uan-lien.* [130]

In employing the clan to help strengthen its control over the countryside, the imperial government treated the kinship group more as a supplementary police organ than as a social body characterized (to borrow the phrase from the Sacred Edict) by the principle of "harmony and affection." In fact, the law which required the *tsu-cheng* to report lawbreakers among their own kinsfolk was in a sense contrary to this principle; it might even conflict with the Confucian idea that the root of human virtue lay in the sanctity of family relationships. [131] Moreover, as has already been suggested, clans often preferred to have erring members dealt with by their own elders rather than to hand them over to government officials. In making the *tsu-cheng* a virtual *pao-chia* agent, therefore, the Ch'ing rulers did some violence both to the basic conception and natural propensities of the clan.

Possibly the imperial government chose this line of action, with full awareness of its implications. Some of the emperors did lip service to the "harmony and affection" that might result from strengthening clan solidarity, but it is doubtful that any of them intended to encourage clans to grow into well-integrated and influential centers of local life. The institution of the *tsu-cheng,* so it seems, not only afforded an intraclan *pao-chia* agent to keep an eye on the clansmen but also introduced a government-sponsored leadership which might counterbalance whatever other leaderships obtained in the kinship group.

Whatever may have been the real intention of the imperial government, it appears certain that owing to government action a duality of clan leadership came into existence. Side by side with the *tsu-chang* or *tsung-tzu*, who may be regarded as "unofficial" clan leaders and whose positions were independent of government authority, were the *tsu-cheng*, who in contradistinction were "official" leaders of the clans. The pattern of village leadership, a duality of official and un- official headmen, was thus repeated in the kinship groups. We do not know the exact relationship between these sets of clan leaders; nor are we sure that in all instances the *tsu-cheng* and *tsu-chang* were different individuals. Probably when they were different individuals the clan heads who were instituted as the result of government action enjoyed less respect and received less active support from their kins- men than those who were chosen by the clansmen of their own accord. For one thing, there was no guarantee that the *tsu-cheng* nominated by their fellow clansmen to meet the government requirement were the most desirable or effective individuals among their respective groups. The fact that they were legally responsible for informing against their own kin tended to make their office a loathsome one to those who were persons of "character and prestige" in their clans. Such persons were likely to refuse to serve as *tsu-cheng*. The im- perial government was aware of the possibility of appointing wrong men to serve as clan heads. In an edict dated 1830 it was admitted that "harm would result if unsuitable persons were nominated" to the post of *tsu-cheng*. Indeed, it was found necessary to threaten with punishment those clan heads who abused their authority. [132] The gov- ernment, in other words, could not have confidence in the *tsu-cheng*, the clan heads whom it established to control the clans. Since these heads did not command the respect of their kinsmen, and since those who did came to their positions independent of government action, the government hardly gained full control of the clans by instituting official leaders in them.

It is easy to see why the imperial government did not achieve such control. Clan interests did not coincide with imperial purposes. Dual- ity of leadership might prevent undue expansion of the former, but it could not make them conform with the latter. The employment of the clan as an auxiliary police organ without sufficient consideration for the basic attitudes and behavior of its members prevented it from acting as a reliable instrument of imperial control or even as a con- sistently stabilizing force in the countryside. The gap between im- perial purposes and clan interests was never bridged and, unfor- tunately for the government, recognition of the clan organization as an instrument of control may have encouraged the clan in some in- stances to expand and operate in directions considered undesirable by the government.

One kind of undesirable behavior exhibited by some clans was making "fraudulent claims" concerning ancestry. Apparently desiring to enhance their prestige or extend their influence, these kinship groups resorted to the dubious expedient of claiming direct descent from well-known celebrated personages (real or imagined) of antiquity. [133] There was often no way to prove either the verity or falseness of the claims. So long as they were not too preposterous or did not have dangerous implications, the pedigrees went unchallenged. But when some clans went so far as to trace their lineage back to ancient emperors, they aroused the suspicion of the government and as a consequence brought suppressive measures upon themselves. For example, the governor of Kiangsi discovered in 1764 that some clans made "absurd claims" concerning their "first ancestors." One clan traced its descent to P'an-ku, the mythical being who "first separated heaven and earth"; another to Ti-huang, the "Earth Emperor," second of the legendary emperors; another to Tung Cho, a traitor minister of the second century of the Christian era; still another to Chu Wen, a usurper of the imperial throne in the tenth century. [134] Perhaps the most curious instance was afforded by a clan which made Lei-chen-tzu, a mythical character in the *Feng-shen chuan* (a popular novel), its "first ancestor." [135] Some years later (1780), the magistrate of I-shui (Shantung) reported that the genealogical records of a Liu clan contained "outrageous and seditious" statements which implied that the kinship group in question had its origin in the imperial family of the Han dynasty. [136] The genealogical records of these clans were destroyed by imperial order.

The government undertook to suppress another offensive practice, misuse of the privilege of establishing ancestral halls and instituting ritual land. Before the sixteenth century, extensive clan organizations and possession of ancestral halls were prerogatives of the gentry. However, upon the advice of a grand secretary, Emperor Shih-tsung, of the Ming dynasty gave express permission to commoners "to join into clans and establish shrines," with the result that "ancestral halls appeared all over the empire."[137] Such a development was not without dangers to the imperial security. When local inhabitants realized that organization spelled influence or power and that the extent of power varied proportionally to the size of the clan organization, they were soon persuaded to extend their kinship groups, by fraudulent means if necessary, and to build "common ancestral halls" as a visible symbol and operational base of their groups. The Ch'ing emperors continued to allow clans to establish ancestral halls and ritual lands, but did not hesitate to curtail these institutions as soon as misuses appeared.

The most flagrant misuse was the establishment of "ancestral halls" by persons who bore the same surname but did not actually belong to the same clan. This was not only a breach of the basic concept of the clan but a practice that might have dangerous consequences from the government's point of view. As early as 1742 the governor of Kiangsi undertook to stamp out what he called "evil practices in connection with ancestral halls." In an official document he said:

> Some persons who perhaps originally inhabited rural areas as clans, gathered together other persons who bore identical surnames but did not belong to the same clans, and built [ancestral] halls in the city, pretending that they were clansmen. The purpose of joining such [ancestral] halls was to obtain illicit gains and to create a power [group] upon which they might rely. No discrimination between the reputable and the menial was made, and genealogical relations were confused.[138]

About two decades later another governor of the same province found the custom of "combining clans and building temples" as rampant as ever. He memorialized the Ch'ien-lung emperor in 1764 that persons who bore identical surnames but did not necessarily belong to the same clans and who lived in different villages, towns, or cities organized themselves into "clans." Funds were collected from those who were interested and "ancestral halls" built (in the prefectural or provincial city), often endowed with a certain amount of ritual land. Ancient emperors, kings, or high officials were usually chosen as the "first ancestors." Persons participating in the organizations sent the tablets of their own ancestors to the common halls; the number of such tablets might amount to hundreds or thousands. The only condition for entering the tablets was the contribution of a certain amount of money. It was altogether immaterial whether the persons in question really had kinship ties with the rest who were combined in the "clans."

The motive behind this behavior has been explained in these words:

> In a current investigation of the ancestral halls [built by persons bearing] identical surnames, although it is impossible to ascertain their ultimate purpose, [it may be supposed that] these arose from the desire of [persons belonging to] inconsequential, humble families to pretend [membership in] prominent clans, or of pettifoggers and rascals to make illicit profits. These persons went from cities to villages, from prefectures to the provincial capital, inviting persons to join them and collecting funds to establish common ancestral halls. They fraudulently identified themselves as descendants of some noblemen or laid false claim to being offspring of some celebrated personages. Unscrupulous persons eagerly imitated them, with the result that the brood became quite numerous. The money left over from the construction of the ancestral halls was used to buy land or put away in cash or grain. Loans were frequently made to simple-minded persons bearing the same surnames. Relying on the influence of the "ancestral halls" [those in control] charged heavy interest rates on the loans, or practiced exorbitant usury on the land rent.[139]

One immediate and perceptible evil consequence that arose from these sham clan organizations was an increase of litigations in Kiangsi province. The governor wrote:

> Investigation reveals that the reason that there have been so many cases at law is that the people of Kiangsi are in the habit of combining into clans and instituting common ancestral halls. . . . Surplus money is used to buy land from which rent is collected. As a consequence, unscrupulous persons, looking at this income with a covetous eye, start litigations on the most ungrounded pretexts. Pretending that they are acting for the entire "clan" on matters of common concern, they defray their expenses from the funds of the ancestral halls. . . . When the funds are exhausted, they make every household contribute money, which they [continue to] appropriate and spend freely. [140]

The imperial government sought to put a stop to such practices. In an edict of 1764 the Ch'ien-lung emperor prohibited them and said by way of explanation:

> In order to give importance to the kinship group and to cultivate affectionate feelings among its members, the people established ancestral halls to perform annual sacrificial rites. If indeed these halls are located in the native villages or cities inhabited by the kinsmen, all of whom are blood relatives of the same clans, [these halls] are not only permitted by law but are encouraged as constituting a good custom. But when remote and unknown persons of an entire prefecture or a whole province are drawn together, fraudulently joining themselves into "clans" and establishing common "ancestral halls," their motive at the beginning may be merely to collect money and to fish for gains, but subsequently their practice may lead to the gathering of bandits and harboring of rogues. The resulting evils would be endless. We fear that [such halls exist] not only in Kiangsi. It is obviously necessary that searching inquiries be made and preventive measures adopted, so that this corruptive custom may be stopped. [141]

Even in provinces where the "custom" referred to by the emperor did not prevail, where the large clans were the result of natural increase of membership and not of fraudulent extension, the very size and strength of these clans gave rise to misuses that were directly detrimental to peace. The Ch'ien-lung emperor said in an edict of 1766:

> According to Wang Chien's memorial, the ritual land attached to the ancestral halls in the eastern part of Kwangtung frequently caused armed feuds [between clans]. . . . It is petitioned that the land be divided up in order to put this wicked custom to a stop. . . . We fear, however, that functionaries may not carry [this proposed measure] out properly, and that clerks and underlings may use it as a pretext and stir up troubles. . . . Moreover, ancestral halls are built and ritual

land instituted normally for the purpose of financing the sacrificial
rites and supplying the needs of the clansmen. If the land is used law-
fully to consolidate and harmonize [kinship relations] . . . it is not
a bad practice at all. But if [it induces people] to rely on the numerical
strength or financial power of their clans, to oppress their fellow
villagers, or even worse, to assemble mobs and fight with weapons,
. . . [such a practice] surely should not be allowed to spread. This
wicked custom is especially prevalent in Fukien and Kwangtung provinces. . . . The governors-general and governors of these provinces
are ordered that hereafter they should rigorously direct local officials
to investigate. If the [practices mentioned above] are discovered . . .
the culprits shall be punished in accordance with law, and all the land
belonging to their ancestral halls . . . distributed to the members of
the clans in question. . . . [It is further] ordered that this edict be
circulated among the governors-general and governors of all provinces and that they direct their subordinates to carry [this measure]
out uniformly and properly. [142]

By then the imperial government was thoroughly convinced of the
dangers of extended clan organizations, whether they were composed
of bona fide clansmen or persons unrelated by blood. It appeared to
the Ch'ien-lung emperor at least that large clans were more likely
to cause trouble than small ones. In an edict of 1768 in reply to a
petition to authorize the establishment of clan heads in large clans,
he said:

Chang Kuang-hsien, imperial censor, memorialized Us, asking
permission to institute clan heads in large clans. His view is extremely perverse and erroneous. . . . When among the people families and
clans become prosperous and contain large numbers of clansmen,
lawless elements are found within these groups, who, relying on their
numerical strength, often raise troubles. Hitherto most of the cases
involving gathering mobs and fighting with weapons have come from
large clans. This is a clear proof [of the danger inherent in large
clans]. . . . Now, if the title *tsu-chang* [clan head] is instituted in
the various clans, it is not sure that unruly sons and younger brothers
[of these clans] will submit themselves to the discipline of their heads;
and worse still, it is possible that the incumbents are not persons
qualified [for the proposed office]. It is certain that [such unqualified
persons] will take advantage of their office to monopolize the control
of their clans, to rely on the strength [of their groups] to oppress the
weak, becoming thus a heavy burden on their native villages. [143]

Thus, before the eighteenth century came to an end, the Ch'ing
rulers had realized that the clan was not necessarily a reliable instrument of rural control and that under adverse conditions it often
became a source of troubles. Their attempt at controlling the clan
and suppressing its undesirable behavior was determined and prompt,
but there is no evidence that they succeeded in making the clan safe

for and useful to the imperial regime. "Evil practices" persisted; at any rate, feuds between kinship groups did not abate in the following century. Some of the clans reacted to the general turbulent circumstances of the middle and late nineteenth century by becoming additional sources of disorder.

Chinese writers convinced of the essentially "evil" nature of the clan condemned in no uncertain terms clans that outgrew their natural dimensions; some of them went so far as to condemn all clans that had tangible organization. A seventeenth-century writer, for example, asserted that the motives for uniting clansmen into a group were purely selfish and that the hidden aim of large kinship organizations was "to ruin the state and harm the people."[144] A nineteenth-century writer voiced the same sentiment in stronger words. He believed that the clan organization involved a disregard of the duties that were due to the sovereign and a friendship that should be shown to all fellow men:[145]

> It is the good fortune of families but a misfortune of the state when [their members] organize and dwell together [as clans. These groups act harmfully] on a small scale when they refuse to pay taxes or maltreat officials, and on a large scale when they plot to rebel or commit acts of sedition. All this [results from the fact that] they capitalize on their numerical strength and *esprit de corps*.[146]

This view may have been too severe and was not shared by all writers of imperial China, but it seems to have contained some truth. Perhaps there was something in the nature of the clan that made it act and react as it did. It was an outgrowth of the family; it was theoretically based on the same natural relationships that gave reality to the family. But since the family group was extended far beyond its natural dimensions, whatever natural sentiments or affection existed in the family were bound to be diluted to the vanishing point in the clan. The clan was therefore held together more often by utilitarian considerations than by sentimental attachments among its members. As our survey of clan activities shows, a good deal of the behavior of kinship groups was not motivated by unselfish principles. In many instances the clan organization was promoted and maintained to advance or protect the interests of a minority of the clansmen. And even where the interests promoted were those of the entire group, these were selfish in that the clansmen assumed that their welfare was paramount to that of the community in general. Clan organization, which integrated a relatively large number of persons and families into a unit, pooling their resources and coordinating their actions, generated a measure of strength that was unknown in the natural family. The clan thus became a power in its locality and sometimes a dominant power in places where it attained greater than ordinary prosperity. "Power tends to corrupt, " and the power enjoyed by clans was no exception. It was indeed easy for some clans to act as predatory groups in the countryside. These clans became, so to speak, group bullies, behaving very much like the individual bullies that plagued many a Chinese village.

Of course not all clans behaved in the same way. In a number of instances the clan was reported as having served as a stabilizing influence in rural life. Even assuming that kinship organizations were generally motivated by selfish purposes, the leaders of some of them might be shrewd enough to see that the welfare of their groups depended upon or was conditioned by the general peace of the larger community, and to refrain from engaging in unlawful or openly antisocial conduct. The behavior exhibited by the Liang clan of Ch'a-k'eng should warn us against a sweeping condemnation of the clan. It should be noted also that since clan leadership was as a rule in the hands of the gentry clansmen, and since the gentry under ordinary circumstances had an interest in recognizing and upholding the imperial order, it was at least as likely that the clan would be a stabilizing social factor as a disruptive one. There is some evidence that leaders of some clans not only willingly submitted their organizations to government control, but even sought to legitimize clan authority by invoking government sanction. The Chu clan of T'ung-ch'eng (Anhwei), for example, sent their *tsung-kuei* (clan regulations) to the local magistrate and requested him to announce publicly that the clan heads were authorized to send any clansman that failed to comply with these regulations. [147] The fact is that the behavior of clans varied under different circumstances and at different times. When clan and government interests definitely clashed, kinship groups might act openly or surreptitiously against the government. It should be borne in mind also that clans were in fact villages or parts of villages, and shared some of the essential characteristics of villages in general. Neither clan organizations nor village organizations operated consistently in harmony with the principle of imperial security.

The upshot of this discussion, then, is that while the clan afforded the imperial government an additional instrument of rural control, it was not a fool-proof one, and even presented additional problems of control for which there was no adequate solution.

DECLINE OF THE CLAN ORGANIZATION

The clan, like any other social institution of nineteenth-century China, underwent a process of decline when the circumstances favoring the growth of the kinship group generally changed. This process went on with varying speeds and in varying degrees in different parts of the empire. Some clans under exceptional conditions suffered no

setback or even enjoyed renewed prosperity. [148] But generally the heyday of the clan passed with the passing of the turbulent mid-nineteenth
century. [149]

An obvious though not necessarily decisive factor that contributed to
the recession of the clan was the vagaries of family fortune. Clans
depended a good deal upon effective leadership for their strength and
prosperity. When such leadership was wanting, no clan could maintain its cohesion for long. [150]

The most definite sign of the decay of the clan was the disintegration
of the visible symbols of its solidarity. Ancestral halls were allowed
to fall into ruins or to be irreverently used; ritual land, the indispensable economic foundation of the kinship organization, was misappropriated or illegally disposed of. Instances of this sort were
readily found even in localities where the clan ordinarily exerted
the greatest influence. A document dated 1830 described the following state of affairs in a locality in Kwangtung:

> Investigation shows that within the limits of Fu-shan Hsiang, the
> ancestral halls of the various clans have been grievously torn down
> and tombs dug open. . . . The reason is that the old materials, wood
> and stone [which were used in the construction of these halls], have
> become increasingly valuable as the prices of them go up. The tomb
> sites arouse interest because they are regarded as desirable accord-
> ing to the principles of geomancy. In their pursuit of gains, unduti-
> ful sons and grandsons forget their ancestors and conceive avaricious
> schemes readily. Local bullies or crafty merchants take advantage
> [of the situation] to reap profits. [151]

Fraudulent selling of clan property occurred equally often in other
localities. As early as in the middle of the eighteenth century, the
governor of Kiangsi memorialized the throne to the following effect:

> Owing to the fact that the price of grain is rising and that land be-
> comes increasingly valuable, greedy and unscrupulous persons some-
> times make schemes to buy [clan land] by fraudulent methods. They
> bribe one or two undutiful sons or grandsons of the clans [that own
> land], instruct them to draw up unauthorized deeds of sale . . . giv-
> ing them half the amount of the price, and tell them to flee to some
> distant places. The purchasers then take possession of the land in
> question, and collect the rent by force. When the cases are brought
> to court, it is often impossible [for the government] to apprehend the
> persons who have received the purchase money. Trials have to be in-
> definitely postponed, leaving the fraudulent buyers in possession of
> the property. [152]

Similar instances were reported in other localities, especially in the
nineteenth century. In some places the property of clans survived the

dynasty, but even there ancestral halls and ritual lands were eventually liquidated in various ways. [153]

Sometimes the land was lost to the clan as a whole but remained in
one of the families that composed it. It was reported, for example,
that "large amounts of land owned collectively by some clans in Kwangtung province are often so appropriated by a few powerful and self-
fattening families in these clans that they become additional causes of
intraclan hatred. "[154]

Since ancestral halls and ritual land were protected by clan regulations and established social custom against disposal, [155] one cannot
resist concluding that the phenomenon described was symptomatic of
some serious disease of the clan organization. The clan, as already
indicated, was normally a gentry-led and gentry-supported organization. Its fortunes were therefore inseparably bound together with
those of its leading gentry kinsmen; its prosperity was conditioned
by the ability, wealth, influence, and personal interest of ranking officials or titled scholars who happened to grace it at a given moment.
Such leaders of the clan, however, did not live forever, nor were
they available at all times. Nor indeed could the leading families of
a clan remain forever prosperous. [156] Without committing ourselves
to the controversial view that family eminence could not extend beyond three or four generations, [157] we must admit that owing to certain characteristics of the Chinese family and society, it was impossible to insure a steady line of capable or ambitious offspring to carry
on whatever "glories" some of the progenitors may have achieved.
This tendency for families to enjoy no more than transient eminence
was eventually reflected in the clan organization which was, after all,
an extended family.

A declining clan either deteriorated as a whole or fell into fragments. The following situation prevailing in a locality in Hunan province in the nineteenth century illustrates some of the outcome of clan
disintegration:

> It has become the custom of Yung-chou for families to live separate-
> ly and be without ancestral halls. Not only do distant branches of the
> same clans not join themselves together; even families of close ties
> treat one another as if they bore different surnames. Being afraid of
> disputes, genealogical records are not kept or revised. Nominally,
> clans may have heads, but these heads give no instructions [to the
> clansmen]. Each individual indulges in the intimate affection of his
> own wife and children, and all clansmen have drifted away from their
> elderly relatives. [158]

Shifting fortunes of families and family heads might not permanently
cripple a clan, if the general socioeconomic environment of the locality in which the clan found itself remained favorable. A kinship group

which suffered an eclipse of its prosperity might regain its former glory when new leaders emerged from one of its component families. But unfortunately for the clans the environment did not remain always favorable. Clans depended for their life and health upon a certain degree of peace and prosperity in the agricultural countryside. A serious disturbance of rural equilibrium was bound to affect them adversely. Recurring natural disasters, frequent uprisings, and military campaigns, especially in the second half of the nineteenth century, resulted in a shrinking economy in many parts of the empire; the aftermath of these misfortunes often delayed recovery. Some of the clansmen may have migrated to more promising lands, while those who remained in their home communities may have found it difficult to afford the luxury of maintaining the ancestral halls. For many of them, there were matters more urgent than the welfare of distant relatives or duties toward departed ancestors.

The Li clan, dwelling in the countryside of Shao-hsing (Chekiang), illustrated how the kinship organization was affected by social conditions and how difficult it was to rejuvenate it after a crushing catastrophe. The first ancestral hall and ritual land (about 200 *mow)* were instituted early in the eighteenth century by one of the clansmen, a *chin-shih* scholar who served as magistrate in a neighboring province. By the mid-nineteenth century the land, which was managed by a number of clansmen, was mostly misappropriated by them, and the ancestral hall was burnt down by the Taiping troops that invaded the locality. After peace was restored, one of the clansmen who had achieved considerable literary fame but little success in the examinations proposed in 1868 to rebuild the ancestral hall and revive the clan organization. His proposal fell on deaf ears. He made known his feelings in these disheartening words: "Among our clansmen the gentry elements are falling apart, and few understand the significance of honoring the ancestors. So when I made the proposal, my lonely voice was drowned by the babble of a hundred objectors. This is profoundly lamentable."[159] His perseverance brought results in 1871, but he had to pay a price. The ritual land was retrieved and mortgaged to a wealthy clansman (an ordinary pennywise merchant, who was so devoid of gentry sentiments that he saw no reason for teaching his three sons to read and write), and the ancestral hall was rebuilt with the funds thus raised. Finding that the resources of the clan were insufficient for maintaining the sacrificial rites, this zealous scholar-clansman (who had recently passed the examinations for the *chü-jen)* contributed twenty-eight *mow* of land belonging to his own branch.[160] In 1885, less than fifteen years after the ritual land was laboriously instituted, an "unworthy" clansman fraudulently sold it again.[161]

This instance is not necessarily typical. There were cases in which clans lost their property permanently, and others in which clans re-

ceived added resources and financial strength even late in the nineteenth century.[162] But whatever were the fortunes of individual clans
in different parts of the empire, it was generally true that the clan
organization depended directly upon effective leadership within and
favorable conditions without for its continued existence and prosperity.[163]

Other factors, of course, affected the clan. Sometimes the very solidarity of the kinship group became a source of trouble which threatened to weaken or destroy the group itself. In some parts of Kwangtung, clansmen often "brought shame to their progenitors" in trying
to evade the payment of taxes. According to an official report:

> The ritual land belonging to the ancestral halls of eastern Kwang-
> tung invariably amounted to several hundred *mow* and the grain [tax]
> collectible on the land to several tens of *shih*. On the days when the
> rent was collected, everyone [came forth] as descendants [of the sev-
> eral clans], but at the time when the tax payments were due, all made
> excuses and backed out. Even [in clans where] there were persons in
> charge of the common property, they were usually appointed to serve
> for one year, and these would by all means dodge and hide. . . . It
> was then that the practice of confiscating ancestral halls and impound-
> ing ancestral tablets arose.[164]

Clan solidarity might bring trouble in another way. It was a common
practice for a clan to stand behind its members in dealing with outsiders, especially when they were involved in some conflict or dispute.[165] Quarrels between individuals, therefore, easily developed
into quarrels between kinship groups. These quarrels were often
settled amicably, but equally often were allowed to develop into feuds,
particularly in Fukien, Kwangtung, and Kiangsi, where the clan organization was very strong.[166] Disputes over land, water rights, ancestral halls, and other matters sometimes flared up into large-scale
fights, which, according to a recent investigator, accounted for a
large number of the armed conflicts that occurred in South China
during the past few centuries.[167] The situation was so grave that it
attracted imperial attention on many an occasion. The Yung-cheng
emperor, for example, said in an edict of 1734:

> We heard in Chang [Chou] and Ch'üan [Chou] of Fukien province,
> the inhabitants have customarily been violent and indulge in fierce
> fights among themselves. Kinship groups with large numbers of male
> members rely on their numerical strength to oppress small and in-
> consequential ones. Quarrels over trivial matters promptly cause
> them to assemble mobs and fight with weapons, resulting in serious
> cases. When officials go to the scene to make arrests and to hear the
> cases, the persons involved either flee and hide themselves, or refuse

to obey the orders. In their eyes there is no such thing as the law.
. . . This is a condition known to all. [168]

Despite imperial prohibition, clan feuds continued in Fukien and
other provinces throughout the nineteenth century. Describing the
conditions in a district in southwest Fukien, a Chinese writer said:

> P'ing-ho is situated near the border of Fukien and Kwangtung. . . .
> The inhabitants dwell on mountainsides divided by streams, each
> household being a stronghold and every man a warrior. The inhab-
> itants gather themselves into clans, each of which occupies a well-
> marked piece of land, and the clansmen fight and rob one another
> from generation to generation. [169]

The same writer related what he saw in Lung-ch'i, another district
in south Fukien:

> The Cheng clan of Ku-hsien [village] and other clans, comprising
> altogether over fifty rural divisions, fight with weapons in the south;
> the Ch'en clan of T'ien-pao [village] and other clans comprising over
> seventy rural divisions, fight in the west; the Wang clan of T'ien-li
> [village] and the Shih clan of Hung-t'ai [village] fight in the east; the
> Tsou clan of Kuei-te [village] and other clans fight in the north. . . .
> [These and many other clans] have been continuously seeking quar-
> rels one with another during past years, murdering and robbing one
> another without end. [170]

A European missionary, writing in the 1840's, summarized the clan
fights in a Fukien village:

> The whole village was inhabited by persons having the same surname
> of *Lim* or *Lin*, who appeared to be united together by the ties of pa-
> triarchal law. . . . They have a common property in the wells and the
> temples within their boundaries, which form subjects of occasional
> dispute with the people of the next village. These quarrels sometimes
> are carried to such an extent that the belligerents on either side reg-
> ularly muster their forces, and an appeal is made to physical vio-
> lence. [171]

A 1766 memorial of the governor of Kwangtung gives a concrete
picture of the situation in that province and throws much light on some
of the features of clan feuds:

> The people of Kwangtung live mostly together in clans, each of
> which has built ancestral halls and each has instituted ritual land and
> attached it to the halls. The land is called *ch'ang-tsu* [sacrificial rent].
> The land of the large clans may amount to as much as several thousand
> *mow;* even small clans may possess several hundred. The rent, paid
> in grain, is collected each year by the various branches of a clan by
> turns. After meeting the expenses for ancestral rites and paying the
> taxes, the surplus [grain] is sold and the money invested. The savings,

accumulating day after day and month after month, may amount to hundreds or thousands [of taels], or even more. The large clans are thus all wealthy. There is not one among them that does not rely on its strength to oppress weak [clans], or does not rely on its numerical superiority to terrorize small ones.

If the strength of two clans [involved in a conflict] is equal and there is doubt with regard to victory, the clansmen on both sides assemble in the ancestral halls, organize, and go out to fight. Arrangements are previously made that clansmen who are wounded in the fight are to be paid handsomely [with funds from] the *ch'ang tsu* . . . and those who die of wounds are to have their tablets entered in the ancestral hall, and their widows and children are to be given a part of the sacrificial land. . . . If someone in the enemy clan is killed [in the fight], the clansman who agrees to take the crime upon himself [and receives punishment] is to have his tablet entered in the ancestral hall and his family given some land, the same as those who die of wounds. Consequently, persons who have no regard for their own lives consider these fights a means to make profit. . . . When [local officials] arrest the culprits and try them, both sides have persons to take the crime upon themselves, [thus allowing the real criminals to go free]. . . . All such cunning and evil practices arise from the ritual land. [172]

The governor went on to recommend that ritual land in excess of one hundred *mow* possessed by one clan be "scattered," hoping thus to put an end to clan feuds. The Ch'ien-lung emperor met his suggestion halfway. [173] Judging from subsequent accounts, the "evil practices" remained uncurtailed, at least in some parts of Kwangtung, as a Westerner observed in 1836:

In each of the villages in the vicinity of Canton and Whampoa, where these feuds are so common, a curious provision has obtained by custom to meet such exigencies. "A band of devoted men" is there found, and a list of them kept, who have voluntarily offered themselves to assume such crimes and to take their chance for life. When complaint is made, therefore, so many of the first on this list as are necessary come forward, confess themselves the perpetrators of the slaughter, and surrender to the government. It then belongs to them and their friends to employ lawyers and bring witnesses to prove it a justifiable homicide, or one which calls for mitigated punishment. . . . The compensation . . . is security for the maintenance of their families in case of capital punishment, and a reward in lands or money, sometimes to the amount of $300. This sum is raised by the voluntary imposition of "taxes" on the inhabitants of that village. [174]

There were a few differences in detail (for example, "rewarding" the "devoted men" with funds raised by *ad hoc* contribution instead of with the resources of the ritual land), but the basic pattern of behavior was unchanged.

Sometimes clan feuds were instigated by unscrupulous clansmen who cast a covetous eye on the clan property. According to a well-known Chinese writer:

> Among the disorders in Fukien and Kwangtung, armed feuds are the most important. All the common ancestral halls of large clans have accumulated immense wealth. Lawless elements who covet this wealth and have no way of getting it, arouse animosity [between their own and] other clans and incite feuds, thus [involving the clans in litigation and creating the necessity of giving] heavy bribes to local officials. Officials are happy to receive bribes as a result of the feuds instigated by the lawless elements, and the latter are happy to take advantage of the necessity to bribe the former to disburse the funds of the common ancestral halls, [thus giving themselves ample opportunity to embezzle]. An old law contained a special provision which required that all the resources of the ancestral halls [of clans engaged in feuds] be divided among clansmen, leaving only enough funds to maintain the sacrificial rites. But this provision was never enforced, for the reason that feuds would cease with the dissipation of [the property belonging to] the ancestral halls; that, so far as the local officials were concerned, would amount to plugging a source of profit for themselves. [175]

It appears, then, that local officials contributed to the rampancy of clan feuds. In fact, the most shameless of them were said to have "regarded a year in which numerous cases of armed conflicts occurred as a year of 'good harvest' and one in which few were reported as a 'lean year.'"[176] Timid magistrates, on the other hand, who "preferred withdrawing from their present posts to dealing with violent clans,"[177] indirectly encouraged feuds by their failure to cope with the situation properly. It should be emphasized, however, that although corrupt and incompetent officials contributed to the sorry state of affairs in many parts of the empire, the leaders of the clan organizations themselves should be held primarily responsible. They organized fights upon the slightest provocation. The fact that they could hire mercenary swordsmen to do the fighting, thus reducing risks to themselves and their clansmen, partly explains their readiness to plunge their groups into the bloody melees. The following statement taken from a memorial written in 1886 by the governor-general of Liang-Kwang will suffice to lend support to our view:

> It often occurs that owing to petty resentment resulting from an angry look or trifling matters concerning hills or land, [clansmen of Kwangtung] without waiting for official action, enlist or hire bad elements from outside [the clans] and set a date for armed conflicts. The leaders of the fights are usually *tsu-shou* [clan heads], *tsu-shen* [clan gentry], or *tz'u-chang* [leaders of ancestral halls] that are unworthy. . . . The men whom they call together may number several hundred

or several thousand [on a given occasion], and the villages that took part [in the fights] may number a few or several dozen. . . . The fights sometimes continue for three to five years.[178]

The gentry dominated the scene in clan feuds as in other activities of the kinship groups, but they did not always take the leadership in these ventures. Commoners might play the role of clan bullies, perhaps somewhat less often than they assumed the doubtful distinction of the village bullies. According to a local official serving early in the nineteenth century in southern Kwangtung, these clan bullies "were not necessarily members of wealthy families or persons holding official titles or academic degrees. They were evil elements [of the clans] to whom low-down blackguards attached themselves. The latter became the talons and teeth of the former, obeying the orders of the former."[179]

In some instances commoner members actually shared the "righteous indignation" of their leaders and took an active part in defending the honor or interests of their group. In such cases hired swordsmen were not employed at all. The following incident was reported in Ching Hsien (Anhwei) in 1785 by a member of the Pao clan:

> Pao Pin-ta was a peasant belonging to our clan. In the *i-ssu* year of Ch'ien-lung [1785] there was a great famine. The distant ancestors of our clan were buried in the Feng-huang hills; [the graveyard] was about ten *li* from the village [where our clan lived], and was in front of the Shui-k'ou-t'ing [village] of the Ts'ao clan. Clansmen of the Ts'ao clan dug bracken roots for food. They refused to stop digging even when they were warned against it, and they almost ruined the tombs. The *tsu-chang* [of our clan] posted a notice in front of the ancestral hall to the effect that men between sixteen and sixty who were not sick should assemble on a designated day in front of the hall, each carrying a stick, to go to the Feng-huang hills [to fight the Ts'ao clan]. Those who failed to appear would have their names deleted from the genealogical records. Clansmen who presented themselves numbered about 1,500. The Ts'ao clan did not have more than three hundred men, and set up their defense at Shui-k'ou-t'ing. The first clash ended in a defeat for our clan. . . . Thereupon Pao Pin-ta said: "Pao is routed by Ts'ao; our face is lost to our fellow inhabitants. Are there any who are willing to fight together with me?" About thirty rallied to his call. Members of the Ts'ao clan were feasting their victorious warriors in their ancestral hall. Pao Pin-ta assigned ten men to block the entrance to Shui-k'ou-t'ing and led the remaining twenty men into the village. They fought in front of the ancestral hall of the Ts'ao clan. [After having defeated the enemy, Pao Pin-ta] secured from them a written promise to refrain from disturbing the graveyard.[180]

Cases like this, however, were comparatively rare. The majority of the recorded instances and opinions point to the conclusion that clan feuds were normally instigated and conducted by the leading members of the groups involved. But whatever may have been the personal status of such members, their action tended to bring more harm than good to their groups. In fact, feuds were frequently so disastrous that they quickly sapped the strength of the clans, if indeed they did not cause their immediate ruin. According to a Western writer reporting conditions in early nineteenth-century Fukien, "The name of one was Tsae [Ts'ai] and of the other Wâng, and a gathering of each having taken place, they fought until many were killed and a number of houses destroyed by fire."[181] The losses sustained by some feuding clans in Kwangtung province late in the nineteenth century were even more serious:

> The fights sometimes continue for three to five years. . . . If a
> village [inhabited by an enemy clan] is taken by storm . . . the houses
> destroyed by fire are counted by hundreds of rooms and persons killed
> by several dozen. . . . The property lost in each of the fights would
> take the owners from one or two years to several dozen years to re-
> store.[182]

The rise and decline of the kinship group under changing circumstances and the impact of fierce feuds on it are strikingly exemplified by a clan in the countryside of nineteenth-century Kwangtung:

> In 1855 the present writer was invited to Quei-shin, the prefecture
> of Weichau-fu [Hui-chou Fu], where, at Ho-au [village], he found a
> wealthy clan of Punti amidst a large Hakka population. On making in-
> quiries respecting their origin, he received the following brief ex-
> tract from their family chronicles:
> "The ancestors of our clan [the Chin] came down from Kiangsi,
> from the prefecture Kieh-ngan [Chi-an], and the district Lo-ling [Lu-
> ling]. When during the reign of Kautsung of the Sung dynasty [in the
> twelfth century], Kiangsi was much disturbed by insurrections; Shi-
> ch'ang and two of his brothers fled to Chu-ki-kiang, in the prefecture
> of Nan-hiung [Nan-hsiung] of this province. After a short time, one
> of them proceeded to Sha-tsing, near the Bogue; one to Yentsan, in
> the same (Sin-ngan district); whilst Shi-ch'ang proceeded to Ho-ya
> (or Ho-au) in the Kwei-shen [sic] district. From the Sung dynasty
> to the middle of the Ming Dynasty our clan increased very little in
> number, and possessed but little wealth. Ho-au was at that time in-
> habited by two clans of the K'ung and Liang names, but who disap-
> peared in the same degree as our number increased. . . .
> "The villages that are descended from these three brothers are
> Sien-jin-ling, Pu-lu-wei and Hwang-ko, and in Sin-ngan, Kiu-tsiun-
> ling, Shang-shi, and Hia-shi, Sha-tsin, etc., altogether fifteen. . . .
> "During the reign of Kien-lung [Ch'ien-lung, 1735-96], Chin-san-
> ming and others accumulated much wealth, and one of them built
> Pu-lu-wei . . . As early as 1737 it was surrounded by a wall of

about 20 feet high, with sixteen parapets. . . . The length of the wall is about half an English mile, and is surrounded by a ditch from 10 to 20 feet deep, and was in 1843 involved in a conflict with the Hakka, which nearly ruined the whole clan. . . ."

About three English miles southwest of Ho-au, there is a market place, which was built by the people of Ho-au [i.e., the Chin clan]. The Hakka, to whom the market was let, refused in that year [1843] to pay their taxes [i.e., rent], and . . . appeal was had to arms. Both parties fought for about six years, when another market place, also belonging to Ho-au, gave occasion to a conflict with even more powerful clans.

In 1850 more than 90 villages united for the extermination of the Chin clan. Pu-lu-wei fell by treachery, and the people were stripped of the last piece of dress they had on their person; but though more than 5,000 men surrounded Ho-au, where only from 300 to 500 fighting men were, the Hakka had not the courage to enter the village, but moved off without any booty. . . .

In 1856 war broke out anew, and frightful murders would have been committed, had not the writer of these lines induced the parties to come once more to terms.

The terrible war that had for so many years raged in those fertile regions had caused the neglect of repairs of embankments necessary for the irrigation of the fields. . . .

In 1855 a terrible epidemic carried off almost all the cattle of the people. . . .

So rapidly did the people fall from their former glory that the late Rev. F. Genahr declared before his death that only about two in fifty [of the clansmen] were competent to read and understand what they read. Women who formerly washed their faces in silver basins, are now reduced to extreme poverty. The young men grow up in ignorance and become vagabonds, and the few left who have any property are not permitted to enjoy it in peace. [183]

Clans might misuse their power and become a disturbing factor in the countryside even where and when they did not indulge in sanguinary feuds. In some localities where the strength of several clans was unequal, the weaker ones frequently became victims of predatory clans. One instance was noted by a Western writer, in the late nineteenth century in Kwangtung:

> On a plain that I have often traversed, north of Swatow, there was a few years ago, a little village inhabited by a small and weak clan, surnamed Stone [Shih]. There were twelve neighboring villages, chiefly of the Plum [Mei] clan, and these all combined against the Stones, whom they far outnumbered. The Stones planted and watered their crops, and the Plums reaped the harvest. There were perpetual raids on the property of the Stones, and they, having no redress for their wrongs, were in danger of utter extinction. [184]

Similar situations were found in other parts of the empire. According to a recent investigator:

> In some communities the weaker *tsu* are often bullied by the powerful ones. . . . In the county of Chao-an, Fukien, the small *tsu* whose fields adjoin the property of the large *tsu*, have to place themselves under the "protection" of the latter, paying one-tenth to one-thirteenth of the produce in order to insure the safety of the crops. . . . A recent account depicts conditions in the county of Li-ch'üan, Shensi: "For three hundred years, the adult males in our *tsu* never exceeded thirty. Living between two big *tsu* and being poor members of the intelligentsia who have been agriculturists for four generations and teachers for three, they could not help being bullied and insulted by the big *tsu*. . . . Year after year, month after month, [members of the big *tsu]* come to borrow money. If you ask for a return of the capital only, you still are abused. If you don't lend money, they come to steal. . . . When they abuse you, bow your head; when they hit you, don't return the blow. Your wife and daughter you have to let them violate. Without money do not go to court."[185]

It may be conjectured that such situations were essentially similar to those which obtained in localities infested with clan feuds, in that they all arose as a result of that "reliance upon superior strength" to which the Ch'ing government had made reference on more than one occasion. Feuds ensued where the strength of conflicting clans was roughly equal, so that there was a good chance for one party to defend against the encroachment of another; exploitation and submission came as a consequence when it was clear to the wronged clan that it was futile to resist the oppressors. Whatever may have been the resulting situations, overbearing or predatory acts committed by powerful clans were bound in the long run to impair the peace and prosperity of their own communities.

Some clans proved themselves detrimental to rural peace in still another way. According to a Western writer of the nineteenth century, clans in certain parts of the empire were known to have engaged in robbery and brigandage.

> To increase the social evils of clanship and systematized thieving, local tyrants occasionally spring up, persons who rob and maltreat the villagers by means of their armed retainers, who are in most cases, doubtless, members of the same clan. . . .
> Clannish banditti often supply themselves with firearms.[186]

In fact, "clannish banditti" might become in some localities a constant threat to rural peace and a constant source of troubles for the government. A mid-nineteenth-century governor-general of Liang-Kwang explained that some of the clans made it difficult to suppress banditry in Kwangtung:

> Whenever somebody wishes to organize and plunder, he merely
> has to hail whomever he meets with the words, "Come and get rich!"
> Few will not gladly join him, including people who till the soil and
> members of well-to-do and eminent clans. . . . In Hui-chou and Ch'ao-
> chou there are clans who made their fortunes through banditry; in
> such cases, the fact that their accomplices are numerous prevents
> [the government] from laying hands on them, since no one dares in-
> form against them and no official dares arrest them. Sometimes entire
> clans or entire villages are bandits. Any attempt to arrest them may
> cause disturbances. . . . This is the reason that it is difficult to check
> the rampancy of banditry. [187]

How powerful and influential bandit clans could become is illustrated
by the Ou clan which dwelt in the hilly countryside of Nan-hai (Kwangtung). According to a report published in 1899:

> The Hsi-ch'iao hills are located in Nan-hai, Kuang-chou. . . .
> Several dozen villages dot the hillsides; the whole area has hitherto
> been infested with robbers and bandits. . . . The most notorious is
> Ou-ts'un village. Ou Hsin, chief of a robber gang, regularly induced
> his clansmen and daring bandits of the neighborhoods to plunder in
> all directions. . . . Last year [1898] Ho Ch'ang-ch'ing, commander
> of river troops . . . went to his village, arrested the named cul-
> prits, sealed up the ancestral hall and put in custody the gentry-elders
> of his clan. One of the gentry clansmen, who was then an official at
> the imperial capital, bribed an imperial censor who promptly mem-
> orialized the emperor, charging Ho Ch'ang-ch'ing with leading his
> troops to vex the people. As a result the commander lost his post.
> Thereafter Ou Hsin became even more unrestrained and unscrupul-
> ous and gathered a band amounting to several hundred men. [188]

As soon as a clan involved itself more or less collectively in overt
antisocial and unlawful activities, it ceased to be what it originally
professed to be—a kinship organization kept together for the benefit
of its members, in conformity with established social and legal rules.
The organization might continue to exist, perhaps with added strength;
but the kinship group, in a true sense, suffered a fatal transformation.

The bandit-clan phenomenon, however, was in all probability a limited one. Clans joined rebel groups or turned themselves into bandit
hordes only in special circumstances. As a rule, clans were more inclined to fight against bandits, "to protect the property, families and
lives" of their members, than to pillage their fellow villagers.

Being essentially a rural group, the clan organization had a good
deal in common with the village organization. The leadership of both
groups was usually in the hands of the same persons in places where
kinship groups dominated the scene. There was a degree of similarity
and a certain amount of overlapping between the activities of the clan

and the village. While the clan was a social group clearly distinguishable from the village as such, it was so entangled with the village that
its fortunes fluctuated with those of the rural community in which it
found itself.

The social and economic inequalities that existed among the individuals and groups in the village were present also in the clan. The
clan organization, in fact, accentuated such inequalities. Veiled by
kinship ties, genuine or imaginary, the domination of the gentry over
commoners was intensified, especially in the large and well-organized
clans. Speaking generally, one can no more regard the clan than the
village as a democratic community.

The clan usually gave the village a higher degree of cohesion among
the inhabitants; monoclan villages in particular showed a degree of
solidarity not observed in villages where the clan was absent or
where more than one clan existed. The imperial rulers perceived
the inherent strength of the kinship groups and made use of them to
supplement the various institutions of rural control. These supplementary instruments of control, however, proved no more reliable
than the rest. Clan organizations exhibited different patterns of behavior under divergent circumstances and engaged in different types
of activities under leaderships of varying qualities. At one time clans
might serve as a stabilizing factor in rural life, but at another time
they might become a source of trouble for the government. Their
compact organization often generated power and influence which might
be used for good or evil. In the latter case, the clan organization
worked to the detriment not only of the imperial security but also of
the welfare of the kinship groups themselves. The imperial government therefore found it necessary to control and curtail the clans,
when it had hoped to use them as instruments of rural control.

Chapter 9

RURAL REACTIONS
TO CONTROL: I

GENERAL CHARACTERISTICS OF RURAL INHABITANTS

The preceding chapters have portrayed rural China as a conglomeration of villages of varying sizes and with varying degrees of organization. They do not take account of the portions of the countryside where organization was virtually absent and the inhabitants were so impoverished that no concerted activities worthy of the term were observed;[1] nor do they deal with those parts of the empire where even the village itself (in the sense of a compact group of rural households dwelling close together and forming a unit recognized as such by being given a definite name) hardly existed.[2] Chapters 9 and 10 supplement this incomplete picture by describing the general circumstances in which rural inhabitants lived, and by identifying their attitudes and behavior as exhibited in diverse situations, without exclusive reference to peasants who were members of organized communities.

The Chinese peasant is familiar to all who are interested in the history of China, but opinions differ as to what sort of human being he was. Two diametrically opposed views have been advanced by various writers at one time or another. The Chinese peasant has appeared to some as a harmless, peace-loving, and politically neutral animal, contented with the simple but not ample life that was his lot.

Examples of this view are readily found; the following statement made by a Western missionary and educator of the late nineteenth century is representative:

> It is said of the Emperor Yao, who lived four thousand years ago, that, being on a tour of inspection, he heard an old man singing to the sound of his lute [sic]:
> "I plough my ground and eat,
> I dig my well and drink;
> For king or emperor
> What use have I?"
> An emperor of the present day, if he made such tours, might in many a place have the same experience.[3]

The political indifference of the peasant, however, did not prevent him from being friendly to his fellow villagers. It was said, for instance, of the villagers of a district in South China that in the "good old days,"

> Whenever a family had some wine, meat, vegetables, or cakes, it usually gave some of the food to all the neighbors. When a family owned a pond, it used only the larger fish, allowing neighbors to take the smaller fish and shrimps. When a guest visited one of the families, neighbors were often invited to join [the party], each of whom brought with him some dishes—a practice known locally as *pang p'an* [assisting the plates]. [4]

The peasant did not lose his patience in the face of calamities or hardships. He was inclined to remain docile and to suffer his lot silently. As a recent Western writer put it:

> Although life is far from easy for him, he accepts it. There is a certain equilibrium between his environment, both physical and social, which apparently is quite stable. He is not agitating against tenancy, although he would like to own a plot of land. He is not indignant against the high rent he has to pay, although he would like to pay less. He is conservative and accepts things as they are. [5]

The extremely passive attitude of the peasantry, indeed, appeared strange in the eyes of some Western observers:

> To a foreigner from the lands of the West, where the revolutionary cry of "Bread, bread, or blood!" has become familiar, it is hard to understand why the hordes of homeless, famishing, and desperate refugees, who roam over the provinces blighted by flood or famine, do not precipitate themselves in a mass upon the district magistrate of the region where they have been ruined, and demand some form of succor. . . . To repeated and pressing inquiries put to the Chinese in the great famines as to the reason why some such plans are not taken, the invariable answer was in the words, "Not dare." [6]

On the other side, an entirely different view has been held. The peasantry is seen as a more or less militant segment of the population. According to some writers, the peasants have struggled violently time and again to overthrow their oppressors, ever since Ch'en She, a farm hand, rose in arms against the dynasty that the First Emperor established. Thus, a well-known fourteenth-century Chinese scholar wrote: "The people began to rise and cause disorder with the Ch'in dynasty. In later times, all who overthrew dynasties were mostly common people." [7] A modern Chinese writer was so impressed by the aggressive role supposedly played by peasants that he produced a sizable volume devoted to what he called "peasant wars" in Chinese history. [8] Another, thinking in a similar vein, argued that the Taiping Rebellion was an "anti-feudal uprising of peasants," which in reality marked the culmination of a long series of similar though smaller uprisings between 1774 and 1849. [9] In the eyes of such writers, "this sort of peasant uprisings and peasant wars alone constituted the real motive force of China's historical progress." [10]

It is safe to say that both these views suffer from oversimplification, and that neither is adequate to describe the actual situation. For each focuses attention on one aspect of the rural scene, without taking into consideration important variations of peasant behavior in diverse historical and local circumstances.

Two general considerations must be kept in mind if the pitfall of oversimplification is to be avoided. First, we must emphasize the obvious but easily overlooked fact that the imperial countryside was not uniform in its economic texture at all times and in all places, but was a vast mosaic of varying local conditions and changing local circumstances, to which the inhabitants of its diverse parts reacted with perceptibly different patterns of behavior. The inhabitants of rural China did not constitute a homogeneous mass, but were divided into two broad segments, the gentry and the common people, each of which again fell into two subcategories, roughly distinguishable by their attitude toward the existing order. Among the gentry those whose attitude or actions were generally in line with imperial purposes and interest were known as *cheng-shen* (upright gentry) while those who deported themselves otherwise were *lieh-shen* (bad gentry). Those among the common people that were generally inclined to be obedient and tractable were known as *liang-min* (good people), whereas those who proved themselves recalcitrant to imperial control or tended to disturb the imperial peace were called *yu-min* (weed people) or were identified by other similar labels.

A word of explanation may be pertinent here. Since the labels "upright," "good," and "bad" were applied to various persons according to whether their behavior tended to enhance or impair imperial security, or whether their attitudes tended to make them amenable or recalcitrant to imperial control, these labels as used by writers of the imperial period reflect the government's point of view. They therefore do not constitute a logical classification of the persons labeled, nor do they necessarily reveal the qualities of these persons, other than their reactions to imperial control. These labels are used here merely because they offer a convenient point of departure and permit us to avoid the inconvenience of using in their stead circumlocutory expressions such as "gentry subservient to imperial purposes," "scholars whose conduct tended to impair imperial security," or "commoners refractory to imperial control."

The "good people" included peasants, craftsmen, peddlers, and all others who earned a living with their limbs or wits, who were largely ignorant of the imperial laws but normally feared and obeyed whatever authority they happened to come into contact with. Their daily attention rarely went beyond the immediate task of keeping their families and themselves alive. They had no conscious desire either to defend or undermine the existing order and were politically indifferent. It was they who lent meaning to the concluding lines of the rustic ditty: "For king and emperor what use have I?" It was they too who gave substance to the observation that "the Chinaman is patient, frugal, laborious, peaceable, law-abiding, and respectful of authority."[11]

The "weed people" were usually without a profession, although some of them might be engaged in occupations (such as mining and squatting on wild, hill land) that tended to toughen them and develop in them gangsterlike attitudes. Under ordinary circumstances and in most of the rural areas they constituted a minority of the local population. But their importance should not be minimized. For although in times of general tranquillity they did not go beyond pestering the "good people" (sometimes even "upright gentry") with blackmail, intimidation, or bullying, they might in turbulent times contribute directly and substantially to the outbreak of "banditry," which might be anything from commonplace highway robbery to full-fledged rebellion.

It should be noted, however, that the "weed people" of the countryside were not alone responsible for uprisings of large dimensions. It was usually the combined action of these elements and some of the "bad gentry" (who for one reason or another found it advisable to challenge the constituted authority) that gave rise to local disorders. In the confusion that resulted from such action, some of the people who were formerly "good" might lose their property or means of living and so be driven by desperation to depart—temporarily at least—from their accustomed behavior; others might be coerced by the invaders to join them, thus augmenting the rebels' ranks and making it more difficult for the government to deal with the situation; still others who had long suffered the oppressive practices of landlords, local officials, and their underlings, and were faced with hunger and destruction, might be readily incited by instigators into acts of violence. Of course, not all of those who were originally regarded as *liang-min* joined the rebels or rioters, or submitted to the power of the latter without a struggle. Some of them who valued their *shen-chia hsing-ming* (person, family, and life) might arm themselves and offer resistance to the invading bands, especially when the local gentry took the leadership. When the emergency was over and order restored, many of these displaced or disturbed rural inhabitants would take the earliest opportunity to return to their former homes and occupations. The "bad" elements again curtailed their activities and kept them

within the bounds prevailing in times of peace. As periods of relative
prosperity alternated with periods of disaster, the "general temperament of the people" appeared to be "morose and lethargic" at one
moment but became "fitfully vehement" at another. [12]

This observation, however, would be inaccurate if by "the people" is
meant the entire rural population or the entire peasantry. For it was
never true that all the inhabitants of the countryside remained docile
under all circumstances, nor did it ever happen that all peasants at any
given instant rose in a single body against the government or another
segment of the population. The Taiping Rebellion, which has been
regarded by some as the best recent instance of "peasant war," certainly did not involve the peasantry as a whole. Were not the Hunan
"braves," who fought the Taipings and helped to save the Ch'ing dynasty, mostly peasants themselves? This great upheaval negates both
the near myth of the incurably placid Chinese rustic and the near myth
of the dynamically revolutionary Chinese peasantry.

The countryside of imperial China did not present a simple picture.
It was a vast, variegated, and variable scene, dotted by villages of
varying sizes and different degrees of organization, and peopled by
persons of dissimilar social, economic, and psychological backgrounds. While the broad historical and environmental background
of all these was roughly identical throughout the empire and remained
essentially unaltered for relatively long stretches of time, various
segments of the rural population reacted quite differently to vicissitudes in their immediate environment. The task of imperial control
resolved itself mainly into the problem of how to deal effectively with
these segments of the rural population so that a maximum of security
could be attained and the danger of insurgency reduced to a minimum,
the problem, in other words, of how to enlist those elements that
were serviceable to the imperial purposes, how to suppress those
that tended to thwart them, and how to protect those that formed the
backbone of the rural economy and were ordinarily inclined to respect authority. The various institutions and measures of rural control were calculated precisely to meet this problem. One is tempted
to think that here the Ch'ing emperors showed a keener insight into
the rural situation than those who subscribed to either of the two near
myths of the Chinese peasantry.

THE RURAL ENVIRONMENT

Economic Conditions

To give more substance to the general observation that the inhabitants of different parts of rural China did not have exactly the same
environment, [13] descriptions of the countryside written by eyewit-
nesses of the nineteenth century may be cited.

The life of some peasants in South China, where the economic conditions were fairly good, was described by a Western writer:

> The farmers in China, as a class, are highly respectable, but, as their farms are all small, they are probably less wealthy than our farmers in England. Each farm-house is a little colony, consisting of some three generations, namely, the grandfather, his children, and his children's children. There they live in peace and harmony together; all who are able work on the farm, and if more labor is required, the stranger is hired to assist them. They live well, dress plainly, and are industrious. . . . Being well known in this part of the country [Chekiang], and having always made it a point to treat the people well, I was welcomed wherever I went. I began to feel quite at home in the farmers' houses. [14]

This may be regarded as a generally correct portrayal of the living conditions and attitudes of the moderately prosperous peasantry, not only of Chekiang but also of other localities where the economic circumstances were comparable. However, such a life was possible only because of a favorable environment. According to the same writer:

> The country through which we passed, and which may be called the plain of Ningpo, is perfectly level, and is not remarkable for any striking features; but it is exceedingly fertile and produces large crops of rice, which is the staple food of the inhabitants. It is thickly covered with small towns, villages and farm-houses; and, like all the fertile plains in China which have come under my observation, it teems with population. . . . Making our boats fast to the river-bank, we stepped on shore and took the first turning which led to the hill on which the [Kong-k'ow-ta] pagoda stands. When we reached the summit of this hill, which appeared to be about 1000 feet above the level of the sea, we were rewarded with one of those splendid views which are, perhaps, more striking in the fertile districts of China than in any other country. . . . Towns and villages were visible in whichever direction our eyes turned, and every part of the extensive plain appeared to be under cultivation. [15]

A somewhat more intimate glimpse of a similar scene was caught by another Western writer of the same period:

> Again we were in the country, among the mulberry-trees and the rice-fields, the patches of tobacco, the sepulchral mounds, with their waving banners of high reeds, the gourds trellised on bamboo framework, and the agricultural population all at work—men and women, with equal energy, treading their irrigation-wheels. Here is the secret of the fertility of this great delta [in the vicinity of Chia-hsing, Chekiang]. Every hundred yards a little family treadwheel, with its line of tiny buckets, is erected over the canal, and the water is thrown up to refresh the mulberry-trees or mature the rice. . . . We must have passed 10,000 people today engaged in this irrigation process. [16]

Since this was written in 1857 when the Taiping Rebellion was raging fiercely in many parts of the empire, the prosperity of this region is the more remarkable. It shows strikingly the decisive influence of the immediate environment upon peasant life and the extent to which local conditions might vary in different parts of the empire.

Such scenes, of course, were not limited to Chekiang or South China. They might be encountered wherever conditions were as favorable. Shantung province as a whole was not noted for the fertility of its soil, but in certain parts of it the life of the peasant was not at all unpleasant. A Western traveler reported what she saw in the vicinity of Ch'ing-chou Fu city (modern I-tu Hsien) in early October, 1907:

> Leaving the city behind us, we passed through open country where every one was still busy harvesting in the fields. Some fields were already ploughed, in others green wheat stood a few inches high. . . . Much of the foliage looked more like spring green than autumn, and many of the villages lay embowered in trees—willows, aspens, cryptomerias, the last-named always belonging to temples or adjoining graves. The threshing-floors were filled with golden grain being prepared for winter storage. Bean pods were being broken up by means of stone rollers, worked by donkeys, blindfolded with neat straw goggles. . . .
> The country was a scene of delightfully cheerful energy, whole families working together; a tiny child lying naked, basking in the sun, the women (despite their bound feet) as busy as the men. Barrows passed along, groaning under loads so heavy that it needed a friend to drag in front. . . . Occasionally a man rode by on a pony, whose coming was heralded by a tinkling of bells. . . .
> Our visit came to rather an abrupt close, as we were warned that we must reach the city before sundown or the gates would be closed. . . . Work in the fields was ended for the day, but for many of the Chinese work is never ended. Until all the grain is housed, watch must be kept by day and night. Small huts are erected in the fields for this purpose, sometimes perched on tall poles, from which a wide outlook can be kept over the country, or on the threshing-floors adjoining the farms. [17]

Another Western traveler reported the following scene which he observed in Chihli province in 1868:

> After leaving Pau-ting-foo [Pao-ting Fu] my road continued through the usual monotony of cultivated plains, villages of considerable size being neither few nor infrequent. I was fortunate enough to pass through the country at the season of the autumn fairs, and I traversed several places where they were going on. Immense quantities of grain of every kind were for sale, and in many places the women were occupied in spinning and selling cotton thread; an employment they were engaged in almost universally in Chih-li. The cotton comes from the south of the province, and what thread is not consumed at home goes up to Peking. Long strips of blue cotton cloth were also abundant, and

fruit, raw cotton, and the rude implements of Chinese agriculture complete the list. [18]

A somewhat less prosperous but equally peaceful rural area was described by an American observer late in 1901:

> Nearly all of the chain of villages that line the road through the Shansi Mountains from the great wall to Tai Yuan [T'ai-yüan Fu], possess certain common characteristics. Few villages have a population of more than three hundred. They are isolated and as lonely, perhaps, as any communities of the same number of human beings anywhere on earth. The villagers have no luxuries, and few comforts, yet they are happy and contented. [19]

These scenes were normal in parts of China where the environment was in general friendly and nature not too harsh. In localities where the circumstances were less fortunate, the rural economy was naturally more stringent, although the life of the peasant was by Chinese standards not necessarily unbearable. This was the picture in some parts of Szechwan as it existed at the beginning of the present century:

> In this part of the country we passed through villages much more frequently, and the people had a busier air. There are markets held every few days in one or other of the villages, so that we continually met people coming from them laden with their spoils. . . . The fields were full of people weeding, and they looked very comfortable, seated on their little stools. . . . Each member of a family seems to share in the toil. . . . The people look well fed and attended to, but their clothing is often a network of rags, and their houses are singularly dark and forbidding. If there is any scarcity through unfavourable crops, they suffer immediately and acutely, as agriculture is the most important industry of the province. [20]

The miserable, tiny villages near Tientsin reported by British officers in the 1870's and 1880's have already been noted. [21] A more concrete impression of this type of rural environment was given by a Western traveler in this same region in May, 1879:

> Certainly the province of Peh-chi-li, so far as I have yet seen it, has no beauty to charm the eye! In every direction, as far as we could see, it is all a vast alluvial plain—not so much as a pebble to represent stone all over the level land. It is a wide expanse of grey dust, and the villages are all built of mud. They are all exactly alike, and all are hideous; only some have dark tiled roofs, and the eye rests with thankful relief where occasional gourds or pumpkins form a blessed trail of green in the poor little gardens.
> Instead of the pale but fully clothed children of the south, these are

really bronzed, and run about in troops quite naked, or lie basking in
the warm wet mud along the edge of the river. . . .

In every direction I noticed toilsome methods of irrigation by hand,
and only where those are diligently practised has the thirsty earth
struggled into greenness. [22]

A British consul reported his impression of some parts of central
China in 1868:

Universal cultivation has long been known to exist in China, but the
cultivators of the land are not in any way remarkable either for the
excellence of their dwellings, the intelligence of their appearance, or
the cleanliness of their persons. . . . Happiness in anything but material matters seems impossible for them, and even that is precarious
and liable to be destroyed by the first bad harvest. [23]

While these descriptions depict fairly accurately the tangible physical aspects of the rural environment, they do not reveal the many
historical factors—economic, social, and political—that decisively
influenced that environment. Any survey of the rural situation of China
in the nineteenth century (or in any other period) must take into account the relationship that existed between the population and the land,
and the problems that arose from it. This is a difficult subject, and
the writer cannot do more than suggest some general points that seem
germane to the inquiry.

Students of Chinese economic history disagree as to the precise rate
or actual extent of the increase of the population of imperial China, but
none of them doubts that since the establishment of the Ch'ing dynasty
the increase was fairly steady up to the middle of the nineteenth century. [24] The amount of land under cultivation also increased during this
same period, but even after allowance is made for the fact that the
figures given in official documents cover only the legally registered
land, the amount of productive farmland did not increase *pari passu*
with population. [25] These unequal rates of increase eventually gave rise
to the problem of population pressure on land. As early as 1710 this
problem had already engaged imperial attention. In an edict of K'ang-
hsi 49, the emperor said:

[The number of] households and mouths has been increasing daily
during the present period of long-continued peace. Since land does
not increase and production [of food] shows no increment, food supplies will fall short of the need. Reason tells us that this is necessarily so. [26]

This sober view was echoed later by the Yung-cheng and Ch'ien-lung
emperors in 1723, 1724, and 1793. They both pointed out the gravity
of the situation and indicated ways and means of ameliorating it—official encouragement of farming, ascertaining the sufferings of peasants and alleviating them, land reclamation in provinces where idle
land was available, and government subsidies to persons who under-

took such reclamation. [27] The Ch'ien-lung emperor confessed that he was awakened to this all-important problem in reading the *Shih-lu* of K'ang-hsi, which gave a population figure of 23,312,200 mouths (1710), and in comparing this figure to the returns of 1792 (307,467,200) an increase, he said, of "over thirteen times" in about eighty years. [28] He did not mention the amount of cultivated land, but was presumably familiar with the official reports, which gave 607,842,992 *mow* for 1685; 683,791,427 *mow* for 1724; and 741,449,550 *mow* for 1766[29]— an increase falling far behind the rate of population increment.

Even when allowance is made for the smaller portion of the total population that lived in cities and towns, [30] it seems safe to conclude that the imperial countryside was "overpopulated," in the sense that the total amount of cultivated land was not sufficient to give the average peasant adequate means of livelihood, even though the number of persons per square mile was not strikingly great. [31] A modern Chinese historian estimated that the amount of land available for cultivation was about 3.86 *mow* per capita in the mid-eighteenth century; in 1812 it was 2.19 *mow;* and in 1833, 1.86 *mow*. [32] This general trend was observed also by a modern Western geographer. [33] Regional differences of course existed, so that inhabitants of some parts of the empire might be better off in this respect than those of other parts. In T'ai-hsing (Kiangsu), for example, the number of *mow* of registered land per capita was approximately 13.31 in the late eighteenth century, and 11.17 around 1830. [34] In Wei Chou (Chihli), it was only 1.71 around 1875; in Po-pai (Kwangsi), 1.69, and in Fu-shun (Szechwan), not quite 1.00. [35] These estimates do not accurately reflect the situation in each case, for they were made on the basis of registered land (which usually represented only a part of the actual amount of cultivated land in a given locality). But since the number of inhabitants reported in a locality often did not include all who actually dwelt there, unreported inhabitants might to some extent offset unregistered land in these estimates. At any rate, it is safe to suppose that a considerable number of peasants in various parts of the empire could not command enough land (i.e., more than three *mow* per capita) for their subsistence. [36] An actual instance will illustrate this point. Commenting on the conditions of Mien-chu (Szechwan), a local historian wrote in the first decade of the present century:

> . . . each person has on the average roughly 2.6 *mow* of land . . . which barely supplies him with food and clothing. If flood, drought, or other disasters occur, or if there is a wedding or funeral [in the family], debts will be incurred, causing him eventually to lose his property and become a vagabond. This is the reason that the people are daily becoming poorer. [37]

There is therefore some justification for the view that "the most outstanding thing in the Far East is the pressure of population upon the means of subsistence."[38] The well-known fact that for a considerable period of time China was faced with varying degrees of food shortage (apart from the famines induced by natural calamities)[39] lends support to this view; the correlated phenomenon of a long-range rise in food prices also tends to give it credence. The words of the Yung-cheng emperor in an edict of 1723 are revealing:

> During recent years different places [in the empire] have [normal] harvests. Those that have bad harvests as a result of floods do not number more than a few *chou* or *hsien*. But rice is becoming gradually ever more expensive. In Fukien and Kwangtung there is a shortage of rice and [the people] look to neighboring provinces for their food supply. The reason for this is that production from the soil remains as of old, whereas consumption by the people has increased. The supply is insufficient to meet the demand. As a result, rice becomes scarce and its price rises. This is inevitable.[40]

This trend, in fact, continued after Yung-cheng times and engaged the attention of many. One writer pointed out that between the closing decades of the eighteenth century and 1820, the price of rice was doubled. Famine, he thought, was a major factor, as in 1707, 1709, 1755, and 1785, when natural disasters in wide areas of Kiangsu (his native province) sent rice prices up to several times the normal rate. But famine was not the only factor. From 1785 onward, no matter whether the harvest was normal or bad, rice prices in these localities remained high, rising up to almost five times the normal rate current in this region prior to the famine of 1707.[41] Another writer, reporting the conditions of Chekiang, stated that while in the 1740's a price of about 1,000 cash per *shih* was regarded as unduly high, 2,000 cash per *shih* had become a "bargain price" by 1790. In the summer of 1794 one *shih* of rice cost as much as about 3,400 cash.[42] A nineteenth-century Catholic priest noted that the average price of rice throughout China in 1862 was ten taels per *shih*.[43] Since the exchange rate in Kiangsu in 1792 was about 1,300 cash per tael,[44] and the price of rice in terms of silver at that time was about two taels per *shih*, the 1862 price level amounted to a fivefold rise, at least in Kiangsu, in a period of seventy years. The rise in rice prices and silver exchange rates was far from uniform in all parts of the empire,[45] but the general trend of rice prices was decidedly and consistently upward.

Meanwhile a trend of rising land prices was observed. A governor of Hunan memorialized the Ch'ien-lung emperor in 1748 that the price of farmland in that province, which formerly was one or two taels per *mow*, rose to seven or eight taels; land of a better quality, which formerly was worth seven or eight taels, sold for over twenty taels.

As a result, he argued, "the land that has gone to wealthy families in recent times has amounted to over 50 per cent [of the total amount of cultivated land in that province]. Persons who formerly owned land have now become tenant farmers."[46] Other writers believed that land was becoming progressively more expensive in many parts of the empire,[47] and that consequently farmers of small means must have found it more and more difficult to buy land.[48] The rise in rice prices did not benefit small peasants much, since the limited quantities of foodstuffs at their disposal usually did not go into the market. Those who had to buy rice to feed their families would be hurt rather than benefited by rising prices. The old Chinese adage *ku chien shang nung* (cheap grain injures farmers) was true only for those who possessed enough grain to sell in the market.

It is clear, therefore, that the economic situation of small land-owners and tenant farmers was by no means attractive, even in normal times; when natural calamities occurred, the life of the people in the localities affected could become extremely miserable. The droughts and floods that so frequently plagued the empire[49] may have tended to ease the population pressure by causing the death of large numbers of people and forcing others to migrate, but their immediate and long-range effects were unmistakably detrimental to the economy and living conditions of the majority of rural inhabitants.

Population pressure and food shortage constituted a difficult enough problem for the empire. This problem was made even more serious by the concentration of landownership, especially noticeable in some regions. The rural population of China was not homogeneous. In every locality there were peasants who owned little or no land, and a relatively small number of persons who owned much; there were families whose heads enjoyed gentry status and others that had no such members. Legally and conceptually, gentry status did not depend upon or imply landownership, but in actual fact social privileges and economic wealth often went to the same persons. The gentry were usually inclined to show a keen interest in fertile land as a sound investment.[50] Their presence in the countryside often accentuated the concentration of landownership in individual families or clan organizations, making it more difficult for families of modest means and inconsequential social position to acquire real property. For while gentry status in itself did not bring economic affluence, the possession of such status (especially if it resulted from the acquisition of a high official rank or scholarly title) facilitated the accumulation of wealth and the protection of property already obtained. We have seen that gentry land-owners had a lighter tax burden than commoner owners.[51] This factor would have been sufficient to tip the economic balance in favor of gentry owners. It is not surprising, therefore, that all inhabitants of a given area did not stand in the same relationship to the land available for cultivation.[52] The gentry did not monopolize the possession of land, but it is reasonable to suppose that there was an affinity between gentry status and landownership. On the one hand, social prestige and political influence made it easier to accumulate capital for buying land, and, on the other hand, owners of large amounts of land could give their children a good education that enabled them to enter the government "schools" or officialdom, or could purchase official ranks or positions for themselves. This factual connection between gentry status and landownership appears to have continued until the second half of the nineteenth century, when the gentry in some parts of the empire acquired their wealth mainly from commercial instead of from agricultural sources.

Whatever may have been the role of the gentry in the concentration of landownership, inequality in landholding had been a familiar phenomenon in imperial China for a long time. In the Ch'ing dynasty it began to attract serious attention in the eighteenth century. A high-ranking official, for instance, memorialized the emperor in 1743 that it was wise to limit the extent of landownership.[53] A governor of Hunan observed with concern in 1748 that 50 or 60 per cent of the land in that province belonged to rich families.[54] An eighteenth-century writer noted that in the 1760's a wealthy family in Chihli province possessed almost a million *mow*.[55]

The situation of course varied in different parts of the empire. A series of investigations made in 1888 by a number of Western writers revealed the conditions in widely separated localities of nineteenth-century China. The results shown in Table 23 are not inclusive or necessarily accurate, but they help us to gain a general impression:[56]

TABLE 23
LAND TENURE AND OWNERSHIP

Locality	Percentage of Tenants	Size of Largest Holdings (in *mow*)
Kweichow Province	Few tenants	
Shansi: P'ing-yang Fu	Few tenants	Seldom over 500 *mow*
Shantung: I-tu Hsien	10	1,000
Wu-ch'ing	30	100,000
Lai Chou	40	100,000
Yunnan: T'ai-ho Valley	20	
Fukien: Foochow	50	Only one over 300
Chekiang: Jen-ho and Shao-hsing	50-60	?
Kwangtung Province	75	1,000
Kiangsu (northern)	70-80	400,000
Hupeh: Kuang-chi	70-90	300

There is some evidence that the concentration of landownership tended to be more pronounced in provinces where the soil was generally more fertile and less pronounced in regions where the land was poorer. One possible explanation of this discrepancy is that fertile soil meant higher agricultural production, which in turn facilitated the accumulation of wealth by some of those who tilled or owned land. At the same time, productive land became an attractive object of investment for those who had the money to invest. Moreover, in the latter part of the nineteenth century, when trade and manufacture in large cities developed rapidly as a result of extensive contact with Western countries as it did in Kwangtung and Kiangsu, part of the wealth accumulated in the cities flowed into the adjacent countryside. Some of the successful merchants or entrepreneurs became owners of productive land. In these places, small landowners were relatively few and tenants numerous. Where the soil was comparatively unproductive, capital was more difficult to accumulate, and land was not a desirable object of investment. There tenant farmers might be outnumbered by small landholders.

From the standpoint of the average villager it is difficult to say which of the two situations was the better. In one, the peasants were freer from the possible oppression of landlords, but had the disadvantage of an unfriendly economic environment. In the other, the natural conditions were more encouraging, but most of the farmers had to depend upon landlords for their precarious livelihood. In either case the tiller of the soil had little assurance of a decent living for any considerable length of time.[57]

Large landowners, it is true, might give certain benefits to the local economy; some of the gentry families and clans were responsible for the construction or maintenance of irrigation systems, bridges, ferries, and so on, in the rural neighborhoods where they held land or resided. But a considerable part of their economic resources realized from landownership must have been used to buy more land or invest in other gainful enterprises, such as commerce in towns or cities, or purchasing official ranks or posts. Probably only a relatively small portion of their wealth was reinvested for the purpose of agricultural improvement in the land they already possessed. At any rate, very little attention was devoted to the welfare of their tenants.

Tenancy arrangements varied in different localities. Fifty per cent of the main crop was not an unusual rate. A compiler (a *chü-jen* of 1882) of the gazetteer of a district in eastern Honan summarized the local practice thus:

> Farmers who till the land of others are called tenants; they show their respect to those from whom they receive the land by calling them *ti-chu* (landlords). [In those cases in which] the lord supplies the tenant with a farmhouse but requires the latter to furnish his own buffalo,

> cart, and seeds, the produce is shared equally [between lord and tenant. If] seeds are supplied by the lord, the tenant keeps 40 per cent of the produce. The tenant receives 30 per cent, if the lord also supplies buffalo, cart, and fodder. Those who merely sow, plant, and cultivate [for the landlord] get no more than 20 per cent. [58]

In a district in Shensi the following arrangement prevailed: In the arrangement known as *tsu-chung* (rent-cultivation) the land was rented for a fixed amount of rent which was to be paid each year after the harvest. In *huo-chung* (partner-cultivation), if the owner supplied the buffalo and seeds, and the tenant the labor, the produce was shared equally between them; if the owners did not supply buffalo and seeds, the tenant kept 60 or 70 per cent. In *yung-chung* (hire-cultivation) the hired tillers received even less. But since the soil in this district was not fertile, tenants usually found it difficult to make a living. "In a year of good harvest they barely had sufficient food and clothing, but in a bad year they could hardly escape becoming vagabonds." [59]

In the south, the following practice prevailed in a district near Canton:

> The land near the hills is usually cultivated by the owners. . . . Practically all other land [which was more fertile than hill land] goes to *ta-nung* [big farmers] who are the landlords. Tenants rent land from them to cultivate, turning over to them one half of the harvest late in the year. But it is a general practice to pay silver to rent land; it is known as *p'i-keng* [lease-cultivation]. The payment varies with degrees of fertility of the land in question. . . . According to a rough estimate, about eight or nine *shih* of grain comes from each *mow* of fertile land, in the early and late harvests; less than six *shih* from stony soil. . . . A family of eight requires at least ten *mow* of fertile land to support itself. This amount of land will not be sufficient if the family tills poor soil. But as available land is scarce and tenants too numerous, the demand always exceeds the supply. Rent rises steadily, with the result that the more [land] a tenant cultivates, the less he receives. [60]

Not only the tenants of South China might become victims of oppressive landowners. Similar situations were found also in parts of North China. The Chihli district gazetteer gave a revealing instance:

> The land is not fertile . . . a slightly bad year drives [tenants] from their homes. But wealthy people possess farmsteads and farmland in abundance. In the two hundred villages [of this district] almost one-third of the cultivators are tenants on these farms. They depend on the landlords for their food and clothing. Unscrupulous landlords may collect excessive profits from them, causing them to toil bitterly for an entire year without getting enough to feed and clothe their wives and children. [61]

Situations like these lend credence to the argument that an over-whelming majority of the rural population of imperial China was "dire-fully in need of land,"[62] and that the existence of a large mass of land-less peasantry was a major cause of the Taiping and other uprisings.[63] Not all peasants, of course, were in the same plight. Where nature was especially kind and landlords were not harsh, or where the tillers themselves owned some land, peasant life could be quite tolerable, even though it had to be earned with continuous labor. When the em-pire was not disturbed by grave catastrophes or misfortunes, the in-fluence of those rural inhabitants who were resigned to their situation outbalanced the disruptive forces engendered by the sufferings of des-titute peasants and the habitually aggressive ways of "weed people." The countryside then remained generally calm.

But eventually calamities occurred. Widespread and long-continued floods or droughts in large areas easily upset the precarious equi-librium of the stagnant rural economy. A variety of other factors gradually but surely undermined the economy, making the environ-ment of the rural inhabitants of many localities less and less satis-factory. Despite the government's efforts at enforcing control and averting disaster, a trend of rural decline became evident, especial-ly in the nineteenth century. Although degrees and effects of decline varied in different regions, the over-all effect on the imperial sys-tem was a weakening of the political foundation and a large contribu-tion to the dynasty's downfall.

The Government and the Land Problem

So far as the fragmentary data on hand show, the Ch'ing emperors were inclined on the whole to uphold the privileges and protect the interests of landowners against the encroachments of tenants, al-though they were not blind to the dangers inherent in the existence of a large mass of dispossessed peasants. These rulers, therefore, af-forded a contrast to the founder of the Ming dynasty, who, according to the historians, "taking warning from the evils resulting from the oppression of the weak and poor by the wealthy and strong during the last years of the Yüan dynasty, established many laws to suppress the wealthy and protect the poor."[64]

The attitude of the Ch'ing emperors, however, is readily understand-able. Property owners in general were presumably a stabilizing ele-ment in the imperial order. Moreover, many of them might be of-ficials, retired or in active service, and scholars who had attained some measure of success in practical life. By giving legal protec-tion to their property the government indirectly strengthened their position in society and at the same time won them over as loyal sup-porters of the regime.

The basic conception of landownership to which the emperors subscribed is revealed in an edict of 1729 (Yung-cheng 7):

> Those scholars and common people who possess property and are wealthy [have come to this condition] either as a result of the accumulation made by their fathers or grandfathers, or through their own labor and enterprise. All these are *liang-min* [good subjects] of the realm. Those who are *hsiang-shen* [gentry in their native communities] and possess surplus wealth either inherit it from former generations or derive it from their own official salaries and remunerations. All these are *liang-li* [good officials] of the state. The state therefore cherishes and protects all the gentry, scholars, and common people whose families are well-to-do. [65]

It is clearly assumed that the distribution of property was rightfully unequal and poverty the consequence of ancestral or personal shiftlessness. Such an assumption made it inexpedient and improper to interfere with the acquisition and possession of landed property.

A policy of noninterference, in fact, was consistently upheld by the imperial government. An edict of 1743 (Ch'ien-lung 8) reaffirmed it in very definite terms, although it was justified by practical instead of moral reasons:

> Previously, Ku Tsung, Director-General of the Grain Transport, petitioned in a memorial that he be permitted to put into practice a system of land restriction, limiting [the ownership of land] to 300 *mow* by each household. He thought that in this way wealth and poverty might be equalized, benefiting people of little means.
>
> We are deeply aware that although this proposal appears correct in principle, it is difficult to implement. Whereupon We have issued this order: "Since you propose 300 *mow* as a limit, [those who own] less than 300 *mow* would still be allowed to buy [additional land]. Even [a family which already owns] 300 *mow* [may in fact acquire more; for] when the land is divided among brothers, sons, and grandsons, each recipient would own no more than a few dozen *mow;* there is nothing to prevent them from buying [more land]. How would [the proposed measure] benefit poor people or reduce [the property of] wealthy persons? Moreover, once a law of land restriction was enacted, it would become a dead letter if it were not [enforced through official] investigation and inspection. It would be necessary to check [the amount of land owned by] each and every family, to question each and every person. That would mean endless annoyance and trouble. . . ."
>
> Ku Tsung, however, still held that [the proposal] was practicable and requested permission to direct local officials to try it out first in Huai-an Fu. We instructed him to deliberate the matter thoroughly again with Yin-chi-shan. Now from the memorial of Yin-chi-shan [We perceive that] the difficulties which he pointed out are identical with

what We have said; [this coincidence of views came about] without any previous exchange of opinions. It is therefore the consensus of all [well-informed] persons that this measure should not and cannot be adopted; it should not be tried [even on a limited scale]. We have ordered Ku Tsung to stop trying it out in Huai-an Fu and the governors-general and governors of other places to acquaint themselves [with Our decision]. [66]

Judging from observations made in the nineteenth century, Huai-an Fu (northern Kiangsu) lay in an area of high concentration of land-ownership. Ku Tsung, it seems, made the proposal with some cogent reason. The Ch'ien-lung emperor himself admitted that it was "correct in principle." The emperor, however, held fast to the view that landownership should be left outside the sphere of government interference. In fact, almost forty years later he reiterated this view with added explicitness in a 1781 edict concerning retrenchment in expenditure:

Since primitive simplicity and purity cannot be revived, ancient principles are now no longer practicable. The *ching-t'ien* [well-field] system of the Three Dynasties, [which maintained equality in land-ownership] is certainly a good institution of the ancient Kingly Rule. This, however, was suitable for ancient times, not for the present age. *Chün-t'ien* [land-equalization] has also been regarded as a good policy. Poverty-stricken scholars often hoped for it, and thought that it certainly should be adopted. But it is also impossible to carry it out at present. Not only is it absolutely unjustifiable to rob the wealthy in order to give more to the poor, but even if we commit ourselves to the principle of reducing the superfluous and adding to the deficient, it is certain that the surplus of the wealthy is eventually not sufficient to make up the shortage of the poor. The inevitable result would be that the poor cannot become rich, while the rich become poor. What benefit, then, would come from this policy of adjusting and evening off?[67]

The emperors, however, were not unaware of the latent danger of allowing large numbers of rural inhabitants to suffer starvation and oppression. They resorted to a variety of measures (or half-measures) to ameliorate rural conditions, taking care at the same time not to impair the legal protection given to landowners. They tried to help landless farmers to acquire property through reclamation. [68] Even as late as the mid-nineteenth century the imperial government was making efforts to enable dispossessed persons to reclaim land. In an edict of 1851 (Tao-kuang 11), for example, the emperor authorized the provincial government of Kwangtung to encourage reclamation of uncultivated land in Kuang-chou, Chao-ch'ing, Shao-chou, Chia-ying, Lo-ting, Nan-hsiung, and Lien-chou. After pointing out that the imperial government had authorized such undertakings in

other localities on many occasions since Ch'ien-lung times, the emperor indicated his desire to make the measure really work by warning local officials against indifference and corruption which would
cause "poor people to suffer much harassment without receiving any
real benefit."[69]

Assistance was sometimes extended to dispossessed farmers to
regain their land as a supplementary measure of rehabilitation after
a local famine. An illuminating instance occurred in 1814. An edict
of that year said:

> Humble people engage themselves in tilling the soil to support [them-
> selves and their families]. Owing to successive bad harvests during
> past years, the people of over thirty *chou* and *hsien* belonging to Ta-
> ming Fu and other prefectures in Chihli sold their farm land at cheap
> prices which were as low as only one-tenth of those prevailing in good
> years. Wealthy families in these localities as well as dealers from
> other places, attracted by the low prices, made extensive purchases
> [of the land]. When, in the present year, the rainfall is just right for
> the crops, these peasants who have lost their property are without land
> to cultivate. They wander and move about, deserving commiseration
> and sympathy.
>
> The government should promptly amend this situation, so that these
> people will be enabled to gain their livelihood. Na-yen-ch'eng, the
> governor-general concerned, is hereby ordered to . . . formulate
> regulations . . . [defining the procedure whereby] the farm land thus
> sold may be bought back [by the original owners] at the original sell-
> ing price. A period of three years should be fixed [for completing
> such purchases]. . . .
>
> In addition, the governors of Shantung and Honan are ordered to
> direct their subordinates to make investigations in those *chou* and
> *hsien* which have suffered from the disturbances and bad harvest last
> year. The same measures [authorized for Chihli] shall be applied uni-
> formly [in these two provinces].[70]

We have no information as to the effectiveness of the measures
outlined above. In view of the general historical circumstances, it
was in all probability very limited. Another government measure,
the postponement or remission of the land taxes in famine-stricken
localities,[71] certainly brought little comfort to tenant farmers. As
an eighteenth-century Chinese official put it,

> Farming people face the greatest of hardships. . . . When they have
> no land of their own to cultivate, they rent the land of others; when
> they have no money to rent land, they live by working as hired hands.
> . . . Such people themselves know that they are in a less desirable
> position than [that of] landowners who can receive the benefit of the
> remission of the land and labor taxes as a result of [imperial] grace;

nor are they equal to families engaged in trade, which can enjoy the exemption of customs dues on rice and beans. [72]

Nor did these acts of imperial generosity bring equal benefits to all landowners. Small owners often shouldered heavier tax burdens than large owners with gentry status. When remissions of tax payments were granted by the government, small owners were on many occasions not informed of the action and therefore had to make the payments as usual, whereas large owners were often able to take advantage of it. [73] The government made little effort to correct this situation. Inequality of tax burdens was allowed to continue and work hardships on petty owners, who might be ruined financially before tax remission actually came their way. According to a local historian writing late in the nineteenth century:

> Everywhere there are cases in which land is annexed by the wealthy and powerful who reap large benefits, live comfortably, and have no taxes to pay. [Those who till] registered land cannot muster enough resources to meet the corvée and other levies even in a year of good harvest; they, in fact, cannot even adequately feed their families. Consequently, some of them become bankrupt, abandon their land, and flee from their homes. [74]

Unequal tax burdens may, in fact, have constituted a cause of unequal landownership in some parts of the empire. According to a Chinese source:

> Concentration of landownership is not the result of powerful owners' oppressing poor ones and taking over [land] by force. The heavy tax burden is not evenly distributed; the frequent labor services are not systematically organized. As a result, while both the powerful owners and weak ones pay taxes, the former pay only small sums whereas the latter pay large sums. Both are called upon for labor services, but the powerful owners can answer the call with ease, whereas weak owners meet it with difficulty. [75]

It may be noted that the imperial government made some attempt to alleviate the lot of tenant farmers without infringing upon the privileges of landowners. On the basis of an edict of 1679 (K'ang-hsi 18) the government laid down the following regulation:

> Lawless gentry and scholars who privately prepare flogging boards and sticks, and [with them] punish their tenants without authorization; and those who appropriate women of tenant families, making them their female slaves or concubines, shall be deprived of their ranks or titles and punished for their offenses. [76]

This might deter tyrannical landlords from indulging in flagrant excesses, but it did not absolve tenants from their obligation to meet the demands of their landlords for the full payment of whatever rent the latter charged them.

The obligation to pay rent, in fact, was usually enforced by the government itself. In 1732, for example, the governor of Kwangtung ordered all tenants to pay their rent in full. [77] In other instances, the government was ready to help landowners to exact rent payments from their tenants. Thus, the following situation was said to prevail in some parts of Chihli province late in the nineteenth century:

> When a wealthy family possesses several hundred or several thousand *mow* of land, tenants are called in to till portions of it. These tenants then depend upon the land for their subsistence. If, however, the rent is not paid in full, they are promptly sent [to the local government] to be tried [for their delinquency]. If the land changes hands and the tenants fail to vacate their farms [which hitherto they have cultivated], they are similarly dealt with. [78]

The unsettled conditions of the second half of the nineteenth century persuaded the imperial government to give special attention to the rights of landowners. For one reason or another many tenants refused to pay their rent and sometimes backed up their refusal by violence or threats of violence. The government found it necessary to reaffirm officially the tenant's obligation to pay rent. An edict of 1854 (Hsien-feng 4) reads in part:

> People of the countryside who assemble in mobs and refuse [to make] tax payments cannot be excused before the law. Local officials should relentlessly impose severe punishment on them. Tenants who fail to pay the full rent due, and whose case has been brought [to court] by the landlords, should also be punished accordingly, so as to warn others against perverse practices. [79]

The obligation to pay rent was thus placed on the same legal level with the duty to pay taxes.

That large landowners took advantage of this imperial order to compel their tenants to perform to the fullest measure their financial obligations is indirectly evinced by the following account of a well-known writer concerning a locality in Kiangsu where in 1865 a reduction of taxes was effected:

> I have heard that fertile land in Soochow is largely in the hands of powerful gentry families. . . . The farmers have little land of their own and have to plow land of the large owners. Rent for each *mow* is over 3,000 cash. If the tenants fail to pay, they will be tied up and sent to the officials to be lashed, receiving the same treatment as if they failed to pay the land taxes. [80]

The Ch'ing government, therefore, was most emphatic and unequivocal in its affirmation, in words and action, of the landlord's right to collect his rent in full. Realizing at the same time, however, that it was as dangerous as it was futile for the owners to press destitute tenants to pay, or to be totally oblivious of the hardships of destitute people in general, the emperors occasionally offered words of counsel to their "good subjects" and "good officials." The Yung-cheng emperor, for one, issued in 1729 an edict addressed to "the wealthy families of the provinces." After having explained the rightfulness of landownership, the emperor went on to say:

> Now, as to the method of preserving one's family and property: to be extravagant and wasteful is of course not the best way to keep one's wealth; nor, however, are miserliness and avidity conducive to self-preservation. . . . For it is usual for the poor and dispossessed, after having become unemployed and bankrupt and having brought themselves into distressing circumstances, to be unaware of their own faults, but to turn their jealousy against well-to-do families. . . . As soon as a famine occurs, destitute people freely plunder and rob. Those families that have made their fortunes by unkindly methods invariably suffer damages before all other [property owners]. For this reason we advise all wealthy families to give, in their everyday life, sympathetic considerations to the poor. They should be reasonable and accommodating toward any tenant family in their neighborhoods that is in need, confronted by a bad harvest, or hard pressed during the season when last year's grain has been exhausted and the new crop is yet to come. They should never refuse to extend a helping hand to it. [81]

Similar advice was offered by the Ch'ien-lung emperor who stressed, in a 1738 edict, that well-to-do persons would be wise to give thought to the needs of the poor, and urged the former not to hoard grain or other foodstuffs with a view to profiteering. The content of this edict was regarded as so important that it was subsequently included among the texts for the *hsiang-yüeh* lectures. [82]

It is noteworthy that these exhortative utterances of the imperial rulers were intended merely to persuade, not to command. The legal right of landownership was never for a moment questioned; practical wisdom was offered to landowners, not to impair their property rights but to promote their own safety and good.

The basic attitude of the Ch'ing rulers is even more apparent in their refusal to compel landowners to give up any part of their rent even in times of distress, although they sought to persuade them to extend to their tenants a part of the benefits which they received from the government. In a revealing edict issued in 1735, the Yung-cheng emperor declared:

> Since we first assumed the imperial rule, we have time and again

conferred favors upon the people. Recently, we have authorized the remission of all taxes collectible in money or grain in the provinces that have become overdue from the people previous to the Yung-cheng 12th year [1734]. . . . As, however, the payments of money or grain are made by landowning households, this act of remission will benefit these households only. Those households that are landless and work diligently the year round still have to pay grain [as rent to their landlords] in proportion to the amount of land involved; they will not receive the favor thus granted by the state.

This is not in accordance with the principle of universality and impartiality. If, however, the rent per *mow* is to be reduced proportionately to the amount of tax remitted, and the rate of reduction is regulated by government decrees . . . confusion and troubles would result.

Landowners are advised to give up [voluntarily] one-half of the benefit which they receive from us, thus to share it with their tenants. . . .

Recently, we have heard that certain landowning families in Chiangnan have shown their charity by cheerfully remitting the rent payments of their tenants. We are pleased with the prevalence of kindly practices in the neighborhoods there. Local functionaries are to be ordered to persuade, in an appropriate and effective manner, landowners [of other localities] to reduce or remit, as they see fit, the rent payments of their tenants—no rates need be fixed by the government—in order that poor people who till the soil will have enough food to support their families. If wealthy landowners truly sympathize with our view and give benefits to their tenants, suitable rewards will be given them. Owners who are unwilling [to do so] should be let alone; no compulsion shall be applied in any case. . . . If perverse and rascally tenants use this [order] as a pretext for delaying [the payment of their rent], they shall be punished for the crime of refusing to pay rent. We regard all in the empire, tenants as well as landowners, as our own children, and wish to have our bounty equally bestowed upon them. [83]

This line of thought was not followed by the Yung-cheng emperor alone. He was anticipated by his immediate predecessor and echoed by his successor. In an undated edict the K'ang-hsi emperor gave the landowners of Shantung province this advice:

The humble people of Shantung depend upon those who possess property, whose land they cultivate. In a good year what the tillers get is not much; in a bad year they, owing to their landless condition, either wander away in all directions if they are physically strong, or fall and die in ditches and valleys when their strength fails. . . . If you officials high and low and all others who own land in this province can reduce their rent, and each of you lend support to your tenants, not only will the tenants be greatly benefited, but also [you, yourselves, will gain much; for by keeping your tenants alive and attached to the soil], your land will not lie uncultivated. [84]

In an edict of 1748 the Ch'ien-lung emperor, after quoting the K'ang-hsi edict, made the following remarks:

> As we took an inspection trip and investigated local conditions, we
> have seen with our own eyes . . . that when occasionally the harvest
> is bad, the people immediately lose their means of subsistence. . . .
> The real cause of this is that landowners do not give support to their
> tenants, causing the latter to lose their livelihood. . . . When many
> [of the tenants] have wandered away, there will be a dearth of tenants
> to till the land [of the owners], which will degenerate into weedy
> wastes. Now since the wealthy cannot cultivate their land themselves,
> would it not be better for the haves and have-nots mutually to help
> each other, so that peasants will not easily leave their home places?
> . . . In short, while the poor depend upon the rich for their food, the
> rich also depend upon the poor for their labor. If the former do not
> supply the latter with food but merely make use of their labor, what
> is there to induce the poor [to remain and work for them]? From now
> on the governor [of Shantung] shall lead all local functionaries to in-
> vestigate and persuade, with a view to making [landowners] clearly
> understand the principle of the interdependence of the rich and the
> poor. [85]

An edict issued by the same ruler in 1790, on the occasion of his eightieth birthday anniversary, repeated substantially the same ideas expressed in the edict of 1735: that landowners should pass on to their tenants the benefits which they received from the imperial government and that reductions of rent should be made by landowners on a completely voluntary basis. [86]

One should not be led to suppose, however, that the Ch'ien-lung emperor was ready to modify the policy of protecting the right of rent collection. Far from it. In an edict issued in 1749, a year after the one addressed to the governor of Shantung, he firmly rejected a proposal that landowners should be made to share equally with their tenants the crops of the current year and to stop demanding payment of all rent overdue in previous years:

> Tenants toil hard throughout the year; they certainly deserve sym-
> pathy. . . . But landowners who manage their property and pay the
> taxes and various levies desire also to support their families and
> themselves. How can [the government] compel them, with decrees
> and injunctions, to give [their income] to others? Moreover, most of
> the tenant farmers are poor, without resources, and shiftless. . . .
> Even during years of good harvest it is not certain that they will not
> bully their landlords, refusing to pay their rent. Now if we issue an
> edict directing local high officials to make pronouncements and re-
> quire [landowners] to obey, the owners cannot be forced to comply
> anyway, whereas rascally tenants will be given a pretext to refuse
> to pay [their rent]. [87]

It is amply clear, then, that the Ch'ing government's basic policy concerning landowners and tenants was to give full legal protection to the rights of ownership and rent collection, and at the same time to prevent the conditions of the landless from becoming too unbearable. There is no evidence that this policy was modified in any tangible way during the eighteenth and nineteenth centuries. It is true that in the nineteenth century the emperors seem to have shown more concern for peasants in distress, as, for example, in 1814, when the Chia-ch'ing emperor ordered a number of provincial officials to help small owners to regain their land, or in 1822, when the Tao-kuang emperor pointed out that it was a mistake to set up one year as the time limit for foreclosure of land mortgages and ordered his servants to allow the people to do "according to their own convenience" (that is, to keep the customary three-year time limit).[88] But the basic idea was still to protect landownership in general.

The imperial rulers had good reasons for maintaining such a policy. It was the landowners who paid the grain and labor service levies that for a considerable period of time constituted the major portion of the imperial revenue. To protect landownership and rent collection was to protect indirectly the major source of that revenue. But since the taxes paid by the landlords came from the rent collected from the tenants, it was to the government's advantage to give the tenants enough protection so that they could continue to produce crops and pay their rent. The fact that in giving relief in a famine-stricken area the imperial government showed preference to peasants who alone, according to law, were entitled to receive the grain from the local granaries, and that other inhabitants, even though they were extremely destitute, were not included among those who were to receive succor,[89] suggests that it was not purely humanitarian motives that prompted the emperors to give consideration to the needs of "humble people." There was also a political reason for their policy. Landowners tended to be a stabilizing element in the empire. The emperors undoubtedly accepted the view of Mencius that persons possessing "fixed property" tended to have "steady purposes."[90] Giving protection to landowners, therefore, was an investment in political security for the benefit of the imperial regime. Moreover, a considerable number of landowners were gentry; they were, in the words of the Yung-cheng emperor, "good officials." There was an even stronger reason for the imperial government to protect their rights and interests as landowners.

Such a policy, however, had in the long run some drawbacks. In allowing the process of concentration of landownership to go on almost unchecked, the government permitted at the same time the number of landless families to multiply. In thus jeopardizing the economic existence of small owners, the government inadvertently reduced

the number of the stabilizing elements and at the same time, made the
conditions of an increasing number of rural inhabitants unsatisfactory.
The measures which it adopted once in a while to ameliorate the lot
of the small owner and tenant farmer ran contrary to the immediate,
selfish interests of large owners, and for that reason produced no
substantial results. With a few exceptions, relations between landlords and tenants were far from cordial. When the economic and
social conditions in any part of the empire deteriorated to a critical
point, or when the rural economy was seriously disturbed by calamities, those elements in the country to whom the government gave
the least protection and in whom it placed the least confidence, might
be driven by desperation into violent demonstrations against their
landlords and perhaps also against their local officials. Imperial
control in the regions thus affected broke down temporarily or for
a considerable period of time.

A long process of fermentation usually preceded the eventual outbreak. Rural inhabitants of imperial China could stand a remarkable
amount of hardship before some of them resorted to extreme measures. In the remaining pages of this chapter we shall describe some
of the salient aspects of the plight in which villagers in various localities found themselves, and the basic patterns of their behavior under such circumstances. This should demonstrate the reality and
meaning of the well-known phrase "the patient Chinaman."

Rural Decline

It has been the opinion of more than one student of modern Chinese
history that especially since the nineteenth century a tendency toward
economic decline was clearly discernible in the countryside,[91] a process partly precipitated by the recurrent disasters that struck wide
regions of the empire, partly by the social disturbances that erupted
with unprecedented fury in mid-century, and partly by the local maladministration that had become increasingly pernicious ever since the
later years of Ch'ien-lung. This process, of course, did not work uniformly in all localities, but it seems certain that rural prosperity became a rarer phenomenon as time went on, and that in areas where
the economy had shrunk drastically, even many of the inhabitants who
were formerly in better positions than tenant farmers could not long
maintain their isolated well-being. In the worst instances rural communities withered away, becoming "ghost towns" or "deserted villages."

The conditions of a village in southern Chihli observed early in
the twentieth century illustrate tellingly some of the salient features
of rural decline:

There are no big landlords in the village because of, among other reasons, the constant division of family property in land. There are now only 18 families with more than 100 *mow* each, 40 with 50 to 100 *mow* each, but as many as 323 with less than 20 *mow* each. . . .

Family deficits are the general rule, even a fairly well-to-do middle peasant having no good future prospects. . . .

During the first ten years of this century [the closing years of the Kuang-hsü reign], there were several seasons of bad harvests and famine, during which most of the young men of the district were killed during clashes with government troops that had been sent to enforce the payment of taxes. . . . After the establishment of the Republic in 1911, there was another year of war and the consequent plague and famine. Then many village families who possessed very little or no land began to migrate. . . .

The sinking economic status of the village is clearly reflected in the decline of education. In the early 1920's there were two boys' schools with nearly 200 pupils and one girls' school with over 40 pupils, but at the present time [around 1935] one of the two boys' schools . . . has closed. . . . half the boys of school age and three-fourths of the girls of school age do not even attend the lower primary schools.[92]

After necessary modifications are made, this account serves as a fairly good example of the "sinking economy" of many villages of nineteenth-century China, which might be encountered in practically every part of the empire, though more frequently in some of the northern provinces where conditions were particularly unfortunate.

A few observations by nineteenth-century writers may be cited to show this general situation. A local historian described conditions in Ting Chou (Chihli) as follows:

Individuals do not have foresight; families do not have savings. There is no other way of making a living than tilling the soil. Once a bad harvest occurs, the inhabitants are utterly helpless. . . . The clans do not have ancestral halls, the graves are without tombstones, and seldom are genealogical records kept.[93]

Irrigation, which was the most indispensable condition for farming in many parts of North China and a matter of more vital practical concern than graves and ancestral halls, was often allowed to break down, as a result of a long rural decay. An instance was supplied by the 1896 edition of the gazetteer of Lu-i (Honan):

The farmers are poor, but not too diligent. After they have sowed the seeds, they leave the rest to heaven, [that is, at the mercy of] droughts or floods. There were formerly within the boundaries [of this district] more than one hundred watercourses, all of which conducted flood water to the trunk river. But recently most of these are blocked and silted up, or are turned into farmland. Every summer when rain falls heavily, half of the low land is submerged in water.

Having no way now to save themselves, farmers merely lament helplessly. The high land, on the other hand, suffers readily from droughts.
Although it is often possible to get water by digging down only a foot
or two into the ground and the utility of irrigation is explained to the
farmers, they refuse to do anything, being generally reluctant to
initiate any task. [94]

Similarly discouraging conditions were found in parts of Central
and South China, where the soil was unproductive. The gazetteer of
Meng-ch'eng (Anhwei) summed up the poverty of the inhabitants in
three sentences: "The soil is barren. The farmers do not have irrigation resources. No family possesses wealth [to last] several generations."[95] Likewise, the 1914 edition of the gazetteer of Ling-shan
(Kwangtung) described the economic situation in the late nineteenth
and early twentieth centuries in these words:

> Ling-shan, since early times, contains much waste land. Its in-
> habitants do not have the habit of maintaining a grain reserve. The
> poor ones among them secure loans in the spring and summer time,
> and sell all their grain in winter to pay their debts. Wealthy people
> keep their grain until the crops of the previous year are gone and the
> new ones are yet to come; then they sell it at good prices. But if
> a serious drought occurs, even they are at a loss as to what is to
> be done. [96]

Conditions of course varied in different localities, even in the same
province. During the late 1850's when large areas of the empire were
devastated by the Taiping Rebellion, a corner of Kwangtung in the
vicinity of Canton enjoyed unbelievable peace and prosperity, unaware
of the commotion outside. According to a British officer:

> On the 20th February a picnic party went out to see a little of the
> country and of the people. . . . Some of the views were charming.
> A striking and pleasing feature in the scenery of this part of China
> is the position of the villages, which, situated on plains cultivated
> in the minutest manner—if such an expression can be used—are sur-
> rounded by luxuriant hedges of the graceful feathery bamboo. . . .
> The people all look busy and contented. In one village there was
> a good deal of gong-beating on our approach, which we did not know
> what to make of; but a man came out and asked us to take tea; so we
> concluded that their intentions were not otherwise than peaceable. [97]

Similarly, during the eighteenth and nineteenth centuries, according
to a Chinese source, many localities in Kiangsu province enjoyed various degrees of prosperity;[98] and, according to other sources, some
parts of Chekiang, Shantung, and Szechwan presented encouraging
scenes between the mid-nineteenth and early twentieth centuries. [99]
Conditions in the same locality might vary a good deal at different
times. Broadly speaking, in the provinces affected by the Taiping

and Nien rebellions, conditions were worst during the fifth and sixth decades of the century. After order was restored, economic recovery in varying degrees could be discerned in places where the circumstances were favorable, but in other portions of the empire either recovery was very slow or a process of economic decay set in. A well-known Western investigator asserted in 1870 that such was the case in some of the northern provinces:

> In Honan and Shansi the drought had been great for several years, and in this present year the first crops were almost a total failure, excepting on those very limited patches of ground which can be irrigated. The poverty of the people has therefore constantly kept increasing, and is now appalling in some districts. All kinds of food commanded an unusually high price. . . . A depression of all trade is the natural consequence of this poverty, and all imports other than breadstuffs diminish in quantity from year to year. This present year will undoubtedly be worse than the preceding ones. A single good wheat crop would change this state of things materially, but only a series of good crops would allow the country to return to its normal state. [100]

The same investigator wrote in another connection:

> The traveller has occasion, at every step, to observe the contrast of the present poverty and inertness of the inhabitants, with the signs of a previously better condition. The large cities, even the villages, the temples, the remnants of magnificent public structures, as well as the history of China, give evidence that the northern provinces have been in a more prosperous state. [101]

He then went on to enumerate what he believed to have been the causes of the economic decay of these provinces. One of these was overpopulation, particularly in the province of Honan:

> The consequence is, that as much as possible of available ground must be retained for raising breadstuffs and clothing for the inhabitants themselves, and the produce which might be exported is restricted in quantity. . . . The cultivation of the fields requires only a limited number of hands; many are therefore unemployed, and the people in general become lazy and indifferent. [102]

Another cause mentioned by this investigator was the wide use of opium by the inhabitants of these provinces, especially in Shansi and Honan. In several places of Shansi, he said, no less than 90 per cent of the adult male population were given to that vice, in villages as well as in cities and largely among the laboring classes. Competition with foreign trade destroyed the market for many articles made in the inland villages and towns, and constituted another factor that quickened the pace of rural decline. Finally, he reckoned the de-

vastation wrought by rebellions among the factors that adversely affected the rural economy of the north. Even though, he argued, the
northern provinces did not suffer more—and perhaps suffered less—
than other regions, they did not recover economically as readily as
the others.

Whatever may have been the causes of rural decay in North China
and in other parts of the empire, and whatever regional differences
in the economic situation existed in the nineteenth century, the crucial
point is that the peasantry as a whole was adversely affected by the
changing circumstances of the time and that it suffered more than
any other segment of the population. The conditions prevailing in some
localities in the second half of the nineteenth century, which in diverse
ways benefited the city or the town, were largely detrimental to the
economy of the village.

It is of course difficult to ascertain the extent of economic damage
the villages thus sustained. However, a number of symptoms of rural
deterioration and factors contributing to it can be discerned. One of
these symptoms was the dislocation of rural manpower as a result
of emigration or abandoning agricultural occupations.

Finding that the local economy no longer afforded them a livelihood,
villagers of many localities left their homesteads to seek opportunities elsewhere, sometimes migrating to distant lands, never to return. It is true that such migration might in some cases prove helpful to the economy of the village. En-p'ing (Kwangtung), a district
where "the land was barren and the people were poor," afforded an
excellent instance. Since no amount of hard work could make farming a dependable livelihood, the inhabitants migrated, temporarily or
permanently, to other places to earn a living. As local historians put
it:

> Those who engaged in farming worked till callouses covered their
> hands and feet. . . . If luckily the harvest was good, they were able
> to supply themselves with some food and clothing; otherwise they
> could hardly escape hunger and cold. Hence no matter whether the
> year was good or bad many of them traveled several hundred *li*, after
> the harvest was done, to Nan-hai, Chiu-chiang, and other places to
> sell their labor. . . . They returned at the end of the year. . . .
> Thus from spring till winter they did not have a single day's rest. [103]

In the 1880's overseas migration began to be considerable and the
hardships of the inhabitants of En-p'ing were further alleviated by
the remittances from native sons who gave up farming and went to
"distant places" to engage in trade. As one expects, the number of
emigrants from the countryside increased with the introduction of
modern means of transportation and the appearance of modern commercial or industrial cities in some parts of the empire. This trend

was clearly reflected in Yang-chiang, another district of Kwangtung, where the inhabitants, reluctant to leave their homes in earlier days, now readily traveled far and wide in search of a more ample life. [104]

It should be noted, however, that although migration might have been economically helpful to the rural communities concerned in some cases, it did not materially improve the rural environment of the empire as a whole. Opportunities to migrate existed only in a relatively small number of regions where outlets to lands of promise were available; moreover, among those who managed to migrate, not all attained economic success. [105] At any rate, emigration, whatever may have been its net effects on the village, remained a testimony to its "shrinking economy."

In one respect at least, the effects of emigration were not salutary. Assuming that the emigrants were in general the more energetic, enterprising elements of the rural economy, their permanent exodus would result in a sort of "negative selection" among the inhabitants. [106] The village was thus deprived of some of its useful and promising elements who might contribute to the life of the community, circumstances permitting. And "because only the less energetic and capable tend to spend their lives under the home conditions," they would be inclined to resign themselves to those very conditions and refuse to struggle for their improvement, even if opportunities presented themselves. [107]

Displacement of agricultural manpower might take the form of change of occupation, the change taking place either in the home villages or elsewhere. Rural inhabitants were often forced to forsake "the fundamental occupation" because a hostile environment made farming decidedly and persistently unproductive. This, according to local historians, was what happened to Pa-ling (Hunan) late in the nineteenth century:

> As this district is very mountainous, farmers have found it difficult to support themselves by cultivating the soil. Many of them go to Hupeh to make a living. Consequently, no less than several ten thousand natives of Pa-ling regularly go to Chien-li, Mien-yang, Chiang-ling, and Ch'ien-chiang, four districts [of Hupeh], to carry on the professions of carpenters, farmhands, brewers, etc. They set out in spring and return in winter. . . . But if these four districts suffer from floods [so that no work is available to them], these workers have to return to their homes and feed themselves [as best as they can]. [108]

A comparable situation existed in Han-tan (Chihli):

> The land being unproductive and the population large, it was impossible [for the peasants] to make a living by farming. The poor supported their families by peddling wares which they carried on their

shoulders. And as this district is adjacent to Wu-an, Honan, where coal mines abound, many of the families [in Han-tan] supplemented their subsistence income by transporting coal, using human labor to perform this service. [109]

Another symptom indicating the "sagging economy" of villages and to some extent helping to bring it about was agricultural unemployment resulting from a variety of causes. The number of "loafing people" in many rural localities appears to have been considerable in the nineteenth century. A Chinese official pointed this out in a memorial which he submitted in 1851:

> In his youthful days Your Majesty's servant heard his seniors say: "Formerly vagrants and the unemployed hardly numbered more than a few individuals in any one village or rural market. At present dozens of them are often encountered in a community of a few hundred households. "
> This statement was made over twenty years ago [in the 1820's]. The number of idlers should be even greater now. [110]

In some cases, the situation created by unemployment was aggravated by a decrease of population consequent upon local disasters. Thus another Chinese official said in a memorial submitted in 1884:

> Recently, owing to the fact that the people suffered in rapid succession various calamities, including wars, floods, droughts, and pestilence, they have sustained countless losses and damages. Added to these, they have found it so difficult to make a living that young men often cannot get married when they come of age. Those who do manage to marry and give birth to girls usually are compelled to practice infanticide by drowning. As a result the rate of population increase is much slower than formerly. It is estimated that in a village where there used to be one hundred persons engaged in agriculture, there are now no more than fifty or sixty. And among these fifty or sixty, those who smoke opium and are too lazy to attend to farming amount to about twenty or thirty individuals. [111]

The phenomenon was fairly widespread and in some localities persisted well into the twentieth century. [112] It is quite conceivable, as a Western writer believed, that taking all the age groups of the rural population in relation to probable productiveness, as much as one half of them depended for support upon the other half. [113]

In depicting the rural environment of imperial China one can hardly overlook the effects of natural disasters, which obviously contributed more directly to the economic hardships of the villagers than did any other single factor.

The imperial government, as we have already seen, undertook to cope with the emergencies created by droughts and floods. [114] The

various measures of flood prevention and famine relief which it adopted were effective only to a limited extent; and these were too often
reduced to something worse than useless by local officials and their
underlings. [115] Frequently, the government was as helpless as the victims of natural calamities. One account describes a flood scene in
a district in Chekiang in 1849. After three months of futile efforts
to save their crops from the inundation, the inhabitants finally decided to abandon their villages:

> Then they began to assemble in great bands, and wander about the
> provinces with bags on their backs, begging here and there for a little
> rice. They were hideous to look at; half covered with rags, their hair
> bristling, their features contracted, their lips livid; and these but
> lately peaceful and industrious peasants were evidently driven by des-
> pair to be ready for every excess. . . . Whole villages were aban-
> doned, and numerous families went to seek a subsistence in the neigh-
> boring provinces. [116]

This picture, ghastly enough, was not the worst created by an extensive calamity. In some parts of North China a sustained drought
or widespread flood readily wrought immeasurable sufferings on the
inhabitants and almost irreparable damage to their villages. The
following account of the appalling conditions resulting from the disasters of 1875-78 in Shantung, Honan, Shansi, Shensi, and northern
Chihli, indicates perhaps the worst that could happen to any part of
rural China:

> It appears that, prior to 1875, an enormous level plain, extending
> inland from Tien-tsin, was famous for its fertility, but in that and
> previous years a succession of overwhelming floods utterly changed
> the face of the country, sweeping away all trace of carefully construct-
> ed irrigation-works, and destroying all vegetation. Here and there
> the banks of the Grand Canal gave way, and the best corn districts
> presented the appearance of great inland lakes. After these years,
> when the prodigal clouds had poured out their precious rain-stores
> in such cruel superabundance, came long years when (in Biblical
> phrase) the heavens were as brass, which here means that they were
> pitilessly blue, and that the rain-bearing clouds wholly vanished from
> the skies.
> Then the great plain became so burnt and hard that the attempt to
> cultivate it became hopeless. Vainly did the farmers sow their fields
> with the precious grain. . . . For months they fed on seeds of wild
> grasses, cotton seeds from which the oil had been expressed, roots
> and bark. . . . Of course the cattle, sheep, asses, poultry, all per-
> ished. . . .
> As Tien-tsin was the port at which the grain-supplies from favoured
> provinces were landed, thence to be forwarded to the famine dis-
> tricts, a multitude of miserable, starved wretches crowded hither.

. . . Men, women, and children, once prosperous, who in the four years of famine had sold all their possessions . . . were subsisting on the sweepings of the quay or the grain-stores, where a few grains of millet were mingled with the dust; others mixed the coarse husks of corn with a soft stone reduced to powder. [117]

The worst immediate effects of a bad famine may be seen from the following report on the conditions of some parts of Shensi in 1901:

To get a better idea of the ravages of famine throughout the province of Shensi, I passed five days in an abandoned mission station in the town of San Yuan, about thirty miles north of Sian. Accompanied by a missionary who had assisted Mr. Duncan in his relief work, we made excursions from San Yuan out across the plain of Sian. The country gave evidence of a former dense population. Every quarter of a mile a mud village rose out of the white, treeless desert, which stretched away to the north, east, and west like a limitless ocean. The vast plain was silent. . . . In some of the villages were groups of half-starved men and children, the only survivors of communities that had perished. The plain was silent because its inhabitants were dead. [118]

There were other instances in which the population of entire villages or towns was wiped out. A Chinese official observed in the spring of 1902 that in the vicinity of Ch'ü-wu and Wen-hsi (both in Shansi) one town and a number of villages were completely depopulated as a result of the great famine of 1897-98, and that at the time when he passed through these places they were still in ruins. [119]

It appears that the loss of lives in the empire as a whole during these various periods of calamity was considerable. We have no reliable figures, but it was estimated in May, 1878, that five million perished in the five northern provinces mentioned above. [120] Over two million were believed to have died in Shensi during the three years that preceded July, 1901. In San-yüan alone the population dwindled from 50,000 to less than 20,000. [121] Other estimates are even more frightening, [122] but perhaps less trustworthy.

The gentry and wealthy families that lived in rural areas presumably survived even the worst adversities and did not perish with villagers of less consequence. It is not certain, however, that they did not migrate to more promising lands. Even before calamities struck their home communities the gentry tended to move from the countryside into towns and cities where they were likely to find a greater degree of comfort and safety or a wider sphere in which to exert their influences. [123] In the event of disaster the rural elite were likely to forsake their ancestral homes and never return. The exodus of these elements must have aggravated the situation created by the decimation of the local population and in some instances contributed to the doom of many villages.

Revolts and rebellions, which were partly a product of misery, [124] contributed in turn to the further deterioration of rural conditions. The military campaigns conducted by the government to quell the uprising often proved to be even more destructive of lives and property than the activities of the "bandits." It is hardly surprising that when "peace and order" were restored, the inhabitants of the villages affected found themselves in a much worse plight than before. In many places few of them survived the ravages of war. It was said, for example, that countless inhabitants of Meng-ch'eng (Anhwei) died during the campaigns of the 1850's or fled their native villages to seek safety in other places. [125] The devastation done to some parts of Anhwei and Chekiang was so extensive that the once prosperous countryside remained in physical and economic ruins many years later. A Western observer, for example, reported what he saw as follows:

> The Fan-sui [Fen-shui] valley is, as regards scenery, among the finest pieces of ground that I have seen in China. . . . There is, however, one drawback. . . . The valleys, notwithstanding the fertility of their soil, are a complete wilderness. In approaching the groups of stately white-washed houses that lurk at some distance from underneath a grove of trees, you get aware that they are ruins. Eloquent witnesses of the wealth of which this valley was formerly the seat, they are now desolation itself. Here and there a house is barely fitted up, and serves as a lodging to some wretched people, the poverty of whom is in striking contrast with the rich land on which they live. The cities which I have mentioned, Tung-lu [T'ung-lu], Chang-hwa [Ch'ang-hua], Yü-tsien [Yü-chien], Ning-kwo-hien [Ning-kuo Hsien, eastern Anhwei] are extensive heaps of ruins, about a dozen houses being inhabited in each of them. Such is the devastation wrought by the Taiping rebels, thirteen years ago. . . .
>
> It is difficult to conceive of a more horrid destruction of life and property than has been perpetrated in these districts, and yet they are only a very small proportion of the great area of country that has shared a similar fate. [126]

The effects of war on the rural environment in North China were equally, if not more, ruinous. Another Western writer related what he learned about the situation in and around Yen-an Fu (northern Shensi) during the third quarter of the nineteenth century, where famine followed upon the heels of war:

> My informant spoke with justifiable enthusiasm as he recalled his city as it was in the days of his youth. "There were eight pawnshops," he exclaimed. This in China is the last word regarding prosperity. . . .

Further, the city was populated in every part; every cave on the Western Hill even was occupied. . . .

And then the spell of peace and prosperity was broken. In the third month of the sixth year of the Emperor Tung Chih (*i. e.*, April, 1866) a large Mohammedan army came. It had devastated all the towns on the route. . . . Happily Yenanfu was then well able to resist the rebels. . . .

This was not done without the total depopulation and robbing of the whole country-side, and the crowding of this city with large numbers of people from other districts, involving a tremendous drain on local resources. . . .

In the tenth Chinese month of the same year (November, 1866) a branch of the Tai-ping rebel army . . . reached Yenanfu. . . . It had completed the depopulation of the country, so thoroughly begun seven months earlier by the Mohammedans. The soldiers had robbed everywhere . . . and the surviving populace had fled. . . .

In the following April (1867) the Mohammedans returned on one of their periodical raids. . . .

And then followed famine. "For this," said my elderly friend . . . "Heaven was not to be blamed." The weather had been seasonable, and so, had there been peace, there would certainly have been prosperity. . . . In 1866 the one rebel army came before the harvest and the other afterwards. . . . The result was that in 1867 there was bigger demand with a smaller supply [of food] than usual. . . .

The second attack by the Mohammedans in April, 1867, had entirely prevented sowing and reaping that year. . . .

. . . Food was ten times its usual cost and therefore 90 per cent. of the people starved. . . .

This small remnant [of the population], however, had a good harvest in 1869, and the prospects consistently improved until 1876, when Yenanfu shared the desolating effects of a real famine [that of 1875-78] which extended over several provinces and caused the death of eight millions of people. . . .

The city has never recovered from the devastating effects of the war and famine, far less has the surrounding country. Wild beasts have taken advantage of the absence of man. While the level country has been recultivated, and by gradual stages the wider mountain valleys are being won back, the narrower gullies are infested with leopards, wild boar, wolves, etc. . . . The whole Yenanfu area is therefore now one of the poorest in the whole of China.[127]

There were many other localities that did not fare so badly as these, but the deterioration of the rural environment in some parts of the empire was bound to exert adverse effects on the other parts. There are no adequate data to indicate the precise extent of deterioration. Some writers pointed to the decrease of the population of the empire during the period of tribulations as an unmistakable symptom of decline.[128] It is safe to suppose that in imperial China a prolonged period of relative prosperity ended in overpopulation which became an economic curse, yet wars and famines cut down the population, thus mitigating a baffling economic problem but inflicting at the same time immeasurable sufferings on the millions that lived in the villages.

WESTERN IMPACT ON RURAL ENVIRONMENT

One can hardly depict the rural environment of nineteenth-century China without indicating the effects on it of the influx of Western commerce and industry. Obviously, the impact of the West was less rapid and more indirect upon rural China than upon the cities and towns, particularly those situated near the seacoast and along the main lines of inland transportation. It is evident also that whatever effects were felt in the countryside were more likely to be economic than intellectual in nature and that they must have varied in degrees of intensity in different parts of the empire.

One direction in which Western influence exerted itself was on the ownership and prices of land. It has been said recently that in provinces little touched by commerce and industry, tenancy had a more or less restricted existence, but where "urban capital" flowed into agriculture, concentration of landownership often became especially noticeable. In the vicinity of modern Shanghai, for example, 95 per cent of the farmers were found to be tenants, and in the Canton delta, 85 per cent; whereas in Shensi, Shansi, Hopei (Chihli), Shantung, and Honan two thirds of the farmers were said to be owners of the land which they tilled.[129]

Such influence was not limited to coastal regions, nor to the twentieth century. A Western writer reported in February, 1870, the conditions of eastern Hunan:

> People in eastern Hunan are, on an average, better dressed than the inhabitants of any other province I have visited. . . . A considerable amount of money flows into the country, in return for tea, tea-oil, hemp, and coal. . . .
>
> This is the first province in which I have seen a considerable number of fine country seats owned by "rich men" who have retired from business. They invest their money in real estate and let this to farmers for rent. . . .
>
> Siang-tan [Hsiang-t'an] has been for a long time the great market of foreign goods and of imports from Canton generally, for Szechuen [Szechwan], Kwei-chau [Kweichow], Hu-peh, Honan, Shan-si, Shen-si, and even for Yunnan and Kansu.[130]

Situations like these, which made land a desirable investment, inevitably resulted in increases in the price of land. In some cases land became valuable not for the agricultural rent which it might yield, but because it was so located as to be useful for commercial purposes.

Such a situation existed in a rural area in San-shui. According to one source:

> San-shui Hsien, Kwangtung, is situated at the important juncture of the West and North rivers. Recently the English are engaged in trade at Wu-chou [Kwangsi]; steamships that come and go must pass through this juncture. The English established a consulate in Kang-keng Hsiang [of San-shui]. The Chinese government also set up a customs house there to collect taxes. When the big merchants of Hong Kong and Canton heard of this news, they rushed to [this place] and purchased land. . . . A *mow* of land which formerly was valued at a few dozen taels, commands now an inflated price of two to three hundred taels. [131]

The effects of such a development (which probably did not obtain in some of the hinterland) were not necessarily beneficial to the rural economy. Persons who bought land for nonagricultural purposes were not interested in increased agricultural production or in improving the livelihood of the peasantry, but primarily in the profits that they might realize from rent or increment in land value. [132] This trend, known long before the nineteenth century, was given a new impetus by the introduction of Western commerce and industry.

Western influence on the rural economy was discernible in another direction. The opening of over forty ports and marts to foreign trade between 1842 and 1906 in various parts of the empire[133] and the establishment of Western-style factories, mostly in provinces with large coastal cities, [134] augmented the trickles of imported goods into an ever increasing stream that overflowed first the cities and eventually the countryside. This meant luxury to many a consumer, more business in towns and cities, and employment for a considerable number of rural inhabitants who would otherwise have remained idle. All these brought prosperity to or eased the stringent economy of some localities. The export of silk, tea, ginger, and other native goods unquestionably benefited the places that produced them. One drawback, however, can hardly be overlooked: the ruin of native handicrafts after the second half of the century. In earlier days handicrafts usually brought additional income to rural families, which alleviated to some extent the financial hardships wrought by their inadequate agricultural income. For a while native manufacture withstood the onslaught of "foreign goods."[135] Rural inhabitants were not slow in recognizing the threat. According to a Western writer, this was the information given the Court of Directors by certain supercargoes in 1831, showing the reaction to the first invasion of imported cotton yarn:

> In two districts in the immediate vicinity of Canton, and in another about twenty miles distant from it, very serious commotions have taken place among the natives at the introduction of cotton yarn. They

loudly complain that it has deprived their women and children, who had previously been employed in the spinning of thread, of the means of subsistence.[136]

Resistance eventually melted away. In time foreign goods became widely used in household consumption and local manufacture, even in the remotest corners of the empire. In the 1870's, for example, a Western traveler found that imported goods were offered for sale in the regular markets of western Yunnan.[137]

This development is well known and needs no elaboration. The disastrous effects of the influx of foreign goods upon the rural economy have also been widely acknowledged.[138] This striking summary of the matter was written at the close of the century by a Western missionary:

> One reads in the reports to the directors of steamship companies of the improved trade with China in cotton goods, and the bright outlook all along the coast from Canton to Tientsin and Newchwang in the line of commerce, but no one reads of the effect of this trade of expansion upon innumerable millions of Chinese on the great cotton-growing plains of China. These have hitherto been just able to make a scant living by weaving cloth fifteen inches wide, one bolt of which requires two days of hard work, realizing at the market only enough to enable the family to purchase the barest necessities of life, and to provide more cotton for the unintermittent weaving. . . . But now, through the "bright outlook" for foreign cotton goods, there is no market for the native product, as there has always been hitherto. . . . In some villages every family has one or more looms. . . . But now the looms are idle. . . .
>
> Multitudes who own no loom are able to spin cotton thread, and thus earn a bare support, —a most important auxiliary protection against the wolf always near to the Chinese door. But lately the phenomenal activity of the mills in Bombay, in Japan, and even in Shanghai itself, had inundated the cotton districts of China with yarns so much more even, stronger, and withal cheaper than the home-made kind, that the spinning-wheels no longer revolve, and the tiny rill of income for the young, the old, the feeble, and the helpless is permanently dried up.[139]

The operators of looms and spinning wheels were among the hardest hit, but they were by no means the only ones who were hurt. The assertion of a recent writer that rural problems in China did not become acute until the handicrafts were largely destroyed is not without cogency.[140]

The effect of the widespread use of opium, which was one item of foreign import, was even more serious than the invasion of consumer goods from foreign countries. It is true, of course, that opium was known in China before it was imported from India, and that native production of opium contributed a good deal to making the drug both an economic and a social menace. Foreign merchants nevertheless must share a substantial part of the blame.[141] At any rate, the importation of the drug increased and "the evils arising from the use of opium became more apparent from year to year."[142] At one point the value of imported opium amounted to one half of the total imports.[143] Expansion and continuation of the opium trade, in addition to causing the waste of a portion of the wealth which otherwise might have been more profitably used, facilitated opium addiction and brought eventual ruin to whole families.

Opium addiction became an empire-wide phenomenon, with some local variations in the degree of intensity. The following situation was reported in some parts of North China around 1890 by a Western medical doctor:

> In the province of Shan Hsi [Shansi] . . . in a number of villages men, women, and children all use the pernicious drug, and . . . on entering such a village you can tell at a glance, by the dilapidated condition of all the houses, temples, etc., that the entire village is composed of opium debauchees.
>
> Nearly every village in Shantung has its opium-shop and it is sold at all the fairs and market-places.[144]

About a decade later a Western traveler wrote:

> Nearly all of the chain of villages that line the road through the Shansi Mountains from the great wall to Tai Yuan [T'ai-yüan], possess certain common characteristics. Few villages have a population of more than three hundred. . . . The villagers have no luxuries, and few comforts, yet they are happy and contented. . . .
>
> I have said nearly all the villages, because in the course of every twenty-four hours, in a progress through Shansi Mountains, one is almost sure to find at least one village whose conditions, no matter by what standards they might be measured, could never be called happy or fortunate. Even from a distance the difference between the sad village and the rest is very marked. The walls at the entrance to it are crumbling. . . . The roofs of the houses are dilapidated and full of holes. A nearer approach reveals windows from which the paper panes are missing and doors supported by only one hinge. No one is selling vegetables in the road, and the one or two shops which the village possessed are closed. In the shadow of the houses a few men and women are lying or squatting—apparently in a stupor. Their faces are drawn and leathery, their eyes glazed and dull. Their clothes are masses of rags. . . . Even some of the babies the women carry in their arms have the same parched skins and wan, haggard faces. And the cause of all this is *opium*.[145]

In some localities opium addiction had become almost universal among the inhabitants. Such was the situation in a prefecture of Shensi. According to a missionary:

> Yenanfu is one of those areas where the opium habit was much more than usually prevalent. It is no exaggeration to say that 90 per cent. of the people of the city were to a smaller or greater extent its victims. . . . It has gone not only along the main highways to the provincial capitals, but also into every prefecture, every county, every town, into numberless villages, and, in the case of Yenanfu, into practically every home. [146]

Since this habit eventually brought "physical as well as financial ruin" to its victims, its adverse effects on the rural economy can readily be imagined.

The importation of opium and consumer goods produced yet another economic effect, which had reverberations in the countryside as well as in cities. The rise of the exchange rate of silver in the early nineteenth century, according to some Western writers, was due partly to this cause. [147] As already noted, the money income of small farmers and tenants was usually in copper cash, whereas tax payments were made in silver taels. A rise in the exchange rate in favor of silver therefore meant hardship on these persons. [148]

In various directions, then, the influence of Western commerce and industry upon nineteenth-century rural China was, for a while at least, more damaging than beneficial. There is some ground for the view that "the most striking fact concerning rural China has been its uninterrupted decline since her open contact with the industrial power of the West." [149] Admittedly certain internal and inherent factors in the historical environment of the empire would have impelled the rural economy to take a downward course without the intrusion of external forces, but these external forces must have hastened the process.

To sum up: Deterioration of the rural environment was partly due to internal factors and partly to the damaging effects of Western commerce and industry. By the middle of the nineteenth century such deterioration had reached a critical point; large numbers of rural inhabitants in various parts of the empire were driven by destitution and hardships to the point of despair. The situation was potentially explosive. Many of the villagers suffered helplessly and died silently. Some of them joined the "bandits" or rallied around rebel leaders who sought to destroy the existing regime.

Chapter 10

●

RURAL REACTIONS
TO CONTROL: II

"THE GOOD PEOPLE"

At the beginning of the previous chapter it was suggested that the inhabitants of rural China exhibited different patterns of behavior at different times and under different circumstances. It has also been said that they were classified by the imperial government into two categories according to the attitudes and reactions which they showed at a given time. Those among them who accepted or supported the existing order were called "the good people," and those who acted so as to endanger the imperial security were stigmatized as "the weed people," "wicked sticks," or "bandits." We have noted the salient features and important changes of the rural environment in the nineteenth century; we propose now to show in some detail how these "types" of rural inhabitants reacted to that environment, with a view to throwing further light on the effects of imperial control.

Various factors contributed to shaping "the good people" into what they were; the social and political milieu that prevailed under the imperial system seems to have been the most crucial. Despotic or autocratic government has always tended to devitalize the people over whom it rules. Even where despotism is truly paternal and benevolent (if ever if could be such),[1] its long-range effect on the subjects could not be other than "the benumbing and debasing of all those faculties which distinguish men from the herd that grazes."[2] And when despotism degenerates into misgovernment, as it often does, it may impair even the people's incentive to make the best of their animal existence.[3] The rural inhabitants of China, well known for their "patience" and "docility," afford a particularly clear demonstration of this truth.

The proverbial timidity of the Chinese peasantry was partly the result of deliberate imperial policy. The entire complex of the institutions of rural control, as we have seen, was designed by the rulers to instill a fear of authority in the minds of the people, to foster in them a willingness to accept the *status quo,* to prevent them from developing capacities of self-help—in short, to make them po-

litically innocuous and intellectually inert. These institutions did
not achieve all the results of which they were theoretically capable,
but their long-range effects, reinforced by contributing factors operating in the historical situation, tended to accentuate those traits of
the average villager that made him the tractable, diffident, and helpless human being he often was. The inhabitants were made to spy
on one another; even though actually few of them reported the misdeeds of their neighbors, most of them were thus deterred from turning their attention to matters beyond their own families. They were
given no protection against arbitrary government and very little against
the oppression of local bullies. For many of them, the best self-
protection consisted in shying away from matters of common concern
and in avoiding coming into contact with government. Most of them
were allowed to remain illiterate, although by means of popular indoctrination some of them absorbed bits of imperial Confucianism
with its emphasis on duties to the sovereign and parents. They were
allowed to dwell in the popular superstitions and to remain convinced
that since the gods dispose, it was futile for men to propose. They
attributed to fate the general insecurity in their material and social
existence which was in part a consequence of inadequate government,
and placed it beyond the pale of human action. They became resigned
to their lot, unsatisfactory as it might be:

> All things are prearranged by Fate; for what shall we pray?
> Today knows not the affairs of tomorrow; how shall we plan? . . .
> My neighbor's wealth and honors were earned in a previous exist-
>   ence; why should I envy him? . . .
> Good luck comes to all who patiently wait for it; do not be over
>   anxious.
> On this earth are few occasions for laughter; why complain of your
>   lot as a specially hard one?
> Patches and rags serve to keep out the cold; why take delight in
>   fine clothing?
> To be diligent and economical is better than to go abroad begging;
>   let us never be wasteful.[4]

Such an attitude of resignation was shared by many villagers in all
parts of the empire, especially when the general conditions were
fairly stable. In periods of unrest some of the villagers might temporarily be driven by desperation into believing that Fate had arranged
for a different order of things and into joining those who offered their
services to bring about that order. But even then a considerable number of rural inhabitants did not change their habitual attitudes and remained in the eyes of the imperial rulers "good people."

Imperial policy was not the only factor that contributed to the persistence of this mentality. Some of the features of the imperial administration itself also bore on the situation. The principle of cen-

tralization of power precluded the development of administrative efficiency in general and that of an efficient local administration in particular. In the first place, no local official was given sufficient discretionary power to perform his prescribed duties properly; the *chou* or *hsien* magistrate, in particular, had to operate within the narrow bounds set by numerous restrictions imposed upon him by imperial laws and superior officials. Local civil functionaries were not permitted to serve in the provinces in which they were residents; they could not hold offices in the same place for more than a few consecutive years. These and similar measures were precautions taken by the imperial rulers against the development of centers of local power or influence. Within certain limits, these measures served the cause of centralization well. But at the same time they prevented the development of an efficient local administration and in fact encouraged local officials to put their personal interests before the welfare of the inhabitants under their care. This is so well known that it hardly requires elaboration. [5]

The quality of local administration was further vitiated by the imperial policy of placing indefinite and extensive responsibilities on the shoulders of the magistrate. This was apparently part of the general policy to place effective restraints on officials who exercised some measure of authority. By assigning them overlapping duties, holding them jointly and severally accountable for anything amiss, making some of them report one against another, the imperial rulers wished to prevent them from gaining too much power or plotting against their sovereigns. Eventually, however, experience taught officials to reduce the perils of assuming responsibilities by evading them as far as possible, with the result that many things which they should have undertaken for the benefit of the local inhabitants were left undone. Even the administration of justice, the protection of law-abiding subjects against the encroachment of lawless elements, which may be regarded as the minimum duty of a magistrate, was often neglected in the desire to evade responsibilities. [6]

Official corruption which became fairly widespread in the nineteenth century rendered an inefficient local administration even less satisfactory. Corruption had some of its roots in the imperial system itself. Officials were notoriously underpaid. [7] "Starving salaries" virtually made it necessary for officials to practice "squeezing." [8] The expenditures of a magistrate were relatively heavy. In addition to personal and household expenses, he must pay his personal secretaries *(mu-yu)*, permanent attendants *(ch'ang-sui)*, household men *(chia-jen)* who assisted him in conducting the routines of the yamen;[9] he was expected to send periodic "gifts" to the secretaries, clerks, and other persons attached to the yamen of his superiors, with a view to making the transaction of official business easier for him, to ex-

pediting his own assignment to a desirable post, or to persuading the
superiors to allow him to remain a little longer in his present post;
he must finance the trip to his post, which might be quite a distance
away, or buy the official vestments if he happened to be serving for
the first time. Many of the magistrates began their careers as men
of very modest financial means. They were compelled by circumstances to raise the necessary funds by taking out loans, which were
readily extended to them by a host of usurers. Among these creditors
were personal servants of higher officials in the provincial capital
or the prefectural city; and to assure repayment of loans, some of
them went with their debtors to their posts, ostensibly as servants
or attendants of the latter, thus placing themselves in a strategic position to take bribes, extortion money, or whatever payments their
nominal master managed to make them. [10]

The practice of selling official posts[11] was perhaps even more conducive to corruption than the low salary scale. It began in the early
days of the dynasty, but the sale became extensive in the Hsien-feng
period, when military campaigns drained the imperial coffers and the
regular revenues did not meet the urgent needs. Its evils were obvious
to many; the attention of the imperial government was called to them
even before the tumultous 1850's. [12]

The deterioration of local officialdom was accompanied by another
unhappy development, the infestation of local yamens by hordes of
unscrupulous underlings—the clerks, runners, and personal attendants of the magistrate. These men knew no rules of decency or propriety and were therefore much more shameless and cruel than the
most corrupt of local officials. Their atrocious deeds are too many
to relate. [13] What is important for us to note is that the average magistrate had no training for his position; he was a stranger in the district where he held office and could not remain there long enough to
understand the needs and problems of the locality. He was unacquainted with the working details of imperial laws and regulations and seldom possessed information on the administrative and judicial matters
of the district in his charge. In all probability, he could not speak the
local dialect, perhaps not even understand it. As a consequence, he
had to depend upon the underlings mentioned above for conducting the
routines of his office and for dealing with the inhabitants. [14] Being
thus at the mercy of his subordinates, he was likely to find it wise
or profitable to connive with them, instead of upholding honesty and
integrity against their wishes. Occasionally, a few particularly capable or experienced magistrates managed to keep their underlings
under control, but they constituted a very small minority and did not
exert sufficient influence to alter the general situation.

One important effect of the degeneration of local administration was
that villagers came to regard the yamen not as a place where they

could apply for justice or protection but a ruinous pit to be avoided as best they could. They learned to prefer letting grievances go un-redressed to running the risk of litigation at court. As a well-known Chinese proverb puts it: "Rather to die of starvation than to be a thief; rather to die of resentment than to bring a lawsuit."[15] Eventually, "not only the government, but the very idea of government," became unpopular in imperial China.[16] As a matter of fact officials were, in the eyes of some villagers, about as frightful as robbers or bandits. The following observation made by a Chinese official on his way to An-ting (Shensi) in the summer of 1904 illustrates this point:

> Ordered that luggage be unloaded in a village inn—a mud building consisting of two rooms; no other furniture besides a table and a brick-bed. Asked for fuel, oil, and candle, but could not get any. Attendants reported that villagers were afraid that officials would not pay for [articles supplied them]; even though they had some in store, they concealed the fact and dared not take them out.
>
> When the people are afraid of officials to such an extent, how far is this fear from their fear of robbers? Those [officials] who created this situation deserve punishment.[17]

Few if any such officials received punishment. It is hardly surprising, therefore, that in the face of persistent misgovernment and widespread corruption, villagers of imperial China became generally timid and diffident, unprepared to defend their interests against the malprac-tices of local officials or the oppression of local bullies.[18]

Such then were the benumbing effects of imperial policy and the circumstances that attended the imperial system. Other factors that worked in the same direction should not be overlooked. The general poverty that prevailed in many parts of rural China was perhaps the most important. It condemned villagers to devote all of their time and energy to the laborious task of keeping themselves and their fam-ilies alive, and thus denied them the opportunity of acquiring an edu-cation which even under autocratic rule might have opened to them a wider vista or better condition of life. Whatever school facilities were provided by the government or the local gentry in the countryside were intended not to be institutions of popular education but rather to serve special purposes. They benefited no more than a very small number of children in any given rural community.[19] Illiterate parents themselves did not show interest in educating their children.[20] There is much evidence to justify the saying current in the nineteenth cen-tury that "the rich never teach school, and the poor never attend one."[21]

Circumstances rather than personal choice accounted for the peas-ant's apparent lack of interest in education. The situation was cogently described in the 1896 edition of the gazetteer of Lu-i:

With the family growing larger daily, those who till the soil merely manage to support themselves with meagre food. Even if there are intelligent sons and younger brothers, these can hardly escape [the lot of growing up] without an education. The teacher in the village school gathers together several tens of boys of various ages in an old house [and gives them instruction]. . . . Every year when the crops are being harvested, they promptly suspend their studies and go away. When they assemble in the ninth month, no more than three or four out of ten boys actually return. The fees collected often are insufficient to support the teacher, who then posts a notice announcing the postponement of instructions. After repeating the same process for a few years, fathers and elder brothers, dissatisfied with the school for its lack of results, decide to have the boys take up farming or engage in handicraft or trade. [22]

A similar situation was observed by a Western writer at about the same time in An-chia Miao, a rural community in Chi-yang (Shantung), on the north bank of the Yellow River:

I found this village to consist of about one hundred adobe houses, an inn, and a school-house. Only ten boys attended school, the rest of the young male population being left to grow up in ignorance. . . . I was informed that if they did [attend school] their parents would have to help contribute to the teacher's salary, and they could not afford it. [23]

It should be noted of course that in prosperous rural communities the situation must have been better than this, and that in places where the clan organization was strong the clan schools provided some educational facilities for their own members. In such localities it may be said that "scholarship has always been a primary social value and therefore an ideal of the village and an object of concerted effort by the village community. "[24] But in the majority of rural areas villagers were compelled by the pressing task of eking out a living under stringent economic conditions to forego schooling. The overwhelming high percentage of illiteracy in China bore out this fact. Illiteracy, which certainly made people inarticulate though not necessarily inept, must have worked jointly with poverty to intensify that general torpor and indifference characteristic of the bulk of the rural inhabitants of the empire.

Thus out of the matrix formed by the convergence of a variety of factors—long-continued autocratic rule, widespread maladministration, general poverty, and illiteracy—a familiar creature, the patient, apathetic, and docile peasant, the "good people" of the imperial rulers, took shape. [25] The rulers did not intentionally bring all these factors to bear on the situation. But by stressing the forces that conditioned the minds of the rural populace so that they would react and behave as they ordinarily did, the Ch'ing emperors as much as their predecessors were to a considerable extent responsible for the evolution of China's passive peasantry.

With the help of whatever gentry elements chose to remain in their home villages and make the lot of the "good people" a little more sat-isfactory or a little less unbearable, the Ch'ing emperors managed to keep the rural situation fairly placid for relatively long periods of time. The occasional disorders that were reported in some localities no more than rippled the imperial peace; for under ordinary circum-stances the bulk of the "peace-loving" elements outnumbered those that were ready to "tread the dangerous path." For one villager that became a "bandit," there was more than one who "preferred dying of starvation to being a thief" or simply remained helpless in des-titution and hard fortune. [26] Under such circumstances it was incon-ceivable that rural inhabitants should rise in a body to challenge the constituted authority or to seek to ameliorate their lot by violence. Herein lies part of the reason for the relative longevity of the Ch'ing dynasty despite the shortcomings of its system of rural control.

"THE WEED PEOPLE"

In the foregoing section we have explained briefly the behavior of "the good people" and its bearing on imperial control. We shall now examine the attitudes and reactions of "the weed people" who by their acts of violence gave the lie to the uncritical view that there was an "unlimited capacity of the Chinese for patient endurance." [27] On the basis of the available information we have been able to identify four types of such acts of violence: feuds, riots, banditry, and rebellions.

Our findings will justify the following conclusions: (1) that the bulk of the peasants were habitually placid, but that some of them might be driven by circumstances into paroxysms of violence, so that they were "good people" at one moment and "weed people" at another; (2) that at all times there were present in rural communities a small number of persons who committed themselves to oppressing their fellow villagers or causing trouble for the government and who under certain conditions might induce or coerce some of the "good people" to take part in mob violence; (3) that members of the local gentry nor-mally identified their interests with those of the government, but under special circumstances some of them might incite or lead the common people to break laws or challenge the constituted authority; (4) that although peasants by themselves were capable of violence, their uprisings could become sustained or large-scale only with the guidance or support of members of the gentry or "literati" who chose to join forces with them; and (5) that inadequate or corrupt local ad-ministration aggravated the unsatisfactory situation which gave rise

to rural unrest, and therefore was partly responsible for the emergence of "the weed people" and for further reducing the effectiveness
of the system of rural control.

Feuds

The word "feud" is here used to describe open conflicts of various
degrees of violence between different rural communities or between
different groups of rural inhabitants. [28] In the more serious conflicts
weapons were extensively used; these miniature wars might develop
into long, drawn-out struggles lasting intermittently for months or
years. These were known in official parlance as *hsieh-tou* (armed
conflicts, fighting with weapons), and were particularly common in
some of the southern provinces—Fukien, Kiangsi, Kwangtung, and
Kwangsi being the most notorious. [29]

Causes of Feuds. The causes of feuds were quite diverse. In some
instances the occasion for sanguinary fights was seemingly trivial.
Quarrels over women, for example, touched off an armed conflict between two villages in Hsieh Hsien (Anhwei) in the 1850's. [30] Most feuds,
however, resulted from conflicts of material interests between individuals or groups. Thus rivalry between different groups promoting "religious fairs" often gave rise to feuds, an instance of which
was reported in Kiangsi in the mid-eighteenth century. Rural bullies
extorted contributions from every household, rich or poor, to finance
religious processions and pageantry, ostensibly to celebrate the new
year. Anyone who failed to meet the demand for money was liable to
be treated in the roughest manner. Various groups organized by the
bullies vied with one another in presenting the most bizarre pageantry and gathering the most noisy rabble. Violent fights readily ensued
when one group allegedly trespassed into the "territory" of another. [31]
Similar "evil practices" also obtained in other parts of the empire
and in later periods. [32]

By far the most important and perhaps also most frequent cause
was disputes over the enjoyment of water rights or control of flood
water. Local gazetteers contain numerous instances of such disputes
that ended in orgies of murder and destruction. The imperial government, obviously realizing the importance of water to the peasantry
and the likelihood that disputes would arise over its use, attempted
to protect water rights against encroachment. Punishment was promised anyone who without authorization drew water to irrigate his own
land from reservoirs, ponds, or water-courses constructed by private parties. [33] But as the need of water often became urgent and some
of the peasants were prevented by their poverty from building "water-
benefit" devices of their own, they might be driven by dire necessity

to diverting water from their neighbor's property, with or without
the consent of the lawful owner. Moreover, even where the irrigation
facilities were not privately owned, as the water from natural rivers
or lakes, the amount available might be inadequate to meet the demand
of all, especially during a drought season. In localities threatened by
floods the problem was either to drain off the unwanted water as soon
as possible, or to construct embankments to prevent it from over-
flowing the fields and farmsteads. Villagers living on high land usually solved the problem by the former method, whereas those living
on low land adopted the latter. The interests of villagers might conflict, if their respective communities were situated on different levels. The flood water released by a neighboring village situated on a
hillside was bound to inundate the farms of a village located near the
foot of the hill, whereas dikes maintained by the latter might, under
special circumstances, be regarded as detrimental to the welfare of
the former. These situations readily gave occasion to bitter feuds.
The experiences of some villages in Ch'ing-yüan (Chihli) may be taken
as typical of many rural communities confronted by similar situations.
According to an account:

> The T'ang-ho flows through this rural area, a river which has defied
> all attempts at diking. All the villages [that dot its banks] seek to es-
> cape damage caused by floods and to avail themselves of whatever
> water benefits [it affords]. Large-scale weaponed feuds often resulted
> [from conflicting interests]. [34]

A few concrete instances may give us a fuller impression of the
situation. Peasants of various rural areas of Po-lo (Kwangtung) were
reported to have fought over irrigation water in the 1850's, with heavy
casualties resulting on both sides. [35] In P'an-yü, another district of
the same province, a struggle over "water benefits" was carried on
intermittently for twenty years. [36] Inhabitants of Pao-ying and Kao-
yu (Kiangsu) resorted to *hsieh-tou* during a serous drought in 1862. [37]
Small-scale fights occurred each year in Tao Chou (Hunan) whenever
rainfall failed to come during the fifth and sixth months, when farmers were in urgent need of water, resulting occasionally in the death
of some of the participants. [38]

Examples of feuds over the control of flood water are also readily
found. The case of Yang-ku and Hsin Hsien (Shantung) is especially
illuminating. It was said that the former, situated on the upper reaches
of a river, wished to break open the dikes in order to allow the flood
water to drain off; the latter, situated down river, desired to maintain the dikes as a defense against flood water. Feuds between the
inhabitants of these two districts had been carried on for centuries
until 1880, when a particularly capable magistrate effected a satisfactory settlement. [39] Bloody feuds broke out in several places in Mien-

yang (Hupeh) in the 1870's when villages inundated by flood water dug open the mud dikes which afforded protection to other villages.[40] Struggles of a similar nature were reported in Hai-ning and Hai-yen (Chekiang)[41] and Nan-hai (Kwangtung). The situation in Nan-hai became so serious around 1885 that the governor had to take drastic action.[42]

In southern provinces where the clan organization was often strong, feuds between rival kinship groups became common. Like feuds between ordinary villages and villagers, feuds between clans arose from divergent causes, petty as well as grave. The real difference between these and village feuds lies mainly in the social relationships of the participants. In one case the mobs were held together simply by a common object, whereas in the other there was an additional tie of kinship, real or imagined.

A number of instances of clashes between clans have already been cited. Two more examples will suffice. According to a censor, writing in 1884 concerning the situation in Hsing-feng (Kiangsi), the Wang clan of Hsiao-yüan (a village), was especially noted for its pugnacity; mobs of as many as a thousand men would gather upon the slightest provocation and fight with weapons in the district city without the least hesitation.[43] A Western observer described a feud between two clans in rural Fukien (1817) as follows:

> The name of one was *Tsae* [Ts'ai] and of the other *Wang*, and, a gathering of each having taken place, they fought until many were killed and a number of houses destroyed by fire. The police seized the most violent; but the worsted clan again attacked the other, and killed several of them, until the government called in the military to restore order.[44]

Another variety of feud resulted from conflicts between rural inhabitants who came from different geographical regions or belonged to different ethnic groups. The distinction between *t'u-cho* (native-settled) and *k'e-hu* (stranger-households) or *k'e-chi* (immigrant registration) was usually maintained in many parts of imperial China. The line of demarcation between the *pun-ti* (natives) and the Hakkas—the *k'e-chia* (stranger-families) or the *k'e-jen* (strangers)—that lived in some parts of Kwangtung, Kwangsi, and Kiangsi, was particularly rigid. Those Hakkas who had migrated to these localities in recent times often faced discrimination by the "natives," and readily engaged in constant disputes with the latter. A local historian, obviously biased in favor of the "natives," made this revealing statement concerning the "stranger-families" recently moved from Hupeh and Hunan to the countryside of Nan-ch'ang (Kiangsi):

> These stranger-people who came from other places are not uniform

in their quality. Owing to the fact that their long wanderings deprive them of education as well as fixed abodes, they become accustomed to employing their superior physical strength to oppress the weak and their superior numerical strength to bully the few. Their presence is a menace to order and security.[45]

Whatever may have been the "quality" of the immigrants and the natives, it is understandable that ill feeling and friction readily developed between the two segments of the populace. When conflicts of material interests commingled with ill feelings, open clashes were bound to result. Occasionally, their strife was kept within the bounds of law, as in the case of the *k'e-hu* and *t'u-cho* of Mien-chu (Szechwan).[46] More often, however, the conflicts took violent forms, as in some localities in Kiangsi, Kiangsu, and Shantung. One of the most ferocious of these feuds was fought between the *k'e-ming* from Shantung, who organized themselves into what were known as *hu-t'uan* on the one side, and native inhabitants of certain districts of northern Kiangsu, on the other side, over reclaimed land in the lake region, during the 1850's and 1860's. According to an official report:

> The *hu-t'uan* are composed of the *k'e-ming* from localities in Ts'ao-chou, Shantung, who reclaim and cultivate land in the lake region near the boundaries of Kiangsu and Shantung provinces. They gather themselves into clans. When their number multiplies as time goes on, they organize themselves into *t'uan*. . . . There are two *t'uan* in Yü-t'ai [Shantung] . . . eight in T'ung-shan [Kiangsu]. . . . All these derive their names from the clan names of their respective leaders.
>
> When the Yellow River broke its embankments at Shang-i in 1855 . . . refugees from Yün-ch'eng, Chia-hsiang, and Chü-yeh migrated from Shantung to Hsü-chou [Kiangsu]. . . . Since the flood [in Hsü-chou] had then already subsided and the inundated areas had recently become dry, mud-covered land, these refugees settled down there and reclaimed the waste land into farms. They constructed wooden sheds to live in, procured weapons to protect themselves, and instituted leaders to make their organizations strong. The natives of T'ung-shan and P'ei Hsien (in Hsü-chou where the Shantung refugees now live) abandoned their land when the flood came, and wandered into other places. On their return a few years later they discovered that this stretch of lowland had become the property of *k'e-ming* from Shantung. Their minds are filled with a feeling of injustice. . . . [When the *k'e-ming* present a hostile attitude toward them], the natives seek to fight them constantly, making the two groups irreconcilable enemies.[47]

This report further relates that in 1859 one of the *hu-t'uan* raided a native family of T'ung-shan. This set off a long series of internecine fights, culminating in the massacre of 1864, in which a number of the natives who dwelt in Liu-chuang Chai, a walled village stronghold, lost their lives.

Feuds between Hakkas and natives in southern provinces were often no less violent. Recurrent fights between these groups broke out in En-p'ing, Ho-shan, and Kao-p'eng (Kwangtung) in the 1850's and 1860's with ever increasing vehemence, with the result that some of the Hakkas became "wandering bandits" or joined the "Red Bandits."[48] Hakka-native feuds were sometimes entangled with clan struggles. A Western source gave the following instance which occurred in the mid-nineteenth century in a number of villages in Kwangtung:

> About three English miles southwest of Ho-au there is a market-place, which was built by the people of Ho-au. The Hakka, to whom the market was let, refused in that year [1843] to pay their taxes [rent], and . . . appeal was had to arms. Both parties fought for about six years, when another market-place, also belonging to Ho-au, gave occasion to a conflict with even more powerful clans.
>
> In 1850 more than ninety villages united for the extermination of the Chin clan [who inhabited Ho-au village]. Pu-lu-wei [a stronghold] fell by treachery, and the people were stripped of the last piece of dress they had on their persons; but though more than 5,000 men surrounded Ho-au, where only from 300 to 500 men were, the Hakka had not the courage to enter the village, but moved off without any booty. Both parties being at last exhausted, peace was concluded, one of the market-places was lost to the Chin clan, the other submitted, and promised to pay further rent.
>
> In 1856 war broke out anew, and frightful murders would have been committed, had not the writer of these lines induced the parties to come once more to terms.
>
> The terrible war that had for so many years raged in those fertile regions had caused the neglect of repairs of embankments necessary for the irrigation of the fields.[49]

Feuds also were fought between different ethnic groups. An instance was reported in Kuei Hsien (Kwangsi). In this district the T'ung tribes were locally known as *t'u* (natives), and those inhabitants who had migrated from Ch'ao-chou and Hui-chou (Kwangtung) were called *lai* (immigrants). It happened that a wealthy person among the latter forced an attractive woman of the former to marry him. A feud ensued, resulting in the utter defeat of the "immigrants." Since all their land was seized by the victorious "natives" and they had no place to live, the vanquished eventually joined the "bandits from Chin-t'ien," the Taiping rebels.[50] A similar instance involving Moslems occurred in the same locality.[51] It was said that ferocious fights between "natives" and Moslem inhabitants of two villages in Hua Chou (Shensi) which resulted from quarrels over some bamboo, touched off the Moslem rebellion of 1862.[52]

Role of the Gentry in Feuds. It is clear, therefore, that whatever
may have been the status or origin of the feuding parties, the fights
were almost always concerned with matters of immediate interest
to the inhabitants of the countryside. These struggles had practically no direct political significance. It would be a mistake, however,
to assume that they were perpetrated by common peasants alone.
There is ample ground for the view that some of the terrible clashes,
especially the more extensive and sustained ones, were instigated,
organized, or directed by the gentry of the rural communities involved. In some cases it was expressly said that they took an active
part in them. The average peasant, being unorganized and habitually
diffident, could seldom act in concert with his fellow villagers without sufficient encouragement and provocation. Hunger, impending
danger, long-felt grudges prepared him for outbursts of violence; but
not having the fuse within itself, this human combustible material had
often to wait for a detonator to touch off the explosion. Moreover, in
many instances the rural elite had more at stake than common peasants, whether it was a matter of impending calamity or of mere "face."
When the gentry deemed it necessary or expedient, they did not hesitate to instigate a fight, even though they preferred to stay behind the
scenes; when the peasants were convinced that their own interests
were involved, they might lend active support to the fight, even though
they did not initiate it. When water rights were in dispute or flood
threatened, tenant farmers would obviously be willing to go along
with their landlords or other landowners. It may also be noted that
since some of the rural inhabitants were quite poor and desperate,
they could be bought or hired at not too high a price to fight and die
for anyone. In such cases the "mercenaries" had no personal interest
in the matter in dispute and perhaps did not even understand the reasons for it. The feud over flood-control embankments in Nan-hai
(1885), already mentioned above, was according to local historians
a struggle between the inhabitants of the area protected by the Ta-
cha-wei (dike) and the group led by Li Hsi-p'ei, a member of the
rural gentry who was responsible for the construction of the troublemaking dike, Sang-yüan-wei. The Ta-cha-wei group first petitioned
the local authorities to stop the construction of Sang-yüan-wei. Without waiting for the official word, however, they took direct action.
In retaliation, the Sang-yüan-wei group burned down some houses and
demolished ships belonging to their enemies.[53] The feud in 1871 in
Mien-yang definitely owed its origin to gentry leadership. According
to a local historian:

> The gentry headman of Ta-hsing Yüan assembled a mob and dug open
> the mud embankment of Sha-yang Ho [river] at Ho-chia-wan, by dint of
> force. A fight ensued, resulting in some dead and a number of houses

demolished or burned down. The case was brought to the attention of superior officials . . . but a decision was not handed down for a long time. [54]

In the feuds between Hakkas and natives in En-p'ing (Kwangtung), in the 1860's, "Hakka gentry" were said to have taken an active part. [55]

As already suggested, the role of the gentry became even more pronounced where clans were involved. In 1886 a high provincial official reported the situation in Kwangtung:

> Owing to petty resentment or minor disputes over hills or fields [the inhabitants] readily call in and hire bad characters from outside, and settle a date for weaponed fights, without waiting for the judgment of the government. Those who direct the fights are usually clan heads, clan gentry *(tsu-shen)*, or elders in charge of ancestral halls *(tz'u-chang)* that are unscrupulous. . . . In some cases the battles have raged for three to five years without coming to an end. . . . If one party takes by storm a village belonging to their adversaries, they indulge freely in looting, massacre, and incendiarism. Houses burned down are numbered by hundreds of rooms, and persons killed by tens. . . . After one such fight the property accumulated in one or two years, or in several tens of years, is totally lost. . . . This evil practice is particularly common in the districts of P'an-yü, Tung-kuan, Tseng-ch'eng, Hsin-ning, and Hsin-hui, all in Kuang-chou Fu. It is, however, quite often found in other prefectures and districts. [56]

The device of hiring "bad characters" to fight the feuds seems to have appeared long before the nineteenth century. A memorial written by the governor of Kwangtung in 1766 contains a lucid description of it:

> Each and every one of the big clans that possess great wealth never fails to rely on its power to oppress the weak and to depend upon its numerical strength to harry the few. But if it is confronted by a family of equal influence and power, and fears that it cannot gain the upper hand over its rival, it promptly gathers the clansmen in the ancestral hall, organizes them and leads them out to fight. It is agreed beforehand that any member of the clan who sustains injuries will be richly compensated out of the funds accrued from the ritual land rent, to enable him to buy medical attention. Anyone who dies of wounds will have a wooden tablet carrying his name entered into the ancestral hall, and some of the ritual land is to be given to his widow and children for their maintenance. If someone in the enemy clan is wounded or killed [and the matter goes to the authorities], anyone who is willing to take the crime upon himself will also "enter the ancestral hall" [after his execution]; his family will be given some land, just like families of those who died of wounds [in battle]. As a consequence, desperadoes and ruffians regard feuds as a means of making profit.

Whenever a fight breaks out, they wave their arms and press forward [to join it], destroying many lives in rapid succession. When the authorities arrest the culprits and bring them to trial, many persons on both sides take the crime upon themselves. The officials undertaking the investigations wish to punish the "offenders" on the basis of their confessions, but the real culprits have always evaded the law. [57]

As time went on this practice seems to have become a regular feature of feuds involving clans, at least in some parts of Kwangtung. According to a Western observer writing in the 1850's:

In each of the villages in the vicinity of Canton and Whampoa, where these feuds are so common, a curious provision has obtained by custom to meet such exigencies. "A band of devoted men" is there found, and a list of them kept, who have voluntarily offered themselves to assume such crimes and to take their chance for life. When a complaint is made, therefore, so many of the first on this list as are necessary come forward, confess themselves the perpetrators of the slaughter, and surrender to the government. It then belongs to them and their friends to employ lawyers and bring witnesses to prove it a justifiable homicide, or one which calls for mitigated punishment. . . . The compensation . . . is security for the maintenance of their families in case of suffering capital punishment, and a reward in lands or money, sometimes to the amount of $300. This sum is raised by the voluntary imposition of taxes on the inhabitants of that village. [58]

Another Western writer pointed out that similar practices prevailed in the nineteenth century in Fukien as well as in Kwangtung; "mercenaries" were used in the clan feuds, "prisoners" were bought when a case went to court, and the maximum price for each "prisoner" was $300. Instigators of the feuds managed to shift not only their criminal responsibility but also the financial burden of buying the substitutes to less robust shoulders than their own. [59]

Evidence compels the conclusion that feuds were not all fought between common peasants, and that some of these struggles, especially when clans were involved, bore the unmistakable mark of the gentry's hand. Peasants often teamed themselves with the gentry, with the latter as planners or leaders. The patterns of feuds thus repeated to some extent that of peaceful village activities.

Conflicts between Different Segments of the Population. This is not to say that peasants might not fight against the gentry when the latter incurred their wrath (although even here we have no assurance that the angry mobs were not encouraged by gentry or wealthy persons who harbored ill feelings against the objects of popular wrath). A very revealing instance was reported in the mid-nineteenth century in Hsiang-ling and Ling-fen (Shansi), two districts which depended upon the Ping-shui River for irrigation. Some "powerful and prominent families" monopolized the use of its water, requiring all others to buy "water tickets" from them. This worked a hardship on the poor peasants, who finally gathered together in a mob; a series of fights resulted in which many were wounded or killed. The situation grew so serious that the case was finally brought to the attention of the imperial government in 1851.[60]

A curious conflict was reported in Chin-t'ien (Kwangsi) at about the same time, an incident that obviously contributed to the Taiping uprising. According to one account, Wei Chih-cheng, who was destined soon to become one of the important leaders of the rebellion, changed his personal name to Ch'ang-huei after having given up his work as yamen runner, and later purchased a low official title for his father in order to "bring honor to his family." A wooden plaque carrying his father's official title was displayed on the occasion of the elder Wei's birthday anniversary. "Bad gentry" from a neighboring village, with the cooperation of yamen runners, swarmed to the Wei residence, loudly crying that since Wei Ch'ang-huei was formerly a yamen runner, his father was barred by law from enjoying any official status. The mob took down the plaque and demanded hush money. Wei Ch'ang-huei pleaded and negotiated with them to no avail. He then went for help to Feng Yün-shan (leader of the God-Worshipers Society), who also failed to settle the affair and was insulted by the mob. The anger of the members of the society was finally aroused. They rushed to the place where the gentry lived and plundered the crops of the wealthy families, in retaliation for the unfriendly action of the latter.[61]

By far the most important conflicts between common peasants and persons in better economic or social positions were the feuds between tenants and landlords reported in many parts of the empire. Perhaps it is useful to dwell upon this matter for a moment. To begin with, we must dispel a misconception that tenants were necessarily and uniformly opposed to their landlords. In many instances under ordinary circumstances the tenant's attitude toward his landlord was one of placid submission or even cordial amiability. The psychological attitude of the tenants differed little from that of peasants in general. The remarks of some tenants of a village in modern Kiangsu, recorded by a Chinese writer, may be regarded as an accurate expression of the sentiment of the bulk of tenants of China, in imperial as well as in modern times. When asked why they continued to pay rent despite their hardships, these tenant farmers said: "We are good people. We never refuse to pay our rent. We cannot steal even when we are poor. How then can we refuse to pay rent? . . . The landlord owns the land. We cultivate his land. We only have the land surface. The surface cannot exist without the subsoil."[62] That it was

possible for tenants to entertain a friendly feeling toward their landlords is clear from these words of a nineteenth-century Chinese writer. He wrote in his diary for 1868 (T'ung-chih 7), when he was residing in his home community in Chekiang:

> Yesterday I procured 731 catties of rice straw from Hsü Kuo-an, a
> farmer of Hui-lung-yen, who sold it to me on credit and refused to
> receive the cash gift I offered him. Kuo-an's grandfather acquired
> moderate wealth as a tenant, but continued to farm for others, with
> added diligence. Twenty years ago [Kuo-an] rented the land of my
> family. Now it has been sold for a long while, and yet he still shows
> such affection and respect to me. The simplicity and sincerity of coun-
> try folk have been proverbial since ancient times, but the generous
> ways in which my forebears treated their tenants may be seen [from
> Hsü Kuo-an's attitude toward me]. [63]

But not all landlords were as "generous" as the ancestors of this
Chinese writer; it is natural that the tenants of harsh landlords did
not show much "affection and respect" to them. Some of the big landlords of Soochow who promptly sent their tenants to the local government to be flogged for their failure to pay the rent[64] must have been
feared and hated by these peasants.

It was, in fact, not uncommon for tenants to refuse to pay rent,
particularly in places where the power and influence of the landlords
were at a minimum.[65] In Pa-ling (Hunan), for example, tenants of the
less accessible parts of the countryside were accustomed to "resisting
rent collection." If their landlord sued them in the local yamen, they
would send their women to demand a subsidy, ostensibly to enable
them to move out; and if yamen runners appeared on the scene, they
would charge the landlords with criminal acts. Sometimes they did
damage to the farm, land and buildings, or wantonly cut down trees,
just to spite their landlords.[66] The situation became so bad in some
localities that the price of land dropped and people were reluctant to
buy land.[67] In Kiangsu province refusal to pay rent became so widespread in 1853 that it affected (so it was claimed) the ability of landowners to pay their taxes.[68]

In such conflicts the tenants enjoyed the advantage of numerical
superiority, whereas the landlords could sometimes enjoy government protection, especially when they had gentry status. When the
local officials for any reason refrained from taking action against the
tenants, the landlords might suffer extensive damages in an unequal
struggle with their opponents. An instance of such a situation was reported by the governor of Kiangsu in 1846 (Tao-kuang 26):

> The rent which tenants of Chao-wen Hsien have to pay the owners of
> wheat land has been for a long time fixed by agreement between the

owners [and their tenants]. Definite rates have thus been established.
. . .

The price of wheat at present is very low. The landlords insist on collecting the usual rent and refuse to reduce the rates.

[Some persons] wrote and posted placards, calling the tenants to assemble with a view to intimidating the landowners into reducing the rent payments, and to organizing a mob to wreck the houses [of the landowners], if their demand was rejected. A series of violent actions broke out. A number of landlords sustained damages.

Order was not restored until after the ringleaders were punished and the inept magistrates dismissed. [69]

Government intervention, however, did not necessarily mean speedy settlement of the conflicts. In localities where the conflict had developed into serious proportions, especially where troublemakers took advantage of the strained relationship between tenants and landlords to embarrass the government, government intervention on behalf of the latter was likely to turn the feuds between local inhabitants into riots against the local government. This was exactly what happened in Yü-yao (Chekiang) in 1858. [70] A writer of the period (a native of the same province) explained the incident as follows:

Heard that "tenant-bandits" of Yü-yao repeatedly killed soldiers and militiamen. The trouble cannot be resolved.

Yü-yao is situated on the seacoast, where the inhabitants are ferocious, and wealthy families are accustomed to oppressing the common people. Last year, some rural inhabitants went to the *hsien* [yamen] to report a famine; they petitioned that rent be reduced. The magistrate, Ts'ui Chia-yin, listened to them. [With his authorization] an association was promptly formed and a bureau established; special dry-measurers were made to be used in rent collection. Three of the "big families," Shao, Hung, and Hsieh, refused to comply [with the new arrangements]. Violent fights broke out immediately.

It happened that at this juncture a new magistrate arrived [at Yü-yao to replace Ts'ui-chia-yin]. The Shao family, in conjunction with others, forced the new magistrate to recruit local militiamen and to order them to arrest the tenants; they increased the rent further, inscribed the new rates on stone tablets, set up special bureaus [to collect the rent], and demanded prompt payment [from the tenants]. The rural inhabitants were infuriated. Hsüan Hsi-wen and Huang Ch'un-sheng, both "bandits," together with some others, incited the tenants to make trouble. After having surrounded and burned down the homes of some of the wealthy people, the mob attacked the *hsien* city in the same evening and set free all [the tenants] that were previously imprisoned [by the new magistrate]. [71]

The uprising, according to the same writer, was eventually quelled, with a good deal of bloodshed.

It should be pointed out that while tenant farmers were capable of violent opposition to landlords, their actions were usually unorganized and on a small scale, unless leadership was supplied them by "bad elements" who ordinarily did not engage in farming. In the instance just mentioned, the uprising was incited by "bandits." In the uprisings of 1846 in Chao-wen (Kiangsu) cited earlier, the instigators were said to be local "sticks," among whom were a Buddhist bonze who had "returned to the laity," a landless fellow who made a living by resorting to foul practices in tribute rice collection, and an unspecified number of local bullies. According to the same official, when the landlords failed to comply with the tenants' demands, Chang Yung-yung (one of the bullies) discussed the situation with the other troublemakers, including Wang Szu-ma-tzu (Pock-marks Wang the Fourth) and Chin San-kuei, and decided that at the sound of the gong all were to assemble. When the appointed moment arrived,

> Chang Yung-yung beat the gong and led the mob. . . . [On their way to the landlords' houses] they saw . . . T'ao Hsiang-hsiang, Huang K'uei, Hsü Huan-ts'ao . . . and others working in the fields. Chang Yung-yung ordered Wang Szu-ma-tzu to tell them, should they refuse to go with them, they would be beaten and their houses destroyed. T'ao Hsiang-hsiang and others were afraid of them and joined them. The mob then numbered twenty-eight men. When they arrived at Kuei-shih and other places, Chang Yung-yung loudly commanded Wang Szu-ma-tzu and others to demolish one house after another, its walls and furniture, belonging to Kuei Ling-yü [apparently a landlord] . . . and those of eight others. . . .
>
> On the twenty-second day since no news of rent reduction came from the landlords, Chang Yung-yung again beat the gong and led [a mob] to deal with them. . . . Perceiving that Chao Hsiao-fu . . . and others were working in the fields, he again sent Wang Szu-ma-tzu to urge them to join. The mob numbering twenty-nine men went to Tung-kuan-shih [village] and other places . . . and destroyed the houses and furniture of Chai Luan . . . [and twenty-seven other landlords].[72]

It is difficult to estimate the extent of tenant enmity against their landlords, for one is not quite sure that the feuds reported between tenants and landowners were not sometimes instigated by elements other than peasants. Two points, however, may be made. It seems clear that when the general social situation became unsettled, as during the mid-nineteenth century, it became easier for oppressed tenants to rise against their landlords and even to challenge the authority of the local government. It also appears that in localities where the concentration of landownership was more pronounced, or where a large number of landless peasants were present, conflicts between tenants and landlords tended to be more frequent and the struggles more violent.

In some parts of the empire tenant-landlord conflicts intertwined with other forms of local struggles. Thus the convergence in some southern provinces of the conflict between Hakka and Punti inhabitants, and between tenants and landlords, often gave rise to bitter feuds. In 1851, for instance, the Punti tenants of Yung shun "engaged them - selves in revengeful killing." One Li K'o-ch'ing together with other "tenant-bandits" initiated the proposal to desist from paying rent to their Hakka landlords. Inhabitants from a number of villages allied themselves in an association, and a mob of several thousand persons was gathered. [73] A comparable situation existed at the same time in En-p'ing (southern Kwangtung), where the positions occupied by the Hakkas and Puntis in relation to land was reversed. In a number of villages "all the tenants who cultivated the land of the Puntis refused by force to pay rent." A series of fights broke out in 1852. In some instances Hakka tenants slaughtered their Punti landlords and put the torch to their houses. The disorder spread, and some of the feuding tenants joined forces with the Red Turbans. Peace was not generally restored until 1866. [74]

Conflict between tenants and landlords might take on the nature of riots, when the local government itself was the landowner. One such instance was afforded by Ch'ien-chou T'ing (Hunan) in 1847. The yamen rented out public land to the inhabitants, including a number of Miao peasants. For some unspecified reason "wicked Miao people" gathered mobs and refused to pay rent. These defiant tenants got the Miao peo- ple of the two adjacent subprefectures of Feng-huang and Yung-sui in league with them, and together they indulged freely in plunder and incendiarism. The disorder was not stopped until the next year, when the governor sent troops to the scene. [75]

A curious conflict between peasants of northern Szechwan and mer- chants of Shensi may be noted. According to a local historian, the inhabitants of a mountainous locality in P'ing-wu Hsien were mostly engaged in farming and were poor. They usually borrowed money in the spring when their food supplies were depleted, and paid their debts with interest in the autumn after the harvest. But in a fam- ine year they were unable to make payments. Their creditors, mer- chants from Shensi, usually brought lawsuits against the defaulters. Thanks to the magistrate's sympathetic understanding of the dif- ficulties of these peasants, the defendants were often leniently dealt with by the government. In 1842, however, a new magistrate ar- rived. The merchants made it known that since this official came from their own province, they would capitalize on this relationship to seek vengeance against their debtors. "Bad people" were alarmed, and in order to protect themselves gathered a huge mob, swearing that they would drive out all the Shensi merchants. The struggle was on the verge of becoming an uprising when a third magistrate captured the ringleaders, put them to death, and restored order.[76]

These occurrences show that feuds arose from a variety of causes and that various segments of the rural population took part in them. While the frequency and magnitude of these local struggles varied with the general social circumstances—that is, in a period of wide-spread economic disasters or of general political disturbances, local conflicts were likely to be serious and recurrent—the quality of local officials was often a decisive factor in a given situation. Inept or cor-rupt officials, so the evidence shows, were in more than one instance responsible for the development of local conflicts. In an edict of 1814 the Chia-ch'ing emperor blamed local officials in the province of Ki-angsi for the prevalence of feuds:

> In various localities in the three prefectures of Chi-an, Kan-chou, and Nan-an in Kiangsi province many unruly and lawless elements gather mobs to engage in armed conflicts over trivial matters. . . . The local functionaries are afraid that [because of their failure to prevent the outbreak of these fights they] would incur punishment [by their superiors]; they [prefer to hush matters up by] bearing with those [who engaged in feuds], refraining from dealing with them, and sometimes resigning their official posts on the pretext of ill health.[77]

According to other reports, local officials of other provinces were from the imperial point of view even more blameworthy than those of Kiangsi. A Chinese governor offered the following explanation for the prevalence of armed feuds in Fukien and Kwangtung:

> Among the evil customs of eastern Kwangtung nothing is worse than *hsieh-tou*. This custom arose in Chang-chou and Ch'uan-chou of Fu-kien, spread into Ch'ao-chou [Kwangtung], and gradually infested Hui-chou, Chia-ying, Kuang-chou, Shao-chou, and Nan-hai. The sit-uation is worst in Ch'ao-chou. The affliction has persisted for many years and there is no end to it. The reason for its appearance is that local afficials know only how to prey upon rural inhabitants and fail to pay attention to the people's affairs. Litigations between inhabit-ants often are allowed to drag on inconclusively for several years. In the worst cases litigants do not even have a glimpse of the mag-istrate's face for several years. Untutored people, having no way to make known their grievances [and obtain redress], are thus com-pelled to resort to feuds. After the fights are over [the local official] still expects [the parties involved to give him] bribes. No attempt is made at distinguishing the wrong from the right. As a result, the people become resentful; incidents arise in which the authority of the government is openly defied. . . .
>
> Investigation shows that there are many reasons why people en-gage in feuds. Some of them are by nature violent and pugnacious. They habitually value money more than their lives, and are ready to die in quarrels over trifles . . . or for a sum of a few taels. . . .

There are rogues who practice the use of fowling pieces, waiting to be hired and making manslaughter their occupation. . . . Some clans possess ample resources with which they easily finance feuds. . . . Large villages often try to oppress small ones and cause feuds between them. Small villages, unwilling to submit to their oppression, ally themselves to fight back and thus engage themselves in feuds also. Powerful clansmen, moreover, take advantage of feuds to fatten themselves . . . pettifoggers instigate feuds, bad gentry stir them up, yamen runners promote them . . . all these are glad to have feuds [which to them constitute a source of illicit profits]. . . .

At present the funds of the clans are exhausted; farms and orchards lie uncultivated; the people have no more money with which to buy gunmen. Many cases, however, remain unresolved. [When the magistrate] leads troops to apprehend the offenders, the inhabitants by now have become accustomed to [the ways of the local official] and are no longer afraid [of him]. As a result, while in former times officials who served in these places regarded feuds as a wonderful opportunity to make money, now those who serve there regard them as a distressing matter. [78]

This shows beyond doubt that incompetent or corrupt local administration contributed to the spread and persistence of feuds. [79] On the other hand, there is conclusive evidence that judicious action by a capable magistrate could resolve serious quarrels, even those over vital interests, and prevent them from developing into sanguinary fights. An excellent instance was reported in Mien-chu (Szechwan) late in the eighteenth century. Many of the rural inhabitants were involved in a long dispute over the use of irrigation water but were glad to accept the settlement arranged by the magistrate in 1798. The water available from three irrigation dikes was apportioned to all who needed it. The quantity of water allotted to each farmer varied with the mount of land he cultivated; and the amount of land in turn determined the amount of money he was required to contribute to the maintenance fund. The arrangement was so reasonable and fair that for more than one hundred years no further disputes arose over the use of water. [80]

Riots

General Significance of Riots. For our purpose "riot" is defined as an uprising of local inhabitants against local officials. [81] Riots are distinguished from feuds by the fact that they arose as a consequence of the hatred of the inhabitants of a given locality toward one or more of the local functionaries, whereas feuds were open conflicts between the inhabitants themselves. In some instances, as indicated previously, feuds might develop into riots; the line of demarcation between these two types of violence is therefore not always distinct. Nevertheless, they are readily distinguishable by the primary object toward which violence was directed.

"Riot" is distinguished from "rebellion" which, for the purpose of the present discussion, is defined as an open, armed resistance to the established government with a view to overthrowing it. [82] Rioters did not oppose the government, central or local, as such. On the contrary, they implicitly or expressly acknowledged the authority of the emperor and officials in general, and did not intend by their violent demonstrations to accomplish anything beyond removing some specific grievances or inflicting insult and injury on the objects of their wrath.

The nature of riots was well understood by a number of writers of the nineteenth century. An American writer on Chinese affairs pointed out:

> The Chinese people have in numberless instances risen in opposition to their local rulers, but it has been an uprising against abuses of the system of government, never against the system itself. They have been known to deal with a local magistrate . . . in a most democratic and unceremonious manner; have gone so far as to pull his queue and slap his face; but it was not because of the exercise on his part of lawful authority, but because he had exceeded it. [83]

This assertion is substantially correct and has been corroborated by the observations of other writers. A British official, for example, who was an eyewitness of the riot of January, 1846, in Canton, noted that when the yamen of the prefect of Kuang-chou was temporarily taken possession of by the tumultuous mob, the portions of it occupied by the local official and his assistants as offices and living quarters were partially burned down, but the division that contained the trial hall and treasury was significantly left untouched, for the obvious reason that the money in the treasury belonged to the emperor and the hall was a court of imperial justice. [84] The description of a "model riot" by an American writer around 1896 is even more illuminating:

> I once saw a procession of country people visit the yamens of the city mandarins. . . . Shops were shut and perfect stillness reigned, as, twenty thousand strong, they wended their way through the streets, with banners flying, each at the head of a company and each inscribed with the name of a temple where that company held its meetings. "What is the meaning of this demonstration?" I inquired. "We are going to reduce the taxes," was the laconic answer. Petitions had been tried in vain, and now, driven to desperation, they were staking everything on a last appeal, with its alternative—revenge. The mandarins did not stay to hear them; and, throwing into heaps the furniture of their oppressors—silken cushions, gauze curtains, carved chairs, and other objects of costly luxury—the rioters applied the torch and

consumed the whole as inexorably as the spoil of Jericho. A man whom I saw making off with something valuable was brought back and his booty thrown into the fire; but he, I believe, escaped the fate of Achan.

Similar scenes were enacted at every yamen in the city, and, strange to say, the peaceful inhabitants were not molested, save that business was interrupted for a day. The conflict was with the mandarins only; the rioters were under strict discipline, and still professed loyalty to the supreme government. Entering the yamen of the *chehien,* or mayor [i. e., *chih-hsien,* magistrate], to watch the proceedings, I noticed a company of rioters guarding a portion of the building while their comrades were eviscerating the rest. Inquiring why they were mounting guard instead of joining the loot, they answered simply, "This is the treasury, and no man shall touch the emperor's money. " Their grievance was not taxation, but excessive charges made by local officers to cover the expense of collection. A month later the provincial governor sent against the rioters a force of fifteen hundred men. Caught in an ambuscade, these troops were beaten with a loss of fifty killed and twice as many wounded. . . .

Force having failed to reduce the rioters to submission, the governor tried persuasion. He dismissed the obnoxious mandarins and promised to put an end to their exactions if the ringleaders were delivered up. These men, Cheo and Chang . . . surrendered themselves to gain their object and stop the plague of war. They were, however, put to death. [85]

The difference between such riots and rebellion against the government itself is clear. It was natural for the people to feel resentment against a corrupt local official rather than against the despotic central government. The latter was so remote from the life of the average villager that any ill-usage it might practice hurt much less directly than the extortions of the former. It should also be recalled that "the emperor cult" had since the time of the Han dynasty been so deeply entrenched in the consciousness of the people that while few acknowledged any positive loyalty toward the dynasty, many felt a vague reverence toward the "son of heaven, " even though he was a Manchu. Moreover, the bulk of the imperial laws and regulations concerning the everyday life of the people, in their letter if not in their application, were by historical standards far from tyrannical or oppressive. Atrocities committed by local functionaries were usually interpreted correctly by the people as misapplications of imperial mandates rather than measures emanating from the throne itself. An old saying heard in many parts of imperial China, "The heavens are high and the emperor is far away, " gives us a clue to the general attitude of the masses toward their rulers and administrators. [86]

If there was relatively little cause for the common people to bear any grudge against the imperial ruler, they often had ample reason to resent the conduct of many of their local officials. The latter and their underlings dealt with the inhabitants directly and frequently. All their acts, kindly or otherwise, had an immediate effect. Responsibility could easily be fixed. Since they enjoyed no awe-inspiring dignity, they could also readily become objects of odium and contempt, should their conduct entail too much hardship upon the people. Indeed, as a Western writer observed,

> The [professed] benevolence of the Emperor, when filtered down through nine grades of officials, may be turned to vexation and sheer tyranny when it reaches the last rank, which is in contact with the people. The question must therefore be never absent from consideration how the people are to defend themselves from arbitrary officials. . . . In the absence of a tribunal they simply take the law into their own hands. . . . In small local questions the populace will sometimes resent an imposition by seizing the official sent to enforce it, dragging him by the heels out of his sedan-chair, pulling his official boots off— a great indignity—and throwing him into the nearest ditch. [87]

It is not at all surprising, therefore, that uprisings against magistrates and their decisions were quite common in China, [88] while rebellions against the imperial government occurred at much longer intervals.

Not all officials of course were bad, nor was the people's attitude toward them invariably hostile. Local inhabitants reacted differently to magistrates of different qualities; they passed judgment upon them and often expressed their judgments with forceful directness. A few instances may be cited here to show that under suitable circumstances local inhabitants might become fairly articulate—perhaps too outspoken to suit some of the magistrates.

Methods of honoring what local inhabitants regarded as a "good official" were various. One of these was to sing his praise in verses, composed presumably by some member of the local gentry. [89] Another was to invite a "good official" to remain in his post after his term had expired or when he was transferred to another post elsewhere. [90] The apparently enthusiastic inhabitants might petition higher authorities to retain their favorite official; and in comparatively rare instances their wish was granted. [91] The presentation of boots or silk umbrellas took place in farewell ceremonies performed by avowedly grateful inhabitants for departing administrators. [92] Cases were known in which shrines were built to commemorate former magistrates whose fine deeds "had won the hearts of the people."[93]

The fine deeds that allegedly endeared magistrates to local inhabitants were those that were calculated to promote the latter's welfare, such as building schools, repairing defense and irrigation works, attention to the needs of the poor during times of famine, and refusing to receive bribes. [94] Such deeds became especially noteworthy when the number of truly "good officials," those who possessed a sense of duty toward their sovereign and a willingness to help the people, tended to be a small minority among thousands of bad or indifferent ones. A survey of the ninety-seven magistrates occupying the post of Hua Hsien (Kwangtung) from 1686 to 1911, as recorded in a local gazetteer, reveals that only eighteen of them were said to have conducted their administrations creditably or won the approval of the people. [95] Among the 131 magistrates of Chiang-ching (Szechwan) who served between 1661 and 1908, only 50 were recognized as "good." [96] The situation was generally no more encouraging in other parts of the empire.

The picture appears even darker if we take into account the fact that popular demonstrations toward supposedly virtuous officials were often the work of local gentry; they did not necessarily represent the spontaneous or genuine sentiment of the common people. It was said by a local historian:

> Writers of the late Ming dynasty indulged in verbiage. Generally speaking, when they wrote about officials who had received appointments, they described them, each and all, as being so loved by the people that they were entreated to remain in their posts; or when these writers penned biographies of scholars [who attained little success], these were invariably represented as literary talents from whom honors in the examinations were unjustly withheld.
>
> These writers, that is to say, wrote in one and the same pattern. What they said, upon investigation, had no ground in fact at all. [97]

Writers of the Ch'ing dynasty might be more reliable than those of this period, but we are not sure that every one of them was free from this shortcoming. It should be borne in mind at least that since stories of "good officials" were without exception written by members of the gentry, in many cases local scholars on friendly or intimate terms with the local officials, there was the likelihood that these did not faithfully reflect the feelings and wishes of the average townsman or villager.

In fact, an exposé was occasionally made, which suggests that not all "good officials" were unquestionably good. It is true that the exposé might be the work of disgruntled gentry, but it is equally possible that the glowing picture of the official in question was the product of gentry favoritism, having nothing to do with popular sentiment. An interesting case was reported in a district of Shantung late in the seventeenth century. Ch'ang Shen, who was appointed magistrate of T'eng Hsien in 1676, was accorded the double honor of having a stone tablet erected to immortalize his benevolent administration and several "living shrines" constructed to express the worshipful affection

of the inhabitants toward him. It was asserted, however, that the
whole affair was simply a stroke of official deceit, a misrepresentation of the character of his administration as well as a falsification
of the sentiment of the populace. According to a local historian:

> [When Ch'ang Shen] first arrived at T'eng Hsien he caused two plac-
> ards to be displayed outside the gate of the drum tower, which bore
> this inscription: "Punishment for the malignant and evil; riddance
> of rowdies and bullies. Never to practice favoritism; never to desire
> money." After a while, however, bribes were received openly, and
> thieves and robbers found ready cover and protection. [98]

This was not a unique instance. Similar official imposture was
encountered in other parts of the empire and in other periods, as the
following document, dated 1800, testified:

> There is one type of magistrates who, upon picking up information
> that they are about to be impeached by their superiors, bribe a num-
> ber of elderly citizens and make them petition the higher authorities to
> the effect that having heard that the officials concerned are about to be
> transferred to other posts, they earnestly beg the government to
> "loan" these functionaries to them for another term. Even impartial
> and keen governors or governors-general are sometimes deceived.
> . . .
> Another type, knowing that they are not much loved or respected
> by the people, secretly instruct yamen underlings to print circulars
> and post them everywhere, stating in effect that the present incum-
> bents are about to resign their offices on account of ill health and
> that all inhabitants should petition the higher authorities to make them
> stay. These officials then ask their relatives and personal advisers
> to collect these circulars and send them [to influential persons]. [99]

The self-made "popularity" of such officials had little to do with
the feeling of the common people or with the opinion of the gentry.
And, it may be noted, the alleged goodness of officials, even when the
judgment actually originated with ordinary townsmen and villagers,
did not usually amount to very much. According to a nineteenth-century Western observer, the difference between them and bad magistrates was merely a matter of degree.

> The people, knowing that the mandarins cannot possibly live on
> their salaries, excuse and acquiesce in what I term "illegal fees,"
> i.e., certain tolerably well ascertained sums, which everyone who
> applies to a yamen must pay; and then as a natural consequence, the
> mandarins take advantage of a system thus endured as a necessary
> evil, to enforce arbitrary extortions, and oblige people to offer bribes.
> Hence in the whole country corruption and injustice abound. I believe,
> in fact, that *all* mandarins take money exclusive of their salary and
> that the grand difference between what the Chinese call the "good"

and the "bad" mandarin is that while the former makes people *pay
for justice,* the latter *sells injustice* to the highest bidder. [100]

Unfortunately for the common people, "good officials" (whatever
may have been the extent of their "goodness") were few, and bad ones
easily outnumbered them. Some of them made the situation so intolerable that even the normally placid inhabitants might be incited into
violent demonstrations against their malpractices, especially when
disgruntled members of the gentry or "bad elements" of the neighborhoods undertook to organize and direct the rioting mobs. The following statement was made by a Chinese writer of the nineteenth century:

> Even though ordinary people do not understand propriety and right-
> eousness, they certainly have regard for their own persons and fam-
> ilies; even though they may not fear the sovereign, they surely are
> afraid of the law. But since local officials have made their conditions
> absolutely unbearable, the timid among them suffer and die, while a
> few who are daring and crafty often rise in noisy violence, unhesitat-
> ingly violate the law and endanger their lives and families, in order
> to save themselves from death [at the hands of tyrannical officials]
> for a brief moment. The uprisings are quelled, but the type of peo-
> ple [liable to riot] cannot be all killed. As a result the people become
> increasingly acquainted with the disgraceful ways of local officials,
> and begin to entertain little fear toward them. . . . This is the origin
> of "unruly people. "[101]

Despite imperial regulations which provided for punishment of any
official whose offensive or tyrannical conduct resulted in riots involving scholars or common people, [102] local uprisings in which magistrates were the target of popular wrath were reported time and again
in all parts of the empire, ever since the early years of the dynasty.
Sometimes the demonstration against hateful officials took the form
of insult, as in one example described by a magistrate writing in the
1690's.

> I have heard recently that when substandard officials are about to
> leave their posts and begin their trip, inhabitants of the localities
> [under their administrations] who bear grudges against them often
> go as far as to block the city gates, refusing to let them pass. The
> mobs may boisterously throng the streets, undress the wives of these
> officials, and maul their attendants and retainers. [103]

At other times, the rioting mobs did not stop at merely insulting the
detested officials. Thus the Ch'ien-lung emperor observed in an edict
issued in 1741:

> In the 4th month of the present year when the submagistrate of P'ing-
> nan Hsien of Fu-chou Fu [Fukien] went to the countryside to collect the

grain tax, villagers tied him with ropes and beat him. In Hsien-yu Hsien of Hsing-hua Fu when the magistrate was about to depart (having resigned from his post for reasons of health) . . . a local inhabitant surnamed Li was angry with him because the official decided to leave without settling a lawsuit brought up to the yamen. The official was waylaid and badly beaten. [104]

In another edict issued a year later, the same emperor said that "recently there has been an incident in Chang-p'u where local inhabitants assassinated the magistrate with a knife."[105] An even more bloody incident was reported in 1870 in a district of Chekiang, where the inhabitants murdered the magistrate together with his wife and daughter. [106] Riots of this description were presumably rare, but they indicate how violent a roused mob could become.

It should be pointed out that rioters did not always gain the upper hand. The magistrate, with the military force at his command, might be able to deal ruthlessly with them. In fact, the imperial government showed its concern about the situation, as an edict dated 1878 (Kuang-hsü 4) clearly reveals:

> Recently, in the *chou* and *hsien* of the various provinces, when [local officials] tried to extort money from the people and failed to get satisfaction, they promptly charged them with opposing [the government] by force and requested that troops be sent to suppress the "uprisings." Military officials, wishing to earn "merits" by the opportunity thus afforded them, indulged in promiscuous killing. . . . Much abuse resulted. [107]

The emperor went on to forbid governors and governors-general to send out troops "to give trouble to the people." Despite such injunction, however, military force remained in more than one case an effective weapon in the hands of local officials who had the support of their immediate superiors.

Types and Causes of Riots: Antiextortion Riots. Having ascertained the general nature of riots, we shall now attempt to analyze them more closely by inquiring into their causes. As we should expect, various factors led to riots. An edict issued in 1747 makes this quite clear:

> According to reports from the provinces, cases in which wicked people gathered mobs [and created disorder] arose from different causes. Those in Su-ch'ien, Kiangsu, and Lan-shan, Shantung, were all due to unsatisfied demand for famine relief; those in Lin-hai, Chekiang, to disputes connected with rain-prayer; those in Shang-hang, Fukien, to refusal to pay the taxes; and those in An-i and Wan-ch'üan, Shansi, to demand for exemption from the land and labor taxes. [Whatever the causes], the eventual outcome was the same: Large mobs

gathered to defy officials and overrun the yamen—sometimes setting buildings on fire and interrupting official business—in short to engage themselves freely in lawless acts. [108]

This document covers fairly well the known causes of riots, with but one important omission. As already suggested above, inequity (alleged or real) in deciding litigation seems to have been a common cause of local uprisings. [109]

By far the most fertile and important source of riots was official extortion in connection with tax collection. It may be worth while to dwell for a moment on these antiextortion riots. Uprisings of this type had occurred before the Ch'ing dynasty, [110] but they appeared more often after the Opium War when the prestige of the imperial government received its first severe blow and when the rise of local corps in many localities emboldened the hitherto unarmed peasants to challenge the authorities. [111]

Antiextortion riots, like riots of other types, were directed against local functionaries rather than against the imperial government itself, but under certain circumstances they might assume formidable proportions. Usually these riots followed a similar pattern including the following steps: (1) petition by the persons concerned to stop the excessive imposts illegally levied by the local agents; (2) failure of higher officials to palliate the grievances, driving the petitioners to desperation; (3) riot, with varying degrees of ferocity; (4) the crushing of the uprising by military force, or the resolving of it by some sort of compromise, often entailing the punishment of the ringleaders; or, under special circumstances, transformation of the riot into a part of a large-scale revolt. [112]

Riots, however, might assume simpler forms when local inhabitants resorted to violence without going through the time-consuming procedure of petitioning higher authorities.

The "model riot" described above affords a fine instance of typical riots. A few additional examples may be given to illustrate the various circumstances under which riots, from the simplest to the more complex forms, actually arose. All these were reported between the 1840's and the end of the century, [113] and will be summarized here in chronological order.

Our first example occurred in 1842, in Hsiu-shui Hsien (Chekiang), in which an abortive riot was quickly put down by the magistrate. According to local historians:

A worthless person who lived in Hsi Hsiang (Western Rural Area) by the name of Yü Ah-nan assembled a mob to resist tax collection. [Under his leadership] inhabitants of neighboring villages were summoned to work together to bail water into the fields and to erect palisades across the streams, with a view to cutting off the passageway of the tax collectors. . . . [Yü] Shih-li [the magistrate] . . . bought some informers who helped him to seize the ringleaders by means of a clever stratagem. In less than ten days all these were tied with ropes and executed in the marketplace. [114]

The riot of Lui-yang (Hunan) which broke out early in 1843 was one of the most violent demonstrations against local officials. Accounts of the incident do not agree as to where the real responsibilities lay. According to the narrative of a writer who had no personal interest in the issue involved and therefore was likely to be impartial, the affair started with the legal action of a local inhabitant against the magistrate who was charged with "levying taxes in excess of the legal rates." Instead of obtaining redress the person in question was found to have "brought an ungrounded charge" against the magistrate and was punished by flogging and imprisonment. His fellow villagers organized a mob and freed him. Inhabitants of all villages in the two adjacent rural areas refused to pay any tax. Under the leadership of two *sheng-yüan* scholars the rioters armed themselves and attacked the *hsien* city. The tumult did not quiet down until several months later. It was thought that "criminal responsibility rested upon the shoulders of officials; the people were free from any guilt."[115]

Riots were especially frequent in some parts of the empire during the turbulent 1850's. The situation in Kiangsu, for example, was summarized by a censor:

> In the *chou* and *hsien* [the inhabitants] were incited into uprisings by the extortionary practices [of local functionaries] who alleged that the disorder was the result of refusal to pay taxes. . . . In the *chou* and *hsien* excessive levies sometimes amounted to as much as twice the legal rates; or the grain which had already been transported [to the collection points] was rejected and payments in silver were demanded instead. As a result the people's resentment flared into riots; incidents occurred in which mobs were gathered and officials murdered. [116]

Riots, according to another contemporary official, were particularly rampant in Sung-chiang Fu:

> [Inhabitants of] Ch'ing-p'u originated the practice of gathering mobs, resisting the authorities and beating officials. In Nan-hui the granary and the official residence were burned down by the people; the officials barely escaped death. In Hua-t'ing, when the personal attendants [of the magistrate] in charge of tribute-rice collection went into the countryside, rural inhabitants heaped firewood around the boat [in which the said agent traveled] and forced yamen runners to set the pyre on fire. . . . Are these rioters to be dealt with according to the law? That would be to drive them quickly into rebellion. Or are they to be left alone? That would be to encourage resistance. [117]

A Western reporter supplied some of the details of the riot in Hua-t'ing, which are illuminating. It was said that the blundering magistrate assembled two hundred volunteers and armed them with guns to compel the inhabitants to pay the taxes. This precipitated the outbreak:

> The people, not being willing to comply with the demand, sounded the gong and assembled the multitudes in a short space of time to the number of several thousands; when they immediately destroyed by fire two mandarin junks and burned to death four of the village braves, the magistrate escaped barefooted to the city. [118]

Antiextortion riots were not restricted to southern provinces. The uprisings in some parts of Honan province in 1854 and 1855 were especially noteworthy. Rising silver exchange rates and continued official extortion drove the inhabitants of large areas of this province to desperation. [119] Rioting villagers soon organized themselves into *lien-chuang she* (associations of allied villages) to resist tax collectors, coming thus into open clashes with local authorities in Hsin-hsiang and Ho-nei. [120]

Riots spread even to the vicinities of the imperial capital. A Grand Secretary memorialized the throne in 1861 that in northern provinces and localities near the capital it was becoming increasingly common for tax collectors to be resisted by organized mobs. The cause was the appointment of "bad magistrates," whose corrupt practices and high-handed measures had made them bitterly hated by the inhabitants. [121]

Our last instance occurred in the 1890's, long after the downfall of the Taiping regime. It transpired in a district city less than one hundred miles from Peking, and was occasioned by unfair official exchange rates between copper cash and silver taels. The land tax of this locality, legally fixed at a certain decimal part of a tael of silver, was usually paid in copper cash, at an official rate of 2,000 cash per tael. At an unspecified date, however, the rate was arbitrarily altered by a magistrate to 4,000 cash, which perhaps meant a clear profit of 100 per cent for himself and some of his underlings. Matters stood thus for quite a few years, and then trouble began to brew:

> A new incumbent increased the rate to five thousand pieces, and this was quietly paid. Misunderstanding the temper of his constituency, after a few months he raised the rate of exchange to six thousand. Then they grumbled, but they paid. A further increase to seven thousand provoked talk of organized opposition, but nothing practical resulted from it. Before the first half of his term of office had expired he raised the rate again, demanding eight thousand cash for an ounce of silver, or about four times the legitimate amount.

This brought matters to a crisis. A mass-meeting was held, at which it was decided to present a petition to the Emperor, through the censorate. . . . The documents were accordingly prepared and a committee of three influential literati carried them to the capital, and there presented them to the Supreme Court of the Censorate. . . .

[The petition] was returned to them unread, they were each favored with fifty blows of the bamboo, and fined a small sum for contempt of court. They returned home sore and crestfallen, and the local magistrate, in too great haste as the event proved, signalized his victory by increasing the official rate of exchange to nine thousand pieces of cash for an ounce of silver. . . .

Another meeting was at once called, papers were more carefully drawn up . . . and another deputation bore them to the capital. This time they were successful. The offending official was degraded, stripped of his rank, and forbidden to apply for future official employment. [122]

This was a highly exceptional case. Events took a much happier turn here than in other places, probably because the scene was so near the capital that the higher officials thought it wiser to be reasonable with the aroused populace than to resort to the usual tactics of armed suppression; or perhaps because effective leadership from the gentry, as the more or less skillful conduct of the affair indicates, was available to the would-be rioters.

Hunger Riots. Another and equally important type of uprising may be designated as "hunger riots," occasioned by the inability of the government to cope with the situation created by famine. When relief was overdue or when relief work was badly handled, starving people were prone to start trouble, especially upon the instigation of some "wicked elements." For when the choice was between immediate death and "treading the dangerous path," the decision was not very difficult to make. As was correctly said by an eighteenth-century Chinese official: "Recently in areas suffering from natural calamities, owing to the fact that the local functionaries are somewhat tardy in their relief work, lawless elements have plundered villages and market towns, or even caused boisterous disturbances in the yamen."[123] Naturally, hunger riots were likely to become a social epidemic in times of widespread disasters and, like other types of riots, tended to assume formidable proportions in a period of general unrest. But they differed from antiextortion riots in at least one respect: while the latter as a rule were directed against local officials, the former might be aimed at wealthy households as well as at local functionaries.

The motive of hunger rioters was sometimes quite simple. Famished mobs often set out to plunder well-to-do families in the neighborhoods simply to get food. Their purpose was merely to satisfy their immediate physical need, rather than to give vent to their wrath against privileged persons or the authorities. The hunger riots reported during a year of famine in the early nineteenth century in a district of Kwangtung were a case in point:

> Due to the generosity of some wealthy families contributions were at first made [voluntarily] to buy food [for the destitute]. But as time went on, the catch phrase, "share the famine" was invented; now whenever rice is expensive, it has become customary for poor people to assemble themselves in groups and beg for rice from door to door. If their wish is not satisfied, they promptly seize rice by force. . . . Even families of modest means sometimes suffer great losses.[124]

A similar situation was observed in some parts of Kiangsu during a bad year late in the nineteenth century. A well-known Chinese official wrote the following in his diary for the *chi-hai* year (1899), third month, sixth day:

> Vagrant people, men and women, numbering over a hundred, noisily demanded food. . . . I heard that three years ago when villagers beat the gong [to warn inhabitants of the presence of such people, a disorder ensued in which] one of the villagers was killed. They nevertheless collected three *tou* of rice before they departed.[125]

Sometimes, however, the situation was complicated by the introduction of motives of revenge against some particular families. An instance was recorded in the diary of another official for the *hsin-hai* year (1911), seventh month, ninth day:

> Chang Chung-li . . . said that in the two districts, Ch'ang-shu and Chao-wen [Kiangsu], rice was being seized by force; none of the wealthy households, in the city as well as in the countryside, were spared. Rice was spilled over streets and lanes, and all the stores were emptied of their contents. Shao Po-ying, owing to the fact that he was in charge of the granaries, became the most hated person. His house, furniture, and household utensils were all demolished, nothing being left intact. . . . As a matter of fact, he was only nominally in charge of the grain stores; it was one person named Ch'i, a relative of his, who actually embezzled and extorted to fatten himself, thereby suddenly transforming himself from a poverty-stricken scholar into a man of substance with considerable land and property.[126]

Hunger riots, however, often involved opposition to local officials. An edict dated 1832 (Tao-kuang 12) summarized the situation that existed in some rural areas thus:

> Owing to the fact that Kiangsi province suffered a flood last year, which wiped out a part of the harvest, the price of grain this year during the gap between the new and old crops is higher than usual. In the prefectures of Nan-an and Kan-chou, where the soil is not fertile and the inhabitants are poor and especially violent in temper, the governor concerned has repeatedly asked [relevant parties] to lower

the price, urged [those who possess grain] to sell it, and arranged
to borrow grain from nearby places to supply the needs. But local
rowdies took advantage of the famine to intimidate their officials. They
even dared to gather mobs, dash into the yamen, and indulge in clamorous disorder freely. [127]

A hunger riot involving both wealthy people and local officials, with
an exceptionally fortunate ending, occurred in Ting Chou (Chihli) in
1801.

In the sixth year of Chia-ch'ing, this locality suffered a big flood; the
people were starving. Chang Lo-kung, Sung Man-tzu, and seven other
inhabitants of Ch'ih-pao village, which is situated south of the city,
knowing that the family of Li T'o was wealthy and hoarded grain, led
a multitude of hungry people to ask Li to "loan" them some of this
grain. After having been refused, they started to loot. Li went to the
city and brought the matter to the attention of the official, surnamed
Chang, who sent yamen underlings to the number of several dozen [to
deal with the mob]. As these failed to put down the disturbance, the
authorities were considering sending troops to the scene. The famished mob, on the other hand, had developed into a crowd of over
1,800 men, ready to resist.

When Liu Fen heard of this, he thought that the reason that hungry
people assembled to seize grain and oppose the officials was that they
had absolutely no other course open to them. If troops were employed
against them, that would simply drive them speedily into revolt. It was
better to send a persuasive person to convince them with high principles, disperse the mob, and lightly punish their offense. The nine
individuals [who instigated the riot] would not pursue a more dangerous
course, the 1,800 men could be saved, and the locality could preserve
its order and peace.

The official was informed of Liu's ideas. He invited Liu to go to the
rioters, and Liu made the trip alone. When he arrived at Ch'ih-pao
village, Chang Lo-kung and the other ringleaders knelt before him,
begging for mercy. After having dispersed the mob, Liu accompanied
Chang and Sung to the city. The official understood their case thoroughly and treated them with leniency. [128]

Ordinarily, however, hunger riots did not end so happily. As the
rioters were usually loosely organized, and as they were mostly starving people without the benefit of able leadership, such uprisings were
often easily quelled by force. The situation in Han-tan (Chihli) in 1857,
for example, showed how helpless were such unorganized rioters:

Calamities and famines have occurred successively in the past years.
In the present year there is a drought. Locusts are so numerous that
they darken the skies. All crops are gone. Hungry people plunder and
pillage. After the magistrate . . . caught and executed several of the
looters, the rest became more cautious. [129]

Hunger riots were not always suppressed without difficulty. When "bandits" capitalized on the hunger of the bulk of the rural population to make trouble for the government, the situation could become quite serious. This seems to have occurred in some provinces in the 1830's. According to an official document:

> In the provinces of Chihli, Honan, and Shantung *chiao-fei* [religious bandits] spread their creeds one to another. . . . Once famine occurs they, relying on their numerical strength, plunder collectively in broad daylight, calling their marauding activities "equalizing the food. " In the south, *hui-fei* [secret-society bandits] are rampant, especially in the prefectures of Yung, Chen, and Kuei of Hunan, the south Kan region of Kiangsi, and the localities near the borders of Kwangsi. . . . Many law-abiding people, merchants, and travelers in these localities contribute money and join the secret societies in order to avoid being robbed. [130]

It is clear, therefore, that disturbances caused by large numbers of hungry villagers were potentially dangerous for the government. The situation often became explosive, and when it was exploited by those who desired to challenge the authorities, rioters prompted by hunger might readily be turned into rebels aiming at destroying the government. At any rate, it was an easy transition from starving villagers to foraging brigands. The "petition" tendered by a leader of an insurgent band in Kwangtung in the mid-nineteenth century, as translated by a Western writer, is revealing:

> We plebians were born in times of plenty, and were once loyal people; our families are reputable in our village, and we practiced welldoing, and regarded property. Owing to a succession of rainy seasons, the farmers were unable to save the crops, and we had no capital for our business, so that people of all occupations were obliged to join themselves to the bandits. We came into the West province [Kwangsi] seeking a place to remain, when we met fellow townsmen in the same trouble with ourselves, so that *nolens volens* we were forced to become bandits to save ourselves from starvation. [131]

The Role of the Gentry in Riots. The materials presented above show that gentry were sometimes involved in riots. In some instances they were objects of popular resentment, in others they played the part of instigators or organizers of the uprisings.

Gentry and wealthy nongentry households might become objects of local riots in two ways. As hoarders of grain they might be attacked by destitute inhabitants in some of the hunger riots; and as landowners and privileged taxpayers they might share with local officials the rough treatment accorded them by irate antiextortion rioters, especially when they were known to have been partners in official injustice or corruption.

The latter situation has been explained in an earlier chapter of this study, [132] but the following statement contained in an 1846 document may be quoted here:

> In the tribute-rice system of Kiangsu province taxpayers with gentry status have hitherto been called "big households," while commoner taxpayers have been called "small households." The deficits resulting from defaulting "big households" are made up by requiring "small households" to pay [taxes in excess of the amounts legally due]. . . . The tax burdens have thus become unequal and unjust. Popular resentment bubbles and boils, and numerous troubles are reported. [133]

This observation was corroborated by a nineteenth-century writer, who attributed to the same cause the violent demonstrations in the form of "smashing grain stores, demolishing yamen, resisting the authorities, and killing local officials" that were reported "every year in every locality of Kiangsu."[134] Similar situations existed in other provinces than Kiangsu. A number of particularly serious uprisings of this description occurred in some districts of Chekiang, Kiangsi, Hunan,[135] and Hupeh[136] during the nineteenth century. In all these incidents the local gentry, often as a result of their odious conduct, became objects of mob violence.

The role of the gentry as instigators or organizers of riots was an important one and therefore calls for close examination. As we shall presently see, they figured prominently in almost all the relatively large-scale uprisings on record. Commoners of course were capable of starting riots on their own, when grievances were keenly felt by a large number of inhabitants. The antiextortion riot reported in Hsiu-shui (Chekiang) in 1842 was led by Yü Ah-nan, a "worthless fellow," whose modest social status is clearly indicated by his personal name.[137] This and other riots that did not enjoy gentry support or guidance, however, were likely to be badly organized and easily quelled. The importance of the gentry in this connection was due not only to their superior status but also to their literacy, which gave them certain knowledge or skills highly useful in the situation. For this reason, scholars who had not as yet earned any examination degree and therefore were not members of the gentry also frequently played a crucial role in many an uprising. For the sake of convenience, we shall refer to such scholars as "literati" in the present discussion to distinguish them from titled scholars, who are considered here as members of the gentry.

As persons to whom their fellow villagers looked for leadership, the gentry and to a somewhat lesser extent the literati often undertook to promote local interests or to defend them when these were threatened. And, as individuals with special social and financial status (as landowners and taxpayers enjoying privileges and immunities), the gentry and literati had special interests of their own, which they were ready to advance or protect when occasion demanded. Naturally, therefore, some of them did not hesitate to resort to mob violence when local officials acted contrary to local or private interests or had a reputation of so acting. Instances are numerous, but the following incident in which a newly appointed magistrate known for his "arbitrary and tyrannical" ways was ejected by a threatened riot before he could take office, is of particular interest. The incident which took place in a district in Hupeh in the 1840's was, according to a Western missionary, as follows:

> A Mandarin had been named governor [magistrate] of the town of whom the inhabitants did not approve. It was known that in the district he had just left his administration had been arbitrary and tyrannical, and that the people had suffered much from his injustice and extortion.
>
> The news of his nomination to Ping-fang therefore excited general indignation, which showed itself at first in the most violent satirical placards. A deputation of the chief citizens set off for the capital of the province, to present to the viceroy [governor-general] a humble petition to have pity on the poor people of Ping-fang, and not to send them a tiger, who would eat them up, instead of a father and mother to take care of them. The petition was refused, and the Mandarin ordered to set off to take possession of his post on the following day.
>
> The deputies returned, bringing this sad news to their fellow citizens. The town was plunged into consternation, but did not confine itself to idle lamentation. The principal people assembled, and held a grand council, to which all the most influential citizens were invited. It was decided that the new governor should not be permitted to install himself, and that he should be civilly ejected from the town.
> . . .
> Scarcely had he entered the tribunal, [when] . . . it was announced to him that the chief citizens of the town requested an audience. . . . The deputation prostrated themselves . . . before their new Prefect [magistrate]; then, one of them stepping forward, announced to him, with exquisite politeness and infinite grace, that they came in the name of the town, to request that he would set off directly to return whence he came, for they would have none of him.
> The Prefect . . . endeavoured first to soothe, and then to intimidate, the rebellious citizens, but all in vain. . . . The spokesman very calmly told him that they had not come there to discuss the matter; that the thing was settled, and they had made up their minds that he should not sleep in the town. In order to leave him no doubt as to their real intention, he added that a palanquin waited before the door, and that the town would pay his traveling expenses, beside providing a brilliant escort to conduct him safely to the capital of the province.
> . . .
> The prefect still endeavoured to raise objections; but a great crowd

had gathered round the house, uttering cries of a far from flattering or reassuring nature, and he saw that it would be imprudent to resist. He yielded, therefore, to his destiny, and signified his willingness to comply with their demand. . . . The cavalcade immediately set off; still accompanied by the chief men of the town.

On reaching their destination, they went straight to the Viceroy's palace. . . . The Viceroy, with some appearance of dissatisfaction, took the roll [containing a petition signed with the names of all the most important people of Ping-fang], read it attentively, and then told the deputies that their arguments were advanced on reasonable grounds, and should be attended to. [138]

"The chief citizens" and "the chief men of the town" were in all probability members of the local gentry and literati, who alone could have written the "satirical placards" as well as the "petition" to the governor-general. (In fact, the "deputation" that went to present the petition to the provincial authorities was probably composed of persons who in imperial times were privileged to visit the yamen.) Perhaps it was owing to their effective leadership that the unacceptable official was prevented from assuming his post in Ping-fang.

Incidents of this sort, however, were relatively rare. More frequently, violent demonstrations against magistrates were promoted by scholars or literati who felt that they had suffered injustice in the local examinations. The riots reported in the 1730's in Ch'ang-li (Chihli) and Fu-an (Fukien) have already been noted in a previous chapter. [139] The riots that repeatedly occurred in some districts of Chekiang in the late 1860's were particularly annoying to the authorities. [140] But since scholars lacked sufficient numerical and physical strength to make their demonstrations really violent, they usually inflicted more insult than injury on the officials involved. When resentful scholars (or gentry) took advantage of popular grievances and enlisted the help of the masses, however, the resulting commotions could be quite terrifying. The riot of scholars who aspired to the *sheng-yüan* degree in Feng-hua (Chekiang) in 1845, for instance, was originally directed against the magistrate who was charged with "gross and flagrant partiality" in conducting previous examinations. But it happened that he also had levied "an unauthorized amount of taxes on the people." The scholars promptly used this also as a *casus belli* against the official. "On the first day of the literary examinations the assembled scholars rose against the authorities, and, being joined by the populace, put the *che-heen* [i. e., *chih-hsien*, magistrate] to flight." [141]

As landowners and taxpayers the gentry might resort to violence when their personal interests were seriously threatened or impaired. Many instances were reported in which scholars with examination degrees or persons possessing official ranks played active roles in local riots. The ringleaders of the mobs from the two rural areas that staged the antiextortion riot in Lui-yang (Hunan) in 1843 were both definitely identified as holders of the *sheng-yüan* degree.[142] A *sheng-yüan* was chiefly responsible for the uprising in Ling-shan (Kwangtung) in 1846, when local inhabitants rose in violent protest against "oppressive levies," gathered mobs and demolished the tax collector's office.[143] The description written by a Western observer of a riot in Chekiang in the mid-nineteenth century is especially revealing:

> It originated in some extortionate proceedings on the part of the officers of government in the collection of taxes, and was, unfortunately for them, joined by the literati, the most influential and powerful class. A deputation of three proceeded from the revolted districts to Ningpo, and repaired with their grievances to the chief magistrate [prefect]. Far from giving ear to them, he questioned the reality of their literary pretensions, and called on them to prove it by quotations from the "Four books." They, however, declined the test, and declared that they came to discuss grievances, not to repeat the classics. The magistrate grew angry; and an assistant unadvisedly suggested that the most forward of the appellants should be visited with the punishment of "face slapping" for contempt of court, this was unfortunately administered. The discomfited deputation indignantly returned to the enraged population of Foong-hwa [Feng-hua], who resolved to be revenged. . . .
>
> An engagement afterwards took place between the rioters and the Ningpo militia, in which six hundred, or, as some said, a thousand, of the latter were defeated. . . . At this time, on the 12th of October [1847] the French minister arrived from Chusan in the Nemesis steamer, which had been placed at his service. At eight o'clock in the morning the acting chief magistrate called on the [British] consul, saying that he was anxious to see the French minister. . . . He appeared very low spirited, stating that there were bad accounts from Foong-hwa; that three mandarins had been killed and the militia defeated; that the Taoutae *[Tao-t'ai,* circuit intendant] was a prisoner with the rebels, who would probably soon advance on Ningpo.[144]

The whole business was finally quieted down after the rioters heard that ten or twelve thousand troops had arrived at Ningpo and several of the local functionaries had been punished.

Gentry participation in riots was not limited to these few provinces. It was discovered, for example, that one of the leaders of *lien-chuang she,* organizations of antiextortion rioters, in some parts of Honan in 1854 and 1855 was a *sheng-yüan.*[145] He was the only one apprehended, but there may have been other leaders with a similar status. The antiextortion uprisings reported in some localities of Shantung in 1858 were led by salaried *sheng-yüan* and military *sheng-yüan.*[146] A *chü-jen* and his associates were responsible for starting the antiextortion riots in a district in Kweichow in 1884-85, which eventually developed into an uprising that resulted in the siege of the prefectural city of T'ung-jen and the death of the prefect. [147] In fact, gentry leadership in antiextortion riots became so common in Kwangsi that a nineteenth-century Chinese writer did not hesitate to say that persons "possessing an official rank or half an official grade readily relied on their influence to resist the government; local officials dared not talk about urging payment of the taxes."[148]

It is clear, therefore, that the gentry were inclined to play an active role in antiextortion riots—perhaps more so than in other types of riots—for the simple reason that as taxpayers their interests were directly at stake when the local magistrate and his underlings overstepped the margin of safety in demanding too much from landowners. Titled scholars or persons with official status were not the only taxpayers; but owing to their literacy and knowledge of the ways of government, they were the logical persons to initiate organized opposition to corrupt officials. Other landowners could be readily persuaded to join them, and it would not be too difficult for the instigators of riots to coax or compel their tenants to march with them to the yamen of the offending functionary.

It was possible, as in some of the feuds in South China, for the gentry leaders to hire substitutes for themselves to receive the punishment intended for them after their uprisings had been quelled. This cowardly device undoubtedly rendered the instigators less hesitant in goading resentful inhabitants to challenge the local authorities, using them as cat's paws for their private purposes. The observations of a Western writer made in the early 1840's is particularly revealing:

> In the department of Ch'au Chou [Ch'ao-chou Fu], in the east of Kwangtung, a substitute may be procured to confess himself guilty of a felony, and suffer certain capital punishment, for about fifty taels of silver. . . . Hence it is, that the murder of mandarins and riots are so frequent there; for when a number of individuals of the richer classes are dissatisfied with the conduct of a mandarin, they are never prevented from instigating the lower classes to make disturbances by the fear of personal punishment. In the autumn of 1843, a district magistrate of the Ch'au Chou department being killed in a disturbance, the provincial judge was, in consequence, despatched from Canton, with a force numerically strong, to seize and punish the criminals. He found, however, on his arrival at the scene of the disturbance, a large body of men assembled in arms to oppose him; and the matter was, as frequently happens in such cases in China, ended by a secret compromise.
>
> The gentry who had instigated the murder of the district magistrate, awed by the force brought against them, bought about twenty substitutes, and bribed the son of the murdered man with, it is said, one hundred thousand dollars, to allow these men to call themselves the instigators, principals, accomplices, etc. The judge, on the other

hand, obliged by the Code of the Board of Civil Service, to execute somebody, or see himself involved in punishment, and knowing that if he attempted to bring the real offenders to justice, they would employ all their means of resistance, which might easily end in the defeat of his force, and his own death, gave way to these considerations, supported by a bribe, and put the twenty innocent substitutes to death. [149]

We have no evidence to show that such a dastardly practice was widespread. But its appearance even in a limited area serves to throw additional light on the relationship between gentry and the common people in local riots.

Banditry

The word "banditry" was loosely used by the Ch'ing government. In official parlance "bandits" might denote any outlaws, from ordinary robbers to outright rebels. In the present discussion we use "banditry" to denote any predatory activity exhibited by individuals or groups that employed physical force to prey upon their fellow inhabitants. Banditry in this sense is distinguishable from "revolt" or "rebellion." Rebels had as their objective the overthrowing of the existing regime, but bandits broke laws without aiming to destroy the government itself. The latter might sometimes openly disobey the established authorities merely as a measure of self-preservation or as a necessary step to carrying out their marauding activities. Thus in actual situations the line between banditry and revolt was not always clear, but the broad distinction between them remains valid.

Banditry had its roots in poverty. [150] It would be inaccurate to say, however, that hungry villagers by themselves were necessarily committed to banditry. Their passivity was so deeply ingrained that hunger alone was not sufficient to stir them up into predatory activities. As we have already noted, destitute peasants often chose to wander, to beg, or to die, rather than "to tread the dangerous path." Two conditions had to exist: the presence of "wicked people" and serious social unrest in a given locality, before some of the normally docile villagers became bandits.

The first-named condition existed almost continuously in many of the villages. The role of "wicked people" in promoting banditry is well known. As a Chinese writer observed in the early nineteenth century:

> When violent people rise, many of them become bandits. The real cause is hunger. At first [hungry people] may engage in burglary or theft, then perhaps in "buying rice" or "borrowing" it by force; and finally in outright plunder. There, however, must be some bullies or evil persons of the neighborhoods who covertly instigate [them to

take such actions]. Untutored people, being destitute and having no way to make a living, are deceived and lured by them; consequently they rob and pillage. Wealthy families that suffered losses sometimes take up arms and defend themselves [against the marauders]. When the latter sustain occasional casualties, they become aroused and desire to take vengeance. They may gather mobs numbering hundreds or thousands, further to rob and plunder.[151]

The truth of this observation may be partly seen from the following account of the developments witnessed in Ling-shan (Kwangtung), where a famished populace was driven first into riots and banditry, and finally into insurrection:

Ling-shan Hsien is situated in a mountainous region where ravines are deep, forests thick, and bandits numerous. Whenever famines occur and the functionaries do not know how to care for and pacify the people, disorders are frequently reported. In the 4th month of Tao-kuang 4th year [1824] Ch'en Chi-tung, a bandit, taking advantage of a famine caused by drought, incited hungry people to rise. . . .

In the 19th year [1839] Ho Yung, a follower of Hung Hsiu-ch'üan, came to this district to recruit members for the *T'ien-ti-Hui* [Heaven-Earth Society]. Disorders started with the plundering of the government revenue stored at Hsi-chiang. . . .

In the 12th month of the 26th year [1846] townsfolk who were pained by obnoxious extortions, assembled a mob and burned down the tax collector's office. . . . [From that point on, banditry flourished.]

In the 4th month of the 28th year [1848] Chang Chia-hsiang [a "wicked man" from Shao-ch'ing], launched the great uprising. . . . His slogan was to rob the rich to succor the poor. Wherever he went he compelled wealthy families to "contribute" money. . . .

In Hsien-feng 1st year [1851] Yen Ta, Ch'en Chi-k'ao . . . and Chou T'ing-ming, gathering several thousand followers, occupied Lu-wu, Chiu-chou, and Sung-t'ai-lien, and robbed wealthy families. . . .

In T'ung-chih 11th year [1872] Liu Hsien led his men, stormed the city, burned down the yamen, and plundered the streets. The price of rice was high that year.[152]

It is evident then that the various disturbances in this unhappy locality were the work of seasoned troublemakers, facilitated by the existence of a large army of starving people. Although in this case it is a little difficult to tell exactly where riots ended and banditry began or where banditry gave place to insurrection, the decisive role of troublemakers is clearly discernible throughout the entire development.

"Wicked People." A brief examination of the behavior of the trouble-makers is therefore necessary for an understanding of the bandit phenomenon. The Ch'ing government, as indicated elsewhere, made a dis-

tinction between *liang-min* (good people) and *yu-min* (weed people) or
chien-min (wicked people). This distinction made by the government
does not necessarily indicate the real qualities of the persons so cat-
egorized, but it does indicate that among the vast population of imperial China there were some elements that ordinarily tended to remain docile and peaceful and other elements that inclined to be unruly and predaceous, thus constituting not only a worry for the authorities but a menace to the security of their fellow inhabitants.

Various types of such "wicked people" were found in almost every
part of the empire. A few of the commonly known may be usefully
described here. There were the *kuang-kun* (bare sticks or beggars),
members of certain secret societies, and "renegade soldiers and
wandering braves." One of the most familiar types, the *kuang-kun*,
was present in almost all markets and villages. The following vivid
description written by a nineteenth-century Western missionary of
what he called "the village bully" serves to show the general behavior
of this species:

> In his simplest form, a Chinese bully is a man of a more or less vi-
> olent temper and strong passions, who is resolved never to "eat loss,"
> and under all circumstances to give as good (or as bad) as he gets.
> . . . A shrewd villager will sometimes adopt the expedient . . . of
> wearing his clothes in a loose and rowdy-like fashion, talking in a
> boisterous tone, and resenting contradiction or any overt lack of com-
> pliance with his opinions. . . .
>
> By persistently following out his peculiar lines of action, he will
> not unlikely succeed in diffusing the impression that he is a danger-
> ous man to interfere with, and will be in consequence let severely
> alone. . . .
>
> Much more to be dreaded is the bully who will not let others alone,
> but who is always inserting himself into their affairs with a view to
> extracting some benefit for himself. The most dangerous type of these
> men is the one who makes very little ado, but whose acts are ruinous
> to those whom he wishes to injure. . . .
>
> It is a useful, but by no means a necessary qualification of the bully,
> that he should be a poor man, with nothing to lose. Poverty in China is
> often a synonym for the most abject misery and want . . . and thou-
> sands of persons never know whence the next meal is to come. Such
> persons would in European countries constitute what are called "the
> dangerous classes." In China, unless their distress is extreme, they
> do not mass themselves, and they seldom wage war against society
> as a whole. But individuals of this type may, if they have other re-
> quisite abilities, become "village kings," and order the course of
> current events much according to their own will.
>
> Such persons, in the figurative language of the Chinese, are called
> "barefoot men," in allusion to their destitute condition, and it is a
> common saying that "the barefoot man (otherwise known as 'mud-
> legs') is not afraid of him who has stockings on his feet," for the

former can at once retreat into the mud, where the latter dare not
follow. In other words, the barefoot man is able to hold in terror the
man who has property to lose, by an open or an implicit threat of
vengeance, against which the man of property cannot safeguard himself.

The forms which this vengeance will take vary according to circumstances. One of the most common is that of incendiary fires. . . .

Another method by which the bully signifies his dissatisfaction with
his enemy, is by injuring his crops. [153]

To increase their fearful influence and power, bullies often organized their comrades into a sort of intangible predatory army, readily
called into action at a moment's notice. These gangster groups were
sometimes responsible for the feuds and riots that time and again
broke out in rural China, and for this reason they may be said to
have been "a formidable foe to the peace of Chinese society." To
quote from the same missionary:

Let us suppose that a man has a violent personal quarrel with an enemy. An outbreak of their feud occurs at a great fair, such as abound
at almost all seasons of the year. One of the men is intimate with
another man who is a professional bully and who has within call a
number of associates who can be depended upon in an emergency. The
man who knows the bully goes to him and tells him of the grievances
and asks his help. The bully lets it be known among his comrades that
a friend is in need of assistance, and that their services will be called
for. The party assembled goes to that section of the fair-ground. . . .
With this lawless band . . . the bully sets upon his victim and wins
an easy victory. . . . It does not follow that there is any regular organization among the rough members of the dangerous classes who
are assembled, except that they are ready to unite in anything which
promises the joy of battle, and a probable reward in the shape of a
complimentary feast. [154]

It should be added, however, that bullies and "sticks" did not limit
their activities to enjoying fights and feasts. They might at different
times engage themselves in a wide variety of rascally enterprises,
ranging from blackmail to burglary. [155] In some localities special
conditions gave rise to specialized forms of troublemaking. It was
said, for example, that the "local sticks" of Kweichow province exhibited the following behavior:

Their comrades are called together, several dozen in a group. On
ordinary days [when there are no markets] they use whatever pretext that suits them to blackmail and extort payments from law-abiding families; with sticks and swords in hand, they insult or beat [those
that fail to satisfy their demands]. In the worst cases they bind [their
victims] with ropes, hang them up and thrash them, stopping [the
torture] only when their desires are fully gratified. On market days

they carry broken vessels, boards of parcels which they promptly drop to the ground after having purposely collided with some hapless person. They then charge [their victim with the responsibility of causing the supposed damage]. If he argues with them, their comrades maul him, robbing him of whatever money or goods he happens to have with him. Nobody dares interfere. Such wicked "sticks" are especially numerous in Tseng-Chou-Ma-ch'ang, Chang-kuan-pao, Shuang-pao-ch'ang of Chen-ning Chou; Chiu-chou-ch'ang and Cha-lung-ch'ang of An-shu Fu. They are found in the markets of other localities [of Kweichow]. [156]

In some parts of South China a different variety of bullies operated. According to a report quoted by a Western writer, these members of the "dangerous classes"

> . . . carry off persons in order to extort ransoms for them; they falsely assume the characters of police officers; they build fast boats professedly to guard the grain-fields, and into these they put from ten to twenty men, who cruise along the rivers, violently plundering the boats of travelers, or forcibly carrying off the wives and daughters of the tanka boat people. The inhabitants of the villages and hamlets fear these robbers as they would tigers, and do not offer them any resistance. The husbandman must pay the robbers a charge, else as soon as his crop is ripe it is plundered and the whole field laid bare. [157]

Troublemakers became a real problem for the authorities when they developed a high degree of physical courage, and, in the words of a Western missionary,

> . . . make it a sport and a matter of pride to defy the laws and the magistrates, and commit all kinds of crimes. To give and receive wounds with composure; to kill others with the most perfect coolness; and to have no fear of death for yourself: this is the sublime ideal of the Kouan-kouen [kuang-kun, bare stick]. [158]

It is not difficult to see that "bare sticks" had not far to go to become lawless marauders. This tendency can easily be demonstrated with a few instances supplied by eighteenth- and nineteenth-century writers. In an official document issued in 1745 by the governor of Shensi, the behavior of the kua-tzu, a northern version of the "sticks," was described as follows:

> It is reported that in the regions around Hu Hsien and Chou-chih [Hsien] there is a band of kua-tzu who . . . "beg" food by force in the day and set [grain stores] on fire in the evening . . . taking advantage of the situation thus created to seize [the grain]. . . .
>
> It is reported by [the magistrate of] Hsien-ning Hsien that there is a band of kua-tzu outside the walls of Hua-wang ts'un [village]—a

total of twenty-six men and women speaking the Shansi dialect. They
bring with them two horses and seventeen mules and donkeys. . . .
Investigation reveals that these wandering people who have come from
other localities . . . rely on their numerical strength to bully, intimidate, and harass [the inhabitants of] villages which they happen to visit. Inevitably, they pillage and plunder whenever opportunities are offered to them. [159]

In another document of the same date, the governor called attention
to the activities of the "sticks" native to Shensi:

In many localities of Shensi pugnacious, violent people abound, who
rely on their strength to tyrannize over their neighbors, induce [in-
nocent people] to join the bandits . . . or gather mobs to engage in
highway robbery. . . . They do not fear the imperial laws, nor do
they submit to the discipline of their fathers or elder brothers. Good
people, being afraid of their vengeance, dare not report [their malpractices to the government]. . . . Untutored people perceive that
these fellows are beyond the reach of the law and that it is profitable
and safe [to follow their course]; as a result, worthless elements in
these localities . . . imitate their wicked ways, doing even greater
damage [to innocent people]. [160]

In some localities, "wicked people" might be "beggars" who made
a living by "begging" but readily extorted money by force or became
outright brigands. A document of the eighteenth century contains this
information:

In cities and villages of various localities of Kiangsi is found a type
of wicked beggars, known as *chien-tzu-hang*, who make a living by
"begging." They are not decrepit or disabled, but are young, robust,
and violent fellows. In groups of three to five men they rush into
houses to demand rice and money. The slightest rebuff sends them
into endless noisy clamor. Their behavior in teahouses and wineshops
is even more unrestrained. . . . They are not so numerous in the cities, but the situation is very bad in villages. [161]

The troublesome conduct of these beggars did not stop at molesting
and extorting money from the inhabitants. Another document dated
a few years later describes the behavior of the marauding "beggars":

The criminals recently arrested, who are guilty of highway robbery
or other crimes punishable by death, are mostly able-bodied "beggars." . . . They lodge at whatever place they may find, in abandoned temples or under arches of bridges. The *pao-chia* cannot control them, nor can militiamen or yamen runners watch over their
doings. They have become outlaws and therefore repeatedly commit
lawless acts. [162]

"Wicked beggars" of a slightly different kind were reported in some parts of Hunan late in the eighteenth century:

> These fellows use as a pretext the fact that neighboring districts have suffered bad harvests in the previous year to enter Ning-yüan; they number no less than six or seven hundred persons. They make troubles in the rural areas. In the worst instances, inhabitants of remote, isolated villages have to move away temporarily [to avoid being molested]. . . . Their chief is designated as *Lao-hou* [The Old Monkey], alias "Sky-flying Centipede"; his wife is nicknamed "Sky-flying Yaksha. " He is only fifty years old, versed in the art of boxing. [The couple] have been living in a cave within the boundaries of this district for sixteen or seventeen years. His comrades, numbering about sixty or seventy men, go out on different routes to "beg" and support the couple with food by daily turns. . . . Any person who incurs the displeasure of the gang will be roughly treated by them; none dare oppose them. [163]

Similar "beggar" bands existed in some parts of the empire in the nineteenth century. An edict dated 1836 (Tao-kuang 16) said:

> Recently, in the mountainous regions lying on the borders of three neighboring provinces . . . namely, in the districts of Shang-jao and Kuang-feng, belonging to Kuang-hsin Fu, Kiangsi; the districts of Ch'ung-an and P'u-ch'eng, belonging to Chien-ning Fu, Fukien; and the districts of Lung-ch'üan and Ching-yüan, belonging to Ch'u-chou Fu, Chekiang, a species of beggar-bandits, known as *hua-tzu-hui* [beggars' associations] have maintained a hold on the land. These are worthless fellows who have come from different places; they organize into groups and harass the local inhabitants. . . . There are in their associations such titles as the "Big Chief, " "Deputy Chief, " "Division Chief, " etc. . . . When they wish to gather a mob to intimidate and extort payments [from the inhabitants], they send a message to their comrades by passing along in all directions a bamboo chopstick upon which a chicken feather and a copper cash have been affixed. Upon seeing this, members belonging to the associations immediately dash to [the rendezvous]. [164]

Obviously, some of the secret societies found in various parts of the empire might practice banditry in times when they were not ready to break out in open revolt. A variety of them, reported in eighteenth-century Szechwan, where they continued to exist in later times in slightly modified forms, was characterized by a contemporary writer as follows:

> Investigation reveals that there are many types of the *kuo-lu*. Generally speaking, they all originate in gambling and end in burglary or robbery, passing through intermediate stages of inebriation, rowdyism, extorting food, and kidnapping. In the worst cases, they may

commit murder and arson, or commit suicide in a group. All those
[who engage in such activities] call themselves "Red-cash brothers."
These types [of *kuo-lu*] do not engage in petty theft. Below these types
are pickpockets. Those [who have been punished by] having their faces
branded are not admitted into the Red-cash [gangs]; they constitute
separately the "Black-cash" [gangs].

One type of the *kuo-lu* is partly composed of dismissed yamen runners. After having committed crimes in one district, they go to another to enlist as yamen runners again. Consequently [the *kuo-lu*]
usually enjoy the connivance of yamen runners; they together are accomplices in crime. "Ko-lao" [Brother-elder] is an incorrect name
derived from *kuo-lu*. [165]

The following statement contained in an official document of the
late nineteenth century serves to indicate the general pattern of the
predaceous activities of some of the secret societies in other regions
of this period:

Hui-fei [society-bandits] have been most rampant in Szechwan, Hunan,
Kweichow, Kwangsi, and Kwangtung. At first they were lawless, wandering people who burned incense and organized societies. When their
organizations have waxed strong and their members become numerous,
they rely on their strength to tyrannize their neighborhoods and vic-
timize the good people. The humble people, being helpless, may join
their societies for self-protection. Such societies assume diverse
names, e. g., *Ko-lao* [Brother-elder], *An-ch'in* [Contentment-affec-
tion], *T'ien-ti* [Heaven-earth], and *San-tien* [Three-dots]. They operate in every *chou* and *hsien*. Each local unit numbers several dozen
or several hundred men. All the units keep in touch one with another. [166]

One should not overlook the fact that under special circumstances
some of the government troops might engage in banditry or become
bandits. Persons who enlisted in the imperial troops were, as is
well known, mostly the unstable elements of their home communities. Even though they were not exactly social riffraff, they were
likely to be persons without regular occupations or means of living.
This lent plausibility to the oft-repeated jingle: "Good iron does not
make nails; good men do not become soldiers." Imperial troops were
notorious for their readiness to engage in looting while they were
supposed to fight bandits. Instances of this behavior are numerous,
but the following one observed in 1861 in Chekiang suffices to illustrate how government troops might be given opportunity to practice
banditry under unsettled conditions:

Atrocities committed by government troops are a hundredfold worse
than those perpetrated by [the Taiping] rebels. In the spring of last
year [1861] the rebels ordered that markets in An-chang and Tou-

men [rural towns in Chekiang] be held as usual. The inhabitants accordingly repaired their houses and set up markets. Merchandise of
every description converged, making these two towns more prosperous then before. But since the winter [of the same year] when the
French . . . led soldiers to advance on Ningpo and Shao-hsing, all
idlers [of these localities] enlisted in the government army. The
number of these ruffians became especially large in the present year
[1862]. Some of the simple-minded peasants helped these enlisted men
to kill a few of the rebels, who angrily set fire to the villages of Sung-
lin, Hsia-fang-ch'iao, Hou-pao, T'ao-yen, Tao-hsü, Tung-kuan, An-
ch'ang, and Tou-men. . . . Government troops evaded the rebels but
practiced brigandage as usual.[167]

These elements did not cease to make trouble in the countryside
even after they were disbanded at the conclusion of a campaign, or
when they were detached from the government forces for one reason
or another. They became, in official parlance, "renegade soldiers
and wandering braves." They presented a serious problem to the government, as for example, after the conclusion of the war against the
Taiping rebels. The following account reveals one of the usual modes
of operation of such bandits:

After the incident of Ling-shan [Kwangsi, i. e., the clash with the
French troops in 1884], when the government forces were disbanded
all weapons were not surrendered [by the soldiers], who often became "wandering braves" and depended on their weapons to rob travelers and merchants. . . . Some of the robber bands numbered as
many as tens of thousands. These "wandering braves" robbed travelers only; they refrained from harming the native inhabitants. As
a result, the latter became friendly to the bandits. When government
troops searched for the marauders, they promptly hid themselves in
the dwellings of the common people . . . coming out after the troops
had left the locality. Consequently, bandits existed virtually everywhere in Kwangsi province.[168]

Another and slightly different mode of operation was described in
an official document dated 1853, depicting the situation in the earlier
stages of the campaign against the Taiping rebels: "Renegade soldiers
and runaway braves, having escaped from the battle fronts, are without the means to return [home] and can find no camp to receive them.
They tarry on their way and plunder as they go."[169]

It is hoped that these instances give substance to the view that while
banditry had its roots in general poverty, it did not flourish without
either the presence in a given locality of "wicked people" or serious
disturbances in the local situation which made it impossible for the
bulk of the peasants to maintain their accustomed way of life.[170] The
average villager was normally inclined to be law-abiding. He might,

when circumstances required, avoid antagonizing the bandits in order
to protect himself and his family, [171] or join his neighbors to fight
them for the same reason. [172] Under special circumstances, however,
some of the ordinarily law-abiding rural inhabitants might be induced
to practice banditry, temporarily or for relatively long periods of
time.

Professional and Occasional Bandits. The foregoing discussion indicates that bandits, properly called, fell into two types which may
be characterized respectively as the professional and the occasional.
The distinction between them is (a) that occasional bandits were often rural inhabitants compelled to join bandit groups for one reason
or another, whereas professional bandits came from habitually predaceous, unruly elements of local communities; and (b) that occasional bandits were usually ready to return to peaceful occupations
as soon as the compulsion which made them bandits was removed,
whereas professional bandits engaged in robbery and pillage regularly
and perhaps permanently.

Instances of professional bandits are readily found. A particularly
interesting one was afforded by nineteenth-century Kwangtung where
banditry was "professionalized" to such an extent as to have become
a highly organized lucrative racket, with several levels of operation.
According to a contemporary Chinese official:

> . . . the evil of banditry obtaining in various localities of Kwang-
> tung owes its origin partly to gamblers and smugglers. But there are
> cases in which it has been carried on as a hereditary occupation, hand-
> ed down from father to son. In other cases the inhabitants of entire
> villages go out to plunder . . . sell their booty openly in front of
> their ancestral halls, and distribute the money thus obtained to mem-
> bers of the entire clan. Then there are village bullies and powerful
> rogues, owners of wealth amounting to millions, who distribute to
> bandits sums of money, amounting to thousands or hundreds, to be
> used as "capital," assuming thus the role of *mi-fan-chu* [rice-hosts,
> to whom presumably the plunderers will pay back the sums lent them,
> with substantial interest]. In addition there are those who issue un-
> authorized flags and arrows [as tokens of authority] and distribute
> them to villagers who wish to have them. These are said to offer
> "protection" to the villagers, but in reality fixed amounts of "gifts"
> are agreed upon between villagers and bandits who [after having re-
> ceived the "gifts"] secretly order their comrades not to molest the
> former. . . . Such big bandits also have contact with scholarly clans
> and maintain social intercourse with them. [173]

The role of "harboring hosts" *(wo-chu* in Chinese official parlance)
in professional banditry should not be minimized. As an eighteenth-
century Chinese official said:

Without "harboring hosts" bandits have no place to lodge; without scouts they have no person to reconnoiter for them. . . . But it is even more difficult to uncover and capture harboring hosts than bandit-scouts. For harboring hosts are either lawless soldiers or yamen runners, or else local bullies or powerful gangsters. The *pao-chia* heads are in their clutches;being keen for their bribes, they refuse to report [the presence of bandits in their houses]. Neighbors and clan heads are afraid of the hosts' malignant power and vengeance and dare not inform against them. As to yamen constables, they have always been conniving with these local bullies and gangsters. Finding their "gifts" attractive, they also let them alone even though they are aware of [their lawless doings]. [174]

The crucial importance of "harboring hosts" may be seen in the following incident occurring in Ch'ang-sha (Hunan) in 1897:

Liu Hsiang-lin of Chang-ch'iao harbored bandits and received their booty. His residence was as formidable as the storehouse of a pawnshop. None dared incur his wrath. The magistrate induced him on some pretext [to visit the yamen, arrested him and] flogged him in the prison till he was dead. . . . His accomplices gathered in large numbers, declaring that they would burn down the entire market. Upon hearing this the magistrate rushed to the scene. The mob was taken by surprise and noisily retreated to a strategic position. [The magistrate led his men] and advanced bravely. Thirteen of the rioters were seized and the remainder beat a hasty retreat. Since then the region lying between Ch'ang-sha and Liu-yang has been free from bandits. [175]

Professional bandits had always existed in the long history of imperial China. They presented a perennial problem to the government, but their existence was actually less dangerous to the dynasty than the periodic appearance of large numbers of occasional bandits. The reason is not difficult to find. Predaceous elements, after all, constituted only a small fraction of the vast population of the empire. No dynasty, even during the years of its maximum stability, was entirely free of them. But peasants who hitherto had been peaceful and law-abiding were forced by man or circumstances to rob and plunder, "to tread the dangerous path," the existing regime was confronted with the possibility of serious unrest involving a large part of the inhabitants.

That possibility was clearly discernible before the middle of the nineteenth century. It was, in fact, perceived by some thoughtful persons in the eighteenth century. For example, it was the opinion of Liang Shang-kuo, a censor, that persons who willingly became bandits (that is, professional bandits) were far outnumbered by those who did so unwillingly (that is, occasional bandits). He said in a memorial dated in 1799:

According to my humble estimate, among the large number of bandits now existing, two in every ten are roused by their hatred toward
local officials, three in every ten are driven to extremity by hunger
and cold, and four in every ten are either constrained to join after
having been captured by a band of robbers or coerced to follow them
after having been driven from their home villages. No more than one
in ten among them have willingly become bandits. [176]

Indeed, it may be surmised that as the conditions of the empire
deteriorated as a result of natural calamities and administrative bung-
ling, the number of rural inhabitants who turned into occasional bandits tended to increase, making it virtually impossible for the government to cope with the situation in any effective way. Such a situation existed in Kwangsi in the 1850's. According to an official document of the period:

The bandits of Kwangsi quickly gather themselves into bands, and all
of a sudden they disperse themselves. At one moment they submit
themselves to the authority of the government, but at another moment
they again become outlaws. It is difficult to count the number of the
marauding bands. Good people may turn into bandits; so may some
of the soldiers. Generally speaking, when they have sufficient food
they are good people, and become bandits when they are hungry; they
are ordinary inhabitants when they dissolve their bands, but when they
come together they are again bandits; when they are defeated they appear as people, and when victorious they are again bandits. [177]

The Role of the Gentry and Local Officials in Banditry. The gentry,
it seems, had relatively little connection with the activities of local
"sticks" and in fact might have been opposed to some of the latter's
annoying practices. An example of such opposition was recorded by
a Chinese official writing at the opening of the nineteenth century:

In recent years sticks and bullies have been making use of diverse
pretexts to collect money, usually to finance theatrical performances
or country fairs from which they expect to derive unlawful profits.
Occasionally the local gentry may petition the authorities to forbid
[them to do so]; sometimes the governor-general or governor, having learned the situation on inquiry, orders the bullies to stop their
racket; the gentry, in this case, have nothing to do with the matter.
The bullies never hesitate to assemble a mob, dash to the homes of
the gentry, and smash the furniture and other effects (when they intend to cause a small damage), or destroy the houses altogether (when
they wish to cause a big one). In the most serious cases as many as
several dozen houses are torn down in rapid succession in broad day-
light. [178]

The relationship between the gentry and bandits, professional or occasional, was ordinarily not much closer. They were quite likely to regard robbers as their own enemies and summon whatever forces were at their command to defend their homes or communities against them. But under special circumstances the gentry of the countryside might become, in various ways, partners or friends of brigands. We have already noted above that some of the gentry families in Kwangtung maintained a cordial relationship with the "big bandits."[179] In other instances members of the local gentry were known to have played the important role of "harboring hosts," as for example, those of Shantung. According to a Chinese official who lived between the last quarter of the eighteenth century and the first half of the nineteenth:

> Bandits are rampant in Shantung. . . . An investigation into the cause of this reveals that there are many regions in this province where bandits are harbored. . . . Among the hosts that harbor bandits are Ma Chan and Chu Li-chiang, both military *chü-jen;* Shih Ta-en, a military *sheng-yüan;* Tung Wu-p'i, son of a petty official; and Chou Yo-feng, yamen clerk. These criminals are either gentry themselves, or offspring of gentry, or functionaries of the government. They are especially detestable for having received shares of the booty in return for harboring the bandits.[180]

This, it may be supposed, was not an isolated instance. Remembering that some of the clans in South China figured quite prominently in banditry,[181] and that there was a close connection between the gentry and the clan organization, we may reasonably assume that some gentry in the countryside were not above conniving with brigands.

Local officials, obviously, stood in an entirely different relationship to bandits. They could hardly become "harboring hosts," or maintain any "cordial relationship" with robbers and looters. They might, however, contribute to the emergence of banditry in an important way, that is, through maladministration. It is hardly necessary to repeat the fact that corrupt officialdom was more or less directly responsible for bringing misery to local inhabitants and giving ample cause for their resentment, thereby making the situation ripe for feuds, riots, or banditry. Official negligence alone often helped banditry spread and made a difficult situation impossible to handle satisfactorily. The following letter, written in 1853 by Tseng Kuo-fan to magistrates of Hunan province, illustrates this point:

> The most urgent business at present is to suppress local bandits. . . . Some of them gather in mountainous regions and muster their comrades. Local officials are informed of their activities, but dare not deal with them firmly. The reason is that if attempts are made to search their strongholds, there is the danger of encountering their resistance by force and the retaliatory action of their comrades. Moreover, [if the cases are reported to superior authorities] there

would be the troublesome task of answering the inquiries and investigations conducted through official dispatches issued by these authorities; or [if some bandits are captured] there would be the burdensome task of satisfying the demands for bribery [by functionaries
in the yamen of the superiors] when the prisoners are sent [to such
yamen], and when they are taken back [to the local yamen]. These
considerations make [local officials] hesitate; they tolerate [the bandits'] presence, hoping that luckily they will operate only covertly
so that no open outbreak occurs. These officials fail to see that it
is these same local bandits who suddenly cause major incidents, who
break open government prisons and kill magistrates. [182]

Higher officials were not above blame. A few years earlier when
Tseng Kuo-fan was still in the imperial capital, he wrote:

Since the spring of the present year bandits in Kwangsi have become
ever more rampant. From the western boundaries of Ssu-ch'eng and
Chen-an to the eastern borders of P'ing-lo and Wu-chou, an area of
two thousand *li*, there is not a single square foot of peaceful territory.
When one traces the cause of this, it turns out to be precisely the fact
that local functionaries have oppressed the people, who after having
been victimized for a long time, are driven to desperation. Meanwhile, high officials above these functionaries, paying little serious
attention to their duties, have for a long while done nothing [to correct the negligence of their subordinates]. [183]

Rebellions

"Rebellion" is defined, for the present purpose, as open armed opposition to the established government, with a view to overthrowing it
and substituting for it a new one. It is one type of "revolution" (as the
term "revolution" is used by some writers) but it is useful to distinguish "rebellion" from "revolution" by reserving the latter term for
movements against the constituted authorities which aim not merely at
a change of rulers but at an alteration of the form of government together with the principles on which it rests. [184]

There was, as is well known, a long tradition in China's intellectual history which upheld what some Western writers have called
"the right of rebellion,"[185] the "right," namely, of the ruled to replace tyrannical rulers with "virtuous and benevolent" ones. It was
given expression by a large number of thinkers and formulated in a
variety of ways. The *Shu-ching*, for example, contains these ring-
ing sentences: "He who soothes us is our sovereign; he who oppresses
us is our enemy."[186] Mencius dwelt emphatically on the same theme
on more than one occasion, holding that it was always justifiable to
destroy "enemies" of the people, even to the extent of practicing tyrannicide. [187] Chia I, an early Han dynasty writer, argued, "The people are the humblest of all, and yet they cannot be slighted; they are
the most ignorant, and yet they cannot be fooled. Therefore, since

antiquity till now any one who makes himself an enemy of the people will sooner or later be vanquished by them. "[188] An early Ming dynasty writer confirmed this view by drawing from historical experience this conclusion: "The people began to rise in revolt in the Ch'in dynasty; since then those who overthrew dynasties were usually the people. "[189] Indeed, throughout the twenty-one and a half centuries of China's imperial history "the right of rebellion" had become a regular feature of all respectable theories of government. Varying emphasis was given to it by different writers, but few were ready to gainsay it.

It is not our concern here to argue for or against the theory that such a right belonged to the people. We cannot deny, however, that this theory may have been suggested to its proponents by actual historical events. In a number of decisive instances "the people" actually were instrumental in one way or another in overthrowing dynasties. One readily recalls Ch'en She, a farm laborer who, when faced with capital punishment, set in motion the rebellion that eventually shattered the formidable Ch'in dynasty; and Chu Yüan-chang, a destitute commoner, who together with other rebel leaders put an end to the oppressive Mongol regime and set up a new dynasty of his own. Many lesser instances occurred between these two, which support the theory that when the vast political sea of the people became too stormy, the boat that was the imperial regime inevitably capsized and sank. [190]

This theory, however, contains a flaw. It refers broadly to "the people" as agents of rebellion without showing the specific circumstances under which revolts broke out; it fails to indicate the fact that rebellions, successful or abortive, resulted from the convergence of different motives and the cooperation of different social classes. The failure to indicate this crucial fact may have been partly responsible for the well-known but mistaken supposition that the peasantry, being the largest segment of the population was by itself prepared to exercise "the right of rebellion," a supposition which makes it difficult to explain how the ordinarily indifferent and passive peasantry could suddenly become an active insurgent force. We propose to examine here the major circumstances that gave rise to rebellions in imperial China and to identify the precise roles played by the diverse segments of the population in these uprisings, in order to help us understand better the nature of rebellions.

Circumstances of Rebellions. The factors that contributed to great upheavals were complex and varied. [191] Circumstances that produced riots and banditry might also produce rebellions. Widespread destitution, economic inequities, maladministration—all these factors figured prominently in the numerous uprisings in the history of imperial China. Whether at a given time these factors led to rebellions or only riots was to a large extent determined by the gravity of the situation. In the matter of maladministration, for instance, the imperial government formulated policies and regulations, and local officials brought them to bear on the life of the common people. The impact of bad local administration was bound to be more directly and keenly felt by the inhabitants of a given locality than the effects of bad central government. Local officials, in particular district magistrates, always bore the brunt of the first waves of popular resentment; they were, as we have seen, the first objects of local riots. When, however, maladministration persisted and the imperial rulers allowed the unhappy state of affairs to continue, when the situation became intolerable and there was no prospect of amelioration, the imperial government itself finally became the target of resentment, and revolts of various dimensions eventually broke out.

In the long history of imperial China resentment against maladministration was always one of the chief reasons advanced by rebels to justify their action and to win popular support. When Ch'en She and his partner discussed their insurrectionary plans, they included as a cogent reason for raising the standard of revolt the fact that the empire had for a long time been bitter toward the oppressive administration of Ch'in.[192] One of the most striking instances in which oppressive administration became the main object of rebellion was the terrible uprising led between 1120 and 1122 by Fang La, who set up a rival government and took almost sixty *chou* and *hsien* before he was annihilated. The emperor's inordinate taste for "fancy plants and rocks" sent some of his servants to the provinces in a mad hunt for the treasured objects. Extortion on a colossal scale ensued, making the situation unbearable. The nature of the resulting upheaval was revealed by the horrible actions of the rebels. "Whenever they captured government officials," the historians said, "they invariably tortured them in every conceivable way—they mutilated their limbs or chopped up their bodies, drew out their entrails, fried them alive in oil, or shot innumerable arrows into their bodies—in order to give vent to their hatred of them."[193] And the fact that Fang La set up a government of his own showed clearly that his aim went beyond the destruction of the hated officials.

The rebellions of the Ch'ing dynasty conformed, in this respect at any rate, to the general historical pattern. It is no surprise that they appeared in the period between the closing decades of the eighteenth century and the middle of the nineteenth, when the entire administrative system had been deteriorating with quickened pace since the later part of the Ch'ien-lung reign. Official and private accounts of these uprisings were for obvious reasons reticent about the grievances of the rebels against the imperial government, but such reticence hardly obscured the fact that their obejctive was to destroy not only corrupt officialdom but the dynasty itself. Many documents of the Taiping Rebellion contain frequent reference to the theme that the Manchus should be destroyed because they had done injustice to the Chinese by their oppressive administration. It is true that in one of the earliest documents in which the Taiping leader assumed the title "general commander" (or "marshall") only the "corrupt officials of the empire" were marked for destruction and no mention was made of the imperial government itself.[194] But in later documents, issued after Hung Hsiu-ch'üan assumed the title *T'ien Wang*, the Manchu dynasty was condemned in the strongest terms.[195] Appeals to "racial" antagonism were frequently and emphatically made by the rebel leaders, but the administrative arguments were seldom omitted.

Some of the opinions voiced by late eighteenth- and nineteenth-century Chinese writers show how bad the local officialdom had become and why opposition to it constituted a cause of rebellions. Perhaps the frankest statement was made by one of these writers with reference to the rampancy of "heretical" rebels in the 1790's. He argued that it was impossible to suppress the insurrections because the wickedness of the magistrates of the *chou* and *hsien* of the time had become "one hundredfold worse than those of ten or twenty years ago."[196] Another writer, discussing the situation that prevailed in Kwangtung during the earlier years of the Taiping uprising, also traced the rebellion to the same basic cause:

> Where does the source of the present day turbulence lie? It lies in those magistrates that are greedy and cruel.
>
> Let us speak of western Kwangtung. When disorder had not yet arisen in western Kwangtung, officials who held posts in this region . . . perceiving that the custom there is primitive and the people are ignorant, treated the latter as if they were birds, beasts, or savages that deserve no affection or care. But since these officials were assigned to this locality and there was no way to escape it, they . . . made monetary gains in the fullest measure their most urgent task. One followed the example of another, with no aim other than to line their private purses and to nourish their own offspring. Their hardhearted and highhanded methods are really unfit for description.
>
> But, one may ask, are there not prefects and intendants above these magistrates, and above these latter the three high provincial officials . . . and the governor and the governor-general? Do these superior officials make no distinction between the worthy and unworthy among their subordinates?
>
> [The answer is, they may be able to make such a distinction] but unfortunately superior officials, too, cannot resist the temptation of that which one does not have to learn to desire [i.e., money]; and in fact the desire of it has soaked deeply into their bones and marrow. They [and their subordinates], one bearing with another, cover and protect one another. . . . Lower officials depend upon higher ones for protection, while higher officials rely on lower ones to serve as their outside agents [in their common malpractices].

> The people have hated them all in the depth of their hearts for a long time. As soon as the crisis comes and the alarm is sounded, wicked elements take advantage of the situation [and start a revolt]. Vagabonds join them; and ignorant, destitute people, after having been subjected to some pressure [applied by the rebels] and having found it impossible to get food, follow them gladly. The conditions for a great upheaval are thus brought to completion. [197]

That such condemnation was not mere gentry sentimentalism without foundation in fact may be seen from the following incident. When Wang San-huai, one of the rebel leaders of the White Lotus in Szechwan, was captured and brought to the capital in 1798, he declared in response to a question put to him during his trial that it was the officials who forced the people to revolt. [198]

Other factors, of course, were also at work. Widespread poverty and inequity, for which the government was at least partially or indirectly responsible, constituted also a fertile breeding ground for insurrectionary movements. It is almost a truism that disorders of various dimensions followed in the wake of serious calamities and the failure of the government promptly and properly to deal with them. The "roaming bandits" of Ming, among whom Li Tzu-ch'eng and Chang Hsien-chung were the most prominent, rose immediately after the great famine of 1628 in Shensi. Li and Chang soon assumed imperial titles, and the former put the dynasty to an official end.[199] The same correlation between economic disasters and political unrest was observable in the Ch'ing dynasty. The most outstanding case was of course the Taiping uprising which developed after a series of famine years.[200]

The connection between glaring economic inequity and rebellions is also obvious. Resentment against overprivileged classes might induce riots against these classes, but when the feeling became sufficiently bitter, it might inspire a rebellion with the avowed or implicit aim of smashing the entire political structure that apparently served as the scaffolding for such inequity. In an agricultural country like China, the resentment of destitute landless peasants was bound to figure most conspicuously in insurrectionary movements.[201] Wang Hsiao-po, who led a revolt in Szechwan between 990 and 994, inspired his comrades with these fiery words: "I hate inequality between the rich and poor: now I am going to effect equalization for you." His followers rapidly multiplied, eventually numbering several tens of thousands. His movement had such an immediate appeal because, as the historians said, Szechwan at that time was a place where "the land was not ample but the population dense, and farming did not yield enough to support life; as a result, monopolizers increased their activity in buying cheap and selling dear to reap profit."[202] Lin Ch'ing and Li Wen-ch'eng, who respectively led the abortive uprisings in

Chihli and Honan early in the nineteenth century, promoted their movement in the following manner:

> All who joined the sect contributed money [to a fund] known as the
> "happiness-sowing fund" or the "root-and-foundation fund." Contrib-
> utors were promised a tenfold reimbursement when the movement
> attained success. All who contributed 100 copper cash would be re-
> warded with 100 *mow* of land. Being deceived by such promises, ig-
> norant people thronged to join. [203]

And it goes without saying that the "communistic" ideas of the Taiping
Rebellion accounted partly for its rapid success. The scheme outlined in the "Land System of the Heavenly Dynasty,"[204] according to
which all were to share equally in the bounties given to mankind by
the "Heavenly Father," undoubtedly had a tremendous appeal to thousands of dispossessed hungry peasants. [205]

These, then, were the usual circumstances that might lead to riots
or rebellions as the situation dictated. In addition to these, there were
a number of special factors that figured only in rebellions. One of
the most obvious was "racial hatred," which the Chinese held for
their Mongol rulers in the thirteenth and fourteenth centuries and
later for their Manchu rulers. The most outstanding example was
Chu Yüan-chang, founder of the Ming dynasty, who used anti-Mongol
arguments in one of his propaganda pieces addressed to inhabitants
of northern provinces still under the Yüan government. [206] The anti-
Manchu ideology of the Taiping leaders was even better known. The
"powerful and vivacious spark that the Tartar government [had] never
been able to extirpate," to borrow the words of a Western writer,
now burst forth into a conflagration with full vehemence. [207]

Personal ambition, especially when reinforced by desperation,
might also contribute to a rebellion. One should not overstress the
personal factor in any important historical development, but it is
safe to admit that ambitious and desperate men often precipitated
historical events that were fermenting. Chinese history contains many
instances of this sort; the most familiar among them are Ch'en She
who initiated the first revolt against the Ch'in dynasty, and Liu Pang
who founded the Han dynasty and, in a different mold, Hung Hsiu-
ch'üan, leader of the Taiping movement. Ch'en betrayed his seemingly incredible ambition when he was a hired farmhand by remark-
ing in effect that despite his poverty and lowly status he had riches
and honor in his mind. Thus primed for unusual action, he was soon
to be prodded by an impending death sentence to start the revolt. [208]
Liu Pang made his great ambition known when he served in the imperial capital as a petty functionary, declaring that it was proper
for a man of parts to live as the Ch'in emperor did. He decided to

challenge the authorities when he, like Ch'en She, was faced with punishment.[209] Hung Hsiu-ch'üan, as is well known, had originally no higher ambition than to attain scholarly success in the examinations. Repeated bitter disappointment drove him into a frame of mind that reacted with explosive force to the troubled circumstances of his time.[210] This is a revealing instance of how personal frustration might contribute to a rebellion.

The Role of Common People. No rebellion could materialize without the cooperation of *shen-shih,* who furnished plans and ideas, and commoners, who supplied physical force. The Taiping Rebellion, the greatest insurrectionary movement of imperial China, serves as a good illustration of this point. As a well-known Western writer of the nineteenth century put it, "War is essentially a contest of physical forces, and the Tae-pings are certain of constant accessions of the best sinew and muscle of the country. Neither does that proportion of cultivated intelligence which is also necessary in war, fail them."[211] Or, in the more precise language of a recent student of Chinese history, the Taiping Rebellion was:

> . . . a peasant movement led by disappointed candidates in the official examinations and unlettered men of native military and organizational genius who capitalized upon the economic distress of the time and the declining ability of the Manchu rulers to take the principal cities of the Yangtze Valley and at one point to threaten Peking itself.[212]

This point is also illustrated by the composition of the secret societies which figured prominently in the uprisings that occurred during the Ch'ing dynasty. These organizations were often known to have recruited their membership from the gentry and literati as well as from common people. The following ditty depicting the "incense meetings" (ritual meetings to initiate new members) of brotherhoods in the mid-nineteenth century throws some light on the situation:

> The happy ties of the brethern are with incense fire solemnized:
> After burning the incense can there still be barriers between you and me?
> Officials, scholars—all into the fold are received;
> Yamen runners, servants, soldiers—none is barred![213]

Perhaps we may add one more instance to show that the cooperation of both *shen-shih* and commoners was indispensable to rebellions. After the downfall of the Ming dynasty there was a movement to "oppose the Ch'ing and restore the Ming," an insurrectionary movement with a clear aim and well-defined ideology, indefatigably sustained by some of the former officials and scholars who survived the defunct regime. Their efforts bore no tangible fruit; so far as evidence shows, the vast populace was completely unconcerned with their cause. In 1728 a Hunan scholar, a particularly ardent supporter of the Ming cause, tried to persuade Yüeh Chung-ch'i, a high military commander, to rebel against the Manchu rulers. His attempt created a sensation but no rebellion. The scholar, apparently realizing that he lacked the physical force to implement his cause, resorted to the desperate move of trying to make a turncoat out of "one of the foremost henchmen of Emperor Shih-tsung."[214] Some of the secret societies, however, kept the anti-Manchu ideology alive.[215] The cause, formerly supported by officials and scholars alone, eventually enjoyed a certain degree of popular support, and in all probability exerted some influence on the Taiping Rebellion in its initial phase.[216]

The crucial importance of the common people in rebellion therefore should not be minimized. "The common people" in the broadest sense would include all the inhabitants who had no gentry status. Thus understood, they can be further divided into various subcategories: first, those who were literate and those who were illiterate. The former included all aspiring scholars who had not as yet taken any of the examinations and frustrated ones who had failed to pass (all of whom were therefore, legally speaking, nongentry) and all others who possessed a certain degree of literacy because of their professions; among these would be such persons as physicians, merchants, and Taoist priests.[217] Although these persons enjoyed less prestige and less influence than the gentry, their literacy gave them advantages which were denied to the huge illiterate population of the countryside. They were likely to have outlooks and to occupy local positions perceptibly different from the rest of their fellow commoners. They tended to be somewhat more sensitive to wrongs or injuries they might suffer, more articulate in expressing their feelings, more ready to devise ways and means to alter unsatisfactory situations. They might be somewhat more intelligent or better informed than ordinary commoners and could therefore supply leadership to the latter when gentry leadership was at the moment not available. Being less bound by the code of conduct which the gentry were expected to honor, and less aware of the allegiance to the existing regime, they might readily assume an active part in promoting local disturbances or full-scale insurrections.

Among the illiterate portion of the common people there might be some who were unusually ambitious, talented, shrewd, or aggressive, such as Ch'en She, the first man to lead a revolt against the Ch'in dynasty. The social status of such persons differed in no perceptible way from that of the average peasant, but their impact on their respective communities or fellow commoners was often so decisive as to make them key figures in the local scene even under ordinary circumstances. It was such men who might under unusual conditions step forward into the limelight of history and startle the world with stirring deeds. They were commoners, but commoners of a special sort, who for want of a better term may be described as "exceptional commoners."

Other commoners distinguished themselves from the inconsequential, innocuous rural inhabitants not by their exceptional capacities but by their habitually unruly, lawless, or shiftless behavior. These were the persons who in normal times were local bullies, idlers, professional beggars—those elements of the population that the government often stigmatized as "wicked" or "weed people." These were the first to start disorders and to challenge the authorities whenever opportunities occurred. [218]

These three types of commoners—literate commoners, "exceptional commoners," and (in official parlance) "wicked people"—constituted the minority of the inhabitants of any given locality. By far the larger part of the population of rural China was made up of plain peasants. These, together with the traders, craftsmen, and a host of others who lived and died in villages or towns, were the truly *common* people, familiarly known in China as *lao-pai-hsing*. It was they who toiled ceaselessly in their occupations, refused to depart from their accustomed pattern of behavior, and earned for the Chinese the reputation of being patient and docile.

In a rebellion, evidently, this type of "common people" figured differently from the other types of "common people." Commoners with special qualifications or attitudes sometimes furnished initiative or leadership, but ordinary inhabitants of the countryside contributed nothing beyond physical force. The former, in other words, played active roles in cooperation with the *shen-shih* elements that chose to join the movement, whereas the latter alone afforded the numerical strength which the *shen-shih* elements could not furnish. It is broadly true, therefore, that the distinctive role of the peasantry in rebellions was to serve as the rank and file of the insurgent armies, making it possible for the rebel leaders to translate their aims or plans into action.

It is useful to scrutinize more closely the behavior of such ordinary peasants and the circumstances under which they lent numerical strength to rebellions. The facts at hand show that villagers took part in insurrectionary movements either as a result of compelling circumstances or of inducement or compulsion exerted upon them by elements in the rebels' camps. Rural inhabitants, like other human beings, reacted differently to varying conditions. When changes in the environment became critical, a dramatic change in peasant psychology might take place. Impending destruction might force placid peasantry into desperation, and thus prepare them for convulsive action.

A Western writer, viewing the matter primarily from the economic standpoint, offered this interesting observation:

> . . . confronted with the overpowering conditions of nature, the Chinese has learned patience. He knows that not everything depends on his power and his industry. He feels himself helplessly dependent on the regularity of celestial events. . . . This endurance . . . arises from the economic conditions of China and in time has become instinctive. It also proves a positive force in situations in which a quiet waiting offers the only way out.
>
> But this attitude also has . . . only a limited validity. . . . As the masses, instead of taking energetic steps of self-help, adapt themselves in docile submission to conditions which go from bad to worse, suffer, and starve, the point is reached eventually when this attitude itself becomes a serious life problem. [219]

The situation became critical. The peasants by themselves, however, were not necessarily ready for action; the inertia of their habitual passivity might linger on. Some of them broke into riots or revolts only when they were incited or guided by leaders who came from the gentry or special categories of commoners. If the general situation worsened further, the unrest would spread; large numbers of ordinary peasants would join the rebel forces and a full-scale rebellion would result. [220] Or if the leadership came from one of the "heretical sects," as sometimes happened in the nineteenth century, charismatic authority would then be pitted against political authority and the hitherto diffident peasant masses might show an incredibly high degree of aggressiveness and intrepidity, fighting fiercely for a cause the significance of which they no more than vaguely understood.

Under the circumstances described above, peasants may be said to have joined the movements more or less willingly. They were compelled by the impossible conditions that confronted them to abandon their habitually peaceful behavior; they joined the rebels because they were lured or attracted by promises of better things to come rather than because they were coerced by the rebels. Under other circumstances, however, peasants were known to have become unwilling participants in rebellions. Rebel leaders were understandably anxious to augment their forces. When persuasion and promises failed to attract would-be recruits, they did not hesitate to coerce or intimidate them into joining their movements. An instance of how this was done was recorded by a Chinese writer in 1798, when the White Lotus uprisings were raging in several provinces:

> The heretics burn down a village after they have entered it, and the same is done to a town. The purpose is to compel good people to be-

come outlaws. . . . During the three successive years when these
heretics bring chaos to a number of provinces, the more villages and
towns are burned down, the more numerous are those who join them,
because they [the inhabitants] are deprived of their homes and means
of living. The heretics have no compassion whatever for these [un-
willing] followers, who are either driven to fight in the front lines or
made to fight rearguard actions against the government troops. Hence
whenever officials report that so many thousand or hundred [rebels]
are killed, these are in fact such homeless people, who were deprived
of their property [by the heretics], not the heretics themselves or
genuine outlaws. [221]

The fact that some of the followers of the rebels were not loyal
comrades was evidently known to their leaders. They did not trust
them and devised various measures to insure against desertion. The
White Lotus tattooed the faces of their men with the picture of a lotus
flower or the characters "White Lotus Sect."[222] The Taiping practice
of requiring their comrades to avoid shaving their heads, which earned
them the nickname "long-hairs," would serve the same purpose.

The method used by the Triads to coerce peasants into following
them is also revealing. According to an official source:

In the south Kan area of Kiangsi province the leaders of the secret
society bandits are malignant and cunning. Whenever they meet with
persons who possess land and are obedient to the law, and refuse to
join the society, they either take away their cattle and horses or destroy their crops, or even kidnap their sons and daughters and hold
them for ransom. The humble people are thus intimidated so that they
realize that if they remain outside the society disaster immediately
descends on them, making it impossible for them to preserve their
families and property; but if they join the society they do no more than
contribute money and will be spared torture and calamities. [223]

The method adopted by the Taiping leaders was especially effective, according to Tseng Kuo-fan. Writing in 1853 in a letter addressed
to "the upright gentry of the *chou* and *hsien* of Hunan" he said:

Wherever they go the rebel-bandits take captives of our good people.
The latter are watched in daytime, forbidden to go out; in the night
they sleep [in rooms] surrounded [by some of the rebels]. No escape
is possible. These captives are invited to become "brothers" and induced to "worship God." Whoever follows them is allowed to live, and
those who refuse to comply are killed. After being held captive by
the rebels for two months their hair grows long. They are then forced
to man the battle lines. In every engagement these captives fight in the
front rows, while the rebels send [trustworthy] men carrying swords
and shields to march behind them. If they turn back or run away they
are killed [by these men]. . . . They have no choice but to close their
eyes and advance, fighting hard. [224]

Rebel leaders did not always employ methods as harsh as these to win the support or help of rural inhabitants. Their slogans and propaganda pieces appealed to the masses, and in addition rebels often treated villagers much better than government troops, with a view, undoubtedly, to inducing these inhabitants to desert the government. This, for example, was what a Chinese official observed in some parts of Honan province in 1853:

> Bandit troops search for provisions, going as far as Chi-yüan and Meng Hsien. The humble people of these localities are helpless. At first they supplied the bandits with rice and fruits. The latter paid them high prices in order to induce [them to bring more]. Ignorant people covet the profits and continuously [send supplies to the rebels].
> . . .
> At present government troops seize men, horses, carts, and goods wherever they go. All villages around the places where they encamp are molested by them. [225]

The observation of a Western writer concerning the situation around Nanking in 1853 is particularly illuminating:

> They [the Taiping rebels] command the personal services of all inhabitants of cities, whether men of wealth or tradesmen, and seize unhesitatingly the whole of their property, and they also press the produce *carriers*, the river boatmen. But while they take possession of government corn stores as theirs by right, and probably do not spare the stores of large corn *merchants* in the towns they enter, it is certain that they purchase from the *farmers*, and make a point of giving liberal prices. The consequence is, that whenever the country people could find an opportunity of slipping unobserved into Chin keang with corn and vegetables they never failed to do so. The people of this village told me that the Imperialists by whom the city was infested subjected them to far more annoyance than the Tae pings had done. [226]

It is clear that when peasants joined rebel movements, whether as a result of inducement or compulsion, they took a subordinate part, acting at the bidding of the rebel leaders, who very rarely were ordinary peasants. These passive followers gave numerical strength to their movements, but in all probability they did not understand either the larger objectives or the immediate plans of their leaders. [227] It is only in a very limited sense, therefore, that any rebellion that occurred in China in the nineteenth century may be said to have been a "peasant movement" pure and simple.

This conclusion may be strengthened by examining more closely the role played by the gentry and literate elements in rebellions. To begin with, the very idea of rebellion, of overthrowing the existing regime by concerted force, must of necessity come from these elements. It was they who developed and transmitted the time-honored theory that rulers rightfully held their authority only when they governed "benevolently," that "the people" had the right to rise against tyrannical rulers,[228] and who, at the suitable moment, put the theory into popular forms and translated it into action by inciting the masses to revolt.

This general relationship between the gentry and literate elements on the one side and the common people on the other in rebellions was aptly revealed by Liu Chi, writing in the last years of the oppressive Mongol dynasty, in one of his parables:

> Once upon a time, there was in the state of Ch'u a person who lived on a group of monkeys which he kept under control. He was called the Monkey Master by his fellow countrymen. Every morning he regimented his monkeys in the courtyard; he ordered the older ones to lead the rest into the hills to collect the fruits of various plants. He took for his own use one-tenth of what they gathered and whipped any monkey that refused to make the tribute. The monkeys hated him bitterly, but they were afraid of him and dared not disobey his commands.
>
> One day a young monkey spoke to the other monkeys thus: "Are the fruits of the hills planted by the Master?" The answer was "No, they are products of nature." "Are these fruits the exclusive property of the Master, so that none but he can take them?" They replied: "No, anybody can take them." "For what, then, do we depend on the Master and what justifies our servitude?"
>
> Hardly had the young monkey finished these words when all the monkeys awoke to the truth of them. That night, after the Monkey Master had gone to bed, they broke open the pens and stockades in which they were confined, took all his hoard and went, arm in arm, into the forest, never to return.
>
> The Monkey Master soon starved to death.

The moral of this tale, according to the author, was simply this:

> Some persons in the world enslave the people with a sort of art but without true principles. Do they not resemble the Monkey Master? His art works so long as the people fail to understand the situation. As soon as somebody enlightens them, his art becomes useless.[229]

That somebody who "enlightened" the people in the rebellions was obviously none other than a member of the gentry or literati—a person possessing the ability to inquire into the justification of political servitude.

Obviously also frustrated scholars, those among the literate persons whose success in the examinations or in officialdom fell short of their ambitions, were more likely to play a decisive role in starting insurrectionary movements than members of the gentry and literati who had fared comparatively well. Such scholars were in one sense more dangerous to the existing regime than the numerous underprivileged, hungry peasants. Their acquaintance with history and literature equipped them not only with the idea of rebellion but in some instances with the sort of knowledge useful in organizing or conducting rebellions—a qualification which the common peasant did not possess. Their resentment against the examiners who "unjustly" denied them due recognition could be easily transformed into a resentment against the existing order, especially when they found their lot extremely unsatisfactory. In times of general peace they became "perverted scholars," and instigators of revolts in times of unrest.

The lot of "the vast army of disappointed candidates" was certainly unenviable; the tendency of these men to act in ways that were detrimental to imperial peace is readily understandable. As a Western observer correctly said of these men:

> Some of them go on trying again and again. . . . But the vast majority drift into petty bread-earning positions, as tutors or school teachers, notaries or clerks, amanuenses or authors, geomancers or physicians, fortune-tellers or *raconteurs*, parasites or beggars. There is much discontent.[230]

One of the few Western observers who had firsthand knowledge of the conditions in the empire in the 1850's described the behavior of such scholars:

> All these [rejected in the provincial examinations] remain members of the non-official commonalty and possess, with hundreds of thousands of candidates who never even attained bachelorships [the *sheng-yüan* degree], as much intellectual power for practical purposes as the bulk of the administrators. Many of the more reckless and daring . . . perform the functions of professional demagogic agitators with us; they for selfish purposes, bully and check the local authorities.[231]

Frustrated scholars, however, did not stop at checking local authorities. Under suitable circumstances some of them might assume leadership in revolts or rebellions. Instances can be readily cited; a few outstanding ones from the nineteenth century will illustrate the point. Miao P'ei-lin, a leader of the Nien rebels, was a *sheng-yüan;* so was Liu Te-p'ei, leader of a rebel band in Shantung. Li Chan, a rebel leader in Honan, was a *chü-jen* who did not enter officialdom.[232] Among the most important leaders of the Taiping Rebellion were Hung Hsiu-ch'üan, who repeatedly failed to obtain the *sheng-yüan* distinction; Wei Ch'ang-huei, who did not go beyond the *chien-sheng* grade; and Yang Hsiu-ch'ing, Hung Jen-kan, and Shih Ta-k'ai, who were literate but possessed no examination degrees.[233]

That the service of literate persons was highly useful and indeed

necessary to rebellions hardly requires explanation. The point is illustrated by the following remarks concerning secret societies, which
were responsible for many of the uprisings of the nineteenth century:

> That the leading members of these organizations have always been
> recruited from the unemployed literati there can be little question.
> In fact, without the co-operation of literati no Chinese society could
> reduce its motives to writing, construct its formulae, compile its
> rituals, and prepare the manifestoes. [234]

The service of literati was even more important in rebellions. Without it no rebellion in the true sense of the term was possible and all
outbreaks of violence ended in futile bloodshed. Peasants, who furnished the numerical strength to all insurrectionary movements in
Chinese history, were not able to organize effective uprisings by
themselves. This is definitely true in the nineteenth century. A Western writer described the Chinese peasants of his time as:

> . . . persons who have either no natural ability, or are too poor to
> procure an education, —persons who, with a moderate proportion of
> talented and educated leaders, would, from their number and their
> desperation, be formidable indeed; but left as they are to themselves,
> only break out into tumults and insurrections, which, like the Jacque-
> rie in France, the insurrection of the common people in the minority
> of Richard II of England, and those that prevailed in the south of Ger-
> many and in Hungary during the end of the fifteenth and the first quar-
> ter of the sixteenth centuries, are ultimately put down with terrible
> loss to themselves, after some well-deserved punishments have been
> inflicted, and some ravages committed by them at the first out-
> break. [235]

It may be added that among the makers of Chinese dynasties an overwhelming majority came from classes other than the illiterate peasantry. Only two, Liu Pang and Chu Yüan-chang, were said to have
sprung from commonalty. Both made extensive use of scholars and
literati to help them give their movements effective form and direction and to consolidate their gains. The author of the parable of the
monkeys was in fact one of the ablest scholars employed by Chu Yüan-
chang. [236]

Between the eminent successes of Liu and Chu on the one side and
the many sad failures of nameless peasant-rebels on the other lay
innumerable uprisings with varying degrees of success (or failure),
including the great rebellion led by Hung Hsiu-ch'üan, all of which
point to the conclusion that the more and better assistance a rebellion secured from the literati, the greater success it was likely to
attain. Even insurgent groups of little consequence derived benefits
from whatever literate or gentry elements they managed to obtain.

It was said of some local "bandits" who were in touch with the Nien rebels:

> When the bandits first rose they comprised not more than several tens of ignorant, brutish fellows. But when more and more persons were coerced into joining them, they included many individuals of notable courage and ability. And when some shameless *chin-shen* and *k'o-mu* [gentry and scholars] were found among them, who directed and guided them, their forces were brought under rigid discipline and clear regulations, and they moved with speed and plenty of cunning tactics. [237]

A few historical instances of this sort may be cited. Ch'en She, a commoner leader, employed the services of effective literati, such as Chang Erh and Ch'en-yü; the former had been magistrate of a district of the state of Wei, and the latter "had a taste for Confucian learning." When later Ch'en She ceased to listen to the counsel of these two men, his fortunes rapidly declined. [238] Huang Ch'ao, who led a terrible uprising in the ninth century and was largely responsible for shortening the life of the T'ang dynasty, was said to have been particularly anxious to enlist the sympathy and service of scholars. According to one Chinese historian, "When Huang Ch'ao entered Fukien all prisoners that he captured were released upon declaring that they were Confucian scholars."[239] Another concurred:

> Emperor Hsi-tsung [of the T'ang dynasty] ascended the throne in his childhood; imperial orders emanated from his servants. . . . As a result . . . factions dominated the court. . . . Talented persons became resentful and remained outside of the political scene. . . . When Huang Ch'ao rose, some of the literati followed him. Whenever Huang Ch'ao sent dispatches and pronouncements to various places, the abuses prevailing at the imperial court were invariably pointed out. These documents were the writings of resentful scholars. [240]

Another revealing instance occurred early in the sixteenth century. Two rebel bands in Shantung competed with each other for ascendance for some time, until one of them made Chao Sui, a *sheng-yüan*, its deputy commander. Then it rapidly gained in power as a result of Chao's leadership. According to one writer, Chao "issued proclamations and sent them to prefectures and districts, directing officials and scholars not to flee when his men arrived; he promised all who welcomed them peace and protection. Hence [the group which he led] traversed the central provinces unopposed, overshadowing the group led by Liu Lu [his rival]. [241]

Li Tzu-ch'eng and Chang Hsien-chung, leaders of the two most important rebel groups in the closing days of the Ming dynasty, afforded even more interesting examples. Being a commoner in very modest circumstances and a fugitive from imperial justice, Li was at first certain that the gentry and literati would not support his movement. When he marched into Shensi in 1643, he "ferreted all of them out, flogged them and confiscated their property. Those who died were buried in a common grave." But he soon realized his mistake and relied on the gentry and literati for assistance and advice. He employed, for instance, Niu Chin-hsing, a disappointed *chü-jen,* and eventually made Niu his "grand secretary." He also used the services of Li Hsing, another *chü-jen,* who was responsible for some of the shrewdest measures which Li Tzu-ch'eng adopted—and for the effective rhymed slogan, "Welcome Prince Ch'uang [Li Tzu-ch'eng]; pay no taxes!"[242]

Chang began as a powerful bandit leader, and was ready to found his own dynasty in 1645 when he gained control of western Szechwan. He appointed a number of gentry to serve in the highest posts of his "imperial government," including at least two *chü-jen* and some holders of lower examination degrees.[243] However, he treated scholar-officials in general as harshly as he treated the common people. It was said that he pretended to hold examinations at Chengtu and massacred all the scholars who appeared to compete therein. He was accustomed to execute any court official whom his dogs happened to sniff.[244] His failure to make profitable use of these elements perhaps accounted partly for his rapid undoing, and for the fact that he attained much less success than Li Tzu-ch'eng.

It may safely be said that the phenomenal, though temporary, success of the Taiping Rebellion was due in part to the help of those gentry elements that joined the movement.[245] It also may reasonably be argued that it enjoyed no more than temporary success because the intellectual leadership at its command was not of a sufficiently high grade to match the leadership available to the opposite camp.

Effects of Rebellion on Villagers. We may now raise a useful question: Did the common peasants gain anything, material or otherwise, from the insurrections in which they had a part or from which they suffered? Did the rebellions bring about any perceptible change in peasant attitudes and reactions?

We have little concrete data concerning rebellions before the Taiping. From what is known of this great uprising it appears that ordinary rural inhabitants received little material benefit from the outbreak. On the contrary, the devastations wrought by battles, looting, and incendiarism committed alternately by bandits, rebels, and government troops, could only have the most depressing and disastrous effect upon the general population. What a Western traveler saw in Honan in 1866 illustrates the conditions prevailing in wartorn areas:

> In places the country had been swept by hordes of rebels, and it was scarcely possible to obtain at any price a chicken or an egg, while rice was out of the question, and coarse millet the only food procurable. Unwalled villages had been reduced to ashes, and their wretched inhabitants, who were living in mat sheds, had their remaining possessions loaded on wheelbarrows, in readiness to fly the moment their sentinel should report the approach of marauders. In one of those villages the most comfortable lodging I could obtain for the night was a mill turned by a buffalo. [246]

A Chinese official understandably may have depicted conditions of some localities in Kiangsu as worse than they actually were, but he throws light on some aspects of the rebels' manner of operation:

> Your servant . . . has personally visited the *chou* and *hsien* which are recently recovered [from the Taiping rebels]. Markets and towns which were formerly famous have all become scorched earth. Devastation is worst in [places] along the highways. Moreover, among the various bandit hordes one does not respect the authority of another. There is no assurance that a place occupied by one horde will not be plundered by another. Therefore even where places occupied by bandits do not border on government-held areas, the countryside has become one continuous expanse of wilderness. . . . Even in remote, hard-to-reach villages the population is now sparse. [247]

A competent Western observer, who certainly had no reason to exaggerate, wrote in the early 1870's that in the parts of Chekiang he visited thirteen years after the invasion of the rebels, several formerly prosperous cities were "extensive heaps of ruins" and the fertile valleys around them constituted "a complete wilderness."[248] Another Western writer well versed in Chinese affairs observed a few decades later that the country was devastated in the years 1853-59 throughout the provinces of Hupeh, Anhwei, Kiangsi, and the western part of Kiangsu, and that about two million people perished. [249] Whatever concern for the immediate welfare of peasants may have been shown by the Taiping rebels in the earlier years of their career, the administration they set up at Nanking was not consistently beneficial to the inhabitants under their rule. According to a well-known Western eyewitness, this was the situation around Nanking in 1861:

> The Taipings rule the country despotically. Unable to obtain the goodwill of the people, they are obliged to obtain their service by force. In addition to the practice of forced and unpaid labour, there is the further evil of frequent foraging raids by bodies of men from the garrisons. . . . The Taiping chiefs often make examples of the worst of their followers, decapitating them, or condemning them to wear the *cangue* for the crimes of robbery and incendiarism. But such instances of just severity do not suffice to restrain from various atroc-

ities a vast number of unprincipled men, who follow the Taiping banner in order to be free from the obligations of honest labour.

What then of the chiefs ? Are they guilty of the anarchy that pre-
vails . . . ? This question must be partly answered by the result.
Should they succeed in establishing an independent kingdom, and reducing their territory to a state of order, their rebellion would become a revolution. At present their prospects are gloomy. . . . But
what efforts do they make to introduce an equitable system of government ? To this it must be answered, that many among them wish
it, and express a strong desire for it, but they want the power and
skill to enforce it. [250]

The behavior of the Taiping rebels, so it seems, fell broadly in
line with the historical tradition of imperial China. As a nineteenth-
century Chinese writer said:

The troops of a new dynasty were always virile at first. . . . They
plundered as they moved on, taking their provisions from the people wherever they found them and dispensing with the trouble of procuring supplies [from fixed logistic posts]. They intimidated and sub-
jugated others by physical force, coercing many persons into following
them. They were thus never worried about getting a sufficient number of recruits. Thieves, robbers, fugitives, and other riffraff flocked
to them. . . . Together they indulged in incendiarism, pillage, and
oppression, at the expense of innocent people. When luckily the leaders of such troops attained success [in establishing a dynasty], official
historians would whitewash the whole matter. [251]

The rebels did not always find support among the rural inhabitants.
In fact, villagers were often afraid of them, as they were afraid of
bandits and government troops; in a few known instances villagers
offered resistance to them. The following graphic account of the attitude and reaction of peasants around Ningpo in 1861 upon hearing
the news that Taiping troops were approaching the place is revealing:

The second rice-crop . . . lay in deep yellow-brown masses covering
the plain and running into the lower hill-valleys, and along the upland
terraces. . . . But nothing could be more pathetic than the expression
of gnawing anxiety and tyrannous suspense which we noticed on all
sides. Every village we visited greeted us with the eager question:
"Are they really coming ?" "Is there any fear ?" "Need we flee ?"
"Whither shall we go to escape the 'long-haired' ?"

After Ningpo and its environs were taken by the Taipings late in the
year, the people reacted to their new rulers in the following way:

The people themselves . . . began to writhe and struggle under the
incubus of their oppressive rulers. On the fine plateau of Ta-lan-shan,

the "Great Mist Mountain," three or four thousand feet high, native patriotic levies, the White Caps, were gathering and drilling. . . . The rebels generally succeeded in breaking up and destroying these combinations, and the acts of vengeance and bloodshed among the beautiful western hills no one can fully describe, for very few survived.[252]

This was not the only instance in which the rebels failed to secure the support of rural inhabitants. In other localities villagers simply resigned themselves to their circumstances, showing neither positive support nor opposition to their new rulers. The following conversation between a Western missionary and a group of villagers dwelling in a locality not far from Nanking illustrates this sort of situation:

Are you happy here under the government of the "long hairs?"

Far from it. We are very wretched. We are called on for contributions of rice or money once a month.

How many men in a hundred have you lost in these parts?

Fifteen to twenty have been killed, and thirty or forty have been carried away to join the rebel army.

Where are the recruits taken to?

To places at a distance. To Sucheu [Soochow, Kiangsu] or Kiahing [Chia-hsing, Chekiang], or some other province.

Are your women also taken away?

Yes. The older and plainer among them are sent back, but the young and good-looking do not return.

If you are wronged, can you not appeal to the nearest magistrates for redress?

Yes; we are told that we can do so; but we dare not.[253]

This conversation took place in 1861, in the vicinity of the "Heavenly Capital." It reveals the interesting fact that after having lived for a decade under Taiping rule many of the rural inhabitants still showed the same timidity and indifference which made them helpless victims of oppression under the Ch'ing government.

It has been said in some quarters that the Taiping Rebellion was a "revolution coming spontaneously from the minds of the multitude of peasant-farmers."[254] In the light of our discussion this view does not appear to square with the known facts. The Taiping movement failed not only to enlist the support of the peasantry as a whole but even to modify the characteristic attitude and behavior of many of the peasants that came under its sway. Much room was left, therefore, for Tseng Kuo-fan and his associates to compete with the Taipings in endeavoring to bring numbers of peasants into their respective camps.[255] And there is no evidence to show that the peasants who fought on the Taiping as well as on the opposite side contributed anything beyond physical force; they all played, in other words, the traditional role of peasants in rebellions and in military campaigns.

WESTERN IMPACT

General Effects

The Chinese empire was confronted with increasingly serious internal troubles after the early decades of the nineteenth century. At about the same time the growing influx of Western religion, technology, commerce, and other elements of European civilization introduced additional disturbing factors which intensified the internal difficulties, and contributed, directly or indirectly, to feuds, riots, and rebellions.

We may begin with a curious instance in which Western religion was involved in local feuds. It was said that the "clan fights between Catholic and Protestant converts" were "common in Chekiang, not uncommon in Kwangtung, and not unknown in other provinces." One such fight, which occurred in Haimen in November, 1906, was particularly revealing. Two versions of this incident are available. According to the Protestant version, the fight broke out on November 9 when between 800 and 2,000 Catholics attacked the little Protestant community. "The Roman Catholic army" was composed of bands of men, each under a leader, and each band had a distinctive badge. The "commander-in-chief" was the native Roman Catholic priest, who was assisted by eleven principal leaders, several of these being "well-known robber-chiefs," and at least two being "only recently liberated from prison." After having been allowed to suffer robbery and assault, the Protestants were sent by local officials to the prefectural city of T'ai-chou for protection. According to the Catholic version, the Protestants provoked the fight by first having schemed to pillage a Catholic inhabitant's house and to deliver from jail by force of arms a criminal arrested by the magistrate (presumably on the advice of the said Catholic inhabitant). Moreover, the Catholic mission owned a piece of land which surrounded the Protestant church. When the mission decided to build a wall around a house (presumably owned by a Protestant) on this lot, the Protestants resisted and a fight ensued in which "pirates and armed Protestants" attacked the Catholic inhabitants with firearms. [256]

Whatever may have been the real situation, this incident shows how, in a small way, rivalry between two foreign religions afforded a new cause for local feuds.

In another and much more momentous way Western religion made its influences felt in nineteenth-century China. The conversion of increasingly large numbers of native inhabitants to Protestantism or Catholicism and the appearance of more and more churches and missions in many parts of the empire were bound to create friction in more ways than one. The conversion of Hung Hsiu-ch'üan and some of his early supporters, in fact, contributed to one of the greatest rebellions in China.[257] The Taiping conception of Christianity was far from orthodox from the viewpoint of any school of theology; but their professed belief gave much of the ideological strength that their movement exhibited, especially during its initial stages. It is certain that without his "visions" which came as a result of his acquaintance with missionary literature, Hung Hsiu-ch'üan would not have become the "Heavenly King," even though he might have started an uprising with another quite different ideology.

Antiforeign Uprisings

One can hardly overlook the numerous antiforeign riots which culminated in the Boxer uprising of 1900. They attracted the attention of many Western writers of the time, and various explanations were offered for them. Misunderstandings arising from cultural differences, Chinese feelings of superiority, the strange and sometimes unscrupulous ways of Westerners that might "leave much bitterness in the minds of the Chinese," "the commercial intrusion," and the spread of opium smoking were generally recognized as important sources of friction. [258] Obviously, the gentry and the common people reacted somewhat differently to these factors. While cultural antipathy was a more decisive cause of antiforeign feelings among the gentry, conflict of immediate economic interests was more likely to incite the enmity of common people. And, as we shall see presently, the former tended to be the instigators or leaders of antiforeign riots, as well as of other types of local disturbances.

That the gentry were usually responsible for most of the demonstrations against foreigners scarcely requires explanation. The introduction of Western thought and religion threatened the traditional values upon which the existence of the gentry as a class depended. The propagation of the religion of the "barbarians" was to professed Confucians of all things the most incredible and insufferable. Consequently, as a modern Western writer put it:

> As soon as it became evident to the Chinese that there was a conflict of more than mere material things in progress, and that there was an actual conflict in civilization types involved, it dawned upon the ruling classes that these new ideas would invalidate a mass of learning which was the property of the ruling literary caste. The gentry and the Confucian scholars were invariably against the foreigners. [259]

The missionaries naturally became the target of antiforeign sentiments. Fantastic stories of abominable doings of missionaries were fabricated and circulated by Chinese writers, some of whom were of no mean scholarly reputation.[260] Local inhabitants were persuaded or coerced by them into refusing to rent houses or sell them for missionary purposes.[261] When the milder forms of antiforeign action failed to dislodge the "foreign devils," more drastic methods were employed. As a Western writer of the nineteenth century correctly observed, many of the *shen-shih* were "accused, on apparently good grounds, with stirring up the people against foreigners and of inciting many of the outbreaks of mob violence, particularly those in which missionaries have been the object of attack,"[262] whereas the common people generally were not hostile to the missionaries.[263]

Opium became one of the major causes of the gentry's antiforeign agitations, although foreigners were not alone responsible for the wide use of the drug with its unfortunate effects. Whatever may have been the share of blame that should be placed upon the foreigners, the fact was that many "among the upper classes" unconditionally ascribed "the real cause of the trouble to the avariciousness of foreigners," and thus looked upon them with hatred. "The ignorant masses" were readily incited to stage antimissionary outbreaks and riots on that score.[264]

Meanwhile, the common people who had to earn a living with their labor or skill realized that the influx of foreign goods and services was detrimental to their economic interests. These, too, entertained antiforeign sentiments and often translated their feelings into overt action. The introduction of cotton yarn, for example, caused riots in some localities of South China around 1830. An officer of the East India Company reported:

> In two districts in the immediate vicinity of Canton, and in another about twenty miles distant from it, very serious commotions have taken place among the natives at the introduction of cotton yarn. They loudly complain that it has deprived their women and children, who had previously been employed in the spinning of thread, of the means of subsistence.[265]

Steamship navigation became another source of friction between the common people and foreigners, wherever it led to the discontinuance of the use of junks and the consequent unemployment of large numbers of persons engaged in river transportation, as on the Yangtze River or along the whole of the Grand Canal.[266]

When and where antiforeign demonstrations were the results of economic conflict, missionaries no longer constituted the primary object of attack. A Western writer, for example, made the following interesting observations concerning the situation in central and western China:

> In 1891 four . . . outbreaks occurred. They were all on the banks

of the Yang-tse, and all at ports of trade. . . . Of the hundreds of missionaries living away from the river, scarcely one was molested. It is morally certain that, among the mixed motives of the excited masses, the diversion of the carrying trade from native junks to foreign steamers was at the bottom of the movement. On the Upper Yang-tse, where two of the riots occurred, so strong was the opposition to steamers ascending the rapids that the British minister felt constrained to waive the exercise of that right. No special effort was made to keep missionaries out of Chungking, but the mandarins moved heaven and earth to prevent the coming of the steamer "Kuling" [for fear that it might precipitate further riots]. [267]

It would be a mistake, however, to suppose that there was a widespread and consistent antiforeign sentiment among the common people. The experiences of many Westerners show that this was not so. Reports from the early nineteenth century down to the time of the Boxer Rebellion compel the conclusion that ordinary villagers were not unfriendly toward foreign visitors until or unless circumstances made them change their basic attitude. A British officer working with the Amherst embassy, for example, described what he experienced in August, 1816, in a village near Tientsin:

> No manner could be more simple and obliging than those of the villagers, when they were satisfied that there was nothing mischievous in my disposition; for, in their first deportment towards me, they evinced the same sort of feeling which is sometimes experienced in approaching an animal whose temper is unknown. This was strikingly displayed by the children, who, observing me much employed in collecting plants [being Naturalist to the Embassy], immediately began to gather them. Then they approached me with caution, step by step, holding their offerings at arm's length, and running off the instant I attempted to take them. When, however, I had once received any part of them, all restraint ceased, and I was presently laden with bundles of flowers. [268]

A British military officer reported that the people of Ningpo showed no evidence of antiforeign feelings even in a time of war:

> The commencement of the year 1842 found the British forces in quiet possession of Ningpo, the inhabitants of which town, although as yet afraid to compromise themselves with the mandarins, so far as to open their shops, and resume their occupations under the auspices of our temporary rule, yet manifested every friendly disposition towards our troops. [269]

A correspondent for the London *Times* confirmed this impression fifteen years later:

> We have passed 400 miles of country not often before traversed. We

have entered four first-class Chinese cities (two of them unknown to European travelers), many second-class cities which in other countries might be classed as first, and innumerable towns and villages. Throughout the whole of our journey we have received from no Chinese an uncivil word or insulting gesture. No mischievous urchin has thrown stones down upon us from any one of the hundreds of bridges we passed through. No one stopped us, and no one waylaid us.

From his experience in this part of the empire, he concluded, "unless excited by the authorities, as they have been at Canton . . . the Chinese people have no objection whatever to the presence of foreigners in their cities."[270]

In fact, even in Canton during the tumultuous days of 1857-58, there were indications that the common people were not all opposed to foreigners, including the British. A lieutenant-colonel of the Royal Engineers recounted this interesting experience in January, 1858:

I judged of the feelings of the common people towards us by a test I think was fair. Of course, on first showing ourselves in a portion of the city where we were rare beasts, the women and children fled in terror; but when they got a little accustomed to us, they did not show the same alarm. It was said by some amongst us, "The treacherous people are only withheld from killing us by fear; they fawn upon us now that we are strong, but hate us in their hearts." Now I believed *that* of the officials who had all their lives traveled along the groove of intolerant and prejudiced exclusiveness, but not of the country people. My test was the behaviour of the little children, old enough to understand their parents' conversation, but too young to be such adepts in dissimulation, or to have such power of self-command as to exhibit towards us the utmost confidence: little children would let me take them out of their fathers' arms, as I rode down the street, and enjoyed a ride with me as much as if I had been their best friend. Now, could we have been stigmatized in those families as barbarians, savage and intractable, unsurpassed in ferocity, or even as a horde of invaders, who, in order to conquer their country, or trade with them against their will, had destroyed a great portion of their city, turned out on the world houseless many unoffending citizens—killing their countrymen, and in reality the main cause of all the trouble and sorrow which of late years had fallen upon them? That would have been a character such as they might be expected to give us; but it would have made the children rather distrustful, had their parents so spoken of us.[271]

It is possible of course to overstress the friendliness of the common people to foreigners. Western travelers in China sometimes encountered hostile villagers or townsfolk whose hostility might come from at least two different sources. In some cases foreigners might travel in localities where "rough characters" happened to be present and active and unhappily come into contact with such elements. Such,

for instance, was the experience of Baron von Richthofen in his journey to Hupeh and Hunan early in 1870. While he had "not met anywhere in China with people more inoffensive and good-natured than
those inhabiting the banks of the Han," he found the inhabitants of
Hunan much less amicable, "due, chiefly, to the existence of a class
of rough characters," especially numerous in that province.[272] In
other cases it appears that inhabitants of inland localities, who had
relatively little previous contact with foreigners, usually were freer
from antiforeign feelings than those of regions where there had been
more contact. Richthofen's journey from Fan-ch'eng (Hupeh) to Huai-
ch'ing Fu (Honan), a total distance of 1,000 li (a region seldom traversed by Westerners in those days), moved him to say that "nowhere
on earth does there exist a more good-natured race than inhabits the
province of Honan." Only in one or two places situated on the Yellow
River did he hear the epithet *Yang-kwei-tsze* (foreign devil).[273] In
his journey through some parts of Chekiang and Anhwei, however,
the experience was less pleasant. He wrote in one of his letters:

> All along my route, the people (as many as there were) were civil
> and kindhearted, until I reached the trading marts in Nganhwei [An-
> hwei] to which the boats of the Yangtse ascend. The rudeness so char-
> acteristic of the people in the trading places all along the great river,
> was here immediately perceptible.[274]

The facts noted by a British civil servant stationed in Hong Kong
lend further support to the view that the antiforeign feelings of the
common people tended to be more pronounced in places where contact with foreigners was likely to be closer than usual. This writer
mentioned thirty-five riots dated from December 7, 1842, to August
15, 1902 (excluding the Boxer uprising), resulting in "destruction of
lives or property or both," and commented that these occurred almost invariably in places where contact with foreigners was most
frequent. In fact, among the twenty-three localities in which these
riots broke out, fifteen were treaty ports and one was a British col-
ony.[275]

Even the Boxer uprising itself, according to another Western observer, did not materialize as the result of any inherent antiforeign
feelings that prevailed among the people of Shantung province.

> Up to the fall of 1897, Shan-tung enjoyed an excellent reputation
> for its treatment of foreigners and native Christians. . . . On the 1st
> of November of that year, however, there was a riot in which two
> German Catholic missionaries were brutally murdered, and Germany
> promptly seized upon the crime as a pretext for what it had long con-
> templated, the seizure of a portion of Chinese territory. On the 14th,
> Admiral Diedrichs landed troops at Kiao Chow [Chiao Chou] . . . On
> the 6th of the following March, a treaty was signed at Peking by which

the country around about the Bay of Kiao Chow, as far inland as the neighboring hills, was ceded to the German Empire for ninety-nine years; the Governor of Shan-tung was dismissed, six other high officials removed, and indemnity of 3,000 taels paid, and a promise made to build three "expiatory" chapels. Germany obtained in addition a concession for two railways in the province, and the right to open mines within a region of territory twenty kilometers wide along them. These were hard terms, but that which was most bitterly resented was the seizure of territory. This high-handed act worked an ominous change in the attitude of the people toward foreigners, and especially Germans. It was not safe for Germans in small companies to travel in the interior, and three who later unwisely did so were attacked, though they fortunately escaped with their lives. To punish the perpetrators of what the German Government chose to consider another unprovoked crime, the commander of Kiao Chow immediately sent troops to the scene of attack, and they burned down two villages. This harsh and indiscriminate retaliation, in which innocent suffered as well as guilty, inflamed the people to madness, and many foreigners predicted serious results. [276]

The Germans precipitated the crisis, but they were not alone to blame for the widespread xenophobia. "The circumstances attending the first introduction of Europeans to the Chinese," a Western writer observed at the end of the nineteenth century, "were such as to give that people the impression that the visitors were little better than pirates and murderers, and not a little has occurred since to deepen that unhappy feeling." And "with Western missionaries preaching peace and Western governments practicing murder, it should not surprise us if the Chinese suspect the former as much as they fear the latter."[277]

The Role of the Gentry and Literati in Antiforeign Uprisings

Owing to the combination of various factors, the course of events moved rapidly to the tragic climax of 1900. So far as the Chinese were concerned, both the gentry and common people were drawn into this catastrophe. As in other types of uprisings, however, they did not play the same role: the former were responsible for supplying the movements with initiative and direction, whereas the latter afforded the physical force. The best illustration of this fact is the incident of San-yüan-li, which occurred in the northern suburb of Canton in May, 1841, and has been regarded by some as "the starting point of rebellious movements in the nineteenth century.[278]

The immediate occasion of the disturbance, according to both Chinese and Western contemporary observers,[279] was local resentment against British troops who reportedly committed some atrocities in villages near Canton. A Chinese writer stated that when these troops

were marching through San-yüan-li on their way to Fu-shan, the inhabitants of this locality rose noisily to drive them away, since they
were reported to have indulged in looting and in violating women.
Suddenly, upon the sound of the gong, people from 103 villages gathered, men and women numbering several thousand, and surrounded
them. [280]

The rioters did not win any victory over the foreigners. [281] Violent
opposition to the "English barbarians," however, persisted and grew.
Resentment against atrocities committed in villages soon was associated with opposition to the British demand to enter Canton. Some
Chinese writers of the time did not hesitate to credit the rioting villagers with patriotic defense of the city. As a Chinese official put it:

> It was really the efforts of rural inhabitants that luckily saved the
> city of Kuang-chou, the provincial capital [from being lost to the Eng-
> lish]. These rural people being aware that the government troops
> cannot be depended upon and aroused by righteous indignation, re-
> sisted [the English] with all their might and main. They rose upon
> the first call, and promptly rendered the English barbarians white-
> livered and frightened them out of their senses. [282]

It is not our task here to ascertain the real cause of the incident, nor
to trace the actual course of its development. One thing, however, is
sure. While the villagers were incited into violent reaction by reports of British atrocities, it was the local gentry who instigated and
directed the uprising.

"Nine antiforeign riots out of ten," opined a British civil servant,
"are directly fomented and instigated from the yamen, possible not
by the mandarin himself, but at any rate by his entourage, or by the
local literati." [283] In the case of San-yüan-li, it was definitely clear
that the riot was from the very beginning guided by local gentry elements. A Chinese educational official of Kwangtung, who in all probability had a hand in the matter, narrated that after the news of British atrocities in the villages reached Ho Yü-ch'eng (a *chü-jen*), he
promptly summoned village leaders in the vicinities of Canton (including Nan-hai, P'an-yü, and Tseng-ch'eng), and instructed them
to send "able-bodied men to protect" San-yüan-li. After two days of
skirmishes between villagers and "barbarians," three local officials
(the magistrates of Nan-hai and P'an-yü, and the prefect of Kuang-
shou) were ordered by the governor-general (Ch'i-kung, who had
just replaced Ch'i-shan) to mediate. These officials "went on foot to
San-yüan-li, courteously saluted the gentry and people, and per-
suasively entreated forgiveness on behalf of the barbarians. A few
hours later, the gentry stealthily departed; the people, owing to the
presence of these officials, dared not do anything." [284]
This narrative is self-explanatory and its general veracity can

hardly be questioned. It is, at any rate, broadly corroborated by the
narrative of a lieutenant of the Madras Engineers, an eyewitness of
the scene:

> . . . the inhabitants of the surrounding villages, bearing arms and
> standards in considerable numbers, began, on the day succeeding the
> commencement of the armistice, to assemble in heavy and threaten-
> ing masses . . . excited, it is believed, by inflammatory addresses
> and placards, circulated among them by influential members of the
> patriotic gentry of the province, and further, it is feared, infuriated
> by some excesses perpetrated by stragglers from the British out-
> posts. . . .
>   During the whole day [May 30] their numbers continued to increase
> until about three P. M. , when from 10, 000 to 12, 000 men appeared
> formed on the hills and preparing for a forward movement. At this
> time the kwang-chow-foo of Canton [the prefect of Kuang-chou] ar-
> rived on the field, and . . . offered to dispatch a mandarin of rank
> to disperse the people. . . . They appeared at first disposed to re-
> sist the mandarin's order to disperse, but after a short discussion
> which he held with their leaders, they began to break up, and . . .
> in the course of half an hour had almost entirely disappeared. [285]

The contents of some of the placards that appeared in this period
may be gathered from an example found in the autumn of 1842, when
the gentry were leading the local inhabitants to oppose any extension
of the area for foreign residence beyond the factories. According to
a contemporary report, this propaganda piece was used to arouse
popular antipathy by reviving all the old causes of complaint against
the English,

> "whose ruler is now a woman and then a man, whose disposition is
> more fierce and furious than the tiger or the wolf, " and charging
> them with breach of faith in continuing hostilities after they had made
> the convention of May 1841; warning the people that, if the English
> were allowed to settle on Chinese soil, "to encroach even to our bed-
> sides, " other nations would follow in their steps. [286]

No untutored commoner or ordinary peasant, certainly, could have
produced such a document.
   There is evidence that some of the local academies *(shu-yüan)* and
"community schools"*(she-hsüeh)* of South China were, in the 1840's,
centers of antiforeign agitation. [287] This of course is no surprise.
Moreover, as some of these schools took leading parts in the local
defense organizations, it was an easy matter for the gentry who controlled *shu-yüan* or *she-hsüeh* to implement their antiforeign actions
by mobilizing the men enlisted in the *t'uan-lien* units that existed in
the villages. Ho Yü-ch'eng, the *chü-jen* mentioned a moment ago,
who summoned "able-bodied men" from the villages near Canton and

precipitated the clash at San-yüan-li, was one of those who established *she-hsüeh* and integrated *t'uan-lien* organizations with them. Similar arrangements sprang up in adjacent localities; the total number of men enlisted was said to have amounted to tens of thousands. These "braves" who were regimented and drilled, "in times of peace engaged themselves contentedly in agricultural pursuits. In an emergency, these farmers promptly became soldiers."[288] It is reasonable to suppose that some of the 10,000 or 12,000 who "appeared from the hills" in San-yüan-li were part of the "braves" that answered the call of their leaders. It is interesting to note that before the incident of 1841 these gentry-controlled organizations received official blessing; those located in the suburbs of Canton were placed, for a little while, under the command of the deputy commander of the government troops stationed in Canton.[289] Apparently, local authorities, including the governor-general, wished to make use of these organizations to convince the English of the imprudence of forcing their demands upon them. But when some of the gentry actually led the drilled villagers to attack the English troops, the local officials found it wise to disavow any connection with the rioters.

As late as 1849, when the English renewed their demand to enter Canton, the persons in charge of some of the *shu-yüan* in the vicinities of the provincial capital took the initiative to organize the gentry in the city and to set up defense forces against the intruders. It was claimed that "within about ten days over 100,000 men were enlisted."[290] Still later, in 1856, when the English forced their way into Canton, according to a contemporary Chinese writer, the ninety-six villages north of the city, which "in years past had inflicted damages on foreigners at San-yüan-li," undertook to revive the *t'uan-lien* under the leadership of three officials then living in retirement in their home communities.[291] Time and circumstances had changed; their efforts proved to be totally abortive. But this development lends additional support to the view that antiforeign movements, in Kwangtung and in other places, were gentry inspired and gentry led.[292]

It should not be assumed, however, that all the gentry in a given locality shared the same views concerning the proper way to deal with foreigners. For one reason or another, some of them found missionary work in China useful and did not hesitate to befriend missionaries. A well-known American missionary, for example, reported in 1836 that the work of the Medical Missionary Society attracted a number of government officials. "Even the official of the Nan hai hsien, the Western district of Canton, sent his card" with the request that medical treatment be given to the child of one of his relatives. Three years later, he reported that an acting judicial commissioner of the province was among the patients of the hospital. "In 1840, the provincial treasurer, Yü, applied for aid but did not dare to come either to the hospital or the Hong merchants, on account of a long standing feud with Lin [Tse-hsü]. "[293] As a matter of fact, there was no unanimous agreement among the gentry of Canton even in the troubled early 1840's. According to a Western observer, when some of the gentry met on December 2, 1842, to discuss antiforeign moves, one of them read a manifesto, "appealing to the reason of those present, and warning them that the only object of the opposite party [that urged violence against the English] was to stir up commotion." As a result "the meeting broke up in confusion. "[294] Apparently, "the opposite party" commanded sufficient support "to go it alone," and succeeded in stirring up trouble.

Nor is it correct to suppose that officials and literati always cooperated in antiforeign movements. Officials who were held accountable for local peace and order could not afford to support the gentry in starting or sustaining riots. Sometimes, as in the episodes occurring around Canton in the 1840's, the local officials who withheld their support became targets of gentry wrath. As a circuit censor said: "In showing enmity to the English barbarians the people of Kwangtung forthwith became hostile to the local functionaries. "[295] The prefect of Kuang-chou, in particular, was odious to the antiforeign gentry on account of his conciliatory attitude toward the "barbarians. "[296] Other officials who had earned the gentry's enmity were made objects of popular derision. Hence the well-known jingle: "The people fear officials; officials fear foreign devils," which, however, was changed into: "Officials fear foreign devils; foreign devils fear the people. "[297] In fact, in some cases antiforeign riots assumed the form of anti-official riots. [298]

Subsequent riots in other localities pointed to the same general situation. A riot broke out in Yang-chou (Kiangsu), August 22, 1868, when a missionary tried to establish a post there:

> Yang Chou was a city of three hundred and sixty thousand inhabitants, situated on the Grand Canal. After making efforts to rent some thirty different houses, one was at last found. But the report of hostility at Chen Chiang stirred up the literati to organized efforts to prevent the occupation of this place. The populace were inflamed, first by small handbills of a defamatory nature, and, these proving insufficient, by larger ones, until the whole city was on the *qui vive*. . . .
> On the 22nd of August the mob attacked the place in earnest, and when it became evident that the repeated messengers sent to the officials would bring no aid, Mr. Taylor [the missionary in charge] and his companion risked their lives in a personal visit to the yamen, where they were kept waiting for three-quarters of an hour, while hearing the shouts of the mob at a distance, destroying the property and not improbably the lives of the ladies left in the house. When at last the magistrate appeared, it was to ask insulting questions about

the imaginary Chinese children alleged to have been kidnapped. . . .
When at length, after two hours of torturing suspense they were allowed to return, the place was in complete ruin, and the remaining
missionaries, who had barely escaped with their lives, were in hiding. [299]

A well-known Western missionary, writing in the late 1890's,
summed up the general situation after 1870:

The minds of the people had been prepared by the dissemination of
false rumors, and when they were wrought up to the required point
the mandarins stood aloof and allowed the storm to take its course.
Since that date [June, 1870, when a Catholic mission in Tientsin was
destroyed] there have been twenty or more anti-foreign—not altogether anti-mission—riots of sufficient magnitude to be visible across
the seas; culminating this year in the expulsion of missionaries from
the capital of Szechuen [Szechwan], and the massacre at Kucheng [Ku-
ch'eng], near Fuchau [Foochow]. Most of these have conformed to
the original type in every particular—beginning with tracts and placards as their exciting cause, followed by studied negligence on the
part of mandarins (who always contrived to come too late when their
aid was invoked), and finishing with an inquiry how many heads and
how much money would satisfy the resulting claims. . . .
    The instigators of mobs are generally mandarins or members of
the student class, who seek to fortify the public mind against the influx of foreign ideas by accusing foreigners of horrible crimes. The
most inflammatory, though not the most revolting, of these accusations is that of kidnapping children, and taking their eyes, blood, and
fat for the preparation of magical drugs. [300]

How effective the antiforeign propaganda could be may be seen from
the following account of another missionary:

For ten years after the Treaty of Tientsin [1860] a salutary dread
of foreign power took the place of the popular contempt for all foreigners on the part of the Cantonese. But in July, 1871, placards
were everywhere circulated throughout the entire region charging
foreigners with the distribution of powders of a supposed wonderful
efficacy in healing disease, which were yet a slow poison. The day
following the posting of these inflammatory sheets a tempest of alarm
and rage spread over the whole city, the violence of which no foreigner had ever seen surpassed. Three-fourths of the people believed
these tales, and a panic seized the whole population. . . .
    The execution of some of the leaders by the friendly Governor-
General put a stop to the excitement, which spread, however, to Amoy,
and even to Fu Chou [Foochow], and almost extinguished mission
work. [301]

As is well known, these and other uprisings, including the great

upheaval of 1900, did not materially impair missionary work. Instead, they brought additional humiliation to the imperial government and further reduced its prestige in the eyes of the native population. Antiforeign riots, no less than other types of local disturbances, contributed to weakening imperial control over rural China.

The importance of these violent outbreaks can hardly be gainsaid.
They constituted the tangible expressions of a virtually empire-wide
antiforeign movement fostered by many of the literati, encouraged
or tolerated by some of the officials, and supported by those commoners who suffered injuries, real or imagined, from foreigners.[302]
It would be inaccurate, however, to regard (as some writers did)
this antiforeign movement of the nineteenth century in general or
the Boxer Rebellion in particular as "a popular war for the maintenance of Chinese nationality,"[303] if by these words it is implied
that the Chinese people as a whole engaged in a concerted struggle
against foreigners. Such an interpretation of this historical development fails to give due emphasis to the role of the gentry and therefore does not square with the facts.

Wars with Western Nations

The disastrous effects of the wars waged by England, France, and
other nations upon China in the nineteenth century can readily be seen.
Besides putting a heavy strain on the economy, these wars exerted
adverse influences on the population (first on the inhabitants of coastal regions and eventually on those of inland provinces) in two important directions. On the one hand, the repeated defeats and the resulting humiliations suffered by the imperial government inevitably impaired whatever prestige it had hitherto enjoyed. On the other hand,
the organization of local forces in some parts of South China to meet
the emergencies arising from the invasion of foreign troops emboldened "wicked people" to challenge openly the authority of government.
The general situation was perhaps most succinctly summarized by
a well-known British official:

> Whatever may be the final result of the internal troubles which now
> [mid-nineteenth century] afflict China, they are, in no small degree,
> the consequences of that disgrace and defeat which the proud and boast-
> ful government of the country sustained in the war with Great Brit-
> ain. . . .
> The change was felt in many parts of the country. The people began
> to oppose the payment of their former exactions, insurrections arose
> in various quarters, and bands of robbers, always a source of trouble,
> now began to defy the government. . . .
> By a long established rule of the government, the possession of
> fire-arms had always, previous to the war with England, been denied

to the common people. . . . But during the war there had been such a liberal distribution of arms to persons of all descriptions, that they remained in the possession of many who were soon ready to make a bad use of them. [304]

After having attributed to this same cause the growth of piracy, banditry, secret societies, and riots in South China, the author went a step further and traced the origin of the Taiping uprising partly to the Opium War:

> There can be no doubt whatever of the existing insurrection in China having been the result of our own war. A Manchu general, in his report, distinctly stated that "the number of robbers and criminal associations is very great in the two Kwang provinces (i.e., Kwang-tung and Kwang-se), and they assemble without difficulty to create trouble; all which arises from that class having detected the inefficiency of the imperial troops during the war with the English barbarians. Formerly they feared the troops as tigers; of late they look on them as sheep. Of the multitudes of irregulars who were disbanded on the settlement of the barbarian difficulty, very few returned to their original occupations—most of them became robbers. [305]

This is obviously an oversimplification. The Taiping uprising had more roots than the circumstances created by the Opium War and its aftermath. Nevertheless it cannot be denied that military defeats contributed directly and powerfully to the weakening of the imperial government, simultaneously lowering the morale of officialdom and encouraging disloyal subjects to rise against the authorities. The following conversation given by a Western missionary may not be a verbatim record, but it indicates the mental attitude that prevailed in the declining years of a dynasty:

> One day, when a military mandarin was relating to us with great naïveté stories of the prowess of the famous Kuoang-ti [Kuan-ti, the god of war], we bethought ourselves to ask him whether he had appeared in the last war that the empire was engaged in with the English. . . . "Don't let us talk any more of that war," said the Mandarin; "Kouang-ti certainly did not appear, and it is a very bad sign. They say," he added, lowering his voice, "that this dynasty is abandoned by Heaven, and that it will be soon overthrown."
> This idea that the Mantchoo dynasty has finished its appointed career, and that another will shortly succeed it, was very widely diffused in China in 1846; during our journey we several times heard it mentioned, and there is little doubt that this kind of vague presentiment, prevailing for several years, was a very powerful auxiliary to the insurrection that broke out in 1851, and since then has made such gigantic progress. [306]

Such a defeatist attitude may not have been very widespread among the officials. But the desperate situation of having to defend the imperial regime against internal rebellion and foreign invasion simultaneously in 1859-60 rendered it difficult even for the ablest statesman of the time to decide on a suitable course of action. In a letter to Hu Lin-i, Tseng Kuo-fan discussed with obvious perplexity the alternatives of remaining where he was to fight the Taipings and of leading his troops to protect the imperial capital against the British and French invaders. [307]

Oddly enough, a contemporary Western writer of a persuasion widely different from the Western official and missionary quoted above, discovered also a direct connection between the Opium War and the Taiping Rebellion:

> Whatever be the social cause, and whatever religious, dynastic, or national shape they may assume, that have brought about the chronic rebellions subsisting in China for about ten years past, and now gathered together in one formidable revolution, the occasion of this outbreak has unquestionably been afforded by the English cannon forcing upon China that soporific drug called opium. Before the British arms the authority of the Manchu dynasty fell to pieces; the superstitious faith in the eternity of the Celestial Empire broke down. [308]

This discussion, it is hoped, has justified the conclusion that the influx of Westerners and Western civilization contributed to the turmoils of the nineteenth century and to the eventual downfall of the Manchu government. It is difficult to determine the precise share which external pressure and internal decay respectively had in putting an end to the Ch'ing dynasty. It may be said, however, that the former reinforced the latter and accelerated the general catastrophic process. [309] By introducing novel conceptions of religion, education, and government, as well as novel methods of manufacture and warfare into China, and by convincing China (through the eloquence of superior military force) that her traditional system was no longer adequate to the changed situation, Western nations had unintentionally helped to put an end to the hitherto seemingly endless dynastic cycle.

Chapter 11

●

SUMMARY AND POSTSCRIPT

THE RATIONALE AND EFFECTS OF RURAL CONTROL

The system of rural control that existed in the Ch'ing dynasty was a product of the circumstances that confronted the imperial rulers and grew out of the nature of the imperial system itself. The government of the Ch'ing dynasty, like preceding regimes, was an autocracy ruling over a society in which the population was stratified into groups of people with unequal political, social, and economic status; and the interests of the ruler and subjects were divergent and to some extent incompatible. [1] The imperial rulers were therefore compelled by practical necessity to maintain as firm as possible a control of the vast realm in order to insure political stability and thus perpetuate their regime. Because they could not have confidence in their subjects or count on their loyalty, they sought to render the latter submissive and subservient by a variety of devices calculated to immunize them against all thought and action that might prove detrimental to imperial security. The fact that the Ch'ing rulers were conquerors from an alien ethnic group made this necessity all the more obvious and urgent.

Imperial control was exercised through an officialdom recruited from the upper strata of the population, reinforced at strategic points by the actual or deterrent power of a military apparatus. The empire, however, was an extensive realm with an immense population and poor means of communication and transportation. It was physically impossible for the administrative and military arms of the imperial government to reach every hamlet or village throughout the countryside. To extend control to the rural level it was necessary to employ what may be described as a subadministrative system of local apparatus. Benefiting from the experiences of preceding dynasties and making use of historical institutions, the early emperors of the Ch'ing dynasty set up such a system with a variety of component devices, each designed to perform a certain function. Every important aspect of rural life was thus theoretically brought under the surveillance and direction of the government.

501

As these devices were first set up, they differed appreciably in their several functions but were operated on similar principles. Local people were extensively employed to assist in the control, but the government took care to maintain close supervision over them. Organizations or groups already existing in rural communities were often used as auxiliary instruments of control, but the government never hesitated to curtail their activities or suppress them altogether. The local gentry and literati were conditioned in such a way that they might be usefully employed in rural control, and were actually often so employed. Being aware that stable economic and political conditions were indispensable to successful control, the imperial rulers undertook to protect the interests of the various sections of the population against undue encroachment, so that the bulk of the inhabitants of any given rural area tended to regard continued acceptance of the existing regime as the surest way to promote or preserve their interests, while "lawless persons" found it generally difficult to extend their activities. The growth of local autonomy was to be prevented by assigning various functions of rural control to a number of separate or partially duplicating apparatus, so that none of them could attain a monopoly of local influence and thereby develop into centers of power at the periphery of the imperial system.

Ingeniously as this system was designed, it did not serve adequately or completely the purposes for which it was intended. It did not assure absolute security to the imperial rulers. Evidence points to the conclusion that rural control attained a measure of success under two conditions: the existence of a fairly reliable and efficient officialdom to direct and supervise its operation, and a generally stable rural environment in which the bulk of the inhabitants could eke out an undisturbed though none too ample livelihood. When these conditions were present, as they were during the first three or four reigns of the Ch'ing dynasty, the instruments of rural control worked relatively well. Even though the *pao-chia,* in some respects the keystone of the control structure, did not in every instance produce positive results, its presence in the countryside had at least a deterrent effect and thus helped to reduce occasions of disorder. Floods, droughts, and other misfortunes occurred time and again, even when the dynasty was at the height of its strength, but owing to the prevalence of order and to a relatively conscientious local administration, they did not result in economic disaster. And thanks perhaps to the good luck of the earlier emperors, natural calamities did not occur too frequently and were not too overwhelming in the early periods. Under such comparatively favorable circumstances a large number of rural inhabitants were poor and some of them hungry, but at any given moment and in any given area not too many of them were driven by poverty or hunger into desperation. Under these same circumstances rural control contributed its share to the general stability of the empire.

Favorable circumstances, however, did not continue indefinitely. By the end of the eighteenth century the dynasty had begun to go downhill. From the latter part of the Ch'ien-lung reign onward, the imperial administration deteriorated with accelerated speed.[2] Meanwhile, as a Western writer remarked, "In the fourteen years since Tao-kuang came to the throne (in 1821) there had not been one prosperous year; inundations, drought, famine, risings, insurrections, and other calamities were constantly occurring in one province or another."[3] With a generally inept and demoralized officialdom the imperial government could no longer meet crises with the same degree of dexterity or determination as it formerly did. It was baffled even in its attempt to preserve a measure of respectability in the eyes of the inhabitants in general. The uncertain tranquillity which formerly prevailed in the countryside was repeatedly broken by rural inhabitants who were driven to desperation by the cumulative effects of prolonged physical want, social inequities, and maladministration, and in particular by those who had come to the conclusion that it was better to challenge the authorities than to continue to submit to them. Under changed conditions the sprawling system of rural control with its diverse auxiliary apparatus became largely ineffectual. In many instances, it became in fact an additional disturbing factor in the rural situation and was therefore worse than useless.

The entire rural system of administration was rapidly breaking down. Amidst discontent and despair—even though these were but vaguely felt by the average peasant—neither the local agents who were supposed to operate the various devices of rural control nor the local officials, who had the responsibility of directing and supervising their operation, were in a condition to fulfill their duties. The morale of the *pao-chia*, *li-chia*, and *hsiang-yüeh*, key institutions of the system, was never high. By the opening decades of the nineteenth century it had declined so far in one institution after another that no amount of imperial effort could revive it. The frequent outbreaks of feuds, riots, banditry, and rebellions in the latter part of that century gave unmistakable proof that the whole structure of rural control had become little more than a skeleton.

LIMITATIONS OF AUTOCRATIC RULE

Without minimizing the importance of other historical forces, one may safely conclude that administrative deterioration was one of the most crucial factors that contributed to the decay of the rural control system. A question naturally suggests itself: could the imperial rulers have averted such deterioration?

It would have been difficult if not impossible to do so. There seem
to have been some weaknesses inherent in the imperial system that
inevitably led to administrative decay. Since the emperors were suspicious of their subjects and as rulers over an alien population could
not wisely take the latter's loyalty for granted, strict administrative
surveillance was exercised. The emperors had to rely to a very large
extent on Chinese scholars and officials to operate, supervise, or assist the administration, but thinking that even these persons were not
necessarily above suspicion, they were consistently careful to keep
their servants on a tight leash. Whenever a choice had to be made,
therefore, the emperors invariably allowed imperial security to over-
rule administrative efficiency. As a result, public functionaries were
rarely given an opportunity to show initiative, independent judgment,
or satisfactory performance of tasks through the exercising of adequate authority. On the contrary, all officials were subjected to a
tight net of regulations, restrictions, and checks, and threatened with
punishment for derelictions or offenses even in matters beyond their
individual control. A situation eventually prevailed in which the most
prudent thing for the average official to do was to assume as little
responsibility as possible—to pay greater attention to formal compliance with written rules than to undertakings that were useful to the
sovereign or beneficial to the people.

Such an imperial policy, while fully consistent with the nature of
autocratic rule, was hardly conducive to efficient government. The
Ch'ing emperors succeeded so well in rendering officialdom politically innocuous that, except during the first and closing years of the
dynasty, no official was known to have harbored treasonable designs
against their regime. At the same time, however, they enervated it
so that few of its members strove to be competent and conscientious
administrators, and many of them were willing to leave vital tasks
of government largely undone.[4] This basic administrative defect was
aggravated by a number of unfortunate imperial practices. The official salary and remuneration scale, which was ridiculously low to
begin with, did not adjust itself to the rising cost of living and thereby
rendered "squeeze," bribery, and extortion inevitable and increasingly
necessary. The large-scale selling of official posts, especially extensive in the second half of the nineteenth century, constituted another invitation to corruption. The thinly veiled discrimination against
the Chinese in appointments to the upper echelons of government prevented the development of a loyal, responsible Chinese officialdom
or the emergence of a competent Manchu bureaucracy recruited according to a strict principle of merit. Thus the Ch'ing administration,
which was never fully efficient, soon showed signs of further deterioration. Despite the presence of the system of universal surveillance
and control, the empire was in fact placed largely at the mercy of

fortuitous circumstances. The imperial government, as well as its subjects, was quite helpless in the face of serious crises or calamities. Inadequacy and inefficient administration was the high price that the Ch'ing emperors paid for the uncertain political stability which they laboriously tried to maintain by means of an otherwise ingenious system of control.

The basic administrative difficulty of the Ch'ing regime may be viewed from another angle. In the Chinese imperial system, which was a form of centralized authoritarianism, the rulers claimed the right to exercise unlimited authority over everything and everyone, and were determined to exercise that right. Their determination, however, did not alter the fact that the existence of a center implies the presence of a periphery and that power emanating from the center diminishes in effectiveness as it approaches the periphery. In an immense political orb like the Chinese empire, the decrement of central power in its empire-wide application was bound to be considerable. Resounding imperial commands, to which officials generally rendered little more than lip service, tended to fade into faint echoes when they arrived at the *chou* and *hsien* level of the administrative structure. In fact, the imperial government was unable even to exercise effective supervision over the fifteen hundred *chou* and *hsien* magistrates who were supposed to keep the various apparatus of rural control in working order and to administer to the needs of the local inhabitants under their "parental care. " The *pao-chia, li-chia, hsiang-yüeh* and other institutions largely fell into desuetude or disrepute; villagers and villages were left to shift for themselves, receiving from the government little beyond occasional token assistance or relief in times of disaster. A partial administrative vacuum thus existed in the countryside, despite the emperors' desire to extend control to every corner of the empire. This vacuum, a consequence of inadequate administration, gave rise to the illusion of rural "autonomy" of which some writers spoke with unfounded enthusiasm. These writers mistook a mirage resulting from incomplete autocratic rule for a true image of democracy. [5]

Another serious flaw of the imperial system, pointed out earlier in the present section, must be underscored: the discrepancy of interests between the rulers on the one side and the various segments of the population on the other, which made it extremely difficult for the former to assure themselves of the loyalty of the latter.

It is important for our purpose here to identify the precise position of the gentry and literati (or potential gentry) in the imperial system. Owing to their personal qualifications and social status, they exerted considerable influence upon the multitude of common people in the villages or towns. It was from this elite group that the imperial rulers recruited their administrative servants. Leadership in their home communities and services in the administration, however, did not make the gentry a part of the ruling class, nor cause their interests to become identical. In fact as well as in theory, scholar-officials remained subjects of the Son of Heaven and, together with commoners, were objects of imperial control. Those who in their capacity as government officials functioned as mediums through which imperial authority was brought to bear on the masses, were at the same time a part of "the people" over whom and ostensibly for whose benefit the emperors ruled.

That the interests of the scholar-officials did not necessarily coincide with the imperial interests can be readily seen. The central aim of the emperors was to maintain their regime for "ten thousand generations." In order, however, to make the conditions of the empire favorable to their continued rule, they sought to make their subjects, both gentry and commoners, generally contented with their lot or at least not seriously dissatisfied with it. Thus while the innermost wish of the dynastic rulers was to perpetuate their regime, their professed intention was, as the time-honored Confucian formula had it, "to benefit the people."[6] Under ordinary circumstances, the gentry and literati were inclined to accept all this quite readily; they had more than one reason to lend their moral or actual support to the imperial regime. For one thing, the Confucian facade of imperial ideology agreed with the intellectual tradition in which they were brought up. Moreover, the continuation of the dynasty promised continued enjoyment (or continued opportunities to secure the enjoyment) of the coveted immunities and privileges of their status. The interests of the gentry who entered officialdom were most closely interwoven with the interests of the existing regime; these men therefore had an even stronger motive to uphold it than the rest of the group. These two sets of interests, however, remained distinct and might drift apart when the circumstances that held them together drastically changed. When a dynastic cycle came to an end, at least as many scholar-officials accepted the new regime as remained loyal to the defunct one.

It should be noted also that only a small fraction of the gentry served in the government at any given time, and that they did not necessarily remain in office for life. Retired functionaries, expectant officials, and degree-holding scholars far outnumbered officials in active government service. These nonadministrative members of the gentry, like commoner literati, were inclined to be more concerned with their personal and family interests than with helping the emperors to control their domain. They had much in common with the ordinary villagers or townsfolk. For besides being gentry, they were heads of households, taxpayers, and perhaps also landowners, with interests that might sometimes be harmed or threatened as a result of imperial policy or local misgovernment. Owing to their status, they were in a better position to protect these interests, but the very necessity for protection revealed their true position in society: they were privileged subjects but not members of the ruling class. One can hardly overlook the significant fact that not a few of the members of the gentry acquired their status precisely to secure better protection of their families and property against encroachment—not to satisfy their wish to serve the imperial cause.

The Confucian theory of benevolent government (which constituted an integral part of imperial ideology and the gentry's political philosophy) was understood in different ways by the imperial rulers on the one hand and by scholar-officials and literati on the other. To the former the concept of benevolent government was essentially a justification of, or a theoretical basis for, "paternalistic," autocratic rule; to the latter it constituted a serviceable ideological armor to guard their own material interests against maladministration and tyranny. The emperors paid high honor to the Ch'eng-Chu school of Neo-Confucianism, which stressed political loyalty and filial duty; scholar-officials, including followers of the Ch'eng-Chu tradition, seldom failed to reiterate Mencius' doctrine of "the paramountcy of the people" and its obverse, the right of tyrannicide, whenever occasion required.

Under ordinary circumstances the gentry tended to use that doctrine to serve their private interests in the name of "the people," without challenging the imperial authority. They equated their own interests with those of "the people" and assumed the role of the latter's spokesmen. The earnest words presenting harrowing pictures of peasant sufferings that were used time and again in petitions for tax relief afford a revealing illustration of this. The petitions were made on behalf of "the people" of the localities affected, but the lion's share of any benefit that might result went to the gentry landowners—if indeed tenants and petty commoner landowners received any at all. The imperial rulers, who were not primarily concerned with "benefiting the people," often allowed their commoner subjects to receive fewer benefits, whenever they made concessions to the interests of "the people," in taxation or other matters. Thus the gentry had another reason for supporting the existing regime and were ready to parrot the platitude that "the profound benevolence of the present dynasty surpasses all," even though they may have actually thought otherwise. A subservient gentry lived symbiotically with a generally submissive rural population, and a measure of political stability prevailed in the empire. The imperial peace was marred by nothing more alarming than sporadic eruptions of local disorder.

This stability, however, was easily upset by serious calamities, natural or man-made, which rendered it difficult for large numbers of the inhabitants to carry on; it was impaired when the government failed or found it impossible to gratify the ambitions and aspirations of exceptional individuals. The members of the gentry or literati who were thus alienated or antagonized might out of resentment or bitter disappointment withdraw their support of the regime. In other words, when the disparity of interests between the imperial rulers and "the people" became apparent, persons who had hitherto remained at least outwardly loyal to the existing dynasty might now find it no longer advantageous to give it obedience or service. Under such circumstances, the Mencian doctrine mentioned above might be put to a different use by resentful members of the gentry and literati. They sought now to promote or protect their interests not by appealing to the principle of benevolent government for the sake of the people but by invoking the principle of "the right of rebellion." They might, like the youthful monkey in Liu Chi's parable,[7] incite villagers and townfolk to rise against "tyrannical government" or offer their skills and services to "bandit" leaders who had already raised their banners of revolt.

It becomes clear, then, that the attitudes of the gentry and literati toward the existing regime tended to vary under changing conditions, just as the reactions of the peasantry to imperial control varied in times of peace and unrest. The effectiveness of imperial control therefore hinged more upon a general confluence of divergent interests of the rulers and the various segments of the subject population than upon the apparatus or technique of control. When such a confluence existed, all segments of the subject population tended to accept the existing order, even though the control apparatus contained inherent shortcomings and operated with less than theoretical efficiency. When, however, the gentry and commoners felt that their vital interests were decidedly incompatible with the continued existence of the regime, no system of control, however ingeniously devised, was able to keep the empire quiet for long.

Apparently aware of this truth, the emperors of the Ch'ing dynasty took steps to induce such a confluence of interests, as we have indicated earlier in this study. Unfortunately for them, however, the differences between the interests of the rulers and the subjects in an autocratic state (particularly in one under alien rule) were too substantial to be completely reconcilable; the best efforts they made under the most favorable circumstances did not bring about more than a temporary, partial concordance of the divergent interests. The incomplete harmony thus attained was soon impaired by the adverse effects of their overshrewd moves to safeguard dynastic interests. Consistently they stressed the control process itself at the expense of constructive efforts to improve the welfare of their subjects. The empire eventually deteriorated administratively and economically, and was further weakened by repeated crises. Thus the Ch'ing dynasty sought to maintain perpetual rule by exercising complete, centralized control over its domain; but it was doomed by the inherent limitations of all autocratic regimes and by the untoward circumstances that prevailed in China from the middle of the nineteenth century to the beginning of the twentieth, to last for less than three centuries and to achieve no more than an incomplete, uncertain control of the vast empire.

In one sense, the imperial government of the Ch'ing may be said to have brought about its own ruin. In so far as it succeeded in keeping the bulk of its subjects passive and docile, it ultimately impaired their capacity for energetic action and rendered them progressively less qualified to cope with the harsh environment in which they had to live. The material foundations of the empire were thus weakened. Even in fairly normal times a large part of the peasantry lived from hand to mouth; some of them were on the verge of destitution. Agricultural improvement was practically impossible, owing to the lack of capital for such improvement and to an inveterate reliance on traditional techniques and on unpredictable luck. Wealthy landowners might possess enough means to furnish the capital, but their interests rarely went beyond collecting as much rent and paying as little tax as they could. They were more likely to use their money to acquire additional land for rent than to spend it to better farm conditions in order to increase production or to improve the livelihood of their tenants. Tillers of the soil (and not a few small landowners) exhausted their energies in eking out a bare subsistence. Little room was left for them to do anything else. Lucky indeed were those among them who managed to hold their own against bankruptcy or starvation resulting from local disasters. They became generally resigned to their physical and social circumstances. In their accustomed reticence they allowed the local gentry or local bullies to dictate matters of the neighborhood, especially the matters that lay beyond the narrow scope of their families or farms. All too readily peasants submitted to predatory acts of rascals and rowdies, to extortions of local functionaries and yamen underlings, and sometimes to the exploitation of the local gentry. Danger lurked behind such a situation. When economic conditions in large parts of the empire took an emphatic turn for the worse, many of the rural inhabitants could not even maintain the marginal existence that had been their lot; they had virtually to choose between "dying in ditches and water channels" and "walking the dangerous path." The choice was often not difficult to make. Enervated and unorganized by themselves, they (as in less stormy times) readily accepted leadership from anyone that offered it, and exhibited different types of behavior largely according to the types of such leadership. Some of them rallied around instigators of riots or rebellions; others were persuaded to follow bandit or insurrectionary groups. Thus, ironically, in so far as the effects of imperial control contributed to keeping peasants generally meek and passive, these very effects ultimately undermined imperial security by turning some of the "ignorant rustics" into material for insurrections—including the great upheavals that characterized the nineteenth century.

THE ROLE OF THE PEASANTRY

The Chinese peasantry, however, did not rise from the ashes of the imperial ruins during or after periods of violent political changes. They of all the inhabitants suffered most in times of peace and in times of turbulence. Economically or psychologically they gained little in the uprisings to which they contributed the main physical force. They were never masters of the movements in which they participated. They did not even choose their leaders, in the sense of freely taking or rejecting them. Many of the rank and file of the rebel armies died as nameless casualties, whether their movements proved fruitful or abortive; and when their movements succeeded in overthrowing the existing government, those that survived the battles and hardships became objects of control under the new regime.

One significant fact which we cannot overlook is that, like local riots and other forms of concerted demonstration of violence, the dynasty-wrecking movements in China's past were brought about by a confluence of human motives and a combination of historical circumstances. These movements were never the exclusive work of any one social class or group in Chinese society. Whatever may have been the precise role played by rural inhabitants in general and the peasantry in particular, it is certain the common villagers were not the only actors in these momentous events. As has already been said, uprisings—especially those that reached sufficient magnitude to be reported and recorded—were often led by persons who were not ordinary peasants, if they were commoners at all. It may also be safely said that in many known instances in which the immediate interests of the peasantry were declared to be a cause for which the movements committed themselves to fight, such interests did not actually constitute the only or central objective of any of these movements. On the contrary, the aim of a more or less important uprising often transcended the interests of the peasantry, which were nevertheless made a part of that aim either because the leaders sincerely believed that these interests should not be ignored or because they felt that by championing the peasants' cause they would gain the support of the masses, even though they were actually concerned with other issues broader than the immediate needs of the peasantry.

Leaders of rebellions or revolutions had good reasons for appealing to the desires of peasants, who, owing to their numbers and strength,

were alone capable of supplying the element of violence indispensable
to the initial success of any uprising. We do not have to go far back
into Chinese history to find pertinent examples. At the end of the Ming
dynasty Li Tzu-ch'eng, an ordinary bandit chief encouraged by circumstances to aspire to the imperial throne, promised universal exemption of grain taxes and consequently enjoyed an increasingly wide
following. [8] In the early 1850's Hung Hsiu-ch'üan and other leaders
of the Taiping Rebellion, which had too broad a significance to be regarded as a simple peasant movement, envisaged a system in which
each tiller of the soil would receive some land to support himself and
his family. [9] More recently, Mao Tse-tung included land redistribution among the first steps in the Communist revolutionary program. [10]
It is important to note that while the appeal to peasant interests secured mass participation in these movements, it does not follow that
such participation turned these movements into peasant movements
in the sense that peasants were actively or exclusively responsible
for them. For it is doubtful that they could have materialized without
the leadership or direction of persons who might have their original
homes in the villages but whose hands probably had never touched a
hoe or a plow and whose first "revolutionary" impulses were imparted
to them through their experiences in cities (e.g., Hung Hsiu-ch'üan
in Canton and Mao Tse-tung in Peking).

It is useful to note also that the Chinese peasants who had been so
long molded by the imperial system and whose characteristic attitudes and behavior had been so firmly established, showed little change
through all the vicissitudes of China's imperial history. Those who
took part in the various political upheavals and those who remained
apart from such events were essentially the same in their outlook and
conduct. One simple desire—the will to live—governed their actions
and reactions; one remitting task, cultivating the soil in order to keep
alive, engaged their attention and energies. Dynastic triumph did not
inject an iota of political enthusiasm into their minds, nor did dynastic
disintegration transform them into revolutionaries resolved to effect
social and political changes. This is not to deny the crucial importance of the peasantry as a factor in imperial history. On the contrary, our inquiry reveals that their superior numerical and physical
strength coupled with their habitual readiness to accept leadership
offered by persons with economic and social status different from
their own rendered the Chinese peasantry an indispensable ingredient
of every uprising against local officials or against the existing regime
itself. It is quite unnecessary to credit them with more than this in
order to account for the momentous role played by the peasants of
imperial China. The phrase "peasant revolution" that has gained favor
in some quarters may be useful or indispensable to propaganda purposes but it can hardly withstand objective historical analysis.

That not even the Communist revolution was a peasant movement pure and simple has become the considered opinion of unbiased writers. "All students of Chinese communism seem to agree," says a recent writer, "that it has been organized and led not by peasants or factory workers but by students, professors, and intellectuals in general."[11] Another writes, "There can be little doubt that the present Communist leaders in China have risen to power by addressing themselves to the immediate felt needs of China's peasant millions. To leap, however, from this fact to the conclusion that they are the embodiment of the aspirations of the Chinese people and that they will automatically continue to express the needs and aspirations of the masses is to construct a myth designed to sanction in advance all their future activities."[12] Facts indeed suggest the conclusion that the Chinese Communist movement, with the exception of its imported ideology, has repeated some of the salient features of the political process prevailing in the imperial past. As just indicated, the revolution was led not by peasants but by "an elite corps of politically articulate leaders organized along Leninist lines but drawn on its top levels from various strata of Chinese society."[13] The educational level of some of these leaders is exceptionally high. A few of them studied in Japan, Germany, France, the United States, and the Soviet Union.[14] Their general position in modern China, indeed, is comparable in certain ways to that occupied by the *shen-shih* of imperial times. They gave expression to their own desires and perhaps also to the inarticulate wishes of the bulk of the common people. Above all, they alone were capable of channeling the latter's unorganized strength into effective force. Marxism replaces Confucianism in their ideology, and "proletarian revolution" supersedes the "right of revolution" as justification for destroying the existing regime. But like the gentry and literati that took active part in the insurrections of old, they are not peasants or workers but come from the intelligentsia. "The Communist Party," an informed observer says,

> had been founded by the intelligentsia. The revolution was shaped by it. Without the intelligentsia the peasant insurrection, which in any case might have happened because of the misery of modern China, would have petered out in banditry like so many expressions of peasant despair in the past. The intelligentsia took hold of it and used it as a means of creating the Communist state.[15]

It is no surprise, therefore, that the Chinese Communist movement achieved victory "where by all Marxist tenets it might have been least expected that it could."[16] The inveterate characteristics of Chinese peasants—political indifference, economic discontent, readiness to follow any who promised change for the better, capacity for spasmodic violence—rendered them particularly suitable material for the

the Communist revolution, or any other type of uprising in which their immediate needs were apparently involved. Ch'en Tu-hsiu, one of the founders of the Chinese Communist movement, once remarked that "the peasantry's cultural level is low, their forces are scattered and they are inclined toward conservatism." These words are, as a recent writer points out, "Marxist-Leninist platitudes."[17] Ch'en, however, was not mistaken in his diagnosis of the mental constitution of Chinese peasants; he erred only in his prognosis that the peasant masses could not under suitable circumstances supply the sinews of a Communist upsurge as they were destined to do less than thirty years after he made these remarks. He fell into this error perhaps because he did not understand the historical position of the peasantry in Chinese society or the true nature of the uprisings in the imperial past. To put it more precisely, he failed to see that the peasantry that survived the imperial system with its essential characteristics unaltered by the revolution of 1911 was in reality a rich legacy for the Communist revolution. With a part of such a peasantry under their banner the Communist leaders came to a relatively easy victory in 1949.

The entire peasantry, however, did not go over to the Communist side deliberately and as a class at the juncture of, or immediately prior to, that victory. Many remained outside the movement up to the eve of the inauguration of the "People's Government." In fact, in places such as western Szechwan, where special conditions prevailed, peasants showed considerable resistance to the new authorities during the period immediately after the region was "liberated" in the winter of 1949. For a number of months suppressing "bandits" constituted a major local problem for the authorities.[18] Moreover, it may be recalled that the rank and file of the army of the National Government at Nanking, like the soldiers of the Red Army, came mostly from the countryside. Both fought many a bloody battle, particularly in the 1930's and 1940's, against their fellow peasants on the opposite side. The situation was not unlike that which prevailed in the 1850's and 1860's when most of China's peasantry was split into two camps, one of which defended the existing regime against the other which undertook to overthrow it.

The outcomes were, of course, totally different in the two situations. In one case the defenders were victorious, while in the other they suffered defeat. But the significant point is that in neither case was the armed conflict a struggle between the peasantry as a whole and a nonpeasant class. The contest was in reality between two heterogeneously composed groups, each mustering whatever number of peasants it could to man its battle lines. Peasant warriors under the leadership of Hung Hsiu-ch'üan and his associates lost the contest, partly because their leadership did not quite match that furnished by

Tseng Kuo-fan and his associates. Peasant comrades under Mao Tse-
tung and his associates conquered China for the Communist cause,
partly because the Kuomintang-controlled government exhibited too
many shortcomings and drifted into too many blunders to survive the
ruthless, shrewdly directed onslaught of the "People's Army." Another fact should also be noted. The Ch'ing government was considerably weakened by its wars with England and other foreign nations,
but the Nanking government suffered even more from the devastating
effects of the war against the Japanese invaders. This long struggle—
longer in duration and greater in dimensions than any of the international wars fought by China in the nineteenth century—contributed
to reducing the National Government's capacity to hold its own against
the Communists.

These facts warn us against taking too simple a view of the matter.
We cannot explain the difference in the outcomes of these events by
simply pointing to the participation of the peasantry or by arguing that
some change of quality had taken place in the peasants between the
middle of the nineteenth and the twentieth centuries. We must examine the various historical circumstances that appear to have affected
these situations in order to find an adequate or correct explanation.

Perhaps it may be added that precisely because the Chinese Communist revolution was not a movement actively directed by peasants
to attain their own objectives, its leaders are not necessarily committed to promoting the peasants' interests as they themselves perceive them. The average Chinese peasant has one dominant desire:
to have sufficient means to keep himself and his family alive and, in
order to insure this, to possess a plot of land and all that it yields.
The Communist program of land redistribution appealed to him because it promised a better livelihood—a better chance to fulfill that
desire. This was the reason, according to an eyewitness report, that
even the peasants of western Szechwan, who at first opposed the new
regime, felt happy with "the progressive elimination of the large landlord's power."[19] The objectives of the Communist leaders, however,
go far beyond the immediate desires of the individual peasant. The
words of Mao Tse-tung and Liu Shao-ch'i have made this especially
clear. Commenting on the proposed "Agrarian Reform Law," June
14, 1950, Liu said:

> The basic reason for and the aim of agrarian reform are different
> from the view that agrarian reform is only designed to relieve the
> poor people. . . . The results of agrarian reform are beneficial to
> the impoverished laboring peasants. . . . But the basic aim of agrarian
> reform is not purely one of relieving the impoverished peasants. It
> is designed to set free the rural productive forces from the shackles
> of the feudal land ownership system of the landlord class in order to

develop agricultural production and thus pave the way for New China's industrialization. [20]

Mao Tse-tung revealed his position in some passages of his "On Coalition Government," dated April 14, 1945, shortly before the conclusion of the Sino-Japanese war:

> "Land to the tillers" means to transfer the land from the hands of the feudal exploiters to those of the peasants, to turn the private property of the feudal landlords into that of the peasants and to free the peasants from feudal agrarian regulations, thereby making it possible to transform an agricultural country into an industrial one. The proposition of "land to the tillers" is therefore a bourgeois-democratic and not a proletarian-socialist one. [21]

Here, in fact, Mao clearly indicated the ideological basis of the Communist program of collectivization—the negation of the peasants' dream of individual ownership—a program which was soon to be relentlessly implemented in many parts of China. [22]

The Communist leaders attached importance to the peasantry not because they were ready to work for the betterment of the peasantry but because they were convinced that the peasantry was indispensable to their revolutionary cause at a certain stage of its progress. In countries where an industrial proletariat did not exist, an "alliance of workers and peasants" was the only feasible means to effect a Communist-directed revolution. Lenin developed this concept (more accurately, the fiction) of the alliance of the "two classes" in 1919, and Mao Tse-tung adroitly applied it in China many years later. [23] As Mao saw it, the peasantry constituted by far the most potent means with which the Communists could accomplish a number of important tasks. "The peasants," he said early in 1945, constituted "the source of the Chinese army," "the mainstay for China's industry," supplying "the largest amount of foodstuffs and raw materials," "the source of China's industrial workers." They constituted, above all, "the main force fighting for a democratic China at the present stage." But the transient importance of the peasantry would be negated with the initial success of the revolution. Then "China will have to undergo a continuous process of transforming the rural inhabitants into urban inhabitants," in order to transform herself from an agricultural country into an industrial one. [24] The Chinese peasant, as we know him and as he wishes himself to be, faces a gloomy prospect in Communist China.

Recent developments have indicated clearly how Chinese peasants are faring under Communist rule. Against their wishes, cooperative and collectivized farms have been instituted in one locality after another during the years 1953 to 1955. [25] Passive resistance was sometimes expressed through the sale or slaughtering of cattle. Agricultural production fell short of the goals set by the Communist rulers. The

intensification of the drive toward collectivization in the latter part
of 1955 served to aggravate peasant discontent which occasionally
expressed itself in acts of resistance. Such resistance, however,
being ill-organized and without effective leadership, proved no more
fruitful than the abortive uprisings under imperial rule. "Peasant
discontent and even passive resistance to whatever degree," a recent
writer observes, "would be of no avail in face of the overwhelming
state power of the regime."[26]

Under imperial rule, as we have seen, uprisings against the established authority attained varying degrees of success under the following
conditions: (1) the movements enjoyed competent leadership furnished
by the gentry or literati, which gave them organization and know-how;
(2) a sufficient number of common people were convinced that their
vital interests could be preserved only by destroying the existing order; and (3) the administrative apparatus of the existing regime deteriorated to a point where it lost the capacity to cope with grave
situations.

It seems that the Communist rulers are taking steps to prevent
the appearance of these conditions. In the first place, they have instituted over the intelligentsia (the modern counterpart of the scholar-official of imperial times) a control far more thoroughgoing and
rigorous than that exercised by the imperial rulers. If by means of
such control the Communists eventually succeed in making the life
of the intelligentsia "like a child's game"—by permitting students,
teachers, government functionaries no "secrets" from the state and
providing an answer for all "the most painful secrets of their conscience,"[27] they will have eliminated the most important and perhaps the sole source of revolutionary leadership. Secondly, they have
undertaken to suppress or curtail private interests by drastically re-
stricting ownership of property and minimizing the influence of the
family.[28] The interests of the family head and landowner, which often persuaded members of the gentry as well as commoners to resist or challenge the authority of government, are thus being liquidated. A "classless" society is set up as the ultimate goal, a society in which there exist no interests other than those of the ruling
class. Thirdly, the Communists have impressed more than one observer with the vigor and efficiency of their administration—qualities,
by the way, which have usually characterized new regimes in the
history of imperial China. The Communist rulers, it seems, have
done away with many of the administrative ills of previous regimes.
By means of a variety of mass organizations and local apparatus[29]
they have gained control of the villages and cities more effectively
than the Ch'ing government ever did.

The Communists are autocratic rulers, and they obviously understand the techniques of autocratic rule. The methods of control which

they have adopted show a decided improvement over those used by the Ch'ing rulers, but the basic aim and underlying principle of control remain essentially the same: to perpetuate the existing regime through ideological, economic, and administrative control. There is even some similarity between the imperial and Communist autocracies in the way they justify their political power: the former professed "to benefit the people," and the latter claims to do everything in the name of "the people."

Will the Communists achieve complete and abiding success in maintaining their control? At the present moment there are indications that they have come short of complete success. It is conceivable, indeed, that they might duplicate, in different ways and under widely different circumstances, some of the frustrating experiences of the Ch'ing rulers. Until quite recently, some of the intelligentsia have still shown signs of ideological insubordination, particularly as their reactions to Mao Tse-tung's fourth "correcting the wind" campaign indicated.[30] Uprisings involving intellectuals and peasants—more or less true to the type known in imperial times—were reported in some localities.[31] Obviously, the Communists face a difficult problem of ideological control unknown to the Ch'ing rulers. The latter were alien conquerors, but by using the established Confucian tradition to implement their ideological control, a tradition in which the bulk of the gentry and literati were brought up and which they accepted with little reservation, the imperial rulers were able to win the support of most of the members of this elite group. The Communists are native conquerors, but they undertake to replace the Chinese traditions with an alien and entirely new ideology which at many points runs contrary to the accustomed ways of thinking and living.[32] Thus they lose an advantage which the Ch'ing rulers had enjoyed. Meanwhile, the gap between the rulers and the ruled has not been closed. The Chinese Communist regime, like other Communist regimes, is "a form of latent civil war between the government and the people."[33] This of course is not new: Han Fei pointed out long ago that in an autocratic system "superior and inferior wage one hundred battles a day."[34] The Chinese Communists have done nothing to put an end to such "battles." The liquidation of private property does not dissolve the discrepancies of interest between the rulers and the people. The attempt to destroy economic classes has not brought about equality, but on the contrary has created new political classes.[35] The *People's Daily* (Peking) calls attention to the existence of "new contradictions between the masses and their leaders," which, it explains, resulted from "offensive distinctions" introduced by the incorrect actions of Party members.[36] If it is true, as an ex-Communist emphatically says, that "wonderful human features were the condition for creating and attracting power for the [Communist] movement; exclusive caste

spirit and complete lack of ethical principles and virtues have become conditions for the maintenance of the movement, "[37] it might
also be true that the Chinese Communist regime, however vigorous
it is at present, will not be permanently immune from administrative
demoralization, an old ailment of all autocratic regimes.

The inhabitants of Huang Village in 1930 felt that the Communists
could not alter the life of the people. [38] A contemporary writer believes
that "the momentum of China's history and organization will in the end
have greater influence upon the future of Chinese society than all the
propaganda, all the dogma, and all the energy the Communists can
bring to bear. "[39] This may well be true. It is too early, however, to
foresee the net effects of the Communist rule. Much depends upon circumstances both behind and beyond the "bamboo curtain," and upon the
Communists' future course of action. [40] It is idle to speculate, and it is
not the task of the present study to prophesy. We hope, however, that
our examination of the conditions of rural China in the nineteenth century has furnished us with a point of departure for interpreting recent
developments. *

*This postscript was written before Mao Tse-tung launched the
"communes." It appears that my conjectures concerning the fate of
the Chinese peasantry have gained some substantiation. --KCH

APPENDIXES

APPENDIX I

VARIATIONS IN THE *LI-CHIA* STRUCTURE

It is impossible to describe all the bewildering variations of the *li-chia* structure in different parts of the empire. It may be helpful, however, to give an account of some of the more important or significant variations; for such an account will not only give us a clearer idea of the *li-chia* system as it actually existed but also shed some light on the character of the imperial administration itself.

The divergent forms of the *li-chia*, including the main types of variations as well as the official form, are classified and presented in Table 24. To facilitate comparison, the divisions in the variation patterns are placed under the corresponding official divisions in the same vertical columns. In cases in which exact correspondence cannot be ascertained, the variation forms are placed where it seems reasonable.

Let us begin with the regular form. The gazetteers of Chao-i and Ch'eng-ku (both in Shensi) gave details of the tax collection divisions of these districts. The former recorded that in Chao-i "generally . . . ten *chia* constituted a *li*. In the sixteenth year of Kuang-hsü (1890), a total of thirty-three *li* were organized."[1] The latter stated that "each *li* contained ten *chia* . . . the number of taxpaying households varied in the different *chia*."[2] These conformed fairly closely to the official pattern. Similarly, according to the 1890 edition of the gazetteer of Ho Hsien (Kwangsi), the eighteen *li* of this locality were each divided into ten *chia*.[3] Practically identical arrangements obtained in Hsin-hua Chou (Kiangsu).[4] Unfortunately, neither of these sources gives the number of *hu* (households) in the *chia*. There is ample reason for suspecting that even in localities where the official scheme of division was adhered to, the number of households in the *chia* was not uniform.

The 1889 edition of the gazetteer of Hsing-kuo Chou (Hupeh) lent support to this conjecture. According to the compiler, each of the two *fang* and thirty-eight *li* of this *chou* contained ten *chia*, as required by law, but the number of *hu* not only varied in these subdivisions but far exceeded the official quota, with an average of 383 *hu* in each *chia*.[5]

TABLE 24
LI-CHIA DIVISIONS AND THEIR VARIATIONS

Forms (level / form)							Localities
Regular form	Li					Chia	Chihli, Shensi, Hupeh, Kiangsu, Kwangsi, Szechwan
Additive forms		Li		Ts'un		Chia	Kweichow, Yunnan
	Hsiang	Li		Ts'un		Chia	Shantung, Hunan
		Li	T'u			Chia	Fukien
Subtractive forms	Hsiang	Li					Shensi, Hupeh, Hunan, Chekiang
	Hsiang = Li						Chihli, Honan, Hupeh, Szechwan, Chekiang
Four- (five-) level	Tu	Pao	T'u			Chia	Kwangtung
	Hsiang	Tu	T'u			Chia	Kiangsu
	Hsiang	P'u	T'u			Chia	Fukien
	Ch'ü	Tu	T'u			Chia	Kiangsu
	Hsiang	Tu	Li		Yüan		Hupeh
	Hsiang	Tu	Li	T'u			Chekiang
	Hsiang	Tu	Li		Ts'un		Kiangsu, Chekiang
		Li	Tu	T'u	Ts'un		Fukien
	Hsiang	Li	Tu	T'u	Pao		Fukien
Three-level	Hsiang	Tu				Chia	Kwangtung, Hupeh, Kiangsu, Anhwei
	Hsiang	Li			Ts'un		Shensi
	Hsiang	Tu			Ts'un		Kiangsi
	Hsiang	Tu	T'u				Kiangsi, Kiangsu, Fukien, Chekiang
	Tu		T'u		Ts'un		Kwangsi, Kwangtung, Chekiang
	Lu	Li			P'u		Fukien
		Tu	T'u			Chia	Fukien
		Pao	T'u			Chia	Kwangtung
		Tu Ch'ü				Chia	Hunan
				T'u Tung Ts'un			Kwangsi
Two-(one-) level	Hsiang	Li					Chekiang
	Hsiang	Tu					Chekiang, Kwangsi, Hupeh
	Lu					Chia	Yunnan
		Hsiang		P'u			Hupeh
	Tu	Li					Kiangsu
	Ch'ü			T'u			Kiangsu
		?		T'u			Kiangsu
	Li	Li					Shensi
		Hsiang		Chuang			Chekiang
		Li		Ts'un			Kwangsi
	Tu			Ts'un			Kwangtung
				Ts'un	Li		Hupeh
				Ts'un		Chia*	Szechwan
		Li					Kwangsi, Hunan, Honan

Variations → Substitutional Forms (vertical labels spanning the variation rows)

*There was a *hsiao-ts'un* division below the *chia*.

In other instances the number of *chia* varied in the *li* divisions. Thus among the forty *li* of Cho Hsien (Chihli), only thirteen had ten *chia* each; those remaining contained less than ten each.[6] The arrangement in Mien-chu Hsien (Szechwan) also deviated from the official quota by giving to each *li* five *chia* instead of ten, with the result that the entire countryside contained only twenty *chia* evenly distributed among its four *li*.[7]

Among the variations which we propose to examine, some deviated from the regular form by adding one or more extra divisions to the *li-chia-hu* pattern, others by omitting one or more from it, and others by substituting one or more divisions not provided by official regulations. These various types of variations are designated respectively: additive variations, subtractive variations, and substitutional variations.

ADDITIVE VARIATIONS

In some cases, the *Hsiang*, and *ts'un* were, like the *pao-chia*, incorporated into the tax collection system, evidently for the sake of convenience. In Yunnan, Kweichow, and Shantung, for example, the *ts'un* (village) was often interposed between the *chia* and the *hu*, from which it may be inferred that the *chia* must have contained a larger number of households than was officially required. According to the 1895 edition of the gazetteer of Jen-huai T'ing (Kweichow), there were in this locality a total of three *li*, one with five *chia* and two with four *chia* each, and an unspecified number of *ts'un* belonging to each of the *chia*.[8] The 1887 edition of the gazetteer of Chen-hsiung Chou (Yunnan) listed the ten *li* of this subprefecture, giving the number of *chia*, *ts'un*, and *hu* in each of them. With the exception of one, all the *li* contained five *chia* each; the number of *ts'un*, however, varied from a dozen to thirty or more.[9] A similar situation existed in another nineteenth-century subprefecture of the same province, with a slightly larger number of *chia* and *ts'un* in its ten *li*.[10] Hsin Hsien (Shantung) presented another comparable picture, differing from the above instances in having the *Hsiang* division over the *li*, and in having an average of less than four villages in each *chia*.[11] The *Hsiang* and the *ts'un* were probably introduced for the sake of convenience. It was for this reason that a seventeenth-century local official of K'un-yang Chou (Yunnan) integrated the *ts'un* into the *li-chia* system. "Since the *li-chia* was united with the village," it was said, "the people found it more convenient to turn in their taxes."[12]

In other cases, divisions other than the *Hsiang* and *ts'un* were introduced. According to the 1870 edition of the gazetteer of Ch'üan-chou Fu (Fukien), An-ch'i Hsien was divided for revenue collection into a total of eighteen *li* arranged into three groups, each of the *li* being subdivided into six *t'u* and each of the *t'u* into ten *chia*.[13] The *t'u* was an item unknown in the official regulations. It may be noted also that the irregularity here involved something more than the addition of a new division. Since the *t'u* contained ten *chia*, it had actually replaced the official *li*. Since each of the eighteen *li* of this locality was divided into six *t'u*, the *li* had become a much larger division (sixty *chia*) than the official *li* (ten *chia*). Finally, since the eighteen *li* were organized into six "groups," there was in reality a higher division above the individual *li*, a division more or less resembling the *Hsiang* of other localities where the latter was brought within the fold of the *li-chia*.

What was the origin of the *t'u* as a tax division? The compiler of the gazetteer cited immediately above describes its development in Hui-an Hsien as follows:

> At the beginning of the Sung dynasty [this *hsien*] was divided into three *Hsiang*, controlling sixteen. *li*. Around the middle of the reign of Wan-li [late sixteenth century] the number of *li* was changed to eighteen. . . . During the Chen-yüan reign of the Yüan dynasty, [the arrangement] was changed to four *Hsiang*, eighteen *li*, controlling thirty-two *t'u*, with ten *chia* in each *t'u*. During Shun-chih times of the Ch'ing dynasty, the number of *t'u* and *chia* decreased slightly; but in the nineteenth year of K'ang-hsi [1680] the original number was restored. [14]

The *t'u* division in this instance appeared therefore to be a survival from the Yüan dynasty, to which the local inhabitants had for some reason clung and with which the government did not bother to interfere.

SUBTRACTIVE VARIATIONS

We have more examples of the subtractive type of variation. According to the gazetteers of Hua Chou, Ch'i-shan Hsien, and I-ch'üan Hsien (all in Shensi), none of the tax collection systems of these localities contained the *chia* division. Hua Chou had a total of forty-one *li*, distributed fairly evenly among the four *Hsiang* of its countryside. [15] Ch'i-shan Hsien also had four *Hsiang*, with a total of twenty-nine *li* unevenly distributed among them. The *li* were not divided into *chia*, but instead each "controlled" a number of villages. There were altogether 610 *ts'un*. Each of the *li* controlled as few as six and as many as forty-six *ts'un*. [16] I-chüan Hsien differed from Hua Chou and Ch'i-shan in that the *chia* division had not completely disappeared. Formerly, the gazetteer said, its countryside was divided into four *Hsiang*, with a total of twenty-four *li*. Some time during the reign of K'ang-hsi the number of *li* was reduced to four. At the time when the gazetteer was compiled there were seventeen *li*, four of which "were not divided into *chia*, owing to the fact that the land was narrow and households were few."[17] This makes it clear that *chia* divisions existed in the remaining thirteen *li*.

Similar situations prevailed in other localities, notably Hupeh, Hunan, and Chekiang. In many *chou* and *hsien* in Hupeh province the *chia* division was consistently absent. In some of these localities only the *Hsiang* and *li* remained (e. g. , Wu-ch'ang Hsien, Ch'i Chou, Huang-mei Hsien, Sui Chou, Hsiang-yang Hsien, Kuei Chou, Pao-k'ang Hsien and Chien-shih Hsien);[18] in others (e. g. , Han-yang Hsien and En-shih Hsien)[19] the *ts'un* was regarded as a tax collection division. Tao Chou and Ch'ing Chou (both in Hunan) afforded examples of the same abbreviated *li-chia* system. In the former each of the eight *Hsiang* was divided into a number of *li*;[20] in the latter there were one *fang* and seven *Hsiang* with nineteen *li* unequally divided among them.[21] *Fang*, the urban equivalent of the rural *li* in official terminology, was here employed to designate a higher division comprising several *li*, on the same level with the *Hsiang*. The same type of shortened version was found in Jen-ho Hsien (Chekiang) in the nineteenth century.[22]

The *li-chia* was further abridged into a single-level arrangement, by omitting the *chia* and at the same time merging the *li* into the *Hsiang* or vice versa. Instances of the former arrangement existed in certain localities of Szechwan. Table 25, compiled from the 1882 edition of the gazetteer of Lu Chou, shows this type of variation clearly:[23]

TABLE 25
LI-CHIA ARRANGEMENT, SZECHWAN

Locality	*Li* Divisions (Ming dynasty)	*Li* Divisions (early Ch'ing)	No. *Hsiang* into which *li* merged, 1729
Lu Chou	67	3	10
Chiang-an-Hsien	20	4	10
Ho-chiang Hsien	7	3	4
Na-ch'i Hsien	3	4	3

An identical situation obtained in a number of *hsien* in Kiangsu province. The 1810 edition of *Yang-chou fu chih*[24] gave this information:

	Hsiang
Chiang-tu Hsien	25
Kuang-ling Hsien	6
Pao-ying Hsien	6
Hai-ling Hsien	8
Kao-yu Hsien	19
Yung-cheng Hsien	10

Instances in which the *Hsiang* division was merged with the *li* were encountered in Chihli, Honan, Chekiang, and Hupeh. The 1877 edition of the gazetteer of Wei Chou (Chihli) stated that the households of this locality were arranged into fifteen *li*, the names of which were still on record at the time the gazetteer was compiled.[25] The 1892 edition of the *Sui chou chih* indicated that the taxes of this locality in Honan province were collected in the *li* divisions, the number of which was increased from forty to seventy-two at an unspecified date.[26] The 1898 edition of the gazetteer of Hang-chou Fu (Chekinag) revealed that the *li* was the sole tax division in some of its *hsien,* such as Yü-ch'ien Hsien. It went on to explain:

> There were only twenty-four *li* during the Yüan dynasty. . . . Some-time after the Ch'eng-hua reign of the Ming dynasty [1465-87], all the [old] *li* names were abolished, and each *Hsiang* was constituted into a *li,* obtaining a total of eleven *li.* . . . This arrangement was followed by the Ch'ing government. [27]

The *Hsiang* was replaced by the *li* in several localities of Hupeh province. The 1921 edition of the provincial gazetteer of Hupeh indicated that Pa-tung Hsien arranged its households into eight *li* and explained:

> . . . the Chia-ch'ing edition [early nineteenth century] of the gazetteer of this *hsien* . . . as well as the Kuang-hsü edition of the *Hu-pei yü-ti chih* made no mention of the *Hsiang.* It has been ascertained that during the Sung dynasty the names of the *Hsiang* were on record, but these disappeared subsequently, at a time now impossible to determine. [28]

The 1900 edition of the Kuei Chou gazetteer afforded a clue to the missing *Hsiang.* This *chou,* it was said, was divided in Sung times first into ten and later into seventeen *Hsiang* which were replaced by *li* in Ming times. [29] There is therefore some ground for surmising that the same process took place in other localities where the *li* had become the sole tax collection division.

This transformation, however, was not universal. In several instances the change was only partially effected, so that the *Hsiang* and the *li* existed in the same locality side by side. This was the situation in Ch'ang-yang Hsien (Hupeh). During the Ch'ing dynasty there were three *Hsiang* in this district, which were constituted into three *li,* "the names of the former being used to designate the latter. [30]

There were a few curious instances in which the entire tax collection system was telescoped into the *chia* division. According to the 1802 edition of the *Yen-an fu chih,* [31] the following changes took place in these localities in Shensi province:

	Original Divisions	Present Divisions
An-chai Hsien	16 *li*	8 *chia*
Pao-an Hsien	8 *li*	6 *chia*
An-ting Hsien	9 *li*	9 *chia*

SUBSTITUTIONAL VARIATIONS

Coming now to "substitutional variations," we are confronted by a bewildering diversity of forms. Ignoring the minor discrepancies that do not seem to have much significance, we can discern some sort of order among these variations. The process of substitution took place most often in the *li* division of the official scheme, where the *li* was either supplanted by the *tu* or the *t'u*. Occasionally, the *Hsiang* gave place to the *ch'ü*. In other instances, usually where the *chia* division was absent, a variety of extralegal divisions, such as the *ts'un*, the *pao*, the *p'u*, and the *yüan*, made their appearance, although we are not sure that these actually replaced the *chia*. Indeed, it should be admitted that since the gazetteers from which we gleaned our data frequently failed to indicate the exact positions of the divisions mentioned, it is difficult to ascertain whether these were substitutions for any given official division or were additions to the system, even though one or more of the official divisions had dropped out.

Four-level Forms

In many instances local deviations from the official scheme consisted in the addition of extra divisions besides the substitution of various divisions for the regulation ones. The following four-level versions may be noted:

1. A *tu-pao-t'u-chia* pattern was said to have existed in Nan-hai Hsien (Kwangtung). According to the 1923 edition of the *Fu-shan Chung-i hsiang chih*, [32] this was the arrangement:

> In our district . . . the *tu* controls the *pao;* the number of *pao* in each *tu* varies. The *pao* controls the *t'u;* since the size of the *pao* varies, the number of *t'u* in each also varies. The *t'u* controls the *chia;* each *t'u* is divided into ten *chia*. The *chia* controls the *hu;* the number of *hu* in each varies.

It should be noted, however, that this statement is at variance with the description contained in the 1910 edition of *Nan-hai hsien chih,* where a three-level pattern prevailed. It is probable that this four-level arrangement was confined to this particular section of Nan-hai.

2. Another four-level pattern was found in Wusih (Kiangsu). The 1908 edition of the *T'ai-pai Mei-li hsiang chih* states that T'ai-pai Hsiang, one of the rural divisions of Wusih Hsien, was divided for revenue purposes into three *tu,* i.e., the fifty-fifth *tu,* containing ten *t'u;* the fifty-sixth, containing ten *t'u;* and fifty-seventh, containing nine *t'u*. Each *t'u* contained a varying number of *chia*. [33] Taking the *Hsiang* as one of the levels, we have here a *Hsiang-tu-t'u-chia* pattern. A similar arrangement obtained in Tung-kuan Hsien (Kwangtung). [34]

3. Hui-an Hsien of Fukien province afforded another instance. The compiler of the 1870 edition of *Ch'üan-chou fu chih* wrote:

At the beginning of the Sung dynasty, [the countryside] was divided into three *Hsiang,* controlling six *li.* . . . In the reign of Yüan-cheng of the Yüan dynasty [1295-96] it was redivided into four *Hsiang* and eighteen *li,* controlling thirty-two *t'u,* and each of the *t'u* controlling ten *chia.* . . . In the thirteenth year of Ch'ien-lung [1748], owing to the fact that the *li-chang* embezzled grain taxes, the *li* division was abolished and new divisions in the form of sixty-seven *p'u* were made. [35]

This explains the origin of the unfamiliar division *p'u* which appeared also in other parts of the empire.

4. Wusih Hsien (Kiangsu) yielded still another four-level variation in a *ch'ü-tu-t'u-chia* pattern. The tax division system there around 1881 was that "the *ch'ü* controlled the *tu,* and the *tu* controlled the *t'u,* which later in turn controlled the *chia.*"[36] The gazetteer containing this statement explained that this was the Ming system which was "followed at the present," but gave no details concerning the number of units in each of these divisions. It is consequently impossible to ascertain whether the *ch'ü* and the *tu* were the equivalents of the *Hsiang* and the *li.*

5. The following four-level variant was found in Hupeh. According to the 1894 edition of the gazetteer of Mien-yang Chou, the rural divisions of this locality were partly as follows. [37]

Hsüan-ch'eng Hsiang (one of five *Hsiang*), 4 *t'u,* 17 *li:*

    1st *T'u:* Huo-fu Li, a total of 19 *yüan;*
            Hsing-jen Li, a total of 13 *yüan;*
            Tou-i Li, a total of 11 *yüan;*
            Tou-erh Li, a total of 20 *yüan;*
            Tou-san Li, a total of 6 *yüan;*

    2nd *T'u:* Shih-pan Li, a total of 8 *yüan* . . .

The pattern that prevailed in one area was the *Hsiang-t'u-li-yüan,* which was novel in two respects. First, it places the *t'u* above the *li;* second, it introduced the *yüan* division seldom found in other localities. The origin of the *yüan* was accounted for by the compiler in these words:

Since the land of this locality is low, the people have built flood dikes to guard their farms. The longer of these encircle areas as wide as several tens of *li,* while the shorter ones embrace areas of more than ten *li.* [The areas surrounded by these dikes] are called *yüan.* There are over one hundred such areas. [38]

The *yüan* therefore seems to have occupied the position of the *ts'un* in those instances in which the village was incorporated into the tax collection sytem.

6. A *Hsiang-tu-t'u-li* pattern existed in several districts in Chekiang province, among which Chien-te Hsien may serve as a typical instance. The following data are from the 1883 edition of *Yen-chou fu chih:*[39]

	Tu	*Li*	*T'u*
Mai-tu Hsiang	2	3	16
Hsin-t'ing Hsiang	3	5	8
Pai-chiu Hsiang	3	5	5
Hsiao-hsing Hsiang	2	7	2
Chien-te Hsiang	4	5	6
Tz'u-shun Hsiang	3	7	5
Lung-shan Hsiang	2	3	4
Jen-hsiang Hsiang	2	3	4
Chih-ch'üan Hsiang	2	2	3

In one instance the number of *t'u* was identical with that of the *li* (Pai-chiu Hsiang), and in another the number of the *li* with that of the *tu*. The compiler of the gazetteer showed beyond doubt that all these divisions were on different levels.

7. The 1875 edition of the gazetteer of T'ung Chou (Kiangsu) contained information concerning the tax collection divisions of T'ai-hsing Hsien, which formed a *Hsiang-tu-li-ts'un* pattern, as follows:[40]

	Tu	*Li*	*Ts'un*
T'ai-p'ing Hsiang	9	35	unspecified
Shun-te Hsiang	6	43	"
Pao-ch'üan Hsiang	3	14	"
I-jen Hsiang	3	14	"

Since, according to this gazetteer, each of the *li* "controlled" a certain number of *ts'un* (villages), both the *li* and the *tu* must have been extensive units, exceeding the size of the official *li*. Similar *Hsiang-tu-li-ts'un* arrangements prevailed in other districts of T'ung Chou,[41] in some districts of Yang-chou Fu (Kiangsu),[42] and possibly also in Ch'ang-hua Hsien of Hangchow (Chekiang).[43]

Chekiang province supplied a variant of this four-level pattern. Yen-yüan Hsiang, a part of Feng-hua Hsien, had a similar arrangement with the difference that the *li* was supplanted by the *t'u*, a division which frequently occurred in southern localities. According to the *Yen-yüan hsiang chih* (1901 edition),[44] this was the situation:

			Ts'un
Yen-yüan Hsiang	47th *Tu*	1st *T'u*	25
	48th *Tu*	1st *T'u*	13

			$Ts'un$
Yen-yüan Hsiang		2nd $T'u$	29
	49th Tu	1st $T'u$	11
		2nd $T'u$	16
		3rd $T'u$	5
	50th Tu	1st $T'u$	45
	51st Tu	1st $T'u$	23
		2nd $T'u$	11
	52nd Tu	1st $T'u$	10

This gazetteer also contains a number of sketches showing the arrangement of the tu and $t'u$ in Yen-yüan Hsiang. (Unfortunately, the arrangement of the $ts'un$ is not shown.) One of these sketches is reproduced here to give us some idea of the situation. The irregular shapes of these divisions may have been due to the topography of the locality or to "gerrymandering" for the purpose of tax evasion—a fraudulent device by which land liable for higher tax rates was registered in low-rate divisions. We shall have occasion to explain this device in more detail.

8. Our last instance of four-level variation, a *Hsiang-li-tu-t'u* pattern, is of special interest, for it was to have been created by adding new divisions in successive dynasties. According to the compilers of the *Fu-chou fu chih* (1756), the tax divisions of Ku-t'ien Hsien (Fukien) began with the four *Hsiang* and thirteen li established in the Sung dynasty. To these were added forty-eight tu (obtained by redividing the li) in the Yüan dynasty and fifty-nine $t'u$ in the Ming dynasty.[45] Each $t'u$ contained a number of $ts'un$, but the $ts'un$ in this locality were natural growths and not an administrative unit for tax collection purposes.

9. A rare instance of what appeared to be a five-level tax collection arrangement may be noted here. According to the 1838 edition of the *Hsia-men chih*[46] the countryside of T'ung-an Hsien (Fukien) was divided into four Hsiang early in the Sung dynasty, with a total of twenty-seven li. These divisions were rearranged into forty-four tu in the Yüan dynasty, which were reduced in Ming times to thirty-seven, controlling a total of fifty-three $t'u$. The li divisions were shuffled once more in 1775 and, at an unspecified later date, forty-five *pao* were placed under the supervision of the $t'u$. The account given by the compiler of this gazetteer is not entirely lucid. The system which he envisaged appeared to contain five different levels: *Hsiang, li, tu, t'u,* and *pao*.

Three-level Forms

1. First, there was the *Hsiang-t'u-chia* pattern in which the li was supplanted by the $t'u$. Nan-hai Hsien (Kwangtung) probably afforded

ARRANGEMENT OF TU AND T'U
Yen-yüan Hsiang, Chekiang
(Each square represents approximately 5 li)

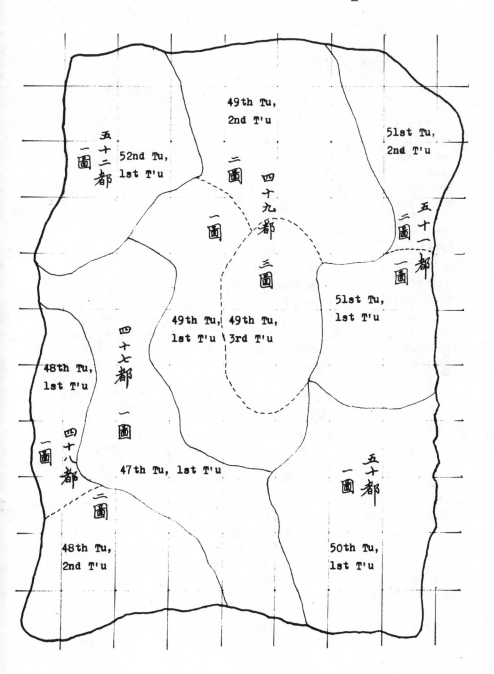

some of the best examples. The number of households *(hu)* in each *chia* varied considerably. In one of its most prosperous rural areas, the Ju-lin Hsiang, the arrangement shown in Table 26 was said to have existed around 1880:[47]

TABLE 26
NUMBER OF *HU* PER *T'U*, JU-LIN HSIANG

	34th T'u	35th T'u	38th T'u	79th T'u	80th T'u
1st Chia	31	36	43	18	39
2nd Chia	23	14	40	32	81
3rd Chia	12	12	48	20·	21
4th Chia	30	39	34	36	15
5th Chia	20	33	86	14	22
6th Chia	19	18	28	133	17
7th Chia	16	10	65	9	79
8th Chia	32	18	54	16	30
9th Chia	26	73	77	21	29
10th Chia	9	16	37	45	31

The compiler did not specify the nature of the *t'u*. It may be inferred, however, that since each of the five *t'u* contained exactly ten *chia*, it must have been the local equivalent of the official *li*. This conjecture is indirectly supported by the 1921 edition of the provincial gazetteer of Hupeh. The compiler of the Chia-ch'ing edition of the *Kuang-chi hsien chih* wrote:

> There were thirty *li* in the original register. Later on the three *t'u* of Ling-ch'üan Hsiang were abolished. In the fifth year of K'ang-hsi [1666] Huang Yü-hsüan, the magistrate, established the three *t'u* of T'ai-p'ing Hsi Hsiang, restoring the original number. In the thirty-fifth year [1696] the seven *t'u* of An-lo Hsiang were added. Since then the seven *Hsiang* of Kuang-chi contained thirty-seven *t'u* and 370 *chia*. The *t'u* was the equivalent of the *li*. [48]

The "original" *li* divisions referred to by this Hupeh gazetteer may have been elements in the *li-chia* system of the Ming dynasty, if credence may be lent to data furnished by the 1810 edition of the gazetteer of Yang-chou Fu (Kiangsu). According to this gazetteer, citing from the Chia-ch'ing edition of the *Pao-ying hsien chih*, the tax collection divisions of this locality underwent changes during the Ming and Ch'ing dynasties as shown below.[49] The *t'u* in this instance definitely replaced the *li*. In other cases, however, it appears that the *t'u* was at first an additional division inserted between the *li* and the *chia*, but later was made to take the place of the *li*. For example,

	Ming Dynasty Divisions *(li)*	Ch'ing Dynasty Divisions *(t'u)*
San-an Hsiang	4	4
Ts'ao-ts'un Hsiang	2	2
Yung-ning Hsiang	2	2
Chün-hsia Hsiang	2	4
Wang-te Hsiang	4	4
Hsiao-i Hsiang	4	4
Hou-ts'un Hsiang	2	2
Pai-ma Hsiang	3	4

according to the 1884 edition of the *Huai-an fu chih*, [50] the situation in T'ao-yüan Hsien (Kiangsu) was as summarized in Table 27:

TABLE 27
NUMBER OF *LI* AND *T'U*, T'AO-YÜAN HSIEN

Hsiang	Original Number of		Present Number of
	Li	*T'u*	*T'u*
Lu-ch'eng Hsiang	15	32	12
Ts'ung-ho Hsiang	12	36	12
En-fu Hsiang	8	33	9
Wu-ch'eng Hsiang	6	30	8
Shun-te Hsiang	7	25	7

The *li* and the *t'u* sometimes coexisted in local terminology. Thus, according to the 1885 edition of the *Lu-chou fu chih*, [51] the tax divisions of Meng-ch'eng Hsien (Anhwei) took the following form:

Tsai-ch'eng Hsiang, divided into 2 *t'u:*
   Tsai-i Li, containing 10 *chia,*
   Tsai-erh Li, containing 10 *chia,*

Hui-an Hsiang, divided into 2 *t'u:*
   Hui-i Li, containing 10 *chia,*
   Hui-erh Li, containing 10 *chia,* etc.

2. The name *li*, however, prevailed in a few instances in which both the *t'u* and *chia* were absent, the latter being replaced by the *ts'un*. In I-ch'eng Hsien (Shansi) and T'ung-kuan Hsien (Shensi), the *Hsiang* was divided into a number of *li*, and each of the latter again into a number of *ts'un*, forming a *Hsiang-li-ts'un* pattern. [52]

3. A southern variant of the above, in the form of a *Hsiang-tu-ts'un* pattern in which the *tu* supplanted the *li*, existed in Min-ch'ing Hsien (Fukien) and T'ai-ho Hsien (Kiangsi). In the former locality the di-

vision made in 1660 by the magistrate were partly as follows:[53]

Ching-liang Hsiang: 3rd *Tu*, containing 7 *ts'un;*
              4th *Tu*, containing 10 *ts'un;*
              5th *Tu*, containing 11 *ts'un;*
              7th *Tu*, containing 9 *ts'un;*
              8th *Tu*, containing 14 *ts'un;*
              9th *Tu*, containing 9 *ts'un*, etc.

In the latter locality, it was said, "The names *fang, 'Hsiang, ' li* originated in Sung times during the reign of Ch'un-hsi [1174-89]. At the
beginning of the Ming dynasty, *fang* was changed into *'Hsiang, '* and
the *Hsiang* was divided into *tu.* Some time later, the *tu* became the
equivalent of *t'u,* and the *t'u* was simply another name for the *li.* "[54]
In the 1870's the tax divisions of T'ao-ho Hsien were partly as follows:

Jen-shan Hsiang: 1st *Tu*, containing 3 *ts'un;*
              2nd *Tu*, containing 4 *ts'un;*
              3rd *Tu*, containing 6 *ts'un;* etc.

4. A *Hsiang-tu-t'u* pattern existed in some places in Kiangsu province. In Wusih, there was the following arrangement as recorded in
the *T'ai-pai Mei-li hsiang chih* (1897 edition):[55]

		T'u
T'ai-pai Hsiang:	33rd *Tu*	7
	34th *Tu*	8
	35th *Tu*	8
	36th *Tu*	4
Mei-li Hsiang:	55th *Tu*	10
	56th *Tu*	10
	57th *Tu*	9

A similar situation existed in Nan-ch'ang Hsien (Kiangsi). It was
said that the five *Hsiang* of this district, when their names first appeared on the register compiled in 1850, controlled a total of sixty-
eight *tu* and 589 *t'u,* distributed unevenly among them.[56] The nature
of the *tu,* as in the previous instance, was not indicated.

The matter, however, was made a little clearer by the 1756 edition
of the *Fu-chou fu chih.* According to its compiler, the rural areas
of Ch'ang-lo Hsien (Fukien) were arranged in part as follows:[57]

		T'u
Nan (South) Hsiang	2nd *Tu* = Ts'ung-sheng Li	4
	3rd *Tu* = Hsing-te Li	2
	4th *Tu* = Sung-p'ing Li	3
	5th *Tu* = Ch'üan yüan Li	2

is evident that the names *tu* and *li* were both used in this locality,
hich suggests that the *tu* may have replaced the *li* in some places,
3 perhaps in Nan-ch'ang Hsien or T'ai-pai Hsiang noted above.

5. A *Hsiang-t'u-ts'un* pattern was found in parts of Kwangsi prov-
ιce. According to the 1908 edition of the *Nan-ning fu chih*,[58] the coun-
·yside of Hsüan-hua Hsien was divided into a number of *Hsiang*, each
ubdivided into one to eight *t'u*, and each *t'u* into a varying number
f *ts'un*. Tha same pattern occurred in Kwangtung and Chekiang,
here the *tu* appears to have been treated as an exact equivalent of
ιe *Hsiang*. According to the 1873 edition of the *Hsiang-shan hsien
hih*,[59] the arrangement in this locality was as partially tabulated
elow:

	T'u	*Ts'un*
Jen-hou Hsiang = Liang-yü Tu	6	37
Te-ch'ing Hsiang= Lung-yen Tu	6	58
Yung-lo Hsiang = Te-leng Tu	6	44
Ch'ang-lo Hsiang = Szu-chih Tu	2	18
Yung-ning Hsiang = Ta-chi Tu	2	30

6. A curious variant was supplied by Fukien province. Instead of
ιe more familiar *Hsiang*, *tu*, and *t'u* divisions, the rural areas of
,o-yüan Hsien took the *lu-li-p'u* pattern:[60]

	Li	Number of *P'u* in each *Li*
Hsi (West) Lu	6	1 to 4
Tung (East) Lu	5	1 to 5
Pei (North) Lu	3	1 to 4

'he compiler offered no explanation as to the meaning and origin of
ιe terms *lu* and *p'u*.

7. Another modification at the *Hsiang* level existed in Chin-chiang
[sien (Fukien) where, so the *Ch'üan-chou fu chih* (1870 edition) stat-
d,[61] the countryside was divided into five *Hsiang* and twenty-three *li*
uring the Sung dynasty. Sometime in the Yüan dynasty the divisions
·ere rearranged, "changing the *Hsiang* and *li* into forty-three *tu*"
·hich, together with the three *yü* (city divisions), contained a total
f 135 *t'u*. The *t'u*, like the *li* in the official form, each had uniformly
ən,*chia*. The Ming government permitted this arrangement to stand,
nd so did the Ch'ing authorities. This *tu-t'u-chia* pattern was found
lso in T'ung-an Hsien and Nan-an Hsien of the same province.[62]

8. Nan-hai Hsien and Hua Hsien (both in Kwangtung) presented a
ιree-level pattern different from the preceding. The *tu* was replaced
y the *pao* (not to be confounded with the *pao* of the *pao-chia* system,
·hich is written differently in Chinese), giving rise to a *pao-t'u-chia*
rrangement as follows:[63]

	Pao	Number of *T'u* in each *Pao*	Number of *Chia* in each *T'u*
Nan-hai Hsien	34	Varying	10
Hua Hsien	3	Varying	Varying

Superficially this resembled the *tu-t'u-chia* pattern of Chin-chiang Hsien (Fukien). But the *pao,* according to the compiler of the *Nan-hai hsien chih* (1910), "was perhaps the vulgar name for the *li.*"[64] It was a relatively small division, it was pointed out, since at the beginning of the Ch'ing dynasty the *pao* on the average contained less than 1,000 persons. The *tu* in Chin-chiang, on the other hand, was a division into which both the *Hsiang* and the *li* had been telescoped. This view was supported by the compiler of the *Fu-shan Chung-i hsiang chih* (1923 edition), who in discussing the system in Fu-shan (Kwangtung), attributed the name *pao* to the Ming dynasty and held that the *li-chang* (head of the *li)* was then the agent in charge of the *pao* division.[65]

9. The *li* division assumed the name *ch'ü* in some localities in Hunan province. In describing the *li-chia* system of Tz'u-li Hsien, the compiler of the 1896 edition of its gazetteer wrote:

> In the Ming dynasty the city and suburban areas were divided into three *fang* and *"Hsiang,"* and the four rural areas into twenty-five *tu.* . . . At first the *tu* was rather extensive, hence each was later partitioned into two or three, or even five or six *li;* each of the latter was in turn divided into ten *chia.* At present, therefore, when the people turn in their grain taxes they simply give them the name of the *tu* to which they belong, or sometimes indicate also the name of their *ch'ü.*[66]

10. Yung-ch'un Hsien (Kwangsi) offered an oddity which may be noted to conclude this list of three-level forms. According to the *Nan-ning fu chih* (1908), the countryside of this district was divided for tax collection purposes into a number of *t'u,* each *t'u* into a number of *tung,* and each *tung* was made to control a number of *ts'un.* The compiler gave no explanation of the unfamiliar term *tung.*[67] Another gazetteer,[68] however, said:

> At the time when the households of this district [Yung Hsien, Kwangsi] were registered, [the lowest division] were called the *tung.* The persons responsible for urging the payment of grain taxes were known as *tung-t'ou* [heads of *tung].* . . . In the twentieth year of K'ang-hsi [1681] Yao P'i, the magistrate, changed for the first time . . . the *tung* to *chia.*

Two-level Forms

These resulted when two or more of the tax collection divisions merged into one another, or when some of them disappeared from the system. With one exception all the instances which will be described below contained two levels, not counting, of course, the *hu* which was a unit instead of a division in the *li-chia*.

1. An instructive instance was afforded by Chekiang province. According to the 1898 edition of the *Hang-chou fu chih*, the main features of the revenue division of Ch'ien-t'ang Hsien were as follows:[69]

The city had eleven *fang*, each controlling a varying number of *li*; the suburb, seven *yü*, each controlling a varying number of *li*; rural areas, nine *Hsiang*, arranged thus:

		Number of *Li* in each *Tu*
Li-t'ai Hsiang		7
Shang T'iao-lu Hsiang		10
Hsia T'iao-lu Hsiang		7
Ling-chih Hsiang	3rd *Tu*	8
	4th *Tu*	4
	5th *Tu*	5
Hsiao-wen Nan Hsiang		5
Hsiao-wen Pei Hsiang		4
Ts'ung-hua Hsiang	7th *Tu*	8
	Upper 8th *Tu*	6
	Lower 8th *Tu*	9
Shang Ch'ing-hsien Hsiang		7
Etc.		

Here we have an example of two different patterns, *Hsiang-li* and *Hsiang-tu-li*, existing side by side in one locality, revealing perhaps a transitional stage in the process of subtractive change. The compiler added in a note that "formerly Ch'ien-t'ang had a total of 160 *li*; the amount of land in each *t'u* varied." It is obvious, therefore, that this district had its *li-chia* system abbreviated from a four-level *Hsiang-tu-li-t'u* pattern to a *Hsiang-tu-li* three-level pattern, and was on its way to a *Hsiang-li* two-level pattern.

2. Another version of the two-level form arose when the *tu* and *li* divisions telescoped. Table 28 shows the divisions that existed in T'eng Hsien, Kwangsi, during the Chia-ch'ing reign (1776-1820).[70] It is interesting to note that in this table each of the five *Hsiang*, Hsiao-i, Hen-feng, Kan-i, I-ch'ang, and T'ai-p'ing, was said to have contained a number of *tu* (the names of which were given by the compiler) and a specified number of *li* (the names of which were not given), the number of *tu* and *li* in each *Hsiang* being exactly equal. In Ning-feng Hsiang there were seven named *tu* and seven named *li*, the num-

TABLE 28
RURAL DIVISIONS OF T'ENG HSIEN, KWANGSI

Hsiang	Tu	Number of Tu in Hsiang	Li	Number of Li in Hsiang
Hsiao-i Hsiang	1st 2nd 3rd 4th A 4th B	5		5
Jen-feng Hsiang	7th 8th 9th 10th 15th	5		5
Kan-i Hsiang	28th 30th 31st 32nd 34th 36th 38th 39th	8		8
I-ch'ang Hsiang	18th 21st 22nd A 22nd B 25th	5		5
T'ai-p'ing Hsiang	41st 42nd 43rd	3		3
Ning-feng Hsiang	46th 47th 48th 49th 52nd 56th 58th	7	Lo-lung Ta-jen Tung-huang San-chiang Sui-hua Yang-t'ung Ta-li	7

ber of both again being equal. There is ample reason for supposing, therefore, that the terms *tu* and *li* were used synonymously in this locality to designate the same tax division and that the arrangement was substantially a two-level one: *Hsiang-tu* = *li*. That the *li* was probably in the process of being replaced by the *tu* was hinted at by the 1921 edition of the provincial gazetteer of Hupeh. The compiler said, citing from the *Kuang-hsü yü-ti chi*, that in the two *Hsiang* of Sung-tzu Hsien there were originally a total of twenty-one *li*, but "at present they were divided into twenty-one *tu*," nine of which were controlled by Kao Hsiang and the remaining twelve by Ti Hsiang. A similar situation existed in Chih-chiang Hsien of the same province. [71]

3. Another type of two-level variation prevailed in some parts of Yunnan, Kwangsi, and Anhwei. The *Ho-ch'ing chou chih* (1894) gave a description of the tax divisions of this locality in Yunnan, which may be partially reproduced as follows: [72]

		Ts'un
Tien-nan Hsiang	Ch'ang-i *Tu*	47
	Ch'ang-erh *Tu*	21
	Ch'ang-san *Tu*	18
	Ch'iu-i *Tu*	13
Tien-pei Hsiang	Feng-i *Tu*	14
	Feng-erh *Tu*	16
	Feng-san *Tu*	11
	Ch'iu-erh *Tu*	10

In its far-flung rural areas (known locally as *Shan-wai*, "Beyond the Hills"), however, a different arrangement was made:

	Name and Number of *Chia*		*Ts'un*
Sung-kuei Nan Lu	Hsi-i	6	17
	Nan-chuang	6	9
	Sung-kuei	6	10
Sung-kuei Pei Lu	San-chuang	6	16
	Tung-shan	6	15
	Po-lo	6	20
	Chung-chiang	6	12
	Pei-ya	4	11
	Chiang-ying	8	27
	To-mei	12	34
	Kuan-ying-shan	?	39

Two points require consideration. First, as is obvious from the above, since the *ts'un* entered the picture here, it is not absolutely certain that these did not constitute one of the levels of the tax collection system. But as these were not said to have been "controlled" by the division above them, as the *ts'un* in other instances, there was a possibility that they were not treated as divisions of this system. Second,

it is not clear whether the various names (Hsi-i, Nan-chuang, etc.)
that preceded the *chia* denoted superior divisions over the *chia,* or
simply indicated different groupings of adjacent *chia* without superior
divisions over them.

At any rate, it is fairly certain that a two-level arrangement, similar to the *Hsiang-t'u* pattern of Ho-ch'ing Chou, existed in some
places of Nan-ning Fu (Kwangsi)[73] as well as in Lu-chou Fu (Anhwei).[74]

4. A close variant of the *Hsiang-t'u* pattern was found in An-yüan
Hsien (Hupeh). The provincial gazetteer (1921) citing from a geographical work of the late nineteenth century, related that the rural
areas of this district were formerly divided into three *li* but later
into three *Hsiang,* with three *p'u* divisions distributed among them
as follows:[75]

Tung (East) Hsiang	Mao-ni P'u
Hsi (West) Hsiang	Lu-yang P'u Pu-kuan P'u Ho-chien P'u
Nan (South) Hsiang	Hsieh-ma P'u Hou-tsai P'u Mu-kua P'u Ch'ing-ch'i P'u Etc.

According to the compiler of the gazetteer, this was one of the few
instances in which the *li* division gave place to the *Hsiang.*

5. There was a curious example in which the *Hsiang* and the *tu* coexisted in one and the same district, while the *li* became synonymous
with the *t'u,* forming a two-level pattern with a sort of bilinear nomenclature. The 1810 edition of the *Yang-chou fu chih* gave this description of the arrangement in I-cheng Hsien (Kiangsu):[76]

Tsai-ch'eng Tu (City)	1st T'u, known as Tsai-i Li 2nd T'u, known as Tsai-erh Li
Hsin-ch'eng Tu	Hsin-ch'eng Li
Huai-i Hsiang	1st T'u, known as 3rd-1st Li 2nd T'u, known as 3rd-2nd Li
Tung Kuang-ling Hsiang, 4th Tu	4th-Tu Li
Kuei-jen Hsiang, 5th Tu	1st T'u, known as 5th-1st Li 2nd T'u, known as 5th-2nd Li 3rd T'u, known as 5th-3rd Li
Kan-lu Hsiang, 6th Tu	1st T'u, known as 6th-1st Li 2nd T'u, known as 6th-2nd Li

Hsi Kuang-ling Hsiang, 7th Tu | 1st T'u, known as 7th-1st Li
2nd T'u, known as 7th-2nd Li
3rd T'u, known as 7th-3rd Li

It is obvious that the rather unusual numerical designations of most of the *li* resulted from referring to the *tu* to which they belonged. Thus "Fifth-First Li" means that this was the first division of the Fifth Tu. Fourth-Tu Li means that this *li* belonged to the Fourth Tu which "controlled" only one division. From this fact it may be surmised that Huai-i Hsiang was probably the Third Tu and that Tsai-ch'eng and Hsin-ch'eng respectively constituted the First Tu and the Second Tu of this district. A second point to note is that in the gazetteer the name "T'ai-p'ing Hsiang" followed immediately the name "Hsi Kuang-ling Hsiang," i.e., "Hsi Kuang-ling Hsiang, T'ai-p'ing Hsiang, Seventh Tu." A possible explanation for this anomaly is that the population of one of these two *Hsiang* (or of both) had dwindled to such an extent that the number of households was insufficient to constitute independent major tax division. Consequently, they were merged into one *tu,* the Seventh.

Two other localities in this general region of Kiangsu presented a similar picture with a slight difference. According to the same gazetteer[77] Chiang-tu Hsien was divided in Ming times into twenty-eight major revenue collection divisions, among which were eight *Hsiang* and one *tu,* controlling together a total of 118 *li.* In the eleventh year of Yung-cheng (1733) the tax divisions were reconstituted into six *tu,* designated as first, second, etc., each of which controlled eleven *t'u,* with the exception of the First Tu which controlled twelve. Likewise, according to the same gazetteer,[78] when Tung-t'ai Hsien was first constituted in the thirty-third year of Ch'ien-lung (1768), it was divided into eight *tu,* each of which controlled a variable number of *t'u* (minimum, 5, maximum, 10).

These two instances point to an interesting conclusion: the Ch'ing government did not consistently observe its own official regulations in making tax divisions. The case of Tung-t'ai is especially interesting, since the arrangement there was fixed as late as 1768. It was possible that the *tu-t'u* nomenclature had become so deeply entrenched in local usage that the officials establishing the system did not deem it wise to uproot it.

6. The four-level *ch'ü-tu-t'u-chia* found in Wusih appeared in an abridged form in Kan-ch'üan Hsien of the same province (Kiangsu). According to the *Yang-chou fu chih* (1810 edition)[79] this was the scheme adopted in the eleventh year of Yung-cheng (1733):

First Ch'ü, controlling 11 *t'u;*
Second Ch'ü, controlling 11 *t'u;*

Third Ch'ü, controlling 10 *t'u;*
Fourth Ch'ü, controlling 10 *t'u;*
Fifth Ch'ü, controlling 10 *t'u.*

7. Kiangsu province produced another two-level variation. Shan-yang Hsien, according to the *Huai-an fu chih* (1884 edition), [80] was partitioned into four major tax divisions, the names of which were Jen-tzu, I-tzu, Li-tzu, and Hsin-tzu. Each of these "controlled" ten *t'u*, designated as first, second, etc. It is impossible to determine, however, whether the major divisions were *tu, li,* or perhaps *ch'ü.*

8. A most curious example of two-level form was recorded in the *Kan-ch'üan hsien hsiang-t'u chih* (undated). According to this gazetteer, [81] *Kan-ch'üan,* a border district of western Shensi, was divided into two *li:*

Tung-tso Li, subdivided into 23 *li;*
Hsi-ch'eng Li, subdivided into 14 *li.*

It may be noted that the character *li* used to designate the higher and lower divisions is written exactly the same in this gazetteer.

9. A *Hsiang-chuang* pattern was encountered in Hsin-ch'eng Hsien (Chekiang). The 1898 edition of *Hang-chou fu chih* [82] stated that this district was divided into fifteen *Hsiang,* each *Hsiang* being the equivalent of one *li* and controlling a variable number of *chuang* (minimum, 5; maximum, 11; total, 123 *chuang*).

10. A related variant existed in Yung Hsien (Kwangsi), where eleven *li* controlled a total of 489 *ts'un* and *chuang.* The compiler of the 1897 edition of its gazetteer explained that "in Ming times the countryside and city areas were arranged into sixteen *t'u* which were later changed into eleven *li.*"[83]

11. In Ch'ing-yüan Hsien (Kwangtung) the *Hsiang* divisions in the countryside were treated as equivalents of the *tu,* giving rise to the following arrangement:[84]

	Ts'un
T'ai-p'ing Hsiang, named Nan-t'ang Tu	25
Shan-hua Hsiang	39
Ch'ing-p'ing Hsiang, named Ch'ing-hu Tu	67
Etc.	

12. In a few isolated instances the *ts'un* became a superior division over the *li,* as in Ching-men Chih-li Chou (Hupeh). According to the provincial gazetteer, [85] Ching-men formerly contained eight *Hsiang* which were divided into fifty-nine *li.* At an unspecified time some change took place, and the tax collection system there assumed this form:

	Li
Wang-hsiang Ts'un	4

	Li
P'ing-t'ai Ts'un	5
Kao-kuan Ts'un	7
Ma-hsien Ts'un	7
Ch'ang-t'i Ts'un	3
Etc.	

13. The *ts'un* also became a superior division in Hsin-fan Hsien (Szechwan), but in a different manner. The *Hsin-fan hsien hsiang-t'u chih* (1907 edition) recorded that this district was "divided into four *ts'un*," with subdivisions distributed among them as follows:[86]

		Number of *Hsiao-ts'un* in each *Chia*
Shui Ts'un	1st Chia	10
	2nd Chia	10
	3rd Chia	7
Han Ts'un	1st Chia	4
	2nd Chia	5
	3rd Chia	4

Etc.

The remaining two *ts'un* contained also three *chia* each, with varying numbers of *hsiao-ts'un* (little villages). The compiler, regrettably, did not explain how small were the *hsiao-ts'un* which comprised the *chia* or how large the *ts'un* which controlled the *chia*. This unique instance seemed to have been a real variant of the three-level form; it is listed here merely because it closely resembles the previous specimen in having the *ts'un* as a superior tax division.

14. Ho Hsien (Kwangsi) furnished a rare instance in which an attempt at standardizing the nomenclature was made. According to the 1934 edition of the *Ho hsien chih*, there were prior to the mid-nineteenth century altogether eighteen *li* in this district, and each of these divisions contained uniformly ten *chia*. Some of the *li*, however, were known as *Hsiang* or *tu*, giving rise to the following rather confusing situation:[87]

Upper six *li*	Tsai-ch'eng Li
	Chiang-tung Li
	Wen-ling Li
	Chiang Seventh Tu
	Chiang Eighth Tu
	Ch'eng Hsiang
Middle six *li*	Chung Li
	Shang Li
	Ying-en Li

Middle six *li*	Kuei-ling Hsiang P'ing-an Li P'ing-chi Li
Lower six *li*	Chao-hsien Li Eighteenth Tu Twentieth Tu Twenty-first Tu (Names of two remaining divisions missing.)

In 1865 (T'ung-chih 14) Liu Tseng-hsiu, the magistrate, "rear-ranged the *li-chia* and the taxpaying households," designating all the above divisions uniformly by the name *li*. This local official, how-ever, secured terminological uniformity but introduced variations in actual arrangement. Instead of assigning ten *chia* to each *li*, as formerly practiced in Ho Hsien and required by official regulations, he attached a varying number of households to each of the eighteen *li*, thereby virtually doing away with the *chia;* and as he retained the old *li* groupings without constituting them into genuine superior di-visions over the *li*, the new arrangement which he effected became in reality a one-level affair.

A similar one-level pattern existed in I-chang Hsien (Hunan), where according to the 1885 edition of the provincial gazetteer,[88] there were seven *li* and six *tu*. These were presumably divisions of the same lev-el, like those in Ho Hsien.

Substantially the same one-level arrangement existed in Lu-i Hsien (Honan). This instance is particularly illuminating, for the *li* divi-sions it contained were said to have been called *t'u* or *Hsiang* indis-criminately in Ming times, but the name *li* became established in the K'ang-hsi reign of the Ch'ing dynasty. The compiler of the 1896 edi-tion of the *Lu-i hsien chih*[89] made this amply clear:

> In the Hung-wu years of Ming [late fourteenth century] the farm-house-holds were arranged into fourteen *t'u*. . . . In Cheng-hua 3rd year [1467] six *t'u* and fourteen *Hsiang* were added . . . making a total of thirty-four *li*. . . . Sometime in the K'ang-hsi reign, ten *ch'ang* and four *li* were added . . . bringing up the total to forty-eight *li*.

CONCLUSIONS AND EXPLANATIONS

The following conclusions suggest themselves:

1. During and even before the nineteenth century the official form of the *li-chia* was actually followed only in a relatively small number of localities.

2. The northern provinces seem to have conformed to the official nomenclature more consistently, whereas in South China a wide va-

riety of names prevailed, the most important of which were *tu* and *t'u*.

3. Southern localities deviated further from the official form by often introducing additional divisions which were superimposed upon or interposed between the official divisions; while northern localities did not meticulously observe the two-level official form, these seldom had more than three levels in their tax collection arrangements.

4. The *chia* (ten-household) division tended to disappear in many localities, and to be replaced by other and usually larger divisions.

There appear to have been two major types of tax divisions actually existing in and before the nineteenth century. Roughly speaking, the northern type had the *li* division as its core, whereas the southern type had the *tu* and *t'u* as basic divisions. It should be noted, of course, that while the *tu-t'u* complex was practically absent from the former, the *li-chia* complex sometimes presented itself in the latter.

It may be of some interest to see how the *li* division was replaced by other divisions in South and Central China. The following will give us a general view of the situation:

Li by *t'u*: Kwangtung, Kiangsi, Kiangsu, Hupeh, Anhwei, and Kwang-si

Li by *tu*: Kiangsu, Chekiang, Fukien, Hupeh, and Kwangsi

Li by *ch'ü*: Hunan

Li by *pao*: Kwangtung

Li by *p'u*: Fukien

Li by *Hsiang*: Hupeh

The present investigator has not yet discovered any instance in the northern provinces where the *li* was replaced by some other division. On the contrary, there is some indication that a reverse process took place in certain localities of North China, where the *li* superseded divisions formerly known by other names. The situation in Lu-i Hsien (Honan), noted shortly before, is a case in point.

The question naturally arises, why did the *li-chia* system in northern localities conform more to the official regulations, whereas wide divergencies appeared in the south? And why did the *tu-t'u* nomenclature, generally absent in the north, often prevail in the south? One cannot do more than conjecture.

As is well known, the *li-chia* system of the Ch'ing dynasty, with its arrangement of divisions and nomenclature, was taken directly from the Ming dynasty official scheme with practically no change. It is clear also that the *tu-t'u* complex originated in all probability in the Sung and Yüan dynasties, [90] but continued to be used in some localities during the Ming dynasty. The lack of uniformity in the tax collection system, therefore, was a phenomenon observed already in Ming times. It was not a special shortcoming of the Ch'ing government. In fact the unofficial nomenclatures had prevailed so widely in the Ming dynasty that some compilers of local gazetteers regarded them (wrongly, of course) as the normal Ming practice. [91]

The *tu-t'u* complex, then, was a historical survival transmitted through the Ming dynasty to the Ch'ing. The Ch'ing government was unable to supplant it with its official scheme, just as the Ming government had failed to do before.

Historical survival accounts for some of the divergencies in terminology but does not explain the structural variations in the tax system. The reasons for the appearance of what we call "additive" and "subtractive" forms of variation seem to lie largely in local circumstances and practical exigencies.

In the first place, the inclusion of the *Hsiang* and the *ts'un* in the system, neither being authorized by the official regulations, may have been a product of practical convenience. The scheme adopted in 1648, as noted before, required the *li-chang* to send the tax registers of the *li* to the local yamen. It must have been much more convenient to group together the various adjacent *li* and present the registers in one batch. One or more persons might be delegated to go to the yamen (which, in certain cases, was quite distant from the far-flung villages), [92] making it unnecessary for all the *li-chang* to make the trip on every occasion. The *Hsiang* (or its equivalent) was a ready division suitable for such a purpose—a grouping of the *li* to facilitate the handling of tax registers. Hence, as early as K'ang-hsi times the head of the *Hsiang* had already been referred to semiofficially as one who "took charge of tax money and grain." [93] The *ts'un*, on the other hand, with its various leaders, [94] would have been a highly serviceable unit for tax collection purposes. Moreover, some villages were so small as to contain very few households (sometimes as few as half a dozen); [95] the *ts'un* in such cases became quite logically the lowest division of the tax system.

Increase or decrease of the local population might have a part in introducing irregularities into the *li-chia* arrangement. Obviously, a substantial increase or decrease of the number of households in any given locality would disturb the size of the original divisions. This would account for the "additive" and "subtractive" variations, and for the disappearance of the *chia* or its replacement by larger divisions. [96] An excellent example of the effect of population change upon the *li-chia* divisions was furnished by An-tsai Hsien, one of the districts of Yen-an Fu (Shensi). According to the *Yen-an fu chih* (1802 edition), [97] An-tsai was

. . . originally divided into twenty *li*. Owing to the fact that the soil was barren and the inhabitants were poor, the number of *li* was reduced to sixteen at the beginning of the Ming dynasty. Each *li* contained ten *chia*, and eleven households were attached to every *chia*. In the reign of Ts'ung-chen [1628-44] more than half of the inhabitants abandoned their homes and went away. When the magistrate (surnamed Wang) received orders to rearrange the divisions, some of the *li* and *chia* had become completely depopulated. He petitioned and was authorized to combine all the existing divisions into one *li* (i. e., Chin-chuang Li). During the Ch'ien-lung reign of the present dynasty, the population increased slightly. I Chia-ch'ien, the magistrate, reconstituted the households into five *li*. . . . Some time later, however, these went out of existence. At present, though there are a total of eight *chia* paying the taxes, actually they are the equivalent of only six *chia*, not quite as populous as a single village in a prosperous district.

We have no actual example to show the effect of population growth on the *li-chia* divisions, but it is safe to assume that it must have been considerable in those instances in which the increase was substantial.

The reason for the unequal distribution of households in the *chia* and consequently also in the *li* or *t'u*, even though the number of *chia* in each of the higher divisions remained constant, appeared to be twofold. On the one hand, owing to the failure of the government periodically to revise the census records as well as the tax divisions,[98] an increase or decrease of local population was bound to render the distribution more and more uneven. On the other hand, tax evasion, a commonplace phenomenon in imperial China, must have played havoc with the decimal pattern of the *li-chia*. The rate of land tax being assessed on the basis of the different grades of the soil and locations of the farms, the transfer of the registration of a piece of land from one *Hsiang* to another, or from one *li* to another, where a lower tax rate applied, would have meant a substantial saving of money to the taxpayer. Such a transfer was, of course, illegal, but could be effected by bribing the local keeper of the tax registers, a practice which eventually reduced the official divisions, in extreme cases, "into mere names."[99] In Chien-ch'ang Hsien (Kiangsi), for instance, it often occurred that

. . . the farm land of certain households was actually in one *Hsiang* but it was registered in the tax records of another *Hsiang*, [with the result that] approximately three of the twenty-one *li* situated in Te, Shou, and Tiao Hsiang appeared as registered divisions of Hsiao-nan Hsiang, whereas about three *li* located in the Hsiao-nan Hsiang became registered divisions of Ta-nan Hsiang.[100]

Special conditions in certain localities sometimes exerted influence on the *li-chia* divisions. An interesting example was found in Mienyang Chou (Hupeh), where the *yüan* became a subdivision of the *li*. As this district was liable to floods during certain months of the year, the inhabitants built dikes to enclose their farms and homesteads for protection. The areas thus enclosed were locally known as *yüan*, which eventually served as a unit of tax collection. [101]

One question still remains: why were there more deviations in nomenclature in southern provinces than in the northern ones? Why, to be more specific, did the names *tu, t'u,* etc., prevail in many southern localities but were practically absent in the north? No definite answer can be offered. One conjecture is that the northern provinces, being nearer to the seat of the central government, presumably came under closer supervision and therefore complied with its orders more strictly. Another conjecture is that the variations in nomenclature and actual arrangement encountered in the south existed already in the previous dynasty, and that these did not constitute a new phenomenon called forth by any special circumstances characteristic of the Ch'ing dynasty.

It may also be speculated that there may have been a political motive behind the use of the *tu-t'u* nomenclature which, as we have seen, was a survival from Sung and Yüan times. Evidence indicates that it was in use early in the Ch'ing dynasty, probably as early as the time when the *li-chia* system was officially adopted by the imperial government, and that it prevailed in the southeastern provinces where the Ming loyalists made their last futile stand, particularly in Chekiang and Fukien. It is possible that the recalcitrant southerners purposely used this extralegal, antiquated nomenclature to show their defiance—somewhat like their refusal to shave their heads. The *tu-t'u* usage persisted and spread, and the government did not think the matter serious enough to deserve action.

Whatever the reason may be for the existence of the bewildering number of variations, one conclusion is certain: the Ch'ing rulers did not succeed in establishing a uniform system of tax collection divisions in rural China. Here, as in many other matters, the great chasm between official forms and actual circumstances points to the fact that, despite its intentions, the Ch'ing government was unable to overcome the diversifying forces inherent in a vast empire with widely different local conditions.

APPENDIX II

HISTORICAL ANTECEDENTS OF THE CH'ING
GRANARY SYSTEM

In order to make clear the full significance of the Ch'ing granary system and incidentally to dispel some confusions, it may be necessary to review the historical development of the concept as well as the institutional forms of this system. [1] The idea of putting aside grain to provide against emergencies—of buying grain when the supply was abundant and selling it when the supply was short with a view to maintaining an equilibrium in grain prices—originated in ancient times. The earliest clear expression of this idea is found in the *Chou-li* [2] and the *Kuan-tzu*. [3] The first granaries designated by the appellation *ch'ang-p'ing* appeared in the Han dynasty (54 B. C.), [4] and were followed by granaries bearing the same name in most of the subsequent dynasties, notably Chin, [5] Sui, [6] T'ang, [7] Sung, [8] and Ming. [9] The Han granaries, usually regarded as the archetype of the *ch'ang-p'ing* of later times, were, however, designed to cope with a general slump of grain prices which resulted from a period of agricultural prosperity and which, ironically, spelled financial disadvantage to persons engaged in agricultural production. They were not intended to serve as insurance against scarcity or disasters; they thus differed in purpose from the *ch'ang-p'ing* of later times.

The first change in this direction occurred in A.D. 583, when the founder of the Sui dynasty decided to set up a number of granaries at suitable points in the newly unified empire, in order "to provide against floods and droughts." Different names were given to these storehouses; the one at Shen-chou (in modern Shensi) alone was called *Ch'ang-p'ing-ts'ang*, the "Ever-normal Granary." It should be noted that such government granaries were established only at more or less important points of the empire. They did not number more than a dozen and were therefore absent in most localities.

This system was followed by the rulers of the T'ang dynasty with very few changes. It was during the Sung dynasty that the *ch'ang-p'ing* system, inaugurated in 992 to give relief to inhabitants of the metropolitan area, and beginning with a few storehouses in the imperial capital, was extended in 1020 practically throughout the entire length and breadth of the empire. The founder of the Ming dynasty further extended the local grain reserve system down to the *chou* and *hsien,* the lowest administrative level. Meanwhile, the practice of encouraging the people to contribute grain (in addition to the reserves bought with government funds) was formally introduced. [10]

Three landmarks stood out most prominently in the development of the *ch'ang-p'ing* granary system: the Han dynasty gave the storehouses their distinctive name, the rulers of Sui defined their ultimate function, and the Ming emperors made them a universal, comprehensive system of famine control, ready for adoption by the builders of the Ch'ing dynasty.

The *i-ts'ang* and *she-ts'ang* made their debut much later than the *ch'ang-p'ing.* In order to make fuller provisions against natural calamities, the government of Sui decided, in 585 (K'ai-huang 5), to encourage the people of various parts of the empire to establish *i-ts'ang* in their own respective *she* divisions. Contributions of rice or wheat were made at the time of harvest. The grain reserve thus realized was stored in the granary of each *she* and entrusted to the headman of the *she* who was held responsible for dispensing it to destitute families in the neighborhoods in the event of famine. [11] These rural granaries were designated as *i-ts'ang,* while they were actually storehouses maintained by and located in the *she* divisions. For this reason, the terms *i-ts'ang* and *she-ts'ang* were sometimes used indiscriminately in later times despite the distinction officially made between these two types of locally managed granaries.

Emperor T'ai-tsung of the T'ang dynasty revived the *i-ts'ang,* but he adopted a new method of procuring the grain reserves. Instead of asking local inhabitants to make contributions voluntarily, he levied a surtax on all landowners, with the exception of those paying the lowest rate of land tax and those belonging to certain ethnic minorities. The reserves thus accrued were either lent to peasants to be used as seed or dispensed to the destitute. [12] When *i-ts'ang* of the Sung dynasty were first instituted in 963 by imperial order, they were to be controlled by local officials, and the grain reserves, as in T'ang times, were procured by the imposition of a surtax on land. [13] The *i-ts'ang* of the T'ang and Sung dynasties, therefore, differed from those of the Sui dynasty in two important respects. First, their grain reserves came from a mandatory surtax instead of from voluntary contributions, and second, they were managed by local officials instead of rural agents. In these respects they were hardly distinguishable from the *ch'ang-p'ing;* they differed from the latter mainly in the fact that their reserves were not used for the purpose of stabilizing the prices of grain.

An abortive attempt to revive the Sui system was made in the closing decade of the eleventh century, shortly before Wang An-shih launched his reforms. [14] About three-quarters of a century later, the first move to establish rural granaries through government action was made by a well-meaning local official. [15] It was, however, Chu Hsi, the famous Sung Confucianist, who set the pattern for the *she-ts'ang* of subsequent times. An experiment made in 1168 in a district of Fukien province convinced him of the soundness of his ideas. He memorialized the Shun-hsi emperor in 1181, and succeeded in persuading his government to "promulgate the system in all parts of the empire."[16] The main features of this system were free contribution, local management, and official supervision, the same features that were so important in the *she-ts'ang* system of the Ch'ing dynasty.

Rulers of the Yüan dynasty reverted to the practice of raising grain reserves by levying a surtax[17] and of designating the rural granaries by the name *i-ts'ang*, although as in Sui times these were located in the *she*, a rural division composed of fifty households. [18] The name *she-ts'ang* prevailed again in Ming times. When provincial governors were ordered in 1925 to establish rural grain storehouses, however, they were instructed to arrange every twenty-five or thirty households into a *she*, in which an "upright and propertied person" was selected as head of the *she*. Each of these heads was assisted by two other suitably chosen persons to manage the granary. Taxpayers were required to deposit varying quantities of grain in proportion to the amounts of the land tax for which they were severally liable. [19]

TABLE 29
PRINCIPAL CHANGES IN GRANARIES
FROM SUI TO CH'ING DYNASTIES

Dynasty	Date Granary Established	Nomenclature	Location	Method of Procuring Reserves	Management and Supervision
Sui	585	*I-ts'ang*	*She*	Contribution	Head of *she*
T'ang	627	*I-ts'ang*	?	Surtax	?
Sung	963	*I-ts'ang*	*Chou,* ihsien	Surtax	Local officials
Sung	1181	*She-ts'ang*	Countryside	Contribution	Local management, official supervision
Yüan	1269	*I-ts'ang*	*She*	Surtax	Local management, official supervision
Ming	1529	*She-ts'ang*	*She*	Surtax	Local management, official supervision
Ch'ing	1654	*I-ts'ang*	Town, market	Contribution	Local management, official supervision
	(1679)	*She-ts'ang*	Villages		

It was left to the Ch'ing government to make a distinction between *she-ts'ang* and *i-ts'ang*, to use them to serve rural communities and towns respectively, to abolish the practice of raising grain reserves through taxation and to place these granaries under local management and official supervision. Table 29 shows the main changes which these granaries underwent from the Sui to Ch'ing dynasties.

APPENDIX III

"VILLAGE ELDERS"

It may be useful to explain the meaning of the much used (and misused) term "village elders." The term "elder" is obviously a translation of *lao-jen* or *ch'i-lao*, appellation for a specific type of village headman obtaining in Ming and early Ch'ing times. According to the history of the Ming dynasty, Emperor T'ai-tsu issued an order to the Hu-pu, at an unspecified date, to the following effect:

> One hundred households of the people are to be joined into one *li*. If marriages, funerals, illness or misfortunes occur in the *li*, wealthy households within it should help [the persons concerned] with money and poor ones with labor. All should co-operate and assist one another in their farming and harvesting during the spring and autumn seasons. This is to teach the people to live in harmony. A *lao-jen* [elderly man] shall be instituted in each *li*, to be selected from virtuous elderly persons who are respected by many. He shall be charged with the task of leading the people to do good and of settling quarrels or [disputes] within the neighborhoods.[1]

The *lao-jen* of Ming times, therefore, were government-instituted rural headmen whose main duty was the maintenance of good order and morals. This Ming institution was accepted by the founders of the Ch'ing dynasty. Imperial lawbooks contained provisions for the selection of elders in the countryside, although their title was changed from *lao-jen* to *ch'i-lao*. It was provided:

> Where *ch'i-lao* are to be appointed, these shall be selected from virtuous elderly persons who are respected by their fellow inhabitants and who live in the same rural areas. Persons who are retired yamen underlings or disbanded yamen runners or who have committed crimes are not eligible. . . . Violators [of this law] shall be punishable by dismissal and sixty blows. . . . The duties of the *ch'i-lao* shall be to influence the people and improve the custom. This is the modern expression of the ancient idea of the *Hsiang-san-lao*.[2]

The *ch'i-lao* of Ch'ing times, therefore, did not differ materially from the *lao-jen* of the Ming dynasty. At a comparatively early date, however, the original functions of the *ch'i-lao* were somehow forgotten, and these elderly leaders of the countryside were treated as if they had been *pao-chia* heads. In a 1646 memorial to the throne the situation was revealed in these words:

> The functions of the *ch'i-lao* should not extend beyond spreading the kingly influence. They should not be held responsible for local affairs. . . . If they are subjected to the system of joint responsibility [as in the *pao-chia* and as is now being done], it would be conformable neither to reason nor to the law. [3]

There is no evidence that the situation ever changed. On the contrary, the so-called *ch'i-lao* ceased to be moral preceptors of the countryside and became rural headmen, policemen, or tax collectors. It was possible that *ch'i-lao* of the kind originally conceived of by the founders of Ch'ing were never regularly or widely appointed but that their appellation was remembered and was indiscriminately used to designate a variety of rural headmen. But whatever the earlier situation may have been, there is no doubt that during the nineteenth century and immediately after it the village headmen who were designated by the title *ch'i-lao* performed tasks totally different from those of a rural preceptor. S. W. Williams wrote late in the nineteenth century: "At the bottom of the judicial scale are the village elders. . . . The elders give character to the village, and are expected to manage its public affairs, settle disputes among its inhabitants, arrange matters with other villages, and answer to the magistrates on its behalf."[4] The elder, in other words, appeared to this writer as a sort of village chief executive, a headman who took general charge of community affairs. Writing a little later than Williams, Arthur H. Smith expressed essentially the same view:

> These headmen are sometimes styled village elders *(hsiang-chang* or *hsiang-lao)* and sometimes they are termed merely managers *(shou-shih jen)*. The theory in regard to these persons is that they are chosen, or rather nominated, by their fellow townsmen, and confirmed in their position by the District Magistrate. [5]

Other writers, however, were convinced that "elders" were *pao-chia* agents. James Legge virtually identified elders with *chia-chang*. "Ten families," he wrote in the 1870's, "make a tithing, called in Chinese a *chia*, over which there is appointed an elder or superintendent."[6] This view was echoed in the 1890's by Sir Robert K. Douglas who observed that "the *ti-pao* or headman [of a village was] held responsible for the peace and well-being of his neighborhoods [and was] commonly assisted in his office by the elders of the village."[7]

An instance in which "elders" discharged tax collecting and other functions was recorded by the compiler of a local gazetteer. According to him:

> Formerly, orders of the government of Cho Hsien [Chihli] did not apply to San-p'o [village]. . . . There was [in this locality] an institution known as the *lao-jen* [elders]. . . . The whole area . . . was arranged . . . into three *li*, each of which contained ten *chia* and for each a *lao-jen* was instituted. . . . The term of office was three years, and no salary was paid. . . . When the term expired, a person whose family was well-to-do, whose conduct was upright and who enjoyed popular esteem . . . was nominated to succeed [the retiring elder]. It was unnecessary that the person be old in age. . . . His powers were very extensive, including the power to press tax payments, to resolve quarrels, and to manage all matters of the community. [8]

The compiler failed to specify the time when this interesting institution prevailed in San-p'o, but he indicated that it did not cease to operate until 1929. It is possible that the "elders" of this locality existed before the opening of the present century.

The term "elder" is sometimes employed to designate village leaders who were not formally instituted; it has been so used, for instance, by James S. Burgess, Daniel H. Kulp, and Martin C. Yang, whose views have been presented in chapter 7. When the term "elder" is used to designate any formally instituted rural headman of Ch'ing times other than the officially appointed *ch'i-lao*, it is, strictly speaking, a misnomer. The term may, however, be legitimately used to denote an elderly man informally recognized as a leader of a rural community, provided the term is not taken to be a specific title conferred on the individual in question.

NOTES

Preface

1. Wen Ch'eng, *Chia-yin chou chih* (1898), 29/68a, quoting from Huang Ch'ao's preface to an earlier edition of the same gazetteer.

2. Mao Ch'i-ling (1623-1716), quoted by En-hsi, in the latter's preface to the 1874 edition of *Hsü-chou fu chih*.

3. Ho Ch'ang-ling (1785-1848), preface to "Tsun-i fu chih," *Wen-ts'un*, 6/12a-b.

4. For example, George W. Cooke, *China* (1858), pp. 391-92, warns against the confusing interpretations offered by the "twenty-years-in-the-country-and-speak-the-language men," and Ernest F. Borst-Smith, *Mandarin and Missionary* (1917), p. 75, against the "authoritative" statements made by "globe-trotters" who wrote books on the Far East.

5. Henry S. Maine, *Village Communities* (3rd ed.; 1876), pp. 6-7, justifies such an inference in these words: "We have a number of contemporary facts, ideas, and customs, and we infer the past form of these facts, ideas, and customs, not only from historical records of that past form, but from examples of it which have not yet died out of the world, and are still to be found in it. . . . Direct observation comes thus to the aid of historical inquiry, and historical inquiry into the help of direct observation."

I do not make use of "direct observation" and am less sanguine than Maine about historical inference made from it.

Chapter 1

1. Han Fei (d. 233 B.C.) was the first Chinese political thinker to give clear expression to this philosophy. See W. K. Liao (transl.), *Complete Works of Han Fei Tzu* (1939), Vol. I.

2. These were the regular divisions. Special divisions were made to suit the circumstances in some localities.

3. The basic reference works for the administrative structure of the Ch'ing dynasty include *Hui-tien, chüan* 1-100, and *Ch'ing t'ung-k'ao, chüan* 77-90. The following works in English are useful: W. F. Mayers, *The Chinese Government;* H. S. Brunnert and V. V. Hagelstrom, *Present Day Political Organization of China;* and Hsieh Pao-ch'ao, *The Government of China, 1644-1911.*

4. K'ang Yu-wei, in a memorial submitted in 1895; in Chien Po-tsan, *Wu-hsü pien-fa tzu-liao,* 2/177.

5. *Ch'ing t'ung-k'ao,* 1/5029, and *Ch'ing hsü t'ung-k'ao,* 1/7761.

6. *Ch'ing t'ung-k'ao,* 1/5619-20, gives definitions of the magistrate's duties and the distribution of magistrates in the eighteen provinces.

7. *Ibid.*, *chüan* 12-13, summarizes the developments from the Chou to the
Sung dynasties; Liu I-cheng, *Wen-hua shih*, 2/265-66, describes the institutions of the Ming dynasty.

8. The *ch'eng* of imperial China was a variable phenomenon, although its main
features are readily and clearly discernible.

Edward T. Williams in his *China Yesterday and Today* (1923), p. 137, wrote:
"In China the word most commonly used as the equivalent of 'city' is *ch'eng*.
Strictly speaking the word means 'a city wall' or 'rampart,' and it is applied as
a rule only to those towns which are surrounded by a substantial brick wall and
a moat. . . . Any town which is the seat of government of an officer of the rank
of a county [i.e., district] magistrate or above it may be called a *ch'eng*. There
are market towns and villages in China which are larger and of greater commercial importance than some cities, but it is political importance that gives a
place the rank of a city." Fei Hsiao-t'ung, *China's Gentry* (1953), p. 95, stressed
the same features, though from a different viewpoint: "To make a wall . . . is
a big enterprise which cannot be accomplished by private means alone; it must
be a public work shared in by the people over a large area. Both political power and political purpose are needed to construct this kind of large wall. A *ch'eng*,
then, is an instrument of the ruling classes in a political system where power
resides in force." Both factors were indeed important but neither was indispensable in the creation of *ch'eng*. There were in exceptional instances *ch'eng* without walls (substantial or otherwise), and there were also some *ch'eng* that had
economic importance independent of their "political importance." For example,
Hsiang-hsiang Hsien (Hunan), T'ao-yüan Hsien (Hunan), and Chen-yüan Hsien
(Kweichow) had no walls. See *Hsiang-hsiang* (1874), 1/8b, and Hua Hsüeh-lan,
Jih-chi (1901), pp. 84 and 100-1. But all these were seats of *hsien* government
and therefore were *ch'eng*. While no place could be a *ch'eng* without the presence of at least a *chou* or *hsien* yamen, some cities had economic as well as
political significance. But sometimes when the economic conditions of a locality
no longer justified the presence of a yamen, the locality was officially deprived
of its status of *ch'eng*. See *Ch'ing hsü t'ung-k'ao*, 135/8952-53. One might say
therefore that there were two main types of *ch'eng* in imperial China: those that
had political or administrative significance primarily or exclusively, and those
that had economic significance in addition to their being seats of local government. Most of the provincial capitals and *fu* (prefectural) cities, and some of
the *chou* and *hsien* cities belonged to the first type. A useful description of this
type was given by a British consul in 1868: "Of natural defences the city seemed
to possess none; but strong, high and thick walls were a sufficient defence against
Chinese artillery. A small mud wall of recent construction surrounded the suburbs. . . . Commercially, the place is of slight importance. . . . As the provincial capital [of Chihli] it is the residence of a Governor-General, a provincial
Treasurer, and a provincial Judge, and from this circumstance derives all its
importance." E. C. Oxenham's report, quoted in Alexander Williamson, *Journeys in North China* (1870), II, 395-96. Instances of the second type are readily
found. Huo-lu Hsien (Chihli), for example, was characterized by a Western traveler thus: "It is apparently a thriving place and is celebrated for its iron-market.
In appearance it reminds one of some Yorkshire towns; the wall is very irregular,
a sort of circle, and only about a mile in circumference. . . . This town [i.e.,
ch'eng] is merely an emporium, no iron being either produced or wrought here.
. . . Why-lu [Huo-lu] is also one of the great centers for the various cooking-
vessels made of sand. One is apt to be misled as to the size of the place by the
number of inns, many of which are of the first class; this arises from the posi-

tion of the town, which is a necessary resting place on the great road to the west. It is here that all needful preparations must be made for passing the mountains; and here, too, those who have just escaped their many dangers generally remain awhile, to repair their shattered carts and to rest their mules." *Ibid.*, I, 279, quoting a report of 1865. An even greater commercial center existed in Chang-te Fu (Honan). According to E. C. Oxenham's report on his journey of 1868: "It is situated on the south bank of a river of some size. . . . On entering the walls I soon perceived that I had arrived at a city very different from the so-called Foos [i. e. , prefectural cities] of Chih-li. Handsome temples in first-rate repair, and stone pailows elegantly carved, bespoke of the piety or the wealth of the inhabitants; whilst a busy and numerous population and the constant succession of shops, gay with the fantastic ornaments of the Chinese, showed the sources whence this wealth was derived. Outside the main street, instead of the bare spaces destitute of houses . . . are here to be seen a constant succession of well-built dwelling-houses reaching up to the very base of the wall." *Ibid.*, II, 402-3. Cities in imperial China varied in their degree of "urbanization." Not a few *chou* and *hsien* cities retained a rustic aspect, even if they were dignified by the presence of city walls. For example, Ting Chou (Chihli) in the 1860's is described as follows: "Within the walls there was little to attract; most of the enclosed space is under cultivation, the only busy quarter being in the centre of the city." Kao-yu Chou (Kiangsu) in 1869 was "an extensive city full of fields." *Ibid.*, I, 268, and II, 286. Even Nanking in 1842 was far from "urban": According to a British officer, "The appearance of the city . . . was somewhat disappointing, --fully four-fifths of the space inclosed by the ramparts revealing to us only a tract of cultivated land, instead of the teeming mass of buildings which we had been led to expect." John Ouchterlony, *The Chinese War* (1844), p. 476. For similar observations made by Chinese writers concerning other cities, see Yü Yin-lin, *I-shu*, 1/27a and 2/23a; and Hua Hsüeh-lan, *Jih-chi*, p. 49. While the imperial countryside was generally an aggregate of villages, hamlets, and rural markets, certain parts of it were devoid of such concentrations of population. Richthofen made these remarks concerning Szechwan in 1872: "In no other province of China is there such a sharp distinction between Country and City as is the case in Sz'-chwan [Szechwan]. . . . In [Szechwan], the country, is dotted everywhere with farms or small groups of them. There the farmer lives, with his numerous family, in the midst of his fields. Those who are given to industrial pursuits or commerce live in market-towns or cities, but the Chinese type of townlike villages is little represented." *Letters* (1903), p. 165. Edward H. Parker, in his *China. Her History, Diplomacy and Commerce* (1901), p. 181, gives a list of names commonly used to designate various local areas and divisions. The book is not definitive but may be profitably consulted.

9. Local gazetteers usually give the number of villages in each *chou* or *hsien*. See, for example, *Po-pai* (1832), 5/16-25; *Feng-chen* (compiled 1881, printed 1916), 1/13-20; *Lu-i* (1896), 3/4b; and *Hsiang-shan* (compiled 1911, printed 1923), 2/1a-b.

10. Daniel H. Kulp II, *Country Life in South China* (1925), I, xxix.

11. *Wei chou* (1877), *chüan shou*, p. 18a-b.

12. The *Hsiang* as an administrative division of rural areas appears to have existed as early as the Chou dynasty. The *Tso-chuan* (564 B.C. [Hsiang-kung 9, 1]) contains a reference to *Hsiang-cheng* (headman of *Hsiang*), implying that such a division existed in the state of Sung. It certainly constituted one level of local administration in Ch'in and Han times, when each *Hsiang* contained ten *T'ing* divisions. Rulers of later dynasties retained the *Hsiang* division in mod-

ified forms. For example, in the Chin dynasty (A. D. 265-419) every hundred households in a district constituted a *Hsiang*, and in T'ang times (A. D. 618-906) one hundred households constituted a *li* and five *li* a *Hsiang*. The Sung dynasty adopted the T'ang arrangement which, some local historians said, persisted in a number of localities down to the Ch'ing dynasty, although the *Hsiang* division disappeared from the official scheme of rural administration in the Ming dynasty when this scheme was formulated in 1381. The term *Hsiang* then became generally used in the sense of "rural areas" *(hsiang)*, in contradistinction to *ch'eng*, "city areas." See *Ming-shih*, 77/2. The *Hsiang* as a rural division did not completely disappear from official usage in Ch'ing times. A few localities, in which actual conditions no longer justified the maintenance of a *hsien* (district) administration, were demoted one level, from hsien to *Hsiang*. In 1796, for example, P'ing-lo Hsien (Shansi) was changed to P'ing-lo Hsiang, and Ma-i Hsien to Ma-i Hsiang. Again, in 1807, Hsin-an Hsien (Chihli) was changed into a Hsiang. In each case the offices of the magistrate and other functionaries were abolished. *Ch'ing hsü t'ung-k'ao* (1936), 135/8952-53.

13. Arthur H. Smith, *Village Life in China* (1899), foreword. Differences might also exist in small areas. See, for example, Cato Young *et al.*, *Ching-ho* (1930), p. 2.

14. Arthur Smith, *Village Life*, p. 30.

15. George W. Browne, *China; the Country and Its People* (1901), p. 195. Cf. Sir Robert K. Douglas, *Society in China* (1894), p. 109, where the village settlement is mistakenly identified with the *ching-t'ien* (well-field) system.

16. E.-R. Huc, *The Chinese Empire* (1855), II, 98.

17. *Ibid.*, II, 297, and I, 289-90.

18. Huc's observation concerning Szechwan was confirmed by a later writer. See Alicia B. Little, *The Land of the Blue Gown* (1902), pp. 113-98, for an intimate description of farm life in Szechwan as the author saw it in July to October, 1898. See also Richthofen's description, *Letters*, p. 181.

19. Parts of Hupeh showed a certain degree of prosperity. Oxenham said in a note on his journey from Peking to Hankow in 1868: "The river increased in breadth. . . . The banks of the river were thickly inhabited; large *ch'ais* (markets) occurring every twenty *li*, with small villages interspersed between." Williamson, *Journeys*, II, 413.

20. George B. Cressey, *China's Geographical Foundations* (1934), p. 13, reports: "There are two Chinas, each with distinct characteristics in sharp contrast to those of the other." He adds on p. 15, however: "The boundary between the North and the South is transitional. Many characteristics overlap or merge gradually from one region to the other. In general, the change takes place midway between the Yangtze Kiang and the Hwang Ho along the thirty-fourth parallel."

21. Wang I-k'o, *Nung-ts'un tzu-wei yen-chiu* (1932), p. 32. It should be pointed out, however, that not a few southern villages were "close-dwelling."

22. This will be discussed in chapter 8.

23. Mark S. Bell, *China* (1884), I, 61.

24. *Ibid.*, p. 78.

25. *Ibid.*, p. 123. See also pp. 62-63 and 118-19. Similar villages were observed by other writers. For example, see Lt. Col. George B. Fisher, *Three Years' Service in China* (1863), pp. 254-55, where an extremely "wretched" group of villages in northern Chihli is described. Li Tzu-ming, *Jih-chi*, vii, 13a, 3rd month, 16th day (1884), noted that between T'ung Chou and Wu-ch'ing (Chihli) the villages gave the impression that "northern land is poor and wretched."

26. Bell, *China*, I, 124. See also pp. 67-68 for descriptions of other prosper-

ous villages. Bell offered the following general characterization of villages of
North China (Chihli and Shantung): "The villages passed generally varied in area
from 30,000 to 10,000 square yards, and consisted of one main street, generally
suited for one line of traffic only. . . . Much space is taken up in every village
for yards. The huts are low, one-storied, and of mud bricks. The exterior is
plastered with mud and chopped straw, which is renewed yearly. . . . Roofs are
thatched or tiled. There are very few buildings of burnt brick in them. . . .
The yards are generally dirty and muddy. No chimneys exist. Each living room
is generally provided with a raised, hollow brick platform capable of being heat-
ed." *Ibid.*, p. 162.

    27. *Ibid.*, p. 123. See also pp. 127 and 168 for other villages threatened with
floods.

    28. *Ibid.*, p. 68.

    29. Samuel W. Williams, *The Middle Kingdom* (1883), I, 280-81.

    30. Ju-lin (1883), 5/1a-4a. The following concrete descriptions of relatively
prosperous villages in South China are useful: 1. Fukien: "The . . . village lies
on the lower slopes of the lofty green mass of Pheasant Mountain. Below the village is a valley cradled by precipitous mountains. Several hundred inhabitants,
whose main occupation is to cultivate the rich soil on the gentle slopes and level
surfaces, dwell in the valley. The black forest stretches up the steep hillsides
above them. Whenever the skies are cloudless and clear, if one looks sharply
amid the verdant splendour on the lower half of Pheasant Mountain, one can detect roof tops covered with grey tiles that overlap one another like the scales of
a fish." Lin Yüeh-hwa, *The Golden Wing* (1948), p. 1. The conditions described
existed in the closing decades of the nineteenth century. 2. Chekiang: "The little
silk-villages at the base of these hills [near Hu Chou, Chekiang] were all visited
by me at this time [June, 1855], and although the natives were much surprised
at the presence of a foreigner amongst them, yet generally they were polite and
hospitable. The same features of wealth and comfort which I had already remarked in other parts of the silk-country were apparent here. The people were
well dressed, had good substantial houses to live in, and judging from their appearance, they were well fed. Nearly all the respectable farmhouses were surrounded with high walls." Robert Fortune, *A Residence among the Chinese* (1857),
p. 360. 3. Kiangsu: "The writer had occasion one summer day, in company with
a friend, to visit a typical farm village among the hills southeast of Nanking.
. . . After winding about for a mile or more, we came upon a little hamlet of
five or six hundred people, known as She-ts'un, or the 'She Village'. . . . Mr.
She . . . the head of the clan and the chief man of the village . . . came to
our assistance. . . . His dress and manners indicated that he was no farmer,
though he lived among farmers. . . . He was indeed the village school-master
as well as the principal landowner of the district. He led us to the village temple, which served as a shelter not only for gods but for guests, though the latter were certainly few and far between. . . . Mr. She invited us to his home,
an extensive pile of buildings constructed of brick. . . . Most of the villagers
were his tenants. Their homes, too, were well-built houses of brick with tile
roofs. The lanes that wound among them, however, were narrow and crooked.
There were no shops in the place, but one of the farmers acted as butcher, when
needed, and sold meat and a few other necessaries to his neighbors. On the whole
the people seemed well fed and clothed, contented and happy. As a rule, however,
the tenant farmers in the region about Nanking do not appear to be so comfort-
able or prosperous as those in She-ts'un. The country was never entirely recovered from the ravages of the Taiping Rebellion." Edward Williams, *China*

Yesterday and Today (1923), pp. 89-91. See John L. Buck, *Chinese Farm Economy* (1930), map i, facing p. 26, for a general impression of the arrangement of farmsteads, farms, paths, ponds, bridges, temple, and school in Tung Chiao village, near Nanking.

31. Leon Donnat, *Paysans en communauté* (1862), p. 8.

32. A few instances will illustrate the situation in North China. Data from the 1880 edition of the gazetteer of Yen-ch'ing Chou (Chihli), 2/5a-59b, show the wide variations in size among the villages in the same locality:

Village	Households	Inhabitants
T'uan-shan-t'un	258	1,392
Hsiao-ho-t'un	224	1,248
Ta-ni-ho	177	960
Ch'ing-an-pao	109	699
Pei-sha-chien	118	642
Shang-pan-ch'iao	95	537
Ch'ien-hei-lung-miao	82	450
Feng-chia-mio	82	423
Hsi-hung-szu	75	414
Shun-feng-t'un	144	395
Hsia-pan-ch'iao	69	375
Chiu-po-chi-ying	62	335
Yen-chia-chuang	63	322
Meng-chia-chuang	50	272
Hsiao-ying-ts'un	48	206
Chu-chia-pao	34	183
Miao-chia-pao	31	173
Ku-chia-ying	27	145
Ch'en-chia-ying	21	114
Wang-chia-chuang	13	93
Shang-shui-mo	19	85
Hsi-sang-yüan	14	73
Hsi-ho-yüan	10	53
Wang-chia-ch'ang	8	41
Ma-chia-chuang	8	35

The following accounts may also be cited for the sake of comparison: According to a report of the Reverend C. Spurgeon Medhurst *(Journal of the Royal Asiatic Society,* North China Branch, N.S., **XXIII** [1888], 86), the population of I-tu Hsien (Shantung) was about 250,000 and the number of villages about 1,000. Since a portion of the inhabitants dwelt in the city, the average number of persons per village was below 250 and probably below 200. According to *Fu-ning* (1877), 8/15a, the population of Fu-ning Hsien (Chihli) was 267,746 and the number of villages 605. Even assuming that all the inhabitants dwelt in the countryside (which was not so), the average size of the village was only 442 persons.

33. *Cheng-ting* (1875), *t'u*, pp. 22b-23a:

Village	Households	Registered Land (in *mow*)
Chu-chia-ho	363	12,141
Tung-t'a-tzu-k'ou	235	7,199
Shih-chia-chuang	211	2,599
Chu-fu-t'un	197	6,532
Hsi-chao-t'ung	181	6,016

Village	Households	Registered Land (in *mow*)
Ling-t'ou-ts'un	164	3,855
Pei-chuang	155	4,036
Nan-ts'un	145	5,189
Nan-yang-chia-chuang	140	5,426
Tung-chao-t'ung	118	12,810
Hsiao-hsi-chang	112	3,694
Nan-niu-t'un	107	4,110
Hei-chia-hsiang-ying	105	2,681
Nan-sheng-pan-ts'un	92	4,116
Ta-feng-t'un	90	2,609
Ta-hsi-chang	86	2,608
Hou-chang	80	1,247
Hsi-chuang	78	1,257
Nan-yung-ku-ts'un	71	1,560
Tien-shang	64	1,192
Tu-chia-chuang	61	1,497
Tung-chuang	56	1,256
Pei-yung-ku-ts'un	52	2,120
Nan-wu-nü-ts'un	47	1,193
Tung-hsin-chia-chuang	44	1,526
Chung-sheng-pan-ts'un	39	593
Tung-kuan-hsiang	30	322
Hsi-chuang-t'un	29	1,115
Hsiao-t'un	25	663
Pei-sheng-pan-ts'un	23	1,461
Wu-chia-chuang	23	124
Tung-yüan-ts'un	15	153
Pei-chung-feng-ts'un	10	228

34. ·*Ting chou* (1850), *chüan* 6 and 7, *passim.*

35. It should be noted that despite the differences, some of which are quite important, Chinese villages had a basically similar organizational pattern and displayed, in varying degrees, activities of a basically similar nature. The differences that existed between them, therefore, did not give rise to distinct types or species of villages, such as the "severalty" and "joint" villages in India. The differences between these two types of Indian villages were indicated by B. H. Baden-Powell, *The Indian Village Community* (1896), pp. 8-9, and *The Origin and Growth of Village Communities* (1899), p. 19, as follows:

Severalty Villages	Joint Villages
1. An influential headman; hereditary;	1. No headman originally, but a council of elders;
2. Separate holding;	2. Joint holdings;
3. No joint liability for revenue;	3. Revenue assessed in lump sums;
4. No joint ownership of waste or "common" land.	4. Village site and usually some wasteland owned in common.

R. Mukerjee, *Democracies of the East* (1923), pp. 265-66, maintained that three types of villages exist in India: (1) the *ryotwari* village, "probably of the most

ancient type," which "owes its original existence to settlement by some tribes
or clans" with a leader; (2) the *zamindari* or landlord system, in which "the
chief men of the village will necessarily be the landlords"; and (3) "the joint
village" in which "some of the villagers claim the ownership not merely of the
fields they cultivate, but of the whole of the village lands." It may be said that
Chinese villages in the nineteenth century and during a long period before it,
were of a type somewhat similar to the "severalty" or *ryotwari* type of India.
Villages that resembled the Indian "joint" type may have existed in ancient China,
although we have no evidence to prove their existence. While modern scholars
doubt the historical truth of Mencius' idea of the "well field" system, this idea
may have reflected roughly a primitive condition of village land distribution no
longer existing in Mencius' time. In the monoclan village of nineteenth-century
China (which we shall discuss later), where the clan was virtually identical with
the village and owned extensive land in common, we encounter a type of village
that bears a faint resemblance to the "joint village" of India. The question arises
whether "village communities" existed in nineteenth-century China. The answer depends to some extent upon what we mean by this term. If it is understood to mean communities with communal property or a communal right to control property, it is certain that these were unknown in China throughout historical times. The nearest approach to them were, as mentioned above, some
of the clan villages. It is therefore difficult to agree with Harold J. E. Peake,
who writes in the *Encyclopedia of the Social Sciences*, XV, 255: "Village communities exist all over China, except in Szechwan, where scattered homesteads
are the rule." In what follows, Peake evidently treats all villages as clan villages. As we shall see in chapter 8, many villages, especially in North China,
did not consist of clans. In the same article (p. 253) Peake characterized the
village community in general as follows: "The village community consists of a
group of related or unrelated persons larger than a single family, occupying
a large house or a number of dwellings placed close together, sometimes ir-
regularly, sometimes in a street, and cultivating, originally in common, a number of arable fields, dividing the available meadowland between them and pas-
turing their cattle upon the surrounding waste land, over which the community
claims rights as far as the boundaries of adjacent communities. In historic times
most such villages were under the rule of a lord, who governed the people and
administered justice, receiving in return the labor of the community for the
cultivation of his share of the land." This definition obviously does not fit the
Chinese villages of historic times. And it is questionable that the relationship
between the "lord" and the people obtained in villages of imperial China. Western authorities on the village community were not agreed upon many important points. For statements of the classical theory, see especially the works of
George Ludwig von Maurer, *Einleitung zur Geschichte der Mark-, Hof-, Dorf-,
und Stadt-verfassung* (2. Auflage, Vienna, 1896); Coulanges, *La cité antique*
(Paris, 1864); Henry S. Maine, *Village-Communities in the East and West* (London, 1871); and Frederic Seebohm, *The English Village Community* (4th ed.,
London & New York, 1890). For criticisms of the classical theory, see Fred-
eric W. Maitland, *Domesday Book and Beyond* (Cambridge, Eng., 1897); Jan
S. Lewinski, *The Origin of Property and the Formation of the Village Community*
(London, 1913); and Charles M. Andrews, "The Theory of the Village Com-
munity," *American Historical Association Papers*, V, Parts I and II, 45-61.
Another aspect of the Indian village community is described by A. S. Altekar,
A History of Village Communities in Western India (1927), pp. ix-x: "From a
careful analysis of the scanty data supplied by the Veda, it would appear that in

the earliest times the village communities enjoyed a practically unlimited autonomy. . . . The state was usually conterminous with the village; so there was no occasion to define the sphere of local and central Government." At another place in the same book, it is said: "This type of a self-contained and self-governing village commune did not, however, last long; larger political units were being evolved and the village soon became their constituent." *Ibid.*, p. xi. Whatever degree of autonomy Chinese villages may have enjoyed in the earliest times, it did not last into the imperial period.

36. Arthur Smith, *Village Life* (1899), p. 148. A rural market *(chi)* should be distinguished from a "fair" *(hui)*, the latter not being a unit of rural division, as Smith correctly pointed out in the same book, p. 149. See also Martin Yang, *A Chinese Village* (1945), pp. 190-91. Rural markets were often well organized centers of commodity exchange. In some of them, at least, qualified persons were appointed to arbitrate disputes concerning prices, measurements, weights, and other matters. See, for example, *Yen-ch'ing* (1880), 2/3b; *Ch'ing-pien* (1899), 4/44a; and Yang Ch'ing-kun, *A North China Local Market Economy* (1944), pp. 18-20. All the instances described were from the nineteenth century.

37. The term *hsü* prevailed especially in Kwangtung and Kwangsi. *Chi* was often used in central China. In Szechwan and Yunnan rural markets were usually called *ch'ang*. See *Fu-shan* (1924), 1/31a-b; *Chia-ying* (1898), 32/18b-19a; *Meng-ch'eng* (1915), 2/8b-10a; *Hsin-hsien* (1887), 1/12b-13a; *Chen-hsiung* (1887), 3/11a; *Hsin-fan* (1907), 6/7b-8b, and other local gazetteers.

38. *Lu-lung* (1931), 4/1b-2b. For a brief survey of the locations and dates of rural markets in the Ch'ing dynasty, see an article by Shigeru Kato, translated into Chinese in *Shih-huo*, V, 51-53. For a few instances, see *Cheng-ting* (1875), 3/5a-b; *Yün-ch'eng* (1893), 2/30a-36b; and *Yü-lin* (1894), 24/4a-5a.

39. Yang Ch'ing-kun, *North China Local Market Economy*, p. 3, explains the general situation as follows: "The length of time intervals differs with local conditions. In general, in rural areas in North China and the Kwangtung province of South China, markets are held every five days, that is, on every fifth day. In Yunnan province of Southwest China, a six-day interval is the rule. But where occupational specialization is highly developed and the necessity of trading is great, such as the conditions in many sizable trading towns where periodic markets continue to exist, they may be held every three or even every two days." Again "Dates of neighboring markets are arranged so that they do not conflict but dovetail each other. If one market is held on the first-sixths, a neighboring one may be held on the seconds-sevenths or other non-conflicting dates. This is to enable villagers to attend more than one market within the five-day interval when emergent or special need arises." *Ibid.*, p. 25. Yang refers to conditions in the early twentieth century, but his statements hold true for the nineteenth century.

40. We have no direct evidence, but Yang Ching-kun's study, *ibid.*, p. 14, gives a clue to nineteenth-century conditions: "The mean radius of service areas of ten basic markets is 1.3 miles (3.6 li), with an average deviation of 0.14 mile. The mean radius for eighteen intermediate markets is 2.5 miles (6.2 li), with an average deviation of 0.2 mile. A central market usually has two service areas, a primary area including nearby villages attending the market regularly or at least frequently, and a secondary area encompassing villages farther away where people come to the market only occasionally for items hard to obtain in their own neighborhood markets. The central market in the County Seat [the city] has a radius of 4.3 miles (12 li) for its primary area and 8.2 miles (23 li) for its secondary area . . . the major factor determining the size of the service area of a market is *walking distance.*"

41. See *Lo-ch'uan* (1944), 9/6a-b, citing the 1806 edition, describing the situation in Lo-ch'uan Hsien (Shensi): ". . . the markets in the various rural areas gathered, either once a year . . . or on three or four days each month. All who exchanged goods there were local residents. Sometimes inhabitants living near the borders of Han-ch'eng and Pai-shui came to trade. No merchants or peddlers came from any great distance."

42. The following table prepared from data furnished by the 1887 edition of *Hsin hsien chih*, 1/12b-13a, will serve to illustrate:

TABLE 30
VARIATION IN MARKETS

Market	Market Days	Distance from City (in *li*)
Yü-huang-miao-chi	2*, 12, 22; 7, 17, 27	12
T'ien-chia-chi	2, 12, 22; 5, 15, 25	12
	7, 17, 27; 10, 20, 30	
Wang-hui-chi	4, 14, 24; 9, 19, 29	20
Tung-wang-chuang-chi	1, 11, 21; 6, 16, 26	12
Tsou-chia-hsiang-chi	3, 13, 23; 8, 18, 28	35

* Refers to second day of the Chinese month.

43. *Cheng-ting* (1875), 6/85a-7/27b; *Fu-ning* (1877), 8/16a; *T'eng hsien* (compiled, 1868; reprinted, 1908), 5/9a-10b; *Nan-yang* (1904), 3/21a; *Sui chou* (1892), 1/5a-6a; and *Yü-lin* (1894), 3/1a-19b. Rural markets were not uniformly distributed among villages. For example, it was said that in Ch'üeh-shan (Honan), while larger villages had one to three markets each, a few villages had none at all. *Ch'üeh-shan* (1931), 1/6b.

44. Bell, *China* (1884), I, 72, 154.

45. *Ting Chou* (1850), *chüan* 6 and 7 *passim*. The following data from this source may be of interest:

	Tung-nei-pao-ts'un	*Hsi-pan-ts'un*
Households	295	411
Inhabitants	2,158	4,046
Stores	10	7
Storekeepers	?	28
Streets	4	8
Registered land *(mow)*	4,100	1,800
Wells	34	350
Temples	6	37
Distance from city *(li)*	75, northwest	20, southeast

TABLE 31
RURAL MARKETS AND TOWNS

Market *(chi)* or Town *(chen)*	House-holds	Inhab-itants	Streets	Stores	Store-keepers	Market Days	Distance from City *(li)*
Wu-nü-ts'un-chi	90	482	1	15	65	5*, 15, 25; 10, 20, 30	40, east
Tzu-wei-ts'un-chi	571	7,288	3	9	?	1, 11, 21; 6, 16, 26	70, southeast
Ming-yüeh-chen	85	592	2	64	250	4, 14, 24; 9, 19, 29	30, southwest
Ch'ing-feng-chen	125	589	2	76	560	2, 12, 22; 7, 17, 27	30, north
Tung-t'ing-chen	196	1,052	3	22	61	1, 11, 21; 6, 16, 26	20, east

Ta-hsin-chuang-chen	161	800	3	30	130	2, 12, 22; 7, 17, 27	40, east
Hsing-i-chen	381	2,160	5	?	?	4, 14, 24; 9, 19, 29	50, south
Chuan-lu-chen	357	1,842	7	?	?	4, 14, 24; 9, 19, 29	35, northwest
Li-ch'in-ku-chen	209	1,630	10	14	?	3, 13, 23; 8, 18, 28	50, south

*Refers to fifth day of Chinese month.

46. Hsin-i Hsien (Kwangtung) had a total of twenty-two *hsü*, of which the following may be regarded as representative. Table 32 is prepared from data given *Hsin-i* (1889), *Chüan* 2, sec. 3, pp. 1a-b.

TABLE 32
SOME *HSÜ* IN HSIN-I HSIEN

Rural Market	Location	Market Days
Chen-lung-hsü	S. across the river	1*, 11, 21; 4, 14, 24; 7, 17, 27
Ta-tung-hsü	E. 10 *li* from city	Not in operation
Ho-shui-hsü	E. 20 *li* from city	Not specified
Pei-chai-hsü	N.W. 35 *li* from city	3, 13, 23; 6, 16, 26; 9, 19, 29
Ch'eng-ching-hsü	E. 45 *li* from city	2, 12, 22; 5, 15, 25; 8, 18, 28
T'an-p'u hsü	E. 50 *li* from city	Not in operation
Pe-shih-hsü	N.E. 80 *li* from city	1, 11, 21; 4, 14, 24; 7, 17, 27
Ta-ch'eng-hsü	N.E. 170 *li* from city	2, 12, 22; 5, 15, 25; 8, 18, 28
Kuei-tzu-hsü	N.E. 180 *li* from city	2, 12, 22; 5, 15, 25; 8, 18, 28

*Refers to first day of Chinese month.

Additional information concerning the *hsü* may be had in *Fu-shan* (1924), 1/31b; *Yang-chiang* (1925), 2/56a-59a; and *En-p'ing* (1934), 7/13a. According to *Fu-shan*, 1/31a, it was customary in Kwangtung to call markets held at ten-day intervals *hsü* and those held daily, *shih*. *Pao-pai* (1832), 5/26a-27b, indicates that the name *hsü* was widely used in Kwangsi also. For example, Pao-pai Hsien had thirty-eight *hsü*, located in villages a few *li* or over one hundred *li* from the city. The market days followed the 1-4-7, 2-5-8, and 3-6-9 patterns. The practice of calling rural markets "ch'ang" seems to have originated in Szechwan. According to *T'ung-jen* (1890), 2/9b, the term *kan-ch'ang* appears in *Shu-yü*, and had come into use in Kweichow "a long time ago." *Shu-yü* is a work on the customs and usages of Szechwan. This nomenclature persisted in Szechwan down to recent times. See, for example, *Hsin-fan* (1907), 6/7b-8b, and *Yen-yüan* (1891), 2/3b-5b. "Ch'ang" was also often used in Yunnan province. For example, *Chen-hsiung* (1887), 3/11a, has: "Buying and selling . . . in the markets is called *kan ch'ang.*"

47. *Ch'u-chou* (1877), 24/2a.

48. See, for example, *Nan-ning* (1852), 3/22a-23a.

49. *Ch'ang-ning* (1901), 2/8a.

50. *Hsiang-shan* (1923), 5/13a-b; *Hua hsien* (1924), 3/15a-b; *Hsin-i* (1889),

Chüan 2, sec. 4, pp. 1a-b; *Ch'ing-yüan* (1880), 2/20a-b; *Po-pai* (1832), 5/26a-b; *Lu-chou* (1882), 1/41a-43b; 2/31b-32b; 2/50a-b; and 2/54a-b; *Mei-t'an* (1899), 2/21a-23b; and *Ch'ang-ning* (1901), 2/8a.

51. *Ch'u-chou* (1877), 24/2a.

52. *Ju-lin* (1883), 4/76a-82a. Other markets in this locality were less prosperous.

53. One more exceptional phenomenon may be noted. In Kwangtung, Szechwan, and a few other provinces in southwest China, rural markets were sometimes held on bridges. See *Tung-kuan* (compiled 1911, printed 1921), 20/1a-4a, for examples in Kwangtung. A few Western writers have left descriptions of scenes which they observed in rural markets in various parts of China. For example, Alexander Williamson wrote in *Journeys in North China* (1870), I, 269: "We spent the evening of September 17 [1865] at the market-town of Min-yue-tien [near Ting Chou, Chihli]. Just outside the houses was a pig-fair, held under the shade of some large trees. A great number of carts were drawn up in a rough circle, the mules tied to the trees, while in the centre lay the pigs. . . . The squealing of the pigs and jabbering of the dealers was something awful; the streets being filled from end to end by a busy throng." E. C. Oxenham narrated what he witnessed in early November, 1868, in rural markets near Pao-ting Fu (Chihli): "Immense quantities of grain of every kind were for sale, and in many places the women were occupied in spinning and selling cotton thread. . . . The cotton comes from the south of the province, and what thread is not consumed at home goes up to Peking. Long strips of blue cotton cloth were also abundant, and fruit, raw cotton, and the rude implements of Chinese agriculture complete the list." Williamson, *Journeys*, II, 398. E. T. Williams writes in *China* (1923), pp. 111-13: "One April morning some years ago, I came into a little village in central Anhui, called 'Great Willow Tree.' The market was already in progress and the street was a busy scene of bargain and sale. . . . As we passed through the gate and entered the village we met a caravan of pack-mules, laden with hemp-oil and making their way to Nanking. Several trains of wheelbarrows followed, carrying opium, oil, cotton, vermicelli or native medicines. . . . Other caravans came in during the day making the return journey, bringing cotton cloth, kerosene, matches, paper, and a varied assortment of other manufactures. . . . Meantime the marketers were busy haggling with their customers over the prices of cabbage and garlic, turnips, chickens and eggs. The shop-keepers within doors were having quite as good a day's trade as the farmers outside. . . . Tables were set by the roadside for the sale of hot tea and a cool smoke with a native hubble-bubble for those who wanted such refreshment, while the usual group of loafers were noisily settling the affairs of the universe in the tea-house. . . . Gradually the crowds in the street began to disperse, and before evening the village had already assumed its wonted aspect of dullness. The farmers could be seen trudging homeward over the hills, each with a pole over his shoulder to which a pair of baskets were suspended, containing the purchases of the day."

54. W. C. Milne, *Life in China* (1857), p. 307. This prosperous town had a well-compiled gazetteer, the 1923 edition of which contains twenty *chüan*.

55. The "four famous interior markets" mentioned by Milne were Fu-shan Chen (Kwangtung), Ching-te Chen (Kiangsi), Han-k'ou Chen (Hankow, Hupeh), and Chu-hsien Chen (Honan).

56. Milne, *Life in China*, pp. 278-79. For a vivid description of a relatively prosperous town in eastern Chekiang during a fair, see Robert Fortune, *A Residence among the Chinese* (1857), pp. 247-59.

Chapter 2
1. Wen Chün-t'ien, *Pao-chia* (1935), p. 204.
2. *China Review*, VIII (1880), 259.
3. Hsiao I-shan, *Ch'ing-tai shih* (3rd ed., 1947), pp. 103-4. Instances of other confused statements are found in L. Richard, *Comprehensive Geography of the Chinese Empire and Dependencies* (1908), pp. 309-10; Pao Shih-ch'en (1775-1855), *Ch'i-min ssu shu, chüan* 4, *shang*, p. 1a-b, "Shuo pao-chia shih-i"; and Tai Ch'ao-ch'en, *Hsüeh-shih lu* (1867), 3/2b, quoting Yang Ming-shih (late 17th century), "Wei-tsai i."
4. *Ch'ing t'ung-k'ao* (1936 reprint), 19/5024.
5. Tu Yu (735-812), *T'ung-tien* (1935 reprint), 3/21-23.
6. *Chou-li*, "Ti-kuan, sui-jen." A different scheme of division is described in "Ti-kuan, ta-ssu-t'u." Later writers on the *pao-chia* usually traced this institution to the *Chou-li*, e.g., those quoted in *K'ang-chi lu*, 2/24a-30b. See also Kung Tzu-chen (1792-1841), *Wen-chi*, 1/90-91, "Pao-chia cheng-ming."
7. *Kuan-tzu, chüan* 4, "Li-cheng"; *chüan* 5, "Ch'en-ma"; *chüan* 20, "Hsiao-k'uang"; and *chüan* 57, "To-ti."
8. See note 6 above. These schemes varied a good deal. Without exception, however, the household *(chia)* was the basic unit of local division, and except in one instance the smallest divisions were formed by five and ten households.
9. For a summary of the schemes adopted by rulers from the Ch'in to Ming dynasties, see Chih-ch'iang (pseud.), "Hsiang-chih ts'ung-shuo," in *Chung-ho*, III (1942), 59-65. The following may also be consulted: Ku Yen-wu (1613-82), *Jih-chih lu, chüan* 8, "Hsiang-t'ing chih chih"; *K'ang-chi lu*, 2/24b-29a; Liu I-cheng, *Chung-kuo wen-hua shih* (1932).
10. Tu Yu, *T'ung-tien*, 3/23.
11. *Ibid.* "One hundred *hu* [households] constituted a *li*, and five *li* a *hsiang*. Four *chia* [families] constituted a *lin*, and three *chia* a *pao*. A *cheng* was instituted in each *li*, [who was placed] in charge of counting and checking the number of households and inhabitants, of urging the planting of farm crops and mulberry trees, of investigating and detecting wrongful or offensive conduct, and of urging the payment of taxes and corvée. Inhabitants of the cities were organized into *fang*; a *fang-cheng* was instituted in each *[fang]*, who was in charge of keeping the key of the gates of the *fang* and of watching for offenders and law-breakers. [Those who served as *fang-cheng]* were exempted from taxes and the corvée. People in the countryside were organized into *ts'un*, in each of which was a *ts'un-cheng* with duties similar to those of *fang-cheng*." Cf. Liu I-cheng, *Chung-kuo wen-hua shih, chüan hsia*, p. 14, quoting from the *T'ang liu-tien*.
12. *Sung-shih*, "Hsiang-p'ing," 3/145. Liang Ch'i-ch'ao, *Chung-kuo wen-hua shih*, p. 56, contended that the *pao-chia* of Sung times owed its origin to Ch'eng Hao (the well-known Neo-Confucian philosopher) who, as magistrate of Chin-ch'eng, set up a *pao-wu* system in which the inhabitants were made to render mutual help and keep watch on the peace and order of the neighborhoods. "Wang An-shih," Liang continued, "took over this system and called it the *pao-chia* system." As a matter of fact, the official system of the Sung dynasty was often designated *pao-wu*. See *Hsü t'ung-k'ao*, 15/2901. Wen Chün-t'ien, *Pao-chia*, p. 9, correctly pointed out that while it is certain that the name *pao-chia* first came into currency in Sung times, its precise meaning is difficult to determine. The difficulty, so far as we can see, lies in two directions. First, different names were often used to indicate the same institution, and second, the institution bearing the same or essentially the same name was given various functions in different periods of history. Failure to take notice of such discrepancies or

variations often led writers to issue confusing statements about the *pao-chia*, e. g. , Robert Lee, "The *Pao-chia* System," *Papers on China*, III, 195-206, especially in his statement that "the principal functions of the *pao-chia* encompassed practically all the things that a village government could be asked to perform. "

13. Wang Shou-jen (1472-1528), *Wang Wen-ch'eng-kung ·chüan-shu, chüan* 16, "Pieh-lu," 8 "kung-i," a set of documents concerning the "ten-household placard" system; and *chüan* 17, "Pieh-lu," 9, "kung-i," three public announcements on the same subject. All these documents were issued between 1517 and 1520. Naturally, the system established by Wang Shou-jen in southern Kiangsi exerted some influence on the *pao-chia* of later times. For example, Ch'en Hung-mou (1696-1771), who was noted for his efforts to develop the *pao-chia* in early Ch'ing times, quoted some of Wang's writings on the "ten-household placard" system in his well-known work on local administration, *Ts'ung-cheng i-kuei(chüan shang*, pp. 31b-32a) and in fact modeled his system on Wang's *(ibid. ,* pp. 33a-b).

14. *Hui-tien* (1908), 17/2a ; *Shih-li* (1908), 158/1a; *Ch'ing t'ung-k'ao* (1936 reprint), 19/5024; *Lü-li pien-lan* (1877), 20/17b; and *Ch'ing-shih kao*, "Shih-huo chih," part 1, pp. 2a-5b. See *Hu-pu tse-li* (1791), 3/4a-10b, for summary of pertinent regulations in force around Ch'ien-lung 50 (1785). A different arrangement is described in *Ch'ing t'ung-k'ao* (1936 reprint), 21/5043. Another official scheme known as *tsung-chia* will be explained in chapter 3.

15. *Nan-ning* (1852), 4/2a.

16. *Liu-yang* (1873), 5/3b, quoting from an earlier (undated) edition of the same gazetteer.

17. Liu Heng (1776-1841), *Yung-yen*, pp. 88 ff.

18. *T'ung chou* (1879), 1/42a.

19. *Lin-chang* (1904), 1/19a-28b.

20. *T'ung-kuan* (1944), 18/4a, quoting from the 1765 edition.

21. *T'eng hsien* (1846), 1/2a.

22. *Ch'ing-pien* (1899), 1/28a-29a.

23. Huang Liu-hung, *Fu-hui* (1699 [1893 reprint]), 21/4a.

24. *T'eng hsien* (1846), 12/8a, quoting K'ung Kuang-kuei, who wrote this statement between 1836 and 1838.

25. Sheng K'ang, *Hsü-pien* (1897), 28/32a, quoting from an essay written by Feng Kuei-fen around 1860.

26. *Li-p'ing* (1891), *chüan* 5, *shang*, pp. 77a-78b.

27. *Nan-yang* (1904), 3/20a-21a. The *Hsiang* division was sometimes replaced by the *lu* division, as for example in Fu-shun Hsien (Szechwan), where a *lu* contained a varying number of *pao*, and each *pao* a varying number of *chia*. *Fu-shun* (1931), 8/12b-15a.

28. In the "second version" of the *pao-chia* arrangement the ten-household division was known as *chia* instead of *p'ai*. This variation may have been due to a confusion (or telescoping) of the police and tax collection systems, the lowest division of the latter being known also as *chia*. The tax collection *chia*, however, contained eleven households, as we shall see when we come to the *li-chia* divisions.

29. *Ming-shih, chüan* 77. "T'ai-tsu followed the *li-she* system of the Yüan dynasty. Inhabitants in the *chou* and *hsien* north of the river were divided into *li-chia*, on the basis of the *she* [division]. Inhabitants of areas under garrison cultivation were divided on the basis of *tun* [divisions]."

30. *Ibid.* See also *Hsü t'ung-k'ao*, 13/2891 and 16/2913.

31. *Ming-shih*, 78/13b. See also *Ch'i-fu* (1884), 96/20b-23b; *Ho hsien* (1934), 2/16b-18a, quoting from the 1890 edition; and Wen Chün-t'ien, *Pao-chia*, p. 275.

32. For instance, see *Yang-chou* (1810), 16/15b-16b.

33. *Shih-li* (1908), 257/1a; *Ch'ing t'ung-k'ao*, 19/5024; and *Ch'ing t'ung-tien* (1935 reprint), 9/2069).

34. This, as indicated elsewhere, accounts partly for the confused statements and inaccurate deductions made by some of the historians.

35. *Lü-li pien-lan* (1877), 8/47a-48b, 20/17b, and 25/99b-100a.

36. *Yung hsien* (1897), 9/2a.

37. *Ch'ang-ning* (1901), 2/1b.

38. *Ho hsien* (1934), 2/17b-18a, quoting from the 1890 edition.

39. Quoted in Orita, *Fen-lun*, I, 19-22. Orita correctly concludes from this: "The *li-chia* was instituted for expediting matters of tax and corvée; the *pao-chia* was established for policing and [detecting] fugitives from the law. "

40. Wen Chün-t'ien, *Pao-chia*, p. 205.

41. One of the worst instances of confusion is found in *Fu-shun* (1931), 8/12a: "When in Shun-chih 17 [1660] *li* and *she* divisions were ordered to be established among the inhabitants, the titles 'li-chang' and 'she-chang' appeared. In southern provinces, [where these divisions] were called *t'u*, there were *t'u-chang;* and [where these] were called *pao*, there were *pao-chang*. The *chia-chang* was also called *p'ai-t'ou*, for he was the head of the ten *p'ai*. . . . Nomenclature differed in various provinces but the service [rendered by the agents] was identical. "

42. Quoted in Orita, *Fen-lun*, I, 479. Orita comments: "This system was based on the *she* system of the Yüan dynasty and on the *li* system of Ming. . . . Was this *li-she* system of agricultural assistance a temporary arrangement made at the inception of the [Ch'ing] dynasty, or was it intended for permanent operation in subsequent generations ? There is no way to answer this question now. A survey of such works as the *Hui-tien* and the *Tse-li* shows that since the *li-she* system was set up in Shun-chih times, there had been no express order to abolish it. . . . Probably it was in operation at the beginning of the dynasty . . . but later died a natural death. "

43. *Chüan* 2, p. 7b.

44. *Luan chou* (1896), 13/12a-50b. Comparable situations existed in Fu-ning Hsien and Pao-ting Fu (both in Chihli). See *Fu-ning* (1877), 8/15b, and *Pao-ting* (1881), 24/1a.

45. *Sui chou* (1892), 2/13a-19a.

46. *Lin-chang* (1904), 1/29b-30a.

47. *Hu-pei* (1921), 34/1041.

48. *Ibid.*, 34/1042, quoting from *Kuang-hua hsien chih;* and 34/1045-46, quoting from *Kuang-hsü yü-ti chi.*

49. *Nan-hai* (1910), *chüan* 3.

50. *Hsia-men* (1839), 2/20b-22a.

51. *Nan-ch'ang* (1919), 3/1a-2a.

52. *Ju-lin* (1883), 1/2b.

53. *Hsin-i* (1889), 1/1a-b.

54. *Nan-ch'ang* (1919), 3/1a-2a.

55. *Tso-chuan*, Chao-kung 25. The religious significance of the *she* has been explained by H. G. Creel thus: "The ancestral temple symbolized the state in so far as the state was conceived as the estate, the patrimony, of its ruling family. But the state was also considered as a territorial entity, a 'fatherland,' and in this sense it was symbolized by the *she*, the so-called 'altar of the land.' Originally this was simply the soil, the giver of crops, to which sacrifices were offered for an abundant harvest; in time of drought it was thought that sacrifices to the land could produce rain. It was not easy to sacrifice to the soil without some symbol, and this symbol was found in a mound which may have been nat-

ural at first. But such mounds came to be thrown up in every village, and since they symbolize the land of the little district they became centers of religious activity in each community." *Birth of China* (1937), pp. 336-37.

56. *Sui-shu*, 7/10b-12b.

57. *T'ung-k'ao*, 21/204.

58. Wittfogel and Feng, *History of Chinese Society: Liao*, p. 379: "These granaries *[i ch'ang]* were local institutions connected with the village altar *[she]*, the center of all local public affairs." For discussion of local granaries, see chapter 4.

59. *Yüan-shih*, 93/3a; *Hsü t'ung-k'ao*, 1/2780.

60. *Ming-shih*, 77/4a.

61. *Lu-chou* (1885), 18/9b; or *Lo-ch'uan* (1944), 13/2a, quoting from the 1806 edition. The oath *(I-ch'iang fu-jo shih-wen)* reads: "All of us who live in the same *li* shall severally comply with the rules of propriety and of law; we shall not rely on superior force to oppress the weak. Any who violate [this oath] will be first restrained by common action and then brought to the officials. Destitute persons who have become helpless will be given relief in their families; those of them who fail to rehabilitate themselves in three years will be excluded from our meetings. Persons who need assistance in weddings and funerals will be given help according to our individual capacities. Those who act contrary to the [wishes of the] group, those who commit adultery, robbery, and fraudulent acts, and all those who do wrong of any description, will not be permitted to join our association. But if any of them are able to repent and reform, these may be allowed to join our association after three years."

62. *Ho hsien* (1934), 2/10b, quoting from the 1890 edition.

63. Chang Shou-yung, *Hui-pien, nei-pien*, 53/14b.

64. *Hsiang-fu* (1898), 8/34a-b.

65. *Han-tan* (1933), 2/8a.

66. Li Yü, *Hsin-shu*, 2nd series, 1/13b, a statement made sometime in 1663-66 by Chou Liang-kung, circuit intendant for Ch'ing-chou (Shantung): "In each *she* there is a *she-chang* who is none other than the *li-chang*. Each *chia* has a *chia-chang*."

67. *Fu-ning* (1877), 8/15b, where the compiler states: "Originally twenty-one *li* were established. At present there remain [in this district] twelve·*she* and five *t'un*, i.e., a total of seventeen *li*."

Chapter 3

1. *Shih-chi* (Chung-hua edition), 97/6, Lu chia's words.

2. *Shih-lu*, Shih-tsu, 6/1b.

3. *Ch'ing t'ung-k'ao*, 19/5024.

4. *Ibid.*, 21/5043; also given in Chang Shou-yung, *Hui-pien, nei-pien*, 53/1a-b.

5. Wen Chün-t'ien, *Pao-chia*, pp. 216-17 and 256, regarded the *pao-chia* and *tsung-chia* as one institution. There is not sufficient evidence to support his view that the *tsung-chia* constituted "the first stage" which covered the years "from Shun-chih 1 to K'ang-hsi 46" (1644-1717) or the development of the *pao-chia*.

6. *Ch'ing t'ung-k'ao*, 22/5055, and *Lü-li pien-lan* (1877), 20/17b. The name *tsung-chia* survived in a few isolated instances. See for example *Li-p'ing* (1891), *chüan* 5, *shang*, pp. 91b-92b, for the situation in some localities in Kweichow.

7. *Shih-li* (1908), 158/1a; *Ch'ing t'ung-k'ao*, 19/5024; *Ch'ing t'ung-tien*, 9/20 and 69; and *Lü-li pien-lan* (1877), 20/17b and 25/99b-100a. See also Pien Pao-ti (1824-92), *Tsou-i*, 3/51; and *Liu-yang* (1873), 24/11b-12a. George Jamieson's article in the *China Review*, VIII (1880), 269 ff, is also useful. For examples of

pao-chia forms, see Wen Chün-tien, *Pao-chia* (1935), pp. 243-50; and Liu Heng, *Yung-yen,* pp. 97 ff. Samuel W. Williams, *Middle Kingdom* (1883), I, 281, quotes Marco Polo's description of the *pao-chia* practice in the thirteenth century (from Yule's translation, II, 152): "It is the custom for every burgess of the city, and in fact for every description of person in it, to write over his door his own name, the name of his wife, and those of his children, his slaves, and all the inmates of his house, and also the number of animals that he keeps. And if any one dies in the house, then the name of that person is erased, and if a child is born its name is added. So in this way the sovereign is able to know exactly the population of the city. And this is the practice throughout all Manzi and Cathay." Williams adds: "This custom was observed long before the Mongol conquest, and is followed at present; so that it is perhaps easier to take a census in China than in most European countries." That Marco Polo and Williams were both somewhat overenthusiastic concerning the *pao-chia* may be seen from this observation made by Dr. Morrison, whom Williams quotes (pp. 282-83): "Every district has its appropriate officers, every street its constable, and every ten houses their tithing man. . . . Every family is required to have a board always hanging up in the house, and ready for the inspection of authorized officers, on which the names of all persons, men, women, and children, in the house are inscribed. This board is called *mun-pai* or 'door tablet.' . . . But it is said that names are sometimes omitted through neglect or design."

8. *Hu-pu* (1791), 3/4a, contains this undated regulation: "In the villages within the five city areas of Shun-t'ien Fu [the metropolitan city areas] and in the cities and villages of the *chou* and *hsien* of the provinces, the local officials in charge shall give to each household a *men-p'ai* [door placard] on which shall be written the name and occupation of the head of the household, and the names and number of tax-paying adult males (women not being included). . . . Any who fail to comply [with this regulation] . . . shall be punished." A regulation dated 1708 (K'ang-hsi 47), given in *Ch'ing t'ung-k'ao,* 22/5051, similarly required the registration of adult males only. This legally prescribed practice of excluding women and children in *pao-chia* registration, however, appears to have prevailed only for a short period, for the law of 1644 (Shun-chih 1), which inaugurated the *pao-chia,* required "adult males and other persons" to register. See *Ch'ing t'ung-k'ao,* 19/5024. By 1740 the imperial government had regarded it as feasible to use the *pao-chia* registers as the sole source of population figures, including all inhabitants. See *Shih-li* (1908), 157/2a. Sometime before this date the practice established by law in 1708 had evidently been abandoned, with or without overt imperial approval. Since then the general practice was to include the names of all persons living in a household in the *pao-chia* door placards. In fact, a well-known official, who was convinced that complete registration made *pao-chia* operation unnecessarily difficult, memorialized the imperial government in 1758 that only adult males should be required to register. See *Tsou-i,* 51/1a. We have no reason to suppose, however, that his proposal was accepted. The regulation given in the *Hu-pu* (1791) was probably in force only briefly in the early decades of the eighteenth century.

9. This regulation was issued in 1644 (Shun-chih 1). See *Ch'ing t'ung-k'ao,* 21/5043; *Hui-tien* (1908), 17/2a; and Chang Shou-yung, *Hui-pien, nei-pien,* 53/3b. For basic regulations of early Ch'ing times, see *Hu-pu* (1791, 3/4a-9b. George Jamieson, *China Review,* VIII (1880), 259-60, is helpful.

10. *Ibid.,* p. 259. ". . . The scholars and people shall elect to this *[chia-chang's]* office men of probity, education and property. The local officials shall not require them to undertake any other public service, so that they be solely

responsible for this duty. If any of the undermentioned offences are committed within the Tithing *[chia]*, the Tithing-man *[chia-chang]* shall be specially responsible for making the necessary inquiries and reporting the fact, viz: theft, corrupt teaching, gambling, hiding and absconding from justice, kidnapping, coining, establishing a secret society, and so on. He shall also be required to report all suspicious characters arriving within his bounds, and see that the necessary alterations are made from time to time in the Register of Individuals in each Family. If constables from a neighboring jurisdiction come in pursuit of offenders in virtue of a warrant, he shall assist in arresting, but if any of the Yamen constables wrongfully arrest an innocent man, he may lay the facts before the district Magistrate for investigation."

11. The word "gentry" used here and elsewhere in this study is a translation of the Chinese expression *shen-shih* or *shen-chin*. The gentry were privileged persons who gained their special status by acquiring an official rank or position, or by passing one or more series of examinations. See Chang Chung-li's volume, *The Chinese Gentry*, for a detailed study of some of the salient aspects of this privileged group. In imperial China during the nineteenth century, persons who had studied for the examinations but had not actually acquired gentry status enjoyed certain advantages denied to other commoners. Legally they were not gentry, but because they were literate and therefore potential future gentry, they were often referred to as *shih* (scholars or literati) and were in some ways treated as a part of the gentry. At any rate, they were regarded as being more closely related to the gentry than to commoners, and usually exhibited attitudes and behavior similar to (though not necessarily identical with) those of the gentry proper. As a result, the Chinese expression *shen-shih*, as it was used on many occasions in the nineteenth century, included not only the gentry proper but also the scholars or literati. We shall therefore generally employ the word "gentry" to translate *shen-shih;* but whenever a distinction between "gentry" and "literati" must be made for the sake of clarity, we shall translate *shen-shih* as "gentry and scholars" or "gentry and literati." Western as well as Chinese writers of the nineteenth century sometimes maintained such a distinction. Meadows, for example, rendered *shen-shih* as "the gentry and scholars." *The Chinese and Their Rebellions* (1856), p. 245.

12. *Liu-pu ch'u-fen tse-li* (1877), 20/1a; and *Lü-li pien-lan* (1877), 8/1b.

13. Huang Liu-hung, *Fu-hui*, 2/14a. James Legge, "Imperial Confucianism," *China Review*, VI (1878), 368-69, quoting from Stubb's *Constitutional History*, I, v., pars. 41-46, pointed out some similarity between the Chinese *pao-chia* and the English tithing system, in which "each householder stood engaged to the King as a pledge for the good behavior of his family, and all the ten families of it were mutually pledges for one another." See also George Burton Adams, *Constitutional History of England* (1921), pp. 24-25, for King Edgar's legislation in the middle of the tenth century, which eventually gave rise to the frankpledge system of Norman times, and pp. 71-72, for a description of the frankpledge system. The Japanese government in the seventeenth century used a system very much like the *pao-chia* for the same purpose. See K. Asakawa, "Notes on Village Government," *Journal of American Oriental Society*, XXXI, 202-3.

14. Samuel Mossman, *China* (1867), p. 278; author's italics.

15. Williams, *Middle Kingdom* (1883), I, 281-83.

16. Leong and Tao, *Village and Town Life* (1915), p. 61.

17. Paul Linebarger, *China* (1938), p. 430. The author defines the *pao-chia* as "a system of local government embodying principles of collective responsibility and mutual aid within interlocking groups of households and neighborhoods."

This definition is intended to apply to the *pao-chia* system under the National Government at Nanking, without any reference to the Ch'ing system. Robert Lee, "The Pao-chia System," *Papers on China*, III, 204-5 and 209, holds that "the principal functions of the *pao-chia* encompassed practically all the things that a village government could be asked to perform," and goes on to argue that "whenever a dynasty collapsed under the weight of its own ineptitude, the peasantry conspicuously failed to capture and command sufficient political power with which to strengthen the embryonic representative features of the *pao-chia* system and make it the necessary stepping-stone to real self-government." It is difficult to see how the *pao-chia* as it really was (at least during the Ch'ing dynasty) could have served the peasantry as a stepping-stone to self-government.

18. *Ch'ing t'ung-k'ao*, 23/5055.

19. *Ibid.*

20. *Ch'ing t'ung-tien*, 9/2072.

21. Chang Shou-yung, *Hui-pien, nei-pien*, 53/7a-b.

22. *Shih-li* (1908), 158/1a. See also *Ch'ing t'ung-tien*, 9/2071.

23. *Shih-li* (1908), 158/8b. See also *P'an-yü* (1911), 44/9b.

24. *Shih-li* (1908), 158/4a-b. This order was reiterated in 1763 and in 1824. See *Ch'ing t'ung-tien*, 9/2071 and Chang Shou-yung, *Hui-pien*, 53/6a-b.

25. *En-p'ing* (1934), 4/12a. See also *Ch'ing t'ung-k'ao*, 23/5055-56.

26. Wen Chün-t'ien, *Pao-chia*, p. 235.

27. *Shih-li* (1908), 158/1a-b. See also *Ch'ing t'ung-k'ao*, 24/5061.

28. *Ch'ing Hsü t'ung-k'ao* (1936 reprint), 25/7755-56.

29. *Ch'ing t'ung-k'ao*, 24/5061-62.

30. *Ibid.*, 19/5033.

31. The major disturbances of this period included the uprising led by Wang Lun (Shantung, 1774); the White Lotus (1793-1802, affecting Chihli, Honan, Shensi, Szechwan, and Kansu); the *chiao-fei* led by Wang San-huai (part of the White Lotus movement); the uprising led by Liu Chih-hsieh (1800-4, in the southwestern part of the empire); and the uprising led by Lin Ch'ing (1813, Peking). See *Chiao-p'ing san-sheng hsieh-fei fang-lüeh (ca.* 1810); *Chiao-pu Lin Ch'ing ni-fei chi-lüeh; Ku-kung chou-k'an*, Nos. 195-236; and I. Inaba, *Ch'ing-ch'ao ch'üan-shih* (Chinese trans.), III, 18-40.

32. *Shih-li* (1908), 158/1a.

33. *Ch'ing hsü t'ung-k'ao*, 25/7757.

34. *Ibid.*

35. *Ibid.*, 25/7758.

36. *Ibid.*, 25/7759.

37. *Ibid.*, 25/7760.

38. *Sheng-hsün*, Jen-tsung, 101/22b-23a.

39. *Ibid.*, 101/25b-26b.

40. *Ibid.*, 101/24b-25a. See also *Ch'ing hsü t'ung-k'ao*, 25/7760.

41. *Ch'ing hsü t'ung-k'ao*, 25/7760.

42. *Ibid.*, 25/7760-61. For *lien-ming hu-pao kan-chieh*, see also *Shih-li* (1908), 158/2b, and Chang Shou-yung, *Hui-pien, nei-pien*, 54/4b.

43. *Ch'ing hsü t'ung-k'ao*, 25/7760.

44. The edict reads in part as follows: ". . . if there are persons practicing heretical religion, anyone in the five-household group is permitted to inform against them. If there are none, the five households are required to furnish a willing bond, which holds them jointly and severally responsible [for any future appearance of heretical persons]." Quoted in Sheng K'ang, *Hsü-pien*, 80/39a-b. Since quite early times Ch'ing emperors had been concerned about "heretical

religions," as shown in the Sacred Edict of K'ang-hsi (Maxim 7) and in the Ch'ien-lung emperor's edict of 1746 instructing provincial officials to tighten the *pao-chia* control in order to suppress those who "advanced erroneous doctrines and collected money for religious festivals." See *Shih-li* (1908), 158/1a. The problem of "heretical religions," however, did not become really serious for the rulers until the closing decades of the eighteenth century.

45. *Shih-li* (1908), 158/3b.

46. *Ch'ing hsü t'ung-k'ao*, 25/7758, compiler's note commenting on an 1810 edict of the Chia-ch'ing emperor. Despite the importance which the imperial rulers attached to the *pao-chia*, they made relatively little effort to maintain uniformity in *pao-chia* structure or consistency in nomenclature. Discrepancies appeared in Shun-chih, K'ang-hsi, Yung-cheng, and Chia-ch'ing times. The Chia-ch'ing emperor apparently was unable to see the distinction between the *li-chia* and *pao-chia* systems; in some of his edicts, notably in those of 1815 and 1816 (given in *Ch'ing hsü t'ung-k'ao*, 25/7760), he spoke as if the *li-chang* had been the equivalent of the *pao-chang*. Table 33, based on data incorporated in previous discussions, shows the fluctuation of official nomenclature from Shun-chih to Chia-ch'ing times:

TABLE 33
CHANGES IN NOMENCLATURE

	1644 (Shun-chih 1)	1708 (K'ang-hsi 47)	1726 (Yung-cheng 4)	1743 (Ch'ien-lung 8) Reaffirmed 1757	1815 (Chia-ch'ing 20)
1,000 *hu*	*pao-chang*	*pao-chang*	*pao-chang*	*pao-chang*	*li-chang*
100 *hu*	*chia-t'ou*	*chia-t'ou*	*chia-chang*	*chia-chang*	*chia-chang*
10 *hu*	*p'ai-t'ou*	*p'ai-t'ou*	?	*p'ai-t'ou*	*p'ai-t'ou*
100 *hu*	*tsung-chia*				
10 *hu*	*chia-chang*				

47. Yü Ch'eng-lung's "Mi-tao an-min t'iao-yüeh," which contains his main ideas on the *pao-chia*, may be found in Ho Ch'ang-ling, *Wen-pien*, 74/24-28, and in Tai Ch'ao-ch'en, *Hsüeh-shih lu*, 2/4b-10b (abridged). For Yü Ch'eng-lung's biographical sketch, see Arthur Hummel, *Eminent Chinese*, II, 937-38.

48. Huang Liu-hung, *Fu-hui*. P'eng P'eng (1637-1704), another well-known magistrate, was credited with fine *pao-chia* work. Tai Ch'ao-ch'en, *Hsüeh-shih lu*, 1/25a-26a, gives P'eng's "Pao-chia shih," a public pronouncement concerning *pao-chia*.

49. Wang Hui-tsu (1731-1807), *I-shuo, chüan hsia*, p. 115.

50. Ch'en Hung-mou (1696-1771), *Ou-ts'un kao*, 43/11a-12a.

51. Quoted in Wen Chün-t'ien, *Pao-chia*, pp. 236-40. Yeh P'ei-sun's *Pao-chia shih-li* was issued by order of the imperial government for use in all provinces, in 1813 (Chia-ch'ing 18). Yang Ching-jen, *Ch'ou-chi pien* (1883 reprint), 17/7b-14b, gives the main features of Yeh's *pao-chia* system. According to Yang Ching-jen, Yeh P'ei-sun formulated a set of *pao-chia* regulations when he was governor of Hunan in the 1780's, known as *Pao-chia kuei-t'iao*. His son (a vice-president of one of the boards of the imperial government) presented this document for imperial consideration in 1813. It was promptly adopted for empire-wide use. Yang also stated that the *hsün-huan ts'e* method of facilitating *pao-chia* registration was worked out by Yeh in 1781 when he was provincial treasurer of Hunan. This constituted a part of Yeh's *pao-chia* system which was officially adopted in 1813. Wang Hui-tsu, quoted in note 49, successfully operated the *pao-chia* in the eighteenth century. See his *Meng-hen lu, chüan hsia*, pp. 9a and 32b, where he recounts his experiences in 1787 and 1788 as magistrate of Ning-yüan Hsien and Tao Chou (both in Hunan).

52. Liu Heng (1776-1841), *Yung-yen*, pp. 91a-96b. The official reports may not, however, have been entirely accurate. Some of the local magistrates may have made overly optimistic reports to their superiors, who in turn may have knowingly or unknowingly made similar reports to the imperial government. What Yü Yin-lin, governor of Honan, revealed in a 1900 memorial should warn us against lending unreserved credence to all the claims made by the officials quoted in these pages: "The established regulations concerning . . . the registration and checking of the inhabitants . . . still stand. Local officials never fail to report that they are doing everything [according to these regulations]. But cases of robbery occur repeatedly. Your humble servant thinks that it is not difficult to have minute regulations but rather to have effective supervision and checking; and that it is not difficult to have detailed laws, but rather to secure earnest application [of these laws]."

53. *Ch'ing-shih lieh-chuan*, 43/34b-35a. Hunan seems to have been one of the few provinces where the *pao-chia* attained some success. In some districts of Hunan *pao-chia* registration was maintained throughout the greater part of the nineteenth century. For example, *Hsiang-hsiang* (1874), 3/52a, contains this information: In 1815 (Chia-ch'ing 20), through *pao-chia* registration and checking, the population of Hsiang-hsiang Hsien was found to be 91,690 *hu*, 583,205 individuals (including women and minors); in 1868 (T'ung-chih 7), *pao-chia* registration and checking gave the population as 85,122 *hu*, 537,218 individuals; and in 1871 (T'ung-chih 10), the *pao-chia* figures were 85,131 *hu*, 537,289 individuals. We need not assume, however, that these figures were accurate.

54. T'ao Chu (1779-1839), *Ch'üan-chi*, 26/4a-6b.

55. *Ibid.*, 26/7a and 8b-9a.

56. *Ibid.*, 26/11a-17a. Cf. *Ch'ing t'ung-k'ao*, 25/7760, Wang Chih-i's memorial concerning riverboats in Fukien province.

57. Quoted in Sheng K'ang, *Hsü-pien*, 80/16a.

58. Chang Shou-yung, *Hui-pien, nei-pien*, 53/12a.

59. Sheng K'ang, *Hsü-pien*, 80/3a.

60. Hsia Hsieh (1799-1875), *Chung-hsi chi-shih*, 4/3b-4a and 9b-11a.

61. *Ibid.*, 8/10b.

62. Ting Jih-ch'ang (1823-82), *Kung-tu*, 32/1b.

63. Pien Pao-ti (1824-92), *Tsou-i*, 3/51 and 9/15a-b.

64. *Ch'ing-pien* (1899), 4/54a-55b. These instances are included because they supply some concrete details on the method of operating the *pao-chia*. There is of course no assurance that the *pao-chia* was operated as successfully as the accounts indicate (see note 52, above). We have refrained, however, from citing official reports couched in general terms, especially reports from high officials to the imperial government, for example, the memorial submitted by Ho Ch'ang-ling (governor of Kweichow) in 1843 reporting "the completion of rechecking the *pao-chia* after the autumn harvest" in Kweichow province, or the memorial of Li Hsing-yüan (governor of Kiangsu) concerning the same matter, submitted in 1846. These were sent to the imperial government as a matter of official routine; their contents should be taken with more than a grain of salt. For these memorials, see Ho Ch'ang-ling (1785-1848), *Tsou-i*, 9/43a-b, and Li Hsing-yüan (1797-1851), *Tsou-i*, 9/30a-31b.

65. Wen Chün-t'ien, *Pao-chia*, p. 25. Huang Liu-hung's system was described by himself in *Fu-hui*, 21/4a.

66. Chang Sheng-chieh, "Pao-chia lun," given in Sheng K'ang, *Hsü-pien*, 80/5a.

67. *Ch'ing t'ung-k'ao*, 24/5061.

68. Tseng Kuo-fan (1811-72), *Tsou-kao*, 2/30a-b. See also his *Shu-cha*, 4/43a,

for a letter "in reply to Lo Chung-ch'eng, " in which Tseng said that he tried in 1853 to put a stop to the undesirable practice of employing *pao-chia* agents to collect the grain taxes.

69. *Shih-li* (1908), 157/1a.

70. *Ibid.*, 157/4a-b.

71. *Ibid.*, 157/1a. Wen Chün-t'ien incorrectly said that the compilation of *hu-k'ou* registers fell into disuse when the *ting-yin* was merged into the *ti-liang* in 1724 (Yung-cheng 2).

72. *Ibid.*, 157/2a.

73. *Ibid.*, 157/2b: "In Ch'ien-lung 37 [1772] it was petitioned by a memorial and imperially approved: 'the practice of compiling population registers every five years in the provinces shall be by imperial edict permanently discontinued.'"

74. *Ibid.*, 157/2a. This edict is also given in *Ch'ing t'ung-k'ao*, 19/5033.

75. See, for example, *Fu-chien* (1871), 48/6a-b. The population figures of other localities of this province, including Hou-kuan, Ku-t'ien, Hsien-yu, and Chin-chiang, were similarly obtained. See *ibid.*, 48/7a ff.; also *Hsin-i* (1889), *chüan* 4, sec. 5, p. 2a, and *Hsi-ning* (1873), 2/12a-16b.

76. *Hui-chou* (1881), 18/7a.

77. *Lin-chang* (1904), 1/19a: "Since the Chang river changed its course several times, many alterations [in the *li-chia*] had been made. A scrutiny of the present tax registers reveals that all the divisions are now designated as *pao* and the [original] names of the *li* divisions as well as the boundaries of these divisions have become impossible to ascertain for a long time." It may be noted that the *pao-chia* of the Sung dynasty was sometimes given tax-collection duties. See *T'ung-k'ao*, 13/137. As, however, evil practices subsequently arose, the government tried to relieve *pao-chia* agents of such duties. *Ibid.*, 13/138-39.

78. *Ch'ing t'ung-k'ao*, 21/5054.

79. *Ibid.*, 24/5062.

80. *T'ung-kuan* (1944), 26/10a.

81. *Yü-lin* (1841), 6/16b-19b. The arrangement in Chia Chou was in part as follows:

> Nan (South) Hsiang: Fou-t'u-yü ti-fang, 71 *ts'un* (villages);
> Pai-kan-yü ti-fang, 51 *ts'un*.
> Hsi (West) Hsiang: Shen-ch'üan-p'u ti-fang, 72 *ts'un;*
> Wu-lung-p'u ti-fang, 60 *ts'un*.

Cf. *Ch'eng-ku* (n. d.), pp. 18b-19a.

82. *Yen-yüan* (1891), 2/7a.

83. *Yung-hsien* (1897), 9/2a.

84. Sheng K'ang, *Hsü-pien*, 80/5a, quoting Chang Sheng-chieh's "Pao-chia lun. "

85. Robert Coltman, *The Chinese* (1891), p. 75.

86. Arthur H. Smith, *Village Life* (1899), p. 228. The *ti-fang* often assumed the duties of assisting the local functionaries in the preparation of tax registers. An instance was given by Weng T'ung-ho in an entry dated Kuang-hsü *jen-yin* (1902), 4th month, 14th day, in his *Jih-chi*, 39/22b: "Ch'en Hsiang-yü came with the *yü-lin-ts'e* [fish-scale register] for the registered land at Ch'en-t'ang-ch'iao. [The register] shows things very clearly; there are small maps showing the various divisions. . . . According to [Ch'en] the register was prepared the day before yesterday by the keeper of the graves and the *ti-fang* [of the division in question]. "

87. Martin C. Yang, *A Chinese Village* (1945), pp. 173-74: "The *ti-fang* was the

policeman of the village. He had to arrest or detain any criminal, report the case to the government, and help the government's commission in making the investigation. He also had to settle petty disputes and to organize the night-patrol system. "

88. Émile Bard, *Chinese Life* (English trans., 1905), p. 107: "The *tepao[ti-pao]*, or dean of the village, elected by universal suffrage, is responsible for the conduct of the families of his domain. " It is hardly necessary to point out that Bard's observation here was not entirely accurate.

89. Hosea B. Morse, *Trade and Administration of China* (1913), pp. 60-61. Leong and Tao, *Village and Town Life* (1915), pp. 61-63, also regarded the *ti-pao* as head of the *chia* division.

90. E. T. C. Werner, *China* (1919), p. 162.

91. George Smith, *A Narrative* (1847), p. 231.

92. Mossman, *China* (1867), p. 191: "There are officials named *Tee-pow [ti-pao]*, in all towns and cities, who register these transfers [of land], and fix the boundaries of the ground by placing stones at the corners, having the name of the purchaser put on them." Cf. Weng T'ung-ho's statement quoted in note 86 above.

93. H. S. Bucklin, *et al.*, *Social Survey* (1924), p. 34.

94. Orita, *Fen-lun*, I, 214-16, quoting from Wang Feng-sheng's *Pao-chia shih-i*, in which the *ti-pao* was said to have functions distinct from those of the *li-chang* and *chia-chang*, the former being responsible for urging payment of the taxes and for assisting the local magistrate in murder trials or other cases, the latter for detecting and reporting crimes. Orita comments that it was impossible to ascertain the precise nature of the *ti-pao*. The *ti-pao* was regarded as a tax-collecting agent (and therefore an agent of the old *li-chia* system), while *li-chang* and *chia-chang* (actual agents in the old *li-chia* system) were regarded as *pao-chia* agents.

95. *Lü-li pien-lan* (1877), 25/100a.

96. Ch'en Hung-mou, *Ou-ts'un kao*, 15/28a-29a. In an official dispatch issued in the spring of 1743 Ch'en, then governor of Kiangsi, in exhorting his subordinates to operate the *pao-chia* in earnest, used the phrase *hsiang-ti pao-chia*, another unfamiliar expression.

97. Wang Hui-tsu, *I-shuo, chüan hsia*, p. 45.

98. Wang Hui-tsu, *Hsü-shuo*, p. 9.

99. Sheng K'ang, *Hsü-pien*, 80/25b.

100. Ting Jih-ch'ang, *Kung-tu*, 28/5b.

101. *Ibid.*, 34/4a.

102. Li T'ang-chieh (1798-1865), *Jih-chi, tse* 10, Tao-kuang ting-hai, 11th moon, 3rd day.

103. Weng T'ung-ho (1830-1904), *Jih-chi*, 38/32a-33a.

104. Sheng K'ang, *Hsü-pien*, 28/32, quoting Feng Kuei-fen (1809-74).

105. In the process of functional shifts the *pao-chia* became entangled with the *hsiang-yüeh*, the "lecture" system which will be explained in chapter 6. One of the earliest instances in which the *hsiang-yüeh* and the *pao-chia* were mentioned as one office occurred in 1799 *(Ch'ing hsü t'ung-k'ao*, 25/7757). Other instances followed and in the nineteenth century *hsiang-yüeh* often became synonymous with *pao-chia*. See, for example, *Ch'eng-ku*, p. 19a; *Ting chou* (1950), 6/1a-b; and *Kuang-chou* (1878), 109/5b. Thus, as with the terms *ti-fang* and *ti-pao*, one cannot be sure of the actual meaning of *hsiang-yüeh* without referring to the context in which it occurs.

106. Including Liu Heng, Chu I-shun, Chou Chin-chang, Wei Li, and Ko Shih-ch'ing. Their views are summarized in Wen Chün-t'ien, *Pao-chia*, pp. 305-25 and 342-47.

107. Tseng Kuo-fan's words, quoted in *ibid.*, p. 310. See Tseng Kuo-fan, *P'i-tu* 1, documents relative to *t'uan-lien* in Feng-huang T'ing, and to *pao-chia* in Heng-yang; *Chou-i* 1, a memorial reporting *t'uan-lien* work, and *Chou-i* 2, a memorial explaining some of the desirable features of *t'uan-lien. (P'i-tu* and *Chou-i* are both included in *Ch'üan-chi.)*

108. See, for example, *Nan-yang* (1904), 8/29a-b; *Ch'ing-pien* (1899), 4/55b; and *Jen-huai* (1895), 4/29a-33b. See also Ko Shih-chün, *Hsü-pien*, 68/15b; Li Huan (1827-91), *Lui-kao*, 5/7b; and Wang Jen-k'an (1849-93), *I-shu*, 5/1a-3b.

109. *Fu-shun* (compiled 1911, printed 1931), 8/15a.

110. Ting Jih-ch'ang (1823-82), *Kung-tu*, 32/1b.

111. Li Tz'u-ming (1830-94), *Jih-chi*, iv, "Keng-chi," 2, p. 38b.

112. *Ch'ing hsü t'ung-k'ao*, 25/7761-62. The traditional *pao-chia* was not entirely forgotten. See, for example, an edict issued in the spring of 1898, in *Shih-lu*, Te-tsung, 416/2b-3a. During the "one hundred days of reform," the provincial authorities of Hunan transformed the *pao-chia* into a modern police system and placed it in charge of Juang Tsun-hsien. Yeh Te-hui, *Chüeh-mi yao-lu* (1905), 1/17a. The National Government at Nanking revived the *pao-chia* with some modifications shortly after 1927. The new *pao-chia* was expected to perform the functions of local police, local defense, and local administration. Failure to discern the functional differences between this and the Ch'ing *pao-chia* system led some writers to erroneous conclusions. See, for example, Wen Chün-t'ien, *Pao-chia*, *passim*, and Ch'en Chih-mai, *Chung-kuo cheng-fu* (1945), 3/77-78.

113. Chang Sheng-chieh, "Pao-chia lun," in Sheng K'ang, *Hsü-pien*, 80/5a.

114. *Shih-lu*, Sheng-tsu, 3/3a, and Shih-tsu, 37/21a-b; and *Ch'ing t'ung-k'ao*, 25/5071, indicate the privileges and immunities accorded to officials and scholars in the early years of the dynasty.

115. *Ch'ing t'ung-k'ao*, 25/5073.

116. *Ibid.*, 21/5043, compilers' note: "According to the *Chou-li* . . . the managing by *shih ta-fu* [scholars and officials] of the affairs of their own home localities constitutes *chih* [function]; the performing of services to the government by common people constitutes *i* [service]. . . . Since the T'ang dynasty, the *chih* . . . became gradually insignificant; from that time on, all tasks done in home localities fell under the rubric *i*. Thus, in Ch'ing times, all services in the *pao-chia* were *i*—services incumbent upon commoner inhabitants but below the dignity of *shen-shih.*

117. Huang Liu-hung, *Fu-hui*, 23/18b.

118. Chang Shou-yung, *Hui-pien, nei-pien*, 53/10a.

119. Ho Ch'ang-ling, *Wen-pien*, 74/25b. For the meaning of "kung-sheng," "chien-sheng," and "sheng-yüan," see Chung-li Chang, *The Chinese Gentry*, especially pp. 4-5.

120. *Ch'ing t'ung-k'ao*, 23/5055.

121. Chang Hui-yen (1761-1802) reflected the view current at the time in a letter on the *pao-chia*, quoted in Tai Ch'ao-ch'ien, *Hsüeh-shih lu*, 13/24a-31b.

122. Liu Heng, *Yung-yen*, p. 88 ff.

123. Hu Lin-i, *I-chi*, 57/11a-19a.

124. Pien Pao-ti, *Tsou-i*, 9/15a-b.

125. *Ch'ing-pien* (1899), 4/54a-55b.

126. *Ibid.*, 1/28b-29b. In this arrangement the sole "chief gentry" resided in the city, and apparently took general charge of the *pao-chia* in the district. No "chief gentry" was appointed in any of the six rural areas. The *pao-chia* probably fared better in cities where the district magistrates' yamen were located and

where the gentry centered their activities than in rural areas. See, for example, Yeh Ch'ang-chih, *Jih-chi*, 2/24b-25a and 32b, where it is said that the *pao-chia* in cities was effectively used to protect gentry interests against the encroachment of local bullies.

127. *Li-p'ing* (1891), *chüan* 5, *shang*, p. 78b.

128. *Ibid.*, 92a-b. A magistrate of Kuang-t'ung Hsien (Yunnan) induced *shen-chih* "willingly" to serve as *pao-chia* heads. Sheng K'ang, *Hsü-pien*, 80/39a.

129. Liu's memorial is given in Sheng K'ang, *Hsü-pien*, 80/52a-b.

130. For example, Wang Yu-po, salt commissioner of Shensi, called attention to some of the ways in which "bad gentry" so used the *pao-chia*. Some of his remarks are given in Legge, *China Review*, VI (1878), 369.

131. *Ch'ing t'ung-k'ao*, 22/5051, an edict issued in 1708 (K'ang-hsi 47).

132. *Ibid.*, 23/5055, an edict issued in 1757 (Yung-cheng 4) see also *Shih-li* (1908), 396/8a.

133. *Ch'ing t'ung-k'ao*, 24/5061, an edict issued in 1757 (Ch'ien-lung 22).

134. *Shih-li* (1908), 158/2b-3b; also 132/1b.

135. *Ibid.*, 158/3b, an edict issued in 1850 (Tao-kuang 30).

136. Huang Liu-hung, *Fu-hui*, 21/4a.

137. *Tsou-i*, 58/1a; also in Chang Shou-yung, *Hui-pien*, *nei-pien*, 53/4a.

138. Wang Hui-tsu, *I-shuo*, *chüan hsia*, p. 42.

139. Quoted in Sheng K'ang, *Hsü-pien*, 80/38a-b. See also *T'eng hsien* (1846), 12/8a-b, for K'ung Kuang-kuei's letter to P'eng Tou-shan, magistrate of T'eng Hsien, 1836-38. Tseng Kuo-fan found the situation in Anhwei no more encouraging. In a memorial (early in 1852) he said: "The regions around Lu, Feng, Ying, and Po have been since antiquity a retreat for bandit hordes. . . . It is reported that recently banditry has become even more rampant. . . . The people are forced to petition the officials [for protection]. When the latter are about to go forth and catch the bandits, they announce their intention beforehand; when they arrive at the scene the *p'ai* and *pao* agents falsely report that the marauders have fled. The officials and their underlings set the houses in the neighborhood on fire; after having thus made a show of their authority they leave the place. Their underlings and runners extort money and goods from the inhabitants who have previously been robbed and reported the robbery. . . . As a matter of fact, the bandits have not fled." *Tsou-kao*, 1/42a.

140. Pien Pao-ti, *Tsou-i*, 2/89a-b, a memorial dated 1863, in which it was said that an inspection of the *pao-chia* in Shun-t'ien Fu revealed that local functionaries of T'ung Chou, Huai-lai, San-ho, and other localities in this metropolitan prefecture either operated the system only halfheartedly or failed to operate it at all.

141. Wang Ting-an, *Ti-tzu chi*, 27/4b.

142. *Ch'ing hsü t'ung-k'ao*, 25/7758, note. Liu Chin-tsao, the compiler, added that "perhaps only by making local divisions and establishing self-government therein can a police system be effectively operated." This view was in general agreement with those of persons favoring reform. An outstanding example was afforded by Huang Tsun-hsien, who abolished the *pao-chia* in Hunan province and set up in its stead a *pao-wei chü* (bureau of protection) in 1898, shortly before the abortive "hundred-day reform." Huang, then salt intendant of the province, subscribed to the doctrines of *p'ing-teng* (equality) and *min-ch'üan* (popular sovereignty). "Thinking that the *pao-chia* was merely an empty word," he decided to establish a *pao-wei chü* modeled after the police systems of Western countries. Ch'en Pao-chen, the governor, approved Huang's plan. See Wang Hsien-ch'ien (1842-1918), *Wen-chi*, 7/7b-8a.

143. The following incident reported by a Western writer of the nineteenth century illustrates this point: "'In very early times,' it was said, the magistrate of a *hsien* in central China was directed by the governor 'to institute a census of the population.' Being dissatisfied with the returns sent in by his subordinates the magistrate undertook to count the inhabitants himself. The population 'alarmed at the pertinacity of the [official] and apprehensive that he was coming to levy some oppressive tax, fled from the city and hid themselves in the fields.' The official was thus frustrated in his efforts, and hanged himself to escape the expected punishment. He left the following note:

'Men . . . . none
Women . . . . none
Children . . under 14 years of age,
_____of both sexes . . . . . none__
Total . . . . none'"

E. C. Baber, "China in Some of Its Physical and Social Aspects," *Proceedings of the Royal Geographical Society*, N.S., V, (1883), 442-43. This story may not be literally true, but the situation which it illustrates is authentic.

144. Chang Shou-yung, *Hui-pien, nei-pien*, 53/10a.

145. *Tsou-i*, 51/1a, memorial submitted in 1758 by Ch'en Hung-mou, then governor of Kiangsu.

146. Ting Jih-ch'ang, *Kung-tu*, 43/8a.

147. Chang Shou-yung, *Hui-pien*, 53/4b, citing an edict of 1799.

148. *Ibid.* The imperial government itself did not insist on absolute accuracy. *Hu-pu* (1791), 3/1a-b, gives the imperial regulation in force at the time as follows: "When the *chou* and *hsien* compile the annual report on the number of inhabitants, each [of the district yamen] shall compile the figures from the original registers made from the current door placards of the *pao-chia*. It shall be unnecessary to check in detail the names [of inhabitants] registered in each household." As an example of inaccurate reports, *Ch'ing t'ung-k'ao*, 19/5033, cites the case of the magistrate of Ying-ch'eng Hsien (Hupeh) who persistently reported an annual population increase of exactly eight persons; and that of the magistrate of Tsao-yang Hsien (Hupeh), who reported about half a dozen. The inaccuracy of the *pao-chia* records was widely noted. See, for example, Tai Ch'ao-ch'en, *Hsüeh-shih lu*, 9/2a-b.

149. Chang Shou-yung, *Hui-pien*, 53/4b, and *Ch'ing t'ung-k'ao*, 25/7757.

150. Ting Jih-ch'ang, *Kung-tu*, 43/9b.

151. Ho Ch'ang-ling, *Wen-pien*, 74/21a.

152. *Ibid.*, 74/10a, quoting T'ao Yüan-ch'un.

153. Sheng K'ang, *Hsü-pien*, 80/52b.

154. Huang Liu-hung, *Fu-hui*, 22/1a.

155. Ho Ch'ang-ling, *Wen-pien*, 74/21a, quoting from P'eng P'eng (1637-1704), magistrate of San-ho Hsien (Chihli), in the early 1680's.

156. *Ibid.*, 74/15b, quoting from Chang Hui-yen (1761-1802), *Lun pao-chia t'iao-li shu*. The same piece is given also in Tai Ch'ao-ch'en, *Hsüeh-shih lu*, 13/25a.

157. *Shih-li* (1908), 158/2b. A few Western observers also came to the conclusion that crime reporting was not practiced by the *pao-chia*. See, for example, G. W. Cooke, *China* (1858), pp. 435-36. Legge, "Imperial Confucianism," *China Review*, VI (1877-78), p. 369, offered a threefold reason for the *pao-chia*'s failure to report crimes and criminals: "First, the local officers are often devoid

of any genuine regard for the people, and care only for their own reputation. They are afraid of having to report to the higher authorities that there are thieves in their districts, lest this should lead to an investigation into their own conduct. . . . The local officers [knowing this] report that their *chia* and pao are free from thieves. . . . Second, all over the country there are many shameless squires, bachelors incapable of making farther progress in the literary career, and pettifoggers, who, all of them, hang on, more or less closely, about the courts. To such men the thieves are as good as clothes and rice. They intentionally conceal them, and go shares with them in their booty. The poor people . . . dare not put out their heads. Third, the people themselves are in many cases, slothful; and though they know that there are thieves in their own tithing, they do not inform against them. They foolishly say, '. . . So long as these fellows do not injure us, why should we be the first to inform against them?' And not only so. There are those, who not only do not inform, but connect themselves with the thieves, that they may buy their booty at a cheap rate, and have a share in their feastings." Legge's observations, it seems, are substantially correct.

158. Chang Ch'i (1765-1833), letter to a friend, in Sheng K'ang, *Hsü-pien*, 80/26a.

159. *Ch'ing hsü t'ung-k'ao*, 25/7759, Wang Chih-i's remark, quoted in an edict issued in 1814.

160. *Ibid.*, 25/7757, an edict issued in 1799 (Chia-ch'ing 4).

161. *Shih-li* (1908), 158/2b-3a.

162. Jamieson, "Translations from the Lü-li," *China Review*, VIII (1880), 261: "The members of a Tithing were no more than perpetual bail for one another. . . . This consisted in the responsibility of ten men, each for the other, throughout the kingdom, so that if one of the ten committed any fault the nine should produce him in justice."

163. Ssu-ma Kuang's memorial written in 1086, quoted in Wen Chün-t'ien, *Pao-chia*, p. 46.

164. *Ch'ing hsü t'ung-k'ao*, 25/7757, the Chia-ch'ing emperor's edict, dated 1799.

165. Ting Jih-ch'ang, *Kung-tu*, 34/2b-4b.

166. Alexander Williamson, *Journeys in North China* (1870), I, 165.

167. Huang Liu-hung, *Fu-hui*, 21/1b and 4a-b.

168. Wu Wen-yung, quoted in Shang K'ang, *Hsü-pien*, 80/23a.

169. *Ch'ing t'ung-k'ao*, 24/5061.

170. Ho Ch'ang-ling, *Wen-pien*, 74/6a-b, an essay by Huang Chung-chien.

171. *Ch'ing hsü t'ung-k'ao*, 25/7760, an edict issued in 1814, quoting Wang Chih-i's memorial.

172. As a well-known magistrate said in an official document: "A special edict was reverently received in Chia-ch'ing 19 [1814], which ordered [*pao-chia*] registration and checking. This humble functionary was then serving in Kwangtung. It was observed that in operating the *pao-chia* the various functionaries very seldom undertook actually to inspect and check [the operations], but merely multiplied the troubles resulting from undue levies and assessments. Consequently, both the gentry and common people regarded the *pao-chia* as a dreadful task, begging not to have their names entered into the registers. Those who had their names entered usually reported smaller numbers of households and inhabitants than there actually were. The reason for this situation is that, being fatigued in attending to official routines, local officials have to rely on clerks and runners [to operate the *pao-chia*]. There are unavoidable expenses incurred in supplying labor, materials, food, and transportation [for those engaged in the work]. Usu-

ally the clerks and runners take the money from *yüeh* or *pao*, the *yüeh* or *pao* demand *chia-chang* to furnish it, the *chia-chang* exact it from *p'ai-t'ou*, and the *p'ai-t'ou* in turn collect if from the registered households. Fees are demanded at each level, as money is required at every turn. But the registers and door placards are written in the most careless manner, with the result that unregistered households are found in every village, and unregistered inhabitants in every household. The people's money is entirely wasted; [the registers and placards] have become useless paper. This is the reason for the unsatisfactory operation [of the *pao-chia*], which holds broadly true in all the provinces." Liu Heng, *Yung-yen*, p. 88a-b.

173. See, for example, P'eng P'eng (seventeenth century), in Ho Ch'ang-ling, *Wen-pien*, 74/21a; Ch'en Hung-mou (eighteenth century), *Ou-ts'un kao*, 12/6a; and Ting Jih-ch'ang (nineteenth century), *Kung-tu*, 28/5b.

174. As Ssu-ma Kuang said in 1086 in a memorial quoted in Wang I-k'o, *Nung-ts'un tzu-wei yen-chiu*, p. 42. It should be borne in mind, however, that the *pao-chia* of the Sung dynasty involved military service.

175. P'eng P'eng, quoted in Ho Ch'ang-ling, *Wen-pien*, 74/21a.

176. *Ibid.*

177. *Shih-li* (1908), 158/1b. The original has "hsien nien keng-tai, i chün lao i."

178. *Lü-li pien-lan* (1877), 25/100a.

179. The compiler of *Li-p'ing* (1891), 5/80a, said in a note: "The method of selection: The *pao-chang* are selected first; then the *pao-chang* and the gentry and elders of the locality should be held responsible for selecting the *pao-cheng* and *chia-chang* from persons who belong to well-to-do families, who are in the prime of their life and strength, who possess outstanding abilities, and who have shown praiseworthy conduct in the past. In each rural area two candidates, a principal and a deputy, are selected and their names are submitted to the *hsien* [yamen]. The local official then carefully investigates [these candidates]. If they prove to be really worthy, they are conducted into the reception room of the yamen, where special courtesy is shown them: they are offered seats, and tea is served to them."

180. *I-ch'eng* (1929), 30/7b-8a, records an instance in which Shih Huai-ying, an inhabitant of Fan-tien village, was honored in 1902 by the magistrate with a tablet, for his untiring and courageous service in rural *pao-chia* work.

181. Sheng K'ang, *Hsü-pien*, 80/25a, Chang Ch'i's letter in reply to Lu Shao-wen.

182. *Tsou-i*, 50/14a; also Chang Shou-yung, *Hui-pien, nei-pien*, 53/4a.

183. Ho Ch'ang-ling, *Wen-pien*, 74/4b.

184. Sheng K'ang, *Hsü-pien*, 80/23a, quoting Wu Wen-yung.

185. *Ibid.*, 80/5b, quoting Chang Sheng-chieh.

186. Wen Chün-t'ien, *Pao-chia*, p. 263.

Chapter 4

1. Wei Yüan (1794-1856), *Nei-chi, chih pien*, 3, 3/9a.

2. These included the salt gabelle, native customs, license and registration fees, and (in the nineteenth century) *likin* and the maritime customs. See *Ch'ing t'ung-k'ao, chüan* 26, and 28-31. For a brief survey of the land tax system of the Ch'ing dynasty, see Huang Han-liang, *The Land Tax in China* (1918), part ii. His treatment of the concepts of taxation and the method of tax collection, however, does not adequately meet our present purpose. Ch'en Shao-kwan, *The System of Taxation in China in the Tsing Dynasty, 1644-1911* (1914), was based

on limited source material and is marred by inaccuracies. George Jamieson's article, "Tenure of Land in China and the Condition of the Rural Population," *Journal of the Royal Asiatic Society,* North China Branch, N.S., XXIII (1888), 65-68, may be usefully consulted.

3. *Shih-li* (1908), 177/6a-b, and *Ch'ing t'ung-tien,* 7/2057.

4. *Shih-li* (1908), 177/6a-b.

5. *Ch'ing t'ung-k'ao,* 1/4859. See also Wang Ch'ing-yün, *Chi-cheng,* 3/15a-b.

6. *Ch'ing t'ung-k'ao,* 1/4857; *Hui-tien* (1908 reprint), 18/1a; *Hu-pu* (1791), 7/1a-13a. Other categories of land included *kuan-t'ien* (government land), *hsüeh-t'ien* (school land), and *ch'i-t'ien* (land allotted to bannermen). See *Hu-pu* (1791), *chüan* 5-6. In some parts of Kiangsu province, for example, a *mow* comprised 240 square *pu* (each *pu* being the equivalent of roughly five local *ch'ih* or feet). In other provinces a *mow* might contain 360 *pu* or as many as 540 *pu*. See Ch'en Ch'i-yüan, *Pi-chi,* 6/11a.

7. *Shih-li* (1908), 162/1a-13a; *Hu-pu* (1791), *chüan* 5-7; and *Ch'ing hsü t'ung-k'ao,* 4/7536. For variations in tax rates, see *Ch'ing hsü t'ung-k'ao,* 3/7521.

8. Feng Kuei-fen (1809-74), *Chi,* 9/2b, pointed out that the excessive rates in these regions dated from the late twelfth century (i.e., in the Shao-hsi reign of the Southern Sung dynasty). Cf. Wei Yüan, *Wai-chi,* 4/47a; Liang Chang-chü (1775-1849), *T'ui-an sui-pi,* 8/2b-3b, and *Lang-chi ts'ung-t'an,* 5/19a-20a.

9. *Ch'ing t'ung-k'ao,* 1/4860 and 4/4891; and *Hui-tien* (1908), 18/1a-b, give the following figures:

Date	*Mow* of land	Tax (in taels)	Tax (in *shih* of grain)
1658	549,357,640	21,576,006	6,479,465
1753	708,114,288	29,611,201	8,406,422
1887	911,976,606	31,184,042	3,624,532

10. According to *Hu-pu ts'ao-yün ch'üan-shu* (1875), 1/1a-8b, these provinces were: Shantung, Honan, Chiang-nan, Chekiang, Kiangsi, Hupeh, and Feng-t'ien. For basic regulations governing tribute rice collection, see *Hu-pu* (1791), *chüan* 34-41. The practice of collecting money in lieu of grain may be traced to the Han dynasty. See Liu Shih-jen, *Chung-kuo t'ien-fu wen-t'i* (1936), pp. 45 and 134. For general accounts of tribute rice, see *Ch'ing t'ung-k'ao,* 25/239 ff., and 43/5251; *Ch'ing hsü t'ung-k'ao,* 31/3095-3102; and Harold C. Hinton, "The Grain Tribute System of the Ch'ing Dynasty," *Far Eastern Quarterly,* XI (1952), 339-54. Hinton's Ph.D. dissertation, The Grain Tribute System of China, 1845-1911 (1950), is a useful introduction to the subject.

11. The rates in force in Shun-chih times are given in *Ch'ing t'ung-k'ao,* 1/4855-57.

12. *Ch'ing t'ung-k'ao,* 3/4872. See Hosea B. Morse, *Trade and Administration of China* (1913), pp. 83-88, for a brief account of surcharges on the land tax. Morse draws heavily on Jamieson's article, "Land Taxation in the Province of Hunan."

13. The matter is clearly explained in *Lo-ch'uan* (1944), 14/8b, quoting from the 1809 edition.

14. The story is briefly related in Wang Ch'ing-yün, *Chi-cheng,* 3/41a-42a. It was illegal, between 1644 and 1724, to levy such surcharges, although the imperial prohibition was often disregarded in practice. See also *Ch'ing t'ung-k'ao,* 2/4863 and 3/4871. For the official rates fixed in 1724, see *Shih-li* (1908), 164/1a-3a and *Hu-pu* (1791), 14/1a-8b.

15. *Hu-pu* (1791), 14/9a.

16. *Shih-li* (1908), 164/3a ff. See also Orita, *Fen-lun,* V, 92-97.

17. *Hu-pu* (1791), *chüan* 110-11 (general exemption) and *chüan* 112-13 (partial exemption). Other pertinent references are: *Shih-li* (1908), *chüan* 276-77 (grain loans), *chüan* 278-81 (exemption), and *chüan* 282-87 (deferment); *Hu-pu ts'ao-yün chüan-shu* (1875), *chüan* 4-6 (tribute rice exemption and deferment); *Wei-chou* (1877), 7/6b-9b; *I-ch'eng* (1929), 13/1b ff. ; *Lo-ch'uan* (1944), 13/7b ff. ; *T'ung-kuan* (1944), 14/2b-3a; *Lu-chou* (1885), *chüan shou*, pp. 1a-31a, and 15/8b-19a; *Meng-ch'eng* (1915), 4/24b ff. ; *Pa-ling* (1891), 16/1a-14b; and *Fu-shun* (1931), 5/7a-8b (exemption and deferment in various localities).

18. The story is summarized in Wang Ch'ing-yün, *Chi-cheng*, 3/15b-16a.

19. *Ch'ing t'ung-k'ao*, 1/4859. See also Orita, *Fen-lun*, V, 76-78. According to Lu Shih-i (1611-72), quoted in *Mu-lin shu*, 3/39b-40a, the yellow registers formerly had households as the main entries, to which was appended information concerning taxable land; this information was used to assess labor service imposts and to facilitate tax collection. The fish scale registers had land as the main entries, to which was appended information concerning the households; these were used to check the boundaries of tax-liable farm land. But as time went on, the fish scale registers were exclusively used for all tax purposes. For the total amount of land in *mow* registered between 1644 and 1908, see *Ch'ing hsü t'ung-k'ao*, 4/7534. Liu Shih-jen, *Chung-kuo t'ien-fu wen-t'i*, p. 68, contains a table giving the amount of land and population in various periods from the beginning of the dynasty to the end of the nineteenth century. The figures, however, cannot be accepted as absolutely accurate.

20. *Hu-pu* (1791), 10/1a: "The *mow* is 1 *pu* in width and 240 *pu* in length"; a note adds, "[namely,] an area 15 *pu* long and 16 *pu* wide." This was the official standard. Actual practice in different parts of the empire seldom conformed to it. For example, *Ch'ing hsü t'ung-k'ao*, 1/7506, gives the information that the "bow" or measuring frame varied from a minimum of 3 feet 2 inches (Chinese measurement), to a maximum of 7 feet 5 inches; and that the *mow* varies from 260 "bows" to 720. Generally speaking, the *mow* in southern provinces was smaller than that in North China. *Ibid.*, 5/7550-51.

21. An illuminating example was afforded by T'ung-ch'eng (Anhwei). *Ch'ing hsü t'ung-k'ao*, 1/7501, cites the opinion of a local writer as follows: "There are over 390,000 *mow* of land in T'ung-ch'eng, the equivalent of nearly 2,000,000 *ch'iu*. One page of the fish-scale register contains over 200,000 sheets of paper. The cost of making each page, including the cost of the paper, of printing the forms, of pen and ink, and of copying, amounts to over 0.01 tael. The total cost of one register is over 2,000 taels. In addition, heavy expenses are incurred in sending copies of the register to the provincial treasurer. . . . The cost of making registers of one prefecture and of the entire province is proportionally heavier [than the cost estimated above, which is for one district]."

22. *Ch'ing hsü t'ung-k'ao*, 1/7507, an edict of 1820 (Chia-ch'ing 25) quotes a censor as saying: "In Kiangsu province poor people who possess no land at all have been known to be paying an annual tax ranging from a few taels to several dozen taels. Inhabitants who own no more than a few *mow* of land are required to pay land taxes many times the quotas [for which they are legally liable]."

23. The term corvée may be used in a strict as well as in a general sense. E. g., *Encyclopaedia of the Social Sciences*, IV, 455-56: "In its general sense the corvée designates a service in labor furnished by one man to another or to a sovereign. . . . The real corvée was an obligation running with the tenancy of land." *Ibid.*, VI, 342: "almost every government had obliged its citizens at one time or another to perform certain services." *Encyclopaedia Britannica* (1947), VI, 481: "Corvée, in feudal law, the term used to designate the unpaid

labour due from tenants, whether free or unfree, to their lord; hence any forced labour, especially that exacted by the State, the word being applied both to each particular service and to the system generally." George Jamieson's article on corvée, *Journal of the Royal Asiatic Society*, North China Branch, N.S., XXIII, 68, may be consulted.

24. *Ch'ing t'ung-k'ao*, 12/123-13/142, contains a summary of the development of the *i* since ancient times.

25. *Ming-shih*, 78, "Shih-huo chih," 2/7b; *Ch'ing hsü t'ung-k'ao*, 16/2912 and 17/2924-25; and Wang Ch'ing-yün, *Chi-cheng*, 3/10b-11a.

26. *Ch'ing t'ung-k'ao*, 21/5043.

27. This was a result of Wang An-shih's reform.

28. *Ming-shih*, 78/1a.

29. *Ch'ing t'ung-k'ao*, 19/5023. Cf. *Hu-pu* (1791), 13/1a-6a, where the different rates for K'ang-hsi 50 (1711) are given. For the various categories of *ting*, see *Ch'ing t'ung-k'ao*, 19/5023 and 21/5044; and *Hui-tien* (1908), 17/9a.

30. *Ch'ing hsü t'ung-k'ao*, 27/7787; and Sheng K'ang, *Hsü-pien*, 38/31a-35a.

31. Orita, *Fen-lun*, V, 69.

32. *Ch'ing t'ung-k'ao*, 25/5071-72. Local gazetteers often give the number of persons exempted from the *ting* service in the places concerned. See, for example, *T'eng hsien* (1846), 4/10b-11a; and *I-ch'eng* (1929), 9/8b-9a. According to the latter source, the total number of *ting* in the late seventeenth century in I-ch'eng Hsien (Shansi) was 19,662, and the number of persons exempted from the *ting* service as a result of their gentry status was 1,001. The net number of *ting* liable for service (or payment of *ting* levies) was therefore 18,661. The *ting* levies of this locality were merged into the land tax in 1745; all *yao* (i.e., miscellaneous labor service imposts in addition to the *ting)* were also so merged in 1825.

33. *Ch'ing t'ung-k'ao*, 19/5024.

34. *Ch'ing hsü t'ung-k'ao*, 27/7788, a note written by the compiler: "In Yungcheng 2 [1724] the *ting* imposts were collected in conjunction with the land tax. Thereafter the *i* was merged into the *fu*. The people paid no other imposts than the *ti* [land tax] and the *ting* [regular corvée imposts]. All government construction work was done by hired labor. Malpractices in revenue administration prevalent since Sung and Yüan times were thus completely eradicated." This statement is too optimistic to fit the facts, as we shall see. Cf. *ibid.*, 24/5066, an edict issued in 1779.

35. *Ch'ing t'ung-k'ao*, *chüan* 21, *passim*, and 27/2789.

36. *Ibid.*, 19/5023. Cf. Orita, *Fen-lun*, V, 60-63, and VII, 62-63. According to *T'ung-k'ao*, 13/139, *ch'ai-i*, or the corvée system, had since ancient times been infested with inequities which no government could completely remove.

37. *Ch'ing t'ung-k'ao*, 27/7790.

38. *Ibid.*, 27/7791.

39. *Ibid.*, 27/7790, a memorial submitted by the provincial treasurer of Chihli in 1822.

40. *Tsou-i*, *hsü-pien*, 3/4b; *Ch'ing t'ung-k'ao*, 28/7797. For an actual instance, see *Lo-ch'uan* (1944), 14/9a.

41. *Ch'ing t'ung-k'ao*, 22/5049-50.

42. *Ibid.*, 21/5045. For an example of local operation, see *T'eng hsien* (1846), 4/11b.

43. *Ch'ing t'ung-k'ao*, 24/5059.

44. *Ibid.*, 24/5061. See also *T'eng hsien* (1846), 4/12a. Hu Ch'ang-tu, Yellow River Administration in the Ch'ing Dynasty (Ph.D. dissertation, Uni-

versity of Washington, 1954), gives additional relevant information.

45. *Ming-shih,* 78/1a, summarizes the Ming system. The yellow registers of Ch'ing times are described in *Ch'ing hsü t'ung-k'ao,* 13/2891 and 13/2893; Liu Shih-jen, *Chung-kuo t'ien-fu wen-t'i,* pp. 87-88; *Huang-ts'e mu-lu,* introduction.

46. Wang Ch'ing-yün, *Chi-cheng,* 3/16a.

47. *Ch'ing hsü t'ung-k'ao,* 2/2786. The first fish-scale registers of the Ming dynasty were completed in 1387 (Hung-wu 20), the first yellow registers in 1381 (Hung-wu 14). The Ming procedure of compiling these registers is described in *ibid.,* 13/2891 and 16/2913. Zenkai Matsumoto's article, "The Establishment of the Li System by the Ming Dynasty," *Tōhōgaku hō* (1941), XII, 109-22, may be consulted.

48. *Shih-li* (1908), 157/1a. *Ch'ing t'ung-k'ao,* 19/5024, gives the additional information that there were four categories of "registration": *chün* (military), *ming* (commoner), *chiang* (artisan), and *tsao* (salt worker), and that each of these was divided into three subgroups according to the rate of taxes for which the persons in question were severally liable. *Ming-shih,* 77/1b, and *Ch'ing hsü t'ung-k'ao,* 16/2913, contain information concerning the Ming practice.

49. *Ch'ing t'ung-k'ao,* 19/5024; *Lü-li pien-lan* (1877), 8/2a-b; Wu Yung-kuang, *Wu-hsüeh lu,* 20/5a-6a. Wu summarizes the penalties as follows:

Offense	Penalty
Omission of entire *hu*	Liable for *ting:* 100 blows with heavy bamboo
	Not liable for *ting:* 80 blows with heavy bamboo
Concealing other *hu* in one's own	Liable for *ting:* 100 blows with heavy bamboo
	Not liable for *ting:* 80 blows with heavy bamboo
Omitting or concealing *ting* and other persons	1-3 *ting:* 60 blows with heavy bamboo
	Over 3 *ting:* up to 100 blows with heavy bamboo
	3-5 minors or aged persons: 40 blows with light bamboo
	Over 5 persons: up to 70 blows with light bamboo

All the *hu, ting,* and other persons omitted or concealed were to be entered in the registers. Penalties for *li-chang* who failed to discover omissions or fraud were as follows:

Offense	Penalty
Involving 1-5 *hu*	50 blows with light bamboo
Involving 6 *hu* or more	Up to 100 blows with heavy bamboo
Involving 1-10 *k'ou*	30 blows with light bamboo
Involving 11 *k'ou* or more	Up to 70 blows with light bamboo

50. *Ch'ing t'ung-k'ao,* 19/5024. The practice of giving rewards was discontinued in 1717. *Ibid.,* 19/5026. *Ibid.,* chüan 19, *passim,* and *Ch'ing hsü t'ung-k'ao,* chüan 25, *passim,* contain figures of the *hu* and *k'ou* reported in various periods of the dynasty. The following may be noted here:

1661 (Shun-chih 18)	21,068,609
1721 (K'ang-hsi 60)	27,621,334 (including 467,850 exempted from the *ting,* being born after the quotas were permanently fixed)

1771 (Ch'ien-lung 36)	214,600,356
1805 (Chia-ch'ing 10)	332,181,403
1844 (Tao-kuang 24)	419,441,336
1851 (Hsien-feng 1)	293,740,282
1860 (Hsien-feng 10)	260,924,675
1901 (Kuang-hsü 27)	426,447,325

51. *Shih-li* (1908), 157/1a.

52. *Ch'ing t'ung-k'ao*, 19/5025.

53. *Ibid.*, 19/5025, a decision of the *Hu-pu* reads: "K'ang-hsi 55 [1716], the *Hu-pu* recommended that wherever vacancies occur in the *ting* quotas of a given locality, these vacancies should be filled by the inhabitants recently born in the same locality. . . . If two or three vacancies occur in one household and the vacancies cannot be filled by members of the same household, surplus *ting* of the clan [to which the household belongs] should be made to fill up the vacancies. If vacancies still remain, households in the same *t'u* and *chia* liable for large tax quotas should be made to fill them."

54. *Shih-li* (1908), 157/1b; *Ch'ing t'ung-k'ao*, 19/5025. In an article, "Land Tax in China and How Collected," signed O. P. C., in *China Review*, VIII (1881), 291, it is said that "the land tax [is] fixed in perpetuity by the emperor K'ang Hi." This writer obviously confounded the *ting* with the *liang;* it was the *ting* or labor service imposts, not the *liang* or land tax, that was so fixed. Morse, *International Relations of the Chinese Empire*, I, 30, suffers from the same confusion. The action taken in 1712 may have made the inhabitants somewhat less hesitant in writing their names on the registers. As Richard Wilhelm puts it in *Chinese Economic Psychology*, p. 17: "Under the emperor Yung Cheng at the beginning of the eighteenth century, a basic law of taxation was adopted which introduced a moderate land tax. . . . The same ruler also abolished the previous head tax. One result of this action was a sudden jump in population increase": from 25,284,818 in the returns of 1724 to 102,750,000 in 1753. The statement that Yung-cheng "introduced a moderate land tax" and that he "abolished the previous head tax" cannot be accepted as accurate.

55. The merging of *ting* (labor service imposts) into *ti* (land tax) began in a number of localities early in the dynasty, although the imperial government did not authorize this practice until Yung-cheng times. Wang Ch'ing-yün, *Chi-cheng*, 3/16a; "Since the amalgamation of the *ting* with the land tax, and since the abolition of the *pien-shen* procedure and the use of the *pao-chia* [registers] as the sole source of population figures, the *huang-ts'e* has become increasingly unimportant and the *yü-lin ts'e* has proportionally gained in importance." It is true that the yellow register lost its significance; but it is doubtful that the fish-scale register gained importance.

56. *Shih-li* (1908), 157/1b; *Shih-lu*, Kao-tsung, 130/1a-3a; *Ch'ing t'ung-k'ao*, 19/5028. The edict of 1740 reads in part: "From now on provincial officials shall submit, in the eleventh month of each year, detailed reports showing the changes in the number of households and inhabitants, and the amount of grain stored in the government granaries [in the localities] under their respective jurisdiction. This will enable us daily to study and familiarize ourselves with these figures, so that [we can] plan in advance and prepare for the eventuality of floods, drought, or famine. It is hereby ordered that after the next quinquennial assessment is made, the provinces shall report the number of households and inhabitants. The *Hu-pu* shall memorialize us, after due consideration, concerning detailed regulations to be uniformly enforced in the provinces." The *Hu-pu* subsequently me-

morialized as follows: "from now on the quinquennial assessment should be carried out as of old and the provincial officials ordered, after the completion of the *[ting]* assessment in 1741, to enumerate all the *ting* of each household [residing] in the *chou* and *hsien*, together with all the adults and children therein. There should be no omissions or evasions." *Shih-lu*, Kao-tsung, 131/4b-5a. After further deliberation by other central officials, the following conclusion was reached: "The recommendation of the *Hu-pu* that the actual number of the population be annually counted . . . can hardly be feasible in actual practice. . . . It is hereby recommended that after the completion of the *[ting]* assessment for 1741 the provincial officials need only to report annually, in the eleventh month, the quantity of grain, and the total number of households and inhabitants in their respective provinces, excluding the *liu-yü* [residents in localities which were not their officially registered ancestral abodes] and aborigines." This recommendation was approved by the emperor. *Ibid.*, Kao-tsung, 133/5b-6a. The following recommendation of the *Hu-pu* also received imperial approval: "It is too troublesome if the annual report on the population figures is to be compiled in accordance with the *pien-shen* [i.e., *ting* assessment] procedure. Since the *chou* and *hsien* of the provinces already have instituted *pao-chia* door placards, the number of native inhabitants and transient residents [in each locality] can readily be ascertained from such records. The actual number of people can be obtained by deducting the *liu-yü* [transients, from the total thus registered]. . . . Regions inhabited by vassal peoples and by aborigines, where no *pien-shen* has ever been applied, should be excluded."

57. *Shih-li* (1908), 157/1b.

58. *Ibid.*, 157/2a.

59. Wang Ch'ing-yün, *Chi-cheng*, 3/9a-10b.

60. The "single-whip" system is briefly explained in *Ming-shih*, 78/6b. This system underwent a period of evolution before it was finally adopted for the empire in 1581 (Wan-li 9). *Hsü t'ung-k'ao*, 2/2793 and 16/2915-19, contains brief descriptions of the system.

61. Wang Ch'ing-yün, *Chi-cheng*, 3/9a.

62. *Ch'ing t'ung-k'ao*, 19/5026. The compiler says in a note that the practice prevailed also in Kwangtung, previous to its imperial authorization in 1723 (Yung-chen 1).

63. *Shih-li* (1908), 157/6a, an edict issued in 1821 (Tao-kuang 1), reads in part: "In the *chou* and *hsien* of Shansi province the labor service imposts and the land tax have hitherto been collected separately. Subsequently, however, owing to the fact that it is difficult for poor people to pay, it has been authorized upon petition that in eighty-one *chou* and *hsien* all the labor service imposts be apportioned to the land tax to be collected together [with the latter].

64. Wang Ch'ing-yün, *Chi-cheng*, 3/19a, contains this information: "Inhabitants registered as 'wealthy people' or 'city people' who have amassed huge fortunes and maintain immense households do not pay the least amount of labor service or land tax, so long as they do not own farm land." Wang wrote before 1862.

65. *Shih-li* (1908), 157/4a; *Ch'ing t'ung-k'ao*, 19/5026.

66. The Nine Ministers and imperial censors, in response to an imperial order, recommended that the governor of Chihli be instructed to survey the registered land in the province with a view to effecting an equitable apportionment of the *ting* imposts, "so that landless, poor people will be spared the hardship of paying the *ting* money." It was eventually decided that a surcharge of approximately 0.207 tael be levied on every tael of the land tax. This surcharge, still

known as *ting* money, was to be collected together with the regular *fu* money. *Ch'ing t'ung-k'ao*, 19/5026.

67. *Shih-li* (1908), 157/4a-6a. The process of integration was largely completed early in the Ch'ien-lung reign. The last localities to receive authorization (in 1821) were about twenty *chou* and *hsien* of Shansi province. For precise dates, see *Ch'ing t'ung-k'ao*, 19/5026. According to Wang Ch'ing-yün, *Chi-cheng*, 3/13a, the *ting* remained a separate levy in a few localities in Feng-t'ien, Shansi, Kwangsi, and Kweichow.

68. *Hu-pu* (1791), 13/7a-b; *Hu-pu hsü-tsuan* (1797), 3/1a-15a; *Shih-li* (1908), 157/4a-6b; *Ch'ing t'ung-k'ao*, 19/5026.

69. See chapter 2, section on "The *Li-chia* Divisions."

70. *Fang-kuo hsiang chih* (1937), 1/2b: "In Hung-wu times the *li* divisions were arranged on the basis of *hu* [households]. Each *li* constituted a *t'u*. These divisions were determined not by the extent of land [in each] but by the number of registered households." Instances illustrative of this point are found in Tai Ch'ao-ch'en, *Hsüeh-shih lu*, 2/27a (quoting Chao Shen-ch'iao, a *chin-shih* of 1670); *Wei chou* (1877), 3/25a and 7/1b; *Hsing-kuo* (1889), 2/6b and 5/2a-7a; *Hu-nan* (1885), *chüan* 48, *passim; Ju-lin* (1883), 5/10a-19a; *Ho hsien* (1934), 2/17a-18a (quoting from the 1890 edition); *Mei-t'an* (1899), 4/1a and 8/53b-54a; *Chen-hsiung* (1887), 3/15b; and *Hsün-tien* (1828), 1/4a.

71. *Hang-chou* (1898), 5/21b.

72. *Huai-an* (1884), 17/3a-4a.

73. *Ch'ang-p'ing* (1886), 11/23a-26a.

74. *Hu-pu hsü-tsüan* (1797), 2/9a-10a.

75. *Shih-lu*, Sheng-tsu, 5/13b-14a.

76. *Ch'ing hsü t'ung-k'ao*, 25/7757, quoting Li Chien-hou, "Wang-kung pien-shen pei-chi."

77. *Ming-shih*, 77/1b. See also *Ch'ing hsü t'ung-k'ao*, 2/2792.

78. Liu Shih-jen, *Chung-kuo t'ien-fu wen-t'i*, p. 109.

79. *Ch'ing hsü t'ung-k'ao*, 25/7755.

80. *Shih-li* (1908), 171/2a-4b, 172/1a-8a, and 173/1a-6b.

81. *Hu-pu*(1791), 11/2a: "In collecting *ti-ting* money and grain, it is required that collection begin in the second month (except in the provinces of Yunnan and Kweichow, where it shall begin in the ninth month) and be completed by the middle of the fourth month (except in the provinces of Shensi and Szechwan, where payments may be deferred until the sixth month). . . . Collection shall be resumed in the eighth month (except in [the province of] Fukien, where collection shall be resumed in the seventh month; and in [the provinces of] Shantung and Honan and in the prefectures of [the province of] Anhwei, namely, Lu-chou, Feng-yang, Ying-chou, and Ssu-chou, where collection shall be resumed in the sixth or seventh month) . . . and be completed in the eleventh month (except in Yunnan and Kweichow, where it shall be completed in the second month of the subsequent year)." *Liu-pu ch'u-fen tse-li* (1877) contains the same regulation. See also Ho Ch'ang-ling, *Tsou-i*, 8/1a-b.

82. *Ch'ing t'ung-k'ao*, 1/4858-59.

83. Feng Kuei-fen (1809-74), *Chi*, 5/37a, a letter to Governor Hsü Nai-chao, written in 1853. According to Feng, "At present, the *i-chih tan* have become a warrant for tax clerks to practice exaction and corruption."

84. Wang Ch'ing-yün, *Chi-cheng*, 3/16b-17a.

85. *Shih-li* (1908), 172/4b-8a, gives some of these basic regulations.

86. *Hu-pu* (1791), 11/3a.

87. *Ibid.*, 11/4a; *Ch'ing t'ung-k'ao*, 2/4867 and 22/5051. Cf. Li Yü, *Hsin-shu, erh chi*, 1/9b.

88. *Hu-pu* (1791), 11/3a.

89. Joseph Edkins, *Revenue and Taxation of the Chinese Empire* (1903), pp. 149-51.

90. *Ch'ing t'ung-k'ao*, 2/4867, a note written by the compiler.

91. *Ibid.*, 4/4885. Under exceptional circumstances, for example, in localities where the official in charge showed particular attention to imperial regulations and the people's welfare, the *kun-tan* device proved workable to some extent. An instance was reported in Ho-p'ing Hsien (Kwangtung) in 1722. *Hui-chou* (1881), 18/6b-7a.

92. *Ch'ing t'ung-k'ao*, 1/4860.

93. *Ibid.*, 22/5051. See also *Chiang-hsi* (1880), *chüan shou*, part 1, p. 9a.

94. *Hu-pu* (1791), 11/7a.

95. Special procedures were devised for absentee landlords owning land in more than one *chou* or *hsien*. See *Ch'ing t'ung-k'ao*, 3/4876, for the *shun-chuang fa*.

96. *Liu-pu ch'u-fen tse-li* (1877), 25/45a: "In paying taxes the people shall be instructed to wrap the money and drop it in person in the chests [provided by the yamen]. Receipts indicating the amounts paid shall be issued to them as evidence [of payment]. If any magistrate of a *chou* or *hsien* prevents the amounts [of tax money paid] from being written [on the receipts] or prevents the receipts from being issued [to the taxpayers], he shall be dismissed from his office, put under arrest, and tried for his offense."

97. Wang Ch'ing-yün, *Chi-cheng*, 5/16b, gives the information that receipts containing four sections were in use between 1725 and 1730. The fourth section was issued to the taxpayer, who was to drop it into a separate chest upon completion of payment as an additional check. This practice was discontinued in 1730.

98. *Hu-pu* (1791), 11/9a, and *Ch'ing t'ung-k'ao*, 2/4866, describe the form and use of the "string receipts."

99. *Ch'ing t'ung-k'ao*, 1/4859. *Hu-pu* (1791), 11/1a-5a, describes further steps and additional paper work.

100. *Hu-pu* (1791), 11/1a. Ts'ai Shen-chih, in an article entitled "Ch'ing-tai chou-hsien ku-shih," *Chung-ho*, II, 53, describes the procedure of tax collection. Documents other than those mentioned here were used. See *Hu-pu* (1791), 11/5a, and *Ch'ing t'ung-k'ao*, 1/4859.

101. *Hu-pu* (1791), 11/10a. See also Orita, *Fen-lun*, V, 109.

102. Ts'ai Shen-chih, "Ch'ing-tai chou-hsien ku-shih," *Chung-ho*, II, 53.

103. *Chou-hsien shih-i* (1851 reprint), pp. 11a-12a; quoted also in Ts'ai Shen-chih, "Ch'ing-tai chou-hsien ku-shih," *Chung-ho*, II, 56.

104. *Ch'ing t'ung-k'ao*, 22/5049, quoting Shen Ch'üan's preface to a book on labor service by Li Fu-hsing, magistrate of Lou Hsien (Kiangsu). The necessity of having rural agents in tax collection was recognized since early times. The *Chou-li* contains some of the basic ideas, especially the *li-tsai, lu-hsü, sui-jen, hsiang-shih*, as described in the section on *ti-kuan*, 3/71, 77; 4/85, 98-99, and 101. The *se-fu* of the Han dynasty *(Han-shu, chüan* 1, *shang*, p. 19a, and *Hou han-shu*, 38/5b-6a); the *li-chang* of the Sui dynasty *(Sui-shu*, 24/6a-b); the *li-cheng, hu-chang*, and *hsiang shu-shou* of the T'ang dynasty *(Chiu T'ang-shu*, 48/3a, and *T'ung-k'ao*, 12/127; and the *liang-chang* and *li-chang* of the Ming dynasty, all had to do with tax collection on the lowest administrative level.

105. *Ming-shih*, 77/3a-b. The *liang-chang* were first instituted in various lo-

calities in 1371 (Hung-wu 4). According to *Ming-shih,* 78/4b, the *liang-chang* were appointed from large landowners whose duty was to "supervise" tax collection in their villages. In the seventh month of each year the magistrates of the *chou* or *hsien* sent deputies to accompany the *liang-chang* to the imperial capital to receive warrants of collection. Cf. *Hsü t'ung-k'ao,* 2/2786.

106. *Ming-shih,* 78/4a-b and 8b; *Hsü t'ung-k'ao,* 2/2785 and 16/2914-15. A *liang-chang* and an assistant were instituted for every 10,000 *shih* of grain. In 1397 an additional *liang-chang* and assistant were instituted for each unit. These agents were abolished in the middle of the fifteenth century. Yukio Yamane, "On the Duty of the Village Headman in the Ming Period," *Tōhōgaku,* January, 1952, pp. 79-80, analyzes the functions of tax agents of the Ming dynasty, using data from local gazetteers published in Ming times. The main conclusion, as stated in the English summary of his article, is as follows: "The headman was responsible for paying as tribute to the Imperial Household and the State, cattle, fruits, drugs, furs, textiles, and the like. It was also his duty to exert himself to raise money for the expenditure of the local government, including among others expenses for religious observances, festivals, social welfare, entertainments, etc."

107. *Chou-hsien shih-i,* pp. 53b-54a. Quoted also in *Chung-ho,* II, 57, by Ts'ai Shen-chih. See *Mu-lin shu,* 3/52a-54a.

108. Li Yü, *Hsin-shu, erh chi,* 1/13b, quoting a report submitted by the circuit intendant of Ch'ing-chou (Shantung) to the governor-general and governor.

109. *Ch'ing t'ung-k'ao,* 21/5045; *Ch'ing-shih kao,* "Shih-huo," p. 11a.

110. *Lü-li pien-lan* (1877), 8/47a: "A *li-chang* and ten *chia-shou* shall be instituted for every hundred households dwelling in each locality; these shall be placed in charge, by annual turns, of tax collection and of arranging other public matters. Any person who without warrant assumes the title of *chu-pao-li-chang, pao-chang, chu-shou* (i. e., *chu-kuan-chia-shou)* or other [titles of authority], and who [taking advantage of such titles] causes trouble and harasses the people, shall receive one hundred blows with the heavy bamboo and be banished [from his native place]." See Jamieson's translation of the same regulation in *China Review,* VIII (1880), 360.

111. *Wu-hsi* (1881), 11/3a-4a.

112. In more recent times even the name *ti-pao* disappeared in some localities. See, for example, Fei Hsiao-t'ung, *Peasant Life in China* (1939), p. 193.

113. *Fu-shan* (1924), 4/2b-3a, quoting from the 1872 edition of *Nan-hai hsien chih.*

114. *Ibid.,* chüan 14, *jen-wu,* sec. 6, p. 32b. See *Hua hsien* (1924), 4/17a.

115. *Fu-chou* (1876), chüan 81, Part 1, p. 23b.

116. *Sheng-hsün,* Shih-tsung, 15/7a-b.

117. *Tao chou* (1878), 3/17a-18b.

118. *Yung hsien* (1897), 28/5a. *Mu-lin shu,* 2/60b-62a.

119. For additional instances, see *Ch'ing-yüan* (1880), 12/14a-b; *Mei-t'an* (1899), 8/35a-b and 37a; *T'eng hsien* (1846), 6/37a. According to Liu Shih-jen, *Chung-kuo t'ien-fu wen-t'i,* p. 91, the *li-shu* kept secret records of the *t'u* and *chia* divisions, of the names of the taxpayers, and of the quotas for which these were liable, thus making themselves indispensable to officials responsible for collecting the taxes. The number of *li-shu* varied, from about ten to as many as sixty in each locality, depending on the size of the tax intake.

120. *Ch'ing t'ung-k'ao,* 21/5047, 22/5049, and 23/5054. In an edict issued in 1724, the Yung-cheng emperor dropped this hint to provincial officials: "If it is thought that the abolition of the *li-chang [ts'ui-t'ou]* will encourage nonpayment

of taxes, other methods of expediting payment may be devised. Perhaps it will be sufficient to require the ten *chia* to urge payment by turns, allowing the registered households to make the remittances themselves."

121. Yü Yüeh, *Hui-tsui pien*, 7/6a.

122. Pai Ching-wei (1831-91), *Chi*, 7/40a-41b.

123. *Tung-kuan* (1921), 51/4a. The statement made by the compiler of this local gazetteer is not entirely clear. Judging from the fact that the *shu-suan* (recorder-accountant) was appointed every five years, this functionary may have been one of the yamen underlings instead of a *li-chia* agent.

124. Orita, *Fen-lun*, V, 110-24, lists three major difficulties that confronted the revenue system of the Ch'ing government: default in payment by taxpayers, unlawful surcharges made by local officials and their underlings, and fraudulent manipulation of procedures. Poverty of the villagers might render collection of the taxes difficult, quite apart from intentional default. A condition prevailing in the twelfth century, described in Wittfogel and Feng, *History of Chinese Society: Liao*, p. 374 (quoting from *Liao-shih*), may well have existed in parts of the empire in the nineteenth century: "At this time what the people were deeply disturbed about were the services for the courier post, horses and oxen, banners and drums, village heads, official attendants, and granary offices. They had reached a state of bankruptcy and were unable to fulfil the obligations."

125. A particularly illuminating instance was reported in 1669 by the prefect of Ch'u Chou (Chekiang): ". . . since the 8th year [of K'ang-hsi] . . . registration of transfers of land titles has been delayed for a long time [after the transactions were completed], so that the true owners cannot be readily ascertained. Tax liabilities are placed upon whomever [the agents] can lay hold of. The land which is legally liable for the taxes cannot be located. How can the *li-chang* know whether a given piece of land is still productive [and therefore liable for the taxes] or remains uncultivated [and is not taxable], if he does not know where it is located? As a result, wicked persons ask recording clerks and yamen runners dealing with tax matters to register their land . . . under the names of households that have been reported as *t'ao-chüeh* (fugitive-extinct), but as a matter of fact the heads of these households live in some other places and return in harvest time to collect their rent. Li Yü, *Hsin-shu, erh chi*, 2/21a-b.

126. Liu Shih-jen, *Chung-kuo t'ien-fu wen-t'i*, pp. 108-9.

127. Ting Jih-ch'ang (1823-82), *Kung-tu*, 20/10a.

128. Feng Kuei-fen (1809-74), quoted in Ko Shih-chün, *Hsü-pien*, 31/6a.

129. *Shih-lu*, Te-tsung, 95/11a-12a; Chu Shou-p'eng, *Tung-hua hsü-lu*, 28/18a-19b; *Ch'ing hsü t'ung-k'ao*, 28/7797, Yen Ching-ming's memorial dated 1880.

130. *Mu-lin shu* (1848 reprint), 11/54a-57a.

131. *Ch'ing hsü t'ung-k'ao*, 27/7790. For explanation of the terms "gentry" and "scholars," see chapter 3, note 11.

132. *Ch'ing hsü t'ung-k'ao*, 27/7791.

133. *Ibid.*, 28/7799.

134. *Shih-lu*, Sheng-tsu, 2/18b-19a. This memorial was dated Shun-chih, 18th year, 3rd month, *wu-hsü* day.

135. *Tsou-i hsü-pien*, 3/4b-5a.

136. *Ch'ing hsü t'ung-k'ao*, 28/7797. Pao Shih-ch'en (1775-1855), *Ch'i-min ssu shu*, 12/11a-b, relates an extreme instance of excessive extortionary practices reported in Wei-yüan (Yunnan) in 1798.

137. *Ch'ing t'ung-k'ao*, 22/5049-50.

138. *Hu-pu hsü-tsuan* (1796), 31/7a.

139. Huang Ang, *Tso-chüan lu, chüan* 2, quoted in *Chung-ho*, II, 132.

140. *Tsou-i, hsü-pien,* 4/12a. The official was Wang Chieh.

141. *Ch'ing hsü t'ung-k'ao,* 28/7799, quoting Kao Yen-ti (writing in the late nineteenth century).

142. *Ch'ing t'ung-k'ao,* 21/5046.

143. *Ibid.,* 21/5046 and 22/5050.

144. *Ibid.,* 22/5051.

145. *Ibid.,* 21/5046.

146. *Ibid.,* 22/5051.

147. See note 103. *Hsüeh-cheng* (1810), 7/6a, may also be consulted.

148. Li Yü, *Hsin-shu, erh chi,* 1/1b. Ch'en Hung-mou (1696-1771) said in an official document: "As regards *tsui-ch'ai* [exaction agents], there are *shun-ch'ai* [regular agents], *t'u-ch'ai* [agents for the *t'u*], and *pan-ch'ai* [accompanying agents]. *Shun-ch'ai* are in charge year after year; *t'u-ch'ai* [are appointed] annually by lot drawn in each *t'u*. . . . These . . . agents do not go into the countryside; hence unscrupulous persons 'buy' [the right to exact tax payment in] the *t'u*. The price is fixed according to the estimated amount of illegal gains obtainable in the *t'u*. These are known as *pan-ch'ai*. Their names do not appear in the official records. When they go to the villages they exact the customary fees [from the paxpayers]."

149. Li Yü, *Hsin-shu,* 1/12a-b.

150. Ch'en Hung-mou, *Ou-ts'un kao,* 18/37a, a directive issued in 1744.

151. Pai Ching-wei (1831-91), *Chi,* 7/42b-43b.

152. *Hsiang-shan* (1873), 22/50a-51a.

153. *Tung-kuan* (1921), 70/9b.

154. Ko Shih-chün, *Hsü-pien,* 32/19a.

155. T'ang Chen (who later changed his name to T'ang Shou-ch'ien), was the author of this passage. *Wei-yen,* 2/25b-26a, quoted in Yü Pao-hsüan, *Wen-pien,* 17/10a-12a. Père Hoang confirmed this view: "The tribute begins to be collected in the eleventh month, and the magistrates, in order to encourage prompt payment, demand 500 cash, in addition to the announced tax, from those who postpone payment until the first month of the following year. Thus it happens that some shrewd collectors do not seek payment of the tribute before the end of the year from peasants who are simple but have the means to pay, but on the contrary refuse payment, or prefer to accept money in commutation and pay the magistrate in advance on behalf of the peasants, so that when the first month comes they may receive an additional 500 cash for themselves." *Notiones* by Harold C. Hinton in "The Grain Tribute System," *Far Eastern Quarterly,* XI, 347.

156. Ting Jih-ch'ang, *Kung-tu,* 18/1a-b. The case occurred in T'ao-yüan Hsien (Kiangsu). Rural taxpayers sometimes set up organizations of their own to prompt payment for the sake of self-protection. See chapter 7, conc.uding pages of section on economic activities, and chapter 8, section on material welfare.

157. Chester Holcombe, *The Real Chinaman* (1895), pp. 348-49.

158. Edward H. Parker, *China* (1901), p. 173.

159. *Fu-shan* (1924), 17/14a-b. Additional tablets were erected in 1778 and 1786.

160. Ting Jih-ch'ang, *Kung-tu,* 3/5a. A similar practice was reported in some localities of Kwangtung. See, for example, *Tung-kuan* (1921), 51/49a, where it is said that the post of *shu-suan* (recorder-accountant) was bought with 1,000 taels for a five-year term.

161. John L. Nevius, *China and the Chinese* (1869), pp. 145-46: "The popular story respecting . . . 'the God of Wealth,' is as follows: He was originally

a tax-gatherer, and once called upon a family who professed their inability to
pay their tax, and determined to stay with them till he obtained it. Before retiring to rest, he was surprised to hear under his window the following address
of an old hen to her young brood: 'My master has a guest in his house, and has
determined to kill me tomorrow to furnish his table. What will become of you,
my dear little nestlings . . . ?' The-tax gatherer was moved by this touching
address. He gave up his post and eventually became the god that dispensed wealth,
riding on the back of a tiger. See *Mu-lin shu*, 2/60b-61a, quoting a public notice
issued by the governor prohibiting the practice of selling posts of *kuei-shu* (chest
recorders) and *li-chang* by magistrates in Honan province, early in the eighteenth century; and *ibid.*, 3/64a-b, a document issued by Ch'en Hung-mou in another province.

162. *Fu-shan* (1924), 17/14a-b.
163. *Tung-kuan* (1921), 51/4a.
164. Ts'ai Shen-chih, in *Chung-ho*, II, 54, quoting from a manuscript entitled
"Ch'ang-sui lun." See *Mu-lin shu*, 3/61b, Ch'en Hung-mou's statement.
165. Feng Kuei-fen, *Chi*, 5/37a.
166. *Yung hsien* (1897), 9/6a-b. See *Chou-hsien shih-i*, pp. 45b-46a, describing the malpractices of *kuan-chiang* (official silversmiths) in charge of
examining and smelting the silver turned in as tax payments.
167. *Tz'u-li'*(1896), 6/3b-4a. Cf. *Mu-lin shu*, 2/60a-b, quoting Yen Ju-yü, a
chü-jen of 1796, serving first as magistrate and finally as provincial judge in
Shensi, on the malpractices known as *chieh-liang* (intercepting tax payments)
similar to the method used by the "brokers" reported in **Tz'u-li** Hsien.
168. *Hui-tien* (1908), 19/1a: "Receipts and expenditures of the empire shall
be in terms of silver."
169. Wang Ch'ing-yün, *Chi-cheng*, 5/8a-10b. See Ch'ien Yung (1759-1844),
Li-yüan ts'ung-hua, 1/14b: "At the beginning of the Ch'ien-lung reign one tael
of silver brought 700 full-sized cash. Later [the rate] increased gradually to
720, 740, 760, 800, and 840 cash. In the days of my youth a tael of silver did
not bring more than 900 full-sized cash. In Chia-ch'ing 1 [1796] the price of silver rose suddenly, one tael of it bringing 1,300 to 1,400 cash. But later the rate
declined gradually." See also Wang Hui-tsu (1731-1807), *Meng-hen lu, chüan
hsia*, pp. 49b-50a: "Before *hsin-ssu* [1761], one *k'u-p'ing* tael of sycee silver
did not bring more than 700 or 800 cash. In *ping-wu* [1786] it was still below
1,000 cash. At present [1792] it may bring 1,300 cash." *Ibid.*, p. 57a: "This
year [1794] one *k'u-p'ing* tael of sycee silver brought 1,440 to 1,450 cash." *K'u-
p'ing* was the official weight used by the *Hu-pu* and generally in northern provinces. It was roughly 0.9872 *kuan-p'ing*, the weight adopted by the maritime
customs. For additional statements on the same matter, see Yeh Ch'ang-chih
(1849-1917), *Jih-chi*, 1/74b, entry of Kuang-hsü *ting-ch'ou* (1877), 10th month,
16th day; and T'ang Chen, *Wei-yen* (1890), 2/24a-28b. In some localities, however, the trend was reversed late in the nineteenth century. For example, Li
Tz'u-ming, *Jih-chi pu, ting chi*, p. 6a-b, entry of 1857 (Hsien-feng 7, 7th month,
23rd day); and Weng T'ung-ho, *Jih-chi*, 26/6a-36a, entries of 1887 (Kuang-hsü
ting-hai, 1st month, 13th day, to 4th month, 4th day). L. Richard, *Comprehensive Geography*, p. 318, gives exchange rates between 1736 and 1907.
170. Wang Ch'ing-yün, *Chi-cheng*, attributed the rise of silver prices to the
oversupply of copper cash in Yung-cheng and Ch'ien-lung times. Li Hsing-yüan,
Chou-i, 3/65a and 10/52a, stressed oversupply of copper cash; so did Ho Ch'ang-
ling, *Tsou-i*, 4/9a. Li Tz'u-ming, *Jih-chi pu, hsin-chi, shang*, p. 67a, entry
of 1861 (Hsien-feng 11, 6th month, 8th day), argued that the rise was due to the

appearance of substandard copper coins on the market, which had resulted from a dearth of copper since the beginning of the Hsien-feng reign. Feng Kuei-fen, however, blamed foreign trade in general and the opium trade in particular for draining China of its silver. Pao Shih-ch'en, *Ch'i-min ssu-shu*, 26/5a, and T'ai-p'ing Shan-jen (pseud.), *Chung-ho*, I, 61-75, held a similar opinion.

171. Li Hsing-yüan, *Tsou-i*, 10/52b: "The authorized practice of collecting 70 per cent of the tax money in silver and 30 per cent in copper cash, traceable to Shun-chih times, was discontinued after a while, although it was indicated in print on the *yu-tan*. " In other words, copper cash were no longer acceptable.

172. *Ch'ing t'ung-k'ao*, 2/7512.

173. Holcombe, *The Real Chinaman*, p. 234.

174. Pao Shih-ch'en, *Ch'i-min ssu-shu*, 2/15a.

175. *T'ung-jen* (1890), 9/40b. A similar situation in Kiangsu was observed by Père Hoang: ". . . the officials prefer to have the rice tribute commuted to an equivalent sum of money. Since, however, the price of rice is subject to constant fluctuations, the value of the rice to be paid for each year's tribute is determined by the provincial treasurer on the basis of the current price of rice, and is announced by the district magistrates. Thus, for example, if the current price of a picul of rice is 2, 300 cash, then the farmers must pay 3, 352 cash for each picul of tribute rice. . . . The people also prefer to pay the rice tribute in money, in order to avoid the difficulties which the agents of the court [i.e., yamen underlings] make when accepting the rice, such as using enlarged instruments of measure and complaining of the quality of the rice. Therefore only powerful proprietors, whom the court's agents do not dare molest, pay in rice." Quoted by Hinton, *Far Eastern Quarterly*, XI, 347.

176. *Ch'ing hsü t'ung-k'ao*, 2/7515.

177. *Ch'ing t'ung-k'ao*, 21/5045, quoting a regulation of early Ch'ing times: "*Li-chang* and *chia-chang* shall be permitted to bring charges against *chou* and *hsien* magistrates who impose levies beyond the quotas without authorization. . . . [These officials] shall be dealt with in accordance with the law."

178. Since early times in Chinese history privileged individuals and families had made tax collection a difficult task for the government. See for example *Shih-chi*, biography of Chao T'u, 81/5a (the Lord of P'ing-yüan's household refused to pay taxes); Chao I, *Cha-chi*, article on the *hsiang-huan* (rural gentry) of Ming times, 34/14a; Chu Chih-yü, quoted in *Shih-huo*, V, 8, 20 (malpractices of the *huan-hu* [official households] of the Ming dynasty).

179. For a fuller discussion, see chapter 3, note 12. Chung-li Chang's *The Chinese Gentry*, pp. 32-43, is very useful.

180. *Lü-li pien-lan* (1877), 11/41b, and *Shih-li* (1736), 383/16a-b.

181. *Hsüeh-cheng* (1810), 32/1a and 2a-b; *Lü-li pien-lan* (1877), 9/2b and 18a. They were also expressly exempted from the services devolving on the *li-chia* agents, which constituted a form of "miscellaneous labor service." See *Ch'ing t'ung-k'ao*, 71/7709, for an order to this effect issued in 1736 (Ch'ien-lung 1).

182. *Chou-li*, "Ti-kuan, hsiang ta-fu, " 3/73: "The duties of the *hsiang ta-fu*: . . . To register every year the number of inhabitants in the households and to ascertain those among them that are capable of rendering services. . . . Exempted from services are those in the state who possess rank, virtue, or talent; those who are performing public functions; and those who are aged or sick." See *T'ung-k'ao*, 13/141, for categories of persons exempted from corvée, from the Han to Sung dynasties.

183. *Shih-lu*, Shih-tsu, 37/21a-b, gives the system of exemptions established at the beginning of the Ch'ing dynasty. See also *Ch'ing t'ung-k'ao*, 25/5071-72.

The regulation of 1648 may be summarized as follows:

Official Rank	Grain Tax Exemption *(shih)*	*Ting* Exemptions
Serving in the capital:		
1st rank	30	30
2nd rank	24	24
3rd rank	20	20
4th rank	16	16
5th rank	14	14
6th rank	12	12
7th rank	10	10
8th rank	8	8
9th rank	6	6
Educational officials		
Chü-jen		
Chien-sheng	2	2
Sheng-yüan		
Local functionaries (nonranking)	1	

Exemptions for those serving in the provinces were 50 per cent, and for retired officials 70 per cent, of the exemptions of those serving in the capital. In 1657, the Shun-chih emperor approved a recommendation of the *Hu-pu* and granted one exemption from the *ting* to each of the officials, from the highest ranking to the lowest, and to scholars of all grades. Nothing was said of exemption from the grain tax; presumably all such exemptions were abolished at that time, so that all owners of land regardless of their status became liable for grain (or land) tax. Local gazetteers usually contain data showing the number of persons exempted from the *ting;* for example, *Ch'u chou* (1897), *chüan* 2, *ting,* p. 11a, gives the information that the total *ting* quota of this locality was 12,292, and that 401 *chü-jen, kung-sheng,* and *sheng-yüan* were exempted.

184. *Ch'ing t'ung-k'ao,* 25/5073. During the closing years of the dynasty, however, the privileges and prestige of *shih* (scholars) tended to disappear. In some localities they became liable for labor service imposts. For example, a petition was submitted in 1881 to Chang Chih-tung, then governor of Shansi, which reads in part: "Since the *ting* has been apportioned into the land tax, the *yao* has become similarly treated. As a result, scholars of Shansi province are no longer exempted from labor service levies. This has now become an established practice." See Wang Jen-k'an, *I-shu,* 3/4a.

185. Chu Hsieh, *Wen-t'i,* pp. 15-16: "Landless adult males no longer paid the *ting* money; the *ting* tax on persons remained in name but actually it had disappeared."

186. Pao Shih-ch'en, *Ch'i-min ssu-shu,* 8/10a, writing in 1822: "Since *shen-shih* are exempted from labor service, and those families that have the means to do so manage to have their names entered in the exemption registers by purchasing some official title, only tillers of the soil who work hard throughout the year are liable for the miscellaneous labor drafts." *Mu-lin shu,* 3/74b-77a, quotes an essay on *ch'ai-yao* by Chang Chieh, a magistrate serving in Chihli in Chia-ch'ing and Tao-kuang times, which reads in part as follows: "In supplying the *ch'ai* [labor] services the practice differs in various localities. In the *chou* and *hsien* of the northern portion of [Chihli] province, in some instances

the banners supply 30 per cent [of the services] and the people supply 70 per cent, while in others the banners supply no service at all so that [the burdens fall on] the people alone. In the southern portion, the gentry supply 30 per cent and the people 70 per cent, but in other instances the gentry supply no service at all, leaving the people alone [to shoulder the burden]. . . . Consequently, families possessing relatively large amounts of land either become nominal yamen functionaries or purchase official titles, in order to obtain exemption from the services. . . . The extensive services rendered year after year in Chihli, there-fore, do not come from the officials and functionaries of the *chou* and *hsien* nor from wealthy gentry and big merchants but from good, poor people who own the smallest amounts of land. "

187. *Ch'ing-shih kao,* "Shih-huo, " 2/3a. The confused situation which resulted from the merging of the *ting* and land taxes occasionally caused scholars to lose their ancient immunity from the *ting,* leaving members of the gentry who pos-sessed official renks or titles the only privileged group in matters of labor serv-ice. See note 184, above. Wang Jen-k'an, *I-shu, chüan shou,* p. 5b and 3/4a, in-dicates that Chang Chih-tung (governor of Shansi) proposed in 1881 that "aged *sheng-yüan* of the first grade, whether possessing land or not, be exempted from labor service imposts to the extent of [the equivalent value of] 200 *mow,* those of the second grade, 100 *mow,* and those of the third grade, 50 *mow.* Those whose grade falls below the third will be given no exemptions. " This proposal was approved by the government, but the exemptions were given only to aged scholars showing relatively high literary accomplishments, not to all scholars. See also Chung-li Chang, *Chinese Gentry,* pp. 43-51.

188. These terms did not constitute a formal or official classification of tax-payers. They were used simply to designate households with various social sta-tus, and the usage varied in different localities. The actual meaning of each of these terms will become apparent in the pages following. The term *ta-hu* may have been applied to nongentry landowners of substantial means, as the following statement made by Ch'en Hung-mou (governor of Kiangsu, 1757-58) suggests: *"Chou* and *hsien* [magistrates], being concerned about their administrative rat-ing, arrest *ta-hu* [who have failed to make the payments] . . . and leave *hsiao-hu* alone. " It is unlikely that magistrates would seize large landowners with gentry status, especially in Kiangsu where the influence of the gentry was considerable.

189. *Shih-li* (1908), 172/4b.

190. *Ibid.,* an action taken in 1660.

191. *Shih-lu,* Sheng-tsu, 3/3a.

192. Hsü K'o, *Ch'ing-p'ai lui-ch'ao,* 8/28-31.

193. Li Yü, *Hsin-shu, erh chi,* 1/14b, quoting Wu Chai, prefect of Chin-hua. Cf. Ch'ien Yung, *Li-yüan ts'ung-hua,* 1/7a. Li Tz'u-ming, *Jih-chi,* iii, *shang chi,* 4b-5a, quoting from Chi Liu-ch'i's narrative of the case of the *sheng-yüan* of Soochow who refused to pay their taxes (1661), indicates that Jen Wei-ch'u, magistrate of Wu Hsien, was partly responsible for the incident. At that time ten similar cases were reported in Chen-chiang, Chin-t'an, Wu-wei, and other localities under the jurisdiction of Chu Kuo-chih; a total of 121 persons incurred the death penalty. The overlenient way in which the Ming dynasty treated schol-ars, according to Chi Liu-ch'i *(Ming-chi pei-lüeh),* rendered the *sheng-yüan* unruly and eventually brought about the calamities of 1661.

194. Li Yü, *Hsin-shu, erh chi,* 3/8a-b.

195. *Liu-pu ch'u-fen tse-li* (1877), 15/28a-29b. The original document has *shen-chin,* which is here translated "members of the gentry and titled scholars. " See chapter 3, note 11.

196. *Shih-li* (1908), 172/5b and 330/1b.

197. *Ibid.*, 172/4b-5b; *Lü-li pien-lan* (1877), 11/8a-b: "The amount of the land tax and grain tribute to be paid [by each household] shall be counted in ten parts. If less than four parts are not paid, [a defaulter who is] a *chü-jen* shall be deprived of his title; a *kung-sheng, chien-sheng*, or *sheng-yüan* shall be deprived of his title and administered sixty blows. If the amount unpaid [exceeds four parts but] is less than seven parts, in addition to having his title taken away from him, a *chü-jen* shall receive eighty blows; a *kung-sheng, chien-sheng*, or *sheng-yüan* shall wear the cangue for two months and receive one hundred blows." See also *ibid.*, 11/11a-b.

198. *Hu-pu* (1791), 11/11a. Tso Tsung-t'ang (1812-85), *Ch'üan-chi*, 19/84a, contains a memorial dated 1866 petitioning the imperial government to restore the *chü-jen* title to salt merchants who had paid their overdue taxes, indicating that this law was actually applied, at least in some localities.

199. Wang Hui-tsu, *Ping-t'a meng-hen lu* (1796), *chüan hsia*, pp. 33a-34a.

200. *Ch'ing t'ung-k'ao*, 22/5049.

201. *Wu-hsi* (1881), 11/1b.

202. "In Tao-kuang 26 [1846] the 'rotating service' system was discontinued and the amount of land became no longer of importance." *Ibid.* It may be recalled that at about the same time scholars in Shansi lost their privileged position and did not even partially regain it until 1881. See notes 184 and 187 above.

203. *Ch'ing t'ung-k'ao*, 22/5051; *Shih-li* (1908), 172/5a.

204. *Ch'ing t'ung-k'ao*, 2/4866.

205. *Ibid.*, 25/5073.

206. *Shih-li* (1908), 172/5a; *Ch'ing t'ung-k'ao*, 2/4867.

207. *Shih-li* (1908), 172/5a; *Ch'ing t'ung-k'ao*, 2/4867.

208. *Shih-li* (1908), 172/5b; *Ch'ing t'ung-k'ao*, 3/4871; *Shih-lu*, Shih-tsung, 16/21b-22a. Shih-tsung reiterated the same prohibition in 1727 and Kao-tsung in 1736. See *Shih-li* (1908), 172/19b, and *Ch'ing t'ung-k'ao*, 71/5510.

209. *Ch'ing hsü t'ung-k'ao*, 1/7505. "Bad scholars and big households" is a translation of *lieh-chin ta-hu* in the original document.

210. *Tung-kuan* (1921), 3/4a, quoting Hung Mu-chi's comment.

211. Li Yü, *Hsin-shu*, 3/1a-2b, quoting Wang Yüan-hsi, governor of Chekiang. Cf. *Ch'ing hsü t'ung-k'ao*, 3/7526, an essay written by Chin An-ch'ing.

212. Wang Hui-tsu, *Ping-t'a meng-hen lu, chüan shang*, pp. 33a-34a, describing the situation in some parts of Kiangsu and Chekiang.

213. Tai Ch'ao-ch'en, *Hsüeh-shih lu*, 11/7b-8a, quoting a memorial submitted by Chiang Yu-t'ien, Grand Secretary of T'i-jen Ko, in 1799. Cf. *Ch'ing hsü t'ung-k'ao*, 2/7511, an edict of 1826 (Tao-kuang 16), in which T'ao Chu's memorial is quoted in part.

214. Tai Ch'ao-ch'en, *Hsüeh-shih lu*, 11/12a.

215. Li Hsing-yüan, *Tsou-i*, 9/37a-38b.

216. *Shih-lu*, Hsüan-tsung, 435/9a-10a; *Shih-li* (1908), 207/4b; *Ch'ing hsü t'ung-k'ao*, 2/7513-14, an edict of 1826 (Tao-kuang 6) and Po-chün's memorial submitted in 1846.

217. Feng Kuei-fen, *Chi*, 2/27b-38a.

218. Wei Yüan, *Wai-chi*, 4/34a-35b. Huang Tsai-chün, *Chin-hu ch'i-mo*, "Lang-mo," 4/6b-7a, gives a briefer account. This uprising should not be confused with the disturbances reported by Tseng Kuo-fan in 1853, in his "Shu-cha," 2/20a-b, in *Ch'üan-chi*.

219. *Shih-li* (1908), 172/7a, an edict of 1842 (Tao-kuang 22).

220. Wei Yüan, *Wai-chi*, 4/35b.

221. *Ch'ing hsü t'ung-k'ao,* 3/7520.

222. *Shih-li* (1908), 172/7b.

223. *Ch'ing hsü t'ung-k'ao,* 3/7522; *Shih-li* (1908), 172/7b.

224. Ting Jih-ch'ang, *Kung-tu,* 22/1a-b and 20/3b. According to Ting, a gentry household paid from 2,000 to 3,000 cash for each *shih* of the tribute rice (if the rice tribute was paid at all), and a commoner household paid from 6,000 to 16,000 cash for each *shih.*

225. *Shih-li* (1908), 172/8a.

226. *Hu-pu* (1791), 12/2a: "Any *kung-sheng, chien-sheng,* or *sheng-yüan* who, taking advantage of the appellation *ju-hu* or *huan-hu,* assumes illegal responsibilities for making tax payments or defalcates the payments collected in localities where land and labor taxes are payable in money or grain, shall be punished in accordance with laws governing defalcation of money or grain from government treasuries or granaries."

227. *Ch'ing t'ung-k'ao,* 24/5062, gives a memorial submitted in 1762 by Li Yin-p'ei: "For a long time scholars, being members of the government schools, have been prohibited by law from performing all categories of *i.* . . . At present, many scholars of Chekiang province engage in *li-chia* services, either as *chuang-shu,* who take charge of the tax registers and records of land titles, or as *yü-chang, tou-chang,* or *t'ang-chang,* who are responsible for repairing dikes and embankments. These are the appellations that prevail in Chekiang; similar ones are found in other provinces. These posts ordinarily are filled by . . . persons nominated by the inhabitants of the countryside."

228. Feng Kuei-fen, *Chi,* 10/1b.

229. *Ch'ing t'ung-k'ao,* 4/4889.

230. *Ibid.,* 2/7510. See *Mu-lin shu,* 3/72a, for a similar view expressed by Ho Shih-ch'i, *chin-shih* of 1822 and assistant prefect of Ch'uan-sha (Kiangsu).

231. Feng Kuei-fen, *Chi,* 9/25a.

232. When private interests conflicted, yamen underlings who usually cooperated with "bad gentry" in fraudulent practices might work against landowners, gentry or otherwise. A case in point was reported in 1854 when a powerful yamen clerk in charge of rice tribute records withheld the news of deferment granted to taxpayers as an act of imperial grace. *Shih-lu,* Wen-tsung, 140/2a-b. According to Feng Kuei-fen, *Chi,* 10/1a-b, there was no equality even among members of the gentry. "The current principle for determining the amounts of tribute rice is that persons with high status and great influence are allowed to pay less, whereas inconsequential and unprivileged persons are required to pay more. There is no uniformity, not only between the gentry *[shen]* and commoners *[min],* but among the members of the gentry and commoners themselves. The tax due from gentry households *[shen hu]* is usually commuted to money equivalents. Those who pay the smallest amounts make their payments at the rate of about 1.3 *shih* for each *shih* [legally due]; others pay progressively more, reaching a maximum rate of about 2 *shih* for each *shih* [legally collectible]. The humblest of commoner households *[min hu]* pay at the rate of 3 or 4 *shih* for each *shih* [due]." Feng Kuei-fen, in the passage quoted in the text, maintained a distinction between gentry *[shen]* and scholars *[chin],* for the simple reason that the gentry and scholars occupied somewhat different positions in matters relative to tax collection. Feng, however, was not the only writer of the nineteenth century who made this necessary distinction; it was made by earlier writers and for purposes beyond tax collection. For example, in *Chou-hsien shih-i,* p. 29a, a handbook compiled by imperial order in the 1720's, it is said that *"Shen* [the gentry] are those to whom an entire district look up; *shih* [scholars] stand at the

head of the four classes of the people." In a sense the imperial government maintained (by implication at least) a distinction between *shen,* who were officials incumbent or retired, and *shih* or *chin,* who were potential or expectant officials. In the earlier days of the dynasty scholars were strictly forbidden to visit the local yamen or to concern themselves with matters relative to local administration. See chapter 3, note 11 and chapter 4, section on "Local Schools."

233. Tai Ch'ao-ch'en, *Hsüeh-shih lu,* 7/7b.

234. Not all of the gentry, however, were involved in the illegal practices described. Instances were known in which the less influential members of the gentry were victimized by local officials and yamen underlings. The extent of extortion varied inversely with the degree of influence or prestige enjoyed by the victims. A revealing instance was reported in Kuei-chi (Shao-hsing, Chekiang) in 1859. The censorate memorialized that the magistrate of this district connived with yamen clerks and collected grain tax in excess of the legal quotas, the illegal levies amounting to over 18,000 *shih,* which gave them a profit of over 100,000 taels. Li Tz'u-ming, a native of the locality, commented in his diary that in collecting the tax from landowners, the official and his underlings had worked out a fixed table of extortion rates. "Big households" usually had to pay a surcharge of between 25 per cent and 30 per cent in excess of the legal quota; the rate increased as the influence or prestige of the taxpayers decreased. "Small households" paid as much as 60 per cent in excess of the legal quotas. The Li family, thanks to the lingering influence of its ancestors and to the fact that it owned a substantial amount of land (over 10,000 *mow),* had to pay an illegal surcharge of only 38 per cent, a moderate rate by local standards. But it compared unfavorably with the Ho, Chang, and T'ao families, which paid the lightest rates, namely under 30 per cent. *Jih-chi pu, ssu chi,* pp. 83a-b.

235. Yü Pao-hsüan, *Wen-pien,* 18/17b, contains a memorial submitted in 1895 by Fu-jin, governor of Anhwei, depicting the situation thus: "Since the registers were lost in the devastations of war, it has become impossible to ascertain the tax liabilities [devolving on the taxpayers]. As a result, gentry families and powerful clans encroach upon [the government's revenues]. They report small liabilities where large quotas should apply, or report their land as uncultivated, whereas it is in fact productive. Local officials dare not question them even though they know the facts. When common people become acquainted with this state of affairs, some of them follow the example [of the gentry families and powerful clans]. As the number of such [tax dodging] persons increases, the officials are afraid to arouse them into making trouble, thereby incurring penalties [upon themselves] for having handled matters badly without achieving any result toward re-establishing tax assessments. They adopt an attitude of patient watching and take no action.

236. Riots are treated in chapter 10. The following, however, may be consulted in this connection: *Ch'ing hsü t'ung-k'ao,* 2/7517, Lui Wei-han's memorial of 1853, and an edict issued in 1861; and Fu I-ling's article in *Ts'ai-cheng chih-shih* (1943), III, 31-39.

237. *Shih-lu,* Sheng-tsu, 1/17a-b, an edict issued in 1661 (Shun-chih 18, 1st month, *chi-mao* day), reads in part as follows: "Revenue from tax money and grain answers the urgent civil and military needs of the empire. . . . Recently in reading memorials submitted to us, we discover that most of the provinces have failed to send in the full amounts of tax money and grain. . . . Hereafter all officials who are responsible for tax collection and who fail to send the money and grain in full and on time, whether their ranks are high or low, shall be punished. . . . Their ranks may be reinstated or their privilege of promotion may

be restored only after they have settled in full the money and grain previously overdue. "

238. Ts'ai Shen-chih, *Chung-ho,* II, 53-54, quoting from *Chou-hsien shih-i.*

239. Wang Hsien-ch'ien, *Tung-hua lu,* Yung-cheng, 12/10b, an edict dated 1728 (Yung-cheng 6, 2nd month, *ping-shen* day), reads: "One who utilizes the land pays taxes: this is an unchanging principle of universal application. Obedience to laws and performance of public duties: these are conformable with the constant nature of the people. There has never been any person who enjoys the benefit of land and yet is unwilling to pay the legitimate taxes, thus voluntarily exposing himself to criminal punishment. Why, then, have the evils of deficit in tax collection and default in tax payment become a long-continued habit which is so difficult to alter? One reason is that the practice of 'satiating the middle' carried on by yamen clerks and runners has not been stamped out. These either take the collection into their own hands and defalcate the revenue, or fraudulently alter the tax receipts, or fish out the money dropped [by taxpayers] into the chests, or give shelter to defaulting taxpayers—their ways being diverse, it is impossible to enumerate them exhaustively." This edict is included also in *Ch'ing t'ung-k'ao,* 3/4875.

240. Li Hsing-yüan, *Tsou-i,* 5/7a-8b, a memorial dated 1844, and 11/40a-41b, a memorial dated 1846. See *Shih-li* (1908), *chüan* 175, *passim,* for official defaults and action taken against them between 1652 and 1884. The collection of the *likin,* a new source of government revenue since the mid-nineteenth century, was not free from embezzlement. Weng T'ung-ho, for example, noted in his *Jih-chi,* 25/43a, entry of 1886 (Kuang-hsü 12, 6th month, 22nd day): "On this day I was summoned to an audience held in the Hsi-luan Ko of Ch'ien-ch'ing Kung, the Empress Dowager sitting with her face to the south and the emperor sitting behind her. . . . Their majesties are of the opinion that governors-general and governors mostly do not wish to perform their responsibilities honestly, and that they appoint irresponsible persons to *likin* [posts]. These persons, usually at the expiration of their terms, [are discovered to have] embezzled [the government's revenue]." See *ibid.,* 30/44b, an entry of 1891 (Kuang-hsü 17, 6th month, 15th day).

241. *Hu-pu hsü-pien* (1795), 23/4a-15b; *Ch'ing t'ung-k'ao,* 41/5232, an edict dated 1827 (Yung-cheng 6); *Ch'ing hsü t'ung-k'ao,* 66/8225 and 66/8228; Ch'en K'ang-ch'i, *Lang-ch'ien chi-wen,* 14/8b-9a; *Shih-li* (1908), 172/6b, an edict of 1807 (Chia-ch'ing 12); *Ch'ing-shih kao,* "Shih-huo, " 2/10b-11a. According to Li Tz'u-ming, *Jih-chi,* vii, *keng-chi hsia,* 86a-b, Anhwei and the Chiang-ning region of Kiangsu showed the greatest amounts of unpaid taxes; Kiangsi and Soochow came next; with the exception of Szechwan, all other provinces reported arrears of at least 20 or 10 per cent of the quotas collectible. The total amount of uncollected taxes of all categories was over 11, 000, 000 taels a year. He quoted from an edict dated 1885 (Kuang-hsü 11, 12th month, 23rd day). Generally speaking, Kiangsu had had a particularly bad record since the early years of the Ch'ing dynasty. See Li Yü, *Hsin-shu, erh chi,* 1/7b, quoting a document issued by Han Shih-ch'i, governor of Chiang-nan, some time before 1667. For the situation of Anhwei in the nineteenth century, see Fu-jun's (governor's) memorial submitted in 1896, in Yü Pao-hsüan, *Wen-pien,* 18/17a. For Kiangsi, see Pao Shih-ch'en, *Ch'i-min ssu-shu,* 3/19a-b, a letter written in 1836. For Kiangsu, see Li Hsing-yüan, *Tsou-i,* 11/12b-14a, 12/30b-32a, memorials submitted in 1846 giving figures for the years 1841-46. Some writers of the period argued that the situation in Kiangsu was due to excessive tax burdens. See Feng Kuei-fen, *Chi,* 9/3a-5a; Ch'en Ch'i-yüan, *Pi-chi,* 6/7a-11a.

242. *Ch'ing t'ung-k'ao, chüan* 27-31, *passim,* and 40/5225-26.

243. Wang Ch'ing-yün, *Chi-cheng,* 3/35a. For the situation in the latter part of the nineteenth century, see Wei Yüan, *Sheng-wu chi,* quoting Li T'ang-chieh, *Jih-chi,* Vol. XIII, Hsien-feng 2, 8th month, 1st day; A. H. Exner, "The Sources of Revenue and the Credit of China," *China Review,* XVII (1888), 276-91; *Chih-hsin pao* (1897), 25/14b, quoting from a German source; Parker, *China* (1901), p. 197; Morse, *Trade and Administration* (1913), p. 111; L. Richard, *Comprehensive Geography* (1908), p. 321, quoting Sir Robert Hart; Joseph Edkins, *Revenue and Taxation* (1903), pp. 55-57 and 66-68, quoting from various sources. *Ch'ing hsü t'ung-k'ao* contains information concerning salt gabelle, *chüan* 35-40, *passim;* miscellaneous levies, *chüan* 29-32 and 41-48, *passim; likin, chüan* 49-50; native customs, *chüan* 29, *passim;* maritime customs, *chüan* 31, *passim.* Weng T'ung-ho, who was in a position to speak authoritatively on the fiscal situation in the 1880's, remarks in his *Jih-chi,* 25/91a, 1886 (Kuang-hsü 12, 12th month, 2nd day): "His Excellency Yen [Yen Ching-ming, president of the *Hu-pu]* had an audience; he made a strong statement to the effect that the *Hu-pu* coffers are short of funds and receipts do not cover expenditures." *Ibid.,* 30/7a, 1891 (Kuang-hsü 17, 2nd month, 1st day). Weng was then president of the *Hu-pu.* "Funds in the *Hu-pu* coffers available for expenditure amount to no more than 60,000 taels, insufficient to meet the expenditure of tomorrow." See also Li Tz'u-ming, *Jih-chi pu, ssu-chi,* p. 89a-b, entry of 1859 (Hsien-feng 9, 11th month, 21st day).

244. For example, Chia Shih-i, *Ts'ai-cheng shih,* I, 4 ff.; and Chu Hsieh, *Wen-t'i,* pp. 9-10, 17-24, and 70-73.

245. Chang Te-chien, *Tse-ch'ing hui-tsuan, chüan* 10, "Lu-chieh."

246. Lo Erh-kang, *Shih-kang,* pp. 90-92.

247. Chang Te-chien, *Tse-ch'ing hui-tsuan, chüan* 10, "K'o-p'ai." Tseng Kuo-fan, *Tsou-kao,* 18/24a, reported the conditions he observed on an inspection trip from Nanking to Anhwei, in a memorial dated 1862 (T'ung-chih 2, 2nd month, 27th day), in these words: "When the *Yüeh-fei* [i.e., Kwangsi bandits] first rose, . . . they were more or less capable of refraining from violating women in order to pacify those that were compelled to follow them; they allowed the people to cultivate the soil, in order to restore peace in localities occupied by them. They shared the harvests with the people, taking one half of what was produced. . . . But now whenever the people hear that the bandits are coming . . . men and women flee to safety, deserting their homesteads and villages. Peasants abandon their farming; not a single grain of rice is harvested."

248. As we have already suggested, the Ch'ing rulers inherited this problem from their Ming predecessors; they tried to solve it but did not achieve any real success. The Ch'ing system repeated some of the experiences of the *liang-chang* system prevailing in the latter part of the Ming dynasty. According to *Ming-shih, chüan* 78, "Shih-huo," 2, "Prior to the Ch'eng-hua [1465-87] and Hung-chih [1488-1505] reigns, the *li-chia* pressed for tax payments, the households paid their taxes, the *liang-chang* received the payments and sent them to the *chou* and *hsien* [yamen], and the magistrates supervised the collection. . . . Recently [in the 1520's], officials no longer hold the *li-chia* agents responsible . . . but flog the *liang-chang* and order them to go into the countryside to demand payments. Those that are ruthless among the *liang-chang* use oversized measures and make collections amounting to twice the legal quotas; they extort money [from the taxpayers] in many ways. . . . Those among them that are weak suffer the oppression of powerful [taxpayers]. They are often compelled to sell their own property to make good the deficits resulting from nonpayment [by such taxpayers]."

Huang Liu-hung, writing in 1694, describes in detail the malpractices prevailing in the earlier years of the Ch'ing dynasty, in his *Fu-hui ch'üan-shu, chüan* 6. Many of these practices persisted and assumed slightly different forms when the historical and institutional background changed in the closing decades of the dynasty. See *Ch'ing hsü t'ung-k'ao,* 5/7540, a memorial submitted by a minor functionary in the *To-chih-pu* (formerly *Hu-pu)* in 1909 (Hsüan-t'ung 1). Liu Shih-jen, *Chung-kuo t'ien-fu wen-t'i,* pp. 85-92, 105-13, and 159-65, indicates that some of the corrupt ways survived the dynasty and continued to plague the republic. Wang Yü-ch'üan's article, "Ch'ing mo t'ien-fu yü nung-min," *Shih-huo* (1936), III, 237-48, represents an attempt to show the effects of the land tax system on peasants in the last years of the Ch'ing dynasty.

Chapter 5

1. *Shih-li* (1908), 166/1a-167/5a, summarizes government action taken between 1644 and 1889. See also *Ch'ing t'ung-k'ao, chüan* 1-14; *Ch'ing hsü t'ung-k'ao, chüan* 1-5; Ko Shih-chün, *Hsü-pien, chüan* 33.

2. *Ch'ing t'ung-k'ao, chüan* 6-9, and *Ch'ing hsü t'ung-k'ao, chüan* 10-14, cover the period 1652-1911.

3. *Shih-li* (1908), *chüan* 278-87, gives the salient points. Local gazetteers usually contain records of such acts of imperial grace, applied in the localities concerned. For basic regulations governing deferment and exemption see *Hu-pu* (1791), especially *chüan* 112-13. One such regulation reads in part: "When flood or drought results in disaster, the local official shall . . . petition for deferment or exemption [of taxes for which the stricken households are liable], according to the degree of loss sustained." *Hu-pu* (1791), 112/4a.

4. According to *Hui-tien* (1908), 19/5a-b, twelve broad measures were designed to cope with famine: (1) "preparation against misfortune," including land reclamation and water works; (2) "eradication of pests," including locusts and "flood dragons"; (3) "emergency measures to relieve the calamity-stricken," including dike repair; (4) "famine relief," namely, giving food or money to the destitute; (5) "retailing grain at reduced prices"; (6) "grain loans"; (7) "exemption from taxes"; (8) "deferment of taxes"; (9) "encouragement to merchants" so that foodstuffs might flow into famine-stricken areas; (10) "solicitation of contributions" to grain reserves or to relief funds; (11) "public works" to give the destitute employment; and (12) "rehabilitation of refugees." Wang Ch'ing-yün, *Chi-cheng,* 1/3b-7b, gives a brief summary of government relief work. *K'ang-chi lu,* compiled in 1739 by imperial order, and *Huang-cheng ts'ung-shu,* compiled in 1690 by Yü Shen (provincial treasurer of Hu-kuang) describe government relief measures adopted before the Ch'ing dynasty.

5. The imperial granaries (officially called *ts'ang-yü)* were located in and near the imperial capital; they totaled thirteen, their reserves being stored in a large number of storehouses. These granaries were administered by two *ts'ang-ch'ang shih-lang,* or superintendents of imperial granaries, one of whom was a Manchu and the other a Chinese, assisted by eighteen *ts'ang-ch'ang chien-tu,* or inspectors of the imperial granaries, half of whom were Manchus. These imperial granaries are described in *Shih-li* (1908), *chüan* 184-88. The local granaries are treated in the same work, *chüan* 189-93, under the title *chi-ch'u* (reserves). Chi Ch'ao-ting's remark *(Key Economic Areas in Chinese History,* p. 6), "Aside from supplying the needs of the capital, the grain tribute was also the source for the accumulation of an indispensable reserve, particularly in order to prevent possible rebellion, or to feed a large force assembled for the purpose of suppressing a rebellion, in case the preventive measures had proved

to be ineffective, or of fighting a foreign war in case of invasion, " was evidently not intended to apply to the local granaries.

6. This term was first used by Henry A. Wallace. See Derk Bodde's article, "Henry A. Wallace and the Ever-Normal Granary, " *Far Eastern Quarterly* V, (1946), 411-26. The local granaries were officially classified as follows: (1) *Ch'ang-p'ing ts'ang;* (2) *Yü-pei ts'ang* (i.e., government granaries in Anhwei, Honan, Szechwan, and Tibet); (3) Banner granaries (in Sheng-ching, Kirin, and Heilungkiang); (4) *She ts'ang;* and (5) *I ts'ang.* See *Hui-tien* (1908), 19/5a.

7. *K'ang-chi lu,* 2/22b.

8. *Shih-li* (1908), 193/4b.

9. *Ibid.*

10. *Ibid.*, 189/1a, regulations formulated in 1655 (Shun-chih 12) and 1679 (K'ang-hsi 18).

11. *Hu-pu* (1791), 31/1a.

12. *Ch'ing t'ung-tien,* 13/2095, regulation of 1679.

13. *Shih-li* (1908), 189/1a, a document says: "The local official concerned shall be in charge of receiving and dispensing" the grain.

14. *Ibid.*, 193/1a.

15. *Hu-pu* (1791), 28/3a-5b and 8a; *Liu-pu ch'u-fen tse-li* (1877), 27/43a. Lu Lien-tching's statement *(Les greniers publics,* p. 152), "Les deux groupes de greniers avaient une même organisation; la seule différence qui les distingue les uns des autres tenait à leur situation géographique, " is therefore inaccurate.

16. Lu Lien-tching wrote *(ibid.,* p. 40), "En réalité, ces deux sortes de greniers n'en font qu'une. Ils sont tantôt appelés greniers de bienfaissance tantôt greniers communaux." John Henry Gray, *China* (1878), II, 58, made no distinction between the two.

17. *Hu-pu* (1791), 28/1a.

18. *Shih-li* (1908), 189/1a-5a; *Ch'ing t'ung-k'ao, chüan* 34-37; *Ch'ing hsü t'ung-k'ao, chüan* 60-61.

19. *Hu-pu* (1791), 27/1a-26a, gives the *ch'ang-p'ing* quotas applicable in the *chou* and *hsien* of the eighteen provinces and in the prefectures of Shun-t'ien, Feng-t'ien, and Ching-chou. See also *Ch'ing t'ung-tien,* 13/2095, and Wang Ch'ing-yün, *Chi-cheng,* 4/20a-23a.

20. *Shih-li* (1908), 190/1a. The quotas established in 1691 for Chihli province were: large *hsien,* 5,000 *shih;* medium *hsien,* 4,000 *shih;* small *hsien,* 3,000 *shih.* The following quotas were fixed in 1704 for all provinces: large *hsien,* 10,000 *shih;* medium *hsien,* 8,000 *shih;* small *hsien,* 6,000 *shih.* Shansi and Szechwan, however, had different quotas. In Shansi, the quotas for the three grades of *hsien* were 20,000, 16,000, and 12,000 *shih,* respectively; in Szechwan these were 6,000, 4,000, and 2,000. In 1748 the quotas for all the provinces amounted to a total of 33,792,330 *shih,* namely, a reduction of 14,318,350 *shih* from the previous total of 48,110,680 *shih.*

21. Lu Lien-tching, *Les greniers publics,* chapter 9. *"Réglementation des sanctions et lois prohibitives, "* conveniently summarizes the main regulations.

22. *Hu-pu* (1791), 28/6a; *Shih-li* (1908), 191/1a.

23. *Shih-li* (1908), 189/1b.

24. *Ch'ing t'ung-tien,* 13/2096. The practice was authorized for Chekiang province in 1710 (K'ang-hsi 49); formerly it had prevailed only in Chiang-nan.

25. *Hu-pu* (1791), 28/5b gives the proportions prescribed for the various provinces. See also Lu Lien-tching, *Les greniers publics,* pp. 109-10.

26. *Hu-pu* (1791), 28/8a, gives the following regulations: "The grain of *ch'ang-p'ing-ts'ang* may be loaned to peasants, to be used for food or as seed. *Chou* and

hsien magistrates shall fix dates for making such loans with due consideration to the time of planting, report [their decisions] to their superiors, and make known the dates by official announcements. In distributing [the grain] they shall investigate and ascertain that the households that apply for the loans are *bona fide* farming families and are able to furnish reliable bonds."

27. *Ibid.*, 28/9a-b.

28. *Ibid.*, 29/19a-20a; *Ch'ing t'ung-tien*, 13/2095. Yang Ching-jen, *Ch'ou-chi pien* (1823), 8/16b-22a, summarizes the regulations and *modus operandi* of the *ch'ang-p'ing* as officially sanctioned in 1660 to 1811.

29. Tai Ch'ao-ch'en, *Hsüeh-shih lu*, 5/20b, gives a good example.

30. Lu Lien-tching, *Les greniers publics*, p. 44, comments on the edicts of 1636, 1657, and 1660: "L'absence de renseignements écrits sur l'institution des greniers publics de cette époque nous fait croire que ces divers textes sont plutôt restés lettre morte."

31. Huang Liu-hung, *Fu-hui*, 27/6b-7a.

32. *Shih-li* (1908), 192/6a.

33. Hsüeh Fu-ch'eng (1838-94), *Yung-an pi-chi*, 3/7b-8b.

34. Especially in edicts issued in 1792, 1800, 1802, 1831, and 1835. *Shih-li* (1908), 189/3a and 6a, and 192/2b.

35. *Ch'ing-shih kao*, "Shih-huo," 2/20a.

36. *Shih-li* (1908), 192/2b, an edict dated 1835 (Tao-kuang 15), gives the following figures:

Grain reserve in all provinces	over 24,000,000 *shih*
Cumulative ullage in past years	over 12,500,000 *shih*
Current spoilage	over 2,700,000 *shih*
Grain sold or loaned and unreplenished	over 3,000,000 *shih*
Total amount of shortage	over 18,000,000 *shih*
Purchasing funds on hand	over 1,100,000 taels

Li Hsing-yüan (1797-1851), *Tsou-i*, 6/2a-b and 8/38b, describes conditions in Shensi province, 1844-1845.

37. Gray, *China* (1878), II, 58.

38. *Shih-lu*, Te-tsung, 416/2b, quotes an edict dated 1898 (Kuang-hsü 24, 3rd month, 4th day), as follows: "Kang-i memorialized that for a long time the *ch'ang-p'ing-ts'ang* of the provinces have been an empty form and that *i-ts'ang* of the people must be established through persuasion. If in any given locality a thousand *shih* of grain is stored each year, [he argues] a total reserve of over ten thousand *shih* would materialize in three years. Even if exceptionally severe famine occurs, the humble people would not be without support. . . . Governors-general and governors are ordered to instruct earnestly their subordinates to persuade the gentry and common people to establish [*i-ts'ang*].

39. Lu Lien-tching, *Les greniers publics*, p. 58: "Les renseignements relatifs aux greniers publics s'arrêtant à la 24e année du même règne, aucune indication ne nous permet de déterminer même approximativement la date òu le régime disparut. Ce qui est certain, c'est qu'il n'a pas été aboli, il s'est éteint de lui-même."

40. *Ch'ing t'ung-tien*, 13/2095, an edict dated 1654 (Shun-chih 11).

41. *Shih-li* (1908), 193/4b; *Ch'ing-shih kao*, "Shih-huo," 2/20a. That this order was not carried out at once in all the provinces may be inferred from the fact that in 1720 a petition was submitted by a high official of the imperial government, requesting that *she-ts'ang* be established in Shansi. Wang Hsien-ch'ien,

Tung-hua lu, K'ang-hsi 59, 108/3b. "Officials, gentry, scholars, and common people" is a translation of *kuan shen shih min* in the original text.

42. *Shih-li* (1908), 193/4b-5b, covers the period from 1679 to 1884.

43. *Ibid.,* 193/5a, a government decision of 1801.

44. *Ibid.; Hu-pu* (1791), 31/5a. It appears, however, that at least in the latter part of the nineteenth century, transporting grain for *ch'ang-p'ing* operations was permitted. Weng T'ung-ho, for instance, wrote in his *Jih-chi,* 1878 (Kuang-hsü 24, 3rd month, 1st day), 16/15b: "Yü Shang-hua requested that various cereals be purchased and transported in Chihli in order to facilitate *p'ing-t'iao* [selling grain at 'normal prices']. Permission was given." Weng was then junior vice-president of the *Hu-pu.*

45. *Hu-pu* (1791), 31/2a-4a.

46. *Ibid.,* 31/1a.

47. *Shih-li* (1908), 193/4b.

48. *Hu-pu* (1791), 32/1b-2a.

49. *Shih-li* (1908), 193/4b, a government decision of 1742.

50. *Hu-pu* (1791), 32/1a. See also Lu Lien-tching, *Les greniers publics,* p. 155.

51. *Shih-li* (1908), 193/5b. The governor in question was T'ao Chu.

52. Ho Ch'ang-ling (1785-1848), *Tsou-i,* 5/58a-59b and 7/15a-16a.

53. *Shih-li* (1908), 193/5b.

54. *Ibid.*

55. *Sui-shu,* 24/9a, an edict of 595 (K'ai-huang 15, 2nd month): "The original purpose of *i-ts'ang* was limited to providing against flood and drought. The people, having no consideration for long-range need, lightly depleted [the reserves], which were eventually exhausted."

56. For example, by Fang Kuan-ch'eng, governor-general of Chihli in the middle of the eighteenth century, and T'ao Chu, governor of Anhwei in the 1820's. See Tai Ch'ao-ch'en, *Hsüeh-shih lu,* 7/27a; *Shih-li* (1908), 193/5b.

57. See note 40, Lu Lien-tching, *Les greniers publics,* p. 129, wrote: "Les greniers communaux des Ts'ing furent créés en même temps que les greniers d'équilibre constant." This statement would be more accurate if "les greniers de bienfaissance" replaced "les greniers d'équilibre constant."

58. *Shih-li* (1908), 193/1a-4a, outlines the measures concerning *she-ts'ang* adopted by the government between 1703 and 1883. Ch'en Hung-mou, *Ou-ts'un kao, chüan* 13, *passim,* narrates his efforts made in Kiangsi, Shensi, Hupeh, Honan, Fukien, Hunan, Kiangsu, Kwangtung, and Kwangsi, in the middle of the eighteenth century.

59. *Shih-li* (1908), 193/1a.

60. *Ibid.,* another edict, dated 1703.

61. *Hu-pu* (1791), 30/1a. "The gentry, scholars, and common people" is a translation of *shen chin shih min* in the original text.

62. *Shih-li* (1908), 193/1a.

63. *Ibid.,* 193/4a.

64. *Liu-pu ch'u-fen tse-li* (1877), 27/43a.

65. *Shih-li* (1908), 193/3b. This policy was reiterated in 1876 by the imperial government in a reply to the memorial of Pao Yüan-shen, governor of Shansi. Li Tz'u-ming, *Jih-chi,* vi, "Ting chi," 2, 89b, 1876 (Kuang-hsü 2, 8th month, 9th day).

66. *Hu-pu* (1791), 30/3a-b; *Shih-li* (1908), 193/1b and 4a; *Tsou-i,* 53/11b-12a, quoting a memorial submitted by Fu-ming-an. In provinces where managers were locally nominated a grain bonus was sometimes given them; for instance, in Ho-

nan and Fukien, as indicated in *Tsou-i*, 50/11b, which quotes T'u-erh-ping-ah's memorial of 1756, when he was serving as governor of Hunan.

67. *Hu-pu* (1791), 30/3b-4a, and *Liu-pu ch'u-fen tse-li*, 27/43a-b. The Yung-cheng emperor said in an edict of 1729: "Officials of Shensi province are not aware that this grain [stored in *she-ts'ang*] is originally from the people's resources." He evidently forgot that the grain reserve stored in the *she-ts'ang* of Shensi came from purchases made with government funds (specifically, from the *hao-hsien)*, and not from contributions as in most other provinces. See *Shih-li* (1908), 193/4b.

68. *Hu-pu* (1791), 31/5a.

69. *Ibid.*, 30/15a.

70. *Ibid.*, 30/6a-b; *Ch'ing t'ung-tien*, 13/2097; *Tsou-i*, 38/21a.

71. *Hu-pu* (1791), 30/7a-8b.

72. *Ibid.*, 30/15a-b. Yang Ching-jen, *Ch'ou-chi pien*, 30/20b-24a, discusses the *she-ts'ang* and *i-ts'ang* of the Ch'ing dynasty.

73. *K'ang-chi lu*, 2/19a; Yü Shen, *Huang-cheng ts'ung-shu*, *chüan* 10, *shang*, p. 1b.

74. *Shih-li* (1908), 191/3a.

75. *Yen-ch'ing* (1880), 5/16b-17a.

76. *Wei chou* (1877), 6/5b.

77. *Ibid.*, 6/6a-b; cf. *chüan shou*, p. 18b.

78. *Ibid.*, 6/5b.

79. *Han-tan* (1933), 2/11b-12a.

80. *Ch'i-fu* (1884), 103/1a-49a, and 104/1a-38b.

81. *Shan-tung* (1915), *chüan* 84. Cf. *T'eng hsien* (1846), 5/4b.

82. *Feng-chen* (1881), *chüan* 3.

83. *I-ch'eng* (1929), 11/1b-3a.

84. *T'ung-kuan* (1944), 14/1a-b.

85. *Lu-i* (1896), 3/8a-b.

86. *Sui chou* (1892), 9/116a-117b.

87. *Hsing-kuo* (1889), 6/6b. See also 6/8a-b, for regulations governing *she-ts'ang* of this locality.

88. *Hu-nan* (1885), 55/1413-23.

89. *Tao chou* (1878), 3/19a.

90. *Pa-ling* (1891), 15/1b-2a.

91. *Tz'u-li* (1896), 4/4b.

92. *Ibid.* According to *Hsiang-hsiang* (1874), 3/9a-b, the original *she-ts'ang* and *i-ts'ang* located in various places in Hsiang-hsiang Hsien (home district of Tseng Kuo-fan) had disappeared long before this edition of the local gazetteer was compiled. In the 1860's, however, local inhabitants rebuilt a few of the *i-ts'ang* in the countryside.

93. *Lu-chou* (1885), 16/1a-8a.

94. *Chien-ch'ang* (1907), 8/3b.

95. *Hang-chou* (1898), *chüan* 69, *passim*.

96. *Chiang-ning* (1880), 2/24a-26b.

97. *Hui-chou* (1881), 18/8b.

98. *Ling-shan* (1914), 10/125a-26b.

99. *Ch'ing-yüan* (1880), 5/20b-21b.

100. *Tung-kuan* (1911), 19/1a-b and 19/5b.

101. *Lu-chou* (1882), 5/5a-b.

102. *Fu-shun*(1931), 2/2a-7a. "*Chi-ts'ang* [reserve granaries] were first built in Kuang-hsü 6 [1880] by order of Ting [Pao-chen], governor of Szechwan. One

per cent of the grain received by [landowners as rent], scholars and common people alike, was collected annually for three years [and stored in these granaries]. In the spring and summer of each year [the grain] was loaned to peasants who repaid their loans in the autumn with an interest charge of 10 per cent. In Kuang-hsü 25 [1899] another collection was made by order." *Ibid.*, 2/26a. The compiler of this gazetteer commented that records did not agree as to the amounts of the grain stored. He tried in 1925 to secure the original documents kept by the local government, but he was shown only copies made from them.

103. *Chiang-ching* (1924), 5/59a-60a.

104. *Chen-hsiung* (1887), 3/42a, affords an example. It is said that in Chen-hsiung Chou (Yunnan) "the *ch'ang-p'ing* and *she-ts'ang* originally built in various places went out of existence during Chia-ch'ing times," i.e., early in the nineteenth century. *Li-p'ing* (1891), *chüan* 3, *shang*, p. 42b, contains information concerning the various localities in Li-p'ing Fu (Kweichow) which is summarized in Table 34:

TABLE 34

RESERVES IN LI-P'ING FU

Locality	Ch'ang-p'ing	I-ts'ang	She-ts'ang
Li-p'ing Fu	Reserve in 1890: 8,480 *shih*	Reserve in 1890: 9,619 *shih*	-
K'ai-t'ai Hsien	Original reserve of 22,055 *shih* exhausted	All abandoned	-
Ku-chou T'ing	All abandoned	Mostly abandoned	Abandoned
Yung-ts'ung Hsien	All reserve disappeared	Reserve in 1890 2,409 *shih*	Reserve disappeared

Yung-ning (1894), 4/5a, describes the conditions in Yung-ning Chou (Kweichow) in these words: "The *i-ts'ang* [i.e., *she-ts'ang*] in this *chou* were formerly built in the various rural areas. After repeated devastations of war not a single grain of rice was left. When peace was restored and the *chou* city walls were reconstructed, contributions were made during the terms [of a number of magistrates], but the amount [of grain received] was small. . . . At present the actual reserve totals less than 800 *shih*. "

105. Gray, *China* (1878), II, 57-58. The writer made no distinction between the various types of local granaries.

106. *Tsou-i*, 58/4a. The acting governor concerned was Li Hu.

107. Wang Jen-k'an (1849-93), *I-shu*, 7/6a and 8a.

108. *Tsou-i*, 57/4b, a memorial submitted by Liang-ch'ing, provincial treasurer of Kweichow. The same practice in slightly different forms was reported in other provinces. See, for example, *Mu-lin shu*, 2/55a-56a, quoting a letter by Chou Hsi-p'u *(chin-shih* of 1775 and a magistrate) describing the procedures of procurement for the *ch'ang-p'ing* in Yung-shun (Hunan), which worked a hardship on people of modest means as well as on wealthy households.

109. *Liu-pu ch'u-fen tse-li* (1877), 27/36a.

110. *Tsou-i, hsü-pien*, 4/2b. The memorial was submitted by Sung Chu, a supervising censor.

111. *Pa-ling* (1891), 15/3a, an essay written by Wu Min-shu, a friend of Tseng

Kuo-fan's. Wu attained *chü-jen* in 1832 and served afterwards as educational official of Liu-yang Hsien.

112. *Shih-li* (1908), 191/1a-2a. ·

113. Huang Liu-hung, *Fu-hui*, 27/6b.

114. *Shih-li* (1908), 189/1b. That such practices were not stopped is evident from a memorial submitted by Li Tien-t'u, governor of Fukien (1802-6), which reads in part: "As time passes evil practices grow. Even in the years when there is no need for relief, the grain reserve is taken out on the pretext of replacing the old with the new crop, or of food shortage during the 'green-yellow gap.' The purpose is to facilitate defalcation and fraud. When grain is taken out of the storehouses, the amounts dispensed [to borrowers] fall short of the quantities specified; but when repayments are made, more than is due [from the borrowers] is exacted. . . . Consequently, honest people who anticipate the trouble and loss involved in borrowing grain and repaying it usually avoid [the *ch'ang-p'ing* granaries]." Quoted in *Mu-lin shu*, 3/21b.

115. Émile Bard, *Chinese Life in Town and Country* (1905), pp, 91-92.

116. Tai Ch'ao-ch'en, *Hsüeh-shih lu*, 2/30a-b, quoting Li Kuang-ti (1642-1718), governor of Chihli.

117. Chao Ju-yü's memorial, quoted in Yü Shen, "She-ts'ang k'ao, " in *Huang-cheng ts'ung-shu*, chüan 10, *shang*, p. 1a, and in *K'ang-chi lu*, 2/19b. Chu Hsi held the same opinion: "What were known in Sui and T'ang times as *she-ts'ang* represented a fine institution which approached that of the ancients. But at present all such [granaries] have fallen into desuetude. Only *ch'ang-p'ing* and *i-ts'ang* remain to carry on the principles that anciently prevailed. The reserves of these [granaries], however, are all kept in [the cities of] *chou* and *hsien*. They benefit only urban loafers; people who live in distant hills and valleys, who work hard in farming and transport [their produce] to faraway places, do not receive any [help], even though they are starving and nearing death. Moreover, the regulations governing the operation [of these granaries] are altogether too minute, so much so that officials who are overcautious are afraid to do too much, lest they should inadvertently break some laws; they choose to watch the people starve and refuse to take out the grain reserves. They usually keep the granaries lockfast, handing them over to their successors, making no inspection for several tens of years. When it becomes necessary and the storehouses are opened, [the grain] has turned into a heap of dust, no longer suitable for food." "Ts'ung-an she-ts'ang chi, " quoted in *K'ang-chi lu*, 4/59a.

118. See, for example, *Fu-shan* (1924), 7/1a-4a.

119. *Tsou-i*, 42/1a-3a, Ch'en Hung-mou's memorial, 1745.

120. *Lu-lung* (1931), 21/3a-b.

121. Huang Chün-tsai, "Chin-hu lang-mo, " in *Chin-hu ch'i-mo*, 5/4b-5a, relates the notorious "relief case of Shan-yang" *(ca.* 1860).

122. Wang Ch'ing-yün, *Chi-cheng*, 1/7a-b.

123. *Hu-pu* (1791), 113/1a; *Liu-pu ch'u-fen tse-li* (1877), 24/4a; *Ch'ing t'ung-k'ao*, 69/5485. According to Ch'en Hung-mou, writing in the late eighteenth century, *kung-sheng* and *chien-sheng* were not ordinarily entitled to relief. They could receive succor as ordinary people only when they became destitute late in life. See Tai Ch'ao-ch'en, *Hsüeh-shih lu*, 9/15a.

124. *Ibid.*, 9/14b-15a. According to *Ch'ing hsü t'ung-k'ao*, 71/5511, the practice authorized by the imperial government was for scholars of limited means to receive assistance from funds and grain reserves accrued from the "school land" of the various provinces. They were precluded from receiving the relief

generally given to destitute commoners. The amounts of money and grain from the school land, however, were small. Hence in 1738 (Ch'ien-lung 3), the emperor ordered governors-general, governors, and provincial educational authorities to instruct local educational officials to prepare lists of destitute scholars so that special relief might be given them fom "public funds."

125. Yü Pao-hsüan, *Hsü-ai wen-pien*, 18/17b-18a. The governor was Fu-jun. See also *Chou-hsien shih-i*, p. 51b, for "selling relief." Gross inequity in deferment of, and exemption from, taxes was sometimes reported. In an essay written by T'ang Ch'en, a late nineteenth-century *chü-jen*, it is said: "When deferment or exemption was granted by the imperial court on occasions of imperial celebration or in the event of serious flood or drought, the transcribed documents invariably ran to thousands of words. The emperor's edict, the decision of the board [i.e., the *Hu-pu*], and the memorials of the governor-general and governor, all contained much verbiage. Illiterate people could not comprehend their meaning, and even those who could read a little were completely at a loss after perusing a few lines. One or two copies of these documents usually had to be posted on the city gates or displayed along main streets. In secluded villages no one had ever seen any of them." *Wei-yen* (1890), 2/26b-27a; cf. *ibid.*, 17/11b. *Ch'ing t'ung-k'ao*, 3/7522, gives the following memorial submitted by Tso Tsung-t'ang in 1865, when he was governor of Chekiang, which reads in part: "In Tao-kuang *kuei-wei* [1823] and again in *hsin-mao* [1831], serious floods occurred [in this province]. . . . Deferment and exemption were repeatedly granted. But humble people failed to receive material benefits, even though the imperial court had showered special favors upon them. For tax-paying households in each district are very numerous. Those that were entitled to deferment or exemption as a result of calamities were reported [to the government] by yamen clerks in charge of the registers, [who were free to include or exclude any person as they wished]. Prominent families and big clans were able to obtain deferment or exemption even though their harvests were good. Commoners and small taxpayers sometimes had to pay the full amounts even though they had suffered losses of crops."

126. *Shih-li* (1908), 189/6a.

127. *Ling-shan* (1914), 10/126a, gives an example.

128. *Tsou-i*, 8/4a.

129. Richard H. Tawney, *Land and Labor in China* (1932), p. 73.

130. *Pa-ling* (1891), 15/2a.

131. *Shih-li* (1908), 189/3a and 6a, and 192/2b.

132. For example, the case of Fukien in 1726, cited above. See also *Shih-li* (1908), 192/6a. A curious instance of liquidating local granaries was reported in Chihli in 1869. According to Weng T'ung-ho, *Jih-chi*, 9/12b-13a, *chi-ssu* (T'ung-chih 8), 2nd month, 16th day, a *chin-shih* of Kuang-p'ing Hsien wrote a letter to Wo-jen, grand secretary, saying that the magistrate had presented granary buildings to "barbarians," who were to use the sites to build churches.

133. *Hsing-kuo* (1889), 6/8a.

134. Ting Jih-ch'ang, *Kung-tu*, 45/12a.

135. Wang Hui-tsu, *Hsü-shuo*, p. 79a.

136. *Fu-shan* (1924), 7/4b-5a.

137. Wang Hui-tsu, *Hsü-shuo*, p. 79a.

138. *Tsou-i*, 42/15a, a memorial submitted by Yen Ssu-shen, 1745.

139. *Shih-li* (1908), 193/3b, an edict dated Yung-cheng 7.

140. *Ibid.*, an edict dated Chia-ch'ing 4.

141. *Pa-ling* (1891), 15/3a, quoting Wu Min-shu, a *chü-jen* of 1832, and junior educational official of Liu-yang Hsien (Hunan).

142. Pai Ching-wei, *Chi*, 1/12a-17b. It may be noted that official management of *ch'ang-p'ing* granaries produced just as many fraudulent practices. According to Chang Shih-ch'eng (1762-1830), writing in 1820, "*Chou* and *hsien* magistrates often take the grain from local granaries and use it for food in their yamens. Some of them even take advantage of routine sale or loan transactions to dispose of more grain than is authorized in order to realize illegal profits. . . . For such unauthorized sale brings high prices, and when they hand over [the grain reserve to their successors] they may convert the grain into money equivalents, at the rate of 0.60 tael per *shih* [which is far below the market price]. As a result, this practice is widely copied by others." *Mu-lin shu* (1868), 10/50b-51a.

143. Wang Ch'ing-yün, *Chi-cheng*, 4/29b-34a.

144. Tai Chao-ch'en, *Hsüeh-shih lu*, 5/27b-38a. "Gentry, scholar, or elder" is a translation of *shen chin shih min* in the original text. Cf. *Hsin-ning* (1893), 12/20b-23a.

145. Yü Shen, *Huang-cheng ts'ung-shu*, *chüan* 10, *hsia*, p. 3a-b, quoting Shen Lan-hsien.

146. *Tsou-i*, 50/10b. The official quoted was T'u-erh-ping-ah, governor of Hunan.

147. *Ibid.*, 53/11b; the writer of the memorial quoted was Fu-ming-an, governor of Kiangsi.

148. Wang Hui-tsu, *Hsü-shuo*, p. 10. Yamen underlings sometimes took advantage of the situation to extort money from timid landowners. Yüan Mei (1716-98), magistrate of several districts in Kiangsu in the 1740's made this observation: "Once *she-chang* [managers of *she-ts'ang*] come into contact with the yamen, they are overwhelmed by the expenses incurred. Wealthy householders prefer to bribe yamen clerks for exemption [from nomination to serve as managers]. Local agents, knowing this, deliberately name a large number of persons in order to exact bribes from them. Thus *she-ts'ang* do not give a jot of benefit to poor people but become a heavy burden on wealthy ones." *Mu-lin shu* (1868), 10/25a.

149. Wang Hsien-ch'ien, *Tung-hua lu*, K'ang-hsi, 108/3b-4a. *Ch'ing shih-lu* does not include this episode. Li Kuang-ti, whom the emperor mentioned in this edict, served as director of education of Chihli in 1690 and again in 1696-98; as governor of the same province, 1699-1705; and as grand secretary, 1705-18. Chang Po-hsing was acting superintendent of government granaries around 1716, was engaged in relief work for the Shun-t'ien and Yung-p'ing prefectures shortly afterward, and became president of the *Li-pu* (Board of Ceremonies) in 1723.

150. Wang Ch'ing-yün, *Chi-cheng*, 4/26a-30a, gives the following dates and actions:

1679 (K'ang-hsi 18), imperial edict authorizing establishment of *she-ts'ang* in villages and *i-ts'ang* in markets and towns.

1703 (K'ang-hsi 42), edict authorizing establishment of *she-ts'ang* in Chihli province.

1711 (K'ang-hsi 50), government order exempting contributors of grain to *she-ts'ang* from *i* (labor service imposts).

1721 (K'ang-hsi 60), imperial edict declaring that *she-ts'ang* lacked success.

Curiously, Wang Ch'ing-yün omits mention of the edict of K'ang-hsi 59 (1720), called forth by Chu Shih's petition. Cf. *Ch'ing-shih kao*, "Shih-huo," 2/20a-22a.

151. The emperor challenged Chu Shih to operate the *she-ts'ang* in Shansi and ordered him to remain there to carry out his own proposal. Chu Shih then admitted his error in judgment and begged to return to the imperial capital. The emperor, however, was inexorable. The reason for the emperor's action was not stated. Wang Hsien-ch'ien, *Tung-hua lu*, K'ang-hsi 59, 9th month, 108/6b-7a.

152. *Tsou-i*, 42/1b. Ch'en Hung-mou was then governor of Shensi; the memorial was submitted jointly with Ch'ing-fu, governor-general of Ch'uan-Shen.

153. *Ibid.*, 42/14b.

154. *Ibid.*, 42/15a.

155. *Ibid.*, 58/6b.

156. *Ibid.*, 58/5a.

157. See notes 139 and 140.

158. *Fu-chien* (1871), 51/18b-19a.

159. Quoted in *K'ang-chi lu*, 4/57b-59a.

160. Yü Shen, *Huang-cheng ts'ung-shu*, *chüan* 10, *shang*, records the following instances: Chin-hua Hsien (Chekiang), P'an-shih *she-ts'ang*, established in 1175; Chien-yang Hsien (Fukien), Ch'ang-t'an *she-ts'ang*, established in 1184; *she-ts'ang* of Kuan-ts'e Hsien (Fukien), date not specified; *she-ts'ang* of I-hsing Hsien (Kiangsu), established in 1194; Nan-ch'eng Hsien (Kiangsi), Wu-shih *she-ts'ang*, established in 1194.

161. Quoted in *K'ang-chi lu*, 2/20a-b.

162. Gray, *China* (1878), II, 58.

163. Wei Hsi, an essay on methods of relief, quoted in Yü Shen, *Huang-cheng ts'ung-shu*, 7/1b. Wei Hsi, a native of Kiangsi, was nominated for *Po-hsüeh hung-tz'u* in 1679 but refused to accept the honor.

164. *Hsing-kuo* (1889), 6/8a, local regulations governing *she-ts'ang*, drawn up in 1879.

165. Yü Shen, *op. cit.*, *chüan* 10, *shang*, p. 14b.

166. *Nan-hai* (1910), 6/9a-10a; *Fu-shan* (1924), 7/1b-5a; *Ju-lin* (1883), 4/3b-7b.

167. Ch'en Hung-mou, *Ou-ts'un kao*, *chüan* 13, *passim*, describing his plans and methods of operating *she-ts'ang* in Kiangsi, Kiangsu, Fukien, Kwangtung, Kwangsi, Hunan, Hupeh, Honan, Shensi, and Shansi, when he was governor of these provinces in 1741-63.

168. Wang Jen-k'an, *I-shu*, 7/107a-108b.

169. Pai Ching-wei, *Chi*, 2/22a-25a.

170. *Ibid.*, 1/14a-b.

171. *Fu-shan* (1924), *chüan* 14, "Jen-wu," sec. 6, p. 38b.

172. *Ling-shan* (1914), 10/126b.

173. Wang Ch'ing-yün, *Chi-cheng*, 4/30a.

174. Wang Hui-tsu, writing in the 1790's summarizes the situation in these words: "With the lapse of time the matter goes into the hands of yamen underlings, and [the granaries] become an empty name and a source of trouble. At first the funds [for purchasing the grain] were kept in the treasuries [of local yamen]; finally even these funds have disappeared. It has become increasingly difficult to speak of any granary system." *I-shuo*, p. 56a. Even the imperial granaries were not free from graft or mismanagement. A deficiency of over 95, 000 *shih* caused by spoilage and fraud was discovered at one of the granaries (Nan-hsin ts'ang) and reported to the emperor early in 1879. (See two imperial edicts con-

cerning the matter quoted in Li Tz'u-ming, *Jih-chi*, vi, "Kuei chi, " 2d ser.,
pp. 69a-b and 83b.) A shortage of almost 170, 000 *shih* was reported in the metropolitan granaries in 1890. See Weng T'ung-ho (president of *Hu-pu*), *Jih-chi*,
29/65a-72a and 30/13a-21a. These incidents were recorded in the *North China
Herald*, quoted by Harold C. Hinton, *The Grain Tribute System* (1956), pp. 97-98.

175. *Ch'ing-shih kao*, "Shih-huo, " 2/22a.

176. *Ibid.; Shih-li* (1908), 191/3a. In a serious famine the effectiveness of any
local granaries that existed in this period was negligible. In the great famine
occurring in Shensi at the turn of the century, for example, relief work was
financed by emergency contributions and "sale of degrees." Francis H. Nichols,
Through Hidden Shensi (1902), pp. 231-32.

177. Walter H. Mallory, *China, Land of Famine* (1926), pp. 65-68: "One of
the first results of the overthrow of the Manchu regime . . . was the abolition
of the public granaries maintained in the provinces. . . . It was said that the contents of the granaries were sold in 1912 in order to 'defray the expenses of the
revolution'; but the granaries have not been restocked by the republican government, and this most important system is now abandoned. . . . Even before the
revolution the effectiveness of the granary system began to fall off, owing to
official corruption." Mallory oversimplified the matter.

178. *Yung hsien* (1897), 10/1b-2a.

179. See Chu Co-Ching, "Climatic Pulsations during Historic Times in China, "
Geographic Review XVI (1920), 274-82, discussing natural calamities from the
first century to 1900; Alexander Hosie, "Droughts in China, A. D. 620-1643, "
Journal of the Royal Asiatic Society, North China Branch, N. S. XII (1878), 51-
89; Tawney, *Land and Labor in China*, pp. 75-76, quoting Hosie's article mentioned above; and Mallory, *China, Land of Famine*, pp. 45-59.

180. Mallory, *China, Land of Famine*, p. 15: "The density of population in
China as a whole is only about 238 to the square mile. This figure, however,
does not show the conditions of the great mass of the people. Half of the total
population of China occupies but a quarter of the total area of the country." *Ibid.*,
p. 17: "This overcrowding on the land makes impossible the collection of any
reserve of foodstuffs. A good crop does not result in a surplus of grain, but
merely provides the people for a short time with a better diet." Mallory spoke
of conditions in the first decades of the twentieth century; to a slightly lesser
extent what he said was true of the nineteenth century also.

181. *Ibid.*, pp. 84-85: "In 1734, according to Professor E. H. Parker's *China*
[London, 1901, p. 27], there were 26, 500, 000 [the figure given by Parker is actually 25, 500, 000] households in all China. If we allow five souls to a household,
this would give us a total population of 130, 000, 000. . . . Professor Parker
goes on to say that the population of China cannot at any time have much exceeded
100, 000, 000 until the beginning of the eighteenth century. By the year 1762 it
had over-topped 200, 000, 000, doubling itself during the next century. This is a
slower rate of increase than the present average for the world." Parker's estimates need not be accurate, but they serve to indicate the general trend.

182. Mallory, *China, Land of Famine*, p. 5. Cf. Tawney, *Land and Labor in
China*, p. 76: "If the meaning of the word [famine] is a shortage of food on a
scale sufficient to cause widespread starvation, then there are parts of the country from which famine is rarely absent." In localities where farming was exceptionally productive, it was of course less difficult to raise a grain reserve,
but there was no guarantee that such a reserve would prove useful. This, for
example, was said of Szechwan early in the nineteenth century: "The original
purpose of making contributions to institute charity farms and to store the grain

thus accrued as reserves was to give relief to destitute people in years of famine. But years of bad harvest are rare in Szechwan. Prior to Tao-kuang 4 [1824] such grain reserves had already amounted to over 200,000 *[shih]*. . . . Upon investigation [it appears that] . . . the regulations governing *she-ts'ang* procedures of borrowing or selling [the grain] are complicated and difficult of application; these merely give rise to opportunities for fraud." Liu Heng, *Yung-yen*, pp. 72a-b. The writer proposed that part of the grain reserves collected after 1825 (Tao-kuang 5) be used for other purposes. *Ibid.*, pp. 73a-74b.

183. Tawney, *Land and Labor in China*, p. 73, quoting John L. Buck.

184. As climatic and social conditions differed in various parts of the empire, the local granary system might prove workable in one region but not in another. Huang K'o-jun, a *chin-shih* of 1739, offered this interesting opinion: "Grain reserves cannot be of much use in the south because the climate is warm and humid, and the grain cannot keep for long. Moreover, the population is dense and the people are inclined to deception. . . . Grain stored in granaries in the north can keep for more than ten years without spoiling. The inhabitants there are simple and honest, and are known to the *pao-chia* and *li-chia* agents. Few of them fail to repay [the grain they have borrowed]." Quoted in *Mu-lin shu* (1868), 4/1a-b. This writer may have been somewhat too optimistic concerning the conditions in North China, but his observations concerning climatic differences are correct. Climate affected the granary system in another way. In regions where nature was more kindly it was easier to realize grain reserves, but ironically, the need for relief there was less urgent than in localities where reserves were difficult to procure. See Liu Heng's remarks concerning Szechwan, quoted in note 182 above.

185. *Ming-shih*, 79/7b.

186. *Mien-yang* (1894), *chüan* 4, "Shih-huo," p. 66b.

187. This document is given in Hsiao I-shan, *T'ai-p'ing t'ien-kuo ts'ung-shu*, 1st. ser., 4/1b-2a, and Hsiang Ta, *T'ai-p'ing t'ien-kuo tzu-liao*, I, 319 ff.

Chapter 6

1. For a summary of actions taken from Shun-chih to Hsüan-t'ung times, see *Ch'ing t'ung-k'ao* (1936), *chüan* 73, and *Ch'ing hsü t'ung-k'ao* (1936), *chüan* 98. An outstanding instance of canonizing, that of Lu Lung-ch'i in 1724, is given in *Ch'ing t'ung-k'ao*, 74/5544.

2. A list of such works is given in *Shih-li* (1908), 32/2b-3a.

3. James Legge's phrase, *China Review*, VI (1878), 147.

4. See Hellmut Wilhelm's article, "The Po-hsüeh hung-ju Examinations of 1679," *Journal of American Oriental Society*, LXXI (1951), 60-66.

5. *Hsüeh-cheng* (1810), 9/1a, indicates that this took place in 1652 (Shun-chih 9).

6. *Ibid.*

7. *Ibid.*, 9/2a-b.

8. *Ibid.*, 9/4a.

9. *Ibid.*, 9/4b; *Shih-li* (1908), 397/9a; Wu Yung-kuang, *Wu-hsüeh lu* (1870), 3/1a-5a. Local gazetteers usually contain information concerning the lecture meetings; e.g., *Yung-chou* (1867), *chüan* 4, *shang*, p. 50a; *Tung-kuan* (1921), 25/2a-b; and *En-p'ing* (1934), 11/5b. According to the last-mentioned source, "The *yüeh-cheng* [of each locality] was selected from elderly and virtuous persons with *chü-jen*, *kung-sheng*, and *sheng-yüan* status. Three or four *chih-yüeh* were selected from honest commoners who serve by turns. . . . The *chih-yüeh* who was on duty [for the current meeting] read aloud the Amplified Instructions . . .; the *yüeh-cheng* then explained the meaning of the passages read. . . .

Those who did not understand were permitted to ask questions." William E. Geil, *Yankee on the Yangtze* (1904), pp. 80-83, contains an account of the origin of the lecture meetings and a description of the proceedings.

10. For example, *Yen-chou* (1883), 5/3b, *"Shen-ming t'ing:* . . . Rebuilt by Liang Hao-jan, the prefect *[ca.* 1668]; now in ruins."

11. *Hsüeh-cheng* (1810), 9/11a-b, and *Shih-li* (1908), 398/2b. According to the former source, these pavilions had generally fallen into desuetude by 1744. Some of them were dilapidated through want of repair, while others were appropriated by yamen runners or local bullies for private use. At that time the government ordered provincial officials to restore as many of these structures as was economical, and to set up wooden bulletin boards wherever restoration was impossible or no pavilions had originally been built.

12. *Shih-li* (1809), 398/1a-2b; *Hsüeh-cheng* (1810), 9/5a-b and 10b; *Sheng-hsün,* Kao-tsung, 262/9b-11a.

13. *Hsüeh-cheng* (1810), 9/13a-b.

14. *Sheng-hsün,* Hsüan-tsung, 78/11a, 17a, and 28a, giving edicts of 1831, 1835, and 1839.

15. *En-p'ing* (1934), 14/18a, quoting the edicts of 1862 and 1865.

16. *Shih-li* (1908), 397/1a, gives the text.

17. The text is given in *Hsüeh-cheng* and in a number of local gazetteers. English translations of this text were made by George T. Staunton in 1812, in his *Miscellaneous Notices* (1822), pp. 1-56, together with the first nine essays of the Amplified Instructions; by William C. Milne, in *Sacred Edict of K'anghi* (1870), quoted by Adele M. Fielde in her *Pagoda Shadows* (1884), pp. 274-76; by Legge in his four lectures on "Imperial Confucianism," *China Review,* VI (1877-78), 147-58, 223-35, 299-310, and 363-74; and by Geil, *Yankee on the Yangtze,* p. 81. A. Théophile Piry in 1876 made a French translation from the Chinese text which was published with the Chinese text, including the Amplified Instructions, in *Le saint édit* (London, 1879).

18. T'ung Kuo-ch'i, governor of Fukien, Kiangsi, and Chekiang between 1653 and 1660, unwittingly let the cat out of the bag when he remarked that "of all the measures to eradicate banditry none are better than the *hsiang-yüeh* which encourages good conduct, and the *pao-chia* which suppresses robbery." An undated memorial quoted Ho Ch'ang-ling, *Wen-pien,* 75/16a.

19. The full text is given in *Shih-li* (1908), 397/1b-8b. The same emperor produced a trilingual edition of this work, including Chinese, Manchu, and Mongolian texts.

20. Legge's translation, *China Review,* VI, 234.

21. After a feast celebrating the sixtieth birthday anniversary (1713), to which a number of elderly men in Chihli province were invited, the K'ang-hsi emperor issued an edict urging these persons to instruct and encourage their neighbors to practice filial and fraternal duties. This edict was printed and copies were distributed to all provinces as an additional text for the semimonthly lectures. *Hsüeh-cheng* (1810), 9/3b.

22. Governors-general and governors were ordered in 1746 to prepare brief accounts of "fine deeds," including performance of filial and fraternal duties, showing respect to superiors, paying due regard to station and duties, to be written in simple language and exhibited in all villages, large and small. The *hsiang-yüeh* lecturers were required to explain these texts at the end of the regular meetings. *Hsüeh-cheng* (1810), 9/12b.

23. *Ch'uan-shan yao-yen* (Essential Words to Exhort Goodness), written by the Shun-chih emperor, was added in 1891.

24. *Hsüeh-cheng* (1810), 9/5b-6a.

25. *Shih-li* (1908), 298/2b.

26. *Hsüeh-cheng* (1810), 9/11b.

27. *Ibid.*, 9/13b-14a.

28. *Shih-li* (1908), 298/3a. Cf. an edict issued in the same year (1758), prohibiting unauthorized sacrifices and superstitious practices, quoted in the same place.

29. *Hsüeh-cheng* (1810), 13/1b.

30. *Shih-li* (1908), 400/3a, gives the text.

31. *Ibid.*, 400/3b. See also *Tung-kuan* (1921), 35/3a and 12b, and *En-p'ing* (1934), 14/7a.

32. For example, an edict dated 1877 (Kuang-hsü 3) says in reply to a memorial proposing that lectures on the Sacred Edict be conducted as a measure to counteract the rampancy of "heretical teachings" in Kiangsu, Chekiang, and other provinces: "Lectures expounding the Amplified Instructions are clearly provided for in the statutes. We hereby order the prefect of Shun-t'ien Fu, censors in charge of the Five City Areas, governors-general, governors, and directors of studies in the provinces to direct officials and the gentry [under their respective jurisdictions] to conduct [the lectures] in earnest, tolerating not even the slightest slackening [in their effort]." Quoted in Li Tz'u-ming, *Jih-chi*, vi, "Wu-chi," 2d ser., 81a. The Ch'ing rulers sometimes sought to suppress "false doctrines" by persuasion in general terms, without referring to Maxim 7. For example, when the imperial government decided to stop the inhabitants of Honan province from practicing boxing, for fear that the skill thus acquired might encourage them to join subversive religious societies, it instructed local officials to explain to townsfolk and villagers who were present in the lecture meetings the legal provisions concerning such matters, in addition to the text of the edict of 1727. *Hsüeh-cheng* (1810), 9/9b-10a. The edict of 1727 (Yung-cheng 5) is given in *Sheng-hsün,* Shih-tsung, 26/18b.

33. In a report submitted by the *Li-pu* (Board of Rites) in 1785 (Ch'ien-lung 50) it was said that "the original purpose of lecturing on the Amplified Instructions . . . is to influence and to convert . . . ignorant villagers who are devoid of knowledge and unacquainted with the proprieties, ceremonies, laws, and regulations." *Hsüeh-cheng* (1810), 9/14b.

34. *Shih-li* (1908), 397/1b.

35. *Nan-hai* (1910), 2/45a.

36. A government decision made in 1746 (Ch'ien-lung 11), given in *Hsüeh-cheng* (1810), 9/12a, and *Shih-li* (1908), 398/2b.

37. *Hsüeh-cheng* (1810), 9/14a-b, and *Shih-li* (1908), 398/3a.

38. *Hsüeh-cheng* (1810), 9/15a.

39. Recommendations submitted by the *Li-pu* in 1785 (Ch'ien-lung 50) and 1808 (Chia-ch'ing 13), given in *Hsüeh-cheng* (1810), 9/14b and 18b-20a.

40. *T'ung-kuan* (1944), 22/2a, and *Po-pai* (1832), 6/1b. According to Meng-ch'eng (1915), 5/8a, these lectures were often given in the *ming-lun t'ang,* a building associated with the local Confucian temple. In all probability this practice obtained in other localities as well.

41. The rationale of this was explained by the imperial government in 1808 in these words: "All youthful scholars have been studying in the *Sheng-yü kuang-hsün* ever since they began to read books in their childhood. They are therefore required to write it from memory when they are admitted to the schools [i.e., when they are granted the *sheng-yüan* status]. The idea is to make them acquaint themselves with it from their childhood days so that they will be deeply steeped in it." The text is given in *Hsüeh-cheng* (1810), 9/9b. Arthur H. Smith,

Village Life (1899), p. 115, and Edward H. Parker, "The Educational Curriculum of the Chinese," *China Review*, IX (1881), 3, may be consulted. A curious incident was recorded in *P'an-yü* (1911), 26/15b. According to the compiler, Fan Feng, a Chinese member of the White Banner in Kwangtung taking the prefectural examinations, felt that he was insulted by an attendant of the examination hall when the latter scolded him for having occupied a wrong booth. Fan requested the commissioner in charge to punish the attendant for his rudeness. Wishing apparently to embarrass Fan, the commissioner ordered him to recite the complete text of the Amplified Instructions, a lengthy document of about 10,000 words. Thereupon the young scholar said: "Sir, since I am going to kneel down and recite it, you will have to kneel down and listen to my recitation." He gave a perfect performance, with the official on his knees. The latter afterwards charged the scholar with disrespect toward superiors and stripped him of his "vestment and button." Sometime later, however, Fan won the admiration of Juan Yüan, governor-general of Liang-kwang (1816-1826), through whose help he was made *fu-kung-sheng* (accessory senior licentiate) by imperial grace.

42. Orita, *Fen-lun*, III, 25. It may be interesting to note that the Sacred Edict and the Amplified Instructions were introduced into premodern Japan. See note 75.

43. Legge, "Imperial Confucianism," *China Review*, VI (1877), 146. Liang occupied this post in 1673-1781. *Sheng-yü hsiang-chieh* (Illustrated Explanations of the Sacred Edict) was a work of twenty *chüan*.

44. *Hsüeh-cheng* (1810), 9/3a.

45. Arthur W. Hummel (ed.), *Eminent Chinese*, I, 329.

46. Legge, *China Review*, VI, 148, quoting from an introduction to Milne's translation of the Sacred Edict, p. xxvi.

47. Huang Liu-hung, *Fu-hui* (1699; 1893 reprint), 25/7a-b.

48. Ho Ch'ang-ling, *Wen-pien*, 74/29a-b.

49. *T'ung-kuan* (1944), 26/9a-10a. The magistrate was Yüan Wen-kuang, appointed to this post in 1763.

50. *Tsou-i* (1936), 65/17b.

51. Wang Hui-tsu (1731-1807), *Hsü-shuo*, p. 84b. *Mu-lin shu* (1868), 6/18a, gives another instance which occurred in the eighteenth century. Wang Chih, a *chin-shih* of 1721, subsequently serving as magistrate of Hsin-hui (Kwangtung), wrote *Shang-yü t'ung-su chieh*, "Popular Explanation of the Imperial Edict," and made the following claim: "Formerly I had developed a method of explaining the Edict, using colloquial language to paraphrase the text of the Amplified Instructions. I ordered the lecturers to preach in the native dialect. Listeners were able to understand and appreciate. . . . Upon arriving at the place where the *hsiang-yüeh* meeting was held I ordered elderly inhabitants over eighty or ninety to sit behind the gentry. All were served tea; but none [of this privileged group of listeners] was permitted to report on public affairs. Commoners were ordered to stand and listen to the *hsiang-yüeh* lectures."

52. *Ch'üeh-shan* (1931), 18/15a-b. The official was Yang Feng-ming, a *chü-jen* of 1844 and a native of Ch'üeh-shan.

53. *Ch'ing-pien* (1899), 4/31a. The magistrate was T'ing Hsi-k'uei.

54. *Yung-chou* (1867), *chüan* 4, *shang*, p. 50b. The magistrate's surname was Tsung; no other information concerning him is given.

55. *Meng-ch'eng* (1915), 5/8a-b. This magistrate is not identified.

56. Ting Jih-ch'ang (1823-1882), *Kung-tu*, 33/9a and 43/10a.

57. *Ibid.*, 29/7b-8a.

58. *Ibid.*, 44/9b.

59. *Wu-hsi* (1881), 6/5b.

60. *Chia-hsing* (1878), 43/79a.

61. *Ju-lin* (1883), 21/21a.

62. *Hsin-i* (1889), *chüan* 3, part 4, pp. 27b-28a.

63. *Hua hsien* (1924), 9/8a. Sung earned his *chü-jen* status in 1808.

64. *Po-pai* (1832), 12/10b. See also 13/1b-2a, where the lecture meeting locally held is described.

65. Lung Ch'i-jui (1814-58), *Wen-chi*, 4/13a. The magistrate was Lung Kuang-tien, the author's father.

66. *Li-p'ing* (1891), *chüan* 5, *shang*, pp. 91b-92b. The magistrate acted in pursuance of an instruction issued by the provincial authorities.

67. *Ibid.*, *chüan* 5, *shang*, pp. 98a-b. Wang Hui-tsu (1731-1801), *Meng-hen lu*, *chüan hsia*, p. 14a, contains this narrative of the author's experience as the magistrate of Ning-yüan Hsien (Hunan) in 1788: "Hsia-tui Hsiang is located seventy *li* northeast of the *hsien* city. The inhabitants are poor and habitually violent; they are engaged in illegal butchering of oxen used to pull the plough. They do not go to the city unless on some business, and officials have not visited the locality for almost one hundred years. As a result they have become accustomed to resisting tax collection [by force]. In the fourth month when I was inspecting the *pao-chia* I took the opportunity to visit this place. I sent an order ahead of my arrival, requiring the people to assemble [at an appointed place] to listen to a lecture on the Sacred Edict. On the designated day I went there, wearing my official vestment and bringing with me a lecturer who gave the lecture. Those who stood in a circle and listened included every person in the neighborhood. . . . They were amazed at [a procedure which] they had never seen before. Thereupon I explained to them with persuasive words the duty of keeping themselves within the bounds of law, urging them to desist from illegal butchering and to pay their taxes. [I could tell from] their faces that they were favorably impressed. Since that day, whenever any of them came into the city, they presented themselves in my office to show their respect for me. Their unruly ways were gradually mended." Wang Hui-tsu was one of the few magistrates of the Ch'ing period who were noted for their administrative ability and personal integrity.

68. *P'an-yü* (1911), 5/25a. The person chiefly responsible for the undertaking was Su Yüan, a *chü-jen*.

69. *Nan-hai* (1910), 6/12a. The status of Chung Ch'in-p'ing, the person chiefly responsible, was not specified beyond the vague phrase *fu shen* (wealthy gentry).

70. *Fu-shan* (1924), 7/5b-6a. The social status of the promotors, including Ho Hsiang-chen and Liang Yeh-hsien, is not indicated.

71. *Hua hsien* (1924), 9/22b. The person in question was Sung Wei-chang, a *fu-kung-sheng* who purchased a minor official post.

72. *Yang-chiang* (1925), 30/23b-24a.

73. *Tung-kuan* (1911), 67/3a and 7a.

74. *Lin-chang* (1904), 9/21b-22a.

75. A similar system obtained in feudal Japan. K. Asakawa, "Notes on Village Government," *Journal of American Oriental Society*, XXXI (1910), 200-1, describes the Japanese practice in these words: "Oral instructions. Besides the regular oral commands delivered through official channels, some Barons followed the historic customs of China of giving the people of the village moral exhortation through teachers. These were usually Confucian scholars. Sometimes they were sent in circuit through the fief, villagers assembling to receive them and listen to their lectures. In the following quotation will be seen the character of the instruction. In 1835, some dozen representative peasants of the Nagoya

fief, regretting that the custom once in vogue had been discontinued, petitioned that it be revived and said: ' . . . If in plain language and with persistence it were taught year after year how high was the virtue of the founder of the regime [i. e. , the Ieyasu], how great was the benefit of the State and its merciful government, and, as regards our daily conduct, how important it was to be frugal, to practise filial piety towards parents and fraternal respect for elder brothers, and to be diligent in agriculture and not to fall into other occupations, it is certain that, by the grace of benevolent ruler, evil customs would be changed, and all the peasants would adopt simple and sincere manners.'"

76. E.- R. Huc, *Chinese Empire* (1855), I, 355, describing what he observed while traveling in Szechwan and Hupeh provinces in the 1840's.

77. Geil, *Yankee on the Yangtze* (1904), p. 82.

78. Huang Liu-hung, *Fu-hui*, 24/2b. In some localities permanent sites for *hsiang-yüeh* lectures were established. Hsiang-fu Hsien (Honan), for example, had eight regular places for lectures in the rural areas. *Hsiang-fu* (1898), 10/28b.

79. Ts'ai Shen-chih, *Chung-ho* (1941), II, 91, quoting from *Chou-hsien shih-i* (compiled early in the eighteenth century).

80. *Shih-li* (1908), 398/1b.

81. *Ibid.*, 399/2b.

82. *Hsüeh-cheng* (1810), 9/21a.

83. *Shih-li* (1908), 398/3b, and *passim;* 399/5a.

84. *Fu-shan* (1924), 11/7a.

85. *Hsüeh-cheng* (1810), 9/10a, a report of the *Li-pu*, 1740.

86. *Ibid.*, 9/4b, and *Shih-li* (1908), 397/9a.

87. *Yung-chou* (1867), *chüan* 4, *shang*, p. 50b. Yung-chou Fu was in Hunan. See also Orita, *Fen-lun*, III, 25-26, where it is said that the provincial treasurer issued commendatory tablets to *hsiang-yüeh* lecturers, who instructed the inhabitants so effectively that not a single case of assault or murder was reported in the locality for three consecutive years.

88. *Hsin-i* (1889), *chüan* 3, part 4, pp. 27b-28a. The *hsiang-yüeh* regulations adopted in 1825 by Huang An-t'ao, prefect of Kao-chou, required among other things that the local official concerned bring with him two lecturers to expound the text of the Amplified Instructions in the local dialect. No mention was made of the *yüeh-cheng* (head of the *hsiang-yüeh)*.

89. *Fu-shan* (1924), 11/7a. A similar practice was adopted in Nan-hai Hsien (Kwangtung) in 1738.

90. Lecturers in Kiangsu province under the governorship of Ting Jih-ch'ang in the 1860's also received monthly stipends of unspecified amounts. *Kung-tu,* 44/9b.

91. Tai Ch'ao-ch'en, *Hsüeh-shih lu* (1867), 7/4a-b. The writer quoted was Jen Ch'i-yün, a *chin-shih* of 1733.

92. Ho Ch'ang-ling (1785-1848), *Tsou-i*, 5/46b.

93. Shen Yüeh-lin, *So-chi*, in Wang Hsi-ch'i (compiler), *Hsiao-fang-hu-chai yü-ti ts'ung-ch'ao*, series 7, 2/181a.

94. *Hsüeh-cheng* (1810), 9/6a-b, gives the Ch'ien-lung emperor's edict, issued in 1738, enjoining wealthy families not to hoard grain with a view to profiteering. This edict was adopted as a supplementary text for *hsiang-yüeh* lectures.

95. *Sheng-hsün*, Hsüan-tsung, 78/16b.

96. *Chinese Repository*, XX (1851), 53.

97. *Ibid.*, XIX (1850), 568. This declaration was issued by the rebels after they scored a temporary victory in the area lying between Ch'ing-yüan and Ying-te.

98. Wang Shih-t'o (1802-89), *Jih-chi*, 2/19a.

99. *Kuang-chou*(1878), 5/10a-b. The emperor quoted from a memorial submitted by Chang Sheng-tsao, a censor. The *hsiang-yüeh* occasionally afforded a pretext for local fraudulent practices. *Mu-lin shu* (1868), 9/2a-b, for example, quotes Wang Chih, a *chin-shih* of 1721 serving as magistrate of Hsin-hui (Kwangtung), as follows: "When I was in Hsin-hui, the accustomed ways of the inhabitants were the most perverse. . . . Huang Tso-cheng, a *sheng-yüan*, schemed with others to appropriate some land belonging to a member of his clan, using the building of a pavilion for the Sacred Edict as a pretext [for taking the coveted land]. I refused to grant permission. . . . Taking advantage of the fact that the provincial treasurer (Mr. Ma) was about to leave his post as a result of promotion, Huang Tso-cheng petitioned him that since the pavilion was nearing completion, an order be issued to the magistrate instructing him to attend the celebration ceremonies. Nothing was said concerning what happened previously [i.e., the fact that the magistrate in question had refused to give permission]. Upon receiving official permission [from the treasurer], Huang promptly gathered a crowd and began the construction work." Wang Chih, however, was able to secure authorization to stop it.

100. The text is given in *Sui-an Hsü-shih ts'ung-shu hsü-pien, Shuo-fu,* and *Ch'ing-chao t'ang ts'ung-shu.* See *Sung-shih, chüan* 340, biography of Lü Ta-fang; *Sung-yüan hsüeh-an, chüan* 31; and Yang K'ai-tao, *Chung-kuo hsiang-yüeh chih-tu,* chapters 3-5. The preamble of *Lü-shih hsiang-yüeh* contains this proposal: "Whoever agrees, please write down his assent." The word *yüeh* is here used apparently in the sense of agreement (i.e., as in the phrase *yao-yüeh)* instead of restraint (as in the phrase *yüeh-shu).* This document was under the signature of Lü Ta-chung. But Chu Hsi, the well-known Sung philosopher, was of the opinion that it was really the work of his younger brother, Lü Ta-chün (1031-82). According to Wen Chün-t'ien, *Pao-chia,* pp. 38-45, the lecture system of Korea was patterned after the *Lü-shih hsiang-yüeh.*

101. Wen Chün-t'ien, *Pao-chia,* pp. 34-36.

102. Fang Hsiao-ju (1357-1402), "Tsung-i," essays 4 and 9, in *Hsün-chih-chai chi, chüan* 1.

103. Wang Shou-jen (1472-1528), "Nan-kan hsiang-yüeh," in *Wang Wen-ch'eng-kung ch'üan-shu, chüan* 17, "Pieh-lu,"part 9, pp. 519-23. Other Ming dynasty writers on this question included Liu Tsung-chou (seventeenth century), "Liu-shih tsung-yüeh," in *Liu-tzu ch'üan-shu, chüan* 17, and "Hsiang-shu," in *ibid., chüan* 24; Lu Shih-i (1611-72, a contemporary of Liu Tsung-chou), "Chih hsiang san yüeh" (written in 1640), in *Chih-hsüeh lu;* and Lü Hsin-wu, "Hsiang-chia yüeh," quoted in Wang I-k'o, *Nung-ts'un tzu-wei yen-chiu,* p. 55.

104. Wang Shou-jen's system was, in a sense, a revival of the *li* organization of Hung-wu times. Emperor T'ai-tsu of Ming ordered the *Hu-pu* to organize every hundred households into one *li,* which constituted a unit of mutual assistance in economic and social needs. (See *Ming-shih, chüan* 3.) Wang Shou-jen extended the scope of *li* activities to include settlement of disputes and determination of right and wrong conduct by the consensus of local opinion within the *yüeh* organization.

105. Wen Chün-t'ien, *Pao-chia,* p. 37.

106. *Fu-shan* (1924), 3/18b, and *Tung-kuan* (1911), 69/1a.

107. Shen Yüeh-lin, *So-chi,* quoted in note 93.

108. Ho Ch'ang-ling, *Wen-pien,* 74/29. Yü Ch'eng-lung was then magistrate of T'ung Chou (Chihli). He later rose to the governorship of Chihli in 1686.

109. Instances are found in the following: *Ting chou* (1850), 6/1a-b and 6/6b-

7/48b; *Yung-chou* (1867), *chüan* 4, *shang*, p. 50b; *Kuang-chou* (1878), 109/5b; *Mien-yang* (1894), *chüan* 3, "Chien-chih," 1a-9a; and *Jen-huai* (1895), 4/39a. There are numerous other instances in local gazetteers in addition to those cited.

110. Quoted in *Chiang-hsi* (1880), *chüan shou*, Part 3, pp. 24a-b.

111. Hsiao I-shan, *Ch'ing-tai shih* (1945), p. 103.

112. *Fu-shan* (1924), 3/3b-4b. See chapter 7 for discussion on local defense.

113. *Ch'ing-yüan* (1880), 12/21a-b. The same source also indicates that when the "Red Turbans" rose in 1854, the magistrate of Ch'ing-yüan Hsien secretly ordered all members of the gentry to join their *yüeh* and to participate in *t'uan-lien* work. *Kuang-chou* (1878), 82/28b and 136/15b, gives similar instances occurring in the mid-nineteenth century.

114. Tseng Kuo-fan (1811-72), *P'i-tu*, 1/2a.

115. Chang Shou-yung, *Hui-pien, nei-pien*, 53/14b.

116. *Po-pai* (1832), 7/5a.

117. *Lo-ch'üan* (1944), 12/1b, quoting from the 1806 edition. Tax collection remained a separate duty in this locality. This is evident from the statement that "each *li* has a *li-cheng.*" See *T'ung-kuan* (1944), 18/1b, "In Ch'ing times each village had a *hsiang-yüeh;* several villages together nominated a *lien-t'ou* [joint head]. "

118. *Hua hsien* (1924), 9/22a-b.

119. Martin C. Yang, *Chinese Village*, p. 173. The change began, in some localities at least, in the eighteenth century, if not earlier. *Mu-lin shu*, 4/4b, quotes Li Tien-t'u (a *chin-shih* of 1765, later governor of Fukien), who made the following remark concerning local granaries and relief work: "The names of the registered households without exception have always been listed and reported by *hsiang-yüeh.* " One more change may be noted. In Chungking (Szechwan) a *hsiang-yüeh* head surnamed Ma set up a private mail and transportation service along the upper Yangtze valley. Ma Hsiang-yüeh's service was so efficient and trustworthy that until the opening decades of the twentieth century even government officials were counted among his satisfied clients.

120. *Ch'ing t'ung-k'ao*, 76/5553-67. *Hu-pu* (1791), 118/28a, gives this regulation: "Local officials shall from time to time give attention to elderly subjects who have reached ninety *sui*. Those among these who are widowers, widows, childless, or whose sons and grandsons are so poor as to be unable to support them, shall receive relief and support; governors-general, governors, and *chou* and *hsien* magistrates shall together devise means to give such relief, or petition the emperor to grant permission to use revenues realized from the regular taxes, so that these subjects will receive actual benefits. " Persons over one hundred *sui* were often given special consideration. Numerous instances were recorded, but two of these suffice here. Wang Hsien-ch'ien, *Tung-hua lu*, Yung-cheng, 9/13a (Yung-cheng 4, 7th month, 29th day), indicates that when the *Li-pu* (Board of Rites) recommended that Hsiao Chün-te, a man who had reached 118 *sui*, be given the customary honor (an imperial gift of thirty taels with which to build a commemorative arch), the emperor ordered that since it was unusual to attain such longevity, the person be given an additional gift of ninety taels, that henceforth persons who reached 110 *sui* were to be given twice the amount of money regularly authorized, and that this sum was to be doubled for each additional ten *sui* above 110. Wu Yung-kuang (1773-1843), *Wu-hsüeh lu*, 3/14a, says that when one Lan Hsiang reached 142 *sui* in 1810, he was given 200 taels, in addition to a quantity of silk fabric and an official button of the sixth rank.

121. In 1688, 1703, 1709, 1723, 1736, 1751, 1761, 1770, 1779, 1782, 1790,

1796, 1800, 1808, 1819, 1821, and 1831. En-p'ing (1934), 13/20a. See also *Hsün-tien* (1828), 12/8a-12a, and *I-ch'eng* (1929), 13/1b-2a.

122. *Ch'ing t'ung-k'ao*, 39/5218; *Sheng-hsün*, Shih-tsung, 49/14a-b; Wang Hsien-ch'ien, *Tung-hua lu*, Yung-cheng, 9/34b; and *T'ai-ho* (1878), *chüan shou*, pp. 7b-8a.

123. *I-ch'eng* (1929), 13/1b-2a. The number of persons receiving the bounty was not specified. The following figures for persons receiving gifts (rice, silk, meat, etc.) are given in *The Chinese Repository*, IX (1840), 259 (quoting from the *Asiatic Journal*, 1826):

Over 70 *sui*	184,086 persons
Over 80 *sui*	169,850 persons
Over 90 *sui*	9,996 persons
Over 100 *sui*	21 persons

Amount of the gift to each and other details are not given.

124. *Sheng-hsün*, Shih-tsung, 15/1a; *Ch'ing t'ung-k'ao*, 76/5556, an edict issued to the *Hu-pu*.

125. Such titles or ranks were, in official parlance, "conferred by imperial grace" *(huang-en ch'in-tz'u)*. See Schuyler Cammann, "The Development of the Mandarin Square," *Harvard Journal of Asiatic Studies*, VIII (1944), 121.

126. *Shih-li* (1908), *chüan* 405, gives these regulations. *Sheng-hsün*, Shih-tsung, 46/32b-33a; and Wang Hsien-ch'ien, *Tung-hua lu*, Yung-cheng, 9/13a, give regulations governing the procedure for honoring persons over 100 *sui*. The practice of *ching-piao* (giving honor and distinction) was extended to other deserving persons besides those who lived to a ripe age. These included (1) persons "taking delight in good and charitable deeds"; (2) persons "prompt in serving public interests and desirous of performing righteous actions"; (3) persons noted for their filial piety or chastity; (4) persons who lived with their kin in the same households for several generations. See *Shih-li* (1908), *chüan* 403 and 404. The various methods of honoring age were summarized in *Lu-chou* (1885), 57/1b-10b, under these headings: (1) invitation to the *hsiang-yin* ceremony; (2) nomination of "Senior Farmers"; (3) presentation of imperial gifts; (4) granting of the privilege of displaying honorific tablets; and (5) conferring of scholarly degrees.

127. *Pa-ling* (1891), 43/1a-2a. According to *Hsün-tien* (1828), 12/10a-11b, an edict issued in 1796 authorized the conferring of buttons of the ninth rank on septuagenarians, of the eighth rank on octogenarians, of the seventh rank on nonagenarians, and of the sixth rank on centenarians. An edict issued in 1820 qualified septuagenarians for receiving official buttons without specifying the rank.

128. *Hsiang-shan* (1923), 14/1a-b. See also *P'an-yü* (1911), 24/22b-28b; *Hua hsien* (1924), 9/26b; *Ju-lin* (1883), 14/18b and 17/7b; *Hsin hsien* (1887), 8/12a-13b; and *Han-tan* (1933), 1/8b and 10/50b.

129. This practice began with the granting of official titles to over forty scholars competing in the metropolitan examinations in 1736, as an act of imperial grace. It soon became established routine and continued down to Kuang-hsü times. The highest degree granted was *chü-jen*, and the highest official title, *kuo-tzu-chien ssu-yeh*. See *K'o-ch'ang* (1885), 53/1a-3b, 6a, 53a. In a number of local gazetteers the names of local scholars who had received the *chü-jen* degree by imperial grace appear in the section on *hsüan-chü*.

130. *Shih-li* (1908), 168/1a-5a, summarizes imperial actions from Shun-chih to Kuang-hsü times. This measure served an ideological purpose, but appears

to have had economic significance also: to encourage diligence in farming with a view to increasing agricultural production. The economic implication of the institution of the Senior Farmer was made clear by the Yung-cheng emperor in an edict issued in 1724. After stressing the urgency of supervising and encouraging farming in order to produce more foodstuffs, the emperor ordered provincial authorities to select in each Hsiang one or two such farmers who were diligent and industrious, and to encourage them further by giving them ample rewards. See *Ch'ing t'ung-k'ao* (1936), 3/4871.

131. *Ibid.*

132. *Ibid.*, 4/4882; *Sheng-hsün*, Kao-tsung, 336/6a.

133. *Hu-pu* (1791), 8/2a. *Ch'ing t'ung-k'ao*, 23/5053. Orita, *Fen-lun*, vol. 1, pp. 479-80, gives a summary covering Yung-cheng and Ch'ien-lung times. *Ch'ing-yüan* (1880), 11/2a-2b, contains this record: "Elderly scholars receiving official buttons of the eighth rank, granted by imperial grace, a total of eighteen persons, among whom two were *sheng-yüan* and one was a *chien-sheng.*" Hsü Ch'ao-chu, status unspecified, was appointed *nung-kuan* (farmer-official, i.e., Senior Farmer). Aged persons (those over ninety *sui)* receiving *ching-piao*, a total of 119, mostly commoners, were distributed geographically as follows:

Inhabitants of villages	103
Inhabitants of the city	9
Residence not indicated	7

The time in which these honors were conferred was not specified.

134. *K'o-ch'ang* (1885), 53/10a-11a, 20a-22b, and 35a-37b.

135. Wang Hsien-ch'ien, *Tung-hua lu*, Yung-cheng, 14/5a.

136. *Ibid.*, 14/36b. See also *Shih-lu*, Shih-tsung, 81/10a-b.

137. *Chinese Repository*, IX (1840), 258-67, gives an account of two festivals given by Emperors Sheng-tsu and Kao-tsung. The elderly men invited were inhabitants of localities near the imperial capital. *Han-tan* (1933), 1/8b, describes the occasion of the sixtieth birthday anniversary of Sheng-tsu, 1713 (K'ang-hsi 52, 3rd month, 18th day), in these terms: "Elderly subjects dwelling near the capital who were over eighty *sui* went to the capital and were entertained at a feast in Ch'ang-ch'un Yüan. Princes of the blood were ordered to pour wine for them. Each guest was presented with a silk suit on the front of which was inscribed the characters *huang-en hao-tang* [Imperial Grace Boundless] and on the back, *wan-shou wu-chiang* [Ten Thousand Birthdays, Limitless]. Five of the elderly men of Han-tan participated: namely, an inhabitant of San-t'i village, aged 89; one of Tung-kuan, aged 83; one of the city, aged 82; one of San-t'i village, aged 82; and one of Wen-chuang village, aged 81."

138. According to *Yung-chou* (1867), *chüan* 4, *shang*, p. 48a-b, the ceremony adopted by the Ch'ing government was similar to that of Ming times. *Ming-shih, chüan* 56, "Li-chih," part 10, pp. 5b-6a, gives the following facts: In 1372 (Hung-wu 5) the Board of Rites, in compliance with an imperial order, established the ceremony in the schools and in the *li-she* in the countryside; in 1379 (Hung-wu 12) persons who had committed crimes or shown offensive conduct were prohibited from sitting with "innocent people" in the ceremony; in 1383 (Hung-wu 16) the *hsiang-yin* ceremony was officially defined, and the details indicated in diagrams. The form adopted by the Ch'ing government resembled the Ming form as fixed in 1383. The earliest origin of *hsiang-yin* may be traced to *Chou-li;* see under *Ti-kuan*, "Tang-cheng," 3/75.

139. *Ch'ing t'ung-k'ao*, 76/5553.

140. For regulations, see *ibid.*, 76/5553-55; *Shih-li* (1908), 30/4a; *Hsüeh-*

cheng (1810), 8/1a-6b. Local gazetteers often contain similar information. See, for example, *Chiang-ching* (1924), *chüan* 4, *shang*, pp. 28b-30a; *Ch'üeh-shan* (1931), 9/9a-b; *Ch'ing-pien* (1899), 2/28b-29b; and *Tung-kuan* (1921), 25/4a. Wu Yung-kuang (1773-1843), *Wu-hsüeh lu*, 3/3a-9b, may also be consulted.

141. *Hsüeh-cheng* (1810), 8/6a-b.

142. *Ibid.*, 8/3a-4b.

143. *Hui-chou* (1881), 9/35a-b; *Yen-chou* (1883), 7/5b-6a; and *I-ch'eng* (1929), 16/8b, quoting from the 1881 edition.

144. *En-p'ing* (1934), 11/6a-10a, and *Meng-ch'eng* (1915), 5/7b.

145. *Lo-ch'uan* (1944), 13/2a-b, quoting the 1806 edition: "In Ch'ien-lung times Ch'en Hung-mou (1696-1771), governor of Shensi, sent a dispatch to all his subordinates, saying, '. . . in out-of-the-way districts where no retired officials are available for nomination to occupy the seats of the Grand Guests, *chü-jen*, *kung-sheng*, or *sheng-yüan* who are elderly and virtuous may be invited instead. *Sheng-yüan*, *chien-sheng*, or good people who are elderly and virtuous and who truly deserve the high opinion which the local inhabitants hold of them, may be nominated as Intermediate and Ordinary Guests.'" Ch'en Hung-mou was governor of Shensi in 1734-46, 1754-55, and 1756-77. This document is given also in Ch'en's *Ou-ts'un kao*, 21/33a-35a. The compilers of the 1944 edition of the Lo-ch'uan gazetteer made this interesting comment: "As late as Hsien-feng times, 'Grand Guest of *Hsiang-yin*' was still a title used by elders in Lo-ch'uan."

146. *Fu-shan* (1924), 17/22a-b, quoting a proclamation issued by the governor-general of Liang-Kuang (i.e., Gio-lo-chi) which reads in part: "The names of persons over eighty *sui*, whether they are native-born or immigrants, may be sent in, provided that they themselves and their families are pure and unstained and have conducted themselves righteously and prudently." The phrase "their own persons and their families are pure and unstained" *(shen-chia ch'ing-pai)* was generally used to indicate that neither the persons in question nor their families belonged to any category of the *chien-min* (base people).

147. Ch'en Hung-mou, *Ou-ts'un kao*, 21/33a-35a.

148. Wu Yung-kuang, *Wu-hsüeh lu*, 3/5b-6a.

149. For instances in which retired officials were honored as Grand Guests, see *Hsin hsien* (1887), 7/19b, a retired magistrate, in 1645; *I-ch'eng* (1929), 29/19b, a *chin-shih* and retired magistrate, in the eighteenth century; *Lu-chou* (1885), 34/11b, a retired subprefect, date unspecified; *Fu-shan* (1924), 6/25a, a submagistrate, in 1801. For scholars so honored, see *Lin-chang* (1904), 9/14a, a *chin-shih* of 1661; *Sui chou* (1892), 7/4a-b, a *sheng-yüan*, date unspecified; *Hsin hsien* (1887), 7/29b, a *kung-sheng*, in 1861; *ibid.*, 7/33a, a *chien-sheng*, in 1884; *Lo-ch'uan* (1944), 21/7b, a *kung-sheng*, in 1849; *Lu-chou* (1885), 57/1b, a *sheng-yüan*, in 1830. For commoners so honored, see *Yün-ch'eng* (1893), 5/42a-b, a village physician, undated; *Hua hsien* (1924), 7/18a-b, a villager who "read books and understood their general meaning, but did not pursue the the work of scholars competing in the examinations," in 1824; *Lu-chou* (1885), 53/38a, a person who "abandoned the scholarly pursuit and followed the medical profession," in 1723.

150. For instances in which scholars were Ordinary Guests, see *Hsin hsien* (1887), 7/27a, a *sheng-yüan*, undated; *I-ch'eng* (1929), 29/17a, a *sheng-yüan*, in 1742; *ibid.*, 29/30a, a *kung-sheng*, date unspecified. For commoners so honored, see *Han-tan* (1933), 10/50a, a merchant, in 1875; *T'ung-kuan* (1944), 28/6b, a person whose family "engaged in farming for generations," in 1721; *Lu-chou* (1885), 50/49b, a person whose family was poor; *ibid.*, 53/19b, a person "accustomed to drudgery and poverty" in his early years, but later "in somewhat

affluent circumstances"—both instances undated. Most of the persons whose social status was not named by the local historians were probably commoners.

151. *Hsiang-shan* (1923), 11/98a-99b.

152. *Hsin-an* (1871), 10/26b-29b.

153. *Ibid.*, 10/7a-b.

154. *Ch'ang-ning* (1901), 11/2b-7a.

155. *Po-pai* (1832), "Chih-yü pei-lan," *chüan hsia, passim*. Cf. *Kan-shui* (1850), 8/71b. The phrase "scholars seeking no government office" was a euphemism for "scholars holding no examination titles."

156. This and the table following are based on data given in *Nan-ch'ang* (1919), 24/3a-16a.

157. *Ibid.*, 21/24b-35b; 22/33a-64a; and 23/19a-38a. A few additional instances: *Po-pai* (1832), "Chih-yü pei-lan," *hsia, passim*, a list of persons who contributed funds for compiling and printing the gazetteer, includes 165 guests in the *hsiang-yin* (dates unspecified), of whom six were persons with scholarly degrees, namely, one *"sheng-yüan* Grand Guest," one *"sheng-yüan* Ordinary Guest," one *"chien-sheng* Intermediate Guest," one *"wu-sheng* Ordinary Guest," and two *"chien-sheng* Ordinary Guests." The rest of the "guests" who contributed (159 persons) were designated by the local historians mostly as "elderly men," "private gentlemen," or "scions of local worthies." *Ho-ch'ing* (1894), 7/24a-b, lists sixteen *hsiang-yin* guests (date unspecified) among whom nine were Grand Guests. One of these Grand Guests was described as a man who had "official experience," another as a man of "outstanding deeds," and a third as a man distinguished in "literary accomplishments." The status of the rest was not even hinted. *Ch'ing-pien* (1899), 3/7b-8a, contains the information that in a ceremony revived by the magistrate in 1896 the following participated: Grand Guest, a *kung-sheng;* Intermediate Guests, two *fu-kung-sheng;* Ordinary Guests, seventeen persons whose status was not indicated.

158. Li Yü (1611-80?), *Hsin-shu, erh chi*, 3/12a.

159. *Ibid.*, 2/13a-b.

160. Huang Liu-hung, *Fu-hui*, 24/23b. Cf. *ibid.*, 3/22a, where it is said that one of the "sordid usages" obtaining in the seventeenth century was to demand "gifts" in return for invitations to the *hsiang-yin* ceremony.

161. Ch'en Hung-mou, *Ou-ts'un kao*, 24/7a-b.

162. *Tsou-i*, 53/13a, a memorial submitted by Li Yin-p'ei in Ch'ien-lung 27 (1762). Cf. *ibid.*, 48/19a-b, a memorial submitted in 1753 by Chang Jo-chen, provincial treasurer at Hsi-an, Shensi, in which the chief difficulties of the *hsiang-yin* are said to have been (1) irregularities in procedure, i.e., that the ceremony was held at irregular intervals and the number of guests varied; (2) invitation of undeserving "guests," some of whom proved to be ex-convicts; and (3) treatment of the ceremony as an "empty formality" by local officials.

163. *Hsüeh-cheng* (1810), 8/2b; *Tung-kuan* (1911), 25/6a, a directive issued by the Board of Rites in Ch'ien-lung 2 (1757).

164. *Sui chou* (1892), 61/24b-25b, gives an early instance in which a *chin-shih* repeatedly refused to accept invitations to the *hsiang-yin*.

165. *Yü-lin* (1894), *hsü*, 1/2b.

166. *Tsou-i*, 53/14a, a memorial submitted in 1762 (Ch'ien-lung 27), by Li Yin-p'ei, director of studies, Chekiang.

167. *Hsüeh-cheng* (1810), 8/5a, a directive issued in 1762 (Ch'ien-lung 27), quoted also in *Po-pai* (1832), 13/9a. The Ch'ing government, it seems, was somewhat less stringent than the Ming government in maintaining the distinction between men with official status and commoners. See *Ming-shih, chüan* 56,

"Li-chih," part 10, p. 10a, for an order of 1379 (Hung-wu 12), forbidding retired officials to occupy in social gatherings seats which were second in honor
to those occupied by commoners, or to return the salute of commoners.

168. In some localities gifts were presented to the guests. For example,
according to *Ch'u chou* (1897), *chüan* 2, *ting*, p. 17b, "gift money" (six taels)
was listed among the *hsiang-yin* expenses.

169. *Hsüeh-cheng* (1810), 8/2a, an imperial order issued in 1723 (Yung-cheng
1); quoted also in *Yün-ch'eng* (1893), 4/19a-b.

170. *Nan-ch'ang* (1919), 11/18a; *Pa-ling* (1891), 14/11b; *Cheng-ting* (1875),
17/24a; *Hsiang-fu* (1898), 8/17a; *Yen-ch'ing* (1880), 3/31a; *Wei chou* (1877),
7/5a; *Hun-yüan* (1880), 2/9b; *Meng-ch'eng* (1915), 4/6b; *Po-pai* (1832), 6/19a;
Ch'ang-ning (1910), 8/10a; *Hsin hsien* (1887), 3/13b; *T'eng hsien* (1846), 4/10b;
T'ung-kuan (1944), 16/4a; *Lo-ch'uan* (1944), 14/7a, quoting the 1806 edition.

171. *Pa-ling* (1891), 14/11b; *Nan-ch'ang* (1919), 11/18a.

172. *Hsiang-fu* (1898), 8/17a.

173. *Yung hsien* (1897), 9/9a.

174. *Tung-kuan* (1911), 25/7a.

175. *Ch'ing-pien* (1899), 3/7b. Cf. *Po-pai* (1832), 13/4b, quoting a government directive issued in 1753 (Ch'ien-lung 18); and *Chen-hsiung* (1887), 2/53a,
where it is said that before 1838 "this ceremony was never held" in that locality.
In some localities the ceremony was so infrequently performed that it became
a rarity, arousing more curiosity than interest on the part of the local inhabitants who watched it. See Wang Hui-tsu, *Meng-hen lu, hsia*, p. 12b, narrating
an occurrence early in Ch'ien-lung 53.

176. *Tung-kuan* (1911), 25/8a, compiler's comment. This, however, may
have been an overstatement. *Hsiang-shan* (1923), 11/98b-99b, records that a
total of twenty guests were invited to the *hsiang-yin* during the Chia-ch'ing period and seven during Tao-kuang times.

177. Ch'en Hung-mou, *Ou-ts'un kao*, 13/17a, an official dispatch issued in
1742 (Ch'ien-lung 7). *Tsou-i*, 48/19a-b, gives a memorial submitted in 1753
(Ch'ien-lung 18) by Chang Jo-chen, in which it is said that the *hsiang-yin* was
being performed in the most careless manner. Huang Liu-hung, *Fu-hui*, 3/23a,
was of the opinion that the malpractices connected with *hsiang-yin* prevailing in
the seventeenth century "brought disgrace to an impressive ceremony instituted
by the imperial court."

178. *Nan-ch'ang* (1919), 24/3a-16a.

179. *Hsing-an* (1871), 10/26b-29b.

180. *Hsiang-shan* (1923), 11/98b-99b. Cf. *Kan-shui* (1850), 8/71b, and *Ho-
ch'ing* (1894), 7/24a-b.

181. *Jung hsien* (1897), 19/23a ff. No entry was made after 1763. Presumably
the ceremony was discontinued, since according to the compiler (9/9a) the expenses for the cermony were officially cancelled at an unspecified date.

182. *Yen-chou* (1883), 17/46a-52b.

183. *Chao-p'ing* (1932), 3/35a-b.

184. *Tung-kuan* (1911), 25/7a.

185. *Fu-shan* (1924), 5/11a, 10/3a-b, and 11/9b.

186. *Nan-hai* (1910), 22/3a. The person in question was Ch'en Ta-nien, who,
"after having repeatedly failed in the examinations, established a private school
and engaged in teaching."

187. *Chen-hsiung* (1887), 2/53a. The Grand Guest was a *sheng-yüan*, the Intermediate Guest also a *sheng-yüan*, and five "elderly people" were invited as
Ordinary Guests.

188. For a full list, see *Hui-tien* (1908), 26/1a-4a; *Shih-li* (1908), *chüan* 427-54; *Ch'ing t'ung-k'ao*, 90/819-24, and 106/5781-83; *Ch'ing hsü t'ung-k'ao*, 79/3493-500. The summary in Wu Yung-kuang, *Wu-hsüeh lu*, *chüan* 9-11, is helpful. J. J. M. de Groot, *Religion in China* (1912), pp. 190-210, covers roughly the same ground. The official classification is given in translation as "Superior Sacrifices," "Middle Sacrifices," and "Collective Sacrifices." The last phrase is an obviously incorrect translation of the term *ch'ün ssu*. The classification was made somewhat differently by the compilers of some local gazetteers. For example, *Fu-shun* (1931), *chüan* 4, Confucius and "Celebrated Officials and Local Worthies," are in category 1; gods of winds, clouds, thunder, rain, mountains, and rivers, in category 2. Cf. *Chiang-ching* (1924), *chüan* 4, part 1; *Han-tan* (1933), 6/8a-20a; and *T'ung-kuan* (1944), 23/3b-4a. Some of the sacrifices were shifted up or down in the official classification during the dynasty. For a brief summary of such changes, see de Groot's *Religion in China*. For temples actually built in various localities, see local gazetteers, which usually have sections on *ts'u-ssu* or on *t'an-miao*.

189. *Hui-tien* (1908), 36/4a.

190. *Ch'ing t'ung-k'ao*, 69/5485. This practice was first established in 1644. See also Wu Yung-kuang, *Wu-hsüeh lu*, 3/12a-b. For local instances see *Lu-chou* (1885), *chüan* 50-54, and *Hua hsien* (1924), 3/6b-7b, and 9/12b-13b. It is noteworthy that T'ang Pin (1627-87), Lu Lung-ch'i (1630-93), and Li Kuang-ti (1642-1718), all orthodox Confucianists of the Ch'eng-chu school, were included in imperial apotheosis. The first had his name entered in the temple of Celebrated Officials in 1733, the second was honored as one of the "Confucians of Former Times" *(Hsien-ju)*, in 1724, and the third received the same honor as the first and in the same year. T'ang and Lu were among the very few scholars of note who participated in the *po-hsüeh hung-tz'u* examinations of 1678 and 1679, thus showing their willingness to submit to Manchu rule. Li helped in the preparation of a number of texts of imperial Confucianism, including the complete works of Chu Hsi, *Chou-li che-chung*, and *Hsing-li ching-i*. For a brief account, see Hummel, *Eminent Chinese*, I, 474. Numerous tablets bearing the names of "loyal, filial, dutiful, and righteous" persons were placed, singly or in groups, in shrines built in various localities. Local gazetteers usually give the sites of such shrines and the names of those honored therein.

191. One of the most frequently performed was rain prayer. Samuel Williams, *Middle Kingdom* (1883), I, 467, notes an instance that occurred in 1832. The invocatory piece as translated by Williams reads in part as follows: "Oh, alas! imperial Heaven, were not the world afflicted by extraordinary changes, I would not dare to present extraordinary services. But this year the drought is most unusual. Summer is past, and no rain has fallen. Not only do agriculture and human beings feel the dire calamity, but also beasts and insects, herbs and trees, almost cease to live. I, the minister of Heaven, am placed over mankind, and am responsible for keeping the world in order and tranquillizing the people. Although it is now impossible for me to sleep or eat with composure, although I am scorched with grief and tremble with anxiety, still, after all, no genial and copious showers have been obtained. . . . Prostrate I beg imperial Heaven . . . to pardon my ignorance and stupidity, and to grant me self-renovation; for myriads of innocent people are involved by me, the One man. My sins are so numerous it is difficult to escape from them. Summer is past and autumn arrived; to wait longer will really be impossible. Knocking head, I pray imperial Heaven to hasten and confer gracious deliverance—a speedy and divinely beneficial rain, to save the people's lives. . . ." The original text is given in *Sheng-hsün*, Hsüan-

tsung, 12/12b-13b. For similar texts, see *ibid.*, Hsüan-tsung, *chüan* 12, *passim;* Sheng-tsu, *chüan* 10, *passim;* Shih-tsung, *chüan* 8, *passim;* Kao-tsung, *chüan* 27-29, *passim;* Jen-tsung, *chüan* 14, *passim;* Wen-tsung, *chüan* 12, *passim;* and Mu-tsung, *chüan* 11, *passim*.

192. In the words of Wu Yung-kuang, *Wu-hsüeh lu*, 11/15b, "Sacrifices offered to the gods who ward off calamities and disasters . . . are calculated to follow the direction of the people's desires, and they constitute one of the methods of governance."

193. *Lu-chou* (1885), 18/8b-9b. The invocatory text reads in part: "If there be among us, people of this district, anyone who is undutiful toward his parents, disrespectful toward persons related to him in the six relationships of the family; or anyone who commits theft, robbery, or fraud, in defiance of public law; or anyone who oppresses good and honest persons; or anyone who evades the corvée, thus shifting the losses to poor families: if there be any such individuals, we beseech you, Spirits, surely to report them to the god of the walls and moats, who will expose their evil deeds and cause them to receive legal punishment of the government. Even if you choose not to expose them, let them surely receive the Unseen Punishment."

194. *Shih-li* (1908), 444/5b. Cf. *Ling-shan* (1914), 9/122b, and *Lo-ch'uan* (1944), 13/2a. According to *Chiang-ning* (1880), 4/1a, the altar of *Hsien-nung* (Farmers of Former Ages) was situated in the east suburb, that of *She-chi* (gods of land and grain) in the west, that of *Shan-ch'uan* (gods of mountains and rivers) in the south, and that of the *li* (unpropitiated spirits) in the north.

195. *Lo-ch'uan* (1944), 13/2a, quoting the 1806 edition.

196. *Nan-ch'ang* (1919), 15/2a, informs us that a total of 410 rural altars of *li* existed in this district of Kiangsi. According to *Yen-yüan* (1910), 7/1a, the 143 rural altars existing in Ming times were all abandoned, leaving only one or two recognizable sites. *Yen-an* (1802), 36/1a, affords this information: *"Li-t'an . . .* in a *fu* or *chou* were *chün-li*, while those in a *hsien* were *i-li*. [Li-t'an]* were occasionally found in towns or walled villages." *Chün-li* and *i-li* may be translated "prefectural altars" and "district altars." The term *hsiang-li* (neglected or unpropitiated spirits of the countryside) was not officially used, but it appears in a number of local gazetteers.

197. This text is not given in *Shih-li* (1908), which was compiled in 1899, but may be found in the following local gazetteers: *K'uei-chou* (1827), 19/37b-39a; *P'u-an* (1889), 8/8b-9b; *Jen-huai* (1895), 2/44b-46a. Another invocatory text beseeching the god of walls and moats to deal justice to the Neglected Spirits reads in part as follows: "Respectfully we have received the emperor's sacred rescript which says that under Heaven and above the earth living persons are everywhere, ghosts and spirits everywhere. Although the ways of men and ghosts differ, the basic principle [governing both] is the same. The state has established rules to govern its subjects and serve the gods. But considering that in the unseen regions there are ghosts and spirits to whom no sacrificial offerings are made, who were formerly living persons that had died for causes unascertained, . . . it is hereby ordered that functionaries in the empire make sacrificial offerings to them at regular intervals. The god of the walls and moats of each locality is appointed master of sacrificial performances, and he shall control the altar and supervise these spirits. If among them there be some who had lived as truly good and upright persons but had met their death innocently through calamity or [unjust] punishment, you, the god, shall report them to the proper [unseen] powers that would cause them to be reborn in the Middle Kingdom and to enjoy lasting blessings of peace. If there be among them some who, although [they had]

escaped lawful punishment and died natural deaths by sheer chance, had been habitually perverse and evil [during their lifetimes], you, the god, shall report them to the proper powers so that they may be banished beyond the four boundaries [of the Middle Kingdom]. Retribution for good and evil [deeds] will surely be administered impartially by you, the god. This is the order contained in the rescript which we have respectfully received; we dare not disobey it. Reverently we set up an altar north of our city and prepare food and drink to offer to the Neglected Ghosts and Spirits of our *fu, (chou,* or *hsien). . . .*" This text is given in *T'ung-jen* (1890), 3/9b-10b; and *Ch'ang-ning* (1901), 3/14b-15b.

198. For example, *Lu-chou* (1885), 18/9a, says that the *li-t'an* sacrifices were "at present generally not offered." *Mien-yang* (1894), 3/1b, records that the city and the rural *li-t'an* were abandoned. *Cheng-ting* (1875), 21/5b indicates that *hsiang li-t'an* (rural altars) "now are mostly not in use." *Ting chou* (1850), 22/47b-48a, informs us that "the *li-t'an* of Ting Chou was formerly situated outside the north city gate. . . . After the great flood at the beginning of Chia-ch'ing [1796], only the site remained. When the sacrificial offerings were made each year, the tablets were placed upon sandy and gravelly ground, amid weeds and thorny bushes." In 1848, however, the altar was restored by the magistrate. This is one of the rare instances in which the *li-t'an* sacrifices were offered in the nineteenth century. Another instance is given in *Hsiang-hsiang* (1874), 4/34a-b, where it is said that the *li-t'an* was rebuilt in 1843 by a member of the local gentry. The invocatory text locally in use at that time differs only in wording from the text which we have quoted. In this and some other localities the *li-t'an* sacrifice ceased to be a government exercise and was taken up by the local gentry. Constance Gordon-Cumming, *Wanderings in China* (1886), I, 315-16, summarizes the matter thus: "Notwithstanding all precautions, the spirit-world does include an incalculable host of miserable beggar-spirits. . . . All these are wholly dependent on the doles of the charitable, who, three times a year, contribute large sums, which they invest in *din,* i.e., paper imitations of coins of diverse value, especially of sycee. . . . Very curious, indeed, are these oft-recurring propitiatory sacrifices, which are offered in every provincial city throughout the vast empire." The "beggar-spirits" here referred to were the *li,* but the sacrifices offered were no longer conducted by the government.

199. *Shih-li* (1908), 164/3a.

200. *Ch'ing-yüan* (1880), 4/32b-35b; *Ch'u chou* (1897), *chüan* 2, *ting,* pp. 17a-b; *Nan-ch'ang* (1919), 11/17b-18a; *Ch'ang-ning* (1901), 8/9b-10a; *Mien-yang* (1894), *chüan* 4, "Shih-huo," p. 48a; *Yen-ch'ing* (1880), 3/30b-31a; *Lo-ch'uan* (1944), 20/5a, quoting from the 1806 edition; *Pa-ling* (1891), 12/1a-33a; *Cheng-ting* (1875), 17/23b-24a; *Hun-yüan* (1880), 5/8b; *T'ung-kuan* (1944), 16/4a; *Po-pai* (1832), 5/1a-13b; *T'eng hsien* (1908), 4/10b. Similar information may be had in many other gazetteers.

201. There are instances in many gazetteers, for example, *Ch'üeh-shan* (1931), 19/4a-13b.

202. De Groot, *Religion* (1912), p. 212. See Daniel Kulp, *Country Life* (1925), p. 292, for local sacrifices in Phoenix Village (Kwangtung).

203. See, for example, *Ch'u-chou* (1877), 24/4a-b.

204. Wang Hui-tsu (1731-1807), *I-shuo, chüan hsia,* pp. 22-23, narrates the following incident which occurred when he was magistrate of Ning-yüan (Hunan) in the 1780's: "Whenever rainprayer was to be said, inhabitants of the *li* divisions carried the images of the gods of their own neighborhoods in sedan chairs, sounding gongs and drums; upon arrival at the main hall of the yamen they requested the local official to genuflect and pray. This was the custom of Hunan province,

Ning-yüan Hsien being no exception. In the fourth month of the *chi-yu* year [1789], when I was leading my subordinates in rainprayer, [the images of] over twenty gods were carried [by rural inhabitants] . . . to the hall of the yamen. Clerks of the *Li-fang* [Division of Rituals] . . . requested me to perform the customary act of worship. I said: 'This is not in accordance with the prescribed ritual form.' . . . Thereupon elders of the villages knelt and beseeched [me to comply with the request]. I told them that . . . 'the government has laid down definite rules prescribing the ritual forms to be followed by officials. . . .' Now the land gods of rural areas [the images of which you carried here] are the counterparts of *ti-pao* [agents of the *pao-chia*]. Local officials cannot treat *ti-pao* as their peers; how can land gods be treated as the equals of local officials?"

205. Even persons who had better social status and more learning than peasants sometimes showed reverence to *ch'eng-huang*. Weng T'ung-ho, a *chin-shih* and a promising official at the imperial court, wrote in his Jih-chi (T'ung-chih 12, 4th month, 21st day), 12/27a, when he was residing in his native city in 1872 mourning the death of his mother: "The *ch'eng-huang* god came out in a religious exercise. When I was a child I had smallpox and was dangerously ill; my mother decided to make votive offerings, by burning incense for ten years. When the time arrived for the annual religious exercise, incense was burned in the temple. Sorrowfully I remembered her wishes and reverently carried on this regular practice."

206. See, for example, *Hsi-ning* (1873), 9/2b; *Feng-chen* (1881), 6/4a; *Luan chou* (1896), 8/22b; *I-ch'eng* (1929), 16/5a; *Lu-lung* (1931), 10/3b-4b. According to the above sources, inhabitants of the countryside "reported" deaths to *Wu-tao miao* instead of to *ch'eng-huang* temples. Cf. *Ting chou* (1850), 19/15b, and Arthur Smith, *Village Life* (1899), p. 137, mentioning only *Wu-tao miao*.

207. See, for example, *Ch'ang-p'ing* (1886), 9/3b; *Lu-i* (1896), 9/4a; *T'ien-ching* (1898), 26/1b; *Han-tan* (1933), 6/5a. The last-mentioned source indicates that "gentry families rarely practice this" (i.e., "reporting" deaths to such temples).

208. *Yen-ch'ing* (1880), 2/65b.

209. See, for example, *Ch'u-chou* (1877), 24/8b, where it is said that the people of Li-shui Hsien "are accustomed to serve fearfully spirits and gods. Persons on trial in a public court who refuse to confess and resort to evasive talk would be greatly frightened if they were ordered to take an oath in some temple." Wang Hui-tsu, *I-shuo, chüan hsia*, pp. 21-22, gives an illuminating instance. Liu K'ai-yang, a bully of the countryside in Ning-yüan Hsien, Hunan, purchased by fraud some hill land belonging to Ch'eng Ta-p'eng. Liu instructed his son to murder a member of the Liu clan who was dying from a natural cause, and charged that the murder was committed by some members of the Ch'eng clan. Wang Hui-tsu, then the magistrate, brought both Liu and Ch'eng to the temple of ch'eng-huang and ordered them to kneel before the image and pray. Ch'eng Ta-p'eng being innocent showed no sign of apprehension, but Liu K'ai-yang trembled all over. In the same night Liu's son, after having imbibed a large amount of liquor, went into the yamen and confessed to the murder. This episode occurred in the 1780's.

210. Cf. de Groot, *Religion*, p. 212: "Not satisfied with the worship of their ancestors, the people freely indulge in the worship of Confucian deities." There is a slight misconception here; the deities which de Groot goes on to enumerate were not all Confucian; some of them were of Taoist or Buddhist origin.

211. The religious attitude thus resulting helped to reduce the possibility of antisocial action in two related ways: by restraining the people from doing "evil"

for fear of the Unseen Punishment, and by encouraging them to do "good" in order to earn "merit." This tended to make ordinary people more amenable to political control. See Charles F. Horne (ed.), *Sacred Books*, Vol. XII, translation of *"T'ai shang* Book of Actions and Their Retribution," especially p. 235; and Mrs. E. T. Williams, "Some Popular Religious Literature of the Chinese," *Journal of the Royal Asiatic Society*, North China Branch, N.S., XXXIII (1899), 20-21.

212. De Groot, *Religion*, p. 214: "What chiefly strikes us in this Universistic Idolatry is its materialistic selfishness. Promotion of the material happiness of the world, in the first place that of the reigning dynasty, is its aim and end."

213. Hence arose the distinction between *kuan ssu* (official sacrifices) and *min ssu* (popular sacrifices) terms which frequently appear in local gazetteers. See, for example, *Fu-shan* (1924), *chüan* 8, *passim*, where temples of each category were listed.

214. Such sacrifices are usually indicated in local gazetteers. In some localities their performance engaged much of the attention of the inhabitants. For example, *Hsia-men* (1838), 15/12a, says of this district of Fukien, "Miscellaneous types of shrines are encountered everywhere one goes; religious exercises and fairs occur in almost one half the days of the year." De Groot, *Religion*, p. 212, writes: "There are gods and goddesses for safety in child-bearing; gods who impart riches, or who, bestowing blessings on various professions, are patrons of the callings of life." In short, there was a god or goddess for virtually every human purpose, need, or undertaking. The same author's larger work, *The Religious Systems of China* (6 vols., 1892-1910), contains a wealth of information concerning popular sacrifices.

215. *Ho hsien* (1934), 2/12a, quoting the 1890 edition. See *T'ung-kuan* (1944), 26/2b; and *Hsia-men* (1839), 15/12a. As pointed out above, the local gentry often showed interest in sustaining "good morals" through promoting religious sacrifices. See, for example, *Kuang-chou* (1878), 67/3a, 13a, and 16b; and *Hsin hsien* (1887), *chüan* 8, "I-wen," *shang*, pp. 41b-42b.

216. Huang Liu-hung, *Fu-hui*, 24/10a-b; see also 24/16b-17a.

217. *Shih-li* (1908), 402/1a.

218. *Ch'ing t'ung-k'ao*, 69/5487.

219. *Shih-li* (1908), 402/1a, an edict dated 1668 (K'ang-hsi 7). Also in *Hsüeh-cheng* (1810), 10/1b.

220. *Shih-li* (1908), 402/1a-b; *Hsüeh-cheng* (1810), 10/3b-4b. Before 1724 (Yung-cheng 2), authorization by provincial authorities was sufficient to confer honors on "local worthies." Since that date, however, all recommendation must be approved by the Board of Rites in order to take effect. *Hsüeh-cheng* (1810), 10/2b.

221. Liang Chang-chü (1775-1849), *Sui-pi*, 6/8b. *Hsüeh-cheng* (1810), contains this revealing information: Between 1775 and 1810, a period of thirty-five years, of the thirty-five names brought up for consideration, thirty-two received imperial approval and were entered either in the shrine of Celebrated Officials or that of Local Worthies. Only three were rejected. Two of these were officials (fourth and seventh rank) and one was a *chien-sheng*. The status of those approved was:

Officials above 2nd rank	26
Officials of 3rd to 5th rank	4
Officials of 8th rank	1
Fu-kung-sheng	1

222. *Shih-li* (1908), 402/2a-b. See also *Chiang-hsi* (1880), *chüan shou*, part 3, pp. 12a-b.

223. Huang Liu-hung, *Fu-hui*, 24/25b-26b.

224. *Kuang-chou* (1878), 131/7a-b.

225. Huang Liu-hung, *Fu-hui*, 24/27a-b.

226. Sheng-hsün, *Kao-tsung*, 34/11a-12b. The emperor added: "As regards the Celebrated Officials and Local Worthies, it is still more difficult to find truly deserving persons to receive the honors. Local officials often fail to carry out the instructions properly, drawing much criticism to themselves." What Emperor Kao-tsung said was not new; in fact he reiterated substantially the words of Emperor Shih-tsung. In 1723 (Yung-cheng), according to *Ch'ing t'ung-k'ao*, 70/5495, "The emperor, realizing that the practice of paying honor to persons noted for their filial piety, righteousness, chastity, or loyalty, has been treated by high-ranking provincial officials as a mere formality, that these officials often fail to make thorough investigations but rely solely on the recommendations of their subordinates, . . . and that the unsung virtues of countless persons living in hilly villages or remote places, who till and weave in poverty, are thus allowed to sink into oblivion, issued a special order to the *Li-pu* [Board of Rites], instructing it to circulate this order to governors-general and governors who shall thereafter seek out [deserving persons] with added care. . . . They shall not suppress any name recommended because the person in question was a commoner, man or woman, nor indiscriminately recommend any name because the individual belongs to a wealthy family or to a powerful clan."

227. *En-p'ing* (1934), 6/17b-18b.

228. For a description of these boisterous affairs, see *Ho hsien* (1934), 2/5a, quoting from the 1890 edition. Similar festivals were observed in most other parts of the empire.

229. De Groot, *Sectarianism and Religious Persecution in China* (2 vols., 1903-4), treats the subject in detail. Chapter 4, "The Law Against Heresy and Sects," is especially pertinent here.

230. *Sheng-hsün*, Kao-tsung, 261/17a-18a; *Shih-li* (1908), 399/2a. Four years later, in 1743, the emperor decreed that it was not necessary to prohibit all religious exercises and fairs organized by "ignorant rural inhabitants." *Sheng-hsün*, Kao-tsung, 262/8b.

231. Ch'en Hung-mou, *Ou-ts'un kao*, 23/9a-11a; see also 24/23a-24a for an imperial edict issued later in the same year reiterating the prohibition of such pilgrimages.

232. *Chinese and Japanese Repository*, III (1865), 275, quoting from the *Indo-Chinese Gleaner*, May, 1818, p. 9, a report sent to the emperor in 1817.

233. Ho Ch'ang-ling (1785-1848), *Kung-tu*, 2/27a-b.

234. *Sheng-hsün*, Hsüan-tsung, 78/13b-14a; *Shih-li* (1908), 400/1a, edicts issued in Tao-kuang 4 and Tao-kuang 14.

235. Li Tz'u-ming (1829-1894), *Jih-chi pu, keng-chi, shang*, p. 33b, Hsien-feng 10, 3rd month, 13th day.

236. *Sheng-hsün*, Kao-tsung, 262/8b, quoted in note 230 above.

237. For example, as reported in some localities of Shensi early in 1843 (Tao-kuang 23), by Li Hsing-yüan, *Tsou-i*, 3/46a-53a. The exercises resulted in gambling, fights, and bodily injuries to yamen underlings. Ting Jih-ch'ang, *Kung-tu*, 32/8a-b, indicates in a public document issued in the late 1860's that gambling, theft, robbery, and fights were reported in localities in Kiangsu, where such religious exercises were held.

238. *Mu-lin shu*, 6/24a-b, gives a public notice issued by T'ien Wen-ching, governor of Honan, in 1724, which says in part: "False doctrines and heretical sects . . . all arise from religious parades and fairs." He explains that this was

so because such activities gave ready cover to persons desiring to mislead the untutored. Therefore, he concludes, "To prevent the rise of heretical sects, we must first maintain a firm policy toward religious fairs. "

239. *Shih-li* (1908), 398/3a, gives one of the earliest of such interdictions issued in 1758 (Ch'ien-lung 23).

240. *Ibid.*, 399/5b, an edict dated 1800 (Chia-ch'ing 5). Sung Chih-ch'ing and Liu Chih-hsieh mentioned in this document were important leaders of the White Lotus. Substantially the same distinction was implied in an edict issued in 1812 (Chia-ch'ing 17), *ibid.*, 399/7a. It says in effect that Confucianism with its emphasis on human virtues and social relationships is the "correct path" for all to follow. Taoism and Buddhism, not valued by followers of Confucius, are tolerated by the government, since these teach men to do good and avoid evil. But heretical sects which have for their chief aim recruiting votaries to collect illegal gains, such as were rampant in Chihli, Kiangsi, Fukien, Kwangtung, Kwangsi, and Kweichow, gave rise to "religious banditry" and should be suppressed.

241. *Ibid.*, 399/7b.

242. Ho Ch'ang-ling, *Tsou-i*, 11/28a-30a.

243. *Luan chou* (1896), 18/28b-29a. The compiler indicates that the White Lotus movement in this locality was brought to light in Tao-kuang times, i. e., after 1821.

244. *Sheng-hsün*, Hsüan-tsung, 78/26a-b. This sect was known to have been active also in Shensi, as memorials submitted in 1833 by Li Hsing-yüan revealed. One of the leaders of these "heretics" worshiped the Old Mother Uncreated, though the sect was called Lung-hua Hui or Ch'ing-lien Hui (Green Lotus Society). Many of its members were from Szechwan; some of them had connections in Hupeh and Hunan. See Li Hsing-yüan, *Tsou-i*, 7/17a-19b, 7/26a-32b, 7/28a-b, and 8/12a-22b. *Shih-li* (1908), 399/6b-7a, refers briefly to another sect whose members worshiped *Wu-wei lao-tsu* (Old Grandfather Nondoing), reported in Szechwan in 1812.

245. *Shih-li* (1908), 400/6a, an edict issued by Emperor Mu-tsung in 1871 (T'ung-chih 10).

246. *Sheng-hsün*, Hsüan-tsung, 78/5b-6a and 22b; *Shih-li* (1908), 400/1a.

247. *Hsüeh-cheng* (1810), 7/18b-19a, edict dated Ch'ien-lung 31.

248. *Jung hsien* (1897), 27/4b and 23b-24a.

249. Wilhelm, *Chinese Economic Psychology* (English trans., 1947), pp. 27-28: "Whenever new trends came into conflict with the system of a completely self-sufficient economy of small farming, deep-going psychic disturbances followed. Among such trends might be mentioned . . . attempts of large capitalists to get hold of the land and to force the peasants as tenants into economic subjection. The misery of the small peasants which such interferences produced invariably had the same consequences. New religious movements appeared among the masses, connected with eschatological concepts—such, for example, as the beginning of an era of rule by a new world god. Peasant leagues formed. A population brought to the edge of destruction and despair, assembled in vast crowds and revolted. . . . But when after a time of unrest a new dynasty had established itself, and the agrarian conditions were again more orderly, always the old psychic equilibrium returned together with the old economic system. " The situation in the nineteenth century was such that after the turmoils of the third quarter of that century neither the establishment of a new dynasty nor the return of the "psychic equilibrium . . . together with the old economic system" was possible. The superstitions of the peasantry and the orthodoxies of the emperors were both destined to be gradually but surely undermined by new historical circumstances.

250. *Shih-li* (1908), *chüan* 394, *passim*.
251. According to Liu I-cheng, *Wen-hua shih* (1932), II, 161, 175, the appellation *shu-yüan* first appeared late in the T'ang dynasty. The institution became
firmly established in the Sung dynasty.
252. In *Ch'ing hsü t'ung-k'ao*, 100/8589, the compiler comments: "In our dynasty since the *Shih-ku shu-yüan* at Heng-yang [Hunan] was restored as the result
of a petition of Yüan Kuo-yü, the governors' *[shu-yüan]* in other provinces were
established, one following another."
253. *Shih-lu*, Shih-tsung, 43/10a-b, an edict issued in 1726 (Yung-cheng 4)
in response to the request of the governor of Kiangsi to set up *shu-yüan* in that
province, says in part: "As to establishing *shu-yüan* and appointing a person to
be the headmaster of each institution, [we think that] if a small number of students attended the schools, the benefit of instruction would be limited. If many
attended, it would be impossible to distinguish the good and bad, the intelligent
and stupid among them; [these institutions would become places] where the un-
clean get shelter and foul persons find cover. Furthermore, if the instruction
of one man [who is to head one of such institutions] can influence many and make
them upright and honorable persons [as is supposed], the virtue and ability of
this man would more than qualify him for the office of imperial assistant or administrator of a province. Is it easy to secure such a man [to head the *shu-
yüan]?* "
254. *Shih-li* (1908), 395/1a; *Hsüeh-cheng*, (1810), 63/1a-b.
255. *Shih-li* (1908), 395/1a.
256. See local gazetteers quoted in notes 261-63.
257. *Lo-ch'uan* (1944), 19/3a, quoting from *Shen-hsi t'ung-chih kao*, an edict
dated 1733 (Yung-cheng 11).
258. *Shih-li* (1908), 395/1b. *Feng-chen* (1916), 3/11a, indicates that in 1724
(Yung-cheng 2), Chu Hsi's rules for his *Pai-lu-tung shu-yüan* were adopted for
the guidance of all local academies.
259. *Lo-chu'an* (1944), 19/3a, an order issued in Ch'ien-lung 30.
260. *Ch'ing hsü t'ung-k'ao*, 100/8589. This opinion was shared by the government and some of the high-ranking officials. For example, *Shih-li* (1908), 395/2b,
gives an edict issued in 1817 (Chia-ch'ing 22), saying in part that instructors
in the *shu-yüan* often were not qualified for their posts, and that some of them
demanded salaries but did not go to the schools to discharge their duties; another,
issued in 1822 (Tao-kuang 2), says that the qualities of headmasters varied widely, some of them not even holding examination degrees, and that they neglected
to go to the institutions which they were supposed to serve. *T'ung-kuan* (1944),
22/3b, quotes a number of edicts commanding provincial authorities to ameliorate
the conditions prevailing in the *shu-yüan*, including those issued in 1733 (Yung-
cheng 11), 1822 (Tao-kuang 2), and 1853 (Hsien-feng 3).
261. *Hsiang-shan* (1923), 6/25b-29a, indicates that Hsiang-shan Hsien (Kwangtung) had seventeen *shu-yüan*, of which five were the results of official-gentry
co-operation, while eight were established by the local officials alone, and the
remaining four by the local gentry alone. Almost all local gazetteers contain
lists of academies, sometimes with descriptions of these institutions. A few
examples: *T'ien-ching* (1898), *chüan* 35; *Yen-ch'ing* (1880), 4/31b-39b; *Yang-
chou* (1810), *chüan* 19; *Ling-shan* (1914), 10/149a-151a; *Chiang-ching* (1924),
8/11b-13a; *T'ung-jen* (1890), *chüan* 14; *Chen-nan* (1892), 3/16a-b.
262. For example, *Chi-chih shu-yüan*, established by "Wang Pi-kung, a villager," in T'ung-chih times, was situated in Sha-ho-pao village. *Han-tan* (1933),
9/4b. *Kuei-lin shu-yüan*, built by Yang Wei-han in 1833, had its site eighty *li*

outside the city of Chiang-ching (Szechwan). *Chiang-ching* (1924), 8/11b. Some well-known *shu-yüan* had scenic locations.

263. For example, *Kuang-chou* (1878), 72/12b-13a, says that *Ying-yüan shu-yüan* received a subsidy of 18,589 taels from the provincial treasury in 1869, and another of 10,800 taels from the same source. About 4,389 taels was spent in constructing the school buildings; the remaining money was turned over to merchants who guaranteed a monthly interest of 10 per cent. An additional 2,760 taels was set aside annually to cover the salaries of the headmaster and the gentry manager who supervised the administration of the institution, stipends of students studying there, and other expenses. *Hsi-hu shu-yüan* (Nan-hai, Kwangtung) received a number of contributions, including 20,000 taels raised by the local gentry in the early 1860's. *Nan-hai* (1910), 14/15b. *Wen-wei shu-yüan* (Wei Chou, Chihli) was established by Tung Hsiang-nien, the magistrate, in 1775, with an endowment of 1,600 *mow* of land, yielding an annual rent of seventy-five *shih*, and twenty-one houses, yielding a rent of 300,000 copper cash. The total annual income from the interest paid on the foregoing amounted to 658,000 cash. *Wei-chou* (1877), 7/17a-b. *Ying-yang shu-yüan* (T'ung-kuan, Shensi) received in 1858 a contribution of 3,000 *shih* of grain from a local *chien-sheng*, which was sold for 3,000,000 cash. This institution, by the way, was converted into the *Ying-yang hsiao-hsüeh-t'ang* (a primary school) in 1907. *T'ung-kuan* (1944), 22/3a. Salaries of headmasters varied widely. The head of *Chung-shan shu-yüan* (an important academy rebuilt by Tseng Kuo-fan after Nanking recovered from the Taipings) received a total of 980 taels yearly. *Chiang-ning* (1880), 5/7a. The head of *Hsin-ch'eng shu-yüan* (Ch'ing-pien, Shensi) received an annual salary of 60,000 cash and "festival gifts" of 6,000 cash (a total of less than 70 taels). *Ch'ing-pien* (1899), 2/3b-4b.

264. *Ch'ing hsü t'ung-k'ao*, 100/8593. These governors included Liao Feng-chou, Chekiang; Wei Kuang-t'ao, Shensi; and Yü Lien-san, Hunan.

265. I. e., *P'eng-nan shu-yüan*, situated in P'an-yü Hsien. It was promoted by the gentry under the leadership of Ho Jo-yao and approved by the authorities. *Kuang-chou* (1878), 66/27b. En-p'ing (Kwangtung), a locality that had suffered heavily in the Hakka uprisings of Hsien-feng times, had two *shu-yüan* built in 1862. *Wu-fu shu-yüan* was the result of the co-operation of all families dwelling within ten *li* of a village. It had, besides the schoolhouse, a walled stronghold *(pao)* and a shrine for honoring "the righteous and the brave." *Sheng-p'ing shu-yüan*, situated in another village, had similar aims and arrangements. *En-p'ing* (1934), 6/18a.

266. *Hsüeh-cheng* (1810), 64/1a. The historical antecedent of *she-hsüeh* may be traced directly to Ming times. According to *Yen-yüan* (1916), 6/7a-b, Emperor Shih-tsu of the Yüan dynasty arranged every fifty rural households into one *she* in which a *she-chang* was instituted to teach the inhabitants in the neighborhood the proper methods of cultivating their land and planting mulberry trees. No rural school in the true sense of the word was included in the *she* of Yüan times. At the beginning of the Ming dynasty the emperor ordered every fifty households to establish a *she-hsüeh* and to engage a *sheng-yüan* of noted learning and good character to teach youngsters of the neighborhood. See also *Fu-shan* (1924), 5/10a, and Liu I-cheng, *Wen-hua shih*, II, 174, 247. Liu's opinion that *she-hsüeh* were already established in Yüan times, however, needs confirmation. *Yüan-shih* makes no mention of such schools either in *shih-huo chih* or in *hsüan-chü chih*.

267. *Hsüeh-cheng* (1810), 64/1a.

268. *Ch'ing t'ung-k'ao*, 69/5489, a government order dated 1670 (K'ang-hsi 9); *T'ung-kuan* (1944), 22/4a, an edict dated 1713 (K'ang-hsi 52).

269. *Shih-li* (1908), 396/1a-2b. *Ch'ing t'ung-k'ao* gives this same document but omits the first two sentences which we quoted. For the law of Shun-chih 9, see note 267.

270. *Shih-li* (1908), 396/2b, indicates that the provincial authorities of Kweichow were ordered in 1736 to establish *she-hsüeh*, "in accordance with the precedent set in Yung-cheng 1." The imperial government reiterated this order in the next year, adding that funds might be drawn from the regular revenue at the discretion of the governor-general concerned. Also in *Ch'ing t'ung-k'ao*, 71/5511.

271. *Hsüeh-cheng* (1810), 64/1b-5b; *Shih-li* (1908), 396/1a-2a; *Ch'ing t'ung-k'ao*, 69/5492.

272. *Hsüeh-cheng* (1810), 64/3a; *Shih-li* (1908), 396/2a-3a; *Ch'ing t'ung-k'ao*, 69/5492, 70/5492, 70/5502, and 72/5523. *Hu-nan t'un-cheng k'ao*, 9/15b, quotes a memorial submitted in 1848 (Chia-ch'ing 28), which reads in part: "Investigation shows that for the Miao were originally set up to teach children of the Miao people. Subsequently, in Chia-ch'ing 15 [1810], twenty more such schools were added, with a view to extending education. For several tens of years the Miao students . . . have mostly been studying diligently."

273. *Shih-li* (1908), 396/2a.

274. *Hsüeh-cheng* (1810), 64/6a-b.

275. *Hsüeh-cheng* (1810), a government compilation, makes no distinction between *she-hsüeh* and *i-hsüeh*, treating them as if they belonged to one system. Orita, *Fen-lun*, III, 5, states that "*she-hsüeh* were promoted and managed by rural communities; *i-hsüeh* were established with funds contributed by the gentry and common people." This does not agree with all the facts.

276. *Yen-chou* (1883), 6/13a-b, for example, records that in local usage *i-hsüeh* were "formerly called *she-hsüeh*."

277. *Li-p'ing* (1891), *chüan* 4, *shang*, p. 115b. The compiler adds: "The distances from different villages to the city vary; not every one of the rural students can go to the city to study. Therefore, additional *she-hsüeh* have been established in large villages and rural towns."

278. *Ch'ing t'ung-k'ao*, 69/5493, an edict dated K'ang-hsi 54.

279. *Hsüeh-cheng* (1810), 64/7a; the document was dated Ch'ien-lung 5.

280. See *ibid.*, 64/7a, for a government order authorizing the establishment of *i-hsüeh* "both in the cities and villages" of Kweichow province. *Mu-lin shu* (1868), 6/25b-27b, quotes Ch'en Hung-mou, who ordered that *i-hsüeh* be set up in *ch'eng* and *hsiang* (city and rural areas).

281. *Ch'üeh-shan* (1931), 14/3a.

282. *Ch'ing-yüan* (1880), 4/30b-32b.

283. *Kuang-chou* (1878), 15/8a.

284. *Hua hsien* (1924), 5/22a.

285. For example, see *Nan-hai* (1910), 8/28a; *P'an-yü* (1911), 10/23b-27a; *T'ung chou* (1875), 5/80a-81b. The gentry, however, often established schools for the exclusive benefit of younger members of their own clans. See, for example, *Liu-shih chia-ch'eng*, 31/3a-b.

286. *Ju-lin* (1883), 3/8a.

287. *Fu-shan* (1924), 5/12b-13a, gives an outstanding instance in which a *she-hsüeh* became a place for local literary contests. The practice began in 1703 and continued till the closing years of the nineteenth century, when the examination system was abolished by the imperial government. *P'an-yü* (1911), 10/27a, contains this information: "The schools of various rural areas usually served as places where public meetings were held. Literary contests and academic lectures were also occasionally held there." The Chinese text has *shu-yüan*, which is

here translated "schools," for these were in reality rural institutions with definitely lower standing than the true *shu-yüan*.

288. *Nan-hai* (1910), 6/31b, gives excellent examples. *Pao-liang she-hsüeh*,
organized in the first years of the nineteenth century by the joint effort of nine
neighboring rural areas, served as headquarters of the local organization for
defense against bandits. In 1854, when the Red Turbans rose, the funds of this
rural institution helped to finance the local *t'uan-lien*.

289. *Wei chou* (1877), 7/17b.

290. *Lu-lung* (1931), 21/2b.

291. *Hsin hsien* (1887), 7/3b, states that Ts'ao Yung, the magistrate, set up
nine *i-hsüeh* in the last quarter of the nineteenth century.

292. *Feng-chen* (1916), 3/10a-b, states that one *she-hsüeh* was established by
the government in Yung-cheng times in the city and that two were set up in the
countryside in Tao-kuang times by local inhabitants.

293. *Ch'üeh-shan* (1931), 7/8b, 14/2b-3a, and 24/14a-b. More than a dozen
i-hsüeh were established between 1694 and 1894 by local officials or the gentry.

294. *Yen-yüan* (1891), p. 1b, says that a total of forty-two rural and city *i-
hsüeh* were set up; the last one was built by the magistrate in 1874. *Hsiang-
hsiang* (1874), 4/17a-18a, gives this interesting information: upon receiving
word in K'ang-hsi 23 that the emperor desired *i-hsüeh* to be established, the
magistrate contributed money and built a school in the city. This school was
reorganized into a *shu-yüan* in Hsien-feng 10.

295. *Ch'ing-pien* (1899), 2/5a-b.

296. Among many local gazetteers that contain relevant information, the following may be cited: *Han-tan* (1933), 14/53a-54b; *Mien-yang* (1894), *chüan* 5,
"Hsüeh-hsiao," p. 6a; *Hsing-kuo* (1889), 9/4a-5a; *Hsü-chou* (1874), 15/4b-15a;
Wu-hsi (1881), 6/16a-23b; *Kuang-chou* (1878), 66/20b; *Tung-kuan* (1911), 17/14b-
15b; *Yang-chiang* (1925), 17/44b-49b; *Hsün-tien* (1828), 7/28a-b; *Chen-nan* (1892),
3/16b-17b; *P'u-an* (1889), 7/1b; and *Yung-ning* (1894), 5/1a-33b.

297. See note 253 for the emperor's reasons for refusal.

298. *Ch'ing t'ung-k'ao*, 70/5495.

299. *Hsü t'ung-k'ao*, 50/3246.

300. *Shih-li* (1908), 331/1a ff., summarizes the regulations first drawn up in
1646 and later modified, especially in 1663, 1668, 1690, and 1723, which fixed
the content and types of questions to be used in the various examinations. Local
gazetteers often give information concerning local practices. See, for example,
En-p'ing (1934), 11/4a; *Meng-ch'eng* (1915), 5/8b; *Ch'u chou* (1897), *chüan* 2,
ting, p. 15a-b; *T'eng hsien* (1846), 4/10b; *I-ch'eng* (1929), 19/5a-b. Parker's
article, "The Educational Curriculum of the Chinese," *China Review*, VI (1877),
67-70, describes the general procedure, from the local to the metropolitan examinations.

301. *Shih-li* (1908), 332/1a. See p. 2b for a regulation of 1758 to the effect that
expositions of the classics should conform to the interpretations set forth in the
writings of Ch'ing emperors and orthodox Confucianists. Any scholar who failed
to follow this regulation disqualified himself in the examinations.

302. For official lists of such books, see *Hui-tien* (1908), 32/2b-3a; *Hsüeh-
cheng* (1810), 12/1a-32b. For lists of books actually received by local schools,
see, for example, *Ch'u chou* (1897), *chüan* 3, *ping*, p. 17b; *Wei chou* (1877),
7/15a-b; *Hsin-ning* (1893), 15/6a-b; *Hsing-an* (1871), *chüan shou*, p. 12a-b;
Nan-ch'ang (1919), 12/4a-6b; *Hsin hsien* (1887), 2/16b; *Lo-ch'uan* (1944), 19/2b.

303. *Hsün-tien* (1828), 7/33a, affords an instance.

304. *Hsüeh-cheng* (1810), 6/1a, action taken in 1652 (Shun-chih 9). This reg-

ulation was reiterated with little material change in Ch'ien-lung 23 (1758). See note 301.

305. *Ch'ing t'ung-k'ao*, 60/5491, action taken in K'ang-hsi 39.

306. *Ibid.*, 70/5495, order issued in 1725 (Yung-cheng 3). Parker, "Education Curriculum of the Chinese," *China Review*, IX (1881), 3, notes the same regulation. With a view to checking the spread of "heretical sects," the government ordered in 1850 (Tao-kuang 30) that the Amplified Instructions be used as one of the essential texts to be studied and expounded in local schools. *Shih-li* (1908), 400/4a.

307. *Hsüeh-cheng* (1810), 13/1a-17a, summarizes the main actions taken between 1686 and 1779. According to the same source (13/13a), in 1776 (Ch'ien-lung 41) the emperor ordered the suppression of the works of Ch'ien Ch'ien-i (1582-1664), Chin Pao (1614-80), and Ch'ü Ta-chün (1630-96), because these authors, "pretending that they belonged to the vanquished dynasty, meaninglessly indulged in mad barks": adverse opinions concerning the new regime. However, the works "of writers of the Southern Sung dynasty, who abused the Chin dynasty, and of writers living in the early years of the Ming dynasty, who disparaged the Yüan dynasty," were to be allowed to circulate, after everything "incompatible with reason and righteousness" had been deleted.

308. *Ibid.*, 14/1a-2a; *Ch'ing t'ung-k'ao*, 69/5486, action taken in Shun-chih 8-9. The Board of Rites, however, was authorized to print certain approved essays, and in 1723 bookstores were permitted to print essays selected by the Board in conjunction with the Hanlin Academy. Upon ascending the throne in 1736, the Ch'ien-lung emperor ordered the Hanlin Academy to select and publish several hundred "eight-legged essays." At the same time the interdiction barring publication of essays written by contemporary scholars was rescinded. *Hsüeh-cheng* (1810), 6/6a.

309. *Sheng-hsün*, Sheng-tsu, 25/22a and 8/14a; *Shih-lu*, Hsien-feng, 38/13a; *Hsüeh-cheng* (1810), 14/1a-14b; Chu Shou-p'eng, *Tung-hua hsü-lu*, Tao-kuang, 29/4a; *Shih-li* (1908), 400/2a and 5b.

310. *Sheng-hsün*, Hsüan-tsung, 78/14b-15a.

311. *Ibid.*, 78/18a-b; *Shih-li* (1908), 400/2b.

312. *Hsüeh-cheng* (1810), 4/1a-13a; *Hui-tien* (1908), 32/3b; *Ch'ing t'ung-k'ao*, 69/5486 ff., give the basic regulations and prohibitions governing the schools and scholars.

313. *Hsüeh-cheng* (1810), 4/3b; *Ch'ing t'ung-k'ao*, 69/5486. The texts of these rules are also found in many local gazetteers, for example, *Kuang-chou* (1878), 66/12b-13a; *Hun-yüan* (1880), 2/8a-9b; *Lu-chou* (1885), 17/5a-6a; *Pa-ling* (1891), 17/1a-b; *Hsin-ning* (1893), 15/5a-6a; *Tung-kuan* (1911), 17/6a-b. Ting Jih-ch'ang (1823-82), *Kung-tu*, 30/8a-b, indicates that as late as the 1860's a prefect of Sung-chiang Fu (Kiangsu) reissued the text of this imperial document to all schools under his jurisdiction and required scholars to write from memory one of the eight rules in each of the monthly tests.

314. *Hsüeh-cheng* (1810), 4/3b-4a; *Shih-li* (1908), 389/2b-3a; *Ch'ing t'ung-k'ao*, 69/5492. The text of this imperial essay is also given in many local gazetteers, including *Kuang-chou* (1878), 1/9a-b and 97/2b; *Hun-yüan* (1880), 2/9b-11b; *Pa-ling* (1891), 17/3b-4b.

315. The Yung-cheng emperor's essay is given in *Hsüeh-cheng* (1810), 4/5a, and the Ch'ien-lung emperor's in 4/11a-12b. These are also found in a number of local gazetteers. According to *Po-pai* (1832), 6/5a, copies of the Yung-cheng emperor's essay were distributed to local schools.

316. *Shih-li* (1908), 383/1a.

317. *Ch'ing t'ung-k'ao,* 70/5498.

318. *Shih-li* (1908), 383/1a.

319. *Ibid.,* 332/1a and 2a. Chu Shou-p'eng, *Tung-hua hsü-lu,* Tao-kuang, 32/1a-b, indicates, however, that the old prohibition was revived in 1836. It is said that in Tao-kuang 16 (first month, *hsin-ch'ou* day) the imperial government punished the director of studies of Hunan province for publishing his own literary works and allowing bookstores to print and sell copies of them. This case, however, involved an official instead of a scholar.

320. *Hsüeh-cheng* (1810), 7/1b, 5a, and 7a; *Shih-li* (1908), 330/1b-2a and 399/6a-b.

321. *Hsüeh-cheng* (1810) and *Shih-li* (1908), 383/1a. See also Orita, *Fen-lun,* III, 44-50, quoting from Kuang-hsu, *Hui-tien.*.

322. *Ibid.,* p. 50.

323. See Chang, *Chinese Gentry,* pp. 165-73.

324. Kung Tzu-chen (1792-1841), *Wen-chi, chüan shang,* "I-pin chih-chi chu-i," p. 9. See biographical sketch in Hummel, *Eminent Chinese,* I, 431-34.

325. Kuan T'ung (1780-1831), *Wen-chi,* "I yen feng-su shu," quoted in Ho Ch'ang-ling, *Wen-pien, chüan* 7; *Chiang-ning* (1880), *chüan* 14, part 8, p. 2a-b. According to Chao I (1727-1814), *Ts'ung-k'ao,* 28/2b, note on "Chien-sheng," scholars of the Ming dynasty were "proud" partly because the founder of the dynasty gave them unprecedented encouragement. Emperor T'ai-tsu in 1343 (Hung-wu 26) selected sixty-four *chien-sheng* from the Imperial College and appointed them to various offices. The following year he sent a number of them to supervise waterworks undertaken by local officials and inhabitants. Some of these were charged with the duty of reporting local conditions and with the authority of hearing cases of litigation not satisfactorily handled by local officials. According to Ku Yen-wu (1613-82), *Wen-chi, chüan* 1, three "Essays on *Sheng-yüan,*" many of the *sheng-yüan* living in the closing years of the Ming dynasty "went in and out of yamen and tyrannized their neighbors." Their conduct, apparently, was one reason that the Ch'ing emperors barred them from yamen visits. It may be added that many scholars of the Ming period had considerable impact on political affairs, a fact which may have been the chief reason for the policy of the Ch'ing government. See Liu I-cheng, *Wen-hua shih,* 2/251-52, for a brief account of the activities of the members of the Tung-lin and Fu-she groups.

326. See note 314.

327. Huang Liu-hung, *Fu-hui,* 3/23b.

328. *Tsou-i,* 51/5b, a memorial submitted in 1759 (Ch'ien-lung 24) by Li Yin-p'ei, provincial director of studies, Kiangsu.

329. Huang Liu-hung, *Fu-hui,* 2/16b-17a.

330. *Shih-li* (1908), 400/2a. *Ibid.,* 400/7a, indicates that in 1876 (Kuang-hsü 2) the imperial government instructed the provincial educational authorities to stiffen their attitude toward unruly scholars, because "pettifoggers in Szechwan province were mostly *kung-sheng, chien-sheng,* and *sheng-yüan* (civil as well as military), and these scholars instigated fights or organized mobs, inflicting serious damages on the people." Similar misbehavior was noticed by the imperial government from time to time. See *Hsüeh-cheng* (1810), 7/1b and 4b-5a, edicts issued in 1659 (Shun-chih 16) and 1727 (Yung-cheng 5). For actual instances, see *Kuang-chou* (1878), 5/17b-18a, 109/25a, 129/23a, and 131/7b; *Nan-hai* (1910), 2/63a and 19/7b; *Kuang-hsi* (1890), 10/17b.

331. *Ch'ing t'ung-k'ao,* 70/5506, an edict dated Yung-cheng 13.

332. *Ibid.,* 24/5062, memorial submitted in Ch'ien-lung 27.

333. Wang Jen-k'an (1849-1893), *I-shu,* 3/13a. As may be expected, military

sheng-yüan often conformed even less with imperial regulations. See, for example, *Nan-hai* (1910), 14/22a-b; *Kuang-chou* (1878), 129/23a. Shen Pao-chen, governor-general of Liang-Chiang, proposed in a memorial in 1878 that the examinations for military "scholars" be abolished. After arguing that such scholars were useless to the government, he wrote: "Those who are not employed and do not live in their home localities usually rely on their examination degrees as a passport to tyrannizing their neighbors. For, while nominally they are scholars, actually they are loafers. . . . Hence, among those who are cited for violation of the rules of the Horizontal Tablet, civil *sheng-yüan* are far outnumbered by military *sheng-yüan;* the latter are thus worse than useless." Ko Shih-chün, *Hsü-pien*, 54/4b.

334. *Shih-li* (1908), 383/3b, an edict dated K'ang-hsi 12. This behavior was as old as the examination system itself. See Chao I, *Ts'ung-k'ao*, 28/12b, note on "Chi-wei."

335. *Ch'ing t'ung-k'ao,* 70/5505, an edict dated Yung-cheng 12.

336. *Nan-hai* (1910), 14/19b-20a, and *Shih-li* (1908), 383/4a.

337. *Shih-li* (1908), 330/4b, an edict dated Hsien-feng 1; quoted also in *Tung-kuan* (1921), 26/9b. Cf. *Nan-hai* (1910), 14/14a, where it is said that scholars in Feng-t'ien exhibited the same pattern of behavior.

338. *Ch'ing t'ung-k'ao,* 69/5487, an edict dated Shun-chih 10. This state of affairs persisted in the nineteenth century. See sources indicated in note 330.

339. *Ibid.*, 70/5501, action taken in Yung-cheng 7.

340. *Hsüeh-cheng* (1810), 7/8a.

341. *Ibid.*, 7/18b.

342. *Ibid.*, 7/15a-16b.

343. *Hsing-an* (1871), *chüan shou,* p. 13a-b.

344. *Ch'ing t'ung-k'ao,* 72/5520.

345. *Ibid.*, 71/5511.

346. *Hsüeh-cheng* (1810), 7/16a.

347. *Ibid.*, 7/16b, quoting a memorial submitted in 1742 (Ch'ien-lung 7) by Te-p'ei, governor-general of Liang-Chiang.

348. *Ibid.*, 7/20b-21a.

349. *Ch'ing-shih kao,* 494/18b. *P'ing-kuei chi-lüeh,* 1/15a-16a, records that Hou Erh-yü, a *sheng-yüan,* and Chang Feng-kang, a military *chü-jen,* both natives of Hsing-an (Kwangsi) dwelling in Nan Hsiang (South Rural Area), oppressed their fellow villagers and eventually joined the Taiping Rebellion in 1853.

350. George Smith, *China* (1847), pp. 251-52. See *Hua hsien* (1924), 2/26a, for a less violent protest against notorious yamen underlings raised by scholars who gathered in the district city to take the examinations.

351. *Hsüeh-cheng* (1810), 16/2a-3a. See also Chang, *Chinese Gentry*, pp. 182-97.

352. *Shih-li* (1908), *chüan* 341-42.

353. *Ibid.*, 383/7b-8a, for example, gives an edict dated 1835 (Tao-kuang 15); Huang Liu-hung, *Fu-hui*, 24/20a, a statement made in the seventeenth century. E. A. Kracke, "Family Versus Merit in Chinese Civil Service Examinations under the Empire," *Harvard Journal of Asiatic Studies* X (September 1947), 103-23, may be consulted. *Nan-hai* (1910), 26/26a, records a curious practice known as *wei-hsing*, a gambling racket resembling betting on race horses, or on candidates in an election, in Western countries. Competent and famed scholars were often prevented from getting the honors they deserved by the method called *chin hsieh* (curbing the crabs), and mediocre, obscure scholars were fraudulently helped to pass the examinations by the method of *kang chi* (carrying the chicks).

354. E. g., in Mei-t'an Hsien (Kweichow), *Mei-t'an* (1899), 3/19a-b, furnishes this information: "Agreement reached through open discussion:-The fees payable by applicants for entering [their names] in the registers [legally qualifying them to take the examinations] are classified into three categories, namely, Upper Households, Middle Households, and Lower Households. Upper Households that possess property valued at over 1,000 taels will each pay 100 taels; if the amount of property is doubled, the fee will also be doubled. Middle Households that possess property valued at over 500 taels will pay 60 taels each. . . . If a household is found upon investigation to be really poor, it does not have to pay more than 20 taels." Cf. *Yung-ning* (1894), 5/32a-b, where it is said that all prospective scholars must qualify themselves by making contributions toward maintaining the local Confucian temple. The amount due from each varied with the degree of affluence of the applicant. Expenses usually incurred in taking the examinations were quite beyond the financial abilities of a poor family. See, for example, *Ch'ing-yüan* (1880), 6/16a-17a; *Mei-t'an* (1899), 3/20a-21b; *Yung-ning* (1894), 5/28a-30b; *T'ung-kuan* (1944), 22/1a. Financial aid was often given to scholars of modest means; such assistance came most frequently from clans.

355. Wang Yu-p'o, quoted by Legge, *China Review*, VI, 231.

356. Quoted in *Kuang-chou* (1878), 5/5b-6a; *Tung-kuan* (1911), 35/12b-13a.

357. Ting Jih-ch'ang, *Kung-tu* 20/6a and 33/10a. According to *Kuang-chou* (1878), 132/15a, the degeneration of local educational officials began as early as the beginning of the eighteenth century. By the last decades of the nineteenth century the process had reached nearly every corner of the empire. See *Nan-hai* (1910), 14/13a; *T'ung-kuan* (1944), 22/1b.

358. See Chang Chung-li, The Gentry in Nineteenth Century China (Ph.D. dissertation, University of Washington, 1953), p. 249, table and discussion concerning the situation in Kwangtung.

359. *Shih-li* (1908), 395/2b, gives an edict dated 1817, in which the Chia-ch'ing emperor said: "Educational officials of the provinces have neglected their duties. Being slothful they fail to keep up the monthly literary tests. Favoritism dictates the appointment of instructors in *shu-yüan* and *she-hsüeh*, some of whom receive salaries without ever making an appearance in the lecture halls." *Han-tan* (1933), 14/51b, indicates that the *shu-yüan* of this district in Chihli province formerly possesses a considerable amount of school land which was illegally disposed of and part of which was not recovered until the 1860's and 1870's. *Hsin hsien* (1887), *chüan* 8, "I-wen," *shang*, pp. 9a-11a, contains this narrative written by the magistrate in 1869: "Upon arrival [at Hsin Hsien, Shantung] I went to *Hsien-chüeh shu-yüan*—only a few rooms, . . . very damp and stuffy. . . . Most of the students do not appear there to receive and write out their assignments. Those that do appear are mostly residents of the city or of places within a few *li* of the city; students living farther away never appear." The compiler of this gazetteer adds this note (p. 8a-b): "Owing to lack of funds [this institution] was in operation at one moment and ceased to operate at another." *Ch'ing-pien* (1899), 4/30b-31a, quotes a report dated 1898 depicting the situation in Ch'ing-pien Hsien (Shensi): "This city has two *shu-yüan*. . . . These two institutions have between them less than twenty students; the rest are youngsters who have just begun their studies, numbering less than thirty. . . . Even these soon take up other vocations." *Nan-ch'ang* (1919), 13/3a, contains this laconic remark: "The *shu-yüan* [of this district in Kiangsi] had ceased to function; many were thus deprived of the opportunity of acquiring knowledge."

360. *Han-tan* (1933), 9/5b.

361. *Yang-chou* (1810), 19/16a ff.

362. Ting Jih-ch'ang, *Kung-tu*, 27/11b, referring to Tan-t'u Hsien and I-hsing Hsien.

363. *T'ung-jen* (1890), 5/19a-b.

364. *Hsüeh-cheng* (1810), 64/1b; *Shih-li* (1908), 396/1a.

365. *T'ien-ching* (1898), 35/32a; *Yen-ch'ing* (1880), 4/39b.

366. See, for example, *Lu-i* (1896), 7/15a; *Hsiang-fu* (1898), 11/70b-71a; *Lo-ch'uan* (1944), 19/4a; *Lu-chou* (1885), 17/70a; *Hsiang-shan* (1873), 6/29a-30a; *Nan-ning* (1909), 20/16b-19b; *Po-pai* (1832), 4/43a; *Ho-ch'ing* (1894), 8/3a-b; *Chen-nan* (1892), 3/16b.

367. *Nan-ch'ang* (1919), 13/1b-2a. *Hsiang-hsiang* (1874), 4/25b-26a, tells this story of Hsiang-hsiang Hsien (Hunan): "Sometime in the reign of Chia-ch'ing [i.e., early in the sixteenth century] Kuei O, the grand secretary, ordered that *she-hsüeh* be built in the city, towns, and villages, to give instruction to the youths of the neighborhoods. . . . This was the origin of *she-hsüeh* in this district. . . . At the beginning of the present dynasty the director of studies corrected examinations for recruiting and appointing *she* instructors, and promoted or dismissed them on the basis of their service records; these were practices that had come down [from Ming times]. In K'ang-hsi 22 [1683] these institutions stopped operation in compliance with a government directive." An old edition of this gazetteer records that the entire district had nineteen such institutions, three of which were in the city. "At present only the site of one of the latter can be identified. . . . The rest can not be traced."

368. *Hsüeh-cheng* (1810), 64/8b-9a.

369. *Lu-i* (1896), 9/2b, quoting a narrative by Fu Sung-ling.

370. A. H. Smith, *Village Life* (1899), p. 74. This tendency persisted in post-dynastic days, in some parts of China at least. Fei Hsiao-t'ung, *Peasant Life* (1939), p. 39: "Illiterate parents do not take school education very seriously. . . . The enrollment [in the village primary school] is more than a hundred, but the actual attendance, as some students told me, rarely exceeds twenty, except when the inspector visits the school."

371. Kulp, *Country Life* (1925), p. 216.

372. *Mencius*, I, vii.

373. *Nan-ch'ang* (1919), 13/1a, indicates that "in Hung-wu 8 [1375] an edict required that *she-hsüeh* be established, one in every fifty households. . . . [This order] was not carried out fully. Hence Emperor T'ai-tsu remarked with a sigh that the task was terribly difficult."

374. *Ibid.*, 13/2b.

375. Hung Liang-chi (1746-1809), "Shou-lin p'ien," an essay on local officials, quoted in Tai Ch'ao-ch'en, *Hsüeh-shih lu* (1867), 11/20a-b.

376. As Knight Biggerstaff summarizes the matter in Hummel, *Eminent Chinese*, I, 289-90: "He [Ho-shen] placed all of his own followers in office, and corrupted the vast majority of others in the official hierarchy by threatening to have them cashiered unless they complied with his demands. . . . The administration went from bad to worse during the last few years of the Ch'ien-lung period, but the state of affairs was even more scandalous in the Chia-ch'ing period during which Emperor Jen-tsung was allowed to have no part in the conduct of affairs of state, control and actual administration of the government remaining entirely in the hands of . . . Ho-shen. . . . The Ch'ing dynasty, which reached its peak during the Ch'ien-lung period, slowly but steadily declined thereafter—the disintegration unquestionably beginning during the period when Ho-shen was in power. See also I. Inaba, *Ch'ing-ch'ao ch'üan-shih* (Chinese trans., 1914), III, 27-28.

377. Weng T'ung-ho (1830-1904), *Jih-chi*, 17/64a, 1878 (Kuang-hsü 4, 10th month, 14th day): "Today an edict sternly upbraids officials of the boards and courts who fail to go to their offices regularly to transact official business." *Ibid.*, 22/9a, 1883 (Kuang-hsü 9, 1st month, 18th day): "Went to office *[Kung-pu*, or Board of Works]; all was quiet in the departments and bureaus; not a single person was in the rooms where documents are kept." *Ibid.*, 22/25b, 3rd month, 2nd day: "Went to office; not a single person there." Li Tz'u-ming (1830-94), *Jih-chi*, vi, *pin-chi*, 14a, T'ung-chih 9 (1870), 12th month, 29th day, quoting an edict printed in the Peking Gazette: "The Sovereign ordered: Censor Hsü Yen-kuei memorialized, requesting that the presidents of the various boards be ordered to go to their offices regularly. . . . Hereafter the presidents of the boards shall appear in their offices every day." *Ibid.*, *jen-chi*, 2nd ser., p. 85a-b, 1878 (Kuang-hsü 4, 10th month, 14th day), quotes the edict to which Weng T'ung-ho referred. These high-ranking officials, it says, often visited the offices only once in several days and remained only momentarily when they did go there. Decisions on official business were secured by their subordinates in their private residences or in the rooms in the imperial palace where they were waiting for an audience. Everything was rapidly and perfunctorily disposed of.

378. Weng T'ung-ho, *Jih-chi*, 15/11b, 1876 (Kuang-hsü 2, 2nd month, 7th day) Weng was newly appointed vice-president of the *Hu-pu*. Weng remarked a few months later (15/58b, 6th month, 4th day): "Went to office; did nothing more than sign the official documents; official business—none of which could be set going."

379. *Ibid.*, 19/87b, 1880 (Kuang-hsü 6, 11th month, 25th day). *Ibid.*, 22/117a, 1883 (Kuang-hsü 9, 11th month, 19th day), hints high-level corruption: "Teng Ch'eng-hsiu . . . impeached Wen-i, associate grand secretary, charging that he deposited over 700,000 taels in *Fu-k'ang* [a big native bank operating in the imperial capital]." A few days later, Weng wrote, (22/119b), "Wen-i replied [to Teng's charge] in a memorial that it was true he had deposited 360,000 taels. Thereupon he was fined 100,000—a contribution to government funds." *Ibid.*, 29/65a-72a, 1890 (Kuang-hsü 16, 8th month, 14th day to 9th month, 5th day), indicates that a very large amount of rice stored in *Lu-mi ts'ang*, one of the imperial granaries located in the capital, was stolen. See 30/12a-21a for the rest of the story. Earlier in his career, Weng had had personal experience with some of the corrupt ways of minor officials serving in the capital. *Ibid.*, 10/86b, 1870 (T'ung-chih 9, 10th month, 19th day): "This year, draw salary of a third-rank official (13.9 *shih* of rice, of which 0.4 *shih* is glutinous rice). Requested the younger brother of [my good friend] Kuei Lien-fang, inspector of *Chung-ts'ang* [the granary issuing the rice], to exercise his influence in my behalf. . . . [The rice] was received only after payment of a 'petty fee' at the rate of 0.50 tael per *shih*. The rice is yellow in color. . . . It is very cheap [at the price paid]." Later, when Weng was one of the young emperor's instructors and enjoyed the confidence of the Empress Dowager, he wrote *(ibid.*, 18/84a, Kuang-hsü 5, 11th month, 13th day) that he still found friendly influence definitely helpful in getting his salary-rice; but he no longer mentioned payment of any "petty fees." Li T'ang-chieh (1798-1865) wrote in his *Jih-chi*, vol. 2, Tao-kuang *chia-wu* (1834), 11th month, 6th day (Li was serving in the *Kuo-tzu chien*, without appreciable influence): "One must ask favor of persons on duty in the granaries in order to get his rice; in addition, there are many sundry expenses. Official business requires bribes at every turn, Alas, the evil has existed for a long time!" That the metropolitan police could not guarantee security even for government property may be surmised from the following edicts printed in the Peking Gazette

and quoted by Li Tz'u-ming, *Jih-chi*, vi, "I-chi," 67b and 79a: 1870 (T'ung-chih 9, 9th month, 29th day), an edict indicating that the treasury of *Nei-wu fu* was burglarized several times; intercalary 10th month, 15th day, another edict, stating that a number of cannons and cannon carriages were stolen from a government arsenal in the imperial capital. See *ibid.*, "Keng chi," p. 47b, T'ung-chih 12, 2nd month, 27th day, where Li quotes an edict revealing that an official seal was stolen; and *ibid.*, "Ken chi," 2nd ser., p. 21a, Kuang-hsü 3 (1877), 8th month, 17th day, an edict revealing that the storerooms of *Nei-ko* were burglarized.

380. Weng T'ung-ho, *Jih-chi*, 15/14a-b, 1876 (Kuang-hsü 2, 2nd month, 14th and 15th day).

381. Twelve years later, Weng recorded another incident. *Ibid.*, 27/6a-b, Kuang-hsü 14, 8th month, 11th day: "Just went to bed; drum beats sounded by the Outer Office . . . heralded the complaint that over four hundred copies of the printed examination questions were missing. I rose and spoke to the supervising official, sharply criticizing him for his improper action. For the functionaries serving in the Outer Office purposely concealed these missing copies; he should have known it, and yet acted thus." Li Tz'u-ming, *Jih-chi*, vi, *ssu-chi*, 2nd series, 60a-b, quotes an edict dated 1877 (Kuang-hsü 3, 5th month, 11th day), stating that the scholars taking the current examination in the imperial palace scrambled noisily for copies of the examination questions, and adds this comment: "According to the established practice, when the examination questions were about to be distributed, the scholars knelt down three times, knocking their foreheads on the ground thrice at each time, and remained kneeling. Under the supervision of high dignitaries, functionaries in charge distributed the questions to the scholars one by one, who rose only after all had received the questions. This year, when the copies of the questions had just arrived, the scholars promptly snatched at them, tearing off the part bearing the first two questions of most of the copies. Scraps of paper littered the entire floor. One hundred and ten of the scholars who did not get their copies argued vehemently with the officials in charge, demanding more copies. The former were thus compelled to write the questions on a large sheet of paper and paste it on one of the pillars for the latter to see. . . . Several tens of scholars could not compose the essays required of them; their friends ghost-wrote for them, and openly passed the ghost-written pieces. . . . The prince and high officials who were supposed to supervise the examination watched and snickered at [what they saw], not appearing to have been surprised or shocked at all.—All respect for law and propriety, all sense of shame, have vanished without a trace." Weng T'ung-ho, *Jih-chi*, 27/70b, 1888 (Kuang-hsü 14, 9th month, 28th day), notes a curious blunder: the Board of Rites announced the date for a sacrificial performance prior to the emperor's wedding one day too early, and repeated the error after it was pointed out by the imperial household authorities.

382. For example, *ibid.*, 16/50a, 1877 (Kuang-hsü 3, 7th month, 7th day), Weng retells a conversation between himself and a local official who described the sorry state of affairs in Honan province in these words: "Most of the local officials do not fulfill the revenue quotas. In years of full harvest one-third of these officials invariably report 'famines.' They report smaller sums than they have actually collected. . . . They are especially inclined to hush up banditry."

Chapter 7
1. Hsiao I-shan, *Ch'ing-tai t'ung-shih* (1923), I, 563. The author tried to fill

this gap in a subsequent shorter work, *Ch'ing-tai shih* (1945); 3rd ed. , Shanghai, 1947.

2. Arthur H. Smith, *Village Life* (1899), p. 226; see also p. 228. Harold E. Gorst, *China* (1899), pp. 82 and 85, states: "There is really no country in which the administrative functions are more completely decentralized than is the case with China. . . . [The people] are accustomed to manage their own affairs, and exercise a measure of local self-government which is unparalleled elsewhere. . . . This leaves an enormous power in the hands of the people. . . . Local affairs are entrusted to village or district councils, and the most worthy person for the office is elected mayor by the suffrages of the community." *Ibid.*, p. 141: "The mayor . . . is elected by popular franchise." This, Gorst thought, "indicates the large measure of self-government which is enjoyed by the Chinese people." E. T. Williams, *China* (1923), pp. 118-36, quoting Maine, "Village Communities," says: "Law is not the command of a superior to inferiors but a declaration by the village elders of immemorial usage," and argues that since the heads of the *p'ai, chia,* and *pao* are "elected" by the inhabitants whom they "represent," the village is a "republic."

3. Radhakamal Mukerjee, *Democracies of the East* (1923), pp. 181-82.

4. Leong and Tao, *Village and Town Life* (1915), pp. 5-6.

5. Hsiao I-shan, *Ch'ing-tai shih,* p. 100: "Although the government had the authority to interfere with affairs of rural and urban self-government, it interfered very little." Paul M. A. Linebarger, *Government* (1938), pp. 138-39: "The governmental superstructure kept the Chinese world together in a formal manner; it did not give it vitality. The family, the village, and the *hui* were fit subjects for imperial attention, but the emperor could not remove his sanction from their existence and thereby annihilate them. No precarious legal personality was attributed to the family, the village, and the *hui,* which could be extirpated by a mere edict." Charles Denby, *China* (1905), II, 6-7: "While China is as autocratic as Russia, nevertheless many principles of democracy enter into her system of government. The emperor is a despot, but he is a patriarchal despot. The head man in every village rules it, but his rule is parental. It is very kindly and gentle, and it dispenses with the costly and troublesome formulas of courts of law."

6. Hosea B. Morse, *Trade and Administration* (1913), p. 59. See also *ibid.*, pp. 32-34: "The government of China is an autocratic rule superposed on a democracy," and "American government stands firm-based on the town meeting. . . . This . . . is true to-day of the country village communities. It is also true, *mutatis mutandis,* of village communities in China today, following the precedent of many centuries."

7. John S. Burgess, *Guilds of Peking* (1928), p. 27.

8. Martin C. Yang, *A Chinese Village* (1945), p. 241.

9. Ch'ien Tuan-sheng, *Government and Politics* (1950), p. 45.

10. George Smith, *China* (1847), p. 23. See also Huc, *Chinese Empire* (1855), I, 88, for a rather confusing statement: "The villages . . . have at their head a mayor called *Sian-yo [hsiang-yüeh],* who is chosen by universal suffrage. . . . The time for which they are elected varies in the different localities; they are charged with the police duties, and serve also as mediators between the Mandarins and the people, in matters beyond their own competence." C. Martin Wilbur, "Village Government in China," p. 40, fails to make any tangible distinction between the two types of leaders.

11. Yang, *A Chinese Village,* pp. 173, 181-82, and 185. Fei Hsiao-t'ung, *China's Gentry* (1953), pp. 83-84, indicates that in some localities of Yunnan province two sorts of leaders were found (1947-48): those locally known as *kung-*

chia, the "better-educated and wealthier family heads" of the neighborhoods, and the *shang-yao,* persons serving in turn as links between the government and the people. These appear to correspond roughly to the "layman" and "official" leaders mentioned by Yang.

12. Yang, *A Chinese Village,* p. 173. Chang Chih-tung, in a memorial dated 1883, indicates that *she-chang* were also found in villages of Shansi. Chang Shou-yung, *Hui-pien, nei-pien,* 53/14b.

13. Huang Liu-hung, *Fu-hui,* 21/5a-b and 22/1a. Huang also stated that *chuang-t'ou* were to be elected even in small hamlets with a population of less than 100 inhabitants each. It is not clear how this requirement was carried out.

14. *Ibid.,* 21/18b-21a.

15. *Ibid.,* 21/4a.

16. *Ting chou* (1850), 7/54b-57a. See also *ibid.,* 7/52a-54a, for regulations issued in 1846 (8th month).

17. Arthur Smith, *Village Life* (1899), p. 228.

18. Yang, *A Chinese Village,* pp. 179-80. L. Donnat, *Paysans en communauté* (1861), pp. 137-38, describes the *chuang-chang* of a village in Ningpo, Chekiang, in these words: "Le village d'Ouang-fu a à sa tête une espèce de maire, élu par les habitants. Ce maire s'appelle tchon-tchiang. C'est le plus vieux ou un des plus vieux chefs de famille (chia tchang) de la localité. Il est nommé à vie. Quand il s'agit de lui donner un successeur, les habitants se réunissent dans la pagode à la première lune de printemps; une affiche émanée de l'un d'entre eux indique le jour et l'heure de la réunion. On ne vote pas; mais on tombe facilement d'accord sur le choix le plus convenable. Les fonctions du tchon-tchiang sont gratuites et quelquefois onéreuses. . . . Le maire n'est pas un personnage officiel; il n'entretient aucun rapport avec le tchi-hien et n'est qu'un agent officieux de la population auprès du pao-tching. C'est le maire qui tient le livre de famille des Ouang *(tsong-tching-bou),* espèce de registre de l'état civil. C'est aussi lui qui administre le trésor du village. Ce trésor est formé des revenus des biens communaux, destinés dès l'origine du village à subvenir à l'entretien de la pagode des ancêtres et aux dépenses de fêtes publiques. Ces biens s'augmentent continuellement de dons de terre faits par les personnes riches qui meurent sans enfants. Dans chaque génération toutes les familles sont chargées successivement d'ordonner, sous la direction du Tchon-tchiang, les fêtes du printemps et de l'automne." Obviously, this village was dominated by a clan.

19. Yang, *A Chinese Village,* pp. 181-84.

20. Burgess, *Guilds,* p. 27.

21. The terms "elders" and "village elders" have been used in a variety of senses. See Appendix III for a brief explanation.

22. Daniel H. Kulp, *Country Life,* I, 110-14.

23. Arthur Smith, *Village Life,* p. 227.

24. Yang, *A Chinese Village,* p. 185.

25. *Ibid.,* p. 186.

26. Samuel Wells Williams, *Middle Kingdom,* I, 483. Williams misnamed these headmen "elders."

27. Yang, *A Chinese Village,* p. 181.

28. Arthur Smith, *Village Life,* pp. 231-32.

29. It may be interesting to compare Chinese village leadership with Japanese and Indian. Kanichi Asakawa's "Notes on Village Government," *Journal of the American Oriental Society,* XXXI (1911), 165 and 167, contains a note on "Village Officials" which is quoted here in part: "The village-head was variously designated. . . . As for the appointment of the village-head, it has been said that

generally in western Japan, the headship was handed down from father to son in old, but not always the wealthiest, families; that in eastern provinces either a general election or an informal selection for life or rotation for an annual term prevailed; and that, as a consequence, the office possessed more dignity and worked with greater ease in the west than in the east. . . . If this was true in a very general way, there were numerous exceptions to this contrast. . . . An official appointment of the head without popular election or choice was not infrequent. . . . Even in cases of election, the authorities sometimes exercised a veto power or ordered reconsideration. . . . It would seem, on the whole, that election or rotation was much less common than appointment, and tended to lapse into the latter." Asakawa, in a note on "Chiefs," *ibid.*, p. 168, gives the following additional information: "In every village, the head was assisted by some half a dozen Chiefs ordinarily called *Kumi-gashira* (group-heads), but also known as *toshi-yori* (elders), *osa byaku-shō* (leading peasants), *otona byaku-shō* (older peasants); . . . *osa-bito* (leading men), and the like. . . . The first name, *kumi-gashira*, suggests that, in some cases, the office originated with the heads of five-man groups. . . . The other titles would seem to indicate that the Chiefs had merely been leading peasants of the village. *Osa byaku-shō*, for example, was the title applied in some parts till a late period to peasants who held no official position, but whose forefathers were large landholders. The Chiefs were usually chosen by the village from among the chief families, for a term of one or more years, and the choice was reported to the authorities. . . . This, however, did not prevent the office from becoming confined to a limited number of persons in a given village. . . . Besides the Head and the Chiefs, the average village had one or more Elders, whose function was to keep an eye on the conduct of the village-officials, to give counsel and admonition, and generally guard and promote the best interest of the village. They were chosen from among the most highly respected of the peasants, and usually served with little or no remuneration. They often enjoyed greater moral influence than the Head, but in public documents his signature and seal followed those of the Head and the Chiefs." Despite obvious differences between Chinese and Japanese village leadership, the differentiation of leaders into two general types, official and informal, obtained in both countries. Much less similarity existed between leaders in Chinese and Indian villages. According to B. H. Baden-Powell, *The Indian Village Community* (1896), p. 19, and *passim,* there were two types of Indian villages: the "severalty village" and the "joint village," which characterized southern and northern India respectively. In a severalty village an influential headman, called *patel* or by other names, occupied his office by heredity succession. There was no headman in a joint village. Community affairs were in the hands of a council of elders, and only in modern times was an official headman instituted.

30. Francis Nichols, *Through Hidden Shensi* (1902), pp. 126-27.

31. *Chinese Repository,* IV (1836), 413-14. Italics are mine.

32. Samuel Mossman, *China* (1867), p. 258.

33. S. W. Williams, *Middle Kingdom* (1863), I, 482.

34. Yang, *A Chinese Village* (1945), pp. 175-76.

35. *Ibid.,* pp. 177-78.

36. *Chinese Repository,* IV, 413-14, and Mossman, *China,* p. 258.

37. Yang, *A Chinese Village,* pp. 178-79.

38. Burgess, *Guilds* (1928), p. 26. Burgess points out on pp. 133-34, that leaders in some of the guilds were similarly "elected": "The elderly and more important shop heads unite to control affairs. To ask . . . how these persons are elected is interjecting a Western conception of a technical process into a sit-

uation where no such process is understood. The status of the elders, determined by generally accepted standards, automatically brings them into leadership."

39. See also Kulp, *Country Life* (1925), I, chapter 5.

40. Smith, *Village Life* (1899), p. 132.

41. Yang, *A Chinese Village*, p. 184.

42. Arthur Smith, *Village Life*, p. 132.

43. Kulp, *Country Life*, p. 115, makes this interesting observation: "Although there are at present two scholars who are recognized as the leaders of the village, yet on some matters they may have to consult as many as twenty-five other men. The extent of consultation and approval varies with different matters."

44. Yang, *A Chinese Village*, p. 185.

45. This holds true for periods long before the Ch'ing dynasty. Wittfogel and Feng, *History of Chinese Society: Liao (907-1125)*, p. 194: "The peasantry of the Chinese villages was stratified. Naturally the village head came from the upper group whose members could well afford to hire a substitute for frontier service; the middle group could barely do so. The position of the villagers below this stratum may be readily imagined; members of their families lived on the fringe of the subsistence level and even hired themselves out to the two upper groups as substitutes. In case of calamity, they must have been the first to be sold, to sell themselves into bondage, or to run off and become vagabonds." Later in the same work, p. 489, note 29, the authors quote from Miao Ch'üan-sun: "A local gazetteer reports that the man who owned the most property in his village was selected as the head of the village."

46. Yang, *A Chinese Village*, p. 240: "The first characteristic of village organization in Taitou is that its purposes are negative. . . . The village has no organized recreation, no village-wide social group, no community means for keeping the streets clean, supplying pure water for drinking, or for any community welfare or betterment." This was broadly true of villages of the nineteenth century. See, however, C. A. Anderson and Mary J. Bowman, *The Chinese Peasant* (1951), pp. 154-73, on "The village as a community center," for a somewhat more optimistic view which does not materially conflict with Yang's opinion.

47. Prepared from data given in *Ting chou* (1850), *chüan* 6 and 7. See tables in chapter 1.

48. See chapter 6.

49. *Ho hsien* (1934), 2/10b, quoting from the 1890 edition.

50. Yang, *A Chinese Village*, p. 197.

51. Wang Jen-k'an (1849-1893), *I-shu*, 3/1a-b, a dispatch to Chang Chih-tung, then governor of Shensi. Wang proposed that such festivities be permitted only in prosperous towns and that villages large and small be prohibited from holding religious fairs. *Nan-hai* (1910), 20/8a, indicates that religious parades in connection with a rural temple in Nan-hai Hsien worked a hardship on the villagers. The managers extorted money from the inhabitants, many of whom had to "pawn their possessions or sell their daughters." If the extortioner was not satisfied, the managers promptly led a mob to the homes of those who could not pay and demolished everything in sight; even the houses were sometimes torn down. Nichols, *Through Hidden Shensi* (1902), p. 136, gives this description of a village theatrical performance in North China, which differed in no appreciable way from similar affairs in other parts of the empire: "The great event in the life of the people of Shensi is the play which is given once a year in the village-theatre. The stage consists of a brick-platform, covered by a roof, supported on poles. At the back is sometimes a stationary scene on which are painted pictures of dragons

and gods. Months in advance a village engages a travelling theatrical company to give a performance. It is paid for by popular subscription, and there are no such things as admission-tickets or reserved seats. The entire population of the village are at liberty to stand around the brick-platform and watch the play, which is usually of an historical character and lasts continuously for five or six days."

52. Arthur Smith, *Village Life* (1899), p. 149.

53. Yen Kia-lok, "Basis of Democracy," *International Journal of Ethics*, XXVIII (1917), 203-7.

54. *Luan chou* (1898), 8/24a-25a.

55. Chang Shou-yung, *Hui-pien, nei-pien*, 53/14b, a memorial submitted by Chang Chih-tung in 1883.

56. Yang, *A Chinese Village*, p. 197. It should be noted, however, that these temples were shared by a number of villages.

57. Arthur Smith, *Village Life*, pp. 136-38.

58. *Ho hsien* (1934), 2/12b, quoting from the 1890 edition. See also chapter 6.

59. See, for example, *Kuang-chou* (1878), *chüan* 67, *passim*. Similar data may be found in the section on altars and temples in many other local gazetteers.

60. *Yung hsien* (1897), 27/4b, 23b, and 24a.

61. *Hsüeh-cheng* (1810), 7/18b-19a.

62. Institute of Pacific Relations, *Agrarian China* (1939), p. 12.

63. Ch'ien Yung, *Ts'ung-hua* (1870), 21/14b-15a.

64. *Lin-chang* (1904), 2/17a.

65. Huc, *Chinese Empire* (1855), II, 292-93. The first statement in this passage is not correct. The imperial government maintained thoroughfares important for military and administrative purposes, and many local officials made efforts to keep in repair the roads in the locality under their jurisdiction.

66. *Hua hsien* (1924), 9/26b-27a. See also *Fu-shan* (1924), 7/12a-15b; *Ju-lin* (1883), 4/69a-74a; *Ling-shan* (1914), 4/51a-b.

67. See among numerous instances *Yen-chou* (1883), 5/13b-25a; *Fu-shan* (1924), 3/58b; *Heng-chou* (1875), 9/4a-19b; *Mien-yang* (1894), *chüan* 3, "Chien-chih," p. 47a; *Lu-chou* (1885), 1/3a-15b; *T'ai-pai* (1897), *chüan* 3, *passim; Hang-chou* (1898), *chüan* 7, *passim*.

68. For example, *Hsin hsien* (1887), *chüan* 2, part 6, pp. 2a-3b; forty-five of the sixty-six bridges serving the rural areas were built by private individuals of gentry status; *K'un-yang* (1839), 7/4a; exactly half of the twenty-eight bridges in the countryside were "built with funds contributed by the gentry and the people." See also *T'ien-ching* (1898), 21/22b-36b; *Ch'ing-yüan* (1880), 4/35a; *Hsün-tien* (1828), 6/8a-b; *Nan-ning* (1852), 2/11a-15b. A few bridges were built by commoners. One example is given in *Chüeh-shan* (1931), 18/18a: "Li Te-yu was a farmer of Hsi-pa-pao. There was in this rural market a bridge called *Tzu-fang Ch'iao*. . . . Perceiving that . . . the two ends of this bridge were damaged by rain . . . Te-yu contributed money from his own pocket to gather workers and to purchase materials, . . . and made it a safe passageway. . . . This took place in Hsien-feng times. . . . Another person, Li Miao, was a native of Nan-shih-pao. His family was poor and he herded swine for others. He did not wear socks or shoes throughout the year; hence he earned the nickname 'Iron-Foot Li.' At the beginning of the Kuang-hsü reign [1875], seeing that the road to Pa-wang-t'ai was interrupted by a small river and that travelers had difficulty in wading across it, he exhausted every bit of his savings to build a stone bridge. Upon its completion he entered the *Pa-t'ai ssu* [a temple] and became a Buddhist bonze." These, obviously, were rare exceptions, which did not alter the general situation.

69. George Smith, *China* (1847), p. 228.

70. *Fu-shan* (1924), 7/10a-12a; *Hsin-i* (1889), *chüan* 2, part 5, p. 2a-b.

71. *Hu-pu hsü-tsuan*(1796), 2/7a, gives this regulation: "On the farm land of the people . . . persons who use without permission the water stored for irrigation purposes in ponds dug, drains constructed, or dikes built by individuals with their own labor, where there are clear boundary lines [marking these off from public rivers, reservoirs, etc.] shall be punished in accordance with the laws governing encroachment upon landed property."

72. *Tsou-i*, 64/20b-21a, quoting a memorial submitted by Pi Yüan in 1776.

73. *T'ung-kuan* (1944), 7/3b, summarizes the local situation: "The people of T'ung-kuan had never known water benefits. . . . In T'ung-chih 11 [1872] Wang Chao-yü, the magistrate, urged the people to construct drains. But these were constructed only in places near the city walls, the South Gate, Hui-tui-pao, and Wang-i-ts'un. None were constructed in the rural areas and towns."

74. Fei Hsiao-t'ung, *Peasant Life* (1939), p. 172; Kulp, *Country Life* (1925), pp. 206-17.

75. *Tung-kuan* (1921), 21/12a-b.

76. *Ch'ing-yüan* (1880), 5/12a-14b.

77. *Lu-chou* (1885), 13/22b.

78. *Kuang-hsi* (1890), 5/32b.

79. *Ibid.*, 9/30b.

80. *I-ch'eng* (1929), 30/6b. No details are given.

81. *Hua hsien* (1924), 2/12b.

82. *Han-tan* (1933), 3/5b-10b.

83. *Hua hsien* (1924), 9/27a.

84. *Tung-kuan* (1921), 70/6a.

85. *Lu-chou* (1885), 28/17b.

86. M. S. Bell, *China* (1884), I, 123.

87. Arthur Smith, *Village Life* (1899), p. 233.

88. *Fu-shan* (1924), 4/50a-66a.

89. *Hua hsien* (1924), 2/14a-b.

90. *Nan-hai* (1910), 2/51a.

91. *Ibid.*, 8/2a-b.

92. *Cheng-ting* (1875), 5/35a-b and 40a-b.

93. *Mien-yang* (1894), *chüan* 3, *chien-chih*, 11a-12a.

94. *Ibid.*, pp. 20b-34b.

95. *Nan-ch'ang* (1919), 6/1a-b.

96. See, for example, *Wei chou* (1877), 4/12b-13b; *Nan-ning* (1852), 2/15b-19b; *Fu-shan* (1924), 3/51a-52a.

97. *Nan-ch'ang* (1919), *Nan-ch'ang chi-shih*, 13/1b-3b.

98. See, for example, *Kuang-chou* (1878), 142/31a; *Tung-kuan* (1911), 56/11a and 67/7b; *Lu-chou* (1885), 54/6a-b, *et passim; Hsü-chou* (1874), *chüan* 22, *hsia*, pp. 9b-10a and 13b; *Han-tan* (1933), 10/32b.

99. *Lu-chou* (1885), 13/46a-47a. Gentry fraud was not limited to Lu-chou Fu. See *Nan-hai* (1910), 8/6a-b, for an instance of a retired official of the sixth rank serving as manager of a bureau organized for directing repair work on a flood embankment, who attempted to embezzle over 3,000 taels in 1908.

100. Huc, *Chinese Empire* (1885), II, 323-25.

101. *Lu-i* (1896), 9/3b.

102. Burgess, *Guilds* (1928), p. 27.

103. Arthur Smith, *Village Life* (1899), pp. 163-64.

104. Robert K. Douglas, *Society in China* (1894), pp. 113-14.

105. Ch'en Hung-mou, *Ou-ts'un kao*, 21/21a-b.

106. Ko Shih-chün, *Hsü-pien*, 32/4b-5a.

107. *Ibid.*, 32/19b, a memorial submitted in 1884 by Wang Peng-hsi, a reader of the Hanlin College.

108. Ting Jih-ch'ang, *Kung-tu*, 45/10b.

109. *Nan-hai* (1910), 22/3a.

110. *Ju-lin* (1883), 21/30a. Other instances will be cited in chapter 8.

111. Douglas, *Society in China* (1894), p. 113.

112. See, for example, *Tung-kuan* (1911), 68/5b, 15a-16a, and 70/8a, 12b, 15b; *Lu-chou* (1885), 54/9a and 57/2b, 4a, 6a; *Hsin hsien* (1887), 7/29a-b.

113. *I-ch'eng* (1929), 30/6b.

114. *P'an-yü* (1911), 22/21a.

115. Cf. Yang, *A Chinese Village* (1945), p. 196: "The market town teahouse is a place where many community disputes and neighborhood quarrels are settled by drinking the so-called 'mediating tea.'"

116. See, for example, Lo Ping-chang's "Essay to Warn against Litigations," written sometime after 1861 when he was appointed governor-general of Ch'uan-Shen. He portrayed vividly the disastrous consequences of litigation and urged all to refrain from lawsuits. This essay begins with two proverbs: "It is better to die of starvation than to become a thief; it is better to be vexed to death than to bring a lawsuit"; and "Runners guarding the yamen: tigers on level ground." Quoted in *Hua hsien* (1890), 10/34a-b.

117. For example, Tu Hung-t'ai, a *chü-jen* of 1801 and magistrate of I-yang and Kan Hsien (Kiangsi), handled all lawsuits in the following fashion: "When litigants brought their petitions, he invariably took great pains to persuade them to go back and listen to the arbitration of their neighbors. When he could not help it [and had to give judgments], he promptly settled the cases, never detaining the plaintiffs or the defendants" for any length of time. *Pa-ling* (1891), 31/6a. According to Huang Liu-hung, *Fu-hui*, 11/16a, "Each year during the season when peasants in the countryside are sowing the seeds, local officials display sign boards on which are written four large characters, 'Farmers busy; litigations suspended'. . . . All cases, with the exception of those involving robbery, fugitives, or manslaughter, are refused hearing. This has been an established practice." Huang Liu-hung wrote in the seventeenth century.

118. Ch'en Ch'i-yüan, *Pi-chi*, 9/15b; quoted in *Chung-ho*, I, 109.

119. Ting Jih-ch'ang, *Kung-tu*, 20/1a-b.

120. See, for example, *Chiang-ching* (1924), *chüan* 1, *shang*, 17a, for description of conditions in a locality in western China, which lent support to a Hakka ditty: "The yamen is as deep as the sea; corruption is as unbounded as the sky."

121. Kulp, *Country Life* (1925), p. 323. Italics are mine.

122. *Fu-shan* (1924), 17/1b. "In an old edition of this gazetteer there was a section dealing with local regulations and prohibitions which were concerned with the welfare and interests of the communities. These were [formulated by] the scholars and the people, and approved by the local official upon petition." See Kulp, *Country Life*, pp. 320-21.

123. *Hua hsien* (1924), 9/26a.

124. Chien Yu-wen, *Shou-i shih* (1945), p. 113.

125. *Nan-hai* (1910), 15/1a. See also Hu Shih, *Tsu-shu* (1933), pp. 4-5, for the statement that whenever the news spread that the author's father was coming home (Chi-ch'i, Anhwei), all gambling and opium dens within a radius of twenty *li* closed down temporarily, to escape the elderly gentleman's scathing criticism.

126. *Hua hsien* (1924), 9/23a.

127. Huc, *Chinese Empire* (1855), II, 80-81.

128. Chang Shou-yung, *Hui-pien, nei-pien,* 53/18a-27a; *Chiang-hsi* (1880), *chüan shou,* part 4, p. 3b; *T'ung-chou* (1879), 7/25a-26a; *Ch'üeh-shan* (1931), 18/19b-20a and 24/16a; *Lu-chou* (1885), 22/2b, 26/27b, 27/1a, 34/11a-12b, 36/1b, and 38, *passim;* *Han-tan* (1933), 10/14b; *Hua hsien* (1924), 6/6a-b. Liu K'un-i, governor-general of Liang-Chiang, thought the *t'uan-lien* so useful that he proposed to use it as the basis for building the empire's modern army. Chang Shou-yung, *Hui-pien, nei-pien,* 53/27a-28b. According to *Ch'ing-shih kao,* "Ping-chih," 4, pp. 1a-8b, "rural militia first appeared in Yung-cheng and Ch'ien-lung times. These local forces, however, were recruited and then disbanded, and did not constitute a permanent army. In Chia-ch'ing times, when religious bandits of Szechwan and Hunan were being suppressed, the merits of rural corps became manifest. In the closing years of Hsien-feng, bandits rose in eastern Kwangtung; *t'uan-lien* were started in various provinces. These were sometimes stationed in their native places to defend them and sometimes employed in the campaigns [in other localities]. Tseng Kuo-fan distinguished between *t'uan* and *lien,* broadly identifying the former with the *pao-chia* and the latter with *yung* (braves). In a letter to Liu Chan-yai written around 1860 he says: *"T'uan-lien* practices vary in different provinces. . . . Speaking briefly, these fall into two types . . . some combine *t'uan* with *lien;* others have *t'uan* but are without *lien.* Those who have *t'uan* without *lien* do not levy money or give pay [to the recruits; they concern themselves] merely with detecting spies and arresting local bandits. This is simply the *pao-chia* system, in use since ancient times. Those who combine *t'uan* with *lien* invariably erect military camps, set up sentinels, and pay their recruits, who can be employed to defend the native provinces or deployed in other provinces to fight [bandits]. This is the *kuan-yung* [government braves] system of today. Tseng Kuo-fan, *Shu-cha,* 13/1b.

129. *Lu-chou* (1885), 49/16a.

130. *Kan-chih* (1935), p. 32a-b and 70b.

131. Quoted by Ch'u-an (pseudonym), in *Chung-ho,* III, 6/128-32. Li Tz'u-ming (1830-94), *Jih-chi,* ii, "Chia chi," *shou-chi, hsia,* 49b, gives a somewhat overenthusiastic account of this case. In a later entry, *ibid.,* "Chia-chi," *wei,* 17b, he adds: "[Pao] Li-sheng was an illiterate villager. . . . When he began the undertaking [of local defense] he claimed to have intercourse with *hsien-jen* [supernatural beings]. . . . Every time he went out to battle, he shouted as he advanced, carrying no weapons. Upon seeing him the bandits promptly ran away. . . . The people of Chekiang, believing that [he had supernatural assistance], sought his protection in increasing numbers. But eventually he was overcome and destroyed [by the bandits. As a result] many of the ancient clans and great families had every one of their members killed. . . . There was a widespread rumor among his fellow villagers that he entertained undue ambitions and was not loyal to the dynasty." Viewed in such a light, Pao Li-sheng was no ordinary peasant but an illiterate practitioner of some "heretical creed," seeking to realize his secret ambitions by using defense against the Taiping rebels as a pretext for organizing his own military force.

132. For example, Chang Shou-yung, *Hui-pien, nei-pien,* 53/22b; *Pa-ling* (1891), 19/10b-20b; *Ch'ing-chou* (1908), 1/25a, 42a-b, 43b, 47a; *Kuang-chou* (1878), 81/30a, 82/5b, 16b, 18b, and 134/25b-26a; *Yü-lin* (1894), 18/1b-73b; *Hsü-chou* (1874), *chüan* 22, *chung chih, hsia,* p. 9a-b; *Ch'u-chou* (1897), *chüan* 7 *wu,* pp. 3b-4a; *Lu-chou* (1885), 48/2b, 53/17a-b, and 54/8a; *Meng-ch'eng* (1915), 6/4b-15a; *Lu-lung* (1931), 19/13a-b; *Han-tan* (1933), 10/35a and 44a-b; *Hsin hsien* (1887), 7/30a and 35b-36a; *Yün-ch'eng* (1893), 10/3a-b and 5b; *Chiang-*

ching (1921), 3/17a-b and 18a; *Fu-shun* (1931), 12/57b. In some localities gentry leadership was in so much demand that directors of *t'uan-lien* did not have to be residents of the communities concerned, for example, in some parts of Kwangsi, where "every town and village had its *t'uan-fang* [i. e. , *t'uan-lien*] defense organization or defense corps" and where "the local gentry had hardly enough members to supply leadership. " *Ku-fei tsung-lu* (1890), 1/8b.

133. See, in addition to references cited in note 132, above, *I-ch'eng* (1929), 29/35a-b; *Ch'üeh-shan* (1931), 18/19b-28a; *Lu-chou* (1885), *chüan* 36-49, *passim;* *Chao-chung lu,* 7/16a, 26a, 31a, 34a, 35a, and 8/3b-64a.

134. See, for example, *Chiang-hsi* (1880), *chüan shou*, part 4, p. 3b, an edict dated Hsien-feng 2; *Lu-chou* (1885), 22/2b, 27/6a, and 34/12a-b, where it is indicated that the government entrusted *t'uan-lien* work to Li Wen-an and others; and *Ch'üeh-shan* (1931), 24/16a, an edict dated 1860 (Hsien-feng 10, 4th month, 16th day), authorizing *shen-shih* of Kiangsu, Anhwei, Chekiang, and Honan, who were then serving in Peking or residing in their home localities, to assist in *t'uan-lien* work. As late as 1898, Liu K'un-i, governor-general of Liang-Chiang, proposed that *t'uan-lien* be placed in the hands of local *shen-shih*. See Chang Shou-yung, *Hui-pien, nei-pien,* 53/27a-28b. Lt. Col. G. B. Fisher, *Three Years' Service in China* (1863), p. 57, gives the following conversation between the emperor and the provincial judge of Kwangtung, referring to the campaign against rebels in Ch'ing-yüan Hsien (Kwangtung): "Question. Which are foremost in action, the regulars or the braves? Answer. The braves, in general. . . . Q. Who command the braves? A. Commanders of braves [come] from the same country as the braves: . . . there are also civilians deputed to take charge of them, such as assistant magistrates, prefects' secretaries, township magistrates, prison masters, and, over all, the district magistrate. " In this locality, therefore, the local officials had the local forces directly under their control.

135. See references cited in notes 132 and 133.

136. See, e. g. , *Fu-shan* (1924), 3/4b, 11/28b-29a, and 14 *jen-wu,* 6/26a-b; *Hsiang-shan* (1923), 4/2b; *P'an-yü* (1911), 5/24b and 42/9b.

137. *Hua hsien* (1924), 5/21b. Other bureaus in this locality performed the same function. See *ibid. ,* 5/22a.

138. *Huai-an* (1884), 3/18b-19a, contains this information: "During the uprising of the Red Brows in Hsi-Han times [A. D. 18-27], Ti-wu Lung, Fan Hung, and others built walls and dug moats to defend themselves. . . . In the last years of the Ming dynasty roving bandits were rampant. People of Shensi and Honan combined small villages into large communities and built walls to defend themselves. When the bandits withdrew, they came out to till [the soil]; when the bandits arrived, they carried arms and manned the ramparts" [to protect their communities against the invaders].

139. *Hsü-chou* (1874), 16/1a-35b.

140. *Lu-chou* (1885), 50/33a-b.

141. *Yü-lin* (1894), 18/20b.

142. *Nan-yang* (1904), 8/29b; *Ch'üeh-shan* (1931), 18/18a.

143. E. C. Oxenham, "Report on a Journey from Peking to Hankow, 1868," quoted in Alexander Williamson, *Journey in North China* (1870), II, 406; Mark S. Bell, *China* (1884), I, 392.

144. Williamson, *Journey in North China,* I, 325; observations made by the author traveling in regions near Chieh-hsiu Hsien, Shansi, in October, 1865.

145. *Fu-shan* (1924), 8/17b-36a. See also *Han-tan* (1933), 14/49b, for description of a *chai* of smaller dimensions built in 1862 jointly by the local gentry of Han-tan Hsien (Chihli).

146. *Huai-an* (1884), 27/84b-85a, gives a good example. Wu T'ang, magistrate of T'ao-yüan Hsien (Kiangsu), upon receiving orders from his superiors in 1853, "recruited local braves . . . and drilled several tens of thousands of them. Seventy-two bureaus were established in the villages and towns, which were kept in close contact one with another. . . . An area of several hundred *li* depended upon [these local forces] for protection."

147. Inaba, *Ch'üan-shih*, III, 21-22, 31-32.

148. The imperial government appointed *t'uan-lien ta-ch'en* in the early 1850's. Tseng Kuo-fan held such a post in 1853. By 1860, however, the government was convinced that these high commissioners for some of the provinces failed to show gratifying results. See, for example, memorials submitted in 1861 by P'an Tsu-yin and Yen Tsung-i, given in Chang Shou-yung, *Hui-pien, nei-pien*, 53/21a-b. After the practice of appointing *t'uan-lien ta-ch'en* was discontinued, the imperial government instructed local officials to rely heavily on the gentry to operate *t'uan-lien*. See, for example, *ibid.*, 53/24b-25a, an edict dated 1862 (T'ung-chih 1, 9th month). The imperial government, however, was aware of the necessity of enlisting the cooperation of local gentry. See, for example, *Chiang-hsi* (1880), *chüan shou chih ssu*, p. 3b, an edict dated Hsien-feng 2, 12th month.

149. Chang Shou-yung, *Hui-pien, nei-pien*, 53/27a. The original text of the last phrase quoted here is *ch'üan i pu chih kuei chih min chien*.

150. Quoted from the Peking Gazette, in Li Tz'u-ming, *Jih-chi pu, keng-chi chung*, pp. 47b-48a, Hsien-feng 10, 4th month, 16th day.

151. *K'uei-chou* (1827), 2/19b, quoting Kung Ching-han, *Chien-pi ch'ing-yeh i.*

152. John Scarth, *Twelve Years in China* (1860), pp. 155-56 and 221.

153. See references cited in note 134.

154. *Chiang-hsi* (1880), *chüan shou*, part 4, p. 6b, quoting an edict dated 1853, which reads in part, "The people of Kiangsi are traditionally known for their timid nature; even gentry-scholars are no exceptions in running away" from the approaching bandits.

155. *I-ch'eng* (1929), 38/25a-b.

156. Chang Shou-yung, *Hui-pien, nei-pien*, 53/22b-23a, quoting a memorial submitted in 1861 by Mao Hung-pin, governor of Hunan. See *ibid.*, 53/17b, an edict dated 1800 (Chia-ch'ing 5).

157. Tseng Kuo-fan, *Shu-cha*, 4/2a, letter in reply to Chia Hsiu-shan (1853). A few years later (1861), Tseng indicated that the gentry alone could not be relied upon. In a letter to another friend, he wrote: *"Hsiang-t'uan* really cannot stand against large bandit hordes. It is particularly difficult to select suitable directors of the *t'uan* from among the gentry-managers. Those of them that are upright cannot keep the bandits in check after having tasted every drudgery and difficulty . . . ; those among them that are unrighteous use the *t'uan* as a pretext to extort money, harass the people and arrogate the control of public affairs." *Ibid.*, 16/34a.

158. Ko Shih-chün, *Hsü-pien*, 68/5b, quoting Lung Ch'i-jui's preface to *Yüeh-hsi t'uan-lien lüeh:* "Speaking generally, well-disciplined and able-bodied *t'uan-lien* were found in localities where bandits were rampant, or where the inhabitants were in prosperous circumstances, or where there were capable functionaries to lead and direct them. . . . Judging from past experiences, capable officials constituted the most crucial" factor in *t'uan-lien* work.

159. See, for example, *Chiang-ching* (1924), 10/5a-6a; *Fu-shen* (1931), 8/15b; *Hsing-kuo* (1889), 2/10b; *Kuang-hsi* (1890), 10/7a; Liu Heng, *Yung-yen*, pp. 102-4. This, as already indicated in note 128 above, agrees partly with the view of Tseng Kuo-fan that local defense could be useful where it was organized on

the *pao-chia* principle. In another letter, dated around 1853, Tseng stated that since *t'uan-lien* was an extremely difficult task, he would stress *t'uan* only, and not concern himself with *lien*. *T'uan*, he continued, was actually the *pao-chia* system, and was completely covered by registering and inspecting *hu-k'ou* (households and inhabitants), permitting no bandits to find lodging in any locality. Tseng Kuo-fan, *Shu-cha*, 2/10a-b, letter in reply to Wen Jen-wu. See *ibid.*, 2/35a, letter to Wu Chen-fu, expressing a nearly identical view.

160. *Tsou-i, hsü-pien*, 3/7a, a memorial submitted in 1800 by Chang P'eng-chan.

161. Ko Shih-chün, *Hsü-pien*, 65/9a, an essay written by Chia Li-shang in 1800, which reads in part as follows: "It is difficult to increase the number of regular soldiers, but it is still more difficult to raise military expenses. . . . [The government] therefore chooses to enlist mercenaries, which entails [only] temporary expenditures, and then adopts *t'uan-lien*, which entails no [government] expenditure at all." A few instances of shifting financial burdens to local inhabitants were noted by Tseng Kuo-fan, *Jih-chi*, 1859 (Hsien-feng 9, 11th month, 3rd day and 5th day); *Shu-cha*, 13/34b, letter in reply to Tso Chi-kao, concerning the practices adopted in some localities in Hupeh and the method to be adopted in Anhwei.

162. Tseng Kuo-fan, *Shu-cha*, 2/10a-b, a letter in reply to Wen Jen-wu; given also in Ko Shih-chün, *Hsü-pien*, 68/9b. It may be noted that, as an edict dated 1800 says, one difference between *hsiang-yung* and *t'uan-lien* was that "when *hsiang-yung* are set up in the provinces the men are called together as occasion demands; they group for defense when bandits come and disband and return to their daily occupations when the bandits depart. . . . Naturally, this [arrangement] is not as good as for the *t'uan-lien* [to regiment and drill] the *hsiang-yung*, to give each recruit regular pay, and to require that all men take positions at strategic points side by side with government troops."

163. Wang I-k'o, *Nung-ts'un tzu-wei* (1932), pp. 82-83, quoting from *Shantung chün-hsing chi-lüeh, chüan* 22, *shang*, memorial submitted by Mao Hung-pin.

164. Ko Shih-chün, *Hsü-pien*, 68/12b, Wu Min-shu, "Biographical Sketch of Huang Te-hsüan."

165. *T'ung-ch'uan* (1897), 17/38a-b, a poem written by Ch'en Ch'ien, in the spring of 1861, during the siege of T'ung-ch'uan city by rebels under Lan Ta-shun, and here paraphrased in part.

166. Wang Shih-t'o (1802-89), *Jih-chi*, 2/1b.

167. Li T'ang-chieh (1798-1865), *Jih-chi, chüan* 13, Hsien-feng *kuei-ch'ou*, 1st month, 19th day.

168. *Ibid., chüan* 15, Hsien-feng *hsin-yu*, 10th month, 20th day, and 11th month, 1st day.

169. Wang Shih-t'o, *Jih-chi*, 3/11a.

170. *Ibid.*, 2/3a.

171. *Ibid.*, 2/1a-b; see also *ibid.*, 1/4a-b. Li Tz'u-ming (1829-94), *Jih-chi pu, keng-chi mo*, p. 57a-b, Hsien-feng 10, 12th month, 26th day, quotes from the Peking Gazette the following memorial submitted by Seng-ko-lin-ch'in: "Scholars and people of Shantung rely on their *hsiang-t'uan*, gather mobs, and refuse to pay taxes."

172. Ch'en Ch'i-yüan, *Pi-chi*, 9/15a. The conditions described prevailed in Chin-hua Hsien and Lan-ch'i Hsien (Chekiang).

173. Sheng K'ang, *Hsü-pien*, 82/44a.

174. *T'ung-jen* (1890), 9/58a-59b. See also *Nan-hai* (1910), 20/6a.

175. Shen Shou-chih, *Pi-chi,* quoted in *Jen-wen,* VII, 8/28-29.

176. *Ku-fei tsung-lu,* 1/8a-11a.

177. Li Tz'u-ming, *Jih-chi pu, hsin-chi shang,* p. 4a, 1861 (Hsien-feng 10, 2nd month, 3rd day): "Heard that Miao P'ei-lin has rebelled. Miao P'ei-lin is a native of Feng-t'ai, Anhwei, a *sheng-yüan* who drilled rural inhabitants to defend against the Nien bandits. When his military strength increased gradually, Sheng-pao induced him [to join the government cause]. Cumulative promotions earned him the title of provincial treasurer and the post of military intendant of Ch'uan-pei. "

178. Ko Shih-chün, *Hsü-pien,* 68/11b, an essay written by Chu Sun-i in 1858.

179. Chang Shou-yung, *Hui-pien, nei-pien,* 53/25a-b, a memorial submitted in 1863 by Seng-ko-lin-ch'in.

180. Pao Shih-ch'en (1775-1855), a letter to Wei Yüan, quoted in Chang Ch'in, *Chung-hua t'ung-shih* (1934), V, 1391.

181. *China Review,* III (1874-75), 63-64, Charles Pitou's note on Chinese government.

182. Yang, *A Chinese Village,* p. 193.

183. See source indicated in note 82.

184. *Hua hsien* (1924), 2/12b-13a.

185. Li T'ang-chieh, *Jih-chi, chüan* 11, Tao-kuang *wu-shen,* 7th month, 13th day, and *passim.*

186. *Ting chou* (1850), 22/58a-b.

187. *Lin-chang* (1904), 2/17a.

188. Arthur Smith, *Village Life* (1899), pp. 164-65.

189. *Nan-hai* (1910), 6/13b-14a.

190. Shigeru Kato, article on rural markets, quoted in *Shih-huo,* V (January 1, 1937), 63-65.

191. Yang Ch'ing-k'un, *North China Local Market* (1944), pp. 18-19.

192. Yang, *A Chinese Village,* pp. 179 and 193.

193. *Chinese Repository,* IV (1836), 414.

194. *Kuang-chou* (1878), 131/21a.

195. *Meng-ch'eng* (1915), 12/9a.

196. Hsien Chin Hu, *Common Descent Group* (1948), p. 123.

197. *Chao-chung lu,* 7/37a-b.

198. *Yü-lin* (1894), 18/21a. For description of other organizations, see *ibid.,* 18/21b-22b. Cf. *Chao-chung lu,* 7/37a-b.

199. *Hsü-chou* (1874), 16/1a-35b.

200. *I-ch'eng* (1929), 20/8a-b.

201. Huc, *Chinese Empire* (1855), II, 81-84.

202. *Chi-an* (1937), *chüan shou,* pp. 10b-22b. The *kung-so* was reorganized in 1935 when the two managements were merged into one.

203. Some Western writers took notice of associations organized for special purposes. See, for example, Burgess, *Guilds,* p. 16, and Paul M. A. Linebarger, *Government,* pp. 136 and 138.

204. *T'ung-kuan* (1944), 26/2b, indicates that the people of this northern locality were "so poor that they valued money as much as their own lives. . . . But when it was a matter of building temples and offering sacrifices to deities, they ungrudgingly paid substantial sums. "

205. *Nan-ch'ang* (1919), 56/11a.

206. Arthur Smith, *Village Life* (1899), pp. 141 ff.

207. See chapter 6, notes 230-34.

208. *Tsou-i, hsü-pien,* 4/28b, memorial submitted in 1805 by Ch'in Ch'eng-en, governor of Kiangsi.

209. *Ibid.*

210. For example, during the first quarter of the nineteenth century the customary interest rate on grain loans in certain localities in Kiangsi was said to have been from 15 to 20 per cent. Later in the century it rose to over 50 per cent in Hunan. See *Chiang-hsi* (1880), *chüan shou,* part 3, p. 16b; *Pa-ling* (1891), 15/3a.

211. Western writers gave it these appellations: "Mutual aid clubs," Kulp, *Country Life,* p. 189; "loan club," John Gray, *China,* II, 84; "money loan association," *China Review,* V, 405; "loan association," Adele Fielde, *Pagoda Shadows,* p. 113; "money lending club," Doolittle, *Social Life,* II, 149; "mutual loan society," Gorst, *China,* p. 117. A modern Chinese sociologist added still another name, "financial aid society." Fei Hsiao-t'ung, *Peasant Life,* p. 267. The procedure of forming such a group was variously called *tso-hui* (making an association), *ta-hui* (striking an association), *ch'ing-hui* (inviting an association), etc.

212. Adele Fielde, *Pagoda Shadows,* pp. 113-15. See Ball, *Things Chinese* (1904), pp. 633-44.

213. *Pa-ling* (1891), 52/3a-b.

214. Arthur Smith, *Village Life,* p. 189.

215. Kulp, *Country Life,* p. 199. Funeral societies persisted, in some localities at least, down to more recent times. In making a survey of villages of Chang-i (Shantung) in 1932, an investigator working for the Institute of Pacific Relations discovered the following: "Owing to the Chinese custom whereby the offspring must mourn their parents with the wearing of coarse, white cloth hats, these societies have assumed various names such as the 'White Hat Society,' the 'White Organization,' etc. Though the exact origin and history of such societies has never been definitely recorded, the objective needs of the village people must be responsible for their existence. The necessity to find outside labor, which is difficult especially during the harvest, together with the necessity of meeting the unavoidable expenditure, evidently made such organizations desirable. In almost every village where there are a considerable number of men with old parents still living, there is always one such 'Filial Mourning Headdress Society.'" *Agrarian China,* pp. 205-6. It is a mistake to suppose that funeral associations were resorted to only by peasants. Scholars of limited means sometimes availed themselves of such convenient devices. An actual instance was afforded by Yeh Ch'ang-chih (1849-1917), who recorded in his *Jih-chi,* 2/25b, Kuang-hsü *chi-mao,* 12th month, 27th day, that in 1879, when he was a *chü-jen* and lived in his native city, Ch'ang-chou, Kiangsu, he formed a "Scholar Funeral Aid Society" which operated in the following manner: "The society has ten principal members, each of whom recruits ten associate members. Only persons belonging to the government school [i.e., holding the *sheng-yüan* title] are accepted into the membership. When a scholar of modest means dies, or when one of his grandparents or parents or his wife dies, and his family is without the money to pay the funeral expenses, such a member will be given assistance amounting to a total of 22,000 cash. There is a total of 110 members; each will pay 200 cash. When a minor dies, the money given in aid will be 5,500 cash, each member paying 50 cash."

216. When the gentry did not live in their home villages, they might exert their influence there through nongentry lieutenants, directing the latter from their residences in towns or cities. This was the situation in modern Shantung where, it was said, "The prestige of what is called 'the big families' still carries influence in all the neighboring districts." Institute of Pacific Relations, *Agrarian China,* p. 15.

217. *Ting chou* (1850), 1/3a.

218. In addition to the references cited in notes 64-98 above, see the following: *Hua hsien* (1924), 9/27a; *Fu-shan* (1924), 7/12-15a; *Ju-lin* (1883), 4/69a-74a; *Ling-shan* (1914), 4/51a-b; *Yen-chou* (1883), 5/13b-25a; *Fu-shun* (1931), 3/58b and 60a-72a; *Heng-chou* (1875), 9/4a-19b; *Hsin-ning* (1893), 17/30a-34b; *Pa-ling* (1891), 11/3a-9b; *Mien-yang* (1894), chüan 3, "Chien-chih," p. 74a; *Chen-nan* (1892), 3/25b-27a; *Hsin hsien* (1887), chüan 8, "I-wen," *shang*, pp. 28a-29b and 30a-b; *T'ien-ching* (1898), 2/22b-36b; *Meng-ch'eng* (1915), 2/13a; *Lu-chou* (1885), 53/11a, 12b, 41a; *Hsü-chou* (1874), chüan 7, *passim; Yung hsien* (1897), 8/8a-10b. Many additional instances may be found in other local gazetteers.

219. *Kuang-chou* (1878), 135/26b, affords an excellent example recorded in the nineteenth century. A retired magistrate, a *chü-jen* of Hsiang-shan Hsien (Kwang-tung), put a stop to extortion practiced by yamen underlings in charge of tax collection, by petitioning first the magistrate and then the provincial treasurer. The absence of effective gentry in a locality might leave it defenseless against oppression. Li Tz'u-ming, *Jih-chi*, vii, "I-chi," *hsia*, 47b, Kuang-hsü 7, 1st month, 23rd day, narrates that a former gatekeeper of the prefect of Wu-ch'ang (Hupeh), serving as commander of the garrison at the town of Lao-ho-k'ou, allowed his soldiers to prey upon the inhabitants. A villager passing through the town with several strings of money was robbed by these soldiers. Angry townspeople noisily demanded redress for this villager in front of the commander's office. Instead of disciplining his soldiers, he reported to his superiors that the inhabitants had rioted. This locality was without titled scholars or gentry with official ranks; the only notables there were a *sheng-yüan* and his father, who was serving as a petty official in a neighboring province. The inhabitants drew up a petition, putting the names of the father and son at the head of the list of petitioners, and sent the document to the prefect. The upshot of this was that these unlucky men were executed by order of the governor-general (Li Han-chang). For additional instances in which the presence of local gentry afforded protection to their home communities, see *Tung-kuan* (1911), 67/6b-7a, where a *chin-shih* secured the abolition of a burdensome levy on incense; *ibid.*, 68/14b-15a, in which another *chin-shih* petitioned the government to eliminate the payment of taxes on land that had ceased to produce crops; *Hsü-chou* (1874), chüan 22, *chung chih, hsia*, p. 20a-b, where two scholars effected the abolition of illegal assessments in connection with riverbank repair work.

220. John Scarth, *Twelve Years* (1860), p. 196.

221. Fei Hsiao-t'ung, *Peasantry and Gentry* (1946), p. 9.

222. Chao I, *Cha-chi*, 34/14a-16a.

223. *Ch'ing-shih kao*, 7/1b.

224. *Sheng-hsün*, Kao-tsung, 263/8b. The measure adopted in Yung-cheng times and referred to in this edict was expressed in an edict dated 1725 in these terms: "If any of the gentry and scholars who live in their native places overstep their rights, oppress good people, or defy government officials and indulge in violent conduct, these persons shall be immediately punished or reported to us." *Sheng-hsün*, Shih-tsung, 26/7b.

225. For a few instances, see *Tung-kuan* (1921), 100/19b-21b; *En-p'ing* (1934), 7/15a.

226. See chapter 4, discussion on the gentry and the revenue system.

227. See, for example, *Ch'ing-shih kao*, 482/15a, where it is indicated that *sheng-yüan* scholars of Li Hsien (Chihli) suffered at the hands of wealthy bullies.

228. *Nan-hai* (1910), 26/9b; *P'an-yü* (1911), 12/11b-12a.

229. *Nan-hai* (1910), 14/6b-7b.

230. *Fu-shan* (1924), 14/13b.

231. *Chiang-hsi* (1880), *chüan shou,* part 2, p. 1b.

232. Wang I-k'o, *Nung-ts'un tzu-wei,* p. 83, quoting from *Shan-tung chün-hsing chi-lüeh, chüan* 22, *shang,* memorial submitted by Mao Hung-ping, governor-general of Liang-Chiang, 1863-65.

233. *Hsiang-shan* (1923), 16/5a-6b.

234. *Tung-kuan* (1921), 100/12b-16a.

235. *Ibid.,* 100/19b-21b.

236. Max Weber, *Social and Economic Organization* (English trans., 1947), p. 136.

237. Fei Hsiao-t'ung, *Peasantry and Gentry,* p. 6: "In a community in which industry and commerce are not developed, in which land has already done its best, and in which the pressure of increasing population is felt, ambitious people have to seek their fortune not through ordinary economic enterprises but through acquiring power legally or illegally. Just the same they must leave their village for good. When they obtain wealth, they may come back to their village to acquire land, but if they retire to live in the village, the pressure of population will be borne upon them and soon wear them out—and after a few generations the big houses will break down into a number of petty owners again. Therefore it is essential for the rich to keep away from the village. The place where they can maintain their power and wealth is the town." This is broadly true, although Fei has somewhat oversimplified and overstated the case.

238. See, for example, *Ku-fei tsung-lu,* 2/25a-27a; *P'an-yü* (1911), 14/13a.

239. The gentry's part in uprisings will be discussed in chapter 10. Fei Hsiao-t'ung, *Peasantry and Gentry,* p. 10, says: "The gentry's interest is not in possessing political power but in maintaining order irrespective of who the monarch is. They will serve him as long as he behaves as a benevolent ruler, but if he becomes despotic and suppresses the peasants too hard, the gentry will exert their pressure against him. On the other hand, if the peasants revolt against the ruler and disturb the social order, they will fight on the side of the monarch." This is hardly an adequate statement of some important facts. As we shall see, the assumption that peasants could by themselves "revolt against the ruler" is a pure abstraction not borne out by the known facts. Fei is on safer grounds when he recognizes the possibility of an undeclared alliance between the gentry and the peasants in a common fight against oppressive government.

240. Chang, *The Chinese Gentry,* pp. 43-51, explains briefly some of these facilities.

241. Weber, *Social and Economic Organization,* pp. 132-33 and 136-37.

242. This will be dealt with more fully in chapters 9 and 10.

Chapter 8

1. Another translation for the term *tsu* is "sib." See Robert H. Lowie, *Social Organization* (1948), pp. 58, 236, and 237, for discussion of terminology. Hu Hsien Chin, *The Common Descent Group in China* (1948), prefers the phrase "common descent group."

2. Ku Yen-wu, *Jih-chih lu,* 10/22b, quoting Ch'en Mei's comment on a passage in the *Chou-li.*

3. Hu Hsien Chin, *The Common Descent Group* (1948), p. 9. She gives another definition on p. 18: "The *tsu* is a group descended from one ancestor who settles in a certain locality or neighborhood." James D. Ball, *Things Chinese* (1904), pp. 172-73, roughly equates the Chinese with the Scottish clan. This is hardly an accurate view.

4. Ch'ü Ta-chün, *Kuang-tung hsin-yü* (1700), 17/5a-6b. This passage is quoted also in *Kuang-chou* (1878), 15/8a-b. Olga Lang, *Chinese Family* (1946), p. 180, supports the view that the clan was essentially a rural phenomenon: "Clans exist only in villages or small towns. There are practically no clan ancestor temples and no clan heads in the cities." This, however, is an overstatement. Ancestral halls existed in such large cities as Peking, Tientsin, Nanking, and Chengtu, as late as the twentieth century. See note 7.

5. Martin C. Yang, *A Chinese Village* (1945), p. 241.

6. Daniel H. Kulp, *Country Life* (1925), p. 135.

7. Hu Hsien Chin, *The Common Descent Group* (1948), p. 10: "The *tsu* is of the greatest importance in rural neighborhoods, in large villages and small towns, although at times its main ancestral hall is located at the county [*hsien* or *chou*] seat or even in the provincial capital. But in the large cities, with their sharp differentiation of the professions and of social classes, it becomes lost." The relatively high degree of mobility among city inhabitants also exerted an adverse influence on the clan. However, the cities, being centers of social and political influence, were often chosen by clans of relatively large size and strong organization as sites for their *ta tsung-tz'u*, that is, common or central clan temples shared and supported by branch halls located in the surrounding countryside. *Chia-ying* (1898), 8/2b, affords an excellent example of such an arrangement: "The local custom attaches importance to the kinship tie. All clans, large and small, have ancestral halls. Inhabitants of villages who dwell together by clans invariably have *chia-miao* [family shrines], which are really ancestral halls. In addition to these halls, there are *ta tsung-tz'u* in the prefectural city. These are built jointly by [the branches of] the clans that dwell in the several districts that compose the prefecture."

8. The affinity that existed between the clan and the village was observed in India. For example, B. H. Baden-Powell, *Village Communities in India* (1899), p. 23, describes one type of "tribe" in the following words: ". . . the existing group remembers only its descent from some one ancestor, and is not numerous enough to be called a 'tribe.' In all probability one man (or two or three brothers) obtained a settlement in some region that was vacant, and the families multiplied into a 'clan,' keeping up the memory of their common descent and acknowledging a certain solidarity. . . . We find a large extent of country containing several hundred square miles, now divided up into 'village' groups, all composed of landowners whose families have a common designation and are reputed descendants of one ancestor; or of two or three families, not more." Cf. the same author's earlier book, *The Indian Village Community* (1896), chapter 6, sec. 3. Radhakamal Mukerjee, *Democracies of the East* (1923), p. 255, indicates an even closer affinity: "In India, since the clans lived in separate villages, and were exogamous and reckoned descent along the male line, they took a special course because their members lived in one or more villages. In the Central Provinces one of the names of the clan is *khera*, which also means a village, and a large number of the clan names are derived from, or the same as, those of villages. Among the Khonds all the members of one clan live in the same locality about some central village." Professor Mukerjee goes on (p. 299) to describe what he believes to have been the Chinese system: "In China the economic association of the village community is obscured by the clan system. The clan jointly possesses property, and indeed the property of the ancestral hall is divided among the poorer members at a very low rental. . . . The ancestral clan fields are inalienable, into whose possession or use it is a sacrilege to bring an intruder." The author seems to have exaggerated the idea of "communal prop-

erty" and forgotten the fact that the clan was not a universal phenomenon in China in the nineteenth century. It is difficult to see what he meant by the statement "the economic association of the village community is obscured by the clan system." George L. Gomme, *The Village Community* (1890), pp. 39-41, suggests that the formation of the village out of the "tribal group" was an early step in the "individuating process of society."

9. Arthur H. Smith, *Village Life* (1899), p. 30.

10. *Cho hsien* (1936), 8/2b.

11. *Hsin-fan* (1907), 5/1a-2b.

12. *Hsiang-shan* (1923), 3/45b.

13. *Ibid.*, 3/1b-36a.

14. *T'ung-kuan* (1944), 25/1a-b.

15. Hu Hsien Chin, *Common Descent Group*, p. 14.

16. *Chinese Repository*, IV (1836), 412. See also Yao Ying (1785-1852), *Wen-chi*, 3/12b.

17. George Smith, *China* (1847), p. 445.

18. John Burgess, *Guilds* (1928), p. 24. Lang, *Chinese Family* (1946), p. 178, echoes this view: "The very appearance of the villages of Central and North China testifies to the diminished importance of the clans. In these parts, especially farther north where wheat and kaoliang fields replace the rice paddies of the South, beautiful and well-kept ancestral temples are rare. . . . Most of the villages in Central and North China are not clan villages."

19. *T'ung-kuan* (1944), 25/1a.

20. *Ch'eng-ku* (n. d.), p. 17a.

21. Arthur Smith, *Village Life* (1899), p. 30.

22. Kao-an (1871), 2/7a-37b; quoted also in Hu Hsien Chin, *Common Descent Group*, p. 14.

23. *Hua hsien* (1924), 2/15a-22a. The largest clan villages in this district were Pi ts'un, inhabited by the Pi clan, with about 10,000 inhabitants; San-hua ts'un, Hsü clan, with about 9,000 inhabitants; and Ya-p'o-lung, Huang clan, with about 8,000 inhabitants. The smallest monoclan villages there contained about a dozen clansmen each.

24. Li Ching-han, *A Survey of the Social Conditions of Ting Hsien* (1933), quoted by Hu Hsien Chin, *Common Descent Group*, p. 15, with this comment" "Here . . . in no locality does the *tsu* play an important part in the village administration. But in agriculturally richer sections of North China, the *tsu* organization appears to be stronger."

25. *Nan-ch'ang* (1919), 27/1b: "One *hsing* [surname] may embrace as many as one hundred clans or several dozen of them. Those that dwell in the *tu* and *t'u* [rural divisions] are so distributed that sometimes one *tu* contains several clans and sometimes one clan is found in several *tu* or *t'u*." *Tu* and *t'u* were rural divisions made for revenue collection purposes but had become territorial units in some parts of the empire.

26. *T'ung-kuan* (1944), 25/1b. See Hu Hsien Chin, *Common Descent Group*, p. 107, for an instance in which a clan dwelt in two villages.

27. L. Donnat, *Paysans en communauté* (1862), p. 85: "Comme celui de Tching-fou, celui de Si-fou et les autres, le village d'Ouang-fou est habité par les descendants d'un même nom. Il a été fondé, il y a plusieurs générations, par une famille de la souche des Ouang, qui abandonna le lieu qu'elle occupait au-dessus de Hang-tcheou pour venir s'établir aux environs de Ning-po. Le livre des ancêtres (Tsong-tching-bou), où sont inscrits depuis plusieurs siècles les naissances et les décès, est déposé entre les mains du Tchong-tchiang, l'ancien

du village, élu par tous les chefs de maison dans la pagode de Oueï-tung-sze, afin de présider à l'administration des affaires communes."

28. Robert K. Douglas, *Society in China* (1894), p. 115: "It often happens that one family becomes the possessor of an entire village, and then we have such names as *Chang-chia chwang*, 'the village of the Chang family' . . . and so on. In such cases the seniors of the clan act as the village elders." See Marion J. Levy, *The Family Revolution in Modern China* (1949), p. 239: "Sometimes the neighborhood consisted of members of only one *tsu*, in which case the neighborhood and the *tsu* organizations were usually conterminous."

29. Burgess, *Guilds*, (1928), p. 25.

30. *Ibid.*

31. Ball, *Things Chinese* (1906), p. 173.

32. Burgess, *Guilds*, p. 24. See Li Chi, *Formation of the Chinese People* (1928), pp. 232-37, indicating the southward migrations since the fourth century, A.D.

33. See, for example, *Yung hsien* (1897), 4/16b. Cf. *T'ai-ho* (1878), 6/3b: "During the turbulent period of the Five Dynasties [907-959] big clans that sought refuge [in T'ai-ho] came from all directions. The Tseng clan came from Ch'ang-sha [Hunan], the Chang clan from Lo-yang [Honan], the Ch'eng, Yen, Wang, Hsiao, Liu, and Ni clans from Chin-ling [i.e., Nanking, Kiangsu]."

34. Hu Hsien Chin, *Common Descent Group*, p. 15.

35. Ch'ü Ta-chün, *Hsin-yü*, 17/5a-6a.

36. *I-ch'uan*(n.d.), p. 12b.

37. *T'ung-kuan* (1944), 26/2a.

38. *Ch'eng-ku* (n.d.), p. 17b.

39. *Ning-ch'iang* (n.d.), p. 23a. It would be interesting to ascertain quantitatively the distribution of clans in various regions of the empire and, in those areas where the clan constituted a regular feature of the local community life, the proportion of clansmen to the inhabitants that did not belong to organized clans. The present investigator regrets that he is not in a position to undertake this task.

40. Fei Hsiao-t'ung, *Peasantry and Gentry* (1946), p. 5.

41. Hu Hsien Chin, *Common Descent Group*, p. 10.

42. Yao Ying, *Wen-chi*, 3/12b, in *Chüan-chi*.

43. Hu Hsien Chin, *Common Descent Group*, p. 112.

44. P'an Kuang-tan, *Wang-tsu* (1947), pp. 98-99, indicates that during the Ming and Ch'ing dynasties, over 67 per cent of the scholars from Chia-hsing who attained the highest successes in the metropolitan examinations belonged to the eminent clans of this locality.

45. Ida Pruitt, *Daughter of Han* (1945), pp. 61-62.

46. Hu Hsien Chin, *Common Descent Group*, Appendix 16, quoting from *T'an-shih hsü-hsiu tsu-p'u*, Vol. I, "Regulations Concerning the Affairs of the Ancestral Hall," pp. 2b-5a and 7b; and Vol. XIV, "On the Ritual Land," pp. 1b-2a.

47. *Ibid.*, Appendix 48, quoting from *Chi-yang Chang-ch'ing Chao-shih tsung-p'u*, Vol. XXII, *chüan* 19, "Rules of the Family," pp. 6a-b.

48. *Ibid.*, p. 29: "The material on hand thus indicates that the poorer the *tsu*, the less the social differentiation." Lang, *Chinese Family* (1946), p. 180, draws a similar conclusion: "The well to do are more clan conscious." We can hardly regard as accurate the following statement in Leong and Tao, *Village and Town Life* (1915), p. 25: "The whole clan then being but a huge family, it follows that all the members of the clan have equal rights and duties towards the ancestral hall."

49. For example, the Fang clan of Nanking (Kiangsu) and the Yang clan of Wusih. See Hu Hsien Chin, *Common Descent Group*, pp. 166-67, quoting from Fang Pao (1668-1749), *Wang-ch'i hsien-sheng wen-chi* (1881), 14/3a, and *Anyang Yang-shih tsu-p'u*, Vol. XVI, *chüan* 23, p. 47a.

50. *Ibid.*, pp. 120-28, quoting from Lu Chiu-kao (1732-94), *Shan-mu chü-shih wen-chi* (1834), 2/1a-4b; T'ung-ch'eng (Anhwei), *Wang-shih tsu-p'u* (1847), Vol. I, *chüan* 1, pp. 34a-35a; Nan-feng (Kiangsi), *T'an-shih hsü-hsiu tsu-p'u*, Vol. I, pp. 1b-2a; and Hunan, *Tseng-shih ssu-hsiu tsu-p'u*, Vol. I, "Wen-i," part 4, pp. 1b-4a.

51. Leong and Tao, *Village and Town Life* (1915), p. 28. Cf. Lang, *Chinese Family* (1946), p. 175: "The clans of Kwangtung and Fukien had two sets of leaders: (1) the clan elders, and (2) the clan executives. The first group, led by the clan head, consisted—theoretically at least—of the eldest men of the eldest generation of the clan. Exceptions, however, were not uncommon. . . . But the clan elders are only venerable figureheads. Real power is in the hands of the clan executives: managers, treasurers, committee members. These men have, of course, to belong to the socially prominent and wealthy families if merely because the well to do alone can afford the degree of education required of them. Most of them were over 50 years of age, but advanced age was not of first importance."

52. Hu Hsien Chin, *Common Descent Group*, pp. 119-20, quoting from *Tseng-shih ssu-hsiu tsu-p'u*, Vol. I, "Wen-i," part 4, pp. 1b-4a.

53. *Ibid.*, p. 131, quoting from *Lu-chiang chün Ho-shih ta-t'ung tsu-p'u*, *chüan* 13, p. 1b.

54. *Ibid.*, p. 127, quoting from T'ung-ch'eng (Anhwei), *Wang-shih tsu-p'u*, Vol. I, *chüan* 1, p. 34b.

55. *Ibid.*, p. 119. Clan heads who had actual charge of practical matters were often chosen primarily for their managerial abilities. See, for example, *Tzuyang Chu-shih ch'ung-hsiu tsung-p'u* (1867), *chüan mo, shang*, p. 44b.

56. Martin C. Yang, *A Chinese Village*, p. 181.

57. Hu Hsien Chin, *Common Descent Group*, p. 29.

58. Some clans engaged in rather extensive activities. Those in Ning-yüan (Hunan), for example, were said to have performed sacrificial rites at the ancestral graveyards on the fifteenth day after the vernal equinox; after these rites they distributed rice and food to the several hundred clansmen who usually attended, gave subsidies to clansmen who married or to whom sons were born, invited to feasts in their honor all clansmen who were fifty *sui* and over, punished erring clansmen by whipping or suspending the privilege of receiving the sacrificial meat, and gave encouragement to scholars who obtained the *sheng-yüan* degree or who taught in the clan schools. *Yung-chou* (1867), *chüan* 5, *shang*, 42a-b.

59. Chao I, *Ts'ung-k'ao*, 17/6a-9a. This well-known historian, writing late in the eighteenth century, traced the origin of genealogical records to the ancient Three Dynasties, but held that such records acquired practical importance only with the adoption in the Wei dynasty (third century, A.D.) of the *chiu-p'in chung-cheng* system of official appointment (i.e., the system of classifying candidates into nine grades, very largely on the basis of family status, and recommending them for appointment by the *chung-cheng*, special functionaries in charge of the matter). During the Six Dynasties (fourth to sixth centuries), when the line between "high" families and commoners became quite rigidly drawn, acquaintance with the *p'u-tieh* (genealogical records) attained the dignity of an independent branch of "learning."

60. Wu Ju-lun (1840-1903), *Jih-chi*, 15/48a.

61. *T'ung-kuan* (1944), 25/9a.

62. *Lo-ch'uan* (1944), 22/7b-8a.

63. *Ch'ing chou* (1908), 2/12a-21b.

64. The following were compiled in the nineteenth century: *Ching-chiang Liu-shih tsung-p'u,* 1825; *K'uai-chi T'ao-shih tsu-p'u,* 1830; *Kui-te Fang-shan Ko-ch'iao Li-shih tsung-p'u,* 1833; *Ta-yüan Yeh-shih tsu-p'u,* 1867; *An-yang Yang-shih tsu-p'u,* 1873; *Wan-t'ung Hu-shih tsung-p'u,* 1880; *Chi-yang Chang-ch'ing Chao-shih tsung-p'u,* 1883. Contents of these are partially quoted in Hu Hsien Chin, *Common Descent Group, passim.*

65. *Nan-hai* (1910), 11/24a-b.

66. The expenditure varied in different clans. For example, in 1771 the Wang clan of Wu Hsien (Kiangsu) revised its *tsu-p'u,* which comprised twenty-six *chüan* and were bound in thirty *ts'e* (volumes). The total expense entailed in compilation and printing one hundred copies amounted to 716 taels. *Tung-t'ing Wang-shih chia-p'u* (1911), *chüan mo,* pp. 42 ff. The Chiang clan of the same locality spent about 312 taels in revising its records in 1803. *Lou-kuan Chiang-shih pen-chih lu* (1846), *chüan mo.* The Tseng clan of Hsiang-hsiang (Hunan) revised its *tsu-p'u* for the fourth time in 1900; the result was a work containing 1,744 *yeh* (leaves), and costing 5,469 dollars. One hundred and fourteen copies were printed. *Tseng-shih tsu-p'u* (1900), *chüan mo.* Assuming that expenditures varied in direct proportion to the size of the records, *Wu-chung Yeh-shih tsu-p'u* (Wu Hsien, 1911), which comprised sixty-six *chüan* bound in fifty-two *ts'e,* must have been an even more expensive affair than the records of the Wang clan as revised in 1771, or those of the Tseng clan as revised in 1900; whereas *P'eng-ch'eng Ch'ien-shih tsung-p'u* (Soochow, 1874), which contained only four *ts'e* and remained in manuscript, must have been comparatively inexpensive to produce.

67. Justus Doolittle, *Social Life,* (1876), I, 225, clarifies the matter thus: "Ancestral halls may be divided into two classes; those in which all the ancestors of families having the same ancestral name and claiming relationship are worshiped, and those in which the ancestors of a particular branch of the families having the same ancestral name and claiming near relationship are worshiped." This explains why in many instances one clan possessed a number of ancestral halls.

68. Edwin D. Harvey, *The Mind of China* (1933), pp. 244-46, quotes from the *Chinese Repository,* I (1832-33), 449 ff., the following description of the sacrificial rites performed in ancestral halls and graveyards: "When there are large clans, which have descended from the same ancestors, living in the same neighborhood, they repair in great numbers for the performance of the sacrificial rites. Rich and poor, all assemble. Even beggars repair to the tombs, to kneel down and worship. This usage is known by the phrase, *sao-fen-mo,* 'sweeping the tombs,' and *pai-shan,* 'worshipping the tumuli. . . .' On some of these occasions . . . even where there are two or three thousand members of a clan, some possessing great wealth, and others holding high ranks in the state—all, old and young, rich and poor are summoned to meet at the *'tsu-tsung-tze-tang,'* or the ancestral hall. Pigs are slaughtered; sheep are slain; and all sorts of offerings and sacrifices are provided in abundance. The processions from the hall to the tombs, on these occasions, are performed in the grandest style which the official rank of the principal persons will admit. . . . Such is the sum of a grand sacrifice at the tombs of ancestors. But to many the best part of the ceremony is to come, which is the feast upon the sacrifice. The roast pigs, rice, fowls, fish, fruits, and liquors are carried back to the ancestral hall; where, according to age and dignity, the whole party sit down to eat and drink and play."

See descriptions in Daniel Kulp, *Country Life,* p. 305, and *Yung chou* (1867), *chüan* 5, *shang,* p. 42a-b.

69. *Tung-kuan* (1911), 68/9a.

70. *Hua hsien* (1924), 9/26a.

71. *Nan-hai*(1910), 16/14b. K'ang Kuo-ch'i, incidentally, was a cousin of K'ang Yu-wei's father.

72. *Kuang-hsi* (1890), 15/13b.

73. *Ibid.,* 4/45a.

74. *Lu-chou* (1885), 50/42b.

75. *Hsü-chou* (1874, *chüan* 22, *chung chih, hsia,* p. 22b.

76. *Fu-ning*(1877), 14/5a. Wealthy persons without gentry status were occasionally known to have instituted ancestral halls. An interesting instance in *Hsü-shih tsung-p'u* (1884), 11/1a ff. : "When our I-chang Kung rose at Pei-ling, he inherited the occupation handed down by Kuan-ch'eng Kung. . . . He transported salt in ships that plied the sea. Within twenty years he was noted for his middle-class wealth." This happened in the middle of the Ming dynasty. Subsequently, the Hsü clan had no less than eight ancestral halls. A wealthy clan like this, however, did not remain long without gentry members, as the following statement hints: "Persons in our clan who have attained eminence and possess high positions and prestige, owe their success, of course, to personal good fortune, but the cumulative efforts of our ancestors are also a contributing factor. These persons should take to their hearts the kind feeling due to all who descend from one common ancestor; they should give aid to destitute clansmen, revise the genealogical records when they become out of date, and do according to their respective abilities everything that benefits the clan." *Ibid.,* 1/17a. Many methods were used to raise funds for building and maintaining ancestral halls, the most commonly employed being voluntary contribution. Sometimes gentry members were required to contribute specific sums, the amounts varying with their official ranks and positions. The Li clan of Ch'ang-chou (Kiangsu), for example, fixed a scale of contribution for its gentry members. A clansman who attained the position of provincial treasurer or judge was to contribute 400 taels; a magistrate, 200; a subordinate local functionary, 20, etc. Occasionally, clans resorted to the ingenious device often known as "loan clubs." In the Li clan just mentioned, a clansman working with his two brothers raised over 2,000 dollars for the ancestral hall by this method. *Li-shih ch'ien-ch'ang chih-p'u* (1894), Appendix, pp. 1a and 6a. Other clans required their members to pay for the privilege of entering the tablets of deceased parents in the ancestral halls, or for registering the names of newborn offspring in the genealogical records. Sons not duly registered were excluded from the sacrificial rites. See, for example, *Wang-shih tsung-p'u* (1840), *chüan* 5. Another method of raising funds was used by the P'u clan of Wusih. In order to meet the expenses of rebuilding the ancestral hall, it required every adult clansman who was not extremely poor to contribute 100 cash each month. *Ch'ien-chien P'u-shih tsung-p'u* (1931), 8/6a ff. These instances indicate that while the clan organization was normally dominated by its gentry members, these did not necessarily shoulder all its financial burdens.

77. Burgess, *Guilds,* p. 25: "There is also throughout North China an absence of the ancestral halls."

78. The information at hand is fragmentary. The following local gazetteers furnish pertinent data: for Kwangtung, *Kuang-chou* (1878), 15/7b; *Ju-lin* (1883), 3/9b, 4/12a-14a; *Hsin-i* (1889), *chüan* 1, part 10, p. 1b; *Ch'ing-yüan* (1880), 2/14a; *Hui-chou* (1881), 45/7a; *Hua hsien* (1924), 2/28a; *Fu-shan* (1924), 9/10a-12a; and *En-p'ing*

(1934), 4/2b-3a. For Chekiang, *Ch'u-chou* (1877), 24/3b; and *Yen-yüan* (1916), 7/7a-12b. For Kiangsu, *Yang-chou* (1810), 60/7b; *T'ung-chou* (1875), 6/51a. For Anhwei, *Ch'u-chou* (1897), *chüan* 2, *shang*, p. 2b. For Hunan, *Pa-ling* (1891), 52/3b; *Hsin-ning* (1893), 19/3b; *Yung-chou* (1867), *chüan* 5, *shang*, pp. 40b-43b; and *Tao chou* (1878), 10/9b. For Hupeh, *Hu-pei* (1921), 21/675-76; *Hsing-kuo* (1889), 4/1b; and *Mien-yang* (1894), *chüan* 9, "I-hsing," *hsia*, p. 22a. For Szechwan, *Fu-shun* (1931), 7/4a; and *Chiang-ching* (1924), *chüan* 11, *shang*, p. 22a. For Kweichow, *T'ung-jen* (1890), 2/4a; *P'ing-yüan* (1890), 5/15a-22a; *P'u-an* (1889), 4/1b-2a; *Li-p'ing* (1891), *chüan* 2, *hsia*, pp. 120b-121b. For Kwangsi, *Po-pai* (1832), "Chih-yü pei-lan," *shang*, pp. 1a-7a; *Yung hsien* (1897), 8/2a-3a; and *Ho hsien* (1934), 4/13a. For Yunnan, *Chen-nan* (1892), 2/26b; *Chen-hsiung* (1887), 3/9a-10a; *K'un-yang* (1839), 5/10a-b; and *Nan-ning* (1852), 1/18b. Doolittle, *Social Life* (1876), I, 226, indicates the situation in the vicinity of Foochow (Fukien): "Many Chinese do not profess to have an interest in any public or common ancestral hall in the vicinity. These are generally the descendants of immigrants from another part of the province or empire, who have not become sufficiently wealthy and numerous to erect an ancestral hall. All such, however, adhere most tenaciously to the worship of ancestral tablets in their houses." For conditions in North China where ancestral halls were generally absent, consult the following: Chihli: *Han-tan* (1933), 6/5b; *Lu-lung* (1931), 10/3b-4b; *T'ien-ching* (1898), 26/1b; *Luan chou* (1896), 8/23b; *Ch'ang-p'ing* (1886), 9/3b; *Shun-t'ien* (1884), 18/10a-13a; *Yen-ch'ing* (1880), 2/65b-66a; *Ting chou* (1850), 19/15b; *Hsi-ning* (1873), 9/2b; and *Tsun-hua* (1794), 11/2b. Shantung: *T'eng hsien* (1908), 3/2b; and *Chi-nan* (1839), 13/5a. Shansi: *I-ch'eng* (1929), 16/5a and 7b; and *Feng-chen* (1881), 6/4a. Shensi: *Yü-lin* (1894), 24/2a-b. Honan: *Nan-yang* (1904), 2/40b; and *Lu-i* (1896), 9/4b.

79. Chen Han-seng, *Landlord and Peasant* (1936), pp. 31-32. Lang, *Chinese Family* (1946), p. 174, states that in Kwangtung, ". . . the proportion of land belonging to the clan varies; among the 24 clans of Kwangtung investigated in 1937 the variation extended from 10% to 90%. These extremes are rather rare. In the majority of cases the clan claimed 50%-70% of the land cultivated by its members, the rest being their private property. This ratio seemed to be typical of Kwangtung. The clans of Fukien possessed less land." Until we have access to adequate data for making a more accurate survey of the situation, all estimates, including those made by Chen and Lang, must be regarded as merely tentative.

80. Theoretically, *i-chuang* or *i-t'ien* was clearly distinguishable from *chü-t'ien* (sacrificial or ritual land) by the purposes which these were each supposed to serve. The ritual land of a clan was designed to maintain the sacrificial rites, whereas welfare farms were used to give aid to needy clansmen. The purpose of the latter is explained in *Wang-shih chia-p'u* (Wu Hsien, 1911), *chüan* 2, *hsia*, p. 35a, in these words: "When *i-t'ien* is instituted, talented ones will not be compelled by the necessity of making a living to neglect their [scholarly] pursuits; those who do not study will not be compelled by hunger and cold to become unworthy; widows, widowers, and orphans will receive support, and all will have the wherewithal for financing weddings and funerals." In actual practice, however, this distinction was not always maintained; the same land might be used for both purposes mentioned above. See, for example, Chang Hsin-t'ai, *Yüeh-yu hsiao-chih*, cited in note 81. Li Tz'u-ming, *Jih-chi*, vi, 82a, gives an instance in Hunan (1870's) where a high-ranking military officer donated 3,600 *mow* of land. Chang Chung-li, The Gentry in Nineteenth-Century China (Ph. D. dissertation, University of Washington, 1953), pp. 167-69, has a table showing

large welfare farms in Wu Hsien, Ch'ang-chou, and Yüan-ho Hsien, based on data given in *Wu hsien chih* (1933), 31/11 ff. The largest of these, totaling 5,300 *mow*, was established by the Fan clan (Wu Hsien); the smallest, barely over 1,000 *mow*, by a member of another clan. The amount of land varied in direct proportion to the size and prosperity of the clan owning it. The following statement from *Chang-shih tsu-p'u* (Kuang-chi, Chekiang, 1841), illustrates this point: "Most of the eminent and great clans institute welfare farms. . . . None is more prosperous than the Tu clan of Shan-yin; the land which it owns amounts to one thousand *mow*. . . . Our clan has a small number of members . . . as a rule, the amount of land it owns does not exceed one hundred *mow*." It is untrue that all or most of the clans in South China had ritual or welfare land. It was said of Wu Hsien (Kiangsu), the place where welfare land was supposed to have originated and where the local economy was fairly affluent, that "wealthy and powerful clans number no less than one hundred, but only about a dozen of them [have welfare farms] as a matter of record." *Wang-shih chih-p'u* (1897), *chüan shou*, "Keng-yin i-chuang chi."

81. Chang Hsin-t'ai, "Yüeh-yu hsiao-chi" (n.d.), in Wang Hsi-ch'i, *Ts'ung-ch'ao*, 4/305a. See *Chia-ying* (1898), 8/7b, for a similar statement.

82. *Kuang-chou* (1878), 15/26b-27a; *Hua hsien* (1924), 9/26b; Kulp, *Country Life* (1925), pp. 86-87.

83. Fei Hsiao-t'ung, *Peasantry and Gentry*, p. 5.

84. For example, "Regulations of the Ancestral Hall," in *T'an-shih hsü-hsiu tsu-p'u*, 1/1b-2a, quoted in Hu Hsien Chin, *Common Descent Group*, Appendix 14, pp. 124-25: ". . . formerly representatives of each branch used to take turns in holding the office of manager of the ancestral hall. Often this person happened to be one who was not wealthy, so that the ancestral rites were neglected and the taxes were unpaid. . . . After deliberations in public, it has been decided that from now on the manager of the ancestral hall must be a wealthy person chosen publicly by the whole *tsu*. . . . The manager of the common granary must be a wealthy man, chosen publicly by the members of the *tsu*. . . . The rice stored at the common granary is to guard against famine, and the post of manager should be filled by a wealthy man."

85. Hu Hsien Chin, *Common Descent Group*, Appendix 58.

86. *Ibid.*, pp. 143-44.

87. Wang Hsien-ch'ien (1842-1918), *Wen-chi*, 13/1a-2b.

88. *Hsiang-shan* (1923), 4/3a-b.

89. *Nan-hai* (1910), 17/8a-b.

90. Hu Hsien Chin, *Common Descent Group*, p. 67, quoting from *An-yang Yang-shih tsu-p'u*, Vol. XVI, *chüan* 23, pp. 47a-48a.

91. *Nan-hai* (1910), 20/20a.

92. *Ibid.*, 4/24a.

93. *Ju-lin* (1883), 21/30a.

94. *China Review*, VIII (1880), 391, a note on "Land Tax in China": "The tax-collector hands a memorandum of the land-tax to the *tsung-hu* or his hereditary representative who is always to be found by going to the *tz'u-t'ang* or ancestral shrine."

95. *Hua hsien* (1924), 2/11b.

96. *Fu-shun* (1931), 3/53b.

97. *Hua hsien* (1924), 10/2b-3a. Another instance was recorded in Chao-wen Hsien (Kiangsu): "The Kuei clan of Chao-wen has been for generations an outstanding kinship group in Wu. During the Chia-ch'ing reign [1522-66] of the Ming dynasty, one of the ancestors, whose personal name was Ch'un, settled down at

Pai-mou. As the village was located on the bank of a river and was marshy, he
. . . constructed drains and sluices; after a while all the land became fertile.
Houses and shops crowded [the village], making it resemble a city." Juan Yüan
(1764-1849), in *Kuei-shih shih-p'u* (1913), 4/9a-10a.

98. *Lo-ch'uan* (1944), 10/2b-3a.

99. *Fang-kuo*(1937), *chüan shou;* Liang Ch'i-ch'ao, *Wen-hua shih,* p. 60; and
Hu Hsien Chin, *Common Descent Group,* p. 120.

100. Hu Hsien Chin, *Common Descent Group,* quoting from *Tseng-shih ssu-
hsiu tsu-p'u*(1900), Vol. I, "Wen-i," pp. 1a-4a, "Chi-kung tz'u kuei-t'iao." The
Huang clan of Shan-hua (Hunan) rewarded clansmen who passed the examinations
with cash prizes ranging from 500 taels for one who won first place in the metropolitan examinations to ten taels or less for one who became *sheng-yüan* of any of
the several grades. *Huang-shih chih-hsi k'ao* (1897), Vol. V. Financial aid was
sometimes given to young scholars merely to enable them to continue their studies. For example, in the middle of the eighteenth century an official-clansman
of the Chang clan of Kuai-chi (Chekiang) instituted "land for scholar aid," the
yields of which—a monthly subsidy of rice (three *tou)* and a quarterly allowance
of money (one-half of a tael)—were used to help needy scholars. *Chang-shih
tsu-p'u* (1841), 19/1b. The effect of clan land on scholarly success was envisaged
by Li Meng-hsiung, who had contributed money to institute "ritual land" for his
clan (Tan-yang, Kiangsu), in these words: "Let me mention the clans in our district that perform extensive common sacrificial rites. The Ching clan of Huang-
t'ang, for instance, where I have personally visited . . . [possesses] ritual land
amounting to several thousand *mow.* . . . The Chiang clan of T'eng-ts'un . . .
has one thousand *mow* of welfare land. . . . The Ho clan of Chiang-shu, though
not as prosperous as it used to be, has several hundred *mow* of ritual land. . . .
The number of clansmen of each of these three clans who have attained scholarly success is greater than that of any other clan in this district." *Li-shih tsung-
p'u*(1883), 3/56 ff.

101. *Tseng-shih ssu-hsiu tsu-p'u* (1900), Vol. I, "Wen-i," part 4, p. 4a.

102. *Lu-chou* (1885), 34/29b and 53/10a.

103. *Hsing-an* (1871), 7/27a.

104. Kulp, *Country Life,* p. 14.

105. *Ju-lin* (1883), 21/18b. The statement quoted is the last line of a little
rhymed piece written by a local poetaster to depict the blissful prosperity of
his home community. The piece runs something like this:

> "In all directions as far as the eye can see kitchen
>   smokes rise;
> Amidst every grove of tall bamboo and ancient banyan
>   trees a village looms.
> Reading and singing, scholars self-confidently thrive:
> Everywhere are ancestral halls used for classrooms."

106. Hu Hsien Chin, *Common Descent Group,* pp. 54-55, quoting from Cheng
T'ai-ho *(ca.* 1277-1367), "Cheng-shih kuei-fan," in *Ts'ung-shu chi-ch'eng,* gives
a pertinent instance: "On the first and fifteenth of the month after the head of the
family has led the members in paying their respects in the ancestral hall, they
come out and he sits in the elevated part of the hall. The male and female members of the family stand below (that is, at the bottom of the steps). Twenty-four
beats are sounded on the drum. Then a young boy chants: 'Listen, listen, listen!
All who are sons must be filial to their parents. Those who are wives must respect
their husbands. Those who are elder brothers must love their younger brothers.

Those who are younger brothers must respect their elder brothers. Listen, listen, listen! Do not attend to your private benefit so as to harm the duty to all! Do not be lazy so as to neglect your affairs! Do not live luxuriously so as to deserve the punishment of Heaven! Do not listen to the words of women, so as to confuse harmonious relations. Do not commit wrongs by violence so as to disturb the peace of the home! Do not become drunk, so as to pervert your nature. . . . Look back at the instructions of the ancestors! To them is tied decay and prosperity.'" Hu Hsien Chin, *Common Descent Group*, p. 186, gives another instance of oral instruction.

107. Leong and Tao, *Village and Town Life*, p. 25.

108. For example, Hu Hsien Chin, *Common Descent Group*, pp. 133-36, quoting from *P'i-ling Ch'eng-shih tsung-p'u*, 1/88b-89a; *Wang-shih tsung-p'u*, Vol. II, *chüan* 1, p. 1b; *I-shih tsung-p'u*, Vol. I, *chüan* 1, pp. 33b-34b; and *T'an-shih hsü hsiu tsu-p'u*, Vol. I, "Regulations," p. 3a-b.

109. *Nan-hai* (1910), 20/19a, gives an instance occurring in the nineteenth century, in which a young man who indulged in gambling, and beat his mother when he was enraged by her scolding, was put to death by order of a gentry clansman. Hu Hsien Chin, *Common Descent Group*, p. 123, describes the practice known as "opening the ancestral hall," that is, convening the clansmen to deal with wayward members.

110. *Tung-kuan* (1911), 98/9b, gives a very interesting instance: "In the Ch'en *ts'un* of Tung-kuan Hsien, Kwangtung, the clansmen number less than five hundred, but the clan regulations are strictly enforced. The villagers regard opium as an enemy. Any person who is addicted to it is severely punished by the *tsu-chang* [clan head] and then ordered to get rid of [the habit]. If the offender proves incorrigible after repeated warning, he is then ostracized from the clan." According to *Chih-hsin pao* (1898), 59/9a-10a, the Chang clan of Sha-wei Hsiang (Hsiang-shan Hsien, Kwangtung), formulated a set of rules prohibiting the use of opium by its members. All addicts were compelled to stop smoking opium within a year. Those who failed to do so were punished by suspension of the privilege of receiving the sacrificial meat (a sort of excommunication). Hu Hsien Chin, *Common Descent Group*, p. 121, quoting from *tsu-p'u* of the Tseng clan of Hunan: "The whole *tsu* [clan] is forbidden to drown girl infants. No matter whether the family be rich or poor, within one month of the birth of a girl it should be reported to the head of the *fang* [branch]." Those who practiced infanticide were punished by fine and flogging.

111. *Tseng-shih ssu-hsiu tsu-p'u* (1900), Vol. I, "Wen-i," part 3, pp. 1a-11b, reprinted forty provisions from the *Ta-ch'ing lü* (the Ch'ing code) governing family relationships, marriage, graves, and payment of taxes. In addition to these, the work gives the clan regulations (a total of twenty-two articles, each with a short note of explanation) which enjoin its members to perform filial duties toward their parents, to revere their superiors and elders, to maintain harmonious relationships with their kinsmen and neighbors, to instruct their offspring, to carry on their own occupations peacefully, to value frugality, to make early payments of their taxes, to do no wrong, etc.

112. Hu Hsien Chin, *Common Descent Group*, p. 133, quoting from *Hsü-shih tsung-p'u*, Vol. I, *chüan* 1, p. 7a-b.

113. *Fu-shan* (1924), 10/10b-12a.

114. In addition to sources cited in notes 109 and 110 above, see *Hua hsien* (1924), 9/23a; Kulp, *Country Life*, pp. 321-22; William Martin, *Cycle of Cathay* (1896), p. 335; and Hu Hsien Chin, *Common Descent Group*, pp. 55-63.

115. Hu Hsien Chin, *Common Descent Group*, p. 132.

116. *Nan-hai* (1910), 4/24a.

117. *En-p'ing* (1934), 6/18a.

118. *China Daily News* (New York), Feb. 8 and 9, 1945, quoted in Hu Hsien Chin, *Common Descent Group*, p. 67.

119. Lin Yüeh-hwa, *Golden Wing* (1947), pp. 1-2.

120. Liang Ch'i-ch'ao, *Wen-hua shih*, pp. 58-60.

121. *Shih-li* (1908), 397/2b.

122. *Shih-shih tsung-p'u* (1900), affords a good instance.

123. Ho Ch'ang-ling, *Wen-pien*, 58/76a. Hu Hsien Chin, *Common Descent Group*, p. 56, summarizes Ch'en Hung-mou's arguments: "Looking at it from the point of view of the state he lists as the most important offenses to be judged by the heads of the *tsu* and the *fang:* (a) unfilial and unbrotherly behavior; (b) robbery; (c) fights. The heads of the *fang* are to make an effort first to persuade the culprit to mend his ways, failing which he is to be reprimanded by the head of the *tsu* in front of the whole group in the ancestral hall. Only if he persists in his misdemeanor is he to be handed over to the authorities. . . . Further, the *tsu* leaders are to be encouraged to arbitrate and settle amicably disputes concerning the sale of land, and of grave land, to compose family quarrels, and also to act on behalf of the *tsu* in the event of difficulties arising with some other group." This official apparently gave some consideration to the essential nature of the clan and did not propose to turn it into a police apparatus.

124. See note 123. The passage upon which Hu bases her summary is given in Ch'en Hung-mou, *Ou-ts'un kao*, 13/40a; cf. *ibid.*, 14/31a-32a. *Chia-ying* (1898), 15/13b, gives an instance in which a magistrate used the clan organization to help maintain local order. This official formulated in the 1850's a set of regulations governing *t'uan-lien*, which reads in part: "Recently, sons and younger brothers do not respect their fathers and elder brothers; fathers and elder brothers, on the other hand, do not behave themselves correctly. . . . The various *hsiang-yüeh* should consult the clans and select persons who are upright and capable of setting [good] examples to serve as *tsu-chang* [clan chiefs]. One chief and one deputy chief should be nominated in each large clan. [All clan chiefs] are responsible for instructing and disciplining the young members [of their respective groups]. . . . Whenever disputes arise in a clan, [*tsu-chang*] should persuade [the parties] with words of reason. Any clansman who dares to act violently or perversely should be promptly reported to the *hsiang-chang* [rural headman], who will summon [the culprit] to his office and admonish him. If the latter persists in challenging the authorities, he will be promptly sent to the government to be dealt with."

125. *Shih-li* (1908), 158/1b. However, Liang Chang-chü (1775-1849), *T'ui-an sui-pi*, 7/21b, obviously quoting from *Ch'ing t'ung-k'ao*, 19/5031-32, recalls that the institution of *tsu-cheng* was not originally intended for universal application. "Investigation shows that a practice was established in Yung-cheng 4 [1726], which required the institution of *tsu-cheng*. Owing to the fact that in the villages of the localities inhabited by the Miao people, where clans numbering over one hundred members live together, it was sometimes impossible for the *pao-chia* to inspect every one of these villages, a *tsu-cheng* was established [in each clan], . . . whose duty was to detect bad elements in the clan. This arrangement was designed to cope conveniently with special local conditions; it was not intended for general adoption." The action taken in 1757 (Ch'ien-lung 22), as indicated in *Shih-li*, 158/1b, cited above, turned it into an empire-wide system.

126. As Orita, *Fen-lun*, I, 213, correctly remarks: "The *Hu-pu tse-li* says that whenever clans live together and their clansmen are numerous, a person with good character and reputation in each clan shall be selected and instituted

as *tsu-cheng*, with the responsibility of investigating and reporting the good and bad elements in the clan. . . . This is also a police arrangement. The office of the *tsu-cheng* does not differ from that of the *pao-cheng* or *chia-chang*. "

127. *Lü-li pien-lan* (1877), 25/100a-b, article on *tao-tse wo-chu* (persons harboring robbers and thieves).

128. Yao Ying (1785-1852), *Wen-chi*, 4/13a-14a.

129. *Chiang-hsi* (1880), *chüan shou*, part 3, p. 28a-b.

130. Feng Kuei-fen (1809-74), *Chi*, 11/23a-26a.

131. For example, *Lun-yü*, 13/18: "The Lord of She informed Confucius, saying, 'Among us here are those who may be styled upright in their conduct; if their fathers have stolen a sheep, they will bear witness to the fact.' Confucius said: 'Among us in our part of the country, those who are upright are different from this. The father conceals the misconduct of the son, and the son conceals the misconduct of the father. Uprightness is to be found in this.'"

132. *Chiang-hsi* (1880), *chüan shou,* part 3, p. 28a-b, gives this edict, which reads in part: "The said governor is hereby ordered to direct all the functionaries under his jurisdiction to select, in earnest, upright *tsu-cheng* and *shen-shih* [clan chiefs and members of the gentry]. . . . If any of the clansmen become bandits or commit unlawful acts, [these men so selected] shall tie the culprits with ropes and send them to the government. . . . If, owing to the fact that members of the robber leagues are numerous and that these men are unable physically to arrest and deliver the culprits [to the government], they shall report to the local officials secretly so that [the latter may make arrests]. But if any of the *tsu-cheng* make false accusations out of personal grudge, such offenders shall be punished according to the law."

133. Hu Hsien Chin, *Common Descent Group*, p. 45: ". . . all *tsu* . . . find a more illustrious ancestor in the earliest historical records of the nation, sometimes a figure of mythical antiquity. The *tsu* of Tseng in Hunan believes it can trace its descent from a prince of the Hsia dynasty, whose father reigned from 2218-2168 B.C., and from Tseng Shen, the disciple of Confucius."

134. In this case the reason for the Ch'ing government's alarm is obvious. Chu Wen was originally a bandit leader; afterward he surrendered to the authorities, achieving official rank and power as a result of "meritorious service" to the T'ang rulers. He usurped the throne in 907 and became the founder of the short-lived Liang dynasty (907-23). *Hsin Wu-tai shih, chüan* 1, gives Chu Wen's early career in detail.

135. *Tsou-i*, 55/3b, a memorial submitted in 1764 by Fu-te, governor of Kiangsi.

136. *Sheng-hsün*, Kao-tsung, 264/19b-20b.

137. *Fu-shan* (1924), 9/8b-9a, quoting from *Hsü t'ung-k'ao.*

138. Ch'en Hung-mou, *Ou-ts'un kao*, 13/21b.

139. *Tsou-i*, 55/3a.

140. *Ibid.*, 55/1a.

141. *Sheng-hsün*, Kao-tsung, 264/5b; *Shih-li* (1908), 399/3b.

142. *Shih-li* (1908), 399/4a; *Sheng-hsün*, Kao-tsung, 264/6a.

143. *Sheng-hsün*, Kao-tsung, 264/10a-b.

144. Ku Yen-wu, *Jih-chih lu*, 23/14a, quoted in Hu Hsien Chin, *Common Descent Group*, p. 50.

145. Wang Shih-t'o (1802-89), *Jih-chi*, 3/21a.

146. *Ibid.*, 3/19b. Cf. Fei Hsiao-t'ung, *Peasantry and Gentry*, p. 4: "An absentee landowner needs political power for his protection. In holding their privileges, the gentry are militant, as they must be. To be politically powerful and

influential, the organization of the gentry has to be big and strong." This, Fei argues, was the rationale of the clan organization.

147. *Tzu-yang Chu-shih ch'ung-hsiu tsung-p'u* (1867), "Tsung-kuei." The pronouncement referred to was issued upon petition by some of the clansmen, including four *sheng-yüan,* seven *chien-sheng,* and one minor official.

148. Lang, *Chinese Family,* . p. 173: "In 1936 a visitor in Kwangtung or Fukien could easily see that the clans were still functioning organizations. The rich villages . . . are usually dominated by three kinds of buildings: ancestor temples in which the ancestors of the clan are worshiped; pawnshops, whose profits serve to increase the clan's fortune, and blockhouses built to protect wealthy clan members from bandits and rebels. Here at least 4 out of every 5 people belong to one of the clans ruling the village." This was broadly true of other localities where the economy was fairly affluent. In less prosperous areas, as already indicated elsewhere in this study, the clan did not do as well. See sources cited in note 78.

149. One obvious reason is that the widespread disturbances of this period reduced many a clan to partial if not complete ruin. This, for example, was said of the Ts'ao clan (Chia-hsing, Chekiang): "Alas, our clan has declined to such an extent! Since . . . Ch'ien-lung times [late in the eighteenth century], when Shou-shan Kung [i.e., Ts'ao Huan] and Ch'iu-yü Kung [i.e., Ts'ao K'un] died in succession, the good fortune of the clan had been gradually waning. After Tao-kuang times [middle of the nineteenth century] the clan unexpectedly suffered the devastations of war, and its decline became daily more apparent. . . . Clansmen now surviving . . . old and young included, number just over ten. . . . In the city there is a place called Wang-tai. Inhabitants of the neighborhood used to tell me that formerly the houses that densely dotted the three sections of this place belonged mostly to the Ts'ao clan. But now the place is desolate, covered with weeds as far as the eye can see. Although it is impossible to identify the clansmen who then dwelt there, [it is certain] that countless among them died of hunger or war, or drifted away to destinations unknown." Quoted in P'an Kuang-tan, *Wang-tsu,* p. 136.

150. *Ibid.,* pp. 116-36, gives three main reasons for the continued existence or prosperity of the ninety-one clans which he studied: (1) the fact that the ancestors of these groups were immigrants from other localities suggests that these persons and their descendants tended to be resourceful. and adaptable; (2) the fact that extensive intermarriage went on between these clans made it possible for whatever good traits the clansmen possessed to be intensified; and (3) the fact that some of the ancestors were long-lived indicates another mark of biological vigor. P'an seems to stress heredity and eugenics; it is probable that he exaggerates the influence of these factors on the clan.

151. *Fu-shan* (1924), 17/29a.

152. *Tsou-i,* 50/9a. The memorial referred to was issued in 1756. Two instances may be cited here. According to *Hua-shih tsung-p'u* (Wusih, Kiangsu, 1894), *chüan-shou, shang,* p. 27a, this clan had at the beginning of the sixteenth century five hundred *mow* of good land, the proceeds from which furnished expenses for sacrificial rites, ancestral hall repair, and financial aid to clansmen. The land, however, soon disappeared. In 1563 a gentry-clansman reinstituted thirty-two *mow,* which again disappeared in about one hundred years. At the beginning of the Ch'ing dynasty seventy *mow* of clan land was again instituted and again was misappropriated. According to *Li-yang nan-men P'eng-shih tsu-p'u* (Li-yang, Kiangsu, 1894), 2/33a, the ritual land dedicated to the "ancestor of the second generation," a total of five hundred *mow,* was so mismanaged that it barely supported the sacrificial rites.

153. See, for example, Hu Hsien Chin, *Common Descent Group*, Appendix 49, pp. 167-68, quoting from *Ching-k'ou Li-shih tsung-p'u,* where it is said that the ancestral hall with ritual land instituted in 1637 suffered mismanagement, and that "in less than one hundred years the descendants had sold all the land to people of different surnames." Ch'en Han-seng, *Agrarian Problem* (1933), pp. 12-13: "The system of community lands in China is also crumbling. . . . Clan land has a high percentage in Kwangtung, Kwangsi, Kweichow, and Fukien. But it is monopolized by a few rent collectors who have thus practically become big landowners." Institute of Pacific Relations, *Agrarian China* (1939), pp. 22-23: "As is well known, the clan land is not subject to sale, nor to division. The land deeds of many a clan, notably in Soochow, Changchow, Shanghsu, and Wusih, do not exist in paper form but are carved on stone tablets which are built into the walls of the clans' ancestral temples. . . . But in recent years, the management of clan land here and there has carried out its sales secretly, which only goes to prove once more that the vital forces of life are stronger than the supposedly binding character of writing on stone. . . . That the Tsao Clan in a village called Ho-tsun in Wusih has had its land reduced from 1,000 *mow* in 1930 to 300 in 1933 is only one example. Clan land has even been divided in some instances, and therefore completely liquidated. . . . Even in the clans whose land has not been officially divided, the rent proceeds are virtually controlled by a tiny minority of the clan." The trend observed by these writers went on at a quickened pace in the twentieth century, but as already indicated, it had become noticeable in the eighteenth century. In isolated instances, determined clansmen might save the clan property from immediate disposal, as, for example, did the Chang clan in Nan-hai Hsien, Kwangtung. *Nan-hai* (1910), 20/8b. While clan organizations generally tended to decline, some clans, for various reasons, remained prosperous for a long time. An outstanding instance was the Fan clan of Wu Hsien, Kiangsu. Wu Hsi-ch'i (1746-1818), quoted in *Ching-chao Kuei-shih shih-p'u* (1913), 4/11b, says: "When I visited Wu Hsien, I climbed the T'ien-p'ing hill and paid respect to the shrine [of Fan Chung-yen, a celebrated official of the Sung dynasty and ancestor of the Fan clan]. There I saw fertile farm land [so extensive that] the paths dividing one field from another formed an unbroken network. On the occasion of the annual sacrificial rites, all the descendants gathered together, numbering as many as several thousand persons." Juan Yüan (1764-1849), quoted in *ibid.*, 4/9b: "A few clans of the *shih-ta-fu* ['scholar-official'] of Wu have instituted welfare farms; that of the Fan clan is the most noted. From the Sung dynasty to the present, a period of seven or eight hundred years have elapsed, but [the clan] has maintained its welfare farm without interruption." Wang Chung-liu, quoted in *Tung-t'ing Wang-shih chia-p'u* (1911), *chüan* 2, *hsia,* p. 35b: "Wen-cheng [i.e., Fan Chung-yen] contributed a thousand *mow* [to the welfare farm of the Fan clan]. . . . I have inquired of the Fan clan [and was told] that the welfare farm originally established by Wen-cheng has now been increased to 8,000 *mow.*" According to this writer, the Ts'ai clan of the same locality began with a welfare farm of modest dimensions but, thanks to efficient management and frequent contributions, the property grew to 1,500 *mow* in less than thirty years. Wang was presumably speaking of the nineteenth century.

154. Francis L. K. Hsü, *Ancestor's Shadow* (1948), p. 130.

155. See initial statements, Institute of Pacific Relations, *Agrarian China,* quoted in note 153. The following are also pertinent: *Hua hsien* (1924), 2/28b: "Ritual land is also called *cheng-ch'ang [t'ien].* It is maintained from generation to generation. . . . When private families sell their own land, no person would care to buy it unless it is expressly declared in the deed of sale that the land is

not clan property." Peter Hoang, "A Practical Treatise on Legal Ownership" (trans.), *Journal of the Royal Asiatic Society*, North China Branch, N.S., XXIII (1888), 147, writes: ". . . ancestral temples and tombs, land belonging to a family or clan generally and set apart for providing funds for general family purposes . . . as also land dedicated to charitable purposes and registered as such in the office of the local authority . . . the original grantor is not permitted to sell. Any person disobeying these laws is liable to punishment." The government protected clans in another way. An undated document issued by the provincial treasurer of Kiangsu to the Yeh clan of Wu Hsien says, "in case wicked persons . . . and unworthy descendants clandestinely and fraudulently sell [the clan land], authorization is given [to the proper persons in the clan] to bring this document [to the local yamen] and enter an accusation against the guilty parties so that they may be punished according to the law." *Wu-chung Yeh-shih tsu-p'u* (1911), 63/90 ff. Special measures were sometimes taken to set up a clear and fixed line between the common property of the clan and the private property of the component families. In the Yeh clan referred to above, clansmen were not allowed to lease any part of the welfare land and till it as tenants. *Ibid.*, 63/91. A similar prohibition existed in the Wu clan of Huai-yin (Kiangsu). *Wu-shih tsung-p'u* (1921), Vol. V, "Clan Regulations." In this instance, however, the prohibition was calculated mainly to avoid embarrassment of forcing defaulting clansmen to pay their rent.

156. It sometimes happened that all the component families of a clan sank to commoner status. Li Tz'u-ming, *Jih-chi pu*, "Jen chi," p. 33a, quotes the following account of the Chang clan of Shan-yin, written by Shih Jun-chang (1619-1683): "The Chang clan of Shan-yin was a first-rate clan of scholar-officials [in Ming times]. . . . Now its offspring are few, and all are common peasants."

157. A Western writer of the nineteenth century summarizes this view in these words: "Wealth is accumulated toilsomely, and there is, as in other countries, an idea that it is dissipated in about four generations. A popular verse says:

> 'One generation toils, and meanly fares;
> The next, broad robes of fur and satin wears;
> The third sells off the fields and pawns the home;
> Its heirs, in tatters, hungry, houseless, roam.'"

Fielde, *Corner of Cathay* (1894), p. 21. Chinese writers frequently voiced the same view. For example, *Tz'u-li* (1896), 2/5a, records that in the third *tu* of Tz'u-li Hsien (Hunan), the Chang, Wang, and Li clans rose and declined in close succession; the prosperity of each "did not last beyond three generations." This view has the support of some recent writers. Yang, *A Chinese Village*, p. 132, says that family prosperity seldom lasts as long as three or four generations. Hsü, *Ancestor's Shadow*, p. 305, concludes that family eminence seldom extends over two generations at a time. The same conclusion is drawn by Hsü in his article in *American Sociological Review*, XIV (1949), 664-771. Other writers, however, appear to question this view. Karl A. Wittfogel, "Public Office in the Liao Dynasty and the Chinese Examination System," *Harvard Journal of Asiatic Studies*, X (1947), 13-40, indicates that there was a tendency for the offspring of privileged families to enjoy special opportunities. Presumably such a tendency would facilitate the perpetuation of their family eminence. P'an Kuang-tan, *Wang-tsu*, *passim*, argues that eminent clans were longer-lived than is ordinarily believed. He questions the truth of a saying by Mencius to the effect that the beneficial influences of a "superior man" could not extend beyond five generations *(Mencius*, IV, part II, xxii, I), and adduces facts to support his view. On pp.

94-96, he presents the story of the ninety-one most eminent clans of Chia-hsing, which may be summarized as follows:

Generations	Clans
4	8
5	15
6	13
7	13
8	8
9	8
10	5
11	4
12	7
14	1
15	2
16	1
17	4
18	1
21	1

In other words, forty-nine of the ninety-one clans endured from four to seven generations, thirty-two from eight to twelve generations, and ten from fourteen to twenty-one generations. The over-all average is 8.3 generations.

The present investigator is in no position to decide between these two views. Fragmentary data suggest the view that *continued* or *uninterrupted* eminence was relatively short-lived in imperial China during the nineteenth century, especially when viewed from the standpoint of financial prosperity (primarily land ownership). The views which appear to support the claim of longevity are themselves open to question. For example, E. A. Kracke, "Family *vs*. Merit in Chinese Civil Examinations Under the Empire,"*Harvard Journal of Asiatic Studies*, X, 103-23, doubts that the influence of family background was as important as Wittfogel supposes. Nor is P'an Kuang-tan's argument conclusive. P'an himself mentions the fact that in the region which he studied there were sixty less eminent clans, and that these clans had as their members only a few individuals of note (i.e., important enough to have their names included in the local gazetteer). As one naturally expects, these clans were relatively short-lived. From the data which P'an gives *(ibid.*, pp. 107-10), it appears that forty of the sixty clans existed for no more than four generations, and twenty-six of them no more than three. These figures lend some support to the popular belief that "family prosperity" seldom survived the fourth generation. But as the prosperity of the clan depended upon the prosperity of some of its component families, so the prosperity of a family depended upon the prosperity of its leading members; conditions being equal, the greater the number of eminent families and the higher the degree of prosperity these families attained, the longer would the clan concerned enjoy its own prosperity. A number of factors in the nineteenth-century Chinese society tended to limit the span of clan prosperity. The division of property often affected the prosperity of a family adversely. Fei Hsiao-t'ung, *Peasantry and Gentry* (1946), p. 6, correctly points out that "after a few generations the big houses will break down into a number of petty owners again." Cf. Fielde, *Journal of the Royal Asiatic Society*, North China Branch, N.S., XXIII (1888), 112. Lack of economic resources did not necessarily prevent families from improving their social position; however, it was often a formidable handicap to maintaining eminence. The instances mentioned in Yeh Ch'ang-chih

(1849-1917), *Jih-chi*, 6/4a-b; Li Tz'u-ming (1830-94), *Jih-chi*, ii, *ping chi*, 13a and 20a; and Lin Yüeh-hwa, *The Golden Wing* (1947), pp. 2-3, illustrate this point. The transitory nature of family prosperity often affected clan leadership directly. When the leadership assumed by a once eminent family (or families) broke down, the clan was bound to suffer a setback unless some other family in the kinship group assumed effective leadership. As is well known, such new leadership did sometimes emerge. This partly explains the continued existence of clans through a number of centuries, the Fan clan of Wu Hsien, mentioned above, being one outstanding example. Another, the Wang clan of Hsin-ho in Shao-hsing, Chekiang, kept genealogical records for a period of about eight centuries, revising them only about once each century. See *Shao-hsing Hsin-ho Wang-shih tsu-p'u* (n. d.). This does not mean, however, that long-lived clans enjoyed uninterrupted prosperity for great lengths of time. They actually went through cycles of prosperity and adversity which broadly corresponded to the vagaries of personal and family fortunes and to general social circumstances. Family fortunes did not constitute the only decisive factor, but they were often a direct and highly important one. When, as in the past century, the general historical circumstances which had previously favored the development and existence of clan organizations gradually disappeared and were replaced by a different set of circumstances, the opportunity for clans to survive or to revive themselves was steadily reduced. Under such conditions, lack of leadership by one of the component families was more than ever likely to spell disaster for a clan.

158. *Yung-chou* (1867), *chüan* 5, *shang*, p. 48b. P'an Kuang-tan, *Wang-tsu* (1947), pp. 133-34, shows that a variety of causes, including premature death, failure to marry, leaving no offspring, migration to other localities, and disappearance, accounted for the loss of membership sustained by the Shen clan of Ch'ing-ch'i (Chia-hsing, Chekiang), from the first to the eleventh generation, covering a period of about four centuries. As time went on, the number of clansmen increased, but the percentage of loss also increased. During the eighteenth and nineteenth centuries (in the eleventh generation), the clan lost over 53 per cent of its membership.

159. Li Tz'u-ming, *Jih-chi*, iii, "Hsia-chi," 76b. See also *Jih-chi pu*, "Pingchi," *shang*, pp. 48a-49a, and "Hsin-chi," *hsia*, p. 35b, for the history of the Li clan since Ming times.

160. Li Tz'u-ming, *Jih-chi*, v, 28a, and vi, "Ping-chi," 5b.

161. *Ibid.*, vii, "Keng-chi," *hsia*, 21a.

162. See Table 22.

163. Commercial prosperity in a locality, however, might introduce new social relationships into a clan-village and perhaps exert adverse influence upon the kinship community. Kulp, *Country Life*, pp. 30-31, observes this situation in a southern village in modern China: "Thus in the market street . . . fifteen of the shop-keepers are not members of the kin group occupying Phenix village. . . . Between the people who have rented shops . . . and the clanspeople themselves, there has arisen a civic relationship. The bond is no longer one of blood but of economic interest."

164. Ko Shih-chün, *Hsü-pien*, 21/17a.

165. Hu Hsien Chin, *Common Descent Group*, pp. 131-32, quoting from *Luchiang-chün Ho-shih tsu-t'ung tsung-p'u* (1921).

166. Samuel Mossman, *China* (1867), p. 257; Samuel Wells Williams, *Middle Kingdom* (1883), I, 484. Peaceful coexistence was of course possible. See, for example, Hu Hsien Chin, *Common Descent Group*, pp. 91 and 121, concerning the Fan clan inhabiting a small town near Wusih, together with several other *tsu* there.

167. Lang Ch'ing-hsiao, "Chin san-pai nien Chung-kuo nan-pu chih hsieh-tou,"
Chien-kuo (1936), Vol. IV, no. 3, pp. 1-10; no. 4, pp. 1-14; and no. 5, pp. 1-12.

168. *Hsüeh-cheng* (1810), 7/8b.

169. Yao Ying, "Wai-chi," 2/10a, in *Ch'üan-chi*.

170. *Ibid.*, 4/9b. Cf. 2/11a-b.

171. George Smith, *China* (1847), p. 445.

172. *Tsou-i*, 56/13b-14a.

173. *Shih-li* (1908), 158/1b.

174. *Chinese Repository*, IV (1836), 413. Pao Shih-ch'eng (1775-1855), *Ch'i-min ssu-shu*, 11/3a, a letter written in 1828, makes a similar observation.

175. *Ibid.*, 8/22a.

176. *Tsou-i, hsü-pien*, 2/12b.

177. *Chiang-hsi* (1880), *chüan shou*, part 3, p. 10a-b.

178. *Tung-kuan* (1911), 36/3a-b, gives this document.

179. *Mu-lin shu* (1868), 9/16b-17a.

180. Pao Shih-ch'eng, *Ch'i-min ssu-shu*, 12/30b.

181. John F. Davis, *China* (1857), II, 459.

182. *Tung-kuan* (1911), 36/3b.

183. *Chinese and Japanese Repository*, III (1865), 282-84.

184. Fielde, *Corner of Cathay* (1894), p. 128.

185. Hu Hsien Chin, *Common Descent Group*, pp. 91-92.

186. Williams, *Middle Kingdom* (1883), I, 486.

187. Lin Tse-hsü (1785-1850), "Liang-kuang tsou-kao," 3/18a, in *Cheng-shu*.

188. *Chih-hsin pao* (1899), 106/1a.

Chapter 9

1. See chapter 1 for description of such villages.

2. E. Colborne Baber, *Travels and Researches in Western China* (1882), p. 9: "Speaking broadly, the purely agricultural parts of Ssu-ch'uan are remarkable for the absence of villages properly so called. In the eastern provinces proprietors, tenants and labourers, with a few shopkeepers and artisans, gather together, apparently for the sake of mutual protection, in an assemblage of houses surrounded by a mud wall, often at some distance from their fields. But in Ssuch'uan the farmer and his workpeople live, it may be said, invariably in farmhouses on their land, and the tendency is to the separation, rather than to the congregation, of dwellings. . . . It thus results that the whole country is dotted over with cottages at a short distance from one another." Ferdinand von Richthofen, in his *Letters* (2nd ed., 1903), p. 181, paints an identical picture of the countryside in the vicinity of Ch'eng-tu Fu in 1872: "The plain is dotted with small groups of houses, in which the country-people live. Each one of them is nestled under a grove of bamboo, ornamental and fruit trees." This remains true of rural Ch'eng-tu in recent times.

3. William Martin, *Cycle of Cathay* (1896), p. 335. This ditty, the *chi-jang ko*, was probably composed at a date much later than the time of Yao. The *jang*, which is here translated "lute," was not a musical instrument but a wooden stick used in a simple game. Cf. James Legge's translation of this piece, quoted in Arthur E. Moule, *Half a Century in China* (1911), p. 292, and Herbert A. Giles's more poetic rendering in his *Gems of Chinese Literature* (2nd ed., 1923), p. 12.

4. *Ling-shan* (1914), 22/311a.

5. A. Doak Barnett, "Notes on Local Government in Szechwan" (unpublished paper, 1948), section on "A Family."

6. Arthur H. Smith, *Chinese Characteristics* (1894), p. 160.

7. Fang Hsiao-ju (1357-1402), *Hsün-chih-chai chi, chüan* 3, "Min Cheng" ("On People's Affairs"). Ch'en She was also known as Ch'en Sheng. See *Shih-chi, chüan* 48, for biographical sketch.

8. Hsüeh Nung-shan, *Chan-cheng, passim.*

9. Hua Kang, *T'ai-p'ing t'ien-kuo ke-ming chan-cheng shih*, pp. 29-50. Lü Chen-yü, *Chung-kuo cheng-chih ssu-hsiang shih*, pp. 521-31, discerns a school of "peasant political thought" in the tenets of Wang Keng (1483-1541), Li Chih (1527-1602), and Yen Yüan (1635-1704). A careful examination of these men's thinking would discourage one from subscribing to Lü's view.

10. Mao Tse-tung, *Chung-kuo ke-ming yü Chung-kuo Kung-ch'ang-tang* (1949), p. 5. This passage as translated in Mao Tse-tung, *Selected Works* (New York, 1954), III, 76, is based on the revised text and therefore differs slightly from our quotation.

11. L. Richard, *Comprehensive Geography of the Chinese Empire* (1908), p. 341.

12. *Ibid.*

13. See chapter 1 on the physical aspects of villages.

14. Robert Fortune, *Residence Among the Chinese* (1857), pp. 98-99.

15. *Ibid.*, pp. 171-73.

16. George W. Cooke, *China* (1858), pp. 111-12.

17. Emily G. Kemp, *Face of China* (1909), pp. 21-26.

18. E. C. Oxenham (British consul), report of a journey from Peking to Hankow, quoted in Alexander Williamson, *Journey in North China* (1870), II, 398. Cf. Williamson's description of a scene in a pig market at Ming-yüeh-tien, near Ting Chou, Chihli, on September 17, 1865. *Ibid.*, I, 269. For commodities usually for sale in rural markets see chapter 1, of this volume.

19. Francis H. Nichols, *Through Hidden Shensi* (1902), p. 56.

20. Kemp, *Face of China*, pp. 158-59.

21. See chapter 1, notes 23 and 24.

22. Constance F. Gordon-Cumming, *Wanderings in China* (1882), II, 134. For brief descriptions of the physical appearance and agricultural methods of the countryside, see L. H. Dudley Buxton, *China* (1929), pp. 59-63 and 65-134. The fact that conditions varied in different parts of the empire was underscored by Clark Abel, a surgeon attached to the Medhurst embassy, in *Journey in the Interior of China*(1818), pp. 75-77: "No country in the world can afford, I imagine, fewer objects of interest to any species of traveler, than the banks of the Pei-ho between those places [Taku and Tientsin]. The land is marshy and sterile, and inhabitants are poor and squalid, their habitations mean, dirty and dilapidated, and the native productions of the soil are few and unattractive. . . . The bank of the river during our first day's journey [August 9, 1816] were not much above its level. . . . The country beyond them was low. . . . Patches of millet, interspersed with a species of bean, occasionally surrounded mud-huts, on the immediate margin of the river; but their produce would hardly be considered equal to the support, even of those people who assembled to see the Embassy pass. Of these, much the greater number were men miserably clad. . . . As we advanced, the country gradually, though slowly, improved. The patches of millet became of greater extent; and we saw a greater number of people perfectly clothed. This alteration of character was still more apparent when we approached within a few miles of Tien-sing. Large fields of corn and pulse were now frequently contiguous, the dwellings more substantial, and the inhabitants more healthy and robust than any we had before observed."

23. E. C. Oxenham, quoted in Williamson, *Journeys in North China*, II, 423.

24. It is impossible to secure reliable figures. Various estimates are to be found in *Ch'ing-shih kao*, 1/5b-6a; Lo Erh-kang, "The Population Pressure in the Pre-Tai-ping Rebellion Years," *Chinese Social and Economic History Review*, VIII, 20-80; L. Richard, *Comprehensive Geography* (1908), p. 346; Edward H. Parker, *China* (1901), pp. 189-92; Archibald R. Colquhoun, *China in Transformation* (1900), p. 9; Martin, *Cycle of Cathay* (1896), p. 459; Hosea B. Morse, *Trade and Administration* (1913), pp. 206-7; William W. Rockhill, "An Inquiry into the Population of China," *Annual Report of the Smithonian Institution*, XLVII (1905), 669-76; Walter F. Willcox, "A Westerner's Effort to Estimate the Population of China and Its Increase Since 1652," *Journal of the American Statistical Association*, 1930. It may be recalled that prior to 1712, official reports of the population of the empire included the *ting* figures only. Later reports gave mouths and households, but the figures were based on *pao-chia* registers which were not consistently trustworthy. Estimates made by modern investigators should be evaluated with this in mind. For a few instances of local population figures, see *Lu-chou* (1885), 14/35a; *Fu-shun* (1931), 5/2b-3b; *Chiang-ching* (1921), 5/1a; *T'ung-ch'uan* (1897), *chüan* 3; *Nan-ning* (1847), 16/19b-25a; *T'eng hsien* (1846), 4/10b-11b; *Lo-ch'uan* (1942), 6/6a-7b; *En-p'ing* (1934), 8/3a-b.

25. Both *Ch'ing t'ung-k'ao*, pp. 4860, 4865, 4872, 4888, and 4890-91, and *Ch'ing hsü t'ung-k'ao*, p. 7534, give the following figures:

Year	Registered Land (in *mow*)
1661	549,357,640
1685	607,842,992
1724	683,791,427
1753	708,114,288
1766	741,449,550
1810's	791,525,100
1880's	918,103,800

26. *Hu-pu* (1791), 110/2a.

27. *Ch'ing t'ung-k'ao*, 3/4871. The provinces mentioned in this connection were Shansi, Honan, and Shantung.

28. *Ch'ing hsü t'ung-kao*, 25/7755. The original has "fifteen times," which is obviously a misprint.

29. *Shih-lu*, Kao-tsung, 405/19b, and Wen-tsung, 50/33b. E. Stuart Kirby, *Introduction to the Economic History of China* (1954), p. 177, summarizes the trend thus: ". . . towards the end of the eighteenth century, there was an increasing tendency towards decline and crisis. . . . For the economic history of the period, some proper census figures and agricultural statistics are fortunately available. The statistics show that the cultivated area did not increase in proportion to the population."

30. Paul Monroe, *China* (1928), p. 50, indicates that about 80-90 per cent of the people of China lived in villages. Cf. C. M. Chang, *A New Government for Rural China* (1936), p. 1: "About eighty percent or more of the Chinese people live in rural districts."

31. L. Richard, *Comprehensive Geography*, p. 8, gives 267 persons per square mile as the average density of population for China proper. The figure should be revised downwards for earlier periods.

32. Lo Erh-kang, "Population Pressure," *Chinese Social and Economic History Review*, VIII, *passim*.

33. George B. Cressey, *China's Geographical Foundation* (1934), p. 90, gives these figures:

Year	Mow of Land Per Capita
1490	7.95
1578	11.55
1661	5.24
1766	4.07
1872	2.49

Chang Chung-li, The Gentry in Nineteenth Century China, Ph.D. dissertation, University of Washington, (1953), pp. 403 ff., may be consulted.

34. *T'ung-chou* (1875), 4/4b-5b, and 4/17a-19a.

35. *Wei chou* (1877), 7/1a; *Po-pai* (1832), 6/21a; *Fu-shun* (1931), 5/4a-b.

36. As studies made in modern times show, varying degrees of food shortage existed in some parts of China. The situation may have been better in the nineteenth century than in the twentieth, but it would be rash to suppose that food supply was then adequate in all localities. The following may be consulted: C. B. Malone and J. B. Taylor, *A Study of Chinese Rural Economy* (1924); C. C. Chang, *China's Food Problem* (1931); Richard H. Tawney, *Land and Labour* (1932), p. 103; Wen-hao Wong, "The Distribution of Population and Land Utilization in China," *China Institute of Pacific Relations*, VI (1933), 3. Tawney made perhaps the most striking statement of all: "The fundamental fact, it is urged, is of a terrible simplicity. It is that the population of China is too large to be supported by existing resources."

37. *Mien-chu* (1908), "Li-shih," *wu*, p. 9b. This view was confirmed substantially by Western observers. George Philips, in *Journal of the Royal Asiatic Society*, North China Branch, N.S., XXIII (1888), 109, reported the situation in a farming family of rural Foochow as follows:

Rice produced from holding of 15 *mow* valued at $160:
Outlay: Land rent (half of the crop) $80
   Rent for bullock, hired labor, cost of
     seeds, etc.   18
  Income: $62

This sum was barely sufficient to keep alive a family of five, assuming that no debt had been incurred. The lot of farmers in more recent times was hardly better. Wong quotes the findings of John Lossing Buck *(Chinese Farm Economy,* p. 4), and draws this conclusion: ". . . the crop yield of wheat in China [i.e., northern provinces] is about the same as in the United States of America, which is 12 bushels per acre. From the three *mow* or 1/2 acre per capita as above calculated, we shall have only 6 bushels or nearly 20 *tou* (. . . one *tou* equals to 10 liters) each year for each person. This is hardly enough for the subsistence of an adult male, and explains the fact that a large proportion of the Chinese peasants cannot get enough food even in ordinary time and great famine occurs whenever there is any excess or deficit of rain or any other cause which decreases the land cultivation or its production."

38. Edward A. Ross, "Sociological Observations in Inner Asia," *Papers and Proceedings of the American Sociological Society*, V, 18.

39. Buxton, *China* (1929), p. 64: "Although China is essentially an agricultural country, somewhat paradoxically it cannot feed itself. Under the conditions which prevailed at the beginning of the nineteenth century and still to a certain extent

exist today, the failure of a crop meant starvation. Efforts were made by the emperors to store up grain against bad times, the old grain being sold annually and replaced by new. But these measures failed in a country where a journey might be of many months' duration, and even intelligence, much more supplies, would necessarily be long on the road." Food supply itself was not adequate. See chapter 5, notes 179-82.

40. *Ch'ing t'ung-kao*, 3/4874. A rise in rice prices attracted wide attention because rice was the most important single agricultural product. According to Chang Chung-li, The Gentry in Nineteenth Century China, p. 408, the percentages of land producing the main crops from 1929 to 1933 were as follows:

Rice-producing	28.3%
Wheat-producing	16.3%
Millet-producing	9.4%
Other	46.0%

The situation in the nineteenth century should not have been radically different.

41. Ch'ien Yung (1759-1844), *Li-yüan ts'ung-hua*, 1/14a-b.

42. Wang Hui-tsu (1731-1807), *Meng-hen lu, hsia,* p. 49b. Wang remarked in 1794 (p. 57a): "In the summer months one *tou* of rice costs 330 or 340 cash. In former times, when the price of rice rose to 150 or 160 cash, there were instances in which people starved to death. At present, however, although rice has become expensive, men still live happily, because rice alone was expensive in past years, while now all the other articles of food—fish, shrimps, vegetables, fruits, etc.—are expensive. Consequently, peddlers and farmers all have means to keep themselves alive."

43. Peter Hoang, *De legali dominio practicae notiones* (1882), p. 24n, quoted by Harold C. Hinton, The Grain Tribute System of China (Ph.D. dissertation, 1950), p. 64.

44. Wang Hui-tsu, *Meng-hen lu*, pp. 49b-50a. Yeh Ch'ang-chih (1849-1917), *Jih-chi*, 1/74b, indicates that the exchange rate in 1877 was over 1,300 cash per tael, but the rise in Chekiang province was less spectacular than in other places.

45. For example, Li Tz'u-ming (1830-94), *Jih-chi*, vi, *keng-chi*, sec. 2, 54a, an entry dated 1877 (Kuang-hsü 3, 10th month, 9th day), indicates that one *shih* (150 catties) of rice cost about 4.5 taels in Peking. Tseng Kuo-fan, *Tsou-kao*, 1/40a, a memorial dated Hsien-feng 1, 12th month, 18th day, indicates that the rise in the exchange rate worked a hardship on taxpayers. We have no information concerning the price of wheat and other staple foodstuffs in North China.

46. See Yang Hsi-fu's memorial explaining why rice becomes expensive, in Ho Ch'ang-ling, *Wen-pien*, 39/5a-6a.

47. Ch'ien Yung, *Li-yüan ts'ung-hua*, 1/14a, indicates that in the eighteenth century a *mow* of land in Kiangsu was valued at about ten taels. The price rose fivefold in the first quarter of the nineteenth century. Li Tz'u-ming, *Jih-chi pu, wu-chi, hsia*, an entry dated Hsien-feng 8, 12th month, 3rd day, shows that he sold some land inherited from his father, to raise money to buy an office. *Ibid., ssu-chi*, the final entry, indicates that he sold 27.7 *mow* of good land suitable for rice culture for a total of 875 taels—in other words, at the rate of about 30 taels per *mow*. This was in northeastern Chekiang. Meanwhile, there had been a general rise in commodity prices since K'ang-hsi and Ch'ien-lung times. See Chang Chung-li, The Gentry, pp. 11-12.

48. *Ibid.*, pp. 33-35. There was also a rise in the prices of articles useful or necessary for farming families. *En-p'ing* (1934), 4/13a-b, gives these figures which prevailed in a district in Kwangtung:

		Price 1860-1900 (in taels)	Price 1930 (in taels)
Buffalo		12-13	over 100
Pig	(100 catties)	6-7	over 20
Rice			
(unhusked)	(100 catties)	below 2	3. 5-4
Salt	(100 catties)	below 3	5-7
Sugar	(100 catties)	below 2	6
(yellow)			

49. Ch'en Kao-yung, *Chung-kuo li-tai t'ien-tsai jen-huo piao, chüan* 10, *t'ung,* p. 4b, a table showing calamities occurring in Ch'ing times; Yao Shan-yu, "The Chronological and Seasonal Distribution of Floods and Droughts in Chinese History," *Harvard Journal of Asiatic Studies,* VI (1942), 273-311; and sources indicated in chapter 5, note 179.

50. Though the gentry did not necessarily depend upon agricultural income for their living, many of them owned land in various amounts. Speaking generally, the gentry regarded land as the safest investment. Chang Ying's essay on the advantages of investing in landed property, quoted in Chang Chung-li, The Gentry, p. 59, note 2, and the "family instructions" of the Yeh clan of Soochow to the effect that "whenever there is fertile land that can be bought, then buy it without regard to its high price," quoted in *ibid.*, p. 19, reflect the typical gentry attitude toward landownership. This attitude was in fact so well known that it was given expression in some of the proverbs, for example, "The character 'wealth' has 'field" for its base; the character 'honor' has 'center' for its apex." *(Fu tzu t'ien tso ti, kuei tzu chung tang t'ou. Chung,* here translated "center," means to hit the center of the target, that is, to score a success in the examinations.) *Fang-kuo* (1937), 3/39b. Land, however, did not remain the most attractive investment. In the last decades of the nineteenth century, the gentry and others showed increasing interest in commercial enterprises. See Yang Chi-hsüan's article on economic trends after the Opium War, *Eastern Miscellany,* XXXI, 5-20.

51. In addition to the material indicated in chapter 4, notes 179-88, we may note here the interesting observation made by Li Tz'u-ming, *Jih-chi,* v, 42a-b, an entry dated T'ung-chih 8 (1869), 7th month, 3rd day, when he was living temporarily in his home village after purchasing a secretarial post in the *Hu-pu:* "Wrote letter to Magistrate Yang of Shan-yin concerning the payment of the grain tax. I do not have a single *mow* of land, [having sold all my land some time ago]. In our Chekiang [the government] collects, over and above the money and grain taxes on land and on labor services, a surtax of two *sheng* [0.01 *shih*] of white rice on each *mow* of land. Last year it was suddenly decided in the provincial capital that all the levies were to be paid in money; one *sheng* of rice was fixed at 50 cash. The current market price of rice is below 30 cash and yet the yamen clerks are collecting the taxes at extortionary rates of as much as 80 or 90 cash per *sheng*. Yamen runners visited the homes of my second brother and Seng-hui yesterday, pressing for payment of the grain taxes. I dickered with the runners, agreeing to pay 64 cash per *sheng*, but they refused to receive the payment. According to the established regulations of the present dynasty, taxes were to be assessed at one part in every twenty parts. Now, tillers of the soil receive their land from landlords. Calculating on the basis of land of medium quality and a year of average harvest, each *mow* yields no more than one *shih* of rice, which

sells at about 2,500 or 2,600 cash. Deducting the expenses entailed in processing the rice . . . which amount to a total of about 500 to 600 cash, the net receipt per *mow* is only 2,000 cash. Out of this sum 200 cash are collected as rice tribute, and another 200 as "white rice." In other words, the government takes from the people one-fifth [of their earnings, namely, four times the legal rate]. Officials and local gentry extend facilities to one another to make illicit profits. The governor-general and the governor fail to uncover and report [their malpractices], and the censors do not openly speak out. How can we expect to end bandit troubles?" Li T'zu-ming did not indicate the rate at which his relatives eventually paid the taxes. Presumably, thanks to his influence with the magistrate, they paid at a more advantageous rate than taxpayers who had no access to gentry protection.

52. The general situation is succinctly described in the Institute of Pacific Relations, *Agrarian China*, pp. 1-2: "During the Ch'ing dynasty, or up to the 1911 Revolution, there were nine categories of landownership in China. These were: (1) Royal land which was scattered in the vicinity of the capital, Peking; (2) Banner land which was bestowed by the emperor on the Manchurian aristocracy and military people . . ., particularly in Chihli . . ., Shantung and Honan; (3) Temple land and land belonging to religious bodies . . .;(4) Educationalist land which was originally owned by Confucian temples for maintenance purposes, but was subsequently used as a means of financing public schools; (5) Military Colonization land, or land that was first opened up by stationed troops; (6) Clan land, . . . particularly common in the lower Yangtze Valley, Fukien and the southern parts of Kiangsi and Hunan, as well as throughout Kwangtung and the eastern part of Kwangsi; (7) Tribe land, . . . practically owned by the chieftains of many of the aboriginal tribes. . . . (8) Governmental land, belonging either to the central, the provincial or the district government, in different forms such as reed land, . . . newly-emerged land, and uncultivated, barren land; (9) The private land of the family, which formed the major part of landownership." *Hui-tien* (1899), 17/3a, gives the official classification of land into twelve partially overlapping categories. We are here concerned particularly with land available for private ownership.

53. *Ch'ing t'ung-k'ao*, 4/4887. More will be said on this matter in a later connection.

54. Ko Shih-chün, *Hsü-pien*, 36/81a-b. Cf. note 46, above.

55. Chao Lien, *Hsiao-t'ing hsü-lu*, 1/63, 64, quoted by Teng Ssu-yü, "New Light on the History of the Taiping Rebellion," p. 42.

56. George Jamieson and others, "Tenure of Land in China," *Journal of the Royal Asiatic Society*, North China Branch, N.S., XXIII (1888), 59-174. Edward T. Williams, *China* (1923), pp. 92-93, summarizes some of their findings. Surveys made in modern times suggest similar conclusions. For example, John L. Buck, *Chinese Farm Economy* (1930), p. 146, Table 1 (2,866 Farms, in 17 Localities of 7 Provinces, 1921-25), gives the following picture:

	Per Cent Owners	Per Cent Part Owners	Per Cent Tenants
North China (Chihli, Honan, Shansi)	76.5	13.4	10.1
East Central China (Anhwei, Chekiang, Fukien, Kiangsi)	48.2	21.3	30.5

Chen Han-seng, in his *Chinese Peasant*, after surveying conditions in various

parts of modern China, concludes that: ". . . there is a general difference between south China and north China. Apparently there is more concentration in
the south than in the north" (p. 14). But, he adds, this does not mean that the
peasant of north China was in a better position. "The typical peasant in north
China is a poor peasant who cultivates his own inadequate piece of land. He usually works on a farm of about ten or fifteen *mow*, whereas it would require twice
that much to feed himself and his family properly. . . . His economic standing
is hardly any better than that of the tenant in south China" (p. 26). Cf. Chen
Han-seng, *Agrarian Problem,* especially pp. 2-7. Institute of Pacific Relations,
Agrarian China, tables on pp. 3 and 4 indicate a similar conclusion.

57. Chen Han-seng, *Chinese Peasant,* .pp. 14-15; Tawney, *Land and Labour,*
p. 37.

58. *Lu-i* (1896), 9/3a, quoting Fu Sung-ling.

59. *Shen-mu* (n. d.), 4/1b.

60. *P'an-yü* (1911), 12/1b-2a. For a few other tenancy arrangements, see,
for example, *Lo-ch'uan* (1944), 8/9a-b; Buck, *Chinese Farm Economy,* p. 148;
and Chen Han-seng, *Agrarian Problem,* p. 52. For additional discussion of tenancy, see Chang Chung-li, The Gentry, pp. 41 ff.

61. *Hsi-ning* (1873), 9/1b.

62. Chen Han-seng, *Agrarian Problem,* p. 1.

63. Wang Ying, "Land Problem on the Eve of the T'ai-p'ing Revolution, " (in
Chinese), *Quarterly Review of the Sun Yat-sen Institute,* Vol. I, no. 1; Hsüeh
Nung-shan, *Chung-kuo nung-min chan-cheng,* pp. 231-55.

64. *Ming-shih,* 77/2b. This policy was partially implemented by the following measure: Emperor Chu Yüan-chang, soon after ascending the throne in 1369,
ordered over 4,300 wealthy families *(fu hu)* of Chekiang and Ying-t'ien (Kiangsu),
to move to the imperial capital, Nanking. Emperor Ch'eng-tsu moved 3,000 additional families of "wealthy people" to Peking and its neighboring districts.
These families were liable for taxes both in their native districts and in the places
of their residence. When some of them eventually became bankrupt and fled, other wealthy families from the same native districts were moved to fill up the vacancies thus created. In 1492 (Hung-chih 5), "fugitive wealthy families" were
no longer to be persecuted, but a levy of three taels was exacted, presumably
from members who remained or from their relatives. This sum was reduced to
two taels in the middle of the sixteenth century, during the Chia-ch'ing reign.
Ibid., 77/2b-3a. Emperor T'ai-tsu instituted another such measure by establishing a *liang-chang* in each rural division to take charge of the collection of
the grain taxes. The "grain-tax headman" was nominated by his fellow villagers.
Ibid., 78/4b; Liu I-cheng, *Wen-hua shih,* II, 265, quoting from Ku Yen-wu, *Jih-
chih lu.* See also chapter 4, note 106. Ming T'ai-tsu's measures, however,
stopped short of the more drastic policy of Wang Mang (reign A. D. 9-23). *Han-
shu, chüan* 99.

65. *Sheng-hsün,* Shih-tsung, 26/19a.

66. *Ch'ing t'ung-k'ao,* 4/4887.

67. *Shih-li* (1908), 399/4b.

68. See chapter 5, note 1.

69. *Sheng-hsün,* Hsüan-tsung, 78/10a-b.

70. *Shih-lu,* Jen-tsung, 296/24a-b. Another government measure, of doubtful
benefit to poor people, was to regulate the interest rates which moneylenders
charged the peasants who pawned their crops. See *Chiang-hsi* (1887), *chüan shou,*
part 3, pp. 16b-17a; *Pa-ling* (1891), 15/3a.

71. See Yang Ching-jen, *Ch'ou-chi pien, chüan shou,* pp. 2a-30b.

72. *Tsou-i*, 42/4b, from a memorial submitted in 1745 (Ch'ien-lung 10) by Liu Fang-ai, supervising censor, *li-k'o* (rites division).

73. See chapter 4, section on gentry and the revenue system, and Chang Chung-li, The Gentry, pp. 25-28.

74. *Mien-yang* (1894), *chüan* 4, "Shih-huo," p. 37a.

75. *Kuei-chou Huang-shih chia-ch'eng, nei-pien hsia,* p. 20b, quoted by Chang Chung-li, The Gentry, p. 26.

76. *Liu-pu ch'u-fen tse-li* (1877), 15/29a. The edict of K'ang-hsi 18 is not given in *Ch'ing shih-lu* and *Tung-hua lu.*

77. *Ch'ing-yüan* (1880), *chüan shou,* pp. 15a-16a.

78. *T'ien-ching* (1898), 26/5a-b. *Ibid.,* 26/6a, gives this interesting information: "The land of the gentry is usually parceled out to tenants to cultivate. [The owners] take one-half of the annual produce [as rent]. When a tenant visits his landlord, he shows roughly the same respect which a servant renders to his master."

79. *Shih-lu,* Wen-tsung, 140/1b-2a.

80. Chang Ping-lin, *Chien-lun,* 7/17a-b.

81. *Sheng-hsün,* Shih-tsung, 26/19a-20b; *Shih-lu,* Shih-tsung, 79/5b-7a; and Wang Hsien-ch'ien, *Tung-hua lu,* 14/20b-21b.

82. *Hsüeh-cheng* (1810), 9/6a-b.

83. Yang Ching-jen, *Ch'ou-chi pien, chüan shou,* pp. 13a-14a. An instance of putting into practice the principle of "charity" urged by the Yung-cheng emperor was afforded by a rural teacher in Wang-chia-chuang, a village in Ch'ing-yüan Hsien, Chihli, late in the nineteenth century. According to Ch'i Shu-k'ai, "Hsi-yin hsüeh-an," quoted in *Chung-ho,* II, 19, "In the fifteenth year of Kuang-hsü [1889], my elder brother and I studied in Wang-chia-chuang. At that time, some families dwelling in villages surrounding Wang-chia-chuang possessed as much as several thousand *mow* of land each. Landless, poor people were many. Our teacher [Wang Hsi-san, a native of Wang-chia-chuang and a *chü-jen* of 1858] earnestly persuaded landowners to take out their grain and give succor to the destitute. Some of these families listened to him, but [his advice] could not reach all. He grieved over [the situation], sighed silently, but could do nothing [more]. When in the twenty-sixth year [1900] the Boxer trouble arose, all the landlords were utterly ruined."

84. Quoted by the Ch'ien-lung emperor in *Sheng-hsün,* Kao-tsung, 263/10a. In an edict dated K'ang-hsi 43rd year, 1st month, *hsin-yu* day, the K'ang-hsi emperor voiced his concern for the "humble people": "We have made several inspection tours to inquire about the condition of the people's livelihood and are thoroughly acquainted with the matter. The humble people toil hard. A person who tills thirty *mow* [of land] receives, after deducting rent payments, less than thirty *shih* [of grain], on which he depends to supply food and clothing and to meet the labor service levies. . . . At present unrestricted, exorbitant demands are made [on cultivators by local officials, who] threaten to take from them all that they have produced by their toils of an entire year. How are humble people to make a living? . . . As to the remission of taxes payable in money or grain, the original purpose [of this measure] was to benefit the humble people. Most of the land, however, has gone to gentry families. The humble people do not own much of it. Edicts authorizing remission have been repeatedly issued in the past, but it is doubtful that poor people who own no land share the benefits [thus conferred]. Estimating roughly, no more than three or four out of every ten of the humble people possess landed property; the rest [who till the soil] rent land and pay rent [for using it]. The grain that remains [to tenant farmers after the rent is paid] barely enables a peasant to keep alive. . . . In recent

years we have toured seven provinces. Only the people of Shensi and Shansi are slightly affluent. Inhabitants in the four prefectures south of the Capital and in the regions traversed en route to Honan find it rather difficult to make a living. In our first tour, the people of Shantung were quite well off, but conditions worsened subsequently and now are very different from those of earlier times. All these [troubles] are due to the fact that local officials, high as well as low, fail to pay serious, sympathetic attention to the inarticulate wishes of the people or remove the distressing circumstances that confront them; on the contrary, [these officials] make up numerous pretexts to impose levies upon them. For this reason the people's strength is impaired and they become daily more destitute." Quoted in Wang Hsien-ch'ien, *Tung-hua lu*, K'ang-hsi, 73/4a-b. It is clear from this document that the emperor had nothing against large landowners.

85. *Sheng-hsün*, Kao-tsung, 263/10a-11a.

86. Yang Ching-jen, *Ch'ou-chi pien, chüan shou*, p. 14a-b.

87. *Sheng-hsün*, Kao-tsung, 263/15a-b.

88. *Chiang-hsi* (1880), *chüan shou*, part 3, pp. 16b-17a.

89. Wang Jen-k'an (1849-93), *I-shu*, 7/31a. Wang formulated a set of regulations to guide the magistrates of Tan-yang Hsien and his other subordinates in doing relief work after the drought of 1892, when he was prefect of Chenkiang, Kiangsu. In one of the regulations, he said: "You must understand that relief extended by the imperial government is for the benefit of farming people injured by the drought, not to give succor to all destitute people in general." This is in perfect agreement with imperial policy as revealed in the regulations concerning local granaries.

90. *Mencius*, III, 3. Legge's translation of this passage reads: "If they have a certain livelihood, they will have a fixed heart." Whether we take the character *ch'an* in the original text as "livelihood" or "property," it is important to bear in mind that Mencius and other Confucians of his time considered farming the basic means of making a living and land the indispensable condition for gaining a livelihood.

91. See, for example, Fu Chu-fu's article in *Eastern Miscellany*, XXXI, 221-28; and K'ung Meng-hsiung's article in *Quarterly Review of the Sun Yat-sen Institute*, II, 1143-58.

92. See, for example, Institute of Pacific Relations, *Agrarian China*, pp. 168-70. The village under survey was Chien-che-chueng, in the district of Kwang-chung, southern Hopei (in Ch'ing times, Chihli).

93. *Ting chou* (1850), 19/12b-13b.

94. *Lu-i* (1896), 9/3a. A few additional instances: *Lu-lung* (1931), 10/1b, "Lu-lung is a district where the soil is not fertile and the people are poor." *Ibid.*, 10/2a, "The population is over 160,000, most of whom earn a living by their own labor. Nine persons out of ten are engaged in farming. The land is scarce and the population dense. [Farmers toil] assiduously and bitterly throughout the year." *Han-tan* (1933), 2/8b: "In recent years rainfall has been deficient, resulting sometimes in disastrous droughts. . . . Although several tens of villages east of the city are situated on the banks of the Fu-shui, where, by building dams across the river each year, [farmers may use the water thus conserved] for irrigation so that even when no rain falls it is still possible to sow the seeds and save some of the crops, [the land thus benefited] is less than 10 or 20 per cent of the land of the entire district. Speaking generally, therefore, Han-tan may be said to be [a place where] the soil is barren and the people are poor." *Lo-ch'uan* (1944), 11/16a, quoting from an undated earlier edition of *Yen-an fu chih*, describes the conditions of the nine *chou* and *hsien* of this prefecture thus: "Un-

trodden mountains extend for a thousand *li;* formidable barriers exist in all directions. Merchants find it difficult to reach these localities, and travelers to pass through them. Since little opportunity is afforded to any type of enterprise, those who possess strength cannot sell their labor to get wages, and those who have grain cannot sell it to obtain money." *Ibid.,* foreword by Li Ching-hsi, p. 3a: "The entire [Lo-ch'uan] *hsien* has less than 60,000 people. The population compares unfavorable with a city ward or a rural town belonging to a large district of the south. There are no forests on the hills or plains, nor water in the rivers and creeks."

95. *Meng-ch'eng* (1915), 1/9b. It was usually difficult for poor villagers to rise in their economic status—a situation which persisted down to comparatively recent times. For example, a survey made in 1935 by S. C. Lee, "Heart of China's Problem," *Journal of Farm Economics,* XXX (1948), 268, quoted in C. Arnold Anderson and Mary Joan Bowman, *The Chinese Peasant,* p. 223, reveals this situation:

Province	Per Cent Rise from Farm Laborer to Tenant	Average Age	Per Cent Rise from Laborer to Part Owner	Average Age	Per Cent Rise from Laborer to Full Owner	Average Age
Honan	6.5	32.8	0.2	40.9	0.9	46.7
Hupeh	6.1	32.2	1.3	42.4	0.3	42.4
Anhwei	9.3	29.8	1.9	40.4	0.8	50.0
Kiangsi	4.7	28.8	1.0	39.5	0.7	46.0
Average	7.0	30.9	1.6	40.9	0.6	48.1

96. *Ling-shan* (1914), 21/297b. Similar conditions persisted in some localities of this comparatively prosperous province. Daniel Kulp, *Country Life,* I, 104-5, summarizes the situation in one of the villages as follows:

Economic Circumstance	No. Families	Per Cent
Good ("well-to-do")	24	18
Fair ("none to spare")	41	31
Poor	68	51

Kulp adds: "The 'poor' live from hand to mouth, at the mercy of nature and the goodwill of their kin. . . . Over half the familist groups are compelled to carry on incessantly the relentless struggle for existence and succeed mainly by virtue of the ideals and organization of the familist system."

97. Lt. Col. George B. Fisher, *Three Years' Service* (1863), pp. 25-27.

98. Feng Kuei-fen, *Chi,* 9/3a-b, ghost-writing for Li Hung-chang, says in a memorial: "Unprecedented prosperity followed a period of peace that extended over one hundred years. Kiangsu in particular, containing the great commercial centers of the southeast, witnessed the greatest concentration of commercial activities. During this period even laborers who carried loads on their shoulders or backs and peddlers of vegetables and fruits shared the prosperity by rendering their services. All cultivated the land, whether as owners or tenants, more as a side line than as the chief means of earning a living. There were consequently no unpaid taxes. Therefore, in the decades after the middle of the Ch'ien-lung reign, full collection of the tribute rice was achieved, for the simple reason that the people were prosperous. But . . . since Tao-kuang *kuei-wei* [1823], when serious floods occurred . . . commercial profits decreased and agricultural prosperity followed suit. As a result, the people gradually descended from prosperity to poverty. . . . After the great flood of *kuei-ssu* [1833],

practically every year was a year of dearth, and deferment [of tax payments] had to be granted in each district.

99. See material indicated in notes 14-17.

100. Von Richthofen, *Letters* (1903), p. 54.

101. *Ibid.*

102. *Ibid.*, p. 56.

103. *En-p'ing* (1934), 4/12b. Both Nan-hai and Chiu-chiang were prosperous districts.

104. See, for example, *Yang-chiang* (1925), 7/4a; *Pa-ling* (1891), 52/6b; and Kulp, *Country Life*, p. 53.

105. Kulp, *Country Life*, I, 104-5: ". . . not more than one-tenth of the emigrants return successful." Worse, those who failed in their adventures became misfits in their home villages (if indeed they managed to return there). At any rate, few of them were willing or able to toil as farm laborers.

106. Ellsworth Huntington, *Character of Races*, pp. 192-93: "[After a famine] the wanderers divide into two groups. One set consists of those who keep trying to go back to the old homes. . . . partly because they have lands there, and partly because their temperament is such that they feel the influence of their ancestral cult and love the old ways even though they be miserable. . . . The other group of wanderers consists of those who have more energy and initiative. . . . The country districts are thereby drained of their best men." Huntington's sweeping conclusions have fallen into discredit, but this observation stands near to the facts.

107. Kulp, *Country Life*, pp. 53-54. See also Wu Wen-hui, "Famine and Rural Migration," *Quarterly Review of the Sun Yat-sen Institute*, VI, 49.

108. *Pa-ling* (1891), 52/6b.

109. *Han-tan* (1933), 6/2b. Cf. *T'ung-kuan* (1944), 10/12b-17b; and Lin Yüeh-hwa, *Golden Wing*, pp. 3-10, the story of Hwang Dunglin.

110. Wang Chih, "Memorial Explaining Eight Matters, in Response to an Edict," quoted in Wu Ju-lun, *Jih-chi*, 6/37a.

111. Wang Pang-hsi, "Memorial Explaining in Detail the Merits and Defects of the *Ting* and *Ts'ao*," in Ko Shih-chün, *Hsü-pien*, 32/20a.

112. For example, *Ch'ing-chou* (1908), 2/21b, gives these figures for Ch'ing Chou (Hunan) in the early years of the twentieth century: Total number of adult males, 44,126. Of these, 2,576 were scholars; 2,550, farmers; and 1,528, merchants, making a subtotal of 33,873. The remaining 10,253 (23 per cent of the total) presumably were mostly unemployed. *Mien-chu* (1908), "Li-shih hsin," p. 15a, gives figures for the early years of the twentieth century: Total male population, 218,580. Of these, 8,900 were scholars; 2,000, school children; 173,900, farmers; 14,500, craftsmen; 11,250, merchants; 4,690, opium smokers; and 3,310, "loafing people." *Lo-ch'uan* (1944), 6/10b, gives figures for the early years of the twentieth century: Persons with occupations (farming, etc.), 1,032, or 3.5 per cent; persons without occupations, 30,122, or 96.5 per cent. Kulp, *Country Life*, p. 90, gives figures for Phoenix Village (Kwangtung) in the 1920's: Total population, 650; persons with occupations, 167; "emigrants," 55; persons without employment, 428, or 65 per cent of the total. Fei Hsiao-t'ung, *Peasant Life*, p. 139, gives figures for Kaishienkung village (Kiangsu) in the 1930's: Total number of families, 360. Of these, 274 were engaged in agriculture, 59 in "special occupations," and 14 in fishing; 13 were unoccupied.

113. Kulp, *Country Life*, p. 38, draws this gloomy conclusion: "If the period of economic productivity in farm life be taken from 20 to 44 years, it is clear that only twenty-nine per cent, or slightly more than one-fourth of the population,

produces the necessary income for maintenance. However, some of these in-cluded in the twenty-nine per cent are ineffective on account of health; others in the range from 45-64 would still be effective producers as women engaged in home industry, or as men in trade. Taking all the age groups in relation to prob-able productiveness, it is safe to say that practically one-half of the population depends for support upon the other half." What Kulp meant by "from 20 to 44 years" is not clear. The argument that many people were not engaged in produc-tive work appears to be generally valid.

114. Yang Ching-jen, *Ch'ou-chi pien*, 16/17b-24a, summarizes the contents of the measures adopted by the government between 1682 and 1802.

115. *Ibid.*, 16/21a-b and 23b. See also chapter 5 of this volume.

116. E.-R. Huc, *Chinese Empire*, II, 324-25. Huc also made this general remark (p. 323): "Not a year passes in which a terrific number of persons do not perish of famine in some part or other of China; and the multitude of those who live merely from day to day is incalculable." Similar scenes were observed in more recent times. See, for example, Institute of Pacific Relations, *Agrarian China*, pp. 248-49, describing villages in Yü-ch'eng Hsien, Shantung.

117. Constance Gordon-Cumming, *Wanderings in China* (1886), II, 137-42.

118. Francis H. Nichols, *Through Hidden Shensi* (1902), p. 242.

119. Yeh Ch'ang-chih (1849-1917), *Jih-chi*, 10/13a.

120. Gordon-Cumming, *Wanderings*, p. 142.

121. Nichols, *Shensi*, p. 228.

122. Wu Wen-hui, in *Quarterly Review of Sun Yat-sen Institute*, IV, 45, esti-mates that over 220,000 persons perished in the floods and droughts that affected Shensi, Shantung, and Kiangsi in 1846; 13,750,000 people were wiped out in 1849 by similar calamities in Chihli, Kansu, Kiangsu, and Chekiang; between 1876 and 1878 about 9,500,000 died in various disasters in Kiangsu, Shantung, Chihli, Shensi, Honan, Anhwei, and Hupei. Cf. *Ch'ing-shih kao*, "Tsai-i," 1/37-41. The following figures given in local gazetteers may also serve to illustrate the point:

Ch'ing-chou (1908), 2/10a-b (include Chinese population only; Miao tribes ex-cluded):

	Families	Persons
1742	23,955	119,328
1757	32,455	153,341
1836	28,378	128,567
1868	16,382	74,152
1908	20,822	79,906

T'ung-kuan (1944), 8/1b:

	Families	
1644	26,685	
1721	31,512	
1800	32,460	
1821-50	32,161	
1851-61	33,080	
1862-74	32,850	
1875-1908	20,860	(Famine, 1877; drought, 1900)
1909-11	32,680	

I-ch'eng (1929), 9/11b-12a, reveals that this district of Shansi suffered a seri-ous drought, as a result of which the population dwindled from 139,985 persons to 45,248, and from 25,957 families to 11,131. The land abandoned by former cultivators was reported to have been 23,087 *mow*.

123. Chang Chung-li, *Chinese Gentry*, pp. 51-52. The following observation

made by Morton H. Fried in modern Ch'u Hsien (Anhwei) reflects broadly the condition of the empire as a whole in the nineteenth century: "The rural gentry in Ch'uhsien has been steadily moving into the city over the past five decades and more. The movement is slow but continuous. The rural gentry located at any great distance removed from city walls find itself in an increasingly hostile environment as civil controls are weakened. . . . The gentry in the country . . . are the exposed victims of such bandit or sporadic rebellious activity as may take place in the locality. Under these conditions the gentry are spurred to move into the city, there to seek the physical protection of the walls and the social protection of such officials as may be approached through ties of kinship and kan-ch'ing [personal understanding or "good will"]. *Fabric of Chinese Society,* p. 224. The gentry, however, did not always seek protection in walled cities. A dictum current in the nineteenth century warned: "Live in the city during minor disturbances; live in the country during a major uprising." The reason is obvious. In a large-scale revolt or rebellion, cities were likely to suffer ravages resulting from determined siege and unsuccessful defense. Hence a higher degree of safety might be afforded by strongholds in the countryside. It is not entirely accurate therefore to suppose that physical protection constituted the sole motive behind the gentry's cityward migration. One should not overlook the fact that the city was a center of social and political influence to which the more active elements of the rural gentry naturally gravitated.

124. As Lin-Le (A. F. Lindley), *Ti-ping Tien-kwok* (1866), I, 101, puts it: "During the years 1838-41, many parts of the empire became plunged in misery and want;—so severe was the famine that many thousands perished, while multitudes were driven to insurrection."

125. *Meng-ch'eng* (1915), 4/2b.

126. Von Richthofen, *Letters* (1903), p. 75.

127. Ernest F. Borst-Smith, *Mandarin and Missionary* (1917), pp. 52-57.

128. *Ch'ing-shih kao,* "Shih-huo," 1/5b-6a. The population was estimated as nearly 413 million in 1849 and as having dwindled to under 334 million in 1875.

129. Tawney, *Land and Labour,* p. 37.

130. Von Richthofen, *Letters,* pp. 13 and 16.

131. *Chih-hsin pao,* Kuang-hsu 23 (1897), 20/11a.

132. Chen Han-seng, "Chinese Peasant," p. 6: "Since the middle of the last century, the steady increase of commercial and industrial influence in the coastal ports and along the railway and steamship lines has become more and more apparent. Money economy, or the use of cash as a means of exchange, has spread further and further into the remotest and interior parts of the country. All this was in contrast with the persistent neglect of irrigation works and the consequent decline of agricultural production."

133. L. Richard, *Comprehensive Geography,* p. 327, lists these ports and marts.

134. John S. Burgess, *Guilds of Peking* (1928), p. 43. Stanley Spector, Li Hung-chang and the Huai-chün (Ph.D. dissertation, University of Washington, 1953), chapter 10, summarizes the beginnings of this development. Morse, *International Relations,* I, 366, Table F, gives figures showing the tea and silk exports in 1843-1860. Tea export, which averaged annually 51,311,000 pounds between 1830 and 1833, rose to 121,388,100 pounds in 1860. Silk export, which averaged annually 5,434 bales between 1830 and 1833 (Canton and Shanghai), rose in 1858 to 85,970 bales (Shanghai).

135. Cotton cloth offered perhaps the best example. A British commercial agent at Canton sent some samples of the native cloth to England in 1844 with

the prices specified. His correspondents assured him that they could not produce the same commodity at the same prices in Manchester. His report deserves quoting in part: "The habits of the Chinese are so thrifty and so hereditary, that they wear just what their fathers wore before them. . . . No working Chinaman can afford to put on a new coat which shall not last him at least three years and stand the wear and tear of the roughest drudgery during that period. . . . When the harvest is gathered, all hands in the farmhouse, young and old together, turn to carding, spinning, and weaving this cotton . . . the manufacture varying in quality . . . all produced in the farmhouse, and costing the producer literally nothing beyond the value of the raw materials." Quoted by Karl Marx, "Trade with China," an article published in the New York *Daily Tribune*, December 3, 1859, from a Blue Book entitled *Correspondence Relative to the Earl of Elgin's Special Mission to China and Japan*. This article is reprinted in *Marx on China*, pp. 89-99.

136. Peter Auber, *China* (1834), p. 64.

137. E. Colborne Baber, *Travels and Researches in West China* (1882), p. 159.

138. For example, Institute of Pacific Relations, *Agrarian China*, p. 225: ". . . after the rural communities of China become linked with the world market, the inevitable trend of the last hundred years has been a desperate struggle for existence on the part of the Chinese handicrafts against foreign economic invasion. . . . The import of cotton cloth, kerosene, cotton yarn, nails and needles, in other words, those articles replacing what was formerly supplied by handicraft products, in an ever-growing quantity, speaks fairly for the general decline of the Chinese handicrafts." Cf. Li Tzu-hsiang, "The Declining Process of the Chinese Handicraft Industries," *Quarterly Review of the Sun Yat-sen Institute*, Vol. IV, no. 3, which relates the story in the early decades of the present century.

139. Arthur Smith, *China in Convulsion* (1901), I, 90-91.

140. Fei Hsiao-t'ung, *China's Gentry* (1953), pp. 113-14.

141. Roswell H. Graves, *Forty Years in China* (1895), pp. 77-78: "While opium was known in China before it was imported from India by foreigners, the habit of opium-smoking was not common. Upon the British East India Company must lie the blame of promoting the cultivation of the poppy in India and encouraging the use of the drug in China. Smuggled in at first, almost forced upon the Chinese as a result of the war of 1842—the so-called 'Opium-War'—and legalized as a legitimate article of commerce by the treaty following the Anglo-French war of 1856, its use soon spread fearfully in the maritime provinces. The cultivation of the native article was also rapidly increased in order to supply the increasing demand for the poison." James D. Ball, *Things Chinese* (1906), pp. 488-90, calls attention to the fact that the importing of opium declined in the closing decades of the century. See the following pamphlets published by the Statistical Department of the Inspectorate General of the Imperial Customs: "Opium," Special Series No. 4, Shanghai, 1881; "Native Opium," Special Series No. 9, 1888; and "Opium: Historical Note, or the Poppy in China," Special Series No. 13, 1889.

142. Morse, *Trade and Administration* (1913), p. 337. Morse gives statistical figures to show the expansion of the opium trade. See also his *International Relations*, I, 209-10, Tables D and E. Morse indicates, however, that his figures are controversial.

143. Burgess, *Guilds of Peking* (1928), p. 38. The time referred to was 1880, when the total import was valued at about 80,000,000 taels.

144. Robert Coltman, *The Chinese* (1891), p. 125.

145. Nichols, *Through Hidden Shensi* (1902), pp. 56-57.

146. Borst-Smith, *Mandarin and Missionary* (1917), pp. 72-73.

147. Morse, *International Relations*, I, 210. Meanwhile silver dollars gained increasingly wide circulation, eventually replacing the silver tael as a medium of exchange. See Wang Hui-tsu (1737-1807), *Meng-hen lu, chüan hsia*, p. 69a-b, writing in 1796, for the story of the introduction of the *yang-ch'ien* (foreign coins) or *fan-yin* (barbarian silver) from Fukien and Kwangtung into Chekiang. Wang noted with apparent regret that "any article that is out of the ordinary is often called 'foreign,'" and that "the prices of such articles are invariably higher than the native products of the provinces." Li Tz'u-ming (1830-94), *Jih-chi*, i, *i-chi*, 3a, writing in the autumn of 1865 when he lived in Shao-hsing, Chekiang, reports that a friend of his, a *sheng-yüan*, remitting fourteen taels from Peking to his wife, paid twenty dollars and eighty cents—the local equivalent—to the lady. Li adds: "What are known as *ying-yang-ch'ien* [English foreign coins] did not appear until about ten years ago. . . . At the end of the Hsien-feng reign [1861] they circulated only in Shanghai and Kwangtung. But now they are used in all localities in Kiangsu and Chekiang."

148. Lo Ping-chang (1793-1867), *Tsou-kao*, 8/13-14. See also an article by Ch'üan Han-sheng on "The Relationship Between the Silver of America and the Revolution in Commodity Prices in China in the Eighteenth Century" (in Chinese), *Bulletin of the Institute of History and Philology*, Academia Sinica, XXVIII, part 2, 517-50.

149. Franklin L. Ho, *Rural Reconstruction in China*, p. 1.

Chapter 10

1. Tscheng Ki-t'ong, "China: a Sketch of Its Social Organization and State Economy," *Asiatic Quarterly Review*, X (1890), 259, represents such an optimistic view of paternal despotism. "The whole empire," Tscheng asserts, "must be regarded as a great family," in which the welfare of the people is served by their rulers.

2. Peter Auber, *China* (1834), p. 51.

3. Thomas T. Meadows, *Rebellions* (1856), pp. 28-29, quotes from John S. Mills, *Political Economy:* "Insecurity paralyzes only when it is such in nature and in degree, that no energy, of which mankind in general are capable, affords any tolerable means of self-protection. And this is a main reason why oppression by the government, whose power is generally irresistible by any efforts that can be made by individuals, has so much more baneful an effect on the springs of national prosperity, than almost any degree of lawlessness and turbulence under free institutions. Nations have acquired some wealth, and made some progress in improvement, in states of social union so imperfect as to border on anarchy; but no countries in which the people were exposed without limit to arbitrary exactions from the officers of government, ever yet continued to have industry or wealth. A few generations of such a government never fail to extinguish both."

4. Mrs. E. T. Williams, "Popular Religious Literature," *Journal of the Royal Asiatic Society*, North China Branch, N.S., XXX (1899-1900), 25-26.

5. E.-R. Huc, *Chinese Empire* (1855), I, 364: "The magistrates and public functionaries, having only a few years to pass at the same post, live in it like strangers, without troubling themselves at all about the wants of the people under their care; no tie attaches them to the population; all their care is to accumulate as much money as possible wherever they go, and continually repeat the operation, till they can return to their native province to enjoy a fortune gained by ex-

tortion in all the rest." William A. P. Martin, *Cycle of Cathay* (1896), p. 334: "The predatory tendencies of provincial [i. e., local] magistrates are aggravated by the fact that they are strangers from abroad, the law forbidding them to take up a post within two hundred miles of their birthplace or to form marriage ties of any kind within their districts. As a device for making the mandarinate wholly dependent on their sovereign nothing could be better. They have no local attachments, no home except a cradle and a grave, and in their perambulatory movements they are not permitted to stop at one post long enough to acquire an influence which might become a danger [to the imperial regime]. . . . It has, however, the disadvantage of delivering [the inhabitants] into the hands of strangers, who, as their tenure is brief, do not scruple to make hay while the sun shines."

6. Thomas Meadows, *Desultory Notes* (1847), pp. 155-57, narrates the story of a magistrate holding a post in Kwangtung in the middle of the nineteenth century. A merchant who was robbed by highwaymen petitioned his yamen for help, but the official refused to take any action. Meadows explains the behavior of the magistrate thus: "For whether the officers be made responsible for the prevention of crime, or for the apprehension of offenders after its commission, the responsibility implies, in both cases, punishment [of the functionaries in question] for want of success; the officers will therefore be constantly on the watch to quash, in the commencement, any proceeding against criminals, in order to prevent the matter coming to light, and thus, though less will be heard of crime, more of it will exist, in consequence of the impunity afforded to the guilty."

7. This was a long-established practice; in fact, there was a time when officials received no regular salaries at all. See Chao I, *Ts'ung-k'ao*, 6/29a-b. Meadows, *Desultory Notes*, p. 100, gives a table showing the official salaries of the Ch'ing dynasty. Local gazetteers usually contain information concerning the remunerations of local officials and yamen underlings.

8. Charles Denby, United States Minister to China, writes in *China and Her People* (1906), II, 6: "China pays wretchedly small wages to its employes, from the highest to the lowest, and each and all are expected to squeeze from the people all the subsidies that can be procured without direct robbery."

9. See Ch'ü T'ung-tsu's forthcoming study on *Local Administration* (Harvard University Chinese Economic and Political Studies), chapter on "Servants and Secretaries."

10. Ting Jih-ch'ang (1823-82), *Kung-tu*, 24/4b. According to a Western observer, some of the "Shansi bankers" were also among the usurers. *China Review*, VIII (1880), 64-65.

11. This practice had its origin in ancient times. In the Ch'ing dynasty it was used probably for the first time to raise revenue in 1677 (K'ang-hsi 16), during the campaign against the three rebel "feudatory princes" (1673-82). Most widely used in the second half of the nineteenth century, it was officially suspended in 1903. See Wang Hsien-ch'ien, *Tung-hua lu*, under relevant years. John Scarth, *Twelve Years in China* (1860), *passim*, describes the method of "buying ranks" as adopted by Tseng Kuo-fan early in 1854.

12. A memorial written by Wang Su, given in *Tsou-i, hsü-pien*, 2/13a, says in part: "Conforming to the established practice in the provinces of Szechwan and Hupeh, district magistrates constitute the largest number of these who have obtained their official status by 'contributions' and are sent to other provinces for assignment. These 'contributors' do not necessarily come from wealthy families. They are usually relatives, personal advisers, or secretaries of government officials. In addition to these there are some whose families do not have even one *shih* of grain in store, but have borrowed enough money to make

'contributions' to obtain district magistracies. Such persons are as a rule clever and shrewd; they have the appearance of being efficient. Their intention differs in no way from that of a peddler or a merchant. Once a post is assigned to one of them, innocent people numbering tens of thousands will have to be handed over to him. How can the people receive beneficial treatment from such officials?" Cf. John F. Davis, *China* (1852), II, 200: "When it was known that civil offices might be eventually obtained by the contribution of certain fixed sums, there was at first no dearth of candidates. As the possession of office might be turned to pecuniary advantage, it was a sort of investment."

13. For a brief description, see Meadows, *Desultory Notes*, No. 9, pp. 101-16, and No. 10, pp. 117-23; Huang Liu-hung, *Fu-hui*, 17/3b; Feng Kuei-fen, in Ko Shih-chün, *Hsü-pien*, 22/5a; and *Kuang-chou* (1878), 129/17a.

14. See, for example, Huc, *Chinese Empire*, I, 366-77, and Justus Doolittle, *Social Life* (1865), I, 322-25.

15. The same sentiment was expressed somewhat differently in another proverb: "The four leaves of the yamen's gate open wide; don't enter if you are out of money, though in the right."

16. Richard R. Tawney, *Land and Labour* (1932), pp. 172-73: "Not only government, but the very idea of government, is unpopular in China. It has every reason to be; it has meant little during the last decade but taxation and war." By omitting the last two words, this statement, made in the 1930's, may be used to depict the situation of the nineteenth century.

17. Yeh Ch'ang-chih (1849-1917), *Jih-chi*, 11/62b-63a.

18. The political indifference of villagers was described by Huc, *Chinese Empire*, I, 97. Huc was traveling on the road from Peking in 1851, shortly after the death of the Tao-kuang emperor. He tried, over the tea table at an inn, to get the reaction of a group of rural inhabitants to the problem of imperial succession. This is the answer he received: "'Listen to me, my friend! Why should you trouble your heart and fatigue your head by all these vain surmises? The Mandarins have to attend to affairs of State; they are paid for it. Let them earn their money, then. But don't let us torment ourselves about what does not concern us. We should be great fools to want to do political business for nothing.' 'That is very conformable to reason,' cried the rest of the company; and thereupon they pointed out to us that our tea was getting cold and our pipes were out." Perhaps the conversation as Huc recorded it is a little too eloquent for the habitually inarticulate Chinese of the nineteenth century. The sentiment which it expresses, however, is unquestionably authentic.

19. John Lossing Buck, *Chinese Farm Economy* (1932), p. 407, indicates that in widely scattered areas of modern China, surveyed in the 1920's, not more than 30 per cent of the children of farm families ever attended school. The percentage was conceivably even lower in the nineteenth century.

20. Fei Hsiao-t'ung, *Peasant Life* (1946), p. 39.

21. Arthur H. Smith, *Village Life* (1899), p. 74.

22. *Lu-i* (1896), 9/2b.

23. Robert Coltman, *The Chinese* (1891), p. 77. Arthur Smith, *Chinese Characteristics* (1894), pp. 152-53, explains the influence of poverty on the mental attitudes of the peasantry in these words: "Among a dense population like that of the Chinese Empire, life is often reduced to its very lowest terms, and those terms are literally a 'struggle for existence.' In order to live, it is necessary to have the means of living, and those means each must obtain for himself as best he can. The Chinese have been well said to 'reduce poverty to a science.' Deep poverty and a hard struggle for the means of existence. . . . these are

the conditions which will tend most effectively to develop industry. The same conditions will also tend to the development of economy. . . . These conditions also develop patience and perseverance. " To forego education was just one way in which the majority of rural inhabitants practiced their "science of poverty. "

24. Daniel H. Kulp, *Country Life* (1925), p. 216.

25. This conclusion is intended to apply to the "native" Chinese of the eighteen provinces only. Exceptions existed among some of the minority ethnic groups; even the Hakkas were far from submissive or docile. Hsieh T'ing-yu, for example, notes the "spirit of fight and 'never-say-die'" of the Hakkas. *Chinese Social and Political Science Review*, XIII (1929), 219. Lo Hsiang-lin similarly asserts that "the Hakka people are most revolutionary in character. " *K'e-chia yen-chiu tao-lun*, p. 490.

26. *Nan-hai* (1910), 22/4b, gives an interesting instance of the influence of traditional morality upon villagers: "Liu Fu-ch'eng was a native of Shih-lung Hsiang, Nan-hai Hsien. His family being poor, he became a hired hand after having studied less than two years in a rural school. He was highly regarded for his honesty. When he attained manhood, he was employed as a letter carrier. He spent all his earnings to support his [widowed] mother. . . . He brought up his younger brothers and sisters, five of them in all. . . . In Hsien-feng *chia-yin* [1854] the Red Turbans caused disturbances. As the roads were blocked, he suspended his work and stayed home, living in extremely difficult financial circumstances. The rebels tried to induce him [to join them], saying, "Your strength is superb and you are skilled in boxing. Come with us and you are sure to achieve wealth and eminence. Why should you torture yourself [in poverty]?" Liu Fu-ch'eng refused [to join them], giving as his reason that his mother was aged and his brothers still young, [and that he must remain at home to look after them]. "

27. Arthur Smith, *Chinese Characteristics* (1894), p. 160.

28. *Webster's International Dictionary*, 2nd ed.: "Feud—(1) Enmity, hostility; obs. (2) A contention or quarrel; bitter mutual ill-feeling and hostility, esp. an inveterate strife between families, clans, or parties marked by bloodshed and alternate outrages in the guise of revenge for former injuries. " The word "feud" is used in this chapter both in the narrower sense ("an inveterate strife"), and in the broader sense ("a contention or quarrel").

29. For a general survey of weaponed fights, see Lang Ch'ing-hsiao, "Chin san pai nien Chung-kuo nan-pu chih hsieh-tou, " *Chien-kuo yüeh-k'an* (1936), Vol. III, no. 3, pp. 1-10; no. 4, pp. 1-14; and no. 5, pp. 1-12.

30. Wang Shih-t'o (1802-1889), *Jih-chi*, 2/8a-b. According to Meadows, *Rebellions* (1856), pp. 139-40: "At that time a very rich kih kea [Hakka] had taken as his concubine a girl who had been promised in marriage to a Punte man; and having agreed to settle the matter with her parents by paying a large sum of money, he peremptorily refused to give her up to the Punte claimant. At the office of the district magistrate numerous petitions and accusations were daily lodged against the kih kea population so that the mandarins were unable to settle all their disputes. . . . The result was, that soon after, between the Puntes and kih keas of the Kwei district, a civil war commenced, in which a number of villages gradually became involved. The fighting began on the 28th of the eighth month (3rd October, 1850), and during the first few days the kih keas had the advantage. . . . Gradually, however, the Puntes grew bolder and more experienced . . . they defeated the kih keas, and burnt their houses, so that the latter had no resting place to which they could resort. In their distress they sought refuge among the worshippers of God [many of whom were kih keas]. "

31. Ch'en Hung-mou, *Ou-ts'un kao*, 15/4a-5a, a proclamation prohibiting the collection of money to finance religious processions, issued in 1742.

32. *Nan-hai* (1910), 20/8a, gives this information: "The Hung-sheng Miao [temple] of our village holds a ritual parade every three years. . . . Persons in charge make exorbitant assessments on taxpayers; some of the latter are thereby forced to pawn their property or sell their daughters. If the exaction is not satisfied, the managers [of the parade] may bring a mob and destroy the house of the defaulter."

33. *Tsou-i, hsü-pien*, 4/5b-6a, a memorial submitted by Chou T'ing-shen in 1803.

34. Ch'i Shu-k'ai, "Hsi-yin hsüeh-an," *Chung-ho* (1941), II, 12.

35. *Chiang-hsi* (1880), 142/36b, biographical sketch of Wen Ch'eng.

36. *P'an-yü* (1911), 14/10b. The feud stopped around 1845.

37. *Lu-chou* (1885), 34/34b.

38. *Tao chou* (1878), 3/16b.

39. *Hsin hsien* (1887), "I-wen," *shang*, pp. 30b-31a.

40. *Mien-yang* (1894), *chüan* 3, "Chien-chih," p. 30a.

41. *Chia-hsing* (1878), 43/36b.

42. *Nan-hai* (1910), 8/3b-4a.

43. *Chiang-hsi* (1880), *chüan shou*, part 3, p. 10a-b.

44. Davis, *China* (1857), I, 459.

45. *Chien-ch'ang* (1907), 1/13a-14a.

46. *Mien-chu* (1908), "Li-shih," 1, p. 7a.

47. Ko Shih-chün, *Hsü-pien*, 33/10a, Tseng Kuo-fan's memorial dated 1866. See also *Hsü-chou* (1874), *chüan* 21, *hsia*, p. 42b.

48. *Yang-chiang* (1925), 20/94a; *En-p'ing* (1934), 14/23a.

49. *Chinese and Japanese Repository*, III (1865), 283-84. The presence of the clan organization often complicated the situation, even though no Hakkas were involved. For example, the Liao clan which dwelt in Huang-mien village in Yung-fu (Kwangsi) was at loggerheads with the "natives." Under their clan chief the clansmen repeatedly harassed their neighbors. They joined the "boat bandits" (pirates from Kwangtung) and gave full vent to their grudge against the "natives." *P'ing-kuei chi-lüeh*, 2/14b.

50. *Ibid.*, 1/2a.

51. Chien Yu-wen, *Shou-i shih*, p. 178.

52. Marshall Broomhall, *Islam in China* (1910), pp. 152-54.

53. *Nan-hai* (1910), 8/4a (cited in note 42 above).

54. *Mien-yang* (1894), *chüan* 3, "Chien-chih," p. 30a (cited in note 40 above).

55. *En-p'ing* (1934), 14/14a (cited in note 48, above).

56. *Tung-kuan* (1911), 36/3a-b.

57. *Tsou-i*, 56/13b-14a.

58. *Chinese Repository*, IV (1836), 413.

59. Samuel W. Williams, *Middle Kingdom* (1883), I, 484-85.

60. *Nan-hai* (1910), 14/6b-7b, biographical sketch of Chu Tz'u-ch'i. The conflict in question was resolved by Chu when serving as acting magistrate of Hsiang-ling in 1859.

61. Chien Yu-wen, *Shou-i shih*, p. 171.

62. Fei Hsiao-t'ung, *Peasant Life*, p. 189.

63. Li Tz'u-ming (1830-94), *Jih-chi*, iii, *hsia chi*, 37b. Morton H. Fried, *Fabric of Chinese Society* (1953), p. 194, describes relationships between tenants and landlords in more recent times: "In Ch'uhsien [Anhwei] it was the fashion for landlords, visiting their tenants in the countryside, to be invited for tea,

wine, or a meal by neighbors of the tenants. These people hoped in this way to widen their circle of influential contacts. Many farmers, when pressed by local tax collectors or representatives of the army, would come to Ch'u [city] where they tried to get their landlords or such influential people as they knew to intercede for them."

64. Chang Ping-lin (1868-1936), Chien-lun, 7/17a-b.

65. Fried, Fabric of Chinese Society (1953), p. 196, describes such a situation existing in more recent times: ". . . in Ch'uhsien [Anhwei], though there was no actual shooting war between landlords and tenants, there were many peripheral areas in the county [district] which, away from the police power of the county seat, defied the landlords and paid no rent."

66. Pa-ling (1891), 52/5a-b.

67. George Jamieson et al., "Tenure of Land in China," Journal of the Royal Asiatic Society, North China Branch, N. S., XXIII (1888), 107 ff. Nonpayment of rent might be the result of dire destitution rather than tenant-landlord conflict. See, for example, a memorial submitted by Pai Pang-hsi in 1884, quoted in Ko Shih-chün, Hsü-pien, 32/20a.

68. Shih-lu, Wen-tsung, 140/1b-2a, an edict addressed to the Grand Councilors, dated 1854 (Hsien-feng 4, intercalary 7th month): ". . . in the winter of the previous year, tenants [in Kiangsu] refused to pay rent; local officials did not compel any of them to pay it. As a consequence, landowners are without the means to pay their grain taxes. . . . The law prohibits rural inhabitants from gathering mobs and resisting the collection of the grain taxes by force. Local officials concerned shall severely punish [those who fail to pay their taxes]. . . . As to tenants who fail to pay their land rent and whose landlords have laid charges against them, [local officials] shall deal with the defaulters in accordance with the established precedents, in order to deter [the people from carrying on] wicked practices."

69. Li Hsing-yüan (1797-1851), Tsou-i, 11/19a-b, and 12/47a-58a. In another memorial (ibid., 12/59a) the governor indicated that since Tao-kuang 22 (1842), similar actions against landlords had been repeatedly instigated by Hsü Erh-man, a "local stick."

70. Wang Hsien-ch'ien, Tung-hua lu, 1859 (Hsien-feng 9, 2nd month), 55/5a.

71. Li Tz'u-ming, Jih-chi pu, ssu-chi, p. 6a, 1859 (Hsien-feng 9, 1st month, 26th day). The fights occurring in 1846 in Chao-wen, mentioned above, also reached the proportions of a riot after the local government intervened. Li Hsing-yüan, Chou-i, 11/19a-b.

72. Ibid., 12/47a-58a. This type of struggle existed in other periods. A striking instance occurred in the Ming dynasty. See Chao I, Cha-chi, 36/14b, for the story of Teng Mou-ch'i; see also Ming-shih, chüan 165, biography of Ting Hsüan.

73. P'ing-kuei chi-lüeh, 1/14b.

74. En-p'ing (1934), 14/8a.

75. Ch'ing-shih lieh-chuan, 43/35a-b, biography of Lu-Fei Ch'üan.

76. Lu-chou (1885), 34/31b-32a.

77. Chiang-hsi (1880), chüan shou, part 3, p. 10a-b.

78. Mu-lin shu, 9/13a-14a, a letter on suppressing feuds, written by Ch'eng Han-chang, one-time governor of Shantung.

79. Weng T'ung-ho (1830-1904), Jih-chi (jen-wu [1882]), 21/12b-13a, supplies an additional instance that lends support to this conclusion. Kang-i, a Manchu official destined to play a part in the Boxer uprising, is quoted as saying that weaponed fights occurred so frequently in some parts of Kwangtung because "law-

suits were not given a hearing" even after the litigants had waited for long periods of time.

80. *Mien-chu* (1908), "Li-shih," I, pp. 7b-8b. The original says, "for more than one hundred and fifty years," an obvious error, since this edition of the gazetteer was printed in 1908. One hundred and fifty years from 1795, the earliest possible year in which the settlement could have been effected, would be 1945.

81. "Riot" is defined in Webster's *International Dictionary* as "(2) disorderly behavior; disorder; uproar; tumult," and "(6) an instance of violent disorder by unruly persons." For the sake of convenience "riot" is used in the present discussion to signify a special type of "violent disorder" as explained in the text.

82. "Rebellion" is here understood substantially as defined in Webster; an "open renunciation of the authority of the government to which one owed obedience, and resistance to its officers and laws, either by levying war or aiding others to do so; an organized uprising of subjects in order to overthrow their lawful ruler or government." This term is not used in the sense, given in the *Encyclopedia of the Social Sciences,* of "an uprising of more or less significant proportions intended to effect territorial autonomy or independence, but not overthrow of the central government." Attention should be called to the fact that riots were not limited to the countryside. Some of the instances cited in this chapter occurred in towns or cities. For convenience's sake these are included in our discussion and the places in which the incidents occurred are indicated wherever these can be ascertained.

83. Chester Holcombe, *Real Chinaman* (1895), p. 33.

84. Meadows, *Desultory Notes* (1847), p. 102n.

85. Martin, *Cycle* (1896), pp. 91-92.

86. Cf. Francis H. Nichols, *Through Hidden Shensi* (1902), p. 141: "To the people of the interior it is not the emperor in Pekin but the mandarins of the province who are government and law and power."

87. Archibald R. Colquhoun, *China in Transformation* (1900), pp. 287-89. According to David Mitrany, *Marx Against the Peasant* (1951), p. 118, a comparable attitude was exhibited by peasants of postwar central Europe: "The peasants were roused, but what were they capable of as a class? Political revolution did not come naturally to them. When peasants rebelled, it was against patent abuses; their quarrels had been with their direct tormentors, landlords and local officials, while they had looked upon king and parliament rather as courts of appeal."

88. Denby, *China* (1906), II, 7.

89. For example, *Hua hsien* (1924), 7/6a-b, tells this story: Ti Shang-chün (a native of Kiangsi) served as magistrate of Hua Hsien in 1800-5. When his term expired, he was entreated by the inhabitants to remain in his post. A rhymed panegyric was composed in his honor which runs somewhat as follows:

"Good official, good official, who desires no money!
To the City of Hua has come Ti, the Blue Sky.
Oh, Ti, the Blue Sky!
After he departs, forever shall we cherish him."

"Blue Sky" was a phrase popularly used to characterize local magistrates believed to have been wise, just, and incorruptible.

90. *Ibid.,* 9/7b, furnishes another instance: Sung T'ing-chen, a native of Kwang-

tung, served as magistrate of Nei-chiang (Szechwan) early in the nineteenth century. When he was ready to leave upon expiration of his term of office, the inhabitants blocked his way, entreating him to remain.

91. For example, *Nan-hai* (1910), 14/8a, relates that Chu Tsi-ch'i, a native of Kwangtung, served as magistrate of Hsiang-ling (Shansi) in the middle of the nineteenth century and was noted for his integrity and kindness. When he was about to leave his post, the inhabitants petitioned the government to retain him. Their request was rejected. District magistrates were very rarely, if ever, allowed to remain in their posts longer than the regulation terms. Other officials, however, might be permitted to do so upon the petition of local inhabitants. An instance is found in *P'an-yü* (1911), 21/17b-18a, in which a river intendant in Honan, appointed in 1873, was so successful in his dike repair work that he was allowed to continue in his post upon the petition of the inhabitants to the governor.

92. Holcombe, *Real Chinaman*, pp. 230-33, describes the "umbrella and boot ceremony." Huc, *Chinese Empire*, II, 73-74, describes a "boot ceremony" honoring a departing military officer. Doolittle, *Social Life* (1865), II, 328, describes the presentation of the "ten-thousand-people umbrella." The boot ceremony involved an allusion to a well-known legend recorded in *Han-shu, chüan* 112, *shang*. Wang Ch'iao, a fine magistrate and a magician of remarkable powers, visited the imperial court from his district every first and fifteenth day of the month. As no one ever saw his carriage or horse, the imperial astrologer got curious and spied upon him. Whenever Wang was about to arrive, a pair of wild ducks were seen to fly from the direction of his district. The astrologer caught them in a hunting net. Miraculously they promptly turned into a pair of shoes, the very ones given to Wang by the emperor four years before! In later times it became accepted literary usage to refer, in a complimentary sense, to a magistrate as *shuang fu* (double wild ducks), or *fu hsi* (wild duck shoes). Thus in the boot ceremony the popular magistrate was impliedly likened to Wang Ch'iao.

93. For example, *Fu-shan* (1924), 12/11a, indicates that a "living shrine," a shrine built to honor a person still living, was dedicated to Hsieh Hsiao-chang in 1855. *P'an-yü* (1911), 20/10a, supplies this information: Yang Yung-hsü, appointed prefect of Hu-chou (Chekiang) in 1863, was reputed to be a kindly administrator. "When he died, scholars and common people wept mournfully. Even peasants dwelling on the shores of the lake went into the city to mourn for his death. Boatmen and sedan-chair carriers all shed tears in grief. His tablet was entered in the Shrine of Celebrated Officials in 1876."

94. The following examples are pertinent. *Huai-an* (1884), 27/82a: A magistrate of Yen-ch'eng built a school and repaired the city walls, early in the nineteenth century. *Ibid.*, 27/84a: A magistrate of Fu-ning who served during the first half of the century took pains to avoid incurring expense to the people and prevented yamen underlings from extorting money from them. *Kuang-chou* (1878), 129/12a: A magistrate of Ting-hsiang (Shansi) risked his position to give relief to the starving inhabitants. *Ch'üeh-shan* (1931), 7/19a: A magistrate of Ch'üeh-shan (Anhwei) completed the city defense work in 1856 just in time to withstand the attack of "bandits."

95. *Hua hsien* (1924), *chüan* 9, *passim*.

96. *Chiang-ching* (1924), 6/3b.

97. *Ch'u-chou* (1897), Hsiung Tsu-i's preface to the 1672 edition.

98. *T'eng hsien* (1846), 6/36a-b. *Chüan* 14, p. 11b, records this rhymed obloquy written in vernacular Chinese:

A tapering, tapering head,
A slender, slender tail,
A mouth hidden under a cover,
A length, from head to tail, of
    less than an inch:
But how much rice of T'eng-yang
    has it consumed?

Apparently, the structure of the Chinese character *ch'ang* (Herbert A. Giles, *Chinese-English Dictionary*, No. 440) induced the native rhymester to liken the loathesome official to a rat. *Chüan* 12, p. 14b, gives a short verse on the theme "Living Shrines" written by an unnamed local scholar and dedicated to this notorious official. The concluding lines are:

Why burn incense to worship a tiger?
Living shrines are built at several places
    in the City!

99. *Tsou-i, hsü-pien*, 2/12b.
100. Meadows, *Desultory Notes*, p. 168. The italics are Meadows'.
101. Feng Kuei-fen (1809-74), *Chi*, 2/35b.
102. *Liu-pu ch'u-fen tse-li* (1877), 15-19b, gives this regulation: "Magistrates of the *chou* and *hsien* who are greedy, cruel, oppressive, habitually disregarding the people's needs; or who are partial and unjust in hearing the people's litigations; or who mistreat and insult the literati, inflicting injuries upon scholars with the *sheng-yüan* degree or scholars aspiring to it; who consequently provoke scholars and common people into shutting up shop and refusing to take the examinations [in protest against such magistrates], or into gathering mobs and beating the local officials, shall be dismissed from their offices, put under arrest, and brought to trial."
103. Huang Liu-hung, *Fu-hui*, 32/30a-b.
104. *Sheng-hsün*, Kao-tsung, 261/24b-25a.
105. *Ibid.*, 262/2b.
106. Li Tz'u-ming, *Jih-chi*, vi, "Chia-chi," 77a, 3rd month, 1st day (T'ung-chih 9), referring to an incident in Ch'eng Hsien.
107. *Ibid.*, "Jen chi," 2nd series, p. 49a, 8th month, 1st day (Kuang-hsü 4), quoting an imperial edict.
108. *Sheng-hsün*, Kao-tsung, 263/1b.
109. Such a situation was described by a president of the Board of Rites in a memorial which he submitted in 1745: "Local officials have the responsibility of hearing and settling litigations. . . . But ruffians and rowdies gather mobs and compel merchants to close down their stores [to protest against the actions taken by local officials]. Such persons even go so far as to insult the officials; they fear and care for nothing whatever." *Tsou-i*, 41/7a.
110. For example, extortions exacted in connection with the collection of "mining taxes" during the Wan-li reign of the Ming dynasty frequently resulted in local uprisings. In 1599 inhabitants of Lin-ch'ing (Shantung) burned down the office of the tax collector and killed thirty-four of his underlings. Uprisings in Wu-ch'ang and Han-yang (Hupeh) resulted in bodily injuries to the regional tax collector. In 1606 inhabitants of Yunnan province rioted and killed the supervisor of tax collection and burned his corpse to ashes. Chao I, *Ts'ung-k'ao*, 20/17a-b. Antiextortion riots in the Ming dynasty eventually led to rebellions. Li Tzu-

ch'eng, as is well known, employed the slogan "Welcome Prince Ch'uang: pay no grain taxes!" to induce people to follow him. *Ming-shih*, 309/6b.

111. Fu I-ling, "T'ai-p'ing t'ien-kuo shih-tai ti ch'üan-kuo k'ang-liang ch'ao," *Ts'ai-cheng chih-shih*, III (1943), 31-39; S. Y. Teng, *New Light*, pp. 41-42.

112. Martin, *Cycle*, p. 336: "The legal imposts are not oppressive, and if a greedy officer ventures to add too much to the burden, the people may petition for his removal or, in extreme cases, band together for armed resistance. Resistance on a large scale becomes rebellion, which may lead to revolution."

113. See note 111. Pao Shih-ch'eng (1775-1855), *Ch'i-min ssu-shu*, *chüan* 7, *hsia*, pp. 25a-31b, records an instance which occurred early in the nineteenth century.

114. *Chia-hsing* (1878), 42/96b.

115. Feng Kuei-fen, *Chi*, 4/36a-b. A somewhat different version, which impliedly places the responsibility on the local inhabitants, is given in *Ch'ing-shih lieh-chuan*, 43/34a-35b.

116. *Ch'ing hsü t'ung-k'ao*, 2/7517.

117. Feng Kuei-fen, *Chi*, 5/33a.

118. *North China Herald*, CLI (1855), 182.

119. Li T'ang-chieh (1798-1865), *Jih-chi*, Vol. XIII, 1854 (Hsien-feng 4, 3rd month, 16th day). According to Li, the official exchange rate was currently fixed at over 4,000 cash to one tael. The old rate was 2,700 to one.

120. *Ibid.*, Vol. XIV, 1854 (Hsien-feng 4, 8th month, 7th day, 26th day, and 27th day); 1855 (Hsien-feng 5, 5th month, 13th day and 25th day; 6th month, 23rd day; 7th month, 6th day, 20th to 25th days inclusive, and 29th day; 8th month, 2nd to 4th days inclusive). Comparable riots were reported at about the same time in remote Kweichow. *T'ung-jen* (1890), 9/40b, records the following: "Investigation reveals that in this district the people of P'o-t'ou Hsiang had always paid their grain taxes promptly and fully. When the time for collecting the taxes of the current year arrived, the inhabitants went to the [designated] granaries to deliver their grain. But the keeper purposely resorted to obstructive tactics; he refused to receive the grain. The taxpayers were asked to hand in money in lieu of grain so that he could embezzle the funds which were to be collected in excess of the real value of the grain. The people were disgusted and rose with an uproar; they broke the door and dashed into his office. The situation now becomes threatening, and grave consequences are impending. . . . According to the old practice, the grain taxes were paid by delivering the grain to the storehouses. After the lapse of a long period of time, however, a new procedure has been set up which requires payment of money equivalents of the grain. At first one *tou* [0.1 *shih]* of grain was converted into 400 or 500 cash. Lately the rate has been progressively raised to over 1,000 or 2,000. The people are very bitter about this."

121. *Ch'ing hsü t'ung-k'ao*, 2/7517.

122. Holcombe, *Real Chinaman* (1895), pp. 234-36. Émile Bard, *Chinese Life* (1905), p. 109, tells of an antiextortion riot staged by opium farmers in Chekiang. "The opium farmers of the district agreed to pay the authorities eight hundred dollars a year *likin* tax, and, in return, they were not to be molested in their occupation. In 1888, a collector's office was installed in Hsiang-Shan, and a tax of twenty-four dollars per *picul* was levied on opium. This tax could not be collected at first because of the opposition of the farmers. Finally, in the spring of 1889, they became resigned and went to pay it. The collector then imprudently added five dollars extra to defray the expenses of collection. The farmers rebelled at this, destroyed the office, and pursued the collector to the door

of the *yamen* in which he took refuge. A mandarin attempting to quiet the mob was also obliged to flee for safety. The people then dispersed. The notables offering afterwards to replace the obnoxious tax by a yearly contribution of two thousand dollars, the farmers accepted; the collector was replaced, the mandarin reduced a grade, and the leaders of the mob were punished."

123. *Tsou-i*, 41/7a, a memorial submitted by Ch'in Hui-t'ien, junior vice-president of the Board of Rites, in 1745.

124. *Yang-chiang* (1925), 7/3a, quoting from the 1822 edition of the same gazetteer.

125. Weng T'ung-ho (1830-1904), *Jih-chi, chi-hai*, 38/13b. Weng was at that time living in his home district (Ch'ang-shu, Kiangsu), after having been dismissed from his office. See also 38/68b, an entry of 11th month, 22nd day.

126. Yeh Ch'ang-chih (1849-1917), *Jih-chi*, 14/33a, an entry of 1911 (Kuang-hsü *hsin-hai*, 7th month, 9th day).

127. *Chiang-hsi* (1880), *chüan shou*, part 3, p. 31a. The situation remained bad. A number of daring robberies, in which rice was seized, were reported in various places of the province in the year following. See *ibid.*, 14/32a-b.

128. *Ting chou* (1850), 11/34a.

129. *Han-tan* (1933), 1/11b.

130. *Sheng-hsün*, Hsüan-tsung, 78/16b, an edict issued in 1833, quoting from a memorial. The uprising in Ling-shan (Kwangtung) in 1848, the objective of which was declared to be "to rob the rich, to succor the poor," and another in 1851 which consistently forced wealthy families to give money and grain to poor people, had substantially the same significance. *Ling-shan* (1914), 8/103a.

131. *Chinese Repository*, XX (1851), 53.

132. See chapter 4, section on the gentry and the revenue system.

133. *Shih-lu*, Hsüan-tsung, 435/9a-10a; *Shih-li*.(1908), 207/4b; *Ch'ing hsü t'ung-k'ao*, 2/7513-14.

134. Feng Kuei-fen, *Chi*, 2/27b.

135. Wei Yüan (1794-1856), *Wai-chi*, 4/35b. The localities in question were Kuei-an and Jen-ho (Chekiang), Tan-yang and Chen-ts'e (Kiangsu), Hsin-yü (Kiangsi), and Lui-yang (Hunan).

136. *Ibid.*, 4/34a-35b. See also Huang Chün-tsai, *Lang-mo*, 4/6b-7a. The locality in which the riot occurred was Ts'ung-yang.

137. *Chia-hsing* (1878), 42/96b. For the Chinese characters of the man's name see Herbert A. Giles, *Chinese-English Dictionary*, Nos. 13608 *(Yü)*, 1 *(A)*, and 8139 *(Nan)*.

138. Huc, *Chinese Empire* (1855), II, 76-78. Huc's description may not have been accurate in every detail, but the incident as narrated appears to be generally authentic.

139. *Hsüeh-cheng* (1810), 7/16a; quoted in chapter 6, note 346, above.

140. Li Tz'u-ming, *Jih-chi*, iv, 49b, T'ung-chih 8th year, 1st month, 10th day. After recording the troubles in Ch'eng Hsien and Shun-an Hsien, Li comments: "Scholars of our prefecture [Shao-hsing Fu] have recently become disrespectful to their teachers and superiors; they vie with one another in exhibiting disorderly and clamorous conduct. Whenever examinations are held in a *hsien* or in the *fu*, they insult the functionaries, demolish walls and doors, and revile [the functionaries] in malicious and hurtful words. In the worst cases they even burn these functionaries' official hats and robes, and search out and seize their wives and children."

141. George Smith, *China*, (1847), pp. 251-52.

142. Feng Kuei-fen, *Chi*, 4/36a-b.

143. *Ling-shan* (1914), 8/103b. The scholar in question was subsequently arrested and tortured, and the disturbance ended with the payment of a "fine" by him.

144. Davis, *China,* (1852), II, 189-96.

145. Li T'ang-chieh, *Jih-chi,* Vol. XIV, 1855 (Hsien-feng *i-mao,* 8th month, 5th day). See also note 120 above, citing from *ibid.,* 1854 (Hsien-feng *chia-yin,* 8th month, 7th day).

146. *Shan-tung chün-hsing chi-lüeh,* 22/3b and 6a, records that in Lo-an a salaried *sheng-yüan* and a military *sheng-yüan* gathered a mob of several thousand men in 1858 and attacked the magistrate's yamen. In Ch'i-ho a salaried *sheng-yüan* led local inhabitants to resist the collection of taxes.

147. *T'ung-jen* (1890), 9/40b-41b.

148. Li Tz'u-ming, *Jih-chi,* V, 53b, 1869 (T'ung-chih 8, 7th month, 27th day). For additional instances in which "bad scholars" instigated or organized riots, see sources indicated in chapter 6, notes 350-54, above.

149. Meadows, *Desultory Notes* (1847), pp. 172-74.

150. George W. Cooke, *China* (1858), p. 190, voices a generally accepted view: "China is a thickly peopled country, peculiarly subject to inundations and failure of crops, with a feeble government and no poor-laws. There must be always bands of hungry men in such a land. . . . Every part of China is rife with 'dangerous classes.'"

151. Yang Ching-jen, *Ch'ou-chi p'ien,* 19/10b.

152. *Ling-shan* (1914), 8/103a-110b.

153. Arthur Smith, *Village Life* (1899), pp. 212-17.

154. *Ibid.,* pp. 220-21. Smith significantly adds that the "village bully" might be a commoner or a "literary man," a *hsiu-ts'ai (sheng-yüan).* Evidence shows, however, that lettered bullies were less common in the countryside than in towns or cities, perhaps because the rural arena was not attractive enough for them. Such persons were more likely to infest cities, including the imperial capital, at least in the second half of the nineteenth century. The following two instances will serve to illustrate: Li Tz'u-ming, *Jih-chi pu,* "Hsin-chi," *hsia,* pp. 59b-60b, 1862, (T'ung-chih 1, 1st month, 13th day), narrates that a young man from a wealthy family of Shansi became the ringleader of a gang of bullies in Peking. He purchased a minor official post and carried on his accustomed violent ways with his comrades, among whom were the son of an unidentified governor and a young Manchu, until he was finally caught by a particularly dutiful censor. He died a painful death in prison. Weng T'ung-ho, *Jih-chi, ting-hai,* 1887 (8th month, 14th day, to 9th month, 14th day, 26/77a-85b), records that some rowdies pummeled his chauffeur for some unknown cause. Because one of the ringleaders was a member of the imperial clan, all his efforts at securing redress for his servant proved futile. Weng was then president of the Board of Revenue.

155. Hsieh Yü-heng, a *chin-shih* of 1820 and magistrate of Chao-hua (Szechwan), identified no less than six varieties of such activities: (1) forcibly extorting money from persons who had recently sold their real property; (2) extorting money from persons who had recently received payments on loans from their debtors; (3) cutting bamboo or trees from private land without permission; (4) forging receipts for borrowed money and demanding payment from persons known to have been inconsequential or helpless; (5) burglary; and (6) robbery. Quoted in *Mu-lin shu,* 9/9b-12a.

156. Ho Ch'ang-ling, *Kung-tu,* 3/14a. Ho was then governor of Kweichow.

157. Cooke, *China* (1858), p. 191. "Sticks" and bullies were given different names in different localities. For example, the "roaming, shiftless people who

blustered and terrorized their fellow villagers and neighbors" in some parts of Kwangtung were referred to locally as *lan-tsai,* literally "rotten kids." *Kuang-chou* (1878), 108/20b. Other names will appear in the discussion that follows.

158. Huc, *Chinese Empire* (1855), II, 251. Huc goes on to say that some of these "bare sticks" formed societies, while others operated individually.

159. Ch'en Hung-mou, *Ou-ts'un kao,* 21/8a-b.

160. *Ibid.,* 21/9a-10b.

161. *Ibid.,* 15/33a-b.

162. *Ibid.,* 43/11a. Such beggars did not stop at molesting local inhabitants. In another document dated 1758 Ch'en Hung-mou indicates: "The criminals recently arrested who are guilty of highway robbery or other crimes punishable by death are mostly able-bodied beggars. . . . They lodge at whatever places they may find, in abandoned temples or under the arches of bridges. The *pao-chia* cannot control them, nor can garrison soldiers or yamen runners check them. They become outlaws and therefore repeatedly commit lawless acts."

163. Wang Hui-tsu, *Meng-hen lu, hsia,* pp. 4b-5a.

164. *Chiang-hsi* (1880), *chiian shou,* part 3, pp. 33b-34a.

165. Ch'ü-mi (pseud.), "Yang-ho-shih sui-pi," *Chung-ho,* I, 121, quoting Ch'iu Hsiang-chou, a *chin-shih* of 1733 and magistrate of Nan-ch'ung (Szechwan). The meaning of the term *kuo-lu* is not clear. It is doubtful that it was the original form of *ko-lao,* as the writer quoted supposes.

166. *Chih-hsin pao,* LXXXII, 1a, quoting a memorial submitted by the governor of Kwangtung in 1899. That secret societies often engaged in banditry may be inferred from the fact that specific regulations were drawn up by the Hung Society to govern such activities among its members and to prevent disputes from arising. E.g., "fifth oath" (British Museum, Oriental 8207D), "twentieth oath" (Oriental 8207E), and "hsing ch'uan yü chieh k'ou-pai" (code language upon encountering pirates), quoted in Hsiao I-shan, *Chin-tai pi-mi she-hui shih-liao,* 3/1b, 3/5b, and 4/38a-b. Secret societies cannot be treated here in any systematic manner. References to them will be made in so far as they bear upon the disorders that were reported in rural China of the nineteenth century. Hsiao I-shan, *Chin-tai,* contains useful primary material. The following well-known works may be consulted: J. S. M. Ward and W. J. Sterling, *The Hung Society,* 3 vols. (1925-26); Gustaaf Schlegel, *Thian-ti-hwui, The Hung League* (1866); chapters in K. S. Latourette, *The Chinese* (1941); and James D. Ball, *Things Chinese* (4th ed., 1906). Henri Cordier, *Bibliotheca Sinica,* III, 1894-1900, gives additional titles.

167. Li Tz'u-ming, *Jih-chi pu, jen chi,* p. 84b, 1862 (T'ung-chih 1, 2nd month, 24th day). *T'ung-ch'uan* (1897), 17/39a, gives the following piece written by a local rhymester in 1861, describing the behavior of both bandits and government troops:

An awesome hush hangs over the entire countryside.
An old man—greedy, ignorant, poor, decrepit—
Rejoicing at the calamity of others, gleefully declares:
"It is well that bandits have come,
Who have pity for my feebleness and poverty,
Who let me enjoy rich food—free from hunger day and
    night!"
For all houses are now deserted by their owners
And all treasures abandoned like worthless dirt.
But soon the troops come—after the bandits have gone.

They seize him, saying, "So you connived with the bandits!"
They take everything from him, valuable or valueless:
The wealth that once filled his eyes vanishes without a trace.

168. *Chih-hsin pao*, 82/2b, quoting a memorial submitted by the governor of Kiangsi.

169. Tseng Kuo-fan, *Tsou-kao*, 2/3b.

170. *Ibid.*

171. See note 168, above.

172. Fried, *Fabric of Chinese Society*, p. 229, gives a recent instance which illustrates this type of peasant reaction: "They [bandits operating in the late 1940's in Ch'u Hsien, Anhwei] had made their living for some time by raiding outlying settlements and robbing the rich peasants or the die-hard rural gentry. For several months they were successful and then, quite suddenly, they were caught. The explanation was simple. . . . During their early patrol, the guerillas' efforts had been confined to the looting of more or less wealthy families. . . . Then, for reasons unknown, the bandits failed to discriminate and began raids on ordinary peasants and tenant villagers, often burning the houses of their victims. . . . The peasantry kept tabs on the location of the bandits and informed the local authorities."

173. Ko Shih-chün, *Hsü-pien*, 21/15b-16a. See also Lin Tse-hsü, *Liang-chiang tsou-kao*, 3/18a, a document describing clans of Hui-chou and Ch'ao-chou (Kwang-tung).

174. T'ien Wen-ching, *Chou-hsien shih-i*, pp. 17b-18a.

175. Wang Hsien-ch'ien, *Wen-chi*, 7/7b.

176. *Tsou-i, hsü-pien*, 2/3a, a memorial submitted by Liang Shang-kuo. Liang used the term "bandit" in the loose sense, as indicated at the beginning of the present section.

177. Lo Ping-chang, *Tsou-kao*, "Hsiang-chung kao," 8/29b.

178. *Tsou-i, hsü-pien*, 2/12a.

179. Ko Shih-chün, *Hsü-pien*, 21/16a.

180. Ho Ch'ang-ling, *Tsou-i*, 1/15a-b.

181. See chapter 8, notes 190-92.

182. Tseng Kuo-fan, *Shu-cha*, 2/1a-b. In this and in the following passage quoted, Tseng Kuo-fan used the term *fei* (bandits) in the customary loose sense. The following passage from von Richthofen's *Letters*, p. 133 (a letter written in May, 1872), throws some light on the behavior of inept and irresponsible officials: "Pingyangfu [Shansi], which I had not entered at the time of my last visit, is completely destroyed. The story is told that, several years ago, a band of rebels, coming from Honan, entered the city quite unexpectedly, but left again after a slight pillage. When they were at some distance, the mandarins, in order to give some substance to their projected report to the Emperor of having saved the city by martial defence, ordered some shots to be fired after them from the walls. The rebels considering this an ungrateful treatment, turned back, and destroyed the whole city, killing a great many people. Since that time, soldiers are stationed among the ruins."

183. Tseng Kuo-fan, *Shu-cha*, 1/27a-b, a letter to Hu Lien-fang, written in 1850-51.

184. These definitions are made from the standpoint of political science. They agree substantially with those given in Webster's *International Dictionary*. The definition of rebellion has already been quoted in note 82, above. The *Dictionary* defines revolution as "a fundamental change in political organization or in gov-

ernment or constitution; the overthrow or renunciation of one government or ruler, and the substitution of another, by the governed." The *Encyclopedia of the Social Sciences* gives a different definition. "Revolution: a major change in the political order—not merely a shift in the personnel of the government or a réorientation of its concrete policies—must be preceded or accompanied by a drastic change in the relations among the different groups and classes in society; . . . a recasting of the social order. . . . This aspect of the revolution distinguishes it . . . from *coup d'état,* rebellion, and insurrection." Cf. Aristotle, *Politics* (Jowett's trans.), I, 1301b: "Two sorts of changes in government: the one affecting the constitution, when men seek to change from an existing form into another, e.g., form democracy into oligarchy . . . the other not affecting the constitution, when without disturbing the form of government . . . they try to get the administration into their own hands." It is obvious that from the establishment of the Ch'in dynasty (246 B.C.) to the establishment of the Ch'ing dynasty (A.D. 1644) all the dynastic changes were, in Aristotle's language, of the type of "revolution" that did not "disturb the form of government." Some of the important uprisings had greater significance than the mere desire of the leaders to "get the administration into their own hands." The Taiping Rebellion is an outstanding example of such movements; it, however, did not deviate from the historical pattern in one respect: the Taiping leaders intended to set up another dynasty and did not envisage a new form of government. Meadows, *Rebellions* (1856), p. 25, offers these interesting remarks: "Revolution is a change of the form of government and of the principles on which it rests; it does not necessarily imply a change of rulers. Rebellion is a rising against the rulers which, far from necessarily aiming at a change of governmental principles and forms, often originates in a desire of preserving them intact. Revolutionary movements are against principles; rebellions against men. . . . Bearing the above distinction clearly in mind, great light may be thrown by one sentence over the four thousand years of Chinese history: *Of all nations that have attained a certain degree of civilization, the Chinese are the least revolutionary and the most rebellious.* Speaking generally, there has been but one great political revolution in China, when the centralized form of government was substituted for the feudal, about two thousand years ago." By defining rebellion as we do and by distinguishing it from revolution, we can include all antigovernment uprisings in Chinese history under the rubric "rebellions" and, at the same time, avoid the delicate problem of ascertaining whether any of these was "revolutionary," which does not directly concern us here.

185. Meadows, *Rebellions,* p. 24: "The Chinese people have no right of legislation . . . they have not the power of voting out their rulers or of limiting or stopping supplies. *They have therefore the right of rebellion.* " The appropriateness of the phrase "right of rebellion" has been questioned by Karl A. Wittfogel. "The term 'right of rebellion' is unfortunate in that it confuses a legal and moral issue. The official discussions on the rise and fall of dynastic power are presented as warnings against rebellious action rather than as guides for it; and they were certainly not incorporated into official 'constitutional' regulations or laws. The 'right of rebellion' could be exercised only when the existing laws are violated and at the risk of total destruction for whoever asserted it." "Oriental Despotism," *Sociologus,* III (1953), 100. The cogency of Professor Wittfogel's argument cannot be denied. However, while there was never a legal right of rebellion in China or anywhere else it was possible for some Chinese writers to speak of something like a moral right of rebellion. In fact, the concepts of the "mandate of Heaven" and "minister of Heaven," especially as stated by Mencius,

implied even a quasi-religious right of rebellion. The "official discussions on the rise and fall of dynastic power" constituted "warnings against rebellions" precisely because such discussions impliedly, if not formally, recognized the principle that "the people" were justified in rising against tyrannical rulers. Rebels, on the other hand, used this principle as a "guide" for their action, exercising the "right of rebellion" at the risk of "total destruction" to themselves. Thus, "right of rebellion," though a legal monstrosity, occupies a legitimate niche in the intellectual and political history of imperial China. It reminds one of the concept of "natural rights," also a legal monstrosity, but occupying a comparable place in European history. In China the Legalists denied the existence of anything like "right of rebellion," moral or legal. Their view, however, was not shared by any other school of thought.

186. *Book of History*, *chüan* 4, *chou-shu*, "T'ai-shih hsia." James Legge, *Chinese Classics*, III, part 3, 296.

187. *Mencius*, I, part 2, iii, 7; xi, 2; II, part 2, viii, 2; VII, part 2, iv, 4-5, xiv, 1. Legge, *ibid.*, II, 157 and 170-71, 223, 480, and 483.

188. Chia I *(ca.* 200-168 B.C.), *Hsin-shu*, *chüan* 9, "Ta-cheng shang."

189. Fang Hsiao-ju (1357-1402), *Hsün-chih-chai chi*, *chüan* 3, "Min-cheng."

190. Walter H. Mallory, *China: Land of Famine*, p. 65: "It seems to the writer that the proper approach to the Chinese monarchical system is that taken by the Chinese themselves—that the people are the sea and the emperor a boat on the sea. If the sea became too stormy, then the boat capsized and that was the end of it."

191. For example, Lo Erh-kang, *Shih-kang*, pp. 1-20, enumerates concentration of landownership, population pressure, unfavorable balance of foreign trade, and recurrent natural calamities as the major factors that led to the Taiping uprising.

192. *Shih-chi*, 48/1b.

193. *Sung-shih*, 468/6b.

194. Lo Yung and Shen Tsu-chi (ed.), *T'ai-p'ing t'ien-kuo shih-wen ch'ao*, pp. 28b-29a. This document, however, may have come from the pen of a person other than Hung Hsiu-ch'üan.

195. *Ibid.*, pp. 32b-34a; Hsiang Ta and others (ed.), *Tzu-liao*, vol. 2, pp. 691-92.

196. *Hung Liang-chi* (1746-1809), letter to Prince Ch'eng, written in 1798; quoted in Inaba, *Ch'ing-ch'ao ch'üan-shih* (Chinese trans.), III, 29. The major rebel movements of this period included those led by Wang Lun, 1774, in Shantung; by Liu Chih-hsieh and Wang San-huai, 1793, in Hupeh, Szechwan, and Shensi; and by Li Wen-ch'eng and Lin Ch'ing, 1813, in Honan and Chihli. Liu and Wang belonged to the White Lotus, Li and Lin to the T'ien-li sect.

197. *Kuang-chou* (1878), 129/24b.

198. *T'ung-ch'uan* (1897), 17/34a.

199. *Ming-shih*, *chüan* 309, *passim.*

200. Lo Erh-kang, *Shih-kang*, pp. 17-20.

201. Paul M. A. Linebarger, *Government in Republican China*, p. 116, puts the matter somewhat too strongly: "Lack of resources caused the loss of the land, and the peasant proprietor found himself a tenant farmer. When economic and political exploitation overreached itself, social upheaval followed, and peasant rebellions tore down the government and the economy together. Most Chinese dynasties met their end as a consequence of the land problem."

202. *Sung-shih*, 276/7a.

203. Hsüeh Nung-shan, *Nung-min chan-cheng*, II, 284, quoting from Lan-i wai-shih (pseud.), *Ch'ing-ni chi.*

204. Hsiao I-shan, *Ts'ung-shu*, 1st series, gives this document.

205. This situation was illustrated in a small way by some of the *p'eng-min* (shack people) in Anhwei. According to *Ch'u chou* (1897), *chüan* 1, *chih* 2, p. 13a, the leaders of these people "obeyed an order of the Heavenly Prince which was issued at a remote place, assembled several thousand comrades, and stormed the walled city of Lai-an." *P'eng-min* were found in the provinces of Chekiang, Kiangsi, Anhwei, and Kwangtung. They were destitute people who migrated from other localities and were "looked down upon by the native inhabitants." Sheng K'ang, *Hsü-pien*, p. 33a, quoting a narrative written by Tai P'an; *Chiang-hsi* (1880), *chüan shou*, part 1, p. 24b.

206. Wang Shih-chen (1526-90), *Yen-shan-t'ang pieh-chi*, *chüan* 85, *chao-ling tsa-k'ao* 1, a proclamation addressed to inhabitants of Shantung, Honan, Chihli, Shensi, and Shansi.

207. Huc, *Chinese Empire*, I, xiii. See Chien Yu-wen, *Tsa-chi*, 1st series, p. 64, for a brief summary of the anti-Manchu ideology of the Taiping uprising. *Ling-shan* (1914), 8/110b, indicates that "all the 'bandits' that swarmed like wasps since the Tao-kuang and Hsien-feng times adopted the slogan 'opposing the Ch'ing, restoring the Ming' of T'ai-p'ing t'ien-kuo."

208. *Shih-chi*, *chüan* 48, biography of Ch'en Sheng.

209. *Ibid.*, 8/2b-4b, Liu Pang was then serving as the *t'ing-chang* of Ssu-shui. A note says: "Ten *li* constituted a *t'ing*, ten *t'ing* a *hsiang*. The *t'ing-chang* was the official who headed a *t'ing*. . . . [This office] was like the present *li-chang*. When the people had litigations, this official . . . settled them." ("The present" refers to the T'ang dynasty.)

210. Theodore Hamberg, *Visions of Hung-Siu-Tshuen* (Yenching University Library reprint, 1935). Meadows, *The Chinese and Their Rebellions* (1856), tended to overrate the moral strength and religious purity of the Taiping leaders. P. M. Yap, "The Mental Illness of Hung Hsiu-ch'üan, Leader of the Taiping Rebellion," *Far Eastern Quarterly*, XIII (1954), 287-304, discusses the psychological aspect of Hung's leadership.

211. Meadows, *Rebellions* (1856), p. 457.

212. Eugene P. Boardman, "Christian Influence upon the Ideology of the Taiping Rebellion," *Far Eastern Quarterly*, X (1951), 115.

213. *T'ung-ch'uan* (1897), 17/42b.

214. Arthur W. Hummel (ed.), *Eminent Chinese*, II, 958, summarizes the incident (Fang Chao-ying).

215. Huc, *Chinese Empire*, I, xiii-xiv. See also Hsiao I-shan, *Chin-tai pi-mi she-hui shih-liao*, *passim*.

216. *Ling-shan* (1914), 8/110b.

217. Such literate rebel leaders figured in some of the uprisings of "heretical sects"; for example, according to *Sung-shih*, 468/6b, the rebel leader Fang La "lured the masses with heretical doctrines." See also *K'uei-chou* (1827), 21/5a-18a, concerning Liu Chih-hsieh; and Yin Chia-pin, *Cheng-chiao chi-lüeh*, 4/23b-24a, concerning Kao Ch'in, a rebel leader executed in 1884.

218. As already noted, the presence of "roaming bandits" in rural China often contributed to the numerical strength of rebellions. A Western missionary, William C. Milne, *Life in China* (1859), p. 431, explains the rapid expansion of the Taiping movement in these words: "The crowd of idle and indolent vagabonds which infested the rural and suburban population found proper aliment in this commotion, and joined the [Taiping] movement in gangs." Naturally, secret societies also contributed to rebellious movements. Cooke, *China* (1858), pp. 433-45, quotes in an appendix some remarks made by Tsang Wang-yen, "a distin-

guished member of the Han-Lin Academy" and one-time commissioner of finance
in Fukien, on "The Origin of the Rebellion" which, while they suffer from oversimplification, are highly revealing: "The reason why brigandage, existing always and in all parts of the province, is now worse in Kwang Tung than it ever
was before, is simply that for a series of years no steps have been taken against
the members of lawless societies; the real criminals have never been apprehended; the facts have been utterly concealed or glossed over. . . . The San-hoh
Hwui (Triad Society) already existed as a denomination before the first year of
Tau-kwang (1820). . . . In the eleventh year of Tau-kwang (1831), the Censor
Fung Tsahhiun reported that he had ascertained that in five provinces this society had its seals, flags, and registers. . . . In the eighth moon of the twenty-
third year of Tau-kwang (1843), a thousand men or more, Triads and members
of the Ngo Lung Hwui (Sleeping Dragon Society) fought together with arms in the
village of Yung-ki, in the district of Shun-teh. . . . In the first moon of the twen-
ty-fourth year of Tau-kwang (December, 1843), the feud revived, and members
of both Triad and Sleeping Dragon societies, natives of several districts, numbering some thousands, had a second fight at the village of Kwei Chau, in Shun-
teh. . . . The magistrate . . . having restored order, hurried to the city and
made his report to the high authorities. They instructed him not to allow the
thing to be noised abroad . . . it was doubtless owing to this [official delinquency]
that the lawless persons in question lost all respect of the law. . . . Hence did
the mischief, weed-like, spread throughout the province, and thence to Kwang
Si, until it included, as at present, both Kiang Nan and Hu Nan. In the autumn of
the 24th year (1844) certain of these vagabonds, belonging to other provinces,
came to the villages of Kiang-k'au and Lung-ta . . . Hsiang-shan, to entice
the people into the society. . . . The military and runners attached to the official
establishments were all members, and while the poor, who knew no better, were
seduced to become so by their eagerness for a trifle of gain [each being paid ten
cash], some even of the orderly agricultural population as well, and respectable
people in trade, were forced to enlist themselves in self-defence against the
persecution to which they were exposed. . . . The authorities dared not utter
the word *hwui*, and the consequence was, that not only throughout the major and
minor districts of the province were other confederacies formed, and Triads enlisted in untold numbers, but even on the White Cloud Mountains, close to the
provincial city, meetings for enlistment were held at all times and seasons; and
from this period not only were merchants, travelling by sea and land, carried
off and plundered, but walled cities and villages were entered, the pawnbrokers'
and other shops, as well as private houses, ransacked, and their proprietors
held to ransom. . . . When these things were complained of to the authorities,
so far from immediately pursuing and capturing the guilty parties, they subjected
the persons robbed to every description of annoyance. . . . When it was known
that these lawless persons were in a particular locality, the military and police
never went there in pursuit of them, but called on the gentry of the place in question to deliver them up; and when the gentry, being without either military or
police at their disposal, were unable to do this, and the real delinquents had
vanished to a distance, the local authorities would bind the spirit-tablet, repre-
senting the progenitor of a tribe [clan] in the ancestral hall, with chains, and
carry it to their official residence, there to be kept in durance. . . . In the 27th
and 28th years of Tau Kwang (1847-8) members of unlawful societies in hundreds
and thousands, carrying tents and armed, took up whatever positions they pleased
. . . throughout districts of Ung-yuen, Jü-yuen, Ying-teh, and Tsing-yuen . . .
in the spring of the present year [1854?] they commenced disturbing in the pre-

fecture of Chan-chau. . . . In the 5th moon the city of Tung-kwan was lost, but subsequently retaken. . . . In the 7th moon the cities of the prefecture of Shau-king, and the districts of Shun-teh, Ho-shan, Tsang, Tsung-hwa, Hwa, and Ying-Teh were all taken. . . . Now, the outlaws from other provinces were not more than a hundred or a few hundred men, while those of Kwang Tung, turbaned in red and with banners of red . . . were in bands of such force as to occupy positions. How could it have come to pass, unless enlistment had been going on for several tens of years before, that a rising in one place should have been responded to in so many other?"

219. Richard Wilhelm, *Chinese Economic Psychology*, pp. 22-23. Fei Hsiao-t'ung, *Peasantry and Gentry*, pp. 10-11: "It is quite natural that the common tendency among the peasants is not to rise on the social ladder but rather to sink toward the bottom. A petty owner may become a tenant when he sells his land as misfortune befalls him. He may further sink from a tenant to a landless farm laborer. He may in the end die disgracefully or disappear from the village. These outcasts are desperate. They have nothing to lose but their life of drudgery. They leave the village and plunge themselves into banditry or smuggling, or join the army, or seek employment as servants in big gentry houses. . . . Thay are the dissatisfied class and thus revolutionary in nature. When the ruling class is strong, they are suppressed. . . . But if the ruling class is degenerate and weak, they are the uprising group aiming at power. In Chinese history there are several instances where new dynasties were inaugurated by such desperate outcasts." Viewed in the light of our discussion, the concluding sentences of this passage can hardly be accepted as accurate. It is being too optimistic to regard the peasantry of imperial China as "revolutionary in nature"; it is historically untrue that several new dynasties were inaugurated by desperate peasants who, by themselves, constituted "the uprising group aiming at power." Wang Shih-t'o (1802-89), *Jih-chi*, 2/18b, asserts: "Among the four classes of people [scholars, peasants, artisans, and merchants], the peasants are most apt to create disturbances." This view can be justified on the ground that, as the most numerous and able-bodied element of the population and as generally in worse economic circumstances than the other classes, the Chinese peasantry were the most likely to exhibit violent behavior. But it would be wrong to infer from Wang's broad observation that the peasantry were therefore "revolutionary in nature."

220. See, for example, Davis, *China* (1852), II, 196; Yin Chia-pin, *Cheng-chiao chi-lüeh*, 2/5b; and *Ku-fei tsung-lu*, 2/17a-b.

221. Hung Liang-chi (1746-1809), letter to Prince Ch'eng, quoted in Inaba, *Ch'üan-shih* (Chinese trans.), III, 28-29.

222. *Chiang-hsi* (1880), *chüan shou*, part 3, p. 9a.

223. *Ibid.*, 3/25a-b.

224. Tseng Kuo-fan, *Shu-cha*, 2/3a.

225. Li T'ang-chieh, *Jih-chi*, Vol. XIII, Hsien-feng 3 (1853), 6th month, 20th day, and 7th month, 1st day.

226. Meadows, *Rebellions*, p. 291. The italics are Meadows'.

227. The Chinese situation as it existed in the nineteenth century may be usefully compared with the Japanese of the same period. See Hugh Borton, "Peasant Uprisings in Japan," *Transactions of the Asiatic Society of Japan*, 2nd series, XVI, 1-219 and K. Asakawa, "Notes on Village Government in Japan," *Journal of the American Oriental Society*, XXX, 259-300, and XXXI, 151-216. Borton's conclusion regarding the significance of these uprisings throws some light on the part played by Chinese peasants in the uprisings of the same period: ". . . most of the peasant uprisings were disconnected, having little concern for the

overthrow of feudalism, as such, but caring more for a rectification of those minor injustices which were inherent in the feudalistic society of the times. True the whole movement among the peasantry aided in the overthrow of the feudal structure, but it is stretching a point to assume that the average peasant was conscious or desirous of taking part in a social revolutionary movement." [p. 20]. Asakawa's estimate of the Japanese peasantry's capacity for rebellion is also illuminating: "Just as the suzerain's policy toward the feudal classes had subdued them at the cost of their true vigor and their genuine loyalty to himself, so his control of the peasants stifled their enterprise, limited their wealth, and levelled down their conditions. If they did not rise in a general revolt, it was because they were thoroughly deprived not only of the opportunity, but also the energy, to protest. When at last the national crisis came in the middle of the nineteenth century, just as the feudal classes chose to make no serious effort to defend the waning power of Tokugawa, but, on the contrary, furnished men to efface it, so the peasants, also proved surprisingly indifferent. The great Revolution was begun and consummated by discontented warriors, with the rural population too weary and too meek to lift a finger in the cause of their own liberation." [XXX, 290]. The differences between the Chinese and Japanese historical situations are obvious. It would be risky to push too far the similarity between the roles played by the peasants of these two countries in socio-political upheavals, but the behavior of the Japanese peasants should warn us against taking too sanguine a view of the "revolutionary" capacity of their counterparts in China.

228. Meadows, *Rebellions*, p. 19.

229. Liu Chi (1311-1475), *Wen-chi, Yü-li-tzu,* "Ku-kuei p'ien."

230. Frank Brinkley, *China* (1902), II, 219.

231. Meadows, *Rebellions*, pp. 27-28. The italics are Meadows'.

232. Li Tz'u-ming (1830-94), *Jih-chi,* i, *chia chi, shou chi chih hsia,* 64b, *kuei-hai* (1863), 11th month, 24th day.

233. Chien Yu-wen, *Shou-i shih, passim.*

234. Brinkley, *China,* XII, 228.

235. Meadows, *Desultory Notes,* p. 191. Instances of uprisings that failed as a result of inadequate leadership are many. The following instance, cited by Hosea Morse, *International Relations,* I, 440-41, from *The Chinese Repository,* May to November, 1832, and March and May, 1833, serves to illustrate such situations: ". . . to us the chief interest attaches to insurrectionary movement in what had always been the most disturbed of all the provinces, Kwangsi, and more especially in the mountainous region where the three provinces, Kwangtung, Kwangsi, and Hunan, join together. Here, on February 5th, 1832, a rebellion broke out under the leadership of Chao Kin-lung (Golden-Dragon Chao), who donned a coat of Imperial yellow, and a robe on which was embroidered 'Prince of the Golden Dragon.' At the outset the rebels took four walled cities and many villages; and the Hunan Titai [military commander] was defeated by them and killed in action. In June it was reported that the rebels, 30,000 in number, defeated the Imperial troops, under the personal lead of the Canton viceroy, with a loss of 2000; in the same month armed bands in Heungshan [Hsiang-shan], south of Canton, also committed many depredations. In July the Canton viceroy was again defeated, and reinforcements were sent from Canton, bringing the Imperial forces up to 15,000. In October the rebellion was reported to have been suppressed, but in November it was as much alive as ever. In March, 1833, the rebellion was actually suppressed, at the cost, it was stated, of large sums of money paid to the leaders in the movement; but five of the relatives of the Prince

of the Golden Dragon were executed by the *ling-ch'ih* [putting to death by slicing the nonvital parts of the body before beheading].

236. Chao I, *Cha-chi*, 36/23a and 25a.

237. *Huai-an* (1884), 29/69b.

238. *Shih-chi* 89/1a-2b. Yü Ying-shih, "The Establishment of the Political Power of the Later Han Dynasty," *The New Asia Journal (Hsin Ya hsüeh-pao)*, I, 209-80, shows in detail that without the participation or guidance of "distinguished clans and notable families," the contenders for power were unable to achieve abiding success, and that the "bands of hungry people" who rallied around these contenders contributed little more than helping to bring about the downfall of the old regime. See the present writer's review of Yü's article in *Journal of Asian Studies*, XVI (1957), 611-12.

239. *Hsin T'ang-shu, chüan* 225, *hsia*, p. 2b.

240. *Chiu T'ang-shu, chüan* 200, *hsia*, pp. 4b-5b.

241. Chao I, *Cha-chi*, 36/17a.

242. *Ming-shih*, 309/6b. See also 309/2a-b and 10a, and Chao I, *Cha-chi*, 20/26a. According to Chao I, "Niu Chin-hsing was a disappointed *chü-jen*. He therefore committed unrestrained atrocities against all officials who had the *chin-shih* degree; however, he ordered the rebel troops not to harm any *chü-jen*."

243. James B. Parsons, "The Culmination of a Chinese Peasant Rebellion: Chang Hsien-chung in Szechwan, 1644-46," *Journal of Asian Studies*, XVI (1957), 391.

244. *Ming-shih, chüan* 309, pp. 17b-18a. Parsons, "Culmination of a Chinese Peasant Rebellion," *Journal of Asian Studies*, XVI, 399, commented on Chang's relationship with the gentry: ". . . he made no carefully planned and effectively executed appeal to the gentry, he chose as his principal adviser [Wang Chao-ling] a man who was the antithesis of traditional gentry viewpoints, and in exasperation he sought to dispose of all opposition by resorting to sheer terror."

245. The following proclamation issued by the rebels operating in Shao-chou (Kwangtung), given in *The Chinese Repository*, XIX (1850), 568, could hardly have been written by peasants: "The present dynasty are only Manchus, people of a small nation, but the power of their troops enabled them to usurp possession of China, and take its revenues, from which it is plain that any one may get money from China, if they are only powerful in warfare. . . . The Manchus get the revenues of the Eighteen Provinces (China proper) and appoint officers who oppress the people; and why should we, natives of China, be excluded from levying money?" It would be a mistake, however, to suppose that all gentry and literati who showed apparent sympathy to "bandits" necessarily took active part in their operations. Some of these did so merely to seek safety; they might at one moment lend help to rebel groups but at another befriend government troops, as the immediate situation demanded. Such behavior was observed by Tseng Kuo-fan, who says in a letter of Lo Ping-chang (in *Shu-cha*, 4/12a: "The *hui fei* of Ch'ang-ning [in western Hunan] number no less than four or five thousand men. In [a recent] engagement only two hundred odd of them were killed. The remainder appear as bandits when they regroup and turn into ordinary people when they disband. The gentry . . . [of this district], like those of Yang-ch'üan and Shan-mu, carry spears and lances to augment the ranks of the bandits when the latter are victorious, and present food and wine to entertain the government troops who become for the moment masters of the situation." Obviously such gentry afforded no useful leadership to the rebels.

246. Martin, *Cycle* (1896), p. 269.

247. Feng Kuei-fen (1809-74), *Chi*, 9/5a.

248. Von Richthofen, *Letters*, p. 75.

249. Morse, *International Relations*, I, 453.

250. Joseph Edkins, "Narrative of a Visit to Nanking," quoted in Mrs. Jane R. Edkins, *Chinese Scenes*, pp. 304-5. Jen Yu-wen (Chien Yu-wen), "Rural Administration of the T'ai-p'ing T'ien-kuo," *Journal of Oriental Studies*, I (1954), 249-312, holds that the Taiping system as it actually obtained in localities under the rebels' control was "certainly better than that of the Ts'ing Dynasty," but concludes, "Ten years of suffering in the course of Revolution brought finally no amelioration of the lot of the people," *(ibid.*, English summary, pp. 311-12), owing partly to the fact that many of the rebels' functionaries were corrupt or in other ways unqualified as administrators. Meadows, *Rebellions*, chapters 12-17, *passim*, paints a generally optimistic picture of the Taiping rule, basing his views on information that referred to conditions not later than 1854.

251. Wang Shih-t'o (1802-89), *Jih-chi*, 1/7b.

252. Arthur E. Moule, *Half a Century in China* (1911), pp. 34 and 55.

253. Edkins, *Chinese Scenes*, pp. 255-56.

254. Chu Ch'i-hua, *Chung-kuo chin-tai she-hui-shih chieh-p'ou*, quoted in Teng Ssu-yü, *New Light*, p. 35.

255. Tseng Kuo-fan tried, for example, to lure away followers of the Taiping leaders by promising all who deserted the rebels' camp unconditional absolution of every "crime," past or present, in a rhymed piece, *Chiai-san ko* (Song of Disbandment), quoted in *Ch'ing hsü t'ung-k'ao*, 199/9482. Robert Lee, "The *Pao-chia* System," *Papers on China*, III, 209, argues that ". . . it was the nature, or the weakness, of peasant leadership that made every successful peasant rebellion also the beginning of a betrayal, as the leaders who rose to power on the crest of agrarian discontent invariably reconstructed the empire on the same principles and framework of government of the overthrown dynasty. . . . The reason for this conspicuous inadequacy of peasant leadership may be surmised from the predominant upper-class background of the *shih-ta-fu*, to whom, because of their monopoly on education, the masses had looked for intellectual, social, and political guidance." This argument has a basis in undeniable facts, but it is not very happily stated.

256. Morse, *Trade and Administration* (1913), Appendix D, pp. 432-41.

257. See Boardman, *Christian Influence Upon the Ideology of the Taiping Rebellion* (1952), and Vincent Y. C. Shih, "The Ideology of the T'ai-p'ing T'ien-kuo" (in manuscript).

258. Arthur Smith, *Convulsion* (1901), chapters 1 to 8.

259. George Danton, *Cultural Contacts of the United States and China*, p. 4.

260. Hsia Hsieh, *Chung-hsi chi-shih*, *chüan* 2, "Hua-hsia chih chien," quoting Wei Yüan, *Hai-kuo t'u-chih*, article on *T'ien-chu chiao*. This work was digested and translated by Edward H. Parker under the title, *China's Intercourse with Europe* (1890).

261. Danton, *Cultural Contacts*, p. 5.

262. Holcombe, *Real Chinaman* (1895), pp. 229-30.

263. Alexander Williamson, *Journeys in North China* (1870), I, viii-ix.

264. Arthur Smith, *Convulsion*, I, 92-93.

265. Auber, *China* (1834), p. 64. See chapter 9 above for additional discussion concerning Western impact on the rural environment.

266. Arthur Smith, *Convulsion*, I, 94-95: "Steam navigation has been known for so long that it might be supposed to have become an integral part of Chinese social, mercantile, and economic life, as indeed it has. But wherever it has

led to the discontinuance of the use of junks, as on the great Yangtze river, or along the whole of the Grand Canal from central China to Tientsin, it has developed an antagonism which is not the less real because it ordinarily finds no vent for expression."

267. Martin, *Cycle,* p. 446.

268. Clarke Abel, *Journey* (1818), pp. 88-89. In another place (p. 233), Abel indicates that the "higher classes" showed a "proneness to falsify"; merchants "generally proved themselves cheats," etc. However, he found the peasant a different sort of human being. "As far as my experience has gone respecting it," he says, "it is all in favor of its simplicity and amiableness."

269. John Ouchterlony, *Chinese War* (1844.), pp. 209-10.

270. Cooke, *China* (1858), p. 128.

271. Fisher, *Three Years' Service* (1863), pp. 13-14.

272. Von Richthofen, *Letters,* pp. 1 and 23.

273. *Ibid.,* p. 26.

274. *Ibid.,* p. 61.

275. James D. Ball, *Things Chinese* (1906), pp. 611-12. Ball enumerates these localities: Canton and Hongkong (Kwang-tung); Ningpo and Wenchow (Chekiang); Shanghai, Tanyang, Soochow, Chinkiang, and Tungchow (Kiangsu); Wuhu, Ankin, and Hoochow (Anhwei); Kiukiang (Kiangsi); Foochow (Fukien); Ichang, Shashi, and Hankow (Hupeh); Tientsin (Chihli); Yenchow (Shantung); Chungking, Yünyang, and Shun-ch'ing Fu (Szechwan), etc. The following were treaty ports: Canton (1842), Ningpo (1842), Foochow (1842), Shanghai (1843), Tientsin (1860), Kiukiang (1861), Chinkiang (1861), Hankow (1861), Soochow (1869), Wuhu (1877), Wenchow (1877), Ichang (1877), Chungking (1891), Shashi (1896), Anching (1904).

276. George B. Smyth, "Causes of Anti-foreign Feeling in China," in *Crisis in China* (1900), pp. 3-32.

277. *Ibid.,* pp. 15 and 28. This view was shared by other Western writers. The editor of *Niles Register* (Philadelphia), February 23, 1822, for example, commented on an imperial edict prohibiting Christianity in these terms: "If the Emperor of China acts from the known conduct of European nations, professing Christianity, he does perfectly right in opposing everything that may introduce such discordant elements into his Empire." Quoted by Danton, *Cultural Contacts,* p. 11, note 16. Wilhelm, *Soul of China,* pp. 226-28, writing in the 1920's, makes this observation: "It is evident that if a man with a limited field of vision comes to a country like China and begins by challenging the whole of its culture . . . even though he has the best intentions in the world he will not find support among the upper intellectual strata. In consequence, the first men who attached themselves to the missions were the people who were outcasts. . . . In addition, the missions . . . interfered in the legal proceedings in which their converts were involved. . . . The missionary . . . used his position as a foreigner, behind whom stood the power of the foreign gunboats, to induce the local magistrates to give judgment in favor of the Christian party against their better knowledge. . . . Naturally enough these methods provided peace neither for the Chinese people nor for the missions. . . . Eventually, when the misdeeds had accumulated, the population would rise in some sort of local revolt; they would burn down the mission buildings, and every now and again they would kill the missionary. Then the foreign powers interfered, dispatched gunboats, executed sanctions—the occupation of Tsingtao [where the author then lived] was, for instance, one of these sanctions—and everything started from the beginning again. The Christians were not, of course, always the only people to be blamed; but

the whole system was to be condemned. St. Paul was beaten, locked up and stoned without any power avenging him.

278. Suzuki Chusei, "The Origin of the Anti-foreign Movements in the Later Ch'ing Period" (English abstract), *Shigaku-Zasshi*, LXII (1953), 1.

279. *Ibid.*, p. 5, quoting from Lo Ping-chang's memorial given in *Wen-hsien ts'ung-pien*. J. L. Shuck, an American missionary, indicates in *Chinese Repository*, X, 340-48, that the invaders actually committed atrocities.

280. Hsia Hsieh, *Chung-hsi chi-shih*, 6/9a. The author adds this comment (6/14b): "The common people do not understand great principles. The hostilities began as the result of the rape of an elderly woman by several [barbarians] in turn."

281. For summaries of the incident, see Morse, *International Relations*, I, 284 ff., and *The Chinese Repository*, X, 340-48 and 536-50.

282. Liang Chang-chü, governor of Kiangsu, in a memorial dated Tao-kuang 21 (1841), 7th month, *pin-yin* day, quoted in *I-wu shih-mo*, Tao-kuang, *chüan* 31.

283. Ball, *Things Chinese*, p. 610. Cf. Holcombe, *Real Chinaman* (1895), pp. 228-30: "These [literati] are the influential men in every community, as would be expected. . . . Since they esteem themselves as belonging to the ruling class, they are generally moderate in their criticisms of those in office; but they mould, control, and guide public opinion. They are invariably the arbitrators in the settlement of disputes among the people, and in all questions at issue between the people and their magistrates. . . . They are bigoted and fanatical. They are accused, on apparently good grounds, with stirring up the people against foreigners and of inciting many of the outbreaks of mob violence, particularly those in which missionaries have been the objects of attack."

284. Liang T'ing-lan (1796-1861), *I-fen chi-wen*, pp. 49-50.

285. Ouchterlony, *Chinese War*, pp. 151-59.

286. Morse, *International Relations*, I, 370-71. Ssu-yü Teng and John K. Fairbank, *China's Response*, p. 36, Document 4, "Cantonese Denunciation of the British, 1841," is an excellent example of anti-British propaganda. Julia Corner, *China* (1853), p. 266, attributes the antiforeign riots to "secret societies and their demagogues" who incited the inhabitants with propaganda. Elements of secret societies may have participated in these uprisings, but the crucial role of the local gentry must be recognized.

287. Suzuki, "Origin of Anti-foreign Movements," *Shigaku-Zasshi*, LXII, 1-28.

288. Liang T'ing-lan, *I-fen chi-wen*, pp. 50-51 and 100.

289. *Ibid.*, pp. 51 and 100.

290. *Ibid.*, pp. 107-8.

291. Hsia Hsieh, *Chung-hsi chi-shih*, 13/6a-7b. The writer goes on to say (13/13b), quoting from a "Western newspaper," that "inhabitants in and immediately outside the city of Kuang-chou entertain no great enmity toward the English. . . . But the inhabitants of the ninety-six villages . . . are difficult to reconcile." He continues (13/17a): "These ninety-six villages are no other than the one hundred and three *Hsiang* of San-yüan-li."

292. *I-wu shih-mo*, 66/40, gives a memorial dated 1823 (Tao-kuang 3) in which Ch'i-ying denies that the local gentry took part in antiforeign riots and blames "rotten kids" *(lan-tsai*, local name for "bare sticks"). In a later document, dated Tao-kuang 26 (75/34), he denies that the local schools *(she-hsüeh)* were involved. These denials were made for understandable reasons and can hardly be accepted as statements of fact.

293. Peter Parker, American missionary doing medical work in Canton, re-

porting the situation in the *Chinese Repository,* V (1836); VIII (1839); and X (1841); quoted by Danton, *Cultural Contacts,* pp. 44-47.

294. Morse, *International Relations,* II, 371, quoting from the *Chinese Repository* of December, 1842.

295. *I-wu shih-mo,* Tao-kuang, 75/13.

296. Hsia Hsieh, *Chung-hsi chi-shih, chüan* 6, *passim.*

297. Hsia Hsieh, *Yüeh-fen chi shih,* 1/1a-b.

298. Hsia Hsieh, *Chung-hsi chi-shih,* 13/1a-2b.

299. Arthur Smith, *Convulsion,* I, 65-66.

300. Martin, *Cycle,* pp. 445-48. See also Arthur Smith, *Convulsion,* I, 77-82.

301. *Ibid.,* pp. 71-72. Antiforeign propaganda sometimes backfired. An instance reported in 1910 is summarized by Yeh Ch'ang-chih, *Jih-chi, keng-shü* year, 3rd month, 1st day, as follows: "Rose in the morning; heard that villagers of Hsiang-shan [near Soochow] demolished the home of Yü P'ei-weng late last night. . . . He barely escaped death. . . . Rumor has it that foreigners in Shanghai are building a bridge and have failed to drive piles [for its foundations]. They resorted to the sorcerous device of using the birth dates of living persons to overcome the evil forces, [thus endangering these persons. The foreigners] bribed Yü, who supplied them with peoples' names [and birth dates], obtained through door-to-door canvassing. It happened that some villagers died suddenly. The popular anger thus aroused was impossible to allay; consequently, he met with this strange disaster. . . . Upon reflection it dawned upon me that Yü served as director in charge of the compilation of the local census registers; for that reason he suffered the calamity [as the result of rustic ignorance]."

302. Harold E. Gorst, *China* (1899), p. 246, makes this observation: "The rebellion which broke out in the province of Kwangsi during the summer of 1898, of little importance in other respects, is chiefly interesting on account of the proof it furnishes that the recent action of foreign Powers has produced some effect upon the people of China. The proclamation issued by the rebel leader Chang appealed solely to antiforeign feeling, and contained the following preamble: 'It is ordained by Heaven that I, Chang, a leader of the Hung Sun Tong and a general of the forces, should expel the foreign element from the country and reform the abuses of China. The barbarian nations are strong in Europe, and are now looking at the country like a tiger on its prey, and they covet it in a sly and underhand manner. In China there is not a place they do not want to swallow up, nor money which they do not covet. Over ten years ago the foreign missionaries came and taught the people to disregard the old gods, and spread poison throughout the land. . . . God and people, Heaven and Earth, unite in anger against these intruders. . . .'" (Quoted from *The London Times,* September 30, 1898.)

303. Friedrich Engels, in "Persia–China," an article originally published in the *New York Daily Tribune,* June 5, 1857, and reprinted in *Marx on China,* pp. 48 and 50, comments on the widespread antiforeign agitation in South China in these terms: ". . . we had better recognize that this is a war *pro aris et focis,* a popular war for the maintenance of Chinese nationality. . . . There is evidently a different spirit among the Chinese now to what they showed in the war of 1840 to '42. Then, the people were quiet; they left the Emperor's soldiers to fight the invaders, and submitted after a defeat with Eastern fatalism to the power of the enemy. But now, at least in the southern provinces, to which the contest has so far been confined, the mass of the people take an active, nay, a fanatical part in the struggle against the foreigners." This view can hardly be accepted as accurate. The "people" of San-yüan-li in 1841, as shown above, were far from

"quiet, " and "the mass of the people" did not show any perceptible change in their behavior toward foreigners between 1840 and 1857, as the following two contemporary observations reveal. John Ouchterlony, lieutenant of the Madras Engineers, reports what he saw near Nanking in 1842 in his volume, *The Chinese War,* pp. 420-21: "Utter licence, therefore, prevailed in the unfortunate suburb, and not a boat's crew of lascars or Europeans bringing provisions ashore for the troops returned to the transports until after they had made a dive into some fresh, untouched-looking corner, or had carried a foray through a whole side of some once flourishing street. Chinamen and Europeans, Indians, Africans, and Malays, were to be seen mixed up together, jostling one another in the common chase, and generally with the greatest good humour; although when a cargo of 'loot' had been collected, it was the general practice to press a gang of Chinamen to carry it off to the destination by means of persuasion not always the most gentle. It was curious, too, to observe with what patience and submission the Chinese lower orders bore all this domineering and rough usage. . . . The news also of the rich harvest soon spread among the villages adjacent, and the numbers of these wretches increased hourly. " George W. Cooke, special correspondent of *The Times,* reports the scene in Canton after the British and French forces occupied the city and took Yeh Ming-chen prisoner, January, 1857, in *China,* p. 339: "The treasury was full of silver. . . . There was also a storehouse of the most costly mandarin fur dresses, lined with sable and rare furs, and there was a room full of copper cash. . . . The instructions were to bring away any bullion, but to touch nothing else. . . . But how to remove the heavy load of bullion? Crowds had assembled in front, and a happy thought occurred to one of the officers, –'A dollar's worth of cash to every coolie who will help to carry the silver to the English camp. ' In a moment the crowd dispersed in search of their bamboo poles, and in another moment there were a thousand volunteer Cantonese contending for the privilege of carrying for an enemy their own city's treasure. " It is difficult to imagine such people fighting a "war *pro aris et focis,"* in 1840 or in 1857. Engels, like many others, failed to pay sufficient attention to the gentry and literate elements in antiforeign movements. Stanley P. Smith (China Inland Mission), *China from Within* (1901), pp. 142-43, correctly says that the Empress Dowager's "pride, ignorance, and superstition" were among the factors that contributed directly to the Boxer Rebellion, the final and most violent expression of imperial China's xenophobia.

304. Davis, *China,* II, 182-83. Davis comments (p. 196) on the riot occurring in Feng-hua (Chekiang) in 1847: "This was a very small sample of the troubles that have prevailed in various quarters since the period of our war; but the worst have occurred in the most southern provinces, where the infection first spread from Canton and became general. The increase of banditti . . . was a subject of universal complaint; and the popular militia, raised by subscription to oppose these, enabled the people to dispute their taxes with the government. "

305. *Ibid.,* p. 412.

306. Huc, *Chinese Empire,* I, 291-92.

307. Tseng Kuo-fan, *Shu-cha,* 13/10b. Sometime later, he indicated in a letter to Tso Tsung-t'ang (13/17a) that whatever might be the outcome, he had decided to go north to the rescue of his sovereign. In a letter to Li Hung-chang, however, he said (13/21b) that he was instructed by an imperial order not to march north.

308. Marx, "Revolution in China and Europe, " *New York Daily Tribune,* June 14, 1853, reprinted in *Marx on China,* pp. 1-2.

309. Mallory, *China, Land of Famine,* p. 66.

Chapter 11

1. Han Fei (280-33 B. C.) was the first writer to indicate clearly that the interests of the ruler and his subjects were inherently opposed; he, however, centered his attention on the relationship between the ruler and the officials rather than on that between the ruler and his subjects in general. For example, *Han-fei-tzu, chüan* 18, no. 48, contains this passage: "He who perceives that the ruler and his servants are opposed in their interests will acquire the kingdom; he who regards them as having identical interests will be robbed of his position." *Ibid.*, *chüan* 2, no. 8 (Liao trans., I, 59): "The Yellow Emperor made this statement: 'Superior and inferior wage one hundred battles a day.'"

2. Hosea B. Morse, *International Relations*, I, 439-40. Morse, however, inaccurately attributed the "legacy of corruption, misgovernment, discontent, and rebellion," inherited by the Hsien-feng emperor, entirely to his father, and described the regime of Ch'ien-lung as a "strong government." In addition to the instances of administrative deterioration cited in other connections in this study, the following observations made in 1859 by Li Tz'u-ming, a well-informed official serving in the capital, may be quoted here. *Jih-chi pu, ssu chi*, pp. 78a-b (Hsien-feng 9th year, 10th month, 25th day): "Last winter I abandoned my scholarly pursuits out of exasperation [after repeated disappointment in the examinations] and contributed grain to obtain an official post. I have since then regretted my action. For when I arrived at the capital, I perceived that the emperor is concerned about [the grave situation] and works diligently, but he is lenient and does not hold high officials responsible for prompt results, all of whom talk leisurely of 'peace and good times' with fine eloquence. Functionaries in and out [of the capital] are busily engaged in sycophantic conduct, showering gifts [upon their superiors] and doing little else. Court officials below the rank of vice-president of the board busily invite one another to feasts and entertainments, paying scant attention to official duties. As I see it, the general condition of the empire has become hopeless; banditry will be daily more rampant. Consequently, I am thinking day and night of returning [to my home in K'uai-chi, Chekiang], where I would serve my mother with modest food and clothing as long as she lives." *Ibid.*, pp. 90a-91a (11th month, 22nd day): "The government maintains a customs office [at Ts'ung-wen Gate] to collect a 10 per cent levy on goods in order to supply the imperial household with funds. A fixed rate is charged every provincial official, from the treasurer up, who visits the imperial capital. All are familiar with this system. In the present year, Prince Cheng [i. e., Tuan-hua] having become supervisor, excessive demands begin to be made. In some cases the sums extorted [from a victim] have amounted to ten thousand [taels]. . . . In the 5th month, when Shu-tzu, Hsiao-huang, and I arrived at the capital, riding in battered carriages and bringing with us nothing but the minimum equipment for travel, customs functionaries made unreasonable extortionary demands, refusing to let us pass unless we paid them fifty taels. . . . We emptied our purses and handed over twenty taels to them, promising to pay them the remainder as soon as we reached our lodging place. They consented only after we had woefully implored them. When we arrived at our lodging place, we borrowed from all our friends and paid the functionaries the required sum. They alleged, however, that the silver was not of sufficient purity and reviled us noisily. Even the servants resented [their action]."

3. Morse, *International Relations*, I, 214, note 2, quoting from *The Chinese Repository*, March, 1834.

4. Kung Tzu-chen (1792-1841), *Wen-chi*, "I-pin-chih-chi chu-i chiu," an essay written in 1815-16, depicting the enervated officialdom and intelligentsia of the

time, is highly revealing. Wei Yüan (1794-1856), *Wai-chi*, 14/13b-14a, an essay written in 1840, describes the effects of centralization in these words: "The affairs of the central government are assigned to the six boards and those of the provinces to the seventeen governors-general and governors. The emperor personally holds the reins of government. Everything is decided from above, and all functionaries respectfully receive the decisions thus made. In the higher echelons of officialdom there have been no unruly civil officials or military commanders who usurp authority, nor are there in the lower ranks any prefects or magistrates who exercise independent power. Even men of less than mediocre abilities are able to lodge their incompetent selves in the government. After having been exposed to such a situation for a long time, officials come to regard those who shirk responsibilities as prudent, those who tread the beaten path as mature and experienced, and those who conform to empty formalities as proper and correct. . . . Ever since the last years of Emperor Jen-tsung, repeated admonition against administrative sluggishness has been issued to officials in and outside the capital, but the free and easy way has become such an established habit that nobody is able to change it." The emphasis on security at the expense of efficiency has been noted by more than one writer. See, for example, Linebarger, Djang Chu, and Burks, *Far Eastern Governments and Politics* (1954), p. 55: ". . . the operation of [the Ch'ing] government was divided so as to insure checks and balances between the central and local governments and between the various branches of administrative service rather than for the application of swift efficient administration. It was more to the interests of the new emperors to remain in power than to give good government. . . . Rarely did constructive policies originate from the central administration in Peking."

5. Karl August Wittfogel prefers to call this phenomenon "the beggars' democracy." See *Oriental Despotism*, p. 108 ff.

6. While Chinese emperors generally professed adherence to the Confucian axiom that rulers were instituted for the sake of the people, many of them knowingly or unconsciously subscribed to the Legalist conception of the state, in which the interests of the rulers constituted the primary concern of government. This double-faced position was revealed for the first time when Emperor Hsüan-ti (reigning 73-49 B. C.) of the Han dyansty remarked to his heir-apparent that "the institutional system of the House of Han" was based on a mixture of the principles of *pa* (hegemonic prince) and those of *wang* (true king), and that it is a mistake to rely exclusively on "virtuous influence." Later emperors were less frank, but they relied as much as did Hsüan-ti on Legalist principles and statecraft.

7. See chapter 10, note 229.

8. *Ming-shih*, 309/6b.

9. See *T'ien-ch'ao t'ien-mou chih-tu* (The Land System of the Heavenly Dynasty), given in Hsiao I-shan, *Ts'ung-shu*, series 1, Vol. I. It has often been said that the revolution of 1911 was a "bourgeois movement." This is true in the sense that it was initiated and led by persons belonging to the "middle classes" instead of by "proletarians." Middle-class leadership, however, was not an exclusive feature of Sun Yat-sen's movement. Its lack of enduring success was due not so much to the fact that the peasantry did not furnish its leadership as to the fact that Sun's followers did not pay sufficient attention to the needs and desires of the masses. Sun Yat-sen's principle that each tiller should own his own land remained a dead letter, leaving to the Communists the opportunity of using "land redistribution" to attract "land-hungry" peasants.

10. The Communists did not maintain a consistent "land policy" but temporized as the immediate situation required. During the late 1920's and prior to the war

with Japan, land redistribution was a salient feature of the Communist movement, as indicated by Mao Tse-tung in his "Report on an Investigation of the
Peasant Movement in Hunan," February, 1927; by the Sixth Congress of the Chinese Communist Party (held in Moscow) in a resolution drawn up in September,
1928; and by the Chinese "Soviet government," in the "Land Law of the Soviet
Republic," November, 1931. See Brandt, Schwartz, and Fairbank, *A Documentary History of Chinese Communism*, documents 7, 12, and 18, especially pp.
80-89, 130-33, and 224-26. This policy was suspended during the war years and
was temporarily replaced by a more moderate policy in the form of reduction of
taxes, rent, and interest rates, which was calculated "to help the peasants in
reducing feudal exploitation but not to liquidate feudal exploitation entirely."
Ibid., documents 20 and 25, especially pp. 244 and 278-81. Shortly after the
conclusion of the war, the old policy was reinstated. Acting on the basis of a
land law passed by a "land conference" on September 13, 1947, and adopted by
the party authorities on October 10, Chu Te, supreme commander of the "People's Liberation Army," and P'eng Te-huai, deputy commander, issued a joint
declaration on the thirty-sixth anniversary of the revolution of 1911 indicating
that to implement the policy whereby "each tiller" should "have his own land"
was one of the eight basic objectives of the Red Army. See *Mu-ch'ien hsing-
shih ho o-men-ti jen-wu (The Present Situation and Our Tasks)*, a compilation
of Communist documents, pp. 8 and 11-16. In a report to the party in December,
1947, Mao Tse-tung summarized these changes and explained the reasons for
them as follows: "During the period of war against Japan our party on its own
initiative suspended the pre-war policy of confiscating land and redistributing
it to peasants, and adopted the policy of reducing rent and interest rates with a
view to establishing a resist-Japan united front with the Kuomintang and to uniting
all persons who at that time were still capable of resisting the Japanese. This
[change of policy] was absolutely necessary. After Japan surrendered, peasants
urgently demanded land. We promptly decided to change our land policy from
that of reducing rent and interest rates to that of confiscating the land of the landlord class and distributing it to peasants. The directives issued by the central
organ of our party on May 4, 1946, indicate this change precisely. In September,
1947, our party called the *ch'üan-kuo t'u-ti hui-i* [nationwide land conference]
which formulated the *Chung-kuo t'u-ti-fa ta-kang [General Principles of the Land
Law of China]*. This law was immediately put into effect in all localities." *Ibid.*,
pp. 23-24. It may be interesting to compare the prewar policy of the Communists
with the land policy of the Taiping leaders. See a passage quoted from Chang
Te-chien, *Tse-ch'ing hui-tsuan*, in chapter 4, note 245, above.

    11. Herrlee G. Creel, *Chinese Thought,* p. 3.
    12. Benjamin I. Schwartz, *Chinese Communism*, p. 258.
    13. *Ibid.*, p. 198. Hugh Seton-Watson, *The Pattern of Communist Revolution*,
pp. 136-37, puts an even greater emphasis on the role of the intellectuals: "Far
the most important communist movement in Asia developed in China. It developed
in spite of the fact that the industrial working class was relatively very weak.
There are two main reasons why communism was so much more successful in
China than elsewhere in Asia. One was the exceptional prestige enjoyed in China
by intellectuals—exceptional in Asia, where . . . intellectuals played a dominant
role in political movements. This exceptional prestige was due to the ancient
Chinese tradition of rule by scholar-administrators *[shen-shih* or *shih ta-fu]*.
The second factor was the breakdown of the machinery of government, the an-
archic condition into which China had relapsed after the overthrow of the Manchu
dynasty. The other factors obviously relevant to Chinese communism—peasant

poverty, nationalist feeling and desire for political change—existed in other countries in Asia. But not being combined with these two special factors, they did not produce the results that were seen in China. The founders of the Chinese communist movement were two professors of Peking University, the Head of the Department of Literature, Ch'en Tu-hsiu, and a historian, Li Ta-chao." The author continues (p. 154): "Successful communist parties are power machines, political elites that draw their members from all social classes, but themselves stand outside social classes. The raw material for the elites can be drawn as well from a peasantry as from a working class, in fact can in a sense be more easily drawn from a peasantry, because peasants are less likely than workers to have formed for themselves ideas that may conflict with communist doctrines." One should not overstress the difference between China and other countries in Asia. Malcolm MacDonald, Commissioner General for Great Britain in Southeast Asia, in answer to the question, "How is public opinion formed?" said: "The public opinion referred to is usually the opinion of the populations who live in cities, large towns and other centers, where there are newspapers, radio, political activity, and so on. The Asian public opinion quoted is often the opinion of the politically conscious citizens in those centers. The peasant population, the agricultural population, haven't got anything like the same chances to form an opinion. They are often apathetic. That's why the Communists have a chance to get at them." *U. S. News and World Report,* December 3, 1954, p. 79.

14. Robert C. North, "The Chinese Communist Elite," *Annals of the American Academy of Political and Social Science, Report on China,* pp. 67-68.

15. Guy Wint, *Spotlight on Asia,* p. 114. Cf. George E. Taylor, "The Intellectual Climate of Asia," *Yale Review,* XLII, 187: "The Chinese Communist movement was a peasant movement only in the sense that it used peasants to get to power." Seton-Watson, *The Pattern of Communist Revolution,* pp. 152-53, makes this observation: "Mao and his faithful comrade Chu Te were brilliant guerilla leaders, and they were brilliant organizers of the peasant masses. . . . The communists' success with the peasants was largely due to their policy of land reform. . . . The emphasis on peasant interests, which not only appeared in communist statements from the early 1930's onwards, but was confirmed by the observations of western correspondents who visited the soviet areas, caused many western commentators to regard the Chinese communists as 'agrarian socialists,' who were 'not real communists at all.' This was a profound error. The Chinese communist movement was a movement of peasants, but not a peasant movement. The masses among whom the communists lived, on whose support their political aims and their very lives depended, were peasants."

16. David Mitrany, *Marx Against the Peasant,* p. 205.

17. Schwartz, *Chinese Communism,* p. 65; Ch'en Tu-hsiu's remarks are also quoted here.

18. G. William Skinner, "Aftermath of Communist Liberation in the Chengtu Plain," *Pacific Affairs,* XXIV, 67, quotes from *Nan-fang jih-pao* (Canton, August 6, 1950), the following remarks made by Liu Po-ch'eng, chairman of the Southwest Military and Administrative Commission, in a speech delivered at the first plenary session of the Commission held in Chungking late in July 1950: ". . . although we have been successful in the work of mopping up bandits in the course of the recent half-year, yet in view of the deep-rooted feudal forces which are behind them, it still behooves us not to underestimate the importance of the problem."

19. *Ibid.,* pp. 68-69, commenting in October, 1950, on the situation in western Szechwan, writes: "The average farmer feels happier about the Communist now

than he did at the time of the liberation. . . . The progressive elimination of the large landlord's power is a concrete development that he can appreciate. . . . The Communists marched into Szechwan with no popular support among the peasantry. In all probability, their program of reform will eventually gain them peasant support in Szechwan, as it did in the North." The author evidently did not take into consideration the possible effects of collectivization on peasants; it was not applied in Szechwan at the time when he wrote. For a summary of the progress of the land redistribution program up to the spring of 1951, see Chao Kuo-chün, "Current Agrarian Reform Policies in Communist China," *Annals of American Academy of Political and Social Science*, 277 (1951), 113-23. For a brief account of Communist rural control, see G. William Skinner, "Peasant Organization in Rural China," *Annals*, CCLXXII, 89-100.

20. Quoted in Peter S. H. Tang, *Communist China Today*, p. 267.

21. Mao Tse-tung, *Selected Works* (London: Lawrence & Wishart, 1956), IV, 291.

22. See Tang, *Communist China Today*, pp. 264-91, for a convenient summary; also Richard L. Walker, *China Under Communism*, pp. 134-53.

23. Tang, *Communist China Today*, pp. 11-12. Douglas S. Paauw, in his review of David Mitrany's *Marx Against the Peasant (Far Eastern Quarterly*, XII, 49-50), describes this "alliance" in these terms: "In the first stage . . . of agrarian revolution, the Communists needed the support of the peasant class to destroy the political and economic power of the 'feudal' elements in the countryside. . . . Thus the peasantry unwittingly became an unnatural partner in the Communist purpose; they were freed from political and economic domination of the landlord class only to fall into the bondage of the new masters. In the second stage of the agrarian revolution of modern Communism, the Communist alliance with the peasantry is dissolved; and the peasantry itself becomes the object of attack."

24. Mao Tse-tung, "On Coalition Government" (April 24, 1945), *Selected Works*, IV, 291 and 294-95.

25. See note 22, above.

26. Tang, *Communist China Today*, p. 291. Party members of peasant origin might find it difficult to accept the "proletarian outlook." S. B. Thomas, *Government and Administration in Communist China* (revised ed., 1955), p. 73, quotes from *The People's Daily* (Peking), June 29, 1951, the following remarks by Po Yi-po, veteran leader and one-time finance minister of "the people's government": ". . . it is a difficult thing to conduct systematic Marxist-Leninist education among party members and cadres of peasant origin, to convince them of socialist and communist principles. . . . Peasant economy is individual and scattered. . . . Party members and cadres of peasant origin essentially show this characteristic of peasant masses."

27. Fyodor Dostoevsky, *The Brothers Karamazov* (Garnett trans.), Modern Library ed., pp. 299-308, the Grand Inquisitor's speech: ". . . No science will give them bread so long as they remain free. In the end they will lay their freedom at our feet, and say to us, 'Make us your slaves, but feed us.' They will understand themselves, at last, that freedom and bread enough for all are incompatible together. . . . Oh, the work is only beginning, but it has begun. It has long to await completion and the earth has yet much to suffer, but we shall triumph and shall be Caesars, and then we shall plan the universal happiness of man. . . . Yes, we shall set them to work, but in their leisure hours we shall make their life like a child's game, with children's songs and innocent dance. . . . We shall tell them that every sin will be expiated, if it is done with our

permission. . . . And they will have no secrets from us. We shall allow or forbid them to live with their wives and mistresses, to have or not to have children—according to whether they have been obedient or disobedient—and they will submit to us gladly and cheerfully. The most painful secrets of their conscience, all, all they will bring to us and we shall have an answer for all." For the Chinese Communists' techniques and institutions of ideological control, see Tang, *Communist China Today*, chapter 9, and Walker, *China Under Communism*, chapter 8.

28. See, for example, Tang, *Communist China Today*, chapter 6, and Walker, *China Under Communism*, chapter 5.

29. See A. Doak Barnett, "Mass Organization in Communist China," *Annals of the American Academy of Political and Social Science, Report on China,* pp. 76-88; Skinner, "Peasant Organization in Rural China," *Annals,* pp. 89-100; Tang, *Communist China Today*, chapter 5; and Walker, *China Under Communism*, chapter 2.

30. A brief account is given in *Time,* May 27, 1957, pp. 33-34.

31. One such uprising was reported by the Associated Press, Hongkong, September 17, 1957: "Red China's official news agency has admitted that violent anti-Communist rioting erupted last July in the South China Province of Kwangtung. A New China News Agency dispatch from Canton said five Communist officials and an unspecified number of other persons were killed in the outbreak July 12. . . .. The dispatch, dated August 27, reached Hongkong only today. It did not give the number of persons taking part in the riots. But it said they attacked a government food station, a tax office, and other buildings. The Communist account confirmed an August 6 report by the official National Chinese Central News Agency from Taipei that students, farmers, and militiamen had staged an armed uprising against the Chinese Reds in Kwangtung July 12."

32. Milovan Djilas, formerly Vice-President of Communist Yugoslavia, points out a significant difference between Communist revolutions and "previous revolutions": "In all previous revolutions, force and violence appeared predominantly as a consequence, as an instrument of new but already prevailing economic and social forces and relationships. The case is entirely different with contemporary Communist revolutions. These revolutions did not occur because new, let us say socialist, relationships were already existing in the economy, or because capitalism was 'overdeveloped.' On the contrary. They did occur because capitalism was not fully developed and because it was not able to carry out the industrial transformation of the country." *The New Class,* p. 19. This also holds true of the Chinese Communist revolution which, in addition, differs from "previous revolutions" (rebellions resulting in new dynasties) in its use of an ideology not already existing in Chinese society.

33. Djilas' phrase, *ibid.,* p. 87.

34. See note 1.

35. Djilas, *The New Class,* pp. 42-43: "When Communist systems are being critically analyzed, it is considered that their fundamental distinction lies in the fact that a bureaucracy, organized in a special stratum, rules over the people. This is generally true. However, a more detailed analysis will show that only a special stratum of bureaucrats, those who are not administrative officials, make up the core of the governing bureaucracy, or, in my terminology, of the new class. This is actually a party or political bureaucracy. Other officials are only the apparatus under the control of the new class." In the case of China, it seems, what Djilas calls "the governing bureaucracy" or "the new class" is the counterpart of "the ruling class" in imperial times, and what he calls "administrative

officials" occupy a position comparable to that occupied by the scholar-officials of the past.

36. Quoted in *Time*, May 27, 1957, p. 33.

37. Djilas, *The New Class*, pp. 152 and 155-56, describes the moral degeneration of communism. Obviously, the well-known maxim, "Power corrupts," holds true here also.

38. Lin Yüeh-hwa, *Golden Wing*, p. 199.

39. Frank A. Kierman, Jr., *The Chinese Communists in the Light of Chinese History*, pp. 40-43.

40. It may be pointed out that even Solomon Adler, who makes no attempt to hide his sympathy with the Chinese Communists and who paints an optimistic picture of their regime, concludes his recent book with the following words in the subjunctive mood: "To carry through the transition from a pre-industrial to an industrial society has been a hard dirty job which exacted heavy sacrifices, whatever the ultimate rewards. So far, perhaps partly because China started from such low levels and was standing on Russia's shoulders, China's growing pains appear to have been relatively mild. If war is avoided and if the socialization of agriculture continues smoothly and if the rate of increase in population does not encroach on the pace of industrialization, the way seems clear for China to do a workmanlike job." *The Chinese Economy*, pp. 237-38.

Appendix I

1. *Chao-i* (n. d.), p. 36b.

2. *Ch'eng-ku* (n. d.), p. 18b.

3. *Ho hsien*(1934), 2/16b, quoting from the 1890 edition.

4. *Hsing-hua* (1852), 2/6b-8b.

5. *Hsing-kuo* (1889), 2/6b and 5/2a-7a.

6. *Cho hsien* (1936), *chüan* 4, sec. 4, pp. 16b-17a, a note on *li-chia* divisions of the past.

7. *Mien-chu* (1908), "Li-shih ping," p. 15b.

8. *Jen-huai* (1895), 1/20a-21a.

9. *Chen-hsiung* (1887), 1/41a-51b.

10. *Hsün-tien* (1828), 1/6b-7a.

11. *Hsin hsien* (1887), 1/14a-27b.

12. *K'un-yang* (1839), 6/12a-b.

13. *Ch'üan-chou* (1870), 5/15b-16a.

14. *Ibid.*, 5/13a-b. According to Wu Yung-kuang (1773-1843), *Wu-hsüeh lu, ch'u pien*, 2/1a-b, the name *t'u* had a different meaning. Quoting from the *Hui-tien*, he wrote: "In compiling the *fu-i ts'e* [revenue registers] in the *fu, chou*, and *hsien* of the provinces, one hundred and ten *hu* are to constitute a *li*. . . . [The *hu* in] each *li* are registered in one *ts'e*. A *t'u* [map, diagram] at the beginning of each *ts'e* summarizes [the entries]."

15. *Hua-chou*(n. d.), pp. 59b-61b.

16. *Ch'i-shan*(n. d.), 3/3b-4a.

17. *I-ch'üan*(n. d.), pp. 7b-8b.

18. *Hu-pei*(1921), 33/1020, quoting from *Wu-ch'ang hsien chih;* 33/1029, quoting from *Ch'i chou chih;* 33/1030, quoting from the Chia-ch'ing edition of *Huang-mei hsien chih;* 33/1033, 34/1039, and 34/1047, quoting from the *Yü-ti chih;* 34/1054, quoting from an unpublished *Kuei chou chih* compiled in Kuang-hsü times; and 34/1058, quoting from *Chien-shih hsien chih*.

19. *Ibid.*, 33/1023-24, quoting from *Han-yang hsien chih*, and 34/1056, quoting from *En-shih hsien chih*.

20. *Tao chou* (1878), 3/23a-b.
21. *Ch'ing chou* (1908), 2/22a-b.
22. *Heng-chou* (1895), 5/22b-23a.
23. *Lu-chou* (1882), 1/2a.
24. *Yang-chou* (1810), 16/1a, quoting from the *T'ai-p'ing huan-yü chi*.
25. *Wei chou* (1877), 3/25a. There were in this *chou* a total of 49,839 *hu* (households).
26. *Sui chou* (1892), 3/2a-3a.
27. *Hang-chou* (1895), 5/31a.
28. *Hu-pei* (1921), 34/1055, quoting from the Chia-ch'ing edition of *Pa-tung hsien chih*. According to the same provincial gazetteer (34/1056), the *Hsiang* division probably did not exist in Hsüan-en Hsien, since no such divisions were mentioned in the Chia-ch'ing edition of the provincial gazetteer nor in the gazetteers of the *hsien* and *fu* concerned.
29. *Kuei chou* (1900), 8/1a-3b.
30. *Hu-pei* (1921), 34/1055.
31. *Yen-an* (1802), 28/3b-15a.
32. *Fu-shan* (1924), 4/2a-3a.
33. *T'ai-pai* (1897), 1/4a-6b.
34. *Tung-kuan* (1911), *chüan* 3, *passim*.
35. *Ch'üan-chou* (1870), 5/13a-b.
36. *Wu-hsi* (1881), 11/3a.
37. *Mien-yang* (1894), *chüan* 4, "Shih-huo," pp. 15a-34a.
38. *Ibid.*, *chüan* 3, "Chien-chih," p. 11a.
39. *Yen-chou* (1883), 4/1a-3a.
40. *T'ung chou* (1875), 1/33b-34b.
41. *Ibid.*, 1/32a and 1/34b-35a, giving arrangements of divisions in T'ung Chou and Ju-kao Hsien.
42. *Yang-chou* (1810), 16/21a.
43. *Hang-chou* (1895), 5/33a-b.
44. *Yen-yüan* (1916), 1/2b-4b.
45. *Fu-chou* (1756), 8/9b-12a.
46. *Hsia-men* (1839), 2/20a-22a.
47. *Ju-lin* (1883), 5/10a-19a.
48. *Hu-pei* (1921), 33/1030.
49. *Yang-chou* (1810), 16/22b-23a.
50. *Huai-an* (1884), 20/1b.
51. *Lu-chou* (1885), 13/46a-b. Cf. *Meng-ch'eng* (1915), 2/7a-b.
52. *I-ch'eng* (1929), 4/4a-b, and *T'ung-kuan* (1944), 2/4a-b. It may be noted that in I-ch'eng Hsien each of the four *Hsiang* was divided uniformly into five *li*, while in T'ung-kuan Hsien each of the four *Hsiang* was divided into six *li*. The compiler of the gazetteer of T'ung-kuan commented that "this was the system existing in Ch'ien-lung times," i. e., in the eighteenth century.
53. *Fu-chou* (1756), 8/13a-14b.
54. *T'ai-ho* (1878), 2/14a-18a.
55. *T'ai-pai* (1897), 1/2b-9b.
56. *Nan-ch'ang* (compiled 1904, printed 1919), 3/3a-5b.
57. *Fu-chou* (1756), 8/15a.
58. *Nan-ning* (1909), *chüan* 10, *passim*.
59. *Hsiang-shan* 1873, 5/1a-12b. See also *Hang-chou* (1895), 5/33a. The arrangement observed by Donnat seems to have been a variant of this pattern: "Cette agglomération [of five villages] fait partie du *tou* de Li-che-tou-ni-dou, qui forme

lui-même avec trois autres . . . le district de Ning-hien.". *Paysans en communauté* (1861), p. 85.

60. *Fu-chou* (1756), 8/18b-20b.
61. *Ch'üan-chou* (1870), 5/1b-9a.
62. *Ibid.*, 5/9a-b and 5/18a-21a.
63. *Nan-hai* (1910), 7/5b-41a, and *Hua hsien* (1924), 10/7a.
64. *Nan-hai* (1910), 26/3a.
65. *Fu-shan* (1924), *chüan* 14, "Jen-wu," sec. 6, p. 32a.
66. *Tz'u-li* (1896), *chüan* 1, "Ti-li," p. 2b.
67. *Nan-ning* (1909), *chüan* 10, *passim*.
68. *Yung hsien* (1897), 28/5a.
69. *Hang-chou* (1895), 5/21a-b.
70. *T'eng hsien* (1908), 3/67a-87a.
71. *Hu-pei* (1921), 34/1053, quoting from *Kuang-hsü yü-ti chi*.
72. *Ho-ch'ing* (1894), 17/2a-7b.
73. *Nan-ning* (1909), *chüan* 10, *passim*.
74. *Lu-chou* (1885), 13/46b.
75. *Hu-pei* (1921), 34/1049-50.
76. *Yang-chou* (1810), 16/11b.
77. *Ibid.*, 16/1a-3a.
78. *Ibid.*, 16/27b.
79. *Ibid.*, 16/8b-9a.
80. *Huai-an* (1884), 17/1b-2a.
81. *Kan-ch'üan* (n. d.), pp. 7a-8a.
82. *Hang-chou* (1895), 5/32a-b.
83. *Yung hsien* (1897), 1/12b-18a.
84. *Ch'ing yüan* (1880), 2/14b-20a.
85. *Hu-pei* (1921), 34/1047, quoting from the Chia-ch'ing edition of *Ching-men chih-li-chou chih*.
86. *Hsin-fan* (1907), 6/3b-7a.
87. *Ho hsien* (1934), 2/16b-17a, quoting from the 1890 edition.
88. *Hu-nan* (1885), 49/1314.
89. *Lu-i* (1896), 3/2a-b.
90. Chao I (1727-1814), a well-known historian, explained in his *Kai-yü ts'ung-k'ao*, 27/22a-b, that during the South Sung dynasty a certain magistrate caused a picture or map *(t'u)* to be made which showed the farmland, hills, rivers, and roads of each *pao* in the district under his administration. In this way the name *t'u* (in the sense of picture or map) came into use. This official then combined a number of *pao* into *t'u* (rural divisions) and a number of *t'u* into *Hsiang*. Chao I added: "Matters concerning tax collection, litigation, and police control were thus made clear by looking at the *t'u* [maps]." According to the compiler of *Chien-ch'ang* (1907), 2/9b-11a, ". . . during the Ming dynasty, when the yellow registers for the grain and corvée imposts were compiled, one hundred and ten households were constituted into a *li*. . . . The *t'u* was a map of the land [attached to the register of each *li*]. For there must be one map for each *li* in order that the amount of the land within the *li* could be ascertained. In Chien-ch'ang . . . [during the Ch'ing dynasty] each *li* was supposed to have a *t'u* [map], but the *t'u* in reality was missing. It may be said that there were *li* but no *t'u*." The *Lü-li pien-lan* (1877), 8/47b-48b, informs us that in compiling the *fu-i ts'e* (tax and corvée registers) each *li* was to make one register which was prefaced by a *t'u* (map). See also note 14 above, where Wu Yung-kuang's statement concerning the *t'u* is quoted. The term *t'u* may have come into use first in Southern Sung times

in the sense of a map showing the location and amount of land in the *li* division, but gradually its original meaning was partly forgotten and it was often used to designate the *li* division itself, in Kwangtung, Kiangsi, Kiangsu, Anhwei, Hupeh, and Kwangsi, during Ch'ing times.

91. See for example *Wu-hsi* (1881), 4/9a, where it is said: "In the Ming system . . . the *Ch'ü* controlled the *tu*, the *tu* controlled the *t'u*, and the *t'u* controlled the *chia*." Similarly, *Fu-shan* (1924), *chüan* 14, "Jen-wu," sec. 6, p. 32a: "In the Ming system the *pao* controlled the *t'u* and the *t'u* controlled the *chia*."

92. The area of a *chou* or *hsien* was in many instances quite extensive. For example, Feng-chen Hsien (Shansi) measured about 270 *li* east to west and 250 *li* north to south (over 7,000 square miles); Wei Chou (Chihli), 120 *li* east to west and 235 north to south (over 3,000 square miles); Po-pai Hsien (Kwangsi), 175 *li* east to west and 250 *li* north to south (over 4,000 square miles); and T'ung-kuan Hsien (Shensi), about 6,875 square *li*. See *Feng-chen* (compiled, 1881; printed, 1916), 1/13a; *Wei chou* (1877), *chüan shou*, p. 18b; *Po-pai* (1832), 6/21a; and *T'ung-kuan* (1944), 1/1a.

93. Huang Liu-hung, *Fu-hui*, 21/4b.

94. The village leaders are discussed in chapter 6.

95. See, for example, Bell, *China* (1884), I, 123, referring to conditions in northeastern China.

96. *I-ch'üan* (n.d.), p. 8b: "The land being limited and households few, no *chia* divisions have been made."

97. *Yen-an* (1802), 47/2a-b. See also *Fu-shan* (1924), 4/2a-b, and *Meng-ch'eng* (1915), 2/7a.

98. It may be recalled that a rule issued in 1648 required that the *hu k'ou* (households and inhabitants) in each locality were to be counted and reported every three years. This rule was modified in 1656, requiring a census in every five years instead of three. A later edict suspended this rule indefinitely, because it had become "no more than empty words." *Shih-li* (1908), 157/1a.

99. *Meng-ch'eng* (1915), 2/7b.

100. *Chien-ch'ang* (1907), 2/9a.

101. *Mien-yang* (1894), *chüan* 3, "Chien-chih," p. 11a.

Appendix II

1. *T'ung-tien* (1935), 12/67-72, gives a historical summary, covering the period from ancient times to A.D. sixth century. *T'ung-k'ao* (1936), 21/203-13, and *Hsü t'ung-k'ao* (1936), 27/3033-42, together bring the story down to the seventeenth century. Lu Lien-tching, *Les greniers publics*, Introduction, contains a brief summary.

2. *Chou-li* (1936), *ti-kuan, hsia*, "I-jen," 4/86.

3. *Kuan-tzu, chüan* 73, 6th essay on *ch'ing-chung*, translated in Lewis Maverick, *Economic Dialogues in Ancient China, Selections from the Kuan-tzu* (1954), pp. 118-20. The idea was actually put into practice by Li K'uei, who helped Wen-hou, ruler of Wei (446-397 B.C.), to make the state "strong and wealthy." *K'ang-chi lu* (1869), 1/7b.

4. *Han-shu, chüan* 24, *shang*, p. 14a-b; quoted in *K'ang-chi lu* (1869), 2/36a, and Yü Shen, *Ch'ang-p'ing-ts'ang k'ao*, 8/36a.

5. *Chin-shu, chüan* 26, "Shih-huo chih," p. 5b. *Ch'ang-p'ing* granaries were instituted in A.D. 268 (T'ai-shih 4).

6. *Sui-shu*, 24/8a. *Li-yang ts'ang* was established in Wei-chou, *ch'ang-p'ing* in Shen-chou, and *kuang-t'ung* in Hua-chou, in A.D. 585 (K'ai-huang 5).

7. *Hsin T'ang-shu,* 51/2b.

8. *Sung-shih,* 176/7b-17a. See also *Yüan-shih,* 96/12a. *Ch'ang-p'ing* granaries were established in 1269 (Chih-yüan 6).

9. *Ming-shih,* 79/6a-7b. See also *K'ang-chi lu,* 2/40b, quoting from *Ta-Ming
hui-tien.*

10. Yü Shen, *Ch'ang-p'ing-ts'ang k'ao,* 9/21a-27a. Four granaries were first
instituted at the beginning of the Hung-wu reign (1368). The practice of encouraging contributions from local inhabitants was initiated in 1440 (Cheng-t'ung 5).

11. *Sui-shu,* 24/8a. See also *K'ang-chi lu,* 2/17a; Yü Shen, *Ch'ang-p'ing-
ts'ang k'ao,* 9/1a-21a; and *T'ung-k'ao,* 21/204. Lu Lien-tching's statement *(Les
greniers publics,* p. 151) that the *i-ts'ang* of Sui had their origin in K'ai-huang
3 of Wen-ti is slightly inaccurate.

12. *Hsin T'ang-shu,* 51/2b; *K'ang-chi lu* (1869), 2/17b; Yü Shen, *op. cit.,*
1/3b; *T'ung-k'ao* (1936), 21/204. According to *Chiu T'ang-shu,* 2/8b, the action
was taken in A.D. 628 (Chen-kuan 2).

13. *Sung-shih,* 176/8a; *K'ang-chi lu* (1869), 2/18a; Yü Shen, *Ch'ang-p'ing-
ts'ang k'ao* 1/5a-b. Ch'en Lung-cheng's opinion, quoted by Yü Shen, that "the
she-ts'ang of Sui and the *i-ts'ang* of T'ang were one and the same thing with two
different names" appears therefore to be questionable.

14. *K'ang-chi lu,* 2/18b-19a. For the *i-ts'ang* system after this period, see
Sung-shih, 176/14b-17a and 178/13a.

15. *K'ang-chi lu* (1869), 2/19b; Yü Shen, *op. cit.,* *chüan* 10, *shang,* p. 1a.

16. *Sung-shih,* 178/13b-14a.

17. *Yüan-shih,* 96/12a. The action was taken in 1269 (Chih-yüan 6). The *she*
of Yüan times was a rural division consisting of fifty households. *Ibid.,* 93/3a.

18. Yü Shen, "She-ts'ang k'ao," in *Huang-cheng ts'ung-shu, chüan* 10, *shang,*
p. 21b, quoting Chang Ta-kuang, a Yüan dynasty writer: "In former times there
were *she-ts'ang* in addition to *i-ts'ang.* The latter were established in *chou* and
hsien [cities], whereas the former were erected in the countryside. . . . In the
present dynasty [the Yüan] . . . *i-ts'ang* are established in *Hsiang* and *tu* [rural
areas]."

19. *Ming-shih,* 79/7b, indicates that a governor of Kiangsi proposed in the
1490's that *ch'ang-p'ing* and *she-ts'ang* be established; the government ordered
in 1529 (Chia-ch'ing 8) that governors of the provinces set up *she-ts'ang.*

Appendix III

1. *Ming-shih,* 77/1b. According to *Hsü t'ung-k'ao,* 16/2914, this decree was
dated 1395 (Hung-wu 28). Ku Yen-wu, *Jih-chih lu* (1735), 8/10b, quoting from
T'ai-tsu shih-lu, dates this document one year earlier. It may be noted *(Ming-
shih,* 77/2b) that Emperor T'ai-tsu's original purpose of setting up the elders
was to give the underprivileged villagers a chance to protect their own interests.
"Wishing," it was said, "to correct the oppression of the poor and weak by the
rich and strong during the last years of the Yüan dynasty, the laws aimed generally at curbing the wealthy to help the poor." Less than forty years later, however, the institution of the *lao-jen* showed definite signs of trouble. Ku Yen-wu
explains the situation *(Jih-chih lu* 8/11b) thus: "In the first year of Hung-hsi
[1425], Ho Wen-yüan, imperial censor of the Szechwan circuit, memorialized
that 'Emperor T'ai-tsu ordered that *lao-jen* be instituted in the *chou* and *hsien*
of the empire. . . . In recent years men appointed to this office are usually
without the necessary qualifications. Some of them come from the servile classes,
or are persons seeking to evade corvée and other labor services. In making the
appointments the magistrates do not ascertain the age and character [of the ap-

pointees], who are thus given an opportunity to use their official connections to
. . . oppress the people of their neighborhoods.'" *Hsü t'ung-k'ao*, 16/2914, contains an almost identical statement.

2. *Lü-li pien-lan* (1877), 8/1a-b; *Ching t'ung-k'ao*, 21/5045. According to the
latter work, 21/5043, *ch'i-lao* were as a rule given official buttons. The *hsiang-
san-lao* mentioned in this law was a Han dynasty institution. Emperor Kao-tsu
appointed "persons over fifty *sui*, noted for fine conduct and capable of leading
the people to do good, as *san-lao*, one in each *Hsiang*." These persons were
responsible for instructing the people, while another agent, *se-fu*, took charge
of local litigations and tax collection, and a third, *yu-chiao*, served as a sort of
sheriff with the duties of detecting and suppressing banditry. *T'ung-k'ao*, 12/124.

3. *Ch'ing t'ung-k'ao*, 21/5044.

4. Samuel W. Williams, *Middle Kingdom* (1883), I, 500.

5. Arthur H. Smith, *Village Life* (1899), p. 227.

6. *China Review*, VI (1877-78), 369.

7. Robert K. Douglas, *Society in China* (1894), pp. 111-12.

8. *Cho hsien* (1936), 3/3a-b.

TABLE OF TRANSLITERATION

An-ch'in hui 安親會

cha 閘

ch'a-t'ing 茶亭

chai 寨

ch'ai 差

ch'ai-yao 差徭

chang 長 . (See cheng)

chang-liang ts'e 丈量冊

ch'ang 場

ch'ang 廠

ch'ang-kan 長幹

ch'ang-p'ing-ts'ang 常平倉

ch'ang-sui 長隨

ch'ang-tsu 嘗租

Ch'ao-hsien hui 朝仙會

che-chia 折價

chen 鎮

chen-chang 鎮長

chen-chieh 賑借

ch'en 臣

cheng 正

cheng-ch'ang t'ien 蒸嘗田

cheng-pin 正賓

cheng-shen 正紳

cheng-ts'e 正冊

ch'eng 城

ch'eng-shih 城市

ch'eng-hu 城戶

ch'eng-huang 城隍

chi 集

chi-chang 集長

chi-ch'u 積儲

ch'i-ke 櫃革

ch'i-lao 耆老

ch'i-lao hui-i 耆老會議

ch'i-pin 耆賓

chi-t'ien 祭田

chia 甲

ch'ia 卡

chia-jen 家人

chia-miao 家廟

chia-shu 家塾

chia-chang 甲長

chia-shou 甲首

chia-t'ou 甲頭

chia-tsung 甲總

chiang sheng-yü 講聖諭

chiang-yüeh so 講約所

chiao fei 教匪

chieh-liang 截糧

chieh p'iao 截票

chieh-pin 介賓

733

chien-min 賤民		*ch'ü-shu* 區書	
chien-min 奸民		*chüan-mien* 蠲免	
chien-sheng 監生		*Ch'üan-shan yao-yen* 勸善要言	
chien-tzu-hang 揀子行		*ch'üeh-e jen-ting* 缺額人丁	
ch'ien liang 欠糧		*chün li* 郡厲	
ch'ien-liang 錢糧		*chün-liang* 均糧	
chih-hsien 知縣		*chün-t'ien* 均田	
chih-li 值理		*chün-yao* 均徭	
chih-yüeh 值月		*ch'ün ssu* 羣祀	
chin hsieh 禁蠍		*fan-yin* 番銀	
chin-shih 進士		*fang* 坊	
ching-piao ch'i-shou 旌表耆壽		*fang* 房	
ching ch'a 警察		*fang-chang* 房長	
ching-t'ien 井田		*fang-teng* 放燈	
ching-ts'ui 經催		*fei* 匪	
ch'ing hui 請會		*fei-shai* 飛灑	
Ch'ing-lien chiao 青蓮教		*fei-t'u* 匪徒	
Ch'ing-miao hui 青苗會		*fen-tz'u* 分祠	
chiu-ch'ing 九卿		*fu* 府	
chou 州		*fu-hsi* 鳧舄	
Chou-i che-chung 周易折中		*fu-i* 賦役	
chu-shih 主事		*Fu-i ch'üan-shu* 賦役全書	
ch'uan-chiao shou-t'u 傳教授徒		*fu-kung-sheng* 附貢生	
ch'uan p'iao 串票		*hao-ch'iang* 豪強	
chuang 莊		*hao-hsien* 耗羨	
chuang-chang 莊長		*hao-wai fou-shou* 耗外浮收	
chuang-t'ou 莊頭		*ho-fu* 河夫	
chung-pao 中飽		*Hsiang* 鄉	
chung-pin 眾賓		*hsiang* 鄉	
chung ssu 中祀		*"Hsiang"* 廂	
chü-chang 局長		*hsiang-chang* 鄉長	
ch'ü 區		*hsiang-hu* 鄉戶	
ch'ü 渠		*hsiang hui* 香會	
chü-jen 舉人		*hsiang kuan* 鄉官	
ch'ü-chang 渠長		*hsiang-kuei* 鄉規	

hsiang-lao 鄉老

hsiang li 鄉厲

hsiang pao 鄉保

hsiang san-lao 鄉三老

hsiang shen 鄉紳

hsiang-t'ou 香頭

hsiang-ts'un 鄉村

hsiang-t'uan 鄉團

hsiang-wei 香尾

hsiang-yin-chiu 鄉飲酒

hsiang-yüeh 鄉約

hsiang-yung 鄉勇

hsiao-hu 小戶

hsiao-i hui 孝義會

hsieh chiao 邪教

hsieh tou 械鬥

hsien 縣

hsien-ju 先儒

hsien-nien 現年

hsien-nung t'an 先農壇

Hsing-li ching-i 性理精義

hsing 姓

hsing-fang 刑房

Hsing-li ta-ch'üan 性理大全

hsing-lü 刑律

hsing shan hui 行山會

hsiu-ts'ai 秀才

hsü 墟

hsüeh-hsiao 學校

hsün-chien 巡檢

hsün-huan ts'e 循環冊

Hsün-ch'ih shih-tsu wen 訓飭士子文

hu 戶

hu-chang 戶長

hu-k'ou 戶口

Hu-lü 戶律

hu-pao kan-chieh 互保甘結

Hu-pu 戶部

hu-shou 戶首

hu-shu 戶書

hu-t'uan 湖團

hua-hu 花戶

hua-tzu hui 花子會

huan-cheng 緩徵

huan-hu 宦戶

Huang-en ch'in-tz'u 皇恩欽賜

Huang-en hao-tang 皇恩浩蕩

Huang-t'ou tsei 黃頭賊

huang ts'e 黃冊

hui-fei 會匪

hui-shou 會首

huo-chung 夥種

huo-hao 火耗

I 夷

i 役

i-chih yu-tan 易知由單

i-chuang 義莊

i-hsüeh 義學

i-hui 義會

i-li 邑厲

i-t'ien 義田

I-ts'ang 義倉

ju-hu 儒戶

juan-t'ai 軟抬

kan-ch'ang 趕場

kan-chieh 甘結

kang chi 杠雞

k'ang-liang 抗糧

"k'ao t'ien ch'ih fan" 靠天吃飯

ke-tso 革胙

ke-yüeh hsiang-yung 各約鄉勇

k'e-chi 客籍

k'e-chia 客家

k'e-hu 客戶

k'e-min 客民

Ko-lao hui 哥老會

k'o-chü hsüeh-hsiao 科舉學校

ku-shih 故事

kua-tzu 卦子

kuan-chiang 官匠

Kuan-hsüeh 官學

kuan ssu 官祀

Kuan-ti 關帝

kuan yü 官圩

kuang-kun 光棍

kuei-hu 鬼戶

kun tan 滾單

kun-t'u 棍徒

kung-ming 功名

kung-sheng 貢生

kung-so 公所

kung-yüeh 公約

kuo li 國厲

kuo-lu 啯嚕

Kuo-tzu-chieh ssu-yeh 國子監司業

Lan-ch'ing hui 闌青會

lan-tsai 爛崽

lao-jen 老人

lao-min 老民

lao-nung 老農

lao-pai-hsing 老百姓

lao-tsung 老總

li 里

li-chang 里長

li-cheng 里正

li-chia 里甲

li-i 里役

li-i 吏役

Li-pu 禮部

li-shu 里書

li t'an 厲壇

liang-ch'ai 糧差

liang-chang 糧長

liang li 良吏

liang-min 良民

liang-shu 糧書

liang-ssu-ma 兩司馬

liang-ti 糧地

liao-hu 寮戶

lieh-shen 劣紳

lieh-sheng 劣生

lien-chang 練長

lien-chuang she 聯莊社

lien-ming hu-pao kan-chieh 聯名互保甘結

lien-tsung 練總

lien-yung 練勇

lin 鄰

ling-sheng 廩生

Liu yü 六諭

Liu-yü yen-i 六諭演義

lu 路

lü-ling an 律令案

Lü-ying 綠營

Lung-hua hui 龍華會

lung-wang miao 龍王廟

men-p'ai 門牌

mi-fen chu 米飯主

Miao 苗

mien-i ch'ien 免役錢

min-fu 民夫

min-hu 民戶

min-k'uai-tsao 民快皂

min ssu 民祀

min yü 民圩

ming-huan hsiang-hsien 名宦鄉賢

Ming-lun T'ang 明倫堂

mu-yu 幕友

nei-ko chung-shu 內閣中書

Nien-fei 捻匪

pa 壩

pa-shih 罷市

pai-i 白役

p'ai 牌

p'ai-chang 牌長

p'ai-men 排門

p'ai-nien 排年

p'ai-t'ou 牌頭

pang-ch'a 幫查

pang p'an 幫盤

pao 保

pao 堡

pao-chang 保長

pao-chang mi 保長米

pao-cheng 保正

pao-chia 保甲

pao-chia chü 保甲局

pao-hu 包戶

pao-lan ch'ien-liang 包攬錢糧

p'eng-min 棚民

P'eng-tang lun 朋黨論

p'i 陂

p'i 鄙

p'i-keng 批耕

P'iao-kao lao-tsu 飄高老祖

pien 匾

pien-shen 編審

Pin-hsing 賓興

Ping-pu 兵部

p'ing-t'iao 平糶

p'u 鋪

p'u-tieh 譜牒

pun-ti 本地

san-lien ch'uan p'iao 三聯串票

San-tien hui 三點會

se-fu 嗇夫

shan-chang 山長

shan-ch'uan 山川

shan hui 山會

shan-shen 散紳

shan-t'ang 善堂

Shang-yü t'ing 上諭亭

she 社

she-chang 社長

she-chi t'an 社稷壇

she-hsüeh 社學

she-t'an 社壇

she-ts'ang 社倉

shen-ch'i 紳耆

shen-chia ch'ing-pai 身家清白

shen-chia hsing-ming 身家性命

shen-chin 紳衿

shen-hu 紳戶

shen min 紳民

shen-ming t'ing 申明亭

shen-shih 紳士

shen-tung 紳董

sheng 升

Sheng-yü 聖諭

Sheng-yü chih-chieh 聖諭直解	*tan-min* 蜑民
Sheng-yü hsiang-chieh 聖諭像解	*tang-nien* 當年
Sheng-yü kuang-hsün 聖諭廣訓	*t'ang* 塘
Sheng-yü kuang-hsün chih-chieh 聖諭廣訓直解	*tao chu* 倒豬
Sheng-yü t'ing 聖諭亭	*t'ao-chüeh hu* 逃絕戶
sheng-yüan 生員	*ti-chu* 地主
shih 士	*ti-fang* 地方
shih 市	*ti-liang* 地糧
shih 石	*ti-lin pao-chia* 地鄰保甲
shih-chia p'ai 十家牌	*ti-pao* 地保
Shih-fu 石佛	*ti-ting* 地丁
shih-tsu 始祖	*t'i* 隄
shou-shih jen 首事人	*tiao-shen lieh-chien* 刁生劣監
shu-min 庶民	*tien-shih* 典史
shu-suan 書算	*T'ien-ti hui* 天地會, 添弟會
shu-yüan 書院	*ting* 丁
shuang-fu 雙鳧	*ting-k'ou* 丁口
shui-shu 稅書	*ting ts'e* 丁冊
shun-ch'ai 順差	*ting-yin* 丁銀
sui 遂	*t'ing* 亭
sui 歲	*t'ing-tso* 停胙
sung-kun 訟棍	*tsa-fan* 雜泛
szu-cheng 四鄉	*tsan* 酇
szu Hsiang 司正	*ts'ang-cheng* 倉正
Szu-yen yin-wen 四言韻文	*ts'ang-ta-shih* 倉大使
ta-chiao 打醮	*ts'ang-yü* 倉庾
ta-hu 大戶	*ts'ao-ts'e* 草冊
ta hui 打會	*tse-ke (tzu-ke)* 資格
ta-nung 大農	*ts'e-shu* 冊書
ta-pin 大賓	*tseng-sheng* 增生
ta ssu 大杞	*tso hui* 做會
ta tsung-tz'u 大宗祠	*tso shan hui* 坐山會
tai-tu 帶肚	*tso ts'ui* 坐催
tai-tu meng-shang 帶肚門上	*tsu* 族
t'ai li 泰厲	*tsu-chang* 族長

tsu-cheng	族正	*tui-t'ien*	兌田
tsu-chung	租種	*tung*	冬
tsu-hsüeh	族學	*tung-t'ou*	冬頭
tsu-p'u	族譜	*T'ung*	獞
tsu-shen	族紳	*tz'u-chang*	祠長
tsu-shou	族首	*Tzu-chih t'ung-chien kang-mu*	資治通鑑綱目
tsu tz'u	族祠	*tz'u-hsüeh*	祠學
ts'uan she t'iao chia	竄社跳甲	*tz'u-ssu*	祠祀
ts'ui k'o	催科	*wan shou chin hsiang*	萬壽進香
ts'ui-t'ou	催頭	*wan-shou wu-chiang*	萬壽無疆
tsun	僎	*wei*	衞
ts'un	村	*wei*	圍
ts'un-chang	村長	*wei-hsing*	闈姓
tsung-chia	総甲	*wo-chu*	窩主
tsung-kuei	宗規	*wo pei*	卧碑
tsung-p'u	宗譜	*wu-chang*	伍長
tsung-shen	総紳	*wu-chü*	武舉
tsung-shu	総書	*wu-sheng*	武生
tsung-tung	総董	*Wu-sheng lao-mu*	無生老母
tsung-tzu	宗子	*wu ssu kuei shen*	無祀鬼神
tsung-tz'u	宗祠	*Wu-tao Miao*	玉道廟
tu	都	*Wu-wei lao tsu*	無爲老主
t'u	圖	*Yao*	猺
t'u-chang	圖長	*Yeh-shih men-p'ai ke-shih*	葉氏門牌格式
t'u-cho	土著	*yen*	堰
t'u-ti miao	土地廟	*yen-i-ts'ang*	鹽義倉
t'u-ti tz'u	土地祠	*yin-p'ai*	印牌
t'uan	團	*yin p'iao*	印票
t'uan-chang	團長	*yin ssu*	淫祠
t'uan-fu	團副	*ying-shen sai-hui*	迎神賽會
t'uan-lien	團練	*ying-t'o*	硬獣
t'uan-lien chang	團練長	*yu-chiao*	游徼
t'uan-lien chü	團練局	*yu-hsing*	游刑
t'uan-ting	團丁	*yu-min*	莠民
t'uan-tsung	團総	*yung-chung*	傭種

yü 圩

yü 隅

yü-chia 漁甲

yüan 圓, 元

yüan 院

yüan-chang 院長

yüeh 約

yüeh-cheng 約正

yüeh-ching shao-hsiang 越境燒香

Yüeh fei 粵匪

REIGNS AND EMPERORS
OF THE CH'ING DYNASTY

Reign		Emperor
T'ien-ming	1616-27	T'ai-tsu (Nurhaci, 1559-1626)
T'ien-ts'ung	1627-36	(Huang-t'ai-chi, i.e., Abahai, joint rule with Daisan, Amin, and Manggultai)
Ts'ung-te	1636-44	(Huang-t'ai-chi)
SHUN-CHIH*	1644-61	Shih-tsu (Fu-lin, 1638-61)
K'ANG-HSI	1662-1722	Sheng-tsu (Hsüan-yeh, 1654-1722)
YUNG-CHENG	1723-35	Shih-tsung (Yin-chen, 1678-1735)
CH'IEN-LUNG	1736-95	Kao-tsung (Hung-li, 1711-99)
CHIA-CH'ING	1796-1820	Jen-tsung (Yung-yen, 1760-1820)
TAO-KUANG	1821-50	Hsüan-tsung (Min-ning, 1782-1850)
HSIEN-FENG	1851-61	Wen-tsung (I-chu, 1831-61)
T'UNG-CHIH	1862-74	Mu-tsung (Tsai-ch'un, 1856-75)
KUANG-HSÜ	1875-1908	Te-tsung (Tsai-t'ien, 1871-1908)
HSÜAN-T'UNG	1909-12 (Feb.)	(P'u-i)

*The dynasty formally inaugurated in Peking, 1644

BIBLIOGRAPHY

This list includes only books and articles of various degrees of usefulness consulted by the writer and, in almost all cases, cited by him in the notes. It is not a systematic or exhaustive bibliography of all works pertinent to the subject.

Group A includes titles of books and articles in Chinese, and of translations into Chinese from works originally written in other languages. Works more conveniently identified by their titles (such as government compilations, local gazetteers, genealogical records) and those whose authors or compilers are not known, are listed alphabetically by titles; other works are arranged by authors or compilers, consecutively with the above. Titles cited in abbreviated form in the notes are given in the bibliography as cited, followed by the titles in full.

Group B contains the titles of books and articles in other languages arranged alphabetically by authors or compilers.

A. BOOKS AND ARTICLES IN CHINESE

Chang Ch'ing, *T'ung-shih: Chung-hua t'ung-shih,* 5 vols. Shanghai, 1934.

章 嶔　中華通史　民國二十三年　上海商務印書館　上版

Ch'ang-ning (1901): *Ch'ang-ning hsien chih,* 1901 ed., 16 *chüan* with *chüan shou.*

長寧縣志　光緒二十七年

Ch'ang-p'ing (1886): *Ch'ang-p'ing chou chih,* 18 *chüan,* compiled 1879, printed 1886.

昌平州志　光緒五年修 十二年刊

Chang Ping-lin (1868-1936), *Chien-lun,* 9 *chüan,* in *Chang-shih ts'ung-shu.* Shanghai, 1924.

章炳麟　檢論　章氏叢書本　上海古書流通處

Chang-shih tsu-p'u: Ch'ung-hsiu Teng-yung Chang-shih tsu-p'u. Shao-hsing, 1841.

重修登榮張氏族譜　浙江會稽　道光辛丑

Chang Shou-yung (1876-1945), *Hui-pien: Huang-ch'ao chang-ku hui-pien; nei-*

pien, 60 *chüan; wai-pien*, 40 *chüan;* 1902.

張壽鏞　皇朝掌故彙編　光緒二十八年

Chang Te-chien (19th century), *Tse-ch'ing hui-tsuan*, 12 *chüan*. Nanking, 1932.

張德堅　賊情彙纂　民國二十一年　南京江蘇省立圖書館

Chao-chung lu: Kuang-hsi chao-chung lu, 8 *chüan*, 1870, in *Kuang-hsi t'ung-chih chi-yao* (see below).

廣西昭忠錄　同治九年　廣西通志輯要本

Chao I (1727-1814), *Cha-chi: Nien-erh-shih cha-chi*, 36 *chüan*, in *Ou-pei ch'üan-chi*, 1877.

趙翼　廿二史劄記　光緒三年重刊甌北全集本

------. *Ts'ung-k'ao: Kai-yü ts'ung-k'ao*, 43 *chüan*, in *Ou-pei ch'üan-chi*, 1877.

　　陔餘叢考　同上

Chao-i: Chao-i hsien hsiang-t'u chih, in *Hsiang-t'u chih ts'ung-pien*, 1st series. Peiping, 1937.

朝邑縣鄉土志　鄉土志叢編第一輯本　民國二十六年　北平刊

Chao-p'ing (1928): *Chao-p'ing hsien chih*, 8 *chüan*, compiled 1928, printed 1932.

昭平縣志　民國十七年修二十一年印

Che-yü pien-lan, Wuchang, preface dated 1850 (see Hsü Nai-p'u below).

折獄便覽　道光庚戌　武昌

Ch'en Ch'i-yüan (19th century), *Pi-chi: Yung-hsien-chai pi-chi*, 12 *chüan*; preface to first 8 *chüan* dated 1872; preface to last 4 *chüan* dated 1875, in *Ch'ing-tai pi-chi ts'ung-k'an*. Shanghai, n. d.

陳其元　庸閒齋筆記　清代筆記叢刊本　上海文明書局

Ch'en Chih-mai, *Chung-kuo cheng-fu*, 3 vols. Shanghai, 1944-45.

陳之邁　中國政府　民國三十三至三十四年　上海商務印書館

Chen-hsiung (1887): *Chen-hsiung chou chih*, 1887 ed., 6 *chüan*.

鎮雄州志　光緒十三年

Ch'en Hung-mou (1696-1771), *Ou-ts'un kao: P'ai-yüan-t'ang ou-ts'un kao*, 48 *chüan*. Wuchang, 1896.

陳宏謀　培遠堂偶存稿　光緒三十三年湖北藩署刊

------. *Tsai-kuan fa-chieh lu*, 4 *chüan*, 1743.

　　在官法戒錄　乾隆八年培遠堂刊

------. *Ts'ung-cheng i-kuei*, 2 *chüan*, preface dated 1742.

　　從政遺規　乾隆壬戌培遠堂刊

Ch'en K'ang-ch'i (19th century), *Lang-ch'ien chi-wen*, 14 *chüan*, preface dated 1880, in *Ch'ing-tai pi-chi ts'ung-k'an*.

陳康祺　郎潛紀聞　清代筆記叢刊本　上海文明書局

Ch'en Kao-yung, *Chung-kuo li-tai t'ien-tsai jen-huo piao*, 10 *chüan*, preface dated 1939.

陳高傭　中國歷代天災人禍表　　上海國立暨南大學叢書

Chen-nan (1892): *Chen-nan chou chih-lüeh*, 1892 ed., 10 *chüan* with *chüan shou*.

鎮南州志略　光緒壬辰

Ch'en-shih tsung-p'u: Wen-ling Ch'en-shih fen-chih Hai-yen tsung-p'u. Soochow, 1909.

溫陵陳氏分支海鹽宗譜　宣統元年蘇州文圃堂刊

Ch'eng-ku: Ch'eng-ku hsien hsiang-t'u chih (n.d.), in *Hsiang-t'u-chih ts'ung-pien*, 1st series. Peiping, 1937.

城固縣鄉土志　鄉土志叢編第一輯本

Cheng-ting (1875): *Cheng-ting hsien chih*, 1875 ed., 46 *chüan* with *chüan shou* and *chüan mo*.

正定縣志　光緒元年

Ch'i-fu (1884): *Ch'i-fu t'ung-chih*, 300 *chüan* with *chüan shou*, compiled 1871, printed 1884.

畿輔通志　光緒十年

Chi-nan (1839): *Chi-nan fu chih*, 1839 ed., 72 *chüan* with *chüan shou*.

濟南府志　道光十九年

Chia-hsing (1878): *Chia-hsing fu chih*, 1878 ed., 88 *chüan* with 3 *chüan shou*.

嘉興府志　光緒四年

Chia I (200-168 B.C.), *Hsin shu*, 10 *chüan*. Shanghai, 1893 reprint.

賈　誼　新書　光緒十九年上海鴻文書局據抱經堂本印

Chia Shih-i, *Ts'ai-cheng shih: Min-kuo ts'ai-cheng shih*, 3rd ed., 2 vols. Shanghai, 1928.

賈士毅　民國財政史　民國十七年上海商務印書館　三版

Chia-ying (1898): *Chia-ying chou chih*, 32 *chüan*, printed 1898.

嘉應州志　光緒辛丑刊　民國二十二年補版

Chiang-ching (1924): *Chiang-ching hsien chih*, 1924 ed., 16 *chüan*, with *chüan shou*.

江津縣志　民國十七年

Chiang-hsi (1880): *Chiang-hsi t'ung-chi*, 1880 ed., 180 *chüan*.

江西通志　光緒六年

Chiang-ning (1811): *Chiang-ning fu chih*, 56 *chüan*, compiled 1811, reprinted 1880.

江寧府志　嘉慶十六年修光緒六年重刊

Chiang-ning (1880): *Hsü tsuan Chiang-ning fu chih*, 15 *chüan*, 1880.

續纂江寧府志　光緒六年

Chiang-shih peng-chih p'u: Lou-kuan Chiang-shih peng-chih p'u. Soochow, 1846.

婁關蔣氏支譜　吳縣　道光二十六年

Chien-ch'ang (1907): *Chien-ch'ang hsien hsiang-t'u chih*. 1907 ed., 12 *chüan* with *chüan shou*.

建昌縣鄉土志　光緒三十三年

Ch'ien-shih tsung-p'u: P'eng-ch'eng Ch'ien-shih tsung-p'u, compiled 1874; in manuscript.

彭城錢氏宗譜　蘇州　同治十三年抄本

Chien Yu-wen (Jen Yu-wen), *Shou-i-shih: T'ai-p'ing t'ien-kuo shou-i shih*. Shanghai, 1945 reprint.

簡又文　太平軍廣西首義史　民國三十四年上海商務印書館

-------. *Tsa-chi: T'ai-p'ing t'ien-kuo tsa-chi*, 1st series. Shanghai, 1936.

　　太平天國雜記　第一輯　民國二十五年　同上

-------. "Rural Administration of the T'ai-p'ing T'ien-kuo," *Journal of Oriental Studies* (Hong Kong), I (1954), 249-308.

　　太平天國鄉治考　香港大學　一九五四年

Ch'ien Yung (1759-1844), *Li-yüan ts'ung-hua*, 24 *chüan*, 1870 reprint.

錢　泳　履園叢話　清代筆記叢刊據同治九年補刻本印

Chih-hsin pao (The Reformer China). Macao, 1897-99 (?).

知新報　光緒二十三年正月二十日澳門創刊

Ch'ing-chou (1908): *Ch'ing-chou hsiang-t'u chih*, 1908 ed., 4 *chüan* with *chüan shou*.

靖州鄉土志　光緒三十四年

Ch'ing hsü t'ung-k'ao: Ch'ing-ch'ao hsü wen-hsien t'ung-k'ao, 400 *chüan*. Shanghai, 1936.

清朝續文獻通考　民國二十五年上海商務印書館

Ch'ing-pien (1899): *Ch'ing-pien hsien chih*, 1899 ed., 4 *chüan*.

靖邊縣志　光緒二十五年

Ch'ing-shih kao, 529 *chüan*. Peking, 1927.

清史稿　民國十六年　北京

Ch'ing-shih lieh-chuan, 80 *chüan* with *chüan shou*. Shanghai, 1928.

清史列傳　民國十七年上海中華書局

Ch'ing t'ung-chih: Ch'ing-ch'ao t'ung-chih, 126 *chüan*. Shanghai, 1935 reprint.

清朝通志　民國二十四年上海商務印書館

Ch'ing t'ung-k'ao: Ch'ing-ch'ao wen-hsien t'ung-k'ao, 300 *chüan*. Shanghai, 1936 reprint.

清朝文獻通考　民國二十五年上海商務印書館

Ch'ing t'ung-tien: Ch'ing-ch'ao t'ung-tien, 100 *chüan*. Shanghai, 1935 reprint.

清朝通典　同上

Ch'ing-yüan (1880): *Ch'ing-yüan hsien chih*, 1880 ed., 16 *chüan* with *chüan shou*.

清遠縣志　光緒庚辰

Chiu T'ang-shu, 200 *chüan*. Shanghai, Chung-hua shu-chü ed.

舊唐書　上海中華書局

Cho hsien (1936): *Cho hsien chih*, 18 *chüan*, compiled 1932, printed 1936.

涿縣志　民國二十五年

Chou-hsien shih-i. Wuchang, 1851 reprint (see Hsü Nai-p'u, below).

州縣事宜　咸豐元年武昌刊本

Chou-li: Chou-li Cheng-shih chu, in *Ts'ung-shu chi-ch'eng*. Shanghai, 1936.

周禮鄭氏注　民國二十五年上海商務印書館叢書集成本

Ch'u-an (pseud.), "Chi-hsüan tsa-chih," in *Chung-ho* (Peiping), III (1942, 128-32.

芻厂　寄軒雜誌　中和月刊第三卷第六期

Ch'u chou (1897): *Ch'u chou chih*, 10 *chüan* with *chüan shou* and *chüan mo*, compiled 1897, printed 1909.

滁州志　光緒二十三年修宣統元年刊

Ch'u-chou (1877): *Ch'u-chou fu chih*, 1877 ed., 30 *chüan* with *chüan shou* and *chüan mo*.

處州府志　光緒五年

Chu Hsieh, *Wen-t'i: Chung-kuo ts'ai-cheng wen-t'i*, 1st series. Nanking, 1933.

朱偰　中國財政問題　第一編　民國二十二年南京　國立編譯館

Chu-shih tsu-p'u: Tzu-yang Chu-shih ch'ung-hsiu tsu-p'u. T'ung-ch'eng, 1867.

紫陽朱氏重修族譜　同治六年安徽桐城

Chu-shih tsung-p'u (1894): *Tou-t'an Chu-shih tsung-p'u*. Shao-hsing, 1894.

陡壇朱氏宗譜　光緒二十年浙江山陰

Chu-shih tsung-p'u (1895): *Shan-yin Pai-yang Chu-shih tsung-p'u*. Shao-hsing, 1895.

山陰白洋朱氏宗譜　光緒二十一年浙江紹興

Chu Shou-p'eng (1868- ?), *Tung-hua hsü-lu*, 220 *chüan*. Shanghai, 1909.

朱壽彭　東華續錄　宣統元年上海圖書集成公司

Ch'ü Ta-chün (17th century), *Kuang-tung hsin-yü*, 28 *chüan*, 1700.

屈大均　廣東新語　康熙三十九年

Ch'ü Tui-chih (Ch'ü Hsüan-ying), *Wang Hui-tsu chuan-shu*. Shanghai, 1935.

瞿兑之　汪輝祖傳述　民國二十四年上海商務印書館

Ch'üan-chou (1870): *Ch'üan-chou fu chih*, 1870 ed., 76 *chüan* with supplement, 1927 reprint.

泉州府志　同治九年　民國十九年補刊

Ch'üeh-shan (1931):*Ch'üeh-shan hsien chih*, 24 *chüan*, compiled 1922-25, printed 1931.

確山縣志　民國十四年修二十年印

En-p'ing (1934): *En-p'ing hsien chih*, 1934 ed., 25 *chüan* with *chüan shou*.

恩平縣志　民國二十三年

Fang Hsiao-ju (1357-1402), *Hsün-chih-chai chi*, 24 *chüan* with appendix, reprint of 1462 ed.

方孝孺　遜志齋集　上海商務印書館覆天順六年本

Fang-kuo hsiang chih (1937): *Chi-an hsien Ho-hsi Fang-kuo hsiang chih*, 1937 ed., 8 *chüan* with *chüan shou*.

吉安縣河西坊廓鄉志　民國二十六年

Feng-chen (1916): *Feng-chen hsien chih-shu*, 8 *chüan* with *chüan shou* and *chüan wei*, compiled 1881, printed 1916.

豐鎮縣志書　光緒七年修民國五年印

Feng Kuei-fen (1809-74), *Chi: Hsien-chih-t'ang chi*, 12 *chüan*, 1876.

馮桂芬　顯志堂集　一名顯志堂稿　光緒二年校邠廬刊

Fu-chien (1871): *Fu-chien t'ung-chih*, 278 *chüan* with *chüan shou*, compiled 1835, printed 1871.

福建通志　道光十五年修同治十年刊

Fu-chou (1756): *Fu-chou fu chih*, 76 *chüan* with *chüan shou*, compiled 1754, printed 1756.

福州府志　乾隆十九年修二十一年刊

Fu-chou (1876): *Fu-chou fu chih*, 1876 ed., 86 *chüan* with *chüan shou*.

撫州府志　光緒二年

Fu Chu-fu, "Chung-kuo ching-chi shuai-lo chih li-shih-ti yüan-yin," *Eastern Miscellany*, XXXI, 221-28.

傅築夫　中國經濟衰落之歷史的原因　東方雜誌
第三十一卷第十四期

Fu-ning (1877): *Fu-ning hsien chih*, 1877 ed., 16 *chüan*.

撫寧縣志　光緒三年丁丑

Fu-shan (1924):*Fu-shan Chung-i hsiang chih*, 19 *chüan* with *chüan shou*, compiled 1923, printed 1924.

佛山忠義鄉志　民國十二年修十三年刊

Fu-shun (1931): *Fu-shun hsien chih,* 1931 ed., 17 *chüan* with *chüan shou.*

富順縣志　民國二十年

Han-fei-tzu, 20 *chüan.* Shanghai, 1893.

韓非子　光緒十九年上海鴻文書局影宋本

Han-shu, 100 *chüan.* Shanghai, Chung-hua shu-chü ed.

漢書　上海中華書局聚珍本

Han-tan (1933): *Han-tan hsien chih,* 17 *chüan* with *chüan shou* and *chüan mo,*
compiled 1931, printed 1933.

邯鄲縣志　民國二十二年

Hang-chou (1895): *Hang-chou fu chih,* compiled 1895, printed 1926.

杭州府志　光緒二十一年修民國十五年印

Heng-chou (1875): *Heng-chou fu chih,* 33 *chüan,* compiled 1763, printed with
additions 1875.

衡州府志　乾隆二十八年修光緒元年補刊

Ho Ch'ang-ling (1785-1848), *Wen-pien: Huang-ch'ao ching-shih wen-pien,* 120
chüan. Shanghai, 1887.

賀長齡　皇朝經世文編　光緒十三年上海點石齋

-------. *'Tsou-i: Nai-an tsou-i ts'un-kao,* 12 *chüan.* (1882?).

耐庵奏議存稿　光緒八年

-------. *Kung-tu: Nai-an kung-tu ts'un-kao,* 4 *chüan.* (1882?).

耐庵公牘存稿　光緒八年

-------. *Wen-ts'un: Nai-an wen-ts'un,* 6 *chüan.* (1861?).

耐庵文存　咸豐十一年

Ho-ch'ing (1894): *Ho-ch'ing chou chih,* 1894 ed., 32 *chüan* with *chüan shou.*

鶴慶州志　光緒二十年

Ho hsien (1934): *Ho hsien chih,* 1934 ed., 10 *chüan.*

賀縣志　民國二十三年

Hsi-ning (1873): *Hsi-ning hsien hsin chih,* 1873 ed., 10 *chüan* with *chüan shou.*

西寧縣新志　同治十二年

Hsia Hsieh (Chiang-shang chien-shou, pseud., 1799-1875), *Chung-hsi chi-shih,*
24 *chüan,* written *ca.* 1851, revised 1860, printed 1881(?).

夏　燮　別署江上蹇叟　中西紀事　光緒七年

-------. (Hsieh-shan chü-shih, pseud.), *Yüeh-fei chih-shih,* 13 *chüan,* n.d.

別署謝山居士　粵氛紀事

Hsia-men (1839): *Hsia-men chih,* 1839 ed., 16 *chüan.*

廈門志　光緒十九年

Hsia Nai, "T'ai-p'ing t'ien-kuo ch'ien-hou Ch'ang-chiang ko-sheng chih t'ien-fu wen-t'i," *Tsing Huo Journal*, X, 409-74.

夏　鼐　太平天國前後長江各省之田賦問題

清華學報　第五卷第二期

Hsiang-fu (1898): *Hsiang-fu hsien chih*, 1898 ed., 24 *chüan* with *chüan shou*.

祥符縣志　光緒二十四年

Hsiang-hsiang (1874): *Hsiang-hsiang hsien chih*, 1874 ed., 23 *chüan* with *chüan shou* and *chüan mo*.

湘鄉縣志　同治十三年

Hsiang-shan (1923): *Hsiang-shan hsien chih hsü-pien*, 1923 ed., 16 *chüan*.

香山縣志　民國十二年

Hsiang Ta *et al*. (ed.), *T'ai-p'ing t'ien-kuo*, 8 vols. Shanghai, 1952, in *Chung-kuo chin-tai-shih tzu-liao ts'ung-k'an*.

向　達等編　太平天國　中國近代史資料叢刊第二種

一九五二年上海神州國光杜

Hsiao I-shan, *Chin-tai pi-mi she-hui shih-liao*, 6 *chüan*. Peiping, 1935.

蕭一山　近代秘密社會史料　民國二十四年北平

國立北平研究院

------- . *Ch'ing-tai shih*, 3rd ed. Shanghai, 1947.

清代史　民國三十六年上海商務印書館三版

------- . *Ch'ing-tai t'ung-shih*, 2 vols. Shanghai, 1928; reprinted 1935.

清代通史　民國十七年上海商務印書館

------- . *T'ai-p'ing t'ien-kuo ts'ung-shu*, 1st series. Nanking, n. d.

太平天國叢書　第一輯　南京國立編譯館

Hsin-fan (1907): *Hsin-fan hsien hsiang-t'u chih*, 1907 ed., 10 *chüan*.

新繁縣鄉土志　光緒二十三年

Hsin-hsien (1887): *Hsin hsien chih*, 1887 ed., 10 *chüan*.

莘縣志　光緒十三年

Hsin-i (1889): *Hsin-i hsien chih*, 8 *chüan* with appendix, compiled 1889, printed 1891.

信宜縣志　光緒十五年修　十七年刊

Hsin-ning (1893): *Hsin-ning hsien chih*, 1893 ed., 26 *chüan*.

新寧縣志　光緒十九年

Hsin T'ang-shu, 225 *chüan*, Shanghai, Chung-hua shu-chü ed.

新唐書　上海中華書局聚珍本

Hsing-an (1871): *Hsing-an hsien chih*, 1871 ed., 16 *chüan* with *chüan shou*.
興安縣志　同治十年

Hsing-hua (1852): *Hsing-hua hsien chih*, 1852 ed., 10 *chüan*.
興化縣志　咸豐二年

Hsing-kuo (1889): *Hsing-kuo chou chih*, 1889 ed., 36 *chüan*.
興國州志　光緒十五年

Hsü-chou (1874): *Hsü-chou fu chih*, 1874 ed., 25 *chüan*.
徐州府志　同治十三年

Hsü K'o (compiler), *Ch'ing-pai lui-ch'ao*, 48 vols. Shanghai, 1917.
徐　珂　清稗類鈔　民國六年上海商務印書館

Hsü Nai-p'u (19th century), *Huan-hai chih-nan*, a collection including *Chou-hsien shih-i*, by T'ien Wen-ching; *Yung-li yung-yen*, by Liu Heng; *Tso-chih yo-yen*; and *Hsüeh-chih i-shuo*, by Wang Hui-tsu; and *Che-yü pien-lan*, anon. Peking, 1859.
許乃普　宦海指南　咸豐九年北京刊本

Hsü t'ung-k'ao: *Hsü wen-hsien t'ung-k'ao*, 250 *chüan*. Shanghai, 1936 reprint.
續文獻通考　民國二十五年上海商務印書館

Hsüeh-cheng (1810): *Hsüeh-cheng ch'üan-shu*, 1810 ed., 60 *chüan*.
學政全書　嘉慶十五年

Hsüeh Fu-ch'eng (1838-94), *Yung-an pi-chi*, 6 *chüan*, in *Ch'ing-tai pi-chi ts'ung-k'an*.
薛福成　庸盦筆記　清代筆記叢刊本

Hsüeh Nung-shan, *Chan-cheng: Chung-kuo nung-min chan-cheng chih shih-ti yen-chiu*, 2 vols. Shanghai, 1935.
薛農山　中國農民戰爭之史的研究　民國二十四年
上海神州國光社

Hsün-tien (1828): *Hsün-tien chou chih*, 1828 ed., 30 *chüan*.
尋甸州志　道光八年

Hu Lin-i (1812-61), *I-chi: Hu Wen-chung-kung i-chi*, 10 *chüan* with *chüan shou*, 1868.
胡林翼　胡文忠公遺集　同治七年醉六堂重刊

Hu-nan (1885): *Hu-nan t'ung-chih*, 1885 ed., 1934 reprint, 288 *chüan* with 8 *chüan shou* and 19 *chüan mo*.
湖南通志　光緒十一年刊民國二十三年影印本

Hu-pei (1921): *Hu-pei t'ung-chih*, 172 *chüan*, compiled 1911, printed 1921.
湖北通志　民國十年

Hu-pu (1791): *Hu-pu tse-li,* 1791 ed., 126 *chüan.*

戶部則例　乾隆五十年續纂

Hu-pu hsü-tsuan (1796): *Hu-pu tse-li hsü-tsuan,* 1796 ed., 31 *chüan.*

戶部則例續纂　嘉慶元年

Hu-pu ts'ao-yün ch'üan-shu, 1875 ed., 96 *chüan* with *chüan shou.*

戶部漕運全書　光緒元年

Hu Shih, *Ssu-shih tsu-shu.* Shanghai, 1933.

胡適　四十自述　民國二十二年上海亞東圖書館

Hua chou (n.d.): *Hua chou hsiang-t'u chih,* in *Hsiang-t'u chih ts'ung-pien,* 1st series.

華州鄉土志　鄉土志叢編第一輯

Hua hsien (1924): *Hua hsien chih,* 1924 ed., 13 *chüan.*

花縣志　民國十三年

Hua Hsüeh-lan (1860-1906), *Jih-chi: Hsin-ch'ou jih-chi.* Shanghai, 1936.

華學瀾　辛丑日記　民國二十五年上海商務印書館

Hua Kang, *T'ai-p'ing t'ien-kuo ke-ming chan-cheng shih.* Shanghai, 1949.

華崗　太平天國革命戰爭史　一九四九年上海海燕書店

Hua-shih tsung-p'u. Wu-hsi, 1894.

華氏宗譜　光緒二十年無錫

Huai-an (1884): *Huai-an fu chih,* 1884 ed., 40 *chüan.*

淮安府志　光緒九年

Huang Chün-tsai (19th century), *Chin-hu ch'i-mo,* 19 *chüan,* in *Ch'ing-tai pi-chi ts'ung-k'an.*

黃鈞宰　金壺七墨　清代筆記叢刊本

Huang Liu-hung (17th century), *Fu-hui: Fu-hui ch'üan-shu,* 32 *chüan,* 1699, 1893 reprint.

黃六鴻　福惠全書　光緒十九年重刊本

Huang-shih chih-hsi k'ao. Shan-hua, 1897.

黃氏支系考　光緒二十三年善化

Huang-ts'e mu-lu: Nei-ko ta-k'u hsien-ts'un Ch'ing-tai han-wen huang-ts'e mu-lu. Peiping, 1936.

內閣大庫現存清代漢文黃冊目錄　民國二十五年北平

故宮博物院

Hui-chou (1881): *Hui-chou fu chih,* 1881 ed., 45 *chüan* with *chüan shou.*

惠州府志　光緒七年

Hui-tien (1899): *Ta-ch'ing hui-tien,* 100 *chüan,* compiled 1899, printed Shanghai, 1908. " (See *Shih-li* below.)

大清會典　光緒二十五年修三十四年上海商務印書館印

Hun-yüan (1880): *Hun-yüan chou hsü-chih,* 1880 ed., 10 *chüan.*

渾源州志　光緒六年

I-cheng (1929): *I-cheng hsien chih,* 1929 ed., 38 *chüan.*

翼城縣志　民國十八年

I-chüan: I-chüan hsien hsiang-t'u chih (n.d.), in *Hsiang-t'u chih ts'ung-pien,* 1st series. Peiping, 1937.

宜川縣鄉土志　鄉土志叢編第一輯

Inaba, Iwakichi, *Ch'ing-ch'ao ch'üan-shih,* Chinese translation by Tan T'ao. 4 vols. Shanghai, 1924.

稻葉岩吉　清朝全史　但燾譯　民國十三年上海

中華書局九版

Jen-huai (1895): *Jen-huai t'ing chih,* 1895 ed., 8 *chüan.*

仁懷廳志　光緒二十一年

Ju-lin (1883): *Chiu-chiang Ju-lin hsiang chih,* 1883 ed., 21 *chüan.*

九江儒林鄉志　光緒九年

Kan-chih (1935): *Kan-chih pu-lu,* 1935 ed.

澉志補錄　民國二十四年

Kan-ch'üan: Kan-ch'üan hsien hsiang-t'u chih (n.d.), in *Hsiang-t'u chih ts'ung-pien,* 1st series. Peiping, 1937.

甘泉縣鄉土志　鄉土志叢編第一輯

Kan-shui (1850): *Kan-shui hsin chih,* 1850 ed., 12 *chüan.*

澉水新志　道光三十年

K'ang-chi lu: Ch'in-ting k'ang-chi lu, 4 *chüan,* compiled 1739, reprinted 1869.

欽定康濟錄　同治八年楚北崇文書局重刊本

Kato, Shigeru, "Ch'ing-tai ts'un-chen ti ting-ch'i-shih." Translated into Chinese by Wang Hsing-jui, in *Shih-huo,* V, 44-65.

加藤繁　清代村鎮的定期市　王興瑞譯　食貨半月刊

第五卷第一期

K'o-ch'ang t'iao-li: Ch'in-ting k'o-ch'ang t'iao-li, 1885 ed., 60 *chüan.*

欽定科場條例　光緒十一年

Ko Shih-chün (19th century), *Hsü-pien: Huang-ch'ao ching-shih wen hsü-pien,* n.d.

葛士濬　皇朝經世文續編

Ku-fei tsung-lu, 3 *chüan,* in *Kuang-hsi t'ung-chih chi-yao,* 1890.

股匪總錄　光緒十五年　廣西通志輯要本

Ku Yen-wu (1613-82), *Jih-chih lu,* 1735 ed., 32 *chüan.*

顧炎武　日知錄　康熙三十四年遂初堂刊本

Kuang-chou (1878): *Kuang-chou fu chih,* 1878 ed., 163 *chüan.*

廣州府志　光緒四年修五年刊

Kuang-hsi (1890): *Kuang-hsi t'ung-chih chi-yao,* 1890 ed., 17 *chüan,* with 5 appendixes, 28 *chüan.*

廣西通志輯要　光緒十六年增輯本

Kuei chou (1900): *Kuei chou chih,* 1900 ed., 17 *chüan.*

歸州志　光緒二十六年

K'uei-chou (1827): *K'uei-chou fu chih,* 36 *chüan* with *chüan shou,* compiled 1827, printed 1891.

夔州府志　道光七年

Kuei-shih shih-p'u: Ching-chao Kuei-shih shih-p'u. Chao-wen, 1913.

京兆歸氏世譜　民國二年昭文縣

K'un-yang (1839): *K'un-yang chou chih,* 1839 ed., 16 *chüan.*

昆陽州志　道光十九年

Kung Tzu-chen (1792-1841), *Wen-chi: Kung-ting-an wen-chi,* 2 vols. Shanghai, reprint, n.d.

龔自珍　定庵文集　上海大達圖書供應社排印本

Lang Ch'ing-hsiao, "Chin san-pai nien Chung-kuo nan-pu chih hsieh-tou," in *Chien-kuo,* Vol. III, no. 3, pp. 1-10; no. 4, pp. 1-14; and no. 5, pp. 1-12.

郎擎霄　近三百年中國南部之械鬥　建國月刊　第四卷　第三至第五期

Li Hsing-yüan (1797-1851), *Tsou-i: Li Wen-kung-kung tsou-i,* 22 *chüan,* in *Li Wen-kung-kung ch'üan-chi,* n.d.

李星沅　李文恭公奏議　李文恭公全集本　同治中　芋香山館刊

Li Huan (1827-91), *Lui-kao: Pao-wei-chai lui-kao,* 82 *chüan,* 1880.

李桓　寶韋齋類稿　光緒六年武林墨寶齋刊

Li Hung-chang (1823-1901), *Ch'üan-chi: Li Wen-chung-kung ch'üan-chi,* 165 *chüan* with *chüan shou.* Nanking, 1908.

李鴻章　李文忠公全集　光緒三十四年金陵刊

Li-p'ing (1891): *Li-p'ing fu chih,* 1891 ed., 8 *chüan* with *chüan shou.*

黎平府志　光緒十八年

Li-shih chih-p'u: Li-shih ch'ien-Ch'ang chih-p'u. Ch'ang-chou, 1894.

李氏遷常支譜　光緒二十年常州

Li-shih tsung-p'u: Tan-yang Li-shih tsung-p'u. Tan-yang, 1883.

李氏宗譜　光緒九年丹陽

Li T'ang-chieh (1798-1865), *Jih-chi: Li Wen-ch'ing-kung jih-chi,* 16 vols. Peking, 1915.

李棠階　李文清公日記　民國四年北京

Li Tzu-hsiang, "Chung-kuo shou-kung-yeh chih mo-lo kuo-ch'eng," *Quarterly Review of the Sun Yat-sen Institute for the Advancement of Culture and Education,* IV, 1013-30.

李紫翔　中國手工業之没落過程　中山文化教育館季刊

第四卷第三期

Li Tz'u-ming (1829-94), *Jih-chi: Yüeh-man-t'ang jih-chi,* 51 vols., in 7 parts: i. *Meng-hsüeh-chai jih-chi;* ii. *Chou-shih-yen-ya-chih-shih jih-chi;* iii. *Shou-li-lu jih-chi;* iv. *Hsiang-ch'ing-shih jih-chi;* v. *Hsi-ch'a-an jih-chi;* vi. *T'ao-hua-sheng-chiai-an jih-chi;* vii. *Hsün-hsüeh-chai jih-chi.* Shanghai, 1920.

李慈銘　越縵堂日記　一孟學齋日記　二籀詩研雅室日記

三受禮廬日記　四祥琴室日記　五息茶庵日記　六桃花聖解庵日記

七荀學齋日記　民國九年上海商務印書館

-------. *Jih-chi pu: Yüeh-man-t'ang jih-chi pu,* 13 vols. Shanghai, 1936.

越縵堂日記補　民國二十五年上海商務印書館

Li Yü (1611-80?), *Hsin-shu: Tzu-chih hsin-shu,* 1st series, 14 *chüan* with *chüan shou* (1663); 2nd series, 20 *chüan;* 3rd series, 20 *chüan* (1667).

李　漁　資治新書　凡三集　康熙二年至六年

Liang Chang-chü (1775-1849), *T'ui-an sui-pi,* 22 *chüan,* 1837. Reprinted in *Ch'ing-tai pi-chi ts'ung-k'an* from 1867 ed.; in *Erh-ssu-t'ang ts'ung-shu,* 1875.

梁章鉅　退庵隨筆　道光十七年　清代筆記叢刊本　二思堂叢書本

-------. *Kuei-t'ien so-chi,* 8 *chüan,* 1845.

歸田瑣記　道光二十五年　北東園刊

-------. *Lang-chi ts'ung-t'an,* 11 *chüan,* 1847.

浪迹叢談　道光二十七年　亦東園刊

Liang Ch'i-ch'ao (1873-1929), *Chung-kuo wen-hua shih,* in *Yin-ping-shih ho-chi, ch'üan-chi,* 86. Shanghai, 1936.

梁啟超　中國文化史　飲氷室合集本　民國二十五年上海　中華書局

Liang T'ing-lan (1796-1861), *I-fen chi-wen,* 5 *chüan.* Shanghai, 1937.

(梁廷枏)　夷氛紀聞　民國二十六年上海商務印書館

Lin-chang (1904): *Lin-chang hsien chih,* 1904 ed., 18 *chüan* with *chüan shou.*

臨漳縣志　光緒三十年

Lin Tse-hsü (1785-1850), *Cheng-shu: Lin Wen-chung-kung cheng-shu,* 37 *chüan*

(1879 ?).

林則徐　林文忠公政書　林氏刊本

Ling-shan (1914): Ling-shan hsien chih, 1914 ed., 22 chüan.

靈山縣志　民國三年

Liu Chi (1311-75), Wen-chi: Ch'eng-i-pai wen-chi, 1572, ed., 20 chüan. Reprinted Shanghai, n.d.

劉　基　誠意伯文集　四部叢刊影明隆慶本

Liu Heng (1776-1841), Yung-yen: Yung-li yung-yen (1831), reprinted in Hsü Nai-p'u, Huan-hai tzu-nan.

劉　衡　庸吏庸言　許乃普置海指南本

-------. Chou-hsien hsü-chih, reprinted in Hsü Nai-p'u, Huan-hai tzu-nan.

　　　州縣須知　同上

Liu I-cheng, Chung-kuo wen-hua shih, 2 vols. Nanking, 1932.

柳詒徵　中國文化史　民國二十一年南京鍾山書局

Liu-pu ch'u-fen tse-li: Ch'in-ting liu-pu ch'u-fen tse-li, 52 chüan, 1877.

欽定六部處分則例　光緒三年金東書行刊

Liu-shih chia-sheng, 32 chüan. Kuang-chou, 1891.

劉氏家乘　光緒十七年廣州

Liu Shih-jen, Chung-kuo t'ien-fu wen-t'i. Shanghai, 1936.

劉世仁　中國田賦問題　民國二十五年上海商務印書館

Liu Hsien-t'ing (1648-95), Tsa-chi: Kuang-yang tsa-chi, 5 chüan, in Ch'ing-tai pi-chi ts'ung-k'an.

劉獻廷　廣陽雜記　清代筆記叢刊本

Liu-yang (1873): Liu-yang hsien chih, 1873 ed., 24 chüan.

瀏陽縣志　同治十二年

Lo-ch'uan (1944): Lo-ch'uan hsien chih, 1944 ed., 26 chüan.

洛川縣志　民國三十三年

Lo Erh-kang, K'ao-cheng: T'ai-p'ing t'ien-kuo shih k'ao-cheng. Shanghai, 1948.

羅爾綱　太平天國史考證　民國三十七年上海獨立出版社

-------. Shih-kang: T'ai-p'ing t'ien-kuo shih-kang. Shanghai, 1936.

　　　太平天國史綱　民國二十五年上海商務印書館

Lo Hsiang-lin, K'e-chia yen-chiu tao-lun. Hsing-ning, 1933.

羅香林　客家研究導論　興寧希山書藏排印

Lo Ping-chang (1793-1867), Tsou-kao: Lo Wen-chung-kung tsou-kao, 27 chüan with appendix, 1878.

駱秉章　駱文忠公奏稿　光緒四年

Lo-ting (1935): *Lo-ting chih,* 1935 ed., 10 *chüan.*

羅定志　民國二十四年

Lo Yung and Shen Tsu-chi (compilers), *Shih-wen ch'ao: T'ai-p'ing t'ien-kuo shih-wen ch'ao,* 2 vols. Shanghai, 3rd printing, 1935.

羅邕　沈祖基　太平天國詩文鈔　民國二十四年上海

商務印書館三版

Lu-chou (1882): *Lu-chou chih-li-chou chih,* 1882 ed., 12 *chüan.*

廬州直隸州志　光緒八年

Lu-chou (1885): *Hsü-hsiu Lu-chou fu chih,* 1885 ed., 100 *chüan* with *chüan shou* and *chüan mo.*

續修廬州府志　光緒十一年

Lu-i (1896): *Lu-i hsien chih,* 1896 ed., 16 *chüan.*

鹿邑縣志　光緒二十二年

Lü-li pien-lan (1877): *Ta-Ch'ing lü-li hui-chi pien-lan,* 40 *chüan,* 1877.

大清律例彙輯便覽　光緒三年

Lu-lung (1931): *Lu-lung hsien chih.* 1931 ed., 24 *chüan* with *chüan shou.*

盧龍縣志　民國二十年

Luan chou (1896): *Luan chou chih,* 1896 ed., 18 *chüan* with *chüan shou.*

灤州志　光緒二十二年修二十四年刊

Lung Ch'i-jui (1814-58), *Wen-chi,* 6 *chüan; Pieh-chi,* 2 *chüan,* in *Ching-te-t'ang ch'üan-chi,* 1878-81.

龍啟瑞　文集　別集　經德堂全集本

Mao Tse-tung, *Chung-kuo ke-ming yü Chung-kuo Kung-ch'an-tang.* Hong Kong, 1949.

毛澤東　中國革命與中國共產黨

Mei-t'an (1899): *Mei-t'an hsien chih,* 1899 ed., 8 *chüan* with *chüan shou.*

湄潭縣志　光緒二十五年

Meng-ch'eng (1915): *Meng-ch'eng hsien chih-shu,* 1915 ed., 12 *chüan.*

蒙城縣志書　民國四年

Mien-chu (1908): *Mien-chu hsien hsiang-t'u chih,* 1908 ed.

綿竹縣鄉土志　光緒三十四年

Mien-yang (1894): *Mien-yang chou chih,* 1894 ed., 12 *chüan* with *chüan shou.*

沔陽州志　光緒二十年

Ming-shih, 332 *chüan.* Shanghai, *Chung-hua shu-chü* ed., n.d.

明史　上海中華書局聚珍本

Mu-ch'ien hsing-shih ho o-men-ti jen-wu. Hong Kong, 1949.

目前形勢和我們的任務　一九四九香港新民主出版社

Mu-lin shu: Mu-lin shu chi-yao, 10 *chüan,* revised and printed, 1868.

牧令書輯要　　同治八年 江蘇書局

Nan-ch'ang (1919): *Nan-ch'ang hsien chih,* 60 *chüan,* with 3 appendixes of 24, 5,
  and 14 *chüan* respectively, compiled 1904, printed 1919.

南昌縣志　光緒三十年修民國八年刊

Nan-hai (1910): *Nan-hai hsien chih,* 1910 ed., 26 *chüan* with *chüan mo.*

南海縣志　宣統二年

Nan-ning (1847): *Nan-ning fu chih,* 1847 ed., 56 *chüan,* reprinted 1909.

南寧府志　道光二十七年修宣統元年續錄重刊

Nan-ning (1852): *Nan-ning hsien chih,* 1852 ed., 10 *chüan* with *chüan shou.*

南寧縣志　咸豐二年

Nan-yang (1904): *Nan-yang hsien chih,* 1904 ed., 12 *chüan* with *chüan shou.*

南陽縣志　光緒三十年

O-sheng ting-ts'ao chih-chang, 10 *chüan,* 1875.

鄂省丁漕指掌　光緒元年湖北藩署

Orita, Yorozu (1868-?), *Fen-lun: Ch'ing-kuo hsing-cheng-fa fen-lun,* Chinese
  translation, 5 vols. Tokyo, 1915-18.

織田　萬　清國行政法分論　大正四年至七年東京
　　東洋印刷株式會社

Pa-ling (1891): *Pa-ling hsien chih,* 1891 ed., 63 *chüan* with an appendix of 16
chüan.

巴陵縣志　光緒十七年

Pai Ching-wei (1831-91), *Chi: Feng-hsi-ts'ao-t'ang chi,* 8 *chüan* with appendix.
  Nanking, 1924.

柏景偉　灃西草堂集　民國十二年思過齋刊

P'an Kuang-tan, *Ming Ch'ing liang tai Chia-hsing wang-tsu.* Shanghai, 1947.

潘光旦　明清兩代嘉興望族　民國三十六年上海商務印書館

P'an-yü (1911): *P'an-yü hsien hsü-chih,* 1911 ed., 44 *chüan.*

番禺縣續志　宣統三年

Pao Shih-ch'en (1775-1855), *Ch'i-min ssu shu,* 15 *chüan,* in *An-wu ssu chung,*
  1888 ed.

包世臣　齊民四術　安吳四種本　光緒十四年重校印

P'eng-shih tsu-p'u: Li-yang nan-men P'eng-shih tsu-p'u. Li-yang, 1894.

溧陽南門彭氏族譜　光緒二十二年

P'eng-shih tsung-p'u. Soochow, 1881.

彭氏宗譜　光緒七年蘇州

P'eng Yüan-jui (18th century), *Fu-hui ch'üan-shu*, 64 *chüan*, 1795.

彭元瑞　孚惠全書　乾隆六十年據彭氏進呈本印

Pien Pao-ti (1824-92), *Tsou-i: Pien chih-chün tsou-i*, 12 *chüan*, 1894.

卞寶第　卞制軍奏議　光緒二十年

P'ing-kuei chi-lüeh, 1889, in *Kuang-hsi t'ung-chih chi-yao*.

平桂紀畧　光緒十五年　廣西通志輯要本

*P'ing-ting Hui-fei fang-lüeh: Ch'in-ting p'ing-ting Shen Kan Hsin-chiang Hui-
fei fang-lüeh*, 320 *chüan* with *chüan shou*, in *Ch'i sheng fang-lüeh*. Peking,
1896.

欽定平定陝甘新疆回匪方畧　七省方畧本

P'ing-yüan (1890): *P'ing-yüan chou hsü-chih*, 1890 ed., 8 *chüan* with *chüan shou*.

平遠州續志　光緒十六年

Po-pai (1832): *Po-pai hsien chih*, 1832 ed., 16 *chüan* with appendix of 2 *chüan*.

博白縣志　道光十二年

P'u-an (1889): *P'u-an chih-li-t'ing chih*, 1889 ed., 22 *chüan*.

普安直隸廳志　光緒十五年

P'u-shih tsung-p'u: Ch'ien-chien P'u-shih tsung-p'u. Wu-hsi, 1831.

前澗浦氏宗譜　民國二十年無錫

Shan-tung chün-hsing chi-lüeh, 22 *chüan*, n.d.

山東軍興紀畧

Shan-tung (1915): *Shan-tung t'ung-chih*, 200 *chüan* with *chüan shou*, compiled
1911, printed 1915.

山東通志　光緒十六年至宣統三年修　民國四年刊成

Shang-Chiang (1874): *Shang-yüan Chiang-ning liang hsien chih*, 1874 ed., 29 *chüan*
with *chüan shou*.

上元江寧兩縣志　同治十三年

Shen Shou-chih (19th century), *Pi-chi: Chieh-ch'ao pi-chi*, 7 *chüan*. Shanghai,
1936.

沈守之　借巢筆記　民國二十五年上海人文月刊社

Shen Yüeh-lin (19th century), *So-chi: Yüeh-hsi so-chi*, in Wang Hsi-ch'i (compiler), *Hsiao-fang-hu-chai yü-ti ts'ung-ch'ao*. Shanghai, 1877-97.

沈日霖　粵西瑣記　王錫祺小方壺齋輿地叢鈔本
　光緒三年至二十三年上海著易堂

Sheng K'ang (19th century), *Hsü-pien: Huang-ch'ao ching-shih-wen hsü-pien*.

Shanghai, 1897.

盛 康　皇朝經文續編　光緒二十三年

Sheng-hsün: Ta-ch'ing shih-ch'ao sheng-hsün, T'ai-tsu, 4 *chüan;* T'ai-tsung 6 *chüan;* Shih-tsu, 6 *chüan;* Sheng-tsu, 60 *chüan;* Shih-tsung, 36 *chüan;* Kao-tsung, 300 *chüan;* Jen-tsung, 110 *chüan;* Hsüan-tsung, 130 *chüan;* Wen-tsung, 110 *chüan;* Mu-tsung, 160 *chüan.* Peking, n. d.

大清十朝聖訓　康熙五年至光緒五年

Shih-chi, 130 *chüan.* Shanghai, Chung-hua shu-chü ed.

史記　上海中華書局聚珍本

Shih-li: Ta-ch'ing hui-tien shih-li, 1899 ed., 1220 *chüan*, with 8 *chüan shou.* Shanghai, 1908.

大清會典事例　光緒二十五年修三十四年上海商務印書館印

Shih-lu: Ta-ch'ing li-ch'ao shih-lu, 4664 *chüan.* Tokyo, *ca.* 1937.

大清歷朝實錄　日本東京大藏出版株式會社

Shun-t'ien (1884): *Shun-t'ien fu chih*, 1884 ed., 130 *chüan.*

順天府志　光緒十年

Sui chou (1892): *Sui chou chih*, 1892 ed., 12 *chüan* with *chüan shou.*

睢州志　光緒十八年

Sui-shu, 85 *chüan.* Shanghai, Chung-hua shu-chü ed.

隋書　上海中華書局聚珍本

Sung-shih, 490 *chüan.* Shanghai, Chung-hua shu-chü ed.

宋史　同上

Tai Ch'ao-ch'en (19th century), *Hsüeh-shih lu*, 16 *chüan*, 1867.

戴肇辰　學仕錄　同治六年

T'ai-ho (1878): *T'ai-ho hsien chih*, 1878 ed., 30 *chüan* with *chüan shou.*

泰和縣志　光緒四年

T'ai-pai (1897): *T'ai-pai mei-li chih*, 1897 ed., 8 *chüan.*

泰伯梅里志　光緒二十三年

Tan Hu-liang (19th century), *Hu-nan miao-fang t'un-cheng k'ao,* 15 *chüan* with supplement, *ca.* 1890.

但湖良　湖南苗防屯政考　光緒十六年(補編序)

T'ang Chen (19th century), *Wei-yen*, 4 *chüan.* Shanghai, 1890.

湯 震　危言　光緒十六年上海

T'ang-fei tsung-lu (1889), in *Kuang-hsi t'ung-chih chi-yao.*

堂匪總錄　光緒十五年廣西通志輯要本

Tao chou (1878): *Tao chou chih*, 12 *chüan* with *chüan shou*, compiled 1877, printed 1878.

道州志　光緒四年

T'ao Chu (1779-1839), *Ch'üan-chi: T'ao wen-i-kung ch'üan-chi*, 64 *chüan* with *chüan shou* and *chüan mo*.

陶　澍　陶文毅公全集　淮北刊本

T'ao Tsung-i (14th century), *Shuo-fu*, 100 *chüan*. Shanghai, 1927 reprint.

陶宗儀　說郛　民國十六年上海商務印書館

T'eng hsien (1846): *T'eng hsien chih*, 14 *chüan* with *chüan shou*, compiled 1832, printed 1846.

滕縣志　道光二十六年

T'eng hsien (1908): *T'eng hsien chih*, 22 *chüan*, compiled 1868, reprinted 1908.

藤縣志　同治七年修光緒三十四年重刊

T'ien-ching (1898): *T'ien-ching fu chih*, 54 *chüan* with *chüan shou* and *chüan mo*, compiled 1895, printed 1898.

天津府志　光緒十七年修二十四年刊

Ting chou (1850): *Ting chou chih*, 22 *chüan*, compiled 1849, printed 1850.

定州志　道光三十年

Ting Jih-ch'ang (1823-82), *Kung-tu: Fu-Wu kung-tu*, 50 *chüan*, 1877.

丁日昌　撫吳公牘　光緒三年

Ting-yüan (1879): *Ting-yüan t'ing chih*, 1879 ed., 26 *chüan* with *chüan shou*.

定遠廳志　光緒五年

Ts'ai Shen-chih, "Ch'ing-tai chou-hsien ku-shih," *Chung-ho*, Vol. II, no. 9, pp. 49-67; no. 10, pp. 72-95; no. 11, pp. 89-101; and no. 12, pp. 100-8.

蔡申之　清代州縣故事　中和月刊第二卷第九至十二期

Tseng Kuo-fan (1811-72), *P'i-tu: Tseng Wen-cheng-kung p'i-tu*, 6 *chüan*; *Shu-cha: Tseng Wen-cheng-kung shu-cha*, 33 *chüan*; *Tsou-kao: Tseng Wen-cheng-kung tsou-kao*, 32 *chüan*; in *Tseng Wen-cheng-kung ch'üan-chi*, 1876.

曾國藩　曾文正公奏稿　批牘書札　光緒二年傳忠書局
曾文正公全集本

Tseng-shih tsu-p'u: *Tseng shih ssu-hsiu tsu-p'u*, 16 *chüan* with appendix. Hsiang-hsiang, 1900.

曾氏四修族譜　光緒二十六年湘鄉

Tso Tsung-t'ang (1812-85), *Ch'üan-chi: Tso Wen-hsiang-kung ch'üan-chi*, 134 *chüan*, 1888-97.

左宗棠　左文襄公全集　光緒十四年至二十三年

Tsou-i: *Huang-Ch'ing tsou-i*, 68 *chüan*, 1936.

皇清奏議　民國二十五年

Tsou-i, hsü-pien: Huang-Ch'ing tsou-i hsü-pien, 14 *chüan,* 1936.

皇清奏議續編　同上

Tsou T'ao (19th century), *Pi-t'an: San-chieh-lu pi-t'an,* 12 *chüan, ca.* 1885, in *Ch'ing-tai pi-chi ts'ung-k'an.* 8th series. Shanghai, Wen-ming shu-chü ed.

鄒弢　三借廬筆談　清代筆記叢刊本

Tsun-hua (1794): *Tsun-hua chou chih,* 20 *chüan,* compiled 1793, printed 1794.

遵化州志　乾隆五十九年刊

T'ung-chou (1875): *T'ung-chou chih-li-chou chih,* 1875 ed., 16 *chüan* with *chüan shou* and *chüan mo.*

通州直隸州志　光緒元年

T'ung chou (1879): *T'ung chou chih,* 1879 ed., 10 *chüan* with *chüan shou* and *chüan mo.*

通州志　光緒五年

T'ung-ch'uan (1897): *T'ung-ch'uan fu chih,* 1897 ed., 30 *chüan.*

潼川府志　光緒二十三年

T'ung-jen (1890): *T'ung-jen fu chih,* 1890 ed., 20 *chüan.*

銅仁府志　光緒十五年

T'ung-k'ao: Wen-hsien t'ung-k'ao, 348 *chüan.* Shanghai, 1936 reprint.

文獻通考　民國二十五上海商務印書館影乾隆戊辰重刊本

Tung-kuan (1911): *Tung-kuan hsien chih,* 102 *chüan* with *chüan shou,* compiled 1911, printed 1921.

東莞縣志　宣統三年修民國十年刊

T'ung-kuan (1944): *T'ung-kuan hsien chih,* 1944 ed., 30 *chüan.*

同官縣志　民國三十三年

T'ung-tien, 200 *chüan.* Shanghai, 1935 reprint.

通典　民國二十六年上海商務印書館影乾隆丁卯重刊本

Tz'u-li (1896): *Tz'u-li hsien chih,* 1896 ed., 10 *chüan.*

慈利縣志　光緒二十二年

Wan-ch'üan (1834): *Wan-ch'üan hsien chih,* 1834 ed., 10 *chüan* with *chüan shou,* 1930 reprint.

萬全縣志　道光十四年修民國十九年重刊

Wang Ch'ing-yün (1798-1862), *Chi-cheng: Hsi-ch'ao chi-cheng* (also known as *Shih-ch'ü yü-chi),* 6 *chüan,* 1898 reprint.

王慶雲　熙朝紀政　一名石渠餘紀　光緒二十四年重校刊本

Wang Hsien-ch'ien (1842-1918), *Tung-hua lu,* 629 *chüan,* 1884. Shanghai, reprint 1899.

王先謙　東華錄　光緒二十五年上海石印本

-------. *Wen-chi: Hsü-shou-t'ang wen-chi*, 15 *chüan*, 1900.

虛受堂文集　光緒庚子校刊

Wang Hui-tsu (1731-1807), *I-shuo: Hsüeh-chih i-shuo*, 2 *chüan*, *ca.* 1793.

汪輝祖　學治臆說　乾隆五十八年刊

-------. *Hsü-shuo: Hsüeh-chih hsü-shuo*, *ca.* 1794.

汪輝祖　學治續說　乾隆五十九年

-------. *Shuo-chui: Hsüeh-chih shuo-chui*, *ca.* 1800.

學治說贅　嘉慶五年

-------. *Meng-hen lu: Ping-t'a meng-hen lu*, 2 *chüan*, *ca.* 1796.

病榻夢痕錄　光緒十二年山東書局重刊

-------. *Meng-hen yü-lu*, *ca.* 1807.

夢痕餘錄　同上

-------. *Tso-chih yo-yen* and *Hsü tso-chih yo-yen*, *ca.* 1775. (This and the preceding five items are to be found in *Wang Lung-chuang hsien-sheng i-shu*, 1882-86.)

佐治藥言　續佐治藥言　乾隆五十年

以上五種收入汪龍莊先生遺書　光緒八至十六年山東書局

Wang I-k'o, *Nung-ts'un tzu-wei yen-chiu*. Hsi Hsien, 1932.

王怡柯　農村自衛研究　民國二十一年汲縣河南村治學院　同學會刊

Wang Jen-k'an (1849-93), *I-shu: Wang Su-chou i-shu*, 12 *chüan* with supplement, 1933.

王仁堪　王蘇州遺書　民國二十二年

Wang Shih-chen (1526-90), *Yen-shan-t'ang pieh-chi*, 100 *chüan*.

王世貞　弇山堂別集　廣雅書局刊本

Wang-shih chia-p'u: Tung-t'ing Wang-shih chia-p'u. Soochow, 1911.

洞庭王氏家譜　宣統三年吳縣

Wang-shih chih-p'u: Wu-ch'u Wang-shih chih-p'u. Soochow, 1897.

吳趨汪氏支譜　光緒二十三年吳縣

Wang Shih-t'o (1802-89), *Jih-chi: Wang Hui-weng i-ping jih-chi*, 3 *chüan*. Peiping, 1936.

汪士鐸　汪梅翁乙丙日記　民國二十五年北平刊

Wang-shih tsu-p'u: Shao-hsing Hsin-ho Wang-shih tsu-p'u, 10 *chüan*, *ca.* 1927.

紹興新河王氏族譜　民國十六年

Wang-shih tsung-p'u, 'I-hsing. 1840.

汪氏宗譜　道光二十年宜興

Wang Shou-jen (1472-1528), *Wang-Wen-ch'eng-kung chüan-shu*, 38 *chüan*, Che-chiang shu-chü ed.

王守仁　王文成公全書　浙江書局刊本

Wang T'ao (1828-?), *Wai-pien: T'ao-yüan wen-lu wai-pien*, 10 *chüan*, 1883.

王韜　弢園文錄外編　光緒九年香海

Wang Ting-an (19th century), *Ti-tzu chi: Ch'iu-ch'üeh-chai ti-tzu chi*, 32 *chüan*, 1876.

王定安　求闕齋弟子記　光緒二年

Wang Yü-ch'üan, "Ch'ing-mo t'ien-fu yü nung-min," *Shih-huo*, III, 237-48.

王毓銓　清末田賦與農民　食貨半月刊 第三卷第五期

Wei chou (1877): *Wei chou chih*, 1877 ed., 20 *chüan* with *chüan shou*.

蔚州志　光緒三年

Wei Yüan (1794-1856), *Nei-chi: Ku-wei-t'ang nei-chi*, 3 *chüan*.

魏　源　古微堂內集　光緒四年淮南書局

-------. *Wai-chi: Ku-wei-t'ang wai-chi*, 7 *chüan*, 1878.

　　　古微堂外集　同上

-------. *Sheng-wu chi*, 14 *chüan*, ca. 1844.

　　　聖武記　道光二十二年

Wen Chün-t'ien, *Pao-chia: Chung-kuo pao-chia chih-tu*. Shanghai, 1935.

聞鈞天　中國保甲制度考　民國二十四年上海商務印書館

Weng T'ung-ho (1830-1904), *Jih-chi: Weng Wen-kung-kung jih-chi*, 40 vols. Shang-hai, 1925.

翁同龢　翁文恭公日記　民國十四年上海商務印書館

Wu-chiang (1917): *Wu-chiang hsien hsiang-t'u chih*, 1917 ed.

吳江縣鄉土志　民國六年

Wu-hsi (1881): *Wu-hsi Chin-kuei hsien chih*, 1881 ed., 40 *chüan* with *chüan shou* and *pu-pien* (6 *chüan*).

無錫金匱縣志　光緒七年

Wu Ju-lun (1840-1903), *Jih-chi: T'ung-ch'eng Wu hsien-sheng jih-chi*, 16 *chüan*, 1928.

吳汝綸　桐城吳先生日記　民國十七年蓮池書社

Wu Wen-hui, "Tsai-huang hsia Chung-kuo nung-ts'un jen-k'ou yü ching-chi chih tung-t'ai," *Quarterly Review of the Sun Yat-sen Institute for the Advancement of Culture and Education*, IV, 43-59.

吳文輝　災荒下中國農村人口與經濟動態　中山文化教育館

季刊第四卷第一期

Wu Yung-kuang (1773-1843), *Wu-hsüeh lu, ch'u pien,* 24 *chüan,* 1870.

吳榮光　吾學錄　初編　同治九年江蘇書局重刊本

Wuo-yang (1924): *Wuo-yang hsien chih,* 1924 ed., 16 *chüan* with *chüan shou.*

渦陽縣志　民國十三年

Yang Chi-hsüan, "Ya-p'ien chan-i i-hou Chung-kuo she-hui ching-chi chuan-pien ti tung-hsiang ho t'e-cheng," *Eastern Miscellany,* XXXII, 5-20.

楊及玄　雅片戰役以後中國社會經濟轉變的動向和特徵　東方雜誌
第三十二卷第四期

Yang-chiang (1925): *Yang-chiang chih,* 1925 ed., 39 *chüan.*

陽江志　民國十四年

Yang Ching-jen (late 18th and early 19th century), *Ch'ou-chi pien,* 32 *chüan,* compiled *ca.* 1823, reprinted 1883.

楊景仁　籌濟編　光緒九年武昌書局重刊

Yang-chou (1810): *Yang-chou fu chih,* 1910 ed., 72 *chüan* with *chüan shou.*

揚州府志　嘉慶十五年

Yang-chou (1874): *Hsü-hsiu Yang-chou fu chih,* 1874 ed., 24 *chüan.*

續修揚州府志　同治十三年

Yao Ying (1785-1852), *Ch'üan-chi: Chung-fu-t'ang ch'üan-chi,* 98 *chüan,* 1867.

姚瑩　中復堂全集　同治六年

Yeh Ch'ang-chih (1849-1917), *Jih-chi: Yüan-tu-lu jih-chi ch'ao,* 16 *chüan.* Shanghai, 1920.

葉昌熾　綠督盧日記鈔　民國九年上海蟬隱廬

Yeh-shih tsu-p'u: Wu-chung Yeh-shih tsu-p'u. Soochow, 1911.

吳中葉氏族譜　宣統三年吳縣

Yeh Te-hui (1864-1927), *Chüeh-mi yao-lu,* 4 *chüan,* 1905.

葉德輝　覺迷要錄　光緒乙巳

Yen-an (1802): *Yen-an fu chih,* 80 *chüan,* compiled 1802, printed 1880.

延安府志　嘉慶七年修光緒十年補刊

Yen-ch'ing (1880): *Yen-ch'ing chou chih,* 1880 ed., 12 *chüan* with *chüan shou* and *chüan mo.*

延慶州志　光緒六年

Yen-chou (1883): *Yen-chou fu chih,* 1883 ed., 38 *chüan* with *chüan shou.*

嚴州府志　光緒九年

Yen-yüan (1891): *Yen-yüan hsien chih,* 1891 ed., 2 *chüan* with *chüan shou,* additional material not arranged into *chüan.*

鹽源縣志　光緒十七年

Yen-yüan (1901): *Yen-yüan hsiang chih,* 24 *chüan,* compiled 1901, printed 1916.

剡源鄉志　光緒二十七年修民國五年刊

Yin Chia-pin (19th century), *Cheng-chiao chi-lüeh,* 4 *chüan,* 1900.

尹嘉賓　征剿紀略　光緒二十六年

Yü-lin (1841): *Yü-lin fu chih,* 1841 ed., 50 *chüan* with *chüan shou.*

榆林府志　道光二十一年

Yü-lin (1894): *Yü-lin chou chih,* 1894 ed., 20 *chüan* with *chüan shou.*

鬱林州志　光緒二十年

Yü Pao-hsüan (19th century), *Wen-pien: Huang-ch'ao hsü-ai wen-pien,* 80 *chüan.* Shanghai, 1903.

于寶軒　皇朝蓄艾文編　光緒二十九年上海官書局

Yü Shen (late 17th and early 18th century), *Ch'ang-p'ing-ts'ang k'ao,* in *Ts'ung-shu chi-ch'eng,* 1st series, vol. CMLXVII. Shanghai, 1936.

俞　森　常平倉考　叢書集成初編　上海商務印書館

——————. *Huang-cheng ts'ung-shu,* 10 *chüan,* compiled 1690, in *Shou-shan-ko ts'ung-shu.*

　　　　荒政叢書　附常平倉義倉社倉考　守山閣叢書

Yü Yin-lin (1838-1904), *I-shu: Yü chung-ch'eng-kung i-shu,* 20 *chüan.* Peking, 1923.

于蔭霖　于中丞遺書　民國十二年北京

Yü Yin-shih, "The Establishment of the Political Power of the Later Han Dynasty and Its Relations with the Distinguished Clans and Notable Families" *(Tung Han cheng-ch'üan chih chien-li yü shih-tsu ta-hsing chih kuan hsi), The New Asia Journal (Hsin-ya hsüeh-pao),* I, 209-80. Hong Kong, 1956.

余英時　東漢政權之建立與士族大姓之關係

　　新亞學報　第一卷第二期

Yü Yüeh (1821-1906), *Hui-tsui pien,* 20 *chüan* (1880), in *Ch'ing-tai pi-chi ts'ung-k'an.*

俞　樾　薈蕞編　清代筆記叢刊

Yüan-shih, 210 *chüan.* Shanghai, Chung-hua shu-chü ed.

元史　上海中華書局聚珍本

Yün-ch'eng (1893): *Yün-ch'eng hsien chih,* 1893 ed., 16 *chüan* with *chüan shou.*

鄆城縣志　光緒十九年

Yung-chou (1867): *Yung-chou fu chih,* 1867 ed., 18 *chüan.*

永州府志　道光五年

Yung hsien (1897): *Yung hsien chih,* 1897 ed., 28 *chüan.*

容縣志　光緒二十三年

Yung-ning (1894): *Yung-ning chou hsü-chih.* 1894 ed. 12 *chüan.*

永寧州續志　光緒二十年

B. BOOKS AND ARTICLES IN OTHER LANGUAGES

Abel, Clarke. *Narrative of a Journey in the Interior of China, and of a Voyage to and from That Country, 1816 and 1817.* London: Longman, Hurst, Rees, Orme, and Brown, 1818.

Adler, Solomon. *The Chinese Economy.* New York: Monthly Review Press, 1957.

Altekar, Anant Sadashiv. *A History of Village Communities in Western India.* (University of Bombay Economic Series, No. 5.) Bombay: Oxford University Press, 1927.

Anderson, Charles Arnold, and Mary Joan Bowman. *The Chinese Peasant: His Physical Adaptation and Social Organization.* Mimeographed. 1951.

Andrews, Charles McLean. "The Theory of the Village Community," *American Historical Association Papers* (New York and London), V (1891), Parts I and II, 45-61.

Asakawa, Kanichi. "Notes on Village Government in Japan after 1600," *Journal of the American Oriental Society* (Boston), XXX (1910), 259-300, and XXXI (1911), 151-216.

Auber, Peter. *China: An Outline of Its Government, Laws, and Policy, and of the British and Foreign Embassies to, and Intercourse with, That Empire.* London: Parbury, Allen and Co., 1834.

Baber, Edward Colborne. *China, in Some of Its Physical and Social Aspects. (Proceedings of the Royal Geographical Society, N.S., V, 441-58.)* London, 1883.

-------. "Travels and Researches in Western China," *Royal Geographical Society, Supplementary Papers* (London), Vol. I (1882), Part I.

Baden-Powell, Baden Henry. *The Indian Village Community, Examined with Reference to the Physical, Ethnographical and Historical Conditions of the Provinces, Chiefly on the Basis of the Revenue-Settlement Records and District Manuals.* London, New York, and Bombay: Longmans, Green and Co., 1896.

-------. *The Origin and Growth of Village Communities in India.* London and New York, 1899.

Ball, James Dyer. *Things Chinese; or, Notes Connected with China,* 4th ed. New York: C. Scribners' Sons, 1904. 5th ed., revised by E. Chalmers Werner, London: John Murray, 1926.

Bard, Emile. *Chinese Life in Town and Country.* Adapted and translated from *Les Chinois chez eux* by Hannah Twitchell. New York and London: G. P. Putnam's Sons, 1905.

Barnett, A. Doak. *Local Government in Szechwan.* New York: Institute of Current World Affairs, 1948.

Bell, Major Mark S. *China. Being a Military Report on the Northeastern Portions of the Provinces of Chihli and Shantung; Nanking and Its Approaches; Canton and Its Approaches; etc., Together with an Account of the Chinese Civil, Naval, and Military Administration.* 2 vols. Simla, 1884.

Boardman, Eugene Powers. *Christian Influence upon the Ideology of the Taiping Rebellion, 1851-1864.* Madison: University of Wisconsin Press, 1952.

-------. "Christian Influence upon the Ideology of the Taiping Rebellion," *Far Eastern Quarterly* (Lancaster), X (1951), 115-24.

Bodde, Derk. "Henry A. Wallace and the Ever-Normal Granary," *Far Eastern Quarterly* (Lancaster), V (1946), 411-26.

Borst-Smith, Ernest Frank. *Mandarin and Missionary in Cathay: the Story of Twelve Years' Strenuous Missionary Work during Stirring Times Mainly Spent in Yenanfu.* London: Seeley, Service & Co., Ltd., 1917.

Borton, Hugh. *Peasant Uprisings in Japan of the Tokugawa Period. (Transactions of the Asiatic Society of Japan,* Series 2, XVI, 1-219.) Tokyo, 1938.

Brandt, Conrad, Benjamin Schwartz, and John King Fairbank. *A Documentary History of Chinese Communism.* Cambridge, Mass.: Harvard University Press, 1952.

Brenan, Byron. "The Office of District Magistrate," *Journal of the Royal Asiatic Society of Great Britain and Ireland,* North China Branch (Shanghai), N.S., XXXII (1897-98), 36-65.

Brinkley, Captain Frank. *China, Its History, Arts and Literature.* Boston and Tokyo: J. B. Millet Co., 1902.

Browne, George Waldo. *China: the Country and Its People.* Boston: D. Estes & Co., 1901.

Brunnert, H. S. and V. V. Hagelstrom. *Present Day Political Organization of China.* Shanghai: Kelly and Walsh, Ltd., 1912.

Buck, John Lossing. *Chinese Farm Economy: A Study of 2866 Farms in 17 Localities and 7 Provinces in China.* Chicago: University of Chicago Press, 1930.

Bucklin, Harold S. *et al. A Social Survey of Sung-ka-hong, China, by Students of the 1923-1924 Social Survey Class at Shanghai College.* Shanghai, 1924.

Burgess, John Stewart. *The Guilds of Peking.* New York: Columbia University Press, 1928.

Buxton, Leonard Halford Dudley. *China, the Land and the People: a Human Geography, with a Chapter on the Climate by W. G. Kendrew.* Oxford: Clarendon Press, 1929.

Chang, C. C. *China's Food Problem.* (Publications and Data Papers of the Fourth Conference of the Institute of Pacific Relations, Vol. III, No. 10.) Shanghai: China Institute of Pacific Relations, 1931.

Chang, Ch'un-ming. *A New Government for Rural China: the Political Aspect of Rural Reconstruction.* Shanghai, 1936.

Chang, Chung-li. *The Chinese Gentry: Studies on Their Role in Nineteenth-Century Chinese Society.* Seattle: University of Washington Press, 1955.

--------. The Gentry in Nineteenth Century China: Their Economic Position as Evidenced by Their Share of the National Product. Unpublished Ph. D. dissertation, University of Washington, 1953.

Chao, Kuo-chün. "Current Agrarian Reform Policies in Communist China," *Annals of the American Academy of Political and Social Science* (Philadelphia), CCLXXVII (1951), 113-23.

Chen, Han-sheng. *The Present Agrarian Problem in China.* Shanghai: China Institute of Pacific Relations, 1933.

--------. *The Chinese Peasant.* (Oxford Pamphlets on Indian Affairs, No. 33.) London, New York, and Bombay: Oxford University Press, 1945.

--------. *Landlord and Peasant in China: a Study of the Agrarian Crisis in South China.* New York: International Publishers, 1936.

Chen, Shao-kwan. *The System of Taxation in China in the Tsing Dynasty, 1644-1911.* New York: Columbia University Press, 1914.

Ch'ien, Tuan-sheng. *The Government and Politics of China.* Cambridge, Mass.: Harvard University Press, 1950.

China. Imperial Maritime Customs. II. Published by order of the Inspector General of Customs. "Opium," Special Ser. No. 4, Shanghai, 1881; "Native Opium, 1887," with an appendix, "Native Opium, 1863," Special Ser. No. 9, Shanghai, 1888; "Opium: Historical Note; or the Poppy in China," Special Series No. 13, Shanghai, 1889.

Chu, Co-Ching. "Climatic Pulsations during Historic Times in China," *Geographic Review* (New York), XVI (1920), 274-82.

Colquhoun, Archibald Ross. *China in Transformation.* Rev. ed., New York and London: Harper & Bros., 1900.

Coltman, Robert. *The Chinese. Their Present and Future: Medical, Political and Social.* Philadelphia and London: F. A. Davis, 1891.

Cooke, George Wingrove. *China: Being "The Times" Special Correspondence from China in the Years 1857-1858.* London, 1858.

Corner, Julia. *China, Pictorial, Descriptive and Historical.* Published anonymously. London, 1853.

Creel, Herrlee Glessner. *Chinese Thought from Confucius to Mao Tse-tung.* Chicago: University of Chicago Press, 1953.

-------. *The Birth of China: a Study of the Formative Period of Chinese Civilization.* New York, Reynal & Hitchcock, 1937.

Cressey, George Babcock. *China's Geographic Foundations: A Survey of the Land and Its People.* New York and London: McGraw-Hill Book Co., Inc., 1934.

Danton, George H. *The Culture Contacts of the United States and China: The Earliest Sino-American Culture Contacts, 1784-1844.* New York: Columbia University Press, 1931.

Davis, Sir John Francis. *China: A General Description of That Empire and Its Inhabitants, with the History of Foreign Intercourse Down to the Events Which Produced the Dissolution of 1857.* 2 vols. London, 1857.

-------. *China During the War and Since the Peace.* 2 vols. London, 1852.

-------. *The Chinese: A General Description of the Empire of China and Its Inhabitants.* 2 vols. New York, 1848.

-------. *Sketches of China, Partly during an Inland Journey of Four Months, between Peking, Nanking and Canton; with Notices and Observations Relative to the Present War.* 2 vols. London, 1841.

Denby, Charles. *China and Her People; Being the Observations, Reminiscences, and Conclusions of an American Diplomat.* Boston: L. C. Page & Co., 1906.

Djilas, Milovan. *The New Class: An Analysis of the Communist System.* New York: Thames and Hudson, 1957.

Donnat, Leon. *Paysans en communauté du Ning-po-fou (Province de Tché-kian).* Paris, 1862.

Doolittle, Justus. *Social Life of the Chinese, with Some Account of Their Religious, Governmental Educational and Business Customs and Opinions. With Special but not Exclusive Reference to Fuhchau.* 2 vols. New York, 1865.

Dostoevsky, Fyodor. *The Brothers Karamazov.* Translated by Constance Garnett. New York: Modern Library, 1950.

Douglas, Sir Robert Kennaway. *Society in China.* London, 1894.

Edkins, Jane R. *Chinese Scenes and People. With Notices of Christian Missions and Missionary Life in a Series of Letters from Various Parts of China. With Narrative of a Visit to Nanking by Her Husband, the Reverend Joseph Edkins of London Missionary Society.* London, 1863.

Edkins, Joseph. *The Revenue and Taxation of the Chinese Empire.* Shanghai: Presbyterian Mission Press, 1903.

Fei, Hsiao-t'ung. *China's Gentry; Essays in Rural-Urban Relations*. Revised and edited by Margaret Park Redfield. Chicago: University of Chicago Press, 1953.

———. *Peasant Life in China: A Field Study of Country Life in the Yangtze Valley*. London: G. Routledge and Sons, 1939.

———. *Peasantry and Gentry: An Interpretation of Chinese Social Structure and Its Changes*. New York: Institute of Pacific Relations, 1946.

Fielde, Adele Marion. *A Corner of Cathay: Studies from Life among the Chinese*. New York, 1894.

———. *Pagoda Shadows: Studies from Life in China*. 3rd ed. Boston, 1884.

Fisher, George Battye. *Personal Narrative of Three Years' Service in China*. London, 1863.

Fortune, Robert. *A Residence among the Chinese: Inland, on the Coast, and at Sea. Being a Narrative of Scenes and Adventures during a Third Visit to China, from 1853 to 1856*. London, 1857.

Fried, Morton H. *Fabric of Chinese Society: A Study of the Social Life of a Chinese County Seat*. New York: Frederick Praeger, 1953.

Geil, William Edgar. *A Yankee on the Yangtze. Being a Narrative of a Journey from Shanghai through the Central Kingdom to Burma*. New York: A. C. Armstrong and Son, 1904.

Giles, Herbert Allen. *Gems of Chinese Literature*. 2nd ed. London: Kelly & Walsh, Ltd., 1923.

Gordon-Cumming, Constance Frederika. *Wanderings in China*. 2 vols. Edinburgh and London, 1886.

Gorst, Harold E. *China*. New York, 1899.

Graves, Roswell Hobart. *Forty Years in China, or China in Transition*. Baltimore, 1895.

Gray, Sir John Henry. *China: A History of the Laws, Manners and Customs of the People*. 2 vols. London, 1878.

Groot, Jan Jakob Maria de. *Religion in China: Universism, a Key to the Study of Taoism and Confucianism*. New York and London: G. P. Putnam's Sons, 1912.

———. *The Religious System of China: Its Ancient Forms, Evolution, History, and Present Aspect: Manners, Customs and Social Institutions Connected Therewith*. 6 vols. Leyden: E. J. Brill, 1892-1910.

———. *Sectarianism and Religious Persecution in China: a Page in the History of Religions*. 2 vols. Amsterdam: Müller, 1903-4.

Gundry, Richard Simpson. *China, Present and Past: Foreign Intercourse, Progress and Resources, the Missionary Question . . .* London, 1895.

Hamberg, Theodore. *The Visions of Hung-Siu-tshuen, and Origin of the Kwangsi Insurrection*. Hong Kong, 1854. Reprinted, Peiping, 1935.

Han, Fei Tzu. *The Complete Works of Han Fei Tzu; a Classic of Chinese Legalism*. Translated from the Chinese with introduction, notes, glossary, and index by Wien Kwei Liao. Vol. I. London: A. Probsthain, 1939.

Harvey, Edwin D. *The Mind of China*. New Haven: Yale University Press; London: Oxford University Press, 1933.

Hinton, Harold C. *The Grain Tribute System of China: 1845-1911: An Aspect of the Decline of the Ch'ing Dynasty*. (Chinese Political and Economic Studies.) Cambridge, Mass.: Harvard University Press, 1956.

———. "The Grain Tribute System of the Ch'ing Dynasty," *Far Eastern Quarterly* (Lancaster), XI (1952), 339-54.

Ho, Franklin Lien. *Rural Economic Reconstruction in China*. (Publications and Data Papers of the 6th Conference of the Institute of Pacific Relations, Vol. I, No. 2.) Tientsin, 1936.

Hoang, Peter. "A Practical Treatise on Legal Ownership," *Journal of the Royal Asiatic Society of Great Britain and Ireland*, North China Branch (Shanghai), N.S., XXIII (1888), 118-74.

Holcombe, Chester, *The Real Chinaman*. New York, 1895.

Horne, Charles F., ed. *The Sacred Books and Early Literature of the East, with Historical Surveys of the Chief Writings of Each Nation. Medieval China*, Vol. XII. New York and London: Parke, Austin, and Lipscomb, Inc., 1917.

Hosie, Sir Alexander. "Droughts in China, A.D. 620-1643," *Journal of the Royal Asiatic Society of Great Britain and Ireland*, North China Branch (Shanghai), N.S., XII (1878), 1-89.

--------. *Three Years in Western China. A Narrative of Three Journeys in Ssu-ch'uan, Kuei-chow and Yün-nan*. London, 1890.

Hsieh, Pao-ch'ao. *The Government of China, 1644-1911*. (Johns Hopkins University Studies in Historical and Political Science, N.S. No. 3.) Baltimore: Johns Hopkins Press, 1925.

Hsieh, T'ing-yü. "The Origin and Migrations of the Hakkas," *Chinese Social and Political Science Review* (Peiping), XIII (1929), 202-27.

Hsü, Francis L.K. *Under the Ancestor's Shadow: Chinese Culture and Personality*. New York: Columbia University Press, 1948.

--------. "Social Mobility in China," *American Sociological Review* (Minosha), XIV (1949), 764-71.

Hu, Chang-tu. Yellow River Administration in the Ch'ing Dynasty. Unpublished Ph.D. dissertation, University of Washington, 1954.

Hu, Hsien Chin. *The Common Descent Group in China and Its Functions*. (Viking Fund Publications in Anthropology, No. 10.) New York, 1948.

Huang, Han Liang. *The Land Tax in China*. New York: Columbia University Press, 1918.

Huc, Evariste-Régis. *The Chinese Empire, Forming a Sequel to the Work Entitled "Recollections of a Journey through Tartary and Thibet."* 2nd ed. 2 vols. London, 1855.

Hummel, Arthur W., ed. *Eminent Chinese of the Ch'ing Period (1644-1912)*. 2 vols. Washington, D.C.: Government Printing Office, 1943-44.

Huntington, Ellsworth. *The Character of Races as Influenced by Physical Environment, Natural Selection and Historical Development*. New York and London: C. Scribner's Sons, 1924.

Institute of Pacific Relations. *Agrarian China: Selected Source Materials from Chinese Authors*. London: G. Allen & Unwin, Ltd., 1939.

Jamieson, George, *et al*. "Tenure of Land in China and the Condition of the Rural Population," *Journal of the Royal Asiatic Society of Great Britain and Ireland*, North China Branch (Shanghai), N.S., XXIII (1888), 59-174.

--------. "Translations from the Lü-li, or General Code of Laws." *The China Review*, VIII (1879-80), 1-18. 193-205, and 259-76; IX (1880-81), 129-36 and 343-50; and X (1881-82), 77-99.

Kemp, Emily Georgiana. *The Face of China: Travels in East, North, Central and Western China*. London, Chatto & Windus, 1909.

Kierman, Frank A. *The Chinese Communists in the Light of Chinese History*. (Communist Bloc Program, China Project B54-1). Cambridge, Mass.: Massachusetts Institute of Technology Center for International Studies, 1954.

Kirby, E. Stuart. *Introduction to the Economic History of China*. London: Allen & Unwin, 1954.

Kracke, E. A. "Family versus Merit in Chinese Civil Service Examinations under the Empire," *Harvard Journal of Asiatic Studies*, X (1947), 103-23.

Kulp, Daniel Harrison II. *Country Life in South China: The Sociology of Familism*. Vol. I. "Phenix Village, Kwangtung, China," New York: Bureau of Publications, Teachers College, Columbia University, 1925.

Lang, Olga. *Chinese Family and Society*. New Haven: Yale University Press, 1946.

Lee, Mabel Ping-hua. *The Economic History of China, with Special Reference to Agriculture*. New York: Columbia University Press, 1921.

Lee, Robert. "The Pao-chia System."*(Papers on China*, III, 193-224.) Mimeographed for private distribution by the East Asia Program, Committee on Regional Studies, Harvard University, Cambridge, 1949.

Legge, James. *The Chinese Classics*. 2nd ed., 5 vols. Oxford: Clarendon Press, 1893-95.

-------. "Imperial Confucianism," *The China Review*, VI (1878), 147 ff., 223 ff., 299 ff., and 363 ff.

Leong [Liang], Y. K., and L. K. Tao. *Village and Town Life in China*. London: G. Allen & Unwin, Ltd.; New York: Macmillan Co., 1915.

Levy, Marion Joseph. *The Family Revolution in Modern China*. Cambridge, Mass.: Harvard University Press, 1949.

Lewinski, Jan S. *The Origin of Property and the Formation of the Village Community*. London: Constable & Co., 1913.

Li, Chi. *The Formation of the Chinese People; An Anthropological Inquiry*. Cambridge, Mass.: Harvard University Press, 1928.

Lin, Yüeh-hwa. *The Golden Wing: A Sociological Study of Chinese Familism*. London: Institute of Pacific Relations, 1948.

Lin-Le (Lindley, A. F.) *Ti-Ping Tien-kwoh: The History of the Ti-Ping Revolution, Including a Narrative of the Author's Personal Adventures*. 2 vols. London, 1866.

Linebarger, Paul Myron Anthony. *Government in Republican China*. New York and London: McGraw Hill Book Co., 1938.

-------, Djang Chu, and Ardath W. Burks. *Far Eastern Governments and Politics: China and Japan*. New York: Van Nostrand, 1954.

Little, Alicia Helen. *The Land of the Blue Gown*. London and Leipzig: T. F. Unwin, 1908.

Little, Archibald John. *Through the Yang-tse Gorges, or Trade and Travel in Western China*. London, 1898.

Lowie, Robert H. *Social Organization*. New York: Rinehart, 1948.

Lu, Lien-tching. *Les greniers publics de prévoyance sous la dynastie des Ts'ing*. Paris: Jouve & Cie., 1932.

Maine, Henry S. *Village Communities*. 3rd ed. London, 1876.

Mallory, Walter Hampton. *China: Land of Famine*. New York: American Geographical Society, 1926.

Malone, C. B. and J. B. Taylor. *The Study of Chinese Rural Economy*. (China International Relief Commission Publications, Ser. B, No. 10.) Peking, 1924.

Martin, William Alexander Parsons. *A Cycle of Cathay; or, China, South and North, With Personal Reminiscences*. Edinburgh, 1896. 3rd ed., New York and Chicago: F. H. Revell and Co., 1900.

Marx, Karl. *Marx on China, 1853-1860. Articles from the New York Daily Tribune*. London: Lawrence & Wishart, 1951.

Matsumoto, Zenkai. "The Establishment of the *Li* System by the Ming Dynasty," *Tōhōgaku hō* (Tokyo), XII (1941), 109-22.

Maverick, Lewis. *Economic Dialogues in Ancient China. Selections from the Kuan-tzu.* Carbondale: University of Illinois Press, 1954.

Mayers, William Frederick. *The Chinese Government. A Manual of Chinese Titles, Categorically Arranged and Explained, with an Appendix,* 3rd ed. Shanghai, 1897.

Meadows, Thomas Taylor. *The Chinese and Their Rebellions, Viewed in Connection with Their National Philosophy, Ethics, Legislation and Administration; to Which is Added an Essay on Civilization and Its Present State in the East and West.* London and Bombay, 1856.

-------. *Desultory Notes on the Government and People of China and on the Chinese Language, Illustrated with a Sketch of the Province of Kwang-Tung . . .* London, 1847.

Michael, Franz H. "Revolution and Renaissance in Nineteenth-Century China: The Age of Tseng Kuo-fan," *Pacific Historical Review,* XVI, 144-51.

Milne, William C. *Life in China.* London, 1857.

Mitrany, David. *Marx Against the Peasant: a Study in Social Dogmatism.* Chapel Hill: University of North Carolina Press, 1951.

Monroe, Paul. *China: A Nation in Evolution.* New York: Chautauqua Press, 1928.

Morse, Hosea Ballou. *The International Relations of the Chinese Empire.* 3 vols. London and New York: Longmans, Green, and Co., 1910-18.

-------. *The Trade and Administration of China.* Rev. ed. London and New York: Longmans, Green, and Co., 1913.

Mossman, Samuel. *China: a Brief Account of the Country, Its Inhabitants and Their Institutions.* London, 1867.

Moule, Arthur Evans. *Four Hundred Millions: Chapters on China and the Chinese.* London, 1871.

-------. *Half a Century in China: Recollections and Observations.* London, New York, and Toronto: Hodder and Stoughton, 1911.

Mukerjee, Radhakamal. *Democracies of the East: a Study in Comparative Politics.* London: P. S. King and Son, Ltd., 1923.

Murdock, George Peter. *Social Structure.* New York: Macmillan, 1949.

Nevius, John Livingston. *China and the Chinese: A General Description of the Country and Its Inhabitants; Its Civilization and Form of Government; Its Religions and Social Institutions; Its Intercourse with Other Nations, and Its Present Condition and Prospects.* New York, 1869.

Nichols, Francis H. *Through Hidden Shensi.* New York: C. Scribner's Sons, 1902.

North, Robert C. "The Chinese Communist Elite," *Annals of the American Academy of Political and Social Science* (Philadelphia), CCLXXVII (1951), 67-75.

Ouchterlony, John. *The Chinese War: An Account of All the Operations of the British Forces from the Commencement to the Treaty of Nanking.* London, 1844.

Oxenham, E. C. "A Report to Sir R. Alcock, on a Journey from Peking to Hankow, through Central Chihli, Honan, and the Han River, November 2 to December 14, 1868," reprinted in Alexander Williamson, *Journey in North China,* II, 393-428. London, 1870.

Parker, Edward Harper. *China: Her History, Diplomacy and Commerce, from the Earliest Times to the Present Day.* London, 1901.

-------. *China's Intercourse with Europe,* adapted and translated from Hsia

Hsieh, *Chung-hsi chi-shih.* Shanghai, 1890.

-------. "The Educational Curriculum of the Chinese," *The China Review* (Hong Kong), IX (1881), 63 ff., 85 ff., 173 ff., 259 ff., and 325 ff.

Parsons, James B. "The Culmination of a Chinese Peasant Rebellion: Chang Hsien-chung in Szechwan, 1644-46," *Journal of Asian Studies,* XVI (1957), 387-99.

Peake, Harold J. E. "Village Community," *Encyclopedia of the Social Sciences,* (New York: Macmillan Co., 1930), XV, 253-58.

Playfair, George MacDonald Home. *The Cities and Towns of China. A Geographical Dictionary.* 2nd ed. Shanghai: Kelly & Walsh, Ltd., 1910.

Pruitt, Ida. *A Daughter of Han: The Autobiography of a Chinese Working Woman, by Ida Pruitt, from the Story Told Her by Nin Lao T'ai-T'ai.* New Haven: Yale University Press; London: Oxford University Press, 1945.

Richard, L. *Comprehensive Geography of the Chinese Empire and Dependencies.* Translated, revised and enlarged from *Geographie de l'empire de Chine,* by M. Kennelly. Shanghai: T'usewei Press, 1908.

Richthofen, Ferdinand Paul Wilhelm von. *Baron Richthofen's Letters, 1870-1872,* 2nd ed. Shanghai: North China Herald, 1903.

Rockhill, William Woodville. "An Inquiry into the Population of China," *Smithsonian Institution Annual Report for 1904,* XLVII, 659-76. Washington, D.C., 1905.

Ross, Edward Alsworth. *Sociological Observations in Inner China.* (Papers and Proceedings of the American Sociological Society, Fifth Annual Meeting, V, 17-29.) Chicago, 1910.

Le saint édit. Translated by A. Théophile Piry. London, 1879.

Scarth, John. *Twelve Years in China: the People, the Rebels and the Mandarins, by a British Resident.* Edinburgh: T. Constable, 1860.

Seton-Watson, Hugh. *The Pattern of Communist Revolution: A Historical Analysis.* London: Methuen, 1953.

Shih, Vincent Y. C. "The Ideology of the Taiping T'ien Kuo," *Sinologica* (Basel), III (1951), 1-15.

Sims, Newell Leroy, ed. *The Rural Community, Ancient and Modern.* New York: C. Scribner's Sons, 1920.

Skinner, G. William. "Aftermath of Communist Liberation in the Chengtu Plain," *Pacific Affairs* (Honolulu), XXIV (1952), 61-76.

-------. "Peasant Organization in Rural China," *Annals of the American Academy of Political and Social Science* (Philadelphia), CCLXXVII (1951), 89-100.

Smith, Arthur Henderson. *China in Convulsion.* 2 vols. New York, Chicago, Edinburgh, and London: Fleming H. Revell Co., 1901.

-------. *Chinese Characteristics.* 2nd ed. New York: Fleming H. Revell Co., 1894.

-------. *Village Life in China: a Study in Sociology.* New York, Chicago, and Toronto: Fleming H. Revell Co., 1899.

Smith, George. *A Narrative of an Exploratory Visit to Each of the Consular Cities of China, and to the Islands of Hong Kong and Chusan, in Behalf of the Church Mission Society in the Years 1844, 1845, 1846.* London, 1847.

Smith, Stanley P. *China from Within, or the Story of the Chinese Crisis.* London: Marshall Bros., 1901.

Smyth, George B. *et al. The Crisis in China.* New York and London: Harper, 1900.

Stanton, W. "The Triad Society or Heaven and Earth Association," *The China Review* (Hong Kong), XXII (1895), 441-43.

Staunton, George Thomas. *Miscellaneous Notices Relating to China, and Our Commercial Intercourse with that Country, Including a Few Translations from the Chinese Language*. London, 1822.

Sun, E-tu Zen, and John De Francis. *Chinese Social History. Translations of Selected Studies*. Washington, D. C. : American Council of Learned Societies, 1956.

Suzuki, Chusei. "The Origin of Anti-Foreign Movements in the Later Ch'ing Period: Studies on the San-yüan-li Incident," *Shigaku-Zasshi* (Tokyo), LXII (1953), 1-28.

Tang, Peter Sheng-hao. *Communist China Today: Domestic and Foreign Policies*. New York: Frederick Praeger, 1957.

Tawney, Richard Henry. *Land and Labour in China*. New York: Harcourt, Brace & Co. , 1932.

Taylor, George E. "The Intellectual Climate of Asia," *Yale Review*, XLII (1952), 184-97.

Teng, Ssu-yü. *New Light on the History of the Taiping Rebellion*. Cambridge, Mass. : Harvard University Press, 1950.

-------, and John King Fairbank. *China's Response to the West. A Documentary Survey, 1839-1923*. Cambridge, Mass. : Harvard University Press, 1954.

Thomas, S. B. *Government and Administration in Communist China*. New York: Institute of Pacific Relations, 1953.

Tscheng, Ki-T'ong. "China: A Sketch of Its Social Organization and State Economy," *Asiatic Quarterly Review* (London), X (1890), 258-72.

Walker, Richard L. *China under Communism: The First Five Years*. New Haven: Yale University Press, 1955.

Wang, Kan-yü. The *Hsien* (County) Government in China. Unpublished Ph. D. dissertation, Harvard University, 1947.

Ward, John Sebastian Marlow, and W. G. Sterling. *The Hung Society, or the Society of Heaven and Earth*. 3 vols. London: Baskerville Press, 1925-26.

Weber, Max. *The Theory of Social and Economic Organization*. Translated and edited, with an introduction, by A. M. Henderson and Talcott Parsons, from Part I of *Wirtschaft und Gesellschaft*. New York: Oxford University Press, 1947.

Werner, Edward Theodore Chalmers. *China of the Chinese*. London and New York: Sir I. Pitman & Sons, Ltd. , 1919.

-------. *Descriptive Sociology, or Groups of Sociological Facts Classified and Arranged by Herbert Spencer: Chinese*. London: Williams and Northgate, 1910.

Wilbur, C. Martin. Village Government in China. Unpublished Master's thesis, Columbia University, 1933.

Wilhelm, Hellmut. "The Po-hsüeh hung-ju Examination of 1679," *Journal of the American Oriental Society* (Boston), LXXI (1951), 60-76.

Wilhelm, Richard. *Chinese Economic Psychology*. Translated by Bruno Lasker from *Chinesische Wirtschaftspsychologie*. New York: Institute of Pacific Relations, 1947.

-------. *The Soul of China*. Text translated by John Holroyd Reece; poems translated by Arthur Waley. New York: Harcourt, Brace & Co. , 1928.

Willcox, Walter F. "A Westerner's Effort to Estimate the Population of China and Its Increase since 1650," *Journal of the American Statistical Association* (Concord), XXV (1930), 255-68.

Williams, Edward Thomas. *China, Yesterday and Today*. New York: Thomas Y. Crowell Co. , 1923.

Williams, Mrs. E. T. "Some Popular Religious Literature of the Chinese,"

Journal of the Royal Asiatic Society of Great Britain and Ireland, North China
Branch (Shanghai), N.S., XXXIII (1899-1900), 11-29.

Williams, Samuel Wells. *The Middle Kingdom: A Survey of the Geography, Government, Literature, Social Life, Arts and History of the Chinese Empire and
Its Inhabitants.* Rev. ed. 2 vols. New York: C. Scribner's Sons, 1883.

Williamson, Alexander. *Journeys in North China, Manchuria and Eastern Mongolia; with Some Accounts of Corea.* 2 vols. London, 1870.

Wint, Guy. *Spotlight on Asia.* Hammondsworth, Eng., and Baltimore: Penguin
Books, 1955.

Wittfogel, Karl August. "Chinese Society: An Historical Survey," *The Journal
of Asian Studies,* XVI (1957), 343-64.

-------. "Oriental Despotism," *Sociologus* (Berlin), III (1953), 96-108.

-------. *Oriental Despotism: A Comparative Study of Total Power.* New Haven:
Yale University Press, 1957.

-------, and Chia-sheng Feng. *History of Chinese Society: Liao (907-1125).*
Philadelphia: American Philosophical Society; New York: Macmillan, 1949.

Wong, Wen-hao. *The Distribution of Population and Land Utilization in China.*
Shanghai, 1933.

Yamane, Yukio. "On the Duty of the Village Headman in the Ming Period," *Tōhōgaku* (Tokyo), III (1952), 79-87.

Yang, Ch'ing-kun. *A North China Local Market Economy: A Summary of a Study
of Periodic Markets in Chowping Hsien, Shantung.* New York: Institute of Pacific Relations, 1944.

Yang, Martin C. *A Chinese Village: Taitou, Shantung Province.* New York: Columbia University Press, 1945.

Yao, Shan-yu. "The Chronological and Seasonal Distribution of Floods and
Droughts in Chinese History," *Harvard Journal of Asiatic Studies* VI (1942),
273-311.

Yen, Kia-lok. "The Basis of Democracy in China," *International Journal of Social, Political and Legal Philosophy* (Philadelphia), XXVIII (1917-18), 197-219.